Fodor's

PACIFIC NORTHWEST

Portions of this book are excerpted from *Fodor's Complete Guide to National Parks of the West*, *Fodor's Oregon*, *Fodor's Seattle*, and *Fodor's Vancouver and Victoria*

WELCOME TO THE PACIFIC NORTHWEST

With its rugged coast, commanding peaks, forested islands, and cool cities, the Pacific Northwest strikes an ideal balance between outdoorsy and cosmopolitan. In Seattle, Portland, and Vancouver, farm-to-table restaurants, sophisticated hotels, and cutting-edge galleries await. Beyond the cities, the wineries of Oregon's Willamette Valley, cute towns of Washington's San Juan Islands, and national parks from Crater Lake to Olympic beg to be explored. Whether your ideal trip involves hiking a trail or window-shopping, the Pacific Northwest delivers.

TOP REASONS TO GO

★ **Hip Cities:** Quirky Portland, eclectic Seattle, and gorgeous Vancouver entice.

★ **Coastal Fun:** Beaches, whale sightings, tidal pools, headland walks.

★ **Mountains:** Mt. Rainier, Mt. Hood, Mt. Olympus, and Mt. St. Helens inspire awe.

★ **Craft Beverages:** Wineries, microbreweries, artisan coffee, and boutique distilleries.

★ **Seafood:** Fresh local crab, razor clams, sea scallops, oysters, and salmon.

★ **Scenic Drives:** On the Oregon Coast, in the Cascade Range, through evergreen forests.

Fodor's PACIFIC NORTHWEST

Editorial: Douglas Stallings, *Editorial Director*; Salwa Jabado and Margaret Kelly, *Senior Editors*; Alexis Kelly, Jacinta O'Halloran, and Amanda Sadlowski, *Editors*; Teddy Minford, *Associate Editor*; Rachael Roth, *Content Manager*

Design: Tina Malaney, *Associate Art Director*

Photography: Jennifer Arnow, *Senior Photo Editor*

Maps: Rebecca Baer, *Senior Map Editor*; Mark Stroud (Moon Street Cartography), David Lindroth, *Cartographers*

Production: Jennifer DePrima, *Editorial Production Manager*; Carrie Parker, *Senior Production Editor*; Elyse Rozelle, *Production Editor*; David Satz, *Director of Content Production*

Business & Operations: Chuck Hoover, *Chief Marketing Officer*; Joy Lai, *Vice President and General Manager*; Stephen Horowitz, *Head of Business Development and Partnerships*

Public Relations: Joe Ewaskiw, *Manager*

Writers: Shelley Arenas, Margot Bigg, Andrew Collins, Chloë Ernst, Jennifer Foden, Adriana Janovich, Lauren Kelley, Sue Kernaghan, Kade Krichko, Chris McBeath, Lesley Mirza, Christina Newberry, Conor Risch, Jonathan Shadel, AnnaMaria Stephens, Naomi Tomky

Editors: Salwa Jabado (lead project editor), Teddy Minford (Seattle editor), Margaret Kelly (Vancouver and Victoria editor)

Production Editor: Jennifer DePrima

Production Design: Liliana Guia

21st Edition

ISBN 978-0-14-754690-6

ISSN 1098–6774

All details in this book are based on information supplied to us at press time. Always confirm information when it matters, especially if you're making a detour to visit a specific place. Fodor's expressly disclaims any liability, loss, or risk, personal or otherwise, that is incurred as a consequence of the use of any of the contents of this book.

PRINTED IN THE UNITED STATES OF AMERICA

10 9 8 7 6 5 4 3 2 1

CONTENTS

Fodor's Features

6 <

MAPS

ABOUT THIS GUIDE

Fodor's Recommendations

Everything in this guide is worth doing—we don't cover what isn't—but exceptional sights, hotels, and restaurants are recognized with additional accolades. **Fodor's Choice** ★ indicates our top recommendations. Care to nominate a new place? Visit Fodors.com/contact-us.

Trip Costs

We list prices wherever possible to help you budget well. Hotel and restaurant price categories from **$** to **$$$$** are noted alongside each recommendation. For hotels, we include the lowest cost of a standard double room in high season. For restaurants, we cite the average price of a main course at dinner or, if dinner isn't served, at lunch. For attractions, we always list adult admission fees; discounts are usually available for children, students, and senior citizens.

Hotels

Our local writers vet every hotel to recommend the best overnights in each price category, from budget to expensive. Unless otherwise specified, you can expect private bath, phone, and TV in your room. For expanded hotel reviews, facilities, and deals, visit Fodors.com.

Top Picks

★ **Fodor's Choice**

Listings

- ✉ Address
- ✉ Branch address
- ☎ Telephone
- 📠 Fax
- 🌐 Website
- 📧 E-mail
- 🎟 Admission fee
- 🕒 Open/closed times
- [M] Subway
- ✥ Directions or Map coordinates

Hotels & Restaurants

- 🏨 Hotel
- 🛏 Number of rooms
- 🍴 Meal plans
- W Restaurant
- ✍ Reservations
- 👔 Dress code
- ▭ No credit cards
- [$] Price

Other

- ⇨ See also
- ☞ Take note
- 🏌 Golf facilities

Restaurants

Unless we state otherwise, restaurants are open for lunch and dinner daily. We mention dress code only when there's a specific requirement and reservations only when they're essential or not accepted.

Credit Cards

The hotels and restaurants in this guide typically accept credit cards. If not, we'll say so.

EUGENE FODOR

Hungarian-born Eugene Fodor (1905–91) began his travel career as an interpreter on a French cruise ship. The experience inspired him to write *On the Continent* (1936), the first guidebook to receive annual updates and discuss a country's way of life as well as its sights. Fodor later joined the U.S. Army and worked for the OSS in World War II. After the war, he kept up his intelligence work while expanding his guidebook series. During the Cold War, many guides were written by fellow agents who understood the value of insider information. Today's guides continue Fodor's legacy by providing travelers with timely coverage, insider tips, and cultural context.

EXPERIENCE THE PACIFIC NORTHWEST

WHAT'S WHERE

1 Portland. With its pedestrian-friendly Downtown and great public transit, Portland is easy to explore. The city has become a magnet for fans of artisanal food, coffee, beer, wine, and spirits, and its leafy parks and miles of bike lanes make it a prime spot for outdoors enthusiasts.

2 The Oregon Coast. Oregon's roughly 300 miles of rugged shoreline are every bit as scenic as the more crowded and famous California coast. Oregon Dunes National Recreation Area, the Oregon Coast Aquarium, Cannon Beach, Astoria, and the Columbia River Maritime Museum are key highlights.

3 The Willamette Valley and Wine Country. Just beyond the Portland city limits and extending south for 120 miles to Eugene, the Willamette Valley is synonymous with exceptional wine-making and an increasingly noteworthy food scene.

4 The Columbia River Gorge and Mt. Hood. Less than an hour east of Portland, the Columbia Gorge extends for about 160 miles along the Oregon-Washington border. Sailboarding, hiking, and wine touring abound. Just 35 miles south of Hood River, Mt. Hood is renowned for hiking and skiing.

5 Central Oregon. The swatch of Oregon immediately east of the Cascade Range takes in a varied landscape, with the outdoorsy city of Bend as the regional hub. Make time for the funky mountain town of Sisters.

6 Crater Lake National Park. The 21-square-mile sapphire-blue expanse is the nation's deepest lake and a scenic wonder. You can drive the loop road around the lake, hike, or take a boat tour.

7 Southern Oregon. Artsy Ashland and Old West–looking Jacksonville have sophisticated restaurants, shops, and wineries. Nearby, Oregon Caves National Monument is a fascinating natural attraction, while the Klamath Falls region has some of the best wildlife-viewing in the state.

8 Seattle. As the Pacific Northwest's hub of arts and culture, this city has a vibrant mix of swanky restaurants and cocktail bars, first-rate coffee shops and brewpubs, and trendy boutique hotels, alongside pedestrian-friendly neighborhoods loaded with indie retail and dining.

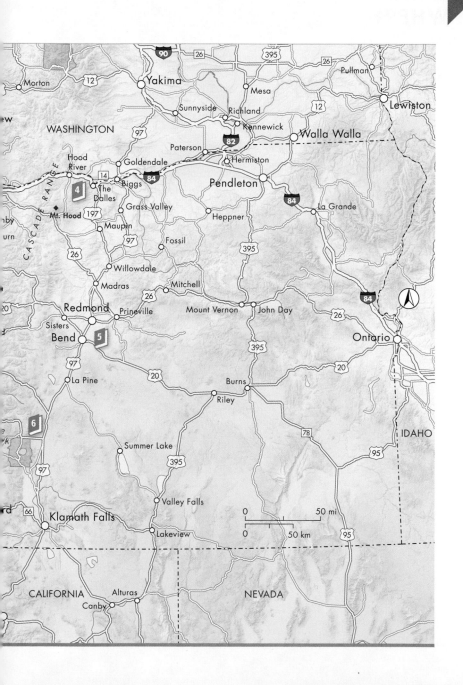

WHAT'S WHERE

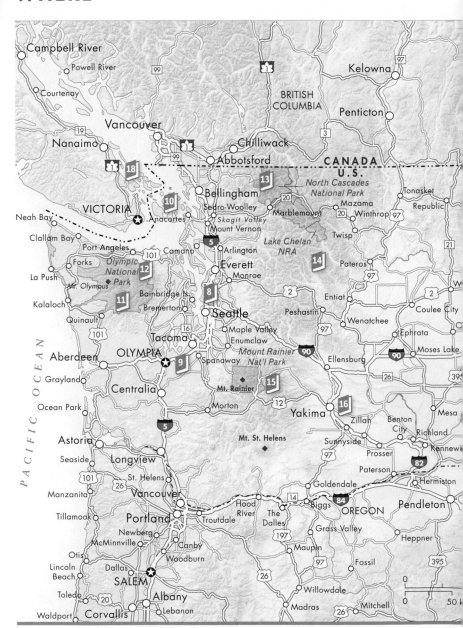

9 Washington Cascade Mountains and Valleys. Outside Seattle, you can tour the waterfront and museums of Tacoma and bike past tulip fields in the Skagit Valley. Olympia is a good base for exploring Mt. Rainier and Mt. St. Helens, and up north, Bellingham is a picturesque waterfront town with a bounty of outdoors activities and great restaurants.

10 The San Juan Islands. This relaxing and stunningly beautiful archipelago is prime whale-watching and kayaking territory, and you'll find art galleries, quirky cafés, and upscale inns amid the islands' largest towns.

11 Olympic National Park. Centered on Mt. Olympus and framed on three sides by water, this 922,651-acre park covers much of Washington's forest-clad Olympic Peninsula.

12 Olympic Peninsula and Washington Coast. Wilderness envelops most of the Olympic Peninsula, with the Olympic Mountains at its core. Rugged terrain and few roads limit interior accessibility, but U.S. Highway 101 offers breathtaking forest, ocean, and mountain vistas.

13 North Cascades National Park. This 505,000-acre expanse of mountain wilderness is part of an area with more than half of the glaciers in America.

14 North Central Washington. Along the beautiful North Cascades Highway, you'll encounter spectacular scenery and logging towns such as Sedro Wooley and Marblemount, as well as Winthrop.

15 Mount Rainier National Park. The fifth-highest mountain in the Lower 48, Mt. Rainier is massive and unforgettable.

16 Washington Wine Country. This fertile valley east of the Cascades has long been known for apple and cherry orchards, and more recently as a prized winemaking area—including the vineyards around Yakima, Zillah, Prosser, and Benton City.

17 Spokane and Eastern Washington. Characterized by rolling, dry, treeless hills and anchored by the state's second-largest city, Spokane, this area takes in the vast Columbia River valley and an eclectic mix of cities and towns, including wine-centric Walla Walla.

18 Vancouver and Victoria. Vancouver is a glorious city with tall fir trees, rock spires, the ocean at your doorstep, and a vibrant atmosphere. Victoria—with its stately Victorian houses, walkable Downtown and waterfront, and hip boutiques and restaurants—is a stunner.

THE PACIFIC NORTHWEST PLANNER

Fast Facts

Currency and Exchange. The units of currency in Canada are the Canadian dollar (C$) and the cent, in almost the same denominations as U.S. currency. A good way to be sure you're getting the best exchange rate is by using your credit card or ATM/debit card. The issuing bank will convert your bill at the current rate. An increasing number of credit card companies offer cards that don't charge exchange fees—if you travel abroad often, it's worth applying for one of these.

Packing. It's all about layers here. The weather can morph from cold and overcast to warm and sunny and back again in the course of a few hours, especially in spring and early fall.

Taxes. Oregon has no sales tax, although many cities and counties levy a tax on lodging and services. Room taxes, for example, vary from 6% to 11.5%. The state retail sales tax in Washington is 6.5%, but there are also local taxes that can raise the total tax to 9.9%, depending on the goods or service and the municipality; Seattle's retail sales tax is 9.6%. A Goods and Services Tax (GST) of 5% applies on virtually every transaction in Canada except for the purchase of basic groceries, and an additional 7% GST is assessed throughout British Columbia.

Border Crossing into Canada

Air and Ferry Travel. You are required to present a passport to enter or reenter the United States. To enter Canada by air you must present a valid passport or an Air NEXUS card; by land or sea you need to present one of the following: (1) passport, (2) a trusted-traveler program card (i.e., Global Entry, NEXUS, SENTRI, or FAST card, (3) a U.S. Passport Card, or (4) an Enhanced Driver's License (issued only in the states of Michigan, New York, Vermont, and Washington).

Car Travel. You will need one of the aforementioned documents (*see above*) to cross the border by car. In addition, drivers must carry owner registration and proof of insurance coverage, which is compulsory in Canada. The Canadian Non-Resident Inter-Provincial Motor Vehicle Liability Insurance Card, available from any U.S. insurance company, is accepted as evidence of financial responsibility in Canada. If you are driving a car that is not registered in your name, carry a letter from the owner that authorizes your use of the vehicle.

The main entry point into British Columbia from the United States by car is on Interstate 5 at Blaine, Washington, 48 km (30 miles) south of Vancouver. Three highways enter British Columbia from the east: Highway 1, or the Trans-Canada Highway; Highway 3, or the Crowsnest Highway; and Highway 16, the Yellowhead Highway, which runs from the Rocky Mountains to Prince Rupert.

Border-crossing procedures are usually quick and simple, although the wait can be trying on weekends and during busy holiday periods. Every British Columbia border crossing is open 24 hours (except the one at Lynden–Aldergrove, which is open from 8 am to midnight). The Interstate 5 border crossing at Blaine, Washington (also known as the Douglas, or Peace Arch, border crossing), is one of the busiest border crossings between the United States and Canada. Listen to local radio traffic reports or check the Washington Department of Transportation (WSDOT) website for information about wait times.

U.S. Passport Information

U.S. Department of State. ☎ *877/487–2778* ⊕ *www.travel.state.gov.*

Getting Around

Car Travel. You'll need a car to get around all but the major cities of the Pacific Northwest. Although a car will also grant you more freedom to explore the outer areas of Portland, Seattle, Vancouver, and Victoria, these four cities have adequate public transportation, taxi fleets, and Uber or similar services (in all but Victoria)—although cabs tend to be expensive. In most other towns in the region, even if bus or train service exists between two points, you'll likely need a car to get around once you arrive.

Interstate 5 is the major north–south conduit in the U.S. part of the region, offering a straight shot at high speeds—when there aren't traffic snarls, of course (these are especially common along the 75-mile stretch from northern Seattle to Olympia)—from Oregon's southern border all the way up to the Canadian border. Seattle and Portland are both along Interstate 5, and Vancouver is about 30 miles across the border from where it ends. This makes driving between the major hubs an easy option, though it's also possible to travel between them by train or bus. Except for the beautiful lower half of Oregon, below Eugene, Interstate 5 is pleasant and green but not especially dramatic as far as scenery goes, at least compared with the rest of the region as a whole.

U.S. 101, on the other hand, is one of the main attractions of the region. It starts in Washington, west of Olympia, makes a very wide loop around Olympic National Park, then heads south through Oregon, hugging the coast almost the whole way down. Most of the road is incredibly scenic, but this is not a very quick way to traverse either state. Make sure you want to commit to the coastal drive, which can be windy and slow going in some parts, before getting on the 101—it takes some time to work your way over from Interstate 5, so jumping back and forth between the two isn't very practical.

The Cascade Range cuts through the middle of Washington and Oregon, which means that east–west journeys often meander over mountain passes and can be either beautiful and relaxing (summer) or beautiful and treacherous (at times, in winter). Interstate 90 is the main east–west artery in Washington, connecting Seattle with Spokane, but Highway 20, which passes through North Cascades National Park, is more scenic. Interstate 84 is Oregon's major east–west artery; not far east of Portland it enters the stunningly picturesque Columbia River Gorge.

See also Car Travel in Travel Smart for driving times to various regions from Seattle and Portland.

When to Go

Hotels in the major tourist destinations often book up early in summer, so it's important to make reservations well in advance. Spring and fall are also excellent times to visit, although rain is more prevalent then. Prices for accommodations, transportation, and tours can be lower and crowds smaller during the off-season in the most popular destinations. In winter, snow is uncommon in the lowland areas but abundant in the nearby mountains, where ski resorts abound and chains and snow tires are often required for driving.

OREGON
TOP ATTRACTIONS

Cannon Beach

(A) The nearest town on the dramatically rocky Oregon coast from Portland also happens to be one of the most idyllic communities in the coastal Northwest. This town, anchored by 235-foot-tall Haystack Rock, is rife with beachside hiking trails, art galleries, and cafés specializing in organic coffee, Oregon wines, and fresh-caught seafood. Nearby Oswald West and Ecola state parks have some of the most stunning beaches and hiking trails in the state.

Columbia River Gorge

(B) The 110-mile section of the Columbia River provides some of the Pacific Northwest's most spectacular vistas. Towering cliffs on both sides of the river form a dramatic backdrop, and meandering highways line both banks. Water and wind sports abound, and a growing wine-making, craft-brewing, and culinary scene has flourished in recent years.

Columbia River Maritime Museum, Astoria

(C) At this dazzling, contemporary facility in the steadily gentrifying town of Astoria, where the northern Oregon Coast meets the Columbia River, you can tour a fully operational U.S. Coast Guard lightship, and check out engaging exhibits on local shipwrecks, marine life, and how the mighty Columbia has driven the economic and cultural development of the Pacific Northwest.

Crater Lake National Park

(D) The deepest lake in the United States is also the clearest, a fact readily grasped as soon as you behold this searing-blue body of water. It's closed much of the year due to snow, but in summer this 21-square-mile lake is southern Oregon's foremost attraction—the nearly century-old Crater Lake Lodge, perched on the southern shore, makes a memorable overnight and dinner venue.

High Desert Museum, Bend
(E) Evocative and intricate walk-through dioramas and an indoor-outdoor zoo with creatures great and tiny convey the high desert's past and present in a delightfully airy and family-friendly space just south of Bend.

Mt. Hood
(F) Just 60 miles east of Portland, the state's highest mountain is the only place in the Lower 48 where you can ski year-round. There are five different facilities, Timberline Lodge Ski Area being the most scenic.

Oregon Sand Dunes
(G) The 41 miles of rolling bluffs that make up Oregon Dunes National Recreation Area bring out the kid in visitors of all ages—there's something inherently happy about frolicking amid these massive mountains of sand, some of them climbing nearly 500 feet higher than the surf. Here you can hike, ride horseback, and race on a dune buggy, and there's great boating and fishing (plus several excellent seafood restaurants) in the nearby town of Florence.

Powell's Bookstore, Portland
(H) The Downtown Portland legend is the world's largest bookstore carrying both new and used titles, and with its coffee-house, late hours, and endless aisles of reading, it's also a prime spot for literary-minded people-watching.

Willamette Valley Wine Country
(I) Within easy day-tripping of Portland, this swath of fertile, hilly countryside is home to more than 500 wineries and has earned a reputation as one of the finest producers of Pinot Noir in the world—some say the best outside Burgundy. Winemakers in these parts also produce first-rate Pinot Gris and Chardonnay.

WASHINGTON TOP ATTRACTIONS

Hurricane Ridge, Olympic National Park

(A) Of the dozens of stunning panoramas within Olympic National Park, this 5,200-foot-high bluff offers the most memorable views—it takes in the vast Olympic mountain range as well as the Strait of Juan de Fuca and, beyond that, Vancouver Island. In summer, rangers lead tours through the wildflower- and wildlife-rich terrain.

Johnston Observatory, Mt. St. Helens

(B) Named for a brave volcanologist who perished in the terrifying 1980 eruption of Mt. St. Helens, this visitor center and observatory affords mind-blowing views of the hulking—often steaming—lava dome that lies deep within the mountain's crater. You reach this spot by driving the scenic Spirit Lake Highway.

LeMay–America's Car Museum, Tacoma

(C) Downtown Tacoma is home to several superb cultural sights, including the Museum of Glass, Washington State History Museum, and Foss Waterway Seaport, but the massive vintage car collection at the LeMay, which occupies a sleek new building on the south edge of downtown, is arguably the city's star attraction. It ranks among the world's most impressive automobile museums.

Long Beach Peninsula

(D) Just two hours by car from Portland and three from Seattle, this 28-mile-long barrier peninsula rises from the mouth of the Columbia River north along the state's southwestern coast, providing visitors with rolling stretches of sand dunes, family-friendly amusements, and endless opportunities to view wildlife, from migrating birds to black bears.

Mount Rainier National Park

(E) Don't be intimidated by Mt. Rainier's 14,411-foot summit. It's true that only highly experienced hikers with guides should attempt this climb, but the national park that surrounds this snow-capped peak has plenty of terrain accessible to everyone, including 260 miles of well-maintained trails. The Skyline Trail is a moderately challenging 5½-mile loop along alpine ridges and wildflower-strewn meadows—it's one of the best Mt. Rainier hikes if you have only one day to explore the mountain.

Orcas Island, San Juan Islands

(F) Of the three main islands in this laid-back and beautiful archipelago between Bellingham and Canada's Vancouver Island, Orcas has the best balance of scenery, seclusion, and diversions. It's home to 2,409-foot Mt. Constitution and surrounding Moran State Park, several picturesque harbors popular for fishing and kayaking, and a sophisticated mix of country inns and farm-to-table restaurants.

Pike Place Market, Seattle

(G) The Pacific Northwest abounds with stellar farmers' markets, but Downtown Seattle's creaky and colorful Pike Place is the mother of them all, established in 1907 and still thriving (despite a near brush with the wrecking ball during the 1960s).

Seattle Center and the Space Needle

(H) Almost every trip includes a stop at Seattle Center, which was built for the 1962 World's Fair and is home to the Space Needle, museums, and performance halls. Most of the city's major events are held here, but even on quiet weekends there's still something for everyone: Pacific Science Center and Children's Museum, Museum of Popular Culture (MoPOP), and the Chihuly Garden and Glass exhibit.

VANCOUVER AND VICTORIA TOP ATTRACTIONS

The Bill Reid Gallery, Vancouver

(A) If First Nations heritage is your thing, be sure to visit this repository of regional art, one of the best of its kind in North America. It is as much a showcase for new artists as it is a showcase of Bill Reid's work, most famous of which is the statue *The Spirit of Haida Gwaii, The Jade Canoe,* on display at the Vancouver International Airport.

Capilano Suspension Bridge, Vancouver

(B) It's just a 20-minute drive across Burrard Inlet from Downtown Vancouver to reach the surprisingly momentous North Shore mountains, home to Grouse Mountain and its aerial tramway, and the famed Capilano Suspension Bridge, a 450-foot cedar-plank swing bridge that crosses 230 feet above the frothy Capilano River.

Dr. Sun Yat-Sen Classical Chinese Garden, Vancouver

(C) "Life is not measured by the number of breaths we take," according to the old saying, "but by the places and moments that take our breath away." That sentiment sums up this elegant Downtown destination. It's the first authentic Ming Dynasty–style garden outside China to incorporate symbolism and design elements from centuries-old Chinese gardens.

Granville Island, Vancouver

(D) Take the foot-passenger ferry across the inlet from Downtown, and bring your appetite. This small island houses an extremely popular indoor market, a marina, a hotel, theaters, restaurants, cafés, parks, and dozens of crafts shops and artist studios. Wander the stalls in the market, then grab a bench outside to get your fill of delicacies and the view.

Museum of Anthropology at UBC, Vancouver

(E) The city's most spectacular museum displays art from the Pacific Northwest and around the world—dramatic totem poles and canoes; exquisite carvings of gold, silver, and argillite; and masks, tools, and textiles from many cultures.

Stanley Park, Vancouver

(F) An afternoon in this gorgeous 1,000-acre wilderness, just blocks from Downtown Vancouver, can include beaches, the ocean, the harbor, Douglas fir and cedar forests, First Nations sculptures, and a view of the North Shore Mountains. Walk, bike, picnic, or just take the trolley tour around the perimeter, but don't miss it.

Butchart Gardens, Victoria

(G) Just 20 minutes from downtown Victoria, the 55-acre Butchart Gardens was planted in a limestone quarry in 1904. Highlights include the Japanese and Italian gardens, as well as the proliferation of roses and 700 other varieties of flowers. On summer nights you can enjoy a fireworks display.

Inner Harbour, Victoria

(H) The lovely capital of British Columbia has a remarkably intimate and pedestrian-friendly Downtown that wraps around the harbor. Street entertainers and crafts vendors—and lots of people—come out to stroll the waterfront walkway in summer.

Royal British Columbia Museum, Victoria

(I) At this superb museum, you can learn about the culture and human history of British Columbia, dating back several thousand years to the earliest First Peoples inhabitants. Other exhibits touch on natural history, European settlement, and maritime heritage.

TOP EXPERIENCES

Shopping at the Portland Saturday Market and Portland Farmers' Market, Portland, OR

The expansive outdoor Saturday market is actually open Saturday and Sunday (from March through Christmas). At the attractive market grounds you'll find every imaginable creation: offbeat patio sculptures, jewelry made from recycled wares, and stylish yet practical housewares to name a few. A 15-minute walk south on Saturday mornings and early afternoons, the unrelated Portland Farmers' Market at PSU campus, on the verdant Park Blocks, is one of the Northwest's most acclaimed foodie gatherings—several vendors sell delish breakfast and lunch fare.

Skiing Mt. Hood, OR

Just 60 miles east of Portland, the state's highest mountain is the only place in the Lower 48 where you can ski year-round (although trails are limited in summer). There are three different facilities on this mammoth, snowcapped mountain. Timberline Lodge Ski Area is the one that remains open year-round, and its runs pass beside the venerable 1930s Timberline Lodge. Nearby Mt. Hood Skibowl has less interesting terrain but the most night-skiing acreage in the country. Around the north side of the mountain, you'll find the most challenging, extensive, and interesting terrain at Mt. Hood Meadows Ski Resort, which offers some 2,000 acres of winter snowboarding and ski fun.

White-Water Rafting on the Rogue River, Grants Pass, OR

Of the many excellent places for white-water rafting in Oregon, the Rogue River offers some of the most thrilling rides. Several outfitters offer trips along this frothy, 215-mile river in the southwestern part of the state, from half-day adventures well suited to beginners to multiday trips that include camping or overnights in local lodges.

Picnicking at Silver Falls State Park, OR

The lush Silver Falls State Park, about 25 miles east of Salem, is so impressive that serious campaigns to admit it to the National Park System have taken place recently. In the meantime, it's something of a secret treasure. The 8,700-acre swath of sky-scraping old-growth Douglas firs climbs into the foothills of the Cascade Range, where rain and melting snow supply the torrent that roars through 14 different waterfalls, several of them more than 100 feet tall.

Driving through the Columbia Gorge, OR/WA

The roughly 110-mile section of the mighty Columbia River that extends from just east of Portland to Goldendale, Washington, provides some of the most stunning scenery in the Pacific Northwest. Towering cliffs on both the Washington and Oregon sides of the river form a dramatic backdrop, and meandering highways line both banks (on the Washington side, Highway 14 is slower but offers better views). There's much to see and do in the Gorge: visit the 620-foot-high Multnomah Falls; stroll among the sophisticated restaurants, shops, and wineries in charming Hood River; or try your luck at sailboarding, a sport well suited to the river's high winds.

Attending the Oregon Shakespeare Festival in Ashland, OR

Sunny, hilly, and attractive Ashland is a charming small city in its own right, with a bustling downtown popping with notable restaurants specializing in farm-to-table cuisine and wines from nearby vineyards. But the Oregon Shakespeare Festival, which presents world-class plays (from Shakespeare to classics to contemporary), on three different stages from mid-February to early November, really put this town on the map.

Consuming Cannabis in Washington and Oregon

Washington and Oregon became two of the first states in the country to legalize the sale and possession of both recreational and medical marijuana in 2012 and 2014, respectively. If you're curious about sampling the local goods, drop by one of the hundreds of dispensaries throughout both states. You'll find an especially strong presence, including many decidedly highbrow artisan retailers, in Portland, Seattle, and other large cities. Not a fan of smoking? Many shops carry a dizzying variety of cannabis-infused topical oils, bath salts, and edibles (from chocolates to taffy). Keep in mind that you must be 21, you can consume recreational pot only on private property, and you can't bring your purchase with you across state borders (even if marijuana is legal in your home state).

Coffeehouse-Crawling in Seattle, WA

Sure, for kicks, it's worth stopping by the original branch of Starbucks, which is across the street from Pike Place Market. But as arguably the nation's coffeehouse capital, Seattle has far more interesting java joints to consider. Especially fertile (coffee) grounds for coffeehouse-hopping include the Capitol Hill, Queen Anne, Ballard, and Fremont neighborhoods—try Espresso Vivace and Victrola Coffee Roasters for stellar espresso.

Biking around Lopez Island, WA

Whether you're an ardent cyclist or an occasional weekender, Lopez Island offers some of the best biking terrain in the West. This laid-back, gently undulating island that's part of Washington's fabled San Juan archipelago is ringed by a beautiful main road and dedicated bike paths. As you cycle past lavender fields, blackberry bushes, horse farms, and occasional patches of woodland, you'll encounter little automobile traffic. There are a couple of bike-rental shops, and Holly B's Bakery is a fine spot for snacks.

Wine Tasting in Walla Walla, WA

Although you'll find super wine-making in several parts of the region, including Oregon's Willamette Valley and Washington's nearby Yakima and Columbia valleys, the dapper college town of Walla Walla has evolved into the Northwest's best overall wine-country hub. The handsomely revived historic downtown abounds with smart boutiques, lively cafés and restaurants, and several prominent tasting rooms. And throughout the surrounding vineyard-studded hills you'll find elegant inns and some of the most critically acclaimed, if still somewhat underrated, wineries in the country.

Riding the Ferry to Victoria, BC

This is a perfectly simple way to admire the region's coastal scenery, from the mountains in Olympic National Park to the meandering shorelines of the San Juan Islands (if you're coming from Port Angeles or Anacortes, Washington) and Gulf islands (if you're coming from mainland British Columbia). Numerous ferries of many sizes ply the waters around Victoria and Vancouver Island, and the trip is best enjoyed on an open deck, while devouring a cup of clam chowder.

FLAVORS OF THE PACIFIC NORTHWEST

Pacific Northwest cuisine highlights regional seafood, locally grown produce, and locally raised meats, often prepared in styles that borrow pan-Asian, French, and Italian influences. All of the region's major and even many smaller cities have top-rated, nationally renowned dining spots, as well as funky, inexpensive little eateries that also pride themselves on serving seasonal and often organic ingredients.

Seafood

The Northwest's dining scene is forever eclectic because of the combined abundance of fresh seafood and the imaginative ways it's cooked. Many restaurants, such as the chain McCormick & Schmick's, which was established in Portland, print menus daily and feature a "fresh list" with more than 30 types of seafood represented, most of which are caught from local waters. And since Dungeness crab, salmon, steelhead, albacore, sole, oysters, spotted prawns, scallops, and rockfish are all within pole's reach, chefs take serious and artful pleasure in discovering ways to fry, grill, bake, stir-fry, sear, poach, barbecue, and sauté the latest catch in new, inventive ways.

Local Ocean Seafoods, Newport, OR. Both a stylish contemporary restaurant overlooking Yaquina Bay and a stellar seafood market, this sophisticated spot is a favorite for lunches and dinners of rockfish tacos, panko-buttermilk-crusted oysters, and other creatively prepared fish and shellfish.

Matt's in the Market, Seattle, WA. Right next to Seattle's prime source of fresh fish, Pike Place Market, Matt's serves a must-try oyster po' boy and Penn Cove mussels with chorizo or Dungeness crab bisque, and pan-roasted fillets of wild salmon and lingcod served with light vinaigrettes.

Blue Water Café, Vancouver, BC. Ask the staff to recommend wine pairings from the BC-focused list, and enjoy exquisitely prepared seafood, which may include overlooked varieties such as mackerel, sardines, and herring.

Locavore Movement

Pacific Northwest chefs are fanatical, in a delicious way, about sustainability, presenting dishes with ingredients raised, grown, or foraged within about 100 miles. Northwest chefs are so determined to maintain an unwavering connection to the land that many hire professional foragers, or on occasion can be found tromping off into the woods themselves. Bounties of morels, chanterelles, and bolete mushrooms (fall), stinging nettles and fiddlehead ferns (spring), and huckleberries and blackberries (summer) now grace the menus of many restaurants. From both Portland and Seattle, farmland immediately surrounds urban boundaries; therefore, daily deliveries of asparagus, eggplant, pears, cherries, and other fruits and vegetables is achievable, along with locally raised game from area ranches and farms.

Higgins, Portland, OR. One of Portland's longtime culinary stars, chef Greg Higgins relies heavily on herbs and produce from nearby farms in such standout dishes as warm beets, asparagus, and artichokes; and venison terrine with dried sour cherries and roasted garlic mustard.

Imperial, Portland, OR. Talented chef Vitaly Paley produces incomparably fresh and complex fare utilizing strictly seasonal and regional ingredients, from local rabbit and duck to peaches and wild mushrooms.

The Herbfarm, Woodinville, WA. Every year the Herbfarm honors mushroom season with the Mycologist's Dream menu, which sees the fungi go into everything from ravioli to flan. The rest of the year, blackberries may mingle with rose geranium in ice cream, or caviar may be accompanied by a jelly flavored with wild ginger and local rhizomes.

Lark, Seattle, WA. Naturally raised veal sweetbreads come with a sunchoke puree, and spring nettles are stuffed into spinach ravioli at Lark, where the small menu names every local farm that contributes to its dishes.

Sitka & Spruce, Seattle, WA. Wild greens and edible flowers always show up in salads or as garnishes alongside fresh seafood or free-range chicken from Vashon Island farms at chef Matt Dillon's tiny temple to the Northwest.

Wineries

Thanks to a mild climate with soil, air, water, and temperature conditions comparable to regions of France, the Northwest is recognized for producing prime varieties of wine. In charming, rural settings, some just outside the cities, petite to larger vineyards offer behind-the-scenes tours where sampling the merchandise is encouraged. The Northwest is also a notable region for its production of organic and biodynamic wines. In keeping with the sustainable food and farm movement, vineyards are developing fertilization, production, harvesting, and fermentation techniques that produce flavorful, eco-friendly varieties that set the standard in the wine world.

Artisanal Cocktails

Thanks to the growing number of craft distilleries that have sprung up in the Northwest, with the bulk of them in Portland (Clear Creek eau de vie, Aviation gin, New Deal vodka), bars and restaurants in Oregon and Washington have begun turning their attention to producing creative, artisanal cocktails, often using local and seasonal ingredients, including fresh juices and herbs garnered from farmers' markets. Bourbon and gin lovers never had it so good, as these drinks seem to be at the base of most creations; for the rest, there are plenty of obscure lavender-infused liqueurs to choose from. Classic drinks are also much appreciated. In Seattle, several bartenders are single-handedly restoring the dignity of the martini, the Manhattan, and the French 75.

Expatriate, Portland, OR. Northeast Portland's cozy Asian-inspired boîte has become renowned for inspired drinks—try the Infante, with Pueblo Viejo Blanco tequila, fresh lime, orgeat, local honey, and nutmeg—and delectable snacks.

Teardrop Lounge, Portland, OR. The expansive cocktail list here changes seasonally and emphasizes interesting mixers, such as basil-lemon soda, marionberry–pink peppercorn honey, and jalapeño syrup.

Zig Zag, Seattle, WA. Zig Zag pours the best martinis in Seattle, along with more exotic fare like the Trident (cynar, aquavit, dry sherry, and peach bitters) and inventive, improvised cocktails.

PORTLAND WITH KIDS

Many of Oregon's best kids-oriented attractions and activities are in greater Portland. Just getting around the Rose City—via streetcars and light-rail trains on city streets and kayaks, excursion cruises, and jet boats on the Willamette River—is fun. For listings of family-oriented concerts, performances by the Oregon Children's Theatre, and the like, check the free *Willamette Weekly* newspaper.

Museums and Attractions

On the east bank of the Willamette River near the new pedestrians-welcome Tilikum Crossing bridge, the **Oregon Museum of Science and Industry** (OMSI) is a leading interactive museum, with touch-friendly exhibits, an Omnimax theater, the state's biggest planetarium, and a 240-foot submarine moored just outside in the river. Along Portland's leafy Park Blocks, both the **Oregon History Museum** and the **Portland Art Museum** have exhibits and programming geared toward kids.

In Old Town, kids enjoy walking amid the ornate pagodas and dramatic foliage of the **Lan Su Chinese Garden**. This is a good spot for a weekend morning, followed by a visit to the **Portland Saturday Market**, where food stalls and musicians keep younger kids entertained, and the cool jewelry, toys, and gifts handcrafted by local artisans appeal to teens. Steps from the market is the **Oregon Maritime Museum**, set within a vintage stern-wheeler docked on the river. And just up Burnside Street from the market, **Powell's City of Books** contains enormous sections of kids' and young adults' literature.

Parks

Portland is dotted with densely wooded parks—many of the larger ones have ball fields, playgrounds, and picnic areas. The most famous urban oasis in the city,

Forest Park (along with adjoining **Washington Park**) offers a wealth of engaging activities. You can ride the MAX light-rail right to the park's main hub of culture, a complex comprising the **Oregon Zoo, Portland Children's Museum**, and **World Forestry Discovery Center Museum**. Ride the narrow-gauge railroad from the zoo for 2 miles to reach the **International Rose Test Garden** and **Japanese Garden**. From here it's an easy downhill stroll to **Northwest 23rd and 21st avenues'** pizza parlors, ice-cream shops, and bakeries.

Outdoor Adventures

Tour boats ply the **Willamette River**, and a couple of marinas near OMSI rent **kayaks** and conduct **drag-boat races** out on the water. There are also several shops in town that rent **bikes** for use on the city's many miles of dedicated bike lanes and trails. There's outstanding **whitewater rafting** just southeast of Portland, along the Clackamas River. On your way toward the Clackamas, check out **North Clackamas Aquatic Park** and **Oaks Amusement Park**, which have rides and wave pools galore.

Nearby **Mt. Hood** has camping, hiking, and biking all summer, and three of the most family-friendly ski resorts in the Northwest—**Timberline** is especially popular for younger and less experienced boarders and skiers. From summer through fall, the pick-your-own berry farms and pumpkin patches on **Sauvie Island** make for an engaging afternoon getaway—for an all-day outing, continue up U.S. 30 all the way to **Astoria**, at the mouth of the Columbia River, to visit the **Columbia River Maritime Museum** and **Fort Stevens State Park**, where kids love to scamper about the remains of an early-20th-century shipwreck.

SEATTLE WITH KIDS

Seattle is great for kids. After all, a place where floatplanes take off a few feet from houseboats, and where harbor seals might be spotted on a routine ferry ride, doesn't have to try too hard to feel like a wonderland. And if the rain falls, there are plenty of great museums to keep the kids occupied. A lot of child-centric sights are easily reached via public transportation, and the piers and the aquarium can be explored on foot from most Downtown hotels. A few spots (Woodland Park Zoo, the Ballard Locks, and Discovery Park) are easier to visit by car.

Museums
Several museums cater specifically to kids, and many are conveniently clustered at the Seattle Center. The Center's winning trio is the **Pacific Science Center,** which has interactive exhibits and IMAX theaters; the **Children's Museum,** which has exhibits on Washington State and foreign cultures plus plenty of interactive art spaces; and, of course, the **Space Needle.** For older, hipper siblings there's a skate park; the Vera Project, a teen music and art space; and the **EMP Museum,** which features exhibits on pop culture and music history.

Downtown there are miles of waterfront to explore along the piers. The **Seattle Aquarium** is here and has touch pools and otters—what more could a kid want?

Parks and Outdoor Attractions
Discovery Park has an interpretive center, a Native American cultural center, easy forest trails, and accessible beaches. **Alki Beach** in West Seattle is lively and fun; a wide paved path is the perfect surface for wheels of all kinds—you can rent bikes and scooters, or take to the water on rented paddleboats and kayaks. **Volunteer Park** has wide lawns and shallow pools made for splashing toddlers.

The **Woodland Park Zoo** has nearly 300 different species of animals, from jaguars to mountain goats, cheap parking, and an adjacent playground; stroller rentals are available. Watching an astonishing variety of boats navigate the ship canal at the **Ballard Locks** will entertain visitors of any age.

Hotels
Downtown, the **Hotel Monaco** offers a happy medium between sophisticated and family-friendly. The colorful, eccentric decor will appeal to kids but remind adults that they're in a boutique property. Fun amenities abound, like optional goldfish in the rooms, and toys in the lobby. Surprisingly, one of the city's most high-end historic properties, the **Fairmont Olympic,** is also quite kid-friendly. The hotel's decor is a little fussy, but the grand staircases in the lobby will awe most little ones, and there's a great indoor pool area. In addition, the hotel offers babysitting, a kids' room-service menu, and toys and board games.

GREAT ITINERARIES

WASHINGTON AND OREGON

Northwest Coast and Cities, 10 days

The hip and urbane cities of Seattle and Portland bookend this itinerary, with the verdant Olympic Peninsula, rugged Oregon Coast, and undulating Willamette Valley Wine Country at the heart, giving you the best of the city and the country in one trip.

Days 1 and 2: Seattle

Start in **Seattle,** where you can spend a couple of nights exploring this picturesque and dynamic city's highlights. Most of the must-see attractions—**Pike Place Market, Seattle Art Museum,** the **Seattle Aquarium**—are steps from Downtown hotels, and it's only a short walk or monorail ride to reach the **Seattle Center,** with its iconic **Space Needle** and such family-friendly draws as the **Pacific Science Center, Children's Museum,** and **EMP Museum.** You could cram several of these attractions into one busy day, but it's better to break them up over two days. Or spend your second day exploring some of the city's lively neighborhoods, including Capitol Hill, with its scenic **Volunteer Park,** and Ballard, where you can check out the **Lake Washington Ship Canal** and **Hiram M. Chittenden Locks** park.

Day 3: Bainbridge Island and Port Townsend

(2 hours by car ferry and car from Seattle)

Take the 35-minute car ferry from Seattle across Puget Sound to laid-back and beautiful **Bainbridge Island,** stopping for lunch and browsing the shops in the village of Winslow and touring **Bloedel Reserve.** Continue on Highways 305, 3, and 104, stopping in the cute Scandinavian town of **Poulsbo,** and continuing to the northeastern corner of the Olympic Peninsula, where the charming towns of **Port Townsend** and **Port Angeles** make good overnight bases and have several fine dinner options.

Days 4 and 5: Olympic National Park

(1 hour by car from Port Townsend, 15 minutes by car from Port Angeles)

The next morning, launch into a full day at **Olympic National Park.** Explore the **Hoh Rain Forest** and **Hurricane Ridge** (the nearest section to Port Angeles) before heading back to Port Angeles or Port Townsend for the evening. Start Day 5 with a drive west on U.S. 101 to **Forks** and on to **La Push** via Highway 110, a total of about 45 miles. Here, an hour-long lunchtime stroll to **Second** or **Third Beach** will offer a taste of the wild Pacific coastline. Back on U.S. 101, head south to **Lake Quinault,** which is about 100 miles from Lake Crescent. Check into the **Lake Quinault Lodge,** then drive up the river 6 miles to one of the rain-forest trails through the lush Quinault Valley.

Days 6 and 7: The Oregon Coast

(3 hours from Lake Quinault to Astoria)

Leave Lake Quinault early on Day 6 for the scenic drive south on U.S. 101. Here the road winds through coastal spruce forests, periodically rising on headlands to offer Pacific Ocean panoramas. Spend your first night in the up-and-coming town of **Astoria,** just across the Columbia River from Washington. The next day, after visiting Astoria's excellent **Columbia Maritime Museum,** continue south on U.S. 101, where small coastal resort towns like **Cannon Beach** and **Manzanita** beckon with cafés, shops, and spectacular beach parks. Be sure to walk out to the gorgeous beach at **Oswald West State Park** just north of Manzanita.

Take a detour onto the **Three Capes Loop,** a stunning 35-mile byway off U.S. 101. Stop in **Newport** (on the loop), 130 miles south of Astoria, for your second night on the coast—this bustling town has several good restaurants and is home to the **Oregon Coast Aquarium.**

Day 8: Eugene and the Willamette Valley

(2½ hours by car from Newport to Eugene or 4 hours by car stopping at Oregon Dunes)

From Newport, continue south along the coast on U.S. 101 for 50 miles, stopping in the charming village of **Florence** for lunch. Then head south another 20 miles to briefly get a look at the soaring mountains of sand that make up **Oregon Dunes National Recreation Area,** before backtracking back to Florence and cutting inland on Highway 126 about 60 miles to the artsy, friendly college town of **Eugene,** which is at the southern end of the Willamette Valley wine region. Eugene has plenty of overnight options, or you could continue north 90 miles on Interstate 5 to spend the night in the heart of the wine country at **Newberg** or **McMinnville,** where you'll find dozens of wineries, several fine restaurants, and a few upscale inns and hotels.

Days 9 and 10: Portland

(1 hour 45 minutes by car from Eugene, 40 minutes by car from Newberg)

On Day 9, visit some of the Willamette Valley's wineries, and then, from either Eugene or Newberg, continue into the hip, outdoorsy, and food-driven city of **Portland.** Be sure to visit the several attractions found at green and beautiful **Washington Park,** the chic shops and restaurants of the **West End** and **Pearl District,** and the **Portland Art Museum,** situated

along Downtown's dapper Park Blocks. Like Seattle, the Rose City is renowned for its quirky, inviting neighborhoods, which abound with locavore-minded restaurants, artisanal-coffee roasters, swanky cocktail lounges, and smart boutiques—the **Central East Side, Hawthorne, Division Street, Mississippi,** and **Alberta** are among the best areas for exploring. From Portland, it's a straight three-hour drive back up to Seattle; if you have an extra day, consider a detour east into the magnificent **Columbia River Gorge.** En route to Seattle, you could also easily detour to **Mt. St. Helens, Mt. Rainier,** and the surprisingly vibrant and engaging city of **Tacoma.**

GREAT ITINERARIES

OREGON

Best of Oregon, 10 days

With 10 days, you can get a taste of Oregon's largest city, eco-conscious Portland, while also getting a nice sense of the state's geographical diversity—the mountainous and sweeping coast, gorgeous Crater Lake, the rugged Cascade Mountains, and the eastern high-desert regions.

Days 1 and 2: Portland

Start by spending a couple of days in Portland, where you can tour the museums and attractions that make up **Washington Park**, as well as the **Lan Su Chinese Garden** in Old Town, and the excellent museums and cultural institutions along Downtown's leafy **Park Blocks.** This city of vibrant, distinctive neighborhoods offers plenty of great urban exploring, with Nob Hill, Hawthorne, Alberta, and the Mississippi Avenue Arts District among the best areas for shopping, café-hopping, and people-watching. If you have a little extra time, consider spending a couple of hours just south of the city in the **Willamette Valley Wine Country**—it's an easy jaunt from Portland.

Days 3 and 4: Oregon Coast

(1½ hours by car from Portland to Cannon Beach)

Leave Portland early on Day 3 for the drive west about 100 miles on U.S. 30 to the small city of **Astoria,** which has several excellent spots for lunch and the **Columbia River Maritime Museum.** Pick the main scenic highway down the Oregon Coast, U.S. 101, and continue south, stopping at **Fort Stevens State Park** and **Fort Clatsop, in Lewis and Clark National Historic Park.** End the day in charming **Cannon Beach** (26 miles south of Astoria), which has a wealth of oceanfront hotels and inns,

many with views of one of the region's seminal features, 235-foot-tall **Haystack Rock.** Be sure to check out the stunning beach scenery at nearby **Ecola State Park** and **Oswald West State Park.**

The following morning, continue south down U.S. 101. In **Tillamook** (famous for its cheese), take a detour onto the **Three Capes Loop,** a stunning 35-mile byway. Stop in small and scenic **Pacific City** (at the south end of the loop) for lunch. Once you're back on U.S. 101, continue south to **Newport,** spending some time at the excellent **Oregon Coast Aquarium** as well as Oregon State University's fascinating **Hatfield Marine Science Center.** Your final stop is the charming village of **Florence,** 160 miles (four to six hours) from Cannon Beach.

Day 5: Eugene

(2½ hours by car from Florence to Eugene with detour at Oregon Dunes)

Spend the morning driving 20 miles south of Florence along U.S. 101 to scamper about the sandy bluffs at **Oregon Dunes National Recreation Area** near Reedsport. Then backtrack to Florence for lunch in Old Town before taking Highway 126 east for 60 miles to the attractive college city of **Eugene,** staying at one of the charming inns or bed-and-breakfasts near the leafy campus of the University of Oregon. Take a walk to the summit of **Skinner Butte,** which affords fine views of the city, and plan to have dinner at one of the top-notch restaurants at the **5th Street Public Market.** Budget some additional time in Eugene the following morning to visit two excellent University of Oregon museums, the **Jordan Schnitzer Museum of Art** and the **Oregon Museum of Natural History.**

1

Days 6 and 7: Crater Lake and Ashland

(3 hours by car from Eugene to Crater Lake National Park or Prospect)

From Eugene, take Interstate 5 south for 75 miles to Roseburg, and then head east along Highway 138 (the Umpqua River Scenic Byway), which twists and turns over the Cascade Range for 85 miles to the northern entrance of **Crater Lake National Park.** Once inside the park, you can continue along Rim Drive for another half hour for excellent views of the lake. Overnight in the park or in nearby **Prospect.**

The following morning, take the lake boat tour to **Wizard Island** and hike through the surrounding forest. In the afternoon, head southwest on Highway 62 to Interstate 5, and then on to **Ashland,** 95 miles (about two hours) from Crater Lake. Plan to stay the night in one of Ashland's many superb bed-and-breakfasts. Have dinner and attend one of the **Oregon Shakespeare Festival** productions (mid-February through October).

Days 8 and 9: Bend

(3½ hours by car from Ashland)

Get an early start out of Ashland, driving east along scenic Highway 140, which skirts picturesque **Upper Klamath Lake,** and then north on U.S. 97, stopping if you have time at **Collier Memorial State Park,** to reach the outdoorsy resort town of **Bend.** Here you can spend two nights checking out the parks, mountain hikes, microbreweries, and restaurants of the state's largest city east of the Cascades. Be sure to visit the outstanding **High Desert Museum,** the **Old Mill District,** and **Mt. Bachelor Ski Area.**

Day 10: Hood River

(3 hours by car from Bend)

From Bend, continue north up U.S. 97, and then northwest up U.S. 26 to **Mt. Hood,** 105 miles total. Have lunch at the historic **Timberline Lodge,** admiring the stunning views south down the Cascade Range. Pick up Highway 35 and drive around the east side of Mt. Hood and then north 40 miles up to the dapper town of **Hood River,** in the heart of the picturesque Columbia Gorge. Spend the night at one of the attractive inns, and try one of this town's stellar restaurants for dinner. From here it's just a 60-mile drive west along a scenic stretch of Interstate 84 to reach Portland.

GREAT ITINERARIES

WASHINGTON

Best of Washington, 10 days

It's hard to say which is more alluring for Washington visitors: the island and sculpted bays of Puget Sound, the volcanic peaks of the Cascade Range, or the lively neighborhoods and first-rate attractions, locavore-minded restaurants, and trendy music clubs of Seattle. Here's a tour that reveals all of the state's charms.

Days 1 and 2: Seattle

Begin with two days of touring this world-class hub of acclaimed arts, culture, and dining, visiting Downtown's must-see sites, including **Pike Place Market**, the **Seattle Art Museum**, and—a bit north—the **Seattle Center** (and its iconic **Space Needle**). Set aside at least a half day to investigate some of the city's liveliest neighborhoods, including **Capitol Hill**, with its indie shops, hipster bars, and diverting cafés, and similarly inviting **Ballard** and **Fremont**. If you have extra time, consider a quick day trip to up-and-coming **Tacoma**, with its several excellent museums (including the **LeMay Car Museum** and **International Museum of Glass**), and to the nearby wine-tasting hub of **Woodinville**, with more than 150 tasting rooms.

Days 3 and 4: Olympic National Park

(3 hours by car ferry and car from Seattle, via Bainbridge Island)

Get an early start from Seattle on Day 3, taking the ferry from Downtown across Puget Sound to scenic **Bainbridge Island** for lunch and shopping in the village of **Winslow**, and perhaps a quick tour of **Bloedel Reserve**, before continuing the drive to historic **Port Angeles**, which you can use as an overnight base for exploring **Olympic National Park**.

Hurricane Ridge is the park's nearest section, but on Day 4, depending on how ambitious you are, you could drive west to the **Hoh Rain Forest** section of the park, as well as the coastal areas out at **La Push**, and possibly all the way down to **Lake Quinault** (125 miles from Port Angeles). Try to visit at least one of the rain forests, where you can hike amid huge stands of Douglas firs and Sitka spruces.

Day 5: Whidbey Island

(1½ hours by car and car ferry from Port Angeles)

Drive from Port Angeles to the Victorian-era town of **Port Townsend**, a good stop for lunch and a look at the **Northwest Maritime Center**, and then catch the ferry to **Whidbey Island**, where there are plenty of sophisticated shops, galleries, restaurants, and inns in the laid-back, friendly hamlets of **Langley**, **Greenbank**, and **Coupeville** (where you disembark the ferry). Nature lovers shouldn't miss **Ebey's Landing National Historic Reserve**. To be closer to where you're headed on Day 6, you might consider staying just north of Whidbey on **Fidalgo Island**, which is home to **Anacortes**, where ferries leave for the San Juan Islands.

Days 6 and 7: The Northern Cascades

(2½ hours by car from Whidbey Island to North Cascades National Park)

Leave the Puget Sound region, perhaps stopping in the picturesque Skagit Valley towns of **La Conner** and **Mount Vernon** for lunch, and head for Washington's stunning, skyscraping Cascades Range, passing through the old logging town of **Sedro-Woolley** and making your way up the dramatic **North Cascades Highway** (Highway 20) into **North Cascades National Park**. You could stay in the park at **Skagit River Resort** or a bit farther east in **Winthrop**.

On Day 7, turn south and follow the upper Columbia River down into **Chelan**

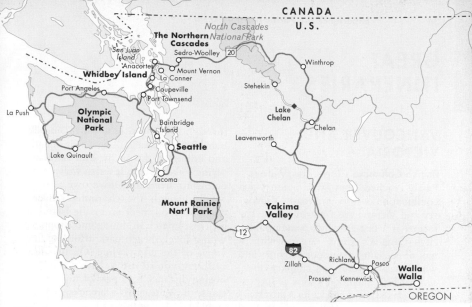

(2½ hours from North Cascades), the base area for exploring fjordlike, 55-mile-long **Lake Chelan**, the state's deepest lake, which you can explore by boat or even floatplane. Stay in Chelan, up at the north end of the lake at **Stehekin** (go by floatplane to save time), or a bit farther south and west in the endearingly cute, if kitschy, Bavarian-style town of **Leavenworth**, with its gingerbread architecture and cozy German restaurants.

Day 8: Walla Walla
(4 hours by car from Chelan)

From the Lake Chelan area, it's a long but pleasant 200-mile drive southeast, much of it along the mighty Columbia River, to reach what's developed into the most impressive of the Pacific Northwest's wine-producing areas, **Walla Walla**. This once-sleepy college and farming town has blossomed with stylish restaurants and shops in recent years, and you'll find dozens of tasting rooms, both in town and in the surrounding countryside.

Day 9: Yakima Valley
(2½ hours from Walla Walla)

The great wine touring continues as you return west from Walla Walla through the **Tri-Cities** communities of Pasco, Kennewick, and Richland, following Interstate 82 to **Yakima**. Good stops for visiting wineries include **Richland, Benton City, Prosser,** and **Zillah.** Yakima itself is a good overnight stop.

Day 10: Mount Rainier National Park
(2½ hours from Yakima)

On the morning of Day 10, take U.S. 12 west from Yakima 102 miles to Ohanapecosh, the southern entrance to **Mount Rainier National Park.** When you arrive, take the 31-mile, two-hour drive on Sunrise Road, which reveals the "back" (northeast) side of Rainier. A room at the **Paradise Inn** is your base for the night. On the following day, energetic hikers could tackle one of the four- to six-hour trails that lead up among the park's many peaks. Or, if it's your last day of traveling, try one of the shorter ranger-led walks through wildflower meadows. It's about a two-hour drive back to Seattle.

Alternatives

You really need a couple of days to enjoy one of Washington's loveliest areas, the **San Juan Islands,** ideally spending a night on two of the three main islands. If you're unable to add two days, you could easily make time by cutting out the Walla Walla–Yakima portion.

GREAT ITINERARIES

VANCOUVER AND VICTORIA

British Columbia's Top Cities, 7 days

Easily reached from Washington via a combination of ferry and roads, Vancouver and Victoria are a pair of gems. The former is a fast-growing, contemporary city—Canada's third largest—with a mix of enchanting outdoor activities and world-class cultural and culinary diversions. Much smaller, Victoria is surprisingly relaxed and compact for a provincial capital—it's renowned for its colorful gardens, well-groomed bike paths, and picturesque Inner Harbour.

Days 1 through 4: Vancouver

Start with two or three days in Vancouver itself. You'll want to dedicate a full day to touring 1,000-acre **Stanley Park,** with its 9-km (5½-mile) seawall for walking, cycling, and skating; and the **Vancouver Aquarium Marine Science Center,** a family favorite. From the park, you're at the edge of Vancouver's bustling **West End,** which is rife with interesting shopping and breezy cafés. Continue up the city's main retail drag, **Robson Street,** to reach some of Vancouver's top museums, including the **Vancouver Art Gallery** and the **Bill Reid Gallery of Northwest Coast Art.**

On additional days in Vancouver, explore the Victorian-era **Gaslamp Quarter** and adjacent **Chinatown,** home to the very interesting **Dr. Sun Yat-Sen Classical Chinese Garden.** Stroll over to hip and exciting **Yaletown,** a trendy warren of dining and shopping, and catch the Aquabus across False Creek to **Granville Island,** a former industrial wasteland that's become arguably—with Stanley Park—Vancouver's premier attraction. Here you can eat and shop your way

through 50,000-square-foot **Granville Island Public Market,** taking a seat outside and admiring the yachts and sailboats plying False Creek. It's also well worth detouring from the Downtown area to stroll through the charming **Kitsilano** neighborhood, near Granville Island, a gentrified patch of dining and shopping with a lovely beach park affording fine views of the city skyline. On this side of town, you're within easy driving or busing distance to a pair of top attractions, the **Museum of Anthropology** on the campus of University of British Columbia, and **Queen Elizabeth Park,** the highest point in the city.

On your final day in Vancouver, explore the mountains and parks of the **North Shore,** hiking across **Capilano Suspension Bridge** and through the adjoining rain forest, and taking the aerial tram to the top of **Grouse Mountain.** You could visit these attractions before catching the ferry from Horseshoe Bay across the Georgia Strait to Nanaimo, and then making the two-hour drive south to Victoria. Or if you're headed to Victoria directly from Downtown Vancouver, you could instead drive south from Vancouver to Tsawwassen, and catch a ferry to Swartz Bay, from which it's a 30-minute drive south to Victoria.

Days 5 through 7: Victoria

(4 hours from Vancouver via Horseshoe Bay–Nanaimo ferry, 3 hours via Tsawwassen–Swartz Bay ferry)

British Columbia's verdant and welcoming capital city, Victoria, is compact enough to explore mostly on foot, although with a car you can more easily reach some of the city's interesting outlying attractions, as well as the wineries of the Saanich Peninsula. Give yourself

1

a couple of days to see the top sites, including the artful architecture of Chinatown; the **Emily Carr House,** dedicated to one of the nation's most celebrated artists; and the fascinating **Royal British Columbia Museum,** where you could easily spend a few hours. Plan to have high tea at the regal **Fairmont Empress** hotel, which overlooks the city's picturesque **Inner Harbour.**

This is a great area for biking, with older residential areas like **Oak Bay, Rockland,** and **Fairfield** popular for touring on foot or on two wheels—highlights include **Abkhazi Garden** and **Craigdarroch Castle.**

Set aside a full day for a side trip outside of Victoria proper to the **Saanich Peninsula,** with its wineries, bike paths, and perhaps the most impressive attraction in the entire region, 55-acre **Butchart Gardens.**

Alternatives
En route from Vancouver to Victoria, many travelers tack on a couple of days in the nearby **Gulf Islands,** which are just off Vancouver Island and bear a strong resemblance in scenery and personality to the **San Juan Islands.**

OUTDOOR ADVENTURES

HIKING

In the Pacific Northwest, hiking is potentially a year-round sport, though only experts should attempt hiking in the snowy higher elevations in winter. One of the greatest aspects of this region is the diverse terrain, from high alpine scrambles that require stamina to flowered meadows that invite a relaxed pace to stunning coastal areas that offer a mix of level and precipitous terrain.

Of course, many of the best trails in the region are in national parks (Crater Lake, Olympic, Mount Rainier, and North Cascades among them). We've focused on trails elsewhere in the region, including some spectacular hidden gems.

Best Hikes

Forest Park, Portland, OR. You can easily walk to the network of more than 80 miles of densely forested trails, many leading to spectacular vistas, from Downtown hotels, making this 5,000-acre urban wilderness one of the most accessible in the country. A good place to start is Washington Park, with its Japanese Garden and International Rose Test Garden.

Oswald West State Park, Manzanita, OR. The trails at this state park, just south of popular Cannon Beach, lead to sweeping headlands, to a sheltered beach popular for surfing, and to the top of Neahkahnie Mountain, from which you have a view of more than 20 miles of coastline.

Smith Rock State Park, Redmond, OR. Although world-famous for rock climbing, this maze of soaring rock formations has a number of trails well suited to casual hikers; the 3-mile Smith Rocks Loop hike is a favorite.

Table Rock, Central Point, OR. Comprising a pair of monolithic rocky peaks outside Medford, Table Rock makes a great quick and relaxing scramble—from the top, you're treated to wonderful views of the Cascades.

Wallowa Mountains, Enterprise, OR. This range of granite peaks in eastern Oregon, near Hells Canyon, is rife with crystalline alpine lakes and meadows, rushing rivers, and thickly forested valleys that fall between mountain ridges. Trails lead from both Enterprise and La Grande.

Beacon Rock State Park, North Bonneville, WA. Although Multnomah Falls, on the Oregon side of the Columbia Gorge, provides access to plenty of cool trails, the hiking at this park across the river provides bigger wows and fewer crowds. Scaling the 848-foot rock for which the park is named is fun and easy, but you can also access longer and more challenging day hikes to Hamilton Mountain and Table Mountain.

Cape Disappointment State Park, Ilwaco, WA. One of the top spots on the Washington coast for a beach hike, Cape Disappointment is at the mouth of the Columbia River and also contains exhibits documenting Lewis and Clark's journey, which ended here.

Moran State Park, Orcas Island, WA. Explore the 14 hiking trails at Moran State Park, which contains the largest mountain in the San Juan Islands, for exhilarating views of the islands, the Cascades, the Olympics, and Vancouver Island.

Snow Lake, Snoqualmie, WA. Relative proximity to Seattle makes this 8-mile trail into the dramatic Alpine Lakes Wilderness a bit crowded on weekends, but don't let that deter you—this hike is one of the state's true stunners.

BEACHES

Unless you're a truly hardy soul, or you've brought your wet suit, taking a trip to the beach in the Pacific Northwest probably won't involve much swimming—water temperatures in these parts rarely exceed 55°F, even in late summer. However, residents of this part of the world love going to the coast. The mountainous coastline in Oregon—which frequently inspires comparisons with everywhere from Big Sur to New Zealand—is home to rugged, curvy, smooth-as-glass beaches ideal for tide pooling, strolling, and surfing. And you'll find similarly spectacular scenery as you continue into Washington, along the Long Beach Peninsula, up around the coast of Olympic National Park, and in the many islands of Puget Sound. Across the border, both Victoria and Vancouver have lovely, graceful beaches set against gorgeous mountain backdrops. Throughout the region, from spring through fall, there's a good chance of spotting whales swimming and diving just offshore (and plenty of tour boats offer cruises that afford better views).

Best Beaches

Cannon Beach, OR. The nearest coastal town to Portland also contains some of the state's most breathtaking beaches, including a stretch that fringes downtown. The 235-foot-tall Haystack Rock rises monumentally above the beach, and on the north side of town, Ecola State Park is a long stretch of rocky headlands punctuated by secluded beaches.

Cape Kiwanda State Natural Area, Pacific City, OR. Yet another formation called Haystack Rock, this one soaring to 327 feet, defines the coast at this dramatic stretch of beach that's part of Oregon's famed Three Capes Loop scenic drive.

Massive waves pound the wide beach here, which has dozens of tidal pools at low tide.

Cape Perpetua Scenic Area, Yachats, OR. This 2,700-acre oceanfront wilderness on the central coast of Oregon is home to an 800-foot-high coastal lookout point, steep and easy hiking trails (including one through a fern-filled rain forest), an educational nature center, and a rocky but beautiful beach.

Oregon Dunes National Recreation Area, Reedsport, OR. Smooth, wind-sculpted dunes—some rising as high as 500 feet—are the highlight of this recreation area near Florence, the largest expanse of coastal sand dunes on the continent.

Port Orford, OR. The westernmost town in the continental United States, this artsy small hamlet along the southern coast is home to several great little beaches, including Battle Rock Park, which is just steps from downtown, and Paradise Point State Beach, a long stretch of sand extending north from Port Orford headland.

Alki Point and Beach, Seattle, WA. The quintessential sunning, beachcombing, and kite-flying stretch of sand, this West Seattle park encompasses 2½ miles of beachfront and is steps from several restaurants.

Second and Third Beaches, Olympic National Park, WA. These national park beaches are ideal for tide pooling, kayaking, surfing, and watching gray whales frolic offshore in spring and fall.

Kitsilano Beach, Vancouver, BC. A lovely urban beach in the quiet and charming Kitsilano neighborhood, the shore here has plenty of diversions (tennis, a huge pool) and gorgeous views of the city skyline and North Shore Mountains in the distance.

BIKING

The Pacific Northwest is ideal for—and hugely popular with—biking enthusiasts. You'll find rental shops, bike-share programs, and a handful of tour operators in Portland and Seattle, and in all of these cities as well as Vancouver, Victoria, Eugene, Tacoma, and other municipalities, dedicated bike lanes and separate multiuse trails (for bikes, runners, and pedestrians) proliferate. And although bikes aren't permitted on many hiking trails, including many of those in national parks, roads in parks and many other scenic regions have wide shoulders and are well suited to cycling adventures.

Best Biking Routes

Columbia Historic Highway, OR. Just 17 miles east of Portland, this narrow, rolling highway climbs through the spectacular Columbia Gorge, past Multnomah Falls, and by the Vista House at Crown Point, a dramatic scenic overlook.

Portland and Sauvie Island, OR. Portland has miles of bike lanes, a bike-share program, and plenty of rental shops. In town, biking is a great way to explore leafy East Side neighborhoods like Hawthorne, Mississippi, and Alberta, which all abound with hip shops and cafés. Nearby are the rural and relatively flat roads of Sauvie Island, with its bounty of pick-your-own berry farms.

U.S. 97, near Bend, OR. The 40 miles or so north from Lava Butte through Bend and on up to Smith Rock State Park have awesome high-desert scenery and receive plenty of sunshine year-round.

Burke-Gilman Trail, Seattle, WA. Extending along an abandoned rail line through Seattle, including part of the lively Ballard community, this 27-mile multiuse trail draws plenty of bikers year-round. The city itself has many miles of bike lanes and paths and a popular bike-share program.

Highway 20, North Cascades National Park, WA. You'll want to be in good shape before tackling the hilly North Cascades Highway, but few roads in the state offer more mesmerizing scenery.

Lopez Island, San Juan Islands, WA. All the islands in Puget Sound, including Whidbey and Bainbridge to the south, are massively popular with cyclists, but rural Lopez Island—with its gently rolling terrain and very little auto traffic—is especially well suited to two-wheel traffic.

Mount Vernon and La Conner, WA. Biking around these two picturesque Skagit County communities is popular year-round, but this activity is especially fun in spring, when Tulip Country Bike Tours arranges trips through the region's glorious tulip fields.

Lochside Regional Trail, Victoria, BC. A fun way to get from the ferry terminal at Swartz Bay to Downtown Victoria, and to access a number of wineries, this 29-km (18-mile) level route is along a former rail track.

Lower Seymour Valley Conservation Reserve, Vancouver, BC. Easily reached from Downtown Vancouver, the reserve in the soaring North Shore Mountains comprises some 25 km (15½ miles) of trails through leafy rain forests, plus an easier, paved, 10-km (6-mile) track.

Seaside Route, Vancouver, BC. The 32-km (20-mile) Seaside Route, which curves around the seawall through False Creek and Stanley Park and then south into Kitsilano, is particularly dramatic.

WHALE-WATCHING
IN THE PACIFIC NORTHWEST

The thrill of seeing whales in the wild is, for many, one of the most enduring memories of a trip to the Pacific Northwest. In this part of the world, you'll generally spot two species—gray whales and killer "orca" whales.

About 20,000 grays migrate up the West Coast in spring and back down again in early winter (a smaller group of gray whales live off the Oregon coast all summer). From late spring through early autumn about 80 orcas inhabit Washington's Puget Sound and BC's Georgia Strait. Although far fewer in number, the orcas live in pods and travel in predictable patterns; therefore chances are high that you will see a pod on any given trip. Some operators claim sighting rates of 90 percent; others offer guaranteed sightings, meaning that you can repeat the tour free of charge until you spot a whale.

COMMON PACIFIC NORTHWEST SPECIES

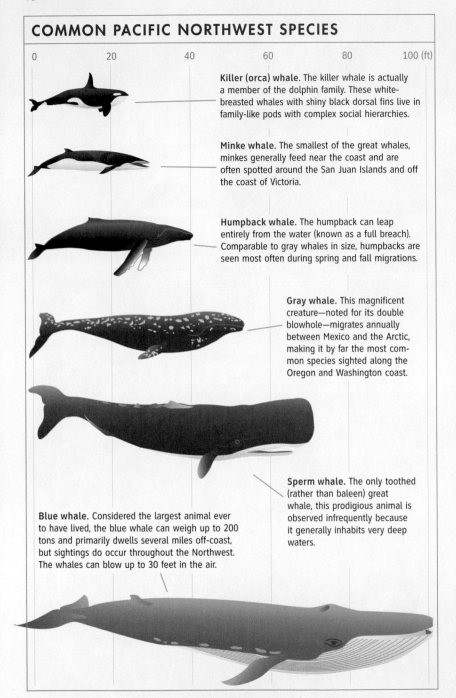

0   20   40   60   80   100 (ft)

Killer (orca) whale. The killer whale is actually a member of the dolphin family. These white-breasted whales with shiny black dorsal fins live in family-like pods with complex social hierarchies.

Minke whale. The smallest of the great whales, minkes generally feed near the coast and are often spotted around the San Juan Islands and off the coast of Victoria.

Humpback whale. The humpback can leap entirely from the water (known as a full breach). Comparable to gray whales in size, humpbacks are seen most often during spring and fall migrations.

Gray whale. This magnificent creature—noted for its double blowhole—migrates annually between Mexico and the Arctic, making it by far the most common species sighted along the Oregon and Washington coast.

Sperm whale. The only toothed (rather than baleen) great whale, this prodigious animal is observed infrequently because it generally inhabits very deep waters.

Blue whale. Considered the largest animal ever to have lived, the blue whale can weigh up to 200 tons and primarily dwells several miles off-coast, but sightings do occur throughout the Northwest. The whales can blow up to 30 feet in the air.

TAKING A TOUR

Spotting an orca in the Haro Strait between British Columbia and Washington

CHOOSING YOUR BOAT

The type of boat you choose does not affect how close you can get to the whales. For the safety of whales and humans, government regulations require boats to stay at least 100 meters (328 feet) from the pods, though closer encounters are possible if whales approach a boat when its engine is off.

Motor Launches. These cruisers carry from 30 to more than 80 passengers. They are comfortable, with washrooms, protection from the elements, and even snack-and-drink concessions. They can be either glass-enclosed or open-air.

Zodiacs. Open inflatable boats, Zodiacs carry about 12 passengers. They are smaller and more agile than cruisers and offer both an exciting ride bouncing over the waves and an eye-level view of the whales. Passengers are supplied with warm, waterproof survival suits. Note: Zodiac tours are not recommended for people with back or neck problems, pregnant women, or small children.

Most companies have naturalists on board as guides, as well as hydrophones that, if you get close enough, allow you to listen to the whales singing and vocalizing. Although the focus is on whales, you also have a good chance of spotting marine birds, Dall's porpoises, dolphins, seals, and sea lions, as well as other marine life. And, naturally, there's the scenery of forested islands, distant mountains, and craggy coastline.

MOTION SICKNESS

Seasickness isn't usually a problem in the sheltered waters of Puget Sound and the Georgia Strait, but seas can get choppy off the Washington and Oregon coasts. If you're not a good sailor, it's wise to wear a seasickness band or take anti-nausea medication. Ginger candy often works, too.

THE OREGON AND WASHINGTON COAST

A full breach in open waters is a thrilling sight

WHEN TO GO

Mid-December through mid-January is the best time for viewing the southbound migration, with April through mid-June the peak period for the northbound return (when whales swim closer to shore). Throughout summer, several hundred gray whales remain in Oregon waters, often feeding within close view of land. Mornings are often the best time for viewing, as it's more commonly overcast at this time, which means less glare and calmer seas. Try to watch for vapor or water expelled from whales' spouts on the horizon.

WHAT IT COSTS

Trips are generally 2 hours and prices for adults range from about $25 to $40.

RECOMMENDED OUTFITTERS

Depoe Bay, with its sheltered, deepwater harbor, is Oregon's whale-watching capital, and here you'll find several outfitters.

Dockside Charters (☏ 800/733–8915 ⊕ www.docksidedepoebay. com) and **Tradewind Charters** (☏ 800/445–8730 ⊕ www.tradewindscharters.com) have excellent reputations. Green-oriented **Eco Tours of Oregon** (☏ 888/868–7733, ⊕ www. ecotours-of-oregon.com) offers full day tours that depart from Portland hotels and include a stop along the coast at Siletz Bay, a 75-minute charter boat tour, lunch, and stops at state parks near Newport and Lincoln City.

Along the Washington coast, several of the fishing-charter companies in Westport offer seasonal whale-watching cruises, including **Deep Sea Charters** (☏ 800/562–0151 ⊕ www.deepseacha-
rters.net) and **Ocean Sportfishing Charters** (☏ 800/562–0105, ⊕ www. oceansportfishing.com).

BEST VIEWING FROM SHORE

Washington: On Long Beach Peninsula, the North Head Lighthouse at the mouth of the Columbia River, makes an excellent perch for whale sightings. Westport, farther up the coast at the mouth of Grays Harbor, is another great spot.

Oregon Coast: You can spot gray whales all summer long and especially during the spring migration—excellent locales include Neahkanie Mountain Overlook near Manzanita, Cape Lookout State Park, the Whale Watching Center in Depoe Bay, Cape Perpetua Interpretive Center in Yachats, and Cape Blanco Lighthouse near Port Orford.

PUGET SOUND AND GEORGIA STRAIT

Killer whales in the Puget Sound

WHEN TO GO

Prime time for viewing the three pods of orcas that inhabit this region's waterways is March through September. Less commonly, you may see minke, gray, and humpback whales around the same time.

WHAT IT COSTS

Trips in the San Juan waters are from 3 to 6 hours and prices range from $60 to $120 per adult. Trips in Canada are generally 4 to 6 hours and prices range from $125 to $175 per adult.

RECOMMENDED OUTFITTERS

Many tours depart from Friday Harbor on San Juan Island, among them **Eclipse Charters** (☎ 360/376–6566 ⊕ www.orcasisland-whales.com), **San Juan Excursions** (☎ 800/809–4253 ⊕ www.watchwhales. com), and **Western Prince Cruises** (☎ 800/757–6722 ⊕ www.orcawhalewatch.

com). **San Juan Cruises** (☎ 800/443–4552 ⊕ www. whales.com) offers both day- and overnight whale-watching cruises between Bellingham and Victoria.

One rather fortuitous approach to whale-watching is simply to ride one of the **Washington State Ferries** (☎ 888/808–7977 ⊕ www. wsdot.wa.gov/ferries) out of Anacortes through the San Juans. During the summer killer-whale season, naturalists work on the ferries and talk about the whales and other wildlife.

In Canada, **Wild Whales Vancouver** (☎ 604/699–2011 ⊕ www.whalesvan-couver.com) departs from Granville Island on both glass-domed and open-air vessels. **Vancouver Whale Watch** (☎ 604/274–9565 ⊕ www.vancouverwhale-watch.com) is another first-rate company.

Victoria has an even greater number of whale-watching outfitters. **Great Pacific Adventures** (☎ 877/733–6722 ⊕ www. greatpacificadventures. com), **Springtide Whale Tours** (☎ 800/470–3474 ⊕ www.victoriawhale-watching.com) and **Prince of Whales** (☎ 888/383–4884 ⊕ www. princeofwhales.com) use boats equipped with hydrophones. The latter also offers trips on a 74-passenger cruiser.

BEST VIEWING FROM SHORE

A prime spot for viewing orcas is Lime Kiln State Park, on the west side of San Juan Island. On the Canadian side, you can sometimes see whales right off Oak Bay in Victoria.

CRUISES

Alaska Cruises

During the Alaska cruise season (May–September), Seattle and Vancouver are among North America's busiest ports of embarkation. Ships debarking from these ports proceed directly to Alaska, with one exception: those leaving from Seattle usually make one stop in Victoria or, occasionally, Prince Rupert, BC. Additionally, many of the cruise lines that sail in Alaska (Carnival, Celebrity, Crystal, Disney, Holland America, Norwegian, Oceania, Princess, Regent Seven Seas, Royal Caribbean, Seabourn, and Silversea are the biggies) stop in Astoria, on the northern Oregon coast, during their seasonal repositioning cruises, when they move ships between Alaska and California, the Mexican Riviera, or even the Caribbean via the Panama Canal. These cruises typically take place in April or May and then again in October, usually starting or ending in Vancouver or Seattle, and sometimes calling in Victoria; additionally, Norwegian Cruise Line often calls on the BC port of Nanaimo during these repositioning cruises. **Cruise Lines International Association** (⊕ *www.cruising.org*) is a good starting point if you don't have a specific carrier in mind.

Pacific Northwest Cruises

From early April through early November, a few cruise lines with smaller ships offer excursions focused specifically on the Pacific Northwest, usually around the San Juan Islands and Puget Sound (leaving from Seattle), or along the Columbia and Snake rivers (leaving from Portland or Clarkston, WA). **UnCruise Adventures** offers seven-day trips exploring Puget Sound, the Olympic Peninsula, the San Juan Islands, the Gulf Islands, Victoria, and other parts of Vancouver Island; and seven-day excursions (some of them wine themed) along the Columbia and Snake Rivers, calling at Richland, Clarkston–Hells Canyon, Walla Walla, Palouse Falls, The Dalles, Hood River, Bonneville Dam, Portland, and Astoria.

American Cruise Lines runs seven-day excursions along the Columbia and Snake Rivers, departing either from Portland or Clarkston (WA), on a Victorian-style stern-wheeler, the *Queen of the West*. The same company offers seven-day Puget Sound cruises out of Seattle that stop at Anacortes, Port Townsend, Poulsbo, Port Angeles, Victoria, BC, and the San Juan Islands. **Bluewater Adventures** provides a number of tours along the coast of British Columbia, with a particular focus on the Gulf Islands and northern Vancouver Island.

Cruise Line Contacts

American Cruise Lines. ☎ *800/460–4518* ⊕ *www.americancruiselines.com.*

Bluewater Adventures. ☎ *888/877–1770* ⊕ *www.bluewateradventures.ca.*

UnCruise Adventures. ☎ *888/862–8881* ⊕ *www.uncruise.com.*

2

PORTLAND

WELCOME TO PORTLAND

TOP REASONS TO GO

★ **Play in the parks:**
Head to Washington Park's Japanese Garden and International Rose Test Garden; stroll along the Willamette in Tom McCall Waterfront Park, or ramble amid the evergreens atop Mt. Tabor.

★ **View works of art:**
Take part in either the First Thursday Pearl District and Last Thursday Alberta Street art walks if you can. Galleries stay open late, often with receptions and openings.

★ **Float on:** Gaze at Portland's gorgeous skyline in the afternoon light, while gently gliding down the Willamette River aboard the *Portland Spirit*.

★ **Sample the liquid assets:** Visit a few of the dozens of superb local producers of craft spirits and beer, artisanal coffee and tea, and fine wine.

★ **Eat locally:** Plenty of visitors to Portland build their entire daily itineraries around eating; food trucks, cafés, and restaurants showcase the city's farm-to-table, locavore ethic.

1 Downtown. At the center of it all, Portland's Downtown boasts the Portland Art Museum, Pioneer Courthouse Square, and the Portland Farmers' Market along with notable restaurants.

2 Old Town/Chinatown. This is the area for Asian-inspired public art and the Lan Su Chinese Garden. It's also home to the Portland Saturday Market, North America's largest open-air handicraft market.

4 Nob Hill. From offbeat to upscale, this neighborhood's shopping, restaurants, and bars draw a sophisticated crowd.

5 Forest Park. Forest Park is the largest forested area within city limits in the nation. Trailheads are easily accessible from Nob Hill.

6 West Hills and Southwest. This neighborhood is home to Washington Park, which contains many must-sees, including the Hoyt Arboretum, International Rose Test Garden, Japanese Garden, and Portland Children's Museum.

7 North. The "fifth quadrant," North Portland sits on the peninsula formed by the joining of the Willamette River and the Columbia River. Part working-class, part trendy, North Mississippi Avenue and North Williams Street are hip dining and drinking destinations.

8 Northeast. Containing the Rose Garden basketball arena, the Lloyd Center Mall, the Alberta Arts District, and some of the city's least and most affluent neighborhoods, Portland's Northeast quadrant is quite diverse.

9 Southeast. The vibrant pockets of foodie-approved restaurants make the Southeast a Portland cultural must-see. This neighborhood is also kid-friendly with the OMSI science museum and Mount Tabor Park.

GETTING ORIENTED

Geographically speaking, Portland is relatively easy to navigate. The city's 200-foot-long blocks are highly walkable, and mapped out into quadrants. The Willamette River divides east and west and Burnside Street separates north from south. "Northwest" refers to the area north of Burnside and west of the river; "Southwest" refers to the area south of Burnside and west of the river; "Northeast" refers to the area north of Burnside and east of the river; "Southeast" refers to the area south of Burnside and east of the river. As you travel around the Portland metropolitan area, keep in mind that named east and west streets intersect numbered avenues, run north to south, and begin at each side of the river. For instance, S.W. 12th Avenue is 12 blocks west of the Willamette. Most of Downtown's streets are one-way.

EAST OF WILLAMETTE RIVER

3 Pearl District. Bordering Old Town to the northwest is Portland's trendy and posh neighborhood teaming with upscale restaurants, bars, and shopping, along with pricey condos and artists' lofts. Don't leave Portland without visiting Powell's City of Books here.

Updated
by Andrew
Collins

What distinguishes Portland, Oregon, from the rest of America's cityscapes? Or from the rest of the world's urban destinations for that matter? In a Northwest nutshell: everything. For some, it's the wealth of cultural offerings and never-ending culinary choices; for others, it's Portland's proximity to the ocean and mountains, or simply the beauty of having all these attributes in one place.

Strolling through Downtown or within one of Portland's numerous neighborhoods, there's an unmistakable vibrancy to this city—one that is encouraged by clean air, infinite trees, and a blend of historic and modern architecture. Portland's various nicknames—Rose City, Bridgetown, Beervana, Brewtopia—tell its story.

Rich cultural offerings, prime historic and modern architecture, endless recreational activities, and a friendly feel make Portland alluring for just about everyone. But it seems that Portland's food scene is one of its biggest attractions these days. It's true that Portland's filled with amazing restaurants—though it's not necessarily the recipes that are causing all the commotion. Rather, it's the locavore movement—using ingredients that are raised, grown, or foraged within a reasonable distance—that's got diners and chefs excited. Often, diners experience savory fish, fowl, or pasta dishes made with seasonal fruit and vegetable accompaniments that have just been plucked from the vine or ground.

PORTLAND PLANNER

WHEN TO GO

Portland's mild climate is best from June through September. Hotels are often filled in July and August, so it's important to book reservations in advance. Spring and fall are also excellent times to visit. The weather usually remains quite good, and the prices for accommodations, transportation, and tours can be lower (and the crowds much smaller) in the most popular destinations. In winter, snow is uncommon in the city but abundant in the nearby mountains, making the region a skier's dream.

Average daytime summer highs are in the 70s; winter temperatures are generally in the 40s. Rainfall varies greatly from one locale to another. In the coastal mountains, for example, 160 inches of rain fall annually, creating temperate rain forests. Portland has an average of only 36 inches of rainfall a year—less than New York, Chicago, or Miami. In winter, however, the rainy days may never seem to end. More than 75% of Portland's annual precipitation occurs from October through March.

GETTING HERE AND AROUND

AIR TRAVEL

It takes about 5 hours to fly nonstop to Portland from New York, 4 hours from Chicago and Atlanta, and 2½ hours from Los Angeles. Flying to Seattle takes just under an hour, and flying to Vancouver takes just over an hour.

Portland International Airport (PDX) is an efficient, modern airport with service to most major national and a handful of international destinations. It's a relatively uncrowded facility, and both check-in and security lines tend to proceed quickly. It's also easily accessible from Downtown Portland, both by car and public transit.

Portland International Airport *(PDX).* This is the city's—and the region's—major airport. You'll find a pretty good selection of local restaurants and shops inside the terminal. ⊠ *7000 N.E. Airport Way, Portland* ☎ *877/739–4636* ⊕ *www.pdx.com.*

GROUND
TRANSPOR-
TATION

Taking the MAX, Portland's light rail train, to and from Portland International Airport is straightforward. The Red Line MAX stops right at the terminal, and the approximately 35- to 45-minute ride to Downtown costs $2.50. Trains run daily from early morning until around midnight—MAX won't be available to some very late-arriving passengers, but it generally runs early enough to catch even the first flights of the day out of Portland, which typically depart around 6 am. You purchase your ticket before boarding at one of the vending machines in the terminal and at every MAX stop; tickets are also good on TriMet buses and the Portland Streetcar, and transfers within 2½ hours of the time of purchase are free.

Contacts TriMet/MAX. ☎ *503/238–7433* ⊕ *www.trimet.org.*

CAR TRAVEL

Portland is a fairly easy city to navigate by car, and if you're planning to explore neighboring regions—such as the coast, Willamette Wine Country, and Columbia Gorge—it's best to do so by car, as public transportation options to these areas, especially the coast, is limited. That said, parking Downtown can get expensive and a car isn't necessary for getting around the city itself. One practical strategy is going without a car during the days you plan to spend in the city center, and then renting a car just for those days when you're venturing outside of the city or exploring some of the East Side neighborhoods, which have ample free parking. Most major rental agencies have Downtown offices, and renting Downtown can save you plenty of money, as you avoid paying the hefty taxes and surcharges that airport agencies charge.

Portland is easily reached via the West Coast's major interstate highway, Interstate 5, which connects Portland to Seattle (which is a three-hour drive north) and Eugene (a little over a two-hour drive south). Interstate 84 begins in Downtown Portland and runs east into the Columbia Gorge and eventually to Idaho. U.S. 26 is the main route to the Oregon Coast west from Downtown, and to Mt. Hood going east. Bypass freeways are Interstate 205, which links Interstate 5 and Interstate 84 before crossing the Columbia River north into Washington, and Interstate 405, which arcs around western Downtown. Most city-center streets are one-way, and some Downtown streets—including 5th and 6th avenues—are limited primarily to bus and MAX traffic (with just one lane for cars, and limited turns).

PARKING Compared with other major U.S. cities, Portland has ample parking, even Downtown, both metered and in garages. The most affordable and accessible option is to park in one of several city-owned "Smart Park" lots. Rates start at $1.60 per hour (short-term parking, two hours or less) to $5 per hour (long-term parking, weekdays 5 am–6 pm), with a $15 daily maximum; weekends and evenings have lower rates. The best part about Smart Park is that hundreds of participating merchants validate tickets, covering the first two hours of parking when you spend at least $25 in their establishments.

There are numerous privately owned lots around the city as well; fees for these vary and can be quite pricey, and Downtown hotels also charge significantly (as much as $30 to $40 nightly).

Downtown street parking is metered only, and enforcement is vigilant. You can use cash or a credit card to pay ($1.60 per hour) at machines located on each block; display your receipt on the inside of your curbside window. Metered spaces are mostly available for one to three hours, with a few longer-term spaces available on certain streets.

Outside of the Downtown core, you'll find plenty of free street parking, although time limits (usually an hour to three hours) are enforced in some busier, commercial parts of town, including the Pearl District and most of Nob Hill. On the east side of the river, unmetered parking is the norm.

TRIMET/MAX TRAVEL

TriMet operates an extensive system of buses, streetcars, and light-rail trains. The North–South streetcar line runs from Nob Hill through the Pearl District, Downtown, and Portland State University campus to South Waterfront. The A and B Loop streetcar lines cross the Willamette River to the East Side via Steel Bridge and the new Tilikum Crossing Bridge.

Metropolitan Area Express, which everybody simply calls MAX, links the eastern and western Portland suburbs with Downtown, Washington Park and the Oregon Zoo, the Lloyd Center district, the Convention Center, and the Rose Quarter. When the Tilikum Crossing Bridge opened in fall 2015, an extension of Downtown's MAX Green line was extended to S.E. Division Street, Sellwood, and the suburbs south of the city. From Downtown, trains operate daily about 5 am–1 am, with a fare of $2.50 for up to 2½ hours of travel (transfers to other MAX trains, buses, and streetcars are free within this time period), and $5 for an unlimited all-day ticket, which is also good system-wide. A 7-day visitor pass is also available for $26, and a 30-day pass costs $100. The ticket for riding without a fare is stiff.

Upon boarding TriMet buses, the driver will hand you a transfer ticket that's good for up to 2½ hours, on all buses, MAX trains, and streetcars. Be sure to hold onto it whether you're transferring or not; it also serves as proof that you have paid your fare. If you're in town for a while, consider downloading the TriMet app, which allows you to buy tickets on your smart phone. The most central bus routes operate every 10 to 15 minutes throughout the day. Bikes are allowed in designated areas of MAX trains, and there are bike racks on the front of all buses that everyone is free to use.

Contacts TriMet/MAX. ⊠ *Ticket Office at Pioneer Courthouse Sq., 701 S.W. 6th Ave., Downtown* ☎ *503/238–7433* ⊕ *www.trimet.org.*

TOURS
BIKE TOURS
Portland is famously bike-friendly, with miles of dedicated bike lanes and numerous rental shops. There are also a couple of great companies that offer guided rides around the city, covering everything from eating and brewpub-hopping to checking out local parks and historic neighborhoods.

Cycle Portland Bike Tours and Rentals. Trust your guide at Cycle Portland to know Portland's popular and lesser-known spots. Tour themes include Essential Portland, Foodie Field Trip, Brews Cruise, and several others. A well-stocked bike shop is on-site and serves beer on tap. Bike and helmet are included with tours. ⊠ *117 N.W. 2nd Ave., Old Town* ☎ *503/902–5035, 844/739–2453* ⊕ *www.portlandbicycletours.com* ⬚ *From $40.*

WALKING TOURS
Walk the Portland beat with guides who share their personal Portland knowledge, including history, food, brews, arts, and sights.

Portland Walking Tours. A slew of tours are offered by this well-established company, but it's the Beyond Bizarre tour that generates the most buzz. Ghost-hunter wannabes and paranormal junkies make this a popular tour that often sells out during the peak season. If it's unavailable, there's also the Underground Portland tour, which highlights the sinister history of Portland, along with a few other options, including tours that focus on the local food scene. Departure points vary depending on the tour. ☎ *503/774–4522* ⊕ *www.portlandwalkingtours.com* ⬚ *From $23.*

VISITOR INFORMATION
Travel Portland Information Center. ⊠ *Pioneer Courthouse Sq., 701 S.W. 6th Ave., Downtown* ☎ *503/275–8355, 877/678–5263* ⊕ *www.travelportland.com.*

EXPLORING

One of the greatest things about Portland is that there's so much to explore. This city rightfully boasts that there's something for everyone. What makes discovering Portland's treasures even more enticing is that its attractions, transportation options, and events are all relatively accessible and affordable.

DOWNTOWN

Portland has one of the most attractive, inviting Downtown centers in the United States. It's clean, compact, and filled with parks, plazas, and fountains. Architecture fans find plenty to admire in its mix of old and new. Whereas many urban U.S. business districts clear out at night and on weekends, Portland's Downtown is decidedly mixed-use, with plenty of residential and commercial buildings, and an appealing mix of hotels, shops, museums, restaurants, and bars. You can easily walk from one end of Downtown to the other, and the city's superb public transportation system—which includes MAX light rail, buses, and the streetcar—makes it easy to get here from other parts of the city. A day pass is recommended.

FAMILY
Fodor's Choice
★

Governor Tom McCall Waterfront Park. Named for a former governor revered for his statewide land-use planning initiatives, this park stretches north along the Willamette River for about a mile from near the historic Hawthorne Bridge to Steel Bridge. Broad and grassy, Waterfront Park affords a fine ground-level view of Downtown Portland's bridges and skyline. Once an expressway, it's now the site for many annual celebrations, among them the Rose Festival, classical and blues concerts, Gay Pride, Cinco de Mayo, and the Oregon Brewers Festival. The arching jets of water at the **Salmon Street Fountain** change configuration every few hours, and are a favorite cooling-off spot during the dog days of summer. ■TIP→ Both the Hawthorne Bridge and Steel Bridge offer dedicated pedestrian lanes, allowing joggers, cyclists, and strollers to make a full loop along both banks of the river, via Vera Katz Eastside Esplanade. ⊠ *S.W. Naito Pkwy. (Front Ave.), from Steel Bridge to south of Hawthorne Bridge, Downtown* ⊕ *www. portlandoregon.gov/parks.*

Oregon Historical Society Museum. Impressive eight-story-high trompe l'oeil murals of Lewis and Clark and the Oregon Trail invite history lovers into this Downtown museum that relates the state's story from prehistoric times to the present. A pair of 9,000-year-old sagebrush sandals, a covered wagon, and an early chainsaw are displayed in "Oregon My Oregon," a permanent exhibit that provides a comprehensive overview of the state's past. Other spaces host large traveling exhibits and changing regional shows. The center's research library is open to the public Tuesday through Saturday; its bookstore is a good source for maps and publications on Pacific Northwest history. ⊠ *1200 S.W. Park Ave., Downtown* ☎ *503/222–1741* ⊕ *www.ohs.org* ☞ *$11.*

Portland/Oregon Information Center. You can pick up maps and literature about the city and the state here at the Portland/Oregon

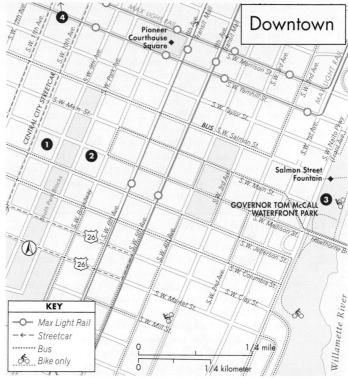

Information Center. Easy to miss, the center is located between the water features, through the glass doors, at Pioneer Courthouse Square. TriMet (⊕ *www.trimet.org*) also operates a desk inside the information center, selling passes and tickets for buses, light rail, and the streetcar. ⊠ *701 S.W. 6th Ave., Downtown* ☎ *503/275–8355, 877/678–5263* ⊕ *www.travelportland.com* ⊙ *Closed Sun. Nov.–Apr.*

Fodor'sChoice **Portland Art Museum.** The treasures at the Pacific Northwest's oldest
★ arts facility span 35 centuries of Asian, European, and American art—it's an impressive collection for a midsize city. A high point is the Center for Native American Art, with regional and contemporary art from more than 200 indigenous groups. The **Jubitz Center for Modern and Contemporary Art** contains six floors devoted entirely to modern art, including a small but superb photography gallery, with the changing selection chosen from more than 5,000 pieces in the museum's permanent collection. The film center presents the annual Portland International Film Festival in February and the Northwest Filmmakers' Festival in early November. Also, take a moment to linger in the peaceful outdoor sculpture garden. Kids under 17 are admitted free. ⊠ *1219 S.W. Park Ave., Downtown* ☎ *503/226–2811, 503/221–1156 film schedule* ⊕ *www.portlandartmuseum.org* ⊠ *$19.99* ⊙ *Closed Mon.*

West End. A formerly rough-around-the-edges section of Downtown, sandwiched between the Pioneer Square area and the swanky Pearl District, this triangular patch of vintage buildings—interspersed with a handful of contemporary ones—has evolved since the early 2000s into one of the city's most vibrant and eclectic hubs of retail, nightlife, and dining. Hip boutique hotels like the Ace, McMenamins Crystal, and Sentinel rank among the city's trendiest addresses. Along Stark Street, formerly the heart of Portland's LGBT scene, there's still a popular gay bar, but now you'll also find noteworthy restaurants and lounges like Clyde Common, Bamboo Sushi, Multnomah Whiskey Library, and Super Bite and connecting bar, Kask. Among the indie-spirited shops, check out Cacao chocolate shop, Frances May clothier, and Union Way—an enclosed pedestrian mall with a handful of upscale boutiques. ⊠ *S.W. 13th to S.W. 9th Aves., between W. Burnside St. and S.W. Alder St., Downtown* ⊕ *www.wepdx.com.*

OLD TOWN/CHINATOWN

The Skidmore Old Town National Historic District, commonly called Old Town/Chinatown, is where Portland was born. The 20-square-block section, bounded by Oak Street to the south and Hoyt Street to the north, includes buildings of varying ages and architectural designs. Before it was renovated, this was skid row. Vestiges of it remain in parts of Chinatown; older buildings are gradually being remodeled, and lately the immediate area has experienced a small surge in development. Portland doesn't have a gay district per se—the scene permeates just about every neighborhood of this extremely LGBT-welcoming city. But you'll find the highest concentration of Portland's gay nightspots in Old Town (and a few others close by in Downtown). MAX serves the area with a stop at the Old Town/Chinatown station.

Fodor's Choice ★ **Lan Su Chinese Garden.** In a twist on the Joni Mitchell song, the city of Portland and private donors took down a parking lot and unpaved paradise when they created this wonderland near the Pearl District and Old Town/Chinatown. It's the largest Suzhou-style garden outside China, with a large lake, bridged and covered walkways, koi- and water lily–filled ponds, rocks, bamboo, statues, waterfalls, and courtyards. A team of 60 artisans and designers from China literally left no stone unturned—500 tons of stone were brought here from Suzhou—in their efforts to give the windows, roof tiles, gateways, including a "moongate," and other architectural aspects of the garden some specific meaning or purpose. Also on the premises are a gift shop and an enchanting two-story teahouse, operated by local Tao of Tea company, overlooking the lake and garden. ⊠ *239 N.W. Everett St., Old Town* ☎ *503/228–8131* ⊕ *www.lansugarden.org* ⌨ *$9.50.*

Fodor's Choice ★ **Pine Street Market.** In a city where restaurants rank among the top sightseeing attractions, the 2016 opening of this bustling food hall in a handsome late-Victorian Old Town building was met with shouts of glee. In one massive room, nine small restaurants with counter service offer visitors the chance to sample the creations of some of Portland's most celebrated chefs. Highlights include one of the first U.S. branches

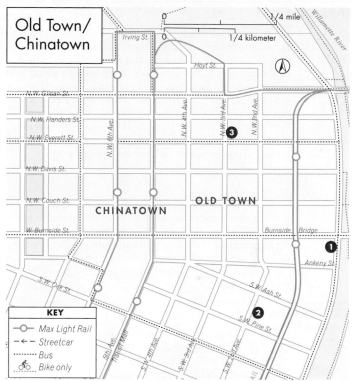

of Tokyo's famed **Marukin Ramen, OP Wurst** gourmet hot dog stand (from Olympia Provisions), Israeli street snacks at **Shalom Y'all** (from John Gorham of Tasty n Sons fame), and a soft-serve ice-cream stand called **Wiz Bang Bar** operated by Salt & Straw. Bring your appetite, and brace yourself for long lines on weekends. ⊠ *126 S.W. 2nd Ave., Old Town* ⊕ *www.pinestreetpdx.com.*

FAMILY **Portland Saturday Market.** On weekends from March to Christmas Eve,
Fodor's Choice the west side of the Burnside Bridge and the Skidmore Fountain area
★ hosts North America's largest ongoing open-air handicraft market. If you're looking for jewelry, yard art, housewares, and decorative goods made from every material under the sun, check out the amazing collection of works by talented artisans on display here. The market also opens for holiday shopping during the three days preceding Christmas Day, a period known as the Festival of the Last Minute. Entertainers and food booths add to the festive feel (although be careful not to mistake this market for the food-centric PSU Portland Farmers' Market, which also takes place on Saturday, on the other side of Downtown). If taking the MAX train to the market, get off at the Skidmore Fountain stop. ⊠ *2 S.W. Naito Pkwy. at foot of S.W. Ankeny, in Waterfront Park, Old Town* ☎ *503/222–6072* ⊕ *www.portlandsaturdaymarket. com* ⊙ *Closed Jan., Feb., and weekdays.*

PEARL DISTRICT

Bordering Old Town to the west and Downtown and the West End to the north, the trendy Pearl District comprises a formerly rough-and-tumble warren of warehouses and railroad yards. Much of the Pearl is new construction, but dozens of the district's historic industrial buildings have been converted into handsome, loft-style housing and commercial concerns, too. You'll find some of the city's most buzzed-about restaurants, galleries, and shops in this neighborhood—the monthly First Thursday evening art walk is an especially fun time to visit. The Portland Streetcar line passes through here, with stops at ecologically themed Jamison Square and Tanner Springs parks.

NOB HILL

Fashionable since the 1880s and still filled with Victorian houses, Nob Hill is a mixed-use cornucopia of old Portland charm and new Portland retail and dining. With its cafés, restaurants, galleries, and boutiques, it's a great place to stroll, shop, and people-watch. At the southern end of 23rd, on the blocks nearest Burnside, you'll mostly encounter upscale chain shops, whereas more independent and generally less pricey retail proliferates farther north.

FOREST PARK

One of the largest city parks in the country, Forest Park stretches 8 miles along the hills overlooking the Willamette River west of Downtown. More than 80 miles of trails through forests of Douglas fir, hemlock, and cedar (including a few patches of old growth) offer numerous options for those looking to log some miles or spend some time outside.

Fodor's Choice ★ **Forest Park.** One of the nation's largest urban wildernesses (5,157 acres), this city-owned, car-free park has more than 50 species of birds and mammals and more than 80 miles of trails through forests of Douglas fir, hemlock, and cedar. Running the length of the park is the 30-mile Wildwood Trail, which extends into adjoining Washington Park (and is a handy point for accessing Forest Park), starting at the Vietnam Veteran's Memorial in Hoyt Arboretum. You can access a number of spur trails from the Wildwood Trail, including the 11-mile Leif Erikson Drive, which picks up from the end of N.W. Thurman Street and is a popular route for jogging and mountain biking. ■ TIP→ You can find information and maps at the Forest Park Conservancy office, at 210 N.W. 17th Avenue, and website. ✉ *Leif Erikson Dr. entrance, end of N.W. Thurman St., Nob Hill* ☎ *503/223–5449* ⊕ *www.forestparkconservancy.org.*

WEST HILLS AND SOUTHWEST

Forming a natural western border of Downtown and Nob Hill, the West Hills extend as a high (up to around 1,000 feet in elevation) ridgeline from Southwest to Northwest Portland. Part of this lofty neighborhood is residential, containing some of the largest and finest homes in the city, many of them with knockout views of the Downtown skyline and Mt.

Lan Su Chinese Garden, Old Town/Chinatown

St. Helens and Mt. Hood in the distance. Technically, Downtown Portland is in the city's Southwest quadrant, as are most of the attractions included in the West Hills section of town. But when locals mention Southwest, they're generally referring to the area south and southwest of Downtown, a mostly middle- to upper-middle-class residential district with a few commercial pockets.

FAMILY
Fodor's Choice
★

International Rose Test Garden. This glorious park within Washington Park comprises three terraced gardens, set on 4½ acres, where more than 10,000 bushes and some 550 varieties of roses grow. The flowers, many of them new varieties, are at their peak in June, July, September, and October. From the gardens you can take in highly photogenic views of the Downtown skyline and, on fine days, the Fuji-shaped slopes of Mt. Hood, 50 miles to the east. Summer concerts take place in the garden's amphitheater. It's a pretty but hilly 30- to 40-minute walk from Downtown, or you can get here via MAX light rail (either to Washington Park or Kings Hill/S.W. Salmon Street stations); then transfer to Bus No. 63 or Washington Park shuttle (May–October only). ⊠ *400 S.W. Kingston Ave., West Hills* ☎ *503/227–7033* ⊕ *www.rosegardenstore.org.*

Fodor's Choice
★

Japanese Garden. One of the most authentic Japanese gardens outside Japan, this serene landscape unfolds over 12½ acres of Washington Park, just a short stroll up the hill from the International Rose Test Garden. Designed by a Japanese landscape master, there are five separate garden styles: Strolling Pond Garden, Tea Garden, Natural Garden, Sand and Stone Garden, and Flat Garden. The Tea House was built in Japan and reconstructed here. An ambitious expansion designed by renowned Japanese architect Kengo Kuma added a tea garden café,

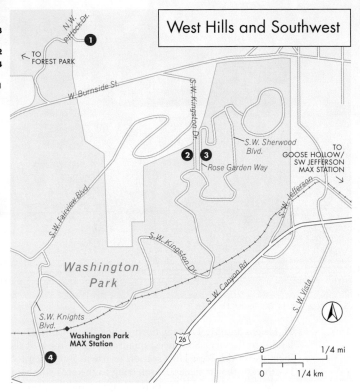

library, art gallery, and a new gift shop in 2017. The east side of the Pavilion has a majestic view of Portland and Mt. Hood. Take MAX light rail to Washington Park station, and transfer to Bus No. 63 or the Washington Park Shuttle (May–October only). ■**TIP→ The noon public tours, given daily March–October and weekends November–February, are given by knowledgeable volunteers.** ⊠ *611 S.W. Kingston Ave., West Hills* ☏ *503/223–1321* ⊕ *www.japanesegarden.com* ⊠ *$9.50.*

FAMILY **Oregon Zoo.** This beautiful animal park in the West Hills, famous for its Asian elephants, is undergoing a two-decade-long series of major improvements and expansions to make the zoo more sustainable and provide more stimulating spaces, education and conservation opportunities, as well as improved guest amenities and event spaces. New in recent years are the Condors of the Columbia habitat, which includes a deep pool for condor bathing, a 30-foot aviary, and an elevated viewing area to see the condors in flight; and the Elephant Lands area, which features feeding stations, mud wallows, varied terrain, and deep pools to keep the elephants active, as well as one of the world's largest indoor elephant facilities. A state-of-the-art Zoo Education Center opened in 2017, and polar bear, primate, and rhino habitats are planned by 2020. Other major draws include an Africa Savanna with rhinos, hippos, zebras, and giraffes. Steller Cove, a state-of-the-art aquatic exhibit, has Steller sea lions and a family of sea otters. Also popular are the chimpanzees, a penguinarium, and habitats for beavers, otters, waterfowl, and reptiles native to the west side of the Cascade Range. In summer a narrow-gauge train operates from the zoo's new train station, chugging along a track past several animal exhibits and through the woods to a station near the International Rose Test Garden and the Japanese Garden. Roughly 15 summer concerts, often featuring nationally known pop stars, take place at the zoo from mid-June through August. Take the MAX light rail to the Washington Park station. ⊠ *4001 S.W. Canyon Rd., West Hills* ☎ *503/226–1561* ⊕ *www.oregonzoo.org* ⊠ *Mar.–Sept., $14.95; Oct.–Feb. $9.95.*

Pittock Mansion. Henry Pittock, the founder and publisher of the *Oregonian* newspaper, built this 22-room, castlelike mansion, which combines French Renaissance and Victorian styles. The opulent manor, built in 1914, is filled with art and antiques. The 46-acre grounds, northwest of Washington Park and 1,000 feet above the city, offer superb views of the skyline, rivers, and the Cascade Range, including Mt. Hood and Mt. St. Helens. The mansion is a half-mile uphill trek from the nearest bus stop. The mansion is also a highly popular destination among hikers using Forest Park's and Washington Park's well-utilized Wildwood Trail. ⊠ *3229 N.W. Pittock Dr., West Hills* ☎ *503/823–3623* ⊕ *www. pittockmansion.com* ⊠ *$10.*

NORTH

Somewhat dismissed historically as the city's "fifth quadrant," North Portland has come into its own in recent years, as the comparatively low cost of real estate has made it popular with young entrepreneurs, students, and other urban pioneers. North Mississippi and North Williams avenues, which are about 10 short blocks apart, have become home to some of the hottest food, drink, and music venues in the city.

Fodor's Choice
★

North Mississippi Avenue. One of North Portland's strips of indie retailers, the liveliest section of North Mississippi Avenue stretches for several blocks and includes a mix of old storefronts and sleek new buildings that house cafés, brewpubs, collectives, shops, music venues, and an excellent food-cart pod, Mississippi Marketplace. Bioswale planter boxes, found-object fences, and café tables built from old doors are some of the innovations you'll see along this eclectic thoroughfare. At the southern end of the strip, stop by the ReBuilding Center, an outlet for recycled building supplies that has cob (clay-and-straw) trees and benches built into the facade. About a 10-minute walk east and running parallel to North Mississippi, the bike-friendly North Williams corridor is an even newer thoroughfare of almost entirely new, eco-friendly buildings and condos rife with trendy restaurants, nightspots, and boutiques. Highlights here include Tasty n Sons, Lark Press letterpress printing studio and shop, the People's Pig barbecue, and Hopworks BikeBar and eco brewpub. You could easily spend a few hours taking in both neighborhoods—both have outstanding food scenes, while North Mississippi is stronger on retail. To get here on MAX light rail, get off at the Albina/Mississippi station. ⊠ *N. Mississippi Ave. between N. Fremont and N. Skidmore Sts., North.*

NORTHEAST

Still the epicenter of the city's relatively small—compared with other U.S. cities the size of Portland—African American community, the inner parts of Northeast have slowly gentrified over the last half century. In the Irvington, Laurelhurst, and Alameda neighborhoods, you'll find some of the largest, most historic homes in town.

FAMILY   **Northeast Alberta Street.** Few of Portland's several hipster-favored East
Fodor's Choice   Side neighborhoods have developed as quickly and as interestingly as
★   N.E. Alberta Street, aka N.E. Alberta, aka the Alberta Arts District, which has morphed from a downcast area into a funky strip of hippie-driven counterculture into a considerably more eclectic stretch of both indie arts spaces and downright sophisticated bistros and galleries. Favorite stops include Pine State Biscuits, Salt & Straw ice cream, the Bye and Bye bar, Tin Shed Garden Cafe, Barista coffee, Aviary restaurant, Bollywood Theater restaurant, Ampersand art gallery and books, the Collective Art Gallery, pedX shoes, and Screaming Sky toys and housewares. Extending a little more than a mile, Northeast Alberta offers plenty of one-of-a-kind dining and shopping; you'll find virtually no national chains along here. The area is also home to some of the best people-watching in Portland, especially during the Last Thursday (of the month) art walks, held May–September from 6 pm until 9:30 pm. The Alberta Street Fair in August showcases the neighborhood's offerings with arts-and-crafts displays and street performances. ■ **TIP→ Northeast Alberta is about a mile from the smaller but similarly intriguing North Mississippi and North Williams corridors; fans of indie dining and shopping could easily spend a full day strolling or biking among both areas.** ⊠ *N.E. Alberta St. between N.E. Martin Luther King Jr. Blvd. and N.E. 30th Ave., Northeast* ⊕ *www.albertamainst.org.*

SOUTHEAST

Bounded on the west by the Willamette River and on the north by Burnside Avenue, the city's Southeast quadrant comprises several of Portland's hottest and hippest neighborhoods. Abundant with shade trees, Craftsman-style houses, and backyard chicken coops, this neighborhood is industrial close in (the river to 7th Avenue)—an increasingly trendy food and retail district known as the Central Eastside, which has also lately blossomed with top-quality artisanal distilleries and urban wineries—and middle- to upper-middle-class residential farther out (8th to 82nd). You'll encounter vibrant pockets of foodie-driven restaurants—as well as bars, coffeehouses, markets, food-cart pods, and boutiques—along east–west running Division, Hawthorne, Belmont, Stark, and Burnside streets, making Southeast a Portland cultural must-see. Other Southeast highlights include the Eastbank Esplanade on the Willamette River (which connects with Downtown via several historic bridges), the kid-focused science museum Oregon Museum of Science and Industry (OMSI), the sleek Tilikum Crossing Bridge, and the beautiful park at Mt. Tabor, an inactive volcanic cinder cone.

Northeast and Southeast

N. E. Killingsworth St.

N. E. Alberta St.

TO AIRPORT →

N. E. Prescott St.

N. E. Fremont St.

N. E. Knott St.

N. E. Russell St.

99E

N. E. Broadway
Weidler St.

HOLLYWOOD

Halsey St.

TO I-205 →

30 84

Laurelhurst
Park

N.E. Glisan St.

E. Burnside St.

S. E. Stark St.

S. E. Belmont St.

S. E. Yamill St.

S. E. Madison St.

S. E. Hawthorne Blvd.

Mt. Tabor
Park

S. E. Division St.

0   1 miles

0   1 kilometers

S. E. Powell Blvd.

26

26

Ross
Island

99E

43

Willamette River

Oaks Bottom
Wildlife
Refuge

S. E. Holgate Blvd.

Lents
Park

S. E. Woodstock Blvd.

205

S. E. Bybee
Blvd.

EASTMORELAND

S. E. Tacoma St.

N.W. Naito Pkwy. (Front Ave.)

N. Mississippi Ave.

Martin Luther King Jr. Blvd.

N. E. 33rd Ave.

N. E. 42nd Ave.

N. E. Cully Blvd.

N. E. 57th Ave.

N. E. Sandy Blvd.

M. L. King Jr. Blvd.

S. E. Grand Ave.

S. E. 20th Ave.

S. E. 28th Ave.

S. E. 39th Ave.

S. E. 60th Ave.

S. E. 50th Ave.

S. E. 72nd Ave.

S. E. 82nd Ave.

S. E. 52nd Ave.

S. E. Milwaukee Ave.

S. E. Mcloughlin Blvd.

S. E. 13th Ave.

S. W. Macadam Ave.

S.W. Naito Pkwy. (Front Ave.)

TOP ATTRACTIONS

Fodor's Choice
★ **Hawthorne District.** Stretching from the foot of Mt. Tabor to S.E. 12th Avenue (where you'll find a stellar food-cart pod), with some blocks far livelier than others, this eclectic commercial thoroughfare was at the forefront of Portland's hippie and LGBT scenes in the '60s and '70s. As the rest of Portland's East Side has become more urbane and popular among hipsters, young families, students, and the so-called creative class over the years, Hawthorne has retained an arty, homegrown flavor. An influx of trendy eateries and shops opening alongside the still-colorful and decidedly low-frills thrift shops and old-school taverns and cafés make for a hodgepodge of styles and personalities—you could easily spend an afternoon popping in and out of boutiques, and then stay for happy hour at a local nightspot or even later for dinner. Highlights include a small (but still impressive) branch of Powell's Books, Bagdad Theater & Pub, Rachel's Ginger Beer, Blue Star Donuts, Gold Dust Meridian bar, Apizza Scholls for stellar thin-crust pizzas, and the Sapphire Hotel for late-night dining, but you'll find every kind of business in Hawthorne, from the airy and contemporary Dosha Aveda day spa to the massive and campy House of Vintage retro fashion and furnishings emporium. ■ TIP→ Bus 14 runs from Downtown along the length of Hawthorne, and there's plenty of free street parking, too. ✉ *S.E. Hawthorne Blvd., between S.E. 12th and S.E. 50th Aves., Buckman, Southeast* ⊕ *www.thinkhawthorne.com.*

Fodor's Choice
★ **House Spirits Distillery.** One of the stalwarts of Distillery Row—a group of eight craft spirits producers mostly clustered together in the Central Eastside—this highly respected outfit opened in 2004, moved into a spacious 14,000-square-foot facility in fall 2014, and has earned international acclaim for its Aviation American Gin and Krogstad Festlig Aquavit. Other favorites include Westward Oregon Straight Malt Whiskey made with locally sourced barley, and—apt in java-loving Portland—coffee liqueur produced using pot-distilled rum and the city's fine Stumptown Coffee beans. In the cozy tasting room, you can also browse a fine selection of barware, books, and other booze-related gifts. Tours are offered daily at 3 pm (and additionally at 1 on Saturday). ■ TIP→ Check out the Distillery Row website (www.distilleryrowpdx. com), where you can view a map of other nearby distilleries and order a Distillery Row Passport, which costs $30 but includes a $5 gift card, complimentary tastings and tours at 11 distilleries (Clear Creek, Bull Run, and Aria in Northwest are included), and discounts at a number of restaurants, hotels, and shops around the city. ✉ *65 S.E. Washington St., Southeast* ☎ *503/235–3174* ⊕ *www.housespirits.com.*

FAMILY
Fodor's Choice
★ **Mt. Tabor Park.** A playground on top of a volcano cinder cone? Yup, that's here. The cinders, or glassy rock fragments, unearthed in the park's construction, were used to surface the respite's roads; the ones leading to the top are closed to cars, but popular with cyclists. They're also popular with cruisers—each August there's an old-fashioned soapbox derby. Picnic tables and tennis, basketball, and volleyball courts make Mt. Tabor Park a popular spot for outdoor recreation, but plenty of quiet, shaded trails and wide-open grassy lawns with panoramic views of the Downtown skyline appeal to sunbathers, hikers, and nature

lovers. The whole park is closed to cars on Wednesday. ■TIP→ Just down the hill on the west side of Mt. Tabor, you'll find the lively cafés and restaurants of the hip Hawthorne District. ⊠ *S.E. 60th Ave. and S.E. Salmon St., Southeast* ⊕ *www.portlandoregon.gov/parks.*

FAMILY
Fodor'sChoice
★
Oregon Museum of Science and Industry (*OMSI*). Hundreds of engaging exhibits draw families to this outstanding interactive science museum, which also has an Omnimax theater and the Northwest's largest planetarium. The many permanent and touring exhibits are loaded with enough hands-on play for kids to fill a whole day exploring robotics, ecology, rockets, animation, and outer space. Moored in the Willamette River as part of the museum is a 240-foot submarine, the USS *Blueback*, which can be toured for an extra charge. OMSI also offers some very cool event programming for adults, including the hugely popular monthly OMSI After Dark nights, where "science nerds" can enjoy food, drink, and science fun, and the twice-monthly OMSI Science Pub nights, where local and national experts lecture on a wide range of topics at theater-pubs in Portland. ■TIP→ OMSI's excellent restaurant, Theory, open for lunch, offers great views of the Willamette River and Downtown skyline. ⊠ *1945 S.E. Water Ave., Southeast* ☎ *503/797–4000, 800/955–6674* ⊕ *www.omsi.edu* 🎫 *Museum $14, planetarium $7.50, Omnimax $8.50, submarine $6.75, parking $5* ⊙ *Closed Mon. early Sept.–mid-June.*

Fodor'sChoice
★
SE Wine Collective. Set along Division Street's white-hot restaurant row, this growing collective houses 11 small wineries and has quickly become the city's leading incubator for vino entrepreneurs. The spacious facility includes a large, light-filled tasting bar with glass roll-up doors (offering a peek at the vinification process) and a main wall and bench seating made from old wine barrels. The tasting bar is also a wine bar, so you can sample the artisanal wines produced on-site, or order a flight, glass, or bottle (to go or to enjoy on-site) as well as tasty small plates from an extensive menu. Although Oregon is chiefly known for Pinot Noir, Pinot Gris, and Chardonnay, the wineries at the collective produce a richly varied assortment of varietals, including a racy Sauvignon Blanc from Pampleau, a supple Gamay Noir from Division Wine Making, and a peppery Cabernet Franc from Willful Wines. ⊠ *2425 S.E. 35th Pl., Southeast* ☎ *503/208–2061* ⊕ *www. sewinecollective.com* ⊙ *Closed Tues.*

WORTH NOTING

Fodor'sChoice
★
Central Eastside. This expansive 681-acre tract of mostly industrial and commercial buildings was largely ignored by all but local workers until shops, galleries, and restaurants began opening in some of the neighborhood's handsome, high-ceilinged buildings beginning in the '90s. These days, it's a legitimately hot neighborhood for shopping and coffeehouse-hopping by day, and dining and clubbing at night, and a slew of high-end apartment buildings have added a residential component to the Central Eastside. The neighborhood lies just across the Willamette River from Downtown—it extends along the riverfront from the Burnside Bridge to south to the Oregon Museum of Science and Industry (OMSI) and Division Street, extending east about a dozen blocks to S.E. 12th Avenue. Businesses of particularly note in these parts include urban-chic

Tilikum Crossing Bridge

coffeehouses (Water Avenue, Coava), breweries (Base Camp Brewing, Cascade Brewing Barrel House, Commons Brewery), shops and galleries, and restaurants (Kachka, Le Pigeon, Revelry, Taylor Railworks, Trifecta Tavern). ⊠ *Willamette River to S.E. 12th Ave. from Burnside to Division Sts., Southeast* ⊕ *www.ceic.cc.*

Tilikum Crossing Bridge. Downtown Portland's collection of striking bridges gained a new member in 2015 with the opening of this sleek, cable-stayed bridge a few steps from Oregon Museum of Science and Industry (OMSI). Nicknamed "the Bridge of the People" and unusual in that it's open only to public transit (MAX trains, buses, and streetcars), bikes, and pedestrians, the 1,720-foot-long bridge connects Southeast Portland with the South Waterfront district and rewards those who stroll or cycle across it with impressive skyline views. ⊠ *Tilikum Crossing, Southeast ✛ Eastbank Esplanade just south of OMSI on the East Side, and S.W. Moody Ave. in South Waterfront.*

WHERE TO EAT

These days, rising-star chefs and the foodies who adore them are flocking to Portland. In this playground of sustainability and creativity, many of the city's hottest restaurants change menus weekly—sometimes even daily—depending upon the ingredients they have delivered to their door that morning from local farms. The combination of fertile soils, temperate weather, and nearby waters contributes to a year-round bountiful harvest (be it lettuces or hazelnuts, mushrooms or salmon) that is within any chef's reach.

2

And these chefs are not shy about putting new twists on old favorites. Restaurants like Le Pigeon, Beast, Ox, Ned Ludd, Tasty n Sons, and Aviary have all taken culinary risks by presenting imaginatively executed, often globally inspired fare while utilizing sustainable ingredients. There's a strong willingness in and around Portland for chefs to explore their creative boundaries.

Most of the city's longtime favorites are concentrated in Nob Hill, the Pearl District, and Downtown. But many of the city's most exciting food scenes are on the East Side, along Alberta Street, Mississippi Avenue, Williams Avenue, Fremont Street, Martin Luther King Jr. Boulevard, Burnside Street, 28th Avenue, Belmont Street, Hawthorne Boulevard, and Division Street, and tucked away in many neighborhoods in between. Serious food enthusiasts will definitely want to make some trips to some of these vibrant, if out-of-the-way neighborhoods.

Reviews have been shortened; for full information visit Fodors.com. Use the coordinate (✣ 1:B2) at the end of each listing to locate a site on the corresponding map.

	WHAT IT COSTS IN U.S. DOLLARS			
	$	$$	$$$	$$$$
At Dinner	under $16	$16–$22	$23–$30	over $30

Restaurant prices are the average cost of a main course at dinner, or if dinner is not served, at lunch.

DOWNTOWN

$ BAKERY FAMILY Fodor's Choice ★ 🍴 **Blue Star Donuts.** The lines outside much-hyped competitor Voodoo Doughnut are longer, but that doesn't mean you should bypass a chance to sample the creative confections at this handsome, light-filled doughnut shop on the street level of a glassy condo tower in the West End. Part of Micah Camden's nouvelle–fast-food empire (that includes Little Big Burger and Boxer Ramen), Blue Star opens at 7 or 8 each morning and remains open until that day's fresh-baked stock of delicious doughnuts is sold out. **Known for:** wildly inventive doughnut flavors; serving Stumptown Coffee. [$] *Average main: $4* ✉ *1237 S.W. Washington St., West End* ☎ *503/265–8410* 🌐 *www.bluestardonuts.com* ✣ *1:B4.*

$$$ PACIFIC NORTHWEST Fodor's Choice ★ 🍴 **Clyde Common.** Gourmands from all walks of life—politicians, rock stars, socialites, and hipsters—eat and drink at this bustling bistro and bar in the Ace Hotel. Long, communal tables dominate the space, which means you never know who you'll end up sitting next to. **Known for:** barrel-aged cocktails; seasonal farm-to-table menu; outstanding weekend brunch. [$] *Average main: $25* ✉ *Ace Hotel, 1014 S.W. Stark St., West End* ☎ *503/228–3333* 🌐 *www.clydecommon.com* ✣ *1:B4.*

$$$ ASIAN FUSION Fodor's Choice ★ 🍴 **Departure Restaurant + Lounge.** This swanky rooftop restaurant and lounge on the top floor of The Nines hotel looks fresh out of L.A.—a look and feel that is, indeed, a departure from Portland's usual no-fuss vibe. The retro-chic interior has an extravagant, space-age, airport-lounge feel, and

Portland's Food Carts

Throughout Portland at any given mealtime, around 850 food carts are dishing up steaming plates of everything from Korean tacos to shawarma to artisanal cupcakes. While food carts have seen a rise in popularity throughout the country, the culture is especially strong in Portland.

Brightly colored and mostly stationary, the carts tend to cluster in former parking lots in pods ranging from 3 to nearly 60 establishments, oftentimes ringing a cluster of picnic tables or a covered awning. A recent construction boom has led to the closure of some key cart pods, but other pods have opened, often farther from the city center, where land costs less.

With plate prices averaging $6 to $10, cart fare provides a quick, inexpensive, and delicious alternative to traditional sit-down restaurants if you don't mind sitting outside. Cart dining is also an easy way to sample Portland's extensive ethnic food offerings.

For up-to-date information on hours and locations, and the latest on openings, moves, and closures, check out the extensive local blog **Food Carts Portland** (⊕ *www. foodcartsportland.com*), the corresponding FoodCartsPDX iPhone and Droid apps FoodCartsPDX, and the Twitter thread @pdxfoodcarts.com.

TOP PODS

Downtown, S.W. 9th (and 10th) and Alder: Covering more than an entire city block, this Downtown pod, home to nearly 60 carts, is the largest in the city. The spot is lively during the workweek but slower on the weekends. We recommend the signature Thai chicken dish at **Nong's Khao Man Gai**; battered fish-and-chips at **The Frying Scotsman**; the Cheesus double cheeseburger with bacon at **Grilled Cheese Grill**; kielbasa and other Polish classics at **EuroDish**; the seductively delicious Chinese-style breakfast crepes at **Bing Mi!**; and kalua pig at the Hawaiian cart **808 Grinds**.

Southeast, Portland Mercado (S.E. 73rd Avenue and Foster Road): A convivial collection of some 40 businesses, including food carts and crafts and gift vendors, the Mercado is devoted to Latin culture and heritage. Feast on *ropa vieja* and other Cuban delicacies at **Que Bola**; shredded-pork and red-mole tamales at **Mixteca**; and cinnamon-dusted churros at **Don Churro**.

Southeast, Tidbit Food Farm and Garden (S.E. Division and 28th): This beautifully designed cart colony has a large central dining area and a fire pit. Try the Heartbreak Hotel hot dog topped with bacon, cheddar, ketchup, and a fried egg at the **DogHouse PDX**; the blistered-crust wood-fired pizzas (the one with fennel salami is killer) at **Paper Bag Pizza**; and the peanut butter, bacon, banana, and honey Dutch-style waffle at **Smaaken**. You can also grab a pint of local IPA or saison to accompany your meal at **Scout Beer Garden**.

Portland's famous food carts

the outdoor patio—furnished with low, white couches and bright-orange tables and chairs—offers panoramic views of the Downtown skyline. **Known for:** big-eye tuna poke; fantastic skyline views. [$] *Average main: $24* ✉ *Nines Hotel, 525 S.W. Morrison St., Downtown* ☎ *503/802–5370* 🌐 *www.departureportland.com* ⏲ *No lunch* ⊕ *1:C5.*

$$$ PACIFIC NORTHWEST Fodor's Choice ★

🍴 **Higgins.** One of Portland's original farm-to-table restaurants, this classic eatery, opened in 1994 by renowned namesake chef Greg Higgins, has built its menu—and its reputation—on its dedication to local, seasonal, organic ingredients. Higgins' dishes display the diverse bounty of the Pacific Northwest, incorporating ingredients like heirloom tomatoes, forest mushrooms, mountain huckleberries, Pacific oysters, Oregon Dungeness crab, and locally raised pork. **Known for:** house-made charcuterie plate; casual bistro menu in adjacent bar. [$] *Average main: $30* ✉ *1239 S.W. Broadway, Downtown* ☎ *503/222–9070* 🌐 *www.higginsportland.com* ⏲ *No lunch weekends* ⊕ *1:B6.*

$ DELI FAMILY

🍴 **Kenny & Zuke's Delicatessen.** The reputation of this Jewish deli beside the hip Ace Hotel is based largely on its much-revered pastrami. Cured for seven days, then smoked for 10 hours and steamed for 3, the rich and flavorful meat is best tasted on a rye bread sandwich or, if your appetite is heartier, the warm, sauerkraut-packed Reuben. **Known for:** best Reuben in town; house-made bagels; breakfast all day. [$] *Average main: $14* ✉ *1038 S.W. Stark St., West End* ☎ *503/222–3354* 🌐 *www.kennyandzukes.com* ⊕ *1:B4.*

$$$ BISTRO

🍴 **Little Bird Bistro.** Celeb-chef Gabriel Rucker of Le Pigeon fame operates this lively Downtown sister restaurant that's gained a following for its deliciously curated charcuterie board and tender seared duck breast. Other notable dishes include a fried-chicken version of coq au vin and classic steak au poivre with frites, and a decadent Brie burger with spiced ketchup. **Known for:** foie gras available a couple of ways; business lunches; late-night menu. [$] *Average main: $26* ✉ *219 S.W. 6th Ave., Downtown* ☎ *503/688–5952* 🌐 *www.littlebirdbistro.com* 🕓 *No lunch weekends* ✥ *1:D4.*

$$ AMERICAN FAMILY 🍴 **Mother's Bistro & Bar.** Chef and cookbook author Lisa Schroeder dedicates her home-style, made-with-love approach to food to the comforting foods prepared by mothers everywhere. Clearly, the theme resonates, as evidenced by the long waits on weekends, and even some weekday mornings for breakfast, which is arguably the best time of the day to sample Schroeder's hearty cooking; try the wild salmon hash with leeks or the French toast with a crunchy cornflake crust. **Known for:** down-home American comfort fare; fantastic breakfasts; drinks in the swanky Velvet Lounge bar. [$] *Average main: $17* ✉ *212 S.W. Stark St., Downtown* ☎ *503/464–1122* 🌐 *www.mothersbistro.com* 🕓 *Closed Mon. No dinner Sun.* ✥ *1:D4.*

$$$$ MODERN AMERICAN 🍴 **Super Bite.** The acclaimed chef duo behind Ox, Greg Denton and Gabi Quiñónez Denton, present an artfully plated selection of globally inspired treats in this refined yet unpretentious West End space. The menu of is divided into smaller bites, shareable plates, and just three quite substantial family-style platters (such as whole fried trout with ginger–black bean sauce, or pork shoulder confit with hazelnut chimichurri). **Known for:** unusual food combinations (beef tongue "spam" musubi, for instance); extensive list of Spanish sherries; plenty of veggie options. [$] *Average main: $35* ✉ *527 S.W. 12th Ave., West End* ☎ *503/222–0979* 🌐 *www.superbitepdx.com* 🕓 *Closed Mon. No lunch* ✥ *1:B4.*

$$$ ECLECTIC 🍴 **Tasty n Alder.** The first Downtown venture of celebrated Portland chef John Gorham, this all-day brunch and evening dinner spot serves some of the most interesting food in the city. Designed for sharing, the tapas-style menu draws on global influences and delivers bold, delicious flavors. **Known for:** "grown-up" milk shakes (with alcohol); deftly prepared cocktails; brunch every day. [$] *Average main: $24* ✉ *580 S.W. 12th Ave., West End* ☎ *503/621–9251* 🌐 *www.tastynalder.com* ✥ *1:B4.*

OLD TOWN/CHINATOWN

$ MEXICAN 🍴 **Mi Mero Mole.** Graffiti and murals decorate one concrete wall of this colorful Old Town–Chinatown eatery dedicated to Mexico City–style street food, proof that superb ethnic food still exists in the Chinatown neighborhood (even if none of it, at the moment, is Chinese). This is some of the most flavorful, authentic Mexican food in town. **Known for:** great afternoon (2–6 pm) happy hour; handcrafted margaritas; lots of veggie options. [$] *Average main: $10* ✉ *32 N.W. 5th Ave., Old Town* ☎ *971/266–8575* 🌐 *www.mmmtacospdx.com* 🕓 *Closed Sun.* ✥ *1:D3.*

$ BAKERY 🍴 **Voodoo Doughnut.** The long lines outside this Old Town 24/7 doughnut shop, marked by its distinctive pink-neon sign, attest to the fact that this irreverent bakery is almost as famous a Portland landmark as Powell's Books. The aforementioned sign depicts one of the shop's biggest sellers, a raspberry-jelly-topped chocolate voodoo-doll doughnut, but all of the creations here, some of them witty, some ribald, bring smiles to the faces of customers—even those who have waited 30 minutes in the rain. **Known for:** offbeat doughnut flavors; the bacon maple bar doughnut; long lines. [$] *Average main: $4* ✉ *22 S.W. 3rd Ave., Old Town* ☎ *503/241–4704* 🌐 *www.voodoodoughnut.com* ✥ *1:D3.*

PEARL DISTRICT

$$$ PERUVIAN Fodor'sChoice ★

🍴 **Andina.** This popular upscale Pearl District restaurant offers an inventive menu—a combination of traditional Peruvian and contemporary "Novoandina" cuisines—served in a large but nook-filled space. The extensive seafood offerings include four kinds of ceviche, grilled octopus, and pan-seared scallops with white and black quinoa. **Known for:** Peruvian-style pisco sours; stylish yet casual lounge; great late-night menu. [$] *Average main: $27* ✉ *1314 N.W. Glisan St., Pearl District* ☎ *503/228–9535* 🌐 *www.andinarestaurant.com* ✥ *1:B2.*

$$$ MODERN AMERICAN Fodor'sChoice ★

🍴 **Irving Street Kitchen.** You might come to this hip Pearl District restaurant set inside a gorgeously transformed warehouse building just because you heard about the rich butterscotch pudding with roasted-banana caramel and peanut butter bonbons (it's available to go, sold in its own adorable canning jar); but chances are, once you see the exposed-brick-and-wood-beam walls, Edison bulb chandeliers, inviting central bar, and patio seats on a converted loading dock, you'll want to stay. And you'll be glad you did. **Known for:** wine by glass dispensed from state-of-the-art taps; terrific weekend brunch; decadent desserts. [$] *Average main: $27* ✉ *701 N.W. 13th Ave., Pearl District* ☎ *503/343–9440* 🌐 *www.irvingstreetkitchen.com* ✥ *1:B2.*

$$ MEDITERRANEAN Fodor'sChoice ★

🍴 **Mediterranean Exploration Company.** Developed by cookbook author and celeb-chef John Gorham, this tribute to Mediterranean cuisine occupies a handsome former warehouse on historic 13th Avenue in the Pearl. MEC (for short) is an energy-filled, open space with a mix of communal and individual tables—it's surprisingly affordable considering the quality and portions, particularly if you opt for the $40 tasting menu. **Known for:** reasonably priced tasting menu; Middle East–inspired cocktails; extensive vegetarian options. [$] *Average main: $22* ✉ *333 N.W. 13th Ave., Pearl District* ☎ *503/222–0906* 🌐 *www.mediterraneanexplorationcompany.com* ⏲ *No lunch* ✥ *1:B3.*

$$$ LATIN AMERICAN

🍴 **Oba!** Many come to Oba! for the upscale bar scene, but this Pearl District salsa hangout with large windows and ample sidewalk seating also serves excellent Latin American cuisine, including coconut prawns, butternut squash enchiladas, achiote braised pork arepas, and filet mignon served with a yuca, gnocchi, and apple cider–molasses reduction. The bar is open late Friday and Saturday. **Known for:** table-side guacamole; flavorful real-fruit margaritas; late-night bar scene on weekends. [$] *Average main: $27* ✉ *555 N.W. 12th Ave., Pearl District* ☎ *503/228–6161* 🌐 *www.obarestaurant.com* ⏲ *No lunch* ✥ *1:B2.*

$ BAKERY

🍴 **Pearl Bakery.** Known for its excellent pastries and fresh baked breads (which are served at many top restaurants around town), this superb café was the first of the city's true artisan bakeries. It offers light breakfasts and delicious sandwiches (the tomato-basil-mozzarella on a puffy pistolet roll is particularly good) for lunch. **Known for:** flaky, buttery croissants; hearty sandwiches. [$] *Average main: $7* ✉ *102 N.W. 9th Ave., Pearl District* ☎ *503/827–0910* 🌐 *www.pearlbakery.com* ⏲ *No dinner* ✥ *1:C3.*

Map 1: Where to Eat and Stay in Central Portland

KEY

- ■ Restaurants
- □ Hotels
- ■ Restaurant in a Hotel
- —— Light Rail / Streetcar
- ↔ following reviews indicates a map-grid coordinate

Willamette River

N.W. 2nd Ave.

Steel Bridge

Hotel Eastlund

N.E. Holladay St.

LLOYD DISTRICT

N.E. Oregon St.

N.E. Irving St.

Northeast Grand Ave.

84

Governor Tom McCall Waterfront Park

N.E. Everett St.

N.E. Davis St.

N.E. Couch St.

S.E. 9th Ave.

Burnside Bridge

E. Burnside St.

Le Pigeon

Jupiter Hotel

S.E. Ankeny St.

BUCKMAN DISTRICT

Willamette River

S.E. Ash St.

Revelry

S.E. 2nd Ave.

Southeast Grand Ave.

S.E. 6th Ave.

S.E. 7th Ave.

S.E. 8th Ave.

S.E. Oak St.

S.E. Stark St.

Olympia Provisions

S.E. Martin Luther King, Junior Boulevard

S.E. Washington St.

S.E. Alder St.

Morrison Bridge

Kachka

S.E. Morrison Street

S.E. Morrison Bridge

S.E. Belmont Street

Afuri Ramen

Governor Tom McCall Waterfront Park

S.E. Yamhill St.

S.E. Taylor St.

CENTRAL EASTSIDE

S.E. Salmon St.

S.E. Water Ave.

S.E. 2nd Ave.

S.E. 3rd Avenue

S.E. Main St.

S.E. 7th Ave.

S.E. 8th Ave.

S.E. 9th Ave.

Hawthorne Bridge

E   F   G   H

1   2   3   4   5   6

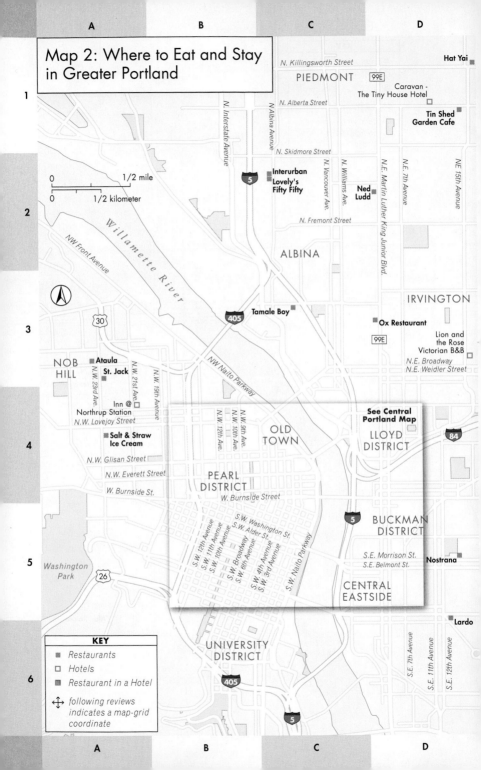

Map 2: Where to Eat and Stay in Greater Portland

A   B   C   D

N. Killingsworth Street

PIEDMONT 99E

Hat Yai

Caravan - The Tiny House Hotel

N. Alberta Street

Tin Shed Garden Cafe

N. Skidmore Street

0   1/2 mile
0   1/2 kilometer

Interurban
Lovely's Fifty Fifty

Ned Ludd

N. Fremont Street

ALBINA

IRVINGTON

Willamette River

Tamale Boy

Ox Restaurant

99E

Lion and the Rose Victorian B&B

N.E. Broadway
N.E. Weidler Street

NOB HILL

Ataula
St. Jack

Inn @ Northrup Station
N.W. Lovejoy Street

Salt & Straw Ice Cream

N.W. Glisan Street

N.W. Everett Street

W. Burnside St.

OLD TOWN

See Central Portland Map

LLOYD DISTRICT

PEARL DISTRICT
W. Burnside Street

BUCKMAN DISTRICT

S.W. Washington St.
S.W. Alder St.

S.E. Morrison St.
S.E. Belmont St.

Nostrana

Washington Park

CENTRAL EASTSIDE

UNIVERSITY DISTRICT

Lardo

KEY

- ■ Restaurants
- ☐ Hotels
- ■ Restaurant in a Hotel
- ✛ following reviews indicates a map-grid coordinate

A   B   C   D

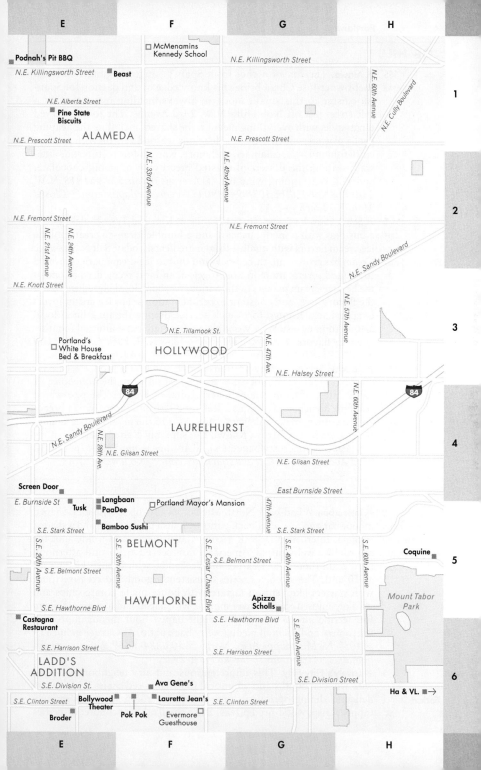

NOB HILL

$$$ TAPAS

🍴 **Ataula.** The son of a chef from Spain's Aragon region, renowned chef-owner Jose Chesa brings his knowledge of and passion for Spanish cuisine to this small, modern, always-bustling restaurant on a side street just off Nob Hill's N.W. 23rd Avenue. The food is served tapas-style, with everything meant to be shared, including the heaping paella platters, which include a delicious seafood version with prawns, cuttlefish, mussels, calamari, and more. **Known for:** picturesque sidewalk seating; the dessert of toasted bread with olive oil, chocolate, and salt; outstanding wine list. [$] *Average main: $29* ✉ *1818 N.W. 23rd Pl., Nob Hill* ☎ *503/894–8904* 🌐 *www.ataulapdx.com* 🕒 *Closed Mon. No lunch* ✣ *2:A3.*

$ CAFÉ FAMILY Fodor's Choice ★

🍴 **Salt & Straw Ice Cream.** In 2011, cousins Kim and Tyler Malek started a business with a small pushcart and a humble idea—to create unique ice-cream flavors with quality, local ingredients. Today, Salt & Straw Ice Cream has grown into three brick-and-mortar ice-cream parlors around town (and several more in Los Angeles), and it is recognized as one of the best ice-cream makers in the nation; seasonal, local ingredients drive the flavors here, and constant experimentation keeps ice-cream lovers coming back. **Known for:** quick service despite the long lines; local artisan toppings, such as Woodblock chocolate bars; unusual monthly specialty flavors. [$] *Average main: $5* ✉ *838 N.W. 23rd Ave., Nob Hill* ☎ *971/271–8168* 🌐 *www.saltandstraw.com* ✣ *2:A4.*

$$$ FRENCH

🍴 **St. Jack.** Serving hearty portions of rich and hearty food, the chic yet cozy Nob Hill restaurant takes its inspiration from the *bouchons*, or rustic cafés, of Lyon, the culinary capital of France. The pan-seared scallops, drenched in a cognac, leek, and Gruyère sauce, with a breadcrumb crunch, make a delicious precursor to the main course, as does the roasted bone marrow. **Known for:** superbly crafted cocktails; mussels (served with crusty baguettes). [$] *Average main: $28* ✉ *1610 N.W. 23rd Ave., Nob Hill* 🌐 *www.stjackpdx.com* 🕒 *No lunch* ✣ *2:A3.*

NORTH

$ MODERN AMERICAN Fodor's Choice ★

🍴 **Interurban.** A laid-back North Mississippi gastropub with an L-shaped indoor bar and a bi-level back patio with lush landscaping and a shaded pergola, Interurban is both a convivial drinkery and a fine spot for affordable, well-crafted American fare served from mid-afternoon until 2 am (hours start earlier on weekends, with brunch kicking off at 10 am). The kitchen creates consistently good and creative food, with starters like venison tartare with house-made potato chips and whiskey-infused chicken-liver mousse with bacon and foie gras. **Known for:** terrific afternoon and late-night happy hour menu; impressive microbrew and cocktail menu; pretty back patio. [$] *Average main: $13* ✉ *4057 N. Mississippi Ave., North* ☎ *503/284–6669* 🌐 *www.interurbanpdx.com* 🕒 *No lunch weekdays* ✣ *2:C2.*

$ PIZZA Fodor's Choice ★

🍴 **Lovely's Fifty-Fifty.** This unpretentious and airy neighborhood spot with wooden booths and whimsical fire-engine-red chairs is really two delicious dining options in one: the dining room serves inventively topped, crisp, wood-fired pizzas, and a small takeout counter dispenses homemade hard and soft-serve organic ice cream. Among the pizzas, you can't go wrong with the pie layered in shaved-and-roasted potatoes, melted leeks, fresh fenugreek, and pancetta, and topped with an egg. **Known for:** innovative flavors of house-made ice cream; perfectly crispy wood-fired pizzas. $\boxed{\$}$ *Average main: $15* ⊠ *4039 N. Mississippi Ave., Mississippi, North* ☎ *503/281–4060* ⊕ *www.lovelysfiftyfifty.com* ⊗ *Closed Mon. No lunch* ✛ *2:C2.*

NORTHEAST

$$$$ ✕ **Beast.** This meat-centric exemplar of Portland's cutting-edge culi-
PACIFIC nary scene occupies a nondescript red building with subtle signage.
NORTHWEST Chef-owner Naomi Pomeroy, who also operates the trendy Expatriate bar across the street, has appeared on TV's *Top Chef Masters* and garnered countless accolades. **Known for:** communal seating overlooking open kitchen; some of the most creative meat-centric food in the city; sublime Sunday brunch. $\boxed{\$}$ *Average main: $102* ⊠ *5425 N.E. 30th Ave., Northeast* ☎ *503/841–6968* ⊕ *www.beastpdx.com* ⊗ *Closed Mon. and Tues.* ✛ *2:E1.*

$ ✕ **Hat Yai.** A new establishment from the acclaimed chef behind Lang-
THAI baan and PaaDee, this cozy and casual counter-service eatery takes its name from a small Thai city near the Malaysian border and its concept from that region's spicy and delicious fried chicken with sticky rice and rich Malayu-style curries with panfried roti bread. Other treats here uncommon to Thai restaurant culture in the States include fiery turmeric curry with mussels and heady lemongrass oxtail soup. **Known for:** the roti dessert with condensed milk; perfectly crunchy free-range fried chicken; good selection of Asian beers. $\boxed{\$}$ *Average main: $12* ⊠ *1605 N.E. Killingsworth St., Northeast* ☎ *503/764–9701* ⊕ *www.hatyaipdx. com* ⊗ *Closed Mon.* ✛ *2:D1.*

$$$ ✕ **Ned Ludd.** Named for the founder of the Luddites, the group that
PACIFIC resisted the technological advances of the Industrial Revolution, this
NORTHWEST Northwest-inspired kitchen prepares its food the most low-tech way
Fodor's Choice possible: in a wood-burning brick oven, over an open flame. Sourcing
★ most of its ingredients locally (or carefully, if they come from afar), Ned Ludd's menu varies completely depending on the season and weather. **Known for:** whole roasted trout with charred leeks; nice selection of craft ciders; earthy and rustic Northwest-inspired interior. $\boxed{\$}$ *Average main: $26* ⊠ *3925 N.E. Martin Luther King Blvd., Northeast* ⊕ *www. nedluddpdx.com* ⊗ *Closed Mon. and Tues. No lunch* ✛ *2:D2.*

$$$$ ✕ **Ox Restaurant.** Specializing in "Argentine-inspired Portland food,"
ARGENTINE Ox is all about prime cuts of meat prepared well. In a dimly lit dining
Fodor's Choice room with hardwood floors, exposed brick walls, and a bar against the
★ front window, the flannel-shirt-and-white-apron clad waitstaff serves beef, lamb, pork, and fish dishes cooked over flames in a large, hand-cranked grill. **Known for:** the asado Argentino platter (lots of amazing meaty grills); creative side dishes, a few of which could make a full meal; vanilla tres leches cake dessert. $\boxed{\$}$ *Average main: $36* ⊠ *2225 N.E. Martin Luther King Blvd., Northeast* ☎ *503/284–3366* ⊕ *www. oxpdx.com* ⊗ *No lunch* ✛ *2:D3.*

$ ✕ **Pine State Biscuits.** Loosen your belt a notch or two before venturing
SOUTHERN   inside this down-home Southern restaurant that's especially beloved for
its over-the-top breakfast biscuit fare. Pat yourself on the back, or belly,
if you can polish off the Reggie Deluxe (a fluffy house-baked biscuit
topped with fried chicken, bacon, cheese, an egg, and sage gravy), a
masterful mélange of calorie-laden ingredients. **Known for:** shrimp and
grits; arguably the best food stall at the Portland Farmers Market; the
massive Reggie Deluxe sandwich. $ *Average main: $7* ⊠ *2204 N.E.*
Alberta St., Alberta District ☎ *503/477–6605* ⊕ *www.pinestatebiscuits.*
com ⊙ *No dinner Mon.–Wed.* ✛ *2:E1.*

$$ ✕ **Podnah's Pit BBQ.** Firing up the smoker at 5 every morning, the pit crew
BARBECUE   at Podnah's spends the day slow cooking some of the best Texas- and Car-
olina-style barbecue in the Northwest. Melt-in-your-mouth, oak-smoked
brisket, ribs, pulled pork, chicken, and lamb are all served up in a sassy
vinegar-based sauce. **Known for:** green-chili mac-and-cheese (when avail-
able); daily specials (fried catfish on Friday, smoked lamb on Thursday);
casual and lively vibe. $ *Average main: $16* ⊠ *1625 N.E. Killingsworth*
St., Northeast ☎ *503/281–3700* ⊕ *www.podnahspit.com* ✛ *2:E1.*

$$ ✕ **Screen Door.** The line that forms outside this Southern cooking restau-
SOUTHERN   rant during weekend brunch and dinner is as epic as the food itself, but
Fodor's Choice   you can more easily score a table if you come for weekday breakfast or
★   lunch. A large, packed dining room with canned pickles and peppers
along the walls, this Portland hot spot does justice to authentic Southern
cooking. **Known for:** fried chicken plate; rotating menu of seasonal side
dishes; breakfast or brunch served daily. $ *Average main: $16* ⊠ *2337*
E. Burnside St., Northeast ☎ *503/542–0880* ⊕ *www.screendoorrestau-*
rant.com ✛ *2:E5.*

$ ✕ **Tamale Boy.** Chef Abel Hernandez hails from Veracruz by way of
MEXICAN   Mexico City, and while he's adept at preparing tamales—both the
Fodor's Choice   Oaxacan style wrapped in banana leaves and the more conventional
★   style wrapped in corn husks (try the version filled with roasted pasilla
peppers, onions, corn kernels, and queso fresco), he also turns out fabulous ceviche and *alambre de camarones* (adobe shrimp with bacon and
Oaxacan cheese over flat corn tortillas). Be sure to start with an order
of table-side guacamole, and the El Diablo margarita with roasted-
habanero-infused tequila and mango puree. **Known for:** the El Diablo
margarita with roasted-habanero-infused tequila and mango puree;
table-side gaucamole; authentic hearty and filling tamales. $ *Average*
main: $7 ⊠ *1764 N.E. Dekum St., Northeast* ☎ *503/206–8022* ⊕ *www.*
tamaleboy.com ⊙ *Closed Mon.* ✛ *2:C3.*

$ ✕ **Tin Shed Garden Cafe.** Sided in metal, this busy restaurant on Alberta
CAFÉ   Street is known for its hearty breakfasts—namely, its biscuits and gravy,
FAMILY   shredded-potato cakes, egg and tofu scrambles, and breakfast burritos;
in fact, it's so well known that there can be a long wait for a table
for breakfast on weekends. The lunch and dinner menus have creative
choices as well, like a creamy artichoke sandwich and a mac and cheese
of the day. **Known for:** dog-friendly patio (and special menu); cozy
ambience with stone fireplace; picturesque and cheerful outdoor seating. $ *Average main: $12* ⊠ *1438 N.E. Alberta St., Alberta District*
☎ *503/288–6966* ⊕ *www.tinshedgardencafe.com* ✛ *2:D1.*

SOUTHEAST

$$ RAMEN Fodor's Choice ★ 🍴 **Afuri Ramen.** When the acclaimed Japanese ramen chain Afuri decided to open an outpost in the United States in 2016, it chose food-obsessed Portland—specifically, a modern, high-ceilinged dining room on the trendy Central East Side. They chose Portland, in part because the exacting culinary team appreciated the city's pristine, glacially fed water supply, which plays a significant part in the steaming, savory bowls of yuzu shio (with chicken broth, yuzu citrus, shimeji mushrooms, seasoned egg, chashu, endive, and nori), one of a half dozen deeply satisfying ramen bowls. **Known for:** relentlessly authentic Japanese ramen; meat and veggie skewers; flights of premium sake. [$] *Average main: $18* ✉ *923 S.E. 7th Ave., Southeast* ☎ *503/468–5001* 🌐 *www.afuri.us* 🕓 *Closed Mon. No lunch* ✣ *1:H6.*

$ PIZZA Fodor's Choice ★ 🍴 **Apizza Scholls.** The pies at Apizza Scholls, lauded by Anthony Bourdain, Rachael Ray, and most any pizza lover who visits, deserve the first-class reputation they enjoy. The greatness of the pies rests not in innovation or complexity, but in the simple quality of the ingredients. **Known for:** exquisitely crisp handmade crusts; the bacon bianca pizza (white, with no sauce); interesting beer list. [$] *Average main: $14* ✉ *4741 S.E. Hawthorne Blvd., Hawthorne District* ☎ *503/233–1286* 🌐 *www.apizzascholls.com* 🕓 *No lunch weekdays* ✣ *2:G5.*

$$$ ITALIAN Fodor's Choice ★ 🍴 **Ava Gene's.** Chef Joshua McFadden's fantastic Roman-inspired Italian eatery ranks among the top tables in town both in popularity and quality. Capsule-shape lamps dangle from the vaulted ceiling of this buzzy dining room with two long rows of banquette seating and several more closely spaced tables. **Known for:** pane flatbreads with creative topping; daily specials, such as rabbit on Thursday and braciole on Saturday; $70 per person family-style option. [$] *Average main: $25* ✉ *3377 S.E. Division St., Southeast* ☎ *971/229–0571* 🌐 *www.avagenes.com* 🕓 *No lunch* ✣ *2:F6.*

$$ SUSHI 🍴 **Bamboo Sushi.** The best sushi spot in Portland is also the most environmentally sustainable, sourcing its fish conscientiously from fishing operations that follow eco-friendly guidelines. Try the black cod with smoked soy and roasted garlic glaze or the house-smoked wild ivory salmon nigiri. **Known for:** sustainable seafood; stylish decor. [$] *Average main: $18* ✉ *310 S.E. 28th Ave., Southeast* ☎ *503/232–5255* 🌐 *www.bamboosushi.com* 🕓 *No lunch* ✣ *2:E5.*

$ INDIAN 🍴 **Bollywood Theater.** Set beneath a soaring beamed ceiling, and with a welcoming mix of worn wooden seating, kitschy decor, bright fabrics, and intoxicating smells, this lively restaurant along Division Street's hoppin' restaurant row specializes in Indian street food and reflects chef-owner Troy MacLarty's colorful, delicious, authentic vision of India as experienced on several trips. Order at the counter, and your food will be brought to you—there's a mix of two-tops and communal tables, with additional seating on a spacious patio. **Known for:** Goan-style shrimp; small Indian gourmet market with spices and curries; lively and fun atmosphere. [$] *Average main: $13* ✉ *3010 S.E. Division St., Division* ☎ *503/477–6699* 🌐 *www.bollywoodtheaterpdx.com* ✣ *2:F6.*

$ RUSSIAN Fodor's Choice ★ 🍴 **Broder.** This delightful neighborhood café—one of the most outstanding brunch spots in town—serves fresh and delicious Scandinavian food with fun-to-pronounce names like *friterade applen* (apple fritter) and *aebleskivers* (Danish pancakes). All of the food—the hashes, the baked egg scrambles, the Swedish breakfast boards—is delicious. **Known for:** aebleskivers (Danish pancakes); Swedish-style hash with smoked trout. [$] *Average main: $11* ✉ *2508 S.E. Clinton St., Southeast* ☎ *503/736–3333* 🌐 *www.broderpdx.com* 🕒 *No dinner* ✥ *2:E6.*

$$$$ PACIFIC NORTHWEST Fodor's Choice ★ 🍴 **Castagna Restaurant.** Enjoy artful Pacific Northwest cuisine—like grilled halibut, kohlrabi, and mussels, or summer beans, chanterelles, wilted sorrel, and roasted-duck jus—at this tranquil Hawthorne restaurant. Dinner options from chef Justin Woodward's monthly changing menu include either a classic 3-course prix fixe for $98 or a lavish 10-course tasting menu that runs $165; opt for the superb wine pairings for an additional $55 or $75 (with the tasting menu). **Known for:** artfully prepared modern fare; outstanding wine pairings with each prix-fixe menu; tasty and less pricey fare at the café next door. [$] *Average main: $98* ✉ *1752 S.E. Hawthorne Blvd., Hawthorne District* ☎ *503/231–7373* 🌐 *www.castagnarestaurant.com* 🕒 *Restaurant: Closed Sun.–Tues. No lunch. Café: No lunch* ✥ *2:E6.*

$$$ FRENCH Fodor's Choice ★ 🍴 **Coquine.** A sunny neighborhood café serving breakfast and lunch daily, Coquine blossoms into a romantic, sophisticated French–Pacific Northwest bistro in the evening. The unfussy storefront space is just steps from Mt. Tabor Park, making it a lovely spot for a meal before or after a leafy stroll. **Known for:** pan-roasted bone-in rib-eye steak for two–three; butterscotch pudding with miso-pumpkin butter and chocolate candied pistachios; cheerful setting near Mt. Tabor. [$] *Average main: $27* ✉ *6839 S.E. Belmont St., Southeast* ☎ *503/384–2483* 🌐 *www.coquinepdx.com* 🕒 *No dinner Mon. and Tues.* ✥ *2:H5.*

$ VIETNAMESE 🍴 **Ha & VL.** This humble, no-frills banh mi shop amid the many cheap and authentic Asian restaurants on S.E. 82nd stands out not just for its filling sandwiches (these crispy-bread creations come with fillings like spicy Chinese sausage, pork meat loaf, or sardines) but also for the daily featured soup, such as peppery pork-ball noodle soup on Wednesday and Vietnamese turmeric soup, with shrimp cake and sliced pork, on Sunday. There's also a diverse selection of thick milk shakes—top flavors include avocado, mango, and durian. **Known for:** milk shakes in unusual flavors; pork-ball noodle soup (on Wednesday only). [$] *Average main: $6* ✉ *2738 S.E. 82nd Ave., No. 102, Southeast* ☎ *503/772–0103* 🕒 *Closed Tues. No dinner* ✥ *2:H6.*

$$ RUSSIAN Fodor's Choice ★ 🍴 **Kachka.** In a city with a sizable population of Russian immigrants, the success of this Central East Side establishment decorated to resemble a *dasha* is hardly surprising, although it's really the devotion of the city's foodies that resulted in Kachka's white-hot popularity. If you are expecting heavy cuisine, you'll be surprised by the wonderfully creative and often quite light fare, including plenty of shareable small plates, like crispy beef tongue with sweet onion sauce, orange, and pomegranate; panfried sour-cherry *vareniki* (Ukranian dumplings), and—of course—caviar with blini and all the usual accompaniments. **Known for:** extensive craft vodka list; classic chicken Kiev; cherry vareniki

(Ukranian dumplings). $ *Average main: $20* ⊠ *720 S.E. Grand Ave., Southeast* ✢ *(moving to 960 S.E. 11th Ave. in 2017)* ☎ *503/235–0059* ⊕ *www.kachkapdx.com* ⊗ *No lunch* ✢ *1:H5.*

$$$$ ✕ **Langbaan.** Guests reach this tiny, wood-paneled, 24-seat gem with an
THAI   open kitchen by walking through the adjoining PaaDee restaurant and
Fodor's Choice   pushing open a faux bookshelf that's actually a door. Of course, you
★   won't even get this far unless you've called ahead to reserve a table: this
very special prix-fixe restaurant, serving the most interesting and consistently delicious Asian food in Portland, is only open Thursday–Sunday, with two seatings per evening. **Known for:** some of the most inventive Thai food in the country; the $30 wine-pairing option is a great value; wonderfully creative and flavorful desserts. $ *Average main: $75* ⊠ *6 S.E. 28th Ave., Southeast* ☎ *971/344–2564* ⊕ *www.langbaanpdx.com* ⊗ *Closed Mon.–Wed. No lunch* ✢ *2:E5.*

$ ✕ **Lardo.** One of several spots around Portland that has become known
AMERICAN   for advancing the art of sandwich making, Lardo offers a steady roster
Fodor's Choice   of about a dozen wonderfully inventive variations, plus one or two
★   weekly specials, along with no-less-impressive sides like maple carrots
and escarole Caesar salads. Sandwiches of particular note include the tender Korean-style braised pork shoulder with kimchi, chili mayo, cilantro, and lime, and grilled mortadella with provolone, marinated peppers, and mustard aioli. **Known for:** inviting covered outdoor seating area at Hawthorne; excellent craft-beer and cocktail selection; "dirty fries" topped with pork scraps, marinated peppers, and Parmesan. $ *Average main: $10* ⊠ *1212 S.E. Hawthorne Blvd., Southeast* ☎ *503/234–7786* ⊕ *www.lardosandwiches.com* ✢ *2:D6.*

$ ✕ **Lauretta Jean's.** Kate McMillen and Noah Cable's pie-focused opera-
CAFÉ   tion began as a stall at Portland's Saturday farmers' market at PSU and
Fodor's Choice   now comprises a couple of charming, homey, brick-and-mortar cafés,
★   one Downtown, but the most atmospheric along Division Street in
Southeast. While it's the delicious pies—with feathery-light crusts and delicious fillings like tart cherry, salted pecan, and chocolate-banana cream—that have made Lauretta Jean's a foodie icon in Portland, these cheerful eateries also serve exceptional brunch fare, including the LJ Classic, a fluffy biscuit topped with an over-easy egg, Jack cheese, bacon, and strawberry jam. **Known for:** salted-caramel apple pie; short but well-curated cocktail list; breakfast sandwich that features the bakery's fluffy biscuits. $ *Average main: $6* ⊠ *3402 S.E. Division St., Division* ☎ *503/235–3119* ⊕ *www.laurettajean.com* ⊗ *No dinner* ✢ *2:F6.*

$$$$ ✕ **Le Pigeon.** Specializing in adventurous Northwest-influenced French
FRENCH   dishes of extraordinary quality, this cozy and unassuming restaurant
Fodor's Choice   consistently ranks among the city's most acclaimed dining venues.
★   The menu changes regularly but often features items like beef-cheek
bourguignon, chicken and oxtail with semolina gnocchi, and seared foie gras with chestnut, raisins, bacon, and cinnamon toast (especially exceptional). **Known for:** open kitchen in which diners at the counter can interact with chefs; one of the best burgers in town; grilled dry-aged pigeon with a seasonally changing preparation. $ *Average main: $33* ⊠ *738 E. Burnside St., Southeast* ☎ *503/546–8796* ⊕ *www.lepigeon. com* ⊗ *No lunch* ✢ *1:H3.*

$$ MODERN ITALIAN

🍴 **Nostrana.** This smart but informal restaurant delivers delicious, thin-crust pizzas and wood-grilled meats and seafood from the large brick oven. Pies carry an assortment of high-quality toppings; the Funghi Verde pizza—topped with shiitake and maitake mushrooms with house mozzarella and garlic—is one of Nostrana's most popular pies. **Known for:** terrific happy hour deals; smoked rotisserie chicken. [$] *Average main: $22* ✉ *1401 S.E. Morrison St., Southeast* ☎ *503/234–2427* 🌐 *www.nostrana.com* 🕓 *No lunch weekends* ✥ *2:D5.*

$$ MODERN AMERICAN Fodor's Choice ★

🍴 **Olympia Provisions.** Salumist Elias Cairo made a name for himself throughout the country with his artisanal charcuterie, such as smoked chorizo, pepper-coated capicola, and pork-pistachio pâté, which is sold in fine grocery stores nationally as well as at numerous Portland farmers' markets and gourmet shops. Now Cairo, alongside chef Alex Yoder, have become known for a pair of stellar, meat-centric restaurants—Olympia Provisions Northwest and Olympia Provisions Southeast—in which you can order platters of charcuterie and cheeses along with more eclectic seasonal American fare. **Known for:** lively happy hours; deeply flavorful charcuterie; interesting cocktail selection. [$] *Average main: $22* ✉ *107 S.E. Washington St., Southeast* ☎ *503/954–3663* 🌐 *www.olympiaprovisions.com* ✥ *1:G5.*

$ THAI Fodor's Choice ★

🍴 **PaaDee.** Adjoining the more celebrated, reservations-only sister restaurant Langbaan, PaaDee serves some of the freshest, most flavorful Thai food in town, and at remarkably fair prices given the complexity of the cooking, the warmth of the staff, and the attractiveness of the dining room, which is on the ground floor of a contemporary condo building at the restaurant-blessed intersection of 28th and Burnside. The kitchen here specializes in traditional Thai comfort fare: grilled squid skewers with chili-lime sauce; wild-caught prawns with lemongrass, scallions, ground rice, and a spicy lime dressing; and sautéed pork belly with basil, chili, green beans, and a fried egg rank among the most popular dishes. **Known for:** fair prices for upscale Thai fare; daily-changing fish entrée, always with a creative preparation. [$] *Average main: $14* ✉ *6 S.E. 28th Ave., Southeast* ☎ *503/360–1453* 🌐 *www.paadeepdx.com* ✥ *2:E5.*

$$ ASIAN Fodor's Choice ★

🍴 **Pok Pok.** Andy Ricker, the owner of one of Portland's most talked-about restaurants, regularly travels to Southeast Asia to research street food and home-style recipes to include on the menu of this always-hopping spot. Ike's Vietnamese chicken wings, deep-fried in caramelized fish sauce and garlic, are legendary. **Known for:** Ike's Vietnamese chicken wings; charcoal-roasted game hen and other meaty fare; fiery-hot food (although there are plenty of milder dishes—you just have to ask). [$] *Average main: $16* ✉ *3226 S.E. Division St., Division* ☎ *503/232–1387* 🌐 *www.pokpokpdx.com* ✥ *2:F6.*

$$ KOREAN FUSION Fodor's Choice ★

🍴 **Revelry.** Portland has long trailed its northerly neighbor Seattle when it comes to Korean cuisine. Happily, in 2016, Seattle's renowned Relay Korean restaurant group opened a stylish, industrial-chic restaurant in Portland's white-hot Central East Side. **Known for:** mochi doughnuts with caramel popcorn for dessert; soju cocktails; dinner till midnight most nights (2 am on weekends). [$] *Average main: $16* ✉ *210 S.E. Martin Luther King Blvd., Southeast* ☎ *971/339–3693* 🌐 *www.relayrestaurantgroup.com* 🕓 *No lunch* ✥ *1:G4.*

$$$ MIDDLE EASTERN 🍴 **Tusk.** With its clean lines and whitewashed walls, Tusk provides a setting for its colorful, beautifully presented modern Middle Eastern fare to shine brightly. Think flatbread with salmon roe, squash, mustard oil, and yogurt, and grilled sweet potato with hazelnut tahini and dukka among the smaller starter plates. **Known for:** extensive selection of vegetarian small plates; fun vibe for late-night drinks and snacking; perfectly grilled flatbreads with house-made toppings. [$] *Average main: $27* ✉ *2448 E. Burnside St., Southeast* ☎ *503/894–8082* 🌐 *www.tusk-pdx.com* 🕘 *No lunch weekdays* ✥ *2:E5.*

WHERE TO STAY

Portland has an unusually rich variety of distinctive, design-driven boutique hotels, historic properties, and charming B&Bs, and while you'll find the usual mix of budget-oriented, mid-range, and upscale chains here, if you'd rather avoid cookie-cutter brand-name properties, you're in the right city.

Hotel reviews have been shortened. For full information, visit Fodors.com. Use the coordinate (✥ B2) at the end of each listing to locate a site on the corresponding map.

	WHAT IT COSTS IN U.S. DOLLARS			
	$	$$	$$$	$$$$
Hotels	under $150	$150–$225	$226–$300	over $300

Hotel prices are the lowest cost of a standard double room in high season.

DOWNTOWN

$$ HOTEL 🏨 **Ace Hotel.** The quintessential Portland hipster hotel, the Ace contains a Stumptown Coffee café and Clyde Common restaurant, is a block from Powell's Books and the Pearl District, and is right in the heart of Downtown's ever-trendy West End neighborhood. **Pros:** prime Downtown location; unique design and artwork in each room; free city bicycles available for guests. **Cons:** offbeat decor and hipster vibe isn't for everybody; rooms with private baths push the Ace into the expensive category; some rooms receive street noise. [$] *Rooms from: $190* ✉ *1022 S.W. Stark St., Downtown* ☎ *503/228–2277* 🌐 *www.acehotel.com* 🛏 *78 rooms* 🍽 *No meals* ✥ *1:C4.*

$$$ HOTEL Fodor's Choice ★ 🏨 **Heathman Hotel.** From the teak-paneled lobby to the marble fireplaces to the rosewood elevators with Warhol prints at each landing, this wonderfully atmospheric, art-filled 1927 hotel exudes refinement. **Pros:** superior service; central location adjoining Portland Center for the Performing Arts, and a block from Portland Art Museum; outstanding art collection; stellar restaurant. **Cons:** some rooms are small; expensive parking. [$] *Rooms from: $269* ✉ *1001 S.W. Broadway, Downtown* ☎ *503/241–4100, 800/551–0011* 🌐 *portland.heathmanhotel.com* 🛏 *110 rooms, 40 suites* 🍽 *No meals* ✥ *1:C5.*

$$$
HOTEL
Fodor'sChoice
★
⊡ **Hotel deLuxe.** This retro-glam 1912 boutique hotel with its original chandeliers, gilded ceilings, black-and-white photography (arranged by movie themes), heavy drapes, and hip cocktail lounge evokes Hollywood's Golden Era, but with welcome modern touches like flat-screen TVs, free Wi-Fi, and iPod docks. **Pros:** fun and artistic vibe; friendly and helpful staff; nice touches like pillow menu, preprogrammed iPods, spiritual book library, and classic movies. **Cons:** standard rooms are a bit compact; location is less central than other Downtown properties. $ *Rooms from: $229* ⊠ *729 S.W. 15th Ave., Downtown* ☎ *503/219–2094, 866/986-8085* ⊕ *www.hoteldeluxeportland.com* ◴ *97 rooms, 33 suites* ⍟⎮*No meals* ✚ *1:A4.*

$$$
HOTEL
⊡ **Hotel Lucia.** Black-and-white celebrity photos from Pulitzer Prize–winner and native Oregonian David Hume Kennerly, comfy leather chairs, and stylish low-slung furniture adorn the rooms of this nine-story, 1909 European-style boutique hotel in the heart of Downtown. **Pros:** prime location; luxurious amenities; two outstanding restaurants. **Cons:** limited shelf and storage space in the small bathrooms; steep rates during busy times. $ *Rooms from: $259* ⊠ *400 S.W. Broadway, Downtown* ☎ *503/225–1717, 866/986-8086* ⊕ *www.hotellucia.com* ◴ *127 rooms, 33 suites* ⍟⎮*No meals* ✚ *1:C4.*

$$$
HOTEL
⊡ **Hotel Modera.** Decorated with local artwork, sleek, contemporary furnishings, and wood-and-marble accents, this boutique property is both upscale and accessible, and offers a location convenient to the Southwest Park Blocks and Portland State University. **Pros:** friendly staff; nice courtyard; great bar-restaurant; individually bagged ice in hand-carved chests in every hall. **Cons:** rooms on the small side; no on-site gym (but free passes to nearby 24-hour gym); a 10- to 15-minute walk from West End and Pearl District dining and nightlife. $ *Rooms from: $234* ⊠ *515 S.W. Clay St., Downtown* ☎ *503/484–1084, 877/484–1084* ⊕ *www. hotelmodera.com* ◴ *167 rooms, 7 suites* ⍟⎮*No meals* ✚ *1:C6.*

$$
HOTEL
⊡ **Hotel Rose.** This dapper but reasonably priced boutique property overlooking the Willamette River affords stellar views of the water, easy access to the waterfront park and the events that take place there (Rose Festival, Blues Festival, Gay Pride, and so on), and—as part of the Pineapple Hospitality chain—complimentary pineapple cupcakes during the daily afternoon reception. **Pros:** central location on the riverfront; typically lower rates than many comparable Downtown hotels; lots of perks for the price; easy access to the MAX. **Cons:** rooms not facing the river have dull views. $ *Rooms from: $179* ⊠ *50 S.W. Morrison St., Downtown* ☎ *503/221–0711, 877/237–6775* ⊕ *www.hotelroseportland.com* ◴ *140 rooms, 2 suites* ⍟⎮*No meals* ✚ *1:D5.*

$$$$
HOTEL
Fodor'sChoice
★
⊡ **Hotel Vintage.** This historic landmark takes its theme from Oregon vineyards, with rooms named after local wineries, complimentary wine served every evening, and an extensive collection of Oregon vintages displayed in the tasting room. **Pros:** terrific on-site Italian restaurant and wine bar; exceptionally helpful and friendly staff; stunning room decor; several over-the-top spectacular suites. **Cons:** pricey parking; some street noise on the lower levels on the Washington Street side. $ *Rooms from: $325* ⊠ *422 S.W. Broadway, Downtown* ☎ *503/228–1212, 800/263–2305* ⊕ *www.vintageplaza.com* ◴ *96 rooms, 21 suites* ⍟⎮*No meals* ✚ *1:C4.*

$$$ HOTEL **Mark Spencer Hotel.** This family-owned hotel, with a prime location in the hip West End near Powell's Books and the Pearl District, is one of the better values in town, with most of its warmly decorated and spacious rooms containing well-equipped kitchenettes. **Pros:** commitment to the arts; afternoon tea and cookies and evening local wine tasting; most rooms have kitchenettes. **Cons:** some rooms are a bit dark; street noise can be a problem. [$] *Rooms from: $249* ✉ *409 S.W. 11th Ave., Downtown* ☎ *503/224–3293, 800/548–3934* 🌐 *www.markspencer.com* 🛏 *36 rooms, 66 suites* 🍴 *Breakfast* ✥ *1:B4.*

$ HOTEL **McMenamins Crystal Hotel.** Travelers who appreciate good music and good beer—especially together—love this West End branch of the McMenamin brothers' unorthodox empire, which is home to three bars and a restaurant and is affiliated with the Crystal Ballroom concert venue a block away. **Pros:** historic building with eccentric, rock-star vibe and decor; lots of bars and dining both on-site and on surrounding blocks; shared-bath rooms are rock-bottom affordable. **Cons:** quirky vibe isn't for everyone; shared bath down the hall in most rooms; no TVs. [$] *Rooms from: $110* ✉ *303 S.W. 12th Ave., Downtown* ☎ *503/972–2670, 855/205–3930* 🌐 *www.mcmenamins.com/crystal-hotel* 🛏 *51 rooms, 9 with bath* 🍴 *No meals* ✥ *1:B3.*

$$$$ HOTEL Fodor's Choice ★ **The Nines.** On the top nine floors of a former landmark department store, this swanky hotel, part of the Starwood Luxury Collection, has the city's poshest accommodations, with luxe decor, great views, and two see-and-be-seen restaurants. **Pros:** stunning views; swanky vibe and cool design; two sceney restaurants. **Cons:** rooms facing the atrium and overlooking the bar and restaurant can be noisy; expensive valet-only parking. [$] *Rooms from: $339* ✉ *525 S.W. Morrison St., Downtown* ☎ *503/222–9996, 866/716–8136* 🌐 *www.thenines.com* 🛏 *318 rooms, 13 suites* 🍴 *No meals* ✥ *1:C5.*

$$$$ HOTEL **RiverPlace Hotel.** With textured wall coverings, pillows made of Pendleton wool, and a color palette of slate blue, mustard yellow, and a variety of browns, this Kimpton-operated boutique hotel on the banks of the Willamette River captures the look and feel of the Pacific Northwest. **Pros:** stellar views and park-side riverfront location; rooms are spacious and airy; some suites have wood-burning fireplaces. **Cons:** not many restaurants or shops within easy walking distance. [$] *Rooms from: $339* ✉ *1510 S.W. Harbor Way, Downtown* ☎ *503/228–3233, 888/869–3108* 🌐 *www.riverplacehotel.com* 🛏 *39 rooms, 45 suites* 🍴 *No meals* ✥ *1:D6.*

$$$ HOTEL Fodor's Choice ★ **Sentinel Hotel.** Formerly known as the Governor Hotel, the grand Sentinel Hotel underwent a $6 million renovation and rebranding in 2014 to take it from historic to hip-historic; all guest rooms and public spaces in the landmark, early-20th-century buildings were brought up-to-date, and the hotel now reflects a very Portland vibe, with locally sourced textiles, furnishings, and goods. **Pros:** indie style meets luxury; central location; spacious, well-designed rooms; well-equipped gym. **Cons:** pricey valet parking. [$] *Rooms from: $259* ✉ *614 S.W. 10th Ave., Downtown* ☎ *503/224–3400, 888/246–5631* 🌐 *www.sentinelhotel.com* 🛏 *76 rooms, 24 suites* 🍴 *No meals* ✥ *1:B4.*

OLD TOWN

$ ⊞ **Society Hotel.** This intimate new boutique hotel with simple, stylish,
HOTEL   and affordable rooms just steps from Old Town nightlife and Lan Su
Fodor'sChoice   Chinese Garden occupies an 1880s former boardinghouse for sailors
★   and retains a quirky and colorful atmosphere. **Pros:** bargain rates; gorgeous rooftop deck; fun and youthful vibe; close to plenty of gay and mainstream bars. **Cons:** rooms are quite basic; neighborhood can get very noisy on weekend evenings. $ *Rooms from: $109* ⊠ *203 N.W. 3rd Ave., Old Town* ☎ *503/445–0444* ⊕ *www.thesocietyhotel.com* ⋗ *39 rooms* ❢❢ *No meals* ⊟ *No credit cards* ✛ *1:D3.*

PEARL DISTRICT

$$$ ⊞ **Residence Inn–Pearl District.** This sleek, six-floor, all-suites hotel is the
HOTEL   trendy Pearl District's first hotel. **Pros:** clean, modern design both inside
Fodor'sChoice   and out; best location for proximity to Pearl District businesses; in-room
★   kitchens; many rooms can sleep four to six guests. **Cons:** a little far from Downtown attractions; pricey overnight parking. $ *Rooms from: $289* ⊠ *1150 N.W. 9th Ave., Pearl District* ☎ *503/220–1339, 888/236–2427* ⊕ *www.marriott.com* ⋗ *224 suites* ❢❢ *Breakfast* ✛ *1:C1.*

NOB HILL

$$ ⊞ **Inn @ Northrup Station.** Bright colors, bold patterns, and retro designs
HOTEL   characterize this Nob Hill hotel containing luxurious suites with full
FAMILY   kitchens or kitchenettes. **Pros:** roomy suites have kitchens and feel like
Fodor'sChoice   home; steps from Nob Hill shopping, dining, and the streetcar; free
★   parking. **Cons:** the bold color scheme isn't for everyone; a 15-minute walk, or slightly shorter streetcar ride, from Downtown core; in demand so it can be hard to get a reservation. $ *Rooms from: $219* ⊠ *2025 N.W. Northrup St., Nob Hill* ☎ *503/224–0543, 800/224–1180* ⊕ *www. northrupstation.com* ⋗ *70 suites* ❢❢ *Breakfast* ✛ *2:A4.*

NORTHEAST

$$ ⊞ **Caravan–The Tiny House Hotel.** In keeping with the artsy, idiosyncratic
B&B/INN   vibe of the surrounding Alberta Arts District, this cluster of itty-bitty custom-built houses-on-wheels offers visitors the chance to experience Portland's unabashed quirky side. **Pros:** a quirky, only-in-Portland experience; in the heart of Alberta's hip retail-dining district; all units have kitchenettes. **Cons:** these houses really are tiny; 15-minute drive or 35-minute bus ride from Downtown; often books up weeks in advance (especially weekends). $ *Rooms from: $155* ⊠ *5009 N.E. 11th Ave., Alberta District* ☎ *503/288–5225* ⊕ *www.tinyhousehotel.com* ⋗ *6 cottages* ❢❢ *No meals* ✛ *2:D1.*

$$$ ⊞ **Hotel Eastlund.** A drab mid-20th-century chain property in Convention
HOTEL   Center/Lloyd District morphed into a stylish and slick boutique hotel
Fodor'sChoice   in 2015. **Pros:** handy location near Moda Center, convention center,
★   and light rail; fashionable rooms with plenty of high-tech perks; see-and-be-seen restaurants with dazzling skyline views. **Cons:** surrounding neighborhood lacks charm and interesting dining options; a bit pricey

for this part of town. [$] *Rooms from: $269* ✉ *1021 N.E. Grand Ave., Lloyd District/Convention Center* ☎ *503/235–2100* 🌐 *www.hoteleastlund.com* 🛏 *168 rooms* 🍴 *No meals* ✣ *1:G1.*

$$ B&B/INN Fodor's Choice ★ 🏨 **Lion and the Rose Victorian B&B.** Oak and mahogany floors, original light fixtures, and a coffered dining-room ceiling set a tone of formal elegance in this 1906 mansion, while the wonderfully friendly, accommodating, and knowledgeable innkeepers—Dusty and Steve—make sure that you feel perfectly at home. **Pros:** gorgeous house; top-notch service; home-cooked meals. **Cons:** young children not allowed in main house; nearest commercial neighborhood, the Lloyd District, is pretty bland. [$] *Rooms from: $170* ✉ *1810 N.E. 15th Ave., Northeast* ☎ *503/287–9245, 800/955–1647* 🌐 *www.lionrose.com* 🛏 *7 rooms, 1 apartment* 🍴 *Breakfast* ✣ *2:D3.*

$$ HOTEL FAMILY Fodor's Choice ★ 🏨 **McMenamins Kennedy School.** In a renovated elementary school on the edge of a trendy Northeast Portland neighborhood, Oregon's famously creative McMenamin brothers hoteliers have created a quirky and fantastical multiuse facility with rooms that feature original schoolhouse touches like chalkboards and cloakrooms and literature-inspired themes, a movie theater, a restaurant, a warm outdoor soaking pool, a brewery, and several small bars. **Pros:** funky and authentic Portland experience; room rates include movies and use of year-round soaking pool; free parking; close to trendy Alberta Arts District. **Cons:** rooms have showers but no tubs; no TVs in rooms; 20-minute drive or 40-minute bus ride from Downtown. [$] *Rooms from: $155* ✉ *5736 N.E. 33rd Ave., Northeast* ☎ *503/249–3983* 🌐 *www.kennedyschool.com* 🛏 *57 rooms* 🍴 *No meals* ✣ *2:F1.*

$$ B&B/INN 🏨 **Portland's White House Bed and Breakfast.** Hardwood floors with Oriental rugs, chandeliers, antiques, and fountains create a warm and romantic mood at this lavish 1910 Greek Revival mansion in the historic Irvington District. **Pros:** over-the-top romantic; excellent service; a short drive or bus ride to several hip East Side restaurant and retail districts. **Cons:** in residential neighborhood a few miles from Downtown; nearest commercial neighborhood is the rather bland Lloyd District. [$] *Rooms from: $165* ✉ *1914 N.E. 22nd Ave., Northeast* ☎ *503/287–7131, 800/272–7131* 🌐 *www.portlandswhitehouse.com* 🛏 *8 suites* 🍴 *Breakfast* ✣ *2:E3.*

SOUTHEAST

$ B&B/INN Fodor's Choice ★ 🏨 **Evermore Guesthouse.** Just a block from the trendy dining along Southeast Portland's hip Division Street, this beautifully restored, 1909 Arts and Crafts–style mansion contains spacious, light-filled rooms, some with private balconies, claw-foot soaking tubs, and good-size sitting areas; one detached suite has a full kitchen, and a cozy and romantic third-floor room has skylights and pitched ceilings. **Pros:** located in hip, charming neighborhood with many bars and restaurants; reasonably priced with free off-street parking; free laundry and breakfast; distinctive, charming decor. **Cons:** some rooms face busy Cesar Chavez Boulevard; a 15-minute drive or 30-minute bus ride from Downtown. [$] *Rooms from: $135* ✉ *3860 S.E. Clinton St., Richmond* ☎ *503/206-6509, 877/600–6509* 🌐 *www.evermoreguesthouse.com* 🛏 *3 rooms, 3 suites* 🍴 *Breakfast* ✣ *2:F6.*

$ ⬛ **Jupiter Hotel.** The hip, creative, and adventurous flock to this contem-
HOTEL porary boutique hotel, formerly a motor inn, adjacent to the Doug Fir
Lounge, a bar and restaurant that's also one of the city's most popular
concert venues. **Pros:** funky decor and vibe; trendy bar and music club
attached; easy access to Downtown. **Cons:** youthful, hipster personality
isn't to everyone's taste; request a room on the "chill side" if you want distance from the noisy patio/bar scene; thin walls between rooms. $ *Rooms
from: $139* ✉ *800 E. Burnside St., Southeast* ☎ *503/230–9200, 877/800–
0004* ⊕ *www.jupiterhotel.com* ⌁ *80 rooms, 1 suite* ❖*No meals* ✛ *1:H3.*

$$ ⬛ **Portland Mayor's Mansion.** More than a century ago, Portland Mayor
B&B/INN H. Russell Albee resided in this stately redbrick Colonial Revival man-
sion on the edge of gracious Laurelhurst Park. **Pros:** beautiful rooms
with rich period details; views of and easy access to Laurelhurst Park.
Cons: two rooms share a bath. $ *Rooms from: $175* ✉ *3360 S.E.
Ankeny St., Laurelhurst* ☎ *503/232–3588* ⊕ *www.pdxmayorsmansion.
com* ⌁ *4 rooms* ❖*Breakfast* ✛ *2:F5.*

NIGHTLIFE AND PERFORMING ARTS

NIGHTLIFE

Portland has become something of a base for up-and-coming alterna-
tive-rock bands, which perform in clubs scattered throughout the city.
Good jazz groups perform nightly in a handful of bars as well.

Portland's most diverting neighborhoods for barhopping are, not surpris-
ingly, its favored dining districts, too—the West End, Pearl District, and
Nob Hill on the west side of the Willamette River, within walking distance
(or a streetcar ride) of Downtown hotels; Alberta Street, North Mississippi
Avenue, and East Burnside Street in the 20s; the Central East Side, Belmont
Street, Hawthorne Boulevard, and Division Street on the East Side.

DOWNTOWN
BARS AND LOUNGES

Fodor's Choice **Driftwood Room.** Once your eyes adjust to the romantically dim lighting,
★ you'll find a curved bar, leather banquette seating, and polished-wood
ceilings and walls in this retro-chic bar in the Old Hollywood–themed
Hotel deLuxe. The trendy cocktails are garnished with herbs culled
from the hotel's garden. ■TIP➜ The happy-hour food menu is one of
the best in the city. ✉ *Hotel deLuxe, 729 S.W. 15th Ave., Downtown*
☎ *503/820–2076* ⊕ *www.hoteldeluxeportland.com.*

Huber's Cafe. The city's oldest restaurant (est. 1879) is notable for its
old-fashioned feel and iconic Spanish coffee cocktail, which is set aflame
at your table. The old bar in the back has great character. Huber's is on
the ground floor of the historic Oregon Pioneer Building, which became
the snazzy Hi-Lo Hotel in fall 2016. ✉ *Hi-Lo Hotel, 411 S.W. 3rd Ave.,
Downtown* ☎ *503/228–5686* ⊕ *www.hubers.com.*

Luc Lac Vietnamese Kitchen. With a reputation as an after-work eating and
drinking hangout among local Portland chefs and restaurant workers, this
always-hopping Vietnamese joint offers well-executed cocktails crafted
with classic liquors and surprising Vietnamese flavors, such as the Single

Knight: Four Roses Single Barrel bourbon, pho syrup, Angostura orange bitters, and Lapsang souchong tea ice cube. The kitchen turns out delicious eats until midnight on weekdays and 4 am on weekends. ⊠ *835 S.W. 2nd Ave., Downtown* ☎ *503/222–0047* ⊕ *www.luclackitchen.com.*

Fodor'sChoice **Multnomah Whiskey Library.** Smartly dressed mixologists roll drink
★ carts around the seductively clubby room—with beam ceilings, wood paneling, leather club chairs, a wood-burning fireplace, and crystal chandeliers—pouring cocktails table-side. The emphasis, of course, is whiskey and bourbon—Multnomah has such an extensive collection in its "library" that bartenders need rolling ladders to access the bottles perched on the tall shelves lining the exposed-brick walls—but don't overlook the impressive food menu. ⊠ *1124 S.W. Alder St., Downtown* ☎ *503/954–1381* ⊕ *www.multnomahwhiskeylibrary.com.*

Saucebox. A sophisticated, often mixed gay/straight crowd flocks here to enjoy colorful cocktails and trendy DJ music, mostly on Friday and Saturday nights. The kitchen turns out consistently good pan-Asian fare. ⊠ *214 S.W. Broadway, Downtown* ☎ *503/241–3393* ⊕ *www.saucebox.com.*

COFFEEHOUSES

Case Study Coffee. A first-rate indie alternative to the scads of chain coffeehouses Downtown, Case Study serves exceptional, house-roasted coffee in a variety of formats, from Chemex to Aeropress; they also make their own syrups and serve delicious drinking chocolates. Nibble delectable sweets from local bakeries Nuvrei and Petunia's (the latter is gluten-free). There are two additional locations, one in Hollywood at 5347 N.E. Sandy Boulevard and another in Alberta at 1422 N.E. Alberta Street. ⊠ *802 S.W. 10th Ave., Downtown* ☎ *503/477–8221* ⊕ *www.casestudycoffee.com.*

Fodor'sChoice **Heart Coffee.** Inside this sleek East Burnside coffeehouse, patrons sip
★ coffees from Central America, South America, and Africa, and feast on affogato (homemade coconut ice cream topped with a shot of espresso) while admiring the rather elegant roasting equipment, which looks like a large-scale art installation. Finnish owner Wille Yli-Luoma brings a modern, minimalist aesthetic to this fiercely popular café. There's another location Downtown at 537 S.W. 12th Avenue. ⊠ *2211 E. Burnside St., Downtown* ☎ *503/206–6602* ⊕ *www.heartroasters.com.*

LIVE MUSIC

McMenamins Crystal Ballroom. With a 7,500-square-foot springy dance floor built on ball bearings to ramp up the energy, this historic former dance hall draws local, regional, and national acts every night but Monday. Past performers include Billy Idol, Jefferson Airplane, Emmylou Harris, Death Cab for Cutie, and the Shins. ⊠ *1332 W. Burnside St., Downtown* ☎ *503/225–0047* ⊕ *www.mcmenamins.com.*

PEARL DISTRICT

BARS AND LOUNGES

Hamlet. This tribute to the finest charcuterie and pork products of Europe, including 48-month-aged melt-in-your-mouth Iberico ham, also serves an impressive roster of craft cocktails, some featuring sherries from this classy, intimate bar's extensive list of fortified wines. ⊠ *232 N.W. 12th Ave., Pearl District* ☎ *503/241–4009* ⊕ *www.hamletpdx.com.*

Fodor's Choice **Teardrop Cocktail Lounge.** A swanky, see-and-be-seen bar in the heart
★ of the trendy Pearl District, Teardrop has earned a loyal following
for its creative cocktail menu. ⊠ *1015 N.W. Everett St., Pearl District*
☎ *503/445–8109* ⊕ *www.teardroplounge.com.*

BREWPUBS AND MICROBREWERIES

Deschutes Brewery & Public House. The Portland branch of the Bend-based
Deschutes Brewery typically has more than 25 beers on tap, including
nationally acclaimed mainstays Mirror Pond Pale Ale, Inversion IPA,
and Black Butte Porter, plus seasonal and experimental brews. There's
an extensive menu of well-prepared pub fare, too. ⊠ *210 N.W. 11th
Ave., Pearl District* ☎ *503/296–4906* ⊕ *www.deschutesbrewery.com.*

OLD TOWN

GAY AND LESBIAN

Fodor's Choice **C.C. Slaughters Nightclub & Lounge.** The most popular gay and lesbian
★ dance club in the city, "C.C.'s" also has a quieter cocktail bar in
front called the Rainbow Room. ⊠ *219 N.W. Davis St., Old Town*
☎ *503/248–9135* ⊕ *www.ccslaughterspdx.com.*

Fodor's Choice **Stag.** Drawing a diverse crowd of hipsters, tourists, and old-school
★ clubbers, this Old Town hot spot cheekily bills itself a "gay gentlemen's
lounge." Mounted antlers, leather chairs, and exposed-brick walls lend
a rustic air, and male strippers dance on a small stage toward the back of
the main room; a side bar contains a pool table. ⊠ *317 N.W. Broadway,
Old Town* ☎ *971/407–3132* ⊕ *www.stagpdx.com.*

LIVE MUSIC

Roseland Theater. This spacious theater holds 1,400 people (standing-
room only except for the 21+ balcony seating area), primarily stages
rock, alternative, and blues shows, plus occasional comedians. Past
performers have included Miles Davis, Pearl Jam, the Police, Bonnie
Raitt, and Prince. ⊠ *10 N.W. 6th Ave., Old Town* ☎ *855/227–8499*
⊕ *www.roselandpdx.com.*

NOB HILL

BARS AND LOUNGES

Fodor's Choice **The Fireside.** Warmed by an open fire pit and a roaring fireplace, and
★ decorated with lots of wood and leather, this cozy campfire-chic spot
on Nob Hill's retail strip offers one of the best happy hours in Northwest, wallet-friendly appetizers made from locally sourced ingredients,
and well-crafted cocktails. Try the Dillicious, made with rye whiskey,
semidry vermouth, dill tincture, Kümmel liqueur, and lemon zest. ⊠ *801
N.W. 23rd Ave., Nob Hill* ☎ *503/477–9505* ⊕ *www.pdxfireside.com.*

Solo Club. The proprietors of this high-ceilinged haunt in a contemporary
apartment building in the up-and-coming Slab Town district like to say
that "if you are awake, chances are we're open." Indeed, you can slip in
here as early as 6 am for coffee, and then wrap up your evening around
1 am most evenings with a nightcap—the bar is know for its "coolers,"
mix-and-match concoctions, such as the radler: your choice of draft
lager with grapefruit, orange, or lemon soda. There's an extensive menu
of nibbles served day and night as well. ⊠ *2110 N.W. Raleigh St., Nob
Hill* ☎ *971/254-9806* ⊕ *www.thesoloclub.com.*

NORTH

BREWPUBS AND MICROBREWERIES

Ecliptic Brewing. Fans of boldly flavored brews flock to this spacious, airy brewery and pub at the south end of the Mississippi strip, which also has a spacious patio that's abuzz with revelers on summer afternoons. Founder John Harris is as obsessed with astronomy as he is with beer, hence the cosmic names of beers, which include Quasar Pale Ale and Phobos Single Hop Red Ale. ✉ *825 N. Cook St., North* ☎ *503/265–8002* ⊕ *www.eclipticbrewing.com.*

Prost! At the northern end of the hip North Mississippi retail and restaurant strip, Prost! is an airy, amber-lit, contemporary bar specializing in old-school German beers like Spaten Lager, Franziskaner Weissbier, and Erdinger Dunkel Weisse. Nosh on Bavarian pretzels and other Euro snacks or venture next door to one of the East Side's best food-cart pods, Mississippi Marketplace. ✉ *4237 N. Mississippi Ave., North* ☎ *503/954–2674* ⊕ *www.prostportland.com.*

LIVE MUSIC

Fodor's Choice ★ **Mississippi Studios.** An intimate neighborhood music venue, with a seated balcony and old Oriental rugs covering the standing-room-only floor, Mississippi Studios offers high-quality live music performances every night of the week in a wide range of genres. Between sets, you can jump back and forth from the adjacent BarBar, a hip, comfortable bar with a delicious hamburger and a covered back patio. ✉ *3939 N. Mississippi, North* ☎ *503/288–3895* ⊕ *www.mississippistudios.com.*

NORTHEAST

BARS AND LOUNGES

Fodor's Choice ★ **The Bye and Bye.** An Alberta go-to specializing in creative drinks (sample the house favorite, the Bye and Bye, a refreshing concoction of peach vodka, peach bourbon, lemon, cranberry juice, and soda served in a Mason jar) and vegan fare, Bye and Bye has a big covered patio and a festive dining room. The owners also operate several other similarly trendy bars around town, including Century Bar and Sweet Hereafter in Southeast, Victoria Bar in North Portland, and Jackknife at Downtown's Sentinel Hotel. ✉ *1011 N.E. Alberta St., Northeast* ☎ *503/281–0537* ⊕ *www.thebyeandbye.com.*

Fodor's Choice ★ **Expatriate.** Operated by Kyle Webster and his wife, celeb-chef partner Naomi Pomeroy of Beast (across the street), this intimate, candlelit spot has a devoted following for its balanced, boozy cocktails and addictively delicious Asian bar snacks, like curried-potato-and-English-pea samosas. Each of the eight nightly cocktails is meticulously crafted, but the Foreign National—a mix of Grey Goose Vodka, Midori Melon Liqueur, Cocchi Americano, fresh lime, ginger syrup, and Pimm's No. 1—is a house favorite. ✉ *5424 N.E. 30th Ave., Northeast* ☎ *503/805–3750* ⊕ *www.expatriatepdx.com.*

Hale Pele. The riotously colorful lighting and kitschy retro-Polynesian decor of this island-inspired tiki bar creates the ideal ambience for sipping tropical cocktails like the fruity Lava Flow (a Hawaiian take on a piña colada) or the potent Cobra's Fang (a mix of grenadine, falernum, dark rum, and mint). The kimchi dog is a highlight among the small plates. ✉ *2733 N.E. Broadway, Irvington* ☎ *503/662–8454* ⊕ *www.halepele.com.*

COFFEEHOUSES

Barista. If you're looking to test-drive a few of Portland's best beans, this dapper café with other locations Downtown, in the Pearl, and on N.E. Alberta is a great option. You'll find Stumptown, Coava, and other fine coffees, as well as a few craft beers and a small selection of high-quality chocolates and desserts. The high-ceilinged Alberta location is the most inviting, with plenty of indoor and outdoor seating. Other locations include 529 S.W. 3rd Avenue (Downtown), 539 N.W. 13th Avenue (Pearl District), and 823 N.W. 23rd Avenue (Nob Hill). ⊠ *1725 N.E. Alberta St., Alberta District* ☎ *503/274–1211* ⊕ *www.baristapdx.com.*

SOUTHEAST
BARS AND LOUNGES

Bar Avignon. Drop by this neighborhood wine bar on S.E. Division for one of the neighborhood's best happy hours, and to check out the impressive European-heavy wine selection; there are plenty of interesting bottles as well as about 15 pours by the glass. The staff is friendly and knowledgeable, and the Northwest-French food menu consistently delivers. ⊠ *2138 S.E. Division St., Southeast* ☎ *503/517–0808* ⊕ *www.baravignon.com.*

Fodor's Choice
★

Coopers Hall. Part of the Central East Side's burgeoning wine scene, this urban winery and taproom is set inside a dramatic and spacious Quonset-hut structure, which was once home to an auto-repair shop. Order any of the outstanding wines produced on-site, or delve into the happily esoteric menu of unusual wines from all over the West Coast, with a few French varieties in the mix. The kitchen turns out seriously good food, too. ⊠ *404 S.E. 6th St., Southeast* ☎ *503/719–7000* ⊕ *www.coopershall.com.*

Fodor's Choice
★

Horse Brass Pub. A laid-back beer-drinking crowd fills the venerable, dark-wood Horse Brass Pub, as good an English-style pub as you will find in Portland, with 59 beers on tap (including some cask-conditioned varieties). ■ TIP➔ Try the fish-and-chips. ⊠ *4534 S.E. Belmont St., Southeast* ☎ *503/232–2202* ⊕ *www.horsebrass.com.*

Loyal Legion. A handsome spot with leather booths and a long central wooden bar, this Central East Side pub carries an eye-opening 99 ales on draft, from local standards to seasonally changing oddballs that delight beer geeks (Ecliptic Orange Giant barley wine, a Yachats Brewing–Loyal Legion collaboration plum-lavender saison). Hefty burgers, Austrian-style wood-smoked pork sausages, and chili-cheddar-smothered fries are among the delicious pub-food accompaniments. ⊠ *710 S.E. 6th Ave., Southeast* ☎ *503/235–8272* ⊕ *loyallegionpdx.com.*

Fodor's Choice
★

Victory Bar. As beloved for its hefty venison burgers, chorizo spaetzle, and other stick-to-your-ribs bar victuals as for its impressive drinks selection, this dark corner bar with a pressed-tin ceiling is the definitive East Side hipster hangout, retaining a happily unfussy—almost divey—ambience in the face of Division Street's rapid transformation into a busy row of contemporary condos and A-list restaurants. ⊠ *3652 S.E. Division St., Southeast* ☎ *503/236–8755* ⊕ *www.thevictorybar.com.*

2

BREWPUBS AND MICROBREWERIES

Cascade Brewing. This laid-back brewpub and pioneer of the Northwest sour-beer movement is a good place for friends and sour-beer lovers to share tart flights of several varieties, including Blackcap Raspberry, Kriek, and potent (9.9% ABV) Sang Noir. You'll find 24 rotating taps, small plates and sandwiches to complement the sour beers, and ample outdoor seating. ✉ *939 S.E. Belmont St., Southeast* ☎ *503/265–8603* ⊕ *www.cascadebrewingbarrelhouse.com.*

Fodor'sChoice ★ **Commons Brewery.** This small, artisanal brewery, born in brewer Mike Wright's garage, maintained its small-batch, hands-on approach as it rapidly outgrew its first and second homes and even more rapidly earned a big reputation for exceptionally flavorful farmhouse-style ales. Wright's brews—inspired by European brewing traditions and crafted with local ingredients—have garnered many accolades; the fruit-forward Flemish Kiss and potent Bourbon Little Brother (aged in Heaven Hill bourbon barrels) are especially popular. A nice selection of cheeses and charcuterie are available in the spacious taproom. ✉ *630 S.E. Belmont St., Southeast* ☎ *503/343–5501* ⊕ *www.commonsbrewery.com.*

Hopworks Urban Brewery. A bicycle-themed microbrewery with deftly crafted beer, sandwiches, and pizzas, Hopworks Urban Brewery (HUB for short) occupies an industrial lodge-inspired building that's 100% renewably powered and water neutral. Hopworks BikeBar, located on the bike highway of North Williams, offers similar fare with the same bikey, eco-friendly vibe. ✉ *2944 S.E. Powell Blvd., Southeast* ☎ *503/232–4677* ⊕ *www.hopworksbeer.com.*

COFFEEHOUSES

Fodor'sChoice ★ **Coava Coffee Roasters.** Located next door to the roastery, the light and open, bamboo wood–filled Coava Coffee Roasters offers some of the highest-quality single-origin, pour-over coffees in the city. There's a second branch in the Hawthorne District. ✉ *1300 S.E. Grand Ave., Southeast* ☎ *503/894–8134* ⊕ *www.coavacoffee.com.*

Stumptown Coffee Roasters. Stumptown Coffee Roasters, which now has locations in several other cities, has three cafés on the east side. At the original site (S.E. Division), organic beans are still roasted on a regular basis. At the Tasting Bar (S.E. Salmon)—adjacent to Stumptown headquarters—patrons can participate in "cuppings," or tastings, at 3 pm each day. Stumptown has other locations around town, including a popular branch inside Downtown's Ace Hotel. ✉ *4525 S.E. Division St., Southeast* ☎ *503/230–7702* ⊕ *www.stumptowncoffee.com.*

GAY AND LESBIAN

Fodor'sChoice ★ **Crush.** A favorite gay and lesbian hangout in Southeast, Crush serves up tasty food, strong cocktails, and DJ-fueled dance parties. The front section is mellow and good for conversation, while the back area contains a small but lively dance floor. ✉ *1400 S.E. Morrison St., Southeast* ☎ *503/235–8150* ⊕ *www.crushbar.com.*

LIVE MUSIC

Fodor'sChoice ★ **Doug Fir Lounge.** Part retro diner and part log cabin, the Doug Fir serves food and booze and hosts DJs and live rock shows from both up-and-coming and established bands most nights of the week. It adjoins the trendy Hotel Jupiter. ✉ *830 E. Burnside St., Southeast* ☎ *503/231–9663* ⊕ *www.dougfirlounge.com.*

Revolution Hall. Southeast Portland's stately early 1900s former Washington High School building was converted into a state-of-the-art concert hall in 2015, featuring noted pop and world-beat music acts and comedians, from Henry Rollins to Tig Notaro, plus film festivals and other intriguing events. There are two bars on-site, including a roof deck with great views of the Downtown skyline. ✉ *1300 S.E. Stark St., Southeast* ☎ *971/808–5094* ⊕ *www.revolutionhall.com.*

PERFORMING ARTS

For a city of this size, there is truly an impressive—and accessible—scope of talent from visual artists, performance artists, and musicians. The arts are alive, with outdoor sculptural works strewn around the city, ongoing festivals, and premieres of traveling Broadway shows. Top-named international acts, such as David Byrne, Arcade Fire, Joan Baez, and Mumford and Sons regularly include Portland in their worldwide stops.

PERFORMANCE VENUES

Fodor's Choice ★ **Arlene Schnitzer Concert Hall.** The 2,776-seat Arlene Schnitzer Concert Hall, built in 1928 in an Italian rococo revival style, hosts rock concerts, choral groups, lectures, and concerts by the Oregon Symphony and others. ✉ *Portland Center for the Performing Arts, 1037 S.W. Broadway, Downtown* ☎ *503/248-4335* ⊕ *www.portland5.com.*

Moda Center. This 21,000-seat facility, formerly known as the Rose Garden, is home to the Portland Trail Blazers basketball team and the site of other sporting events and rock concerts. It's right on the MAX light-rail line, just across from Downtown. ✉ *Rose Quarter, 1 Center Ct., Lloyd District, Northeast* ☎ *503/745-3000* ⊕ *www.rosequarter.com.*

Portland'5 Centers for the Arts. The city's top performing arts complex hosts opera, ballet, rock shows, symphony performances, lectures, and Broadway musicals in its five venues. ✉ *1111 S.W. Broadway, Downtown* ☎ *503/248-4335* ⊕ *www.portland5.com.*

CLASSICAL MUSIC

The Oregon Symphony, established in 1896, is Portland's largest classical group—and one of the largest orchestras in the country.

OPERA

Portland Opera. This well-respected opera company performs five productions a year at Keller Auditorium. ✉ *Keller Auditorium, 222 S.W. Clay St., Downtown* ☎ *503/241-1802, 866/739-6737* ⊕ *www.portlandopera.org.*

ORCHESTRAS

FAMILY Fodor's Choice ★ **Oregon Symphony.** Established in 1896, the symphony is Portland's largest classical group—and one of the largest orchestras in the country. Its season officially starts in September and ends in May, with concerts held at Arlene Schnitzer Concert Hall, but throughout the summer the orchestra and its smaller ensembles can be seen at Waterfront Park and Washington Park for special outdoor summer performances. It also presents about 40 classical, pop, children's, and family concerts each year. ☎ *503/228-1353, 800/228-7343* ⊕ *www.orsymphony.org.*

DANCE

Portland has a wonderful variety of both progressive and traditional dance companies. As part of their productions, many of these companies bring in international talent for choreography and guest performances.

Fodor's Choice ★ **Northwest Dance Project.** Founded in 2004, this first-rate contemporary-dance company performs several shows—typically including a world premier or two—each season at different venues around town, including the Newmark Theatre and PSU's Lincoln Performance Hall. ☏ 503/828–8285 ⊕ www.nwdanceproject.org.

Oregon Ballet Theatre. This respected company produces several classical and contemporary works a year, including a much-loved holiday *Nutcracker*. Most performances are at Keller Auditorium and the Portland Center for the Arts' Newmark Theatre. ☏ 503/222–5538, 888/922–5538 ⊕ www.obt.org.

FILM

The McMenimans "brew theaters" are a great place to catch a flick while chowing down and sipping on local beer. They are not-to-be-missed Portland landmarks when it comes to movie viewing in uniquely renovated buildings that avoid any hint of corporate streamlining.

If you're a film buff, be sure to check out the Northwest Film Center's calendar of events for special screenings and film festivals, with genres that include international, LGBT, and animation.

Fodor's Choice ★ **Bagdad Theater.** Built in 1927, the stunningly restored, eminently quirky Bagdad Theater shows first-run Hollywood films on a huge screen and serves pizza, burgers, sandwiches, and McMenamins ales. The Bagdad is a local favorite. ✉ 3702 S.E. Hawthorne Blvd., Hawthorne District, Southeast ☏ 503/249–7474 ⊕ www.mcmenamins.com.

Hollywood Theatre. A landmark movie theater that showed silent films when it opened in 1926, the not-for-profit Hollywood Theatre screens everything from obscure foreign art films to old American classics and second-run Hollywood hits, and hosts an annual Academy Awards viewing party. ✉ 4122 N.E. Sandy Blvd., Northeast ☏ 503/281–4215 ⊕ www.hollywoodtheatre.org.

Fodor's Choice ★ **Kennedy School Theater.** Furnished with couches and end tables, the Kennedy School theater, which is located in a renovated elementary school that also contains a hotel, a restaurant, several bars, and a soaking pool, screens second-run and occasional indie movies. ✉ 5736 N.E. 33rd Ave., Concordia, Northeast ☏ 503/249–3983 ⊕ www.mcmenamins.com.

THEATER

From the largest of productions to the smallest of venues, theater comes to life in Portland year-round.

Artists Repertory Theatre. The theater company performs seven to nine productions a year including regional premieres, occasional commissioned works, and classics. ✉ 1515 S.W. Morrison St., Downtown ☏ 503/241–1278 ⊕ www.artistsrep.org.

FAMILY
Fodor's Choice ★ **Northwest Children's Theater.** This long-running company presents four shows during its fall–spring season, geared to both the toddler and teen set. Performances are staged in the handsome Northwest Neighborhood

Cultural Center in Nob Hill. ⊠ *1819 N.W. Everett St., Nob Hill* ☎ *503/222–4480* ⊕ *www.nwcts.org.*

Fodor's Choice
★
Portland Center Stage. Housed in a handsomely restored 1891 armory, Portland Center Stage puts on contemporary and classical works in the LEED-certified green building between September and June. ⊠ *Gerding Theater at the Armory, 128 N.W. 11th Ave., Pearl District* ☎ *503/445–3700* ⊕ *www.pcs.org.*

SPORTS AND THE OUTDOORS

Portlanders avidly gravitate to the outdoors and they're well acclimated to the elements year-round. Once the sun starts to shine in spring and into summer, the city fills with hikers, joggers, and mountain bikers, who flock to Portland's hundreds of miles of parks, paths, and trails. The Willamette and Columbia rivers are popular for boating and water sports.

As for competitive sports, Portland is home to the Timbers, a major league soccer team with a devout local fan base, and NBA basketball's beloved Trail Blazers.

BASKETBALL

Portland Trail Blazers. The NBA's Portland Trail Blazers play their 82-game season in the Moda Center, which can hold up to 20,000 spectators. The MAX train pulls up just a couple blocks from the arena's front door. ⊠ *Moda Center, 1 N. Center Ct., Rose Quarter, North* ☎ *503/797–9600* ⊕ *www.nba.com/blazers.*

BIKING

Biking is a cultural phenomenon in Portland—likely the most beloved mode of transportation in the city. Besides the sheer numbers of cyclists you see on roads and pathways, you'll find well-marked bike lanes and signs reminding motorists to yield to cyclists.

There are more than 340 miles of bicycle boulevards, lanes, and off-street paths in Portland, and the city ushered in the long-anticipated BIKETOWN Portland bike-share program in 2016. Accessible maps, specialized tours, parking capacity (including lockers and sheltered racks Downtown), and bicycle-only traffic signals at confusing intersections make biking in most neighborhoods easy. Cyclists can find the best routes by following green direction-and-distance signs that point the way around town, and the corresponding white dots on the street surface.

Cycling in Portland has evolved into a medium for progressive politics and public service. Several bike co-ops in the city are devoted to providing used bikes at decent prices, as well as to teaching bike maintenance and the economic and environmental benefits of becoming a two-wheel commuter. Check out the helpful Bike Portland (⊕ *www.bikeportland. org*) website for information on regularly scheduled bike events, cycling-related local news and advice, and referrals to reliable bike rental, sales, and repair shops.

BIKE RENTALS

BIKETOWN Portland. Portland's bike-share program, in partnership with Nike and begun in 2016, is affordable and easy to use. There are more than 100 stations throughout the city, and some 1,000 bikes, each with a small basket (helmets are not provided, however, so consider bringing your own). Just choose a plan (single rides start at $2.50 for 30 minutes, and day passes are $12), sign up, and you'll receive an account and PIN number that allows you to take out a bike. ⊠ *Portland* ☎ *866/512–2453* ⊕ *www.biketownpdx.com.*

Waterfront Bicycle Rentals. For jaunts along the Willamette River, Waterfront Bicycles has everything a visiting bicyclist needs. There is a variety of styles and sizes of bikes to outfit the entire family, including balance bikes for the little rider. To reserve online, book at least 48 hours ahead. Guided bike tours are available as well. ⊠ *10 S. W. Ash St., Suite 100, Downtown* ☎ *503/227–1719* ⊕ *www.waterfrontbikes.com.*

BIKE ROUTES

If you're a social rider, group rides set out from several local shops. Check the events pages of **Bike Gallery** (⊕ *www.bikegallery.com*), **River City Bicycles** (⊕ *www.rivercitybicycles.com*), and **Bike Portland** (⊕ *www. bikeportland.org*).

Bike paths line both sides of the **Willamette River** through Downtown, so you can easily make a mild, several-mile loop through Waterfront Park via the Steel, Hawthorne, Tilikum Crossing, or Sellwood bridges.

Though much of **Forest Park's** 80-plus miles of trails are reserved for hiking and nonbiking activities, there are more than 30 miles of single-track mountain-biking trails and fire lanes open to biking, including Leif Erikson Drive, an 11-mile ride whose dense canopy occasionally gives way to river views. Along the park's trails you may come across old-growth forest as well as some of the park's more than 175 species of animals and birds. To reach the Leif Erikson trailhead, bike up steep Thurman Street or shuttle there via TriMet Bus 15. Maps and information on the trails can be found at ⊕ *www. forestparkconservancy.org.*

PARKS

The variety of Portland's parks ensures that there's something for just about everyone, from the world's smallest park (Mill Ends) to one of the largest urban natural areas in the country (Forest Park). ⇨ *See Exploring for details about other favorite Portland green spaces, including Laurelhurst, Mt. Tabor, and Washington parks.*

Fodor's Choice ★ **Council Crest Park.** The highest point in Portland, at 1,073 feet, this 43-acre bluff-top patch of greenery is a superb spot to take in sunsets and sunrises. Along with nearly 180-degree views of the Portland metro area, a clear day also affords views of the surrounding peaks—Mt. Hood, Mt. St. Helens, Mt. Adams, Mt. Jefferson, and Mt. Rainier. A bronze fountain depicting a mother and child has been erected in the park twice; first in the 1950s and the second in the 1990s. The peaceful piece was stolen in the 1980s, uncovered in a narcotics bust 10 years later, and then returned to the park. Trails connect Council Crest with Marquam Nature Park and Washington Park. ■TIP→ It's quite busy on weekends so visit on a weekday, if possible. ⌂ *3400 Council Crest Dr., West Hills ⊕ www.portlandoregon.gov/parks.*

FAMILY
Fodor's Choice
★
Sauvie Island. If it's a day to take advantage of gorgeous weather then drive about a half hour northwest of Downtown to Sauvie Island. The island has a wildlife refuge, three beaches (including Collins Beach, which is clothing-optional), superb biking and hiking trails, and several farms offering "u-pick" bounty. To get to the beaches, take U.S. 30 north to Sauvie Island bridge, and turn right; follow N.W. Sauvie Island Road to Reeder Road and follow signs. There's plenty of parking at the beaches, but a permit is required ($10 for a one-day permit, available at the general store at the base of the bridge). ⌂ *N.W. Sauvie Island Rd., Sauvie Island ⊕ www.sauvieisland.org.*

SOCCER

Portland Timbers. Portland's major-league soccer team plays their 34-game season at the Downtown Jeld-Wen Field from March through October. The city has many ardent soccer fans known as the Timbers Army. Sitting near this group means a raucous time with drumming, chanting, and cheers. The MAX stops right by the stadium. ⌂ *Jeld-Wen Field, 1844 S.W. Morrison St., Downtown ☎ 503/553–5555 ⊕ www.portlandtimbers.com.*

SHOPPING

The shopping landscape in Portland has changed significantly in recent years, perhaps not quite as dramatically as the much-buzzed-about culinary scene, but in similar (pardon the pun) fashion. Specifically, those same hip and indie-spirited neighborhoods around the city that have become hot spots for food and drink—areas like the Pearl District, Downtown West End, Alberta, North Mississippi, North Williams, and Central East Side—are also enjoying a steady influx of distinctive, well-curated boutiques specializing in edgy fashion and jewelry, handcrafted home accessories and household goods, and artisanal foods.

DOWNTOWN

CLOTHING

Fodor's Choice
★
Frances May. Located in the hip West End section of Downtown, this grandmother-and-granddaughter-owned clothing store is a favorite of stylish local men and women who come for that cool, understated, high-quality look (casual to dressy) that Portlanders are known for. You'll find made-in-America labels like Steven Alan and Rachel Comey as well as European faves like Acne and APC. The Alex Mill cashmere beanies and Carven women's pullovers and sweaters are especially popular during Portland's cool winters. ⌂ *1003 S.W. Washington St., Downtown ☎ 503/227–3402 ⊕ www.francesmay.com.*

Nike Portland. It's safe to assume that Nike's flagship retail store, just a short drive from the company's mammoth HQ campus in Beaverton, has the latest and greatest in swoosh-adorned products. The high-tech setting has athlete profiles, photos, and interactive displays. ⊠ *638 S.W. 5th Ave., Downtown* ☎ *503/221–6453* ⊕ *www.nike.com.*

FOOD

Cacao. Chocolate fiends and sweet-tooths get their fix at this inviting storefront shop and café in the West End, which also has a branch inside Downtown's natty Heathman Hotel. Browse the huge selection of ultra-fine, single-origin, artisanal chocolates from around the world, or order a cup of luscious and satisfying house-made drinking chocolate. ⊠ *414 S.W. 13th Ave., West End* ☎ *503/241–0656* ⊕ *www.cacaodrinkchocolate.com.*

Moonstruck Chocolate Cafe. Even without getting a nod from Oprah in her magazine, Moonstruck would still be known as a chocolatier extraordinaire. There are three cafés in the Portland metro area, including another Downtown location at Pioneer Place Mall. All offer made-to-order hot chocolate, cocoa, shakes, and mochas, as well as truffles, chocolate bars, and dynamic holiday treats. ⊠ *608 S.W. Alder St., Downtown* ☎ *503/241–0955* ⊕ *www.moonstruckchocolate.com.*

FAMILY
Fodor's Choice
★

Portland Farmers' Market. Running on Saturday mornings and early afternoons year-round, this astoundingly large and diverse farmers' market carries not only Oregon's bounty of flowers and produce (look especially for berries in summer and stone fruits in fall) but also hazelnuts, cheese, delectable baked goods, wines and ciders, and other goodies. It's great for people-watching and souvenir shopping, and several stalls sell great food to eat on-site—be sure to come hungry. If you can't make the Saturday market, check the website for locations of smaller but still very popular versions of the market, held most days during the warmer months at various locations around town. ⊠ *South Park Blocks at S.W. Park Ave. and Montgomery St., Downtown* ☎ *503/241–0032* ⊕ *www. portlandfarmersmarket.org.*

GIFTS

Made in Oregon. This eclectic retail tribute to the Beaver State sells books, smoked salmon, artisan chocolates, local wines, Pendleton woolen goods, carvings made of myrtle wood, and other products made in the state. There are numerous branches around the area, including Portland International Airport and all of the larger shopping malls. ⊠ *Pioneer Place Mall, 340 S.W. Morrison St., Downtown* ☎ *503/241– 3630, 866/257–0938* ⊕ *www.madeinoregon.com.*

HOUSEHOLD GOODS AND FURNITURE

Boys Fort. If the name of this colorful Downtown emporium brings back memories of hanging out with friends in a rad basement rec room, you'll likely love this offbeat store curated by designers R. Rolfe and Jake France. They've stocked this high-ceilinged shop with a mix of artful items for the hip dude's urban nest, including earthy-hued terra-cotta planters, model sailboats, and mounted wooden faux deer heads, plus old posters and games. ⊠ *902 S.W. Morrison St., Downtown* ☎ *503/567–1015* ⊕ *www.boysfort.com.*

Fodor's Choice **Canoe.** Form meets function at this stylish, contemporary boutique
★ with a carefully curated selection of clean-lined, modern goods and
gifts for every room in the home. You'll find curvy thick-glass bowls,
modern lamps with sheer paper shades, polished-stone trays, Bigelow
natural-bristle toothbrushes, and Chemex coffee kettles, with some
goods produced locally and exclusively for Canoe, and others imported
from Asia and northern Europe. ⊠ *1233 S.W. 10th Ave., Downtown*
☎ *503/889–8545* ⊕ *www.canoeonline.net.*

MALLS AND DEPARTMENT STORES

Fodor's Choice **Union Way.** A modern take on an old-fashioned European shopping
★ arcade, this indoor alley spans one block from Stark to Burnside streets
(right across the street from Powell's Books) and contains about a
dozen diverting boutiques, plus a branch of Little T Bakery and the
trendy Asian restaurant Boxer Ramen. Most of these shops specialize
in apparel and accessories, including Will Leather Goods, Steven Alan
eyewear, and Danner sports and outerwear, but you'll also find Quin
Candy shop and Spruce Apothecary. ⊠ *1022 W. Burnside St., Downtown* ☎ *503/922–0056* ⊕ *www.facebook.com/UnionWayPDX.*

PEARL DISTRICT

BOOKS

Fodor's Choice **Oblation Papers.** Employing antique presses and old-world processes, this
★ dapper shop in the Pearl District houses a paper mill, letterpress shop, and
retail store where you can find one-of-a-kind cards, stationery, albums,
and journals. The quality, handcrafted cards featuring vintage posters or
images of local wildlife make wonderful keepsakes and gifts. ⊠ *516 N.W.
12th Ave., Pearl District* ☎ *503/223–1093* ⊕ *www.oblationpapers.com.*

Fodor's Choice **Powell's City of Books.** The largest retail store of used and new books in
★ the world (with more than 1.5 million volumes), covers an entire city
block and rises three stories on the edge of the Pearl District. A local
legend, and rightfully so, Powell's also carries rare and collectible books
and contains a popular coffeehouse, World Cup. There are also branches
in Portland International Airport as well as a large outpost in the heart
of the Hawthorne District, with its own coffeehouse, Fresh Pot. ⊠ *1005
W. Burnside St., Pearl District* ☎ *503/228–4651* ⊕ *www.powells.com.*

CLOTHING

Nau. Specializing in men's and women's sustainable clothing, from rugged hoodies and urbane down jackets to dressier threads made with
cotton, Tencel, and other breathable fabrics, Portland-based Nau ships
all over the world, but you can try on products and ask questions at this
sleek flagship retail store in the Pearl District. ⊠ *304 N.W. 11th Ave.,
Pearl District* ☎ *503/224–9697* ⊕ *www.nau.com.*

FOOD

Fodor's Choice **Smith Teamaker.** Tea drinkers rejoice: you don't have to resort to coffee
★ just because you're in Portland. The late founder and legendary tea guru
Steve Smith launched two renowned companies, Stash Tea and Tazo,
before opening his own company inside a former blacksmith shop on the
northwestern edge of the Pearl District. At this handsome tea shop, you

can see how the tea is made and packaged, shop teas and accessories, and then sample different varieties at a small tasting bar. Select a tea flight from a menu, try a tea latte, or work your work through an oxidation spectrum—from white to black. The sturdy, pastel-hued boxes in which Smith packages his exquisite, carefully sourced teas make great gifts. ⊠ *1626 N.W. Thurman St., Pearl District* ☎ *503/719–8752* ⊕ *www.smithtea.com.*

GALLERIES

Fodor'sChoice
★

First Thursday. This gallery walk the first Thursday of every month gives art appreciators a chance to check out new exhibits while enjoying music and wine. Typically, the galleries, which are largely located in the Pearl District, are open in the evening from 6 to 9, but hours vary. Be prepared for a lively scene including throngs of people, street musicians, and local art vendors, with much of the action along N.W. 13th Avenue between Hoyt and Kearney streets, which is pedestrian only during this event. ⊠ *Pearl District* ☎ *503/227–8519* ⊕ *www.explorethepearl.com.*

NOB HILL

CLOTHING

Sloan Boutique. Set among the several fine clothiers on the 700 and 800 blocks of N.W. 23rd Avenue, Sloan Boutique carries a good mix of affordable women's casual and fashion brands, including Kensie, Free People, Kut, and Franco Sarto. The boutique's adjoining space—PlaTform—carries a good selection of trendy shoes and accessories. Sloan has a second branch across the river in Hawthorne. ⊠ *738 N.W. 23rd Ave., Nob Hill* ☎ *503/222–6666* ⊕ *www.sloanpdx.com.*

GALLERIES

Twist. This huge space in Nob Hill is well stocked with contemporary American ceramics, glass, furniture, sculpture, and handcrafted jewelry often with a whimsical touch. ⊠ *30 N.W. 23rd Pl., Nob Hill* ☎ *503/224–0334* ⊕ *www.twistonline.com.*

JEWELRY

Gem Set Love. Portland's premier estate and vintage jewelry destination, known formerly as Gilt, occupies a dapper Craftsman bungalow along a fashionable stretch of Nob Hill's N.W. 23rd. Inside you'll find an ever-changing inventory of radiant gold and silver rings, bracelets, earrings, and necklaces, many inlaid with dazzling gems. The antique wedding and engagement rings are especially popular. ⊠ *720 N.W. 23rd Ave., Nob Hill* ☎ *503/226–0629* ⊕ *www.gem-set-love.com.*

WEST END

MUSIC

Tender Loving Empire. The retail shop of the eponymous Portland indie record label founded by Jared and Brianne Mees carries not only music but also cool hand-printed cards, posters, and T-shirts, along with a hipster-favored selection of lifestyle goods, from coffee-infused soaps and beard oils to do-it-yourself goat-cheese-making kits and screen-printed tote bags. You'll find additional locations on Hawthorne and in Nob Hill. ⊠ *412 S.W. 10th Ave., West End* ☎ *503/243–5859* ⊕ *www.tenderlovingempire.com.*

NORTH

FOOD

Fodor'sChoice   **The Meadow.** Food writer Mark Bitterman knows a thing or two about
★   salt—he's written two popular books on the subject, and he's the owner
of this tiny purveyor of gourmet finishing salts, some of them smoked or
infused with unusual flavors, like cherry and plums, or saffron. At this
flagship location (there's a second Meadow in Nob Hill, and a third in
Manhattan's West Village) you can also purchase the additional magical
touches you might need to create the perfect dinner party, from Oregon
and European wines and vermouths, to fresh-cut flowers, aromatic
cocktail bitters, and high-quality, single-origin chocolates. ⊠ *3731 N.
Mississippi Ave., North* ☎ *503/974–8349* ⊕ *www.atthemeadow.com.*

HOUSEHOLD GOODS AND FURNITURE

Fodor'sChoice   **Beam & Anchor.** Set on a busy street corner several blocks from the North
★   Side's trendy North Mississippi strip, this once-dilapidated warehouse
houses an upstairs workshop for makers of artisanal goods and an
inspiring downstairs retail space where proprietors Robert and Jocelyn
Rahm sell a carefully curated selection of lifestyle goods for every room
in the home, many of them produced locally—some as local as upstairs.
Among the hipster treasures, look for warm and soft camp blankets and
Navajo rugs with vibrant prints, women's jewelry in a variety of simple-
but-beautiful styles, Portland Apothecary bath salts and soaps, and
quite a few larger pieces of distinctive furniture. ⊠ *2710 N. Interstate
Ave., North* ☎ *503/367–3230* ⊕ *www.beamandanchor.com.*

TOYS

Fodor'sChoice   **Paxton Gate.** Here, science and biology mix with whimsy and imagina-
★   tion. You'll find everything from taxidermied scorpions and baby goats
to ostrich eggs and ceramic chimes. It's a fascinating and strangely
beguiling mix of goods, and not for the faint of heart. ⊠ *4204 N. Mississippi Ave., North* ☎ *503/719–4508* ⊕ *www.paxtongate.com.*

NORTHEAST

FOOD

Providore Fine Foods. This sleek gourmet market features the artisan
and local fare of several notable Portland purveyors, including Little
T Baker, Rubinette Produce, Flying Fish Company, Arrosto (which
turns out delicious Mediterranean-style rotisserie chicken), and
Pastaworks. It's a terrific source for picnic supplies, and there's table
seating. The owners also operate Pastaworks at City Market in Nob
Hill. ⊠ *2340 N.E. Sandy Blvd., Northeast* ☎ *503/232–1010* ⊕ *www.
providorefinefoods.com.*

GALLERIES

Ampersand Gallery & Fine Books. Part art gallery, part media store, this
minimalist white-wall space on Alberta Street has monthly shows
featuring edgy, contemporary art, and stocks a fascinating trove of
photography and art books, vintage travel brochures, curious photography, pulp-fiction novels, and other printed materials of the sort
you might find in a chest in a mysterious neighbor's attic. The owners

also operate the cute Cord boutique next door, which stocks artfully designed household goods, from handcrafted soaps to aerodynamic coffeepots. ⊠ *2916 N.E. Alberta St., Alberta District* ☎ *503/805–5458* ⊕ *www.ampersandgallerypdx.com.*

FAMILY
Fodor'sChoice
★

Last Thursday Arts Walk. The Alberta Arts District hosts an arts walk on the last Thursday of each month. This quirky procession along 15 blocks of one of the city's favorite thoroughfares for browsing art galleries, distinctive boutiques, and hipster bars and restaurants features street performers and buskers, crafts makers, and food vendors. The street is closed to traffic from 6 to 9:30 pm. ⊠ *N.E. Alberta St., Alberta District* ⊕ *www.lastthursdayonalberta.com.*

MUSIC

Fodor'sChoice
★

Music Millennium. The oldest record store in the Pacific Northwest, Music Millennium Northwest stocks a huge selection of new and used music in every possible category, including local punk groups. The store also hosts a number of in-store performances, often by top-name artists like Lucinda Williams, Richard Thompson, Sheryl Crow, and Randy Newman. ⊠ *3158 E. Burnside St., Laurelhurst* ☎ *503/231–8926* ⊕ *www. musicmillennium.com.*

SOUTHEAST

CLOTHING

Fodor'sChoice
★

Altar. A tiny but impressively stocked boutique in a charming, old, Craftsman-style house that also houses the excellent Hazel Room café, Altar is devoted to decorative items, fashion, jewelry, and crafts made by Portlanders. The selection is eclectic and fun—everything from handcrafted soaps made with local beer to geometric-shape brass necklaces. Clothing at Altar is geared mostly to women. ⊠ *3279 S.E. Hawthorne Blvd., Hawthorne District* ☎ *503/236–6120* ⊕ *www. altarpdx.com.*

Herbivore Clothing. An animal-rights-minded shop in the Central East Side, Herbivore is a terrific resource if you're seeking clothing and accessories—from cotton-rayon tees and sweaters to braided canvas belts and wallets fashioned out of reclaimed bike and truck tubes—that have been created without the harm or use of animals. There's also a great selection of books on veganism, plus food, health-care products, and gifts. ⊠ *1211 S.E. Stark St., Southeast* ☎ *503/281–8638* ⊕ *www. herbivoreclothing.com.*

Union Rose. For distinctive women's fashion and accessories designed and made in Portland, check out this boutique in up-and-coming Montavilla. Though there are scores of dresses for any season, including a very good selection of dresses and skirts in plus sizes, there's also plenty of everyday wear, like hoodies and hats. ⊠ *7909 S.E. Stark St., Southeast* ☎ *503/287–4242* ⊕ *www.unionrosepdx.com.*

Fodor'sChoice
★

Wildfang. This edgy fashion label and shop run by self-proclaimed "tomboys" and "modern-day female Robin Hoods" has earned an international reputation for its gender-bending styles, from brocade lapel blazers and matching trousers to slouchy-fit hoodies. You'll also find beanies, briefs, ties, and trademark "Wild Feminist" snapback caps that make a statement on the street or in the club. ⊠ *1230 S.E. Grand Ave., Portland* ☎ *503/208–3631* ⊕ *www.wildfang.com.*

HOUSEHOLD GIFTS AND FURNITURE

House of Vintage. This mammoth 13,000-square-foot shop, just down the street from one of the better Goodwill shops in the city, is de rigueur among vintage aficionados. Inside, you can rifle through the wares of some 60 dealers; bell-bottom jeans and plaid blazers are a big draw, but this time capsule also brims with kitschy ceramic ashtrays, Naugahyde couches, '50s magazines, old-school lunchboxes, and pretty much anything else you might recall from your childhood. ⊠ *3315 S.E. Hawthorne Blvd., Hawthorne District* ☎ *503/236–1991* ⊕ *www. houseofvintagenw.com.*

OUTDOOR SUPPLIES

Next Adventure Sports. It all about the gear here. Next Adventure Sports carries new and used sporting goods, including camping gear, snowboards, kayaks, and mountaineering supplies. Kayak classes and Outdoor School provide plenty of opportunities to get out and enjoy Oregon like a local. They also operate The Paddle Sports Center, just a few blocks southeast at 624 S.E. 7th Avenue. ⊠ *426 S.E. Grand Ave., Southeast* ☎ *503/233–0706* ⊕ *www.nextadventure.net.*

TOYS

FAMILY

Fodor's Choice

★

Cloud Cap Games. There's more than just run-of-the-mill board games at Cloud Cap. For children and grown-ups alike, the games here challenge the mind and provide hours of entertainment. There's a room with tables to play or try out a game. The knowledgeable owners and staff may sit down and join in the fun and are always happy to answer questions and offer suggestions. ⊠ *1226 S.E. Lexington St., Sellwood* ☎ *503/505–9344* ⊕ *www.cloudcapgames.com.*

OREGON COAST

WELCOME TO OREGON COAST

TOP REASONS TO GO

★ **Beaches:** The Oregon Coast has breathtaking beaches, from romantic stretches to creature-teeming tide pools and stunning cliffs that flank many of the beaches.

★ **Shop for blown glass:** Artisanal glass shops dot the coastline—at some, you can even craft your own colorful creations.

★ **Oregon Dunes National Recreation Area:** Whether you're screaming in a dune buggy or scrambling over them on foot, southern Oregon's mountainous sand dunes bring out the kid in anyone who traverses them.

★ **Small-town charms:** You'll find some of the state's most quirky and charming communities along the coast, from hipster-approved Astoria to arty and secluded Port Orford to rustic yet sophisticated Yachats.

★ **Wine and dine:** You don't have to spend a lot to enjoy creatively prepared seafood, artisanal microbrews, and local wines.

1 North Coast. As the primary gateway for both Portlanders and those visiting from neighboring Washington, the north coast is the busiest stretch of Oregon coastline, although it's still rife with secluded coves and funky seaside hamlets. Its lighthouse-dotted shoreline stretches from the mouth of the Columbia River south to Pacific City. The 90-mile region includes the historic working-class fishing town of Astoria and its recent influx of hip cafés, indie boutiques, and restored hotels; family-friendly Seaside with its touristy but bustling boardwalk; art-fueled and refined Cannon Beach; laid-back and stunningly situated Manzanita Beach; and tiny Pacific City, where a colorful fleet of dories dots the wide, deep beach.

2 Central Coast. The 75-mile stretch from Lincoln City to Florence offers whale-watching, incomparable seafood, shell-covered beaches, candy confections, and close-up views of undersea life. At the north end, in Lincoln City visitors can indulge in gaming, shopping, golfing, and beachcombing. The harbor town of Depoe Bay is a center for whale-watching, and nearby Newport offers a stellar aquarium and science center. It's also home to one of Oregon's largest fishing fleets. The less-developed town of Yachats is a true seaside gem with astounding coastal views, where the only demands are to relax and enjoy an increasingly noteworthy restaurant scene. The cute town of Florence and its bustling downtown hugs the Siuslaw River—it's also the northern access point for the Oregon dunes.

3 South Coast. From the heart of Oregon dunes country in Reedsport to the southernmost Oregon town of Brookings, the 134-mile stretch of U.S. 101 is less touristy than points north, but still has mesmerizing beaches, headlands, and coastal rain forests in abundance. Coos Bay and adjacent North Bend make up the region's largest population center. The beach town of Bandon is a world-class golfing destination that's also popular for beachcombing and lighthouse gazing. Ruggedly situated and low-key Port Orford has gorgeous beach landscapes and a growing arts scene, while Gold Beach and Brookings, farther south, are bathed in sunshine.

GETTING ORIENTED

3

Oregon's coastline begins in the north in the town of Astoria, which lies at the mouth of the Columbia River on the Washington state line. It's a slow-going but spectacular 363-mile drive south along U.S. Highway 101 to the small town of Brookings at Oregon's southwestern corner, several miles from the California border. The rugged Coast Range flanks the entire coast to the east, providing a picturesque barrier between the ocean and the lush Willamette, Umpqua, and Rogue valleys, where you'll find Oregon's larger communities, including Portland and Eugene.

EXPLORING OREGON'S BEST BEACHES

Oregon's 300 miles of public coastline is the backdrop for thrills, serenity, rejuvenation, and romance. From yawning expanses of sand dotted with beach chairs to tiny patches bounded by surf-shaped cliffs, the state's shoreline often draws comparisons to New Zealand.

(above) Surfing the Oregon Coast; (opposite page, top) Oregon Dunes National Recreation Area; (opposite page, bottom) Cannon Beach Sandcastle Contest

Most awe inspiring are the massive rock formations just offshore in the northern and southern sections of the coast, breaking up the Pacific horizon. Beaches along the north coast, from Astoria to Pacific City, are perfect for romantic strolls on the sands. The central-coast beaches, from Lincoln City to Florence, are long and wide, providing perfect conditions for sunbathers, children, clam diggers, horseback riders, and surfers. The southern-coast beaches from Reedsport to Brookings are less populated, ideal for getting away from it all.

In late July and August the climate is kind to sun worshippers. During the shoulder months, keep layers of clothing handy for the unpredictable temperature swings. Winter can be downright blustery, a time that many seaside inns optimistically call "storm-watching season."

GLASS FLOATS: FINDERS KEEPERS

Since 1997, between mid-October and Memorial Day, more than 2,000 handcrafted glass floats made by local artists have been hidden along Lincoln City's 7½-mile public beach. If you happen to come upon one, call the local tourism office (*800/452–2151*) to register it, and find out which artist made it. While antique glass floats are extremely rare, these new versions make great souvenirs.

THE OREGON COAST'S BEST BEACHES

Cannon Beach. In the shadow of glorious **Haystack Rock**, this beach is wide, flat, and perfect for bird-watching, exploring tide pools, building sand castles, and romantic walks in the sea mist. Each June the city holds a **sand-castle contest**, drawing artists and thousands of visitors. The rest of the year the beach is far less populated. The dapper beachfront town has several of the region's swankiest hotels and finest restaurants, as well as spots for surfing, hiking, and beachcombing.

Pacific City. This beach is postcard perfect, with its colorful fleet of dories sitting on the sand and massive Cape Kiwanda dune flanking the shore to the north. Like Cannon Beach, this town also has a huge (less famous) Haystack Rock that provides the perfect scenic backdrop for horseback riders, beach strollers, and people with shovels chasing sand-covered clams. With safe beach breaks that are ideal for beginners and larger peaks a bit to the south, this is also a great spot for surfers. Winter-storm-watchers love Pacific City, where winds exceeding 75 mph twist Sitka spruce, and tides deposit driftwood and logs on the beach.

Winchester Bay. One reason the Pacific Northwest isn't known for its amusement parks is because nature hurls

more thrills than any rattling contraption could ever provide. This certainly is true at **Oregon Dunes National Recreation Area.** Here riders of all-terrain vehicles (ATVs) will encounter some of the most radical slips, dips, hills, and chills in the nation. It is the largest expanse of coastal sand dunes in North America, extending for 40 miles, from Florence to Coos Bay. More than 1.5 million people visit the dunes each year. For those who just want to swim, relax, hike, and marvel at the amazing expanse of dunes against the ocean, there are spaces off-limits to motorized vehicles. Overlooking the beach is the gorgeous **Umpqua River Lighthouse.**

Samuel H. Boardman State Scenic Corridor. It doesn't get any wilder than this—or more spectacular. The 12-mile strip of forested, rugged coastline between Gold Beach and Brookings is dotted with smaller sand beaches, some more accessible than others. Here visitors will find the amazing **Arch Rock** and **Natural Bridges** and can hike 27 miles of the **Oregon Coast Trail.** Beach highlights include **Whaleshead Beach, Secret Beach,** and **Thunder Rock Cove,** where you might spot migrating gray whales. From the 345-foot-high **Thomas Creek Bridge** you can take a moderately difficult hike down to admire the gorgeous, jagged rocks off **China Beach.**

3

Updated
by Andrew
Collins

If you aren't from the Pacific Northwest, Oregon's spectacular coastline might still be a secret: it's less visited and talked about than California's coast, but certainly no less beautiful. But in recent decades, the state's reputation for scenic drives and splendid hikes, reasonably priced oceanfront hotels and vacation rentals, low-key towns with friendly, creative vibes, and consistently fresh and well-prepared seafood has garnered increased attention. The true draw here is the beaches, where nature lovers delight at their first sight of a migrating whale or a baby harbor seal sitting on a rock.

Oregon's coastline is open to all; not a grain of its more than 300 miles of white-sand beaches is privately owned. The coast's midsize towns and small villages (you won't find any large cities) are linked by U.S. 101, which runs the length of the state. It winds past sea-tortured rocks, brooding headlands, hidden beaches, historic lighthouses, and tiny ports. This is one of the most picturesque driving routes in the country, and it should not be missed. Embracing it is the vast, indigo-blue Pacific Ocean, which presents a range of moods with the seasons. On summer evenings it might be glassy, and reflect a romantic sunset. In winter the ocean might throw a thrilling tantrum for storm watchers sitting snug and safe in a beachfront cabin.

Active visitors indulge in thrills from racing up a sand dune in a buggy to making par at Bandon Dunes, one of the nation's finest links-style golf courses. Bicyclists pedal along misty coastline vistas, cruising past historic lighthouses. Hikers enjoy breezy, open trails along the sea as well as lush, evergreen-studded treks into the adjoining Coast Range. Boaters explore southern-coast rivers on jet boats while the more adventuresome among them shoot rapids on guided raft trips. If the weather turns, don't overlook indoor venues like the Oregon Coast Aquarium and Columbia River Maritime Museum.

Shoppers appreciate the several art galleries in Newport and Cannon Beach; for more family-oriented shopping fun, giggle in the souvenir shops of Lincoln City and Seaside while eating fistfuls of caramel corn or chewing saltwater taffy.

OREGON COAST PLANNER

WHEN TO GO

November through May are generally rainy months (albeit with sporadic stretches of dry and sometimes even sunny days), but once the fair weather comes, coastal Oregon is one of the most gorgeous places on earth. July through September offer wonderful, dry days for beachgoers. Autumn is also a great time to visit, as the warm-enough weather is perfect for crisp beachcombing walks followed by hearty harvest meals paired with ales from the growing crop of craft breweries up and down the coast.

Even with the rain, coastal winter and spring do have quite a following. Many hotels are perfectly situated for storm watching, and provide a romantic experience. Think of a toasty fire, a smooth Oregon Pinot, and your loved one, settled in to watch the waves dance upon a jagged rocky stage.

FESTIVALS

Astoria Music Festival. Fans of opera and classical works flock to this increasingly popular festival, which mounts more than 20 performances, over 16 days in late June and early July. ⊕ *www.astoriamusicfestival.org.*

Cannon Beach Sandcastle Contest. It can be tough to find a room—or parking spot—during this single-day mid-June festival that's been going strong for more than 50 years and showcases the amazingly detailed sand constructions of both professional and amateur teams. ⊕ *www.cannonbeach.org.*

Cranberry Festival. In Bandon each September this festival in celebration of the town's most famous product (well, after seafood) comprises a fair and parade. ⊕ *www.bandon.com/cranberry-festival.*

Newport Seafood and Wine Festival. This renowned foodie gathering takes place the last full weekend in February and bills itself the premier seafood and wine event of the Oregon Coast. Dozens of wineries are represented at this expansive celebration, which also features myriad crafts and eateries. ⊕ *www.seafoodandwine.com.*

GETTING HERE AND AROUND

By far the most practical way to reach and to explore the coast is by car. There's only one small regional airport with limited commercial service, the regional bus lines provide fairly slow and infrequent service from other parts of the state, and there's zero train service. Several two-lane state highways connect the central and northern sections of the coast with the state's two largest cities, Portland and Eugene; the southern portion of the coast is more remote and requires a longer drive.

AIR TRAVEL

From Portland, which has Oregon's largest airport, the drive is about 2 hours to Astoria and Cannon Beach, and 2½ hours to Lincoln City and Newport. If you're headed farther south, you have a few other options, including flying into the regional airport in Eugene, which is served by most major airlines and is a 90-minute drive from Florence; flying into the tiny Southwest Oregon Regional Airport in the coast town of North Bend, which is an hour south of Florence and 2½ hours north of Brookings; flying into Rogue Valley International Airport in Medford, which is a 2½-hour drive from Brookings and a 3-hour drive from Bandon; and flying into Del Norte County Airport in Crescent City, California, which is just a 30-minute drive south of Brookings.

Southwest Oregon Regional Airport has flights to Portland on PenAir (a partner with Alaska Airlines) and to San Francisco and Denver on United Express. The airport has Hertz and Enterprise car-rental agencies as well as cab companies serving the area, including Coos Bay and Bandon.

There are a few shuttle services connecting the airports in Portland and Eugene to the coast, but these tend to be far less economical than renting a car. Caravan Airport Transportation runs a daily shuttle service from Portland International Airport to Lincoln City and on down to Yachats. OmniShuttle provides door-to-door van service from the Eugene airport to the central coast, from Florence down to around Bandon.

Contacts Caravan Airport Transportation. ☏ *503/288–5102* ⊕ *www.caravanairporttransportation.com.* **OmniShuttle.** ☏ *541/461–7959, 800/741–5097* ⊕ *www.omnishuttle.com.* **PenAir.** ☏ *800/448–4226* ⊕ *www.penair.com.* **Southwest Oregon Regional Airport.** ✉ *1100 Airport La., North Bend* ☏ *541/756–8531* ⊕ *www.cooscountyairportdistrict.com.*

BUS TRAVEL

There is bus travel to the coast from Portland and Eugene, but this is a fairly slow and cumbersome way to explore the area. North by Northwest Connector is a nonprofit organization that coordinates travel among five rural transit services in the northwestern corner of the state. From its website, you can plan and book trips from Portland to Astoria, with connecting service between the two along the coast, stopping in Seaside, Cannon Beach, Manzanita, and other communities. Additionally, Northwest Point, operated by MTR Western bus line, has twice-daily bus service from Portland to Cannon Beach, and then up the coast to Astoria; Greyhound handles the company's reservations and ticketing. Pacific Crest Bus Lines connects Florence, Coos Bay, and Reedsport with Eugene every day except Saturday.

Contacts North by Northwest Connector. ⊕ *www.nworegontransit. org.* **Northwest Point.** ☏ *800/231–2222 ticketing through Greyhound, 541/484–4100 information* ⊕ *www.oregon-point.com.* **Pacific Crest Bus Lines.** ☏ *541/344–6265* ⊕ *www.pacificcrestbuslines.com.*

CAR TRAVEL

Beautiful U.S. 101 hugs the entire Oregon coastline from Brookings near the California border in the south to Astoria on the Columbia River in the north. The road can be slow in places, especially where it passes through towns and curves over headlands and around coves. In theory, you could drive the entire 345-mile Oregon stretch of U.S 101 in a little under eight hours, but that's without stopping—and, of course, the whole point of driving the coast is stopping regularly to enjoy it.

If you want to do a full road trip of the Oregon Coast, give yourself at least three days and two nights; that's enough time to see a few key attractions along the way, enjoy the many scenic viewpoints, and stop to eat and overnight in some small towns along the route.

Several two-lane roads connect key towns on the coast (Astoria, Cannon Beach, Tillamook, Lincoln City, Newport, Waldport, Florence, Reedsport, and Bandon) with the major towns in the Willamette and Rogue valleys (Portland, Eugene, Roseburg). All these roads climb over the Coast Range, meaning the drives tend to be winding and hilly but quite picturesque. Keep in mind that winter storms in the mountains occasionally create slick conditions and even road closures. Always use numbered, paved state roads when crossing the mountains from the valley to the coast, especially in winter; what might appear to be a scenic alternative or shortcut on a map or GPS device is likely an unmaintained logging or forest road that leads through a secluded part of the mountains, without cell service.

RESTAURANTS

Deciding which restaurant has the best clam chowder is just one of the culinary fact-finding expeditions you can embark upon along the Oregon Coast. Chefs here take full advantage of the wealth of sturgeon, chinook, steelhead, and trout that abound in coastal rivers as well as the fresh rockfish, halibut, albacore, and lingcod caught in the Pacific. You'll find fresh mussels, bay shrimp, and oysters throughout as well as Dungeness crab in Newport. Restaurants still tend to be casual, low-key, and affordable here. *Restaurant reviews have been shortened. For full information visit Fodors.com.*

HOTELS

Compared with other coastal destinations in the United States, the Oregon Coast offers a pretty good value. You can typically find clean but basic motels and rustic inns, often with beachfront locations, that have nightly rates well below $150, even in high season. Spring and fall rates often drop by 20% to 30% and the value is even greater in winter. The lodging landscape is dominated by family-owned or independent motels and hotels, vacation rentals, and a smattering of distinctive B&Bs.

Properties in much of the north and central coast fill up fast in the summer, so book in advance. Many lodgings require a minimum two-night stay on a summer weekend. *Hotel reviews have been shortened. For full information, visit Fodors.com.*

WHAT IT COSTS IN U.S. DOLLARS			
$	$$	$$$	$$$$
Restaurants	under $16	$16–$22	$23–$30	over $30
Hotels	under $150	$150–$200	$201–$250	over $250

Restaurant prices are the average cost of a main course at dinner, or if dinner is not served, at lunch. Hotel prices are the lowest cost of a standard double room in high season.

VISITOR INFORMATION
Central Oregon Coast Association. ☎ *541/265–2064, 800/767–2064*
⊕ *www.coastvisitor.com.*

Eugene, Cascades & Coast Visitor Center. ✉ *3312 Gateway St., Springfield*
☎ *541/484–5307, 800/547–5445* ⊕ *www.eugenecascadescoast.org.*

Oregon Coast Visitors Association. ☎ *541/574–2679, 888/628–2101*
⊕ *www.visittheoregoncoast.com.*

NORTH COAST

This is the primary beach playground for residents of Portland, and in recent years, increasing numbers of sophisticated cafés, craft breweries and wine bars, colorful art galleries and indie retailers, and smartly restored boutique hotels have opened along this stretch of the Oregon Coast. What distinguishes the region historically from other areas of the coast are its forts, its graveyard of shipwrecks, historic sites related to Lewis and Clark's early visit, and a town—Astoria—that is closer in look and misty temperament to Monterey, California, than any other city in the West. Just south, Cannon Beach and its several high-end hotels feels a bit swankier than any other town in the area.

Every winter Astoria celebrates fisherman poets: hardworking men and women who bare their souls as to what makes their relationship to Oregon's north-coast waters so magical. It's easy to understand their inspiration, whether in the incredibly tempestuous ocean or the romantic beaches.

ASTORIA

96 miles northwest of Portland.

The mighty Columbia River meets the Pacific at Astoria, the oldest city west of the Rockies and a bustling riverfront getaway with a creative spirit and urbane vibe. In recent years the city has reinvented itself, with a greater variety of trendy dining and lodging options, as well as a superb museum dedicated to the Columbia River. Astoria also now cultivates a bit of Portland's hipster vibe, especially when it comes to shopping and nightlife.

It is named for John Jacob Astor, owner of the Pacific Fur Company, whose members arrived in 1811 and established Fort Astoria. In its early days, Astoria was a placid amalgamation of small town and hardworking port city. With rivers rich with salmon, the city relied on its fishing and canning industries. Settlers built sprawling Victorian houses on the flanks of Coxcomb Hill; many of the homes have since been restored and used as backdrops in movies or been converted into bed-and-breakfast inns. Astoria still retains the soul of a fisherman's town, celebrated each February during its FisherPoets Gathering. The town of about 9,500 also has wonderful views from most areas and a richly forested backdrop to the east, yet it remains a working waterfront. There is little public beach access in the town proper; to reach the Pacific, you have to drive a few miles west to Fort Stevens in Warrenton.

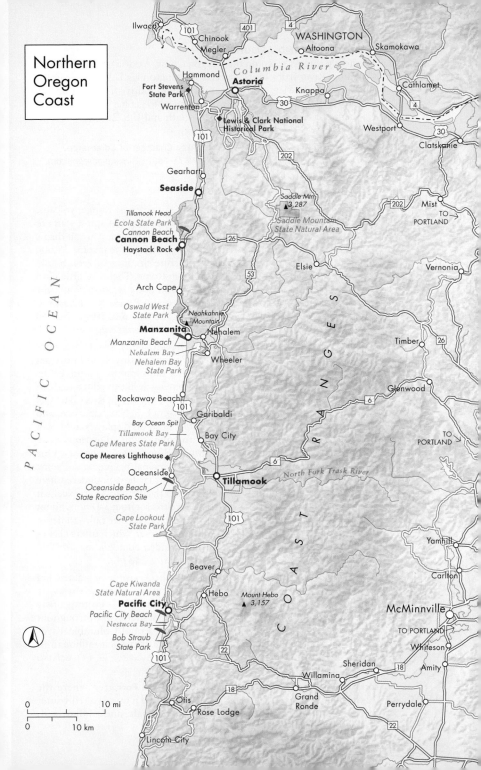

GETTING HERE AND AROUND

The northernmost town on the Oregon Coast, Astoria is just across the Columbia River from southwestern Washington via U.S. 101 (over the stunning Astoria-Megler Bridge) and a two-hour drive from Portland on U.S. 30. It only takes about 20 extra minutes to get here from Portland via the more scenic route of U.S. 101 south and U.S. 26 east.

ESSENTIALS

Visitor Information Astoria-Warrenton Area Chamber of Commerce.
⊠ *111 W. Marine Dr.* ☎ *503/325–6311, 800/875–6807* ⊕ *www.oldoregon.com.*

EXPLORING

TOP ATTRACTIONS

Fodor'sChoice
★
Astoria Column. For the best view of the city, the Coast Range, volcanic Mt. Helens, and the Pacific Ocean, scamper up the 164 spiral stairs to the top of the Astoria Column. When you get to the top, you can throw a small wooden plane and watch it glide to earth; each year some 35,000 gliders are tossed. The 125-foot-high structure sits atop Coxcomb Hill, and was patterned after Trajan's Column in Rome. There are little platforms to rest on if you get winded, or, if you don't want to climb, the column's 500 feet of artwork, depicting important Pacific Northwest historical milestones, are well worth a study. ⊠ *16th St. S* ☎ *503/325–2963* ⊕ *www.astoriacolumn.org* 🖼 *$5 parking (good for an entire yr).*

FAMILY
Fodor'sChoice
★
Columbia River Maritime Museum. One of Oregon's best coastal attractions illuminates the maritime history of the Pacific Northwest and provides visitors with a sense of the perils of guiding ships into the mouth of the Columbia River. Vivid exhibits recount what it was like to pilot a tugboat and participate in a Coast Guard rescue on the Columbia River Bar. You can tour the actual bridge of a World War II–era U.S. Navy destroyer and the U.S. Coast Guard lightship *Columbia.* Also on display is a 44-foot Coast Guard motor lifeboat, artifacts from the region's illustrious riverboat heyday, and details about Astoria's seafood-canning history. One especially captivating exhibit displays the personal belongings of some of the ill-fated passengers of the 2,000 ships that have foundered here since the early 19th century. In addition, the theater shows an excellent documentary about the river's heritage as well as rotating 3-D films about sea life. At the east end of the property, the city's former railroad depot now houses the museum's Barbey Maritime Center, which offers classes and workshops on maritime culture and wooden boatbuilding. ⊠ *1792 Marine Dr.* ☎ *503/325–2323* ⊕ *www.crmm.org* 🖼 *$14.*

Flavel House. The Queen Anne–style mansion helps visitors imagine what life was like for the wealthy in late-19th-century Astoria. It rests on parklike grounds covering an entire city block and has been gorgeously restored, with its three-story octagon tower visible from throughout town. It was built for George Flavel, an influential Columbia River bar pilot and businessman who was one of the area's first millionaires. Visits start in the Carriage House interpretive center. ⊠ *441 8th St.* ☎ *503/325–2203* ⊕ *www.cumtux.org* 🖼 *$6.*

FAMILY
Fodor'sChoice
★
Fort Clatsop at Lewis and Clark National Historical Park. See where the 30-member Lewis and Clark Expedition endured a rain-soaked winter in 1805–06, hunting, gathering food, making salt, and trading with

the local Clatsops, Chinooks, and Tillamooks. This memorial is part of the 3,200-acre Lewis and Clark National Historical Park and is a faithful replica of the log fort depicted in Clark's journal. The fort lies within a forested wonderland, with an exhibit hall, gift shop, film, and trails. Park rangers dress in period garb during the summer and perform such early-19th-century tasks as making fire with flint and steel. Hikers enjoy the easy 1½-mile Netul Landing trail and the more rigorous but still fairly flat 6½-mile Fort to Sea trail. ⊠ *92343 Fort Clatsop Rd.* ☎ *503/861–2471* ⊕ *www.nps.gov/lewi* ⊠ *$5.*

3

WORTH NOTING

FAMILY **Astoria Riverfront Trolley.** Also known as "Old 300," this is a beautifully restored 1913 streetcar that travels for 4 miles along Astoria's historic riverfront, stopping at several points between the Astoria River Inn and the foot of 39th Street (although you can easily flag it down at any point along the route by offering a friendly wave). The hour-long ride gives you a close-up look at the waterfront from the Port of Astoria to the East Morring Basin; the Columbia River; and points of interest in between. ☎ *503/325–6311, 800/875–6807* ⊕ *www.old300.org* ⊠ *$1 per boarding, $2 all-day pass.*

Hanthorn Cannery Museum. Drive or walk over the rickety-seeming (but actually completely sturdy) bridge onto historic Pier 39, which juts out into the Columbia River on the east side of downtown, to visit this small but interesting museum that occupies the oldest extant cannery building in Astoria. It was once operated by Bumble Bee Seafood, and some 30,000 cans of salmon were processed here annually during the plant's late-19th-century heyday. Exhibits and artifacts, including three vintage gill-net boats, some wonderful old photos, and equipment and cans tell the story of the town's—and facility's—canning history. Also on the pier is Coffee Girl café and Rogue Ales Public House. ⊠ *100 39th St.* ☎ *503/325–2502* ⊕ *www.canneryworker.org* ⊠ *Free.*

NEED A BREAK

✕ **Coffee Girl.** This cozy café inside a 19th-century cannery building on historic Pier 39 has big windows overlooking the river—you can always take your well-crafted espresso or latte with you for a stroll around the pier. Open until late afternoon each day, Coffee Girl also serves tasty quiches, pastries, soups, and grilled panini sandwiches. ⊠ *100 39th St.* ☎ *503/325–6900* ⊕ *www.thecoffeegirl.com.*

FAMILY **Fort Stevens State Park.** This earthen fort at Oregon's northwestern tip was built during the Civil War to guard the Columbia River against attack. None came until World War II, when a Japanese submarine fired upon it. The fort still has cannons and an underground gun battery, of which tours are available in summer (call for details). The park has year-round camping, with full hookup sites, 11 cabins, and 15 yurts. There are also bike paths, boating, swimming, hiking trails, and a short walk to a gorgeous, wide beach where the corroded skeleton—or the tiny bit that remains of it—the *Peter Iredale* pokes up through the sand. This century-old English four-master shipwreck is a reminder of the nearly 2,000 vessels claimed by these treacherous waters. ⊠ *100 Peter Iredale Rd., Hammond* ☎ *503/861–3170, 800/551–6949* ⊕ *www. oregonstateparks.org* ⊠ *Day use $5 per vehicle.*

FAMILY **Oregon Film Museum.** Housed in the old Clatsop County Jail, this small but engaging museum celebrates Oregon's long history of filmmaking and contains artifacts from and displays about prior productions. The location is apt because it was featured prominently in the famous cult film *The Goonies*. The state's film productions date back to 1908 for *The Fisherman's Bride*. Since then, Oregon has helped give birth to such classics as *The General*, *The Great Race*, *One Flew Over the Cuckoo's Nest*, *Paint Your Wagon*, *Animal House*, and *Twilight*, leading some to call the state Hollywood North. *Kindergarten Cop*, *The Ring II*, *Free Willy I* and *II*, and *Short Circuit* are among those filmed in Astoria. You can download an audio tour of filmed sites (or buy a tour CD for $2) from the Astoria-Warrenton Chamber of Commerce—it's a fun way to see the city's oft-unsung landmarks, especially during the annual Goonies festival, held in June. ✉ *732 Duane St.* ☎ *503/325–2203* 🌐 *www.oregonfilmmuseum.org* 🎟 *$6.*

WHERE TO EAT

$$ ECLECTIC Fodor's Choice ★ 🍴 **Astoria Coffeehouse & Bistro.** A source of fine coffee drinks and baked goods, this cheerful storefront café has both sidewalk seating and a living-room-like interior decorated with old photos. The always-bustling restaurant serves consistently well-prepared food, a mix of American classics and international treats. **Known for:** local-rockfish tacos; superb drinks, from coffees to cocktails; Monte Cristo sandwiches. [$] *Average main: $19* ✉ *243 11th St.* ☎ *503/325–1787* 🌐 *www.astoriacoffeehouse.com.*

$ CAFÉ FAMILY 🍴 **Blue Scorcher Bakery Café.** "Joyful work, delicious food, and strong community" is this family-friendly café's rallying cry. It serves everything from *huevos scorcheros* (poached eggs with rice, beans, cheese, and salsa) and organic, handcrafted breads to a variety of foods using local, fair trade, and organic ingredients. **Known for:** vegan and gluten-free options; children's play area. [$] *Average main: $8* ✉ *1493 Duane St.* ☎ *503/338–7473* 🌐 *www.bluescorcher.com* 🕒 *No dinner.*

$$ PACIFIC NORTHWEST 🍴 **Bridgewater Bistro.** In the same complex as the Cannery Pier Hotel, this stylish restaurant has great views of the river and bridge to Washington. Inside, high ceilings are supported by ancient fir timbers, and an extensive menu is strong on creative seafood and meat grills, including roasted spice-encrusted duck breast with orange marmalade glaze, and seared wild local salmon with an arugula-strawberry salad and a star anise–balsamic vinaigrette. **Known for:** Sunday brunch; Columbia River views. [$] *Average main: $22* ✉ *20 Basin St., Suite A* ☎ *503/325–6777* 🌐 *www.bridgewaterbistro.com.*

$ AMERICAN 🍴 **Buoy Beer Co.** One of the most acclaimed craft brewers on the coast, Buoy Beer also serves exceptionally tasty contemporary pub fare in its warm and inviting taproom, set in a converted 1920s grain warehouse on the Astoria's riverfront walk—huge windows afford dramatic views of the Columbia. Seafood figures prominently in many dishes here, including rockfish-and-chips and bacon-clam chowder, but you'll also find delicious burgers and meat and cheese boards. **Known for:** hoppy handcrafted IPAs and strong German-style beers; river views. [$] *Average main: $15* ✉ *1 8th St.* ☎ *503/325–4540* 🌐 *www.buoybeer.com.*

$ ECLECTIC 🍴 **Columbian Cafe & Voodoo Room.** Locals love this funky diner-and-nightclub complex that defies categorization by offering inventive, fresh seafood, spicy vegetarian dishes, and meats cured and smoked on the premises. Located next to the historic Columbian Theater, the café serves simple food, such as crepes with broccoli, cheese, and homemade salsa for lunch. **Known for:** cocktails and very good pizza in the Voodoo Room bar; good people-watching. [$] *Average main: $12* ✉ *1114 Marine Dr.* ☎ *503/325–2233* 🌐 *www.columbianvoodoo.com/cafe* 💳 *No credit cards.*

3

WHERE TO STAY

$$$$ HOTEL Fodor's Choice ★ 🏨 **Cannery Pier Hotel.** From every room in this captivating property there's a gorgeous view of the mighty Columbia River flowing toward the Pacific Ocean, and it's almost hypnotic to watch the tugboats shepherding barges to and fro. **Pros:** amazing river views; great in-room amenities; hotel hot tub and day spa. **Cons:** pricey; a bit of a walk from downtown. [$] *Rooms from: $309* ✉ *10 Basin St.* ☎ *503/325–4996, 888/325–4996* 🌐 *www.cannerypierhotel.com* 🛏 *46 rooms, 8 suites* 🍴 *Breakfast.*

$ B&B/INN 🏨 **Clementine's B&B.** This painstakingly restored 1888 Italianate Victorian home is just a couple of blocks up the hill from Flavel House Museum and a short walk from several fine restaurants and shops. **Pros:** superb, multicourse breakfast included; handy downtown location. **Cons:** the traditional lacy room decor isn't for everyone. [$] *Rooms from: $122* ✉ *847 Exchange St.* ☎ *503/325–2005* 🌐 *www.clementines-bb.com* 🛏 *4 rooms, 1 suite* 🍴 *Breakfast.*

$ HOTEL Fodor's Choice ★ 🏨 **Commodore Hotel.** An economical but stylish downtown boutique hotel, the Commodore has become a favorite with young and artsy souls from Portland and Seattle thanks to its vintage-chic aesthetic, large wall murals and photos, and hip Street 14 Cafe off the lobby. **Pros:** hip ambience; wallet-friendly rates; excellent Street 14 Cafe on-site. **Cons:** least expensive rooms share a bath; simple decor. [$] *Rooms from: $89* ✉ *258 14th St.* ☎ *503/325–4747* 🌐 *www.commodoreastoria.com* 🛏 *18 rooms, 10 with shared bath* 🍴 *No meals.*

$$ HOTEL 🏨 **Hotel Elliott.** This atmospheric, five-story hotel stands in the heart of Astoria's historic district and retains the elegance of yesteryear, updated with modern comforts like cozy underfloor heating in the bathrooms. **Pros:** captures the city's historic ambience beautifully; every effort made to infuse the rooms with upscale amenities; popular wine bar. **Cons:** no on-site dining. [$] *Rooms from: $179* ✉ *357 12th St.* ☎ *503/325–2222* 🌐 *www.hotelelliott.com* 🛏 *21 rooms, 11 suites* 🍴 *Breakfast.*

$ HOTEL 🏨 **Norblad Hotel & Hostel.** Formerly a boardinghouse until its recent renovation, the offbeat Norblad occupies a stately two-story 1920s building a few steps from Fort George Brewery. **Pros:** distinctive and quirky vibe; short walk from downtown shopping and dining; bargain-priced rooms. **Cons:** very basic; front desk isn't staffed overnight; most rooms share a bath. [$] *Rooms from: $69* ✉ *443 14th St.* ☎ *503/325–6989* 🌐 *www.norbladhotel.com* 🛏 *12 rooms with shared bath, 1 suite, 2 hostel rooms* 🍴 *No meals.*

NIGHTLIFE

Fodor's Choice ★ **Fort George Brewery.** The spacious taproom and brewery set in a former 1920s auto showroom has plenty of indoor and outdoor seating where you can sample some of the best craft beers on the coast, including the Belgian-style Quick Wit or the oatmeal-infused Sunrise OPA, a light

American pale ale. Plenty of seasonal brews appear on the menu as well, along with tasty pub fare. ✉ *1483 Duane St.* ☎ *503/325–7468* ⊕ *www.fortgeorgebrewery.com.*

Inferno Lounge. Just about every seat in this hip bar situated on a pier that juts into the Columbia River offers stupendous water views. Catch the sunset with a well-crafted cocktail and perhaps a few nibbles—Thai shrimp tacos, pork potstickers—from the tapas menu. This place known for house-infused spirits buzzes until midnight or later. ✉ *77 11th St.* ☎ *503/741–3401.*

SHOPPING

Doe & Arrow. This beautifully curated purveyor of urbane women's and men's fashion as well as arty jewelry, hip home accessories, and eco-friendly grooming products occupies a large corner space in downtown's Historic Astor Hotel building. ✉ *380 14th St.* ☎ *503/741–3132* ⊕ *www.doeandarrow.com.*

Josephson's. One of the Oregon Coast's oldest commercial smokehouses, Josephson's uses alder for all processing and specializes in Pacific Northwest chinook and coho salmon. The mouthwatering fish that's smoked on the premises includes hot smoked pepper or wine-maple salmon, as well as smoked halibut, sturgeon, tuna, oysters, mussels, scallops, and prawns by the pound or in sealed gift packs. ✉ *106 Marine Dr.* ☎ *503/325–2190* ⊕ *www.josephsons.com.*

SEASIDE

12 miles south of Astoria on U.S. 101.

As a resort town, Seaside has somewhat spruced up its kitschy, arcade-filled reputation and now supports a bustling tourist trade, with hotels, condominiums, and restaurants lining a traditional promenade. It still has fun games, candy shops, and plenty of carny noise to appeal to young people, but it has added more in the way of shopping and dining that appeals to adults, and it's home to some of the most affordable lodging options on this stretch of the coast. Only 90 miles from Portland, Seaside is often crowded, so it's not the place to come if you crave solitude. Peak times include mid- to late March, when hordes of teenagers descend on the town during spring break; and late June, when the annual Miss Oregon Pageant is in full swing. Just south of town, waves draw surfers to the Cove, a spot jealously guarded by locals, and the dramatic hike along the Oregon Coast Trail to Tillamook Head connects with Cannon Beach's famous Ecola State Park.

GETTING HERE AND AROUND

Seaside is about a 90-minute drive from Portland via U.S 26 and a 20-minute drive south of Astoria on coastal U.S. 101.

VISITOR INFORMATION

Seaside Visitors Bureau. ✉ *7 N. Roosevelt Ave.* ☎ *503/738–3097, 888/306–2326* ⊕ *www.seasideor.com.*

3

EXPLORING

FAMILY **Seaside Aquarium.** The first thing you hear at this relatively small but fun 1930s-era aquarium is the clapping and barking of the harbor seals just inside the door. Located on the 1½-mile beachfront Promenade, the aquarium has jellyfish, giant king crab, octopus, moray eels, wolf eels, and other sea life swimming in more than 30 tanks. The discovery center draws curious kids and grown-ups alike for its hands-on touch tanks of starfish, anemones, and urchins, as well as for a close-up exploration of the most miniature marine life. No restrooms on-site. ✉ *200 N. Promenade* ☎ *503/738–6211* 🌐 *www.seasideaquarium.com* 🎟 *$8.*

WHERE TO EAT

$ DINER 🍴 **Firehouse Grill.** This bustling diner-style café in a former firehouse in downtown Seaside hits the mark with its hearty breakfast fare, including fluffy biscuits with gravy, cinnamon French toast, meat-loaf scrambles, and a couple of lighter options, such as house-made granola with fresh fruit. The excellent Sleepy Monk coffee from Cannon Beach is served, too, as are eye-opening Bloody Marys. **Known for:** hearty breakfasts; halibut tacos at lunch. [$] *Average main: $10* ✉ *841 Broadway* ☎ *503/717–5502* 🕒 *Closed Tues. and Wed. No dinner.*

$$ HAWAIIAN 🍴 **Lilikoi Grill.** You'll find bamboo mats, tropical plants, and knickknacks at this festive Hawaiian-themed restaurant set amid downtown Seaside's souvenir stores and candy shops. The menu mixes island-inspired recipes with both local and Hawaii ingredients. **Known for:** Kona coffee–braised short ribs; tropical cocktails. [$] *Average main: $19* ✉ *714 Broadway St.* ☎ *503/738–5232* 🌐 *www.lilikoigrill.com* 🕒 *Closed Tues. and Wed. No lunch.*

SPORTS AND THE OUTDOORS

HIKING

Fodor's Choice ★ **Saddle Mountain State Natural Area.** One of the most accessible mountain peaks in the Coast Range, 3,283-foot Saddle Mountain is reached via a challenging but beautiful 2½-mile climb, with a 1,603-foot elevation gain—the reward, on clear days, is a view of the ocean to the west and the Cascade peaks—including Mt. Hood—far to the east. Wear sturdy shoes, and be prepared for sections with steep upgrades. There's a zippy change in the altitude as you climb higher, but the wildflowers make it all worthwhile. The trailhead is well signed off U.S. 26, the main highway from Portland to Cannon Beach and Seaside. ✉ *Saddle Mountain Rd., off U.S. 26, 20 miles east of Seaside and 70 miles west of Portland* ☎ *800/551–6949, 503/368–5943* 🌐 *www.oregonstateparks.org.*

Tillamook Head. A moderately challenging 7½-mile loop from U.S. 101, south of Seaside, brings you through lushly forested Elmer Feldenheimer Forest Reserve and into the northern end of Cannon Beach's Ecola State Park to a 900-foot-high viewing point, a great place to see the **Tillamook Rock Light Station,** which stands a mile or so off the coast. The lonely beacon, built in 1881 on a straight-sided rock, towers 41 feet above the ocean and was abandoned in 1957. You can also reach this viewing area by hiking north from Indian Beach in Ecola State Park. ✉ *End of Sunset Blvd.* 🌐 *www.oregonstateparks.org.*

CANNON BEACH

25 miles south of Astoria.

Cannon Beach is a mellow but relatively affluent town where locals and part-time residents—many of the latter reside in Portland—come to enjoy shopping, gallery-touring, and dining, the sea air, and the chance to explore the spectacular state parks at either end of the area: Ecola to the north and Oswald West to the south. Shops and galleries selling surfing gear, upscale clothing, local art, wine, coffee, and candies line Hemlock Street, Cannon Beach's main thoroughfare. In late June the town hosts the Cannon Beach Sandcastle Contest, for which thousands throng the beach to view imaginative and often startling works in this most transient of art forms. On the downside, this so-called Carmel of the Oregon Coast is more expensive and often more crowded than other towns along U.S. 101.

GETTING HERE AND AROUND

It's a 90-minute drive east from Portland on U.S. 26 to reach Cannon Beach, which is a 10-minute drive south of Seaside. To make a scenic loop, consider returning to Portland by way of Astoria and U.S. 30 (about 2¼ hours) or Tillamook and Highway 6 (about 2½ hours).

ESSENTIALS

Visitor Information Cannon Beach Chamber of Commerce. ✉ *207 N. Spruce St.* ☎ *503/436–2623* 🌐 *www.cannonbeach.org.*

EXPLORING

EVOO: Cannon Beach Cooking School. School never tasted this good. EVOO Cooking School performs advanced feats of culinary education for large and small groups, set around seasonal or specific food themes. EVOO holds cooking demonstrations, or you can sign up for hands-on courses—both always based on what's local, in season, and tantalizing. They call them dinner shows for a reason: whether or not you remember how to duplicate these recipes at home, you'll have a great time sampling them here. Classes start at $79 per person and include a full meal, with wine pairings for the dinner classes. ✉ *188 S. Hemlock St.* ☎ *503/436–8555, 877/436–3866* 🌐 *www.evoo.biz.*

Fodor's Choice ★ **Haystack Rock.** Towering over the broad, sandy beach is a gorgeous, 235-foot-high dome that is one of the most photographed natural wonders on the Oregon Coast. For safety and to protect birding habitats, people are not allowed to climb on the rock, but you can walk right up to its base at low tide. ✉ *Access beach from end of Gower St.*

WHERE TO EAT

$$ IRISH Fodor's Choice ★ 🍴 **Irish Table.** Adjacent to the Sleepy Monk café, this cozy restaurant with a timber-beam ceiling and warm lighting serves seasonal food with an Irish twist, such as potato-kale soup and its heralded Irish lamb stew. Other offerings include a perfect steak and delicate fresh halibut. **Known for:** Irish whiskey selection; friendly service; addictive hot soda bread. [$] *Average main: $19* ✉ *1235 S. Hemlock St.* ☎ *503/436–0708* 🕒 *Closed Wed. and Jan. No lunch.*

$ CAFÉ 🍴 **Sleepy Monk.** In a region renowned for artisan coffee, this small roaster brews some of the best espresso and coffee drinks in the state. Sleepy

Monk attracts java aficionados on caffeine pilgrimages from near and far eager to sample its certified-organic, fair-trade beans. **Known for:** outstanding coffee. [$] *Average main: $5* ✉ *1235 S. Hemlock St.* ☎ *503/436–2796* 🌐 *www.sleepymonkcoffee.com* 🕓 *Closed Wed. No dinner.*

$$$$ | PACIFIC NORTHWEST | Fodor's Choice ★

🍴 **Stephanie Inn Dining Room.** As diners enjoy a romantic view of Haystack Rock, this luxe hotel's sophisticated, supremely romantic dining room prepares a new menu nightly, crafting exquisite dinners using fresh, local ingredients. Diners can expect dishes such as cedar plank–roasted salmon, rack of lamb with chanterelle risotto, and a lemon-curd tart with wild berry sauce. **Known for:** one of the best wine lists on the coast; deft and attentive service; spectacular four-course prix-fixe menu option. [$] *Average main: $46* ✉ *2740 S. Pacific St.* ☎ *503/436–2221, 800/633–3466* 🌐 *www.stephanie-inn.com* 🕓 *No lunch.*

$$$ | AMERICAN

🍴 **Wayfarer Restaurant.** The dazzling beach and ocean views, especially at sunset, are just part of the story at this casually elegant restaurant at the Surfsand Resort; it's also the top destination in town for a leisurely meal of American food, including plenty of local seafood options, such as sesame-breaded Pacific razor clams with jalapeño-lime jelly, and Oregon-hazelnut-seared sole with a berry beurre blanc. If fish isn't your game, consider the prodigious 22-ounce "tomahawk" rib-eye steak with a Cabernet butter. **Known for:** juicy steaks; razor clams; delicious crab cakes. [$] *Average main: $29* ✉ *1190 Pacific Dr.* ☎ *503/436–1108* 🌐 *www.wayfarer-restaurant.com.*

WHERE TO STAY

$ | HOTEL

🏨 **Ecola Creek Lodge.** With a quiet, shady courtyard just off the main road leading into the north side of town, this small, reasonably priced 1940s hotel offers 22 suites and rooms with a mix of configurations, from two-bedroom units with kitchens to cozy standard rooms. **Pros:** quiet setting; rooms come in wide range of layouts; good value. **Cons:** not on the beach; slight walk from downtown shopping. [$] *Rooms from: $136* ✉ *208 5th St.* ☎ *503/436–2776, 800/873–2749* 🌐 *www.ecolacreeklodge.com* 🛏 *9 rooms, 13 suites* 🍽 *No meals.*

$$$$ | RESORT

🏨 **Ocean Lodge.** Designed to capture the feel of a 1940s beach resort, this rustic but upscale lodge is perfect for special occasions and romantic getaways. **Pros:** beachfront location; spacious rooms; warm cookies delivered to rooms. **Cons:** expensive; balconies are shared with neighboring rooms. [$] *Rooms from: $289* ✉ *2864 S. Pacific St.* ☎ *503/436–2241, 888/777–4047* 🌐 *www.theoceanlodge.com* 🛏 *45 rooms* 🍽 *Breakfast.*

$$$$ | RESORT | Fodor's Choice ★

🏨 **Stephanie Inn.** One of the coastline's most beautiful views is paired with one of its most splendid hotels, where the focus is firmly on romance, superior service, and luxurious rooms. **Pros:** incredibly plush accommodations; lots of little extras included; top-notch service. **Cons:** among the highest rates of any hotel in the state; not for families with younger children; some minimum-night stay requirements. [$] *Rooms from: $479* ✉ *2740 S. Pacific St.* ☎ *503/436–2221, 800/633–3466* 🌐 *www.stephanie-inn.com* 🛏 *27 rooms, 14 suites* 🍽 *Breakfast.*

$ | HOTEL | FAMILY

🏨 **Tolovana Inn.** Set on the beach at the quieter southern end of town, the large, rambling Tolovana Inn is one of the better-priced options in this tony seaside community, especially considering that most rooms enjoy partial or full views of the Pacific. **Pros:** panoramic beach views;

3

good mix of layouts and room sizes; some units have kitchens. **Cons:** a 10-minute drive from downtown shops; some rooms are relatively small; economy rooms have no water view. [$] *Rooms from: $134* ✉ *3400 S. Hemlock St.* ☎ *503/436–2211, 800/333–8890* 🌐 *www.tolovanainn.com* 🛏 *74 rooms, 103 suites* 🍴 *No meals.*

SHOPPING

Cannon Beach Art Galleries. The numerous art galleries that line Cannon Beach's Hemlock Street are an essential part of the town's spirit and beauty. A group of about a dozen galleries featuring beautifully innovative works in ceramic, bronze, photography, painting, and other mediums have collaborated to form the Cannon Beach Gallery Group. You'll find information about exhibits and special events on the website. ✉ *Hemlock St.* 🌐 *cbgallerygroup.com.*

SPORTS AND THE OUTDOORS

BEACHES

FAMILY Fodor's Choice ★ **Cannon Beach and Ecola State Park.** Beachcombers love Cannon Beach for its often low foamy waves and the wide stretch of sand that wraps the quaint community, making it ideal for fair-weather play or for hunting down a cup of coffee and strolling in winter. This stretch can get feisty in storms, however, which also makes Cannon Beach a good place to curl up indoors and watch the show. Haystack Rock rises 235 feet over the beach on the south side of downtown, one of 1,853 protected rocks that's part of the Oregon Ocean Island Wildlife Refuge, providing a nesting habitat for birds. Continue south past Tolovana Park—a playground located in the flood plain—to find the quiet side of Cannon Beach with a bevy of tide pools and few other souls. To the north of town, the beach gives way to Ecola State Park, a breathtakingly beautiful series of coves and rocky headlands where William Clark spotted a beached whale in 1806 and visitors still come to view them offshore during the twice-yearly migrations. From here, Sitka spruce and barbecues feature along the sands. There are a few excellent trails that hug the sometimes steep cliffs that rise above sand, including a 6½-mile trail first traced by Lewis and Clark, which runs from this spot past the Tillamook Head lookout and all the way to Seaside. **Amenities:** parking; toilets. **Best for:** partiers; sunset; walking. ✉ *Ocean Ave.* ☎ *503/436–2844, 800/551–6949* 🌐 *oregonstateparks.org* 🎟 *Ecola State Park day use $5 per vehicle.*

MANZANITA

15 miles south of Cannon Beach.

Manzanita is a secluded and gorgeously situated seaside community with only a few more than 500 full-time residents—but a growing following among weekenders from the Willamette Valley means there's one of the highest number of vacation rentals along the northern Oregon Coast here. The village is on a sandy peninsula, peppered with tufts of grass, on the northwestern side of Nehalem Bay, a noted windsurfing destination. It's a fairly laid-back town, but its growing crop of notable restaurants and boutiques has made it increasingly popular with visitors, as does its proximity to beautiful Oswald West State Park.

GETTING HERE AND AROUND

Tiny Manzanita is an easy and picturesque 20-minute drive south of Cannon Beach on coastal U.S. 101; from Portland, it takes just less than two hours to get here.

WHERE TO EAT AND STAY

$$$ MODERN AMERICAN Fodor's Choice ★ 🍴 **Blackbird.** Laid-back and decidedly causal downtown Manzanita received a significant culinary boost with the opening of this sophisticated, locavore-driven bistro. The menu changes often but might feature fried cauliflower with lemon and harissa aioli; ricotta gnocchi with lamb bacon, shaved fennel, basil, and tarragon pesto; or steamed clams with prawns, smoked cippolini onions, and white wine cream—the fresh, uncomplicated food is attractively presented and sings with flavor. **Known for:** dark-chocolate pot de crème; intimate and romantic setting. [$] *Average main: $27* ✉ *503 Laneda Ave.* ☎ *503/368–7708* 🌐 *www.blackbirdmanzanita.com* 🕒 *Closed Sun. No lunch.*

$$ AMERICAN 🍴 **Bread and Ocean Bakery.** This small bakery with a simple, cheerful dining room and several more tables on the sunny patio is hugely popular for breakfast and lunch with the many folks who rent cottages in the friendly beach town. Start the morning with slice of quiche or breakfast frittata; tuck into a hefty deli sandwich at lunch. **Known for:** to-go picnic lunches that are great for the beach; craft beers and local wines; decadent cinnamon rolls. [$] *Average main: $16* ✉ *154 Laneda Ave.* ☎ *503/368–5823* 🌐 *www.breadandocean.com* 🕒 *No dinner Sun.–Thurs.*

$ AMERICAN 🍴 **San Dune Pub.** Once a neighborhood dive bar, this 1930s pub has upped its game and become a local magnet for delicious seafood, burgers, sweet-potato fries, grilled-cod tacos, oyster po'boys, and, on Tuesday, baby back ribs. Desserts are worth saving room for here—a few different fresh-fruit and cream pies are always featured. **Known for:** pet-friendly patio; extensive beer selection; live music some evenings. [$] *Average main: $14* ✉ *127 Laneda Ave.* ☎ *503/368–5080* 🌐 *www.sandunepub.com.*

$$ B&B/INN FAMILY 🏨 **Inn at Manzanita.** Shore pines around this 1987 Scandinavian structure give upper-floor patios a tree-house feel, and it's just half a block from the beach. **Pros:** tranquil ambience with a Japanese garden atmosphere; very light and clean; several rooms good for families. **Cons:** two-night minimum stay on weekends; can book up fast in summer. [$] *Rooms from: $179* ✉ *67 Laneda Ave.* ☎ *503/368–6754* 🌐 *www.innatmanzanita.com* 🛏 *13 rooms, 1 suite* 🍽 *No meals.*

SPORTS AND THE OUTDOORS

BEACHES

FAMILY **Manzanita Beach and Nehalem Bay State Park.** The long stretch of white sand that separates the Pacific Ocean from the town of Manzanita is as loved a stretch of coastline as the next, its north side reaching into the shadows of Neahkanie Mountain, right where the mountain puts its foot in the ocean (the mountain itself, which makes for a great hike, lies within Oswald West State Park). The beach is frequented by vacationers, day-trippers, kite flyers, and dogs on its north end, but it extends a breezy 7 miles to the tip of Nehalem Bay State Park, which is accessible on foot over sand or by car along the road. At the south end of the park's parking lot, a dirt horse trail leads all the way to a peninsula's tip, a flat walk behind grassy dunes—you can book horseback rides from **Oregon Beach Rides** (☎ 971/237–6653 ⊕ *www. oregonbeachrides.com*), which has a stable inside the park. Cross to the right for a secluded patch of windy sand on the ocean, or to the left for a quiet, sunny place in the sun on Nehalem Bay, out of the wind. **Amenities:** toilets. **Best for:** sunset; walking. ✉ *Foot of Laneda Ave.* ☎ *503/368–5154, 800/551–6949* ⊕ *www.oregonstateparks.org* 💳 *Nehalem Bay State Park day use $5 per vehicle.*

RECREATIONAL AREAS

Fodor's Choice **Oswald West State Park.** Adventurous travelers will enjoy a sojourn at one
★ of the best-kept secrets on the Pacific coast, at the base of Neahkahnie Mountain. Park in one of the two free lots on U.S. 101 and hike a half-mile trail to dramatic Short Sand Beach, aka "Shortys," one of the top spots along the Oregon Coast for surfing. It's a spectacular beach with caves and tidal pools. There are several trails from the beach, all offering dazzling scenery; the relatively easy 2½-mile trail to Cape Falcon overlook joins with the Oregon Coast Trail and offers impressive views back toward Shortys Beach. The arduous 5½-mile trail to the 1,680-foot summit of Neahkahnie Mountain (access the trailhead about 2 miles south of the parking lots marked only by a "hikers" sign, or get there via Short Sand Beach) provides dazzling views south for many miles toward the surf, sand, and mountains fringing Manzanita and, in the distance, Tillamook. Come in December or March and you might spot pods of gray whales. ✉ *U.S. 101, 5 miles north of downtown Manzanita, Arch Cape* ☎ *800/551–6949, 503/368–3575* ⊕ *www. oregonstateparks.org* 💳 *Free.*

HORSEBACK RIDING

FAMILY **Oregon Beach Rides.** Saddle up for horseback rides at Nehalem Bay State Park, available Memorial Day through Labor Day weekends. Guides take you on a journey along the beach in Manzanita, and reserved rides can last from one to several hours. There's even a romantic sunset trot. It's appropriate for ages six and up. ✉ *Nehalem Bay State Park, 9500 Sandpiper La., Nehalem* ☎ *971/237–6653* ⊕ *www.oregonbeachrides. com* 💳 *Reservations essential.*

TILLAMOOK

27 miles south of Manzanita.

More than 100 inches of annual rainfall and the confluence of three rivers contribute to the lush green pastures around Tillamook, probably best known for its thriving dairy industry and cheese factory. The Tillamook County Cheese Factory ships about 50 million pounds of cheese around the world every year. The town itself lies several miles inland from the ocean and doesn't offer much in the way of beachy diversions, but it is the best jumping-off point for driving the dramatic Three Capes Loop, which passes over Cape Meares, Cape Lookout, and Cape Kiwanda and offers spectacular views of the ocean and coastline. The small village of Oceanside, just north of Cape Lookout, has several cute restaurants and shops.

GETTING HERE AND AROUND

Tillamook is a 90-minute drive from Portland on U.S. 26 to Highway 6. It's a winding, pretty, 45-minute drive south of Cannon Beach on U.S. 101, and a one-hour drive north of Lincoln City along the same coastal highway.

VISITOR INFORMATION

Visitor Information Tillamook Coast Tourism. ✉ *4301 3rd St.* ☎ *503/842–2672, 844/330–6962* 🌐 *www.tillamookcoast.com.*

EXPLORING

FAMILY **Tillamook Cheese Factory.** In high season, hundreds of visitors stop by the largest cheese-making plant on the West Coast to watch the cheese-making process, enjoy free samples, and order delicious ice cream (try the marionberry) from the on-site parlor. Here the rich milk from the area's thousands of Holstein and brown Swiss cows becomes ice cream, butter, and cheddar and Monterey Jack cheeses. The self-guided cheese-making tours don't allow much interaction—you view the operations from a glassed-in mezzanine—but they're free. The store carries a variety of other specialty-food products, including smoked meats, chocolates, jams, and honeys. ✉ *4175 U.S. 101 N* ☎ *503/815–1300, 800/542–7290* 🌐 *www.tillamookcheese.com.*

Tillamook Naval Air Station Museum. In the world's largest wooden structure, a former blimp hangar south of town displays a fine collection of vintage aircraft from World War II, including a vast trove of artifacts and memorabilia, including war uniforms, photos, and remains from the Hindenburg. The 20-story-high building is big enough to hold half a dozen football fields. ✉ *6030 Hangar Rd.* ☎ *503/842–1130* 🌐 *www.tillamookair.com* 🎟 *$9.50.*

WHERE TO EAT

$$ SEAFOOD 🍴 **Roseanna's Cafe.** In a rustic 1915 building on the beach, this café is right opposite Three Arch Rock, a favorite resting spot for sea lions and puffins. The calm of the beach is complemented in the evening by candlelight and fresh flowers. **Known for:** marionberry cobbler; baked Washington oysters; lovely water views. [$] *Average main: $21* ✉ *1490 Pacific Ave., Oceanside* ☎ *503/842–7351* 🌐 *www.roseannascafe.com.*

SPORTS AND THE OUTDOORS

The **Three Capes Loop,** an enchanting 35-mile byway off U.S. 101, winds along the coast between Tillamook and Pacific City, passing three distinctive headlands—Cape Meares, Cape Lookout, and Cape Kiwanda. Bayocean Road heading west from Tillamook passes what was the thriving resort town of Bayocean, which washed into the sea more than 50 years ago. A road still crosses the levee to Bayocean, and along the beach on the other side you can find the remnants of an old hotel to the north. The panoramic views from the north end of the peninsula are worth the walk. A warm and windless road returns hikers on the bay side.

BEACHES

Oceanside Beach State Recreation Site. This relatively small, sandy cove is a great stop at the midpoint of the cape's loop. It's especially popular with beachcombers in summer for both its shallow, gentle surf and the low-tide bowls and tide pools that make it a great play beach for youngsters. When the water recedes, it also uncovers a tunnel through the north rock face ensconcing the beach, allowing passage to a second, rocky cove. Oceanside's few eateries cater to the crowds: ice cream and quick bites are easily found. Parking in summer, however, is tough. The small lot fills quickly, and a walk through the hilly side streets is sometimes required. **Amenities:** none. **Best for:** walking; partiers. ⊠ *Pacific Ave. at Rosenberg Loop, off Hwy. 131, 3 miles south of Cape Meares, Oceanside* ☎ *800/551–6949, 503/842–3182* ⊕ *www.oregonstateparks.org.*

RECREATIONAL AREAS

Cape Kiwanda State Natural Area. Huge waves pound the jagged sandstone cliffs and caves here, and the much-photographed, 327-foot-high **Haystack Rock** (not to be confused with the 235-foot-tall rock of the same name up in Cannon Beach) juts out of the Pacific Ocean to the south. Surfers ride some of the longest waves on the coast, hang gliders soar above the shore, and beachcombers explore tidal pools and massive sand dunes, and take in unparalleled ocean views. ⊠ *Cape Kiwanda Dr., 1 mile north of Pacific City, Pacific City* ☎ *503/842–3182, 800/551–6949* ⊕ *www.oregonstateparks.org.*

Fodor's Choice
★

Cape Lookout State Park. Located about 8 miles south of the beach town Netarts, this park includes a moderately easy (though often muddy) 2-mile trail—marked on the highway as "wildlife viewing area"—that leads through giant spruces, western red cedars, and hemlocks, and ends with views of Cascade Head to the south and Cape Meares to the north. Wildflowers, more than 150 species of birds, and occasional whales throughout the summer months make this trail a favorite with nature lovers. The section of the park just north of the trail comprises a long, curving stretch of beach with picnic areas and campsites. ⊠ *Cape Lookout Rd. at Netarts Bay Rd.* ☎ *503/842–4981* ⊕ *www.oregonstateparks.org* ▦ *Day use $5.*

Cape Meares State Park. On the northern tip of the Three Capes Loop is Cape Meares State Park. The restored **Cape Meares Lighthouse,** built in 1890 and open to the public April through October, provides a sweeping view over the cliff to the caves and sea lion rookery on the rocks below. A many-trunked Sitka spruce known as the Octopus Tree grows near the lighthouse parking lot. ⊠ *3500 Cape Meares Loop, 10 miles west of Tillamook, Oceanside* ☎ *503/842–3182* ⊕ *www.oregonstateparks.org* ▦ *Free.*

PACIFIC CITY

24 miles south of Tillamook.

There's a lot to like about Pacific City, not the least of which is that it's 3 miles off Oregon's busy coastal highway, U.S. 101. That means there's no backup at the town's only traffic light—a blinking-red, four-way stop in the center of town. There's just the quiet, happy ambience of a town whose 1,000-or-so residents live the good life in the midst of extraordinary beauty. There are a few notable dining and hotel options here, along with some wonderful opportunities for recreation. The beach at Pacific City is one of the few places in the state where fishing dories (flat-bottom boats with high, flaring sides) are launched directly into the surf instead of from harbors or docks. Pacific City's windy climes tend to keep even the summer months quieter than most.

GETTING HERE AND AROUND

Between Tillamook and Lincoln City, the unincorporated village of Pacific City is just off U.S. 101 on the south end of the beautiful Three Capes Loop. It is a two-hour drive from Portland on U.S. 26 to Highway 6, or a 75-minute drive from Salem via Highway 22.

ESSENTIALS

Visitor Information Pacific City-Nestucca Valley Chamber of Commerce. ☎ *503/392–4340* 🌐 *www.pcnvchamber.org.*

WHERE TO EAT AND STAY

$$ AMERICAN FAMILY 🍴 **Grateful Bread Bakery & Restaurant.** This airy and bright café uses the cod caught by the local dories for its fish-and-chips. Everything it makes is fresh and from scratch, including delicious breads, pastries, breakfasts, and pizzas. **Known for:** made-from-scratch pastries; filling breakfasts of smoked-salmon scrambles and gingerbread pancakes. [$] *Average main: $16* ✉ *34805 Brooten Rd.* ☎ *503/965–7337* 🌐 *www.gratefulbreadbakery.com* 🕒 *Closed Tues. and Wed. No dinner Mon.*

$ AMERICAN FAMILY 🍴 **Pelican Pub & Brewery.** This beer-lover's favorite stands on the oceanfront by Haystack Rock. The microbrewery has garnered considerable kudos for its beers, including the Kiwanda Cream Ale and deep, rich Tsunami Stout, while the pub excels with creative comfort fare. **Known for:** occasional brewers dinner with international food and house beer pairings; good children's menu; root beer floats. [$] *Average main: $15* ✉ *33180 Cape Kiwanda Dr.* ☎ *503/965–7007* 🌐 *www.pelicanbrewing.com.*

$$$ RESORT 🏨 **Inn at Cape Kiwanda.** You won't find a weather-beaten beach cottage here—each of the 35 deluxe, fireplace-warmed rooms has a gorgeous view of Haystack Rock. **Pros:** great views; light and contemporary rooms; terrific restaurants nearby. **Cons:** some rooms have only partial water views. [$] *Rooms from: $219* ✉ *33105 Cape Kiwanda Dr.* ☎ *888/965–7001, 503/965–7001* 🌐 *www.yourlittlebeachtown.com/inn* 🛏 *33 rooms, 2 suites* 🍽 *No meals.*

SPORTS AND THE OUTDOORS

BEACHES

Fodor's Choice ★ **Pacific City beach.** The town's public beach sits between Cape Kiwanda State Natural Area and Bob Straub State Park. Adjacent to Cape Kiwanda's massive 240-foot-tall dune, it's a favorite for kids who often climb its bulk just for the thrill of sliding back down again. Hikers also get a thrill from the top, where the view opens on a tiny cove and tide pools below, and the walk down is infinitely easier than the climb. The beach is also popular with tailgaters—it's one of the few places on the Oregon Coast where it's legal to park your vehicle on the sand. Other parking is available off Cape Kiwanda Drive, near the Pelican Pub. For quieter outings, try the Bob Straub. **Amenities:** none. **Best for:** partiers; walking. ✉ *Cape Kiwanda Dr.* 🌐 *www.pcnvchamber.org.*

RECREATIONAL AREAS

Bob Straub State Park. An often sand-blasting walk along the flat white-sand beach leads down to the mouth of the Nestucca River, considered by many to be the best fishing river on the north coast. The beach along the Pacific is frequently windy, but it's separated from the stiller, warmer side of the peninsula by high dunes. Multiple trails cross the dunes into a forest that leads to small beaches on the Nestucca. Relax here with a book, and easily find stillness and sunshine. It's possible to skip the Pacific stroll all together, and find trails to the Nestucca straight from the parking lot, but it's hard to resist the views from the top of the dunes at the Bob Straub. If you choose the ocean side, pitch your beach-camp in the dunes, not the flat sand, and you'll find respite from the some-times unrelenting wind. ⊠ *Sunset Dr., just south of where Pacific Ave. crosses river* ☎ *503/842–3182* ⊕ *www.oregonstateparks.org.*

CENTRAL COAST

This is Oregon's coastal playland, drawing families, shoppers, kite fly-ers, deep-sea fishing enthusiasts, surfers, and dune-shredding daredevils. Although it's a bit touristy and bisected by a rather tatty commercial stretch of U.S. 101, Lincoln City offers a wealth of shops devoted to souvenirs and knickknacks, and visitors can even blow their own glass float at a few local studios. Depoe Bay is popular for whale-watching excursions, and New-port is designated the Dungeness crab capital of the world. As you venture farther south, you'll roll through gorgeous and less developed Yachats and charming Florence to reach the iconic mountains of sand that fall within Oregon Dunes National Recreation Area. Even if you're not intent on making tracks in the sand, the dunes provide vast, unforgettable scenery.

LINCOLN CITY

16 miles south of Pacific City, 90 miles southwest of Portland.

Lincoln City is a captivating destination for families and couples who want to share some time laughing on the beach, poking their fingers in tide pools, and trying to harness wind-bucking kites. Once a series of small villages, Lincoln City is a sprawling town without a center. But the endless tourist amenities make up for a lack of a small-coastal-town ambience. Clustered like barnacles on the offshore reefs are fast-food restaurants, gift shops, supermarkets, candy stores, antiques markets, dozens of motels and hotels, a factory-outlet mall, and a busy casino. Lincoln City is the most popular destination city on the Oregon Coast, but its only real geographic claim to fame is the 445-foot-long D River, stretching from its source in Devil's Lake to the Pacific; *Guinness World Records* lists the D as the world's shortest river.

GETTING HERE AND AROUND

Lincoln City is a 2-hour drive from Portland on Highway 99W and High-way 18, and a 2½-hour drive south of Astoria along coastal U.S. 101.

ESSENTIALS

Visitor Information Lincoln City Visitors & Convention Bureau. ⊠ *801 S.W. U.S. 101, Suite 401* ☎ *541/996–1274, 800/452–2151* ⊕ *www.oregoncoast.org.*

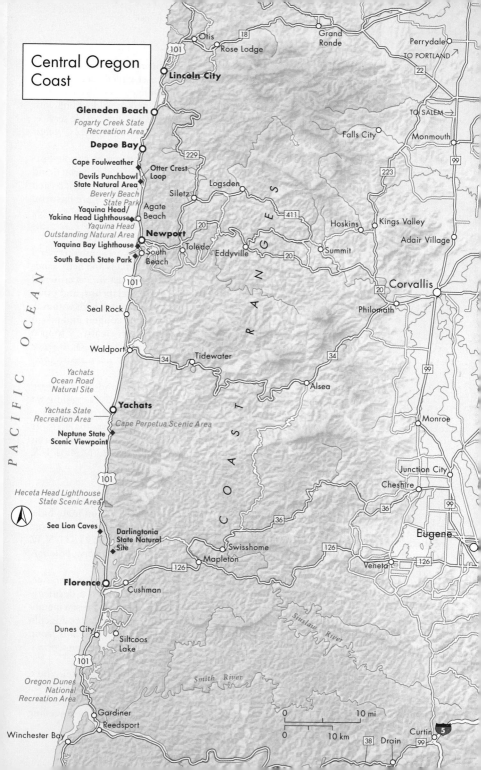

Central Oregon Coast

Otis
Rose Lodge
101
18
Grand Ronde
Perrydale
TO PORTLAND
22
Lincoln City
TO SALEM
Gleneden Beach
Fogarty Creek State Recreation Area
Falls City
Monmouth
99
Depoe Bay
229
Cape Foulweather
Otter Crest Loop
223
Devils Punchbowl State Natural Area
Beverly Beach State Park
Logsden
Siletz
411
Hoskins
Kings Valley
Yaquina Head/ Yakina Head Lighthouse
Agate Beach
20
Summit
Adair Village
Yaquina Head Outstanding Natural Area
Newport
Yaquina Bay Lighthouse
South Beach State Park
Toledo
South Beach
Eddyville
20
Corvallis
20
101
Philomath
99
Seal Rock
Waldport
34
Tidewater
34
Alsea
Yachats Ocean Road Natural Site
Yachats State Recreation Area
Yachats
Cape Perpetua Scenic Area
Monroe
Neptune State Scenic Viewpoint
Junction City
Cheshire
99
Heceta Head Lighthouse State Scenic Area
36
Sea Lion Caves
36
Darlingtonia State Natural Site
Swisshome
Eugene
126
Florence
Mapleton
Cushman
126
Veneta
126
Dunes City
Siltcoos Lake
101
Siuslaw River
Oregon Dunes National Recreation Area
Smith River
Gardiner
Reedsport
0   10 mi
0   10 km
Winchester Bay
38
Drain
99
Curtin
5

PACIFIC OCEAN

COAST RANGES

WHERE TO EAT

$$$$ PACIFIC NORTHWEST

🍴 **Bay House.** Inside a charming bungalow, this restaurant serves meals to linger over while you enjoy views across sunset-gilded Siletz Bay. The seasonal Pacific Northwest cuisine includes Dungeness crab cakes with roasted-chili chutney, fresh halibut Parmesan, and roast duckling with cranberry compote. **Known for:** extensive wine list; impeccable service. [$] *Average main: $35* ✉ *5911 S.W. U.S. 101* ☎ *541/996–3222* 🌐 *www.thebayhouse.org* 🕒 *Closed Mon. and Tues. No lunch.*

$$ SEAFOOD Fodor's Choice ★

🍴 **Blackfish Café.** Owner and chef Rob Pounding serves simple-but-succulent dishes that blend fresh ingredients from local fishermen and gardeners. His skillet-roasted, "ocean trolled" chinook salmon, basted with fennel lime butter, and Oregon blue-cheese potatoes are flavorful and perfect. **Known for:** chinook salmon; Ding Dong dessert. [$] *Average main: $22* ✉ *2733 N.W. U.S. 101* ☎ *541/996–1007* 🌐 *www.blackfish-cafe.com* 🕒 *Closed Tues.*

$ AMERICAN

🍴 **Hearth & Table Kitchen.** The fragrant dishes at this artisan bakery and pizzeria look as delicious as they taste—bountiful salads and hefty sandwiches packed with seasonal ingredients; crispy-crust pizzas crowned with roasted tomatoes, dry-cured salami, pickled jalapeños, and other gourmet ingredients; and fluffy cakes and cupcakes piled high with rich icing. It's a simple, cheerful space: you order at the counter and take a seat at one of the plain wooden tables. **Known for:** creatively topped pizzas; decadent desserts; good beer and wine selection. [$] *Average main: $15* ✉ *660 S.E. U.S. 101* ☎ *541/614–0966* 🌐 *www.hearthandtablekitchen.com* 🕒 *Closed Sun. and Mon.*

$ MEXICAN

🍴 **Puerto Vallarta.** Decorated with colorful tapestries and hand-painted booths depicting whimsical scenes of Mexico, this festive restaurant consistently prepares some of the best Mexican fare on the coast. Dishes ranges from fairly authentic (tongue tacos, carne asada) to those geared toward American tastes (fajitas, burgers). **Known for:** tortas and tacos; fresh-fruit margaritas. [$] *Average main: $12* ✉ *3001 U.S. 101* ☎ *541/994–0300.*

WHERE TO STAY

$ HOTEL FAMILY Fodor's Choice ★

🏨 **Coho Oceanfront Lodge.** Set on a romantic cliff, the renovated Coho is a perfect hybrid of family-friendly lodging and a quiet, intimate hideaway for couples. **Pros:** great value; family-friendly; lots of nice in-room amenities. **Cons:** no restaurant. [$] *Rooms from: $145* ✉ *1635 N.W. Harbor Ave.* ☎ *541/994–3684, 800/848–7006* 🌐 *www.thecoholodge.com* 🛏 *33 studios, 32 suites* 🍽 *Breakfast.*

$ B&B/INN

🏨 **Historic Anchor Inn.** This quirky bungalow might not be for everyone, but for those who appreciate a warm, spirited inn with a decidedly inventive and whimsical touch, this is a remarkable find. **Pros:** a memorable, truly unique property; everything you need to explore Lincoln City. **Cons:** not on the beach; very quirky and rustic. [$] *Rooms from: $99* ✉ *4417 S.W. U.S. 101* ☎ *541/996–3810* 🌐 *www.historicanchorinn.com* 🛏 *19 rooms* 🍽 *Breakfast.*

$$$ RESORT

🏨 **Inn at Spanish Head.** Driving up to this upscale resort hotel, you'd think it might be a fairly intimate place, but on further investigation you'll see that the property takes up the entire side of a bluff like a huge staircase. **Pros:** sweeping views of the ocean through floor-to-ceiling windows; good restaurant; easy beach access via elevator; great place to watch winter storms. **Cons:** pricey; isolated setting not within walking distance of many restaurants or shops. [$] *Rooms from: $209* ✉ *4009 S.E. U.S. 101* ☎ *541/996–2161, 800/452–8127* 🌐 *www.spanishhead.com* 🛏 *68 rooms, 52 suites* 🍴 *Some meals.*

$$ HOTEL 🏨 **Surftides.** Built in the 1940s and given a retro-cool makeover in recent years, this angular five-story hotel enjoys direct access to a wide expanse of beach and is within walking distance of several restaurants along U.S. 101. **Pros:** ocean views; distinctive whimsical decor; good on-site restaurant. **Cons:** not everybody will appreciate the quirky decor. [$] *Rooms from: $179* ✉ *2945 N.W. Jetty Ave.* ☎ *541/994–2191, 800/452–2159* 🌐 *www.surftideslincolncity.com* 🛏 *153 rooms* 🍴 *No meals.*

NIGHTLIFE

Chinook Winds Casino Resort. Oregon's only beachfront casino has a great variety of slot machines, blackjack, poker, keno, and off-track betting. The Rogue River Steakhouse serves a great fillet and terrific appetizers. There's also the Siletz Bay Buffet, the Chinook Seafood Grill, a snack bar, and a lounge. An arcade keeps the kids busy while you are on the gambling floor. Big-name entertainers perform in the showroom. Players can take a break from the tables and enjoy a round of golf at the Chinook Winds Golf Resort next door. ✉ *1777 N.W. 44th St.* ☎ *541/996–5825, 888/244–6665* 🌐 *www.chinookwindscasino.com.*

SHOPPING

Fodor's Choice ★ **Alderhouse Glassblowing.** The imaginative crafts folk at this studio turn molten glass into vases and bowls, which are available for sale. It is the oldest glass-blowing studio in the state. ✉ *611 Immonen Rd.* ☎ *541/996–2483* 🌐 *www.alderhouse.com.*

Culinary Center. Whether she's conducting a small, hands-on class or orchestrating a full-blown cooking demonstration for dozens, executive chef Sharon Wiest loves sharing her passion for Pacific Northwest ingredients. The classes, some of which are led by other noted chefs in the area, offer all sorts of culinary adventures, from baking pizza to making sushi. ✉ *801 S.W. U.S. 101, Suite 401* ☎ *541/557–1125* 🌐 *www.oregoncoast.org/culinary.*

Jennifer L. Sears Glass Art Studio. Blow a glass float or make a glorious glass starfish, heart, or fluted bowl of your own design (prices start at $65 for a glass float). The studio's expert artisans will guide you every step of the way. It's a fun, memorable keepsake of the coast. ✉ *4821 S.W. U.S. 101* ☎ *541/996–2569* 🌐 *www.jennifersearsglassart.com.*

SPORTS AND THE OUTDOORS

BOATING

Devil's Lake State Recreation Area. Canoeing and kayaking are popular on this small lake just inland from the coast, also loved by coots, loons, ducks, cormorants, bald eagles, and grebes. Visitors can sign up in advance for popular kayaking tours in the summer, for which bird guides are provided. A campground has tent and RV sites as well as yurts. ✉ *N.E. 6th St., just east of U.S. 101* ☎ *541/994–2002, 800/551–6949* 🌐 *www.oregonstateparks.org.*

GLENEDEN BEACH

7 miles south of Lincoln City.

Gleneden Beach is a small vacation town known primarily for the famed Salishan Resort, which is perched high above placid Siletz Bay. This expensive collection of guest rooms, vacation homes, condominiums, restaurants, golf fairways, tennis courts, and covered walkways blends into a forest preserve; if not for the signs, you'd scarcely be able to find it.

GETTING HERE AND AROUND

Little Gleneden Beach is a 10-minute drive south of Lincoln City via U.S. 101.

WHERE TO EAT AND STAY

$$$ PACIFIC NORTHWEST 🍴 **Side Door Café.** This dining room, set in an old brick and tile factory with a high ceiling, exposed beams, a fireplace, and many windows, shares its space with Eden Hall performance venue. The menu changes often—fresh preparations have included fire-roasted rack of lamb with vegetable risotto and Northwest bouillabaisse with a lemongrass-saffron-tomato broth. **Known for:** funky and historic industrial setting; creatively prepared seasonal cuisine. [$] *Average main: $28* ✉ *6675 Gleneden Beach Loop Rd.* ☎ *541/764–3825* 🌐 *www.sidedoorcafe.com* 🕑 *Closed Mon. and Tues.*

$$ RENTAL FAMILY 🏨 **Beachcombers Haven vacation rentals.** This cluster of properties is right off the beach, and features spacious one-, two-, or three-bedroom accommodations, some with a hot tub or in-room Jacuzzi. **Pros:** very friendly; well-equipped units with full kitchens; near the beach. **Cons:** some decor is a bit dated; two-night minimum. [$] *Rooms from: $189* ✉ *7045 N.W. Glen* ☎ *541/764–2252, 800/428–5533* 🌐 *www.beachcombershaven.com* 🛏 *14 units* 🍽 *No meals.*

$$$ RESORT 🏨 **Salishan Lodge and Golf Resort.** Secluded and refined, this upscale resort in a hillside forest preserve has long been revered as a luxury weekend getaway as well as a destination for tony corporate retreats, with plenty of reasons to stay on the property. **Pros:** very elegant; secluded resort with a terrific golf course; plenty of activities on the property. **Cons:** ocean views are few; service a bit hit-or-miss considering the steep prices. [$] *Rooms from: $229* ✉ *7760 N. U.S. 101* ☎ *541/764–3600, 800/452–2300* 🌐 *www.salishan.com* 🛏 *205 rooms* 🍽 *No meals.*

SPORTS AND THE OUTDOORS

GOLF

Salishan Golf Resort. With a layout designed by Peter Jacobsen, this par-71 course is a year-round treat for hackers and aficionados alike. The front nine holes are surrounded by a forest of old-growth timber, while the back nine holes provide old-school, links-style play. There's an expansive pro shop and a great bar and grill for relaxing after a "rough" day out on the links. High-season greens fees are $99–$119. ✉ *7760 N. U.S. 101* ☎ *541/764–3600, 800/452–2300* 🌐 *www.salishan.com.*

DEPOE BAY

5 miles south of Gleneden Beach.

Depoe Bay calls itself the whale-watching capital of the world. The small town was founded in the 1920s and named in honor of Charles DePoe of the Siletz tribe, who was named for his employment at a U.S. Army depot in the late 1800s. With a narrow channel and deep water, its tiny harbor is also one of the most protected on the coast. It supports a thriving fleet of commercial and charter fishing boats. The Spouting Horn, a natural cleft in the basalt cliffs on the waterfront, blasts seawater skyward during heavy weather.

GETTING HERE AND AROUND

Depoe Bay lies right between Newport and Lincoln City along U.S. 101—it's a 20-minute drive to either town.

ESSENTIALS

Visitor Information Depoe Bay Chamber of Commerce. ⊠ *223 S.W. U.S. 101, Suite B* ☎ *541/765–2889, 877/485–8348* ⊕ *www.depoebaychamber.org.*

EN ROUTE Five miles south of Depoe Bay off U.S. 101 (watch for signs), the **Otter Crest Loop,** another scenic byway, winds along the cliff tops. Only parts of the loop are open to motor vehicles, but you can drive to points midway from either end and turn around. The full loop is open to bikes and hiking. British explorer Captain James Cook named the 500-foot-high **Cape Foulweather,** at the south end of the loop, on a blustery March day in 1778—a small visitor center and gift shop at this site affords mesmerizing views, and opportunities to spot whales and other marine life. Backward-leaning shore pines lend mute witness to the 100-mph winds that still strafe this exposed spot. At the viewing point at the **Devil's Punchbowl,** 1 mile south of Cape Foulweather, you can peer down into a collapsed sandstone sea cave carved out by the powerful waters of the Pacific. About 100 feet to the north in the rocky tidal pools of the beach known as **Marine Gardens,** purple sea urchins and orange starfish can be seen at low tide. The Otter Crest Loop rejoins U.S. 101 about 4 miles south of Cape Foulweather near **Yaquina Head,** which has been designated an Outstanding Natural Area. Harbor seals, sea lions, cormorants, murres, puffins, and guillemots frolic in the water and on the rocks below the gleaming, white tower of the **Yaquina Bay Lighthouse.**

WHERE TO EAT AND STAY

$$$
PACIFIC
NORTHWEST
Fodor's Choice
★

✕ **Restaurant Beck.** Immensely talented chef-owner Justin Wills presents a short but memorable menu of creatively prepared, modern, Pacific Northwest cuisine each night in this romantic, contemporary dining room at the Whale Cove Inn. The menu changes regularly, with chef Wills sourcing largely from local farms, ranches, and fisheries. **Known for:** panoramic views of Whale Cove; exceptional desserts. $ *Average main: $29* ⊠ *Whale Cove Inn, 2345 U.S. 101* ☎ *541/765–3220* ⊕ *www. restaurantbeck.com* ⊗ *No lunch.*

$$
SEAFOOD

✕ **Tidal Raves Seafood Grill.** An outstanding purveyor of modern seafood fare, Tidal Raves uses local and sustainable fish and shellfish in preparations inspired by places far and near. A few steaks and vegetarian dishes round out the lengthy menu, which also includes such local classics as Dungeness crab cakes, panko-crusted razor clams, and grilled wild salmon. **Known for:** local Dungeness crab cakes; ocean views. [$] *Average main: $22* ⊠ *279 U.S. 101* ☎ *541/765–2995* ⊕ *www. tidalraves.com.*

$
HOTEL
🖥 **Clarion Surfrider Resort.** The economical Clarion Surfrider Resort comprises a few two-story clapboard buildings perched on a bluff overlooking the ocean and Fogarty Creek State Park. **Pros:** impressive ocean views; reasonable rates; decent seafood restaurant and bar on-site. **Cons:** rooms have pleasant but perfunctory furniture; not within walking distance of town. [$] *Rooms from: $142* ⊠ *3115 N.W. U.S. 101* ☎ *541/764–2311* ⊕ *www.choicehotels.com* ⇨ *55 rooms* ❁ *Breakfast.*

$
B&B/INN
🖥 **Depoe Bay Inn.** This pet-friendly bed-and-breakfast overlooking tiny Depoe Bay Harbor provides a dreamy setting for watching boats and relaxing in a quaint atmosphere. **Pros:** intimate and quite; great breakfasts; peaceful and scenic location. **Cons:** on the bay but no beach. [$] *Rooms from: $129* ⊠ *235 S.E. Bay View Ave.* ☎ *541/765–2322, 800/228–0448* ⊕ *www.depoebayinn.com* ⇨ *13 rooms* ❁ *Breakfast.*

$$$$
B&B/INN
Fodor's Choice
★
🖥 **Whale Cove Inn.** This small and exquisitely decorated high-end inn overlooks the picturesque cove for which it's named and contains just eight spacious suites, each with a dazzling view of the water. **Pros:** astoundingly good restaurant; stunning building with cushy and spacious suites; terrific ocean views. **Cons:** not a good fit for kids (only those 16 and over are permitted); pricey; not within walking distance of town. [$] *Rooms from: $455* ⊠ *2345 U.S. 101* ☎ *541/765–4300, 800/628–3409* ⊕ *www.whalecoveinn.com* ⇨ *8 suites* ❁ *Breakfast.*

SPORTS AND THE OUTDOORS
RECREATIONAL AREAS
Fogarty Creek State Recreation Area. Bird-watching and viewing the tidal pools are the key draws here, but hiking and picnicking are also popular at this park found along U.S. 101. Wooden footbridges wind through the dense forest and tall cliffs rise above the beach. ⊠ *U.S. 101, 3 miles north of Depoe Bay* ☎ *800/551–6949, 541/265–4560* ⊕ *www.oregon-stateparks.org* 🎟 *Free.*

NEWPORT

12 miles south of Depoe Bay.

Known as the Dungeness crab capital of the world, Newport offers accessible beaches, a popular aquarium, the coast's premier performing-arts center, and a significant supply of both elegant and affordable accommodations and restaurants. Newport exists on two levels: the highway above, threading its way through the community's main business district, and the old Bayfront along Yaquina Bay below (watch for signs on U.S. 101). With its high-masted fishing fleet, well-worn buildings, seafood markets, art galleries, and touristy shops, Newport's Bayfront is an ideal place for an afternoon stroll. So many male sea lions in Yaquina Bay loiter near crab pots and bark from the waterfront piers that locals call the area the Bachelor Club. Visit the docks to buy fresh seafood or rent a kayak to explore the bay. In 2010 Newport was designated the National Oceanic and Atmospheric Administration's (NOAA) Pacific Marine Operations Center and a $38 million, 5-acre facility (and a port for four ships) opened a year later.

GETTING HERE AND AROUND

Newport is a 2½-hour drive from Portland by way of Interstate 5 south to Albany and U.S. 20 west; the town is a 40-minute drive south along U.S. 101 from Lincoln City, and a 75-minute drive north of Florence.

ESSENTIALS

Visitor Information Destination Newport. ⊠ *555 S.W. Coast Hwy.* ☎ *503/262–8801, 800/262–7844* ⊕ *www.discoverynewport.com.*

TOURS

Marine Discovery Tours. Sea-life cruises, priced from $40 and departing throughout the day, are conducted on a 65-foot excursion boat *Discovery*, with inside seating for 49 people and two viewing levels. The cruise season is March through October. ⊠ *345 S.W. Bay Blvd.* ☎ *800/903–2628, 541/265–6200* ⊕ *www.marinediscovery.com* ➥ *From $36.*

EXPLORING

The Flying Dutchman Winery. Occupying a bluff by the sea, this small, family-owned winery on the Otter Crest Loop enjoys one of the most spectacular locations on the Oregon Coast. Owner Danielle Cutler buys grapes from five Oregon vineyards, and brings them over the Coast Range to its salt-air environment for fermenting. Guests can enjoy its eclectic vintages in the cozy tasting room, or take a quick tour of the oak barrels next door. ⊠ *915 1st St., Otter Rock* ☎ *541/765–2553* ⊕ *www.dutchmanwinery.com.*

FAMILY **Hatfield Marine Science Center.** Interactive and interpretive exhibits at Oregon State University appeal to the kid in everyone. More than just showcasing sea life, the center contains exhibits and holds classes that teach the importance of scientific research in managing and sustaining coastal and marine resources. The staff regularly leads guided tours of the adjoining estuary. ⊠ *2030 S. Marine Science Dr.* ☎ *541/867–0100* ⊕ *www.hmsc.oregonstate.edu* ➥ *$5 suggested donation.*

FAMILY **Oregon Coast Aquarium.** This 4½-acre complex brings visitors face to face with the creatures living in offshore and near-shore Pacific marine habitats: frolicking sea otters, colorful puffins, pulsating jellyfish, and even a 60-pound octopus. There's a hands-on interactive area for children, including tide pools perfect for "petting" sea anemones and urchins. The aquarium houses one of North America's largest seabird aviaries, including glowering turkey vultures. Permanent exhibits include Passages of the Deep, where visitors walk through a 200-foot underwater tunnel with 360-degree views of sharks, wolf eels, halibut, and a truly captivating array of sea life. Large coho salmon and sturgeon can be viewed in a naturalistic setting through a window wall 9 feet high and 20 feet wide. The sherbet-colored nettles are hypnotizing. ⊠ *2820 S.E. Ferry Slip Rd.* ☎ *541/867–3474* ⊕ *www.aquarium.org* ➥ *$22.95.*

FAMILY **Yaquina Bay Lighthouse.** The state's oldest wooden lighthouse was only in commission for three years (1871–74), because it was determined that it was built in the wrong location. Today the well-restored lighthouse with a candy-apple top shines a steady white light from dusk to dawn.

Oregon Coast Aquarium, Newport

Open to the public, it is thought to be the oldest structure in Newport, and the only Oregon lighthouse with living quarters attached. ✉ *S.W. Government St. at S.W. Martin St.* ☎ *541/265–5679* 🌐 *www.yaquinalights.org* 🎟 *Free, donations suggested.*

FAMILY Fodor's Choice ★ **Yaquina Head Lighthouse.** The tallest lighthouse on the Oregon Coast has been blinking its beacon since its head keeper first walked up its 114 steps to light the wicks on the evening of August 20, 1873. Next to the 93-foot tower is an interpretive center. Bring your camera and call ahead to confirm tour times. ✉ *N.W. Lighthouse Dr., off U.S. 101, 4 miles north of Newport* ☎ *541/574–3100* 🌐 *www.yaquinalights.org* 🎟 *Free, donations suggested.*

WHERE TO EAT

$$ SEAFOOD FAMILY Fodor's Choice ★ 🍴 **Georgie's Beachside Grill.** This stand-alone restaurant for the Hallmark Inns and Resorts serves up some wonderfully innovative dishes. From the sea scallops blackened in house-mixed herbs to flame-broiled halibut with pineapple salsa, the food here lives up to the ocean view. **Known for:** ocean views; excellent breakfasts. [$] *Average main: $20* ✉ *744 S.W. Elizabeth St.* ☎ *503/265–9800* 🌐 *www.georgiesbeachsidegrill.com.*

$$ SEAFOOD FAMILY Fodor's Choice ★ 🍴 **Local Ocean Seafoods.** At this fish market and sleek grill on picturesque Yaquina Bay, the operators purchase fish directly from more than 60 boats in the fishing fleet right outside and take the mission of locally sourced, sustainable seafood seriously. This is also one of few restaurants on the Oregon Coast that doesn't own a deep fryer—even the fish-and-chips are panfried. **Known for:** market with fresh-caught seafood to go; outdoor seating overlooking the bay; flavorful and

fragrant Fishwives Stew. $ *Average main: $21* ⊠ *213 S.E. Bay Blvd.* ☎ *514/574–7959* ⊕ *www.localocean.net.*

$ ✕ **Panini Bakery.** The owner, who operates this local favorite bakery
CAFÉ and espresso bar, prides himself on hearty and home-roasted meats, hand-cut breads, sourdough pizza, and friendly service. The coffee's organic, the eggs free range, the orange juice fresh-squeezed, and just about everything is made from scratch. **Known for:** made-from-scratch breakfast fare; outdoor seating. $ *Average main: $8* ⊠ *232 N.W. Coast Hwy.* ☎ *541/265–5033* ▭ *No credit cards.*

$$ ✕ **Tables of Content.** The well-plotted prix-fixe menu at the restaurant of
PACIFIC the outstanding Sylvia Beach Hotel changes nightly. Chances are that the
NORTHWEST main dish will be fresh local seafood, perhaps a moist grilled salmon fillet in a Dijonnaise sauce, served with sautéed vegetables, fresh-baked breads, and rice pilaf; a decadent dessert is also included. **Known for:** convivial family-style dining; rich desserts. $ *Average main: $18* ⊠ *267 N.W. Cliff St.* ☎ *541/265–5428, 888/795–8422* ⊕ *www.sylviabeachhotel.com.*

WHERE TO STAY

$$$ ⊡ **Inn at Nye Beach.** With a prime beachfront location in the historic Nye
HOTEL Beach section of Newport, this chic, eco-friendly, boutique hotel contains
Fodor's Choice 22 rooms and suites. **Pros:** direct beach access and great views; smartly
★ furnished; contemporary rooms. **Cons:** the complimentary breakfast is very limited (a full one costs extra); views not great from some rooms. $ *Rooms from: $216* ⊠ *729 N.W. Coast St.* ☎ *541/265–2477, 800/480– 2477* ⊕ *www.innatnyebeach.com* ⤳ *6 rooms, 16 suites* ⦿ *Breakfast.*

$$ ⊡ **Newport Belle B&B.** This fully operational stern-wheeler is permanently
B&B/INN moored at the Newport Marina, where guests have front-row seats to all the boating activity around Yaquina Bay. Rooms are cozy and decorated with nautical memorabilia and Victorian-style furnishings. **Pros:** one-of-a-kind lodging experience; great harbor views. **Cons:** not suitable for kids; need a car to get into town. $ *Rooms from: $160* ⊠ *Dock H, 2126 S.E. Marine Science Dr.* ☎ *541/867–6290* ⊕ *www. newportbelle.com* ☽ *Closed Nov.–early Feb.* ⤳ *5 rooms* ⦿ *Breakfast.*

$ ⊡ **Sylvia Beach Hotel.** At this offbeat 1913-vintage beachfront hotel,
HOTEL reading, writing, and conversation eclipse technological hotel-room isolation. **Pros:** distinctive decor; great place to disconnect. **Cons:** no TV, telephone, or Internet access; sharing tables with other guests at mealtimes doesn't suit everyone; least expensive rooms don't have ocean views. $ *Rooms from: $130* ⊠ *267 N.W. Cliff St.* ☎ *541/265–5428, 888/795–8422* ⊕ *www.sylviabeachhotel.com* ⤳ *20 rooms* ⦿ *Breakfast.*

NIGHTLIFE AND PERFORMING ARTS

Fodor's Choice **Newport Symphony Orchestra.** The only year-round, professional sym-
★ phony orchestra on the Oregon Coast plays at the 400-seat Newport Performing Arts Center, just a few steps away from the seashore in Nye Beach. Adam Flatt is the music director and conductor, and actor and narrator David Ogden Stiers serves as associate conductor. The orchestra performs a popular series of concerts in the Newport Performing Arts Center September through May, and special events in the summer, including its popular free community concert every July 4. ⊠ *777 W. Olive St.* ☎ *541/574–0614* ⊕ *www.newportsymphony.org.*

SPORTS AND THE OUTDOORS
RECREATIONAL AREAS

Beverly Beach State Park. Seven miles north of Newport, this beachfront park extends from Yaquina Head, where you can see the lighthouse, to the headlands of Otter Rock. It's a great place to fly a kite, surf the waves, or hunt for fossils. The campground is well equipped, with a wind-protected picnic area and a yurt meeting hall. ⊠ *N.E. Beverly Dr., off U.S. 101, 6 miles north of Newport* ☎ *541/265–9278, 800/551–6949* ⊕ *www.oregonstateparks.org* 🖅 *Free.*

Devil's Punchbowl State Natural Area. A rocky shoreline separates the day-use area from the surf. It's a popular whale-watching site and has excellent tidal pools. ⊠ *1st St., off U.S. 101, 8 miles north of Newport, Otter Rock* ☎ *541/265–4560, 800/551–6949* ⊕ *www.oregonstateparks.org* 🖅 *Free.*

South Beach State Park. Fishing, crabbing, boating, windsurfing, hiking, and beachcombing are popular activities at this park that begins just across the Yaquina Bay Bridge from Newport and contains a lovely stretch of beach. Kayaking tours are available for a fee. There's a popular campground, too. ⊠ *U.S. 101 S, 3 miles south of Newport* ☎ *541/867–4715, 800/452–5687* ⊕ *www.oregonstateparks.org.*

Yaquina Head Outstanding Natural Area. Thousands of birds—cormorants, gulls, common murres, pigeon guillemots—make their home just beyond shore on Pinnacle and Colony rocks, and nature trails wind through fields of sea grass and wildflowers, leading to spectacular views. There is also an interpretive center and the historic Yaquina Head Lighthouse. ⊠ *750 N.W. Lighthouse Dr.* ☎ *541/574–3100* ⊕ *www.yaquinalights.org* 🖅 *Free, donations suggested.*

YACHATS

24 miles south of Newport.

The small town of Yachats (pronounced "yah-*hots*") is at the mouth of the Yachats River, and from its rocky shoreline, which includes the highest point on the Oregon Coast, trails lead to beaches and dozens of tidal pools. A relaxed alternative to the more touristy communities to the north, Yachats has all the coastal pleasures without the traffic: B&Bs and oceanfront hotels, some terrific restaurants, deserted beaches, tidal pools, surf-pounded crags, fishing, and crabbing.

GETTING HERE AND AROUND
Yachats lies between Newport and Florence on coastal U.S. 101—it's a 40-minute drive from either town, and a three-hour drive via Interstate 5 and Highway 34 from Portland.

ESSENTIALS
Visitor Information Yachats Visitors Center. ⊠ *241 U.S. 101* ☎ *800/929–0477* ⊕ *www.yachats.org.*

WHERE TO EAT

$ ✕ **Bread and Roses Baking.** Artisan breads are handmade in small batches
BAKERY here, along with pastries, muffins, scones, cookies, cinnamon rolls, and desserts. In the bright, yellow-cottage bakery you can also try the daily soup and sandwiches at lunchtime, or just while away the morning

with pastries and good coffee. **Known for:** proximity to Yachats State Recreation Area; delicious pastries and baked goods. $ *Average main: $9* ✉ *238 4th St.* ☎ *541/547–4454* ✆ *No dinner.*

$ ✗ **Luna Sea Fish House.** The freshest Dungeness crab around is one of the
SEAFOOD   seasonal attractions in this small weathered restaurant, coming straight
FAMILY   from owner Robert Anthony's boat—he catches much of the fish served here using sustainable hook-and-line methods for salmon, cod, and albacore tuna. And in season, he pots the crab seen bubbling in outdoor kettles. **Known for:** on-site market with fresh fish; slumgullion (a rich clam-and-shrimp chowder baked with cheese). $ *Average main: $14* ✉ *153 N.W. U.S. 101* ☎ *541/547–4794, 888/547–4794* ⊕ *www.lunaseafishhouse.com.*

$$ ✗ **ONA Restaurant.** Relatively snazzy for such a laid-back town, this
MODERN   popular downtown bistro overlooking the confluence of the Yachats
AMERICAN   River and the Pacific is nonetheless unpretentious and relaxed. The specialty is locally and seasonally sourced Oregon seafood (try the sole over Dungeness crab and bay shrimp with a rosé cream reduction). **Known for:** sticky toffee pudding; rockfish-and-chips; great regional wine. $ *Average main: $22* ✉ *131 U.S. 101 N* ☎ *541/547–6627* ⊕ *www. onarestaurant.com* ✆ *Closed Wed.–Thurs. in winter.*

$ ✗ **Yachats Brewing and Farmstore.** Inside this lively establishment with
ECLECTIC   pitched timber ceilings, skylights, and a solarium-style beer garden,
Fodor's Choice   you'll find one of the state's most impressive young craft breweries
★   as well as a taproom specializing in house-fermented ingredients—everything from kimchi to sauerkraut. It may sound like a slightly odd concept, but it works. **Known for:** unusual craft beers and probiotic drinks; house-fermented foods. $ *Average main: $14* ✉ *348 U.S. 101 N* ☎ *541/547–3884* ⊕ *www.yachatsbrewing.com.*

WHERE TO STAY

$ ⌂ **Deane's Oceanfront Lodge.** This simple single-story, family-run motel
HOTEL   is set on a sweeping stretch of beachfront midway between downtown Yachats and Waldport. **Pros:** charming rooms; motel has direct ocean views and beach access; reasonable rates. **Cons:** small rooms; not within walking distance of dining and shopping. $ *Rooms from: $75* ✉ *7365 U.S. 101 N* ☎ *541/547–3321* ⊕ *www.deaneslodge.com* ⌫ *18 rooms.*

$$$ ⌂ **Overleaf Lodge.** On a rocky shoreline at the north end of Yachats,
HOTEL   this rambling romantic three-story hotel enjoys spectacular sunsets and
Fodor's Choice   contains splendidly comfortable accommodations. **Pros:** best hotel in
★   one of the coast's best communities; one of the best full-service spas on the coast. **Cons:** no restaurant; a bit of a walk from the action. $ *Rooms from: $225* ✉ *280 Overleaf Lodge La.* ☎ *541/547–4885, 800/338–0507* ⊕ *www.overleaflodge.com* ⌫ *54 rooms, 4 suites* ⦿*Breakfast.*

$$ ⌂ **SeaQuest Inn.** Friendly and knowledgeable innkeeper Sherwood
B&B/INN   Heineman prepares lavish two-course breakfasts as well as an evening wine-and-cheese hour at this beautifully designed contemporary B&B situated along a quiet stretch of U.S. 101 with mesmerizing views of the sea. **Pros:** tranquil setting; smartly furnished rooms; delicious breakfast included; all rooms have full or partial ocean views. **Cons:** a 10- to 15-minute drive from the village of Yachats. $ *Rooms from: $180* ✉ *95354 U.S. 101 S* ☎ *541/547–3782, 800/341–4878* ⊕ *www. seaquestinn.com* ⌫ *5 rooms, 1 suite* ⦿*Breakfast.*

3

SPORTS AND THE OUTDOORS
RECREATIONAL AREAS

Fodor's Choice **Cape Perpetua Scenic Area.** The highest vehicle-accessible lookout on
★ the Oregon Coast, Cape Perpetua towers 800 feet above the rocky
shoreline. Named by Captain Cook on St. Perpetua's Day in 1778,
the cape is part of a 2,700-acre scenic area popular with hikers, campers, beachcombers, and naturalists. General information, educational
movies and exhibits, and trail maps are available at the **Cape Perpetua
Visitors Center,** on the east side of the highway, ½ mile south of Devil's
Churn. The easy 1-mile **Giant Spruce Trail** passes through a fern-filled
rain forest to an enormous 600-year-old Sitka spruce. Easier still is the
marked Auto Tour; it begins just north of the visitor center and winds
through Siuslaw National Forest to the ¼-mile **Whispering Spruce Trail.**
Views from the rustic rock shelter here extend 50 miles north to south,
and some 40 miles out to sea. For a more rigorous trek, hike the **St.
Perpetua Trail** to the shelter. Other trails lead from the visitor center
down along the shore, including a scenic pathway to **Devil's Churn,**
next to which a small snack bar sells sandwiches, sweets, and coffee.
✉ *2400 U.S. 101, 3 miles south of Yachats* ☎ *541/547–3289* ⊕ *www.
fs.usda.gov/siuslaw* ⌘ *Parking fee $5.*

Neptune State Scenic Viewpoint. Visitors have fun searching for animals,
watching the surf, or hunting for agates. The benches set above the
beach on the cliff provide a great view of Cumming Creek. It's also a
terrific spot for whale-watching. At low tide, beachcombers have access
to a natural cave and tidal pools. ✉ *U.S. 101, 4 miles south of Yachats*
☎ *800/551–6949, 541/547–3416* ⊕ *www.oregonstateparks.org* ⌘ *Free.*

Yachats Ocean Road State Natural Site. Drive this 1-mile loop just across
the Yachats River from downtown Yachats, and discover one of the
most scenic viewpoints on the Oregon Coast. Park along Yachats Ocean
Road and scamper out along the broad swath of sand where the Yachats River meets the Pacific Ocean. There's fun to be had playing on
the beach, poking around tide pools, and watching blowholes, summer sunsets, and whales spouting. ✉ *Yachats Ocean Rd., just south of
U.S. 101 bridge over Yachats River* ☎ *800/551–6949, 541/867–7451*
⊕ *www.oregonstateparks.org.*

Yachats State Recreation Area. The public beach in downtown Yachats is
more like the surface of the moon than most other places, and certainly
most beaches. A wooden platform overlooks the coastline, where the
waves roll in sideways and splash over the rocks at high tide. As is
the case throughout most of the town, the beach itself is paralleled by
an upland walking trail and dotted with picnic tables, benches, and
interpretive signs. Visit to spot the sea lions that frequent this stretch
of coast. Or join the intrepid beachcombers who climb the rocks for a
closer look at tide pools populated by sea urchins, hermit crabs, barnacles, snails, and sea stars. **Amenities:** parking; toilets. **Best for:** walking;
sunset. ✉ *Ocean View Dr., off 2nd St. and U.S. 101* ☎ *800/551–6949,
541/867–7451* ⊕ *www.oregonstateparks.org.*

FLORENCE

25 miles south of Yachats; 64 miles west of Eugene.

The closest beach town to Oregon's second-largest city, Eugene, charming and low-keyed Florence delights visitors with its restored riverfront Old Town and proximity to one of the most remarkable stretches of Oregon coastline. Some 75 creeks and rivers empty into the Pacific Ocean in and around town, and the Siuslaw River flows right through the historic village center. When the numerous nearby lakes are added to the mix, it makes for one of the richest fishing areas in Oregon. Salmon, rainbow trout, bass, perch, crabs, and clams are among the water's treasures. Fishing boats and pleasure crafts moor in Florence's harbor, forming a pleasant backdrop for the town's restored buildings. Old Town has notable restaurants, antiques stores, fish markets, and other diversions. South of town, miles of white sand dunes lend themselves to everything from solitary hikes to rides aboard all-terrain vehicles.

GETTING HERE AND AROUND

It's a 75-minute drive west to Florence on Highway 126 from Eugene and a stunningly scenic 40-minute drive south on U.S. 101 from Yachats. It takes about an hour to drive U.S. 101 south to Coos Bay, a stretch that takes in all of Oregon Dunes National Recreation Area.

ESSENTIALS

Visitor Information Florence Area Chamber of Commerce. ✉ *290 U.S. 101* ☎ *541/997–3128* ⊕ *www.florencechamber.com.*

EXPLORING

Darlingtonia State Natural Site. Six miles south of Sea Lion Caves, on the east side of U.S. 101, is an example of the rich plant life found in the marshy terrain near the coast. It's also a surefire child pleaser. A short paved nature trail leads through clumps of insect-catching cobra lilies, so named because they look like spotted cobras ready to strike. This area is most interesting in May, when the lilies are in bloom. ✉ *U.S. 101, at Mercer Lake Rd.* ☎ *541/997–3851* ⊕ *www.oregonstateparks.org.*

FAMILY **Sea Lion Caves.** In 1880 a sea captain named Cox rowed a small skiff into a fissure in a 300-foot-high sea cliff. Inside, he was startled to discover a vaulted chamber in the rock, 125 feet high and 2 acres in size. Hundreds of massive sea lions—the largest bulls weighing 2,000 pounds or more—covered every available surface. Cox's discovery would become one of the Oregon Coast's premier attractions, if something of a tourist trap. An elevator near the cliff-top ticket office and kitschy gift shop descends to the floor of the cavern, near sea level, where vast numbers of Steller's and California sea lions relax on rocks and swim about (their cute, fuzzy pups can be viewed from behind a wire fence). This is the only known hauling-out area and rookery for wild sea lions on the mainland in the Lower 48, and it's an awesome sight and sound when they're in the cave, typically only in fall and winter (in spring and summer the mammals usually stay on the rocky ledges outside the cave). You'll also see several species of seabirds here, including migratory pigeon guillemots, cormorants, and three varieties of gulls. Gray whales are sometimes visible during their October–December and March–May migrations. ✉ *91560 U.S. 101* ✣ *10 miles north of Florence* ☎ *541/547–3111* 🌐 *www.sealioncaves.com* 🎟 *$14.*

NEED A BREAK

🍴 Siuslaw River Coffee Roasters. This small, homey business serves cups of drip-on-demand coffee—you select the roast and they grind and brew it on the spot. Beans are roasted on-site, muffins and breads are freshly baked, and a view of the namesake river can be savored from the deck out back. ✉ *1240 Bay St.* ☎ *541/997–3443* 🌐 *www.coffeeoregon.com.*

WHERE TO EAT AND STAY

$$ SEAFOOD

🍴 **Bridgewater Fishhouse.** Freshly caught seafood—20 to 25 choices nightly—is the mainstay of this creaky-floored, Victorian-era restaurant in Florence's Old Town. Whether you opt for patio dining during summer or lounge seating in winter, the eclectic fare of pastas, burgers, salads, and seafood-packed stews is consistently well prepared. **Known for:** live music; happy hour deals; lighter fare in Zebra Lounge. [$] *Average main: $19* ✉ *1297 Bay St.* ☎ *541/997–1133* 🌐 *www.bridgewaterfishhouse.com* 🕓 *Closed Tues.*

$ MODERN AMERICAN

🍴 **Homegrown Public House.** This bustling, intimate gastropub in Old Town Florence—a couple of blocks north of the riverfront—specializes in locally sourced, creatively prepared American fare and offers a well-chosen list of Oregon beers on tap, plus local spirits, iced teas, and kombucha. Stop by for lunch to enjoy the lightly battered albacore fish and hand-cut fries with tartar sauce, or a cheeseburger topped with Rogue blue and served with marinated vegetables and local greens. **Known for:** Sunday brunch; daily market fish special. [$] *Average main: $15* ✉ *294 Laurel St.* ☎ *541/997–4886* 🌐 *www.homegrownpub.com* 🕓 *Closed Mon.*

$$ SEAFOOD Fodor's Choice ★

🍴 **Waterfront Depot Restaurant and Bar.** The detailed chalkboard menu says it all: from the fresh, crab-encrusted halibut to classic duck-and-lamb cassoulet to Bill's Flaming Spanish Coffee, this is a place serious about fresh food and fine flavors. Originally located in the old Mapleton train station, moved in pieces and reassembled in Old Town Florence, the atmospheric tavern has a great view of the Siuslaw River and the Siuslaw River Bridge. **Known for:** patio seating on the river; creative daily specials. [$] *Average main: $20* ✉ *1252 Bay St.* ☎ *541/902–9100* 🌐 *www.thewaterfrontdepot.com* 🕓 *No lunch.*

$$$ B&B/INN Fodor's Choice ★

🏨 **Heceta Head Lighthouse B&B.** On a windswept promontory, this unusual late-Victorian property is one of Oregon's most remarkable bed-and-breakfasts; it is located at Heceta Head Lighthouse State Scenic Viewpoint and owned by a certified executive chef. **Pros:** unique property with a magical setting; exceptionally good food. **Cons:** remote location; expensive, especially considering some rooms share a bath; tends to book up well in advance. [$] *Rooms from: $215* ✉ *92072 U.S. 101, 12 miles north of Florence* ☎ *541/547–3696, 866/547–3696* 🌐 *www.hecetalighthouse.com* 🛏 *6 rooms, 4 with bath* 🍽 *Breakfast.*

$ B&B/INN

🏨 **River House Inn.** On the beautiful Siuslaw River, this property has terrific accommodations and is near quaint shops and restaurants in Florence's Old Town. **Pros:** spacious rooms; great views from most rooms; close proximity to dining and shopping. **Cons:** not on the beach. $ *Rooms from: $119* ⊠ *1202 Bay St.* ☎ *541/997–3933, 888/824–2454* ⊕ *www.riverhouseflorence.com* ⊃ *40 rooms* ⦿ *Breakfast.*

SPORTS AND THE OUTDOORS

RECREATIONAL AREAS

Fodor'sChoice ★ **Heceta Head Lighthouse State Scenic Viewpoint.** A ½-mile trail from the beachside parking lot leads to the oft-photographed Heceta Head Lighthouse built in 1894, whose beacon, visible for more than 21 miles, is the most powerful on the Oregon Coast. More than 7 miles of trails traverse the rocky landscape north and south of the lighthouse, which rises some 200 feet above the ocean. For a mesmerizing view of the lighthouse and Heceta Head, pull over at the scenic viewpoint just north of Sea Lion Caves. ⊠ *U.S. 101, 11 miles north of Florence, Yachats* ☎ *541/547–3416, 800/551–6949* ⊕ *www.oregonstateparks.org* ⊠ *Day use $5, lighthouse tours free.*

FAMILY Fodor'sChoice ★ **Oregon Dunes National Recreation Area.** The Oregon Dunes National Recreation Area is the largest expanse of coastal sand dunes in North America, extending for 40 miles, from Florence to Coos Bay. The area contains some of the best ATV riding in the United States and encompasses some 31,500 acres. More than 1.5 million people visit the dunes each year, and about 350,000 are ATV users. **Honeyman Memorial State Park,** 515 acres within the recreation area, is a base camp for dune-buggy enthusiasts, mountain bikers, hikers, boaters, horseback riders, and dogsledders (the sandy hills are an excellent training ground). There's a campground, too. The dunes are a vast playground for children, particularly the slopes surrounding cool **Cleawox Lake.** If you have time for just a quick scamper in the sand, stop by the Oregon Dunes Overlook off U.S. 101, 11 miles south of Florence and 11 miles north of Reedsport—it's on the west side of the road, just north of Perkins Lake. ⊠ *Office, 855 U.S. 101, Reedsport* ☎ *541/271–6000* ⊕ *www. fs.usda.gov/siuslaw* ⊠ *Day use $5.*

FAMILY Fodor'sChoice ★ **Sandland Adventures.** This outfitter provides everything you need to get the whole family together for the ride of their lives. Start off with a heart-racing dune-buggy ride with a professional that will take you careening up, over, down, and around some of the steepest sand in the Oregon Dunes National Recreation Area. After you're done screaming and smiling, Sandland's park has bumper boats, a go-kart track, a miniature golf course, and a small railroad. ⊠ *85366 U.S. 101* ☎ *541/997-8087* ⊕ *www.sandland.com.*

SANDBOARDING

FAMILY **Sand Master Park.** Everything you need to sandboard the park's private dunes is right here: board rental, wax, eyewear, clothing, and instruction. The staff is exceptionally helpful, and will get beginners off on their sandboarding adventure with enthusiasm. However, what must be surfed must first be hiked up, and so on. ⊠ *5351 U.S. 101* ☎ *541/997-6006* ⊕ *www.sandmasterpark.com.*

SOUTHERN COAST

Outdoors enthusiasts find a natural amusement park along this gorgeous stretch of coast from Reedsport to Brookings. The northern portion has a continuation of the Oregon Dunes National Recreation Area, and is the location of its visitor center. The Umpqua Discovery Center is a perfect trip with (or without) the kids, to learn about the region's history and animals. In Bandon golfers flock to one of the most celebrated clusters of courses in the nation at Bandon Dunes. Lovers of lighthouses, sailing, fishing, crabbing, elk viewing, camping, and water sports may wonder why they didn't venture south sooner.

BAY AREA: COOS BAY AND NORTH BEND

27 miles south of Reedsport on U.S. 101.

The Coos Bay–Charleston–North Bend metropolitan area, collectively known as the Bay Area (population 27,000), is the gateway to rewarding recreational experiences. The town of Coos Bay lies next to the largest natural harbor between San Francisco Bay and Seattle's Puget Sound. A century ago, vast quantities of lumber cut from the Coast Range were milled in Coos Bay and shipped around the world. Coos Bay still has a reputation as a rough-and-ready port city, but with mill closures and dwindling lumber reserves it now looks to tourism and other industries for economic growth. The waterfront is now dominated by an attractive boardwalk with interpretive displays, a casino, and the new home of the Coos History Museum, which opened in 2015.

To see the most picturesque part of the Bay Area, head west from Coos Bay on Newmark Avenue for about 7 miles to **Charleston.** Though it's a Bay Area community, this quiet fishing village at the mouth of Coos Bay is a world unto itself. As it loops into town, the road becomes the Cape Arago Highway and leads to several stunning oceanfront parks.

GETTING HERE AND AROUND
The area lies along a slightly inland stretch of U.S. 101 that's a 40-minute drive south of Reedsport and a 30-minute drive north of Bandon; from the Umpqua Valley and Interstate 5 corridor, Coos Bay is just under two hours' drive west from Roseburg on Highway 42.

Southwest Oregon Regional Airport in North Bend has commercial flights from Portland, Denver, and San Francisco.

ESSENTIALS
Visitor Information Coos Bay—North Bend Visitors & Convention Bureau.
⊠ *50 Central Ave., Coos Bay* 🕾 *541/269–0215, 800/824–8486* ⊕ *www.oregonsadventurecoast.com.*

EXPLORING
FAMILY **Cape Arago Lighthouse.** On a rock island just offshore from Charleston near Sunset Bay State Park, this lighthouse has had several iterations; the first lighthouse was built here in 1866, but it was destroyed by storms and erosion. A second, built in 1908, suffered the same fate. The current white tower, built in 1934, is 44 feet tall and towers 100 feet above the ocean. If you're here on a foggy day, listen for its unique

Umpqua Sand Dunes in Oregon Dunes National Recreation Area

foghorn. The lighthouse is connected to the mainland by a bridge. Neither is open to the public, but there's an excellent spot to view this lonely guardian and much of the coastline. From U.S. 101, take Cape Arago Highway to Gregory Point, where it ends at a turnaround, and follow the short trail. ✉ *Cape Arago Hwy., just north of Sunset Bay State Park, Charleston* ⊕ *www.oregonstateparks.org.*

Charleston Marina Complex. At this bustling marina 8 miles west of Coos Bay, there's a launch ramp, a store with tackle and marine supplies, an RV park, a motel, restaurants, and gift shops. Fishing charters also set out from here. ✉ *63534 Kingfisher Dr., Charleston* ☎ *541/888–2548* ⊕ *www.charlestonmarina.com.*

FAMILY **Coos History Museum & Maritime Collection.** This modern 11,000-square-foot museum with expansive views of the Coos Bay waterfront contains an exhaustive collection of memorabilia related to the region's history, from early photos to vintage boats, all displayed in an airy, open exhibit hall with extensive interpretive signage. You'll also find exhibits on Native American history, agriculture, and industry such as logging, shipping, natural history, and mining. ✉ *1210 N. Front St., Coos Bay* ☎ *541/756–6320* ⊕ *www.cooshistory.org* 🖃 *$7.*

FAMILY **South Slough National Estuarine Research Reserve.** The 5,000-acre reserve's fragile ecosystem supports everything from algae to bald eagles and black bears. More than 300 species of birds have been sighted at the reserve, which has an interpretive center with interesting nature exhibits, guided walks (summer only), and nature trails that give you a chance to see things up close. ✉ *61907 Seven Devils Rd., 4 miles south of Charleston, Coos Bay* ☎ *541/888–5558* ⊕ *www.oregon.gov/dsl/ssnerr* 🖃 *Free.*

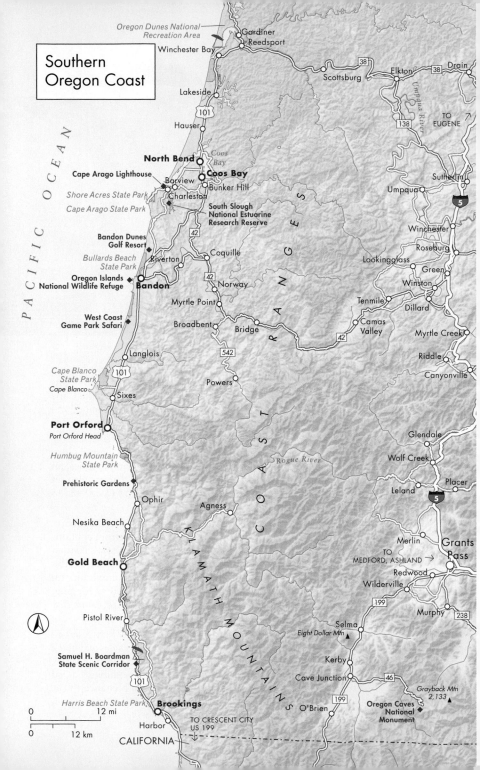

WHERE TO EAT AND STAY

$$ GERMAN 🍴 **Blue Heron Bistro.** The specialty at this bustling downtown bistro is hearty German fare, but you'll also find a number of local seafood items, as well as sandwiches and lighter dishes, from panfried oysters to meatball sandwiches. The skylit, tile-floor dining room seats about 70 amid natural wood and blue linen. **Known for:** great beer selection; outdoor seating. [$] *Average main: $18* ✉ *100 W. Commercial St., Coos Bay* ☎ *541/267–3933* 🌐 *www.blueheronbistro.net.*

$ SEAFOOD 🍴 **Miller's at the Cove.** Often packed with local fishing and dock workers as well as tourists en route to and from Sunset Bay and nearby state parks, this lively and fun—if at times raucous—sports bar and tavern makes a great dinner or lunch stop for fresh seafood, and watching a game on TV. Favorites here include the fish-and-chips (available with local snapper or cod), oyster burgers, Dungeness crab melts, meatball subs, clam chowder, and Baja-style fish or crab tacos. **Known for:** laid-back ambience; tasty fish tacos; craft beer by the pitcher. [$] *Average main: $11* ✉ *63346 Boat Basin Rd., Charleston* ☎ *541/808–2404* 🌐 *www.millersatthecove.rocks.*

$ B&B/INN FAMILY 🏨 **Coos Bay Manor.** Built in 1912 on a quiet residential street, this 15-room Colonial Revival manor contains original hardwood floors, detailed woodwork, high ceilings, and antiques and period reproductions. **Pros:** very nicely kept and decorated; family-friendly. **Cons:** in busy downtown Coos Bay; a 15-minute drive from the ocean. [$] *Rooms from: $145* ✉ *955 S. 5th St., Coos Bay* ☎ *541/269–1224, 800/269–1224* 🌐 *www.coosbaymanor.com* 🛏 *5 rooms, 1 suite* 🍽 *Breakfast.*

$ RESORT 🏨 **Mill Casino Hotel.** Even if you're not a big fan of gambling, this attractive hotel near the waterfront in North Bend (a short distance north of downtown Coos Bay) makes a handy and fairly economical base for exploring this stretch of the coast. **Pros:** attractive, contemporary rooms; location close to downtown dining and shopping; nice views from rooms in tower. **Cons:** casino can be noisy and smoky. [$] *Rooms from: $114* ✉ *3201 Tremont Ave., North Bend* ☎ *541/756–8800, 800/953–4800* 🌐 *www.themillcasino.com* 🛏 *207 rooms, 10 suites* 🍽 *No meals.*

SPORTS AND THE OUTDOORS

RECREATIONAL AREAS

Cape Arago State Park. The distant barking of sea lions echoes in the air at a trio of coves connected by short but steep trails. The park overlooks the **Oregon Islands National Wildlife Refuge,** where offshore rocks, beaches, islands, and reefs provide breeding grounds for seabirds and marine mammals, including seal pups (the trail is closed in spring to protect them). ✉ *End of Cape Arago Hwy., 1 mile south of Shore Acres State Park, Coos Bay* ☎ *800/551–6949, 541/888–3778* 🌐 *www.oregonstateparks.org* 🎟 *Free.*

Fodor's Choice ★ **Shore Acres State Park.** An observation building on a grassy bluff overlooking the Pacific marks the site that held the mansion of lumber baron Louis J. Simpson. The view over the rugged wave-smashed cliffs is splendid, but the real glory of Shore Acres lies a few hundred yards to the south, where an entrance gate leads into what was Simpson's private garden. Beautifully landscaped and meticulously maintained, the gardens incorporate formal English and Japanese designs. From March to mid-October the grounds are ablaze with blossoming daffodils, rhododendrons, azaleas, roses, and dahlias. In December the garden is decked out with a dazzling display of holiday lights. ✉ *89526 Cape Arago Hwy., 1 mile south of Sunset Bay State Park, Coos Bay* ☎ *800/551–6949, 541/888–2472 info center, 541/888–3732* ⊕ *www. oregonstateparks.org* ✉ *$5 per vehicle day-use fee.*

BANDON

25 miles south of Coos Bay.

Referred to by some who cherish its romantic lure as Bandon-by-the-Sea, Bandon is both a harbor town and a popular vacation spot, famous for its cranberry products and its artists' colony, complete with galleries and shops. Two national wildlife refuges, Oregon Islands and Bandon Marsh, are within the town limits, and a drive along Beach Loop Road, just southwest of downtown, affords mesmerizing views of awesome coastal rock formations, especially around Coquille Point and Face Rock State Scenic Viewpoint. The Bandon Dunes links-style golf courses are a worldwide attraction, often ranked among the top courses in the nation.

Tiny Bandon bills itself as Oregon's cranberry capital—10 miles north of town you'll find acres of bogs and irrigated fields where tons of the tart berries are harvested every year. Each September there's the Cranberry Festival, featuring a parade and a fair.

GETTING HERE AND AROUND
Bandon, on U.S. 101, is a half-hour drive south of Coos Bay and North Bend, and a 2-hour drive north up the coast from the California border; allow 4½ hours to get here from Portland.

ESSENTIALS
Visitor Information Bandon Chamber of Commerce. ✉ *300 2nd St.* ☎ *541/347–9616* ⊕ *www.bandon.com.*

EXPLORING
Bandon Historical Society Museum. In the old city hall building, this museum depicts the area's early history, including Native American artifacts, logging, fishing, cranberry farming, and the disastrous 1936 fire that destroyed the city. The well-stocked gift shop has books, knick-knacks, jewelry, myrtlewood, and other little treasures. ✉ *270 Fillmore St.* ☎ *541/347–2164* ⊕ *www.bandonhistoricalmuseum.org* ✉ *$3.*

FAMILY
Fodor's Choice
★

Oregon Islands National Wildlife Refuge. Each of the colossal rocks jutting from the ocean between Bandon and Brookings is protected as part of this 19-acre refuge, in total comprising a string of 1,853 rocks, reefs, islands, and two headland areas spanning 320 miles. Thirteen species of seabirds, totalling 1.2 million birds, nest here, and harbor seals, California sea lions, Steller sea lions, and Northern elephant seals also breed within the refuge. Coquille Point, a mainland unit of Oregon Islands Refuge, is one of many places to observe seabirds and harbor seals. The point overlooks a series of offshore rocks, and a paved trail that winds over the headland ends in stairways to the beach on both sides, allowing for a loop across the sand when tides permit. Visitors are encouraged to steer clear of harbor seals and avoid touching seal pups. A complete list of viewpoints and trails is available online. ✉ *11th St. W and Portland Ave. SW, drive west to road's end for Coquille Point and parking* ☎ *541/347–1470* ⊕ *www. fws.gov/oregoncoast/oregonislands.*

FAMILY **West Coast Game Park Safari.** The "walk-through safari" on 21 acres has free-roaming wildlife (it's the visitors who are behind fences); more than 450 animals and about 75 species, including lions, tigers, snow leopards, lemurs, bears, chimps, cougars, and camels, make it one of the largest wild-animal petting parks in the United States. The big attractions here are the young animals: bear cubs, tiger cubs, whatever is suitable for actual handling. ✉ *46914 U.S. 101, 8 miles south of Bandon on U.S. 101* ☎ *541/347–3106* ⊕ *www.westcoastgamepark-safari.com* 🎟 *$17.50.*

WHERE TO EAT

$$ ✗ **Edgewaters Restaurant.** This second-story bar above Edgewaters Res-
SEAFOOD taurant has some of the best west-facing views of the ocean from Bandon, and is among few properties in Old Town that don't face north toward the Coquille River. You can sometimes see whales from this spot during whale-watching season. **Known for:** sushi; impressive river and sunset views. 💲 *Average main: $18* ✉ *480 1st St.* ☎ *541/347–8500* ⊕ *www.edgewaters.net* ⊙ *Closed Mon. in winter. No lunch Tues.–Thurs.*

$$$ ✗ **The Loft Restaurant & Bar.** This hip eatery in Bandon's Old Town is
PACIFIC notable for chef-owner Kali Fieger's innovative, modern spin on French
NORTHWEST basics. On the second floor of an old Port of Bandon property, The
Fodor'sChoice Loft's vaulted, wood-trimmed ceilings, three-sided view of the Coquille
★ River, and classic wooden tables are all ingredients for an enjoyable meal. **Known for:** gourmet deli and market for to-go goods; artfully presented food. 💲 *Average main: $25* ✉ *315 1st St.* ☎ *541/329–0535* ⊕ *www.theloftofbandon.com* ⊙ *Closed Sun. and Mon. No lunch.*

$$$ ✗ **Lord Bennett's.** His lordship has a lot going for him: a cliff-top setting,
AMERICAN a comfortable and spacious dining area in a dramatic contemporary
Fodor'sChoice building, sunsets visible through picture windows overlooking Face
★ Rock Beach, and occasional live music on weekends. The modern American menu features plenty of local seafood; try the nut-crusted halibut, blackened red snapper with potato-horseradish crust, or wild prawns with garlic butter and sherry. **Known for:** weekend brunch; some of the best steaks in the area. 💲 *Average main: $27* ✉ *1695 Beach Loop Rd.* ☎ *541/347–3663* ⊕ *www.lordbennetts.com* ⊙ *No lunch Mon.–Sat.*

$$ ✗ **Tony's Crab Shack & Seafood Grill.** Started in 1989 as a bait and tackle
SEAFOOD shop, Tony's Crab Shack has since become a staple of the Bandon boardwalk, popular with locals and visitors for its crab cakes, fish tacos, crab and bay shrimp sandwich, and smoked Alaskan sockeye. Open only until 6 pm, it's a reliable bet for lunch or perhaps very early dinner. **Known for:** handy boardwalk location; to-go lunch fare that's perfect for a picnic at the beach. 💲 *Average main: $16* ✉ *155 1st St.* ☎ *541/347–2875* ⊕ *www.tonyscrabshack.com.*

WHERE TO STAY

$

HOTEL

Fodor's Choice

★

Bandon Beach Motel. As its owners like to proclaim, it's all about the view at this low-frills, exceptionally well-kept seaside motel set high on a bluff on Coquille Point and overlooking the smooth beach and rugged offshore rock formations below. **Pros:** terrific value; gorgeous beach views; run by a friendly and helpful family. **Cons:** basic rooms with few bells and whistles; 20-minute walk to downtown; often books up weeks in advance in summer. $ *Rooms from: $130* ⊠ *1090 Portland Ave. SW* ☎ *541/347–9451, 866/945–0133* ⊕ *www.bandonbeachmotel. com* ⌁ *20 rooms* ⊚ *No meals.*

$$$

RESORT

Fodor's Choice

★

Bandon Dunes Golf Resort. This golfing lodge provides a comfortable place to relax after a day on the links, with accommodations ranging from single rooms to four-bedroom condos, many with beautiful views of the famous golf course. **Pros:** if you're a golfer, this adds to an incredible overall experience; if not, you'll have a wonderful stay anyway. **Cons:** the weather can be wet and wild in the shoulder-season months. $ *Rooms from: $230* ⊠ *57744 Round Lake Dr.* ☎ *541/347–4380, 888/345–6008* ⊕ *www.bandondunesgolf.com* ⌁ *186 rooms* ⊚ *Some meals.*

SPORTS AND THE OUTDOORS

RECREATIONAL AREA

Bullards Beach State Park. At this rugged park along the north bank of the Coquille River (just across from downtown Bandon but reached via a 3½-mile drive up U.S. 101), you can tour the signal room inside the octagonal **Coquille Lighthouse,** built in 1896 and no longer in use; due to safety concerns, visitors can no longer tour the tower. From turnoff from U.S. 101, the meandering 2-mile drive to reach it passes through the Bandon Marsh, a prime bird-watching and picnicking area. The 4½-mile stretch of beach beside the lighthouse is a good place to search for jasper, agate, and driftwood—the firm sand is also popular for mountain biking. There's a campground with a wide variety of tent and RV sites as well as pet-friendly yurts. ⊠ *52470 U.S. 101, 2 miles north of Bandon* ☎ *800/452–5687, 541/347–2209* ⊕ *www.oregonstate-parks.org* ⌁ *Free.*

GOLF

Fodor's Choice

★

Bandon Dunes Golf Resort. This windswept, links-style playland for the nation's golfing elite is no stranger to well-heeled athletes flying in to North Bend on private jets to play on the resort's four distinct courses, including the beloved Pacific Dunes layout, many of whose rolling, bunker-laced fairways meander atop high bluffs with breathtaking ocean views. The steep greens fees vary a good bit according to season; they drop sharply during the November–April off season. The expectations at Bandon Dunes are that you walk the course with a caddy—adding a refined, traditional touch. Caddy fees are determined by the player, but it's recommended that you pay $100 per bag, per round. ⊠ *57744 Round Lake Dr.* ☎ *541/347–4380, 888/345–6008* ⊕ *www.bandond-unesgolf.com* ⌁ *$240–$325* ⚑. *Bandon Dunes Course: 18 holes, 5716 yards, par 72; Bandon Trails Course: 18 holes, 5751 yards, par 71; Old Macdonald Course: 18 holes, 5658 yards, par 71; Pacifc Dunes Course: 18 holes, 5775 yards, par 71.*

PORT ORFORD

30 miles south of Bandon.

The westernmost incorporated community in the contiguous United States, Port Orford is surrounded by forests, rivers, lakes, and beaches. The jetty at Port Orford offers little protection from storms, so every night the fishing boats are lifted out and stored on the docks. Commercial fishing boats search for crab, tuna, snapper, and salmon in the waters out of Port Orford, and diving boats gather sea urchins for Japanese markets. Visitors can fish off the Port Orford dock or the jetty for smelt, sardine, herring, lingcod, and halibut. Dock Beach provides beach fishing. The area is a favorite spot for sport divers because of the near-shore, protected reef, and for whale-watchers in fall and early spring.

GETTING HERE AND AROUND

Port Orford is a 30-minute drive south of Bandon and a one-hour drive north of Brookings along U.S. 101.

ESSENTIALS

Visitor Information Port Orford Visitors Center. ✉ *520 Jefferson St.* ☎ *541/332–4106* 🌐 *www.enjoyportorford.com.*

EXPLORING

OFF THE BEATEN PATH

Prehistoric Gardens. As you round a bend between Port Orford and Gold Beach, you'll see one of those sights that make grown-ups groan and kids squeal with delight: a huge, open-jawed tyrannosaurus rex, with a green brontosaurus peering out from the forest beside it. You can view 23 other life-size dinosaur replicas on the trail that runs through the property. ✉ *36848 U.S. 101* ☎ *541/332–4463* 🌐 *www.prehistoric-gardens.com* 🎟 *$12.*

WHERE TO EAT AND STAY

$ SEAFOOD FAMILY

🍴 **Crazy Norwegians Fish and Chips.** This quirky and casual hole-in-the-wall in Port Orford excels at what they do: good old-fashioned fish-and-chips. With everything from shrimp to cod to halibut paired with fries, the Crazy Norwegians serve it up with a side of pasta salad or coleslaw. **Known for:** to-go meals to take to the beach or park. [$] *Average main: $11* ✉ *259 6th St.* ☎ *541/332–8601* 🕒 *Closed Mon.*

$$$ MODERN AMERICAN Fodor's Choice ★

🍴 **Redfish.** Two walls of windows allow diners at the stylish Redfish in downtown Port Orford spectacular ocean vistas, but the views inside are pretty inviting, too, from the modern artwork provided by sister establishment Hawthorne Gallery to the artfully presented and globally influenced food. Start with the Manila clams in lemongrass-coconut red-curry broth or the daily ceviche, before graduating to cedar-plank chinook salmon with mushroom risotto, or organic chicken with truffle grits, garlic-tomato marmalade, and broccoli rabe. **Known for:** crab cakes Benedict at weekend brunch. [$] *Average main: $25* ✉ *517 Jefferson St.* ☎ *541/366–2200* 🌐 *www.redfishportorford.com.*

$ HOTEL FAMILY

🏨 **Castaway by the Sea.** This old-school motel operated by friendly proprietor Rockne Berge offers fantastic views from nearly every room, most of which have enclosed sun porches—the simplest and least expensive rooms open to an enclosed breezeway that takes in these same views. **Pros:** within walking distance of local restaurants; panoramic ocean views; reasonable rates. **Cons:** decor is a bit dated; not actually on the beach. [$] *Rooms from: $95* ✉ *545 5th St.* ☎ *541/332–4502* 🌐 *www.castawaybythesea.com* 🛏 *9 rooms, 4 suites* 🍴 *No meals.*

$$$$ B&B/INN Fodor's Choice ★ 🏨 **WildSpring Guest Habitat.** This rustic outpost in the woods above Port Orford blends all the comforts and privacy of a vacation rental with the services of a resort. **Pros:** relaxing, secluded, and private; gorgeous rooms; eco-conscious management. **Cons:** need to drive to the beach and stores. [$] *Rooms from: $298* ✉ *92978 Cemetery Loop Rd.* ☎ *541/332–0977, 866/333–9453* 🌐 *www.wildspring.com* 🛏 *5 cabins* 🍴 *Breakfast.*

THE FAB 50

U.S. 101 between Port Orford and Brookings, often referred to as the "fabulous 50 miles," soars up green headlands, some of them hundreds of feet high, and past a seascape of cliffs and sea stacks. The ocean is bluer and clearer—though not appreciably warmer—than it is farther north, and the coastal countryside is dotted with farms, grazing cattle, and small rural communities.

SPORTS AND THE OUTDOORS

RECREATIONAL AREAS

FAMILY **Battle Rock Park and Port Orford Heads State Park.** Stroll the mocha-color sand and admire pristine Battle Rock right in the heart of downtown Port Orford. Named for a battle between white settlers and the Dene Tsut Dah that took place here in 1850, this spot sits just below Port Orford Heads State Park. Atop the bluff that is Port Orford Heads, a trail loops the rocky outcropping between the Pacific and the Port Orford Lifeboat Station, taking in the hillside below, from which crews once mounted daring rescues on the fierce sea. The lifeboat station and adjoining museum is open for tours Wednesday–Monday, 10–3:30. Their motto? "You have to go out... you don't have to come back." ✉ *Port Orford Hwy., follow signs from U.S. 101* ☎ *800/551–6949, 541/332–6774* 🌐 *www.oregonstateparks.org* 🎟 *Free.*

FAMILY **Cape Blanco State Park.** Said to be the westernmost point in Oregon and perhaps the windiest—gusts clocked at speeds as high as 184 mph have twisted and battered the Sitka spruces along the 6-mile road from U.S. 101 to the **Cape Blanco Lighthouse.** The lighthouse, atop a 245-foot headland, has been in continuous use since 1870, longer than any other in Oregon. **Huges House** is all that remains of the Irish settler Patrick Hughes's dairy farm complex built in 1860. No one knows why the Spaniards sailing past these reddish bluffs in 1603 called them *blanco* (white). One theory is that the name refers to the fossilized shells that glint in the cliff face. Campsites at the 1,880-acre park are available on a first-come, first-served basis. Four cabins are available for reservation. ✉ *91814 Cape Blanco Rd., off U.S. 101, 6 miles north of Port Orford, Sixes* ☎ *541/332–2973, 800/551–6949* 🌐 *www.oregonstateparks.org* 🎟 *Day use and Hughes House tour free; lighthouse tour $2.*

Humbug Mountain State Park. This secluded, 1,850-acre park, especially popular with campers, usually has warm weather, thanks to the nearby mountains that shelter it from ocean breezes. A 6-mile loop leads to the top of 1,756-foot Humbug Mountain, one of the highest points along the state's coastline. It's a pretty, moderately challenging hike, but the summit is fairly overgrown and doesn't provide especially panoramic views. The campground has tent and RV sites. ✉ *U.S. 101, 6 miles south of Port Orford* ☎ *541/332–6774, 800/551–6949* 🌐 *www.oregonstateparks.org.*

GOLD BEACH

28 miles south of Port Orford.

The fabled Rogue River is one of about 150 U.S. rivers to merit Wild and Scenic status from the federal government. From spring to late fall an estimated 50,000 visitors descend on the town to take one of the daily jet-boat excursions that roar upstream from Wedderburn, Gold Beach's sister city across the bay, into the Rogue River Wilderness Area. Black bears, otters, beavers, ospreys, egrets, and bald eagles are seen regularly on these trips.

Gold Beach is very much a seasonal town, thriving in summer and rather quiet the rest of the year because of its remote location. It marks the entrance to Oregon's banana belt, where mild, California-like temperatures take the sting out of winter and encourage a blossoming trade in lilies and daffodils.

GETTING HERE AND AROUND

It's a 90-minute drive south along U.S. 101 from Coos Bay and North Bend to reach Gold Beach, which is a one-hour drive north of the California border.

ESSENTIALS

Visitor Information Gold Beach Visitors Center. ✉ *94080 Shirley La.* ☎ *541/247–7526, 800/525–2334* 🌐 *www.visitgoldbeach.com.*

WHERE TO EAT

$$$ MODERN AMERICAN Fodor's Choice ★

🍴 **Anna's by the Sea.** Dining at Anna's by the Sea is like stepping into one man's artisan universe: bowed and wood-trimmed ceilings, handmade cheeses, and blackberry honey lemonade, even a hydroponic herb garden, crafted by owner/head cook Peter Dower. Diners get a dash of personality with their meal service, which offers such choices as rack of lamb with ginger and mint and seared albacore and chicken thighs in chanterelle gravy. **Known for:** outstanding selection of Oregon wines and craft spirits; live music; intimate setting. [$] *Average main: $26* ✉ *29672 Stewart St.* ☎ *514/247–2100* 🌐 *www.annasbythesea.com* 🕒 *Closed Sun.–Tues. No lunch.*

$ AMERICAN

🍴 **Barnacle Bistro.** At this quirky tavern on the main road in downtown Gold Beach, try the fish-and-chips with Asian-style coleslaw and sweet-potato fries, the Dungeness crab–and–bay-shrimp cakes with lemon-dill aioli, the shellfish tacos with a Brazilian coconut-peanut sauce, or any of the enormous burgers. It's reliably good pub fare using produce, meat, and seafood sourced locally, and serving beer from nearby Arch Rock Brewery. **Known for:** beer from nearby Arch Rock Brewery; very reasonable prices. [$] *Average main: $14* ✉ *29805 Ellensburg Ave.* ☎ *541/247–7799* 🌐 *www.barnaclebistro.com* 🕒 *Closed Sun. and Mon.*

$ AMERICAN FAMILY 🍴 **The Port Hole Café.** A local staple in the old cannery building at the Port of Gold Beach since 1995, this family business has been passed down a generation, and many of the employees are friends and relations who have been tied to it for years. The café overlooks the mouth of the Rogue River, an area with great views but too blustery for outdoor dining. **Known for:** local people-watching; first-rate blueberry pie; fish-and-chips. [$] *Average main: $15* ✉ *29975 Harbor Way* ☎ *541/247–7411* 🌐 *www.portholecafe.com.*

WHERE TO STAY

$ HOTEL FAMILY 🏨 **Pacific Reef and Resort.** This resort offers a little something for everyone: from comfy, clean, economical rooms in the original renovated 1950s hotel to modern two-story condos with expansive ocean views, king-size beds, full kitchens, and outdoor patios. **Pros:** luxurious condos; full kitchens; glorious water views from the best units. **Cons:** rocky beach; on a busy road. [$] *Rooms from: $89* ✉ *29362 Ellensburg Hwy.* ☎ *541/247–6658* 🌐 *www.pacificreefhotel.com* 🛏 *39 units* 🍽 *Breakfast.*

$$$$ RESORT Fodor's Choice ★ 🏨 **Tu Tu' Tun Lodge.** Pronounced "too- *too*-tin," this renowned and rather lavish resort is a slice of heaven on the Rogue River, and owner Kyle Ringer is intent on providing his guests with a singular Northwest experience. **Pros:** luxurious, beautifully outfitted rooms; exceptional dining; peaceful location overlooking river. **Cons:** no TV; not well suited for young kids; 15-minute drive from downtown and the ocean. [$] *Rooms from: $255* ✉ *96550 N. Bank Rogue River Rd., 7 miles east of Gold Beach* ☎ *541/247–6664, 800/864–6357* 🌐 *www.tututun.com* 🛏 *16 rooms, 2 suites, 2 cottages* 🍽 *Breakfast.*

SPORTS AND THE OUTDOORS

BOATING

FAMILY Fodor's Choice ★ **Jerry's Rogue Jets.** These jet boats operate from May through September in the most rugged section of the Wild and Scenic Rogue River, offering 64-, 80-, and 104-mile tours, starting at $50 per person. Whether visitors choose a shorter, six-hour lower Rogue scenic trip or an eight-hour white-water trip, folks have a rollicking good time. Its largest vessels are 40 feet long and can hold 75 passengers. The smaller, white-water boats are 32 feet long and can hold 42 passengers. ✉ *29985 Harbor Way* ☎ *541/247–4571, 800/451–3645* 🌐 *www.roguejets.com.*

FISHING

Five Star Charters. Fishing charter trips range from a five-hour bottom-fish outing to a full-day salmon, steelhead, or halibut charter. They offer all the tackle needed, and customers don't even need experience—they'll take beginners and experts. The outfit has four riverboats, including two drift boats and two powerboats, as well as two ocean boats. They operate year-round. ✉ *29957 Harbor Way* ☎ *541/247–0217, 888/301–6480* 🌐 *www.goldbeachadventures.com.*

RECREATIONAL AREAS

Cape Sebastian State Scenic Corridor. The parking lots at this scenic area are more than 200 feet above sea level. At the south parking vista you can see up to 43 miles north to Humbug Mountain. Looking south, you can see nearly 50 miles toward Crescent City, California, and the Point Saint George Lighthouse. A deep forest of Sitka spruce covers most of the park. There's a 1½-mile walking trail. ✉ *U.S. 101, 6 miles south of Gold Beach* ☎ *541/469–2021, 800/551–6949* ⊕ *www. oregonstateparks.org.*

EN ROUTE

Samuel H. Boardman State Scenic Corridor. This 12-mile corridor through beach forests and alongside rocky promontories and windswept beaches contains some of Oregon's most spectacular stretches of coastline, though seeing some of them up close sometimes requires a little effort. About 27 miles of the Oregon Coast Trail weaves its way through this area, a reach dominated by Sitka spruce trees that stretch up to 300 feet and by rocky coast interspersed with sandy beaches. Starting from the north, walk a short path from the highway turnoff to view Arch Rock. The path travels a meadow that blooms in spring time. Down the road, find **Secret Beach**—hardly a secret—where trails run from two parking lots into three separate beaches below. Visit at low tide to make your way through all three, including through a cave that connects to the third beach close to Thunder Rock. At **Thunder Rock,** just north of milepost 345 on U.S. 101, walk west for a 1-mile loop that traces inlets and headlands, edging right up to steep drops. Find the highest bridge in Oregon just south—the **Thomas Creek Bridge**—from which a moderately difficult trail extends to wide, sandy **China Beach.** Find some sun on China Beach, or continue south to walk the unusual sculpted sandstone at **Indian Sands.** Easy beach access is at Whaleshead Beach, where shaded picnic tables shelter the view. From farther south at **Lone Ranch,** climb the grassy hillside to the top of **Cape Ferrelo** for a sweeping view of the rugged coastline, also a great spot for whale-watching in fall and summer. ✉ *U.S. 101 between Gold Beach and Brookings* ☎ *800/551–6949, 541/469–2021* ⊕ *www. oregonstateparks.org* ✉ *Free.*

BROOKINGS

27 miles south of Gold Beach on U.S. 101.

The coastal gateway to Oregon if you're approaching from California, Brookings is home to a pair of sterling state parks, one overlooking the ocean and another nestled amid the redwoods a bit inland. It's also a handy base, with some reasonably priced hotels and restaurants—your only overnight option along the 55-mile stretch between Gold Beach and Crescent City. A startling 90% of the pot lilies grown in the United States come from a 500-acre area inland from Brookings. Mild temperatures along this coastal plain provide ideal conditions for flowering plants of all kinds—even a few palm trees, a rare sight in Oregon.

The town is equally famous as a commercial and sportfishing port at the mouth of the turquoise-blue Chetco River. Salmon and steelhead weighing 20 pounds or more swim here.

GETTING HERE AND AROUND

Brookings is the southernmost town on Oregon's coastal 101, just 10 miles north of the California border and a half-hour drive from Crescent City; it's a 2½-hour drive south on U.S. 101 from the Coos Bay and North Bend area. Allow about six hours to get here from Portland via Interstate 5 to Grants Pass and U.S. 199 to Crescent City.

VISITOR INFORMATION

Brookings Harbor Chamber of Commerce. ✉ *97900 Shopping Center Ave., Suite 14* ☎ *541/469–3181, 800/535–9469* 🌐 *www.brookingsharbor-chamber.com.*

WHERE TO EAT AND STAY

$ AMERICAN 🍴 **Superfly Martini Bar & Grill.** The unusual name of this stylish little bar and grill has nothing to do with the Curtis Mayfield '70s funk anthem—rather, owner Ryan Webster named this establishment, which is also an artisanal-vodka distillery, after a fishing fly. Appropriately, the bar serves first-rate cocktails, including a refreshing lemon-basil martini. **Known for:** first-rate cocktails; high-quality pub fare. [$] *Average main: $11* ✉ *623 Memory La.* ☎ *530/520–8005* 🌐 *www.superflybooze.com.*

$$ HOTEL 🏨 **Best Western Plus Beachfront Inn.** This spotlessly clean three-story Best Western across the street from the Brookings boat basin has direct beach access and ocean views, making it one of the best-maintained and most appealingly located lodging options along the southern coast. **Pros:** fantastic ocean views; quiet location away from busy U.S. 101; very well kept. **Cons:** rooms don't have much personality; not many restaurants within walking distance. [$] *Rooms from: $169* ✉ *16008 Boat Basin Rd.* ☎ *541/469–7779* 🌐 *www.bestwesternoregon.com* 🛏 *102 rooms* 🍽 *Breakfast.*

SPORTS AND THE OUTDOORS

RECREATIONAL AREAS

Fodor's Choice ★ **Harris Beach State Park.** The views from the parking areas, oceanfront trails, and beaches at this popular tract of craggy rock formations and evergreen forest are some of the prettiest along the southern Oregon Coast. The proximity to downtown Brookings makes this an easy place to head for morning beachcombing or a sunset stroll. You might see gray whales migrate in spring and winter. Just offshore, Bird Island, also called Goat Island, is a National Wildlife Sanctuary and a breeding site for rare birds. The campground here, with tent and RV sites, is very popular. ✉ *1655 Old U.S. 101* ☎ *541/469–2021, 800/551–6949* 🌐 *www.oregonstateparks.org* 🎟 *Free.*

4

WILLAMETTE VALLEY AND WINE COUNTRY

Visit Fodors.com for advice, updates, and bookings

WELCOME TO WILLAMETTE VALLEY AND WINE COUNTRY

TOP REASONS TO GO

★ **Swirl and sip:** Each region in the Willamette Valley offers some of the finest vintages and dining experiences found anywhere.

★ **Soar through the air:** Newberg's hot-air balloons will give you a bird's-eye view of Yamhill County's wine country.

★ **Run rapids:** Feel the bouncing exhilaration and the cold spray of white-water rafting on the wild, winding McKenzie River outside Eugene.

★ **Walk on the wild side:** Hillsboro's Jackson Bottom Nature Preserve gives walkers a chance to view otters, beavers, herons, and eagles.

★ **Back the Beavers or Ducks:** Nothing gets the blood pumping like an Oregon State Beaver or University of Oregon Ducks football game.

1 **North Willamette Valley.** Most visitors begin their journey into wine country here, an area rich with upscale dining, shopping, the arts, and wineries. Close to Portland, North Willamette's communities provide all the amenities of urban life with a whole lot less concrete. Wine enthusiasts will relish the excellent vineyards in Hillsboro and Forest Grove.

2 **Yamhill County.** This part of the state has undergone a renaissance in the past 20 years, as the world has beaten a path to its door, seeking the perfect Pinot. Many of the Willamette's highest-rated wineries are here. There are gorgeous inns, wine bars, and unforgettable restaurants providing a complete vacation experience.

3 **Mid-Willamette Valley.** Agriculture is the mainstay of this region; roadsides are dotted with fruit and veggie stands, and towns boast farmers' markets. The flat terrain is ideal for bicycle trips and hikes. The state capitol is Salem, and Oregon State University is in Corvallis.

4 **South Willamette Valley.** Here visitors soak in natural hot springs, hike in dense forest, run the rapids. Eugene, home to the University of Oregon, has a friendly, youthful vibe, which is enhanced by the natural splendor of the region.

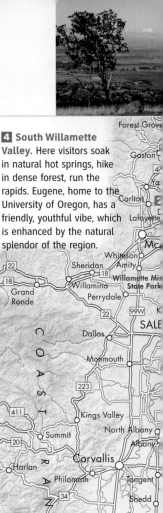

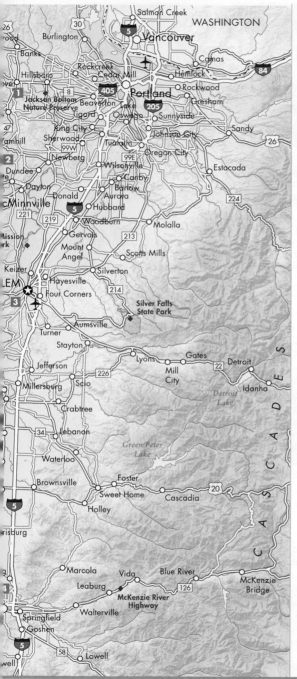

GETTING ORIENTED

4

The Willamette Valley is a fertile mix of urban, rural, and wild stretching from Portland at the north to Cottage Grove at the south. It is bordered by the Cascade Range to the east and the Coast Range to the west. The Calapooya Mountains border it to the south and the mighty Columbia River runs along the north. Running north and south, Interstate 5 connects communities throughout the valley. In the mid-1800s the Willamette Valley was the destination of emigrants on the Oregon Trail, and today is home to about two-thirds of the state's population. The Willamette Valley is 150 miles long and up to 60 miles wide, which makes it Oregon's largest wine-growing region.

Updated by
Margot Bigg

The Willamette (pronounced "wil- *lam*-it") Valley has become a wine lover's Shangri-La, particularly in the northern Yamhill and Washington counties between Interstate 5 and the Oregon Coast, a region that is not only carpeted with vineyards but encompasses small hotels and inns, cozy restaurants, and casual wine bars.

The valley divides two mountain ranges (the Cascade and Coast), and contains more than 500 wineries. The huge wine region is made up of six subappellations: Chehalem Mountains, Ribbon Ridge, Dundee Hills, Yamhill-Carlton, Eola-Amity Hills, and McMinnville. With its incredibly rich soil perfect for growing Pinot Noir, Pinot Gris, Chardonnay, and Riesling, the valley has received worldwide acclaim for its vintages. The region's farms are famous for producing quality fruits, vegetables, and cheeses that are savored in area restaurants. During spring and summer there are many roadside stands dotting the country lanes, and farmers' markets appear in most of the valley's towns. Also delicious are the locally raised lamb, pork, chicken, and beef. The valley also is a huge exporter of plants and flowers for nurseries, with a large number of farms growing ornamental trees, bulbs, and plants.

The valley definitely has an artsy, expressive, and fun side, with its wine and beer festivals, theater, music, crafts, and culinary events. Many residents and visitors are serious runners and bicyclists, particularly in Eugene, so pay close attention while driving.

There's a longstanding collegiate football rivalry between the Oregon State Beavers in Corvallis and University of Oregon Ducks in Eugene; getting a ticket to the annual "Civil War" game between the two teams is a feat in itself. Across the state, but particularly in the Willamette Valley, Oregonians are passionate fans of one team or the other. If you happen to be visiting the area during the event (usually held in October or November), be prepared for some serious traffic and some closed businesses.

THE WILLAMETTE VALLEY AND WINE COUNTRY PLANNER

WHEN TO GO

July to October are the best times to wander the country roads in the Willamette Valley, exploring the grounds of its many wineries. Fall is spectacular, with leaves at their colorful peak in late October. Winters are usually mild, but they can be relentlessly overcast and downright rainy. Visitors not disturbed by dampness or chill will find excellent deals on lodging. In the spring rains continue, but the wildflowers begin to bloom, which pays off at the many gardens and nature parks throughout the valley.

FESTIVALS

International Pinot Noir Celebration. During the International Pinot Noir Celebration in late July and early August, wine lovers flock to McMinnville to sample fine regional vintages along with Pinot Noir from around the world. ⊠ *Box 1310800, McMinnville* ☎ *800/775–4762* ⊕ *www.ipnc.org.*

Oregon Bach Festival. Eugene hosts the world-class Oregon Bach Festival, with 18 summer days of classical music performances. ⊠ *1257 University of Oregon, Eugene* ☎ *541/346–5666, 800/457–1486* ⊕ *oregonbachfestival.com.*

Oregon Country Fair. Every July, the weekend after Independence Day, a small patch of fields and forest right outside of Eugene transforms into an enchanting community celebration known as the Oregon Country Fair. This annual event has been going on since the 1960s and maintains much of its flower-child vibe, with all sorts of parades, live music, puppet shows, face painting, and excellent craft shopping. ⊠ *24207 Oregon 126, Veneta* ☎ *541/343–4298* ⊕ *www.oregoncountryfair.org.*

Wooden Shoe Tulip Fest. Every spring from the end of March through April, visitors to Woodburn's Wooden Shoe Tulip Farm can tiptoe (or walk, or take a hayride) through spectacular fields of brightly hued tulips. Other festival features include wine-tastings, cut-out boards for photos, food booths, and a play area for kids. ⊠ *33814 S. Meridian Rd., Woodburn* ☎ *503/634–2243* ⊕ *www.woodenshoe.com/events/tulip-fest/.*

GETTING HERE AND AROUND

AIR TRAVEL

Portland's airport is an hour's drive east of the northern Willamette Valley. The **Aloha Express Airport Shuttle** and the **Beaverton Airporter** provide shuttle service. **Eugene Airport** is more convenient if you're exploring the region's southern end. It's served by Delta, Alaska/Horizon, American, and United/United Express. The flight from Portland to Eugene is 40 minutes. Smaller airports for private aircraft are scattered throughout the valley.

Rental cars are available at the Eugene airport from Budget, Enterprise, and Hertz. Taxis and airport shuttles will transport you to downtown Eugene for about $22. **Omni Shuttle** will provide shuttle service to and from the Eugene airport from anywhere in Oregon.

Air Contacts Aloha Express Airport Shuttle. ☎ *503/356–8848* ⊕ *www.aloha-expressshuttle.com.* **Beaverton Airporter.** ☎ *503/760–6565, 866/665–6965* ⊕ *www.beavertonairporter.com.* **Omni Shuttle.** ☎ *541/461–7959, 800/741–5097* ⊕ *www.omnishuttle.com.*

BUS TRAVEL

Buses operated by Portland's **TriMet** network connect Forest Grove, Hillsboro, Beaverton, Tigard, Lake Oswego, and Oregon City with Portland and each other; light-rail trains operated by MAX run between Portland and Hillsboro. Many of the **Lane Transit District** buses will make a few stops to the outskirts of Lane County, such as McKenzie Bridge. All buses have bike racks. **Yamhill County Transit Area** provides bus service for Yamhill County, with links to Hillsboro/MAX, Sherwood/TriMet, and Salem/SAMT.

Bus Contacts Lane Transit District (*LTD*). ☎ *541/682–6100* ⊕ *www.ltd.org.* **Yamhill County Transit Area** (*YCTA*). ☎ *503/472–0457* ⊕ *www.yctransitarea.org.*

CAR TRAVEL

Interstate 5 runs north–south the length of the Willamette Valley. Many Willamette Valley attractions lie not too far east or west of Interstate 5. Highway 22 travels west from the Willamette National Forest through Salem to the coast. Highway 99 travels parallel to Interstate 5 through much of the Willamette Valley. Highway 34 leaves Interstate 5 just south of Albany and heads west, past Corvallis and into the Coast Range, where it follows the Alsea River. Highway 126 heads east from Eugene toward the Willamette National Forest; it travels west from town to the coast. U.S. 20 travels west from Corvallis. Rental cars are available from Budget (Beaverton), Enterprise, and Hertz (both Beaverton, Salem).

RESTAURANTS

The buzzwords associated with fine dining in this region are "sustainable," "farm-to-table," and "local." Fresh salmon, Dungeness crab, mussels, shrimp, and oysters are harvested just a couple of hours away on the Oregon Coast. Lamb, pork, and beef are local and plentiful, and seasonal game appears on many menus. Desserts made with local blueberries, huckleberries, raspberries, and marionberries should not be missed. But what really sets the offerings apart are the splendid local wines that receive worldwide acclaim.

Restaurants in the Willamette Valley are low-key and unpretentious. Expensive doesn't necessarily mean better, and locals have a pretty good nose for good value. Reasonably priced Mexican, Indian, Japanese, and Italian do very well. Food carts in the cities are a growing phenomenon. But there's still nothing like a great, sit-down meal at a cozy bistro for some fresh fish or lamb, washed down with a stellar Pinot Noir. *Restaurant reviews have been shortened. For full information visit Fodors.com.*

HOTELS

One of the great pleasures of touring the Willamette Valley is the incredible selection of small, ornate bed-and-breakfast hotels sprinkled throughout Oregon's wine country. In the summer and fall they can fill up quickly, as visitors come from around the world to enjoy wine tastings at the hundreds of large and small wineries. Many of these have exquisite restaurants right on the premises, with home-baked goods available day and night. There are plenty of larger properties located closer to urban areas and shopping centers, including upscale resorts with expansive spas, as well as national chains that are perfect for travelers who just need a place to lay their heads. *Hotel reviews have been shortened. For full information, visit Fodors.com.*

WHAT IT COSTS IN U.S. DOLLARS			
$	**$$**	**$$$**	**$$$$**
Restaurants	under $16	$16–$22	$23–$30	over $30
Hotels	under $150	$150–$200	$201–$250	over $250

Restaurant prices are the average cost of a main course at dinner or, if dinner is not served, at lunch. Hotel prices are the lowest cost of a standard double room in high season.

4

TOURS

Oregon Wine Tours and **EcoTours of Oregon** provide informative guided outings across the Willamette Valley wine country.

Contacts EcoTours of Oregon. ☎ 503/245–1428 ⊕ www.ecotours-of-oregon. com. **Oregon Wine Tours.** ☎ 503/681–9463 ⊕ www.orwinetours.com.

VISITOR INFORMATION

Contacts Chehalem Valley Chamber of Commerce. ⊠ 115 N. College St., Newberg ☎ 503/538–2014 ⊕ www.chehalemvalley.org. **Oregon Wine Country/ Willamette Valley Visitors Association.** ☎ 866/548–5018 ⊕ www.oregon-winecountry.org. **Travel Lane County.** ⊠ 754 Olive St., Eugene ☎ 541/484–5307, 800/547–5445 ⊕ www.eugenecascadescoast.org. **Travel Yamhill Valley.** ⊕ www.travelyamhill.com. **Washington County Visitors Association.** ⊠ 12725 S.W. Millikan Way, Suite 210, Beaverton ☎ 503/644–5555, 800/537–3149 ⊕ www.oregonswashingtoncounty.com.

NORTH WILLAMETTE VALLEY

Just outside Portland the suburban areas of Tigard, Hillsboro, and Forest Grove have gorgeous wineries, wetlands, rivers, and nature preserves. The area has a wealth of golfing, biking, and trails for running and hiking, and, appropriately, is home to the headquarters of Nike. From wetlands to residential neighborhoods, it's not unusual to spot red-tail hawks, beavers, and ducks on your route. Shopping, fine dining, and proximity to Portland make this a great area in which to begin your exploration of the Willamette Valley and the wine country.

EN ROUTE

Vineyard and Valley Scenic Tour. A 60-mile driving route through the lush Tualatin Valley runs between the city of Sherwood in the southern part of the valley and Helvetia at the northern end. The rural drive showcases much of Washington County's agricultural bounty, including many of the county's wineries and farms (some with stands offering seasonal fresh produce and/or U-pick), along with pioneer and historic sites, wildlife refuges, and scenic viewpoints of the Cascade Mountains. For more information, visit the Washington County Visitors Association's tourist center. ⊠ *Washington County Visitors Association, 12725 S.W. Millikan Way , Suite 210, Beaverton* ☎ *503/644–5555* ⊕ *tualatinvalley.org* ☉ *Closed weekends.*

HILLSBORO

20 miles southwest of Portland.

Hillsboro offers a wealth of eclectic shops, preserves, restaurants, and proximity to the valley's fine wineries. In the past 20 years Hillsboro has experienced rapid growth associated with the Silicon Forest, where high-tech business found ample sprawling room. Several of Intel's industrial campuses are in Hillsboro, as are the facilities of other leading electronics manufacturers. Businesses related to the town's original agricultural roots remain a significant part of Hillsboro's culture and economy. Alpaca ranches, nurseries, berry farms, nut and fruit orchards, and numerous wineries are among the area's most active agricultural businesses.

GETTING HERE AND AROUND

Hillsboro is about a 45-minute drive west from Portland International Airport. The **Aloha Express Airport Shuttle** and the **Beaverton Airporter** provide shuttle service.

From Downtown Portland it's a short 20-minute car ride, or visitors can ride the MAX light rail. The TriMet Bus Service connects to the MAX light rail in Hillsboro, with connections to Beaverton, Aloha, and other commercial areas.

EXPLORING

Hillsboro Saturday Market. Fresh local produce—some from booths, some from the backs of trucks—as well as local arts and crafts are on sale Saturdays from May through October. Live music is played throughout the day. The market is just a block from the light-rail line. ⊠ *Main St. between 1st and 3rd Aves.* ☎ *503/844–6685* ⊕ *www. hillsboromarkets.org.*

Fodor's Choice **Ponzi Vineyards.** One of the founding families of Willamette Valley wine,
★ Dick and Nancy Ponzi planted their original estate vineyard in 1970. While you can still visit the historic estate that looks out over these old vines, your best bet is to drop in at their new visitors facility at the winery just 12 miles south of Hillsboro. Here you'll find red and white flights of the current releases, as well as the occasional older vintage from the library. Enjoy table-side wine service indoors around the fireplace, or out on the covered terrace. Antipasti plates are a nice accompaniment to the wine. Pictures on the walls and displays provide a wonderful visual history of this winery that is still family owned and operated. The Ponzi family also launched the BridgePort Brewing Company in 1984, and runs a wine bar and restaurant in Dundee. ⊠ *19500 S.W. Mountain Home Rd., Sherwood* ✛ *12 miles south of Hillsboro* ☎ *503/628–1227* ⊕ *www.ponziwines.com* ▨ *Tastings $20.*

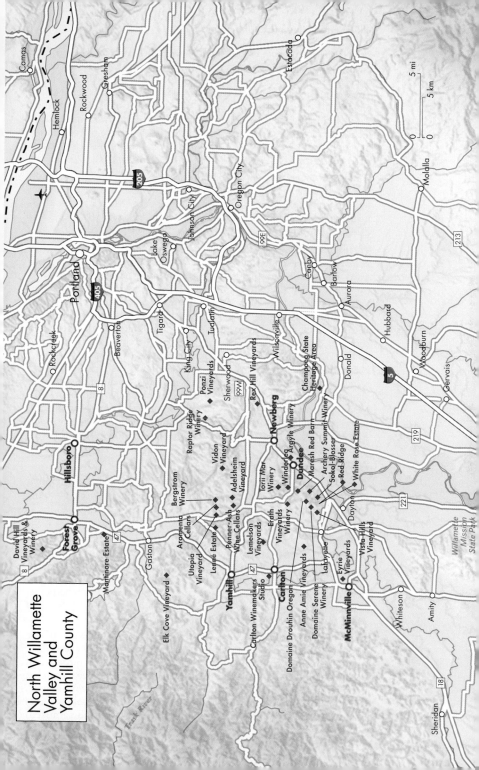

North Willamette Valley and Yamhill County

Camas
Hemlock
Rockwood
Gresham
205
Rockcreek
Portland
405
Beaverton
Tigard
Johnson City
Lake Oswego
Oregon City
99E
Wilsonville
Canby
Barlow
Aurora
213
Donald
Hubbard
Woodburn
Gervais
Molalla
5
219
221
Willamette Mission State Park
Whiteson
Amity
Sheridan
18

Hillsboro
8
47
Forest Grove
David Hill Vineyards & Winery
Mountinore Estate
Gaston
Elk Cove Vineyard
Trask River

King City
Sherwood
99W
Ponzi Vineyards
Rex Hill Vineyards
Tualatin

Raptor Ridge Winery
Vidon Vineyard
Adelsheim Vineyard
Bergstrom Winery
Aramenta Cellars
Penner-Ash Wine Cellars
Lemelson Vineyards
Utopia Vineyard
Leafé Estate
Yamhill
47
Carlton Winemakers Studio
Carlton
Domaine Drouhin Oregon
Anne Amie Vineyards
Domaine Serene Winery
Lafayette

Newberg
Argyle Winery
Winderlea
Dundee
Maresh Red Barn
Archery Summit Winery
Sokol-Blosser
Red Ridge
White Rose Estate
Dayton
Torii Mor Winery
Erath Vineyards Winery
Eyrie Vineyards
Vista Hills Vineyard
McMinnville

Champoeg State Heritage Area

5 mi
5 km

FAMILY **Rice Northwest Museum of Rocks and Minerals.** Richard and Helen Rice began collecting beach agates in 1938, and over the years they developed one of the largest private mineral collections in the United States. The most popular item here is the Alma Rose rhodochrosite, a 4-inch red crystal. The museum (in a ranch-style home) also displays petrified wood from all over the world and a gallery of Northwest minerals—including specimens of rare crystallized gold. Tours are offered Saturday at 2 pm. ✉ *26385 N.W. Groveland Dr.* ☎ *503/647–2418* 🌐 *www.ricenorthwestmuseum.org* 🎫 *$10* 🕒 *Closed Mon. and Tues.*

Washington County Museum and Historical Society. This impressive space on the second floor of the Hillsboro Civic Center houses a range of exhibits focusing on the history and culture of the area. Most of the exhibits include activities for children. ✉ *120 E. Main St.* ☎ *503/645–5353* 🌐 *www.washingtoncountymuseum.org* 🎫 *$6.*

WHERE TO EAT

$ MEXICAN FAMILY 🍴 **Mazatlan Mexican Restaurant.** Although this popular spot is hidden away in a small shopping mall, once you're inside and surrounded by stunning murals and ceramics you'll feel like you're in a charming village. Try the Mazatlan Dinner, a house specialty with sirloin, a chili relleno, and an enchilada, or *arroz con camarones,* prawns sautéed with vegetables. **Known for:** the Mazatlan Dinner; hidden gem in a shopping mall. [$] *Average main: $13* ✉ *20413 S.W. TV Hwy., Aloha* ☎ *503/591–9536* 🌐 *www.mazatlanmexicanrestaurant.com.*

$ JAPANESE 🍴 **Syun Izakaya.** A large assortment of sushi and sashimi, soups, and salads are served in quiet surroundings in the basement of the old Hillsboro Library. Wonderful grilled and fried meats and vegetables are also available, accompanied by a vast sake selection. **Known for:** unique daily specials; a delicious variety of sushi and sashimi. [$] *Average main: $11* ✉ *209 N.E. Lincoln St.* ☎ *503/640–3131* 🌐 *www.syun-izakaya.com* 🕒 *No lunch Sun.*

SPORTS AND THE OUTDOORS

The Tualatin, a slow, meandering river, flows into Hillsboro and along its length offers fantastic opportunities for paddlers who are new to the sport, as well those who are experienced.

RECREATIONAL AREAS

Cook Park. On the banks of the Tualatin River in Tiagrd, east of Hillsboro, this 79-acre park is where local suburbanites gather to enjoy a variety of outdoor activities, and plays host to the annual Festival of Balloons in June. The park has horseshoe pits, a fishing dock, a small boat ramp, picnic shelters, and several walking trails and bike paths. Wildlife includes great blue herons and river otters. ✉ *17005 S.W. 92nd Ave., Tigard* ☎ *503/718–2641* 🌐 *www.tigard-or.gov.*

Jackson Bottom Wetlands Preserve. Several miles of trails in this 710-acre floodplain and woods are home to thousands of ducks and geese, deer, otters, beavers, herons, and eagles. Walking trails allow birders and other animal watchers to explore the wetlands for a chance to catch a glimpse of indigenous and migrating creatures in their own habitats. The **Education Center** has several hands-on exhibits, as well as a real bald eagle's nest that has been completely preserved (and sanitized) for public display. No dogs or bicycles are allowed. ✉ *2600 S.W. Hillsboro Hwy.* 🕿 *503/681–6206* ⊕ *www.jacksonbottom.org* 🖃 *$2 suggested donation.*

FAMILY **L.L. "Stub" Stewart State Park.** This 1,654-acre, full-service park has hiking, biking, and horseback riding trails for day use or overnight camping. There are full hookup sites, tent sites, small cabins, and even a horse camp. Lush rolling hills, forests, and deep canyons are terrific for bird-watching, wildflower walks, and other relaxing pursuits. An 18-hole disc golf course winds its way through a dense forest. In case you don't know, in disc golf players throw a disc at a target and attempt to complete the course with the fewest throws. ✉ *30380 N.W. Hwy. 47, Buxton* 🕿 *503/324–0606* ⊕ *www.oregonstateparks.org* 🖃 *$5 for day use permit.*

Tualatin River Wildlife Refuge. This sanctuary for indigenous and migrating birds, waterfowl, and mammals is in Sherwood (about 18 miles south of Hillsboro). It is one of only a handful of national urban refuges in the United States and has restored much of the natural landscape common to western Oregon prior to human settlement. The refuge is home to nearly 200 species of birds, 50 species of mammals, 25 species of reptiles and amphibians, and a variety of insects, fish, and plants. It features an interpretive center, a gift shop, photography blinds, and restrooms. This restoration has attracted animals back to the area in great numbers, and with a keen eye, birders and animal watchers can catch a glimpse of these creatures year-round. In May the refuge hosts its Migratory Songbird Festival. ✉ *19255 S.W. Pacific Hwy., Tigard* 🕿 *503/625–5944* ⊕ *www.fws.gov/tualatinriver.*

FOREST GROVE

24 miles west of Portland on Hwy. 8.

This small town is surrounded by stands of Douglas firs and giant sequoia, including the largest giant sequoia in the state. There are nearby wetlands, birding, the Hagg Lake Recreation Area, a new outdoor adventure park, and numerous wineries and tasting rooms. To get to many of the wineries, head south from Forest Grove on Highway 47 and watch for the blue road signs between Forest Grove, Gaston, and Yamhill. To the west of town, you'll find some of the oldest Pinot Noir vines in the valley at David Hill Winery.

GETTING HERE AND AROUND

Forest Grove is about an hour's drive west from Portland International Airport. The **Aloha Express Airport Shuttle** and the **Beaverton Airporter** provide shuttle service.

From Downtown Portland it's a short 35-minute car ride with only a few traffic lights during the entire trip. TriMet Bus Service provides bus service to and from Forest Grove every 15 minutes, connecting to the MAX light rail 6 miles east in Hillsboro, which continues into Portland. Buses travel to Cornelius, Hillsboro, Aloha, and Beaverton.

ESSENTIALS

Forest Grove Chamber of Commerce. ✉ *2417 Pacific Ave.* 🕿 *503/357–3006* ⊕ *www.visitforestgrove.com.*

David Hill Vineyards and Winery, Forest Grove

EXPLORING

David Hill Vineyards and Winery. In 1965 Charles Coury came to Oregon from California and planted some of the Willamette Valley's first Pinot Noir vines on the site of what is now the David Hill Winery. The original farmhouse serves as the tasting room and offers splendid views of the Tualatin Valley. They produce Pinot Noir, some of which comes from the original vines planted by Coury, along with Chardonnay, Gewürztraminer, Merlot, Tempranillo, Pinot Gris, and Riesling. The wines are well made and pleasant, especially the eclectic blend called Farmhouse Red and the estate Riesling. ✉ 46350 N.W. David Hill Rd. ☎ 503/992–8545 ⊕ www.davidhillwinery.com ✉ Tastings from $10.

Elk Cove Vineyard. Founded in 1974 by Pat and Joe Campbell, this well-established winery covers 600 acres on four separate vineyard sites. The tasting room is set in the beautiful rolling hills at the foot of the coast range overlooking the vines. The focus is on Willamette Valley Pinot Noir, Pinot Gris, and Pinot Blanc. Be sure to also try the limited bottling of their Pinot Noir Rosé if they're pouring it. ✉ 27751 N.W. Olson Rd., Gaston ☎ 503/985–7760, 877/355–2683 ⊕ www.elkcove. com ✉ Tastings from $10.

Montinore Estate. Locals chuckle at visitors who try to show off their French savvy when they pronounce it "Mont-in-or-ay." The estate, originally a ranch, was established by a tycoon who'd made his money in the Montana mines before he retired to Oregon; he decided to call his estate "Montana in Oregon." Montinore (no "ay" at the end) has 232 acres of vineyards, and its wines reflect the high-quality soil and fruit. Highlights include a crisp Gewürztraminer, a light Müller-Thurgau, an off-dry Riesling, several lush Pinot Noirs, and a delightful white blend called Borealis that's a perfect partner for Northwest seafood. The tasting-room staff is among the friendliest and most knowledgeable in Oregon wine country. ⊠ *3663 S.W. Dilley Rd.* ☎ *503/359–5012* ⊕ *www.montinore.com* ▭ *Tastings $10.*

Pacific University. Founded in 1849, this is one of the oldest educational institutions in the western United States. Concerts and special events are held on the shady campus in the Taylor-Meade Performing Arts Center. ⊠ *2043 College Way* ☎ *503/352–6151, 877/722–8648* ⊕ *www. pacificu.edu.*

SakéOne. After the founders realized that the country's best water supply for sake was in the Pacific Northwest, they built their brewery in Forest Grove in 1997. It's one of only six sake brewing facilities in America and produces award-winning sake under three labels, in addition to importing from partners in Japan. The tasting room offers three different flights, including one with a food pairing. Be sure to catch one of the tours, offered daily, where your guide will walk you through every phase of the sake-making process, from milling the rice to final filtration and bottling. ⊠ *820 Elm St.* ☎ *503/357–7056, 800/550–7253* ⊕ *www.sakeone.com* ▭ *Tastings $5.*

WHERE TO STAY

$ 🏨 **McMenamins Grand Lodge.** On 13 acres of pastoral countryside, this
HOTEL converted Masonic rest home has accommodations that run from bunk-bed rooms to a three-room fireplace suite, with some nice period antiques in all. **Pros:** relaxed, friendly brewpub atmosphere. **Cons:** most rooms have shared bathrooms. $ *Rooms from: $50* ⊠ *3505 Pacific Ave.* ☎ *503/992–9533, 877/992–9533* ⊕ *www.mcmenamins.com/ grandlodge* ⟿ *77 rooms* ¶*No meals.*

SPORTS AND THE OUTDOORS

RECREATIONAL AREAS

FAMILY **Scoggin Valley Park and Henry Hagg Lake.** This beautiful area in the Coast
Fodor's Choice Range foothills has a 15-mile-long hiking trail that surrounds the lake.
★ Bird-watching is best in spring. Recreational activities include fishing, boating, waterskiing, picnicking, and hiking, and a 10½-mile, well-marked bicycle lane parallels the park's perimeter road. ⊠ *50250 S.W. Scoggins Valley Rd., Gaston* ☎ *503/846–8715* ⊕ *www.co.washington. or.us/hagglake* ▭ *$6.*

FAMILY **Tree to Tree Adventure Park.** At the first public aerial adventure park in the Pacific Northwest—and only the second of its kind in the United States—the aerial adventure course features 19 zip lines and more than 60 treetop elements and obstacles. You can experience the thrills of moving from platform to platform (tree to tree) via wobbly bridges, tight ropes, Tarzan swings, and more. The courses range from beginner to extreme, with certified and trained instructors providing guidance to adventurers. "Woody's Ziptastic Voyage" zip-line tour features six extreme zip lines (including one that is 1,280 feet long), a bridge, and a 40-foot rappel. Harnesses and helmets are provided, and no open-toed shoes are allowed. Reservations are required. ⊠ *2975 S.W. Nelson Rd., Gaston* ☎ *503/357–0109* ⊕ *tree2treeadventurepark.com* ▭ *Aerial park $49, zip tour $75* ⟿ *Closed mid-Nov.–Feb.*

YAMHILL COUNTY

Yamhill County, at the northern end of the Willamette Valley, has a fortunate confluence of perfect soils, a benign climate, and talented winemakers who craft world-class vintages. In recent years several new wineries have been built in Yamhill County's hills, as well as on its flatlands. While vineyards flourished in the northern Willamette Valley in the 19th century, viticulture didn't arrive in Yamhill County until the 1960s and 1970s, with such pioneers as Dick Erath (Erath Vineyards Winery), David and Ginny Adelsheim (Adelsheim Vineyard), and David and Diana Lett (The Eyrie Vineyards). The focus of much of the county's enthusiasm lies in the Red Hills of Dundee, where the farming towns of Newberg, Dundee, Yamhill, and Carlton have made room for upscale bed-and-breakfasts, spas, wine bars, and tourists seeking that perfect swirl and sip.

The Yamhill County wineries are only a short drive from Portland, and the roads, especially Route 99W and Route 18, can be crowded on weekends—that's because these roads link suburban Portland communities to the popular Oregon Coast.

NEWBERG

24 miles south of Portland on Hwy. 99W.

Newberg sits in the Chehalem Valley, known as one of Oregon's most fertile wine-growing locations, and is called the Gateway to Oregon Wine Country. Many of Newberg's early settlers were Quakers from the Midwest, who founded the school that has become George Fox University. Newberg's most famous resident, likewise a Quaker, was Herbert Hoover, the 31st president of the United States. For about five years during his adolescence, he lived with an aunt and uncle at the Hoover-Minthorn House, now a museum listed on the National Register of Historic Places. Now the town is on the map for the nearby wineries, fine-dining establishments, and a spacious, spectacular resort, the Allison. St. Paul, a historic town with a population of about 325, is about 8 miles south of Newberg, and every July holds a professional rodeo.

GETTING HERE AND AROUND

Newberg is just under an hour's drive from Portland International Airport; **Caravan Airport Transportation** (⊕ *541/994–9645* ⊕ *www.caravanairporttransportation.com*) provides shuttle service. The best way to visit Newberg and the Yamhill County vineyards is by car. Situated on Highway 99W, Newberg is 90 minutes from Lincoln City, on the Oregon Coast. Greyhound provides bus service to McMinnville.

EXPLORING
TOP ATTRACTIONS

Fodor'sChoice
★
Adelsheim Vineyard. David Adelsheim is the knight in shining armor of the Oregon wine industry—tirelessly promoting Oregon wines abroad, and always willing to share the knowledge he has gained from his long viticultural experience. He and Ginny Adelsheim founded their pioneer winery in 1971. They make their wines from grapes picked on their

230 acres of estate vineyards, as well as from grapes they've purchased. Their Pinot Noir, Pinot Gris, Pinot Blanc, and Chardonnay all conform to the Adelsheim house style of rich, balanced fruit and long, clean finishes. They also make a spicy cool-climate Syrah from grapes grown just outside the beautiful tasting room. Tours are available by appointment. ⊠ *16800 N.E. Calkins La.* ☎ *503/538–3652* ⊕ *www.adelsheim. com* 🍷 *Tastings from $15.*

Bergstrom Winery. Focusing on classic Oregon Pinot Noir and Chardonnay, this family-owned winery produces elegant and refined wines that represent some of the best the Willamette Valley has to offer. The tasting room is surrounded by the Silice Vineyard, and offers beautiful views of several neighboring vineyards as well. French-trained winemaker Josh Bergstrom sources fruit from his estate vineyards and from several other local sites to produce a wide range of single-vineyard Pinots. Enjoy your tasting on the deck on a warm summer day. ⊠ *18215 N.E. Calkins La.* ☎ *503/554–0468* ⊕ *www.bergstromwines.com* 🍷 *Tastings $20.*

Penner-Ash Wine Cellars. Lynn Penner-Ash brings years of experience working in Napa and as Rex Hill's winemaker to the winery that she and her husband Ron started in 1998. Although focused primarily on silky Pinot Noir, Penner-Ash also produces very good Syrah, Viognier, and Riesling. From its hilltop perch in the middle of the Dussin vineyard, this state-of-the-art gravity-flow winery and tasting room offers commanding views of the valley below. ⊠ *15771 N.E. Ribbon Ridge Rd.* ☎ *503/554–5545* ⊕ *www.pennerash.com* 🍷 *Tastings $15.*

Rex Hill Vineyards. A few hundred feet off the busy highway, surrounded by conifers and overlooked by vineyards, Rex Hill seems to exist in a world of its own. The winery opened in 1982, after owners Paul Hart and Jan Jacobsen converted a former nut-drying facility. It produces first-class Pinot Noir, Pinot Gris, Chardonnay, Sauvignon Blanc, and Riesling from both estate-grown and purchased grapes. The tasting room has a massive fireplace, elegant antiques, and an absorbing collection of modern art. Another highlight is the beautifully landscaped garden, perfect for picnicking. ⊠ *30835 N. Hwy. 99W* ☎ *503/538–0666, 800/739–4455* ⊕ *www.rexhill.com* 🍷 *Tastings $15.*

WORTH NOTING

Aramenta Cellars. Owners Ed and Darlene Looney have been farming this land for more than 40 years. In 2000, they planted grape vines after keeping cattle on the property. The winery and tasting room are built on the foundation of the old barn, and Ed makes the wine while Darlene runs the tasting room. Of the 27 acres planted in vines, 20 acres are leased to Archrey Summit for their Looney Vineyard Pinot Noir, and the Looneys farm 7 acres for their own wines which have very limited distribution. If you're looking for a break from all the Pinot Noir, try the Tillie Claret—a smooth Bordeaux blend made with grapes from eastern Washington and southern Oregon. Aramenta offers a great opportunity to interact with farmers who have worked the land for several generations and to taste some great small-production wine. ⊠ *17979 N.E. Lewis Rogers La.* ☎ *503/538–7230* ⊕ *www.aramentacellars.com* 🍷 *Tastings $10.*

Bravura Cellars. One of the newest additions to the Newberg tasting-room scene, this boutique winery eschews the Pinot Noir prevalent throughout the region in favor of hot-climate varietals—including Zinfandel, Cab, and even a Ruby Port—all produced in small batches of around 40 to 60 cases. Bravura's wines are only available at the tasting room or online, and every bottle is individually numbered. ✉ *108. S. College St.* ☎ *503/822–5116* ⊕ *www.bravuracellars.com.*

Champoeg State Heritage Area. Pronounced "sham- *poo*-ee," this 615-acre state park on the south bank of the Willamette River is on the site of a Hudson's Bay Company trading post, granary, and warehouse that was built in 1813. This was the seat of the first provisional government in the Northwest. The settlement was abandoned after a catastrophic flood in 1861, then rebuilt and abandoned again after the flood of 1890. The park's wide-open spaces, groves of oak and fir, modern visitor center, museum, and historic buildings provide vivid insight into pioneer life. Tepees and wagons are displayed here, and there are 10 miles of hiking and cycle trails. ✉ *8239 Champoeg Rd. NE, St. Paul* ☎ *503/678–1251* ⊕ *www.oregonstateparks.org* 🎫 *$5 per vehicle.*

Hoover-Minthorn House Museum. In 1885 Dr. Henry Minthorn invited his orphan nephew Herbert "Bertie" Hoover to come west and join the Minthorn family in Newberg. Built in 1881, the restored frame house, the oldest and most significant of Newberg's original structures, still has many of its original furnishings, including the president's boyhood bed and dresser. Hoover maintained his connection to Newberg, and visited several times after his presidency. ✉ *115 S. River St.* ☎ *503/538–6629* ⊕ *hooverminthorn.org* 🎫 *$5* 🕑 *Closed Jan.; Mar.–Nov., Mon. and Tues.; Dec. and Feb., weekdays.*

Raptor Ridge Winery. The huge windows in the new tasting room look out over the vines of their estate vineyard on the northeast slope of the Chehalem Mountains. If you keep a sharp eye, you may even catch a glimpse of the many raptors (red-tail hawks, sharp-shinned hawks, and kestrels) that give this small winery its name. Raptor Ridge specializes in single-vineyard Pinot Noirs that capture the sense of place of their estate vineyard as well as several other vineyards throughout the Willamette Valley. They also produce Chardonnay, Pinot Gris, and a very nice Tempranillo. During the summer, enjoy your tasting at a table on the outside deck that overlooks the vineyards. Tours of the wine-making facility are available by appointment. ✉ *18700 S.W. Hillsboro Hwy.* ☎ *503/628–8463* ⊕ *www.raptoridge.com* 🎫 *Tours with tastings $25* 🕑 *Closed mid-Jan.–mid May and mid-Oct.–mid-Dec., Tues. and Wed.*

Utopia Vineyard. Take a trip back in time to when the Oregon wine industry was much smaller and more intimate. Utopia owner and winemaker Daniel Warnhius moved north from California looking for a vineyard site that would produce world-class Pinot Noir, and he found this location with the right combination of location, climate, and soil structure. In the tasting room, you're likely to be served by Daniel himself. In addition to several great Pinot Noirs, they also produce a bright, crisp Chardonnay, and a Pinot Noir Rosé. ✉ *17445 N.E. Ribbon Ridge Rd.* ☎ *503/687–1671* ⊕ *utopiawine.com* 🎫 *Tastings $15* 🕑 *Closed weekdays Dec.–Apr.*

Vidon Vineyard. This small Newberg-area winery produces seven varieties of Pinot Noir along with small batches of Chardonnay, Pinot Gris, Viognier, Tempranillo, and Syrah. While the wines are enough to merit a visit to Vidon's hilltop tasting room, those with an interest in the science of wine-making will likely get a kick out of chatting with physicist-turned-winemaker Donald Hagge, who has applied his background to come up with some innovative ways to make and store wine. ✉ *17425 N.E. Hillside Dr.* ☎ *503/538–4092* 🌐 *www.vidonvineyard.com* 🎟 *Tastings $20.*

WHERE TO EAT AND STAY

$$$$ MODERN AMERICAN 🍴 **Jory.** This exquisite hotel dining room is named after one of the soils in the Oregon wine country. Chef Sunny Jin sources the majority of his ingredients locally, many from the on-site garden. **Known for:** Oregon-centric wine list; locally sourced ingredients. [$] *Average main: $35* ✉ *The Allison Inn, 2525 Allison La.* ☎ *503/554–2525, 877/294–2525* 🌐 *www.theallison.com.*

$$$$ RESORT 🏨 **The Allison Inn & Spa.** At this luxurious, relaxing base for exploring the region's 200 wineries, each bright, comfortable room includes a gas fireplace, original works of art, a soaking tub, impressive furnishings, bay-window seats, and views of the vineyards from the terrace or balcony. **Pros:** outstanding on-site restaurant; excellent gym and spa facilities; located in the middle of wine country. **Cons:** not many nearby off-property activities other than wine tasting. [$] *Rooms from: $405* ✉ *2525 Allison La.* ☎ *503/554–2525, 877/294–2525* 🌐 *www.theallison.com* 🛏 *85 rooms.*

$$$ B&B/INN 🏨 **Le Puy A Wine Valley Inn.** This beautiful wine country retreat caters to wine enthusiasts with amenities that include wine bars in each individually decorated room, along with hot tubs and gas fireplaces in some. **Pros:** beautiful surroundings; lots of nice architectural and decorative touches. **Cons:** a distance from sights other than wineries. [$] *Rooms from: $235* ✉ *20300 N.E. Hwy. 240* ☎ *503/554–9528* 🌐 *lepuy-inn.com* 🛏 *8 rooms* 🍽 *Breakfast.*

NIGHTLIFE AND PERFORMING ARTS

FAMILY **99W Drive-in.** Ted Francis built this drive-in in 1953, and operated it until his death at 98; the business is now run by his grandson. The first film begins at dusk. ✉ *3110 Portland Rd. (Hwy. 99W)* ☎ *503/538–2738* 🌐 *www.99w.com* 🎟 *$8; vehicles with single occupant $12* ⏰ *Closed Mon.–Thurs.*

SPORTS AND THE OUTDOORS

BALLOONING

Hot-air balloon rides are nothing less than a spectacular, breathtaking thrill—particularly over Oregon's beautiful Yamhill County.

Fodor's Choice ★ **Vista Balloon Adventures.** Enjoy floating gently above beautiful Oregon wine country as the sun rises behind the vines. Your FAA-licensed pilot will take the balloon up about 1,500 feet and can often steer the craft down to skim the water, then up to view hawks' nests. A brunch is served upon returning to the ground. ✉ *1050 Commerce Pkwy.* ☎ *503/625–7385, 800/622–2309* 🌐 *www.vistaballoon.com* 🎟 *$220 per person.*

DUNDEE

3 miles southwest of Newberg on Hwy. 99W.

Dundee used to be known for growing the lion's share (more than 90%) of the U.S. hazelnut crop. Today, some of Oregon's top-rated wineries are just outside Dundee, and the area is now best known for wine tourism and wine bars, bed-and-breakfast inns, and restaurants.

GETTING HERE AND AROUND

Dundee is just under an hour's drive from Portland International Airport; **Caravan Airport Transportation** provides shuttle service.

What used to be a pleasant drive through quaint Dundee on Highway 99W now can be a traffic hassle, as it serves as the main artery from Lincoln City on the Oregon Coast to suburban Portland. Others will enjoy wandering along the 25 miles of Highway 18 between Dundee and Grande Ronde, in the Coast Range, which goes through the heart of the Yamhill Valley wine country.

Contacts Caravan Airport Transportation. ☎ *541/994–9645* ⊕ *www.caravanairporttransportation.com.*

EXPLORING
TOP ATTRACTIONS

Fodor's Choice ★ **Archery Summit Winery.** The winery that Gary and Nancy Andrus, owners of Pine Ridge winery in Napa Valley, founded in the 1990s has become synonymous with premium Oregon Pinot Noir. Because they believed that great wines are made in the vineyard, they adopted such innovative techniques as narrow spacing and vertical trellis systems, which give the fruit a great concentration of flavors. In addition to the standard flight of Pinot Noirs in the tasting room, you can call ahead and reserve a private seated tasting or a tasting paired with small bites or a tour of the winery and, weather permitting, a walk out to the vineyard. You're welcome to bring a picnic, and as at many Oregon wineries, you can bring your dog, too. ⊠ *18599 N.E. Archery Summit Rd., Dayton* ☎ *503/864–4300* ⊕ *www.archerysummit.com* ⊠ *Tastings $20.*

Argyle Winery. A beautiful establishment, Argyle has its tasting room in a Victorian farmhouse set amid gorgeous gardens. The winery is tucked into a former hazelnut processing plant—which explains the Nuthouse label on its reserve wines. Since Argyle opened in 1987, it has consistently produced sparkling wines that are crisp on the palate, with an aromatic, lingering finish and bubbles that seem to last forever. And these sparklers cost about a third of their counterparts from California. The winery also produces Chardonnay, dry Riesling, Pinot Gris, and Pinot Noir. ⊠ *691 Hwy. 99W* ☎ *503/538–8520, 888/427–4953* ⊕ *www.argylewinery.com* ⊠ *Tastings $15.*

Fodor's Choice ★ **Domaine Drouhin Oregon.** When the French winery magnate Robert Drouhin ("the Sebastiani of France") planted a vineyard and built a winery in the Red Hills of Dundee back in 1987, he set local oenophiles abuzz. His daughter Veronique is now the winemaker and produces silky and elegant Pinot Noir and Chardonnay. Ninety acres of the 225-acre estate has been planted on a hillside to take advantage of the natural coolness of the earth and to establish a gravity-flow winery. No appointment is needed to taste the Oregon wines, but if you can plan ahead for the tour (reservations required), you can taste Oregon and Burgundy side-by-side. ✉ *6750 N.E. Breyman Orchards Rd., Dayton* ☎ *503/864–2700* ⊕ *www.domainedrouhin.com* ✉ *Tastings $15* ⊙ *Closed mid-Oct.–May, Mon. and Tues.*

Winderlea. The tasting room looks over the acclaimed former Gold-schmidt vineyard, first planted in 1974, and the view can be enjoyed on the outside deck on a warm summer day. Winemaker Robert Brittan crafts lush Pinot Noir and Chardonnay from several nearby vineyards in both single-vineyard offerings and blends from multiple vineyards. Proceeds from the tasting fee are donated to Salud, a partnership between Oregon winemakers and local medical professionals to provide health-care services for Oregon's seasonal vineyard workers and their families. ✉ *8905 N.E. Worden Hill Rd.* ☎ *503/554–5900* ⊕ *www.winderlea.com* ✉ *Tastings $20.*

WORTH NOTING

Dobbes Family Estate. Joe Dobbes makes a lot of wine, but he's definitely not a bulk winemaker. He provides custom wine-making services to many Oregon wineries that are too small to have their own winery or winemaker. But he also makes several lines of his own wine, ranging from his everyday "Wine By Joe" label to the premium Dobbes Family Estate label featuring great Pinot Noir, Syrah, Sauvignon Blanc, Viognier, and Grenache Blanc. In addition to a few single vineyard Pinot Noir bottlings, Dobbes focuses on blends from multiple vineyards to provide consistent, balanced, and interesting wines. Two different tasting fights are available in the tasting room, and seated tastings and tours can be arranged by appointment. ✉ *240 S.E. 5th St.* ☎ *503/538–1141* ⊕ *www.joedobbeswines. com* ✉ *Tastings $15.*

Domaine Serene. This world-class winery in Dundee's Red Hills is a well-regarded producer of Oregon Pinot Noir and Chardonnay. Bring a picnic and enjoy the beautiful grounds of the estate. As an alternative to the standard drop-in tasting in the high-ceiling tasting room, call ahead to reserve a tour or private seated tasting, which includes an extended flight of rare wines. ✉ *6555 N.E. Hilltop La., Dayton* ☎ *503/864–4600, 866/864–6555* ⊕ *www.domaineserene. com* ✉ *Tastings $20.*

The Dundee Bistro's Wine and Bubble Bar. Located right on the main highway between Portland and wine country, The Dundee Bistro's Wine and Bubble Bar offers the opportunity to sample wines from both the Ponzi Winery and small local producers without straying far from the beaten path. The tasting menu features current releases of Ponzi wines, as well as a rotating selection of other local wines. If you've had enough wine for a while, you can also get snacks, Italian coffee, or a craft beer to enjoy in the comfortable tasting room. ✉ *100 S.W. 7th St.* ☎ *503/554–1500* ⊕ *www.dundeebistro.com.*

Continued on page 184

The Willamette Valley is Oregon's premier wine region. With a milder climate than any growing area in California, cool-climate grapes like Pinot Noir and Pinot Gris thrive here, and are being transformed into world-class wines.

There may be fewer and smaller wineries than in Napa, but the experience is often more intimate. The winemaker himself may even pour you wine.

Touring is easy, as most wineries are well marked, and have tasting rooms with regular hours. Whether you're taking a day trip from Portland, or staying for a couple of days, here's how to get the most out of your sipping experience.

By Dave Sandage and John Doerper

Above and right, Willamette Valley

Wine Tasting
in the
Willamette
Valley

OREGON'S WINES: THEN AND NOW

Rex Hill Vineyards

THE EARLY YEARS

The French made wine first—French Canadians, that is. In the 1830s, retired fur trappers from the Hudson's Bay Company started to colonize the Willamette Valley and planted grapes on the south-facing buttes. They were followed by American settlers who made wine.

Although wine-making in the region-languished after these early efforts, it never quite vanished. A few wineries hung on, producing wines mainly for Oregonians of European descent.

It wasn't until the 1970s that the state's wine industry finally took off. Only after a group of young California winemakers started making vinifera wines in the Umpqua and Willamette Valleys and gained international acclaim for them, did Oregon's wines really take hold.

WINEMAKING TODAY

Today, Oregon's wine industry is racing ahead. Here the most prolific white and red grapes are Pinot Gris and Pinot Noir, respectively. Other prominent varietals include Riesling, Gewürztraminer, Viognier, Chardonnay, Carbernet Franc, and Syrah.

The wine industry in Oregon is still largely dominated by family and boutique wineries that pay close attention to quality and are often keen to experiment. That makes traveling and tasting at the source an always-interesting experience.

OREGON CERTIFIED SUSTAINABLE WINE

The latest trend in Oregon winemaking is a dedication to responsible grape growing and winemaking. When you see the Oregon Certified Sustainable Wine (OCSW) logo on the back of a wine bottle, it means the winery ensures accountable agricultural and winemaking practices (in conjunction with agencies such as USDA Organic, Demeter Biodynamic, the Food Alliance, Salmon-Safe, and Low Input Viticulture and Enology) through independent third-party certification. For more information on Oregon Certified Sustainable wines and participating wineries, check ⊕ www.ocsw.org.

WINE TOURING AND TASTING

Wine tasting at Argyle and Rex Hill

WHEN TO GO

In high season (June through October) and on weekends and holidays during much of the year, wine-country roads can be busy and tasting rooms are often crowded. If you prefer a more intimate tasting experience, plan your visit for a weekday.

To avoid the frustration of a fruitless drive, confirm in advance that wineries of interest will be open when you plan to visit.

Choose a designated driver for the day: Willamette wine-country roads are often narrow and curvy, and you may be sharing the road with bicyclists and wildlife as well as other wine tourists.

IN THE TASTING ROOM

Tasting rooms are designed to introduce newcomers to the pleasures of wine and to the wines made at the winery. At popular wineries you'll sometimes have to pay for your tasting, anything from a nominal $2 fee to $30 and up for a tasting that might include a glass you can take home. This fee is often deducted if you buy wine before leaving.

WHAT'S AN AVA?

AVAs (American Viticultural Areas) are geographic winegrowing regions that vaguely reflect the French concept of terroir, or "sense of place." The vineyards within a given AVA have similar characteristics such as climate, soil types, and/or elevation, which impart shared characteristics to the wines made from grapes grown in that area. AVAs are strictly geographic boundaries distinct from city or county designations. AVAs can also be subdivided into sub-AVAs; each of the AVAs mentioned here is actually part of the larger Willamette Valley AVA.

Each taste consists of an ounce or two. Feel free to pour whatever you don't finish into one of the dump buckets on the bar. If you like, rinse your glass between pours with a little water. Remember, those sips add up, so pace yourself. If you plan to visit several wineries, try just a few wines at each so you won't suffer from palate fatigue, when your mouth can no longer distinguish subtleties. It's also a good idea to bring a picnic lunch, which you can enjoy on the deck of a winery, taking in the surrounding wine country vistas.

DAY TRIP FROM PORTLAND

With nearly 150 vineyards, the Chehalem Mountain and Ribbon Ridge AVAs offer widely varied soil types and diverse Pinot Noirs. The region is less than an hour away from Portland.

Ponzi Vineyards

CHEHALEM MOUNTAIN AND RIBBON RIDGE AVAS

❶ PONZI VINEYARDS

First planted in 1970, Ponzi has some of Oregon's oldest Pinot Noir vines. In addition to current releases, the tasting room sometimes offers older library wines. **Try:** *Arneis, a crisp Italian white varietal.*

- ✉ 19500 SW Mountain Home Rd., Sherwood
- ☎ 503/628-1227
- 🌐 www.ponziwines.com

❷ REX HILL VINEYARDS

Before grapevines, the Willamette Valley was widely planted with fruits and nuts. Enjoy classic Oregon Pinot Noir in this tasting room built around an old fruit and nut drying facility. **Try:** *dark and spicy Dundee Hills Pinot Noir.*

- ✉ 30835 N. Hwy. 99W, Newberg
- ☎ 800/739-4455
- 🌐 www.rexhill.com

❸ BRAVURA CELLARS

Newberg's newest winery features small-batch wines made from hot-climate grapes, including Zinfandels, Cabernets Sauvignons, and even port. **Try:** *bright and full-bodied Petit Sirah.*

- ✉ 108 S. College St., Newberg
- ☎ 503/822-5116
- 🌐 www.bravuracellars.com

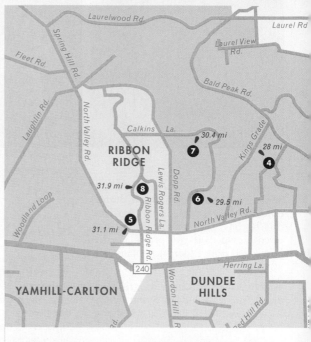

❹ VIDON VINEYARD

Run by a particle physicist-turned-winemaker, this hilltop vineyard features a low-key tasting room plus a covered outdoor seating area for taking in bucolic vineyard views. **Try:** *rich but fruity Pinot Noir Maresh.*

- ✉ 17425 NE Hillside Dr., Newberg
- ☎ 503/538-4092
- 🌐 www.vidonvineyard.com

❺ UTOPIA VINEYARD

The tasting room at this small Oregon winery is quite intimate—you'll likely be served by the winemaker himself. **Try:** *light and slightly sweet Rosé.*

- ✉ 17445 N.E. Ribbon Ridge Rd., Newberg
- ☎ 503/298-7841
- 🌐 www.utopiawine.com

Vercingetorix (VX) Vineyard

Adelsheim Vineyard   Rex Hill   Pinot Gris grapes

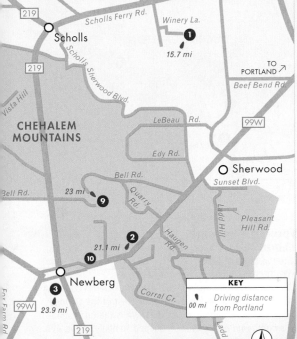

KEY

● / 00 mi Driving distance from Portland

❽ ARAMENTA CELLARS

A small, family-run operation that offers tastings in its winery, built on the foundation of an old barn. The on-site vineyard grows primarily Pinot Noir and Chardonnay. **Try:** *smooth and structured Tillie Claret.*

✉ 17979 N.E. Lewis Rogers La., Newberg
☎ 503/538-7230
⊕ www.aramentacellars.com

STOP FOR A BITE

❾ JORY RESTAURANT

Located within the luxurious Allison Inn and Spa, Jory serves creative dishes that highlight the bounty of the Willamette Valley.

✉ 2525 Allison La., Newberg
☎ 503/554-2526
⊕ www.theallison.com

❿ SUBTERRA

Casual fine dining in a wine cellar atmosphere underneath the Dark Horse wine bar. The menu features global cuisine and a good selection of local wines.

✉ 1505 Portland Rd., Newberg
☎ 503/538-6060
⊕ www.subterrarestaurant.com

❻ ADELSHEIM VINEYARD

One of Oregon's older Pinot Noir producers, Adelsheim has just opened a new tasting room inside its modern winery, with friendly, knowledgeable employees. **Try:** *dark and smoky Elizabeth's Reserve Pinot Noir.*

✉ 16800 N.E. Calkins La., Newberg
☎ 503/538-3652
⊕ www.adelsheim.com

❼ BERGSTROM WINERY

A beautiful tasting room, but the real high point here is the classic Oregon Pinot Noir sourced from several of its estate vineyards as well as other local sites. **Try:** *earthy Bergstrom Pinot Noir.*

✉ 18215 N.E. Calkins La., Newberg
☎ 503/554-0468
⊕ www.bergstromwines.com

TWO DAYS IN WINE COUNTRY

DAY 1

DUNDEE HILLS AVA

The Dundee Hills AVA is home to some of Oregon's best known Pinot Noir producers. Start your tour in the town of Dundee, about 30 miles southwest of Portland, then drive up into the red hills and enjoy the valley views from many wineries.

❶ ARGYLE WINERY

If you don't want to drive off the beaten path, this winery is right on Highway 99W in Dundee. They specialize in sparkling wines, but also make very nice still wines. Try: *crisp Brut Rosé.*

✉ 691 Hwy. 99 W, Dundee
☎ 503/538–8520
🌐 www.argylewinery.com

❷ PONZI WINE BAR

This tasting room close to Argyle has a nice selection of local wines. It's a good choice for those who want to sample a large selection side-by-side. **Try:** *bright and fruity Ponzi Pinot Gris.*

✉ 100 S.W. 7th St., Dundee
☎ 503/554–1500
🌐 www.ponziwines.com

❸ ARCHERY SUMMIT

An Oregon Pinot Noir pioneer, Archery Summit features memorable wines and equally pleasing views. Call in advance to schedule a tour of the winery and aging caves. **Try:** *dark and rich Premier Cuvée Pinot Noir.*

✉ 18599 NE Archery Summit Rd., Dayton
☎ 503/864–4300
🌐 www.archerysummit.com

❹ DOMAINE DROUHIN OREGON

Started in the late 1980s by the Drouhin family of Burgundy fame, this winery makes notable Oregon Pinot Noir, as well as Chardonnay. **Try:** *smooth and earthy Willamette Valley Pinot Noir.*

✉ 6750 Breyman Orchards Rd., Dayton
☎ 503/864–2700
🌐 www.domainedrouhin.com

❺ VISTA HILLS VINEYARD

The so-called Treehouse is arguably the most stunning tasting room in Oregon. Sample wine made from estate fruit on a deck that overlooks the vineyards of the Dundee Hills. **Try:** *fruity Treehouse Pinot Noir.*

✉ 6475 N.E. Hilltop La., Dayton
☎ 503/864–3200
🌐 www.vistahillsvineyard.com

DAY 2

YAMHILL-CARLTON AVA

To the west of the Dundee Hills AVA is the horseshoe-shaped Yamhill-Carlton AVA. Vineyards here are found on the slopes that surround the towns of Yamhill and Carlton. Carlton has become a center of wine tourism, and you could easily spend a day visiting tasting rooms in town.

❻ PENNER-ASH WINE CELLARS

This state-of-the-art winery and tasting room is atop a hill with an excellent view of the valley below. **Try:** *smooth and dark Shea Vineyard Pinot Noir.*

✉ 15771 N.E. Ribbon Ridge Rd., Newberg
☎ 503/554–5545
🌐 www.pennerash.com

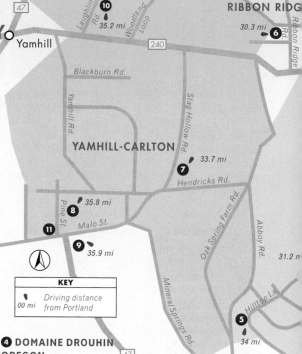

RIBBON RIDG

Yamhill

❿ 35.2 mi

30.3 mi ❻

240

Blackburn Rd.

YAMHILL-CARLTON

❼ 33.7 mi

Hendricks Rd.

❽ 35.8 mi

❺

❾ 35.9 mi

34 mi

31.2 m

KEY

❙ 00 mi — Driving distance from Portland

Penner-Ash Wine Cellars

Ponzi Wine Bar

STOP FOR A BITE

7 LEMELSON VINEYARDS
Although it specializes in single-vineyard Pinot Noir, Lemelson also makes several crisp white wines. The deck overlooking the vineyards is perfect for picnics. **Try:** *crisp and fruity Riesling.*
- ✉ 12020 N.E. Stag Hollow Rd., Carlton
- ☎ 503/852–6619
- 🌐 www.lemelsonvineyards.com

8 TYRUS EVAN WINE
Well-known winemaker Ken Wright's second label features big reds. The tasting room is in the historic Carlton train station. **Try:** *bold and spicy Del Rio Claret.*
- ✉ 120 N. Pine St., Carlton
- ☎ 503/852–7070
- 🌐 www.tyrusevanwine.com

9 SCOTT PAUL WINES
In addition to making Oregon Pinot Noir, Scott Paul Wines also runs a Burgundy import company, allowing you to taste locally grown Pinot Noir alongside some of the best Burgundies. **Try:** *structured and elegant La Paulée Pinot Noir.*
- ✉ 128 S. Pine St., Carlton
- ☎ 503/852–7300
- 🌐 www.scottpaul.com

10 LENNÉ ESTATE
Lenné specializes in highly regarded Pinot Noir, although it's often pouring a couple of non-Pinot wines from other wineries as well. The tasting room in a small stone building overlooks the vineyards. **Try:** *complex and earthy Estate Pinot Noir.*
- ✉ 18760 Laughlin Rd., Yamhill
- ☎ 503/956–2256
- 🌐 www.lenneestate.com

11 THE HORSERADISH WINE AND CHEESE BAR
Located in downtown Carlton, The Horseradish offers a wide selection of local wines as well as cheese from around the world. The sandwiches and small plates make for a great quick lunch.
- ✉ 211 W. Main St., Carlton
- ☎ 503/852–6656
- 🌐 www.thehorseradish.com

12 DUNDEE BISTRO
A favorite of winemakers, Dundee Bistro serves seasonal local ingredients paired with Willamette Valley wines. Enjoy outdoor seating, or watch chefs work in the open kitchen inside.
- ✉ 100-A S.W. 7th St., Dundee
- ☎ 503/554–1650
- 🌐 www.dundeebistro.com

13 TINA'S
The warm and intimate Tina's features dishes made with seasonal ingredients, organic vegetables, and free-range meats. Stop by for lunch Tuesday–Friday, or nightly dinner.
- ✉ 760 Hwy. 99 W, Dundee
- ☎ 503/538–8880
- 🌐 www.tinasdundee.com

Erath Vineyards Winery. When Dick Erath opened one of Oregon's pioneer wineries more than a quarter century ago, he focused on producing distinctive Pinot Noir from grapes he'd been growing in the Red Hills since 1972—as well as full-flavored Pinot Gris, Pinot Blanc, Chardonnay, Riesling, and late-harvest Gewürztraminer. The wines are excellent and reasonably priced. In 2006 the winery was sold to Washington State's giant conglomerate Ste. Michelle Wine Estate. The tasting room is in the middle of the vineyards, high in the hills, with views in nearly every direction; the hazelnut trees that covered the slopes not so long ago have been replaced with vines. The tasting-room terrace, which overlooks the winery and the hills, is a choice spot for picnicking. Crabtree Park, next to the winery, is a good place to stretch your legs after a tasting. ⊠ *9409 N.E. Worden Hill Rd.* ☎ *503/538–3318, 800/539–9463* ⊕ *www.erath.com* ▧ *Tastings $15.*

Maresh Red Barn. When Jim and Loie Maresh planted 2 acres of vines in 1970, theirs became the fifth vineyard in Oregon and the first on Worden Hill Road. The quality of their grapes was so high that some of the Dundee Hills' best and most famous wineries soon sought them out. When the wine industry boomed in the 1980s, the Mareshes decided they might as well enjoy some wine from their renowned grapes, now planted on 45 acres of their land. They transformed their old barn into a tasting room, where you can taste and purchase exceptional Chardonnay, Pinot Noir, Pinot Gris, Riesling, and Sauvignon Blanc made by several acclaimed local winemakers from Maresh family grapes. ⊠ *9325 N.W. Worden Hill Rd.* ☎ *503/537–1098* ⊕ *www.vineyardretreat.com* ☉ *Closed Dec.–Feb. and Mar.–Thanksgiving, Mon.–Thurs.*

Red Ridge. A good place to clean your palette after all that wine tasting is Red Ridge, home to the first commercial olive mill in the Pacific Northwest. Stop by the gift shop to taste some of the farm's signature oils or head out back to see an old-fashioned (and not-in-use) olive press imported from Spain. Free tours are available June through September, daily at 11; if you're in town in November, don't miss the annual Olio Nuovo Festival, where you can taste extra virgin oil in its freshly milled and unfiltered state. ⊠ *5510 N.E. Breyman Orchards Rd., Dayton* ☎ *503/864–8502* ⊕ *redridgefarms.com.*

Fodor's Choice   **Sokol Blosser.** One of Yamhill County's oldest wineries (it was estab-
★   lished in 1971) makes consistently excellent wines and sells them at reasonable prices. Set on a gently sloping south-facing hillside and surrounded by vineyards, lush lawns, and shade trees, it's a splendid place to learn about wine. A demonstration vineyard with several rows of vines contains the main grape varieties and shows what happens to them as the seasons unfold. Winery tours are available daily at 11. ⊠ *5000 Sokol Blosser La.* ✛ *3 miles west of Dundee off Hwy. 99 W* ☎ *503/864–2282, 800/582–6668* ⊕ *www.sokolblosser.com* ▧ *Tastings $15, tours $40.*

Torii Mor Winery. One of Yamhill County's oldest vineyards, established in 1993, makes small quantities of handcrafted Pinot Noir, Pinot Gris, and Chardonnay and is set amid Japanese gardens with breathtaking views of the Willamette Valley. The gardens were designed by Takuma

Tono, the same architect who designed the renowned Portland Japanese Garden. The owners, who love all things Japanese, named their winery after the distinctive Japanese gate of Shinto religious significance; they added a Scandinavian mor, signifying "earth," to create an east-west combo: "earth gate." Jacques Tardy, a native of Nuits Saint Georges, in Burgundy, France, is the current winemaker. Under his guidance Torii Mor wines have become more Burgundian in style. ✉ *18323 N.E. Fairview Dr.* ☎ *503/538–2279* 🌐 *www.toriimorwinery.com* 🎫 *Tastings $15.*

Vista Hills Vineyard. The Treehouse tasting room here is arguably the most beautiful in Oregon. Step out onto the deck and enjoy the view from underneath the towering trees. Vista Hills is a bit different from its neighbors in that there is no winery but several well-known local winemakers create wine from the vineyard grapes to sell under the Vista Hills label. The result is a range of distinctive wine styles, all made from the same vineyard. Also available are Hawaiian chocolate and coffee from their sister farm in Kona. ✉ *6475 Hilltop La., Dayton* ☎ *503/864–3200* 🌐 *www.vistahillsvineyard.com* 🎫 *Tastings $15.*

White Rose Estate. Like many of its better-known neighbors in the Dundee Hills, White Rose Estate produces elegant Pinot Noir that reflects the land where it is grown. In addition to their own estate vineyard, they purchase grapes from several highly regarded vineyards around the Willamette Valley. They describe their wines as "neoclassical," using traditional techniques in the vineyard, and state-of-the-art equipment and handling in the winery. Somewhat unusual for Oregon, most of the wines have a fairly high percentage of whole clusters included during fermentation, giving the wines more complexity and a bit of spice. ✉ *6250 N.E. Hilltop La., Dayton* ☎ *503/864–2328* 🌐 *www.whiteroseestate.com* 🎫 *Tastings $15.*

WHERE TO EAT

$$$ CONTEMPORARY

🍴 **Dundee Bistro.** The Ponzi wine family are capable restaurateurs as well and use Northwest organic foods such as Draper Valley chicken, Carlton Farms pork, and locally produced wines, fruits, vegetables, nuts, mushrooms, fish, and meats. Vaulted ceilings provide an open feeling inside, warmed by abundant fresh flowers and the works of local Oregon artists. **Known for:** part of the Ponzi wine family. [$] *Average main: $25* ✉ *100-A S.W. 7th St.* ☎ *503/554–1650* 🌐 *www.dundeebistro.com.*

$ PACIFIC NORTHWEST FAMILY

🍴 **Red Hills Market.** Serving great sandwiches, salads, and pizza, this is the perfect stop for a quick lunch in the middle of a day of wine tasting, or a casual no-frills dinner at the end of the day. Many of the sandwiches feature locally made charcuterie and cheeses, and the pizzas range from traditional Margarita to a spicy chorizo, blue cheese, and arugula. **Known for:** great stop during wine tasting; takeout options. [$] *Average main: $12* ✉ *155 S.W. 7th St.* ☎ *971/832–8414* 🌐 *www.redhillsmarket.com.*

$$$$ FRENCH Fodor's Choice ★

🍴 **Tina's.** Chef–proprietors Tina and David Bergen bring a powerful one-two punch to this Dundee favorite that often lures Portlanders away from their own restaurant scene. The couple shares cooking duties—Tina does the baking and is often on hand to greet you, and David brings his experience as a former caterer and employee of nearby Sokol Blosser Winery to the table, ensuring that you have the right glass of wine to match your course. **Known for:** attracting Portland foodies; delicious homemade soups. [$] *Average main: $35* ✉ *760 Hwy. 99W* ☎ *503/538–8880* 🌐 *www.tinasdundee.com* ⏲ *No lunch Sun. and Mon.*

WHERE TO STAY

$$$ B&B/INN Fodor's Choice ★ 🏨 **Dundee Manor Bed and Breakfast.** This 1908-built traditional home on expansive grounds is filled with treasures and collectibles that add intrigue to each themed room: African, Asian, European, and North American. **Pros:** terrific amenities; lots of activities; attentive staff. **Cons:** few rooms; closed January and February. [$] *Rooms from: $225* ✉ *8380 N.E. Worden Hill Rd.* ☎ *503/554–1945, 888/262–1133* 🌐 *www.dundeemanor.com* ⏲ *Closed Jan. and Feb.* 🛏 *4 rooms* 🍴 *Breakfast.*

$$ HOTEL 🏨 **The Inn at Red Hills.** These spacious and extremely comfortable rooms, each with its own layout, offer plenty of local flavor, from the materials in the building, to the wines served and the ingredients used in the kitchen. **Pros:** contemporary, stylish surroundings; close to many wineries. **Cons:** located on the main highway through town rather than the country. [$] *Rooms from: $179* ✉ *1410 N. Hwy. 99W* ☎ *503/538–7666* 🌐 *www.innatredhills.com* 🛏 *20 rooms* 🍴 *No meals.*

YAMHILL-CARLTON

14 miles west of Dundee.

Just outside the small towns of Carlton and Yamhill are neatly combed benchlands and hillsides, an American Viticultural Area (AVA) established in 2004, and home to some of the finest Pinot Noir vineyards in the world. Carlton has exploded with many small tasting rooms in the past few years, and you could easily spend an entire day tasting wine within three or four blocks. The area is a gorgeous quilt of nurseries, grain fields, and orchards. Come here for the wine tasting, but don't expect to find too much else to do.

GETTING HERE AND AROUND

Having your own car is the best way to explore this rural region of Yamhill County, located a little more than an hour's drive from Portland International Airport. The towns of Yamhill and Carlton are about an hour's drive from Downtown Portland, traveling through Tigard, to Newberg and west on Highway 240.

EXPLORING

TOP ATTRACTIONS

Lemelson Vineyards. This winery was designed from the ground up to be a no-compromises Pinor Noir production facility with an eye to Willamette Valley aesthetics, and the highlight is a diverse range of single-vineyard Pinot Noirs. But don't neglect the bright Pinot Gris and Riesling, perfect with seafood or spicy fare. The spacious high-ceiling tasting room is a great place to relax and take in the view through the floor-to-ceiling windows, or bring a picnic and enjoy the deck on a warm summer day. ✉ *12020 N.E. Stag Hollow Rd., Carlton* ☎ *503/852–6619* 🌐 *www.lemelsonvineyards.com.*

Lenné Estate. The small stone building that houses the tasting room is surrounded by the estate vineyard and looks like something right out of Burgundy. Steve Lutz was looking for the perfect site to grow Pinot Noir and bought the property in 2000. In addition to offering his own rich and elegant estate Pinot Noirs for tasting, he often pours other varietals from other wineries. ✉ *18760 N.E. Laughlin Rd., Yamhill* ☎ *503/956–2256* ⊕ *www.lenneestate.com* 🖃 *$10* ☾ *Closed Mon.–Wed.*

WORTH NOTING

Anne Amie Vineyards. Early wine country adopters Fred and Mary Benoit established this hilltop winery as Chateau Benoit in 1979. When the winery changed hands in 1999, it was renamed Anne Amie and has been concentrating on Pinot Blanc, Pinot Gris, and Pinot Noir, but still makes a dry Riesling. In addition, they also make Syrah and a Bordeaux blend from eastern Washington grapes. Both the tasting room and the picnic area have spectacular views across the hills and valleys of Yamhill County. ✉ *6580 N.E. Mineral Springs Rd., Carlton* ☎ *503/864–2991* ⊕ *www.anneamie.com* 🖃 *Tastings $15.*

Carlton Winemakers Studio. Oregon's first cooperative winery was specifically designed to house multiple small premium wine producers. This gravity-flow winery has up-to-date wine-making equipment as well as multiple cellars for storing the different makers' wines. You can taste and purchase bottles from the different member wineries: Andrew Rich, Asilda, Bachelder, Dukes Family Vineyard, Hamacher Wines, Lazy River Vineyard, Merriman Wines, Mad Violets, Omero, Retour Wine Co., Trout Lily Ranch, Utopia Vineyard, and Wahle Vineyards and Cellars. The emphasis is on Pinot Noir, but more than a dozen other types of wines are poured, from Cabernet Franc to Gewürztraminer to Mourvèdre on a rotating basis. The selection of wines available to taste changes every few days. ✉ *801 N. Scott St., Carlton* ☎ *503/852–6100* ⊕ *www.winemakersstudio.com* 🖃 *Tastings from $22.*

Ken Wright Cellars Tasting Room. Carlton's former train depot is now the tasting room for Ken Wright Cellars and his warm-climate label, Tyrus Evan. The winery specializes in single-vineyard Pinot Noirs, each subtly different from the next depending on the soil types and grape clones. The wines are poured side by side, giving you an opportunity to go back and forth to compare them. The Tyrus Evan wines are quite different from the Ken Wright Pinots: they are warm-climate varieties like Cabernet Franc, Malbec, Syrah, and red Bordeaux blends, from grapes Wright buys from vineyards in eastern Washington and southern Oregon. You can also pick up cheeses and other picnic supplies, as well as wine country gifts and souvenirs. ✉ *120 N. Pine St., Carlton* ☎ *503/852–7010* ⊕ *www.kenwrightcellars.com* 🖃 *Tastings from $20.*

Scott Paul Tasting Room and Winery. Pinot Noir fans, listen up: this small spot in the center of Carlton not only makes Pinot Noir from Oregon grapes, but it also imports and sells Pinot Noirs from Burgundy (as well as grower Champagne). The mainstay Pinot Noirs made from local grapes are Audrey, the finest wine of the vintage, and La Paulée, a selection of the best lots of each vintage. In addition, they'll make several other Pinots customized to the widely variable growing conditions each year in

Oregon. All are splendid examples of the wines that can be made from this great, challenging grape. The tasting room, a quaint redbrick building, is across the street from the winery. Tours are by appointment only. Wine seminars are offered periodically, and private guided tastings are available by appointment. ⊠ *128 S. Pine St., Carlton* ☎ *503/852–7300* ⊕ *www.scottpaul.com* ⬜ *Tastings $10* ⊙ *Closed Mon. and Tues.*

WHERE TO EAT

$

PACIFIC
NORTHWEST

✕ **The Horse Radish.** The perfect stop in the middle of a day of wine tasting offers a wide selection of artisan cheese and meats, as well as a great lunch menu. Pick up some sandwiches and a soup or salad to go, and you're all set for a picnic at your favorite winery. **Known for:** live music on Friday and Saturday nights; tasting room featuring Marshall Davis wines. $ *Average main: $8* ⊠ *211 W. Main St., Carlton* ☎ *503/852–6656* ⊕ *www.thehorseradish.com* ⊟ *No credit cards.*

MCMINNVILLE

11 miles south of Yamhill on Hwy. 99 W.

The Yamhill County seat, McMinnville lies in the center of Oregon's thriving wine industry. There is a larger concentration of wineries in Yamhill County than in any other area of the state. Among the varieties are Chardonnay, Pinot Noir, and Pinot Gris. Most of the wineries in the area offer tours and tastings. McMinnville's downtown area has a few shops worth a look; many of the historic district buildings, erected 1890–1915, are still standing, and are remarkably well maintained.

GETTING HERE AND AROUND

McMinnville is a little more than an hour's drive from Downtown Portland; **Caravan Airport Transportation** provides shuttle service to Portland International Airport. McMinnville is just 70 minutes from Lincoln City on the Oregon Coast, and 27 miles west of Salem.

ESSENTIALS

Visitor Information Visit McMinnville. ⊠ *328 N.E. Davis St., Suite 1* ☎ *503/857–0182* ⊕ *visitmcminnville.com.*

EXPLORING

FAMILY
Fodor's Choice
★

Evergreen Aviation and Space Museum and Wings and Waves Waterpark. Howard Hughes' *Spruce Goose,* the largest plane ever built and constructed entirely of wood, is on permanent display, but if you can take your eyes off the giant you will also see more than 45 historic planes and replicas from the early years of flight and World War II, as well as the postwar and modern eras. Across the parking lot from the aviation museum is the space museum with artifacts that include a German V-2 rocket and a Titan missile, complete with silo and launch control room. The adjacent Wings and Waves Waterpark (separate admission) has 10 waterslides, including one that starts at a Boeing 747-100 that sits on *top* of the building. The IMAX theater is open daily and features several different films each day. There's a museum store and two cafés, as well as ongoing educational programs and special events. ⊠ *500 N.E. Michael King Smith Way* ☎ *503/434–4185* ⊕ *www.evergreenmuseum. org* ⬜ *$27, includes IMAX movie; $33 waterpark.*

The Eyrie Vineyards. When David Lett planted the first Pinot Noir vines in the Willamette Valley in 1965, he was setting in motion a series of events that has caused Willamette Valley Pinot Noir to be recognized as among the best in the world. Affectionately known as Papa Pinot, Lett, along with several other pioneering winemakers nurtured the Oregon wine industry to what it is today. Today David's son Jason Lett is now the winemaker and vineyard manager, and continues to make Pinot Noir, Pinot Gris, and Chardonnay that reflect the gentle touch that has always characterized Eyrie wines. In recent years, many small wineries have sprung up in the neighborhood around this historic winery. ✉ *935 N.E. 10th Ave.* ☎ *503/472–6315, 888/440–4970* 🌐 *www.eyrievineyards.com* 🎫 *Tastings $10.*

4

NEED A BREAK

🍴 Serendipity Ice Cream. Historic Cook's Hotel, built in 1886, is the setting for a true, old-fashioned ice-cream-parlor experience. Try a sundae, and take home cookies made from scratch. Known for: locally made ice cream (dairy- and sugar-free varieties). ✉ ***502 N.E. 3rd St.*** ☎ ***503/474–9189*** 🌐 ***serendipityicecream.com.***

WHERE TO EAT AND STAY

$$$$ CONTEMPORARY

🍴 **Joel Palmer House.** Wild mushrooms and truffles are the stars at this 1857 home, named after an Oregon pioneer, that is now on the National Register of Historic Places. There are three small dining rooms, each seating about 15 people. **Known for:** mushrooms, mushrooms, mushrooms; three-course prix-fixe menu; chef Christopher's Mushroom Madness Menu. [$] *Average main: $50* ✉ *600 Ferry St., Dayton* ☎ *503/864–2995* 🌐 *www.joelpalmerhouse.com* 🕒 *Closed Sun. and Mon. No lunch.*

$$$ ITALIAN Fodor's Choice ★

🍴 **Nick's Italian Cafe.** Famed for serving Oregon's wine country enthusiasts, this fine-dining venue is a destination for a special evening or lunch. Modestly furnished but with a voluminous wine cellar, Nick's serves spirited and simple food, reflecting the owner's northern Italian heritage. **Known for:** five-course prix-fixe with wine pairings; expansive wine cellar. [$] *Average main: $26* ✉ *521 N.E. 3rd St.* ☎ *503/434–4471* 🌐 *nicksitaliancafe.com.*

$ HOTEL

🏨 **Hotel Oregon.** Rooms in the former Elberton Hotel, built in 1905, have tall ceilings and high windows, are outfitted in late-Victorian furnishings, and filled with whimsical art—sometimes serene, often bizarre—as well as photos and sayings scribbled on the walls. **Pros:** inexpensive; casual and lively; plenty of food and drink on the premises. **Cons:** shared baths for most rooms; those seeking upscale ambience should look elsewhere. [$] *Rooms from: $60* ✉ *310 N.E. Evans St.* ☎ *503/472–8427, 888/472–8427* 🌐 *www.mcmenamins.com* 🛏 *42 rooms* 🍽 *No meals.*

$$ B&B/INN Fodor's Choice ★

🏨 **Joseph Mattey House Bed & Breakfast.** The four upstairs rooms in this Queen Anne Victorian mansion are whimsically named after locally grown grape varieties and are decorated in keeping with the character of those wines: crisp white furnishings in the Chardonnay Room, dark-wood pieces and reddish wine accents in the Pinot Noir room. **Pros:** refined bed-and-breakfast atmosphere. **Cons:** not many modern amenities in the rooms. [$] *Rooms from: $175* ✉ *10221 N.E. Mattey La.* ✧ *Off Hwy. 99 W, ¼ mile south of Lafayette* ☎ *503/434–5058* 🌐 *www.matteyhouse.com* 🛏 *4 rooms* 🍽 *Breakfast.*

NIGHTLIFE AND PERFORMING ARTS

Spirit Mountain Casino and Lodge. Located 24 miles southwest of McMinnville on Highway 18, this popular gambling getaway is owned and operated by the Confederated Tribes of the Grande Ronde Community of Oregon. The 90,000-square-foot casino has more than a thousand slots, as well as poker and blackjack tables, roulette, craps, Pai Gow poker, keno, bingo, and off-track betting. Big-name comedians and rock and country musicians perform in the 1,700-seat concert hall, and there's an arcade for the kids. Complimentary shuttle service from Portland and Salem is available. Dining options include an all-you-can-eat buffet, a deli, and a café. ⊠ *27100 S.W. Salmon River Hwy., Grand Ronde* ☏ *503/879–2350, 800/760–7977* ⊕ *spiritmountain.com.*

MID-WILLAMETTE VALLEY

While most of the wineries are concentrated in Washington and Yamhill counties, there are several finds in the mid–Willamette Valley that warrant extending a wine enthusiast's journey. There are also flower, hops, berries, and seed gardens scattered throughout Salem, Albany, and Corvallis. The huge number of company stores concentrated on Interstate 5 will have you thinking about some new Nikes, and Oregon State University will have you wearing orange and black long after Halloween is over. Be aware that many communities in this region are little more than wide spots in the road. In these tiny towns you might find only a gas station, a grocery store, a church or two, and a school. Watch out for any "School Crossing" signs: Oregon strictly enforces its speed-limit laws.

SALEM

24 miles from McMinnville, south on Hwy. 99 W and east on Hwy. 22, 45 miles south of Portland on I–5.

The state capital has a rich pioneer history, but before that it was the home of the Calapooia Indians, who called it Chemeketa, which means "place of rest." Salem is said to have been renamed by missionaries. Although trappers and farmers preceded them in the Willamette Valley, the Methodist missionaries had come in 1834 to minister to Native Americans, and they are credited with the founding of Salem. In 1842 they established the first academic institution west of the Rockies, which is now known as Willamette University. Salem became the capital when Oregon achieved statehood in 1859 (Oregon City was the capital of the Oregon Territory). Salem serves as the seat to Marion County as well as the home of the state fairgrounds. Government ranks as a major industry here, while the city's setting in the heart of the fertile Willamette Valley stimulates rich agricultural and food-processing industries. More than a dozen wineries are in or near Salem. The main attractions in Salem are west of Interstate 5 in and around the Capitol Mall.

GETTING HERE AND AROUND

Salem is located on Interstate 5 with easy access to Portland, Albany, and Eugene. **Hut Portland Airport Shuttle** provides transportation to Portland International Airport, which is one hour and 15 minutes away. Salem's McNary Field no longer has commercial airline service, but serves general aviation aircraft.

Bus transportation throughout Salem is provided by **Cherriots**. Amtrak operates regularly, and its train station is located at 500 13th Street SE.

ESSENTIALS

Contacts Cherriots. ⊕ *www.cherriots.org.* **Hut Portland Airport Shuttle.** ☎ *503/364–4444* ⊕ *www.portlandairportshuttle.com.*

Visitor Information Salem Convention & Visitors Center. ⊠ *181 High St. NE* ☎ *503/581–4325, 800/874–7012* ⊕ *www.travelsalem.com.*

EXPLORING

TOP ATTRACTIONS

Oregon Garden. Just outside the town of Silverton, a 25-minute drive from Salem, the Oregon Garden showcases the botanical diversity of the Willamette Valley and Pacific Northwest. Open 365 days a year, the 80-acre garden features themed plots ranging from a conifer forest to medicinal plants. There is also a whimsical children's garden complete with a model train, and another garden featuring the agricultural bounty of the area. A free narrated tram tour operates from April to October allowing visitors an overview of the garden before exploring on their own. ⊠ *879 W. Main St., Silverton* ☎ *503/874–8100, 877/674–2733* ⊕ *www.oregongarden.org* ▣ *$12* ☉ *Closed Jan.–Mar., Mon.–Thurs. and Nov.–Dec., Mon.–Wed.*

FAMILY **Willamette Heritage Center at The Mill.** Take a trip back in time to experience the story of Oregon's early pioneers and the industrial revolution. The **Thomas Kay Woolen Mill Museum** complex (circa 1889), complete with working waterwheels and millstream, looks as if the workers have just stepped away for a lunch break. Teasel gigging, napper flock bins, and the patented Furber double-acting napper are but a few of the machines and processes on display. The **Jason Lee House,** the **John D. Boon Home,** and the **Methodist Parsonage** are also part of the village. There is nothing grandiose about these early pioneer homes, the oldest frame structures in the Northwest, but they reveal a great deal about domestic life in the wilds of Oregon in the 1840s. ⊠ *1313 Mill St. SE* ☎ *503/585–7012* ⊕ *www.willametteheritage.org* ▣ *$7* ☉ *Closed Sun.*

Witness Tree Vineyard. Named for the ancient oak that towers over the vineyard (it was used as a surveyor's landmark in the 1850s), this winery produces premium Pinot Noir made entirely from grapes grown on its 100-acre estate nestled in the Eola Hills northwest of Salem. The vineyard also produces limited quantities of estate Chardonnay, Viognier, Pinot Blanc, Dolcetto, and a sweet dessert wine called Sweet Signé. Tours are available by appointment. ⊠ *7111 Spring Valley Rd. NW* ☎ *503/585–7874* ⊕ *www.witnesstreevineyard.com* ▣ *Tastings from $5* ☉ *Closed May–Oct., Mon. and Mar. and Apr., Nov.–mid-Dec., Mon.–Wed.*

WORTH NOTING

Bethel Heights Vineyard. Founded in 1977, Bethel Heights was one of the first vineyards planted in the Eola Hills region of the Willamette Valley. It produces Pinot Noir, Chardonnay, Pinot Blanc, and Pinot Gris. The tasting room has one of the most glorious panoramic views of any winery in the state; its terrace and picnic area overlook the surrounding vineyards, the valley below, and Mt. Jefferson in the distance. ⊠ *6060 Bethel Heights Rd. NW* ☎ *503/581–2262* ⊕ *www.bethelheights.com* ▧ *Tastings $10* ☉ *Closed Mon.*

Bush's Pasture Park. These 105 acres of rolling lawn and formal English gardens include the remarkably well-preserved Bush House, an 1878 Italianate mansion at the park's far-western boundary. It has 10 marble fireplaces and virtually all of its original furnishings, and can be visited only on informative tours. Bush Barn Art Center, behind the house, exhibits the work of Northwest artists and has a sales gallery. ⊠ *600 Mission St. SE* ☎ *503/363–4714* ⊕ *www.salemart.org* ▧ *House $6.*

Elsinore Theatre. This flamboyant Tudor Gothic vaudeville house opened on May 28, 1926, with Edgar Bergen in attendance. Clark Gable (who lived in nearby Silverton) and Gregory Peck performed on stage. The theater was designed to look like a castle, with a false-stone front, chandeliers, ironwork, and stained-glass windows. It's now a lively performing arts center with a busy schedule of bookings, and there are concerts on its Wurlitzer pipe organ. ⊠ *170 High St. SE* ☎ *503/375–3574* ⊕ *www.elsinoretheatre.com.*

FAMILY **Gilbert House Children's Museum.** This is a different kind of kids' museum; an amazing place to let the imagination run wild. Celebrating the life and the inventions of A.C. Gilbert, a Salem native who became a toy manufacturer and inventor, the historic houses included many themed interactive rooms along with a huge outdoor play structure. In addition to the children's activities, many beloved toys created by A.C. Gilbert are on display, including Erector sets and American Flyer trains. The wide range of indoor and outdoor interactive exhibits will appeal to children (and adults) of all ages. ⊠ *116 Marion St. NE* ☎ *503/371–3631* ⊕ *www.acgilbert.org* ▧ *$8* ☉ *Closed Mon. in fall and winter.*

Mount Angel Abbey. This Benedictine monastery on a 300-foot-high butte was founded in 1882 and is the site of one of two Modernist buildings in the United States designed by Finnish architect Alvar Aalto. A masterpiece of serene and thoughtful design, Aalto's library opened its doors in 1970, and has become a place of pilgrimage for students and aficionados of modern architecture. ⊠ *1 Abbey Dr., St. Benedict* ✛ *18 miles from Salem; east on Hwy. 213 and north on Hwy. 214* ☎ *503/845–3030* ⊕ *www.mountangelabbey.org* ▧ *Free* ☉ *Closed Sun.*

Oregon Capitol. A brightly gilded bronze statue of the *Oregon Pioneer* stands atop the 140-foot-high Capitol dome, looking north across the Capitol Mall. Built in 1939 with blocks of gray Vermont marble, Oregon's Capitol has an elegant yet austere neoclassical feel. East and

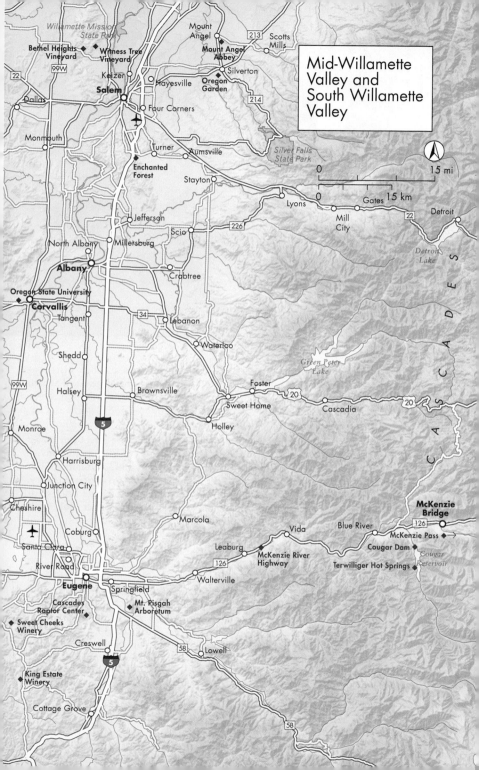

Mid-Willamette
Valley and
South Willamette
Valley

0   15 mi

0   15 km

Willamette Mission State Park

Mount Angel

Scotts Mills

213

Bethel Heights Vineyard

Witness Tree Vineyard

Mount Angel Abbey

Silverton

Keizer

Hayesville

Oregon Garden

Salem

214

Dallas

22

99W

Four Corners

Monmouth

Turner

Aumsville

Enchanted Forest

Silver Falls State Park

Stayton

Lyons

Gates

Detroit

Jefferson

Mill City

22

226

Detroit Lake

Scio

North Albany

Millersburg

Albany

Crabtree

Oregon State University

Corvallis

Tangent

34

Lebanon

Shedd

Waterloo

Green Peter Lake

Halsey

Brownsville

Foster

99W

Sweet Home

20

Cascadia

20

Monroe

Holley

Harrisburg

Junction City

Cheshire

Marcola

McKenzie Bridge

Coburg

Vida

Blue River

126

Santa Clara

Leaburg

McKenzie River Highway

McKenzie Pass

River Road

Eugene

126

Walterville

Cougar Dam

Terwilliger Hot Springs

Cougar Reservoir

Springfield

Cascades Raptor Center

Mt. Pisgah Arboretum

Sweet Cheeks Winery

Creswell

58

Lowell

King Estate Winery

5

Cottage Grove

58

C A S C A D E S

Oregon Capitol building in Salem

west wings were added in 1978. Relief sculptures and deft historical murals soften the interior. Tours of the rotunda, the House and Senate chambers, and the governor's office leave from the information center under the dome. ⊠ *900 Court St. NE* ☎ *503/986–1388* ⊕ *www.oregon-legislature.gov* 🎟 *Free* ⏾ *Closed weekends.*

Willamette University. Behind the Capitol, across State Street but half a world away, are the brick buildings and grounds of Willamette University, the oldest college in the West. Founded in 1842, Willamette has long been a breeding ground for aspiring politicians. **Hatfield Library,** built in 1986 on the banks of Mill Stream, is a handsome brick-and-glass building with a striking campanile; tall, prim **Waller Hall,** built in 1867, is one of the oldest buildings in the Pacific Northwest. ⊠ *900 State St.* ☎ *503/370–6300* ⊕ *www.willamette.edu* ⏾ *Closed weekends.*

EN ROUTE

Enchanted Forest. South of Salem, the Enchanted Forest is the closest thing Oregon has to a major theme park. The park has several attractions in forestlike surroundings, including a Big Timber Log Ride. On it, you ride logs through flumes that pass through a lumber mill and the woods. The ride—the biggest log ride in the Northwest—has a 25-foot roller-coaster dip and a 40-foot drop at the end. Other attractions include the Ice Mountain Bobsled roller coaster, the Haunted House, English Village, Storybook Lane, the Fantasy Fountains Water Light Show, Fort Fearless, and the Western town of Tofteville. ⊠ *8462 Enchanted Way SE, Turner* ✛ *7 miles south of Salem at Exit 248 off I–5* ☎ *503/363–3060, 503/371–4242* ⊕ *www.enchantedforest.com* 🎟 *$11.75, rides cost extra* ⏾ *Closed Apr. and Labor Day–end of Sept., weekdays, and Nov.–Mar.*

WHERE TO EAT AND STAY

$$ ITALIAN Fodor's Choice ★ 🍴 **DaVinci.** Salem politicos flock to this two-story downtown gathering spot for Italian-inspired dishes cooked in a wood-burning oven. No shortcuts are taken in the preparation, so don't come if you're in a rush. **Known for:** pasta made in-house; good wines by the glass; live music. [$] *Average main: $24* ✉ *180 High St. SE* ☎ *503/399–1413* 🌐 *www.davincisofsalem.com* 🕒 *No lunch.*

$$ HOTEL 🏨 **Grand Hotel in Salem.** Large rooms, with comfortable and luxurious furnishings, are the best in town, a good base for guests attending shows and meetings at Salem Conference Center or touring the region. **Pros:** spacious rooms; centrally located. **Cons:** some street noise; lacks character. [$] *Rooms from: $169* ✉ *201 Liberty St. SE* ☎ *503/540–7800, 877/540–7800* 🌐 *www.grandhotelsalem.com* 🛏 *193 rooms* 🍽 *Breakfast.*

$ RESORT 🏨 **Oregon Garden Resort.** Bright, spacious, and tastefully decorated rooms, each with a fireplace and a private landscaped patio or balcony, neighbor the Oregon Garden (admission is included in the rates). **Pros:** gorgeous grounds; luxurious rooms; pool and plenty of other amenities. **Cons:** a distance from other activities. [$] *Rooms from: $115* ✉ *895 W. Main St., Silverton* ☎ *503/874–2500* 🌐 *www.oregongardenresort.com* 🛏 *103 rooms* 🍽 *Breakfast.*

SHOPPING

Reed Opera House. These days the 1869 opera house in downtown Salem contains an eclectic collection of locally owned stores, shops, restaurants, bars, and bakeries, everything from art galleries to tattoo parlors. Its Trinity Ballroom hosts special events and celebrations. ✉ *189 Liberty St. NE* ☎ *503/391–4481* 🌐 *www.reedoperahouse.com.*

Woodburn Company Stores. Located 18 miles north of Salem just off Interstate 5 are more than 100 brand-name outlet stores, including Nike, Calvin Klein, Bose, Gymboree, OshKosh B'Gosh, Ann Taylor, Levi's, Chico's, Fossil, The North Face, and Columbia Sportswear. There's also a small playground and a couple of places to eat. ✉ *1001 Arney Rd., Woodburn* ☎ *503/981–1900, 888/664–7467* 🌐 *www.premiumoutlets.com/outlet/woodburn.*

SPORTS AND THE OUTDOORS

RECREATIONAL AREAS

Silver Falls State Park. Hidden amid old-growth Douglas firs in the foothills of the Cascades, this is the largest state park in Oregon (8,700 acres). South Falls, roaring over the lip of a mossy basalt bowl into a deep pool 177 feet below, is the main attraction here, but 13 other waterfalls—half of them more than 100 feet high—are accessible to hikers. The best time to visit is in the fall, when vine maples blaze with brilliant color, or early spring, when the forest floor is carpeted with trilliums and yellow violets. There are picnic facilities and a day lodge; in winter you can cross-country ski. Camping facilities include tent and trailer sites, cabins, and a horse camp. ✉ *20024 Silver Falls Hwy. SE, Sublimity* ☎ *503/873–8681, 800/551–6949* 🌐 *www.oregonstateparks.org* 🎟 *$5 per vehicle.*

Willamette Mission State Park. Along pastoral lowlands by the Willamette River, this serene park holds the largest black cottonwood tree in the United States. A thick-barked behemoth by a small pond, the 275-year-old tree has upraised arms that bring to mind J.R.R. Tolkien's fictional Ents. Site of Reverend Jason Lee's 1834 pioneer mission, the park also offers quiet strolling and picnicking in an old orchard and along the river. The Wheatland Ferry, at the north end of the park, began carrying covered wagons across the Willamette in 1844 and is still in operation today. ⊠ *Wheatland Rd.* ✛ *8 miles north of Salem, I–5 Exit 263* ☎ *503/393–1172, 800/551–6949* ⊕ *www.oregonstateparks.org* ⬛ *$5 per vehicle.*

ALBANY

20 miles from Salem, south on I–5 and west on U.S. 20.

Known as the grass-seed capital of the world, Albany has some of the most historic buildings in Oregon. Some 700 buildings, scattered over a 100-block area in three districts, include every major architectural style developed in the United States since 1850. The area is listed on the National Register of Historic Places. Eight covered bridges can also be seen on a half-hour drive from Albany. Oregon has the largest collection of covered bridges in the western United States, and the Willamette Valley has more than 34 of the wooden structures.

GETTING HERE AND AROUND

Albany is located on Interstate 5 with easy access to Portland, Salem, and Eugene. Portland International Airport is one hour, 40 minutes away, and the Eugene airport is one hour away to the south. Several shuttle services are available from both airports.

Albany Transit System provides two routes for intercity travel. The Linn-Benton loop system provides for transportation between Albany and Corvallis. Albany is served by Amtrak.

ESSENTIALS

Visitor Information Albany Visitors Association. ⊠ *110 3rd Ave. SE* ☎ *541/928–0911, 800/526–2256* ⊕ *www.albanyvisitors.com.*

EXPLORING

Albany Historic Carousel and Museum. It's not often that you get to watch a carousel being built, but that's exactly what's happening here. Craftsmen and volunteers from the Albany area have come together to contribute thousands of hours to carving and painting a huge array of whimsical carousel creatures ranging from traditional horses to giant frogs and dragons. They hope to have the carousel in operation in 2017, but there have been plenty of delays in the project so it's best to call ahead. In the meantime you can enjoy watching the creations come together, as well as viewing many historical carousel artifacts in the museum. ⊠ *250 S.W. Broadalbin St.* ☎ *541/791–3340* ⊕ *albanycarousel.com.*

WHERE TO EAT

$ ✕ **Novak's Hungarian.** Since 1984, the Novak family has been a delightful
HUNGARIAN   fixture in Albany's dining scene. Whether you're ordering Hungarian hash and eggs in the morning or chicken paprika served over homemade Hungarian pearl noodles for dinner, you can't go wrong in this

establishment. **Known for:** good, hearty Hungarian fare; locally sourced ingredients; familial atmosphere. $ *Average main: $14* ✉ *208 2nd St. SW* ☎ *541/967–9488* ⊕ *www.novakshungarian.com.*

$$ ✗ **Sybaris.** A rotating menu at this fine bistro in Albany's historic downtown changes monthly and features flavorful cuisine at reasonable prices. The restaurant strives to ensure that most of the ingredients, including the lamb, eggs, and vegetables, are raised within 10 miles. **Known for:** reasonable prices; menu changes monthly; locally sourced products. $ *Average main: $20* ✉ *442 1st Ave. W* ☎ *541/928–8157* ⊕ *www.sybarisbistro.com* ☾ *Closed Sun. and Mon. No lunch.*

ECLECTIC

Fodor's Choice

★

CORVALLIS

4

10 miles southwest of Albany on U.S. 20.

Corvallis is a small city that's best known as the home of Oregon State University and its Beavers athletic teams. Driving the area's economy are a growing engineering and high-tech industry, a burgeoning wine industry, and more traditional local agricultural crops, such as grass and legume seeds. The town and its environs offer plenty of outdoor activities as well as scenic attractions, from covered bridges to wineries and gardens.

GETTING HERE AND AROUND

Corvallis Transit System (CTS) operates eight bus routes throughout the city. **Hut Shuttle** provides transportation between Corvallis and the Portland airport, located one hour, 53 minutes away. **OmniShuttle** provides transportation between Corvallis and the Eugene airport, 50 minutes away. Corvallis Municipal Airport is a public airport 4 miles south of the city.

ESSENTIALS

Visitor Information Corvallis Tourism. ✉ *420 N.W. 2nd St.* ☎ *541/757–1544, 800/334–8118* ⊕ *www.visitcorvallis.com.*

EXPLORING

Oregon State University. It's a thrill to be on campus on game day, when students are a sea of orange and black cheering on their beloved Beavers. This 400-acre campus, west of the city center, was established as a land-grant institution in 1868. OSU has more than 26,000 students, many of them studying the university's nationally recognized programs in conservation biology, agricultural sciences, nuclear engineering, forestry, fisheries and wildlife management, community health, pharmacy, and zoology. ✉ *15th and Jefferson Sts.* ☎ *541/737–1000* ⊕ *oregonstate.edu.*

WHERE TO EAT AND STAY

$$$ ✗ **Del Alma.** This multilevel waterfront eatery gives every table a nice view of the river and puts a modern spin on tapas, bringing unexpected flavors and textures to classic Latin food. The menu features both tapas and larger dishes, with a strong emphasis on seafood and beef. **Known for:** tapas; Latin-inspired cocktails; great river views. $ *Average main: $28* ✉ *136 S.W. Washington Ave.* ☎ *541/753–2222* ⊕ *delalmarestaurant.com* ☾ *Closed Sun. No lunch.*

LATIN AMERICAN

$$$
MODERN
AMERICAN
Fodor's Choice
★

✕ **Gathering Together Farm.** When spring arrives, it means that the organic farmers outside of Philomath are serving their bounty. Fresh vegetables, pizzas, local lamb, pork, and halibut are frequent highlights on a menu that features simple fresh ingredients impeccably prepared. **Known for:** coppa; organic produce from collective of local farms. $ *Average main: $25* ⌖ *25159 Grange Hall Rd., Philomath* ☎ *541/929–4270* ⊕ *www. gatheringtogetherfarm.com* ⊗ *No dinner Tues. or Wed.*

$
HOTEL
Fodor's Choice
★

⌂ **Boulder Falls Inn.** One of the chicest places to stay in the area, this business-boutique hotel features sleek rooms and suites filled with locally produced furniture, many of which look out on a huge koi pond surrounded by an authentic Japanese garden. **Pros:** sleek rooms; excellent dining; on-site Japanese garden. **Cons:** location somewhat removed from area attractions. $ *Rooms from: $120* ⌖ *505 Mullins Dr., Lebanon* ☎ *541/405–7025* ⊕ *boulderfallsinn.com* ⇝ *84 rooms* ⦿ *Breakfast.*

SPORTS AND THE OUTDOORS
RECREATIONAL AREAS

Fodor's Choice
★

Siuslaw National Forest. The forest, starting just 2 miles from Corvallis and extending to the coast, includes the Oregon Dunes National Recreation Area and the Cape Perpetua Interpretive Center. Within the park is the highest point in the Coast Range, Mary's Peak (4,097 feet), offering panoramic views of the Cascades, the Willamette Valley, and the rest of the Coast Range. On a clear day you can see as far as the Pacific Ocean. There are several picnicking areas, more than 10 miles of hiking trails, and a small campground, as well as stands of noble fir and alpine meadows. You can access Mary's Peak from Highway 34 between Corvallis and Newport and the central coast. Several other major highways (Highways 26, 6, 18, 26, and 126) also run through the forest between the Willamette Valley and the coast, providing access to recreation areas. ⌖ *Forest office, 3200 S.W. Jefferson Way* ☎ *541/750–7000* ⊕ *www.fs.fed.us/r6/siuslaw* ⌖ *$5 per vehicle at some recreation sites.*

SWIMMING

FAMILY
Osborn Aquatic Center. This is not your ordinary lap pool. There are waterslides, a water channel, water cannons, and floor geysers. The indoor pools are open all year. ⌖ *1940 N.W. Highland Dr.* ☎ *541/766–7946* ⊕ *www.corvallisoregon.gov/index.aspx?page=57* ⌖ *$6.*

SOUTH WILLAMETTE VALLEY

Lane County rests at the southern end of the Willamette Valley, encompassing Eugene, Springfield, Drain, McKenzie Bridge, and Cottage Grove. Visitors can enjoy a wide range of outdoor activities such as running, fishing, swimming, white-water rafting, and deep-woods hiking along the McKenzie River, while Eugene offers great food, shopping, and the arts. There are plenty of wineries to enjoy, too, as well as cheering on the Oregon Ducks. To the west lies the Oregon Dunes Recreation Area, and to the east are the beautiful central Oregon communities of Sisters, Bend, and Redmond.

EUGENE

63 miles south of Corvallis on I–5.

Eugene was founded in 1846, when Eugene Skinner staked the first federal land-grant claim for pioneers. Eugene is consistently given high marks for its "livability." As the home of the University of Oregon, a large student and former-student population lends Eugene a youthful vitality and countercultural edge. Full of parks and oriented to the outdoors, Eugene is a place where bike paths are used, pedestrians *always* have the right-of-way, and joggers are so plentiful that the city is known as the Running Capital of the World. Shopping and commercial streets surround the Eugene Hilton and the Hult Center for the Performing Arts, the two most prominent downtown buildings. During football season you can count on the U of O Ducks being the primary topic of most conversations.

4

GETTING HERE AND AROUND
Eugene's airport has rental cars, cabs, and shuttles that make the 15-minute trip to Eugene's city center. By train, Amtrak stops in the heart of downtown. Getting around Lane County's communities is easy with **Lane Transit District** public transportation. Eugene is very bicycle-friendly.

ESSENTIALS
Visitor Information Travel Lane County. ⊠ *754 Olive St.* ☎ *541/484–5307, 800/547–5445* ⊕ *www.eugenecascadescoast.org.*

EXPLORING
TOP ATTRACTIONS
FAMILY **Cascades Raptor Center.** This birds-of-prey nature center and hospital hosts more than 30 species of birds. A visit is a great outing for kids, who can learn what owls eat, why and where birds migrate, and all sorts of other raptor facts. Some of the full-time residents include turkey vultures, bald eagles, owls, hawks, falcons, and kites. ⊠ *32275 Fox Hollow Rd.* ☎ *541/485–1320* ⊕ *www.eraptors.org* ⊴ *$8* ⊙ *Closed Mon.*

Eugene Saturday Market. Held every Saturday from April through the middle of November, the Saturday Market is a great place to browse for handicrafts, try out local food carts, or simply kick back and people-watch while listening to live music at the Market Stage. ⊠ *126 E. 8th Ave.* ☎ *541/686–8885* ⊕ *www.eugenesaturdaymarket.org.*

King Estate Winery. One of Oregon's largest producers is known for their crisp Pinot Gris and silky Pinot Noir and boasts the world's largest organic vineyard. The visitors center offers wine tasting and production tours, and the restaurant highlights local meats and organic produce grown in the estate gardens. ⊠ *80854 Territorial Rd.* ☎ *541/942–9874* ⊕ *www.kingestate.com* ⊴ *Tastings $10* ⊙ *Closed Mon. and Tues. in winter.*

Lane County Farmers' Market. Across the street from the Eugue Saturday Market, the Lane County market offers produce grown or made in Oregon. Hours and days vary throughout the year. ⊠ *Corner of 8th Ave. and Oak St.* ☎ *541/431–4923* ⊕ *www.lanecountyfarmersmarket.org/markets* ⊙ *Closed Jan.*

Fresh produce at a farmers' market in Eugene

Ninkasi Brewing Company. Named after the Sumerian goddess of fermentation, Ninkasi has grown from a little start-up in 2006 to a major supplier of craft beer. Its flagship beer, Total Domination IPA, is signature Northwest, with bold flavor and lots of hops. Visit the tasting room and enjoy a tasting flight or a pint, either indoors or on the patio. The beer menu changes often and includes a few hard-to-find limited-production beers. If you'd like a little food to go with your beer, you'll usually find one of Eugene's many food carts right there on the patio. Free brewery tours are offered daily. ⊠ *272 Van Buren St.* ☎ *541/344–2739* ⊕ *www. ninkasibrewing.com.*

WORTH NOTING

Alton Baker Park. This parcel of open land on the banks of the Willamette River is named after the late publisher of Eugene's newspaper, the *Register-Guard,* and is the site of many community events. Live music is performed in summer at the Cuthbert Amphitheater. There's fine hiking and biking on a footpath that runs along the river for the length of the park, and an 18-hole disc golf course. Also worth seeing is the Whilamut Natural Area, an open space with 13 "talking stones," each with an inscription. ⊠ *200 Day Island Rd.* ☎ *541/682–4906* ⊕ *www. altonbakerpark.com/.*

Jordan Schnitzer Museum of Art. Works from the 20th and 21st centuries are a specialty in these handsome galleries on the University of Oregon campus. They feature works by many leading Pacific Northwest artists, and European, Korean, Chinese, and Japanese works are also on view, as are 300 works commissioned by the Works Progress Administration in the 1930s and '40s. You can also view an ever-changing collection of important works from private collections by internationally recognized artists through the museum's Masterworks On Loan program. ✉ *1430 Johnson La.* ☎ *541/346–3027* ⊕ *jsma.uoregon.edu* 🎫 *$5* ⊘ *Closed Mon. and Tues.*

FAMILY **Mount Pisgah Arboretum.** This beautiful nature preserve near southeast Eugene includes extensive all-weather trails, educational programs for all ages, and facilities for special events. Its visitor center holds workshops and features native amphibian and reptile terraria; microscopes for exploring tiny seeds, bugs, feathers, and snakeskins; "touch me" exhibits; reference books; and a working viewable beehive. ✉ *34901 Frank Parrish Rd.* ☎ *541/747–3817* ⊕ *www.mountpisgaharboretum. org* 🎫 *Parking $4.*

FAMILY **Science Factory.** Formerly the Willamette Science and Technology Center (WISTEC), and still known to locals by its former name, Eugene's imaginative, hands-on museum assembles rotating exhibits designed for curious young minds. The adjacent **planetarium,** one of the largest in the Pacific Northwest, presents star shows and entertainment events. ✉ *2300 Leo Harris Pkwy.* ☎ *541/682–7888* ⊕ *www.sciencefactory.org* 🎫 *$4 for exhibit hall or planetarium, $7 for both* ⊘ *Closed Oregon Ducks home football games; exhibit hall Mon. and Tues.; planetarium weekdays.*

Sweet Cheeks Winery. This estate vineyard lies on a prime sloping hillside in the heart of the Willamette Valley appellation. It also supplies grapes to several award-winning wineries. Bring a picnic and enjoy the amazing view from the lawn outside the tasting room, or take advantage of the food available for purchase. Friday-night tastings are embellished with cheese pairings and live music. ✉ *27007 Briggs Hill Rd.* ☎ *541/349–9463, 877/309–9463* ⊕ *www.sweetcheekswinery.com* ⊘ *Closed Sun. and Mon.*

University of Oregon. The true heart of Eugene lies southeast of the city center at its university. Several fine old buildings can be seen on the 250-acre campus; **Deady Hall,** built in 1876, is the oldest. More than 400 varieties of trees grace the bucolic grounds, along with outdoor sculptures that include *The Pioneer* and *The Pioneer Mother.* The two bronze figures by Alexander Phimster Proctor were dedicated to the men and women who settled the Oregon Territory and less than a generation later founded the university. ✉ *1585 E. 13th Ave.* ☎ *541/346–1000* ⊕ *www.uoregon.edu.*

University of Oregon Museum of Natural and Cultural History. Relics on display are devoted to Pacific Northwest anthropology and the natural sciences. Highlights include the fossil collection of Thomas Condon, Oregon's first geologist, and a pair of 9,000-year-old sandals made of sagebrush. ✉ *1680 E. 15th Ave.* ☎ *541/346–3024* ⊕ *natural-history. uoregon.edu* 🎫 *$5* ⊘ *Closed Mon.*

WHERE TO EAT

$ ✕ **The CiderHouse at WildCraft Cider Works.** With the laid-back atmosphere of a brewpub and a long list of house-crafted ciders, this casual spot is a great place to try out WildCraft's locally celebrated dry ciders. The menu is equally impressive with Oregon-style comfort food ranging from mac and cheese with truffle oil to sesame tofu brochettes. **Known**

PACIFIC
NORTHWEST
Fodor's Choice
★

for: house-crafted ciders; Oregon-style comfort food. [$] *Average main: $14* ✉ *390 Lincoln St.* ☎ *541/735–3506* 🌐 *wildcraftciderworks.com* 🕒 *Closed Sun. and Mon.*

$$ PACIFIC NORTHWEST 🍴 **Grit Kitchen and Wine.** You know you're in for local, seasonal ingredients when the chalkboard in this intimate place right across the street from the Ninkasi Brewery in Eugene's eccentric Whiteaker neighborhood lists nearly 20 local farmers and purveyors who are suppliers. The menu changes often, depending on what's in season. **Known for:** the weekly changing four-course feast; Northwest cuisine; products and ingredients come from 20 local farmers and purveyors. [$] *Average main: $21* ✉ *1080 W. 3rd St.* ☎ *541/343–0501* 🌐 *gritkitchen.com* 🕒 *No lunch.*

$$$ FRENCH 🍴 **Marché.** Located in the bustling Fifth Street Market, this renowned Eugene restaurant works with more than a dozen local farmers to bring fresh, local organic food to the table. Specialties include salmon, halibut, sturgeon, and beef tenderloin, braised pork shoulders, and outstanding local oysters paired with an extensive wine list featuring lots of Oregon wines. **Known for:** fresh Sunday beignets; sourced from a dozen local farmers; located in Fifth Street Market. [$] *Average main: $30* ✉ *296 E. 5th Ave.* ☎ *541/342–3612* 🌐 *www.marcherestaurant.com.*

$$$ ITALIAN 🍴 **Ristorante Italiano.** The chef uses fresh local produce from the restaurant's own farm, but this bistro-style café across from the University of Oregon is best known for its authentic Italian cuisine, with a heavy emphasis on fresh local seafood. The menu changes according to the season, but staples include delicious salads and soups, ravioli, grilled chicken, pizza, and sandwiches. **Known for:** seasonal menus; outdoor seating. [$] *Average main: $26* ✉ *Excelsior Inn, 754 E. 13th Ave.* ☎ *541/342–6963, 800/321–6963* 🕒 *No lunch Sat.*

WHERE TO STAY

$ B&B/INN 🏨 **Campbell House.** One of the oldest structures in Eugene, built in 1892, combines architectural details and a mixture of century-old antiques and reproductions to lend each of the rooms a distinctive personality. **Pros:** classic architecture; comfortable rooms; well-kept grounds. **Cons:** rooms lack some of the amenities of nearby hotels. [$] *Rooms from: $129* ✉ *252 Pearl St.* ☎ *541/343–1119, 800/264–2519* 🌐 *www.campbellhouse.com* 🛏 *18 rooms* 🍽 *Breakfast.*

$$ B&B/INN Fodor'sChoice ★ 🏨 **C'est la Vie Inn.** Listed on the National Register of Historic Places, this 1891 Queen Anne Victorian bed-and-breakfast provides Old World comfort and modern-day amenities in its luxurious and romantic guest rooms. **Pros:** outstanding service and value. **Cons:** few rooms. [$] *Rooms from: $160* ✉ *1006 Taylor St.* ☎ *541/302-3014* 🌐 *cestlavieinn.com* 🛏 *4 rooms* 🍽 *Breakfast.*

$ B&B/INN Fodor'sChoice ★ 🏨 **Excelsior Inn.** Quiet sophistication, attention to architectural detail, and rooms furnished in a refreshingly understated manner, each with a marble-and-tile bath and some with fireplaces, suggest a European inn. **Pros:** romantic accommodations; excellent service and restaurant. **Cons:** formal in a casual town. [$] *Rooms from: $135* ✉ *754 E. 13th Ave.* ☎ *541/342–6963, 800/321–6963* 🌐 *www.excelsiorinn.com* 🛏 *14 rooms* 🍽 *Breakfast.*

$$$$ HOTEL **Inn at the 5th.** This upscale boutique hotel, set among the shops and restaurants of the trendy Fifth Street Public Market, features subtly elegant rooms and suites. **Pros:** most rooms have fireplaces; great location surrounded by boutiques and restaurants. **Cons:** no self-parking. [$] *Rooms from: $259* ✉ *205 E. 6th Ave.* ☎ *541/743–4099* 🌐 *www.innat5th.com* 🛏 *69 rooms* 🍴 *No meals.*

NIGHTLIFE AND PERFORMING ARTS

Hult Center for the Performing Arts. This is the locus of Eugene's cultural life. Renowned for the quality of its acoustics, the center has two theaters that are home to Eugene's symphony and opera. ✉ *1 Eugene Center* ☎ *541/682–5087 administration, 541/682–5000 tickets* 🌐 *www.hultcenter.org.*

Fodor's Choice ★ **Oregon Bach Festival.** Conductor Helmuth Rilling leads the internationally known Oregon Bach Festival every summer. Concerts, chamber music, and social events—held mainly in Eugene at the Hult Center and the University of Oregon School of Music but also in Corvallis and Florence—are part of this three-week event. ✉ *1 Eugene Center* ☎ *541/682–5000 for tickets, 800/457–1486 for information* 🌐 *oregonbachfestival.com.*

SPORTS AND THE OUTDOORS

BIKING AND JOGGING

The **River Bank Bike Path,** originating in Alton Baker Park on the Willamette's north bank, is a level and leisurely introduction to Eugene's topography. It's one of 120 miles of trails in the area. **Prefontaine Trail,** used by area runners, travels through level fields and forests for 1½ miles.

RECREATIONAL AREAS

FAMILY **Dexter State Recreation Site.** A 20-minute drive southeast of Eugene on the western shores of Dexter Reservoir, this recreation site offers disc golf, picnic areas, boat launches, and plenty of hiking. ✥ *Hwy. 58, between mileposts 11 and 12.*

FAMILY **Skinner Butte Park.** Rising from the south bank of the Willamette River, this forested enclave provides the best views of any of the city's parks; it also has the greatest historic cachet, since it was here that Eugene Skinner staked the claim that put Eugene on the map. Children can scale a replica of Skinner Butte, uncover fossils, and cool off under a rain circle. Skinner Butte Loop leads to the top of Skinner Butte, traversing sometimes difficult terrain through a mixed-conifer forest. ✉ *248 Cheshire Ave.* ☎ *541/682–4800* 🎟 *Free.*

SHOPPING

Fifth Street Public Market. Tourists coming to the Willamette Valley, especially to Eugene, can't escape without experiencing the Fifth Street Public Market in downtown Eugene. There are plenty of boutiques and crafts shops, a large gourmet food hall with a bakery, and restaurants serving sushi, pizza, and seafood. ✉ *296 E. 5th Ave.* ☎ *541/484–0383* 🌐 *www.5stmarket.com.*

Valley River Center. The largest shopping center between Portland and San Francisco has five department stores, including Macy's and JCPenney, plus 130 specialty shops and a food court. ✉ *293 Valley River Center* ☎ *541/683–5513* 🌐 *www.valleyrivercenter.com.*

MCKENZIE BRIDGE

58 miles east of Eugene on Hwy. 126.

On the beautiful McKenzie River, lakes, waterfalls, and covered bridges surround the town of McKenzie Bridge and wilderness trails in the Cascades. Fishing, skiing, backpacking, and rafting are among the most popular activities in the area.

GETTING HERE AND AROUND

McKenzie Bridge is about an hour from Eugene, on Highway 126. It is just 38 miles from Hoodoo Ski Area, but its proximity can be deceiving if the snow is heavy. Bend also is close at 64 miles to the east.

EXPLORING

McKenzie River Highway. Highway 126, as it heads east from Eugene, is known as the McKenzie River Highway. Following the curves of the river, it passes grazing lands, fruit and nut orchards, and the small riverside hamlets of the McKenzie Valley. From the highway you can glimpse the bouncing, bubbling, blue-green McKenzie River, one of Oregon's top fishing, boating, and white-water rafting spots, against a backdrop of densely forested mountains, splashing waterfalls, and jet-black lava beds. The small town of McKenzie Bridge marks the end of the McKenzie River Highway and the beginning of the 26-mile McKenzie River National Recreation Trail, which heads north through the Willamette National Forest along portions of the Old Santiam Wagon Road. ✉ *McKenzie Bridge.*

OFF THE BEATEN PATH

McKenzie Pass. Just beyond McKenzie Bridge, Highway 242 begins a steep, 22-mile eastward climb to McKenzie Pass in the Cascade Range. The scenic highway, which passes through the Mt. Washington Wilderness Area and continues to the town of Sisters, is generally closed November through June because of heavy snow. Novice motorists take note, this is not a drive for the timid: it's a challenging exercise in negotiating tight curves at quickly fluctuating, often slow speeds—the skid marks on virtually every turn attest to hasty braking—so take it slow, and don't be intimidated by cars on your tail itching to take the turns more quickly. The route is closed to trucks and large trailers and motor homes. ✉ *McKenzie Bridge.*

WHERE TO EAT AND STAY

$ AMERICAN FAMILY

🍴 **Takoda's Restaurant.** A popular roadside café serves burgers, sandwiches, great soups, salads, pizza, and daily specials. The burger selection includes not only beef, but seafood, chicken, turkey, and veggie options. **Known for:** great burger options; video game room for kids. [$] *Average main: $11* ✉ *91806 Mill Creek Rd., Milepost 47.5 McKenzie Hwy., Blue River* ☎ *541/822–1153* 🌐 *www.takodasrainbow.com.*

$ RESORT FAMILY

🏨 **Belknap Hot Springs Resort.** A pleasant lodge, with comfortable though not luxurious rooms, and a campground with both tent trailer sites, are nestled onto the banks of the beautiful McKenzie River. **Pros:** hot springs; wooded location. **Cons:** 14-day cancellation policy; two-night minimum on weekends; trailers and motor homes detract from the rustic atmosphere. [$] *Rooms from: $120* ✉ *59296 Belknap Springs Rd.* ☎ *541/822–3512* 🌐 *www.belknaphotsprings.com* 🛏 *19 rooms, 7 cabins* 🍽 *Breakfast.*

$ B&B/INN Fodor's Choice ★ **Eagle Rock Lodge.** These wood-paneled rooms filled with quilts and gorgeous custom furniture are surprisingly luxurious and provide a romantic, relaxing riverside retreat in the woods. **Pros:** great location on the McKenzie River; comfortable atmosphere. **Cons:** a distance from nonoutdoor activities. [$] *Rooms from: $130* ✉ *49198 McKenzie Hwy., Vida* ☎ *541/822–3630, 888/773–4333* 🌐 *www.eaglerocklodge.com* 🛏 *8 rooms* 🍴 *Breakfast.*

SHOPPING

Organic Redneck. On the way to McKenzie Bridge from Eugene, this farm stand offers seasonal, certified organic produce grown right on the family's farm. Blueberries are the specialty here, and they've got dried versions available for those who visit out of season. ✉ *44382 Mckenzie Hwy., Leaburg* ☎ *541/896–3928* 🌐 *www.ogredneck.com.*

SPORTS AND THE OUTDOORS

GOLF

Tokatee Golf Club. Ranked one of the best golf courses in Oregon by *Golf Digest*, this 18-hole beauty is tucked away near the McKenzie River with views of the Three Sisters Mountains, native ponds, and streams. *Tokatee* is a Chinook word meaning "a place of restful beauty." The course offers a practice range, carts, lessons, rentals, a coffee shop and snack bar, and Wi-Fi. ✉ *54947 McKenzie Hwy.* ☎ *541/822–3220, 800/452–6376* 🌐 *www.tokatee.com* 🎟 *18 holes $49; 9 holes $29* ⛳ *9 or 18 holes, 6806 yards, par 72.*

RECREATIONAL AREAS

Cougar Dam and Reservoir. Four miles outside of McKenzie Bridge is the highest embankment dam ever built by the Army Corps of Engineers—452 feet above the streambed. The resulting reservoir, on the South Fork McKenzie River, covers 1,280 acres. The dam generates 25 megawatts of power, and includes a fish collection and sorting facility, and a temperature control tower to keep the downstream water at a suitable temperature for spawning. The public recreation areas are in the Willamette National Forest. You can visit the dam year-round, but some campgrounds are open only from April to September. ✉ *Willamette National Forest, Forest Rd. 19* ☎ *541/822–3381* 🎟 *Free.*

Terwilliger Hot Springs (Cougar Hot Springs). Bring a towel and enjoy the soaking pools in this natural hot-springs area. Located an hour east of Eugene off of Highway 126, the pools are a short hike from the parking area, and include a changing area. Soaking aficionados will find Terwilliger to be rustic, which many regard as an advantage, though the popularity of this beautiful spot can be a drawback. The pools are in a forest of old-growth firs and cedars, and just downstream is a beautiful lagoon complete with waterfall that is also suitable for swimming. Clothing is optional. ✉ *Off Forest Rd. 19, Blue River* ☎ *541/822–3381* 🎟 *$6.*

Fodor's Choice ★ **Willamette National Forest.** Stretching 110 miles along the western slopes of the Cascade Range, this forest boasts boundless recreation opportunities, including waterfall exploration, camping, hiking, boating, ATV riding, and winter sports. It extends from the Mt. Jefferson area east of Salem to the Calapooya Mountains northeast of Roseburg, encompassing 1,675,407 acres. ⊠ *3106 Pierce Pkwy., Suite D, Springfield* 🕾 *541/225–6300* ⊕ *www.fs.usda.gov/willamette.*

WHITE-WATER RAFTING

FAMILY **High Country Expeditions.** Raft the white waters of the McKenzie River on a guided full- or half-day tour. You'll bounce through rapids, admire old-growth forest, and watch osprey and blue herons fishing. The outfit provides life jackets, splash gear, wet suits, booties (if requested), boating equipment, paddling instructions, river safety talk, a three-course riverside meal, and shuttle service back to your vehicle. Full-day trips are $90, half-day trips $60. ⊠ *Belknap Hot Springs Resort, 59296 N. Belknap Springs Rd.* 🕾 *541/822–8288, 888/461–7238* ⊕ *www.highcountryexpeditions.com.*

COLUMBIA RIVER GORGE AND MT. HOOD

WELCOME TO COLUMBIA RIVER GORGE AND MT. HOOD

TOP REASONS TO GO

★ **Orchards and vineyards:** Dozens of farm stands selling apples, pears, peaches, cherries, and berries, and wine-tasting rooms are open to visitors around Hood River.

★ **Outdoor rec mecca:** From kiteboarding in the Columbia River to mountain biking the slopes of Mt. Hood to hiking among the roaring waterfalls of the Gorge, this is a region tailor-made for adventure junkies.

★ **Historico-luxe:** Grand dames like Timberline Lodge and the Columbia Gorge Hotel exude history and architectural distinction.

★ **Road-tripping:** From Portland, you can make a full 250-mile loop through the Gorge out to Goldendale, Washington, returning to Hood River and then circling Mt. Hood to the south.

★ **Hop havens:** The Gorge/Hood area has a fast-growing proliferation of taprooms, from Stevenson's tiny Walking Man Brewing to Pfriem, in Hood River.

1 Columbia River Gorge. The dams of the early 20th century transformed the Columbia River from the raging torrent that vexed Lewis and Clark in 1805 to the breathtaking but comparatively docile waterway that hosts kiteboarders and windsurfers today. Auto visitors have been scoping out the Gorge's picturesque bluffs and waterfalls for quite a while now—the road between Troutdale and The Dalles, on which construction began in 1913, was the country's first planned scenic highway.

2 Mt. Hood. Visible from 100 miles away, Mt. Hood (or simply "the Mountain," as some Portlanders call it) is the kind of rock that commands respect. It's holy ground for mountaineers, more than 10,000 of whom make a summit bid each year. Sightseers are often shocked by the summer snows, but skiers rejoice, keeping the mountain's resorts busy year-round. Mingle with laid-back powderhounds and other outdoorsy types in the hospitality villas of Welches and Government Camp.

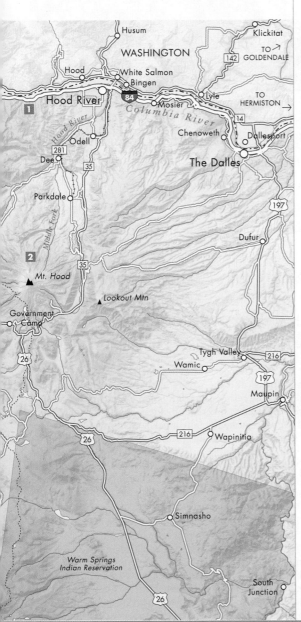

GETTING ORIENTED

The mighty Columbia River flows west through the Cascade Range, past the Mt. Hood Wilderness Area, to Astoria. It's a natural border between Oregon and Washington to the north, and bridges link roads on both sides of the Gorge at Biggs Junction, The Dalles, Hood River, and Cascade Locks. The Gorge's watery recreation corridor stretches from Portland's east-ernmost suburbs past Hood River and The Dalles out to Maryhill and Goldendale, Washington. For portions of that drive, Mt. Hood looms to the southwest. While the massive peak feels remote, the snowcapped heights are just 60 miles east of Portland. Hood River drains the mountain's north side, emptying into the Columbia at its namesake town. Follow the river upstream and you'll trade the warm, low-elevation climes of the Gorge for the high country's tall pines and late-season snows.

Updated
by Andrew
Collins

Volcanoes, lava flows, Ice Age floodwaters, and glaciers were nature's tools of choice when carving a breathtaking, nearly 100-mile landscape now called the Columbia River Gorge. Proof of human civilization here reaches back 31,000 years, and excavations near The Dalles have uncovered evidence that salmon fishing is a 10,000-year-old tradition in these parts. In 1805 Lewis and Clark discovered the Columbia River, the only major waterway that leads to the Pacific. Their first expedition was a treacherous route through wild, plunging rapids, but their successful navigation set a new exodus in motion.

Today the river has been tamed by a comprehensive system of hydro-electric dams and locks, and the towns in these parts are laid-back recreation hamlets whose residents harbor a fierce pride in their shared natural resources. Sightseers, hikers, and skiers have long found contentment in this robust region, officially labeled a National Scenic Area in 1986. They're joined these days by epicures scouring the Columbia's banks in search of farm-to-table cuisine, artisanal hop houses, and top-shelf vino. Highlights of the Columbia River Gorge include Multnomah Falls, Bonneville Dam, the rich orchard and vineyard land of Hood River, and Maryhill Museum of Art. Sailboaters, windsurfers, and kiteboarders take advantage of the blustery Gorge winds in the summer, their colorful sails decorating the waterway like windswept confetti.

To the south of Hood River are all the alpine attractions of the 11,250-foot-high Mt. Hood. With more than 2.2 million people living just up the road in greater Portland, you'd think this mountain playground would be overrun, but it's still easy to find solitude in the 300,000-acre wilderness surrounding the peak. Some of the world's best skiers take advantage of the powder on Hood, and they stick around in summertime for the longest ski season in North America at Palmer Snowfield, above Timberline Lodge.

COLUMBIA RIVER GORGE AND MT. HOOD PLANNER

WHEN TO GO

Winter weather in the Mt. Hood area is much more severe than in Portland and the Willamette Valley, and occasionally rough conditions permeate the Gorge, too. Rarely, Interstate 84 closes because of snow and ice. If you're planning a winter visit, be sure to carry plenty of warm clothes. High winds and single-digit temps are par for the course around 6,000 feet—the elevation of Timberline Lodge on Mt. Hood—in January. Note that chains are sometimes required for traveling over mountain passes.

Temperatures in the Gorge are mild year-round, rarely dipping below 30°F in winter and hovering in the high 70s in midsummer. As throughout Oregon, however, elevation is often a more significant factor than season, and an hour-long drive to Mt. Hood's Timberline Lodge can reduce those midsummer temps by 20–30 degrees. Don't forget that the higher reaches of Mt. Hood retain snow year-round.

In early fall, look for maple, tamarack, and aspen trees around the Gorge, bursting with brilliant red and gold color. No matter the season, the basalt cliffs, the acres of lush forest, and that glorious expanse of water make the Gorge one of the West's great scenic wonders.

GETTING HERE AND AROUND

The Columbia Gorge, which is easily accessed from Portland, is best explored by car. The same is generally true for the Mt. Hood area, but in season, the area ski resorts do have shuttle services from Portland and the airport. Even light exploring of the region, however, requires an automobile—take heart that the driving in these parts is scenic and relatively free of traffic. Just keep in mind that winter storms can result in road closures around Mt. Hood and, occasionally, even in the Gorge. It's just a 20-minute drive east of Portland to reach the beginning of the Columbia Gorge, in Troutdale. From Portland it's a one-hour drive to Hood River, a 90-minute drive to Mt. Hood, and a two-hour drive to Goldendale, Washington *(the farthest-away point covered in this chapter)*.

CAR TRAVEL

Interstate 84 is the main east–west route into the Columbia River Gorge, although you can also reach the area on the Washington side via slower but quite scenic Highway 14, which skirts the north side of the river. U.S. 26, which leads east from Portland, is the main route into the Mt. Hood area.

The scenic Historic Columbia River Highway (U.S. 30) from Troutdale to just east of Oneonta Gorge passes Crown Point State Park and Multnomah Falls. Interstate 84/U.S. 30 continues on to The Dalles. Highway 35 heads south from Hood River to the Mt. Hood area, intersecting with U.S. 26 near Government Camp. From Portland, the Columbia Gorge–Mt. Hood Scenic Loop is the easiest way to fully explore the Gorge and the mountain. Take Interstate 84 east to Troutdale and then follow U.S. 26 east to Mt. Hood, then take Highway 35 north to Hood River and Interstate 84 back to Portland. Or make the loop in reverse.

RESTAURANTS

A prominent locavore mentality pervades western Oregon generally, and low elevations around the Gorge mean long growing seasons for dozens of local producers. Fresh foods grown, caught, and harvested in the Northwest dominate menus in the increasingly sophisticated restaurants in the Gorge, especially in the charming town of Hood River, and up around Mt. Hood. Columbia River salmon is big, fruit orchards proliferate around Hood River, delicious huckleberries flourish in Mount Hood National Forest, and the Gorge nurtures a glut of excellent vineyards. Additionally, even the smallest towns around the region have their own lively brewpubs with consistently tasty pub fare and tap after tap of craft ales. In keeping with the region's green and laid-back vibe, outdoor dining is highly popular. *Restaurant reviews have been shortened. For full information visit Fodors.com.*

HOTELS

The region is close enough that you could spend a day or two exploring the Gorge and Mt. Hood, using Portland hotels as your base. The best way to fully appreciate the Gorge, however, is to spend a night or two—look to Hood River and The Dalles for the largest selections of lodging options, although you'll also find some noteworthy resorts, motels, and B&Bs in some of the towns between Portland and Hood River, on both sides of the river.

WHAT IT COSTS IN U.S. DOLLARS			
$	**$$**	**$$$**	**$$$$**
Restaurants under $16	$16–$22	$23–$30	over $30
Hotels under $150	$150–$200	$201–$250	over $250

Restaurant prices are the average cost of a main course at dinner or, if dinner is not served, at lunch. Hotel prices are the lowest cost of a standard double room in high season.

TOURS

EverGreen Escapes. The energetic crew at this highly respected tour operator provides both regularly scheduled and customizable tours of the Gorge (with themes that range from wine to hiking) and Mt. Hood, where options include hiking and snowshoeing. ☎ *503/252–1931, 866/203–7603* ⊕ *www.evergreenescapes.com* ✉ *From $135.*

Explore the Gorge. Customizable tours of the Gorge, Mt. Hood, and the Hood River Valley explore everything from the Lewis and Clark Trail to the region's microbreweries. ☎ *800/899–5676* ⊕ *www.explorethegorge. com* ✉ *From $180.*

Martin's Gorge Tours. Wine tours, waterfall hikes, and spring wildflower tours are among the popular trips offered by this Portland-based guide. ☎ *503/349–1323* ⊕ *www.martinsgorgetours.com* ✉ *From $49.*

Mt. Hood Adventure. The only outfitter on Mt. Hood that rents snowmobiles and offers snowmobile tours is also a well-respected tour company for snowshoe tours and sleigh rides in winter, and mountain hikes, biking trips, and boat excursions on area rivers—the shop is also a good place to buy gear and ask for advice on outdoorsy activities in the area. ✉ *88335 Government Camp Loop Rd., Government Camp* ☎ *503/715–2175* ⊕ *www.mthoodadventure.com* ✉ *From $111; snowmobile tours from $189.*

VISITOR INFORMATION

Columbia River Gorge Visitors Association. ☎ *509/427–8911* ⊕ *www.crgva.org.*

Mt. Hood Territory. ☎ *800/424–3002, 503/655–8490* ⊕ *www.mthoodterritory.com.*

COLUMBIA RIVER GORGE

When glacial floods carved out most of the Columbia River Gorge at the end of the last Ice Age, they left behind massive, looming cliffs where the river bisects the Cascade mountain range. The size of the canyon and the wildly varying elevations make this small stretch of Oregon as ecologically diverse as anyplace in the state. In a few days along the Gorge you can mountain bike through dry canyons near The Dalles, hike through temperate rain forest in Oneonta Gorge, and take a woodland wildflower stroll just outside Hood River. At night you'll be rewarded with historic lodging and good food in one of a half dozen mellow river towns and one very bustling one, Hood River. The country's second federally designated National Scenic Area remains exceptionally inviting.

HISTORIC COLUMBIA RIVER HIGHWAY

U.S. 30, paralleling I–84 for 22 miles between Troutdale and Interstate Exit 35.

The oldest scenic highway in the United States is a construction marvel that integrates asphalt path with cliff, river, and forest landscapes. Paralleling the interstate, U.S. 30 climbs to forested riverside bluffs, passes half a dozen waterfalls, and provides access to hiking trails leading to still more falls and scenic overlooks. Completed in 1922, the serpentine highway was the first paved road in the Gorge built expressly for automotive sightseers. Technically, the Historic Columbia River Highway extends some 74 miles to The Dalles, but much of that is along modern Interstate 84—the 22-mile western segment is the real draw.

GETTING HERE AND AROUND

U.S. 30 heads east out of downtown Troutdale, but you can also access the route from Interstate 84 along the way, via Exit 22 near Corbett, Exit 28 near Bridal Veil Falls, Exit 31 at Multnomah Falls, and Exit 35, where it rejoins the interstate.

ESSENTIALS

Visitor Information Multnomah Falls Visitor Center. ✉ *53000 E. Historic Columbia River Hwy., Exit 31 off I–84, 15 miles east of Troutdale, Bridal Veil* ☎ *503/695–2372* ⊕ *www.multnomahfallslodge.com.*

EXPLORING

FAMILY
Fodor's Choice
★

Multnomah Falls. A 620-foot-high double-decker torrent, the second-highest year-round waterfall in the nation, Multnomah is by far the most spectacular of the Gorge cataracts east of Troutdale. You can access the falls and Multnomah Lodge via a parking lot at Exit 31 off Interstate 84, or via the Historic Columbia River Highway; from the parking area, a paved path winds to a bridge over the lower falls. A much steeper, though paved, 1.1-mile trail climbs to a viewing point overlooking the upper falls, and from here, unpaved but well-groomed trails join with others, allowing for as much as a full day of hiking in the mountains above the Gorge, if you're up for some serious but scenic trekking. Even the paved ramble to the top will get your blood pumping, but worth it to avoid the crowds that swarm the lower falls area in every season. ✉ *53000 E. Historic Columbia River Hwy., 15 miles east of Troutdale, Bridal Veil* ☎ *503/695–2376* ⊕ *www.multnomahfallslodge.com.*

Oneonta Gorge. Following the old highway east from Multnomah Falls, you come to a narrow, mossy cleft with walls hundreds of feet high. Oneonta Gorge is most enjoyable in summer, when you can walk up the streambed through the cool green canyon, where hundreds of plant species—some found nowhere else—flourish under the perennially moist conditions. At other times of the year, take the trail along the west side of the canyon. The clearly marked trailhead is 100 yards west of the gorge, on the south side of the road. The trail takes you to Oneonta Falls, about ½ mile up the stream, where it links with an extensive regional trail system exploring the region's bluffs and waterfalls. Bring boots or submersible sneakers—plus a strong pair of ankles—because the rocks are slippery. On hot days, many hikers wade or swim in the creek at the base of the falls. ✉ *E. Historic Columbia River Hwy., Cascade Locks* ✛ *2 miles east of Exit 31 off I–84 and Multnomah Falls* ☎ *541/308–1700* ⊕ *www.fs.usda.gov/crgnsa.*

Fodor's Choice
★

Vista House at Crown Point. A two-tier octagonal structure perched on the edge of this 730-foot-high cliff offers unparalleled 30-mile views up and down the Columbia River Gorge. The building dates to 1917, its rotunda and lower level filled with displays about the Gorge and the highway. Vista House's architect Edgar Lazarus was the brother of Emma Lazarus, author of the poem displayed at the base of the Statue of Liberty. The property is part of the Crown Point State Scenic Corridor, which is administered by the Oregon State Parks office. ✉ *40700 E. Historic Columbia River Hwy., Corbett* ✛ *10 miles east of Troutdale* ☎ *503/344–1368* ⊕ *www.vistahouse.com* 🎫 *Free.*

WHERE TO EAT AND STAY

$$
AMERICAN

✗ **Multnomah Falls Lodge.** Vaulted ceilings, stone fireplaces, and exquisite views of Multnomah Falls are complemented by friendly service and reliably good American fare at this landmark restaurant, which is listed on the National Register of Historic Places. Consider the smoked salmon starter with apple-huckleberry compote, cod fish-and-chips, or the elk burger with aged Tillamook cheddar and garlic-sesame mayo. **Known for:** amazing waterfall views; champagne Sunday brunch.

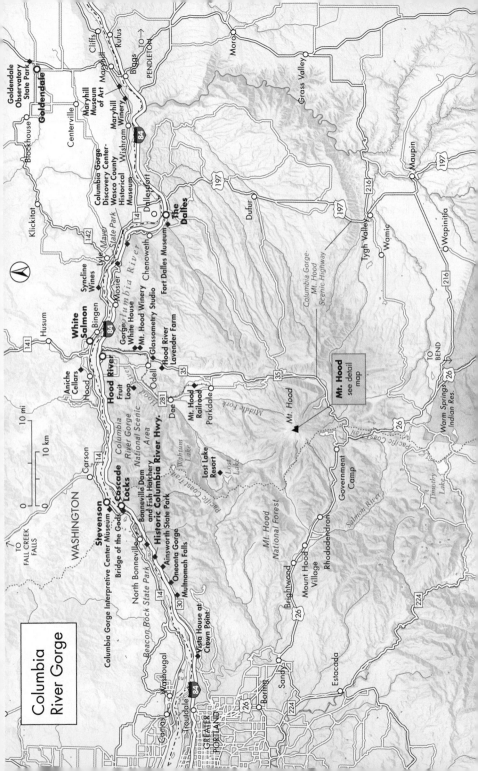

Columbia River Gorge

WASHINGTON

Goldendale Observatory State Park
Goldendale
Blockhouse
Centerville
Klickitat
Husum
Carson
TO FALL CREEK FALLS

Maryhill Museum of Art
Maryhill Winery
Wishram
Cliffs
Rufus
Biggs
TO PENDLETON
Moro
Grass Valley
Maupin

Columbia Gorge Discovery Center-Wasco County Historical Museum
Dallesport
The Dalles
Fort Dalles Museum
Dufur
Tygh Valley
Wamic
Wapinitia

Syncline Wines
Bingen
Lyle Mayer State Park
Mosier
Chenoweth
Mt. Hood Winery
White House

Columbia Gorge-Mt. Hood Scenic Highway

Aniche Cellars
White Salmon
Hood River
Glassometry Studio
Hood River Lavender Farm
Odell
Hood River Fruit Loop
Dee
Mt. Hood Railroad
Parkdale

Mt. Hood
see detail map

Mt. Hood
TO BEND

Columbia Gorge National Scenic Area
Columbia River Gorge

Lost Lake Resort
Lost Lake
Wahtum Lake

Pacific Coast Trail

Mt. Hood National Forest

Middle Fork
Hood River

Warm Springs Indian Res.
Timothy Lake

Government Camp
Salmon River
Rhododendron
Mount Hood Village
Brightwood
Sandy
Boring

Estacada

Columbia Gorge Interpretive Center Museum
Stevenson
Cascade Locks
Bridge of the Gods
Bonneville Dam and Fish Hatchery
Historic Columbia River Hwy.
North Bonneville
Ainsworth State Park
Oneonta Gorge
Multnomah Falls
Beacon Rock State Park
Washougal
Camas
Troutdale
Vista House at Crown Point

GREATER PORTLAND

84 14 141 142 35 281 197 216 26 224 30

N

10 mi
10 km

WASHINGTON

[$] *Average main: $21* ✉ *53000 Historic Columbia River Hwy., Bridal Veil* ✣ *Exit 31 off I–84, 15 miles east of Troutdale* ☎ *503/695–2376* 🌐 *www.multnomahfallslodge.com.*

$ RESORT Fodor's Choice ★ 🏨 **McMenamins Edgefield.** Set in 74 acres of gardens, murals, orchards, and vineyards, this Georgian Revival manor that once housed the county poor farm is now operated by Northwest brewers and hospitality innovators par excellence Mike and Brian McMenamin. **Pros:** plenty of eating and drinking choices; large variety of rooms and prices; great spa; on-site movie theater; live music events. **Cons:** this busy place can get pretty crowded; no TVs, phones, or air-conditioning in the rooms; most rooms share baths. [$] *Rooms from: $110* ✉ *2126 S.W. Halsey St., Troutdale* ☎ *503/669–8610, 800/669–8610* 🌐 *www.mcmenamins.com* 🛏 *114 rooms* 🍴 *No meals.*

SPORTS AND THE OUTDOORS

RECREATIONAL AREAS

Rooster Rock State Park. The most famous beach lining the Columbia River is right below Crown Point. Three miles of sandy beaches, panoramic cascades, and a large swimming area makes this a popular spot. True naturists appreciate that one of Oregon's two designated nude beaches is at the east end of Rooster Rock, and that it's not visible to conventional sunbathers—the area is especially popular with Portland's LGBT community. Rooster Rock is 9 miles east of Troutdale, and it's accessible only via the interstate. ✉ *I–84, Exit 25, 9 miles east of Troutdale, Corbett* ☎ *503/695–2261* 🌐 *www.oregonstateparks.org* 🎟 *Day use $5 per vehicle.*

CASCADE LOCKS

7 miles east of Oneonta Gorge on Historic Columbia River Hwy. and I–84; 30 miles east of Troutdale on I–84.

In pioneer days, boats needing to pass the bedeviling rapids near the town of Whiskey Flats had to portage around them. The locks that gave the town its new name were completed in 1896, allowing waterborne passage for the first time. In 1938 they were submerged beneath the new Lake Bonneville when the Bonneville Lock and Dam became one of the most massive Corps of Engineers projects to come out of the New Deal. The town of Cascade Locks hung on to its name, though. A historic stern-wheeler still leads excursions from the town's port district, and the region's Native American tribes still practice traditional dip-net fishing near the current locks.

GETTING HERE AND AROUND

Cascade Locks is 45 miles east of Portland and 20 miles west of Hood River on Interstate 84. The town is also home to Bridge of the Gods ($2 toll), which featured prominently in the 2014 movie *Wild* and is the only auto bridge crossing the Columbia River (it connects with Stevenson, Washington) between Portland and Hood River.

5

Dog Mountain Trail, Columbia River Gorge National Scenic Area

EXPLORING

FAMILY **Bonneville Dam.** President Franklin D. Roosevelt dedicated the first federal dam to span the Columbia in 1937. Its generators (visible from a balcony on a self-guided tour or up close during free guided tours offered daily in summer and on weekends the rest of the year) have a capacity of more than a million kilowatts, enough to supply power to more than 200,000 single-family homes. There's an extensive visitor center on Bradford Island, complete with underwater windows where gaggles of kids watch migrating salmon and steelhead as they struggle up fish ladders. The best viewing times are between April and October. In recent years the dwindling runs of wild Columbia salmon have made the dam a subject of much environmental controversy. ⊠ *I–84, Exit 40, follow signs 1 mile to visitor center* ☎ *541/374–8820* ⊕ *www.nwp.usace.army.mil.*

Cascade Locks Marine Park. This riverfront park is the home port of the 500-passenger stern-wheeler *Columbia Gorge*, which churns upriver, then back again, on one- and two-hour excursions through some of the Columbia River Gorge's most impressive scenery, mid-May to early October; brunch and dinner cruises are also available. The ship's captain discusses the Gorge's fascinating 40-million-year geology and pioneering spirits and legends, such as Lewis and Clark, who once triumphed over this very same river. The park itself, which includes a pedestrian bridge to leafy and tranquil Thunder Island, is a lovely spot for picnicking, and Thunder Island Brewing—at the west end of the park—serves first-rate craft beers. ⊠ *Marine Park, S.W. Portage Rd.* ☎ *541/224–3900, 800/224–3901* ⊕ *www.portlandspirit.com* ⚓ *Cruises from $28* ⛵ *Reservations essential.*

WHERE TO EAT AND STAY

$ ✕ **Thunder Island Brewing.** Hikers, boaters, and others exploring the Gorge
AMERICAN gather at this laid-back, funky brewpub with several tables inside, as
well as a large patio with picnic tables overlooking the Columbia River,
Marine Park, and the little island for which the brewery is named. Order
a glass of hoppy Pacific Crest Trail Pale Ale or malty Scotch Porter, and
enjoy it with one of the light dishes from the short menu. **Known for:**
great beer from on-site brewery; smoked-fish and charcuterie platters;
stellar river views from outdoor dining area. $ *Average main: $8 ⊠ 515
S.W. Portage Rd.* ☏ *971/231–4599* ⊕ *www.thunderislandbrewing.com.*

$$ ⛉ **Best Western Plus Columbia River Inn.** The draw here is an enviable set-
HOTEL ting with great views of the Columbia River and Bridge of the Gods—
many rooms, which are done in soft tans and grays and hung with
framed black-and-white photos of the Gorge, overlook the river, as
does a deck in back and the breakfast room. **Pros:** excellent river views;
handy location midway between Portland and Hood River; spotless,
modern rooms. **Cons:** cookie-cutter furnishings; some rooms face away
from the river. $ *Rooms from: $159 ⊠ 735 Wa Na Pa St.* ☏ *541/374–
8777, 800/780–7234* ⊕ *www.bwcolumbiariverinn.com* ⟿ *62 rooms*
⑩ *Breakfast.*

SPORTS AND THE OUTDOORS
HIKING
Pacific Crest Trail. Cascade Locks bustles with grubby thru-hikers refuel-
ing along the 2,650-mile Canada-to-Mexico Pacific Crest Trail, which
was immortalized in the 2014 movie, *Wild* starring Reese Witherspoon.
Check out a scenic and strenuous portion of it, heading south from the
trailhead at Herman Creek Horse Camp, just east of town. The route
heads up into the Cascades, showing off monster views of the Gorge.
Backpackers out for a longer trek will find idyllic campsites at Wahtum
Lake, 14 miles south. You can also access the trail from the free parking
area at Toll House Park, by the Bridge of the Gods. ⊠ *Off N.W. Forest
La., 1 mile east of downtown* ☏ *541/308–1700* ⊕ *www.pcta.org.*

STEVENSON, WASHINGTON

*Across the river from Cascade Locks via the Bridge of the Gods and 1
mile east on Hwy. 14.*

With the Bridge of the Gods toll bridge spanning the Columbia River
above the Bonneville Dam, Stevenson acts as a sort of "twin city" to
Cascade Locks on the Oregon side. Tribal legends and the geologic
record tell of the original Bridge of the Gods, a substantial landslide that
occurred here sometime between AD 1000 and 1760, briefly linking the
two sides of the Gorge before the river swept away the debris. The land-
slide's steel namesake now leads to tiny Stevenson, where vacationers
traverse quiet Main Street, which has a few casual eateries and shops.
Washington's Highway 14 runs through the middle of town, and since
the cliffs on the Oregon side are more dramatic, driving this two-lane
highway actually offers better views.

GETTING HERE AND AROUND

From the Oregon side of the Gorge, cross the Columbia River at the Bridge of the Gods ($2 toll).

ESSENTIALS

Visitor Information **Skamania County Chamber of Commerce.** ✉ *167 N.W. 2nd St., Stevenson* ☎ *509/427–8911, 800/989–9178* 🌐 *www.skamania.org.*

EXPLORING

Bridge of the Gods. For a magnificent vista 135 feet above the Columbia, as well as a short and quick (despite its 15 mph speed limit) route between Oregon and Washington, $2 will pay your way over the grandly named bridge that Reese Witherspoon memorably strolled across in the 2014 movie, *Wild*. Hikers cross the bridge from Oregon to reach the Washington segment of the **Pacific Crest Trail**, which picks up just west of the bridge. ✉ *Off Hwy. 14, Stevenson* 🌐 *portofcascadelocks.org/bridge-of-the-gods/.*

FAMILY **Columbia Gorge Interpretive Center Museum.** A petroglyph whose eyes seem to look straight at you, "She Who Watches" or "Tsagaglalal" is the logo for this museum. Sitting among the dramatic basaltic cliffs on the north bank of the Columbia River Gorge, the museum explores the life of the Gorge: its history, culture, architecture, legends, and much more. Younger guests enjoy the reenactment of the Gorge's formation in the Creation Theatre, and the 37-foot-high fish wheel, a device like a mill wheel equipped with baskets for catching fish, from the 19th century. Historians appreciate studying the water route of the Lewis and Clark Expedition. There's also an eye-opening exhibit that examines current environmental impacts on the area. ✉ *990 S.W. Rock Creek Dr., Stevenson* ☎ *509/427–8211, 800/991–2338* 🌐 *www.columbiagorge.org* 🎟 *$10.*

WHERE TO EAT AND STAY

$ AMERICAN 🍴 **Big River Grill.** A tradition with hikers, bikers, fishermen, and scenic drivers out exploring the Gorge, especially for weekend breakfast but also at lunch and dinnertime, this colorful roadhouse in the center of town is festooned with license plates, vintage signs, and kitschy artwork. Grab a seat at the counter or in one of the high-back wooden booths, and tuck into grilled wild salmon sandwich, chicken-fried chicken with eggs, home-style meat loaf with buttermilk-garlic mashed potatoes, and other hearty, reasonably priced fare. **Known for:** grilled wild salmon sandwiches; weekend breakfast; hiker and biker crowd. [$] *Average main: $16* ✉ *192 S.W. 2nd St., Stevenson* ☎ *509/427–4888* 🌐 *www.thebigrivergrill.com.*

$$$ PACIFIC NORTHWEST Fodor's Choice ★ 🍴 **Cascade Room at Skamania Lodge.** At Skamania Lodge's signature restaurant, with its stunning views of sky, river, and cliff scapes, the chef draws on local seafood and regionally sourced meats. Try dishes like a Dungeness crab tower with avocado, beet coulis, and basil oil; and bacon-cured Carlton Farms pork chops. **Known for:** stunning Gorge views; lavish Sunday brunch. [$] *Average main: $26* ✉ *Skamania Lodge, 1131 S.W. Skamania Lodge Way, Stevenson* ☎ *509/427–7700* 🌐 *www.skamania.com.*

$ AMERICAN 🍴 **Red Bluff Tap House.** With exposed-brick walls, varnished wood tables, and a sleek long bar, this downtown gastropub excels both with its extensive craft-beer and drinks selection and its modern take on comfort food. Snack on shareable starters like deep-fried brussels sprouts with pork belly and apple-cider reduction and smoked salmon flatbread. **Known for:** ample selection of craft beers and Columbia Gorge wines; fish-and-chips. [$] *Average main: $13* ✉ *256 2nd St., Stevenson* ☎ *509/427–4979* 🌐 *www.redblufftaphouse.com.*

$$$ RESORT FAMILY Fodor's Choice ★ 🏨 **Skamania Lodge.** This warm, woodsy lodge on an expansive, verdant swath of forest and meadows impresses with a multitude of windows overlooking in the surrounding mountains and Gorge, an outstanding array of recreational facilities, and handsome, Pacific Northwest–chic accommodations, many with fireplaces and all with views. **Pros:** just a 45-minute drive from Portland but feels secluded and totally relaxing; plenty of fun outdoorsy activities; first-rate spa and dining facilities. **Cons:** expensive for a large family; can get crowded—sometimes there's a wait for a table in the dining room. [$] *Rooms from: $229* ✉ *1131 S.W. Skamania Lodge Way, Stevenson* ☎ *509/427–7700, 800/221–7117* 🌐 *www.skamania.com* 🛏 *254 rooms* 🍴 *No meals.*

5

NIGHTLIFE

Walking Man Brewing. This sunshiny patio and cozy interior are great spots for creative pizzas and a sampling the dozen-or-so craft ales. After a couple of pints of the strong Homo Erectus IPA and Knuckle Dragger Pale Ale, you may go a little ape. Live music on summer weekends skews twangy and upbeat. ✉ *240 S.W. 1st St., Stevenson* ☎ *509/427–5520* 🌐 *www.walkingmanbeer.com.*

SPORTS AND THE OUTDOORS

RECREATIONAL AREA

Fodor's Choice ★ **Beacon Rock State Park.** For several hundred years this 848-foot rock was a landmark for river travelers, including Native Americans, who recognized this point as the last rapids of the Columbia River. Lewis and Clark are thought to have been the first white men to see the volcanic remnant. Even most casual hikers can make the steep but safe trek up to the top of the rock—allow about 45–60 minutes round-trip. More serious hikers should head to the trailhead for Hamilton Mountain, which is reached via a beautiful, though arduous, 8-mile ramble over a roaring waterfall, through dense temperate rain forest, and finally up to 2,400-foot summit with breathtaking views up and down the Gorge. ✉ *34841 Hwy. 14, Skamania* ✣ *7 miles west of Bridge of the Gods* ☎ *509/427–8265* 🌐 *www.parks.wa.gov* 🎟 *$10.*

Falls Creek Falls. You'll find one of the most spectacular waterfalls hikes in the Northwest in the Wind River section of 1½-million-acre Gifford Pinchot National Forest. The large, free parking area (with restrooms) is at the end of graded, unpaved forest road off paved Wind River Road, about 20 miles north of Stevenson. The trail meanders through dense forest and crosses a couple of sturdy suspension bridges en route to the more spectacular Lower Falls (a relatively easy 3½-mile round-trip). If you're up for more of an adventure, continue to the Upper Falls overlook, which adds about 3 more miles and makes it a loop hike—parts of this section are quite steep. ✉ *End of NF 057, Carson* ✣ *16 miles north of Carson via Wind River Rd. and NF 3062* ☎ *509/395–3400* 🌐 *www.fs.usda.gov/main/giffordpinchot.*

HOOD RIVER

20 miles east of Cascade Locks and 60 miles east of Portland on I–84.

This picturesque riverside community of about 7,200 residents affords visitors spectacular views both of the Columbia River and snowcapped Mt. Hood. More than 40 civic and commercial buildings date from 1893 to the 1930s, some of which are listed in the National Register of Historic Places.

Hood River is the dining and lodging hub of the Gorge, with an increasingly respected bounty of urbane farm-to-table restaurants, up-and-coming craft breweries and wine-tasting rooms, and nicely curated shops and art galleries. Little wonder this is one of the most popular weekend getaways among Portlanders, all the more so since the surrounding countryside abounds with orchards and vineyards, making it a favorite destination for fans of U-pick farmsteads and tasting rooms. Hood River wineries grow a broader range of grapes than Oregon's more famous Willamette Valley, and wine touring has become a favorite activity in the area.

GETTING HERE AND AROUND

Reach Hood River from Portland by driving 60 miles east on Interstate 84, or from Mt. Hood by heading 40 miles north on Highway 35.

ESSENTIALS

Visitor Information Hood River County Chamber of Commerce. ⊠ *720 E. Port Marina Dr.* ☎ *541/386-2000, 800/366-3530* ⊕ *www.hoodriver.org.*

EXPLORING ·

Cathedral Ridge Winery. Run by fourth-generation winemaker Michael Sebastiani, this vineyard has racked up countless ribbons and awards from wine festivals and publications, and *Wine Press Northwest* called it one of the region's best wine-country picnic spots. Popular varietals include Riesling, Pinot Gris, and Syrah. ⊠ *4200 Post Canyon Dr.* ☎ *800/516–8710* ⊕ *www.cathedralridgewinery.com.*

Fruit Loop. Either by car or bicycle, tour the quiet country highways of Hood River Valley, which abounds with more than 25 fruit stands, a handful of U-pick berry farms, and about 10 wineries. You'll see apples, pears, cherries, and peaches fertilized by volcanic soil, pure glacier water, and a conducive harvesting climate. Along the 35 miles of farms are a host of outlets for delicious baked goods, wines, flowers, and nuts. While on the loop, consider stopping in the small town of **Parkdale** to lunch, taste beer at Solera Brewery, and snap a photo of Mt. Hood's north face. ⊠ *Hood River* ✛ *Begins just east of downtown at State St. and Hwy. 35* ⊕ *www.hoodriverfruitloop.com.*

Glassometry Studios. Artist and teacher Laurel Marie Hagner operates this colorful gallery and sculpture garden just off the Hood River Fruit Loop, near the village of Odell. You can admire the larger-than-life, riotously vibrant glass sculptures with a walk through the garden, watch live glass-blowing demonstrations (and take classes) in the studio, and browse the fanciful yet absolutely functional vases, bowls, drinking glasses, decanters, and decorative glass art in the studio. ⊠ *3015 Lower Mill Dr.* ☎ *541/354-3015* ⊕ *www.glassometry.com* ☉ *Closed Mon.–Wed.*

Fodor'sChoice **Gorge White House.** You'll find pretty much everything the Hood River
★ Valley is famous for growing and being produced at this picturesque,
century-old farm anchored by a Dutch Colonial farmhouse and surrounded by acres of U-pick flowers, apple and peach trees, and blackberry and blueberry bushes. After strolling through the farm fields,
stop inside the main house to sample wines—the tasting room carries
one of the largest selections of Columbia River wines in the region.
Out back, there's a farm store, another tasting room serving local craft
beer and cider, and a garden patio with seating and a food-truck-style
café serving delicious strawberry salads, pulled-pork sandwiches, pear
pizzas, and other light fare. ⊠ *2265 Hwy. 35* ☎ *541/386–2828* ⊕ *www.*
thegorgewhitehouse.com.

Hood River Lavender Farm. Part of the joy of visiting this organic U-pick
lavender farm that harvests some 75 varieties of the plant is the beautiful drive up the hill from Odell's orchards and vineyards. Stroll through
the fields of lavender, relax in a chair taking in mesmerizing views of
Mt. Hood and Mt. Adams, or peruse the huge selection of lavender
products in the gift shop—everything from lip balms and shampoo
to infused teas and dried lavender bouquets. ⊠ *3801 Straight Hill Rd.*
☎ *541/354–9917* ⊕ *www.hoodriverlavender.com.*

OFF THE **Lost Lake Resort.** One of the most-photographed sights in the Pacific
BEATEN Northwest, this lake's waters reflect towering Mt. Hood and the thick
PATH forests that line its shore. Cabins and campsites are available for overnight stays, and because no motorboats are allowed on Lost Lake,
the area is blissfully quiet. ⊠ *9000 Lost Lake Rd., Dee* ⟊ *25 miles*
southwest of Hood River via Hwy. 35 and Hwy. 281 ☎ *541/386–6366*
🖅 *Day use $8.*

Fodor'sChoice **Marchesi Vineyards.** Somewhat unusual for the Pacific Northwest, this
★ boutique winery with a small, airy tasting room and a verdant garden
patio specializes in Italian varietals—Moscato, Primitivo, Dolcetto, Sangiovese, Barbera, Nebbiolo, and a few others. Owner Franco Marchesi
hails from Italy's Piemonte region, and he's earned serious kudos for his
finesse as a winemaker. ⊠ *3955 Belmont Dr.* ☎ *541/386–1800* ⊕ *www.*
marchesivineyards.com.

FAMILY **Mt. Hood Railroad.** Scenic passenger excursions along a small rail line
established in 1906 offer a picturesque and relaxing way to survey
Mt. Hood and the Hood River Valley. Chug alongside the Hood River
through vast fruit orchards before climbing up steep forested canyons,
glimpsing Mt. Hood along the way. There are several trip options, from
$30: a four-hour excursion (serves light concessions), dinner, brunch,
and several themed trips, like murder-mysteries and Old West rob-
beries, and a family-popular holiday-inspired Polar Express train runs
throughout much of November and December. Exceptional service is
as impressive as the scenery. ⊠ *110 Railroad Ave.* ☎ *541/386–3556,*
800/872–4661 ⊕ *www.mthoodrr.com* ☉ *Closed Jan.–Apr.*

Mt. Hood Winery. In addition to producing increasingly acclaimed wine—
with particularly impressive Pinot Gris, dry Rosé, Zinfandel (which is
seldom bottled in these parts), Pinot Noir, Barbera, and Syrah—this
winery adjacent to the long-running Fruit Company (fruit and gift

baskets) has a beautiful, contemporary tasting room with gorgeous Mt. Hood views from inside and the expansive patio. ✉ *2882 Van Horn Dr.* ☎ *541/386–8333* 🌐 *www.mthoodwinery.com* 🕒 *Closed Dec.–Feb.*

Viento Wines. Focused more on whites than most of the winemakers in the Gorge region, Viento has a stunning tasting room with vaulted ceilings, soaring windows, and a large patio overlooking the on-site vineyard of Riesling grapes. This is a lovely space for tasting and chatting with fellow oenophiles. Notable wines here include a crisp Grüner Veltliner, a food-friendly Brut Rosé, and one of the better Oregon Pinot Noirs you'll find in the Hood River region. ✉ *301 Country Club Rd.* ☎ *541/386–3026* 🌐 *www.vientowines.com.*

FAMILY **Western Antique Aeroplane and Automobile Museum.** Housed at Hood River's tiny airport (general aviation only), the museum's impressive, meticulously restored, propeller-driven planes are all still in flying condition. The antique steam cars, Model Ts, and sleek Depression-era sedans are road-worthy, too. Periodic car shows and an annual fly-in draw thousands of history buffs and spectators. ✉ *1600 Air Museum Rd., , off Hwy. 281* ☎ *541/308–1600* 🌐 *www.waaamuseum.org* 🎟 *$14.*

WHERE TO EAT

$ SCANDINAVIAN 🍴 **Broder Øst.** Portland's wildly popular modern Scandinavian restaurant Broder has opened a branch just off the lobby of downtown's historic Hood River Hotel. Breakfast and lunch are the main event, although dinner is served during the busy summer months. **Known for:** Danish favorites like pancakes with lingonberry sauce; covered sidewalk tables overlooking bustling Oak Street. [$] *Average main: $11* ✉ *Hood River Hotel, 102 Oak St.* ☎ *541/436–3444* 🌐 *www.brodereast.com* 🕒 *No dinner Mon. and Tues. or Sept.–May.*

$$$ PACIFIC NORTHWEST 🍴 **Celilo Restaurant.** Refined and relaxing, this high-ceilinged restaurant in a contemporary downtown building is popular both for dinner and enjoying a glass of local wine in the bar. Deftly crafted Pacific Northwest fare—order the cast-iron-skillet seafood-and-chorizo roast or duck-leg confit if it's on the menu. **Known for:** one of the best local wine lists in the Gorge; attractive sidewalk seating. [$] *Average main: $25* ✉ *16 Oak St.* ☎ *541/386–5710* 🌐 *www.celilorestaurant.com* 🕒 *No lunch Mon.–Thurs.*

$$ ECLECTIC 🍴 **Kin.** Several Czech dishes have been added to the otherwise farm-to-table Northwest menu that includes orecchiette pasta with merguez sausage, mint, and fava beans, and hearty goulash with potato gnocchi. Kin doesn't serve lunch, but is justly popular for Sunday brunch. **Known for:** Sunday brunch; impressive Eurocentric wine list. [$] *Average main: $19* ✉ *110 5th St.* ☎ *541/387–0111* 🌐 *www.kineatery.com* 🕒 *Closed Mon. and Tues. No lunch.*

$$ PIZZA Fodor's Choice ★ 🍴 **Solstice Wood Fire Cafe.** It can be hard to score a table on weekends in this snazzy space along the Hood River waterfront. Wood-fire-grilled pizzas with unusual toppings—such as the Cherry Girl, layered with local cherries, spicy chorizo, goat cheese, mozzarella, and marinara sauce—bring the crowds. **Known for:** creative pizzas; wood-fired mac-n-cheese; s'mores. [$] *Average main: $17* ✉ *501 Portway Ave.* ☎ *541/436–0800* 🌐 *www.solsticewoodfirecafe.com.*

Vineyards in the Hood River Valley

$$ ✕ **Stonehedge Gardens.** Each of the four dining rooms in the restored
AMERICAN   1898 home has a distinct personality, from cozy to verdant to elegant,
but the tiered patio is where summer diners gather. The kitchen tends
toward the traditional side, specializing in classics like steak Diane and
filet mignon. Just when you think your meal is complete, along comes
the Flaming Bread Pudding. **Known for:** gorgeous outdoor seating amid
lovely gardens; flaming bread pudding. $ *Average main: $23* ⊠ *3405
Wine Country Ave.* ☎ *541/386–3940* ⊕ *www.stonehedgeweddings.com*
🕐 *Closed Mon. No lunch.*

WHERE TO STAY

$$ 🏨 **Best Western Plus Hood River Inn.** This low-slung, rambling hotel beside
HOTEL   the Hood River Bridge offers some of the best river views of any hotel
in the Gorge, and many units have private balconies or patios on the
water; the deluxe accommodations have full kitchens, fireplaces, and
Jacuzzi tubs. **Pros:** riverfront location with great views; good restaurant
and lounge. **Cons:** a little pricey in summer; downtown shopping and
dining not within walking distance. $ *Rooms from: $179* ⊠ *1108 E.
Marina Way* ☎ *541/386–2200, 800/828–7873* ⊕ *www.hoodriverinn.
com* 🛏 *194 rooms* ⊙| *Breakfast.*

$$ 🏨 **Columbia Cliff Villas Hotel.** This elegant condo-style compound on
HOTEL   a sheer cliff overlooking the Columbia River contains some of the
FAMILY   plushest accommodations in the region—units have one to three bed-
Fodor's Choice   rooms, fireplaces, terraces or patios, stone-and-tile bathrooms, and
★   fine linens. **Pros:** private apartment-style accommodations; great river
views; sophisticated decor and top-flight amenities. **Cons:** no restau-
rant or fitness center on-site. $ *Rooms from: $189* ⊠ *3880 Westcliff*

Dr. ☎ *541/490–8081, 866/912–8366* 🌐 *www.columbiacliffvillas.com* 🛏 *37 suites* 🍴 *No meals.*

$$$$ HOTEL 🏨 **Columbia Gorge Hotel.** Charming though somewhat dated-looking period-style rooms at this grande dame of Gorge hotels are fitted out with plenty of wood, brass, and antiques and overlook the Gorge, impeccably landscaped formal gardens, or a 208-foot-high waterfall. **Pros:** historic structure built by Columbia Gorge Highway visionary Simon Benson; unbeatable Gorge views; full-service spa. **Cons:** smallish rooms with rather dated decor; rooms facing away from river pick up noise from nearby Interstate 84; often books up with weddings on summer and fall weekends. [$] *Rooms from: $255* ✉ *4000 Westcliff Dr.* ☎ *541/386–5566, 800/345–1921* 🌐 *www.columbiagorgehotel.com* 🛏 *40 rooms* 🍴 *No meals.*

$ HOTEL 🏨 **Hood River Hotel.** In the heart of the lively and hip business district, steps from great restaurants and shops, this handsomely restored building has a grand, Old West facade, behind which are simple rooms with tasteful period-style antiques and a few larger suites that have kitchenettes and large sitting rooms. **Pros:** excellent downtown location; good-value rafting and ski packages; antiques-heavy interiors have feel of a European inn. **Cons:** smallish rooms; no king-size beds; rooms in back have great river views but tend to receive some freeway noise. [$] *Rooms from: $129* ✉ *102 Oak St.* ☎ *541/386–1900, 800/386–1859* 🌐 *www.hoodriverhotel.com* 🛏 *41 rooms* 🍴 *Breakfast.*

$$$ B&B/INN Fodor'sChoice ★ 🏨 **Sakura Ridge.** The five warm but sleekly furnished rooms of this contemporary lodge-style B&B on a 72-acre farm on the south side of town offer magical panoramas of Mt. Hood amid a welcome absence of clutter. **Pros:** spectacular mountain views; rustic yet urbane decor; lush gardens and orchards on the grounds. **Cons:** secluded location is a 15-minute drive from downtown; closed in winter. [$] *Rooms from: $205* ✉ *5601 York Hill Rd.* ☎ *541/386–2636, 877/472–5872* 🌐 *www.sakuraridge.com* 🕒 *Closed Nov.–Mar.* 🛏 *5 rooms* 🍴 *Breakfast.*

NIGHTLIFE

Brian's Pourhouse. A cute downtown cottage with a spacious deck serves excellent, eclectic food, but is even better known as a later-in-the-evening spot. It's the favored place in town to enjoy a cocktail or glass of wine and perhaps a sweet nosh—the Dutch apple pie with caramel sauce, whipped cream, and ice cream is memorable. ✉ *606 Oak St.* ☎ *541/387–4344* 🌐 *www.brianspourhouse.com.*

Double Mountain Brewery & Taproom. Notable for its European-style beers, including the rich Black Irish Stout and the refreshing Kölsch, Double Mountain also produces seasonal cherry-infused Kriek ales and a hoppy India Red Ale. The bustling, homey downtown taproom is also a great source for pizzas, salads, and sandwiches. ✉ *8 4th St.* ☎ *541/387–0042* 🌐 *www.doublemountainbrewery.com.*

Full Sail Tasting Room and Pub. A glass-walled microbrewery with a windswept deck overlooking the Columbia, Full Sail was a pioneer brewpub in Oregon, helping to put Hood River on the map as a major beer hub. Free, on-site brewery tours are given daily at 1, 2, 3, and 4 pm. ✉ *506 Columbia St.* ☎ *541/386–2247* 🌐 *www.fullsailbrewing.com.*

Fodor's Choice **Pfriem Family Brewers.** Inside a striking new building on the Columbia
★ River, Pfriem (pronounced "freem") is all about the marriage of Belgium's
brewing traditions and Oregon's decidedly hoppy style. The brewery has
quickly vaulted to the top echelon of Northwest craft beer makers, earning accolades for its heady Belgian Strong Blonde and one of the best IPAs
in the state. The on-site restaurant serves stellar pub fare, too, including
mussels and fries, vegan Moroccan stew, and house-made bratwurst.
⌧ *707 Portway Ave.* ☏ *541/321–0490* ⊕ *www.pfriembeer.com.*

SPORTS AND THE OUTDOORS
KAYAKING
Gorge Paddling Center. Whether you want to practice your Eskimo roll
in the safety of a pool, run the Klickitat River in an inflatable kayak, or
try out a stand-up paddleboard on the Columbia, the Gorge's premier
kayak guides can arrange the trip. Book online, by phone, or at the
Kayak Shed downtown. ⌧ *101 N. 1st St.* ☏ *541/806–4190* ⊕ *www.
gorgekayaker.com.*

WINDSURFING
Big Winds. The retail hub for Hood River's windsurfing and kiteboarding
culture also rents gear and provides windsurfing lessons for beginners.
Lessons and clinics begin at $79. ⌧ *207 Front St.* ☏ *541/386–6086,
888/509–4210* ⊕ *www.bigwinds.com.*

WHITE SALMON, WASHINGTON

5 miles north of Hood River on Hwy. 14.

Tiny White Salmon, which sits on a bluff with commanding views of
the Columbia River as well as the town of Hood River, is a good base
for exploring the Washington side of the eastern end of the Gorge. A
few noteworthy restaurants and shops in the village center cater to hikers, kayakers, and wine- and beer-tasting aficionados checking out this
quieter but similar scenic counterpart to Hood River. Several first-rate
wineries have opened in the rural communities just west and east of
White Salmon along Highway 14.

The Coyote Wall trail, accessed about 5 miles east of town off Highway
14 at Courtney Road, affords hikers unobstructed views of the Columbia
River and the surrounding mountains, including Mt. Hood. The trail
leads from a disused section of roadway up a gradual slope, through tall
grass and wildflower meadows, from sea level to an elevation of 1,900
feet. You can descend the way you came up or by looping back down
through an intriguing valley of basalt rock formations—the full round-
trip is about 8 miles, but you could hike part of the way up the trail and
back, taking in the impressive vistas, in less than an hour. Drive north of
town about 20 miles on Highway 141 to reach secluded Trout Lake, the
access point for hiking and recreation in and around 12,281-foot Mt.
Adams, which is visible from many points in the Gorge.

GETTING HERE AND AROUND
You reach White Salmon by driving across the Hood River Bridge (toll
$1), turning east onto Highway 14, and then north in the small village
of Bingen onto Highway 141—it's a 10-minute drive from Hood River.

5

ESSENTIALS

Mt. Adams Chamber of Commerce. ✉ *1 Heritage Plaza, off Hwy. 14, just west of Hood River Bridge, White Salmon* ☎ *509/493–3630* 🌐 *www.mtadamschamber.com.*

EXPLORING

Aniche Cellars. Just a short drive west of White Salmon, this friendly boutique winery has one of the prettiest tasting-room settings in the area—it's high on Underwood Mountain, with outdoor seating that affords spectacular views looking east toward Hood River and deep into the Gorge. The cleverly named wines here—Puck, an Albarino–Pinot Gris blend; Three Witches, a Rhône-style blend of Cinsault, Carignan, and Counoise—are paired with little amuse-bouche-style nibbles, typically chocolate, prosciutto, or fruit. The winery also has a tasting room in downtown Hood River. ✉ *71 Little Buck Creek Rd., Underwood* ☎ *360/624–6531* 🌐 *www.anichecellars.com.*

Fodor's Choice ★ **Syncline Wines.** The focus at this intimate winery is predominantly on elegant, full-bodied Rhône-style wines. The friendly, knowledgeable tasting-room has garnered plenty of awards for its aromatic Cuvée Elena Grenache-Syrah-Mourvedre blend, as well as a first-rate standalone Syrah, and several racy, dry whites—Picpoul, Grenache Blanc, Gruner Veltliner—that seem tailor-made for the Gorge's warm summer nights. Note that several other outstanding small wineries—Domaine Pouillon, Memaloose, and COR Cellars among them—are in the same rural town, 10 miles east of White Salmon. ✉ *111 Balch Rd., Lyle* ☎ *509/365–4361* 🌐 *www.synclinewine.com* 🕒 *Closed Mon.–Wed.*

WHERE TO EAT

$$ PACIFIC NORTHWEST Fodor's Choice ★

🍴 **Henni's Kitchen & Bar.** It's well worth venturing across the Columbia from Hood River to this jewel of a neighborhood tavern, which serves well-priced, creatively prepared international fare with a decided Northwest focus—think kale fritters with romesco sauce, Thai red curry with local flat-iron steak, and classic fish-and-chips. This is hearty comfort food, but with healthy and fresh ingredients. **Known for:** good cocktails; eclectic menu. [$] *Average main: $18* ✉ *120 E. Jewett Blvd., White Salmon* ☎ *509/493–1555* 🌐 *www.henniskitchenandbar.com* 🕒 *No lunch.*

NIGHTLIFE

Everybody's Brewing. Head to this festive downtown brewpub for seriously impressive beers, with the potent Big Brother Imperial IPA (7.7% ABV) and orange-peel-enhanced Daily Bread Common Ale leading the way. There's live music many evenings, and tasty pub fare, too. ✉ *151 E. Jewett Blvd., White Salmon* ☎ *509/637–2774* 🌐 *www.everybodysbrewing.com.*

SPORTS AND THE OUTDOORS

Wet Planet Whitewater. This outfitter just outside White Salmon offers half- and full-day white-water rafting trips on the White Salmon, Wind, Klickitat, Hood, and Tieton rivers, which rank among some of the top waterways for this activity in the region. The Wind and Hood rivers contain stretches of hairy Class IV–Class V rapids (previous experience is required), but the other trips are suitable for beginners. The company also offers kayaking instruction and trips. ✉ *860 Hwy. 141, Husum* ☎ *509/493–8989, 877/390–9445* 🌐 *www.wetplanetwhitewater.com.*

THE DALLES

20 miles east of Hood River on I–84.

The Dalles lies on a crescent bend of the Columbia River where it narrows and once spilled over a series of rapids, creating a flagstone effect. French voyagers christened it *dalle,* or "flagstone." The Dalles is the seat of Wasco County and the trading hub of north-central Oregon. It gained fame early in the region's history as the town where the Oregon Trail branched, with some pioneers departing to travel over Mt. Hood on Barlow Road and the others continuing down the Columbia River. This may account for the small-town, Old West feeling that still permeates the area. Several historic Oregon moments as they relate to The Dalles' past are magnificently illustrated on eight murals painted by renowned Northwest artists, located downtown within short walking distance of one another.

GETTING HERE AND AROUND

From Hood River, it's a 22-mile drive east on Interstate 84 to reach The Dalles. Alternatively, you can take the slightly slower and more scenic Highway 14, on the Washington side of the Columbia, from White Salmon to U.S. 197, which leads you into town via The Dalles Bridge.

ESSENTIALS

Visitor Information The Dalles Area Chamber of Commerce. ⊠ *404 W. 2nd St.* ☎ *541/296–2231, 800/255–3385* ⊕ *www.thedalleschamber.com.*

EXPLORING

FAMILY **Columbia Gorge Discovery Center–Wasco County Historical Museum.** Exhibits and artwork at this expansive, contemporary museum just off Interstate 84 as you approach The Dalles from the west highlight the geological history of the Columbia Gorge, back 40 million years when volcanoes, landslides, and floods carved out the area. History exhibits focus on 10,000 years of Native American life and exploration of the region by white settlers, from Lewis and Clark to the early-20th-century engineers who developed the Historic Columbia River Highway. ⊠ *5000 Discovery Dr.* ☎ *541/296–8600* ⊕ *www.gorgediscovery.org* ⌦ *$9.*

Fort Dalles Museum. The 1856-vintage Fort Dalles Surgeon's Quarters ranks among the state's oldest history museums. The first visitors came through the doors in 1905. On display in authentic hand-hewn log buildings, originally part of a military base, are the personal effects of some of the region's settlers and a collection of early automobiles. The entrance fee gains you admission to the Swedish log-style **Anderson Homestead** museum across the street, which also displays pioneer artifacts. ⊠ *500 W. 15th St.* ☎ *541/296–4547* ⊕ *www.fortdallesmuseum. org* ⌦ *$5.*

Sunshine Mill Winery. You won't find many wineries situated in more unusual buildings than Quenett, which operates out of a early 1900s flour mill with huge grain elevators that soar over the southern end of The Dalles's downtown. Inside this dramatic old structure that nearly fell to the wrecking ball before winemakers James and Molli Martin bought it, you'll find the tasting room for Quenett, which produces first-rate Grenache, Viognier, Barbera, and a

Chardonnay–Viognier–Sauvignon–Blanc–Semillon blend. You can also order cheese boards and other snacks, and sample wines from the company's other line, Copa Di Vino, an inexpensive brand of single-serving table wines sold throughout the country. ⊠ *901 E. 2nd St.* ☎ *541/298–8900* ⊕ *www.sunshinemill.com.*

WHERE TO EAT AND STAY

$ ✕ **Baldwin Saloon.** The walls of this historic downtown watering hole
AMERICAN   and restaurant are an engagingly authentic mix of landscape art and early American oil-painting erotica. The immense, traditional menu runs the gamut from pastas to fish-and-chips to burgers—portions are substantial. **Known for:** conversation-starting art; dinner accompanied by the saloon's 1894 piano; delicious bouillabaisse. $ *Average main: $13* ⊠ *205 Court St.* ☎ *541/296–5666* ⊗ *Closed Sun.*

$ ✕ **Petite Provence.** This popular downtown bistro-bakery-dessertery,
CAFÉ   which also has branches in Portland, serves delicious eggs, crepes, and croissants for breakfast; hot and cold sandwiches and salads for lunch, and fresh-baked pastries and breads (you can take a loaf home). For lunch, consider the Columbia River steelhead fillet with hazelnut crust, served over sautéed leeks and roasted artichokes. **Known for:** delicious French pastries; nice selection of wines. $ *Average main: $11* ⊠ *408 E. 2nd St.* ☎ *541/506–0037* ⊕ *www.provencepdx.com* ⊗ *No dinner.*

$ ▦ **Celilo Inn.** A prototypical retro motor lodge gone high-design, with
HOTEL   exterior-entry rooms and a '50s light-up motel sign that disguise a slick,
Fodor'sChoice   boutique feel, commands a hilltop overlooking the Columbia River and
★   Dalles Dam. Flat-screen TVs, pillow-top mattresses, and smart decorating come standard, and the outdoor pool and patio are mighty inviting during The Dalles' dry summers. **Pros:** sexy design; terrific wine-touring packages; most rooms have great views. **Cons:** not all rooms have views; those on the far end feel very away from the front desk. $ *Rooms from: $119* ⊠ *3550 E. 2nd St.* ☎ *541/769–0001* ⊕ *www.celiloinn.com* ⌐ *46 rooms* ⏀ *No meals.*

SPORTS AND THE OUTDOORS

RECREATIONAL AREAS

Celilo Park. Named for the falls that challenged spawning salmon here in the pre-dam days, this favorite spot for windsurfers also has swimming, sailboarding, fishing, and both tent and RV camping. ⊠ *The Dalles* ✛ *13 miles east of The Dalles, off I–84 Exit 97* ☎ *541/296–1181* ▦ *Free.*

Fodor'sChoice   **Mayer State Park.** Views from atop the park's Rowena Crest bluff are
★   knockout, especially during the March and April wildflower season, and there are a couple of fairly short and scenic hikes that lead from the bluff parking lot (off U.S. 30, 13 miles west of The Dalles, and 6 miles east of Mosier). The 3½-mile (round-trip) trek up to McCall Point is especially scenic—it affords great views of Mt. Hood. The lower part of the park hugs the Columbia River and is accessed from Interstate 84; here the activities include swimming, boating, fishing, and picnicking. ⊠ *Exit 76 off I–84 , Lower Mayer State Park access* ☎ *800/551–6949* ⊕ *www.oregonstateparks.org* ▦ *Day use $5 per vehicle.*

GOLDENDALE, WASHINGTON

34 miles northeast of The Dalles via Hwy. 14 and U.S. 97.

Although the actual town of Goldendale lies about 12 miles north of the Columbia River, this easygoing community is a good base for exploring the eastern end of the Gorge. It's home to one of the few notable restaurants in this vast but sparsely populated section of the Columbia River Valley, and it also has a couple of basic motels, a small downtown with a few funky cafés and shops, and the small but excellent Goldendale Observatory State Park. Views on the drive to Goldendale and in town itself are some of the most dramatic in the drier, eastern reaches of the Gorge—you'll see soaring white wind turbines lining the grassy bluffs and cliffs on both sides of the river, and along U.S. 97 as it leads into Goldendale, you can see the snowcapped summit of Washington's 12,281-foot Mt. Adams, which receives a little less attention than its southerly twin, Mt. Hood, but is actually taller and every bit as dramatic.

GETTING HERE AND AROUND

Although it's quickest to drive east along Interstate 84 and then north on U.S. 97 to reach Goldendale (a total of 34 miles) and the attractions around Maryhill, it takes only a few extra minutes and is far more scenic to cross the Columbia via The Dalles Bridge into Washington and drive east on Highway 14 to U.S. 97.

ESSENTIALS

Greater Goldendale Chamber of Commerce. ⊠ *903 E. Broadway St., Goldendale* ☎ *509/773–3400* ⊕ *www.goldendalechamber.org.*

EXPLORING

FAMILY **Goldendale Observatory State Park.** This 5-acre park on a 2,100-foot-elevation bluff just north of Goldendale's compact downtown contains one of the nation's largest public telescopes, and the town's remote location, far from the lights of any cities, is ideal. Fascinating astronomy programs and sky-watching events are held during the day and evening, year-round. ⊠ *1602 Observatory Dr., Goldendale* ☎ *509/773–3141* ⊕ *www.goldendaleobservatory.com* ⊠ *$10 day pass* ⊙ *Closed Apr.–Sept., Mon. and Tues.; Oct.–Mar., Mon.–Thurs.*

Fodor's Choice **Maryhill Museum of Art.** A wonderfully eclectic mix of artworks, including
★ the largest assemblage of Rodin works outside France; posters, glasswork, and ephemera related to the modern-dance pioneer Loïe Fuller; an impressive cache of Native American artifacts; furniture and art that belonged to another Hill companion, Queen Marie of Romania; an art nouveau glass collection; and a large collection of mostly Victorian-era European and American landscape paintings: they're all housed within the walls of a grandiose mansion built rather improbably in the middle of nowhere by Sam Hill, the man who spearheaded the development of a scenic highway through the Columbia Gorge. The main Beaux Arts building dates to 1914, and a daring, beautifully executed, LEED-certified modern wing, extends from the back, with a terraced slope overlooking the Columbia River—it contains the museum café, a lovely spot for lunch. The extensive, harmoniously landscaped grounds

include a sculpture garden and pathways along the Gorge rim. ✉ *35 Maryhill Museum of Art Dr., Goldendale ✣ Off Hwy. 14, 3 miles west of junction with U.S. 97* ☎ *509/773–3733* 🌐 *www.maryhillmuseum.org* 🎟 *$9* ⏲ *Closed mid-Nov.–mid-Mar.*

Fodor's Choice ★ **Maryhill Winery.** Just down the road from Maryhill Museum, this large winery enjoys the same phenomenal views up and down the Gorge. The largest tasting room in the Gorge has a good-size gift shop as well as a market selling cheese, charcuterie, and other gourmet goodies. Maryhill produces dozens of wines at a variety of prices—the reserves, including stellar Cabernet Franc, Cabernet Sauvignon, Malbec, and Chardonnay, tend to earn most acclaim. In summer, the outdoor amphitheater on the grounds hosts a series of pop concerts. ✉ *9774 Hwy. 14, Goldendale* ☎ *509/773–1976, 877/627–9445* 🌐 *www.maryhillwinery.com.*

WHERE TO EAT

$ MODERN AMERICAN Fodor's Choice ★ 🍴 **Glass Onion.** Visitors to small, unpretentious Goldendale will be surprised to find one of the culinary gems of the Columbia Gorge in the center of town, set within a cozy, beautifully restored house hung with local artwork. Chef Matt McGowan sources seasonal ingredients from local farms and purveyors, serves a great selection of local beers and wines, and keeps the price of everything on his menu at least $10 below what you'd pay in Hood River or Portland. **Known for:** homemade desserts; reasonable prices; nice selection of Gorge wines and beers. [$] *Average main: $13* ✉ *604 S. Columbus Ave., Goldendale* ☎ *509/773–4928* 🌐 *www.theglassonionrestaurant.com* ⏲ *Closed Sun.–Tues.*

MT. HOOD

Today Mt. Hood is known for the challenge it poses to climbers, its deep winter snows, and a dozen glaciers and snowfields that make skiing possible nearly year-round. Resort towns and colorful hospitality villages are arranged in a semicircle around the mountain, full of ski bars and rental cabins that host hordes of fun-loving Portlanders each weekend. In every direction from the postcard-perfect peak, the million-acre Mount Hood National Forest spreads out like a big green blanket, and more than 300,000 acres of that are designated wilderness. Mule deer, black bears, elk, and the occasional cougar share the space with humans who come to hike, camp, and fish in the Pacific Northwest's quintessential wild ecosystem.

AROUND THE MOUNTAIN

About 60 miles east of Portland on I–84 and U.S. 26, and 42 miles south of Hood River via Hwy. 35 and U.S. 26.

Majestically towering 11,245 feet above sea level, Mt. Hood is what remains of the original north wall and rim of a volatile crater. Although the peak no longer spews ash or fire, active vents regularly release steam high on the mountain. The mountain took its modern moniker in 1792, when a crew of the British Royal Navy, the first recorded Caucasians sailing up the Columbia River, spotted it and named it after a famed British naval officer by the name of—you guessed it—Hood.

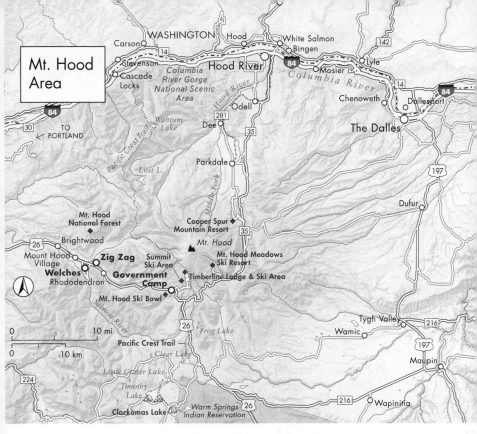

Mt. Hood offers the longest ski season in North America, with three major ski areas and some 30 lifts, as well as extensive areas for cross-country skiing and snowboarding. Many of the ski runs turn into mountain-bike trails in summer. The mountain is also popular with climbers and hikers. In fact, some hikes follow parts of the Oregon Trail, and signs of the pioneers' passing are still evident.

GETTING HERE AND AROUND

From Portland, U.S. 26 heads east into the heart of Mount Hood National Forest, while Highway 35 runs south from Hood River along the mountain's east face. The roads meet 60 miles east of Portland, near Government Camp, forming an oblong loop with Interstate 84 and the Historic Columbia Gorge Highway. It's about a 75-minute drive from Downtown Portland to Government Camp via U.S. 26. **Sea to Summit**—call for timetables and pickup and drop-off sites—offers shuttle service from Portland International Airport and Downtown Portland hotels to all of the Mt. Hood resorts; the fare is $50 each way, with discounted lift-ticket and ski-rental packages available. Additionally, the **Mt. Hood Express** bus line operates daily and links the villages along the corridor—including Welches, Government Camp, and Timberline Lodge—to the Portland suburb of Sandy, which you can get to via TriMet commuter bus. This option is slower (it takes

2½ to 3 hours each way from the airport or Downtown to Timberline Lodge, for example) than a direct shuttle but costs just $2, plus $2.50 for TriMet bus fare to Sandy.

Contacts Mt. Hood Express. ☎ *503/668–3466* ⊕ *www.mthoodexpress.com.* **Sea to Summit.** ☎ *503/286–9333* ⊕ *www.seatosummit.net.*

ESSENTIALS

Visitor Information Mt. Hood Area Chamber of Commerce. ☎ *503/622–3017* ⊕ *www.mthoodchamber.com.* **Mount Hood National Forest Headquarters.** ✉ *16400 Champion Way, Sandy* ☎ *503/668–1700* ⊕ *www.fs.usda.gov/ mthood.*

EXPLORING

Fodor's Choice ★ **Mount Hood National Forest.** The highest spot in Oregon and the fourth-highest peak in the Cascades, "the Mountain" is a focal point of the 1.1-million-acre forest, an all-season playground attracting around 3 million visitors annually. Beginning 20 miles southeast of Portland, it extends south from the Columbia River Gorge for more than 60 miles and includes more than 311,400 acres of designated wilderness. These woods are perfect for hikers, horseback riders, mountain climbers, and cyclists. Within the forest are more than 80 campgrounds and 50 lakes stocked with brown, rainbow, cutthroat, brook, and steelhead trout. The Sandy, Salmon, Clackamas, and other rivers are known for their fishing, rafting, canoeing, and swimming. Both forest and mountain are crossed by an extensive trail system for hikers, cyclists, and horseback riders. The **Pacific Crest Trail,** which begins in British Columbia and ends in Mexico, crosses at the 4,157-foot-high Barlow Pass. As with most other mountain destinations within Oregon, weather can be temperamental, and snow and ice may affect driving conditions as early as October and as late as June. Bring tire chains and warm clothes as a precaution.

Since this forest is close to the Portland metro area, campgrounds and trails are potentially crowded over the summer months, especially on weekends. If you're planning to camp, get info and permits from the Mount Hood National Forest Headquarters. Campgrounds are managed by the U.S. Forest Service and a few private concessionaires, and standouts include a string of neighboring campgrounds on the south side of Mt. Hood: Trillium Lake, Still Creek, Timothy Lake, Little Crater Lake, Clackamas Lake, Summit Lake, Clear Lake, and Frog Lake. Each varies in what it offers and in price. The mountain overflows with day-use areas. From mid-November through April, all designated Winter Recreation Areas require a Sno-Park permit, available from the U.S. Forest Service and many local resorts and sporting goods stores. ✉ *Headquarters, 16400 Champion Way, Sandy* ☎ *503/668–1700* ⊕ *www.fs.usda.gov/mthood* 🖘 *Day pass $5.*

WHERE TO EAT AND STAY

$$$$
PACIFIC
NORTHWEST

✕ **Cascade Dining Room.** Vaulted wooden beams and a wood-plank floor, handcrafted furniture, handwoven drapes, and a lion-size stone fireplace set the scene in Timberline Lodge's esteemed restaurant, from which views of neighboring mountains are enjoyed, except when snow drifts cover the windows. The atmosphere is traditional and historic, but chef

Jason Stoller Smith is a former wine-country *wunderkind* whose resume includes orchestrating a salmon bake at the White House. **Known for:** taste of Oregon lunch buffet; chef demonstrations; historic setting. $ *Average main: $38* ✉ *27500 E. Timberline Rd., Timberline Lodge* ☎ *503/272–3104* ⊕ *www.timberlinelodge.com.*

$$

RESORT

FAMILY

Fodor's Choice

★

🛏 **Timberline Lodge.** Guest rooms are simple, rustic, and charming (a handful of them lack private baths), but don't expect a cushy experience—the reason for staying here is the location and setting. **Pros:** a thrill to stay on the mountain itself; great proximity to all snow activity; amazing architecture. **Cons:** rooms are small and the least expensive ones have shared bathrooms; views from rooms are often completely blocked by snow in winter; carloads of tourists. $ *Rooms from: $160* ✉ *27500 E. Timberline Rd., Timberline Lodge* ☎ *503/272–3311, 800/547–1406* ⊕ *www.timberlinelodge.com* ↯ *70 rooms* ⦿| *Some meals.*

SPORTS AND THE OUTDOORS
DOWNHILL SKIING

FAMILY **Cooper Spur Mountain Resort.** On the northern slope of Mt. Hood, Cooper Spur caters to families and has one double chair and a tow rope. The longest run is 2/3 mile, with a 350-foot vertical drop. Facilities and services include rentals, instruction, repairs, and a ski shop, day lodge, snack bar, and restaurant. Call for hours. ✉ *10755 Cooper Spur Rd., Mount Hood* ✛ *Follow signs from Hwy. 35 for 2½ miles to ski area* ☎ *541/352–6692* ⊕ *www.cooperspur.com.*

Timberline Lodge & Ski Area. The longest ski season in North America unfolds at this full-service ski area, where the U.S. ski team conducts summer training. Thanks to the omnipresent Palmer Snowfield, it's the closest thing to a year-round ski area in the Lower 48 (it's typically closed for just a few weeks in September). Timberline is famous for its Palmer chairlift, which takes skiers and snowboarders to the high glacier for summer skiing. There are five high-speed quad chairs, one triple chair, and one double. The top elevation is 8,500 feet, with a 3,700-foot vertical drop, and the longest run is 3 miles. Facilities include a day lodge with fast food and a ski shop; lessons and equipment rental and repair are available. Parking requires a Sno-Park permit. The Palmer and Magic Mile lifts are popular with both skiers and sightseers. ✉ *27500 E. Timberline Rd., Timberline Lodge* ☎ *503/272–3311* ⊕ *www.timberlinelodge.com.*

GOVERNMENT CAMP

54 miles east of Portland on I–84 and U.S. 26, and 42 miles south of Hood River via Hwy. 35 and U.S. 26.

This alpine resort village with a bohemian vibe has several hotels and restaurants popular with visitors exploring Mt. Hood's ski areas and mountain-biking and hiking trails. "Govy" is also just a 12-mile drive up the hill from Welches, which also has restaurants and lodging.

GETTING HERE AND AROUND

Government Camp is on U.S. 26, which is often called the Mt. Hood Corridor. It's about 55 miles east of Portland and just down the hill from Timberline Lodge.

5

WHERE TO EAT AND STAY

$ AMERICAN 🍴 **Charlie's Mountain View.** Old and new ski swag plasters the walls, lift chairs function as furniture, and photos of famous (and locally famous) skiers and other memorabilia are as abundant as the menu selections. Open-flame-grilled steaks and hamburgers are worthy here, and the happy hour crowd shares plates piled high with waffle fries. **Known for:** live music on weekends; apple dumplings (in season); rowdy and fun vibe. [$] *Average main: $9* ✉ *88462 E. Government Camp Loop* ☎ *503/272–3333* 🌐 *www.charliesmountainview.com/eats.*

$$ EASTERN EUROPEAN 🍴 **Glacier Haus Bistro.** This lively, family-operated spot in the center of Government Camp is a good bet for a snack. Locals love the Eastern European standards, such as Hungarian beef goulash, Wiener schnitzel, and Bavarian sausages with sauerkraut and garlic-mashed potatoes. **Known for:** hearty Eastern European fare; family-friendly ambience. [$] *Average main: $17* ✉ *88817 E. Government Camp Loop Rd.* ☎ *503/272–3471* 🌐 *www.glacierhaus.com* 🕒 *Closed Mon. and Oct.*

$ AMERICAN 🍴 **Mt. Hood Brewing.** Producing finely crafted beers—Multorporter Smoked Porter, Ice Axe IPA, Highland Meadow Blond Ale, and others—since the early '90s, this casual brewpub with stone walls, a fireplace, and both booth and table seating buzzes in the early evening for après-ski dining and drinking. It's popular for its creative comfort food, including poutine with fontina cheese and peppercorn demi-glace, cast-iron-skillet-baked fondue, Alsatian pizza topped with smoked ham and crème fraîche, barbecue pulled-pork-and-porter sandwiches. **Known for:** root-beer—and beer—ice-cream floats; cast-iron fondue. [$] *Average main: $13* ✉ *87304 E. Government Camp Loop* ☎ *503/272–3172* 🌐 *www.mthoodbrewing.com.*

$$ RESORT FAMILY Fodor's Choice ★ 🏨 **Collins Lake Resort.** Comprising 66 poshly furnished chalets with fireplaces and dozens of other amenities, scattered around an alpine lake, this contemporary, 28-acre compound is the cushiest accommodations option in the Mt. Hood area. **Pros:** within walking distance of Government Camp restaurants and bars; spacious layouts are ideal for groups and families. **Cons:** steepest rates in town. [$] *Rooms from: $190* ✉ *88149 E. Creek Ridge Rd.* ☎ *503/928–3498, 800/234–6288* 🌐 *www.collinslakeresort.com* 🛏 *66 condos* 🍽 *No meals.*

SPORTS AND THE OUTDOORS

DOWNHILL SKIING

Fodor's Choice ★ **Mt. Hood Meadows Ski Resort.** The mountain's largest resort has more than 2,150 skiable acres, 85 runs, five double chairs, six high-speed quads, a top elevation of 9,000 feet, a vertical drop of 2,777 feet, and a longest run of 3 miles. If you're seeking varied, scenic terrain with plenty of trails for all skiing abilities, this is your best choice among the region's ski areas. Facilities include a day lodge, nine restaurants, two lounges, a ski-and-snowboard school, a children's learning center with daycare, and two ski shops with equipment rentals. ✉ *Hwy. 35* ✣ *10 miles east of Government Camp* ☎ *503/337–2222* 🌐 *www.skihood.com.*

FAMILY **Mt. Hood Skibowl.** The ski area closest to Portland is also known as "America's largest night ski area," with 34 runs lighted each evening. It has 960 skiable acres serviced by four double chairs and five surface tows, a top elevation of 5,100 feet, a vertical drop of 1,500 feet, and a longest run of 3 miles. You can take advantage of two day lodges, a mid-mountain warming hut, four restaurants, and two lounges. Sleigh rides are conducted, weather permitting, and a hugely popular tubing and adventure park has several tubing hills, plus music, LED lights, and a laser show. In summer the resort morphs into the Adventure Park at Skibowl, with mountain biking, zip lines, bungee jumping, a five-story free-fall Tarzan Swing, disc golf, and kid-friendly tubing and alpine slides. ⊠ *87000 E. U.S. 26* ☎ *503/272–3206* ⊕ *www.skibowl.com.*

SHOPPING

Govy General Store. Good thing this is a really nice grocery store, because it's the only one for miles around. Govy General stocks all the staples, plus a nice selection of gourmet treats like cheeses and chocolates. It's also a full-service liquor store and your one-stop shop for Mt. Hood sweatshirts, postcards, and other keepsake tchotchkes. ∎TIP➔ Grab your Sno-Park permit here in winter. ⊠ *30521 E. Meldrum St.* ☎ *541/272–3107* ⊕ *www.govygeneralstore.com.*

WELCHES AND ZIGZAG

12 miles west of Government Camp and 40 miles east of Portland.

One of a string of small communities known as the Villages at Mt. Hood, Welches's claim to fame is that it was the site of Oregon's first golf course, built at the base of Mt. Hood in 1928. Another golf course is still going strong today, and summer vacationers hover around both towns for access to basic services like gas, groceries, and dining. Others come to pull a few trout out of the scenic Zigzag River or to access trails and streams in the adjacent Salmon–Huckleberry Wilderness.

GETTING HERE AND AROUND

Most of Welches is found just off U.S. 26, often called the Mt. Hood Corridor here, about 45 miles east of Portland.

WHERE TO EAT AND STAY

$$ ✕**The Rendezvous Grill & Tap Room.** "Serious food in a not-so-serious

AMERICAN place" is the slogan of this casual roadhouse with surprisingly sophisti-

Fodor'sChoice cated food—it's been a locals' favorite since it opened back in mid-'90s.

★ For a joint many miles from the coast, the 'Vous sure does a nice job with seafood, turning out appetizing plates of sautéed shrimp, Willapa Bay oysters, Dungeness crab, and char-grilled wild salmon. **Known for:** surprisingly sophisticated menu; house-infused vodkas; great outdoor seating. $ *Average main: $21* ⊠ *67149 E. U.S. 26, Welches* ☎ *503/622–6837* ⊕ *www.thevousgrill.com* ☉ *Closed Mon.*

$ 🏚**The Cabins Creekside at Welches.** Affordability, accessibility to rec-

RENTAL reational activities, and wonderful hosts make these cabins with knotty-pine vaulted ceilings, log furnishings, and full-size kitchens a great lodging choice in the Mt. Hood area. **Pros:** family-run; quiet, off-highway location; anglers will benefit from the Thurmans' fly-fishing savvy. **Cons:** no dining within walking distance; no cabin-side parking; simple but clean, functional furnishings. $ *Rooms from: $109* ⊠ *25086 E. Welches Rd., Welches* ☎ *503/622–4275* ⊕ *www.mthoodcabins.com* ⬐ *10 cabins* ☉❘ *No meals.*

5

$$ RESORT

🏨 **Resort at The Mountain.** In the evergreen-forest foothills of Mt. Hood, this expansive resort is popular year-round both with outdoorsy sorts and couples seeking romantic hideaways. **Pros:** every sport available; plenty of choices in room size. **Cons:** there will be crowds; may not appeal to those who are not fans of golf. [$] *Rooms from: $188* ✉ *68010 E. Fairway Ave., Welches* ☎ *503/622–3101, 877/439–6774* 🌐 *www.theresort.com* 🛏 *157 rooms* 🍴 *No meals.*

SPORTS AND THE OUTDOORS

FISHING

The Fly Fishing Shop. This heritage shop full of self-proclaimed "fish-aholics" has been peddling flies and guiding trips for three decades. Drop in to ask about the huge variety of customizable float trips (from $500), clinics, and by-the-hour walking trips for seasonal steelhead and salmon ($50 an hour). Great nearby rivers include the glacial-fed Sandy and its tributary the Zigzag, which hides some native cuthroat. ✉ *67296 E. U.S. 26, Welches* ☎ *503/622–4607, 800/266–3971* 🌐 *www.flyfishusa.com.*

Ron Lauzon's Fly Fishing School. Knowledgeable and highly respected fishing expert Ron Lauzon offers private and group lessons and instruction, and also leads guided float and wading trips. He knows the top trout- and steelhead-fishing sites in the region like no other. ✉ *Sandy* ☎ *503/622–3634* 🌐 *www.theflyfishinginstructor.com.*

GOLF

The Courses. The three 9-hole tracks at the Resort at the Mountain include the Pine Cone Nine, Oregon's oldest golf course, built on a rented hayfield in 1928—you can mix any combination of the three courses to complete a full 18-hole round. There's also a lighted 18-hole putting course that's popular with families and adults working on their short game. ✉ *68010 E. Fairway Ave., Welches* ☎ *503/622–3151, 800/669–4653* 🌐 *mthood-resort.com* 🎟 *$50–$70 for 18 holes* 🏌 *Pine Cone: 9 holes, 3299 yards, par 36. Foxglove: 9 holes, 3106 yards, par 36. Thistle: 9 holes, 2956 yards, par 34.*

CENTRAL
OREGON

WELCOME TO CENTRAL OREGON

TOP REASONS TO GO

★ **Become one with nature:** Central Oregonians live on the flanks of the Cascade Range and are bracketed by rock formations, rivers, lakes, forests, ancient lava flows, and desert badlands. Bring your golf clubs, carabiners, snowboard, or camera, and explore deeper.

★ **Visit Bend:** Downtown Bend is lively and walkable, with a variety of appealing restaurants, galleries, and stores.

★ **Kick back at Sunriver:** This family-oriented resort has bike paths, river trails, horse stables, tennis courts, a golf course, and several restaurants.

★ **Check out the craft-brewing scene:** With nearly three dozen breweries—and more on the horizon—you can discover nearly any type of beer that fits your tastes.

★ **Discover the Old West:** Cowboy towns, such as Sisters, offer a glimpse into what life was like when the West was wild.

1 West Central Oregon. The western portion of central Oregon ranges from lush and green in the Cascades to dry and full of conifers down to the Deschutes River. It's the side with the ski areas, the high mountain lakes, most of the resorts, and the rushing waters. The region's largest town is Bend, and it straddles the forested west and the harshly beautiful east.

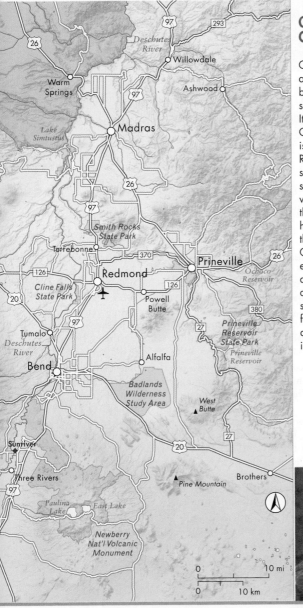

GETTING ORIENTED

Central Oregon provides a natural meeting place between the urban west side and the rural east side. It nestles neatly below the Columbia River basin and is drained by the Deschutes River, which flows from south to north. Skiers and snowboarders flock to winter sports areas on the western edge, anglers head to the Deschutes, the Metolius, and the Cascade Lakes, and climbers, campers, rockhounds, and wanderers explore the arid landscapes on the east side. Bend, the largest town for more than 120 miles in any direction, sits roughly in the center of this region.

6

Updated
by Jonathan
Shadel

After a day on the Sunriver bike paths, a first-time visitor from Europe shook her head. "This place is paradise," she declared. It's easy to see why she thought so. Central Oregon has snowfields so white they sharpen the edges of the mountains; canyons so deep and sudden as to induce vertigo; air so crisp that it fills the senses; water that ripples in mountain lakes so clear that boaters can see to the bottom, or rushes through turbulent rapids favored by rafters.

A region born of volcanic tumult is now a powerful lure for the adventurous, the beauty-seeking, and even the urbane—Bend has grown into a sophisticated city of 87,000-plus, a magnet for people retreating from larger, noisier city centers. For most visitors Bend is the sunny face of central Oregon, a haven for hikers, athletes, and aesthetes, but with the charm and elegance of much larger cities.

From Bend it's easy to launch to the attractions that surround it. To the northwest, Camp Sherman is a stunning place to fish for rainbow trout or kokanee. The Smith Rocks formation to the north draws climbers and boulderers, and, to the south, Lava Lands and the Lava River Caves fascinate visitors more than 6,000 years after they were chiseled out of the earth. The Oregon Badlands Wilderness to the east draws hikers and horseback riders wanting to connect with the untamed landscape. Lake Billy Chinook to the north is a startling oasis, where summer visitors drift in houseboats beneath the high walls of the Deschutes River canyon. The Deschutes River itself carries rafters of all descriptions, from young families to solo adventurers.

The area's natural beauty has brought it a diverse cluster of resorts, whether situated on the shores of high mountain lakes or cradling golf courses of startling green. They dot the landscape from the dry terrain around Warm Springs to the high road to Mt. Bachelor.

CENTRAL OREGON PLANNER

WHEN TO GO

Central Oregon is a popular destination year-round. Skiers and snow-boarders come from mid-December through March, when the powder is deepest and driest. During this time, guests flock to the hotels and resorts along Century Drive, which leads from Bend to Mt. Bachelor. In summer, when temperatures reach the upper 80s, travelers are more likely to spread throughout the region. But temperatures fall as the elevation rises, so take a jacket if you're heading out for an evening at the high lakes or Newberry Crater.

You'll pay a premium at the mountain resorts during ski season, and Sunriver and other family and golf resorts are busiest in summer. It's best to make reservations as far in advance as possible; six months in advance is not too early.

GETTING HERE AND AROUND

AIR TRAVEL

Visitors fly into **Redmond Municipal Airport–Roberts Field** (RDM), about 17 miles north of downtown Bend. Rental cars are available for pickup at the airport from several national agencies. The **Redmond Airport Shuttle** provides transportation throughout the region (reservations requested); a ride from the airport to addresses within Bend costs about $40. Taxis are available at curbside, or can be summoned from the call board inside the airport. Portland's airport is 160 miles northwest of Bend, and daily flights connect the two cities.

Air Contacts Redmond Airport Shuttle. ☎ *541/382–1687, 888/664–8449* ⊕ *www.redmondairportshuttle.net.* **Redmond Municipal Airport–Roberts Field** (RDM). ✉ *2522 S.E. Jesse Butler Circle, Redmond* ☎ *541/548–0646* ⊕ *www.flyrdm.com.*

BUS TRAVEL

The **Central Oregon Breeze,** a regional carrier, runs one bus a day each way between Portland and Bend, with stops in Redmond and Madras. **Cascades East Transit** is Bend's intercity bus service, and connects Redmond, La Pine, Madras, Prineville, Bend, and Sisters. Trips from the airport require reservations. **Greyhound** also serves the area with direct routes from Bend to Eugene and Salem, with connections onward to Portland.

Bus Contacts Cascades East Transit. ✉ *334 Hawthorn Ave., Bend* ☎ *541/385–8680, 866/385–8680* ⊕ *www.cascadeseasttransit.com.* **Central Oregon Breeze.** ✉ *2045 N.E. Hwy. 20, Bend* ☎ *541/389–7469, 800/847–0157* ⊕ *www.cobreeze.com.* **Greyhound Bend.** ✉ *334 N.E. Hawthorne Ave., Bend* ☎ *541/923–1732* ⊕ *www.greyhound.com.*

CAR TRAVEL

U.S. 20 heads west from Idaho and east from the coastal town of Newport into central Oregon. U.S. 26 goes southeast from Portland to Prineville, where it heads northeast into the Ochoco National Forest. U.S. 97 heads north from California and south from Washington to Bend. Highway 126 travels east from Eugene to Prineville; it connects with

U.S. 20 heading south (to Bend) at Sisters. Major roads throughout central Oregon are well maintained and open throughout the winter season, although it's always advisable to have tire chains in the car. Some roads are closed by snow during winter, including Oregon 242. Check the **Oregon Department of Transportation's TripCheck** (⊕ *www.trip-check.com*) or call **ODOT** (☎ *800/977–6368*).

FESTIVALS

Bend Film Festival. This popular local film festival takes place in October. ⊠ *1000 N.W. Wall St., Suite 260, Bend* ☎ *541/388–3378* ⊕ *www. bendfilm.org.*

Bend Summer and Fall Festival. Downtown Bend is blocked off with food, crafts, art booths, and music in July and September. ⊠ *Box 1424, Bend* ☎ *541/508–4280* ⊕ *www.bendfestivals.com.*

Oregon Winterfest. February brings music, food, brews, wine, ice carving, and other winter sports to Bend's Old Mill District. ⊠ *Bend* ⊕ *www. oregonwinterfest.com.*

Pole, Pedal, Paddle. Bend's popular ski, bike, run, and kayak or canoe race is held in May. ⊠ *Bend* ☎ *541/388–0002* ⊕ *www.pppbend.com.*

Sisters Folk Festival. A celebration of American music is held in September. ⊠ *Sisters* ☎ *541/549–4979* ⊕ *www.sistersfolkfestival.org.*

Sisters Outdoor Quilt Show. The second Saturday in July, Sisters transforms into a Western town covered with colorful quilts hanging from building exteriors. ⊠ *Sisters* ☎ *541/549–0989* ⊕ *www.sistersout-doorquiltshow.org.*

Sisters Rodeo. Multiple rodeo and community events, held annually for more than 70 years, take place over a weekend in June. ⊠ *67637 U.S. 20, south of Sisters, Sisters* ☎ *541/549–0121, 800/827–7522* ⊕ *www. sistersrodeo.com.*

RESTAURANTS

The center of culinary ambition is in downtown Bend, but good restaurants also serve diners in Sisters, Redmond, Prineville, and the major resorts. Styles vary, but many hew to the Northwest preference for fresh foods grown, caught, and harvested in the region.

Central Oregon also has many down-home places and family-friendly brewpubs, and authentic Mexican restaurants have emerged to win faithful followings in Prineville, Redmond, Madras, and Bend. *Restaurant reviews have been shortened. For full information visit Fodors.com.*

HOTELS

Central Oregon has lodging for every taste, from upscale resort lodges to an in-town brewpub village, eclectic bed-and-breakfasts, rustic Western inns, and a range of independent and chain hotels and motels. If you're drawn to the rivers, stay in a pastoral fishing cabin along the Metolius near Camp Sherman. If you came for the powder, you'll want a ski-snowboard condo closer to the mountain. For soaking up the atmosphere, you might favor one of downtown Bend's luxurious hotels, or Old St. Francis, the Catholic school–turned-brewpub village. *Hotel reviews have been shortened. For full information, visit Fodors.com.*

WHAT IT COSTS IN U.S. DOLLARS				
	$	**$$**	**$$$**	**$$$$**
Restaurants	under $16	$16–$22	$23–$30	over $30
Hotels	under $150	$150–$200	$201–$250	over $250

Restaurant prices are the average cost of a main course at dinner, or if dinner is not served, at lunch. Hotel prices are the lowest cost of a standard double room in high season.

TOURS

Cog Wild Bicycle Tours. One- and multiday mountain bike tours are offered for people of all skill levels and interests. ✉ *255 S.W. Century Dr., Suite 201, Bend* ☎ *541/385–7002* ⊕ *www.cogwild.com* 🖅 *From $170.*

Sun Country Tours. A longtime provider of raft and tube trips on central Oregon rivers offers rafting excursions that range from two hours to full days May through September. ✉ *531 S.W. 13th St., Bend* ☎ *541/382–6277* ⊕ *www.suncountrytours.com* 🖅 *From $59.*

Fodor's Choice ★ **Wanderlust Tours.** Popular and family-friendly half-day or evening excursions are offered around Bend, Sisters, and Sunriver. Options include kayaking, canoeing, snowshoeing, and caving. ✉ *61535 S. Hwy. 97, Suite 13, Bend* ☎ *541/389–8359* ⊕ *www.wanderlusttours.com* 🖅 *From $75.*

VISITOR INFORMATION

Central Oregon Visitors Association. ✉ *57100 Beaver Dr., Bldg. 6, Suite 130, Sunriver* ☎ *541/389–8799, 800/800–8334* ⊕ *www.visitcentraloregon.com.*

WEST CENTRAL OREGON

Sunshine, crisp pines, pure air, rushing waters, world-class skiing and snowboarding at Mt. Bachelor, destination golf resorts, a touch of the frontier West at Sisters, an air of sophistication in Bend—the forested side of central Oregon serves up many recreational flavors. The area draws young couples, seniors, families, athletes, and adventurers, all of whom arrive with a certain sense of purpose, but also with an appreciation for the natural world. Travelers will have no problem filling a week in central Oregon's western half with memorable activities, from rafting to enjoying some sensational meals.

BEND

160 miles southeast of Portland.

Bend, Oregon's largest city east of the Cascades, is once more one of the fastest-growing cities in the state, recovering abundantly from the hard-hitting recession. Construction is booming and new businesses seem to open every day. The people of Bend continue to enjoy an enviable climate, proximity to skiing, dynamic lifestyle, and a reputation as a playground and recreational escape. At times it seems that everybody in Bend is an athlete or a brewer, but it remains a tolerant, welcoming town, conscious of making a good first impression. Bend's heart is an

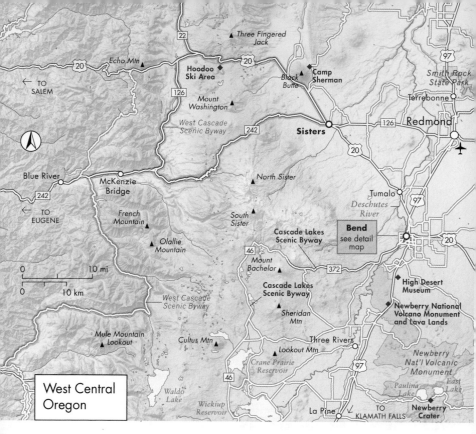

West Central Oregon

area of about four square blocks, centered on Wall and Bond streets. Here you'll find boutique stores, galleries, independent coffee shops, brewpubs, fine restaurants, lively nightlife establishments, and historic landmarks such as the Tower Theatre, built in 1940. A few traditional barbershops and taverns are also spread around, keeping it real.

Neighboring Mt. Bachelor, though hardly a giant among the Cascades at 9,065 feet, is blessed by an advantage over its taller siblings—by virtue of its location, it's the first to get snowfall, and the last to see it go. Inland air collides with the Pacific's damp influence, creating skiing conditions immortalized in songs by local rock bands and raves from the ski press.

GETTING HERE AND AROUND
Portlanders arrive via car on U.S. 20 or U.S. 26, and folks from the mid–Willamette Valley cross the mountains on Oregon 126. Redmond Municipal Airport, 17 miles to the north, is an efficient hub for air travelers, who can rent a car or take a shuttle or cab into town. **Greyhound** also serves the area with direct routes to Eugene and Salem. The **Central Oregon Breeze**, a privately operated regional carrier, runs daily between Portland and Bend, with stops in Redmond and Madras. Bend is served by a citywide bus system called **Cascades East Transit**, which also connects to Redmond, La Pine, Sisters, Prineville, and Madras. To take a Cascades East bus between cities in central Oregon, reservations are

not required but recommended. *For more on bus travel to and from Bend, see Getting Here and Around in the Central Oregon Planner.*

If you're trying to head out of or into Bend on a major highway during the morning or 5 pm rush, especially on U.S. 97, you may hit congestion. Parking in downtown Bend is free for the first two hours (three hours at the centrally located parking garage), or park for free in the residential neighborhoods just west of downtown. In addition to the car-rental counters at the airport, Avis, Budget, Enterprise, and Hertz also have rental locations in Bend.

ESSENTIALS

Visitor Information Bend Chamber of Commerce. ✉ *777 N.W. Wall St., Suite 200* ☎ *541/382–3221* ⊕ *www.bendchamber.org.* **Visit Bend/Bend Visitor Center.** ✉ *750 N.W. Lava Rd., Suite 160* ☎ *541/382–8048, 877/245–8484* ⊕ *www.visitbend.com.*

EXPLORING

FAMILY **Des Chutes Historical Museum.** The Deschutes County Historical Society operates this museum, which was originally built as a schoolhouse in 1914. Exhibits depict historical life in the area, including a pioneer schoolroom, Native American artifacts, and relics from the logging, ranching, homesteading, and railroading eras. ✉ *129 N.W. Idaho Ave.* ☎ *541/389–1813* ⊕ *www.deschuteshistory.org* 🎫 *$5.*

Deschutes Brewery. Central Oregon's first and most famous brewery produces and bottles its beer in this facility separate from the popular brewpub. Take a free tour at 1 pm every day and learn from the beer-obsessed staff; be sure to make reservations online or by phone since groups fill quickly. The tour ends in the tasting room and gift shop, where participants get to try samples of the fresh beer. ✉ *901 S.W. Simpson Ave.* ☎ *541/385–8606* ⊕ *www.deschutesbrewery.com.*

Drake Park and Mirror Pond. At its western edge, downtown Bend slopes down to these 13 acres of manicured greensward and trees lining the edge of the Deschutes, attracting flocks of Canada geese as well as strollers from downtown. Various events, such as music festivals, occur in the park during the summer months. Note the 11-foot-high wheel log skidder, harkening back to Bend's logging industry in the early 20th century, when four draft horses pulled the wheel to move heavy logs. ✉ *Bounded on the west by N.W. Brooks St. and Drake Park; N.W. Lava Rd. on the east; N.W. Franklin Ave. to the south; and N.W. Greenwood Ave. to the north* ⊕ *www.downtownbend.org.*

FAMILY **High Desert Museum.** The West was actually wild, and this combo
Fodor's Choice museum/zoo proves it. Kids will love the up-close-and-personal encoun-
★ ters with Gila monsters, snakes, porcupines, birds of prey, Vivi the bobcat, and Snowshoe the lynx. Characters in costume take part in the Living History series, where you can chat with stagecoach drivers, boomtown widows, pioneers, homesteaders, and sawmill operators. Peruse the 110,000-square-feet of indoor and outdoor exhibits, such as Spirit of the West and a historic family ranch, to experience how the past can truly come alive. ✉ *59800 S. Hwy. 97, 7 miles south of downtown Bend* ☎ *541/382–4754* ⊕ *www.highdesertmuseum.org* 🎫 *$15 May–Oct., $12 Nov.–Apr.*

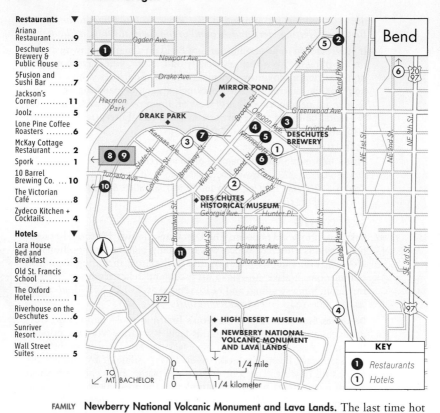

FAMILY **Newberry National Volcanic Monument and Lava Lands.** The last time hot lava flowed from Newberry Volcano was about 13 centuries ago. The north end of the monument has several large basalt flows, as well as the 500-foot **Lava Butte** cinder cone—a coal-black and scorched-red, symmetrical mound thrust from the depths 7,000 years ago. The cone is now home to the **Lava Lands Visitor Center,** which features interpretive exhibits that explain the volcanic and early human history of the area. **Lava River Cave,** a 1-mile-long lava tube, takes about 90 minutes to explore on your own with a lantern (available for rent, $5). On the south end of the monument, an unpaved road leads to beautiful views from **Paulina Peak.** Along the shores of **Paulina Lake** and **East Lake,** you can hike, fish, camp, or stay at the rustic resorts. You can also hike a trail to **Paulina Falls,** an 80-foot double waterfall. The monument offers 100 miles of summer trails, and may be accessible during winter months, depending on snowmelt, for snowmobiling, snowshoeing, and skiing. ⊠ *58201 S. Hwy. 97* ☎ *541/593–2421* ⊕ *www.fs.usda.gov/ centraloregon* ➘ *$5 per vehicle* ⊙ *Lava River Cave closes Oct. 1 to protect bat population.*

EN ROUTE **Cascade Lakes Scenic Byway.** For 66 miles, this nationally designated Scenic Byway meanders past a series of high mountain lakes and is good for fishing, hiking, and camping in the summer months. (Much of the road

Paulina Falls in Newberry National Volcanic Monument

beyond Mt. Bachelor is closed by snow during the colder months.) To find, take Century Drive/Oregon 372 out of Bend and follow it around Mt. Bachelor. To complete as a loop, take U.S. 97 to return. ⊠ *Bend* ⊕ *www.visitbend.com.*

WHERE TO EAT

$$$
AMERICAN
Fodor's Choice
★

✕ **Ariana Restaurant.** Bendites craving a fine-dining experience flock to this upscale New American restaurant, housed in a Craftsman bungalow just west of downtown. Top Northwest ingredients are transformed into French-, Italian-, and Spanish-inspired dishes, which pair perfectly with the extensive wine list. **Known for:** intimate atmosphere; special-occasion meals; decadent desserts. Ⓢ *Average main: $30* ⊠ *1304 N.W. Galveston Ave.* ☎ *541/330–5539* ⊕ *www.arianarestaurantbend.com.*

$
AMERICAN

✕ **Deschutes Brewery & Public House.** Established in 1988, Bend's original brewpub remains a happening spot to get a taste of the city's beer scene. The menu includes a diverse lineup of craft brews, including rotating seasonals, and pub food, such as hearty burgers on house-made brioche rolls. **Known for:** central Oregon–inspired brews; crowded dining room. Ⓢ *Average main: $15* ⊠ *1044 N.W. Bond St.* ☎ *541/382–9242* ⊕ *www. deschutesbrewery.com.*

$$$
ASIAN FUSION

✕ **5 Fusion and Sushi Bar.** Elegant combinations of sushi and other dishes fill the senses with color, texture, and tastes and are presented as pieces of art. Everything about this dining experience is exciting, from the background music to the IPA sushi roll to the horizontal waterfall hanging from the ceiling. **Known for:** inventive sushi; craft cocktails. Ⓢ *Average main: $25* ⊠ *821 N.W. Wall St.* ☎ *541/323–2328* ⊕ *www.5fusion. com* ☾ *No lunch.*

CLOSE UP

Central Oregon Brewery Boom

With nearly three dozen breweries and counting, central Oregon rivals the Portland metro area for brewpubs per capita, but it only hit the map as a beer travel destination in recent years.

Since the first microbrewery opened its doors in 1988 (Deschutes Brewery in downtown Bend), the industry has continued to grow and expand. Each brewery and brewpub approaches the craft beer experience in an original manner, often supported by locals and a combination of live music, good food, unique marketing, experimental brews, and good ole standbys that keep pint glasses and growlers filled.

Residents may buoy the industry, but breweries in turn support the community. Local artists design labels, many beer proceeds go to neighborhood causes, and brews are continually concocted with local events and culture in mind.

BEND ALE TRAIL

Pick up a Bend Ale Trail brochure, or download the app, to guide you through 15 of Bend's breweries. Stop at each brewery, have a taste or a pint, and receive a stamp in your passport. Once you've visited 10 locations, drop by the Bend Visitor Center to receive the prize: a durable silicone pint glass.

$ AMERICAN FAMILY 🍴 **Jackson's Corner.** This family-friendly community restaurant is housed in an unassuming vintage building tucked into a neighborhood near downtown. The eclectic menu leans heavily on locally grown and organic dishes, such as seasonal market salads, house-made pasta dishes, and brick-oven pizza. **Known for:** pasta made fresh daily; kid-friendly table-side service. [$] *Average main: $12* ✉ *845 N.W. Delaware Ave.* ☎ *541/647–2198* 🌐 *www.jacksonscornerbend.com/.*

$$ MIDDLE EASTERN 🍴 **Joolz.** Joolz offers vibrant Middle Eastern food with an Oregon flair; try the small plates like Oregon lamb meatballs and cauliflower with tahini dipping sauce, or mains such as a local free-range longhorn beef burger or Pacific seafood tagine. The chef, raised in Beirut, is the son of a Lebanese father and Oregonian mother (who is rumored to still make the family's melt-in-your-mouth spiced date cake). **Known for:** extensive small plates menu; happy hour cocktail deals (4–9 pm at the bar). [$] *Average main: $17* ✉ *916 N.W. Wall St.* ☎ *541/388–5094* 🌐 *www.joolzbend.com* 🕒 *No lunch.*

$ CAFÉ Fodor's Choice ★ 🍴 **Lone Pine Coffee Roasters.** Tucked down Tin Pan Alley, just paces from The Oxford Hotel, this micro-roaster and café crafts espresso drinks with single-origin coffee and house-made syrups. A hip crowd descends on the shop mid-morning for a light breakfast of pastries delivered daily from Bend's Sparrow Bakery; show up early to snatch a flaky Ocean Roll. **Known for:** skilled baristas; house-roasted coffee; breakfast sweets. [$] *Average main: $5* ✉ *845 Tin Pan Alley* ☎ *541/306–1010* 🌐 *www.lonepinecoffeeroasters.com* 🕒 *No lunch or dinner.*

$ AMERICAN 🍴 **McKay Cottage Restaurant.** This breakfast and lunch spot is housed in a 1916 pioneer cottage, where locals relax throughout its cozy rooms and spill over onto the porch and patio below. The menu is long on comfort food, including fresh scones and sticky buns, and servers are friendly and attentive. **Known for:** cheesy omelets and scrambles; gluten-free options. $ Average main: $12 ⊠ 62910 O.B. Riley Rd. ☎ 541/383–2697 ⊕ www.themckaycottage.com ☾ No dinner.

$ ✕ **Spork.** Bend's favorite food cart–turned–restaurant offers a glob-
INTERNATIONAL ally inspired and healthy menu with an intimate and trendy decor. Try Peruvian stir-fry, Thai steak salad, coconut green curry, or organic tofu tacos. **Known for:** eclectic, wide-ranging menu; globally inspired house cocktails; popular for takeout. $ Average main: $12 ⊠ 937 N.W. Newport Ave. ☎ 541/390–0946 ⊕ www.sporkbend.com.

$ ✕ **10 Barrel Brewing Co.** This trendy brewpub supplies good beer and
AMERICAN compatible food. Pizzas are hand tossed daily, salads are fresh, and sandwiches are varied. **Known for:** innovative brews; comfort pub food; noisy crowds. $ Average main: $12 ⊠ 1135 N.W. Galveston Ave. ☎ 541/678–5228 ⊕ www.10barrel.com.

$ ✕ **The Victorian Café.** In a renovated house on the west side of Bend, this
AMERICAN breakfast and lunch place offers a wide selection of surprising combinations of egg Benedict, such as the Caribbean Benedict with Cuban seasoned ham, mango, and black beans. There's often a long wait on weekends, so order a Bloody Mary or a "Man-mosa" (a mimosa in a pint glass) to enjoy around the outdoor fireplace. **Known for:** extensive menu of conventional brunch fare; big, boozy breakfast cocktails. $ Average main: $16 ⊠ 1404 N.W. Galveston Ave. ☎ 541/382–6411 ⊕ www.victoriancafebend.com ☾ No dinner.

$$$ ✕ **Zydeco Kitchen & Cocktails.** The blended menu of Northwest spe-
AMERICAN cialties and Cajun influences has made this trendy but welcoming restaurant (named after a style of Creole music) a popular lunch and dinner spot. On the menu, fillet medallions, chicken, and pasta sit alongside jambalaya and redfish dishes. **Known for:** gluten-free menu; well-curated wine list; expert bartenders. $ Average main: $23 ⊠ 919 N.W. Bond St. ☎ 541/312–2899 ⊕ www.zydecokitchen. com ☾ No lunch weekends.

WHERE TO STAY

$$ ⌂ **Lara House Bed and Breakfast.** Located in a manicured residential
B&B/INN neighborhood across from Drake Park, guests will feel at home at this historically grand and cherished Bend house. **Pros:** clean lines and an uncluttered feel; downtown is a short walk away; wine hour every evening. **Cons:** no pets or kids; can be crowded during peak travel times; check-in only 4–6 or by prior arrangement. $ Rooms from: $200 ⊠ 640 N.W. Congress St. ☎ 541/388–4064, 800/766–4064 ⊕ www.larahouse. com ⤳ 6 rooms ⦿ Breakfast.

$$ ⌂ **Old St. Francis School.** Part of the eclectic McMenamins brand of
RESORT pubs, movie theaters, and hotels, this charming and fun outpost in a restored 1936 Catholic schoolhouse has classrooms turned into lodging quarters, restaurant and bars, a brewery, a stage, a mosaic-tile soaking pool, and a movie theater with couches and food service. **Pros:** a self-contained destination village, yet only footsteps from downtown Bend and Drake Park; quirky, unique stay; kids and pets welcome. **Cons:** few modern appliances. $ Rooms from: $155 ⊠ 700 N.W. Bond St. ☎ 541/382–5174, 877/661–4228 ⊕ www.mcmenamins.com ⤳ 60 rooms ⦿ No meals.

6

$$$$ HOTEL Fodor's Choice ★ 🏨 **The Oxford Hotel.** Stepping into the sleek, high-ceilinged lobby tells you you've found a new kind of accommodation in central Oregon, with stylish Northwest interiors and elegantly spacious rooms. **Pros:** generous and environmentally sustainable amenities; luxurious spa and fitness room; loaner bikes in summer months; exceptional service. **Cons:** on the exterior, property appears inconspicuously wedged into a half block on the edge of downtown. [$] *Rooms from: $349* ✉ *10 N.W. Minnesota Ave.* ☎ *877/440–8436* 🌐 *www.oxfordhotelbend.com* 🛏 *59 rooms* 🍴 *No meals.*

$$ HOTEL FAMILY 🏨 **Riverhouse on the Deschutes.** Freshly renovated, this lodge-inspired hotel and convention center overlooks the Deschutes River and appeals to family travelers with its indoor and outdoor pools, hot tubs, and on-site dining. **Pros:** large, simply decorated standard rooms and suites; convenient facilities for family and business travelers; dining and shopping nearby. **Cons:** rooms lack character; not ideal for those looking to walk downtown. [$] *Rooms from: $189* ✉ *3075 N. Business Hwy. 97* ☎ *541/389–3111* 🛏 *221 rooms* 🍴 *No meals.*

$$$$ RESORT FAMILY Fodor's Choice ★ 🏨 **Sunriver Resort.** Central Oregon's premier family playground and luxurious destination resort encapsulates so many things that are distinctive about central Oregon, from the mountain views and winding river, to the biking, rafting, golfing, skiing, and family or romantic getaways. **Pros:** many activities for kids and adults; much pampering in elegant lodge facilities; close to The Village at Sunriver. **Cons:** when visitors throng the shops, restaurants, and bike paths, it can feel as if an entire city has relocated here. [$] *Rooms from: $259* ✉ *17600 Center Dr., 15 miles south of Bend on Hwy. 97, Sunriver* ☎ *800/801–8765* 🌐 *www.sunriver-resort.com* 🛏 *245 rooms, 284 houses* 🍴 *No meals.*

$$$ HOTEL 🏨 **Wall Street Suites.** Built in the 1950s as a motel and renovated with stunning pine, hardwood, tile, and iron a few years ago, these spacious suites and rooms are both stylishly contemporary and cozy. **Pros:** close to downtown; pet-friendly; nice amenities and TVs. **Cons:** next to a busy and complicated intersection. [$] *Rooms from: $224* ✉ *1430 Wall St.* ☎ *541/706–9006* 🌐 *www.wallstreetsuitesbend.com* 🛏 *4 suites, 13 rooms* 🍴 *No meals.*

NIGHTLIFE

The Astro Lounge. Bend's take on a space-age cocktail haven comes complete with specialty martinis and cosmic-looking interior. ✉ *939 N.W. Bond St.* ☎ *541/388–0116* 🌐 *www.astroloungebend.com* 🕒 *Closed Sun.*

Bend Brewing Company. A long-standing brewery, founded in 1995, BBC (as it is affectionately called by locals) offers about 10 different types of beers on tap. It's located on the second floor above the brewpub, where diners and drinkers can look up through windows to the tanks above. Because space is limited for brewing, BBC focuses not on the quantity of beer, but the quality. ✉ *1019 N.W. Brooks St.* ☎ *541/383–1599* 🌐 *www.bendbrewingco.com.*

Crux Fermentation Project. Housed in a converted auto repair shop, this industrial-chic and experimental brewery has no flagship beer. Instead, the brewmaster, a Deschutes Brewery alum, produces an ever-changing variety of pale ales and other craft brews, all of which are on tap

Sunriver Resort

in the lively tasting room. On-site food carts and a sprawling patio make this a popular hangout in summer months. ⊠ *50 S.W. Division St.* ☏ *541/385–3333* ⊕ *www.cruxfermentation.com.*

Level 2. After a day of shopping, or before concertgoing at the amphi-theater, sip on a perfectly mixed cocktail at this trendy Old Mill District urban-esque lounge. The rich chai martini is a delectable winter treat. ⊠ *360 S.W. Powerhouse Dr.* ☏ *541/323–5382.*

900 Wall Restaurant and Bar. In a historic corner brick building on a downtown Bend crossroads, this sophisticated restaurant and bar serves hundreds of bottles and about 50 different wines by the glass, earn-ing it the Wine Spectator Award of Excellence. ⊠ *900 N.W. Wall St.* ☏ *541/323–6295* ⊕ *www.900wall.com.*

SPORTS AND THE OUTDOORS
BIKING
U.S. 97 north to the Crooked River Gorge and Smith Rock and the route along the **Cascade Lakes Highway** out of Bend provide bikers with memorable scenery and a good workout. **Sunriver** has more than 30 miles of paved bike paths.

Hutch's Bicycles. Road, mountain, and kids' bikes can be rented at this shop as well as a location at 725 N.W. Columbia Street. ⊠ *820 N.E. 3rd St.* ☏ *541/382–6248 3rd St. shop, 541/382–9253 Columbia St. shop* ⊕ *www.hutchsbicycles.com.*

BOATING AND RAFTING
A popular summer activity is floating the Deschutes River at your own pace.

Bend Whitewater Park. The first white-water park in Oregon, at McKay Park in the Old Mill District, is the result of an extensive renovation to a 1915 dam, which previously made this section of the Deschutes River impassable. Three separate channels below the dam cater to rafters, kayakers, tubers, and even surfers. ⊠ *166 S.W. Shevlin Hixon Rd.* ☎ *541/389–7275* ⊕ *www.bendparksandrec.org.*

Riverbend Park. In Bend, rent an inner tube at Riverbend Park from a kiosk operated from Memorial Day to Labor Day by **Sun Country Tours** and float an hour and a half downriver to Drake Park, where you can catch a shuttle back for a minimal cash fee. ⊠ *799 S.W. Columbia St.* ☎ *541/389–7275* ⊕ *www.bendparksandrec.org.*

Tumalo Creek Kayak & Canoe. Rent a kayak or stand-up paddleboard and enter the river from the store's backyard, but be prepared to paddle upriver before a leisurely float downstream. ⊠ *805 S.W. Industrial Way, Suite 6* ☎ *541/317–9407* ⊕ *tumalocreek.com.*

RECREATIONAL AREAS

Deschutes National Forest. This 1½-million-acre forest has 20 peaks higher than 7,000 feet, including three of Oregon's five highest mountains, more than 150 lakes, and 500 miles of streams. If you want to park your car at a trailhead, some of the sites require a Northwest Forest Pass; day-use passes are also needed May through September at many locations for boating and picnicking. Campgrounds are operated by a camp host. ⊠ *63095 Deschutes Market Rd.* ☎ *541/383–5300* ⊕ *www. fs.usda.gov/centraloregon* ⚑ *Park pass $5.*

SKIING

Many Nordic trails—more than 165 miles of them—wind through the Deschutes National Forest.

FAMILY **Mt. Bachelor.** This is alpine resort area has 60% of downhill runs that are rated advanced or expert, with the rest geared for beginner and intermediate skiers and snowboarders. One of 10 lifts takes skiers all the way to the mountain's 9,065-foot summit. One run has a vertical drop of 3,265 feet for thrill-seekers, and the longest of the 88 runs is 4 miles. Facilities and services include equipment rental and repair, a ski school, retail shop, and day care; you can enjoy seven restaurants, three bars, and six lodges. Other activities include cross-country skiing, a tubing park, sled-dog rides, snowshoeing, and in summer, hiking, biking, disc-golfing and chairlift rides. The 35 miles of trails at the **Mt. Bachelor Nordic Center** are suitable for all abilities.

During the off-season, the lift to the **Pine Marten Lodge** provides sightseeing, stunning views, and fine sunset dining. Visitors can play disc golf on a downhill course that starts near the lodge. At the base of the mountain, take dry-land dogsled rides with four-time Iditarod musher Rachael Scdoris. ⊠ *13000 S.W. Century Dr.* ☎ *541/382–7888, 800/829–2442* ⊕ *www.mtbachelor.com* ⚑ *Lift tickets $52–$92 per day; kids 5 and under free.*

SHOPPING

In addition to Bend's compact downtown, the Old Mill District draws shoppers from throughout the region. Chain stores and franchise restaurants have filled in along the approaches to town, especially along U.S. 20 and U.S. 97.

Cowgirl Cash. This funky Western outfitter buys and sells vintage boots and Western apparel. You never know exactly what you'll find, but you can expect a fair share of leather, turquoise, silver, and, always, boots. It's a quirky and welcome feature of the downtown scene but closed Thursday–Sunday in the winter. ✉ *924 N.W. Brooks St.* ☎ *541/678–5162* ⊕ *www.cowgirlcashbend.com.*

Dudley's BookShop Cafe. This independent bookseller offers Wi-Fi, a small café, and seating areas that attract interesting people who meet amidst new and used books to participate in all kinds of activities, from tango classes to philosophical debates. ✉ *135 N.W. Minnesota Ave.* ☎ *541/749–2010* ⊕ *www.dudleysbookshopcafe.com.*

Goody's. If the aroma of fresh waffle cones causes a pause on your downtown stroll, you've probably hit one of central Oregon's favorite soda fountain and candy shops. Try the Oreo cookie ice cream, a local favorite, or the homemade chocolate. If you purchase a stuffed toy animal that calls the store home, expect for it to smell sweetly for weeks to come. ✉ *957 N.W. Wall St.* ☎ *541/389–5185* ⊕ *www.goodyschocolates.com.*

Hot Box Betty. This fun, lively shop sells high fashion for women, carrying boutique clothing and designer handbags. ✉ *903 N.W. Wall St.* ☎ *541/383–0050* ⊕ *www.hotboxbetty.com.*

Newport Avenue Market. In business for more than 20 years, this favorite local grocer not only offers a large selection of organic and gourmet foods, but also sells items such as high-end kitchen supplies and humorous gifts. Pick up a pair of squirrel underwear—it's as small as you might expect. ✉ *1121 N.W. Newport Ave.* ☎ *541/382–3940* ⊕ *www.newportavemarket.com.*

Old Mill District. Bend was once the site of one of the world's largest sawmill operations, with a sprawling industrial complex along the banks of the Deschutes. In recent years the abandoned shells of the old factory buildings have been transformed into an attractive shopping center, a project honored with national environmental awards. National chain retailers can be found here, along with restaurants, boutiques, a 16-screen multiplex and IMAX movie theater, and the Les Schwab Amphitheater that attracts nationally renowned artists, local bands, and summer festivals. ✉ *450 S.W. Powerhouse Dr.* ☎ *541/312–0131* ⊕ *www.theoldmill.com.*

Oregon Body & Bath. If adventures in the high desert's arid climate have left your skin feeling dry and dehydrated, head to this body and bath boutique in downtown Bend for locally made soaps, lotions, bath bombs, and body butters. The store also stocks home goods, such as fragrant candles and scents. ✉ *1019 N.W. Wall St.* ☎ *541/383–5890* ⊕ *www.oregonbodyandbath.com.*

6

Patagonia@Bend. A helpful staff sells stylishly comfortable and environmentally friendly outdoor clothing, equipment, and footwear at a Patagonia concept store that is locally owned. ✉ *1000 N.W. Wall St., Suite 140* ☎ *541/382–6694* ⊕ *www.patagoniabend.com.*

Pine Mountain Sports. Part of Bend's fleet of outdoors stores, this shop sells high-quality clothing, energy bars, and the locally famous Hydro Flask water bottles. Recreation equipment such as mountain bikes, backcountry skis, and snowshoes are also available for rent or purchase. ✉ *255 S.W. Century Dr.* ☎ *541/385–8080* ⊕ *www.pinemountainsports.com.*

Silverado Jewelry Gallery. Showcasing dazzling pieces of silver, turquoise, pearls, and everything in between, it will be difficult not to exit the store without being moved by a stunning piece of jewelry that appeals to all tastes. ✉ *1001 N.W. Wall St., Suite 101* ☎ *541/322–8792* ⊕ *www. silveradogallery.com.*

SISTERS

21 miles northwest of Bend.

If Sisters looks as if you've stumbled into the Old West, that's entirely by design. The town strictly enforces an 1800s-style architecture. Rustic cabins border ranches on the edge of town, and you won't find a stoplight on any street. Western storefronts give way to galleries, the century-old hotel now houses a restaurant and bar, and a bakery occupies the former general store. Although its population is just a little more than 2,000, Sisters increasingly attracts visitors as well as urban runaways who appreciate its tranquillity and charm. If you're driving over from the Willamette Valley, note how the weather seems to change to sunshine when you cross the Cascades at the Santiam Pass and begin descending toward the town.

Black Butte, a perfectly conical cinder cone, rises to the northwest. The Metolius River/Camp Sherman area to the west is a special find for fly-fishermen and abounds with springtime wildflowers.

GETTING HERE AND AROUND

Travelers from Portland and the west come to Sisters over the Santiam Pass on Oregon 126. This is also the route for visitors who fly into Redmond Municipal Airport, rent a car, and drive 20 miles west. Those coming from Bend drive 21 miles northwest on U.S. 20. **Cascades East,** a regional bus carrier, runs routes between Sisters and the Redmond airport by reservation.

ESSENTIALS

Visitor Information Sisters Chamber of Commerce. ✉ *291 E. Main Ave.* ☎ *541/549–0251* ⊕ *www.sisterscountry.com.*

EXPLORING

Camp Sherman. Surrounded by groves of whispering yellow-bellied ponderosa pines, larch, fir, and cedars and miles of streamside forest trails, this small, peaceful resort community of about 250 full-time residents (plus a few stray cats and dogs) is part of a designated conservation area. The area's beauty and natural resources are the big draw: the spring-fed Metolius River prominently glides through the community. In the early 1900s Sherman County wheat farmers escaped the dry summer heat by migrating here to fish and rest in the cool river environment, making Camp Sherman one of the first destination resorts in central Oregon. As legend has it, to help guide fellow farmers to the spot, devotees nailed a shoebox top with the name "camp sherman" to a tree at a fork in the road. Several original buildings still stand from the early days, including some cabins, a schoolhouse, and a tiny railroad chapel. Find the source of local information at the Camp Sherman Store & Fly Shop, built in 1918, adjacent to the post office. ✉ *25451 S.W. Forest Service Rd. 1419, 10 miles northwest of Sisters on U.S. 20, 5 miles north on Hwy. 14* ☎ *541/595–6711* 🌐 *www.campshermanstore.com.*

NEED A BREAK

🍴 **Sisters Bakery. In a rustic Western-looking former general store built in 1925, Sisters Bakery turns out high-quality pastries, doughnuts, and specialty breads from 5 am to 5 pm. The bakery serves Bend's Strictly Organic coffee, and harkens back to a time when doughnuts were simple and tasty.** ✉ ***251 E. Cascade St.*** ☎ ***541/549-0361*** 🌐 ***www.sistersbakery.com.***

WHERE TO EAT

$ AMERICAN FAMILY Fodor's Choice ★

🍴 **The Cottonwood Cafe.** Formerly the much-celebrated Jen's Garden, the owners opened this new breakfast and lunch concept in the same cute cottage in 2015. The new family-oriented menu focuses on comfortable café standbys, such as eggs Benedict and slow-roasted pulled pork sandwiches. **Known for:** festive brunch ambience; pup-friendly patio. [$] *Average main: $12* ✉ *403 E. Hood Ave.* ☎ *541/549–2699* 🌐 *www.intimatecottagecuisine.com* 🕓 *Closed Wed. fall and winter.*

$ AMERICAN

🍴 **The Depot Café.** A railroad theme prevails at this main-street rustic café. A miniature train circles above as the kitchen dishes out sandwiches, salads, and dinner specials. **Known for:** minitrain. [$] *Average main: $12* ✉ *250 W. Cascade St.* ☎ *541/549–2572* 🌐 *www.sistersdepot.com* 🕓 *No breakfast Mon.–Thurs.*

$$$ AMERICAN

🍴 **Kokanee Café.** The remarkable restaurant near the banks of the Metolius River draws diners from across the mountains to sample artful Northwest dishes at this homey hideaway with a paneled dining room and warm-weather porch. Local lamb, fresh fish, and vegetarian options are presented with creative elegance. **Known for:** menu focused on local and sustainably sourced meat; extensive wine list. [$] *Average main: $30* ✉ *25545 S.W. Forest Service Rd. 1419, Camp Sherman* ☎ *541/595–6420* 🌐 *www.kokaneecafe.com* 🕓 *Closed Oct.–Apr. No lunch.*

$ ITALIAN

🍴 **The Open Door.** Serving simple and light Italian fare, such as panini and flatbread pizzas, this quaint and cozy restaurant and wine bar offers a different homemade pasta dish every night for dinner. The interior is an eclectic mix of mismatched tables and chairs, which opens into a gallery displaying Northwest artwork. **Known for:** romantic, artsy ambience; good wine list. [$] *Average main: $16* ✉ *303 W. Hood Ave.* ☎ *541/549–6076* 🌐 *www.theclearwatergallery.com* 🕓 *Closed Sun.*

$ AMERICAN 🍴 **Sno Cap Drive In.** Since 1945, this burger joint has been serving iconic burgers, sandwiches, fries, milk shakes, and ice cream to residents and visitors. Be prepared for long lines out the doors, as travelers driving across the mountain often plan to stop here for lunch. **Known for:** authentic drive-in fare; creamy and thick milk shakes; long lines in summer months. [$] *Average main: $8* ✉ *380 W. Cascade Ave.* ☎ *541/549–6151.*

WHERE TO STAY

$$ RESORT FAMILY Fodor's Choice ★ 🏨 **FivePine Lodge.** At this luxurious Western-style resort resembling a forest lodge, high-end furnishings were built by Amish craftsmen. **Pros:** top-quality amenities, like the Kohler waterfall tubs; peaceful atmosphere, but conveniently located on the fringes of downtown Sister. **Cons:** slightly set back from U.S. 20, where traffic is sometimes heavy; some cabins are close to neighbors. [$] *Rooms from: $189* ✉ *1021 Desperado Trail* ☎ *541/549–5900, 866/974–5900* 🌐 *www.fivepinelodge.com* 🛏 *8 rooms, 24 cabins* 🍽 *Breakfast.*

$$$$ RENTAL 🏨 **Metolius River Resort.** Each of the immaculate, individually owned cabins that nestle amid the pines and aspen at this peaceful resort has splendid views of the sparkling Metolius River, decks furnished with Adirondack chairs, a full kitchen, and a fireplace. **Pros:** privacy; cabins feel like home—a very luxurious home; fall asleep and wake up to the sound of the river. **Cons:** no additional people (even visitors) allowed; no cell-phone service; bring supplies on winter weekdays when Camp Sherman closes down. [$] *Rooms from: $265* ✉ *25551 S.W. Forest Service Rd. 1419, Camp Sherman* ✣ *Off U.S. 20, northeast 10 miles from Sisters, turn north on Camp Sherman Rd., stay to left at fork (1419), and then turn right at only stop sign* ☎ *800/818–7688* 🌐 *www.metoliusriverresort.com* 🛏 *11 cabins* 🍽 *No meals.*

$$$$ RENTAL 🏨 **Metolius River Resort.** Each of the immaculate, individually owned cabins that nestle amid the pines and aspen at this peaceful resort has splendid views of the sparkling Metolius River, decks furnished with Adirondack chairs, a full kitchen, and a fireplace. **Pros:** privacy; cabins feel like home—a very luxurious home; fall asleep and wake up to the sound of the river. **Cons:** no additional people (even visitors) allowed; no cell-phone service; bring supplies on winter weekdays when Camp Sherman closes down. [$] *Rooms from: $265* ✉ *25551 S.W. Forest Service Rd. 1419, Camp Sherman* ✣ *Off U.S. 20, northeast 10 miles from Sisters, turn north on Camp Sherman Rd., stay to left at fork (1419), and then turn right at only stop sign* ☎ *800/818–7688* 🌐 *www.metoliusriverresort.com* 🛏 *11 cabins* 🍽 *No meals.*

$$$ RESORT 🏨 **Suttle Lodge.** The hospitality company behind the hip Ace Hotel Portland reopened this lakefront resort in 2016 after an extensive renovation, enhancing the whimsical charm of the grand light-flooded lodge and rustic cabins. **Pros:** hip accommodations in a peaceful setting; on-site restaurant and bar; year-round accessibility to outdoor sports. **Cons:** no air-conditioning; cell reception is spotty. [$] *Rooms from: $248* ✉ *13300 U.S. Hwy. 20, 13 miles northwest of Sisters* ☎ *541/638–7001* 🌐 *www.thesuttlelodge.com* 🛏 *11 rooms, 14 cabins* 🍽 *Breakfast.*

NIGHTLIFE

Fodor'sChoice **Sisters Saloon & Ranch Grill.** Pass through the swinging saloon doors
★ into this Old West watering hole, originally built more than a century
ago as the Hotel Sisters. Head to the bar, which is decorated with a
mural of cancan dancers, weathered saddles hanging on the wall, and
a mounted stuffed buffalo head. Under new ownership, the menu
remains rooted in ranch favorites but gets updated with vegetarian-
friendly offerings. ⊠ *190 E. Cascade Ave.* ☎ *541/549–7427* ⊕ *www.*
sisterssaloon.net.

Three Creeks Brewing Co. Currently Sisters' only brewery, Three Creeks
offers a selection of beers at its brewing facility and brewpub that play
on Northwest culture and the outdoor lifestyle. The brewery is visible from the brewpub, which serves a wide range of burgers, pizzas,
salads, and other bar mainstays. Order a frothing pint of the popular
Knotty Blonde, or try one of their seasonal brews. ⊠ *721 Desperado*
Ct. ☎ *541/549–1963* ⊕ *www.threecreeksbrewing.com.*

SHOPPING

Hop in the Spa. America's first beer spa takes advantage of the medicinal, nonintoxicating, and detoxifying qualities of hops and other beer
ingredients. Call ahead to schedule a microbrew soak and massage,
or one of the other beer-centric spa packages. ⊠ *371 W. Cascade Ave.*
☎ *844/588–6818* ⊕ *www.hopinthespa.com.*

Paulina Springs Books. Select a book from the discounted staff recommendation table, or from categories such as history, outdoor recreation, field guides, regional, science, and fiction. Sisters' leading
independent bookstore also sells toys and games, and has a substantial
young readers section. ⊠ *252 W. Hood Ave.* ☎ *541/549–0866* ⊕ *www.*
paulinasprings.com.

Stitchin' Post. Owned by a mother-and-daughter team, the famous
knitting, sewing, and quilting store opened its doors in 1975. The
spacious store not only inspires the senses with colorful fabric, patterns and yarns, but also conducts classes throughout the year. The
Sisters Outdoor Quilt Show, annually held the second Saturday of
July, is the largest in the world and intertwines its origins with the
store's early years. ⊠ *311 W. Cascade St.* ☎ *541/549–6061* ⊕ *www.*
stitchinpost.com.

SPORTS AND THE OUTDOORS
FISHING

Fly-fishing the Metolius River attracts anglers who seek a challenge.

Camp Sherman Store & Fly Shop. This local institution, center of life in
the tiny riverside community, sells gear and provides information about
where and how best to fish. ⊠ *25451 Forest Service Rd. 1419, Camp*
Sherman ☎ *541/595–6711* ⊕ *www.campshermanstore.com.*

Fly and Field Outfitters. This large Bend-based supplier of gear also sets
anglers up with expert guides. ⊠ *35 S.W. Century Dr., Bend* ☎ *866/800–*
2812 ⊕ *www.flyandfield.com.*

6

RECREATIONAL AREAS

Metolius Recreation Area. On the eastern slope of the Cascades and within the 1.6-million-acre Deschutes National Forest, this bounty of recreational wilderness is drier and sunnier than the western side of the mountains, giving way to bountiful natural history, outdoor activities, and wildlife. There are spectacular views of jagged, 10,000-foot snow-capped Cascade peaks, looming high above the basin of an expansive evergreen valley clothed in pine.

Five miles south of **Camp Sherman** (2 miles to head waters), the dark and perfectly shaped cinder cone of **Black Butte** rises 6,400 feet. At its base the **Metolius River** springs forth. Witness the birth of this "instant" river by walking a short paved path embedded in ponderosa forest, eventually reaching a viewpoint with the dramatic snow-covered peak of **Mt. Jefferson** on the horizon. At this point, water gurgles to the ground's surface and pours into a wide trickling creek cascading over moss-covered rocks. Within feet it funnels outward, expanding its northerly flow; becomes a full-size river; and meanders east alongside grassy banks and a dense pine forest to join the Deschutes River downstream. Within the 4,600-acre area of the Metolius and along the river, there are ample resources for camping, hiking, biking, and floating. Enjoy fly-fishing for rainbow, brown, and bull trout in perhaps the best spot within the Cascades. ⊠ *Off Hwy. 20, 9 miles northwest of Sisters, Camp Sherman* ⊕ *www.metoliusriver.com.*

SKIING

Hoodoo Ski Area. On a 5,703-foot summit, this winter sports area has more than 800 acres of skiable terrain. With 32 runs and five lifts, skiers of all levels will find suitable thrills. Upper and lower Nordic trails are surrounded by silence, and an inner tube run and night skiing round out the range of activities. At a 60,000-square-foot lodge at the mountain's base you can take in the view, grab a bite, shop, or rest your weary feet. The ski area has kids' activities and child-care services available. Lift tickets range from $10 to $51, depending on the type and day. ⊠ *U.S. 20, 20 miles northwest of Sisters* ☎ *541/822–3799* ⊕ *www.hoodoo.com.*

CRATER LAKE
NATIONAL PARK

WELCOME TO CRATER LAKE NATIONAL PARK

TOP REASONS TO GO

★ **The lake:** Cruise inside the caldera basin and gaze into the extraordinary sapphire-blue water of the country's deepest lake, stopping for a ramble around Wizard Island.

★ **Native land:** Enjoy the rare luxury of interacting with totally unspoiled terrain.

★ **The night sky:** Billions of stars glisten in the pitch-black darkness of an unpolluted sky.

★ **Splendid hikes:** Accessible trails spool off the main roads and wind past colorful bursts of wildflowers and cascading waterfalls.

★ **Lake-rim lodging:** Spend the night perched on the lake rim at the rustic yet stately Crater Lake Lodge.

1 Crater Lake. The park's focal point, this nonrecreational, scenic destination is known for its deep blue hue.

2 Wizard Island. Visitors can take boat rides to this protruding landmass rising from the western section of Crater Lake; it's a great place for hiking and picnicking.

3 Mazama Village. About 5 miles south of Rim Drive, the village is your best bet for stocking up on snacks, beverages, and fuel.

4 Cleetwood Cove Trail. The only designated trail to hike down the caldera and reach the lake's edge is on the rim's north side off Rim Drive; all boat tours leave from the dock at trail's end.

GETTING ORIENTED

Crater Lake National Park covers 183,224 acres, and only a relatively small portion of it encompasses the lake for which it's named. In southern Oregon less than 75 miles from the California border, the park is surrounded by several Cascade Range forests, including the Winema and Rogue River national forests. The town of Klamath Falls, 50 miles south of the park, has the most convenient Amtrak stop; Ashland and Medford, to the southwest, are 73 miles and 85 miles, respectively, from the park's southern (Annie Spring) entrance. Roseburg is 85 miles northwest of the park's northern entrance, which is open only seasonally.

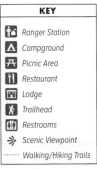

KEY	
👤	Ranger Station
⛺	Campground
🧺	Picnic Area
🍴	Restaurant
🏨	Lodge
🚶	Trailhead
🚻	Restrooms
⇝	Scenic Viewpoint
-----	Walking/Hiking Trails

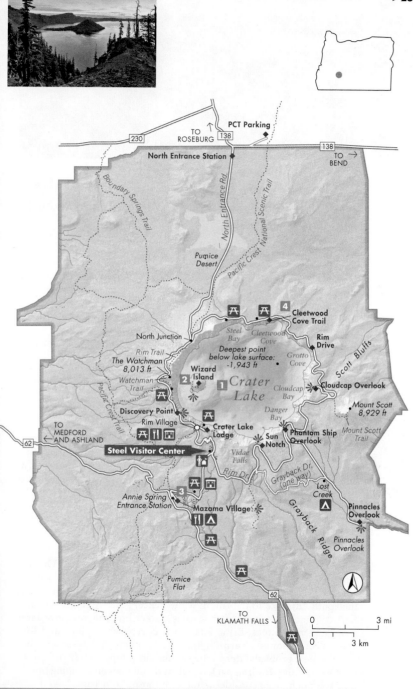

Updated by Andrew Collins

The pure, crystalline blue of Crater Lake astounds visitors at first sight. More than 5 miles wide and ringed by cliffs almost 2,000 feet high, the lake was created approximately 7,700 years ago, following Mt. Mazama's fiery explosion. Days after the eruption, the mountain collapsed on an underground chamber emptied of lava. Rain and snowmelt filled the caldera, creating a sapphire-blue lake so clear that sunlight penetrates to a depth of 400 feet (the lake's depth is 1,943 feet). Crater Lake is both the clearest and deepest lake in the United States—and the ninth deepest in the world.

For most visitors, the star attractions of Crater Lake are the lake itself and the breathtakingly situated Crater Lake Lodge. Although it takes some effort to reach it, Wizard Island is another outstanding draw. Other park highlights include the natural, unspoiled beauty of the forest and the geological marvels you can access along the Rim Drive.

CRATER LAKE PLANNER

WHEN TO GO

The park's high season is July and August. September and early October tend to draw smaller crowds. From October well into June, nearly the entire park closes due to heavy snowfall. The road is kept open just from the South Entrance to the rim in winter, except during severe weather. Early summer snowmelt often creates watery breeding areas for large groups of mosquitoes. Bring lots of insect repellent in June and July, and expect mosquito swarms in the early morning and at sunset. They can also be a problem later in the summer in campgrounds and on the Cleetwood Cove Trail, so pack repellent if you plan on camping or hiking. You might even consider a hat with mosquito netting.

FESTIVALS AND EVENTS

Oregon Shakespeare Festival. More than 400,000 Bard lovers descend on charming downtown Ashland (85 miles from Crater Lake) for this nearly yearlong festival that presents works by Shakespeare and other past and contemporary playwrights. ⊠ *Ashland* ☎ *541/482–4331* ⊕ *www.osfashland.org.*

PLANNING YOUR TIME

CRATER LAKE IN ONE DAY

Begin at the **Steel Visitor Center,** a short drive from Annie Spring, the only park entrance open year-round. The center's interpretive displays and a short video describe the forces that created the lake and what makes it unique. From here, begin circling the crater's rim by heading northeast on **Rim Drive,** allowing an hour to stop at overlooks—be sure to check out the Phantom Ship rock formation in the lake—before you reach the trailhead of **Cleetwood Cove Trail,** the only safe and legal way to access the lake. If you're game for a good workout, hike down the trail to reach the dock at trail's end and hop aboard a **tour boat** for a two-hour ranger-guided excursion. If you'd prefer to hike on your own, instead take the late-morning shuttle boat to **Wizard Island** for a picnic lunch and a trek to the island's summit.

Back on Rim Drive, continue around the lake, stopping at the **Watchman Trail** for a short but steep hike to this peak above the rim, which affords a splendid view of the lake and a broad vista of the surrounding southern Cascades. Wind up your visit at **Crater Lake Lodge.** Allow time to wander the lobby of this 1915 structure that perches right on the rim. Dinner at the lodge's restaurant, overlooking the lake, caps the day.

7

GETTING HERE AND AROUND

Rogue Valley International–Medford Airport (MFR) is the nearest commercial airport. About 75 miles southwest of the park, it is served by Alaska, Allegiant, Delta, and United airlines and has rental cars. Amtrak trains stop in downtown Klamath Falls, 50 miles south of the park. Car rentals are available.

Crater Lake National Park's South Entrance, open year-round, is off Highway 62 in southern Oregon. If driving here from California, follow Interstate 5 north to Medford and head east on Highway 62, or take U.S. 97 north past Klamath Falls, exiting northwest on Highway 62. From Portland, Oregon, allow from 5½ to 6 hours to reach the park's South Entrance, via Interstate 5 through the city of Grants Pass. In summer, when the North Entrance is open, the drive from Portland takes just 4½ hours via Interstate 5, Highway 58 (through Oakridge), U.S. 97, and Highway 138. If coming from Portland in summer, staying at an Oakridge or Chemult motel the night before your arrival will have you fairly close to the park the following morning.

Most of the park is accessible only from late June or early July through mid-October. The rest of the year, snow blocks park roadways and entrances except Highway 62 and the access road to Rim Village from Mazama Village. Rim Drive is typically closed because of snow from mid-October to mid-July, and you could encounter icy conditions at any time of year, particularly in the early morning.

PARK ESSENTIALS
PARK FEES AND PERMITS
Admission to the park is $15 per vehicle, good for seven days. For all overnight trips, backcountry campers and hikers must obtain a free wilderness permit at Canfield Ranger Station, which is at the park headquarters adjacent to Steel Visitor Center and open daily 9–5 from mid-April through early November, and 10–4 the rest of the year.

PARK HOURS
Crater Lake National Park is open 24 hours a day year-round; however, snow closes most park roadways from October to June. Lodging and dining facilities usually are open from late May to mid-October. The park is in the Pacific time zone.

CELL-PHONE RECEPTION
Cell-phone reception in the park is unreliable, although generally it works around Crater Lake Lodge and Mazama Village, which also have public phones.

EDUCATIONAL OFFERINGS
RANGER PROGRAMS
FAMILY **Boat Tours.** The most popular way to tour Crater Lake itself is on a two-hour ranger-led excursion aboard a 37-passenger launch. The first narrated tour leaves the dock at 9:30 am; the last departs at 3:45 pm. Four of the 10 daily boats stop at Wizard Island, where you can get off and reboard three or six hours later. Two of these trips act as shuttles, with no ranger narration. They're perfect if you just want to get to Wizard Island to hike. The shuttles leave at 8:30 and 11:30 and return to Cleetwood Cove at 12:45 and 3:35 respectively. To get to the dock you must hike down Cleetwood Cove Trail, a strenuous 1.1-mile walk that descends 700 feet in elevation along the way; only those in excellent physical shape should attempt the hike. Bring adequate water with you. Purchase boat-tour tickets at Crater Lake Lodge, at the top of the trail, or through reservations. Restrooms are available at the top and bottom of the trail. ⊠ *Crater Lake National Park* ⚓ *Access Cleetwood Cove Trail off Rim Dr., 11 miles north of Rim Village* ☎ *541/594–2255, 888/774–2728 reservations* ⊕ *www.craterlakelodges.com/activities* ⊠ *$32 shuttle, $40 guided tour, $57 guided tour with island drop-off.*

FAMILY **Junior Ranger Program.** Kids ages 6–12 learn about Crater Lake while earning a Junior Ranger patch in daily sessions during summer months at the Rim Visitor Center, and year-round they can earn a badge by completing the Junior Ranger Activity Booklet, which can be picked up at either visitor center. ☎ *541/594–3100* ⊕ *www.nps.gov/crla/learn/kidsyouth.*

TOURS
Main Street Adventure Tours. This Ashland-based outfitter's guided tours in southern Oregon include seven-hour ones to Crater Lake. During these tours, available year-round, participants are driven around part of the lake and, seasonally, given the chance to take a boat tour. Along the way to the park there are stops at the Cole M. Rivers Fish Hatchery, the Rogue River Gorge, and Lake of the Woods. ⊠ *Ashland* ☎ *541/482–9852* ⊕ *www.ashland-tours.com* ⊠ *From $179.*

RESTAURANTS

There are just a few casual eateries and convenience stores within the park, all near the main (southern) entrance. For fantastic upscale dining on the caldera's rim, head to the Crater Lake Lodge. Outside the park, Klamath Falls has a smattering of good restaurants, and both Medford and Ashland abound with first-rate eateries serving farm-to-table cuisine and local Rogue Valley wines. *Restaurant reviews have been shortened. For full information visit Fodors.com.*

HOTELS

Crater Lake's summer season is relatively brief, and Crater Lake Lodge, the park's main accommodation, is generally booked up a year in advance. If you are unable to get a reservation, check availability as your trip approaches—cancellations do happen on occasion. The other in-park option, the Cabins at Mazama Village, also books up early in summer. Outside the park there are a couple of options in nearby Prospect, and numerous lodgings in Klamath Falls, Medford, Ashland, and Roseburg. Additionally, if visiting the park via the North Entrance in summer, you might consider staying in one of the handful of motels in Oakridge and Chemult. Even Bend is an option, as it's just a two-hour drive from North Entrance, which is only slightly longer than the drive from Ashland to the main entrance. *Hotel reviews have been shortened. For full information, visit Fodors.com.*

WHAT IT COSTS				
	$	**$$**	**$$$**	**$$$$**
Restaurants	under $12	$12–$20	$21–$30	over $30
Hotels	under $100	$100–$150	$151–$200	over $200

Restaurant prices are the average cost of a main course at dinner, or if dinner is not served, at lunch. Hotel prices are the lowest cost of a standard double room in high season.

VISITOR INFORMATION

Park Contact Information Crater Lake National Park. ☎ *541/594–3000* ⊕ *www.nps.gov/crla.*

Park Literature and Information Crater Lake Natural History Association. ☎ *541/594–3111* ⊕ *www.craterlakeoregon.org.*

VISITOR CENTERS

Rim Visitor Center. In summer you can obtain park information at the center, take a ranger-led tour, or stop into the nearby Sinnott Memorial, which has a small museum and a 900-foot view down to the lake's surface. In winter, snowshoe walks are offered on weekends and holidays. A short walk away, the Rim Village Gift Store and cafeteria are the only services open in winter. ✉ *Rim Dr., 7 miles north of Annie Spring entrance station* ☎ *541/594–3000* ⊕ *www.nps.gov/crla.*

Steel Visitor Center. Open year-round, the center, part of the park's headquarters, has restrooms, a first-aid station, a small post office, and a shop that sells books, maps, and postcards. There are fewer exhibits

Wildlife in Crater Lake

Wildlife in the Crater Lake area flourishes in the water and throughout the surrounding forest.

SALMON AND TROUT

Two primary types of fish swim beneath the surface of Crater Lake: kokanee salmon and rainbow trout. Kokanees average about 8 inches in length, but they can grow to nearly 18 inches. Rainbow trout are larger than the kokanee but are less abundant in Crater Lake. Trout—including bull, Eastern brook, rainbow, and German

brown—swim in the park's many streams and rivers.

ELK, DEER, AND MORE

Remote canyons shelter the park's elk and deer populations, which can sometimes be seen at dusk and dawn feeding at forest's edge. Black bears and pine martens—cousins of the short-tailed weasel—also call Crater Lake home. Birds such as hairy woodpeckers, California gulls, red-tailed hawks, and great horned owls are more commonly seen in summer in forests below the lake.

than at comparable national park visitor centers, but you can view an engaging 22-minute film, *Crater Lake: Into the Deep*, which describes the lake's formation and geology and examines the area's cultural history. ⊠ *Rim Dr., 4 miles north of Annie Spring entrance station* ☎ *541/594–3000* ⊕ *www.nps.gov/crla.*

EXPLORING

SCENIC DRIVES

Fodor's Choice **Rim Drive.** Take this 33-mile scenic loop for views of the lake and its cliffs
★ from every conceivable angle. The drive takes two hours not counting frequent stops at overlooks and short hikes that can easily stretch this to a half day. Rim Drive is typically closed due to heavy snowfall from mid-October to mid-June, and icy conditions can be encountered any month of the year, particularly in early morning. ⊠ *Crater Lake National Park* ✛ *Drive begins at Rim Village, 7 miles from (Annie Spring) South Entrance; from North Entrance, follow North Entrance Rd. south for 10 miles* ⊕ *www.nps.gov/crla.*

HISTORIC SITES

Fodor's Choice **Crater Lake Lodge.** Built in 1915, this imposing log-and-stone structure
★ was designed in the classic style of Western national park lodges, and the original lodgepole-pine pillars, beams, and stone fireplaces are still intact. The lobby, fondly referred to as the Great Hall, serves as a warm, welcoming gathering place where you can play games, socialize with a cocktail, or gaze out of the many windows to view spectacular sunrises and sunsets by a crackling fire. Exhibits off the lobby contain historic photographs and memorabilia from throughout the park's history. ⊠ *Rim Village, just east of Rim Visitor Center* ⊕ *www.craterlakelodges.com.*

SCENIC STOPS

Cloudcap Overlook. The highest road-access overlook on the Crater Lake rim, Cloudcap has a westward view across the lake to Wizard Island and an eastward view of Mt. Scott, the volcanic cone that is the park's highest point. ⊠ *Crater Lake National Park* ✛ *2 miles off Rim Dr., 13 miles northeast of Steel Visitor Center* ⊕ *www.nps.gov/crla.*

Discovery Point. This overlook marks the spot at which prospectors first spied the lake in 1853. Wizard Island is just northeast, close to shore. ⊠ *West Rim Dr., 1½ miles north of Rim Village* ⊕ *www.nps.gov/crla.*

Mazama Village. In summer, a campground, cabin-style motel, amphitheater, gas station, and small store are open here. No gasoline is available in the park from mid-October to mid-May. Snowfall determines when the village and its facilities open and close for the season. Hours vary; call ahead. ⊠ *Mazama Village Rd., off Hwy. 62, near Annie Spring entrance station* ☎ *541/594–2255, 888/774–2728* ⊕ *www.craterlakelodges.com.*

Phantom Ship Overlook. From this point you can get a close look at Phantom Ship, a rock formation that resembles a schooner with furled masts and looks ghostly in fog. ⊠ *East Rim Dr., 7 miles northeast of Steel Visitor Center* ⊕ *www.nps.gov/crla.*

Pinnacles Overlook. Ascending from the banks of Sand and Wheeler creeks, unearthly spires of eroded ash resemble the peaks of fairy-tale castles. Once upon a time, the road continued east to a former entrance. A path now replaces the old road and follows the rim of Sand Creek (affording more views of pinnacles) to where the entrance arch still stands. ⊠ *Pinnacles Rd., 12 miles east of Steel Visitor Center* ⊕ *www.nps.gov/crla.*

Sun Notch. It's a relatively easy ¼-mile hike through wildflowers and dry meadow to this overlook, which has views of Crater Lake and Phantom Ship. Mind the cliff edges. ⊠ *East Rim Dr., about 4½ miles east of Steel Visitor Center* ⊕ *www.nps.gov/crla.*

Fodor'sChoice
★
Wizard Island. The volcanic eruption that led to the creation of Crater Lake resulted in the formation of this magical island a quarter mile off the lake's western shore. The views at its summit—reached on a somewhat strenuous 2-mile hike—are stupendous.

Getting to the island requires a strenuous 1-mile hike down (and later back up) the steep Cleetwood Cove Trail to the cove's dock. There, board either the shuttle boat to Wizard Island or a Crater Lake narrated tour boat that includes a stop on the island. If you opt for the latter, you can explore Wizard Island a bit and reboard a later boat to resume the lake tour.

The hike to Wizard Summit, 763 feet above the lake's surface, begins at the island's boat dock and steeply ascends over rock-strewn terrain; a path at the top circles the 90-foot-deep crater's rim. More moderate is the 1¾-mile hike on a rocky trail along the shore of Wizard Island, so called because William Steel, an early Crater Lake booster, thought its shape resembled a wizard's hat. ⊠ *Crater Lake National Park* ✛ *Access Cleetwood Cove Trail off Rim Dr., 11 miles north of Rim Village* ☎ *541/594–2255, 888/774–2728* ⊕ *www.craterlakelodges.com/activities* ⌦ *Shuttle boat $32, tour boat $57.*

SPORTS AND THE OUTDOORS

HIKING

EASY

Castle Crest Wildflower Trail. This short half-mile loop that passes through a spring-fed meadow is one of the park's flatter hikes. Wildflowers burst into full bloom here in July. *Easy.* ⊠ *Crater Lake National Park* ✛ *Trailhead: East Rim Dr., across street from Steel Visitor Center parking lot.*

Godfrey Glen Trail. This 1-mile loop trail is an easy stroll through an old-growth forest with canyon views. Its dirt path is accessible to wheelchairs with assistance. *Easy.* ⊠ *Crater Lake National Park* ✛ *Trailhead: Mission Valley Rd., 2½ miles south of Steel Visitor Center.*

MODERATE

Annie Creek Canyon Trail. This somewhat challenging 1½-mile hike loops through a deep stream-cut canyon, providing views of the narrow cleft scarred by volcanic activity. This is a good area to look for flowers and deer. *Moderate.* ⊠ *Mazama Campground, Mazama Village Rd.* ✛ *Trailhead: behind amphitheater between D and E campground loops.*

Boundary Springs Trail. If you feel like sleuthing, take this moderate 5-mile round-trip hike to the headwaters of the Rogue River. The trail isn't well marked, so a detailed trail guide is necessary. You'll see streams, forests, and wildflowers along the way before discovering Boundary Springs pouring out of the side of a low ridge. *Moderate.* ⊠ *Crater Lake National Park* ✛ *Trailhead: pullout on Hwy. 230, near milepost 19, about 5 miles west of Hwy. 138.*

Watchman Peak Trail. This is one of the park's best and most easily accessed hikes. Though it's just more than 1½ miles round-trip, the trail climbs more than 400 feet—not counting the steps up to the actual lookout, which has great views of Wizard Island and the lake. *Moderate.* ⊠ *Crater Lake National Park* ✛ *Trailhead: at Watchman Overlook, Rim Dr., about 4 miles northwest of Rim Village, west side of lake.*

DIFFICULT

Cleetwood Cove Trail. This strenuous 2¼-mile round-trip hike descends 700 feet down nearly vertical cliffs along the lake to the boat dock. Be in very good shape before you tackle this well-maintained trail—it's the hike back up that catches some visitors unprepared. Bring along plenty of water. *Difficult.* ⊠ *Crater Lake National Park* ✛ *Trailhead: on Rim Dr., 11 miles north of Rim Village, north side of lake.*

Fodor's Choice
★

Mt. Scott Trail. This strenuous 4½-mile round-trip trail takes you to the park's highest point—the top of Mt. Scott, the oldest volcanic cone of Mt. Mazama, at 8,929 feet. The average hiker needs 90 minutes to make the steep uphill trek—and nearly 60 minutes to get down. The trail starts at an elevation of about 7,679 feet, so the climb is not extreme, but the trail is steep in spots. The views of the lake and the broad Klamath Basin are spectacular. *Difficult.* ⊠ *Crater Lake National Park* ✛ *Trailhead: 14 miles east of Steel Visitor Center on Rim Dr., across from road to Cloudcap Overlook.*

CLOSE UP

Best Campgrounds in Crater Lake

Tent campers and RV enthusiasts alike will enjoy the heavily wooded and well-equipped setting of Mazama Campground. Lost Creek Campground is much smaller, with minimal amenities and a more "rustic" Crater Lake experience. Pack bug repellent and patience if camping in the snowmelt season.

Lost Creek Campground. The 16 small, remote tent sites here are usually available on a daily basis; in July and August arrive early to secure a spot. The cost is $10 nightly. ✉ *3 miles south of Rim Rd. on Pinnacles Spur Rd. at Grayback Dr.* ☎ *541/594–3100.*

Mazama Campground. This campground is set well below the lake caldera in the pine and fir forest of the Cascades not far from the main access road (Highway 62). Drinking water, showers, and laundry facilities help ensure that you don't have to rough it too much. About half the 200 spaces are pull-throughs, some with electricity and a few with hookups. The best tent spots are on some of the outer loops above Annie Creek Canyon. Tent sites cost $22, RV ones $31. ✉ *Mazama Village, near Annie Spring entrance station* ☎ *541/594–2255, 888/774–2728* 🌐 *www.craterlakelodges.com.*

Pacific Crest Trail. You can hike a portion of the Pacific Crest Trail, which extends from Mexico to Canada and winds through the park for 33 miles. For this prime backcountry experience, catch the trail off Highway 138 about a mile east of the North Entrance, where it heads south and then toward the west rim of the lake and circles it for about 6 miles, then descends down Dutton Creek to the Mazama Village area. You'll need a detailed map for this hike; check online or with the PCT association (*www.pcta.org*). *Difficult.* ✉ *Crater Lake National Park* ✥ *Trailhead: at Pacific Crest Trail parking lot, off Hwy. 138, 1 mile east of North Entrance.*

7

WHERE TO EAT

$$ AMERICAN FAMILY

🍴 **Annie Creek Restaurant.** This family-friendly dining spot in Mazama Village serves hearty if unmemorable comfort fare, and service can be hit or miss. Blue cheese–bacon burgers, Cobb salads, sandwiches, pizzas, lasagna, and a tofu stir-fry are all on the menu. **Known for:** large portions. [$] *Average main: $13* ✉ *Mazama Village Rd. and Ave. C, near Annie Spring entrance station* ☎ *541/594–2255* 🌐 *www.craterlakelodges.com/dining-shopping* ⏲ *Closed late Sept.–early Apr.*

$$$$ PACIFIC NORTHWEST Fodor's Choice ★

🍴 **Dining Room at Crater Lake Lodge.** The only sophisticated dining option inside the park, the dining room is magnificent, with a large stone fireplace and views of Crater Lake's clear-blue waters. Breakfast and lunch are enjoyable here, but the dinner is the main attraction, with tempting dishes such as smoked salmon crostini with roasted beets and goat cheese, elk chops with a huckleberry-walnut glaze, and bison meat loaf with a mushroom-Merlot sauce. **Known for:** well-prepared steak; rustic and historic atmosphere; views of the lake. [$] *Average main: $33* ✉ *Crater Lake Lodge, 1 Lodge Loop Rd.* ☎ *541/594–2255* 🌐 *www.craterlakelodges.com* ⏲ *Closed mid-Oct.–mid-May.*

PICNIC AREAS

Godfrey Glen Trail. In a small canyon abuzz with songbirds, squirrels, and chipmunks, this picnic area has a south-facing, protected location. The half dozen picnic tables here are in a small meadow; there are also a few fire grills and a pit toilet. ⊠ *Crater Lake National Park ✛ 2½ miles south of Steel Visitor Center* ⊕ *www.nps.gov/crla.*

Rim Drive. About a half dozen picnic-area turnouts encircle the lake; all have good views, but they can get very windy. Most have pit toilets, and a few have fire grills, but none have running water. ⊠ *Rim Dr.* ⊕ *www.nps.gov/crla.*

Rim Village. This is the only park picnic area with running water. The tables are set behind the visitor center, and most have a view of the lake below. There are flush toilets inside the visitor center. ⊠ *Rim Dr., south side of lake, by Crater Lake Lodge, Rim Village* ⊕ *www.nps.gov/crla.*

Vidae Falls. In the upper reaches of Sun Creek, the picnic tables here enjoy the sound of the small falls across the road. There is a vault toilet, and a couple of fire grills. ⊠ *Rim Dr., 3 miles east of Steel Visitor Center, near Crater Peak turnoff* ⊕ *www.nps.gov/crla.*

Fodor's Choice
★
Wizard Island. The park's best picnic venue is on Wizard Island; pack a lunch and book yourself on one of the early-morning boat tour departures, reserving space on an afternoon return. There are no formal picnic areas and just pit toilets, but you'll discover plenty of sunny and shaded spots where you can enjoy a quiet meal and appreciate the astounding scene that surrounds you. The island is accessible by boat only, and to get to the boat dock you must hike down about 1 mile. The hike back up is strenuous. ⊠ *Crater Lake ✛ To get to boat dock, access Cleetwood Cove Trail, off Rim Dr., 11 miles north of Rim Village* ⊕ *www.craterlakelodges.com/activities/volcano-boat-cruises.*

WHERE TO STAY

$$$
HOTEL
🏨 **The Cabins at Mazama Village.** In a wooded area 7 miles south of the lake, this complex is made up of several A-frame buildings and has modest rooms with two queen beds and a private bath. **Pros:** clean and well-kept facility. **Cons:** lots of traffic into adjacent campground. Ⓢ *Rooms from: $152* ⊠ *Mazama Village, near Annie Spring entrance station* ☎ *541/594–2255, 888/774–2728* ⊕ *www.craterlakelodges.com* ☯ *Closed mid-Oct.–late May* ⚑ *40 rooms* ⦿⧘ *No meals.*

$$$
HOTEL
Fodor's Choice
★
🏨 **Crater Lake Lodge.** The period feel of this 1915 lodge on the caldera's rim is reflected in its lodgepole-pine columns, gleaming wood floors, and stone fireplaces in the common areas. **Pros:** ideal location for watching sunrise and sunset reflected on the lake; exudes rustic charm; excellent restaurant. **Cons:** books up far in advance; some rooms have tubs only, no shower; relatively simple furnishings and basic amenities; small rooms; no air-conditioning. Ⓢ *Rooms from: $180* ⊠ *1 Lodge Loop Rd., Rim Village, east of Rim Visitor Center* ☎ *541/594–2255, 888/774–2728* ⊕ *www.craterlakelodges.com* ☯ *Closed mid-Oct.–mid-May* ⚑ *71 rooms* ⦿⧘ *No meals.*

SOUTHERN
OREGON

WELCOME TO SOUTHERN OREGON

TOP REASONS TO GO

★ **Discover Oregon's other wine regions:** The underrated Umpqua and Rogue River wine regions offer picturesque pastoral views and numerous tasting rooms.

★ **Go underground:** Explore deep into mysterious underground chambers and marble caves at Oregon Caves National Monument.

★ **Shakespeare Festival:** The acclaimed Oregon Shakespeare Festival draws drama lovers to Ashland nine months a year, presenting a wide variety of both classic and contemporary theater.

★ **Enjoy quaint towns:** Southern Oregon's own throwback to the Old West, Jacksonville abounds with well-preserved buildings while Ashland claims one of the prettiest downtowns in the state.

★ **Get wet and wild:** Each fall more than 1 million waterfowl descend upon Klamath Basin National Wildlife Refuge Complex. The Rogue River is Oregon's white-water-rafting capital, and the entire region is laced with stunning hiking trails.

1 Umpqua Valley. Known increasingly for its up-and-coming wineries, including superb Abacela, this valley is home to tiny and historic Oakland, bustling Roseburg and its family-friendly Wildlife Safari park, and the Umpqua River Scenic Byway, a particularly scenic route to the northern (summer only) entrance of Crater Lake.

2 Rogue Valley. This fertile, mild-temperature region that extends from Grants Pass southeast through Medford and down to Ashland takes in the most populous communities in the area—it's also the gateway for reaching Klamath Falls, to the east, and the remote but fascinating Oregon Caves National Monument to the southwest. The Oregon Shakespeare Festival and an abundance of historic buildings have turned Ashland into a hub of arts, dining, and fine bed-and-breakfasts. Grants Pass, which also has a lively downtown restaurants and boutiques district, is the launch point for some of the best white-water rafting around, while Medford and historic Jacksonville are surrounded by vineyards and farms that produce some of the state's tastiest local edibles, from pears to Pinot Gris.

GETTING ORIENTED

To locals, southern Oregon really refers to the southwestern corner of the state, encompassing the Rogue and several other river valleys that lie between the Coast and Cascade mountain ranges, from a little north of Roseburg down to the California border. The area is due south of Eugene and the Willamette Valley, and has a lush, hilly, and fertile terrain that lends itself perfectly to agriculture and wine-making. Towns in the valleys, such as Ashland and Roseburg, have elevations ranging from about 500 to 2,000 feet, while peaks to the east, in the Cascade Range, rise as high as 9,000 feet. This area is also the gateway to Crater Lake National Park—many visitors to that park overnight in Medford or Ashland, which are about 85 miles away.

8

Updated by Andrew Collins

Southern Oregon begins where the verdant lowlands of the Willamette Valley give way to a complex collision of mountains, rivers, and ravines. The intricate geography of the "Land of Umpqua," as the area around Roseburg is somewhat romantically known, signals that this is territory distinct from neighboring regions to the north, east, and west.

Wild rivers—the Rogue and the Umpqua are legendary for fishing and boating—and twisting mountain roads venture through the landscape that saw Oregon's most violent Indian wars and became the territory of a self-reliant breed. "Don't-Tread-on-Me" southern Oregonians see themselves as markedly different from fellow citizens of the Pacific Wonderland. In fact, several early-20th-century attempts to secede from Oregon (in combination with northern California) and proclaim a "state of Jefferson" survive in local folklore and culture. That being said, Ashland and parts of the surrounding area have steadily become more progressive and urbane in recent decades, as wineries, art galleries, and farm-to-table restaurants continue to proliferate. The mix of folks from all different political, social, and stylistic bents is a big part of what makes southern Oregon so interesting—and appealing.

Some locals describe this sun-kissed, sometimes surprisingly hot landscape as Mediterranean; others refer to it as Oregon's banana belt. It's a climate built for slow-paced pursuits and a leisurely outlook on life, not to mention agriculture—the region's orchards, farms, and increasingly acclaimed vineyards have lately helped give southern Oregon cachet among food and wine aficionados. The restaurant scene has grown partly thanks to a pair of big cultural draws, Ashland's Oregon Shakespeare Festival and Jacksonville's open-air, picnic-friendly Britt Festivals concert series.

Roseburg, Medford, and Klamath Falls are also all popular bases for visiting iconic Crater Lake National Park *(see Chapter 7)*, which lies at the region's eastern edge, about two hours away by car. Formed nearly 8,000 years ago by the cataclysmic eruption of Mt. Mazama, this stunningly clear-blue lake is North America's deepest.

SOUTHERN OREGON PLANNER

WHEN TO GO

Southern Oregon's population centers, which all lie chiefly in the valleys, tend to be warmer and quite a bit sunnier than Eugene and Portland to the north, receiving almost no snow in winter and only 2 to 3 inches of rain per month. In summer, temperatures regularly climb into the 90s, but the low humidity makes for a generally comfortable climate. This makes most of the region quite pleasant to visit year-round, with spring and fall generally offering the best balance of sunny and mild weather.

The exceptions, during the colder months, are southern Oregon's mountainous areas to the east and west, which are covered with snow from fall through spring. Some of the roads leading from the Umpqua and Rogue valleys up to Crater Lake are closed because of snow from mid-October through June, making summer the prime time to visit.

Fodor's Choice ★ **Oregon Shakespeare Festival.** Ashland's biggest attraction is this festival of Shakespeare and other plays, which runs mid-February through early November. Book tickets and lodging well in advance. ⊠ *15 S. Pioneer St., Ashland* ☎ *541/482–4331* ⊕ *www.osfashland.org.*

Winter Wings Festival. Each February, nature enthusiasts flock to the Klamath Basin for the Winter Wings Festival, the nation's oldest birding festival. ⊠ *Box 354, Klamath Falls* ☎ *877/541–2473* ⊕ *winterwingsfest.org.*

GETTING HERE AND AROUND

AIR TRAVEL

Medford's Rogue Valley International Airport (MFR) is the state's third-largest facility, with direct flights to Denver, Los Angeles, Portland, Salt Lake City, San Francisco, and Seattle, and service by Allegiant, Alaska, Delta, and United. Most national car-rental branches are at the airport. A few taxi and shuttle companies provide transportation from the airport to other towns in the area; these are used mostly by locals, as a car is the only practical way to explore this relatively rural part of Oregon. The one exception is Ashland, where many attractions, restaurants, and accommodations are within walking distance. Cascade Airport Shuttle offers door-to-door service from the airport to Ashland for about $30 to $35. Among taxi companies, Valley Cab serves the Rogue Valley region, with fares costing $2.75 base per trip, plus $2.75 per mile thereafter.

Roseburg is a 75-mile drive from Oregon's second-largest airport, in Eugene (EUG). Ashland is about 300 miles south of the state's largest airport, in Portland, and 350 miles north of San Francisco. Although it's often cheaper to fly into these larger airports than it is to Medford, what you lose in gas costs, time, and inconvenience will likely outweigh any savings.

Contacts Cascade Airport Shuttle. ☎ *541/488–1998, 888/760–7433* ⊕ *www.cascadeshuttle.com.* **Rogue Valley International Airport.** ☎ *541/772–8068* ⊕ *www.jacksoncountyor.org/airport.* **Valley Cab.** ☎ *541/772–1818* ⊕ *www.myvalleycab.com.*

8

CAR TRAVEL

Unquestionably, your best way to explore the region is by car, although most of Ashland's key attractions, hotels, and dining are downtown and within walking distance of one another. Interstate 5 runs north–south the length of the Umpqua and Rogue river valleys, linking Roseburg, Grants Pass, Medford, and Ashland. Many regional attractions lie not too far east or west of Interstate 5. Jacksonville is a short drive due west from Medford. Highway 138 winds scenically along the Umpqua River east of Roseburg to the less-visited northern end of Crater Lake National Park. Highway 140 leads from Medford east to Klamath Falls, which you can reach from Bend via U.S. 97.

RESTAURANTS

Southern Oregon's dining scene varies greatly from region to region, with the more tourism-driven and upscale communities of Ashland, Jacksonville, and Grants Pass leading the way in terms of sophisticated farm-to-table restaurants, hip coffeehouses, and noteworthy bakeries and wine bars. Other larger towns in the valleys, including Roseburg and Medford, have grown in culinary stature and variety of late, while Klamath Falls and Cave Junction have few dining options of note. In the former communities you'll find chefs emphasizing Oregon-produced foods; regional wines, including many from the Rogue and Umpqua valleys, also find their way onto many menus. *Restaurant reviews have been shortened. For full information visit Fodors.com.*

HOTELS

Ashland has the region's greatest variety of distinctive lodgings, from the usual low- to mid-priced chain properties to plush B&Bs set in restored Arts and Crafts and Victorian houses. Nearby Jacksonville also has several fine, upscale inns. Beyond that, in nearly every town in southern Oregon you'll find an interesting B&B or small hotel, and in any of the key communities along Interstate 5—including Roseburg, Grants Pass, and Medford—a wide variety of chain motels and hotels. Rooms in this part of the state book up earliest in summer, especially on weekends. If you're coming to Ashland or Jacksonville, try to book at least a week or two ahead. Elsewhere, you can usually find a room in a suitable chain property on less than a day's notice. *Hotel reviews have been shortened. For full information, visit Fodors.com.*

WHAT IT COSTS IN U.S. DOLLARS			
	$	$$	$$$	$$$$
Restaurants	under $16	$16–$22	$23–$30	over $30
Hotels	under $150	$150–$200	$201–$250	over $250

Restaurant prices are the average cost of a main course at dinner or, if dinner is not served, at lunch. Hotel prices are the lowest cost of a standard double room in high season.

TOURS

FAMILY **Hellgate Jetboat Excursions.** You'll see some of Oregon's most magnificent scenery on these excursions, which depart from the Riverside Inn in Grants Pass. The 36-mile round-trip runs through Hellgate Canyon and takes two hours. There is also a five-hour, 75-mile round-trip from Grants Pass to Grave Creek, with a stop for a meal on an open-air deck (cost of meal not included). Trips are available May through September, conditions permitting. ☎ *541/479–7204, 800/648–4874* ⊕ *www. hellgate.com* 🍽 *From $31.*

Wine Hopper Tours. Getting to know the region's more than 125 wineries can be a challenge to visitors, especially when you factor in having to drive from tasting room to tasting room. This outfitter with knowledgeable guides leads seven-hour tours leaving daily from Ashland, Medford, and Jacksonville—the day includes a tour of a winery, picnic lunch, and tasting at a few of the area's top producers. ☎ *541/476–9463, 855/550–9463* ⊕ *www.winehoppertours.com* 🍽 *From $89.*

VISITOR INFORMATION
Southern Oregon Visitors Association. ⊕ *www.southernoregon.org.*

UMPQUA VALLEY

The northernmost part of southern Oregon, beginning about 40 miles south of Eugene and the Willamette Valley, the rural and sparsely populated Umpqua Valley is the gateway to this part of the state's sunny and relatively dry climate. As you drive down Interstate 5 you'll descend through twisting valleys and climb up over scenic highlands. In summer you can follow the dramatic Umpqua River Scenic Byway (Highway 138) east over the Cascades to access Crater Lake from the north—it's the prettiest route to the lake. Within the Umpqua Valley, attractions are relatively few, but this area has several excellent wineries, some of the best river fishing in the Northwest, and one of the region's top draws for animal lovers, the Wildlife Safari park.

ROSEBURG

73 miles south of Eugene on I–5.

Fishermen the world over hold the name Roseburg sacred. The timber town on the Umpqua River attracts anglers in search of a dozen popular fish species, including bass, brown and brook trout, and chinook, coho, and sockeye salmon. The native steelhead, which makes its run to the sea in the summer, is king of them all.

The north and south branches of the Umpqua River meet up just north of Roseburg. The roads that run parallel to this river provide spectacular views of the falls, and the North Umpqua route also provides access to trails, hot springs, and the Winchester fish ladder. White-water rafting is also popular here, although not to the degree that it is farther south in the Rogue Valley.

About 80 miles west of the northern gateway to Crater Lake National Park and in the Hundred Valleys of the Umpqua, Roseburg produces innovative, well-regarded wines. Wineries are sprouting up throughout the mild, gorgeous farm country around town, mostly within easy reach of Interstate 5.

GETTING HERE AND AROUND

Roseburg is the first large town you'll reach driving south from Eugene on Interstate 5. It's also a main access point into southern Oregon via Highway 138 if you're approaching from the east, either by way of Crater Lake or U.S. 97, which leads down from Bend. And from the North Bend–Coos Bay region of the Oregon Coast, windy but picturesque Highway 42 leads to just south of Roseburg. It's a 75-mile drive north to Eugene's airport, and a 95-mile drive south to Rogue Valley Airport in Medford.

ESSENTIALS

Visitor Information Roseburg Visitors & Convention Bureau. ⊠ *410 S.E. Spruce St.* ☎ *541/672–9731, 800/440–9584* ⊕ *www.visitroseburg.com.*

EXPLORING

Fodor'sChoice   **Abacela Vineyards and Winery.** The name derives from an archaic Span-
★   ish word meaning "to plant grapevines," and that's exactly what this winery's husband-wife team did not so very long ago. Abacela released its first wine in 1999 and has steadily established itself as one of the best wineries outside the Willamette Valley. Hot-blooded Spanish Tempranillo is Abacela's pride and joy, though inky Malbec and torrid Sangiovese also highlight a repertoire heavy on Mediterranean varietals, which you can sample in a handsome, eco-friendly tasting room. ⊠ *12500 Lookingglass Rd.* ☎ *541/679–6642* ⊕ *www.abacela.com.*

Douglas County Museum. One of the best county museums in the state surveys 8,000 years of human activity in the region. The fossil collection is worth a stop, as is the state's second-largest photo collection, numbering more than 24,000 images, some dating to the 1840s. ⊠ *123 Museum Dr.* ☎ *541/957–7007* ⊕ *www.umpquavalleymuseums.org* ☞ *$8.*

FAMILY   **Wildlife Safari.** Come face-to-face with some 500 free-roaming animals
Fodor'sChoice at the 600-acre drive-through wildlife park. Inhabitants include alliga-
★   tors, bobcats, cougars, gibbons, lions, giraffes, grizzly bears, Tibetan yaks, cheetahs, Siberian tigers, and more than 100 additional species. There's also a petting zoo, a miniature train, and elephant rides. The admission price includes two same-day drive-throughs. This nonprofit zoological park is a respected research facility with full accreditation from the American Zoo and Aquarium Association, with a mission to conserve and protect endangered species through education and breeding programs. ⊠ *1790 Safari Rd., Winston* ☎ *541/679–6761* ⊕ *www. wildlifesafari.net* ☞ *$18.*

WHERE TO EAT AND STAY

$$ ✕ **Brix.** This handsome downtown American bistro with exposed-brick
AMERICAN   walls, curving leather banquettes, and high ceilings serves reasonably priced breakfast and lunch fare daily, and somewhat more upscale dinners. Start the day with blueberry–lemon zest pancakes or eggs Benedict

topped with wild salmon. **Known for:** mix of affordable and upscale dishes; impressive wine and cocktail list. [$] *Average main: $19* ✉ *527 S.E. Jackson St.* ☎ *541/440–4901* ⏲ *No dinner Sun.*

$$ AMERICAN FAMILY 🍴 **Tolly's.** Most folks head to this sweetly nostalgic restaurant in the center of tiny and historic Oakland—18 miles north of Roseburg—for inexpensive lunch (including exceptionally good burgers) or to enjoy an old-fashioned soda or malt downstairs in the Victorian ice-cream parlor. Most nights, however, you can dine upstairs in the oak- and antiques-filled dining room on deftly prepared creative American cuisine. **Known for:** Sunday brunch; historic vibe. [$] *Average main: $18* ✉ *115 N.E. Locust St., Oakland* ☎ *541/459–3796* 🌐 *www.tollysgrill.com* ⏲ *No dinner Mon.–Wed.*

$$$ B&B/INN Fodor's Choice ★ 🏨 **The Steamboat Inn.** The world's top fly-fishermen converge at this secluded forest inn, high in the Cascades above the North Umpqua River; others come simply to relax in the reading nooks or on the decks of the riverside guest cabins nestled below soaring fir trees. **Pros:** good option if en route to Crater Lake; access to some of the best fishing in the West; peaceful escape. **Cons:** far from any towns or cities. [$] *Rooms from: $205* ✉ *42705 N. Umpqua Hwy., 38 miles east of Roseburg on Hwy. 138, near Steamboat Creek, Idleyld Park* ☎ *541/498–2230, 800/840–8825* 🌐 *www.thesteamboatinn.com* 🛏 *8 cabins, 5 cottages, 2 suites, 5 houses* 🍽 *No meals.*

SPORTS AND THE OUTDOORS

FISHING

You'll find some of the best river fishing in Oregon along the Umpqua, with smallmouth bass, shad, steelhead, salmon (coho, chinook, and sockeye), and sturgeon—the biggest reaching 10 feet in length—among the most prized catches. In addition to the Steamboat Inn, several outfitters in the region provide full guide services, which typically include all gear, boats, and expert leaders. There's good fishing in this region year-round, with sturgeon and steelhead at their best during the colder months, chinook and coho salmon thriving in the fall, and most other species prolific in spring and summer.

Big K Guest Ranch. Set along a 10-mile span of the upper Umpqua River near Elkton (about 35 miles north of Roseburg), Big K is a 2,500-acre guest ranch. Accommodations are geared primarily to groups and corporate retreats, but the ranch offers individual eight-hour fishing trips starting at $400 for one or two anglers, and two-day/three-night fishing and lodging packages (meals included) for around $900 per person. Adventures include fly-fishing for smallmouth bass and summer steelhead, as well as spin-casting and drift-boat fishing. ✉ *20029 Hwy. 138 W, Elkton* ☎ *541/584–2295, 800/390–2445* 🌐 *www.big-k.com.*

Oregon Angler. One of the state's most respected and knowledgeable guides, Todd Hannah, specializes in jet-boat and drift-boat fishing excursions along the famed "Umpqua Loop," an 18-mile span of river that's long been lauded for exceptional fishing. Full-day trips start at $200 per person. ✉ *1037 Maupin Rd., Elkton* ☎ *800/428–8585* 🌐 *www.theoregonangler.com.*

RAFTING

There's thrilling Class III and higher white-water rafting along the North Umpqua River, with several outfitters providing trips ranging from a few hours to a few days throughout the year.

North Umpqua Outfitters. Since 1987, this trusted provider has offered half-, full-, and two-day rafting and kayaking trips, starting at $105 per person, along the frothy North Umpqua. ⊠ *Box 158, Idleyld Park* ☎ *888/454–9696* ⊕ *www.umpquarivers.com.*

ROGUE VALLEY

Encompassing the broad, curving, southeasterly swath of towns from Grants Pass through Medford down to Ashland, the mild and sun-kissed Rogue Valley is southern Oregon's main population center, and also where you'll find the bulk of the region's lodging, dining, shopping, and recreation.

Interstate 5 cuts through the valley en route to northern California, but venture away from the main thoroughfare to see what makes this part of Oregon so special, including the superb—if underrated—wineries. With warmer temperatures, this area is conducive to many more grape varieties than the Willamette Valley—from reds like Syrah, Tempranillo, and Cabernet Sauvignon to increasingly well-known Old World whites like Viognier and Pinot Gris. Foodies are drawn to the region's abundance of local food producers, from nationally acclaimed cheese makers and chocolatiers to farms growing pears, blackberries, and cherries. Access to excellent food has helped turn the small but artsy city of Ashland into one of Oregon's top restaurant destinations, with nearby communities also growing in culinary cachet. Additionally, the area's reputation for performing arts, which manifests itself in the famed Oregon Shakespeare Festival in Ashland and Britt Music Festival in historic Jacksonville, continues to grow.

Flanked by about a 2-million-acre Rogue–Siskiyou National Forest, which has rangers' offices near Grants Pass and Medford, the Rogue Valley is a hub of outdoor recreation, from fishing and white-water rafting along its clear rivers to mountain biking, hiking, and even skiing in the higher elevations—peaks in the Cascade Range, to the east, rise to nearly 10,000 feet. Klamath Falls lies technically a bit east of the Rogue Valley but shares the region's abundance of unspoiled wilderness and opportunities for getting in touch with nature.

GRANTS PASS

70 miles south of Roseburg on I–5.

"It's the Climate!" So says a confident 1950s vintage neon sign presiding over Josephine County's downtown. Grants Pass bills itself as Oregon's white-water capital: the Rogue River, preserved by Congress in 1968 as a National Wild and Scenic River, runs right through town. Downtown Grants Pass is a National Historic District, a stately little enclave of 19th-century brick storefronts housing a mix of folksy businesses harking back to the 1950s and newer, trendier cafés and boutiques. It's all

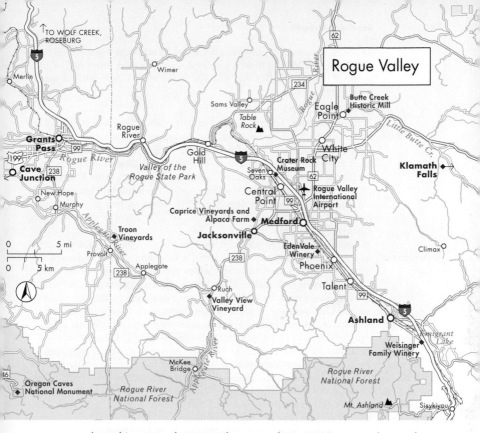

Rogue Valley

that white water, however, that compels most visitors—and not a few moviemakers (*The River Wild* and *Rooster Cogburn* were both filmed here). If the river alone doesn't serve up enough natural drama, the sheer rock walls of nearby Hellgate Canyon rise 250 feet.

GETTING HERE AND AROUND

Grants Pass is easily reached via Interstate 5, and it's also where U.S. 199 cuts southwest toward Oregon Caves National Monument and, eventually, the northernmost section of California's coast (and Redwood National Park). Many visitors to the southern Oregon coastline backtrack inland up U.S. 199 to create a scenic loop drive, ultimately intersecting with Interstate 5 at Grants Pass. Medford's airport is a 30-mile drive south.

ESSENTIALS

Visitor Information Grants Pass Tourism. ✉ *198 S.W. 6th St.* ☎ *541/476–7574* ⊕ *travelgrantspass.com.*

EXPLORING

Fodor's Choice **Troon Vineyards.** Few winemakers in southern Oregon have generated
★ more buzz than Troon, whose swank tasting room and winery is patterned after a French country villa. Troon produces relatively small yields of exceptional wines more typical of Sonoma than Oregon (Malbec and Zinfandel are the heavy hitters), but they also plant less typical U.S. varietals, such as Vermentino and Sangiovese. The winery is

14 miles southeast of downtown Grants Pass, in the northern edge of the Applegate Valley; there's a second Troon tasting room in Carlton, in the Willamette Valley. ✉ *1475 Kubli Rd.* ☎ *541/846–9900* 🌐 *www.troonvineyard.com.*

WHERE TO EAT

$$ ECLECTIC 🍴 **Blondie's Bistro.** Sophisticated but affordable Blondie's serves globally inspired food and cocktails in a dapper downtown space with high ceilings and hardwood floors—the lone aesthetic drawback is the sometimes boisterous acoustics. The kitchen, however, prepares first-rate food, including an especially good list of starters, from Portuguese-style steamed clams with herbed sausage to a substantial Mediterranean antipasto platter. **Known for:** live music some nights; popular happy hour. [$] *Average main: $19* ✉ *226 S.W. G St.* ☎ *541/479–0420* 🌐 *www.blondiesbistro.com.*

$ LATIN AMERICAN 🍴 **Gtano's.** Set in a nondescript downtown shopping center, this cozy and welcoming restaurant is cheerful inside, and the kitchen turns out superb Nuevo Latino cuisine. Specialties include the starter of Puerto Rico "nachos," with Jack cheese, black beans, chicken, grilled pineapples, and mango salsa; and hearty main dishes, many of them focused on seafood, such as Colombian-style prawns with butter, garlic, and a tropical sauce. **Known for:** fresh-fruit margaritas; guacamole prepared table-side. [$] *Average main: $13* ✉ *218 S.W. G St.* ☎ *541/507–1255* ⏲ *Closed Sun.*

$ AMERICAN Fodor's Choice ★ 🍴 **Ma Mosa's.** Sustainability is the name of the game at this lively café in downtown Grants Pass, with a cozy dining room of colorfully painted tables and mismatched chairs, and a large adjacent patio with picnic tables and lush landscaping. The kitchen sources from local farms and purveyors to create beer-battered fried chicken and waffles, kale Caesar salads, and line-caught-fish tacos with seasonal slaw and house-made salsa. **Known for:** refreshing mimosa cocktails at brunch; pet-friendly patio. [$] *Average main: $10* ✉ *118 N.W. E St.* ☎ *541/479–0236* 🌐 *www.mamosas.com* ⏲ *Closed Mon. No dinner.*

$ WINE BAR Fodor's Choice ★ 🍴 **Twisted Cork Wine Bar.** With a mission to showcase southern Oregon's fast-growing reputation for acclaimed vino, this dapper, art-filled space lends a bit of urbane sophistication to downtown Grants Pass. In addition to pouring varietals from throughout the Umpqua and Rogue valleys, Twisted Cork carries wines from more than 115 wineries throughout the Northwest, along with a few from California. **Known for:** local ports and dessert wines; shareable platters of cheese and charcuterie; reasonably priced food. [$] *Average main: $15* ✉ *210 S.W. 6th St.* ☎ *541/295–3094* 🌐 *www.thetwistedcorkgrantspass.com* ⏲ *Closed Sun. and Mon.*

WHERE TO STAY

$$ HOTEL 🏨 **Lodge at Riverside.** The pool and many rooms overlook the Rogue River as it passes through downtown, and all but a few rooms, furnished with stylish country house–inspired armoires, plush beds, and oil paintings, have private balconies or patios; suites have river-rock fireplaces and Jacuzzi tubs. **Pros:** central location; attractive modern furnishings; landscaped pool overlooks Rogue River. **Cons:** no restaurant on-site. [$] *Rooms from: $155* ✉ *955 S.E. 7th St.* ☎ *541/955–0600, 877/955–0600* 🌐 *www.thelodgeatriverside.com* 🛏 *29 rooms, 4 suites* 🍴 *Breakfast.*

$$$
B&B/INN
Fodor's Choice
★

⊡ **Weasku Inn.** Pacific Northwest–inspired art, handmade furnishings, and fine fabrics fill a rambling timber-frame home overlooking the Rogue River, 11 handsomely outfitted cabins, and an A-frame bungalow to comprise the most luxurious accommodations between Ashland and Eugene. **Pros:** set directly on the Rogue River; impeccably decorated; fireplaces in many rooms. **Cons:** 10-minute drive east of downtown; among the highest rates in the region. $ *Rooms from: $209* ✉ *5560 Rogue River Hwy.* ☎ *541/471–8000, 800/493–2758* ⊕ *www. weaskuinn.com* ⤳ *5 rooms, 12 cabins* ❑ *Breakfast.*

SPORTS AND THE OUTDOORS
RAFTING
More than a dozen outfitters guide white-water rafting trips along the Rogue River in and around Grants Pass. In fact, this stretch of Class III rapids ranks among the best in the West. The rafting season lasts from about July through August and often into September, and the stretch of river running south from Grants Pass, with some 80 frothy rapids, is exciting but not treacherous, making it ideal for novices, families, and others looking simply to give this enthralling activity a try.

Morrisons Rogue Wilderness Adventures. If you're up for an adventure that combines rafting with overnight accommodations, consider booking one of these exciting excursions that run along a 34-mile stretch of the Rogue River. They last for four days and three nights, with options for both lodge and camping stays along the way. Half- and full-day trips are also available. ✉ *8500 Galice Rd., Merlin* ☎ *800/336–1647, 541/476–3825* ⊕ *www.rogueriverraft.com* ✑ *From $65.*

Orange Torpedo Trips. One of the most reliable operators on the Rogue River offers half-day to several-day trips, as well as relaxed dinner-and-wine float trips along a calmer stretch of river. Klamath and North Umpqua river trips are also available. ✉ *210 Merlin Rd., Merlin* ☎ *541/479–5061, 800/635–2925* ⊕ *www.orangetorpedo.com* ✑ *From $49.*

RECREATIONAL AREAS
Rogue River–Siskiyou National Forests, Grants Pass. In the Klamath Mountains and the Coast Range of southwestern Oregon, the 2-million-acre forest contains the 35-mile-long Wild and Scenic section of the Rogue River, which races through the Wild Rogue Wilderness Area, and the Illinois and Chetco Wild and Scenic rivers, which run through the 180,000-acre Kalmiopsis Wilderness Area. Activities include white-water rafting, camping, and hiking, but many hiking areas require trail-park passes. ✉ *Off U.S. 199* ☎ *541/618–2200* ⊕ *www.fs.usda. gov/rogue-siskiyou.*

Valley of the Rogue State Park. A 1¼-mile hiking trail follows the bank of the Rogue, the river made famous by novelist and fisherman Zane Grey. There's a campground along 3 miles of shoreline with full RV hookups as well as yurts (some of them pet-friendly). There are picnic tables, walking trails, playgrounds, and restrooms. The park is 12 miles east of downtown Grants Pass. ✉ *3792 N. River Rd., Gold Hill* ☎ *541/582–1118, 800/551–6949* ⊕ *www.oregonstateparks.org.*

8

MEDFORD

30 miles southeast of Grants Pass on I–5.

Medford is the professional, retail, trade, and service hub for eight counties in southern Oregon and northern California. As such, it offers more professional and cultural venues than might be expected for a city of its size (with a population of about 80,000). The workaday downtown has shown signs of gentrification and rejuvenation in recent years, and in the outskirts you'll find several major shopping centers and the famed fruit and gourmet-food mail-order company Harry & David.

Lodging tends to be cheaper in Medford than in nearby (and easily accessible) Ashland or Jacksonville, although cookie-cutter chain properties dominate the hotel landscape. It's also 71 miles southwest of Crater Lake and 80 miles northeast of the Oregon Caves, making it an affordable and convenient base for visiting either.

GETTING HERE AND AROUND

Medford is in the heart of the Rogue Valley on Interstate 5, and is home to the state's third-largest airport, Rogue Valley International. A car is your best way to get around the city and surrounding area.

ESSENTIALS

Visitor Information Medford Visitors & Convention Bureau. ⊠ *1314 Center Dr.* ☎ *541/776–4021, 800/469–6307* ⊕ *www.travelmedford.org.*

EXPLORING

Crater Rock Museum. Jackson County's natural history and collections of the Roxy Ann Gem and Mineral Society are on display at this quirky, 12,000-square-foot museum in Central Point (6 miles northwest of Medford). Fossils, petrified wood, fluorescent rocks, and precious minerals from throughout Oregon and elsewhere in the West are included, plus works of glass by renowned artist Dale Chihuly. ⊠ *2002 Scenic Ave., Central Point* ☎ *541/664–6081* ⊕ *www.craterrock.com* ☜ *$7.*

EdenVale Winery. Four miles southwest of downtown Medford amid a bucolic patch of fruit orchards, this winery and tasting room, called the Rogue Valley Wine Center, adjoins a rather grand 19th-century white-clapboard farmhouse surrounded by flower beds and vegetable gardens. Inside the tasting room you can sample and buy not only EdenVale's noted reds and late-harvest whites but also other respected labels from vineyards throughout the region. ⊠ *2310 Voorhies Rd.* ☎ *541/512–2955* ⊕ *www.edenvalewines.com.*

Ledger David Cellars. Sandwiched handily between Rogue Creamery and Lillie Belle Chocolates in the small downtown of Central Point, this boutique winery produces an interesting portfolio of wines that have rapidly begun to earn praise at competitions and from critics. Standouts include a bright, balanced Chenin Blanc and a berry-forward, medium-body Sangiovese. Enjoy your tasting on the patio if it's a nice day. ⊠ *245 N. Front St., Central Point* ☎ *541/664–2218* ⊕ *www.ledgerdavid.com.*

WHERE TO EAT AND STAY

$$ TAPAS 🍴 **Elements Tapas Bar.** A stylish ambience and a taste of impressively authentic Spanish fare—these are the draws of this handsome tapas restaurant in downtown Medford's turn-of-the-20th-century "Goldy" building. Pass around plates of mussels in romesco sauce, apricot-braised-pork empanadas, chorizo-studded Andalucian paella, and lamb-sausage flatbread, while sampling selections from the lengthy beer and cocktail menus. **Known for:** late-night dining; Sunday brunch; extensive beer, wine, and cocktail selection. [$] *Average main: $20* ✉ *101 E. Main St.* ☎ *541/779–0135* 🌐 *www.elementsmedford.com* 🕑 *No lunch.*

$ BURGER 🍴 **Jaspers Cafe.** This cute roadhouse-style building a few miles northwest of downtown Medford has made a name for itself serving obscenely large, decadently topped, and deliciously crafted burgers. Polish off the Jasperado, with chorizo, salsa verde, and a fried egg, and you probably won't be experiencing any hunger pains for the rest of the day. **Known for:** unusual game burgers (such as kangaroo and antelope); tasty sides—sweet potatoes, pork pot stickers. [$] *Average main: $7* ✉ *2739 N. Pacific Hwy.* ☎ *541/776–5307* 🌐 *www.jasperscafe.com.*

$ HOTEL 🏨 **Inn on the Commons.** This recently revamped and rebranded (formerly a Red Lion) mid-price hotel is within walking distance of downtown Medford's restaurants and shops. **Pros:** prettier and more distinctive decor than most of Medford's chain properties; a branch of Ashland's excellent Larks restaurant is on-site; guests receive free passes to health club across the street. **Cons:** some rooms have street and freeway traffic noise. [$] *Rooms from: $99* ✉ *200 N. Riverside Ave.* ☎ *541/779–5811, 866/779–5811* 🌐 *www.innatthecommons.com/* 🛏 *118 rooms* 🍽 *Breakfast.*

$ HOTEL 🏨 **Rodeway Inn–Medford.** If you're on a budget and seeking a simple and immaculately clean base camp, check into this friendly, family-run '50s vintage motor court on the city's south side. **Pros:** vintage charm; convenient to sights in Medford as well Jacksonville and Ashland; super low rates. **Cons:** few amenities and luxuries; rather dated (though that's part of the charm). [$] *Rooms from: $60* ✉ *901 S. Riverside Ave.* ☎ *541/776–9194, 877/424–6423* 🌐 *www.rodewayinnmedford.com* 🛏 *40 rooms* 🍽 *Breakfast.*

NIGHTLIFE AND PERFORMING ARTS

Jefferson Spirits. This hip nightspot has helped to spur downtown Medford's ongoing renaissance by creating a swanky environment for hobnobbing and enjoying creating craft cocktails, like the locally inspired Rogue Pear, with whiskey, pear, and a splash of lemon juice. Barrel-aged cocktails are a specialty, and you'll also find local and international wines and mostly Oregon beers. ✉ *404 E. Main St.* ☎ *541/622–8190* 🌐 *www.jeffersonspirits.com.*

SPORTS AND THE OUTDOORS

FISHING

With close access to some of the best freshwater fishing venues in the Northwest, Medford has several companies that lead tours and provide gear.

Carson's Guide Service. Based 22 miles north of Medford along Highway 62 (toward Crater Lake), Carson's provides expert instruction and knowledge of many of the area's rivers, including the Rogue, Sixes, Umpqua, Coquille, Elk, and Chetco, as well as several lakes. Steelhead, salmon, shad, and smallmouth bass are the most common catches. ⊠ *595 Ragsdale Rd., Trail* ☎ *541/261–3279* ⊕ *www.fishwithcarson.com.*

Fishing The Rogue. These experienced outfitter offers half- and full-day guided steelhead and salmon fishing trips in heated boats, with all gear provided, on the Rogue and Umpqua rivers as well as some of the waterways that flow down toward the southern Oregon Coast. These trips are great for all skill and experience levels, even beginners—expert instruction is included. ☎ *541/326–9486* ⊕ *www.fishingtherogue.com.*

HIKING

Fodor's Choice
★ **Table Rock.** One of the best venues for hiking in the Rogue Valley comprises a pair of monolithic rock formations that rise some 700 to 800 feet above the valley floor about 10 miles north of Medford and just a couple of miles north of TouVelle State Park. Operated by a partnership between the Bureau of Land Management and the Nature Conservancy, the Table Rock formations and surrounding 4,864 acres of wilderness afford panoramic valley views from their summits. You reach Lower Table Rock by way of a moderately challenging 5½-mile round-trip trail, and Upper Table Rock via a shorter (about 3miles round-trip) and less-steep route. The trailheads to these formations are a couple of miles apart—just follow the road signs from Table Rock Road, north of TouVelle State Park (reached from Exit 33 of Interstate 5). ⊠ *Off Table Rock Rd., Central Point* ☎ *541/618–2200* ⊕ *www.blm.gov.*

RECREATIONAL AREAS

Rogue River–Siskiyou National Forest, Medford. Covering 2 million acres, this immense tract of wilderness woodland has fishing, swimming, hiking, and skiing. Motorized vehicles and equipment—even bicycles—are prohibited in the 113,000-acre Sky Lakes Wilderness, south of Crater Lake National Park. Its highest point is the 9,495-foot Mt. McLoughlin. Access to most of the forest is free, but there are fees at some trailheads. ⊠ *Forest Office, 3040 Biddle Rd.* ☎ *541/618–2200* ⊕ *www.fs.fed.us/r6/rogue-siskiyou.*

OFF THE
BEATEN
PATH **Rogue River Views.** Nature lovers who want to see the Rogue River at its loveliest can take a side trip to the Avenue of the Boulders, Mill Creek Falls, and Barr Creek Falls, off Highway 62, near Prospect, which is about 45 miles northeast of Medford—it's a scenic one-hour drive, and it's on the way to Crater Lake. Here the wild waters of the upper Rogue foam past volcanic boulders and the dense greenery of the Rogue River National Forest. ⊠ *Hwy. 62, Prospect.*

FAMILY **Rogue Valley Family Fun Center.** You'll find an impressive array of kids' games and recreation at this complex just off Exit 33 of Interstate 5 (about 5 miles north of Medford). Miniature golf, batting cages, a golf driving range, bumper boats, and go-karts are among the offerings, and there's also a video arcade and game room. ⊠ *1A Peninger Rd., Central Point* ☎ *541/664–4263* ⊕ *www.rvfamilyfuncenter.com.*

SHOPPING

Harry & David. Famous for their holiday gift baskets, Harry & David is based in Medford and offers hour-long tours of its huge facility on weekdays at 9:15, 10:30, 12:30, and 1:45. The tours cost $5 per person, but the fee is refunded if you spend a minimum of $40 in the mammoth Harry & David store, great for snagging picnic supplies to carry with you on any winery tour. Reservations are recommended, as space is limited. ⊠ *1314 Center Dr.* ☎ *541/864–2278, 877/322–8000* ⊕ *www.harryanddavid.com.*

Fodor'sChoice
★ **Lillie Belle Farms.** Next door to Rogue River Creamery, this artisan chocolatier handcrafts outstanding chocolates using local, often organic ingredients. A favorite treat is the Smokey Blue Cheese ganache made with Rogue River blue, but don't overlook the dark-chocolate–marionberry bonbons (made with organic marionberries grown on-site) or the delectable hazelnut chews. Most unusual, however, is the chocolate-covered bacon, coated in chipotle and brown sugar, hand-dipped in chocolate, and sprinkled with sea salt. ⊠ *211 N. Front St., Central Point* ☎ *541/664–2815* ⊕ *www.lilliebellefarms.com.*

Fodor'sChoice
★ **Rogue Creamery.** Just a few miles up the road from Medford in the little town of Central Point, you'll find one of the nation's most respected cheese makers, started in 1935 by Italian immigrants. Current owners Cary Bryant and David Gremmels bought the company in 2002, and promptly won one of the highest honors for cheese making, the London World Cheese Award. You can purchase any of the company's stellar cheeses here, from Smokey Blue to a lavender-infused cheddar, and you can watch the production through a window on most days. Delicious grilled-cheese sandwiches and local wines and beers are also available—enjoy them at one of the sidewalk tables outside. ⊠ *311 N. Front St., Central Point* ☎ *541/664–1537, 866/396–4704* ⊕ *www.roguecreamery.com.*

8

JACKSONVILLE

5 miles west of Medford on Hwy. 238.

This perfectly preserved town founded in the frenzy of the 1851 gold rush has served as the backdrop for several Western flicks. It's easy to see why. Jacksonville is one of only a small number of towns corralled into the National Register of Historic Places lock, stock, and barrel. These days, living-history exhibits offering a glimpse of pioneer life and the world-renowned Britt Festivals of classical, jazz, and pop music are the draw, rather than gold. Trails winding up from the town's center lead to the festival amphitheater, mid-19th-century gardens, exotic madrona groves, and an intriguing pioneer cemetery.

GETTING HERE AND AROUND

Most visitors to Jacksonville come by way of Medford, 5 miles east, on Highway 238—it's a scenic drive over hilly farmland and past vineyards. Alternatively, you can reach the town coming the other way on Highway 238, driving southeast from Grants Pass. This similarly beautiful drive through the Applegate Valley takes about 45 minutes.

ESSENTIALS

Visitor Information Jacksonville Visitor Center. ⊠ *185 N. Oregon St.* ☎ *541/899–8118* ⊕ *www.jacksonvilleoregon.org.*

EXPLORING

FAMILY **Caprice Vineyards and Alpaca Farm.** Among the many vineyards through-out the Rogue Valley, Caprice stands out both for producing well-bal-anced wines (including a quite tasty oak-aged Cabernet Sauvignon) and for having a herd of curious, friendly alpacas, which makes this a fun stop for the entire family. You can admire and even pet the alpacas; shop for sweaters, scarves, and fiber art in the small boutique; and sip wine while snacking on cheese and charcuterie on the tasting room or on the shaded patio. Although technically in the town of Central Point, the vineyard is just over a mile up the road from Jacksonville's his-toric downtown. ⊠ *970 Old Stage Rd., Central Point* ☎ *541/499–0449* ⊕ *www.capricevineyards.com.*

FAMILY
Fodor's Choice
★
Jacksonville Cemetery. A trip up the winding road—or, better yet, a hike via the old cart track marked Catholic access—leads to the resting place of the clans (the Britts, the Beekmans, and the Orths) that built Jacksonville. You'll also get a fascinating, if sometimes unattractive, view of the social dynamics of the Old West: older graves (the cem-etery is still in use) are strictly segregated, Irish Catholics from Jews from Protestants. A somber granite plinth marks the pauper's field, where those who found themselves on the losing end of gold-rush economics entered eternity anonymously. The cemetery closes at sun-down. ⊠ *Cemetery Rd. at N. Oregon St., follow signs from downtown* ☎ *541/826–9939* ⊕ *www.friendsjvillecemetery.org.*

Valley View Vineyard. Perched on a bench in the scenic Applegate Valley, you can sample acclaimed Chardonnay, Viognier, Rousanne, Merlot, Tempranillo, Pinot Noir, and Cabernet Franc while soaking up some of the best views in southern Oregon. The valley's especially sunny, warm climate produces highly acclaimed vintages. Founded in the 1850s by pioneer Peter Britt, the vineyard was reestablished in 1972. A restored pole barn houses the winery and tasting room. ⊠ *1000 Upper Applegate Rd., 10 miles southwest of downtown* ☎ *541/899–8468, 800/781–9463* ⊕ *www.valleyviewwinery.com.*

WHERE TO EAT AND STAY

$$
BARBECUE
✕ **Back Porch Bar & Grill.** For an excellent, mid-priced alternative to Jacksonville's more upscale eateries, head to this roadhouse-style clapboard building six blocks northeast of the town's historic main drag. Authentic central Texas–style barbecue is served here: char-grilled red-hot sausage, slow-cooked pork ribs, chicken-fried steak, and ½-pound burgers, plus a few seafood and pasta dishes. **Known for:** tangy slow-cooked barbecue; laid-back atmosphere. Ⓢ *Average main: $18* ⊠ *605 N. 5th St.* ☎ *541/899–8821* ⊕ *www.backporch-jacksonville.com.*

$$
PACIFIC
NORTHWEST
✕ **Déjà Vu Bistro.** This classy but unpretentious wine bar and bistro resides inside downtown Jacksonville's historic McCully House Inn. Seasonal dishes include a summertime starter of pan-roasted brussels sprouts, heirloom cherry tomatoes, crumbled goat cheese, and balsamic vinegar, and the entrée of coffee-rubbed flat iron steak with local green beans, roasted red potatoes, and stone-ground mustard sauce. **Known for:** predinner wine tasting; delicious house-made gelato for dessert. $ *Average main: $20* ⊠ *McCully House Inn, 240 E. California St.* ☎ *541/899–1942* ⊕ *www.dejavubistrowinebar.com* ☯ *Closed Mon. and Tues. No lunch.*

$$$
ECLECTIC
Fodor's Choice
★
✕ **Gogi's.** Visitors sometimes miss this small, low-key restaurant just down the hill from Britt Gardens—it's a favorite of foodies and locals, though, for sophisticated international cuisine. The menu changes regularly, but has featured a tower of roasted beets and chèvre topped with toasted walnuts and a balsamic-truffle reduction, followed by prosciutto-wrapped quail with cauliflower, asparagus, and roasted mushrooms. **Known for:** terrific Sunday brunch; artful and innovative dishes; discerning wine list. $ *Average main: $26* ⊠ *235 W. Main St.* ☎ *541/899–8699* ⊕ *www.gogisrestaurant.com* ☯ *Closed Mon. and Tues. No lunch Wed.–Sat.*

$$
B&B/INN
⊡ **Jacksonville Inn.** The spotless pioneer period antiques and the wealth of well-chosen amenities (fireplaces, saunas, whirlpool tubs, double steam showers) at this 1861-vintage inn evoke what the Wild West might have been had Martha Stewart been in charge. **Pros:** in heart of downtown historic district; one of the town's most historically significant buildings; very good restaurant on-site. **Cons:** rather old-fashioned decor for some tastes. $ *Rooms from: $159* ⊠ *175 E. California St.* ☎ *541/899–1900, 800/321–9344* ⊕ *www.jacksonvilleinn.com* ⇆ *8 rooms, 4 cottages* ⦿ *Breakfast.*

$$
B&B/INN
Fodor's Choice
★
⊡ **TouVelle House B&B.** This six-bedroom inn set inside a grand 1916 Craftsman-style home a few blocks north of Jacksonville's tiny commercial strip manages that tricky balance between exquisite and comfy. **Pros:** situated on a gentle bluff surrounded by beautiful gardens; downtown dining is a five-minute walk away; knowledgeable and friendly hosts. **Cons:** a couple of rooms require climbing two flights of stairs to third floor. $ *Rooms from: $159* ⊠ *455 N. Oregon St.* ☎ *541/899–8938* ⊕ *www.touvellehouse.com* ⇆ *6 rooms* ⦿ *Breakfast.*

SHOPPING

Jacksonville's historic downtown has several engaging galleries, boutiques, and gift shops. It's best just to stroll along California Street and its cross streets to get a sense of the retail scene.

Jacksonville Company. Drop by to browse the stylish selection of handbags, footwear, and women's apparel. MOTO Jeans, Brighton, Nicole Shoes, Kersh sweaters, and Bernardo Footwear are among the top brands carried here. ⊠ *115 W. California St.* ☎ *541/899–8912.*

Jacksonville Mercantile. The racks of this gourmet-food store abound with sauces, oils, vinegars, jams, and tapenades. Watch for Lillie Belle Farms lavender–sea salt caramels, and the shop's own private-label Merlot-wine jelly. ⊠ *120 E. California St.* ☎ *541/899–1047* ⊕ *www.jacksonvillemercantile.com.*

8

ASHLAND

20 miles southeast of Jacksonville and 14 miles southeast of Medford on I-5.

As you walk Ashland's hilly streets, it seems like every house is a restored Victorian or Craftsman operating as an upscale B&B, though that's not nearly all there is to this town: the Oregon Shakespeare Festival attracts thousands of theater lovers to the Rogue Valley every year, from late February to early November (though tourists don't start showing up en masse until June). That influx means that Ashland is more geared toward the arts, more eccentric, and more expensive than its size (about 21,000 people) might suggest. The mix of well-heeled theater tourists, bohemian students from Southern Oregon University, and dramatic show folk imbues the town with some one-of-a-kind cultural frissons. The stage isn't the only show in town—skiing at Mt. Ashland and the town's reputation as a secluded getaway and growing culinary destination keep things hopping year-round.

GETTING HERE AND AROUND

Ashland is the first town you'll reach on Interstate 5 if driving north from California, and it's the southernmost community in this region. You can also get here from Klamath Falls by driving west on winding but dramatic Highway 66. Cascade Airport Shuttle offers door-to-door service from the airport to Ashland for about $30 to $35. A car isn't necessary to explore downtown and to get among many of the inns and restaurants, but it is helpful if you're planning to venture farther afield or visit more than one town, which most visitors do.

ESSENTIALS

Visitor Information Ashland Chamber of Commerce and Visitors Information Center. ⊠ *110 E. Main St.* ☎ *541/482–3486* ⊕ *www.ashlandchamber.com.*

EXPLORING

FAMILY

Fodor's Choice

★

Lithia Park. The Allen Elizabethan Theatre overlooks this park, a 93-acre jewel that is Ashland's physical and psychological anchor. The park is named for the town's mineral springs, which supply a water fountain by the band shell as well as a fountain on the town plaza—be warned that the slightly bubbly water has a strong and rather disagreeable taste. Whether thronged with colorful hippie folk and picnickers on a summer evening or buzzing with joggers and dog walkers in the morning, Lithia is a well-used, well-loved, and well-tended spot. On weekends from March through early November, the park plays host to a lively artisans' market, and free concerts take place Thursday evenings in summer. Each June the Oregon Shakespeare Festival opens its outdoor season by hosting the Feast of Will in the park, with music, dancing, bagpipes, and food. Tickets (📧 $15) are available through the festival box office (☎ *541/482–4331* ⊕ *www.osfashland.org*). ⊠ *W. Fork and S. Pioneer Sts.* ⊕ *www.ashland.or.us.*

Schneider Museum of Art. At the edge of the Southern Oregon University campus, this museum includes a light-filled gallery devoted to special exhibits by Oregon, West Coast, and international artists. The permanent collection has grown considerably over the years, and includes pre-Columbian

Lithia Park, Ashland

ceramics and works by such notables as Alexander Calder, George Inness, and David Alfaro Siqueiros. Hallways and galleries throughout the rest of the 66,000-square-foot complex display many works by students and faculty. ⊠ *1250 Siskiyou Blvd.* ☎ *541/552–6245* ⊕ *www.sou.edu/sma.*

FAMILY **ScienceWorks Hands-On Museum.** Geared toward kids but with some genuinely fascinating interactive exhibits that will please curious adults, too, this 26,000-square-foot science museum is close to Southern Oregon University campus. In the main hall, you can explore touch-friendly exhibits on nanotechnology and sports science, and Discovery Island has curious games and puzzles geared to tots under age five. There's outdoor fun amid the plantings and pathways in the xeriscape Black Bear Garden, as well as a weather station, solar-power nursery, and kid-appropriate climbing wall. ⊠ *1500 E. Main St.* ☎ *541/482–6767* ⊕ *www.scienceworksmuseum.org* 🎟 *$10.*

Weisinger Family Winery. Just a short drive from downtown Ashland's wine bars and tasting rooms, Weisinger occupies a leafy hilltop with broad views of the surrounding mountains. Specialties here include a fine Malbec, a well-respected Viognier, and a nicely balanced Tempranillo. ⊠ *3150 Siskiyou Blvd.* ☎ *541/488–5989, 800/551–9463* ⊕ *www.weisingers.com.*

WHERE TO EAT

$$$
PACIFIC
NORTHWEST
Fodor's Choice
★

✕ **Alchemy.** Meticulous attention to detail, with regard both to preparation and presentation, are hallmarks of this refined contemporary Pacific Northwest restaurant inside the plush Winchester Inn, just a few blocks from the Shakespeare Festival theaters. Typically artful creations from the seasonal menu include a starter of goat cheese gnocchi seared in brown butter with chorizo and apricots and a tender 14-day dry-aged

8

Oregon filet mignon cooked *sous vide* with sunchoke puree. **Known for:** lighter and less spendy fare in the bistro; the best filet mignon in town. $ *Average main: $28* ✉ *Winchester Inn, 35 S. 2nd St.* ☎ *541/488–1115* ⊕ *www.alchemyashland.com* ☾ *No lunch.*

$$$$
ECLECTIC
Fodor's Choice
★

✕ **Amuse.** Northwest-driven French cuisine here is infused with seasonal, organic meat and produce. You might sample braised cheek and grilled tenderloin of pork with herb spaetzle, Savoy cabbage, and pomegranate molasses, or charcoal-grilled ruby trout with pole beans, heirloom tomatoes, and horseradish. **Known for:** amazing desserts; terrific coffee and pastries at sister establishment, Mix Sweet Shop. $ *Average main: $31* ✉ *15 N. 1st St.* ☎ *541/488–9000* ⊕ *www.amuserestaurant.com* ☾ *Closed Mon. No lunch.*

$$$
AMERICAN

✕ **Larks.** In a swanky yet soothing dining room off the lobby of the historic Ashland Springs Hotel, Larks pairs the freshest foods from local farms with great wines, artisan chocolate desserts, and drinks. Modern interpretations of comfort food are the order of the day, with servings such as homemade meat loaf with grilled-onion ketchup and smoked Brie–and–cheddar grits; Southern fried chicken with bacon pan gravy; and double-cut pork chops with grilled peach compote. **Known for:** cheesecake with daily-rotating flavor; outstanding Sunday brunch; pretheater dining. $ *Average main: $25* ✉ *Ashland Springs Hotel, 212 E. Main St.* ☎ *541/488–5558* ⊕ *www.larksrestaurant.com.*

$
AMERICAN
Fodor's Choice
★

✕ **Morning Glory.** Breakfast reaches new heights in an eclectically furnished, blue Craftsman-style bungalow across the street from Southern Oregon University. The extraordinarily good food emphasizes breakfast fare—omelets filled with crab, artichokes, Parmesan, and smoked-garlic cream; Tandoori tofu scrambles with cherry-cranberry chutney; lemon-poppy waffles with seasonal berries; and cranberry-hazelnut French toast with lemon butter. **Known for:** large portions; long lines; crab omelet and crab melt. $ *Average main: $12* ✉ *1149 Siskiyou Blvd.* ☎ *541/488–8636.*

$$$
PACIFIC
NORTHWEST
Fodor's Choice
★

✕ **New Sammy's Cowboy Bistro.** The loyal legion of foodies fond of this cult favorite a few miles northwest of Ashland, in the small town of Talent, have been known to make reservations weeks in advance, especially on weekends. The stucco Southwest-style roadhouse is surrounded by orchards and gardens, whose bounty finds its way into the exquisite—and mostly organic—Northwestern fare. **Known for:** artful desserts; funky yet romantic ambience; farm-to-table ingredients. $ *Average main: $27* ✉ *2210 S. Pacific Hwy.* ☎ *541/535–2779* ⊕ *www.newsammyscowboybistro.com* ☾ *Closed Sun.–Tues.*

$$
MODERN
AMERICAN

✕ **Peerless Restaurant & Bar.** This cosmopolitan, neighborhood bistro and wine bar anchors the up-and-coming Railroad District, on the north side of downtown, just a few blocks from Main Street and the Shakespeare theaters. It's adjacent to the Peerless Hotel, a stylish little property with the same creative spirit and hipster vibe of the restaurant. **Known for:** delicious desserts; first-rate cocktails; farm-to-table American fare. $ *Average main: $19* ✉ *265 4th St.* ☎ *541/488–6067* ⊕ *www.peerlesshotel.com* ☾ *Closed Sun. and Mon. No lunch.*

WHERE TO STAY

The Oregon Shakespeare Festival has stimulated one of the most extensive networks of B&Bs in the Northwest—more than 30 in all. High season for Ashland-area bed-and-breakfasts is June–October.

Ashland B&B Network. The network provides referrals and has an online booking system for about two dozen of the town's top inns. ⊕ *www.stayashland.com.*

$$$$
B&B/INN
Ashland Creek Inn. Every plush suite in this converted late-19th-century mill has a geographic theme—the Normandy is outfitted with rustic country French prints and furniture, while Moroccan, Danish, and New Mexican motifs are among the designs in other units—and each sitting room–bedroom combo has its own entrance, a full kitchen or kitchenette, and a deck just inches from burbling Ashland Creek. **Pros:** exceptionally good breakfasts; peaceful but central location; enormous suites. **Cons:** expensive for this part of the state; limited common areas. $ *Rooms from: $295* ✉ *70 Water St.* ☎ *541/482–3315* ⊕ *www.ashlandcreekinn.com* ↙ *10 suites* ⍑ *Breakfast.*

$
HOTEL
Fodor's Choice
★
Ashland Hills Hotel & Suites. Hoteliers Doug and Becky Neuman (who also run the excellent Ashland Springs Hotel and Lithia Springs Resort) transformed this long-shuttered '70s-era resort into a stylish yet affordable retro-cool compound, retaining the property's fabulous globe lights, soaring lobby windows, and beam ceilings while adding many period-style furnishings. **Pros:** great value; terrific restaurant on-site; attractive grounds, including patio and sundeck. **Cons:** just off the interstate; a 10-minute drive from downtown; some rooms face parking lot. $ *Rooms from: $140* ✉ *2525 Ashland St.* ☎ *541/482–8310, 855/482–8310* ⊕ *www.ashlandhillshotel.com* ↙ *152 rooms, 70 suites* ⍑ *Breakfast.*

$$
HOTEL
Ashland Springs Hotel. Ashland's stately 1925 landmark hotel towers seven stories over the center of downtown, with 70 rooms done with a preponderance of gentle fall colors and unconventional decor—think French-inspired botanical-print quilts and lampshades with leaf designs. **Pros:** rich with history; upper floors have dazzling mountain views; the excellent Larks restaurant is on-site. **Cons:** central location translates to some street noise and bustle; some rooms are on the small side. $ *Rooms from: $185* ✉ *212 E. Main St.* ☎ *541/488–1700, 888/795–4545* ⊕ *www.ashlandspringshotel.com* ↙ *70 rooms* ⍑ *Breakfast.*

$$
B&B/INN
Fodor's Choice
★
Chanticleer Inn. At this courtly, 1920 Craftsman-style bed-and-breakfast, owner Ellen Campbell has given the rooms a tasteful, contemporary flair with muted, nature-inspired colors and Arts and Crafts furnishings and patterns. **Pros:** rooms all have expansive views of the Cascade Mountains; only eco-friendly products are used; exceptional breakfasts. **Cons:** it's intimate and homey, so fans of larger and more anonymous lodgings may prefer a bigger inn or hotel. $ *Rooms from: $175* ✉ *120 Gresham St.* ☎ *541/482–1919* ⊕ *www.ashland-bed-breakfast.com* ↙ *6 rooms* ⍑ *Breakfast.*

$$$
B&B/INN
FAMILY
The Winchester Inn. Rooms and suites in this upscale Victorian have character and restful charm—some have fireplaces, refrigerators, and wet bars, and private exterior entrances, and most are well suited to having one or two children in the room. **Pros:** the adjacent Alchemy

8

wine bar and restaurant serve outstanding international fare; one of the more child-friendly B&Bs in town; surrounded by lush gardens. **Cons:** among the more expensive lodgings in town. $ *Rooms from: $225* ⊠ *35 S. 2nd St.* ☎ *541/488–1113, 800/972–4991* ⊕ *www.winchesterinn.com* ⇩ *11 rooms, 9 suites* ⦿| *Breakfast.*

NIGHTLIFE AND PERFORMING ARTS

With its presence of college students, theater types, and increasing numbers of tourists (many of them fans of local wine), Ashland has developed quite a festive nightlife scene. Much of the activity takes place at bars inside some of downtown's more reputable restaurants in the center of town.

Fodor's Choice ★ **Caldera Tap House.** In addition to operating a full-service restaurant at their brewing facility out at 590 Clover Lane, just off Interstate 5, Exit 14, this highly acclaimed Ashland craft-beer maker with wide distribution throughout the Northwest also has this tap room downtown. Here you can sample the signature Hopportunity Knocks IPA, Old Growth Imperial Stout, and an extensive selection of tasty apps, burgers, and pub fare. ⊠ *31 Water St.* ☎ *541/482–7468* ⊕ *www.calderabrewing.com.*

Liquid Assets. Popular early in the evening and late at night with those attending Shakespeare Festival plays up the street, this handsome wine bar and restaurant serves delicious modern-American food, from truffled popcorn and beef tartare to substantial fare. But as the name suggests, the favorite assets here are drinkable, including wines by the glass and a huge selection of bottles priced at retail (there's a modest $5 cork fee). Creative cocktails and local microbrews are also served. ⊠ *96 N. Main St.* ☎ *541/482–9463* ⊕ *www.liquidassetswinebar.com.*

Fodor's Choice ★ **Oregon Shakespeare Festival.** From mid-February to early November, more than 100,000 Bard-loving fans descend on Ashland for some of the finest Shakespearean productions you're likely to see outside of London—plus works by both classic (Ibsen, O'Neill) and contemporary playwrights. Eleven plays are staged in repertory in the 1,200-seat Allen Elizabethan Theatre, an atmospheric re-creation of the Fortune Theatre in London; the 600-seat Angus Bowmer Theatre, a state-of-the-art facility typically used for five different productions in a single season; and the 350-seat Thomas Theatre, which often hosts productions of new or experimental work. The festival, which dates to 1935, generally operates close to capacity, so it's important to book ahead. ⊠ *15 S. Pioneer St.* ☎ *541/482–4331, 800/219–8161* ⊕ *www.osfashland.org.*

SPORTS AND THE OUTDOORS

MULTISPORT OUTFITTERS

Adventure Center. This respected Ashland company offers "mild to wild" outdoor expeditions, including white-water rafting, fishing, and bike excursions. ⊠ *40 N. Main St.* ☎ *541/488–2819, 800/444–2819* ⊕ *www.raftingtours.com.*

RAFTING

Noah's River Adventures. This long-running outfitter provides white-water rafting and wilderness fishing trips throughout the region—the company can lead single- or multiple-day adventures along the mighty Rogue River as well as just across the border, in northern California, on the Salmon and Scott rivers. ⊠ *53 N. Main St.* ☎ *541/488–2811* ⊕ *www.noahsrafting.com.*

SKIING

Mt. Ashland Ski Area. This winter-sports playground in the Siskiyou Mountains is halfway between San Francisco and Portland. The ski runs average more than 265 inches of snow each year. There are 23 trails, virtually all of them intermediate and advanced, in addition to chute skiing in a glacial cirque called the bowl. Two triple and two double chairlifts accommodate a vertical drop of 1,150 feet; the longest of the runs is 1 mile. Facilities include rentals, repairs, instruction, a ski shop, a restaurant, and a bar. A couple of days a week, usually Thursday and Friday, there's also lighted twilight skiing until 9 pm. Anytime of year the drive up the twisting road to the ski area is incredibly scenic, affording views of 14,162-foot Mt. Shasta, some 90 miles south in California. ⊠ *Mt. Ashland Access Rd., off Exit 6 from I–5, 18 miles south of downtown* ☎ *541/482–2897* ⊕ *www.mtashland.com* ☜ *Lift ticket $48.*

SHOPPING

Dagoba Organic Chocolate. A few miles' drive south of town you'll find the retail outlet of this company that produces those small, handsomely packed, superfine chocolate bars sold in fancy-food shops and groceries throughout the country. Although Hershey Company now owns the company, Dagoba was founded in Ashland, and its operation remains here, where a small retail shop—open weekdays only—sells its goods. ⊠ *1105 Benson St.* ☎ *866/608–6944* ⊕ *www.dagobachocolate.com.*

8

KLAMATH FALLS

65 miles east of Ashland via Hwy. 66, 75 miles east of Medford via Hwy. 140.

The Klamath Basin, with its six national wildlife refuges, hosts the largest wintering concentration of bald eagles in the contiguous United States and the largest concentration of migratory waterfowl on the continent. Each February nature enthusiasts from around the world flock here for the Winter Wings Festival, the nation's oldest birding festival.

GETTING HERE AND AROUND

Klamath Falls lies along U.S. 97, one of the Northwest's main north–south routes—it's a prime stop between Bend, 140 miles north, and Weed, California, about 70 miles south. You can also get here from the Rogue Valley, either by way of Highway 66 from Ashland or Highway 140 from Medford, which is home to the nearest airport (about a 90-minute drive).

ESSENTIALS

Visitor Information Meet Me In Klamath. ⊠ *205 Riverside Dr.* ☎ *541/882–1501, 800/445–6728* ⊕ *www.meetmeinklamath.com.*

EXPLORING

Fodor's Choice ★ **Klamath Basin National Wildlife Refuge Complex.** As many as 1,000 bald eagles make Klamath Basin their rest stop, amounting to the largest wintering concentration of these birds in the contiguous United States. Located along the Pacific Flyway bird migration route, the nearly 40,000 acres of freshwater wetlands in this complex of six different refuges serve as a stopover for nearly 1 million waterfowl in the fall. Any time of year is bird-watching season; more than 400 species of birds—including about 15 types of raptors—have been spotted in the Klamath Basin. For a leisurely excursion by car, follow the tour routes in the Lower Klamath and Tule Lake refuges—the latter has a superb bookstore and visitor center and is also a short drive from Lava Beds National Monument. ✉ *Tule Lake Refuge Visitor Center, 4009 Hill Rd., Tulelake* ✥ *27 miles south of Klamath Falls via Hwy. 39* ☎ *530/667–2231* 🌐 *www.fws.gov/refuge/tule_lake* 🎟 *Free.*

Klamath County Museum. The anthropology, history, geology, and wildlife of the Klamath Basin are explained at this extensive museum set inside the city's historic armory building, with special attention given to the hardships faced by early white settlers. Also part of the museum's domain are the Baldwin Hotel Museum and Fort Klamath Museum. ✉ *1451 Main St.* ☎ *541/883–4208* 🌐 *museum.klamathcounty.org* 🎟 *$5.*

WHERE TO EAT AND STAY

$$ AMERICAN 🍴 **Basin Martini Bar.** Although the name of this elegant storefront spot in the heart of the downtown historic district suggests an option for evening cocktails, the bar is just as well regarded for its reliably tasty dinner fare—New York strip steaks, burgers topped with Crater Lake blue cheese, and bacon-wrapped scallops are among the highlights. There's seating in a handful of comfy booths or at stools along the modern bar. **Known for:** well-prepared craft cocktails; decadent mac-and-cheese. [$] *Average main: $17* ✉ *632 Main St.* ☎ *541/884–6264* ⏲ *Closed Sun. No lunch.*

$ CAFÉ 🍴 **Gathering Grounds Cafe.** Although this bustling coffeehouse with comfortable seating and exposed-brick walls is a hot spot for espresso drinks made from house-roasted coffee beans, it's also a great option for grabbing healthful, flavorful picnic items. Fresh-fruit parfaits and croissant and English muffin sandwiches are popular for breakfast. **Known for:** delicious panini sandwiches at breakfast and lunch; best coffee in town, roasted in-house. [$] *Average main: $9* ✉ *116 S. 11th St.* ☎ *541/887–8403* 🌐 *www.gatheringgroundscafe.com* ⏲ *Closed Sun. No dinner.*

$ RESORT FAMILY 🏨 **Running Y Ranch Resort.** Golfers rave about the Arnold Palmer–designed course at this 3,600-acre resort in a juniper-and-ponderosa–shaded canyon overlooking Upper Klamath Lake. **Pros:** kids enjoy indoor pool; walkers and joggers have 8 miles of paved trails. **Cons:** may be too far off the beaten path for some. [$] *Rooms from: $149* ✉ *5500 Running Y Rd., 8 miles north of Klamath Falls* ☎ *541/850–5500* 🌐 *www.runningy.com* 🛏 *82 rooms, 43 houses* 🍽 *No meals.*

SPORTS AND THE OUTDOORS
MULTISPORT OUTFITTERS

The Ledge Outdoor Store. For advice, gear, clothing, books, and maps for hiking, birding, mountaineering, canoeing, camping, and fishing throughout the area, visit this extensively stocked shop in downtown Klamath Falls, which carries all kinds of equipment, and also offers guided fly-fishing trips. ☒ *369 S. 6th St.* ☎ *541/882–5586* ⊕ *www.yetiledge.wordpress.com.*

CAVE JUNCTION

30 miles southwest of Grants Pass via U.S. 199, 60 miles west of Jacksonville via Hwy. 238 and U.S. 199.

One of the least populated and most pristine parts of southern Oregon, the town of Cave Junction and the surrounding Illinois Valley attract outdoors enthusiasts of all kinds for hiking, backpacking, camping, fishing, and hunting. Expect rugged terrain and the chance to view some of the tallest Douglas fir trees in the state. Other than those passing through en route from Grants Pass to the northern California coast via U.S. 199, most visitors come here to visit the Oregon Caves National Monument, one of the world's few marble caves (formed by erosion from acidic rainwater). Sleepy Cave Junction makes an engaging little base camp, its main drag lined with a handful of quirky shops, short-order restaurants, and gas stations.

GETTING HERE AND AROUND

Cave Junction lies along U.S. 199, the main road leading from Grants Pass. You can also reach Cave Junction by heading west from Jacksonville on Highway 238 to U.S. 199. From Cave Junction, head east on Highway 46 to reach Oregon Caves National Monument. Cave Junction is about a 75-minute drive southwest of Medford's regional airport. Alternatively, the small airport (served by PenAir, with service from Portland) in Crescent City, California, is the same distance.

ESSENTIALS

Visitor Information Illinois Valley Chamber of Commerce. ☒ *201 Caves Hwy. (Hwy. 46), just off U.S. 199* ☎ *541/592–3326* ⊕ *www.cavejunction.com.*

EXPLORING

Bridgeview Vineyard and Winery. The producers of the well-distributed and reasonably priced Blue Moon wines (known especially for Riesling, Chardonnay, Pinot Gris, and Merlot), as well as more premium vintages such as Black Beauty Syrah and a very nice reserve Pinot Noir, established the winery in 1986, and—despite skepticism from observers—have gone on to tremendous success. There's a second tasting room, open summer only, in the Applegate Valley, near Grants Pass. ☒ *4210 Holland Loop Rd.* ☎ *541/592–4688* ⊕ *www.bridgeviewwine.com.*

Fodor's Choice ★ **Oregon Caves National Monument.** Marble caves, large calcite formations, and huge underground rooms shape this rare adventure in geology. Guided cave tours take place on the hour in late spring and fall, and every half hour in June, July, and August. The 90-minute half-mile tour is moderately strenuous, with low passageways, twisting turns, and

8

more than 500 stairs; children must be at least 42 inches tall to participate. Cave tours aren't given in winter. Above ground, the surrounding valley holds an old-growth forest with some of the state's largest trees. ⚠ **GPS coordinates for the caves often direct drivers onto a mostly unpaved forest service road meant for four-wheel-drive vehicles. Instead, follow well-signed Highway 46 off U.S. 199 at Cave Junction, which is also narrow and twisting in parts; RVs or trailers more than 32 feet long are not advised.** ✉ *19000 Caves Hwy. (Hwy. 46), 20 miles east of U.S. 199, 140 miles southwest of Crater Lake* ☎ *541/592–2100* 🌐 *www.nps.gov/orca* 🎟 *Park free, tours $10.*

WHERE TO STAY

$ HOTEL FAMILY 🏨 **Oregon Caves Chateau.** This six-story wood-frame lodge, virtually unchanged since it was built in 1934, has a rustic authenticity and steep gabled roofs, while the simple rooms, all with their original furnishings, have canyon or waterfall views. **Pros:** on the grounds of the national monument; historic and funky personality; wonderfully tranquil setting. **Cons:** no-frills rooms; no Internet or phones (and very limited cell reception); location well out of the way if you aren't visiting the caves. [$] *Rooms from: $109* ✉ *20000 Caves Hwy.* ☎ *541/592–3400* 🌐 *www.oregoncaveschateau.com* 🕒 *Closed early Nov.–early May* 🛏 *23 rooms* 🍴 *No meals.*

$ B&B/INN FAMILY 🏨 **Out 'n' About.** You sleep among the leaves in the tree houses of this extraordinary resort—the highest is 37 feet from the ground, one has an antique claw-foot bath, and another has separate kids' quarters connected to the main room by a swinging bridge. **Pros:** kids love the Swiss Family Robinson atmosphere; it truly feels at one with the surrounding old-growth forest; amazingly quiet and peaceful. **Cons:** accommodations are extremely rustic; some units don't have bathrooms; two-night minimum during week and three-night minimum weekends during spring to fall. [$] *Rooms from: $140* ✉ *300 Page Creek Rd.* ☎ *541/592–2208* 🌐 *www.treehouses.com* 🛏 *15 tree houses, 1 cabin* 🍴 *Breakfast.*

SEATTLE

WELCOME TO SEATTLE

TOP REASONS TO GO

★ **Examine Seattle's architecture:** From the skyline-defining Space Needle to the starchitect-designed Seattle Center Library, the city offers aficionados plenty to admire.

★ **Appreciate art:** Visit the Seattle Art Museum and make time for a stroll in SAM's Olympic Sculpture Park on the Elliott Bay waterfront.

★ **Drink coffee:** Seattle may be the birthplace of Starbucks, but this is a city that takes coffee snobbery seriously, so be sure to explore.

★ **Cheer beer:** Tap into Seattle's craft beer scene, regularly ranked one of the best in the country.

★ **Indulge in fresh seafood:** First gawk at all the fabulous local produce and seafood at the Pike Place Market, and then visit some of Seattle's renowned restaurants to eat it.

1 **Downtown and Belltown.** Skyscrapers are here, along with most of the city's hotels and many popular spots, including the waterfront, Pike Place Market, and Seattle Art Museum. Just north of Downtown, Belltown is home to the Olympic Sculpture Park.

2 **Seattle Center, South Lake Union, and Queen Anne.** Queen Anne, north of Belltown, rises up from Denny Way to the Lake Washington Ship Canal. At the bottom are the Space Needle, the Seattle Center, and MoPOP. South Lake Union has the REI superstore, lakefront, and some eateries and hotels.

3 **Pioneer Square.** Seattle's oldest neighborhood has classic redbrick and sandstone buildings, plus numerous galleries and a burgeoning food scene.

4 **International District.** This is a fun place to shop and eat. The stunning Wing Luke Museum and Uwajimaya shopping center anchor the neighborhood.

5 **First Hill.** There is one must-see here: the Frye Art Museum.

6 **Capitol Hill.** The Hill has two faces: young and hip and elegant and upscale. It has fantastic restaurants and nightlife.

7 **Fremont.** There is a mix of pricey boutiques and notable restaurants here; up the hill, residential Phinney Ridge includes the Woodland Park Zoo.

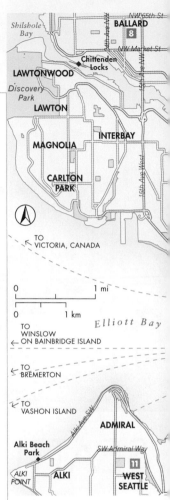

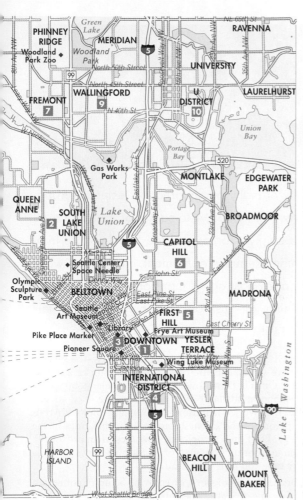

GETTING ORIENTED

Hemmed in by mountains, hills, and multiple bodies of water, Seattle is anything but a linear, grid-lined city. Twisty, turny, and very long, the city can be baffling to navigate, especially if you delve into its residential neighborhoods—and you should. Water makes the best landmark. Both Elliott Bay and Lake Union are pretty hard to miss. When you are trying to get your bearings Downtown, Elliott Bay is a much more reliable landmark than the Space Needle. Remember that Interstate 5 bisects the city (north–south). The major routes connecting the southern part of the city to the northern part are Interstate 5, Aurora Avenue/Highway 99, 15th Avenue NW (Ballard Bridge), and Westlake (Fremont Bridge) and Eastlake avenues. Streets in the Seattle area generally travel east to west, whereas avenues travel north to south.

8 Ballard. The main attraction is the Hiram M. Chittenden Locks. This historically Scandinavian neighborhood is beloved for its eateries, trendy shops, and year-round farmers' market.

9 Wallingford. At the ship canal is the wonderful waterfront Gas Works Park. Its booming commercial strip along North 45th Street has a few excellent restaurants.

10 The "U District." The university's surrounding neighborhood can be both gritty and charming, with loads of ethnic restaurants and a large student population.

11 West Seattle. West Seattle's California Avenue has some lovely shops and restaurants. Gorgeous Alki Beach offers views of the Seattle skyline.

Updated by
Lauren Kelley,
Kade Krichko,
Conor Risch,
AnnaMaria
Stephens, and
Naomi Tomky

Seattle is a city of many neighborhoods: eclectic, urban, outdoorsy, artsy, gritty, down-to-earth, or posh—it's all here, from the quirky character of the Seattle Waterfront and the eccentric "Republic of Fremont," to hipsters walking baby carriages past aging mansions on Capitol Hill. There's something for just about everyone within this vibrant Emerald City.

The city owes much of its appeal to its natural features—the myriad hills that did survive settlement offer views of mountain ranges and water, water, water. Outside Downtown and other smaller commercial cores, Seattle's neighborhoods fan out in tangles of tree-lined streets. Massive parks like Discovery, Magnuson, and Washington Park Arboretum make Seattle one of the greenest and most livable cities in the nation. From the peaks of the Olympics or Cascades to an artistically landscaped garden in front of a classic Northwest bungalow, nature is in full effect every time you turn your head.

Taking a stroll, browsing a bookstore, or enjoying a cup of coffee can feel different in every one of Seattle's neighborhoods. It's the adventure of exploring that will really introduce you to the character of Seattle.

SEATTLE PLANNER

WHEN TO GO

Unless you're planning an all-indoor museum trip, Seattle is most enjoyable May through October. June can be surprisingly rainy, but July through September is almost always dry, with warm days reaching into the mid-70s and 80s; nights are cooler, though it doesn't get dark until 9 or 10 pm. Although the weather can be dodgy, spring (particularly April) and fall are also excellent times to visit, as lodging and tour costs are usually much lower (and the crowds much smaller). In winter, the days are short, dark, and wet, but temperatures rarely dip below the low 40s and winter events—especially around the holidays—are plentiful.

FESTIVALS

The Seattle Convention and Visitors Bureau has a full calendar of events at ⊕ *www.visitseattle.org/cultural*. Foodies will want to hit up **Taste Washington** (spring ⊕ *www.tastewashington.org*) for the best of food and wine, as well as **Bite of Seattle** (July ⊕ *www.biteofseattle.com*), the Northwest Chocolate Festival (September ⊕ *www.nwchocolate.com*) and Seattle International Beer Fest (July ⊕ *www.seattlebeerfest.com*). The **Seattle International Film Festival** presents more than 200 features (May and June ⊕ *www.siff.net*).

Music lovers have three major events to keep them happy: **Bumbershoot** (September ⊕ *bumbershoot.org*) is Seattle's premier music festival, packed with major acts, as well as dance and theater, while Northwest Folklife Festival (May ⊕ *www.nwfolklife.org*) is a free, family-friendly event featuring folk music and dance from around the globe. Hipsters will want to check out Capitol Hill Block Party (July ⊕ *www.capitolhill-blockparty.com*) for the best indie pop, rock, hip-hop, and alt-country.

The **Seattle Pride Festival** (June ⊕ *www.seattlepride.org*) has the Northwest's biggest gay, lesbian, and transgender pride parade. A local favorite, the quirky Fremont Fair Summer Solstice Parade (June ⊕ *www. fremontfair.org*) provides a glimpse into the true character of the city. **Seafair** (July and August ⊕ *www.seafair.com*) is the biggest summer festival; hydroplane races are just one major event.

GETTING HERE AND AROUND

GETTING HERE

The major gateway is Seattle–Tacoma International Airport (SEA), known locally as Sea-Tac. The airport is south of the city and reasonably close to it—non-rush-hours trips to Downtown sometimes take less than a half hour. Sea-Tac is a midsize, modern airport that is usually pleasant to navigate. You can take Sound Transit's **Link light-rail** (⊕ *www.soundtransit.org*), which will take you right to Downtown or beyond in 35 minutes for just $3.

GETTING AROUND

Biking is a popular but somewhat tricky endeavor, thanks to a shortage of safe bike routes and some daunting hills. Walking is fun, though distances and rain can sometimes get in the way. Several neighborhoods—from Pioneer Square to Downtown, or from Belltown to Queen Anne, for example—are close enough to each other that even hills and moisture can't stop walkers.

The bus system will get you anywhere you need to go, although some routes require a time commitment and several transfers. Within the Downtown core, however, the bus is efficient and affordable. Another option for public transport is the bright red streetcars that connects Downtown to South Lake Union and Pioneer Square to Capitol Hill.

Access to a car is *almost* a necessity if you want to explore the residential neighborhoods beyond their commercial centers, but parking can cost upwards of $50 per night in the urban center. Alternatives like Car2Go, Lyft, or Uber are great options, and many high-end hotels offer complimentary town-car service around Downtown and the immediate areas.

9

Ferries are a major part of Seattle's transportation network, and they're the only way to reach Vashon Island and the San Juans. You'll get outstanding views of the skyline and the elusive Mt. Rainier from the ferry to Bainbridge.

VISITOR INFORMATION

Contact the **Seattle Visitors Bureau and Convention Center** (⊕ *www. visitseattle.org* ☎ *206/461–5800*) for help with everything from sightseeing to booking spa services. You can also follow its Twitter feed (⊕ *twitter.com/seattlemaven*). The main visitor information center is Downtown, at the Washington State Convention and Trade Center on 8th Avenue and Pike Street; it has a full-service concierge desk open daily 9 to 5 (in summer; weekdays only in winter). There's also an info booth at Pike Place Market.

EXPLORING

Each of Seattle's neighborhoods has a distinctive personality, and taking a stroll, browsing a bookstore, or enjoying a cup of coffee can feel different in every one. It's the adventure of exploring that will really introduce you to the character of Seattle.

DOWNTOWN AND BELLTOWN

Except for the busy areas around the Market and the piers, and the always-frenetic shopping district, a lot of Downtown can often seem deserted, especially at night. Still, while it may not be the soul of the city, it's definitely the heart, and there's plenty to do—nearly all of it easily reachable by foot.

Belltown is Downtown's younger sibling, just north of Virginia Street (up to Denny Way) and stretching from Elliott Bay to 6th Avenue. Today, Belltown is increasingly hip, with luxury condos, trendy restaurants, bustling bars, and a number of boutiques. (Most of the action happens between 1st and 4th avenues and between Bell and Virginia streets.)

Fodor's Choice **Olympic Sculpture Park.** An outdoor branch of the Seattle Art Museum
★ is a favorite destination for picnics, strolls, and quiet contemplation. Nestled at the edge of Belltown with views of Elliott Bay, the gently sloping green space features native plants and walking paths that wind past bigger-than-life public artwork. On sunny days, the park frames an astounding panorama of the Olympic Mountains, but even the grayest afternoon casts a favorable light on the site's sculptures. The grounds are home to works by such artists as Richard Serra, Louise Bourgeois, and Alexander Calder, whose bright-red steel "Eagle" sculpture is a local favorite (and a nod to the bald eagles that sometimes soar above). "Echo," a 46-foot-tall elongated girl's face by Spanish artist Jaume Plensa, is a beautiful and bold presence on the waterfront. The park's PACCAR Pavilion has a gift shop, café, and information about the artworks. ✉ *2901 Western Ave., between Broad and Bay Sts., Belltown* ☎ *206/654–3100* ⊕ *www.seattleartmuseum.org/visit* 🎟 *Free.*

FAMILY
FodorsChoice
★

Pike Place Market. One of the nation's largest and oldest public markets dates from 1907, when the city issued permits allowing farmers to sell produce from parked wagons. At one time the market was a madhouse of vendors hawking their produce and haggling with customers over prices; now you might find fishmongers engaging in frenzied banter and hilarious antics, but chances are you won't get them to waver on prices. There are many restaurants, bakeries, coffee shops (including the flagship Starbucks), lunch counters, and ethnic eateries. Go to Pike Place hungry and you won't be disappointed. The flower market is also a must-see—gigantic fresh arrangements can be found for around $10. It's well worth wading through dense crowds to enjoy the market's many corridors, where you'll find specialty-food items, quirky gift shops, tea, honey, jams, comic books, beads, eclectic crafts, and cookware. In spring 2017, Pike Place Market debuted a significant expansion, fulfilling a decades-long vision for Seattle's Market Historic District. The market's new digs feature artisanal-food purveyors, an on-site brewery, four public art installations, and a 30,000-square-foot open public space with a plaza and a viewing deck overlooking Elliott Bay. ⊠ *Pike Pl. at Pike St., west of 1st Ave., Downtown* ☎ *206/682–7453* ⊕ *www.pikeplacemarket.org.*

FAMILY
FodorsChoice
★

Seattle Aquarium. Located right at the water's edge, the Seattle Aquarium is one of the nation's premier aquariums. Among its most engaging residents are the sea otters—kids, especially, seem able to spend hours watching the delightful antics of these creatures and their river cousins. In the Puget Sound Great Hall, "Window on Washington Waters," a slice of Neah Bay life, is presented in a 20-foot-tall tank holding 120,000 gallons of water. The aquarium's darkened rooms and large, lighted tanks brilliantly display Pacific Northwest marine life. The "Life on the Edge" tide pools re-create Washington's rocky coast and sandy beaches—kids can touch the starfish, sea urchins, and sponges. Huge glass windows provide underwater views of the harbor seal exhibit; go up top to watch them play in their pools. If you're visiting in fall or winter, dress warmly—the Marine Mammal area is outside on the waterfront and catches all of those chilly Puget Sound breezes. The café serves Ivar's chowder and kid-friendly food like burgers and chicken fingers; the balcony has views of Elliott Bay. ⊠ *1483 Alaskan Way, Pier 59, Downtown* ☎ *206/386–4300* ⊕ *www.seattleaquarium.org* ⊠ *$24.95.*

9

FodorsChoice
★

Seattle Art Museum. Sculptor Jonathan Borofsky's several-stories-high "Hammering Man" greets visitors to SAM, as locals call this pride of the city's art scene. SAM's permanent collection surveys American, Asian, Native American, African, Oceanic, and pre-Columbian art. Collections of African dance masks and Native American carvings are particularly strong. SAM's free floors have the best attractions for kids, including an installation of cars hanging upside down from the ceiling and the WaMu OpenStudio. ⊠ *1300 1st Ave., Downtown* ☎ *206/654–3100* ⊕ *www.seattleartmuseum.org* ⊠ *Suggested donation $20; fee for special exhibitions; free 1st Thurs. of month.*

FAMILY

Seattle Great Wheel. Want to hitch a ride to a soaring Seattle vantage point? At the end of Pier 57, just steps from Pike Place Market and the Seattle Aquarium, the Seattle Great Wheel is a 175-foot (about 17 stories tall) Ferris wheel. As you round the top, enjoy views of the

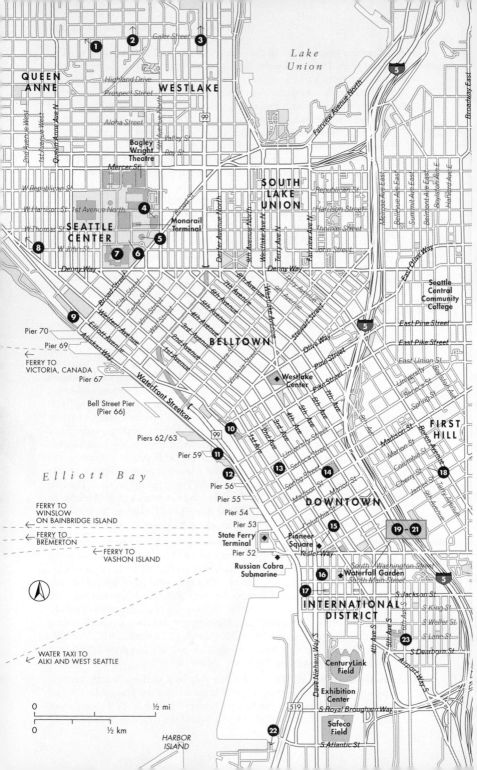

Downtown Seattle and Environs

city skyline, the Puget Sound, and the Olympic and Cascade mountain ranges (on a clear day, of course). Rides are slow and smooth, lasting 15 to 20 minutes, with three revolutions total. Each gondola can hold six people (up to eight if some are children) and, generally speaking, parties get to stick together. The Seattle Great Wheel also lights up the waterfront after dark with dazzling colors, making it a romantic option for date night. Advance tickets are recommended—you'll still have to wait in line, but the line is a lot shorter. ■ TIP➔ If you're afraid of heights, you should definitely skip this attraction. ⊠ *1301 Alaskan Way (Pier 56), Downtown* ☎ *206/623–8600* ⊕ *www.seattlegreatwheel. com* ⊠ *$13; $50 for VIP Gondola.*

Fodor's Choice
★
The Seattle Public Library. The hub of Seattle's 27-branch library system is a stunning jewel of a building that stands out against the concrete jungle of downtown. Designed by renowned Dutch architect Rem Koolhaas and Joshua Ramus, this 11-story structure houses more than 1 million books, a language center, terrific areas for kids and teens—plus hundreds of computers with Internet access, an auditorium, a "mixing chamber" floor of information desks, and a café. The building's floor plan is anything but simple; stand outside the beveled glass-and-metal facade of the building and you can see the library's floors zigzagging upward. Tours are self-guided via a laminated sheet you can pick up at the information desk; there's also a number you can call on your cell phone for an audio tour. The reading room on the 10th floor has unbeatable views of the city and the water, and the building has Wi-Fi throughout. Readings and free film screenings happen on a regular basis; check the website for more information. ⊠ *1000 4th Ave., Downtown* ☎ *206/386–4636* ⊕ *www.spl.org/locations/central-library.*

SEATTLE CENTER, SOUTH LAKE UNION, AND QUEEN ANNE

Almost all visitors make their way to Seattle Center at some point, to visit the Space Needle or other key Seattle sites like MoPOP, the Pacific Science Center, or the stunning new Chihuly Garden and Glass. The neighborhoods that bookend Seattle Center couldn't be more different: Queen Anne is all residential elegance (especially on top of the hill), while South Lake Union, once completely industrial, is quickly becoming Seattle's next hot neighborhood.

Fodor's Choice
★
Chihuly Garden and Glass. Just steps from the base of the Space Needle, fans of Dale Chihuly's glass works will be delighted to trace the artist's early influences—neon art, Native American Northwest Coast trade baskets, and Pendleton blankets, to name a few—to the vibrant chandelier towers and architectural glass installations he is most known for today. There are eight galleries total, plus a 40-foot-tall "Glasshouse," and an outdoor garden that serves as a backdrop for colorful installations that integrate with a dynamic Northwest landscape, including native plants and a 500-year-old western cedar that washed up on the shores of Neah Bay. Chihuly, who was born and raised in Tacoma, was actively involved in the design of the exhibition as well as the whimsical Collections Cafe, where you'll find Chihuly's quirky personal collections on display—everything from tin toys to vintage cameras to antique shaving brushes. Indeed,

A steel sculpture by Richard Serra at the Olympic Sculpture Park

so many of his personal touches are part of the exhibition space, you can almost feel his presence in every room (look for the guy with the unruly hair and the black eye patch). Chihuly is kid-friendly for all but the littlest ones. ⊠ *305 Harrison St., under Space Needle, Central District* ☎ *206/753–4940* ⊕ *www.chihulygardenandglass.com* ▱ *$22.*

9

FAMILY
Fodor'sChoice
★

Discovery Park. You won't find more spectacular views of Puget Sound, the Cascades, and the Olympics. Located on Magnolia Bluff, northwest of Downtown, Seattle's largest park covers 534 acres and has an amazing variety of terrain: shaded, secluded forest trails lead to meadows, saltwater beaches, sand dunes, a lighthouse, and 2 miles of protected beaches. The North Beach Trail, which takes you along the shore to the lighthouse, is a must-see. Head to the South Bluff Trail to get a view of Mt. Rainier. The park has several entrances—if you want to stop at the visitor center to pick up a trail map before exploring, use the main entrance at Government Way. The North Parking Lot is much closer to the North Beach Trail and to Ballard and Fremont, if you're coming from that direction. First-come, first-served beach parking passes for the disabled, elderly, and families with small children are available at the Learning Center. Note that the park is easily reached from Ballard and Fremont. It's easier to combine a park day with an exploration of those neighborhoods than with a busy Downtown itinerary. ⊠ *3801 W. Government Way, Magnolia* ✛ *From Downtown, take Elliot Ave. W (which turns into 15th Ave. W), and get off at Emerson St. exit and turn left onto W. Emerson. Make a right onto Gilman Ave. W (which eventually becomes W. Government Way). As you enter park, road becomes Washington Ave.; turn left on Utah Ave.* ☎ *206/386–4236* ⊕ *seattle.gov/parks/environment/discovery.htm* ▱ *Free.*

FAMILY

Fodor's Choice

★

Museum of Pop Culture (MoPOP). Formerly EMP, Seattle's most controversial architectural statement is the 140,000-square-foot complex designed by architect Frank Gehry, who drew inspiration from electric guitars to achieve the building's curvy metallic design. It's a fitting backdrop for rock memorabilia from the likes of Bob Dylan and the grunge-scene heavies. Two permanent exhibits provide a primer on the evolution of Seattle's music scene, focusing on Nirvana and Jimi Hendrix, respectively. In the Science Fiction Museum and Hall of Fame—now a permanent exhibit—you'll find iconic artifacts from sci-fi literature, film, television, and art, including an Imperial Dalek from *Doctor Who,* the command chair from the classic television series *Star Trek,* and Neo's coat from *The Matrix Reloaded.* ⊠ *325 5th Ave. N, between Broad and Thomas Sts., Central District* ☎ *206/770–2700* ⊕ *www.mopop.org* ⊠ *$25.*

FAMILY

Fodor's Choice

★

Pacific Science Center. If you have kids, this nonprofit science center in the heart of Seattle is a must-visit, home to more than 200 indoor and outdoor hands-on exhibits, two IMAX theaters, a Laser Dome, a butterfly house, and a state-of-the-art planetarium. The dinosaur exhibit—complete with moving robotic reproductions—is a favorite, and tots can experiment with water at the ever-popular stream table. Machines analyze human physiology in the *Body Works* exhibit. When you need to warm up, the Tropical Butterfly House is 80°F and home to colorful butterflies from South and Central America, Africa, and Asia; other creatures live in the Insect Village and saltwater tide-pool areas. IMAX movies, planetarium shows, Live Science Shows, and Laser Dome rock shows run daily. Look for the giant white arches near the Space Needle and make a day of the surrounding sights. ■TIP➔ Pacific Science Center offers a number of lectures, forums, and "Science Cafes" for adults, plus a variety of educational programs for kids, including camp-ins, monthly parents' night outs, workshops, and more. See website for schedule information. ⊠ *200 2nd Ave. N, Central District* ☎ *206/443–2001* ⊕ *www.pacsci.org* ⊠ *Center $19.75, IMAX $10–$15.50, laser shows $7–$10.50, combined museum/IMAX $31.25.*

FAMILY

Space Needle. More than 50 years old, Seattle's most iconic building is as quirky and beloved as ever. The distinctive, towering, 605-foot-high structure is visible throughout much of Seattle—but the view from the inside out is even better. A less-than-one-minute ride up to the observation deck yields 360-degree vistas of Downtown Seattle, the Olympic Mountains, Elliott Bay, Queen Anne Hill, Lake Union, and the Cascade Range. Built for the 1962 World's Fair, the Needle has educational kiosks, interactive trivia game stations for kids, and the glass-enclosed SpaceBase store and Pavilion spiraling around the base of the tower. The top-floor SkyCity restaurant is "revolutionary" (literally—watch the skyline evolve as you dine) and the elevator trip and observation deck are complimentary with your reservation. If the forecast says you may have a sunny day during your visit, schedule the Needle for that day! If you can't decide whether you want the daytime or nighttime view, for an extra 10 bucks you can buy a ticket that allows you to visit twice in one day. (Also look for package deals with Chihuly Garden and Glass.) ⊠ *400 Broad St., Central District* ☎ *206/905–2100* ⊕ *www. spaceneedle.com* ⊠ *$22.*

The stunning Seattle Public Library.

PIONEER SQUARE

The Pioneer Square district, directly south of Downtown, is Seattle's oldest neighborhood. It attracts visitors with elegantly renovated (or in some cases replica) turn-of-the-20th-century redbrick buildings and art galleries. It's the center of Seattle's arts scene, and the galleries in this small neighborhood are a large part of the sights. In recent years, a growing number of new restaurants and businesses have opened, giving the neighborhood fresh appeal to locals and tourists alike.

Bill Speidel's Underground Tour. Present-day Pioneer Square is actually one story higher than it used to be. After the Great Seattle Fire of 1889, Seattle's planners regraded the neighborhood's streets, which had been built on filled-in tide lands and regularly flooded. The result? There is now an intricate and expansive array of subterranean passageways and basements beneath Pioneer Square, and Bill Speidel's Underground Tour is the only way to explore them. Speidel was an irreverent historian, PR man, and former *Seattle Times* reporter who took it upon himself to preserve historic Seattle, and this tour is packed with his sardonic wit and playful humor. It's very informative, too—if you're interested in the general history of the city or salty anecdotes about Seattle's early denizens, you'll appreciate it that much more. Younger kids will probably be bored, as there's not much to see at the specific sites, which are more used as launching points for the stories. Comfortable shoes, a love for quirky historical yarns, and an appreciation of bad puns are musts. Several tours are offered daily, and schedules change month to month: call or visit the website for a full list of tour times. ⊠ *608 1st Ave., Pioneer Square* ☎ *206/682–4646* ⊕ *www.undergroundtour.com* ✉ *$20.*

MARIJUANA LEGALIZATION

In 2012, Washington voted to legalize recreational marijuana, one of the first two states in the United States to blaze the trail. Since 2014, when the first handful of legal locations opened in Washington, pot shops have cropped up in every Seattle neighborhood. Just two years after the initial roll out, state residents and visitors had consumed more than $1 billion in marijuana products, which generated roughly $250 million for the state through a 37% excise tax at the point of purchase. Steep taxes mean legal weed doesn't come as cheap as black-market goods, but as demand has grown, average prices have dropped significantly, from $25 per gram in 2014 to $10 per gram in 2016. That's good news for tourists who'd like to try it!

If you're inclined to explore the legal scene, it's a good idea to do a bit of research first. Shopping options range from hole-in-the-wall storefronts to upscale boutiques that stock impressive selections of marijuana along with various accessories. Check sites like ⊕ leafly.com or ⊕ weedmaps.com to locate stores and check on what strains they carry. You must be 21 or up with a valid ID to purchase marijuana in Washington. You can buy or possess an ounce of weed at a time, or up to 6 ounces of solid marijuana-infused edibles. When it comes to consumption, treat it like booze. Don't partake in public, and don't get high and drive. If you'd like a guided introduction to Emerald City's green offerings, check out Kush Tourism (⊕ www.kushtourism.com).

Foster/White Gallery. One of the Seattle art scene's heaviest hitters has digs as impressive as the works it shows: a century-old building with high ceilings and 7,000 square feet of exhibition space. Works by internationally acclaimed Northwest masters Kenneth Callahan, Mark Tobey, Alden Mason, and George Tsutakawa are on permanent display. ⊠ *220 3rd Ave. S, Pioneer Square* ☎ *206/622–2833* ⊕ *www. fosterwhite.com* ⊠ *Free.*

Fodor's Choice ★ **G. Gibson Gallery.** Vintage and contemporary photography is on exhibit in this elegant corner space, including work by the likes of Michael Kenna, Walker Evans, Jule Blackman, Lori Nix, and JoAnn Verburg. The gallery also shows contemporary paintings, sculpture, and mixed-media pieces. The gallery's taste is always impeccable and shows rotate every six weeks. ⊠ *300 S. Washington St., Pioneer Square* ☎ *206/587–4033* ⊕ *www.ggibsongallery.com* ⊠ *Free.*

Fodor's Choice ★ **Greg Kucera Gallery.** One of the most important destinations on the First Thursday gallery walk, this gorgeous space is a top venue for national and regional artists. Be sure to check out the outdoor sculpture deck on the second level. If you have time for only one gallery visit, this is the place to go. You'll see big names that you might recognize—along with newer artists—and the thematic group shows are always thoughtful and well presented. ⊠ *212 3rd Ave. S, Pioneer Square* ☎ *206/624–0770* ⊕ *www.gregkucera.com* ⊠ *Free.*

Occidental Park. This shady, picturesque cobblestone park is the geographical heart of the historic neighborhood—on first Thursdays it's home to a variety of local artisans setting up makeshift booths. Grab a sandwich or pastry at the Grand Central Bakery (arguably the city's finest artisanal bakery) and get in some good people-watching at the outdoor patio. Note that this square is a spot where homeless people congregate; you're likely to encounter more than a few oddballs. The square is best avoided at night. ⊠ *Occidental Ave. S and S. Main St., Pioneer Square.*

Stonington Gallery. You'll see plenty of cheesy tribal art knockoffs in tourist-trap shops, but this elegant gallery will give you a real look at the best contemporary work of Northwest Coast and Alaska tribal members (and artists from these regions working in the Native style). Three floors exhibit wood carvings, paintings, sculpture, and mixed-media pieces from the likes of Robert Davidson, Joe David, Preston Singeltary, Susan Point, and Rick Barto. ⊠ *119 S. Jackson St., Pioneer Square* ☎ *206/405–4040* ⊕ *www.stoningtongallery.com* ☒ *Free.*

INTERNATIONAL DISTRICT

Bright welcome banners, 12-foot fiberglass dragons clinging to lamp-posts, and a traditional Chinese gate confirm you're in the International District. The I.D., as it's locally known, is synonymous with delectable dining—it has many inexpensive Chinese restaurants, but the best eateries reflect its Pan-Asian spirit: Vietnamese, Japanese, Malay, Filipino, Cambodian.

Kubota Garden. A serene 20 acres of streams, waterfalls, ponds, and rock outcroppings were created by Fujitaro Kubota, a 1907 emigrant from Japan. The gardens on the Seattle University campus and the Japanese Garden at the Bloedel Reserve on Bainbridge Island are other examples of his work. The garden, a designated historical landmark of the city of Seattle, is free to visitors and tours are self-guided, though you can go on a docent-led tour on the fourth Saturday of every month, April through October, at 10 am. ⊠ *9817 55th Ave. S, Mt. Baker* ⊹ *From I–5, take Exit 158 and turn left toward Martin Luther King Jr. Way; continue up hill on Ryan Way. Turn left on 51st Ave. S, then right on Renton Ave. S and right on 55th Ave. S to parking lot* ☎ *206/684–4584* ⊕ *www.seattle.gov/parks/find/parks/kubota-garden* ☒ *Free.*

FAMILY
Fodor'sChoice
★

Uwajimaya. This huge, fascinating Japanese supermarket is a feast for the senses. A 30-foot-long red Chinese dragon stretches above colorful mounds of fresh produce and aisles of delicious packaged goods—colorful sweets and unique savory treats from countries throughout Asia. A busy food court serves sushi, Japanese bento-box meals, Chinese stir-fry combos, Korean barbecue, Hawaiian dishes, Vietnamese spring rolls, and an assortment of teas and tapioca drinks. You'll also find authentic housewares, cosmetics (Japanese-edition Shiseido), toys (Hello Kitty), and more. There's also a fantastic branch of the famous Kinokuniya bookstore chain, selling many Asian-language books. The large parking lot is free for one hour with a minimum $7.50 purchase or two hours with a minimum $15 purchase—don't forget to have your ticket validated by the cashiers. ⊠ *600 5th Ave. S, International District* ☎ *206/624–6248* ⊕ *www.uwajimaya.com.*

Continued on page 320

PIKE PLACE MARKET
Nine Acres of History & Quirky Charm

With more than a century of history tucked into every corner and plenty of local personality, the Market is one spot you can't miss. Office workers hustle past cruise-ship crowds to take a seat at lunch counters that serve anything from pizza to piroshkies to German sausage. Local chefs plan the evening's menu over stacks of fresh, colorful produce. At night, couples stroll in to canoodle by candlelight in tucked-away bars and restaurants. Sure, some residents may bemoan the hordes of visitors, and many Seattleites spend their dollars at a growing number of neighborhood farmers' markets. But the Market is still one of Seattle's best-loved attractions.

The Pike Place Market dates from 1907. In response to anger over rising food prices, the city issued permits for farmers to sell produce from wagons parked at Pike Place. The impromptu public market grew steadily, and in 1921 Frank Goodwin, a hotel owner who had been quietly buying up real estate around Pike Place for a decade, proposed to build a permanent space.

More than 250 businesses, including 90 eateries. Breathtaking views of Elliott Bay. A pedestrian-friendly central shopping arcade that buzzes to life each day beginning at 6:30 AM. Strumming street musicians. Cobblestones, flying fish, and the very first Starbucks. Pike Place Market—the oldest continuously operated public market in the United States and a beloved Seattle icon—covers all the bases.

The Market's vitality ebbed after World War II, with the exodus to the suburbs and the rise of large supermarkets. Both it and the surrounding neighborhoods began to deteriorate. But a group of dedicated residents, led by the late architect Victor Steinbrueck, rallied and voted the Market a Historical Asset in the early 1970s. Years of subsequent restoration turned the Market into what you see today.

Pike Place Market is many buildings built around a central arcade (which is distinguished by its huge red neon sign). Shops and restaurants fill buildings on Pike Place and Western Avenue. In the main arcade, dozens of booths sell fresh produce, cheese, spices, coffee, crafts, and seafood—which can be packed in dry ice for flights home. Farmers sell high-quality produce that helps to set Seattle's rigorous dining standards. The shopkeepers who rent store spaces sell art, curios, clothing, beads, and more. Most shops cater to tourists, but there are gems to be found.

EXPLORING THE MARKET

TOP EATS

❶ THE PINK DOOR. This adored (and adorable) Italian eatery is tucked into Post Alley. Whimsical decor, very good Italian food (such as the scrumptious *linguine alla vongole*), and weekend cabaret and burlesque make this gem a must-visit.

❷ LE PANIER. It's a self-proclaimed "Very French Bakery" and another Seattle favorite. The pastries are the main draw, but sandwiches on fresh baguettes and stuffed croissants offer more substantial snacks.

❸ PIROSHKY PIROSHKY. Authentic piroshky come in both standard varieties (beef and cheese) and Seattle-influenced ones (smoked salmon with cream cheese). There are plenty of sweet piroshky, too, if you need a sugar fix.

❹ CAMPAGNE. This French favorite and its charming attached café have you covered, whether you want a quick Croque Madame for lunch, a leisurely and delicious weekend brunch, or a white-tablecloth dinner.

❺ BEECHER'S. Artisanal cheeses—and mac-n-cheese to go—make this a spot Seattleites will brave the crowds for.

❻ THREE GIRLS BAKERY. This tiny bakery turns out piles of pastries and sandwiches on their fresh-baked bread (the baked salmon is a favorite).

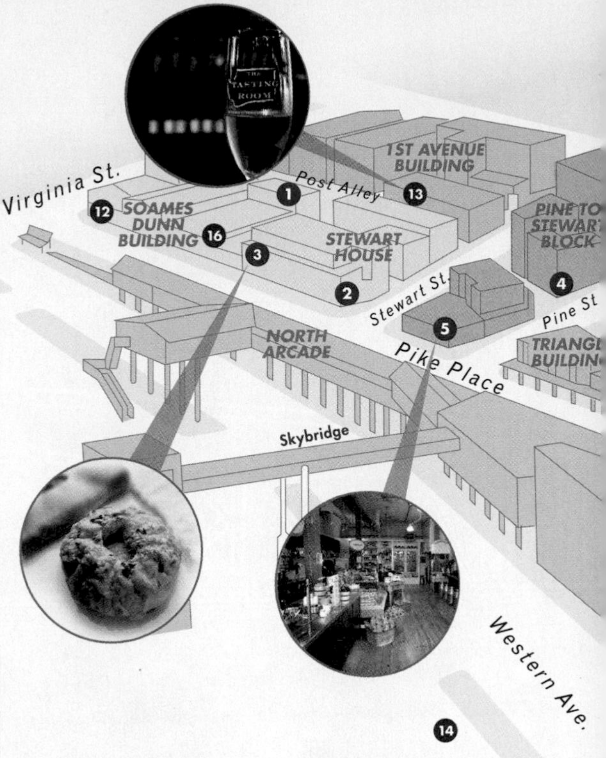
Virginia St.
12
SOAMES DUNN BUILDING
16
3
1
Post Alley
1ST AVENUE BUILDING
13
STEWART HOUSE
2
PINE TO STEWAR BLOCK
4
Stewart St.
5
Pine St
NORTH ARCADE
Pike Place
TRIANGL BUILDIN
Skybridge
Western Ave.
14

❼ MATT'S IN THE MARKET. Matt's is the best restaurant in the Market, and one of the best in the city. Lunch is casual (try the catfish po'boy), and dinner is elegant, with fresh fish and local produce showcased on the small menu. Reservations are essential.

❽ DAILY DOZEN DONUTS. Mini-donuts are made fresh before your eyes and are a great snack to pick up before you venture into the labyrinth.

❾ MARKET GRILL. This no-frills counter serves up the market's best fish sandwiches and a great clam chowder.

❿ CHUKAR CHERRIES. Look for handmade confections featuring—but not restricted to—local cherries dipped in all sorts of sweet, rich coatings.

TOP SHOPS

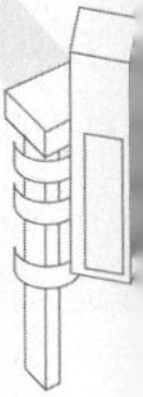

⓫ MARKET SPICE TEA. For a tin of the Market's signature tea, Market Spice Blend, which is infused with cinnamon and clove oils, seek out Market Spice shop on the south side of the main arcade.

⓬ PIKE & WESTERN WINE SHOP. The Tasting Room in Post Alley may be a lovely place to sample Washington wines, but Pike and Western is the place where serious oenophiles flock.

⓭ THE TASTING ROOM. With one of the top wine selections in town, the Tasting Room offers Washington wines for the casual collector and the experienced connoisseur. Stop by the bar for

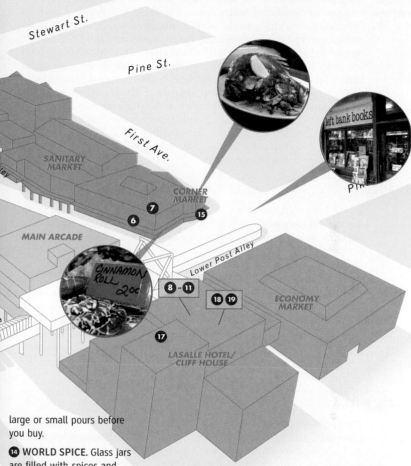

Stewart St.

Pine St.

First Ave.

SANITARY MARKET

CORNER MARKET

MAIN ARCADE

Lower Post Alley

7

6

15

8 - 11

18 19

ECONOMY MARKET

17

LASALLE HOTEL/ CLIFF HOUSE

large or small pours before you buy.

⑭ WORLD SPICE. Glass jars are filled with spices and teas from around the world here: Buy by the ounce or grab a pre-packaged gift set as a souvenir.

⑮ LEFT BANK BOOKS. A collective in operation since 1973, this tiny bookshop specializes in political and history titles and alternative literature.

⑯ THE ORIGINAL STAR-BUCKS. At 1912 Pike Place, you'll find the tiny store that opened in 1971 and started

an empire. The shop is definitely more quaint and old-timey than its sleek younger siblings, and it features the original, uncensored (read: bare-breasted) version of the mermaid logo.

⑰ RACHEL'S GINGER BEER. The flagship store for Seattle's wildly popular ginger beer serves up delicious variations on its homemade brew, including boozy cocktails.

⑱ PAPPARDELLE'S PASTA. There's no type of pasta you could dream up that isn't already in a bin at Pappardelle's.

⑲ DELAURENTI'S. This amazing Italian grocery has everything from fancy olive oil to digestifs and wine to meats and fine cheeses.

FAMILY
Fodor's Choice
★

Wing Luke Museum of the Asian Pacific American Experience. The only museum in the United States devoted to the Asian Pacific American experience provides a sophisticated and often somber look at how immigrants and their descendants have transformed (and been transformed by) American culture. The evolution of the museum has been driven by community participation—the museum's library has an oral history lab, and many of the rotating exhibits are focused around stories from longtime residents and their descendants. Museum admission includes a guided walk-and-talk tour through the East Kong Yick building, where scores of immigrant workers from China, Japan, and the Philippines first found refuge in Seattle. ⊠ *719 S. King St., International District* ☎ *206/623–5124* ⊕ *www.wingluke.org* ✉ *$14.95, free 1st Thurs. and 3rd Sat. of month.*

FIRST HILL

Smack between Downtown and Capitol Hill, First Hill is an odd mix of sterile-looking medical facilities (earning it the nickname "Pill Hill"), old brick buildings that look like they belong on a college campus, and newer residential towers.

Frye Art Museum. In addition to its beloved permanent collection—predominately 19th- and 20th-century pastoral paintings—the Frye hosts eclectic and often avant-garde exhibits, putting this elegant museum on par with the Henry in the U-District. No matter what's going on in the stark, brightly lighted back galleries, it always seems to blend well with the permanent collection, which is rotated regularly. Thanks to the legacy of Charles and Emma Frye, the museum is always free, and parking is free as well. ⊠ *704 Terry Ave., First Hill* ☎ *206/622–9250* ⊕ *www.fryemuseum.org* ✉ *Free.*

CAPITOL HILL

The Hill has two faces: on one side, it's young and edgy, full of artists, musicians, and students. Tattoo parlors and coffeehouses abound, as well as thumping music venues and bars. On the other side, it's elegant and upscale, with tree-lined streets, 19th-century mansions, and John Charles Olmsted's Volunteer Park. Converted warehouses, modern high-rises, colorfully painted two-story homes, and brick mansions all occupy the same neighborhood.

Volunteer Park. Nestled among the grand homes of North Capitol Hill sits this 45-acre grassy expanse that's perfect for picnicking, sunbathing (or stomping in rain puddles), and strolling. You can tell this is one of the city's older parks by the size of the trees and the rhododendrons, many of which were planted more than a hundred years ago. The Olmsted Brothers, the premier landscape architects of the day, helped with the final design in 1904; the park has changed surprisingly little since then. In the center of the park is the **Seattle Asian Art Museum (SAAM, a branch of the Seattle Art Museum)**, housed in a 1933 art moderne–style edifice; note the museum is closed for renovations until 2019.

A focal point of the park, at the western edge of the hill in front of the Asian Art Museum, is Isamu Noguchi's sculpture, *Black Sun,* a natural frame from which to view the Space Needle, the Puget Sound, and the Olympic Mountains. ⊠ *Park entrance, 1400 E. Prospect St., Capitol Hill* ☎ *206/654–3100 museum.*

FAMILY
Fodor's Choice
★

Washington Park Arboretum. As far as Seattle's green spaces go, this 230-acre arboretum is arguably the most beautiful. On calm weekdays, the place feels really secluded. The seasons are always on full display: in warm winters, flowering cherries and plums bloom in its protected valleys as early as late February, while the flowering shrubs in Rhododendron Glen and Azalea Way bloom March through June. In autumn, trees and shrubs glow in hues of crimson, pumpkin, and lemon; in winter, plantings chosen specially for their stark and colorful branches dominate the landscape. In 2016, as part of a 20-year master plan, the arboretum broke ground on a 1¼ mile trail that connects to an existing path to create a 2½-mile loop, giving guests access to areas that were previously hard to reach. March through October, visit the peaceful **Japanese Garden,** a compressed world of mountains, forests, rivers, lakes, and tablelands. The pond, lined with blooming water irises in spring, has turtles and brightly colored koi. An authentic Japanese teahouse is reserved for tea ceremonies and instruction on the art of serving tea (visitors who would like to enjoy a bowl of tea and sweets can purchase a $10 "Chado" tea ticket at the Garden ticket booth). The Graham Visitors Center at the park's north end has descriptions of the arboretum's flora and fauna (which include 130 endangered plants), as well as brochures, a garden gift shop, and walking-tour maps. Free tours are offered most of the year; see website for schedule. ⊠ *2300 Arboretum Dr. E, Capitol Hill* ☎ *206/543–8800 arboretum, 206/684–4725 Japanese garden* ⊕ *www.depts.washington.edu/uwbg* 🎟 *Free, Japanese garden $6.*

> **GALLERY WALKS**
>
> It's fun to simply walk around Pioneer Square and pop into galleries. South Jackson Street to Yesler between Western and 4th Avenue South is a good area. The first Thursday of every month, galleries stay open late for First Thursday Art Walk, a neighborhood highlight. Visit ⊕ *www.firstthursdayseattle.com.*

9

FREMONT

For many years, Fremont enjoyed its reputation as Seattle's weirdest neighborhood, home to hippies, artists, bikers, and rat-race dropouts. But Fremont has lost most of its artist cachet as the stores along its main strip turned more upscale, and rising rents sent many longtime residents reluctantly packing (many to nearby Ballard).

FAMILY
Theo Chocolate factory tour. If it weren't for a small sign on the sidewalk pointing the way, you'd never know that Fremont has its own chocolate factory. Theo has helped to boost the Northwest's growing artisanal chocolate scene and has taken the city by storm, thanks to high-quality chocolate creations. Theo uses only organic, fair-trade cocoa beans, usually in high percentages—yielding darker, less sweet, and more complex

flavors than some of their competitors. You'll see Theo chocolate bars for sale in many local businesses, from coffee shops to grocery stores. Stop by the factory to buy exquisite "confection" truffles—made daily in small batches—with unusual flavors like basil-ganache, lemon, fig-fennel, and burnt sugar. The super-friendly staff is known to be generous with samples. You can go behind the scenes as well: informative, hour-long tours are offered daily; reservations aren't always necessary, but it's a good idea to reserve ahead, particularly on weekends. ⊠ *3400 Phinney Ave. N, Fremont* ☎ *206/632–5100* ⊕ *www.theochocolate.com* 🎫 *Tour $10.*

BALLARD

Ballard is Seattle's sweetheart. This historically Scandinavian neighborhood doesn't have major sights outside of the Hiram M. Chittenden Locks, though it's also home to one of Seattle's most beloved and beautiful public beaches, Golden Gardens Park, which looks out at panoramic views of the Puget Sound and Olympic Mountains. The Ballard Avenue Historic District is a place to check out lovely old buildings, along with a happening nightlife, shopping, and restaurant scene. Every Sunday, rain or shine, Ballard hosts one of the best farmers' markets in town.

FAMILY **Hiram M. Chittenden Locks.** There's no doubt—there's something intriguing Fodor's Choice and eerie about seeing two bodies of water, right next to each, at different ★ levels. The Hiram M. Chittenden Locks (also known as "Ballard Locks") are an important passage in the 8-mile Lake Washington Ship Canal that connects Puget Sound to freshwater Lake Washington and Lake Union. In addition to boat traffic, the Locks see an estimated half-million salmon and trout make the journey from saltwater to fresh each summer, with the help of a fish ladder. Families picnic beneath oak trees in the adjacent 7-acre Carl S. English Botanical Gardens; various musical performances (from jazz bands to chamber music) serenade visitors on summer weekends; and steel-tinted salmon awe spectators as they climb a 21-step fish ladder en route to their freshwater spawning grounds—a heroic journey from the Pacific to the base of the Cascade Mountains. Guided tours of the Locks are available departing from the visitor center; however, plaques by the locks will give you plenty of information if you don't have time for a tour. ⊠ *3015 N.W. 54th St., Ballard* ✛ *From Fremont, head north on Leary Way NW, west on N.W. Market St., and south on 54th St.* ☎ *206/783–7059* ⊕ *www.seattle.gov/tour/locks.htm* 🎫 *Free.*

WALLINGFORD

The laid-back neighborhood of Wallingford is directly east of Fremont—the boundaries actually blur quite a bit. There are several lovely parks and residential streets brimming with colorful Craftsman houses. The main drag, 45th Street NW, has an eclectic group of shops, from a gourmet beer store to an erotic bakery to a Hawaiian merchant, along with a few great coffeehouses, and several notable restaurants.

FAMILY **Gas Works Park.** Far from being an eyesore, the hulking remains of an Fodor's Choice old 1907 gas plant actually lends quirky character to the otherwise ★ open, hilly, 20-acre park. Get a great view of Downtown Seattle while seaplanes rise up from the south shore of Lake Union; the best vantage point is from the zodiac sculpture at the top of a very steep hill, so be sure to wear appropriate walking shoes. This is a great spot for couples and families alike; the sand-bottom playground has monkey bars, wooden platforms, and a spinning metal merry-go-round. Crowds throng to picnic and enjoy outdoor summer concerts, movies, and the July 4th fireworks display over Lake Union. ■TIP→ Gas Works can easily be reached on foot from Fremont Center, via the waterfront Burke-Gilman Trail. ⊠ *2101 N. Northlake Way, at Meridian Ave. N (the north end of Lake Union), Wallingford.*

UNIVERSITY DISTRICT

The U District, as everyone calls it, is the neighborhood surrounding the University of Washington (UW or "U Dub" to locals). The campus is extraordinarily beautiful (especially in springtime, when the cherry blossoms are flowering), and the Henry Art Gallery, on its western edge, is one of the city's best small museums. Beyond that, the appeal of the neighborhood lies in its variety of cheap, delicious ethnic eateries, its proximity to the waters of Portage and Union Bays and Lake Washington, and its youthful energy.

Fodor's Choice
★

Henry Art Gallery. This large gallery is perhaps the best reason to take a side trip to the U-District and consistently presents sophisticated and thought-provoking contemporary work. Exhibits pull from many different genres and include mixed media, photography, and paintings. Richard C. Elliott used more than 21,500 bicycle and truck reflectors of different colors and sizes in his paintings that fit into the sculpture alcoves on the exterior walls of the museum; in another permanent installation, *Light Reign,* a "Skyspace" from artist James Turrell, an elliptical chamber allows visitors to view the sky. More than a few people have used this as a meditation spot; at night the chamber is illuminated by thousands of LED lights. ⊠ *University of Washington campus, 15th Ave. NE and N.E. 41st St., University District* ☎ *206/543–2280* ⊕ *www.henryart.org* ⚟ *$10.*

WEST SEATTLE

Cross the bridge to West Seattle and it's another world altogether. Jutting out into Elliott Bay and Puget Sound, separated from the city by the Duwamish waterway, this out-of-the-way neighborhood covers most of the city's western peninsula—and, indeed, it has an identity of its own.

FAMILY
Fodor's Choice
★

Alki Point and Beach. In summer, this is as close to California as Seattle gets—and some hardy residents even swim in the cold, salty waters of Puget Sound here (water temperature ranges from 46°F to 56°F). This 2½-mile stretch of sand has views of the Seattle skyline and the Olympic Mountains, and the beachfront promenade is especially popular with skaters, joggers, strollers, and cyclists. Year-round, Seattleites come to build sand castles, beachcomb, and fly kites; in winter, storm-watchers come to see the crashing waves. Facilities include drinking water, grills, picnic tables, phones, and restrooms; restaurants line the street across from the beach. To get here from Downtown, take either Interstate 5 south or Highway 99 south to the West Seattle Bridge (keep an eye out, as this exit is easy to miss) and exit onto Harbor Avenue SW, turning right at the stoplight. Alki Point is the place where David Denny, John Low, and Lee Terry arrived in September 1851, ready to found a city. The Alki Point Lighthouse dates from 1913. One of 195 Lady Liberty replicas found around the country lives near the 2700 block of Alki Avenue SW. Miss Liberty (or Little Liberty) is a popular meeting point for beachfront picnics and dates. ⊠ *1702 Alki Ave. SW, West Seattle.*

WHERE TO EAT

Use the coordinate (✛ B2) at the end of each listing to locate a site on the corresponding map.

Thanks to inventive chefs, first-rate local produce, adventurous diners, and a bold entrepreneurial spirit, Seattle has become one of the culinary capitals of the nation. Fearless young chefs have stepped in and raised the bar. Nowadays, fresh and often foraged produce, local seafood, and imaginative techniques make the quality of local cuisine even higher.

Seattle's dining scene has been stoked like a wildfire by culinary rock stars who compete on shows like *Iron Chef* and *Top Chef* and regularly dominate "best of" lists. Seattle chefs have won big in the prestigious James Beard competition—empire-builder Tom Douglas has even been named the national "Best Restaurateur." The city is particularly strong on New American, French, and Asian cuisines. Chefs continuously fine-tune what can best be called Pacific Northwest cuisine, which features fresh, local ingredients. Think nettles and mushrooms foraged in nearby forests; colorful berries, apples, and cherries grown by Washington State farmers; and outstanding seafood from the cold northern waters of the Pacific Ocean, like wild salmon, halibut, oysters, Dungeness crab, and geoduck. Seattle boasts quite a few outstanding bakeries, too, whose breads and desserts you'll see touted on many menus.

For a truly local experience, be sure to try at least one of Seattle's famous food trucks—the city's roving casual restaurants routinely make national "best of" lists. They're parked all over the city and serve up everything from authentic po'boys to Native American flatbreads to sushi, crepes, and vegan fare. Among the very best are El Camion, Marination Nation, Maximus/Minimus, and Where Ya At Matt.

Prices in the reviews are the average cost of a main course at dinner or, if dinner is not served, at lunch.

WHAT IT COSTS IN U.S. DOLLARS			
$	**$$**	**$$$**	**$$$$**
RESTAURANTS under $16	$16–$24	$25–$32	over $32

Restaurant prices are the average cost of a main course at dinner or, if dinner is not served, at lunch.

DOWNTOWN AND BELLTOWN

$$$ MEDITERRANEAN 🍴 **Lola.** Tom Douglas dishes out his signature Northwest style, spiked with Greek and Mediterranean touches—another huge success for the local celebrity chef. Try a sensational tagine of Northwest seafood; a variety of meat kebabs; and scrumptious spreads including hummus, tzatziki, and *harissa* (a red-pepper concoction). **Known for:** Greek food; breakfast; doughnuts. [$] *Average main: $25* ✉ *2000 4th Ave., Belltown* ☎ *206/441–1430* ✣ *E4.*

$ BAKERY 🍴 **Macrina Bakery.** One of Seattle's favorite bakeries is also popular for breakfast and brunch and an excellent place to take a delicious break on your way to or from the Olympic Sculpture Park. With its perfectly executed breads and pastries—from Nutella brioche and ginger cookies to almond croissants and dark-chocolate, sugar-dusted brownies—it's become a true Belltown institution. **Known for:** baguettes; pastries. [$] *Average main: $7* ✉ *2408 1st Ave., Belltown* ☎ *206/448–4032* 🌐 *www.macrinabakery.com* ✣ *D4.*

$$$$ PACIFIC NORTHWEST Fodor's Choice ★ 🍴 **Matt's in the Market.** One of the most beloved of Pike Place Market's restaurants, Matt's is now owned by Dan Bugge, who continues to value intimate dining, fresh ingredients, and superb service. You can perch at the bar for pints and the signature deviled eggs or be seated at a table—complete with vases filled with flowers from the market—for a seasonal menu that synthesizes the best picks from the restaurant's produce vendors and an excellent wine list. **Known for:** view; seafood. [$] *Average main: $35* ✉ *94 Pike St., Downtown* ☎ *206/467–7909* 🌐 *www.mattsinthemarket.com* 🕒 *Closed Sun.* ✣ *D4.*

$$$ PACIFIC NORTHWEST 🍴 **Palace Kitchen.** The star of this chic yet convivial Tom Douglas eatery may be the 45-foot bar, but the real show takes place in the giant open kitchen at the back. Wood-grilled chicken wings, olive poppers, Penn Cove mussels, roast-pork ravioli, and a nightly selection of cheeses vie for your attention on the ever-changing menu of small plates. **Known for:** late-night dining; burger. [$] *Average main: $25* ✉ *2030 5th Ave., Belltown* ☎ *206/448–2001* 🌐 *www.tomdouglas.com* 🕒 *No lunch* ✣ *D4.*

$$$$ SUSHI Fodor's Choice ★ 🍴 **Sushi Kashiba.** After decades spent earning a reputation as one of Seattle's top sushi chefs, Shiro Kashiba opened his own spot in a location as iconic as his skill with seafood deserves. Diners in the spare-but-elegant Pike Place Market space can opt for the *omakase* (chef's choice) selection of the best fish from around the world and just up the street, or order from the menu of Japanese classics and sashimi. **Known for:** omakase; fresh fish. [$] *Average main: $85* ✉ *86 Pine St., Suite 1, Downtown* ✣ *Inn at the Market* ☎ *206/441–8844* 🌐 *www.sushikashiba.com* 🕒 *No lunch* ✣ *D4.*

SOUTH LAKE UNION AND QUEEN ANNE

$$$$ PACIFIC NORTHWEST 🍴 **Canlis Restaurant.** Canlis has been setting the standard for opulent dining in Seattle since the 1950s and although there are no longer kimono-clad waitresses, the food, the wine, the practically clairvoyant service, and the views overlooking Lake Union are still remarkable. Executive chef Brady Williams (formerly of New York's acclaimed Roberta's and

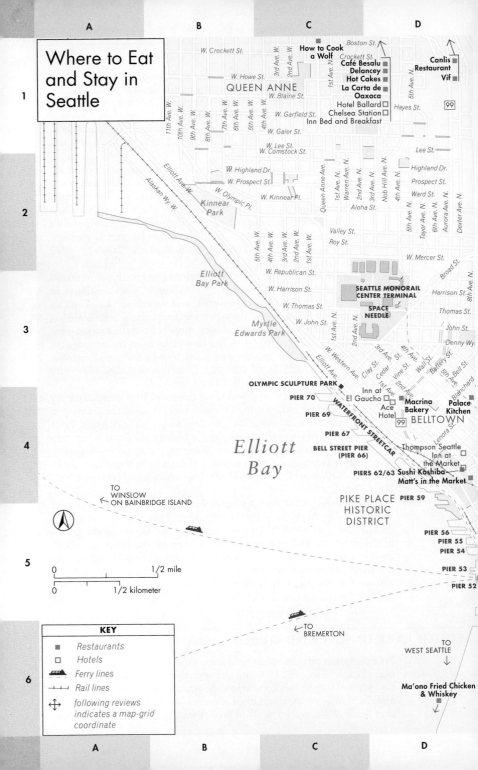

Where to Eat and Stay in Seattle

A **B** **C** **D**

W. Crockett St.

W. Howe St.

QUEEN ANNE

W. Blaine St.

W. Garfield St.

W. Galer St.

W. Lee St.
W. Comstock St.

W. Highland Dr.
W. Prospect St.

W. Kinnear Pl.

Kinnear
Park

Valley St.
Roy St.

W. Republican St.

W. Harrison St.

W. Thomas St.

W. John St.

Myrtle
Edwards Park

Elliott
Bay Park

Elliott Ave. W.

Alaskan Wy. W.

11th Ave. W.
10th Ave. W.
9th Ave. W.
8th Ave. W.
7th Ave. W.
6th Ave. W.
5th Ave. W.
4th Ave. W.
3rd Ave. W.
2nd Ave. W.
1st Ave. W.

Boston St.

W. Crockett St.
How to Cook a Wolf ■
Crockett St.
Café Besalu ■
Delancey ■
Hot Cakes ■
La Carta de Oaxaca ■
Hotel Ballard □
Chelsea Station □
Inn Bed and Breakfast

Hayes St.

Canlis Restaurant
Vif ■

99

Lee St.

Highland Dr.
Prospect St.
Ward St.

Aloha St.

5th Ave.
5th Ave. N.
4th Ave. W.
3rd Ave. W.
2nd Ave. W.
1st Ave. W.

Queen Anne Ave.
Warren Ave. N.
2nd Ave. N.
3rd Ave. N.
Nob Hill Ave. N.
4th Ave. N.

Taylor Ave. N.
Aurora Ave. N.
Dexter Ave. N.

W. Mercer St.

Broad St.

SEATTLE MONORAIL CENTER TERMINAL

SPACE NEEDLE

Harrison St. N.
8th Ave. N.

Thomas St.

John St.

Denny Wy.

W. Western Ave.

W. Mercer St.

3rd Ave. St.
4th Ave. St.

Clay St.
Cedar
Vine St.
Wall St.
2nd Ave.
Battery St.
5th Ave.
Bell St.
Blanchard
Lenora St.

Elliott Ave.

OLYMPIC SCULPTURE PARK ■

PIER 70

WATERFRONT STREETCAR

PIER 69

PIER 67

BELL STREET PIER (PIER 66)

PIERS 62/63

Inn at
El Gaucho □
Ace
Hotel □
99

Macrina Bakery ■

Palace Kitchen ■

BELLTOWN

Thompson Seattle
Inn at
the Market □
Sushi Kashiba ■
Matt's in the Market ■

Elliott Bay

TO
WINSLOW
ON BAINBRIDGE ISLAND

PIKE PLACE HISTORIC DISTRICT

PIER 59

PIER 56
PIER 55
PIER 54

PIER 53

PIER 52

0 ————— 1/2 mile
0 ————— 1/2 kilometer

TO
BREMERTON

TO
WEST SEATTLE
↓

Ma'ono Fried Chicken & Whiskey ■
↓

A **B** **C** **D**

1
2
3
4
5
6

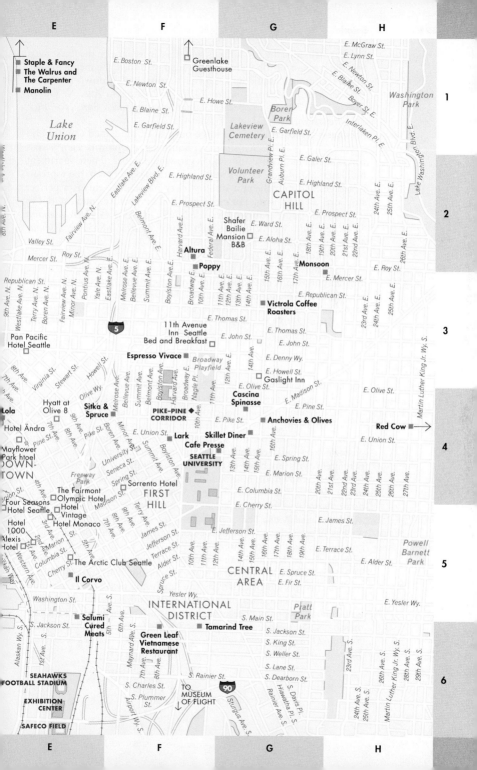

E   F   G   H

1

■ Staple & Fancy
■ The Walrus and
   The Carpenter
■ Manolin

E. Boston St.
Greenlake
Guesthouse

E. McGraw St.
E. Lynn St.
E. Newton St.
E. Blaine St.
E. Newton St.
Boyer St. E.
E. Howe St.
Washington
Park

Lake
Union

E. Blaine St.
E. Garfield St.

Boren
Park
Lakeview
Cemetery

E. Garfield St.
Interlaken Pl. E.

Lake Washington Blvd. E.

2

Valley St.
Mercer St.
Roy St.

Volunteer
Park

E. Highland St.

E. Galer St.

E. Highland St.

Republican St.

E. Prospect St.

CAPITOL
HILL

E. Prospect St.

Shafer
Bailie
Mansion
B&B
E. Ward St.

E. Roy St.

■ Altura

E. Aloha St.

■ Poppy

Monsoon ■

Pan Pacific
Hotel Seattle

11th Avenue
Inn Seattle
Bed and Breakfast

E. Mercer St.

E. Republican St.

3

■ Victrola Coffee
   Roasters

E. Thomas St.

E. Thomas St.

E. John St.

E. John St.

Espresso Vivace ■
Broadway
Playfield

E. Denny Wy.

E. Howell St.
Gaslight Inn

Lola

Hyatt at
Olive 8

Sitka &
Spruce ■

E. Olive St.

Cascina
Spinasse

E. Olive St.

Hotel Ändra

PIKE–PINE
CORRIDOR

E. Pine St.

Mayflower
Park hotel
DOWN-
TOWN

■ Lark

E. Pike St.

Anchovies & Olives ■

Red Cow ■ →

E. Union St.
Skillet Diner

E. Union St.

4

Cafe Presse

SEATTLE
UNIVERSITY

E. Spring St.

Sorrento Hotel

E. Marion St.

The Fairmont
Olympic Hotel

FIRST
HILL

E. Columbia St.

Four Seasons
Hotel Seattle

Hotel
Vintage
Hotel Monaco

E. Cherry St.

Hotel
1000

E. James St.

Alexis
Hotel

Powell
Barnett
Park

5

■ Il Corvo

The Arctic Club Seattle

CENTRAL
AREA

E. Terrace St.

E. Alder St.

E. Spruce St.
E. Fir St.

Washington St.

Yesler Wy.

E. Yesler Wy.

INTERNATIONAL
DISTRICT

Pratt
Park

S. Jackson St.

S. Main St.

■ Salumi
   Cured
   Meats

Tamarind Tree ■

S. Jackson St.

Green Leaf
Vietnamese
Restaurant

S. King St.

S. Weller St.

S. Lane St.

S. Rainier St.

S. Dearborn St.

6

SEAHAWKS
FOOTBALL STADIUM

S. Charles St.

TO
MUSEUM
OF FLIGHT

S. Plummer
St.

EXHIBITION
CENTER

SAFECO FIELD

E   F   G   H

Blanca) maintains the restaurant's signature insistence on the finest meat and the freshest produce, but he has also refreshed the menu—which offers traditional multicourse and tasting options. **Known for:** view; service; wine. [$] *Average main: $48* ✉ *2576 Aurora Ave. N, Queen Anne* ☎ *206/283–3313* 🌐 *www.canlis.com* 🕒 *Closed Sun. No lunch* 👔 *Jacket required* ✥ *D1.*

$ CAFÉ 🍴 **Espresso Vivace.** A cozy and large outpost of the famed Capitol Hill roaster, the Vivace coffee shrine in South Lake Union is right across from the REI megastore and amid a growing number of new apartment buildings and offices. Grab a seat, order an expertly prepared espresso beverage, and munch on a small variety of snacks—this is a perfect stop after an exhausting jaunt through REI and before you head out to the next adventure. **Known for:** café Nicos; espresso. [$] *Average main: $3* ✉ *227 Yale Ave. N, South Lake Union* ☎ *206/388–5164* 🌐 *www.espressovivace.com* ✥ *F3.*

$$ ITALIAN 🍴 **How to Cook a Wolf.** This sleek eatery—complete with loads of trendy young couples perched at its tables—"pays homage to M.F.K. Fisher and her philosophy of taking simple ingredients and transforming them into culinary splendor." As you would expect then, fresh, artisanal ingredients are the focus. **Known for:** small plates; pasta. [$] *Average main: $16* ✉ *2208 Queen Anne Ave. N, Queen Anne* ☎ *206/838–8090* 🌐 *www.ethanstowellrestaurants.com* 🕒 *No lunch* ✥ *C1.*

PIONEER SQUARE

$ ITALIAN Fodor's Choice ★ 🍴 **Il Corvo.** It may be a Pioneer Square hole-in-the-wall, but Il Corvo serves up some of the best pasta in town. Experienced chef Mike Easton left the cooking line at higher-end restaurants to found this lunch-only (11 am to 3 pm), cash-only collection of family-style tables where he prepares a few inexpensive handmade dishes each day using antique pasta makers and artisanal, seasonal ingredients—perhaps squid-ink perciatelli with anchovy-toasted bread crumbs or pappardelle *alla Bolognese*. **Known for:** house-made pasta; affordable prices. [$] *Average main: $9* ✉ *217 James St., Pioneer Square* ☎ *206/538–0999* 🌐 *www.ilcorvopasta.com* 🕒 *Closed weekends. No dinner* ✥ *E5.*

$ ITALIAN Fodor's Choice ★ 🍴 **Salumi Cured Meats.** The lines are long for hearty, unforgettable sandwiches filled with superior house-cured meats and all other sorts of goodies at this shoebox shop owned by Gina Batali—sister of famed New York chef Mario Batali—and founded by their dad Armandino. The oxtail sandwich special is unbeatable, but if it's unavailable or sold out (as specials often are by the lunchtime peak) order a salami, bresaola, porchetta, meatball, sausage, or lamb prosciutto sandwich with onions, peppers, cheese, and olive oil. **Known for:** cured meats; meatballs. [$] *Average main: $10* ✉ *309 3rd Ave. S, Pioneer Square* ☎ *206/621–8772* 🌐 *www.salumicuredmeats.com* 🕒 *Closed weekends. Take-out only, limited hrs on Mon. No dinner* ✥ *E5.*

INTERNATIONAL DISTRICT

$ VIETNAMESE 🍴 **Green Leaf Vietnamese Restaurant.** Locals pack this friendly café for the expansive menu of fresh, well-prepared Vietnamese staples. The quality of the food—the spring rolls, *báhn xèo* (the Vietnamese version of an omelet), and lemongrass chicken are just a few standouts—and reasonable prices would be enough to make it an instant I.D. favorite. **Known for:** báhn xèo; spring rolls. [$] *Average main: $11* ✉ *418 8th Ave. S, International District* ☎ *206/340–1388* 🌐 *www.greenleaftaste.com* ⊕ *F6.*

$$ VIETNAMESE 🍴 **Tamarind Tree.** Wildly popular with savvy diners from all across the city, this Vietnamese haunt on the eastern side of the I.D. *really* doesn't look like much from the outside, especially because the entrance is through a grungy parking lot (which it shares with Sichuanese Cuisine restaurant), but once you're inside, the elegantly simple, large, and warm space is extremely welcoming. The food is the main draw—try the spring rolls, which are stuffed with fresh herbs, fried tofu, peanuts, coconut, jicama, and carrots; authentic bánh xèo; spicy pho; the signature "seven courses of beef"; and, to finish, grilled banana cake with warm coconut milk. **Known for:** spring rolls; cocktails. [$] *Average main: $21* ✉ *1036 S. Jackson St., International District* ☎ *206/860–1404* 🌐 *www.tamarindtreerestaurant.com* ⊕ *F6.*

CAPITOL HILL

$$$$ ITALIAN Fodor's Choice ★ 🍴 **Altura.** A hand-carved cedar angel statue watches over diners at this lively spot, where chef-owner Nathan Lockwood lends a Northwest focus to Italian cuisine. The set tasting menu weaves rare, intriguing, and fascinating local and global ingredients into classic Italian techniques. **Known for:** tasting menu; interesting ingredients. [$] *Average main: $137* ✉ *617 Broadway E, Capitol Hill* ☎ *206/402–6749* 🌐 *www.alturarestaurant.com* ⏲ *Closed Sun. and Mon. No lunch* ⊕ *F2.*

$$ SEAFOOD 🍴 **Anchovies & Olives.** Artful lighting, an exposed kitchen, a well-edited Italian and Northwest wine list, and a lively small bar are the backdrop for elegant seafood dishes at this sophisticated Ethan Stowell restaurant on the ground floor of a residential high-rise at the eastern end of the Pike–Pine Corridor. Appetizer plates and crudos are small and easily shared, while mains focus on seasonal fish. **Known for:** seafood; pasta. [$] *Average main: $24* ✉ *1550 15th Ave., at Pine St., Capitol Hill* ☎ *206/838–8080* 🌐 *ethanstowellrestaurants.com/anchoviesandolives* ⏲ *No lunch* ⊕ *G4.*

$ FRENCH 🍴 **Café Presse.** Two distinct rooms create plenty of space at this French bistro just off the Pike–Pine Corridor, where you can get such Parisian fare as pressed chicken with greens; a *croque madame*; mussels with french fries; pan-roasted quail with sautéed potatoes and apples; and simple cheese platters with slices of baguette. This is the spot to order some red table wine and people-watch. **Known for:** chicken; french fries; magazine rack. [$] *Average main: $15* ✉ *1117 12th Ave., Capitol Hill* ☎ *206/709–7674* 🌐 *www.cafepresseseattle.com* ⊕ *F4.*

$$$ ITALIAN Fodor's Choice ★ 🍴 **Cascina Spinasse.** Squeeze into this postage-stamp-size eatery with its cream-colored lace curtains and true Italian soul—and come hungry, because chef Stuart Lane knows how to make pasta. It's made fresh daily and comes with such sauces and fillings as short rib ragu,

9

eggplant and anchovies, or simply, as in their signature dish, dressed in butter and sage. *Secondi* options can range from braised pork belly with cabbage to stewed venison served over polenta. **Known for:** handmade pasta; amaro. [$] *Average main: $26* ✉ *1531 14th Ave., Capitol Hill* ☎ *206/251–7673* 🌐 *www.spinasse.com* ⏲ *Closed Tues. No lunch* ✣ *G4.*

$$$ MODERN AMERICAN Fodor's Choice ★

🍴 **Lark.** The Central Agency Building, a converted 1917 warehouse with 25-foot ceilings, is the setting for mouthwateringly delicious small plates to share and seasonally inspired main dishes—you'll want to sample as much as possible. The expert servers can help you choose from an impressive wine list, and will happily help you decide from a menu divided into cheese; vegetables and grains; charcuterie; fish; meat; and, of course, dessert. **Known for:** small plates; local ingredients. [$] *Average main: $30* ✉ *952 E. Seneca St., Capitol Hill* ☎ *206/323–5275* 🌐 *www.larkseattle.com* ⏲ *Closed Mon. No lunch* ✣ *F4.*

$$$ VIETNAMESE

🍴 **Monsoon.** With an elegant bar and laid-back roof deck, this serene Vietnamese restaurant on a tree-lined residential stretch of Capitol Hill is a better bet than ever. Upscale fare blends Vietnamese and Pacific Northwest elements, including wild gulf prawns with lemongrass, catfish clay pot with fresh coconut juice and green onion, and lamb with fermented soybeans and sweet onions. **Known for:** crab; wine. [$] *Average main: $25* ✉ *615 19th Ave. E, Capitol Hill* ☎ *206/325–2111* 🌐 *www.monsoonrestaurants.com* ✣ *G3.*

$$$ MODERN AMERICAN

🍴 **Poppy.** Jerry Traunfeld's bright, airy restaurant on the northern end of Broadway is a feast for the senses, with funky design details, friendly staff, and a happening bar area. Start with one of the many interesting cocktails and an order of eggplant fries with sea salt and honey; then peruse the menu, which offers small plates and thali of various sizes—the idea is inspired by the Indian thali meal, in which a selection of different dishes is served in small compartments on a large platter, though the food here is mainly seasonal new American cuisine with occasional Asian accents. **Known for:** thali plates; cocktails; Indian spices. [$] *Average main: $30* ✉ *622 Broadway E, Capitol Hill* ☎ *206/324–1108* 🌐 *www.poppyseattle.com* ⏲ *No lunch* ✣ *F2.*

$$$ BRASSERIE

🍴 **Red Cow.** One of the latest from restaurateur Ethan Stowell—and a well-received departure from his usual Italian fare—this new French brasserie in beautiful tree-lined Madrona serves up excellent house-made charcuterie and expertly prepared grass-finished beef. A 10-minute trip from Downtown or Capitol Hill, Red Cow is a bustling modern space with knowledgeable, personable servers. [$] *Average main: $30* ✉ *1423 34th Ave., Madrona* ☎ *206/454–7932* ⏲ *No lunch* ✣ *H4.*

$$$ MODERN AMERICAN

🍴 **Sitka & Spruce.** James Beard Award–winner Matthew Dillon helms this popular restaurant at Capitol Hill's Melrose Market; it's romantic, chic, friendly, and cutting-edge all at once. Diners choose from seasonally rotating offerings such as king bolete mushrooms with blistered fava beans, whole baby turnips in tarragon with house-made yogurt with za'atar spice, and deliciously tender charcoal-grilled chicken served with rye berries grown in nearby Winthrop. **Known for:** small plates; vegetables; wood-fired dishes. [$] *Average main: $29* ✉ *1531 Melrose Ave., Capitol Hill* ☎ *206/324–0662* 🌐 *www.sitkaandspruce.com* ✣ *E4.*

$

AMERICAN

✕ **Skillet Diner.** Diner fare takes a modern turn on Capitol Hill at this stylishly retro, brick-and-mortar version of one of the city's pioneering food trucks. Skillet's hot, strong coffee is made with beans from neighboring Caffé Vita, while their burgers are ridiculously savory, on a beef tallow bun, topped with signature "bacon jam" and blue cheese (max out the decadence with a side of cheesy poutine). **Known for:** bacon jam; burgers; fried chicken. $ *Average main: $14* ⊠ *1400 E. Union, Capitol Hill* ☎ *206/512–2000* ⊕ *www.skilletstreetfood.com* ✛ *G4.*

$

CAFÉ

✕ **Victrola Coffee Roasters.** Victrola is one of the most loved of Capitol Hill's many coffeehouses, and it's easy to see why: the sizable space is lovely—the walls are hung with artwork by local painters and photographers—the coffee and pastries are fantastic, the baristas are skillful, and everyone, from soccer moms to indie rockers, is made to feel like this neighborhood spot exists just for them. If 15th Avenue East is too far off the beaten path for you, there are also branches at 310 East Pike Street (*206/462–6259*), between Melrose and Bellevue, as well as in Beacon Hill. **Known for:** espresso; fresh-roasted beans. $ *Average main: $3* ⊠ *411 15th Ave. E, Capitol Hill* ☎ *206/462–6259* ⊕ *www.victrolacoffee.com* ✛ *G3.*

FREMONT

$$$

SEAFOOD

Fodor'sChoice

★

✕ **Manolin.** Walking into the light-filled dining room of Manolin, with its horseshoe-shape bar framing the open kitchen, transports you straight to the sea. Blue tiles, the wood-fired oven in the center, the cool marble bar, and the seafood-laden menu all bring diners to the ambiguous maritime destination, where ceviches are inspired by coastal Mexico, plantain chips come from the Caribbean, smoked salmon has vaguely Scandinavian flavors, and the squid with black rice and ginger is as if from Asia, all mingling on the menu. **Known for:** ceviche; cocktails. $ *Average main: $28* ⊠ *3621 Stone Way N, Fremont* ☎ *206/294–3331* ⊕ *www.manolinseattle.com* ⊘ *No lunch. Closed Mon.* ⊟ *No credit cards* ✛ *E1.*

$

BISTRO

Fodor'sChoice

★

✕ **Vif.** Part coffee shop, part casual snack restaurant, and part wine retailer, Vif is all magic. The brainchild of a former pastry chef and wine director of one of Seattle's bygone restaurants, the menu brings the kind of nuance and skill that you'd expect from a pastry chef, but the elegance of a wine expert. **Known for:** wine; snacks. $ *Average main: $8* ⊠ *4401 Fremont Ave. N, Fremont* ☎ *206/557–7357* ⊕ *www. vifseattle.com* ⊘ *No dinner. Closed Mon.* ✛ *D1.*

BALLARD

$

BAKERY

✕ **Café Besalu.** A slice of France here in Ballard, this small, casual bakery gets patrons from across the entire city, thanks to its *I-swear-I'm-in-Paris* croissants—they are buttery, flaky perfection. Weekend lines are long, but if you score a table, you'll be in heaven. **Known for:** croissants; jam. $ *Average main: $8* ⊠ *5909 24th Ave. NW, Ballard* ☎ *206/789–1463* ⊕ *www.cafebesalu.com* ⊘ *Closed Mon. and Tues.* ✛ *D1.*

$

PIZZA

Fodor'sChoice

★

✕ **Delancey.** Brandon Pettit spent years developing his thin-but-chewy pizza crust, and the final product has made him a contender for the city's best pies. Pettit himself is occasionally manning the wood-fired oven at this sweetly sophisticated little spot north of downtown Ballard

9

that he owns with partner Molly Wizenberg (author of the popular "Orangette" food blog). **Known for:** quality pizza toppings; desserts. [$] *Average main: $16* ✉ *1415 N.W. 70th St., Ballard* ☎ *206/838–1960* 🌐 *www.delanceyseattle.com* ⏲ *Closed Mon. No lunch* ✣ *D1.*

$ CAFÉ 🍴 **Hot Cakes.** A few savory dishes are available at this Ballard "cakery," but consider passing on the chicken potpie in favor of the grilled chocolate sandwich. Autumn Martin, formerly head chocolatier at Theo Chocolate, specializes in creative, high-quality desserts (including vegan options) such as a "s'mores" molten chocolate cake with house-made marshmallows and caramel, and cookies with house-smoked chocolate chips. **Known for:** molten chocolate cakes; extravagant shakes. [$] *Average main: $9* ✉ *5427 Ballard Ave. NW, Ballard* ☎ *206/420–3431* 🌐 *www.getyourhotcakes.com* ✣ *D1.*

$ MEXICAN 🍴 **La Carta de Oaxaca.** True to its name, this low-key, bustling Ballard favorite serves traditional Mexican cooking with Oaxacan accents. The *mole negro* is a must, served with chicken or pork; another standout is the *albondigas* (a spicy vegetable soup with meatballs). **Known for:** margaritas; albondigas; mole. [$] *Average main: $15* ✉ *5431 Ballard Ave. NW, Ballard* ☎ *206/782–8722* 🌐 *www.lacartadeoaxaca.com* ⏲ *Closed Sun. No lunch Mon.* ✣ *D1.*

$$$ MODERN ITALIAN Fodor's Choice ★ 🍴 **Staple & Fancy.** The "Staple" side of this Ethan Stowell restaurant at the south end of Ballard Avenue might mean ethereal gnocchi served with corn and chanterelles, or a whole grilled branzino. But visitors to the glam, remodeled, historic brick building are best served by going "Fancy," meaning the chef's choice dinner where diners are asked about allergies and food preferences, then presented with several courses (technically four, but the appetizer usually consists of a few different plates) of whatever the cooks are playing with on the line that night—cured meats, salads made with exotic greens, handmade pastas, seasonal desserts. **Known for:** multicourse menu; pasta. [$] *Average main: $30* ✉ *4739 Ballard Ave. NW, Ballard* ☎ *206/789–1200* 🌐 *www.ethanstowellrestaurants.com* ⏲ *No lunch* ✣ *E1.*

$$$ SEAFOOD 🍴 **The Walrus and the Carpenter.** Chef-owner Renee Erickson was inspired by the casual oyster bars of Paris to open this bustling shoebox of a restaurant on the south end of Ballard Avenue (in the rear of a historic brick building, behind Staple & Fancy). Seats fill fast at the zinc bar and the scattered tall tables where seafood fans slurp on fresh-shucked kusshis and shigokus and other local oysters, but the menu also offers refined small plates like grilled sardines with shallots and walnuts or roasted greengage plums in cream. **Known for:** oysters; small plates. [$] *Average main: $27* ✉ *4743 Ballard Ave. NW, Ballard* ☎ *206/395–9227* 🌐 *www.thewalrusbar.com* ✣ *E1.*

WEST SEATTLE

$$ PACIFIC NORTHWEST Fodor's Choice ★ 🍴 **Ma'ono Fried Chicken & Whiskey.** A quietly hip vibe pervades this culinary beacon in West Seattle, where the vast bar surrounds an open kitchen. Diners of all stripes relish the Hawaiian spin on fresh and high-quality Pacific Northwest bounty. **Known for:** fried chicken; whiskey. [$] *Average main: $18* ✉ *4437 California Ave. SW, West Seattle* ☎ *206/935–1075* 🌐 *www.maono.springhillnorthwest.com* ⏲ *No lunch weekdays* ✣ *D6.*

WHERE TO STAY

Hotel reviews have been shortened. For full information, visit Fodors. com. Use the coordinate (⊕ B2) at the end of each listing to locate a site on the corresponding map. Prices in the reviews are the lowest cost of a standard double room in high season.

Much like the eclectic city itself, Seattle's lodging offers something for everyone. There are grand, ornate vintage hotels; sleek and elegant modern properties; green hotels with yoga studios and enough bamboo for an army of pandas; and cozy bed-and-breakfasts with sweet bedspreads and home-cooked breakfasts. Travelers who appreciate the anonymity of high-rise chains can comfortably stay here, while guests who want to feel like family can find the perfect boutique inn to lay their heads.

WHAT IT COSTS IN U.S. DOLLARS			
$	**$$**	**$$$**	**$$$$**
HOTELS under $180	$180–$265	$266–$350	over $350

Hotel prices are the lowest cost of a standard double room in high season.

DOWNTOWN AND BELLTOWN

$
HOTEL
Fodor's Choice
★
Ace Hotel. The Ace is a dream come true for both penny-pinching hipsters and folks who appreciate unique minimalist decor, with such touches in the rooms as army-surplus blankets, industrial metal sinks, and street art breaking up any notion of austerity; the cheapest rooms share bathrooms, which have enormous showers. **Pros:** ultratrendy but with some of the most affordable rates in town; good place to meet other travelers; free Wi-Fi. **Cons:** half the rooms have shared bathrooms; not for people who want pampering; neighborhood rife with panhandlers; lots of stairs to get to lobby. $ *Rooms from: $129* ⊠ *2423 1st Ave., Belltown* ☎ *206/448–4721* ⊕ *www.acehotel.com* ↗ *14 standard rooms, 14 deluxe rooms* ⭘ *No meals* ⊕ *D4.*

$$
HOTEL
Alexis Hotel. Two historic buildings near the waterfront use exposed brick, walls of windows, and nouveau-baroque touches to appeal to aesthetes and modern romantics, and ornate leather chairs and wood-burning fireplaces recall a different era. **Pros:** great service; close to waterfront; unique, beautiful rooms; suites aren't prohibitively expensive. **Cons:** small lobby; not entirely soundproofed against old building and city noise; some rooms can be a bit dark. $ *Rooms from: $229* ⊠ *1007 1st Ave., Downtown* ☎ *206/624–4844, 888/850–1155* ⊕ *www. alexishotel.com* ↗ *88 rooms, 33 suites* ⭘ *No meals* ⊕ *E5.*

$$$
HOTEL
Fodor's Choice
★
The Arctic Club Seattle. From the Alaskan-marble-sheathed foyer and the antique walrus heads to the Northern Lights Dome room with its leaded-glass ceiling to explorer-chic touches like steamer trunks for bedside tables, the Arctic Club pays homage to an era of gold-rush opulence (the early 1900s building was once a gentlemen's club). **Pros:** cool, unique property; great staff; light-rail and bus lines just outside the door. **Cons:** not in the heart of Downtown; rooms are a bit

9

dark; style may be off-putting for travelers who like modern hotels; charge for Wi-Fi. $ *Rooms from: $275* ✉ *700 3rd Ave., Downtown* ☎ *206/340–0340, 800/445–8667* ⊕ *thearcticclubseattle.com* ⤳ *118 rooms, 2 suites* ❍ *No meals* ✛ *E5.*

$$$$
HOTEL
FAMILY
Fodor's Choice
★

⛫ The Fairmont Olympic Hotel. With marble floors, soaring ceilings, massive chandeliers, and sweeping staircases, the lobby of this hotel personifies old-world elegance, while guest rooms have a modern twist. **Pros:** great location; excellent service; fabulous on-site dining and amenities. **Cons:** not much in the way of views; a lot of construction nearby. $ *Rooms from: $379* ✉ *411 University St., Downtown* ☎ *206/621–1700, 888/363–5022* ⊕ *www.fairmont.com/seattle* ⤳ *232 rooms, 218 suites* ❍ *No meals* ✛ *E4.*

$$$$
HOTEL
FAMILY
Fodor's Choice
★

⛫ Four Seasons Hotel Seattle. Just south of the Pike Place Market and steps from the Seattle Art Museum, this Downtown gem is polished and elegant, with Eastern accents and plush furnishings in comfortable living spaces in which Pacific Northwest materials, such as stone and fine hardwoods, take center stage. **Pros:** fantastic location with amazing water views; large rooms with luxurious bathrooms with deep soaking tubs; lovely spa. **Cons:** Four Seasons regulars might not click with this modern take on the brand; street-side rooms not entirely soundproofed; some room views are partially obscured by industrial sites. $ *Rooms from: $679* ✉ *99 Union St., Downtown* ☎ *206/749–7000, 800/332–3442* ⊕ *www.fourseasons.com/seattle* ⤳ *134 rooms, 13 suites* ❍ *No meals* ✛ *E5.*

$$$$
HOTEL
FAMILY
Fodor's Choice
★

⛫ Hotel 1000. Chic and modern yet warm and inviting, these luxurious tech-savvy rooms are full of surprising touches, including large soaking tubs that fill from the ceiling—and a cute yellow rubber ducky and bubbles for bath time. **Pros:** useful high-tech gadgets; virtual golf club and spa; hotel is hip without being alienating. **Cons:** rooms can be dark; a small percentage of rooms without views look out on a cement wall. $ *Rooms from: $445* ✉ *1000 1st Ave., Downtown* ☎ *206/957–1000, 877/315–1088* ⊕ *www.hotel1000seattle.com* ⤳ *101 rooms, 19 suites* ❍ *No meals* ✛ *E5.*

$$$
HOTEL
Fodor's Choice
★

⛫ Hotel Ändra. Scandinavian sensibility and clean, modern lines define this sophisticated hotel on the edge of Belltown, where rooms have dark fabrics and woods, with a few bright accents and geometric prints. **Pros:** hangout-worthy lobby lounge; hip vibe; excellent service; spacious rooms. **Cons:** some street noise; not family-friendly. $ *Rooms from: $295* ✉ *2000 4th Ave., Belltown* ☎ *206/448–8600, 877/448–8600* ⊕ *www.hotelandra.com* ⤳ *93 rooms, 4 studios, 22 suites* ❍ *No meals* ✛ *E4.*

$$
HOTEL
FAMILY
Fodor's Choice
★

⛫ Hotel Monaco. It only takes one glimpse of the gorgeous modern-global lobby to know that this stylish boutique hotel in the heart of Downtown is a standout, and rooms carry on the image, with a palette of soft reds and gunmetal grays, beds topped with Frette linens, floor-to-ceiling drapes in a Turkish motif, and floor lamps that recall telescopes. **Pros:** near Pike Place Market and the Space Needle; welcoming public spaces; daily hosted wine reception with savory snacks. **Cons:** some street-facing rooms can be a little noisy; small gym. $ *Rooms from: $249* ✉ *1101 4th Ave., Downtown* ☎ *206/621–1770, 800/715–6513* ⊕ *www.monacoseattle.com* ⤳ *152 rooms, 37 suites* ❍ *No meals* ✛ *E5.*

WHERE SHOULD I STAY?

	Neighborhood Vibe	Pros	Cons
Down-town and Belltown	Downtown is central, with the hottest hotels with water views. If you're a fan of galleries and bars, stay in Belltown.	A day in Downtown and Belltown can take you from the Seattle Art Museum to Pike Place Market.	Parking can be pricey and hard to come by. This is not your spot if you want a quiet, relaxing respite.
Seattle Center, South Lake Union, and Queen Anne	Queen Anne boasts great water views and easy access to Downtown. South Lake Union can feel industrial.	Seattle Center's many festivals (such as Bumber-shoot) means you'll have a ringside seat.	You'll be away from the key Downtown sights. Parking can be difficult.
Capitol Hill	One of Seattle's oldest and quirkiest neighbor-hoods, Capitol Hill has cozy accommodations.	A great place to stay if you want to mingle with creative locals in great bookstores and cafés.	If you're uncomfortable with the pierced, tat-tooed, or LGBT set, look elsewhere.
Fremont and Ballard	From the Woodland Park Zoo to the locks, these funky neighborhoods are excellent jumping-off points.	These quintessential Seattle 'hoods are a short trek from Downtown and have restaurants and shops.	The only lodgings to be found in Fremont are B&Bs—book ahead.
Green Lake	Laid-back and wonder-fully situated near the Woodland Park Zoo and Gas Works Park.	Outdoorsy types will love the proximity to Green Lake, a great place to stroll or jog.	You won't find anything trendy here, and, after a few days, you'll have seen everything.
University District	It offers everything you'd expect from a college area—from bookstores to ethnic food.	If you're renting a car, this area offers centrality with a lower price tag for parking.	The homeless and college kids populate University Avenue ("The Ave."). Not much in the way of sightseeing.
West Seattle	In summer, West Seattle can feel a lot like South-ern California: it's a fun place to stay.	Alki Beach and Lincoln Park are fun, plus great restaurants and shopping on California Avenue.	You'll need a car to stay in this very removed 'hood. The only way in or out is over a bridge.
The Eastside	Proximity to high-end malls, Woodinville winer-ies, and Microsoft.	Woodinville is wine HQ; Kirkland offers cute bou-tiques; and Bellevue is a shopping mecca.	If you're here to experi-ence Seattle, stick to the city. Traffic is a total nightmare.

$$ HOTEL 🏨 **Hotel Vintage.** Each of the stylish rooms—some of which boast marvelous views of Seattle's iconic public library—feature a vineyard-inspired palette of burgundy, taupe, and green hues, with a focus on unique interior design. **Pros:** friendly staff; beautiful, quiet rooms; caters to wine lovers; close to shopping, theaters, and the Convention Center. **Cons:** a short-but-steep uphill walk from Downtown could be tough on some travelers; small lobby; small bathrooms. [$] *Rooms from: $249* ✉ *1100 5th Ave., Downtown* ☎ *206/624–8000, 800/853–3914* 🌐 *www.hotelvintage-seattle.com* 🛏 *124 rooms, 1 suite* 🍴 *No meals* ⊕ *E5.*

$$$$ HOTEL Fodor's Choice ★ 🏨 **Hyatt at Olive 8.** In a city known for environmental responsibility, being the greenest hotel in town is no small feat, and green is rarely this chic—rooms have floor-to-ceiling windows flooding the place with light along with enviro touches like dual-flush toilets, fresh-air vents, and low-flow showerheads. **Pros:** central location; superb amenities; environmental responsibility; wonderful spa. **Cons:** standard rooms have showers only; guests complain of hallway and traffic noise; translucent glass bathroom doors offer little privacy; fee for Wi-Fi. [$] *Rooms from: $359* ✉ *1635 8th Ave., Downtown* ☎ *206/695–1234, 800/233–1234* 🌐 *www.olive8.hyatt.com* ⛾ *331 rooms, 15 suites* 🍴 *No meals* ✣ *E4.*

$$ B&B/INN Fodor's Choice ★ 🏨 **Inn at El Gaucho.** Hollywood Rat Pack enthusiasts will want to move right in to these swank, retro-style suites done in dark wood with buttery leather furniture. **Pros:** unique aesthetic; some rooms have great views; location; warm, helpful staff. **Cons:** steep stairs with no elevator; some rooms only have showers; no outdoor spaces; rooms are (purposely) dark; no on-site fitness center. [$] *Rooms from: $249* ✉ *2505 1st Ave., Belltown* ☎ *206/728–1133, 866/354–2824* 🌐 *www.elgaucho.com* ⛾ *17 suites* 🍴 *No meals* ✣ *D4.*

$$$$ HOTEL Fodor's Choice ★ 🏨 **Inn at the Market.** From its heart-stopping views to the fabulous location just steps from Pike Place Market, this is a place you'll want to visit again and again. **Pros:** outstanding views from most rooms; half a block from Pike Place Market; fantastic service; complimentary town-car service for Downtown locations. **Cons:** little common space; being in the heart of the action means some street noise. [$] *Rooms from: $390* ✉ *86 Pine St., Downtown* ☎ *206/443–3600, 800/446–4484* 🌐 *www.innatthemarket.com* ⛾ *63 rooms, 7 suites* 🍴 *No meals* ✣ *D4.*

$$ HOTEL Fodor's Choice ★ 🏨 **Mayflower Park Hotel.** Comfortable, old-world charm in the center of the action comes with sturdy antiques, Asian accents, brass fixtures, and florals. **Pros:** central Downtown location; quiet; good value; direct connection to the airport via light-rail and Seattle Center via the Monorail; great service. **Cons:** rooms are small; no pool. [$] *Rooms from: $229* ✉ *405 Olive Way, Downtown* ☎ *206/623–8700, 800/426–5100* 🌐 *www.mayflowerpark.com* ⛾ *160 rooms, 29 suites* 🍴 *No meals* ✣ *E4.*

$$$$ HOTEL Fodor's Choice ★ 🏨 **Sorrento Hotel.** Opened in 1909 for the Alaska-Yukon-Pacific Exposition, the Sorrento features carved wood moldings, period fixtures, and restored antique furniture. **Pros:** serene and classy; fantastic service; great restaurant; fabulous beds; free Downtown car service. **Cons:** not central; rooms are a bit small (though corner suites are commodious). [$] *Rooms from: $424* ✉ *900 Madison St., First Hill* ☎ *206/622–6400, 800/426–1265* 🌐 *www.hotelsorrento.com* ⛾ *34 rooms, 42 suites* 🍴 *No meals* ✣ *F4.*

$$$ HOTEL Fodor's Choice ★ 🏨 **Thompson Seattle.** Designed by local starchitects Olson Kundig, the 12-story Thompson Seattle is the most stylish newcomer to Seattle's hotel scene, with a contemporary glass exterior and sophisticated guest rooms that feature floor-to-ceiling windows, hardwood floors, a crisp white-and-navy palette, and leather and smoked-glass accents. **Pros:** perfect for the style obsessed; very close to Pike Place Market; top-notch on-site dining and drinks. **Cons:** blazing afternoon sun in some

rooms; some small rooms; floor beneath rooftop bar can be noisy. [$] *Rooms from: $279* ✉ *110 Stewart St., Downtown* ☎ *206/623–4600* 🌐 *www.thompsonhotels.com/hotels/thompson-seattle* 🛏 *151 rooms, 7 suites* ✣ *D4.*

SOUTH LAKE UNION AND QUEEN ANNE

$$$ HOTEL Fodor's Choice ★ 🏨 **Pan Pacific Hotel Seattle.** One of the best-looking hotels in Seattle is a chic treat for travelers, from the attractive and comfortable modern rooms to the impressive views of the Space Needle and Lake Union. **Pros:** no touristy vibe like Downtown hotels; feels more luxurious than it costs; award-winning sustainability efforts. **Cons:** long walk to Downtown (though streetcar access and the hotel's free car service help with that); bathroom design isn't the most private. [$] *Rooms from: $285* ✉ *2125 Terry Ave., South Lake Union* ☎ *206/264–8111* 🌐 *www.panpacific.com/seattle* 🛏 *131 rooms, 22 suites* 🍴 *No meals* ✣ *E3.*

CAPITOL HILL

$ B&B/INN Fodor's Choice ★ 🏨 **11th Avenue Inn Seattle Bed & Breakfast.** The closest B&B to Downtown offers all the charm of a classic bed-and-breakfast (exquisitely styled with antique beds and Oriental rugs) with the convenience of being near the action. **Pros:** unpretentious take on classic B&B; free on-site parking; oozes vintage charm; wonderful owner and staff. **Cons:** although most guests are courteous, sound does carry in old houses; no kids under 12; minimum three-night stay. [$] *Rooms from: $169* ✉ *121 11th Ave. E, Capitol Hill* ☎ *206/720–7161* 🌐 *www.11thavenueinn.com* 🛏 *9 rooms* 🍴 *Breakfast* ✣ *F3.*

$ B&B/INN 🏨 **Gaslight Inn.** Rooms here range from a crow's nest with peeled-log furniture and Navajo-print fabrics to a more traditional suite with Arts and Crafts–style furnishings, a fireplace, and stained-glass windows. **Pros:** great art collection; house and rooms are quite spacious; in-ground heated pool; free Wi-Fi. **Cons:** breakfast is unimpressive; street parking not always easy to find; minimum two-night stay. [$] *Rooms from: $168* ✉ *1727 15th Ave., Capitol Hill* ☎ *206/325–3654* 🌐 *www.gaslight-inn.com* 🛏 *6 rooms with private bath; 2 rooms with shared bath* 🍴 *Breakfast* ✣ *G3.*

$$ B&B/INN Fodor's Choice ★ 🏨 **Shafer Baillie Mansion Bed & Breakfast.** The opulent guest rooms and suites on the second floor are large, with private baths, antique furnishings, Oriental rugs, huge windows, and lush details like ornate four-poster beds; third-floor rooms, while lovely, have a more contemporary country feel, but still have private baths and large windows. **Pros:** wonderful staff; great interior and exterior common spaces; free Wi-Fi; location. **Cons:** no elevator and the walk to the third floor might be hard for some guests; while children are allowed, some guests say the mansion isn't kid-friendly; three-night minimum stay during summer weekends; two nights otherwise. [$] *Rooms from: $199* ✉ *907 14th Ave. E, Sea-Tac* ☎ *800/985–4654* 🌐 *www.sbmansion.com* 🛏 *6 rooms, 2 suites* 🍴 *Breakfast* ✣ *G2.*

FREMONT

$$$ B&B/INN Fodor's Choice ★ 🏨 **Chelsea Station Inn Bed & Breakfast.** The four 900-square-foot suites in this 1920s brick colonial have distressed hardwood floors with colorful rugs, decorative fireplaces, sleeper sofas, contemporary furnishings, and a soft, modern color palette, and are a convenient and luxurious jumping-off point for all the north end has to offer. **Pros:** great, unobtrusive host; huge rooms and 1½ bathrooms per suite; fabulous breakfasts and complimentary snacks. **Cons:** far from Downtown; no TVs; no elevator. [$] *Rooms from: $287* ✉ *4915 Linden Ave. N, Fremont* ☎ *206/547–6077* 🌐 *www.chelseastationinn.com* 🛏 *4 suites* 🍴 *Breakfast* ✣ *D1.*

GREEN LAKE

$$ B&B/INN Fodor's Choice ★ 🏨 **Greenlake Guest House.** Outdoorsy types, visitors who want to stay in a low-key residential area, and anyone who wants to feel pampered and refreshed will enjoy this lovely B&B across the street from beautiful Green Lake. **Pros:** views; thoughtful amenities and wonderful hosts; can accommodate kids over four years old; short walk to restaurants. **Cons:** 5 miles from Downtown; on a busy street. [$] *Rooms from: $229* ✉ *7630 E. Green Lake Dr. N, Green Lake* ☎ *206/729–8700, 866/355–8700* 🌐 *www.greenlakeguesthouse.com* 🛏 *5 rooms* 🍴 *Breakfast* ✣ *F1.*

BALLARD

$$ HOTEL Fodor's Choice ★ 🏨 **Hotel Ballard.** A historic sandstone building features a modern gray-and-yellow palette that melds historical details with design accents that nod to the neighborhood's Scandinavian heritage, and many rooms include views of waterways and the Olympic Mountains; eight rooftop suites are especially inviting. **Pros:** in the heart of Ballard; $15 self park; free use of large gym with saltwater pool; fireplaces and soaking tubs in suites. **Cons:** not close to the majority of Seattle attractions. [$] *Rooms from: $239* ✉ *5216 Ballard Ave. N.W., Ballard* ☎ *206/789–5012* 🌐 *www.hotelballard.com* 🛏 *20 rooms, 8 suites* 🍴 *No meals* 💳 *No credit cards* ✣ *D1.*

NIGHTLIFE

Seattle's amazing musical legacy is well known, but there's more to the arts and nightlife scenes than live music. In fact, these days, there are far more swanky bars and inventive pubs than music venues in the city. To put it bluntly, Seattle's a dynamite place to drink. You can sip overly ambitious and ridiculously named specialty cocktails in trendy lounges, get a lesson from an enthusiastic sommelier in a wine bar or restaurant, or swill cheap beer on the patio of a dive bar. Though some places have very specific demographics, most Seattle bars are egalitarian, drawing loyal regulars of all ages.

In addition to its bars, Downtown and Belltown in particular have notable restaurants with separate bar areas. Most restaurants have impressive bar menus, and food is often served until 11 pm, midnight, or even 1 am in some spots.

DOWNTOWN AND BELLTOWN

BARS AND LOUNGES

Alibi Room. Well-dressed locals head to this hard-to-find wood-paneled bar to sip double martinis while taking in views of Elliott Bay or studying the scripts, handbills, and movie posters that line the walls. The lower level is more crowded and casual. It's an ever-cool yet low-key, intimate place. Stop by for a drink or a meal, or stay to listen and dance to live music. Happy hour—daily from 11:30 am to 6 pm—is quiet and a good respite from the Market. ☒ *85 Pike St., in Post Alley, at Pike Place Market, Downtown* ☎ *206/623–3180* ⊕ *www.seattlealibi.com.*

Black Bottle. This sleek and sexy gastro-tavern makes the northern reaches of Belltown look good. The interior is simple but stylish, with black chairs and tables and shiny wood floors. It gets crowded on nights and weekends with a laid-back but often dressed-up clientele. A small selection of beers on tap and a solid wine list (with Washington, Oregon, California, and beyond well represented) will help you wash down the sustainably sourced pub snacks, including house-smoked wild boar ribs, pork belly with kimchi, and oysters on the half shell. ☒ *2600 1st Ave., Belltown* ☎ *206/441–1500* ⊕ *www.blackbottleseattle.com.*

Oliver's. The most important question here: Shaken or stirred? This bar in the Mayflower Park Hotel is famous for its martinis. In fact, having a cocktail here is like having afternoon tea in some other parts of the world. Wing chairs, low tables, and lots of natural light make it easy to relax after a hectic day. The likes of Frank Sinatra or Billie Holiday may be playing in the background; expect an unfussy crowd of regulars, hotel guests, and older Manhattan-sippers who appreciate old-school elegance. ☒ *405 Olive Way, Downtown* ☎ *206/623–8700* ⊕ *oliverstwistseattle.com.*

Purple Café and Wine Bar. Wine lovers come for the massive selection—the menu boasts 90 wines by the glass and some 600 bottles—but this place deserves props for its design, too. Despite the cavernous quality of the space and floor-to-ceiling windows, all eyes are immediately drawn to the 20-foot tower ringed by a spiral staircase that showcases thousands of bottles. Full lunch and dinner menus feature American and Pacific Northwest fare—the lobster mac 'n' cheese is especially tasty—and servers know their ideal pairings. ☒ *1225 4th Ave., Downtown* ☎ *206/829–2280* ⊕ *www.thepurplecafe.com.*

Fodor's Choice ★ **Zig Zag Café.** A mixed crowd of mostly locals hunts out this unique spot at Pike Place Market's Street Hill Climb (a nearly hidden stairwell leading down to the piers). In addition to pouring a perfect martini, Zig Zag features a revolving cast of memorable cocktails. A Mediterranean-inspired food menu offers plenty of tasty bites to accompany the excellent cocktails. A small patio is the place to be on a summery happy-hour evening. Zig Zag is friendly—retro without being obnoxiously ironic—and very Seattle, with the occasional live music show to boot. ☒ *1501 Western Ave., Downtown* ☎ *206/625–1146* ⊕ *zigzagseattle.com.*

9

LIVE MUSIC

Fodor'sChoice

★

The Crocodile. The heart and soul of Seattle's music scene since 1991 has hosted the likes of Nirvana, Pearl Jam, and Mudhoney, along with countless other bands. There's a reason *Rolling Stone* once called the 525-person Crocodile one of the best small clubs in America. Nightly shows are complemented by cheap beer on tap and pizza at the Back Bar. All hail the Croc! ⊠ *2200 2nd Ave., Belltown* ☎ *206/441–7416* ⊕ *www.thecrocodile.com.*

Dimitriou's Jazz Alley. Seattleites dress up to see nationally known jazz artists at Dimitriou's. The cabaret-style theater, where intimate tables for two surround the stage, runs shows nightly. Those with reservations for cocktails or dinner, served during the first set, receive priority seating. ⊠ *2033 6th Ave., Downtown* ☎ *206/441–9729* ⊕ *www.jazzalley.com.*

Showbox. Just across from Pike Place Market, this venue—which turned 75 in 2014—is a great spot to see some pretty big-name acts. The room's small enough that you don't feel like you're miles away from the performers, and the terraced bar areas flanking the main floor provide some relief if you don't want to join the crush in front of the stage. Another branch, **Showbox SoDo** (*1700 1st Ave. S, SoDo*), is named for its location south of Downtown; the converted warehouse, larger than the original, features big national acts, but has little of the charm of the original. ⊠ *1426 1st Ave., Downtown* ☎ *888/929–7849* ⊕ *www. showboxpresents.com.*

THEATER

Paramount Theatre. Built in 1928 as a venue for early talkies and vaudeville acts, this lovely beaux arts movie palace—which features an original Wurlitzer theater pipe organ—now mostly hosts concerts, as well as the occasional comedy, dance, or Broadway event. Seattle Theatre Group (STG Presents) also operates the Moore and the Neptune, both old Seattle theaters with terrific music-and-beyond lineups. ⊠ *907 Pine St., Downtown* ☎ *206/682–1414* ⊕ *www.stgpresents.org.*

QUEEN ANNE

MUSIC CLUBS

Teatro ZinZanni. There's dinner theater, and then there's Seattle's famous, over-the-top—and totally entertaining—five-course feast with a circus on the side. Featuring vaudeville, comedy, music, and dance, the themed shows change every few months, but ZinZanni, in the heart of Seattle Center, remains a reliable favorite for locals and tourists alike. Tickets start at $99. ⊠ *222 Mercer St., Queen Anne* ☎ *206/802–0015* ⊕ *www.zinzanni.com.*

PIONEER SQUARE

BARS AND LOUNGES

Collins Pub. The best beer bar in Pioneer Square features 22 rotating taps of Northwest (including Boundary Bay, Chuckanut, and Anacortes) and California beers and a long list of bottles from the region. Its upscale pub menu features local and seasonal ingredients. ⊠ *526 2nd Ave., Pioneer Square* ☎ *206/623–1016* ⊕ *www.thecollinspub.com.*

Sake Nomi. Whether you're a novice or expert, you'll appreciate the authentic offerings here. The shop and tasting bar is open until 10 pm Tuesday through Saturday and from noon to 6 on Sunday. Don't be shy—have a seat, try a few of the rotating samples, and ask a lot of questions. Sake can be served up in a variety of temperatures and styles. ⊠ *76 S. Washington St., Pioneer Square* ☎ *206/467–7253* ⊕ *www.sakenomi.us.*

CAPITOL HILL

BARS AND LOUNGES

Garage Billiards. Built in 1928, this former auto-repair shop is now a large, happening, chrome-and-vinyl pool hall, restaurant, and bar. The large garage doors are thrown wide open on warm evenings, making it a pleasurable alternative to other, more cramped places. There are 18 tournament pool tables and a small bowling alley, and you must be 21 to enter the bowling and billiards areas. ⊠ *1130 Broadway Ave., Capitol Hill* ☎ *206/322–2296* ⊕ *www.garagebilliards.com.*

Linda's Tavern. Welcome to one of the Hill's iconic dives—and not just because it was allegedly the last place Kurt Cobain was seen alive. The interior has a vaguely Western theme, but the patrons are pure Capitol Hill indie-rockers and hipsters. The bartenders are friendly, the burgers are good (brunch is even better), and the always-packed patio is one of the liveliest places to grab a happy-hour drink. ⊠ *707 E. Pine St., Capitol Hill* ☎ *206/325–1220* ⊕ *www.lindastavern.com.*

The Pine Box. The clever name is just one reason to visit this beer hall housed in a former funeral home on the corner of Pine Street. The churchlike interior is stately, with soaring ceilings, dark woodwork, and custom furniture made from huge Douglas fir timbers found in the basement—they were supposedly used to shelve coffins many years ago. The place is rumored to be haunted, but that doesn't stop a trendy crowd from congregating to sample from 30-plus taps of craft beer and a menu of wood-fired pizza and meatballs and pulled-pork tacos. Or get your morning drink on at the weekend brunch. ⊠ *1600 Melrose Ave., Capitol Hill* ☎ *206/588–0375* ⊕ *www.pineboxbar.com.*

Quinn's. Capitol Hill's original gastropub has friendly bartenders, an *amazing* selection of beers on tap (with the West Coast and Belgium heavily represented), an extensive list of whiskey, and an edgy menu of good food, which you can enjoy at the long bar or at a table on either of the two floors of the industrial-chic space. Spicy fried peanuts and country-style rabbit pâté are good ways to start—then you can choose from Painted Hills beef tartare with pumpernickel crisps, perfect marrow bones with baguette and citrus jam, or a cheese plate. Heartier mains, like the signature wild boar sloppy Joe are available at dinnertime. A pared-down pub menu is also available from 3 pm to midnight or later. The folks here take their libations seriously, so feel free to chat up the bartenders about their favorites. ⊠ *1001 E. Pike St., Capitol Hill* ☎ *206/325–7711* ⊕ *www.quinnspubseattle.com* ☾ *No lunch* ⌕ *Reservations not accepted.*

9

Fodor's Choice
★
Sun Liquor Lounge. If you adore creative handcrafted cocktails, add this intimate Capitol Hill haunt to your must-visit list. Friendly bartenders sling exceptional drinks mixed with fresh-squeezed juices and house-made ingredients like shrubs—flavorful "drinking vinegars" that first became popular in colonial America—and aromatic bitters. They even make and sell their own hooch. A few years ago, Sun Liquor opened a nearby distillery, which produces the company's flagship Hedge Trimmer Gin, among others. ■TIP➜ The lounge is a much cozier place to hang out, but the same specialty cocktails are served up at the distillery, along with a lunch menu (512 East Pike). ⊠ *607 Summit Ave. E, Capitol Hill* ☎ *206/860–1130* ⊕ *www.sunliquor.com.*

BREWPUBS

Elysian Brewing Company. Worn booths and tables are scattered across the bi-level warehouse space of this Capitol Hill mainstay, where the beers are a good representation of the thriving brewing scene in the Northwest. Always on tap are the hop-heavy Immortal IPA, the rich Perseus Porter, and the crisp Elysian Fields Pale Ale. The food (burgers, fish tacos, sandwiches, salads) is decent, too. This is a favorite of Seattleites and Capitol Hill residents and a laid-back alternative to the more trendy haunts and lounges in the area. ⊠ *1221 E. Pike St., Capitol Hill* ☎ *206/860–1920* ⊕ *www.elysianbrewing.com.*

LIVE MUSIC

Neumos. One of the grunge era's iconic clubs (when it was Moe's) has managed to reclaim its status as a staple of the Seattle rock scene, despite being closed for a six-year stretch. And it is a great rock venue: acoustics are excellent, and the roster of cutting-edge indie rock bands is one of the best in the city. Other genres of music are also represented among the acts coming through Neumos. Their intimate downstairs venue, Barboza, often brings in great, lesser-known acts. ⊠ *925 E. Pike St., Capitol Hill* ☎ *206/709–9467* ⊕ *www.neumos.com.*

FREMONT AND GREENWOOD

BARS AND LOUNGES

Brouwer's. It may look like a trendy Gothic castle, but in fact this is heaven for Belgian-beer lovers. A converted warehouse is home to a top selection of suds, which are provided by the owners of Seattle's best specialty-beer shop, Bottleworks. Brouwer's serves plenty of German and American/Northwest beers, too, as well as English, Czech, and Polish selections. Surprisingly good sandwiches, frites, and Belgian specialties help to lay a pre-imbibing foundation (remember that most Belgian beers have a higher alcohol content). Before settling on a seat downstairs, check out the balcony and the cozy parlor room. ⊠ *400 N. 35th St., Fremont* ☎ *206/267–2437* ⊕ *www.brouwerscafe.com.*

Chuck's Hop Shop. Were it not for the picnic tables and rotating food trucks routinely parked outside, this place might look like just another corner convenience store. In fact, that's precisely what it used to be before owner Chuck transformed it into one of North Seattle's favorite spots for sampling craft beer and hanging out for hours. With nearly 40 taps, Chuck's features an especially good selection of IPAs and ciders on draft, many of local origin. Families love this extremely kid-friendly spot—there's an ice-cream counter, ample seating, and a stack of board games inside—and so do the dogs that get plenty of head pats and a big cookie, if you ask. Chuck's also offers a huge selection of bottled beers from all over the world, including gluten- and alcohol-free options. Sticking to the Capitol Hill area? Chuck's now has a second location (2001 East Union Street). ⊠ *656 N.W. 85th St., Greenwood* ☎ *206/297–6212* ⊕ *www.chucks85th.com.*

Quoin. Even if you're not staying for dinner at the neighboring Revel— a Korean-fusion restaurant that's won raves for its dumplings, rice, and noodle dishes—this sliver of a bar is worth a visit, and you can order food from next door. Bartenders make a fantastic cocktail, and it offers a much more intimate and stylish experience than other Fremont spots. There's also an outdoor deck with bench seating around a fire pit. Happy hour runs 4–6 pm daily. ⊠ *403 N. 36th St., Fremont* ☎ *206/547–2040.*

Über Tavern. At what many serious aficionados claim may be one of the best beer bars on the planet, there's a constantly changing lineup of drafts—everything from Belgian imports to hop-heavy California DIPAs (double IPAs)—as well as a big list of bottles from around the globe. A digital menu shows what's on tap (and what's almost out) and there are Scrabble and checkerboards built into the bar tables—perfect for lazy afternoons. Über doesn't offer food, but you're free to order from a stack of takeout menus. ⊠ *7517 Aurora Ave. N, Green Lake* ☎ *206/782–2337* ⊕ *www.uberbier.com.*

BREWPUBS

Hale's Ales. One of the city's oldest craft breweries, opened in 1983, produces unique English-style ales, cask-conditioned ales, and nitrogen-conditioned cream ales, plus a popular Mongoose IPA. The pub serves a full menu and has a great view of the fermenting room. Order a taster's flight if you want to try everything. ⊠ *4301 Leary Way NW, Fremont* ☎ *206/706–1544* ⊕ *www.halesbrewery.com.*

BALLARD

BARS AND LOUNGES

The Noble Fir. A rotating selection of great beer, cider, and wine and a truly varied crowd are just part of the appeal of this popular bar. Like many (most?) Seattleites, the husband-and-wife owners are outdoorsy— and it shows in the rustic-modern interior, which includes a library-like seating area stocked with large trail maps, as well as hundreds of travel books. The Noble Fir serves a few simple snacks, like cheese, charcuterie, fish, and vegan and vegetarian options, in case you feel like settling in and planning your next big adventure. ⊠ *5316 Ballard Ave., Ballard* ☎ *206/420–7425* ⊕ *www.thenoblefir.com.*

Ocho. Blink and you'll miss it, and that would be a shame, because this tiny corner hot spot crafts some of the finest cocktails in town. Dimly lit and loud, Ocho only has a few tables and bar seats, and it fills up fast with a mixed crowd that flocks here for the drinks

9

and top-notch Spanish tapas. It's usually possible to snag a table without a wait during the weekend happy hour from noon to 6. Come summer, the slender sidewalk patio is an ideal spot for soaking up the sun and people-watching. ✉ *2325 N.W. Market St., Ballard* ☎ *206/784–0699.*

The Peoples Pub. Head to this Ballard institution to see what locals love about this unpretentious neighborhood. The pub (a dining room and a separate bar in the back) isn't much to look at—a lot of wood paneling, simple wood tables and chairs, and some unfortunate floral uphol-stery—but it has a *Prost*-worthy selection of German beers and one delicious fried pickle. True to its name, Peoples draws an interesting cross section of the neighborhood, from the young and trendy to old-school fishermen. ✉ *5429 Ballard Ave. NW, Ballard* ☎ *206/783–6521* ⊕ *www.peoplespub.com.*

LIVE MUSIC

Tractor Tavern. Seattle's top spot for roots music and alt-country has a large, dimly lighted hall with all the right touches—wagon-wheel fixtures, exposed-brick walls, and a cheery staff. The sound system is outstanding. ✉ *5213 Ballard Ave. NW, Ballard* ☎ *206/789–3599* ⊕ *www.tractortavern.com.*

SPORTS AND THE OUTDOORS

The question in Seattle isn't "do you exercise?" Rather, it's "how do you exercise?" Athleticism is a regular part of most people's lives here, whether it's an afternoon jog, a sunrise rowing session, a lunch-hour bike ride, or an evening game of Frisbee.

PARKS INFORMATION

King County Parks and Recreation. This agency manages many of the parks outside city limits. ✉ *201 S. Jackson, Suite 700, Downtown* ☎ *206/477–4527 information* ⊕ *www.kingcounty.gov/services/ parks-recreation/parks.*

Seattle Parks and Recreation Department. To find out whether an in-town park baseball diamond or tennis court is available, contact the Seattle Parks and Recreation Department, which is responsible for most of the parks, piers, beaches, playgrounds, and courts within city limits. The department issues permits for events, arranges reservations for facilities, and staffs visitor centers and naturalist programs. ✉ *100 Dexter Ave. N, Central District* ☎ *206/684–4075* ⊕ *www.seattle.gov/parks.*

Washington State Parks. The state manages several parks and camp-grounds in greater Seattle. ✉ *1111 Israel Rd. SW, Olympia* ☎ *360/902–8844 for general information, 888/226–7688 for campsite reservations* ⊕ *www.parks.wa.gov.*

BIKING

Biking is probably Seattle's most popular sport. Thousands of Seattleites bike to work, and even more ride recreationally, especially on weekends. In the past, Seattle wasn't a particularly bike-friendly city. But the city government has adopted a sweeping Bicycle Master Plan that calls for 118 new miles of bike lanes, 19 miles of bike paths, and countless route signs and lane markings throughout the city by 2017. The plan can't erase the hills, though—only masochists should attempt Queen Anne Hill and Phinney Ridge. Fortunately, all city buses have easy-to-use bike racks (on the front of the buses, below the windshield) and drivers are used to waiting for cyclists to load and unload their bikes. If you're not comfortable biking in urban traffic—and there is a lot of urban traffic to contend with here—you can do a combination bus-and-bike tour of the city or stick to the car-free Burke-Gilman Trail.

Seattle drivers are fairly used to sharing the road with cyclists. With the exception of the occasional road-rager or clueless cell-phone talker, drivers usually leave a generous amount of room when passing; however, there are biking fatalities every year, so be alert and cautious, especially when approaching blind intersections, of which Seattle has many. You must wear a helmet at all times (it's the law) and be sure to lock up your bike—bikes do get stolen, even in quiet residential neighborhoods.

The Seattle Parks Department sponsors Bicycle Sundays on various weekends from May through September. On these Sundays, a 4-mile stretch of Lake Washington Boulevard—from Mt. Baker Beach to Seward Park—is closed to motor vehicles. Many riders continue around the 2-mile loop at Seward Park and back to Mt. Baker Beach to complete a 10-mile, car-free ride. Check with the **Seattle Parks and Recreation Department** (☎ *206/684–4075* ⊕ *www.seattle.gov/parks/bicyclesunday*) for a complete schedule.

The trail that circles **Green Lake** is popular with cyclists, though runners and walkers can impede fast travel. The city-maintained **Burke-Gilman Trail**, a slightly less congested path, follows an abandoned railroad line 14 miles roughly following Seattle's waterfront from Ballard to Kenmore, at the north end of Lake Washington. (From there, serious cyclists can continue on the Sammamish River Trail to Marymoor Park in Redmond; in all, the trail spans 42 miles between Seattle and Issaquah.) **Discovery Park** is a very tranquil place to tool around in. **Myrtle Edwards Park**, north of Pier 70, has a two-lane waterfront path for biking and running. The **islands of the Puget Sound** are also easily explored by bike (there are rental places by the ferry terminals), though keep in mind that Bainbridge, Whidbey, and the San Juans all have some tough hills.

King County has more than 100 miles of paved and nearly 70 miles of unpaved routes, including the Sammamish River, Interurban, Green River, Cedar River, Snoqualmie Valley, and Soos Creek trails. For more information, contact the **King County Parks and Recreation** office (☎ *206/296–8687*).

RENTALS

Montlake Bicycle Shop. This shop a mile south of the University of Washington and within easy riding distance of the Burke-Gilman Trail rents mountain bikes, road bikes, basic cruisers, and tandems. Prices range from $50 to $110 for the day, with discounts for longer rentals (credit card hold required). If you find yourself on the Eastside, you can rent a bike from its Kirkland branch. ⊠ 2223 24th Ave. E, Montlake ☎ 206/329–7333 ⊕ www.montlakebike.com ⊠ Kirkland Bicycle Shop, 208 Kirkland Ave., Kirkland ☎ 425/828–3800 ⊕ www.montlakebike.com.

BOATING AND KAYAKING

Fodor's Choice
★

Agua Verde Cafe & Paddle Club. Start out by renting a kayak and paddling along either the Lake Union shoreline, with its hodgepodge of funky-to-fabulous houseboats and dramatic Downtown vistas, or Union Bay on Lake Washington, with its marshes and cattails. Afterward, take in the lakefront as you wash down some Mexican food (halibut tacos, anyone?) with a margarita. Kayaks and stand-up paddleboards are available March through October and are rented by the hour—$18 for single kayaks, $24 for doubles, and $23 for SUPs. It pays to paddle midweek: the third hour is free on weekdays. ⊠ 1303 N.E. Boat St., University District ☎ 206/545–8570 ⊕ www.aguaverde.com.

Alki Kayak Tours & Adventure Center. For a variety of daylong guided kayak outings—from a Seattle sunset sea kayak tour to an Alki Point lighthouse tour—led by experienced, fun staff, try this great outfitter in West Seattle. In addition to kayaks, you can also rent stand-up paddleboards, skates, fishing boats, and longboards here. Custom sea-kayaking adventures can be set up, too. To rent a kayak without a guide, you must be an experienced kayaker; otherwise, sign up for one of the fascinating guided outings (the popular sunset tour is $69 per person). ⊠ 1660 Harbor Ave. SW, West Seattle ☎ 206/953–0237 ⊕ kayakalki.com.

The Center for Wooden Boats. Located on the southern shore of Lake Union, Seattle's free maritime heritage museum is a bustling community hub. Thousands of Seattleites rent rowboats and small wooden sailboats here every year; the center also offers workshops, demonstrations, and classes. Rentals for nonmembers range from $24 to $40 per hour. There's also a $25 skills-check fee for sailing. Free half-hour guided sails and steamboat rides are offered on Sunday from 11 am to 4 pm (arrive an hour early to reserve a spot). ⊠ 1010 Valley St., Lake Union ☎ 206/382–2628 ⊕ www.cwb.org.

Green Lake Boathouse. This shop is the source for canoes, paddleboats, sailboats, kayaks, stand-up paddleboards, and rowboats to take out on Green Lake's calm waters. On beautiful summer afternoons, however, be prepared to spend most of your time dealing with traffic, both in the parking lot and on the water. Fees are $20 an hour for paddleboats, single kayaks, rowboats, and stand-up paddleboards, $30 an hour for sailboats. Don't confuse this place with the Green Lake Small Craft Center, which offers sailing programs but no rentals. ⊠ 7351 E. Green Lake Dr. N, Green Lake ☎ 206/527–0171 ⊕ www.greenlakeboatrentals.net.

Northwest Outdoor Center. This center on Lake Union's west side rents one- or two-person kayaks (it also has a few triples) by the hour or day, including equipment and basic or advanced instruction. The hourly rate is $16 for a single and $23 for a double (costs are figured in 10-minute increments after the first hour). For the more vertically inclined, the center also rents out stand-up paddleboards for $18 an hour. In summer, reserve at least three days ahead. NWOC also runs sunset tours near Golden Gardens Park and moonlight tours of Portage Bay. ⊠ *2100 Westlake Ave. N, Lake Union* ☎ *206/281–9694* ⊕ *www.nwoc.com.*

GOLF

Gold Mountain Golf Complex. Most people make the trek to Bremerton to play the Olympic Course, a beautiful and challenging par 72 that is widely considered the best public course in Washington. The older, less-sculpted Cascade Course is also popular; it's better suited to those new to the game. There are four putting greens, a driving range, and a striking clubhouse with views of the Belfair Valley. Prime-time greens fees are $29 to $45 for the Cascade and $40 to $70 for the Olympic. Carts are $16.50 prior to twilight and $10 after. You can drive all the way to Bremerton via Interstate 5, or you can take the car ferry to Bremerton from Pier 52. The trip will take roughly 1½ hours no matter which way you do it, but the ferry ride (60 minutes) might be a more pleasant way to spend a large part of the journey. Note, however, that the earliest departure time for the ferry is 6 am, so this option won't work for very early tee times. ⊠ *7263 W. Belfair Valley Rd., Bremerton* ☎ *360/415–5433* ⊕ *www.goldmt.com.*

Jefferson Park. This golf complex has views of the city skyline *and* Mt. Rainier. The par-27, 9-hole course has a lighted driving range with heated stalls that's open from dusk until midnight. And the 18-hole, par-72 main course is one of the city's best. Greens fees are $35 on weekends and $30 on weekdays for the 18-hole course; you can play the 9-hole course for $8.50 daily. Carts are $28 and $18, and $6 buys you a bucket of 34 balls at the driving range. You can book tee times online up to 10 days in advance or by phone up to 7 days in advance. ⊠ *4101 Beacon Ave. S., Beacon Hill* ☎ *206/762–4513* ⊕ *www.seattlegolf.com.*

HIKING

■TIP➔ Within Seattle city limits, the best nature trails can be found in Discovery Park, Lincoln Park, Seward Park, and at the Washington Park Arboretum. Some trailheads require parking permits, but they're marked and you can usually pay on-site.

Cougar Mountain Regional Wildland Park. This spectacular park in the "Issaquah Alps" has more than 36 miles of hiking trails and 12 miles of bridle trails within its 3,000-plus acres. The Indian Trail, believed to date back 8,000 years, was part of a trade route that Native Americans used to reach North Bend and the Cascades. Thick pine forests rise to spectacular mountaintop views; there are waterfalls, deep caves, and the remnants of a former mining town. Local residents include deer, black bears, bobcats, bald eagles, and pileated woodpeckers, among many other woodland creatures. ⊠ *18201 S.E. Cougar Mountain Dr., Issaquah ✛ From Downtown Seattle take I–90 E; follow signs to park beyond Issaquah.*

Mt. Si. This thigh-buster is where mountaineers train to climb grueling Mt. Rainier. Mt. Si offers a challenging hike with views of a valley (slightly marred by the suburbs) and the Olympic Mountains in the distance. The main trail to Haystack Basin, 8 miles round-trip, climbs some 4,000 vertical feet, but there are several obvious places to rest or turn around if you'd like to keep the hike to 3 or 4 miles. Note that solitude is in short supply here—this is an extremely popular trail thanks to its proximity to Seattle. On the bright side, it's one of the best places to witness the local hikers and trail runners in all their weird and wonderful splendor. ⊠ *North Bend ✛ Take I–90 E to Exit 31 (toward North Bend). Turn onto North Bend Way and then make left onto Mt. Si Rd. and follow that road to trailhead parking lot ⊕ www.mountsi.com.*

Fodor's Choice **Snow Lake.** Washington State's most popular wilderness trail may be
★ crowded at times, but the scenery and convenience of this hike make it a classic. Though very rocky in stretches—you'll want to wear sturdy shoes—the 8-mile round-trip sports a relatively modest 1,300-foot elevation gain; the views of the Alpine Lakes Wilderness are well worth the sweat. The glimmering waters of Snow Lake await hikers at the trail's end; summer visitors will find abundant wildflowers, huckleberries, and wild birds. ⊠ *Snoqualmie Pass ✛ Take I–90 E to Exit 52 (toward Snoqualmie Pass West). Turn left (north), cross under freeway, and continue on to trailhead, located in parking lot at Alpental Ski Area ⊕ www.wta.org/go-hiking/hikes/snow-lake-1.*

SHOPPING

To find many of the stores that are truly special to Seattle—such as boutiques featuring handmade frocks from local designers, independent record stores run by encyclopedic-minded music geeks, cozy used-book shops that smell of paper and worn wood shelves—you'll have to branch out to Capitol Hill, Queen Anne, and northern neighborhoods like Ballard. Shopping these areas will give you a better feel for the character of the city and its quirky inhabitants, all while you score that new dress or nab gifts for your friends.

DOWNTOWN AND BELLTOWN

BOOKS AND PRINTED MATERIAL

Fodor's Choice **Peter Miller Architectural & Design Books and Supplies.** Aesthetes and archi-
★ tects haunt this shop, which is stocked floor to ceiling with all things design. Rare, international architecture, art, and design books mingle with high-end products from Alessi and Iittala; sleek notebooks, bags, portfolios, and drawing tools round out the collection. This is a great shop for quirky, unforgettable gifts, like a Black Dot sketchbook, an Arne Jacobsen wall clock, or an aerodynamic umbrella. ⊠ *2326 2nd Ave., Belltown* ☎ *206/441–4114* ⊕ *www.petermiller.com.*

TOP SPOTS TO SHOP

Shopping becomes decidedly less fun when it involves driving around and circling for parking. You're better off limiting your all-day shopping tours to one of several key areas than planning to do a citywide search for a particular item. The following areas have the greatest concentration of shops and the greatest variety.

5th and 6th Avenues, Downtown. Depending on where you're staying, you may not need to drive to this area, but if you do, the parking garage at Pacific Place mall (at 600 Pine Street) always seems to have a space somewhere. Tackling either Pacific Place or the four blocks of 5th and 6th avenues between Olive Way and University Street will keep you very busy for a day.

1st Avenue, Belltown. From Wall Street to Pine Street, you'll find clothing boutiques, shoe stores, and some sleek home- and architectural-design stores. First Avenue and Pike Street brings you to the Pike Place Market. There are numerous pay parking lots on both 1st and 2nd avenues.

Pioneer Square. Walk or bus here if you can. Art galleries are the main draw, along with some home-decor and rug shops. If you do drive, many pay lots in the neighborhood participate in the "Parking Around the Square" program, which works with local businesses to offer shoppers validated parking; the website ⊕ www.pioneersquare.org lists the lots and stores that offer it.

International District. Parking in the I.D. can be hit or miss depending on the time of day. It's best if you can walk here from Downtown or take a quick bus ride over. If you do drive, go directly to the Uwajimaya parking lot. It validates for purchases, and it's a safe bet you'll be buying something here.

Pike–Pine Corridor, Capitol Hill. The best shopping in the Hill is on Pike and Pine Streets between Melrose Avenue and 10th Avenue East. Most of the stores are on Pike Street; Pine's best offerings are clustered on the western end of the avenue between Melrose and Summit. There are pay lots on Pike Street (near Broadway) and one on Summit by East Olive Way (next to the Starbucks).

Fremont and Ballard. Start in Fremont's small retail center, which is mostly along 36th Street. You may be able to snag street parking. After you've exhausted Fremont's shops, it's an easy drive over to Ballard. Ballard Avenue and N.W. Market Street are chockablock with great boutiques. Finding parking in Ballard can be tricky on weekends, but it's possible.

9

CHOCOLATE

Fodor's Choice ★ **Fran's Chocolates.** A Seattle institution (helmed by Fran Bigelow) has been making quality chocolates for decades. Its world-famous salted caramels are transcendent—a much-noted favorite of the Obama family, in fact—as are delectable truffles, which are spiked with oolong tea, single-malt whiskey, or raspberry, among other flavors. This shop is housed in the Four Seasons on 1st Avenue—how very elegant, indeed! ⊠ *1325 1st Ave., Downtown* ☎ *206/682–0168* ⊕ *www.franschocolates.com.*

CLOTHING

Pirkko. Fans of Scandinavian fashion and home decor will adore this little boutique just outside Pike Place Market. Specializing in Finnish design, Pirkko stocks a covetable selection of Marimekko—the brand's iconic graphic prints adorn clothing, handbags, and home accessories—along with Ilse Jacobsen, Iittala, Hasbeens, and more. ⊠ *1407 1st Ave., Seattle* ☎ *206/223–1112* ⊕ *www.pirkko.com.*

DEPARTMENT STORES

Fodor'sChoice ★ **Nordstrom.** Seattle's own retail giant sells quality clothing, accessories, cosmetics, jewelry, and lots of shoes—in keeping with its roots in footwear—including many hard-to-find sizes. Peruse the various floors for anything from trendy jeans to lingerie to goods for the home. A sky bridge on the store's fourth floor will take you to Pacific Place Shopping Center. Deservedly renowned for its impeccable customer service, the busy Downtown flagship has a concierge desk and valet parking. ■**TIP**➜ The Nordstrom Rack store at 1st Avenue and Spring Street, close to Pike Place Market, has great deals on marked-down items. ⊠ *500 Pine St., Downtown* ☎ *206/628–2111* ⊕ *shop. nordstrom.com.*

MUSIC

Singles Going Steady. If punk rock is more to you than anarchy symbols sewn on Target sweatshirts, then stop here. Punk and its myriad subgenres on CD and vinyl are specialties, though they also stock rockabilly, indie rock, and hip-hop. It's a nice foil to the city's indie-rock-dominated record shops, and a good reminder that Belltown is still more eclectic than its rising rents may indicate. ⊠ *2219 2nd Ave., Belltown* ☎ *206/441–7396.*

WINE AND SPECIALTY FOODS

Fodor'sChoice ★ **DeLaurenti Specialty Food and Wine.** Attention foodies: clear out your hotel minibars and make room for delectable treats from DeLaurenti. And, if you're planning any picnics, swing by here first. Imported meats and cheeses crowd the deli cases, and packaged delicacies pack the aisles. Stock up on hard-to-find items like truffle-infused olive oil or excellent Italian vintages from the wine shop upstairs. Spring travelers will also want to stop by DeLaurenti's nosh nirvana, called Cheesefest, in May. ⊠ *Pike Place Market, 1435 1st Ave., Downtown* ☎ *206/622–0141* ⊕ *www.delaurenti.com.*

Pike and Western Wine Shop. These folks have spent nearly four decades carving out a reputation as one of the best wine markets in the city. With more than 1,000 wines personally selected from the Pacific Northwest and around the world, this shop offers expert advice from friendly salespeople. ⊠ *1934 Pike Pl., Downtown* ☎ *206/441–1307* ⊕ *www. pikeandwestern.com.*

SOUTH LAKE UNION AND QUEEN ANNE

BOOKS AND MUSIC

FAMILY **Queen Anne Book Company.** This beloved Seattle bookstore is well-known for its friendly, knowledgeable staff and extensive book selection. Pop in for children's storytelling sessions on the third Sunday of every month, or browse at night and catch one of the many author events. After you grab your new books, slip into El Diablo, the cute coffee shop adjacent to the bookstore. ✉ *1811 Queen Anne Ave. N, Queen Anne* ☎ *206/283–5624* ⊕ *www.queenannebooks.com.*

CLOTHING

Peridot Boutique. Strapless animal-print pocket dresses, retro gingham tops, and ruffly skirts abound in this contemporary women's boutique in lower Queen Anne. The prices are reasonable, the accessories are abundant, and local designers are represented as well. ✉ *2135 Queen Anne Ave. N, Queen Anne* ☎ *206/687–7130* ⊕ *www.peridotboutique.wordpress.com.*

OUTDOORS CLOTHING AND EQUIPMENT

Fodor'sChoice **REI.** The enormous flagship for Recreational Equipment, Inc. (REI) has
★ an incredible selection of outdoor gear—polar-fleece jackets, wool socks, down vests, hiking boots, raingear, and much more—as well as its own 65-foot climbing wall. The staff is extremely knowledgeable; there always seems to be enough help on hand, even when the store is busy. You can test things out on the mountain-bike test trail or in the simulated rain booth. REI also rents gear such as tents, sleeping bags, skis, snowshoes, and backpacks. Bonus: the outdoor behemoth offers an hour of free parking. ✉ *222 Yale Ave. N, South Lake Union* ☎ *206/223–1944* ⊕ *www.rei.com.*

PIONEER SQUARE

ART AND GIFTS

Agate Designs. Amateur geologists, curious kids, and anyone fascinated by fossils and gems should make a trip to this store that's almost like a museum (but a lot more fun). Between the 500-million-year-old fossils and the 250-pound amethyst geodes, there's no shortage of eye-popping items on display. ✉ *120 1st Ave. S, Pioneer Square* ☎ *206/621–3063* ⊕ *www.agatedesigns.com.*

Glass House Studio. Seattle's oldest glassblowing studio and gallery lets you watch fearless artisans at work in the "hot shop." Some of the best glass artists in the country work out of this shop, and many of their impressive studio pieces are for sale, along with around 40 other Northwest artists represented by the shop. ✉ *311 Occidental Ave. S, Pioneer Square* ☎ *206/682–9939* ⊕ *www.glasshouse-studio.com.*

CLOTHING AND ACCESSORIES

Velouria. The ultimate antidote to mass-produced, unimaginative women's clothes can be found in this exquisitely feminine shop where independent West Coast designers rule. Much on offer is one of a kind: handmade, '70s-inspired jumpsuits; romantic, demure eyelet dresses; and clever screen-printed tees. Superb bags, delicate jewelry, and fun cards and gifts are also on display. It's worth a look just to check out all the wearable art. ✉ *145 S. King St., Pioneer Square* ☎ *206/788–0330* ⊕ *shopvelouria.com.*

9

CAPITOL HILL

BOOKS AND MUSIC

Fodor'sChoice **Elliott Bay Book Company.** A major reason to visit this landmark book-
★ store—formerly a longtime haunt in Pioneer Square, hence the name—is
the great selection of Pacific Northwest history books and fiction titles
by local authors, complete with handwritten recommendation cards
from the knowledgeable staff. A big selection of bargain books, underground parking, lovely skylights, and an appealing café all sweeten the
deal—and the hundreds of author events held every year mean that
nearly every day is an exciting one for dropping by. ⊠ *1521 10th Ave.,
Capitol Hill* ☎ *206/624–6600* ⊕ *www.elliottbaybook.com.*

Wall of Sound. If you're on the hunt for Japanese avant-rock on LP,
antiwar spoken word, spiritual reggae with Afro-jazz undertones, or old
screen-printed show posters, you've found the place. Obscure, experimental, adventurous, and good? Wall of Sound probably has it. ⊠ *315
E. Pine St., Capitol Hill* ☎ *206/441–9880* ⊕ *www.wosound.com.*

CLOTHING

Le Frock. It may look like just another overcrowded consignment shop,
but among the racks of Seattle's classiest vintage and consignment store
you'll find classic steals for men and women from Burberry, Fendi,
Dior, Missoni, and the like. Contemporary looks from Prada, Gucci,
and Chanel round out the collection. ⊠ *613 E. Pike St., Capitol Hill*
☎ *206/623–5339* ⊕ *www.lefrockonline.com.*

Totokaelo. Style mavens (including men) who wouldn't be caught dead
in fleece flock to this fashion-forward cult boutique, which stocks edgy
lines like Marni, Maison Martin Margiela, Rachel Comey, Acne Studios, and Dries Van Noten. The gorgeously spare space—a converted
1940s auto shop—plays blank canvas for the covetable clothing and
shoes, as well as the store's smartly curated selection of "art-objects,"
such as lighting, textiles, ceramics, linens, and art, along with eye-catch-
ing pieces from Totokaelo's in-house furniture brand. ⊠ *1523 10th Ave.,
Capitol Hill* ☎ *206/623–3582* ⊕ *www.totokaelo.com.*

GIFTS AND HOME DECOR

NuBe Green. An emphasis on recycled goods and sustainability is the mission of this well-presented store anchoring a corner of the Oddfellows
Building. All items are sourced and made in the United States, including
linens, candles, glass art, and even dog beds made from old jeans. Our
favorite items are by local **Alchemy Goods** (*www.alchemygoods.com*),
which recycles bicycle tubes, reclaimed vinyl mesh, and seatbelts into
distinctively cool wallets and messenger bags. ⊠ *921 E. Pine St., Capitol
Hill* ☎ *206/402–4515* ⊕ *www.nubegreen.com.*

SPECIALTY FOODS

Melrose Market. Seattle is famously foodie-friendly, and this historic triangular building packs several of the city's best culinary shops under
one roof. Browse and sample artisanal meats, cheeses, shellfish, and
liquor, all with locavore leanings. Unlike Pike Place, the relatively
pint-size Melrose is more a hipster haunt than a tourist trap: Anthony
Bourdain and the Seattle *Top Chef* contestants have been spotted here.
⊠ *1501–1535 Melrose Ave., Capitol Hill* ⊕ *melrosemarketseattle.com.*

FREMONT

OUTDOOR CLOTHING

evo. For outdoor gear with an edgy vibe, locals head to evo, which specializes in snow sports gear and also carries a solid selection of hip street clothes for men and women. You'll find everything you need to shred Washington's big mountains in style, from fat powder skis and snowboards with wild graphics to flashy ski jackets and thick woolen beanies. Occupying a two-level space at the Fremont Collective building, evo also has a gallery space that hosts art shows. Traveling with skateboarders? Seattle's only indoor skate park, All Together Skate Park, is right next door. ✉ *3500 Stone Way N, Fremont* ☎ *206/973–4470* ⊕ *www.evo.com.*

BALLARD

BOOKS AND MUSIC

FAMILY **Secret Garden Bookshop.** Named after the Francis Hodgson Burnett classic, this cozy shop has been delighting readers for 34 years. A favorite of teachers, librarians, and parents, the store stocks a wide array of imaginative literature and thoughtful nonfiction for all ages; their children's section is particularly notable. ✉ *2214 N.W. Market St., Ballard* ☎ *206/789–5006* ⊕ *www.secretgardenbooks.com.*

CLOTHING AND ACCESSORIES

FAMILY **Clover.** What's easily the cutest children's store in town carries wonderful handcrafted wooden toys, European figurines, works by local artists, and a variety of swoon-worthy, perfectly crafted little clothes. Even shoppers without children will be smitten—it's hard to resist the vintage French Tintin posters, knit-wool cow dolls, and classic figurines. ✉ *5333 Ballard Ave. NW, Ballard* ☎ *206/782–0715* ⊕ *www.clovertoys.com.*

SIDE TRIPS FROM SEATTLE: THE PUGET SOUND ISLANDS

The islands of Puget Sound—particularly Bainbridge, Vashon, and Whidbey—are easy and popular day trips for Seattle visitors, and riding the Washington State ferries is half the fun. There are a few classic inns and B&Bs in the historic towns of Langley and Coupeville if you want to spend the night. It's definitely worth planning your trip around mealtimes, because the islands of Puget Sound have top-notch restaurants serving local foods—including locally grown produce, seafood, and even island-raised beef. On Vashon Island, Sea Breeze farm's restaurant La Boucherie is at the top of the locavore pack; Bainbridge, Whidbey, and the San Juans also have a myriad of small farms and charming restaurants worth a visit. Seafood is a big draw: local crab, salmon, and shellfish should be on your not-to-miss list, including the world-renowned Penn Cove mussels from Whidbey Island.

Whidbey Island has the most spectacular natural attractions, but it requires the biggest time commitment to get to (it's 30 miles northwest of Seattle). Bainbridge is the most developed island—it's something of a moneyed bedroom community—with higher-end restaurants and shops supplementing its natural attractions. It's also the easiest to get to—just hop on a ferry from Pier 52 on the Downtown Seattle waterfront. Vashon is the most pastoral of the islands—if you don't like leisurely strolls, beachcombing, or bike rides, you might get bored there quickly. Bainbridge and Whidbey get tons of visitors in summer. Though you'll be able to snag a walk-on spot on the ferry, spaces for cars can fill up, so arrive early. Whidbey is big, so you'll most likely want to tour by car (you can actually drive there, too, as the north end of the island is accessible via Deception Pass), and a car is handy on Bainbridge as well, especially if you want to tour the entire island or visit spectacular Bloedel Reserve. Otherwise, Bainbridge is your best bet if you want to walk on the ferry and tour by foot.

BAINBRIDGE ISLAND

10 minutes west of Seattle by ferry.

Of the three main islands in Puget Sound, Bainbridge has by far the largest population of Seattle commuters. Certain parts of the island are dense enough to have rush-hour traffic problems, while other areas retain a semirural, small-town vibe. Longtime residents work hard to keep parks and protected areas out of the hands of condominium builders, and despite the increasing number of stressed-out commuters, the island still has resident artists, craftspeople, and old-timers who can't be bothered to venture into the big city. Though not as dramatic as Whidbey or as idyllic as Vashon, Bainbridge always makes for a pleasant day trip.

The ferry, which departs from the Downtown terminal at Pier 52, drops you off in the charming village of Winslow. Along its compact main street, Winslow Way, it's easy to while away an afternoon among the antiques shops, art galleries, bookstores, and cafés. There are two bike-rental shops in Winslow, too, if you plan on touring the island on two wheels. Getting out of town on a bike can be a bit nerve-racking, as the traffic to and from the ferry terminal is thick, and there aren't a lot of dedicated bike lanes, but you'll soon be on quieter country roads. Be sure to ask for maps at the rental shop, and if you want to avoid the worst of the island's hills, ask the staff to go over your options with you before you set out.

Many of the island's most reliable dining options are in Winslow, or close to it. You'll also find the delightful Town & Country supermarket on the main stretch if you want to pick up some provisions for a picnic, though you can also easily do that in Seattle at the Pike Place Market before you get on the ferry.

GETTING HERE AND AROUND

Unless you're coming from Tacoma or points farther south, or from the Olympic Peninsula, the only way to get to Bainbridge is via the ferry from Pier 52 Downtown. Round-trip fares start at $7.70 per person; round-trip fare for a car and driver is $32.80. Crossing time is 35 minutes. If you confine your visit to the village of Winslow, as many visitors do, then you won't need anything other than a pair of walking shoes. Out on the island, besides driving or biking, the only way to get around is on buses provided by Kitsap Transit. Fares are only $2 one way, but note that since routed buses are for commuters, they may not drop you off quite at the doorstep of the park or attraction you're headed to. Be sure to study the route map carefully or call Kitsap at least a day in advance of your trip to inquire about its Dial-A-Ride services.

Contacts Kitsap Transit. ☎ 800/501–7433 ⊕ *www.kitsaptransit.com.*

ESSENTIALS

Visitor Information Bainbridge Chamber of Commerce. ☎ *206/842–3700* ⊕ *www.bainbridgechamber.com.*

EXPLORING

Bainbridge Island Studio Tour. Twice a year (the second weekend in August and the first weekend in December), the island's artists and craftspeople are in the spotlight when they put their best pieces on display for these three-day events, and you can buy anything from watercolors to furniture directly from the artists. Even if you can't make the official studio tours, check out the website, which has maps and information on studios and shops throughout the island, as well as links to artists' websites. Many of the shops have regular hours, and you can easily put together your own tour. ✉ *Bainbridge Island* ⊕ *www.bistudiotour.com.*

Bainbridge Vineyards. Bainbridge Vineyards has 8 acres of grapes that produce small batches of Pinot Noir, Pinot Gris, and Siegerrebe; it's the only winery in the Seattle area that grows all of its own grapes. Fruit wines are made from the seasonal offerings of neighboring farms. It's open for tastings Friday–Sunday noon–5. ✉ *8989 Day Rd. E, Bainbridge Island* ☎ *206/842–9463* ⊕ *www.bainbridgevineyards.com.*

Fodor's Choice
★

Bloedel Reserve. This 150-acre internationally recognized preserve is a stunning mix of natural woodlands and beautifully landscaped gardens—including a moss garden, Japanese garden, a reflection pool, and the impressive former Bloedel estate home. Dazzling rhododendrons and azaleas bloom in spring, and Japanese maples colorfully signal autumn's arrival. Picnicking is not permitted, and you'll want to leave the pooch behind—pets are not allowed on the property, even if they stay in the car. Check the website's events page for special events, lectures, and exhibits. ✉ *7571 N.E. Dolphin Dr., 6 miles west of Winslow, via Hwy. 305, Bainbridge Island* ☎ *206/842–7631* ⊕ *www.bloedelreserve.org* ✍*$15.*

Fort Ward Park. On the southwest side of the island is this lovely and tranquil 137-acre park. There are 2 miles of hiking trails through forest, a long stretch of (sometimes) sun-drenched rocky beach, several picnic tables, and even a spot for scuba diving. Along with views of the water and the Olympic Mountains, you might be lucky and get a peek of Mt. Rainier—or of the massive sea lions that frequent the near-shore waters. A loop trail through the park is suitable for all ability levels, and will take you past vestiges of the park's previous life as a military installation. ✉ *Fort Ward Hill Rd. NE, Bainbridge Island* ✛ *Take Hwy. 305 out of Winslow; turn west on High School Rd. and follow signs to park* ☎ *206/842–3931* ⊕ *www.biparks.org/parksandfacilities/pkftward.html.*

9

WHERE TO EAT

$ ✕ **Blackbird Bakery.** A great place to grab a cup of coffee and a snack
BAKERY   before exploring the island serves up rich pastries and cakes along
with quiche, soups, and a good selection of teas and espresso drinks.
Though there is some nice window seating that allows you to watch the
human parade on Winslow Way, the place gets very crowded, especially
when the ferries come in, so you might want to take your order to go.
Ⓢ *Average main: $5* ✉ *210 Winslow Way E, Winslow* ☎ *206/780–1322*
⊕ *www.blackbirdbakery.com* ▭ *No credit cards* ☯ *No dinner.*

$$ ✕ **Café Nola.** This is the best option on the island for something a little
BISTRO   fancier than pub grub or picnic fare. The bistro setting is pleasant, with
pale yellow walls, white tablecloths, and jazz music, and there's a small
patio area for alfresco dining. Ⓢ *Average main: $22* ✉ *101 Winslow
Way E, Winslow* ☎ *206/842–3822* ⊕ *www.cafenola.com.*

$ ✕ **Harbor Public House.** An 1881 estate home overlooking Eagle Harbor
SEAFOOD   was renovated to create this casual pub and restaurant at Winslow's
Harbor Marina, where a complimentary boat tie-up is available for pub
patrons. Local seafood—including steamed mussels, clams, and oyster
sliders—plus burgers, fish-and-chips, and poutine are typical fare, and
there are 12 beers on tap. Ⓢ *Average main: $16* ✉ *231 Parfitt Way SW,
Winslow* ☎ *206/842–0969* ⊕ *www.harbourpub.com.*

VASHON ISLAND

20 minutes by ferry from West Seattle.

Vashon is the most peaceful and rural of the islands easily reached from
the city, home to fruit growers, commune-dwelling hippies, rat-race
dropouts, and Seattle commuters.

Biking, beachcombing, picnicking, and kayaking are the main activi-
ties here. A tour of the 13-mile-long island will take you down country
lanes and past orchards and lavender farms. There are several artists'
studios and galleries on the island, as well as a small commercial district
in the center of the island, where a farmers' market is a highlight every
Saturday from May to October. The popular Strawberry Festival takes
place every July.

GETTING HERE AND AROUND

Washington State Ferries leave from Fauntleroy in West Seattle (about 9
miles southwest of Downtown) for the 20-minute ride to Vashon Island.
The ferry docks at the northern tip of the island. Round-trip fares are
$5.20 per person or $22.05 for a car and driver. A water taxi also goes
to Vashon from Pier 50 on the Seattle waterfront, but it's primarily
for commuters, operating only on weekdays during commuter hours.
One-way fares are $5. There's limited bus service on the island; the
best way to get around is by car or by bicycle (bring your own or rent
in Seattle. Note that there's a huge hill as you immediately disembark
the ferry dock and head up to town). The site ⊕ *www.vashonchamber.
com* is also a good source of information.

ESSENTIALS

Visitor Information Vashon-Maury Island Chamber of Commerce. ✉ *17141 Vashon Hwy. SW, across from Ober Park, Vashon* ☎ *206/463–6217* 🌐 *www.vashonchamber.com.*

EXPLORING

Jensen Point and Burton Acres Park. Vashon has many parks and protected areas. This park, on the lush Burton Peninsula overlooking Quartermaster Harbor, is home to 64 acres of secluded hiking and horseback-riding trails. The adjacent Jensen Point, a 4-acre shoreline park, has picnic tables, a swimming beach, and kayak and paddleboard rentals (May through September). ✉ *8900 S.W. Harbor Dr., Vashon* ✣ *From ferry terminal, take Vashon Hwy. SW to S.W. Burton Dr. and turn left. Turn left on 97 Ave. SW and follow it around as it becomes S.W. Harbor Dr.* 🌐 *www.vashonparks.org.*

Point Robinson Park. You can stroll along the beach, which is very picturesque thanks to **Point Robinson Lighthouse.** The lighthouse is typically open to the public from noon to 4 on Sunday during the summer; call to arrange a tour or rent out the keeper's quarters by the week. ✉ *3705 S.W. Pt. Robinson Rd., Vashon* ☎ *206/463–9602* 🌐 *www.vashonparks.org.*

Vashon Allied Arts. The best representative of the island's diverse arts community presents monthly exhibits and events that span all mediums, including dance, chamber music, and art lectures. The gallery's exhibits rotate monthly, featuring local and Northwest artists, and Heron's Nest (17600 Vashon Highway SW, 206/463–5252), the affiliated gift shop in town, is where you'll find fine art and handcrafted items by local artists. ✉ *19704 Vashon Hwy.* ☎ *206/463–5131* 🌐 *www.vashonalliedarts.org.*

WHERE TO EAT

$$ AMERICAN 🍴 **Hardware Store.** This all-day restaurant's unusual name comes from its former life as a mom-and-pop hardware shop—it occupies the oldest commercial building on Vashon, and certainly looks like a relic from the outside. Inside, you'll find a charming restaurant that's a cross between a bistro and an upscale diner. [$] *Average main: $17* ✉ *17601 Vashon Hwy. SW, Vashon* ☎ *206/463–1800* 🌐 *www.thsrestaurant.com.*

$$$$ FRENCH 🍴 **La Boucherie and Sea Breeze Farm.** La Boucherie, the restaurant at the "beyond organic" Sea Breeze Farm, is a much-discussed outpost of local cuisine serving meats, poultry, and produce grown on or very close to the property. As a result, the menu is highly seasonal, but it always highlights Vashon's growers and farmers. [$] *Average main: $125* ✉ *17635 100th Ave. SW, Vashon* ☎ *206/567–4628* 🌐 *www.seabreezefarm.net.*

$ THAI Fodor's Choice ★ 🍴 **May Kitchen + Bar.** Here's another reason for city dwellers to hop a ferry to come to Vashon for dinner. This is where sophisticated foodies swoon over delectable and highly authentic Thai dishes. [$] *Average main: $15* ✉ *17614 Vashon Hwy. SW, Vashon* ☎ *206/408–7196* 🌐 *www.maykitchen.com* 🕓 *Closed Mon. and Tues. No lunch.*

9

WHIDBEY ISLAND

20 minutes by ferry from Mukilteo (20 miles north of Seattle) to Clinton, at the southern end of Whidbey Island, or drive north 87 miles to Deception Pass at the north end of the island.

Whidbey is a blend of low pastoral hills, evergreen and oak forests, meadows of wildflowers (including some endemic species), sandy beaches, and dramatic bluffs with a few pockets of unfortunate suburban sprawl. It's a great place for a scenic drive, viewing sunsets over the water, taking ridge hikes that give you uninterrupted views of the Strait of Juan de Fuca, walking along miles of rugged seaweed-strewn beaches, and for boating or kayaking along the protected shorelines of Saratoga Passage, Holmes Harbor, Penn Cove, and Skagit Bay.

The best beaches are on the west side, where wooded and wildflower-bedecked bluffs drop steeply to sand or surf—which can cover the beaches at high tide and can be unexpectedly rough on this exposed shore. Both beaches and bluffs have great views of the shipping lanes and the Olympic Mountains. Maxwelton Beach, with its sand, driftwood, and amazing sunsets, is popular with the locals. Possession Point includes a park and a beach, but it's best known for its popular boat launch. West of Coupeville, Ft. Ebey State Park has a sandy spread and an incredible bluff trail; West Beach is a stormy patch north of the fort with mounds of driftwood. At 35 miles long, Whidbey's island vibe is split between north and south; the historic southern and central towns of Langley and Coupeville are quaint and offer the most to do; Clinton (near the ferry terminal) isn't much of a destination, nor is the sprawling navy town of Oak Harbor farther north. Yet Deception Pass at the island's northern tip offers the most jaw-dropping splendor, so plan enough time to visit both ends of the island. One fun way to see it all is to arrive via the Clinton ferry and drive back to Seattle via Deception Pass, or vice versa.

GETTING HERE AND AROUND

You can reach Whidbey Island by heading north from Seattle on Interstate 5, west on Route 20 onto Fidalgo Island, and south across Deception Pass Bridge. The Deception Pass Bridge links Whidbey to Fidalgo Island. From the bridge it's just a short drive to Anacortes, Fidalgo's main town and the terminus for ferries to the San Juan Islands. It's easier—and more pleasant—to take the 20-minute ferry trip from Mukilteo (30 miles northwest of Seattle) to Clinton, on Whidbey's south end, as long as you don't time your trip on a Friday evening, which could leave you waiting in the car line for hours. Fares are $4.80 per person for walk-ons (round-trip) and $10.30 per car and driver (one way). Be sure to look at a map before choosing your point of entry; the ferry ride may not make sense if your main destination is Deception Pass State Park. Buses on Whidbey Island, provided by Island Transit, are free. Routes are fairly comprehensive, but keep in mind that Whidbey is big—it takes at least 35 minutes just to drive from the southern ferry terminal to the midway point at Coupeville—and if your itinerary is far-reaching, a car is your best bet.

Contact Island Transit. ☎ *800/240–8747* ⊕ *www.islandtransit.org.*

ESSENTIALS

Visitor Information **Central Whidbey Chamber of Commerce.** ✉ *107 S. Main St., Coupeville* ☎ *360/678–5434* 🌐 *www.centralwhidbeychamber.com.*
Langley Chamber of Commerce. ✉ *208 Anthes Ave., Langley* ☎ *360/221–6765* 🌐 *www.visitlangley.com.*

LANGLEY

The historic village of Langley, 7 miles north of Clinton on Whidbey Island, is above a 50-foot-high bluff overlooking Saratoga Passage, which separates Whidbey from Camano Island. A grassy terrace just above the beach is a great place for viewing birds on the water or in the air. On a clear day you can see Mt. Baker in the distance. Upscale boutiques selling art, glass, jewelry, books, and clothing line 1st and 2nd streets in the heart of town.

WHERE TO EAT AND STAY

$$ BISTRO 🍴 **Prima Bistro.** Langley's most popular gathering spot occupies a second-story space on 1st Street, right above the Star Store Grocery. Northwest-inspired French cuisine is the headliner here; classic bistro dishes like steak frites, salade nicoise, and confit of duck leg are favorites. [$] *Average main: $21* ✉ *201½ 1st St., Langley* ☎ *360/221–4060* 🌐 *www.primabistro.com.*

$$$ B&B/INN Fodor's Choice ★ 🏨 **Inn at Langley.** Perched on a bluff above the beach, this concrete-and-wood Frank Lloyd Wright–inspired structure is just steps from the center of town. **Pros:** island luxury; lovely views; amazing restaurant. **Cons:** some rooms can be on the small side; decor is starting to feel slightly dated. [$] *Rooms from: $335* ✉ *400 1st St., Langley* ☎ *360/221–3033* 🌐 *www.innatlangley.com* 🛏 *28 rooms* 🍽 *Breakfast.*

$$ B&B/INN 🏨 **Saratoga Inn.** At the edge of Langley, this cedar-shake, Nantucket-style inn features cozy decor and fireplaces in every room. **Pros:** breathtaking views; cozy interiors. **Cons:** a bit rustic; some small bathrooms; minimum two-night stay. [$] *Rooms from: $195* ✉ *201 Cascade Ave., Langley* ☎ *360/221–5801, 800/698–2910* 🌐 *www.saratogainnwhidbeyisland.com* 🛏 *15 rooms, 1 carriage house* 🍽 *Breakfast.*

SHOPPING

Brackenwood Gallery. At this gallery known for its fine art and well-known Pacific Northwest artists, you can see pieces by Georgia Gerber, a famed island sculptor whose bronze pieces are regionally famous; Western-themed paintings and prints by Bruce Morrow; exquisite stone sculpture by Sharon Spencer; and Northwest landscape paintings by Pete Jordan. ✉ *302 1st St., Langley* ☎ *360/221–2978* 🌐 *www.brackenwoodgallery.com.*

Moonraker Books. Langley's independent bookshop, an institution since 1972, stocks a wonderful and eclectic array of fiction, nonfiction, cookbooks—and, according to the owners, "books you didn't even know you wanted until you stepped inside." ✉ *209 1st St., Langley* ☎ *360/221–6962.*

Museo. This contemporary fine art gallery focused on Northwest and regional artists is known for its glass art, sculpture, and handcrafted jewelry. Artist receptions are held on the first Saturday of each month from 5 to 7 pm. ✉ *215 1st St., Langley* ☎ *360/221–7737* 🌐 *www.museo.cc.*

GREENBANK

About halfway up Whidbey Island, 14 miles northwest of Langley, is the hamlet of Greenbank, home to a loganberry farm encircled by views of the Olympic and Cascade Ranges.

EXPLORING

FAMILY **Greenbank Farm.** You can't miss the huge, chestnut-color, two-story barn with the wine vat out front—the centerpiece to this picturesque, 150-acre property. Greenbank's loganberry wines and dessert wines (for which they are famous) can be sampled daily in the tasting room. The adjacent Whidbey Pies Café creates gourmet sandwiches, soups, and pies, all of which disappear quickly as visitors head for the scattered picnic tables. There's also a specialty cheese shop. Bring your dog (or horse!) and walk the scenic meadow trails. The 1904 barn, which once housed a winery, is now a community center for farmers' markets, concerts, flea markets, and other events, including the famous Loganberry Festival each September. ✉ *765 Wonn Rd., Greenbank* ☎ *360/678–7700* 🌐 *www.greenbankfarm.com* 🎟 *Free.*

Meerkerk Rhododendron Gardens. The 53-acre Meerkerk Rhododendron Gardens contain 1,500 native and hybrid species of rhododendrons and more than 100,000 spring bulbs on 10 acres of display gardens with more than 4 miles of nature trails (a guided tour is available for $10). The flowers are in full bloom in April and May; summer flowers and fall color provide interest later in the year. The 43 remaining acres are kept wild as a nature preserve. Leashed pets are permitted on the gravel paths. ✉ *Hwy. 525 and Resort Rd., Greenbank* ☎ *360/678–1912* 🌐 *www.meerkerkgardens.org* 🎟 *$5.*

WHERE TO STAY

$ B&B/INN 🏨 **Guest House Cottages.** Surrounded by 25 secluded wooded acres, each of these six private cabins, resembling cedar-sided barns with towering stone chimneys, comes with a feather bed, a Jacuzzi, country antiques, a kitchen, and a fireplace. **Pros:** lots of privacy and amenities; good location between Langley and Coupeville. **Cons:** strict cancellation policy of 21 days; basic breakfast foods are provided but you have to make your own. [$] *Rooms from: $165* ✉ *24371 State Rte. 525 E, Christianson Rd., Greenbank* ☎ *360/678–3115, 800/997–3115* 🌐 *www.guesthouselogcottages.com* 🛏 *6 cabins* 🍴 *Some meals.*

9

COUPEVILLE

Restored Victorian houses grace many of the streets in quiet Coupeville, Washington's second-oldest city, on the south shore of Penn Cove, 12 miles north of Greenbank. It also has one of the largest national historic districts in the state, and has been used for filming movies depicting 19th-century New England villages. Stores above the waterfront have maintained their old-fashioned character. Captain Thomas Coupe founded the town in 1852. His house was built the following year, and other houses and commercial buildings were built in the late 1800s. Even though Coupeville is the Island County seat, the town has a laid-back, almost 19th-century air.

EXPLORING

FAMILY **Ebey's Landing National Historic Reserve.** The reserve encompasses a sand-
Fodor'sChoice and-cobble beach, bluffs with dramatic views down the Strait of Juan
★ de Fuca, two state parks (Ft. Casey and Ft. Ebey; see separate listings), and several privately held pioneer farms homesteaded in the
early 1850s. The first and largest reserve of its kind holds nearly 400
nationally registered historic structures (including those located within
the town of Coupeville), most of them from the 19th century. Miles
of trails lead along the beach and through the woods. Cedar Gulch,
south of the main entrance to Ft. Ebey, has a lovely picnic area in a
wooded ravine above the beach. ⊠ *Coupeville* ✛ *From Hwy. 20, turn
south on Main St. in Coupeville. This road turns into Engles Rd. as
you head out of town. Turn right on Hill Rd. and follow it to reserve*
⊕ *www.nps.gov/ebla.*

Ft. Casey and Keystone State Park. The 467-acre Ft. Casey State Park,
on a bluff overlooking sweeping views of Strait of Juan de Fuca and
the Port Townsend ferry landing, was one of three forts (the "Triangle
of Death") built after 1890 to protect the entrance to Admiralty Inlet
from a naval invasion. Look for the concrete gun emplacement and a
couple of 8-inch "disappearing" guns. The charming Admiralty Head
Lighthouse Interpretive Center is north of the gunnery emplacements.
There are also grassy picnic sites, rocky fishing spots, waterfront campsites, and a boat launch. A Washington State Discover Pass is required
($30/year or $10/day; see *www.discoverpass.wa.gov*). Once you're
done exploring the park, take the ferry from here to Port Townsend
for a quick side trip or long lunch. ⊠ *2 miles west of Rte. 20, Coupeville* ☎ *360/678–4519* ⊕ *www.parks.wa.gov/parks* ⊠ *Discover Pass
required; $30/year or $10/day.*

Ft. Ebey State Park. In late May and early June, Ft. Ebey State Park
blazes with native rhododendrons. West of Coupeville on Point Par-
tridge, it has 3 miles of shoreline, campsites in the woods, trails to the
headlands, a freshwater lake for fishing, World War II gun emplacements, wildflower meadows, spectacular views down the Strait of
Juan de Fuca, and miles of hiking and biking trails. A Washington
State Discover Pass is required. ⊠ *3 miles west of Rte. 20, Coupeville*
☎ *360/678–4636* ⊕ *www.parks.wa.gov* ⊠ *Washington State Discover
Pass required ($30/year or $10/day).*

FAMILY **Island County Historical Museum.** Collections include Ice Age relics, mammoth remains, and a strong Native American collection, including cedar
dugout canoes. The square-timber **Alexander Blockhouse** outside dates
from 1855. Note the squared logs and dovetail joints of the corners—no
overlapping log ends. This construction technique was favored by many
western Washington pioneers. ⊠ *908 N.W. Alexander St., Coupeville*
☎ *360/678–3310* ⊠ *$4.*

WHERE TO EAT AND STAY

$$ ✕ **Christopher's on Whidbey.** This warm and casual place is in a house one
PACIFIC block from the waterfront. The menu features many Whidbey favorites,
NORTHWEST including local mussels and clams, and such flavorful fare as raspberry
barbecued salmon, bacon-wrapped pork tenderloin with mushrooms,

CLOSE UP

Woodinville Wineries

Walla Walla wine country is too far to go from Seattle if you've only got a few days; instead, check out Woodinville's excellent wineries. It's only about 22 miles from Seattle's city center. You'll need a car unless you sign up for a guided tour. Check out ⊕ www.woodinvillewinecountry.com for a full list of wineries and touring maps.

WINERIES

There are more than 50 wineries in Woodinville, though most of them don't have tasting rooms. This list provides a good survey, from the big guys to the smallest boutique producers:

Chateau Ste. Michelle (14111 N.E. 145th St. ⊕ www.ste-michelle.com) is the grande dame of the Woodinville wine scene, and perhaps the most recognizable name nationwide. Guided tours of the winery and grounds (which do include a château) are available daily 10:30–4:30. The tasting room is open daily 10–5. Check the website for special events like dinners and concerts.

Columbia Winery (14030 N.E. 145th St. ⊕ www.columbiawinery.com) is another major player with a grand house anchoring its winery. Columbia's tasting room is open Sunday–Tuesday 11–6 and Wednesday–Saturday 11–7. Regular tastings are $10 and private tastings are available for $25 per person.

Novelty Hill-Januik (14710 Woodinville-Redmond Rd. NE ⊕ www.noveltyhilljanuik.com) is often described as the most Napa-esque experience in Woodinville. The tasting room (open daily 11–5) for these sister wineries is sleek and modern. Themed tastings are $7–$10 per person. Brick-oven pizza is available on weekends.

Ross Andrew (14810 N.E. 145th St., No. A-2 www.rossandrewwinery.com) is a newcomer that is already at the top of many enthusiasts' lists for Cabs and Syrah from Columbia Valley grapes and Pinot Blanc and Pinot Gris from Oregon grapes. The tasting room is open Thursday–Monday noon–5 (Saturday until 6).

9

Penn Cove seafood stew, and linguine with a smoked-salmon cream sauce. Ⓢ *Average main: $22* ⊠ *103 N.W. Coveland, Coupeville* ☎ *360/678–5480* ⊕ *www.christophersonwhidbey.com* ⊗ *Closed Mon.*

$$$
SEAFOOD
Fodor'sChoice
★

✕**The Oystercatcher.** A dining destination for foodies from across the Northwest is renowned for its local-inspired cuisine. The simple menu is heavily influenced by fresh, in-season ingredients. Ⓢ *Average main: $30* ⊠ *901 Grace St. NW, Coupeville* ☎ *360/678–0683* ⊕ *www.oystercatcherwhidbey.com* ⊗ *Closed Mon. and Tues. No lunch weekdays.*

$
B&B/INN

🏨**Captain Whidbey Inn.** Over a century old, this venerable historic lodge on a wooded promontory offers a special kind of old-world romance and charm now rarely found, with gleaming log-walled rooms and suites. **Pros:** private cabins with hot tubs; rustic yet comfortable. **Cons:** poor soundproofing in the main motel; shared bathrooms. Ⓢ *Rooms from: $103* ⊠ *2072 Captain Whidbey Inn Rd., off Madrona Way, Coupeville* ☎ *360/678–4097, 800/366–4097* ⊕ *www.captainwhidbey.com* ⇆ *29 rooms, 2 suites, 4 cabins.*

$ B&B/INN 🏨 **Compass Rose Bed and Breakfast.** Inside this stately 1890 Queen Anne Victorian on the National Register of Historic Places, a veritable museum of art, artifacts, and antiques awaits you. **Pros:** wonderful hosts; great breakfast; full of interesting antiques and collectibles. **Cons:** only two rooms, so it gets booked up fast. [$] *Rooms from: $140* ✉ *508 S. Main St., Coupeville* ☎ *360/678–5318, 800/237–3881* 🌐 *www.compassrosebandb.com* 💳 *No credit cards* 🛏 *2 rooms* 🍴 *Breakfast.*

OAK HARBOR

Oak Harbor, about 10 miles north of Coupeville, is the least attractive and least interesting part of Whidbey—it mainly exists to serve the Whidbey Island Naval Air Station, and has none of the historic or pastoral charm of the rest of the island. It is, however, the largest town on the island and the one closest to Deception Pass State Park. If you need to stock up on provisions, you'll find all the big-box stores here, in addition to major supermarkets. In town, the marina, at the east side of the bay, has a picnic area with views of Saratoga Passage and the entrance of Penn Cove.

FAMILY **Deception Pass State Park.** The biggest draw of the park is the historic two-lane Deception Pass Bridge connecting Whidbey Island to Fidalgo Island, about 9 miles north of Oak Harbor. Park the car and walk across in order to get the best views of the dramatic saltwater gorges and churning whirlpools below. Then, spend a few hours walking the 19 miles of rocky shore and beaches, exploring three freshwater lakes, or walking along the many forest and meadow trails. ✉ *Rte. 20, 9 miles north of Oak Harbor, Oak Harbor* ☎ *360/675–2417* 🌐 *www.parks.wa.gov* 🎟 *Daily Discover pass $10 per vehicle; annual $30 (valid at all state parks); campsite fees vary.*

WASHINGTON CASCADE MOUNTAINS AND VALLEYS

With Tacoma, Olympia, and Mt. St. Helens

WELCOME TO WASHINGTON CASCADE MOUNTAINS AND VALLEYS

TOP REASONS TO GO

★ **Take flight:** See a Boeing in mid-construction or a World War II chopper up close at Everett's Paine Field.

★ **Tiptoe through the tulips:** Bike past undulating fields of tulips and other spring blooms in La Conner and Mount Vernon.

★ **Hang in glass houses:** Check out Dale Chihuly's biomorphic sculptures at Tacoma's Museum of Glass.

★ **View a volcano:** Visit Johnston Ridge Observatory, for an eerily close view of Mt. St. Helens.

★ **Paddle around Puget Sound:** Rent a kayak to explore the charming seaside communities of Poulsbo or Gig Harbor.

1 Cascade Foothills and Snohomish County. Short jaunts off the Interstate 5 highway include attending a county fair in Puyallup and winding down a day of hiking or biking near Snoqualmie Pass with a snack in the cute town of Snoqualmie. North of Seattle are two notable port towns, Edmonds and Everett. Edmonds has more of a seaside vibe, with waterfront parks and trendy downtown restaurants, and a ferry terminal serving the islands of Puget Sound. Everett, on the other hand, is devoted to flight, with a Boeing factory tour and a collection of vintage airplanes its main attractions.

2 Bellingham and Skagit Valley. The laid-back, outdoorsy college town of Bellingham is about as close as this area comes to bustle. Although not as tranquil as the central part of the state, the area is about picturesque roads less traveled: the farm roads that connect La Conner and Mount Vernon and the bike and hiking paths that wind through state parks.

3 Kitsap Peninsula. The smaller, less industrial port towns provide beach parks plus glimpses of the region's Scandinavian and logging pasts—a nice snapshot of coastal Washington life that's more accessible than the Olympic Peninsula.

4 Tacoma and Olympia. Immortalized in song by Neko Case as the "dusty old jewel in the South Puget Sound," Tacoma is shining far more brightly these days, with a walkable waterfront that includes several impressive museums and a burgeoning restaurant scene. Farther south is the capital city Olympia, which is the perfect mix of quirky and stately.

5 Mt. Rainier Environs. Washington's rugged southern Cascades region is famous for two massive volcanic peaks, Mt. Rainier and Mt. St. Helens. Small, remote towns are strung along winding, forested country highways that meander through this dramatic area within day-tripping distance of Olympia and Tacoma, even Seattle.

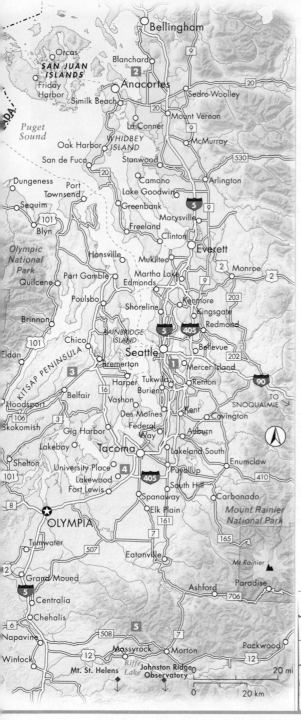

GETTING ORIENTED

Most of the major towns are along—or not far from—the Interstate 5 corridor, stretching from the capital city of Olympia, 60 miles south of Seattle, and on north to Bellingham, 90 miles north of Seattle and the last city of any size before the Canadian border. Many of the cities along the route are ports on Puget Sound. There's even more waterfront out on the Kitsap Peninsula, which is sandwiched between this corridor and the Olympic Peninsula. Three other outlying areas include the western edge of the Skagit Valley, an important agricultural area; Snoqualmie, in the foothills of the Cascades east of Seattle via Interstate 90; and the towns around Mt. Rainier and Mt. St. Helens, which are south of Seattle and just east of the Interstate 5 corridor.

10

Updated by Andrew Collins

The San Juan Islands, the Olympic Peninsula, and the great swaths of midstate wilderness provide Washington's favorite photo ops, but there are plenty of adventures that don't require traveling on ferries or bumping along Forest Service roads.

Up and down Interstate 5 you'll find most of the state's major cities: the ports of Tacoma, Olympia, and Bellingham each have enough cultural and outdoorsy attractions to warrant an overnight or two.

Slightly farther afield you'll find smaller towns with some very specific draws: Poulsbo's proud Norwegian heritage, Port Gamble's painstakingly preserved mill-town vibe, Everett's enthusiasm for all things flight related, whether crafted by Boeing or not, and North Bend and Snoqualmie's breathtaking alpine scenery and friendly feel. And south of Mt. Rainier, towns like Packwood and Ashford in the Cascades offer rugged scenery and jumping-off points for visiting both Rainier and Mt. St. Helens.

Exploring this part of the state, encompassing so many distinct geographical areas like the Kitsap Peninsula and the western fringe of the Skagit Valley, can bring you from industrial areas to tulip fields in one day. From naval warships to thundering falls, there's a lot to see within two hours of Seattle.

WASHINGTON CASCADE MOUNTAINS AND VALLEYS PLANNER

WHEN TO GO

The climate throughout the Interstate 5 corridor, from the Skagit Valley down through Tacoma and Olympia, largely matches that of Seattle, with cool and damp winters (with low temperatures in the upper 30s) and largely dry and sunny summers, with temperatures in the 70s and low 80s. The more favorable weather of late spring through mid-October brings the largest crowds to the region. Rainy winter brings lower hotels rates—and on the Kitsap Peninsula or up in Bellingham and the

Skagit Valley, can be charmingly stormy—ideal for cozying up by the fireplace in a toasty room. In the Snoqualmie area, skiing and other winter sports are popular from December through April, when heavy snows come, although the towns in the foothills receive more rain than snow. In the towns up around Mt. Rainier and Mt. St. Helens, winter snow often brings temporary road closures, and many restaurants, lodges, and attractions are closed or have limited hours from mid-fall through mid-spring; check forecasts and call ahead if venturing into the Cascades at this time.

FESTIVALS AND EVENTS

Skagit Valley Tulip Festival. April brings a monthlong celebration of these iconic flowers that bloom in their millions throughout Mount Vernon and La Conner. ☎ 360/428–5959 ⊕ www.tulipfestival.org.

Fodor'sChoice **Washington State Fair.** This fair in September brings thousands of visi-
★ tors daily over three weeks to Puyallup, a suburb just south of Seattle and southeast of Tacoma, and features concerts, a rodeo, art and cultural exhibits, agricultural shows, and amusement rides. There's also a shorter four-day version of the fair held in Puyallup each April. ☎ 253/845–1771 ⊕ www.thefair.com.

GETTING HERE AND AROUND

AIR TRAVEL

Seattle-Tacoma International Airport (Sea-Tac), 15 miles south of Seattle, is the hub for this region. There are several regional airports, but the only one that sees much action is Bellingham's International Airport, which has direct flights to and from Seattle as well as Maui, Las Vegas, Los Angeles, Oakland, Portland, and several other cities. This small airport is a hub between northwestern Washington and Canada and serves as link to Bellingham's ferry terminal for cruises to British Columbia and beyond.

Contacts Bellingham International. ✉ 4255 Mitchell Way, Bellingham
☎ 360/676–2500 ⊕ www.portofbellingham.com.

AIRPORT TRANSFERS

10

Shuttle Express provides scheduled ride-share service hourly from Sea-Tac Airport to all the cities and larger towns in the region. Bremerton–Kitsap Airporter shuttles passengers from Sea-Tac to points in Tacoma, Bremerton, Port Orchard, Gig Harbor, and Poulsbo ($16–$27 one-way). The Airporter Shuttle/Bellair Charters makes numerous trips daily between Sea-Tac and Bellingham ($39 one-way), with a few stops in between; and between Sea-Tac and North Bend ($25 one way), continuing on to Yakima.

Contacts Airporter Shuttle/Bellair Charters. ☎ 866/235–5247
⊕ www.airporter.com. **Bremerton–Kitsap Airporter.** ☎ 360/876–1737
⊕ www.kitsapairporter.com. **Shuttle Express.** ☎ 425/981–7000
⊕ www.shuttleexpress.com.

BOAT AND FERRY TRAVEL

Washington State Ferries ply Puget Sound, with routes between Seattle and Bremerton and between Edmonds and Kingston on the Key Peninsula.

BUS TRAVEL

Greyhound Lines and Northwestern Trailways cover Washington and the Pacific Northwest. From Seattle, Greyhound connects to Tacoma, Olympia, Bellingham, and several other cities in the region. Pierce County Transit provides bus service around Tacoma. *For more on bus travel throughout the region, see Travel Smart.*

Contacts Pierce County Transit. ☎ *253/581–8000* ⊕ *www.piercetransit.org.*

CAR TRAVEL

Interstate 5 runs south from the Canadian border through Seattle, Tacoma, and Olympia to Oregon and California. Interstate 90 begins in Seattle and runs east through North Bend all the way to Idaho. U.S. 2 meanders east, parallel to Interstate 90, from Everett to Spokane. Highways 7 and 167 connect the Tacoma area with the Puyallup suburbs and towns around Mt. Rainier. U.S. 101 begins northwest of Olympia and traces the coast of the Olympic Peninsula.

TRAIN TRAVEL

Amtrak's Cascades line serves Centralia, Tacoma, Olympia, Seattle, Edmonds, Everett, Mount Vernon, and Bellingham. Sound Transit's Sounder trains (commuter rail, weekdays only) connect Seattle with Edmonds, Mukilteo, and Everett; and Seattle with Tacoma and Puyallup as well as a few other suburbs.

TRAVELING FROM SEATTLE

Tacoma and Everett are good choices for day trips. Tacoma is only 30–40 minutes by car or train from Seattle; Everett are also easy to reach in under an hour, plus seeing their major attractions (exhibits on flight history) doesn't require an overnight. Just don't get stuck driving the Interstate 5 corridor during weekday rush hours or on Sunday night in summer—the chaotic and heavy traffic will sour any outing.

Snoqualmie is also easily visited in a day, as it's close to Seattle, but because it's a popular base for outdoor recreation, many visitors overnight here.

Olympia is far enough from Seattle—it's only about 60 miles, but during the day you'll nearly always hit traffic, so expect a solid 1½ hours in the car—that it's often better for an overnight visit or as a stop on the way to the southern part of the Olympic Peninsula (Ocean Shores or Moclips, for example). You can pick up U.S. 101 on the outskirts of the city. Olympia is also a good leg-stretch between Seattle and Portland and can be part of an itinerary to Mount Rainier National Park or Mount St. Helens National Volcanic Monument—it's a good idea to spend the night near these parks if planning a visit, as they're a good drive from Seattle, and you'll want to get an early start if planning a hike or driving along these winding, narrow forest roads.

RESTAURANTS

Olympia and especially Tacoma have increasingly hip and sophisticated dining scenes, with everything from laid-back cafés to seasonally driven restaurants with water views. After those cities, Gig Harbor and Bellingham have the best food scenes—they're not terribly big, but support fine little crops of notable restaurants. You'll also find good brewpubs and indie coffeehouses in most of the larger towns in the area. Edmonds also has a growing bounty of exceptional eateries.

On the road, refueling takes place at country-style cafés, farm stands, and kitschy or specialty shops like the '50s-style sweets shops of Port Gamble and Snoqualmie or the Norwegian bakeries of Poulsbo. None of these is in short supply, and many eateries, however small, pride themselves on using local ingredients.

HOTELS

Many of the towns listed are easy day trips from Seattle, so staying there is always an option. On the other hand, hotel rates are nearly always lower outside Seattle. Tacoma, Olympia, and Bellingham have the widest variety of accommodations, with pricey hotels, midrange chains, and bed-and-breakfasts. Almost all but the smallest rural towns have midrange chain motels; towns lacking those, like Port Gamble, have at least one B&B. The only truly great luxury resort in the region is the Salish Lodge in Snoqualmie. There are a few other noteworthy hotels in these parts—the Murano in Tacoma, the Chrysalis Inn in Bellingham, and some fine B&Bs elsewhere—but relatively prosaic chains dominate the lodging landscape. *Hotel reviews have been shortened. For full information, visit Fodors.com.*

WHAT IT COSTS IN U.S. DOLLARS				
	$	$$	$$$	$$$$
Restaurants	under $16	$16–$22	$23–$30	over $30
Hotels	under $150	$150–$200	$201–$250	over $250

Restaurant prices are the average cost of a main course at dinner, or if dinner is not served, at lunch. Hotel prices are the lowest cost of a standard double room in high season.

CASCADE FOOTHILLS AND SNOHOMISH COUNTY

10

Flanking the Interstate 5 corridor are gateway towns to the scenically beautiful areas north and east of Seattle: Snoqualmie and North Bend are tried-and-true pit stops for hikers, bikers, and skiers heading over Snoqualmie Pass. The town of Snoqualmie is itself day-trip-worthy, with its stuck-in-time downtown full of vintage railroad cars, and beautiful, easily accessed falls.

The towns north of Seattle are a mixed bag. Edmonds and Everett, both close to Seattle, are important commuter hubs. Edmonds has a major ferry terminal and the more sophisticated dining and shopping scenes. Everett has slightly more tourist appeal because of its connection to Boeing and the great airplane-related attractions its Paine Field supports.

SNOQUALMIE

28 miles east of Seattle.

Although it's just a 30-mile drive from downtown Seattle, much of the densely wooded town of Snoqualmie (sno- *qual*-mie) feels as though it could be hours away. Indeed, the rustic scenery and famed Snoqualmie Falls inspired David Lynch to film many of the exterior shots for *Twin Peaks* in and around the town. Although it's growing quickly (the population has skyrocketed from about 1,600 in 2000 to more than 13,000 today) and becoming more suburban, it's still a popular getaway because of the falls, the luxurious Salish Lodge resort, and the impressive Northwest Railway Museum.

GETTING HERE AND AROUND

To reach Snoqualmie from Seattle, take Interstate 90 east to Exit 27. The Old Town area of Snoqualmie is very compact and walkable; the falls and Salish Lodge are a mile north of Old Town.

EXPLORING

FAMILY **Northwest Railway Museum.** Vintage cars line a paved path along Railroad Avenue, with signs explaining the origin of each engine, car, and caboose on display, with more history and memorabilia exhibited inside several different buildings, including the former waiting room of the stunning restored Snoqualmie depot and the train-shed building. The Railway Education Center, at this writing scheduled to open in summer 2017, will display photographs and historical documents related to the region's rail history. Several times a day, on weekends only, a train made of cars built in the mid-1910s for the Spokane, Portland, and Seattle Railroad travels between Snoqualmie Depot and North Bend. The 75-minute (round-trip) excursion passes through woods, past waterfalls, and around patchwork farmland. Crowds of families pack the winter Santa Train journeys and the midsummer Railroad Days rides, when a helicopter drops balloons and prizes over the annual parade. ⊠ *Snoqualmie Depot, 38625 S.E. King St.* ☎ *425/888–3030* ⊕ *www.trainmuseum.org* 🖭 *Depot free; rides $20* ⊗ *No rides weekdays or Nov.–Apr. except during certain holidays periods.*

Fodor's Choice ★ **Snoqualmie Falls.** Spring and summer snowmelt turn the Snoqualmie River into a thundering torrent at Snoqualmie Falls. These sweeping cascades provided the backdrop for the *Twin Peaks* opening montage. The water pours over a 268-foot rock ledge (100 feet higher than Niagara Falls) to a 65-foot-deep pool. These cascades, considered sacred by the Native Americans, are Snoqualmie's biggest attraction. A privately owned 2-acre park with a gift shop and observation platform affords some of the best views of the falls and the surrounding area, as does the elegant Salish Lodge hotel. The 3-mile round-trip River Trail winds through trees and over open slopes to the base of the cascades. ⊠ *Observation Deck and Park, 6351 Railroad Ave. SE* ☎ *831–6525* ⊕ *www.snoqualmiefalls.com.*

WHERE TO EAT AND STAY

$ ✕ **Snoqualmie Taproom & Brewery.** This bustling, spacious Old Town

AMERICAN brewpub and casual restaurant is renowned for its craft beers, including a much-acclaimed Steam Train Porter, named for the town's historic rail line. Expect a range of hearty hot and cold sandwiches (the smoked turkey, provolone, jalapeño, and chipotle mayo on rosemary bread has plenty of kick), plus a variety of 12-inch pizzas and flatbreads. **Known for:** Black Frog stout; house-brewed root beer; Washington apple flatbread. $ *Average main: $12* ✉ *8032 Falls Ave. SE* ☎ *425/831–2357* ⊕ *www.fallsbrew.com.*

$$$

RESORT

Fodor'sChoice

★

⊡ **Salish Lodge.** The stunning, chalet-style lodge—which you may recognize from the opening credits of *Twin Peaks*—sits right over Snoqualmie Falls. **Pros:** right on the falls; exceptional, sophisticated restaurants; great spa. **Cons:** resort fee; not within easy walking distance of Old Town. $ *Rooms from: $229* ✉ *6501 Railroad Ave. SE* ☎ *206/888–2556* ⊕ *www.salishlodge.com* ⤳ *80 rooms, 4 suites* ⦿| *No meals.*

SPORTS AND THE OUTDOORS

FAMILY

Fodor'sChoice

★

The Summit at Snoqualmie. This winter sports destination, 53 miles east of Seattle and about 25 miles east of Snoqualmie, combines the Alpental, Summit West, Summit East, and Summit Central ski areas along Snoqualmie Pass. Spread over nearly 2,000 acres at elevations of up to 5,400 feet, the facilities include 65 ski trails (86% of them intermediate and advanced), 26 chairlifts, and two terrain parks. Those seeking tamer pursuits can head to the Summit Nordic Center, with groomed trails and a tubing area. Shops, restaurants, lodges (none of which are slope-side), and ski schools are connected by shuttle vans; there's even child care. For a different take on the mountains, head up to the pass after dinner; this is one of the nation's largest night-skiing areas. Full-day lift tickets, good for any of the four mountains, start at $66. ✉ *1001 Hwy. 906, Snoqualmie Pass* ✚ *Exit 52 off I–90* ☎ *425/434–7669, 206/236–1600 snow conditions* ⊕ *www.summitatsnoqualmie.com.*

EDMONDS

45 miles northwest of Snoqualmie, 15 miles north of Seattle.

This charming, somewhat suburban small city just north of Seattle has a waterfront lined by more than a mile of boutiques and restaurants, seaside parks and attractions, and a string of broad, windswept beaches. Just beyond is the small but lively downtown area, where you can wander into hip cafés and wine shops, peruse attractive antiques stores and chic galleries, and browse the colorful Summer Market, which runs Saturday 9 to 3 from July through September. The early-evening Third Thursday Art Walk—one of the state's largest such events—shows off the work of local artists, and numerous events and festivals take place year-round. On the east side of Puget Sound, Edmonds is also a gateway to the Kitsap Peninsula, as ferries from here connect to Kingston.

GETTING HERE AND AROUND

From Seattle, take Interstate 5 north to Highway 104 west, which leads downtown and to the ferry terminal.

ESSENTIALS

Visitor Information Edmonds Chamber of Commerce. ✉ *121 5th Ave. N* ☎ *425/776–6711* ⊕ *www.edmondswa.com.*

10

The Summit at Snoqualmie

EXPLORING

Edmonds Historical Museum. The lower level of this museum is the place to find out about local legends and traditions; rotating exhibits upstairs touch on everything from local art to regional and maritime history. The museum's Summer Garden Market sells handmade and hand-grown items on Saturdays from 9 to 3 from July through September. ⊠ *118 5th Ave. N* ☎ *425/774–0900* ⊕ *www.historicedmonds.org* ⊠ *$5* ⊗ *Closed Mon. and Tues.*

Edmonds Underwater Park. Perhaps the best-known dive site in Puget Sound besides the Narrows Bridge area has 27 acres of sunken structures and developed dive trails. It's immediately north of the ferry landing at the foot of Main Street. The adjacent Brackett's Landing Park—where there's parking—has trails, picnic areas, and restrooms. ⊠ *Brackett's Landing Park, Main St. and Railroad Ave., next to ferry terminal* ☎ *425/771–0230* ⊕ *www.edmondswa.gov.*

FAMILY **Olympic Beach.** Get your dinner to go and watch the sun go down behind Whidbey Island and the Olympic Mountains at this lovely waterfront park. The Olympic Beach fishing pier attracts anglers all year and public art dots the landscape. In summer, a visitor station (open weekends noon–5) is a great place to pick up local info; kids like exploring the marine touch tank. ⊠ *200 Admiral Way* ☎ *425/775–1344* ⊕ *www.edmondswa.gov.*

WHERE TO EAT

$$ **✕ Bar Dojo.** Although it's a couple of miles east of downtown in a strip
ASIAN FUSION mall, this trendy place has quickly established itself as a hot spot for creative, often complex modern Asian fare, with an emphasis on local ingredients. The early-evening and late-night happy hours are hugely

popular, with great bargains on food and drinks. **Known for:** great deals during late-night happy hour; banana tarte tatin for dessert. [$] *Average main: $20* ✉ *8404 Bowdoin Way* ☎ *425/967–7267* 🌐 *www.bardojo.com* 🕓 *No lunch weekdays.*

$$ MEDITERRANEAN Fodor's Choice ★ 🍴 **Epulo Bistro.** Darkly lighted, smartly furnished, and urbane, this hip spot in the heart of downtown serves seasonally driven Mediterranean food with plenty of Northwestern influences. It's very easy to make a meal here of several tantalizing small plates, like sautéed brussels sprouts with bacon, chili, and garlic and Penn Cove mussels with saffron, orange, and leeks. **Known for:** fig-and-Gorgonzola wood-fired pizza; extensive wine list. [$] *Average main: $22* ✉ *526 Main St.* ☎ *425/678–8680* 🌐 *epulobistro.com* 🕓 *Closed Mon. No lunch.*

$$ ITALIAN 🍴 **Girardi's Osteria Italiana.** Coming here is like walking into an elegant yet comfortable Italian kitchen, where every space beneath the high, peaked ceiling glows with warm country colors and muted light. The menu is an induction into the Italian dining experience, with such entrées as *anitra della casa* (pan-seared duck breast on herb polenta) and *vitello del capitano* (veal medallions in a Madeira wine sauce). **Known for:** half-price bottled wine on Monday and Tuesday; house-made tiramisu. [$] *Average main: $19* ✉ *504 5th Ave. S* ☎ *425/673–5278* 🌐 *www.girardis-osteria.com.*

WHERE TO STAY

$ HOTEL 🏨 **Best Western Plus Edmonds Harbor Inn.** In downtown Edmonds, this inn has as much country style and luxury as you're likely to find in a chain property, with comfortable rooms updated in modern, easy-on-the-eyes beiges and earth tones; some have fireplaces, kitchens, or oversize jetted bathtubs. **Pros:** proximity to the waterfront and downtown dining; only 1½ blocks from the Kingston ferry terminal. **Cons:** no beach views. [$] *Rooms from: $134* ✉ *130 W. Dayton St.* ☎ *425/771–5021, 800/441–8033* 🌐 *www.bwedmondsharborinn.com* 🛏 *91 rooms* 🍽 *Breakfast.*

SPORTS AND OUTDOORS

DIVING

Underwater Sports. This in-town shop offers scuba instruction, equipment rentals, and underwater tours of the park. ✉ *264 Railroad Ave.* ☎ *425/771–6322* 🌐 *www.underwatersports.com.*

EVERETT

19 miles north of Edmonds.

Everett is best known for the Boeing Aircraft plant and for having the second-largest Puget Sound port (after Seattle). The naval station here is home to the U.S.S. *Nimitz* aircraft carrier and a support flotilla of destroyers and frigates. Much of this industrial town, the county seat of suburban Snohomish County, sits high on a bluff above Port Gardner Bay and the Snohomish River. The waterfront was once lined by so many lumber, pulp, and shingle mills that Everett proudly called itself "the city of smokestacks." Downtown Everett has many elegant old commercial buildings dating from the period when John D. Rockefeller heavily invested in the fledging town, hoping to profit from the nearby Monte Cristo mines—which turned out to be a flop. Another scheme failed when James J. Hill made Everett the western terminus of the Great Northern Railroad, hoping to turn it into Puget Sound's most important port.

The pleasant waterfront suburb of Mukilteo, about 5 miles southeast of Everett, is the main departure point for ferries to Clinton, on Whidbey Island. The old lighthouse and waterfront park are fun to explore. An important Native American treaty was signed in 1855 at nearby Point Elliott.

Marysville, 6 miles north of Everett, was set up as a trading post in 1877. Pioneers exchanged goods with the Snohomish people, who once occupied southeastern Whidbey Island and the lower Snohomish Valley. Settlers drained and diked the lowlands, raised dairy cows, planted strawberry fields, cleared the forests, and in no time a thriving community was established. Marysville kept to itself for a century, until the Interstate 5 freeway was built; today it's a thriving community and the home of the popular Tulalip (Too- *lay*-lip) Casino.

GETTING HERE AND AROUND

Everett is best explored by car; take Interstate 5 north to Exit 192.

Contact **Sound Transit.** ☎ 800/201–4900 ⊕ www.soundtransit.org.

ESSENTIALS

Visitor Information **Snohomish County Tourism Bureau.** ✉ *Visitor Center at Future of Flight, 8415 Paine Field Blvd., Mukilteo* ☎ 425/348–5802, 888/338–0976 ⊕ www.snohomish.org.

EXPLORING

The Flying Heritage Collection. Housed within a 51,000-square-foot airport hangar, this spectacular gathering of unique vintage aircraft belongs to local tycoon Paul Allen, who began collecting and restoring rare planes in 1998. The selections run the full length of 20th-century military history, including pieces from the two world wars and other international battles. A favorite plane is the P-51D Mustang from World War II. Tours are self-guided; exhibits help to explain the collection. In summer, try to time your visit for one of the Free Fly Days, when pilots are on-site to fly some of the craft as part of monthly maintenance. ✉ *Paine Field, 3407 109th St. SW* ☎ *206/342–4242* ⊕ *www.flyingheritage.com* 🎟 *$14.*

FAMILY **Imagine Children's Museum.** This engaging spot for kids is on a pioneer homestead built in the 1800s. Interactive exhibits and crafts are part of the fun; wee ones love the magic school bus as well. ✉ *1502 Wall St.* ☎ *425/258–1006* ⊕ *www.imaginecm.org* 🎟 *$10.20* ⊗ *Closed Mon.*

Fodor's Choice ★ **Institute of Flight.** This facility showcases the Boeing Everett line (747, 777, and 787), and the 98-acre site holds the world's largest building—so big that it often creates its own weather system inside. You can see planes in various stages of production on a 90-minute tour of the Boeing factory and spend time in the Boeing Centennial Exhibit, with cutaways of airplane fuselages, exhibits on the inner workings of navigation and hydraulic systems, and interactive exhibits that let you design your own commercial airliner. There's also a café, a kid-oriented family zone, and a number of other exhibit areas, and from the Strato Deck atop the building, you're treated to views of test flights taking off and landing as well as impressive views of the surrounding mountains and Puget Sound. Note that no purses, backpacks, cameras, cell phones, or children under 48 inches tall are permitted on the factory tour (free lockers are provided); they are allowed on the Strato Deck and in the Centennial Exhibit. Reserving tour tickets a day in advance is recommended if you need a specific tour time, but same-day tickets are always available. ✉ *8415 Paine Field Blvd., Mukilteo* ☎ *425/438–8100, 888/467–4777* 🌐 *www.futureofflight.org* 🎟 *$25.*

FAMILY **Jetty Island.** Open in summer only, this is a 2-mile-long, sand-fringed offshore haven full of wildlife and outdoor opportunities. Seasonal programs include guided walks, bonfires, and midsummer Jetty Island Days festivities. A ferry (reservation recommended to avoid lines) provides round-trip transportation. ✉ *West end of 10th St., off W. Marine View Dr.* ☎ *425/257–8304* 🌐 *everettwa.gov/jettyisland* 🎟 *$2 ferry fare, $3 parking* 🕓 *Closed early Sept.–early July.*

Museum of Flight Restoration Center. At this branch of Seattle's Museum of Flight, vintage planes are restored by a volunteer staff who simply love bringing vintage aircraft back to life. You can wander among the mix of delicate and behemoth planes on a leisurely, self-guided tour at Paine Field. ✉ *2909 100th St. SW, Bldg. C-72* ☎ *425/745–5150* 🌐 *www.museumofflight.org/restoration* 🎟 *$5* 🕓 *Closed Mon. and Tues. in summer and Sun.–Wed. and Fri. in winter.*

WHERE TO EAT AND STAY

$$$ SEAFOOD 🍴 **Anthony's Homeport.** Tucked into chic Marina Village, this elegant waterfront outlet of a popular Washington-based seafood chain has large windows opening to a panorama of Port Gardner Bay. The specials, which change daily, might include meaty Dungeness crab, wild chinook salmon, and other sea creatures caught just offshore, and the clam chowder is justly renowned. **Known for:** great views of Port Gardner Bay; weekday-evening four-course "sunset dinners" for $23.95; clam chowder. [$] *Average main: $24* ✉ *1726 W. Marine View Dr.* ☎ *425/252–3333* 🌐 *www.anthonys.com.*

$ AMERICAN 🍴 **The Sisters.** This funky breakfast and lunch café in Everett Public Market is as popular now as when it opened in 1983. Perhaps that's because the blueberry or pecan hotcakes, rich soups, and overflowing sandwiches are as good as ever. **Known for:** breakfast served all day; sweet-potato pie. [$] *Average main: $7* ✉ *2804 Grand Ave.* ☎ *425/252–0480* 🌐 *www.thesistersrestaurant.com* 🕓 *Closed weekends. No dinner.*

$ HOTEL 🏨 **Inn at Port Gardner.** Stroll along the marina and you'll encounter this gray, warehouselike structure, which wraps around a cozy, contemporary-style hotel where accommodations are enhanced by water views. **Pros:** right on the waterfront; close to area restaurants; nice patio and lobby. **Cons:** no pool or on-site gym (although guests receive free passes to nearby gym); rooms are lovely but of the standard chain-hotel variety. [$] *Rooms from: $139* ✉ *1700 W. Marine Dr.* ☎ *425/252–6779, 888/252–6779* 🌐 *www.innatportgardner.com* 🛏 *27 rooms, 6 suites* 🍽 *Breakfast.*

PUYALLUP

35 miles south of Seattle, 10 miles southeast of Tacoma.

Set before the towering forests and snowfields of Mt. Rainier is Puyallup (pyoo- *al*-lup), one of western Washington's oldest towns. The Puyallup Fair attracts all of western Washington to its carnival rides, performers, produce, and animals. The annual event is held at the fairgrounds on the northwest end of town each September. The Spring Fair and Daffodil Festival (known as "The Little Puyallup") is another beloved event that takes place each April. These special events are really the only reason to make a detour to Puyallup unless you need a leg-stretch or a bite to eat on your way elsewhere. The downtown area is pleasant enough, though, and has a few boutiques, antiques dealers, and restaurants.

GETTING HERE AND AROUND

To reach Puyallup, take Interstate 5 south to Interstate 405 north and then Route 167 south.

EXPLORING

FAMILY **Northwest Trek Wildlife Park.** This spectacular, 435-acre wildlife park 35 miles south of Puyallup is devoted to native creatures of the Pacific Northwest. Walking paths wind through natural surroundings—so natural that a cougar once entered the park and started snacking on the deer (it was finally trapped and relocated to the North Cascades). See beavers, otters, and wolverines; get close to wolves, foxes, coyotes; and observe several species of big cats and bears in wild environments. Admission includes a 50-minute tram ride through fields of wandering moose, bighorn sheep, elk, bison, and mountain goats. The most adventurous way to see the park is via one of five ziplines, which traverse the park canopy—rides are available early May through late September. ✉ *11610 Trek Dr. E, Eatonville* ☎ *360/832–6117* 🌐 *www.nwtrek.org* 🎟 *$22.25* 🕑 *Closed Mon.–Thurs. in Oct.–mid-Mar. (except holidays).*

FAMILY **Pioneer Farm Museum and Ohop Indian Village.** This living-history museum, 23 miles south of Puyallup, provides a look at pioneer and Native American life. Kids can learn how to hunt and fish in a realistic tribal village, grind grain, milk a cow, churn butter, and do other old-fashioned chores. A trading post shows the commodities of earlier eras. One-hour tours are available through both the farm and village. ✉ *7716 Ohop Valley Rd. E, Eatonville* ☎ *360/832–6300* 🌐 *www.pioneerfarmmuseum.org* 🎟 *Farm $9, village $8.50* 🕑 *Closed late Nov.–mid-Mar. and weekdays spring and fall.*

WHERE TO EAT

$ CAFÉ 🍴 **Anthem Coffee & Tea.** Drop by this spacious, modern café to kick off the day with a well-crafted espresso drink and breakfast sandwich, or linger later in the day over a naan flatbread pizza and a pint of craft beer or local wine. Tall windows let in plenty of sunlight, and on warm days you can stroll across the street and enjoy your coffee on a park bench in verdant Pioneer Park. **Known for:** sweet-cream cold brew; bacon-cheddar scones; wine and beer happy-hour deals in the evening. [$] *Average main: $7* ✉ *210 W. Pioneer Ave.* ☎ *253/256–8140* 🌐 *www.facebook.com/anthemcoffeepuyallup.*

BELLINGHAM AND SKAGIT VALLEY

Some people drive right past places like La Conner, Mount Vernon, or Bellingham on their way west to the San Juans, east to the Cascades, or north to the Canadian border. But between Everett and Canada are some lovely miles of coastline, some impressive parkland, and charming farm towns—all of which are fairly easy to access from Interstate 5. Collectively, the towns that anchor the northwestern edge of the state are seriously underappreciated: La Conner is a pleasantly laid-back agrarian community, and Mount Vernon is a riverfront town with some great festivals. Between the two towns are the best of the Skagit Valley flower farms, which do draw big crowds in spring when the tulips bloom. Bellingham is a progressive, scenic university town with a fun and quirky vibe that appeals to artists, outdoorsy types, and hipsters. Any one of these towns makes a good stopover on other itineraries.

LA CONNER

14 miles southeast of Anacortes, 68 miles north of Seattle.

Morris Graves, Kenneth Callahan, Guy Anderson, Mark Tobey, and other painters set up shop in La Conner in the 1940s, and the village on the Swinomish Channel (Slough) has been a haven for artists ever since. In recent years the community has become increasingly popular as a regional weekend escape—it's a fairly short drive from Seattle, but it feels refreshingly far from the bustle.

La Conner has several historic buildings near the waterfront or a short walk up the hill—use the stairs leading up the bluff, or go around and walk up one of the sloping streets—as well as several inviting shops and restaurants. In summer the village can become a bit congested with people and cars, and parking can be hard to find. The flat land around La Conner makes for easy biking along levees and through the tulip fields. You'll see plenty of fields and farms, and a major attraction in fall and summer are farm stands selling local produce.

GETTING HERE AND AROUND

The center of La Conner is roughly 12 miles west of Interstate 5 (from Seattle, take Exit 221 for Highway 534). The town is very close to both Anacortes, where ferries depart for the San Juan Islands, and the northern tip of Whidbey Island. A car is by far the best way to reach and explore the area. In summer bike rentals ($30 for a half day; $40 per day) are available in La Conner from Tulip Country Bike Tours, which can deliver bikes to your hotel.

Contact La Conner Chamber of Commerce. ⌧ 413 Morris St. ☎ 360/466–4778, 888/642–9284 ⊕ www.lovelaconner.com.

EXPLORING

Museum of Northwest Art. Here in this striking, modern building you can view some 2,500 works of regional creative minds past and present, painters, sculptors, photographers, and other artists. Soaring spaces, circular exhibit rooms, a glass gallery, and a broad spiral staircase add

10

to the free-form feeling of the displays. The small shop sells examples of what you see in the exhibits. ⊠ *121 S. 1st St.* ☎ *360/466–4446* ⊕ *www. museumofnwart.org* ✉ *Free.*

Skagit County Historical Museum. This hilltop museum surveys domestic life in early Skagit County and Northwest Coastal Native American history. There's an interesting gallery showcasing goods commonly found in the region's early general stores, and rotating exhibits interpret the different aspects of the community's rich heritage. ⊠ *501 4th St.* ☎ *360/466–3365* ⊕ *www.skagitcounty.net/museum* ✉ *$5* ⊗ *Closed Mon.*

WHERE TO EAT

$ ✕ **Calico Cupboard.** A local favorite, this storefront bakery, with branches
CAFÉ nearby in Anacortes and Mount Vernon, turns out some of the best pastries in Skagit County, plus big portions of breakfast and lunch fare. Lunches focus on fresh and creative salads, soups, and burgers; huge and hearty breakfasts may leave you with little need for lunch—the roasted-butternut-squash hash and *migas* are a couple of favorites. **Known for:** riverfront seating on the deck; filling and delicious breakfasts. $ *Average main: $10* ⊠ *720 S. 1st St.* ☎ *360/466–4451* ⊕ *www. calicocupboardcafe.com* ⊗ *No dinner.*

$$ ✕ **The Oyster and Thistle.** A couple of blocks from the river on a bluff
PACIFIC with expansive views of the village, this homey restaurant with a
NORTHWEST rustic dark-wood interior serves some of the best seafood in the
Fodor's Choice area, plus a few well-prepared French classics, such as cassoulet with
★ duck confit and house-cured bacon, and fall-off-the-bone pork shank with wild-mushroom risotto. Simpler fare—caramelized-onion flatbread, shepherd's pie—is served in the adjoining pub. **Known for:** extensive selection of regional oysters; impressive list of Northwest and French wines; filet mignon with crab-stuffed prawn. $ *Average main: $22* ⊠ *205 E. Washington St.* ☎ *360/766–6179* ⊕ *www. theoysterandthistle.com.*

WHERE TO STAY

$$ 🛏 **Channel Lodge.** Most of the smartly furnished contemporary rooms
HOTEL here, done in subdued gray tones with wooden trim and gas fireplaces,
Fodor's Choice overlook the narrow Swinomish Channel. **Pros:** big stone fireplace
★ in lobby; rustic charm wrapped around sleek modern amenities; lovely waterfront setting and views. **Cons:** some rooms don't overlook water. $ *Rooms from: $159* ⊠ *205 N. 1st St.* ☎ *360/466–1500, 888/466–4113* ⊕ *www.laconnerchannellodge.com* 🛏 *39 rooms, 3 suites* ❄ *Breakfast.*

$ 🛏 **Hotel Planter.** This smartly renovated hotel, the oldest in La Con-
B&B/INN ner, is on the National Register of Historic Places, and its homey rooms, furnished with handmade country-style furniture, have fine views of the hill or the waterfront. **Pros:** reasonably priced; most rooms overlook attractive courtyard; historic charm. **Cons:** old-fashioned decorative scheme isn't for everybody. $ *Rooms from: $119* ⊠ *715 1st St.* ☎ *360/466–4710* ⊕ *www.hotelplanter.com* 🛏 *12 rooms* ❄ *No meals.*

$ 🛏 **La Conner Country Inn.** At this rambling motel-style property all the
HOTEL   spacious rooms have private outdoor entrances, high, vaulted ceilings,
FAMILY   gas fireplaces, refrigerators, and pleasant country-style furnishings;
several have whirlpool baths. **Pros:** spacious rooms, most with more
than one bed; good value; quiet but central location. **Cons:** rooms are
a slightly odd mix of country coziness and chain hotel. $\boxed{\$}$ *Rooms from:
$149* ✉ *107 S. 2nd St.* ☎ *360/466–1500, 888/466–4113* ⊕ *www.lacon-
nercountryinn.com* 🛏 *27 rooms, 1 suite* ⦿ *Breakfast.*

$ 🛏 **Wild Iris.** The garden-laced exterior is a sprawling model of a Vic-
B&B/INN   torian-style inn, and the elegantly decorated interior begins with a
Fodor's Choice   river-rock fireplace and extends to spacious rooms done with soft,
★   colorful fabrics and polished wood accents. **Pros:** beautiful and tastefully decorated rooms; great in-room amenities (plush linens, DVD
library) considering the decent rates; excellent breakfast. **Cons:** the
least expensive rooms are quite small. $\boxed{\$}$ *Rooms from: $134* ✉ *121
Maple Ave.* ☎ *360/466–1400, 800/477–1400* ⊕ *www.wildiris.com*
🛏 *4 rooms, 12 suites* ⦿ *Breakfast.*

MOUNT VERNON

11 miles northeast of La Conner.

This attractive riverfront town, the county seat of Skagit County and
founded in 1871, is surrounded by dairy pastures, vegetable fields, and
bulb farms—the town is famous for its annual Tulip Festival in April,
when thousands of people visit to admire the floral exuberance. After a
giant logjam on the lower Skagit was cleared, steamers began churning
up the river, and Mount Vernon soon became the major commercial
center of the Skagit Valley, a position it has never relinquished. Rising
above downtown and the river, 972-foot-high Little Mountain is a city
park with a view. It used to be an island until the mudflats were filled
in by Skagit River silt. Glacial striations in rocks near the top of the
mountain, dating from the last continental glaciation (10,000–20,000
years ago), were made when the mountain (and all of the Puget Sound
region) was covered by some 3,500 feet of ice.

GETTING HERE AND AROUND

The best way to reach Mount Vernon is by car, taking Interstate 5
north to any of several exits right in town. In Mount Vernon Interstate
5 connects with Highway 536, which then merges with Highway 20
toward Anacortes.

Tulip Country Bike Tours arranges spring trips through the tulip fields,
starting around $70 per person. In summer, tours take in other Skagit
Valley sights like berry farms and Padilla Bay. You can also rent bikes
for $40 per day.

Contacts Mount Vernon Chamber of Commerce. ✉ *301 W. Kincaid St.*
☎ *360/428–8547* ⊕ *www.mountvernonchamber.com.* **Tulip Country Bike Tours.**
☎ *360/424–7461* ⊕ *www.countrycycling.com.*

10

EXPLORING

Bay View State Park. Adjoining the small waterfront community of the same name, this scenic 25-acre park has a campground with cabins in the woods and picnic tables on the low grassy bluff above Padilla Bay, a national estaurine sanctuary. Canoers and kayakers take note: Padilla Bay runs almost dry at low tide, when water is restricted to a few creek-like tidal channels. ✉ *10905 Bay View–Edison Rd.* ☎ *360/757–0227* 🌐 *www.parks.wa.gov* 🎫 *$10 per vehicle.*

Little Mountain Park. Atop the eponymous mountain at the southeastern edge of town, this 522-acre park, which rises to nearly 1,000 feet above sea level, has great views of the Skagit Valley (especially in March and April, when the daffodils and tulips are in full bloom), the San Juan Islands, and the distant Olympic Mountains. It's a lovely spot for a picnic. ✉ *Little Mountain Rd., off E. Blackburn Rd., 4 miles southeast of downtown* ☎ *360/336–6213* 🌐 *www.mountvernonwa.gov* 🎫 *Free.*

Fodor's Choice ★ **Padilla Bay National Estuarine Reserve.** At this serene wildlife preserve adjacent to Bayview State Park, the Breazeale Interpretive Center has great birding: there are black Brant (or Brent) geese, raptors, peregrine falcons, and bald eagles. Trails lead into the woods and to a rocky beach, with more good bird-watching opportunities. The 2¼-mile Shore Trail starts at the south end of Bayview; look for signs directing you to the parking area, which is away from the water off the east side of the road. ✉ *10441 Bayview–Edison Rd.* ☎ *360/428–1558* 🌐 *www.padillabay.gov* 🎫 *Free* 🕓 *Interpretive center closed Sun. and Mon.*

Roozengaarde. This 1,200-acre estate was established by the Roozen family and Washington Bulb Company in 1985—it's the world's largest family-owned tulip-, daffodil-, and iris-growing business. Sixteen acres of greenhouses are filled with multicolored blossoms, and more than 200,000 bulbs are planted in the show gardens each fall. The Skagit Valley Tulip Festival, held in April, is the main event, when the flowers pop up in neat, brilliant rows across the flat land, attracting thousands of sightseers. The garden and store are open year-round, and the staff and website are full of helpful advice for both novice and experienced gardeners. ✉ *15867 Beaver Marsh Rd.* ☎ *360/424–8531, 866/488–5477* 🌐 *www.tulips.com* 🎫 *Free.*

WHERE TO EAT

$ MEXICAN 🍴 **COA Mexican Eatery.** You'll find some of northern Washington's tastiest Mexican food, from wild-cod ceviche to chicken in a complex 30-ingredient mole sauce, at this cheerful and unpretentious downtown eatery that also specializes in made-to-order premium margaritas (try the smooth "top shelf" with Jimador Blanco tequila, lime juice, and agave nectar). There are additional locations in La Conner and Snohomish. **Known for:** deep-fried ice cream; chiles rellenos; margaritas made with premium tequila. [$] *Average main: $15* ✉ *102 S. 10th St.* ☎ *360/840–1938* 🌐 *www.coaeatery.com* 🕓 *Closed Sun.*

$$$ ITALIAN 🍴 **Il Grainaio.** Tucked deep into the town's historic Old Granery, amid displays of century-old farming equipment, is this cozy and rustic place where dark-wood floors, small tables, and lanternlike lighting provide

the authentic ambience of a local trattoria. The waitstaff is quick and knowledgeable, bringing out enormous pasta bowls, seafood salads, and panfried eggplant or salmon. **Known for:** extensive selection of Italian and Northwest wines; saltimbocca alla romana. $ Average main: $25 ⊠ 100 E. Montgomery St. ☎ 360/419–0674 ⊕ www.granaio.com ⊗ No lunch weekends.

$ ✕ **Rexville Grocery.** From local artisanal chocolates to local microbrews,
AMERICAN Rexville is one well-stocked country store, with a great mix of every-
FAMILY day and gourmet snacks and drinks. There's a small café with a patio
Fodor's Choice encircled by trees, vines, and blooming thistle. **Known for:** "upsid-
★ edown" apple pie; Thursday burger nights; biscuits-and-gravy breakfasts. $ Average main: $9 ⊠ 19271 Best Rd. ☎ 360/466–5522 ⊕ www.
rexvillegrocery.com.

BELLINGHAM

29 miles northwest of Mount Vernon.

The fishing port and college community of Bellingham has steadily transformed itself from a rough-and-tumble blue-collar town to the arts, retirement, and pleasure-boating capital of Washington's northwest corner. Downtown abounds with cafés, microbreweries, specialty shops, and galleries, and the waterfront—dominated by lumber mills and shipyards in the early 1900s—is gradually morphing into a string of parks with connecting trails. College students and professors from Western Washington University make up a sizable part of the town's population and contribute to its laid-back intellectual climate. The lushly green bay front, creeks meandering through town, and Lakes Whatcom and Padden attract wildlife like deer, raccoons, river otters, beavers, ducks, geese, herons, bald eagles, and the occasional cougar.

GETTING HERE AND AROUND
From Seattle, Bellingham is nearly a straight shot on Interstate 5 north (Exit 253 gets you into the center of town).

Amtrak's Cascades train stops in Bellingham on its way to Vancouver, BC. Greyhound buses also serve Bellingham from Seattle, as does the Airporter Shuttle from Sea-Tac and Downtown Seattle. The low-cost Bolt Bus is another handy option, connecting with both Seattle and Vancouver, BC.

Biking is popular in and around Bellingham, which has a series of designated bike paths and park trails. The city of Bellingham has a good high-res bike-route map that can be downloaded from its website.

The Coast Millennium Trail will eventually connect Skagit and Whatcom counties to British Columbia. So far, about 15 miles of the 50-mile trail are open to bikes and walkers. Fairhaven Bike & Ski rents road bikes, full-suspension bikes, and standard mountain bikes starting at $40 per day.

Contacts Bellingham Whatcom County Tourism. ⊠ 904 Potter St.
☎ 360/671–3990, 800/487–2032 ⊕ www.bellingham.org. **City of Bellingham Bike Routes.** ⊕ www.cob.org/services/transportation. **Fairhaven Bike & Ski.**
⊠ 1108 11th St. ☎ 360/733–4433 ⊕ www.fairhavenbike.com.

10

EXPLORING
TOP ATTRACTIONS

Fodor'sChoice
★

Chuckanut Drive. Highway 11, also known as Chuckanut Drive, was once the only highway accessing Bellingham from the south. The drive begins in Fairhaven, reaches the flat farmlands of the Samish Valley near the village of Bow, and joins up with Interstate 5 at Burlington, in Skagit County; the full loop can be made in a couple of hours. For a dozen miles this 23-mile road winds along the cliffs above beautiful Chuckanut and Samish bays. It twists its way past the sheer sandstone face of Chuckanut Mountain and crosses creeks with waterfalls. Turnouts are framed by gnarled madrona trees and pines and offer great views of the San Juan Islands. Bald eagles cruise along the cliffs or hang out on top of tall firs. Drive carefully: the cliffs are so steep in places that closures resulting from rock slides occasionally occur in winter. ⊠ *Hwy. 11, starting in Fairhaven at 12th St. and Old Fairhaven Pkwy.*

Fairhaven. Just shy of 3 miles south of downtown Bellingham and at the beginning of Chuckanut Drive (Highway 11), this historic district was an independent city until 1903 and still retains its distinct identity as an intellectual and artistic center. The beautifully restored 1890s redbrick buildings of the Old Fairhaven District, especially on Harris Avenue between 10th and 12th streets, house restaurants, galleries, and specialty boutiques. On the north side of the district, Boulevard Park is a beautiful swath of greenery fronting Bellingham Bay, with access to the South Bay biking and pedestrian path. ⊠ *Bellingham* ⊕ *www.fairhaven.com.*

Fairhaven Marine Park. This long, sandy beach at the foot of Harris Avenue a few blocks south of Bellingham Cruise Terminal is a good place to launch sea kayaks. A rough trail runs south from the park along the railroad tracks to pebble beaches and rocky headlands, where you'll find clams, summer blackberries, and splendid views of Lummi Island. ⊠ *Foot of Harris Ave.*

Larrabee State Park. South of Chuckanut Bay along the Whatcom–Skagit county line, this rugged 2,683-acre tract is one of the state's most scenic and popular parks. It straddles an 8,100-foot stretch of rocky shore that has quiet, sandy coves and runs high up along the slopes of Chuckanut Mountain. Even though the mountain has been logged repeatedly, some of it is still wilderness. Miles of trails lead through ferny fir and maple forests to hidden lakes, caves, and cliff-top lookouts from which you can see all the way to the San Juan Islands. At the shore there's a sheltered boat launch; you can go crabbing here or watch the birds—and the occasional harbor seal—that perch on the offshore rocks. The area west of Chuckanut Drive has picnic tables as well as tent and RV sites with hookups, which are open all year. ⊠ *245 Chuckanut Dr.* ☎ *360/676–2093* ⊕ *www.parks.wa.gov* 🗟 *$10 per vehicle.*

FAMILY
Fodor'sChoice
★

Whatcom Museum. Bellingham's art and history museum comprises three buildings near one another downtown. At its centerpiece is the Lightcatcher, a LEED-certified (Leadership in Energy and Environmental Design) building with an 180-foot-long translucent wall. Rotating shows are presented here, as are permanent collections of contemporary Northwest artists. The second building, Bellingham's 1892 former city hall, is a redbrick structure that was converted into a museum in

1941—it completed a dramatic renovation in 2010 and contains historic exhibits. The third building, the Syre Education Center, contains a photographic archive. The museum's restaurant, Artifacts Café & Wine Bar, is in the Lightcatcher and garners raves for its creative farm-to-table lunch and dinner fare. ✉ *250 Flora St.* ☎ *360/778–8930* ⊕ *www.whatcommuseum.org* 🏷 *$10* ⊗ *Closed Mon. and Tues.*

NEED A BREAK

✗ **Woods Coffee Boulevard Park.** This bay-front outpost of a popular northwestern Washington coffeehouse chain has a cozy dining room with high-back chairs and large windows overlooking Bellingham Bay—in warm weather, you can enjoy your vanilla latte, yogurt parfait, breakfast sandwich, or white-chocolate–raspberry scone on the patio. With its peaceful setting in leafy Boulevard Park, this is a popular spot with bikers and strollers using the Bay Trail, which passes right outside the door. **Known for: waterfront setting in Boulevard Park; white-chocolate–raspberry scones.** ✉ *470 Bayview Rd.* ☎ *360/738-4771* ⊕ *www.woodscoffee.com.*

WORTH NOTING

Bellingham Cruise Terminal. In Fairhaven, this massive brick building surrounded by gardens dispatches daily ferries to Alaska as well as tour boats to the San Juan Islands and whale-watching ships. There's terrific wildlife-watching right off the docks and adjacent shoreline, where sea lions and otters frolic out in the water as great blue herons, cormorants, and harlequin ducks bob on the surface. The Community Boating Center right by the terminal is a good place to launch sea kayaks. ✉ *355 Harris Ave.* ☎ *360/676–2500* ⊕ *www.portofbellingham.com.*

Bloedel Donovan Park. The only public access in Bellingham to rippling, 14-mile-long Lake Whatcom is at its north end, in this park about a 10-minute drive east of downtown. Locals swim in the sheltered waters of a cove, but you might find the water a bit cold. If so, spend some time trying to spot beavers, river otters, ducks, great blue herons, and yellow pond lilies at Scudder Pond, which is another 100 feet west (reached by trail from a parking area at Northshore and Alabama). ✉ *2214 Electric Ave.* ☎ *360/778–7000* ⊕ *www.cob.org/services/recreation.*

FAMILY **Maritime Heritage Park.** Down a flight of steps behind the Whatcom Museum's 1892 City Hall building, this park pays tribute to Bellingham's fishing industry. Self-guided Marine Heritage Center tours take you through a salmon's life cycle, winding past hatcheries, aquarium tanks, and fish ladders. A boardwalk route from Holly Street leads to the ponds and a waterfall, where Bellingham was founded in 1852, when it was then known Whatcom, and the Salmon Art Trail showcases 10 different salmon-related public art installations, from sculptures to murals. Note that salmon runs occur annually around September and October. ✉ *500 W. Holly St.* ☎ *360/778–7000* ⊕ *www.cob.org/services/recreation* 🏷 *Free.*

FAMILY **Squalicum Harbor Marina.** A good place to fish, lounge, picnic, or walk, the marina holds more than 1,200 commercial and pleasure boats. Zuanich Point Park, at the end of the spit, has a telescope for close-up views of the water and a marine-life center with touch tanks. ✉ *722 Coho Way* ☎ *360/676–2542* ⊕ *www.portofbellingham.com.*

10

WHERE TO EAT

$

AMERICAN

Fodor'sChoice

★

✕ Boundary Bay Brewery & Bistro. Long a top venue in downtown Bellingham, both for sampling distinctive, well-crafted microbrews and enjoying big portions of delicious pub fare, this convivial spot occupies a vintage former garage—the huge central door is rolled open in warm weather, and there's also a good-size side patio. Boundary garners high marks among beer lovers for its ruby-red Scottish ale, smooth oatmeal stout, and rotating seasonal ales. **Known for:** Bavarian-style pretzels; Imperial oatmeal stout; pecan brownie sundae. $ *Average main: $15* ⊠ *1107 Railroad Ave.* ☎ *360/647–5593* ⊕ *www.bbaybrewery.com.*

$

AMERICAN

FAMILY

✕ Chuckanut Brewery & Kitchen. Even if you're not a beer aficionado, this spacious, chatter-filled brewpub in a modern industrial building near Whatcom Creek and the Maritime Heritage Center is a terrific, affordable option for lunch or dinner, and the good kids' menu makes it a family-friendly choice. The brewery's acclaimed beers play a role in many of the kitchen's top dishes, from the Reuben sandwich with beer-braised corned beef to the "beerbq" chicken pizzas. **Known for:** dark and heady German- and British-style beers; red-chili pork posole; hand-tossed pizzas. $ *Average main: $12* ⊠ *601 W. Holly St.* ☎ *360/752–3377* ⊕ *www. chuckanutbreweryandkitchen.com.*

$$$

AMERICAN

✕ Chuckanut Manor. The old-fashioned, glassed-in dining room and bar overlook the mouth of the Samish River, Samish Bay, and the mudflats, where great blue herons hang out. It's a popular spot for sunset- and bird-watching: bird feeders outside the bar's picture windows attract finches, chickadees, red-winged blackbirds, and other songbirds. **Known for:** Sunday champagne brunch; sunset views of Samish Bay; Dungeness crab–and–bay shrimp salad. $ *Average main: $29* ⊠ *3056 Chuckanut Dr., Bow* ☎ *360/766–6191* ⊕ *www.chuckanutmanor.com* ◷ *Closed Mon. No lunch Tues.–Thurs.*

$$$

PACIFIC

NORTHWEST

Fodor'sChoice

★

✕ Fork at Agate Bay. It's a scenic 20-minute drive east from downtown to reach this intimate but lively contemporary bistro near the north shore of Lake Whatcom, where chef-owners John and Gina Russell emphasize local, seasonal ingredients in creating some of the most creative and artfully presented fare in the region. In the evening, you might start with an heirloom-tomato-and-lump-crab salad with chèvre, mizuna greens, and balsamic vinaigrette, before continuing on to a perfectly grilled hanger steak with roasted-garlic-and-cauliflower puree, kale "lollipops," and a cherry-shallot demi-glace. **Known for:** barbecue pulled pork with eggs and a biscuit; wood-fired flatbread pizza; strong commitment to sourcing locally. $ *Average main: $25* ⊠ *2530 N. Shore Rd.* ☎ *360/733–1126* ⊕ *www.theforkatagatebay.com* ◷ *Closed Mon. and Tues. No lunch Wed.–Fri.*

$

CAFÉ

✕ Harris Avenue Café. Occupying a light-filled, cheerfully painted late-Victorian building a few blocks from the port and train station in Fairhaven, this hugely popular breakfast and lunch spot adjoins an inviting little coffeehouse (Tony's), which is a nice option for lighter snacking and fueling up on espresso. In the main café, which has patio dining in summer, you can kick off a day of exploring with a filling Sitka omelet (smoked salmon, feta, roasted garlic, tomatoes, and pesto). **Known for:** Sitka omelet with smoked salmon and feta;

strong coffee drinks; pleasant patio for warm-weather dining. $ *Average main: $10* ✉ *1101 Harris Ave.* ☎ *360/738–0802* ⊕ *www.theharrisave.com* ☾ *No dinner.*

$ ✕ **Homeskillet.** This decidedly offbeat breakfast and lunch spot in a

AMERICAN quiet neighborhood just north of downtown stands out both for

Fodor'sChoice its prodigious portions of rib-sticking all-day breakfast fare and its

★ funny (and often freaky) decorative elements, from dozens of clown paintings and figurines to its psychedelic color scheme. Prepare for a wait, especially on weekend mornings, and if you can possibly save room for dessert, the seasonal fruit (peach-blueberry, for example) bread puddings are to die for. **Known for:** wonderfully bizarre and kitschy decor; chicken-fried steak with chorizo gravy; homemade cinnamon-roll French toast. $ *Average main: $10* ✉ *521 Kentucky St.* ☎ *360/676–6218* ⊕ *www.homeskilletinsunnyland.com* ☾ *Closed Mon. No dinner.*

$ ✕ **Old World Deli.** Epicureans flock to this bustling, high-ceilinged deli

DELI and specialty market in the heart of downtown for generously portioned sandwiches, salads, and charcuterie and cheese plates fashioned out of Portland's famed Olympic Provisions and Seattle's vaunted Salumi. The hot-pressed sub with mortadella, capicola, sopressata, fontina cheese, tomato, pepperoncini, and arugula on an Italian roll tastes right out of the best Little Italy neighborhoods of any big East Coast city. **Known for:** artisanal charcuterie and cheeses; excellent wine selection; muffaletta sandwiches. $ *Average main: $9* ✉ *1228 N. State St.* ☎ *360/738–2090* ⊕ *www.oldworlddeli1.com* ☾ *Closed Sun.*

$$$$ ✕ **Oyster Bar.** Above the shore on a steep, wooded bluff, this intimate

SEAFOOD restaurant in the village of Bow is regionally famous for what may be

Fodor'sChoice the best marine view from any Washington restaurant. People come

★ here to dine and watch the sun set over the islands to the west or to watch the full moon reflect off the waters of Samish Bay. **Known for:** outstanding water views; oyster fry with Parmesan–bread crumb crust; steak-and-lobster combo. $ *Average main: $37* ✉ *2578 Chuckanut Dr., 22 miles south of Bellingham, Bow* ☎ *360/766–6185* ⊕ *www. theoysterbar.net.*

WHERE TO STAY

$$$ ⬚ **Chrysalis Inn and Spa at the Pier.** In a long, gray, gabled building rising

HOTEL above the waterfront between downtown and Fairhaven, the lobby is

Fodor'sChoice warmed by dark woods and a large fireplace, and light-filled, contem-

★ porary rooms have fireplaces and offer the cushiest accommodations in town. **Pros:** utterly relaxing; great water views from most rooms; first-rate on-site restaurant and spa. **Cons:** some noise from train track behind the hotel. $ *Rooms from: $219* ✉ *804 10th St.* ☎ *360/756–1005, 888/808–0005* ⊕ *www.thechrysalisinn.com* ⤴ *34 rooms, 9 suites* ❖❘ *Breakfast.*

$$$ ⬚ **Fairhaven Village Inn.** On a slight bluff overlooking Fairhaven Village

B&B/INN Green and just up the street from Port of Bellingham's south terminal, this charming, historic inn overlooks Bellingham Bay; the bay-view rooms have balconies and gas fireplaces, and a suite has French doors dividing a bedroom and sitting area. **Pros:** interesting part of town with good shops, galleries, and restaurants; convenient for Chuckanut Scenic

10

Drive and the university; staff is helpful and knowledgeable. **Cons:** two-night minimum stay at certain times. [$] *Rooms from: $209* ✉ *1200 10th St.* ☎ *360/733–1311, 877/733–1100* 🌐 *www.fairhavenvillageinn.com* 🛏 *21 rooms, 1 suite* 🍴 *Breakfast.*

$$$ HOTEL **Hotel Bellwether.** Bellingham's original waterfront hotel overlooks the entrance to bustling Squalicum Harbor, and its luxurious rooms have gas fireplaces, plush bathrooms with jetted tubs and separate glassed-in showers, and private balconies for lounging and dining. **Pros:** beautiful bay views; large private dock; wide variety of room configurations. **Cons:** can get crowded with groups and weddings; one of the more expensive options in town. [$] *Rooms from: $219* ✉ *Squalicum Harbor Marina, 1 Bellwether Way* ☎ *360/392–3100, 877/411–1200* 🌐 *www.hotelbellwether.com* 🛏 *50 rooms, 16 suites* 🍴 *Breakfast.*

$ B&B/INN **MoonDance B&B.** This handsomely restored 1930s lodge-style home with tastefully and quirkily furnished guest rooms is surrounded by colorful gardens and sits on the western shore of pristine Lake Whatcom—it's one of the most tranquil settings of any lodging in the area. **Pros:** expansive lake views; kayaks on-site; one family-friendly room can accommodate two adults and two children. **Cons:** 5 miles east of downtown; two-night minimum during busy times. [$] *Rooms from: $145* ✉ *4737 Cable St.* ☎ *360/927–2599* 🌐 *www.bellinghambandb.com* 🛏 *4 rooms, 1 suite* 🍴 *Breakfast.*

$ RESORT **Silver Reef Hotel Casino and Spa.** This modern casino hotel just outside the small town of Ferndale—10 miles northwest of Bellingham—has spacious and well-maintained rooms and a slew of amenities that include a full-service spa, an indoor pool, slots and table games, a showroom, and nearly a dozen restaurants and bars. **Pros:** lots of entertainment and dining options on-site; pretty favorable rates considering the nice rooms. **Cons:** a 20-minute drive from downtown Bellingham; casino vibe not for everyone; many rooms face a large parking lot. [$] *Rooms from: $149* ✉ *4876 Haxton Way, Ferndale* ☎ *866/383–0777, 360/543–7169* 🌐 *www.silverreefcasino.com/* 🛏 *199 rooms, 5 suites* 🍴 *No meals.*

NIGHTLIFE AND PERFORMING ARTS

Aslan Brewing. One of the newer of Bellingham's fast-growing number of highly regarded craft breweries occupies a sleek downtown building with soaring glass walls, an open floor plan, and plenty of sidewalk seating. The brewmasters here specialize in flavorful, small-batch beers, like faintly ginger-accented Irie Eyes Red Ale, and a rich, chocolaty dark lager called Cascadian. Part of the fun here is the bar food, including a rather decadent waffle-fry poutine, hefty bacon-bison burgers, and Chocolate Stout soft-serve ice cream topped with candied barley. ✉ *1330 N. Forest St.* ☎ *360/778–2088* 🌐 *www.aslanbrewing.com.*

Fodor's Choice ★ **The Local.** This old-school downtown pub with a modern vibe and first-rate beer and food was opened by a trio of Western Washington University graduates who also happen to be talented beer makers (they own Menace Brewing). As you might guess, this laid-back spot with a conversation-friendly decibel level has a great list of rotating taps, featuring craft beers from throughout the Northwest. The locally driven food is tasty, too, from fried chicken and waffles during the popular weekend brunches to late-night pork-belly tacos and fish-and-chips. ⊠ *1427 Railroad Ave.* ☎ *360/306–3731* ⊕ *www.facebook.com/ thelocalpublichousebellingham.*

Mt. Baker Theatre. The state's largest performing arts center north of Seattle occupies a restored vaudeville-era (1927) theater with a 110-foot-tall Moorish tower and a lobby fashioned after a Spanish galleon. It's home to the Whatcom Symphony Orchestra and is also a venue for movies, musicals, and headline performers. ⊠ *104 N. Commercial St.* ☎ *360/734–6080* ⊕ *www.mountbakertheatre.com.*

SPORTS AND THE OUTDOORS
WHALE-WATCHING
San Juan Cruises. This popular whale-watching excursion company sails around Bellingham Bay and out to the San Juan Islands, where there's a stop for lunch and exploring in Friday Harbor on San Juan Island. Under the right conditions, the views of whales and sunsets cannot be beat. They also offer cruises with craft-beer and Northwest wine themes. ⊠ *Bellingham Cruise Terminal, 355 Harris St., Suite 104* ☎ *360/738–8099, 800/443–4552* ⊕ *www.whales.com.*

KITSAP PENINSULA

Branching off the southeastern edge of the Olympic Peninsula, the Kitsap Peninsula has Puget Sound on one side and the Hood Canal on the other. Though the Kitsap doesn't possess the great, wild beauty of the Olympic Peninsula, it does have several charming waterfront towns with beach parks, kayaking and sailing opportunities, and a serene setting. Gig Harbor's marinas are full of pretty sailboats—it's the town that has the most to offer in terms of tourist amenities. Poulsbo is a pilgrimage point for anyone interested in tracing the Norwegian influence in the Pacific Northwest, and Port Gamble is a twee little town made up mostly of historic buildings.

GIG HARBOR

10

10 miles northwest of Tacoma.

One of the prettiest and most accessible waterfront communities on Puget Sound, Gig Harbor has a neat, circular bay dotted with sailboats and fronted by hills of evergreens and million-dollar homes. Expect spectacular views all along the town's winding, 2-mile, bay-side walkway, which is intermittently lined by boat docks, quirky shops, cozy cafés, and broad expanses of open water.

The bay was a storm refuge for the 1841 survey team of Captain Charles Wilkes, who named the area after his small gig (boat). A decade later Croatian and Scandinavian immigrants put their fishing, lumber, and boatbuilding skills to profitable use, and the town still has strong seafaring traditions. By the 1880s, steamboats carried passengers and goods between the harbor and Tacoma, and auto ferries plied the narrows between the cities by 1917.

The town winds around the waterfront, centering at the intersection of Harborview Drive and Pioneer Way, where shops, art galleries, and restaurants often attract more foot traffic than vehicles. From here, Harborview makes a long, gentle curve around the bay toward the renovated Finholm Market building, which has shops, docks, a restaurant, kayak rentals, and more views. A Gig Harbor Historical Society self-guided walk brochure covers 49 sights (see if you can spot the 16 metal salmon sculptures, designed by local artists, placed in front of sights around town).

Surrounding Gig Harbor, pine forests and open woods alternate with rolling pastures; it's enjoyable scenery (even on rainy days) during the 10-minute drive to Fox Island. Crossing the Fox Island Bridge over Echo Bay, you'll see stunning views of the Olympic Mountains to the right and the Tanglewood Lighthouse against a backdrop of Mt. Rainier to the left. Tanglewood Island, the small drop of forest on which the Tanglewood Lighthouse sits, was once a Native American burial ground known as Grav Island. At low tide the boat ramp and boulder-strewn beach next to the bridge are scattered with stranded saltwater creatures.

GETTING HERE AND AROUND

From Seattle, the fastest way (if there's no traffic) to Gig Harbor is to take Interstate 5 south through Tacoma to Highway 16 toward Bremerton. A slightly longer approach—in minutes, not miles—is to take the ferry from the West Seattle terminal to the Southworth landing on the Kitsap Peninsula and take Highway 160 west to Highway 16 south. Taking the ferry from Seattle to Bremerton also works—you take Highway 3 south to Highway 16.

ESSENTIALS

Visitor Information Gig Harbor Chamber of Commerce. ⊠ *3125 Judson St.* 🕿 *253/851–6865* ⊕ *www.gigharborchamber.com.*

EXPLORING

Gig Harbor Museum. An excellent collection of exhibits here describes the city's maritime history, and there are photo archives, video programs, and a research library focusing on the area's pioneer and Native American ancestors. The facilities include a one-room, early-20th-century schoolhouse and a 65-foot, 1950s purse seiner, a type of fishing vessel from the community's famous seafaring fleets. News clippings and videos about "Galloping Gertie," a bridge over the Tacoma Narrows that famously collapsed in 1940, are particularly eerie. ⊠ *4121 Harborview Dr.* 🕿 *253/858–6722* ⊕ *www.harborhistorymuseum.org* 🗃 *$7* 🕾 *Closed Mon.*

Kopachuck State Park. A 10-minute drive from Gig Harbor, this is a wonderful beachcombing area at low tide. Native American tribes once fished and clammed here, and you can still see people trolling the shallow waters or digging deep for razor clams in season. Children and dogs alike delight in discovering huge Dungeness crabs, sea stars, and sand dollars. Picnic tables and walking trails are interspersed throughout the 109 acres of steep, forested hills, and the campground is popular all summer. ⊠ *11101 56th St. NW* 🕿 *253/265–3606* ⊕ *www.parks.wa.gov* 🗃 *$10 per vehicle.*

Gig Harbor

WHERE TO EAT

$$$ MODERN AMERICAN Fodor's Choice ★

🍴 **Brix 25.** Simple seafood dishes and classic European fare are beautifully presented in this cozy, glass-fronted setting at the base of Harborview Drive and the Gig Harbor bay. Dinners are elaborate affairs that feature seafood—perhaps Thai curry and coconut-steamed mussels—and rich classics such as grilled filet mignon with pink-peppercorn sauce. **Known for:** terrific happy hour; decadent desserts; Thai curry with steamed mussels. [$] *Average main: $26* ✉ *7707 Pioneer Way* ☎ *253/858–6626* 🌐 *www.harborbrix.com* 🕒 *No lunch.*

$ MEXICAN

🍴 **El Pueblito.** The mariachi music, cilantro-and-chili-pepper scents from the kitchen, and a waitstaff that chats in Spanish are reminiscent of a compact cantina south of the border. Huge portions of better-than-average Mexican dishes and frothy margaritas are served amid much gaiety. **Known for:** lively bar scene; strong margaritas; tacos al pastor. [$] *Average main: $13* ✉ *3226 Harborview Dr.* ☎ *253/858–9077* 🌐 *www.elpueblitorestaurant.com.*

$$ PACIFIC NORTHWEST

🍴 **JW.** This elegant yet unfussy downtown bistro is one of Gig Harbor's top picks for memorable dinners. The kitchen turns out creative, seasonally driven fare—starters of honey-almond prawns, and duck-confit sliders, followed by seared sea scallops with candied bacon, and wild boar Bourguignon with sweet onions, carrots, fennel, and peppercorn sauce. **Known for:** flourless dark-chocolate torte; nice selection of Washington and Oregon wines; wild salmon with daily rotating preparation. [$] *Average main: $22* ✉ *4107 Harborview Dr.* ☎ *253/858–3529* 🌐 *www.jwgigharbor.com* 🕒 *Closed Mon. No lunch.*

WHERE TO STAY

$$ HOTEL **Inn at Gig Harbor.** The city's largest hotel is a four-story midrange property that looks and feels a bit like a cookie-cutter chain, but many of its rooms have Mt. Rainier views, and suites have a fireplace or jetted tub. **Pros:** lodge-style ambience; professional staff; good, affordable restaurant on-site. **Cons:** no pool; rates can get steep during busy summer periods. [$] *Rooms from: $154* ✉ *3211 56th St. NW* ☎ *253/858–1111, 800/795–9980* 🌐 *www.innatgigharbor.com* 🛏 *52 rooms, 12 suites* 🍴 *Breakfast.*

$ HOTEL **Maritime Inn.** On a hill across from Jersich Park and the docks, these individually decorated and themed rooms have unfussy, contemporary furnishings and gas fireplaces, and nearly every one overlooks the water; several have decks. **Pros:** right on the waterfront; friendly staff and highly personal service. **Cons:** front rooms absorb traffic noise. [$] *Rooms from: $149* ✉ *3112 Harborview Dr.* ☎ *253/858–1818, 888/506–3580* 🌐 *www.maritimeinn.com* 🛏 *15 rooms* 🍴 *Breakfast.*

SPORTS AND THE OUTDOORS

SAILING AND BOATING

Emerald Yachts. This outfitter close to downtown Gig Harbor rents individual and tandem kayaks as well as stand-up paddleboards. ✉ *3419 Harborview Dr.* ☎ *253/358–3491* 🌐 *www.harborkayaks.com.*

POULSBO

19 miles north of Bremerton, 12 miles northwest of Bainbridge Island.

Velkommen til Poulsbo (*pauls*-bo), a charming village on lovely Liberty Bay. Soon after it was settled by Norwegians in the 1880s, shops and bakeries sprang up along Front Street, as did a cod-drying facility to produce the Norwegian delicacy called lutefisk. Although it's no longer produced here commercially, lutefisk is still served at holiday feasts. Front Street is crammed with authentic Norwegian bakeries, eclectic Scandinavian crafts shops, small boutiques and bookstores, and art galleries. Norwegian flags flutter from the eaves of the town's chalet-style buildings. Grassy Liberty Bay Park is fronted by a network of slender docks where seals and otters pop in and out of the waves. One of the town's biggest events is the annual May Viking Festival (🌐 *www.vikingfest.org*), complete with Viking tents and weapons, costumed locals, and a lively parade.

GETTING HERE AND AROUND

To reach Poulsbo from Seattle, it's easiest to take the Washington State Ferries to Bainbridge Island and drive 12 miles from there via Highway 305 north across the Agate Pass Bridge. If you're driving up the Kitsap Peninsula, head north from Bremerton about 19 miles up Highway 3.

ESSENTIALS

Visitor Information **Greater Poulsbo Chamber of Commerce.**
✉ *19735 10th Ave. NE, Suite S100* ☎ *360/779–4848, 877/768–5726*
🌐 *www.poulsbochamber.com.*

EXPLORING

FAMILY **Poulsbo Marine Science Center.** Right along the shoreline and the edge of Liberty Bay Park, the center operated by Western Washington University is raised above the water and jam-packed with exhibits of local sea creatures. An intertidal touch tank lets kids feel sea anemones, sea urchins, and starfish, while other displays house crabs, jellyfish, and plants. Puppets, puzzles, murals, and videos help youngsters learn more about what they see. Don't miss the giant Pacific octopus in a 2,000-gallon tank beneath the center. A small gift shop fronts the building, and the center organizes special activities during Poulsbo festivals. ✉ *18743 Front St. NE* ☎ *360/598–4460* 🌐 *www.poulsbomsc.org* 🎟 *Free* 🕒 *Closed Mon.–Wed.*

WHERE TO EAT AND STAY

$$ TAPAS 🍴 **Paella Bar.** This warmly lighted, inviting downtown spot for Pacific Northwest–inspired Spanish tapas is adjacent to similarly excellent Burrata Bistro and is popular for both afternoon and late-night happy hour as well as for lunch and dinner. Paella is, of course, the big star here—it's studded with fresh local seafood. **Known for:** sangria and Spanish wines; seafood and chicken paella; potato tortillas with artichokes and aioli. [$] *Average main: $18* ✉ *19006 Front St.* ☎ *360/930–8446* 🌐 *www.burratabistro-paellabar.com.*

$ B&B/INN 🏨 **Green Cat Guest House.** A few miles north of downtown Poulsbo on the way to Port Gamble, this dashing B&B with steep gabled roof has a funky vibe, whimsical artwork, and a striking design, along with rooms decorated with a mix of Mission and Arts and Crafts pieces. **Pros:** completely peaceful and enchanting setting; distinctive furnishings; good proximity both to Poulsbo and Port Gamble. **Cons:** not within walking distance of downtown; a bit remote. [$] *Rooms from: $119* ✉ *25819 Tytler Rd. NE* ☎ *360/779–7569* 🌐 *www.greencatbb.com* 🛏 *3 rooms, 1 suite* 🍽 *Breakfast.*

$$ RESORT 🏨 **Suquamish Clearwater Casino Resort.** Whatever your feeling about casinos, this large contemporary resort just across the bridge to Bainbridge Island and a 10-minute drive from downtown Poulsbo offers some of the most attractive and well-equipped rooms in the region, especially considering the reasonable rates and views (from many rooms) of Puget Sound's Agate Pass strait. **Pros:** plenty of on-site entertainment and dining options; most rooms have sweeping water views; easy access to both Poulsbo and Bainbridge Island. **Cons:** not especially relaxing on busy weekends; casino on-site can be a drawback for nongamers. [$] *Rooms from: $159* ✉ *15347 Suquamish Way NE* ☎ *360/598–8700, 866/609–8700* 🌐 *www.clearwatercasino.com* 🛏 *186 rooms* 🍽 *No meals.*

SHOPPING

Fodor's Choice ★ **Sluys Bakery.** Rhyme it with "pies" and you'll sound like a local when you enter the town's most famous bakery. Gorgeous Norwegian pastries, braided bread, and *lefse* (traditional Norwegian round flatbread) line the shelves. Kids often beg for one of the decorated cookies or frosted doughnuts displayed at eye level. There's only strong coffee and milk to drink, and there are no seats, but you can grab a bench along busy Front Street or take your goodies to the waterfront at Liberty Bay Park. ✉ *18924 Front St.* ☎ *360/779–2798* 🌐 *www.sluyspoulsbobakery.com.*

PORT GAMBLE

6 miles northeast of Poulsbo.

Residents from the opposite side of America founded Port Gamble around a sawmill in 1853; hence its New England–style architecture mimicking founder Captain William Talbot's hometown of East Machias, Maine. Its setting amid the Kitsap Peninsula's tall stands of timber brought in great profits, but the mill was later destroyed by fire, and much of the forest has disappeared. A walk through town takes you past the 1870 St. Paul's Episcopal Church as well as the Thompson House, thought to be the state's oldest continuously lived-in home, and a handful of shops and restaurants. The town also stages a popular medieval-inspired June Faire each summer. This is also an excellent hiking area, with numerous backcountry trails throughout.

GETTING HERE AND AROUND

Port Gamble is just 6 miles from Poulsbo via Highway 3 and Highway 104.

EXPLORING

FAMILY
Fodor's Choice ★
Port Gamble Historic Museum. Beneath the town's quaint General Store, the Smithsonian-designed Port Gamble Historic Museum takes you through the region's timber heyday. Highlights include artifacts from the Pope and Talbot Timber Company, which built the town, and realistic ship's quarters. Above the General Store, the **Of Sea and Shore Museum** is open daily and houses more than 25,000 shells as well as displays on natural history. Kids love the weird bug exhibit. In between visits stop at the General Store for souvenirs or a huge ice-cream cone or hand-dipped milk shake, or stay for lunch or dinner in the acclaimed restaurant in the back of the building. ✉ *32400 Rainier Ave. NE* ☎ *360/297–8078* 🌐 *portgamble.com/visitin/museum* 🎟 *Historic Museum $4, Shell Museum free* 🕒 *Closed Mon.–Thurs. in Oct.–Apr.*

WHERE TO EAT AND STAY

$$
DELI
Fodor's Choice ★
🍴 **Butcher & Baker Provisions.** You'll find everything from thoughtfully curated aritsanal groceries and prepared foods to a selection of creative contemporary American and international fare in the cheerful dining room of this stylish market set inside a retrofitted auto repair shop a short walk from the Port Gamble Museum and General Store. Try the fried chicken and waffles at breakfast. **Known for:** fried chicken and waffles; pecan sticky buns; great selection of gourmet picnic provisions. [$] *Average main: $17* ✉ *4719 Hwy. 104* ☎ *360/297–9500* 🌐 *www.butcherandbakerprovisions.com* 🕒 *Closed Mon. and Tues.*

$
HOTEL
🏨 **Point Casino & Hotel.** This contemporary hotel is adjacent to the local S'Klallam Tribe's Point Casino with spacious rooms brightly decorated in patterns, artwork, and materials consistent with the tribe's aesthetic. **Pros:** modern, attractively furnished rooms; nongamers can easily avoid the casino; interesting tribal artwork and totem poles throughout property. **Cons:** common areas and casino can be noisy and crowded on weekends; 15- to 20-minute drive from Port Gamble and Poulsbo. [$] *Rooms from: $124* ✉ *7980 Salish La. NE* ☎ *360/340–9700* 🌐 *www.the-point-casino.com* 🛏 *94 rooms* 🍽 *No meals.*

TACOMA AND OLYMPIA

A trip south down Interstate 5 quickly yields two important port cities: Tacoma, and Olympia, the state capital. Although Olympia is more practiced in winning over visitors with its tidy legislative campus and laid-back charms, Tacoma has steadily followed suit with an ambitious revitalization plan and a growing number of hip restaurants, lounges, and shops. Both have the same good foundation to work with: beautiful waterfront locations with historic cores and lots of adjacent parkland, and Tacoma has an especially notable bounty of first-rate museums.

TACOMA

25 miles southeast of Gig Harbor, 34 miles southwest of Seattle.

After decades of decline, Tacoma has been steadily undergoing a renaissance in recent years, with development around the waterfront and in other parts of downtown showing dramatic progress—a number of urbane galleries, bars, and restaurants have popped up around Union Station and nearby blocks. Several of the Victorian homes in the charming Stadium Hill neighborhood, high on a hill overlooking Commencement Bay, have been converted to bed-and-breakfast inns. Still, even on the busiest nights, Tacoma can seem a little quiet considering its population of 204,000. In this sense, proximity to Seattle is both a blessing and a curse, as locals still tend to drive there for a big night on the town.

Tacoma's got character, however, and it does have plenty to fill a day or two. The museums (which are vastly underrated), waterfront promenade, lush and expansive Point Defiance Park, and attractive old neighborhoods make for a very pleasant side trip or overnight adventure. The waterfront stretches west from the busy port, past the city and Puget Sound islands to the cliff-lined Tacoma Narrows. Renovated 19th-century homes, pretty beaches, and parks pocket the outskirts, and a young, diverse population gives the city a spirited character. The city's convenient setting provides easy access to Seattle to the north; Mt. Rainier to the southeast; Olympia to the south; and the Kitsap and Olympic Peninsulas to the west.

Tacoma was the first Puget Sound port connected by train to the East, and its economy was once based on the railroad. Old photos show tall-masted windjammers loading at the City Waterway, whose storage sheds were promoted by local boosters as the "longest warehouse under one continuous roof in the world." The city's shipping industry certainly weathered the tests of time, as Tacoma is roughly tied with both Portland and Seattle as the busiest container port in the Northwest.

GETTING HERE AND AROUND

Tacoma is close enough to Seattle that many people commute in both directions. It's a straight 30-mile shot down Interstate 5 to Exit 133 toward the city center. The city is served by Greyhound and Amtrak, with connections north to Seattle and beyond, as well as south to Olympia. Tacoma is also served by Sound Transit's commuter rail, though trains are limited to rush hours.

10

If you're not planning to go too far out of the downtown core—just seeing
the museums and the waterfront—you don't absolutely need a car to get
around, as Amtrak and Greyhound let you off within a few blocks of each
other in the Dome district (by the Tacoma Dome, on Puyallup Avenue).
From here, you can catch Sound Transit's free Link light-rail, which will
get you to the museums, restaurants, and hotels of the downtown core.

ESSENTIALS

Visitor Information Tacoma Tacoma + Pierce County. ⊠ *1516 Commerce St.*
☎ *253/284–3254, 800/272–2662* ⊕ *www.traveltacoma.com.*

EXPLORING

TOP ATTRACTIONS

Fodor's Choice **Foss Waterway Seaport.** With its beautiful setting right along the Thea
★ Foss waterfront, the turn-of-the-20th-century, wharf-style structure—
with a dashing modern glass facade—is easily reached along a walk by
the bay. Inside the enormous timber building, a museum devoted to the
city's waterfront heritage contains displays about the history of Tacoma's
brisk shipping business. Extensive exhibits cover boat making, vintage
scuba and diving gear, importing and exporting, and the development of
the waterfront. Photos and relics round out the exhibits, and children's
activities are staged regularly. ⊠ *705 Dock St.* ☎ *253/272–2750* ⊕ *www.
fosswaterwayseaport.org* ⊿ *$10* ☉ *Closed Mon. and Tues.*

FAMILY
Fodor's Choice
★

LeMay—America's Car Museum. About 350 meticulously restored auto-mobiles, from some of the world's earliest models to brassy muscle cars from the late '60s, are displayed in this sleek, striking museum on the south side of downtown. It's one of the most impressive car museums in the country, with engaging exhibits on Route 66, alternative-fuel cars, NASCAR, and other aspects of automobile culture and history. The cars here were collected by the late Harold LeMay, whose entire inventory of some 4,000 autos is recognized by the *Guinness Book of World Records* as the largest privately owned collection in the world. Highlights include a 1906 Cadillac Model M, a 1926 Rolls-Royce Silver Ghost, a 1930 Lincoln L Brougham, a 1953 Citroen 2CV, a 1960 Corvette, and a 1963 Studebaker Avanti. The café serves diner classics, including very tasty banana splits. If you're an ardent car enthusiast, it's worth making the 15-minute drive south to the related LeMay Family Collection Foundation at the Marymount Event Center in the Spanaway neighborhood of south Tacoma (⊕ *www.lemaymarymount. org*), which displays another 1,500 classic autos and trucks from the collection, along with all sorts of additional memorabilia, from antique dolls and toys to farming equipment. ✉ *2702 E. D St.* ☎ *253/779–8490, 877/902–8490* ⊕ *www.lemaymuseum.org* ⛶ *$18.*

Fodor's Choice
★

Museum of Glass. The showpiece of this spectacular, 2-acre combination of delicate and creative exhibits is the 500-foot-long Chihuly Bridge of Glass, a tunnel of glorious color and light that stretches above Interstate 705. Cross it from downtown to reach the building grounds, which sit above the bay and next to a shallow reflecting pool dotted with large modern-art sculptures. Inside, you can wander through the quiet, light-filled galleries, take a seat in the theaterlike Hot Shop—with its soaring conical roof—to watch glass-blowing artists, or try your own hand at arts and crafts in the studio. You'll also find a souvenir shop and café. ✉ *1801 E. Dock St.* ☎ *253/284–4750, 866/468–7386* ⊕ *www. museumofglass.org* ⛶ *$12.*

FAMILY
Fodor's Choice
★

Point Defiance Park. Jutting into Commencement Bay, this hilly, 760-acre park surrounds Five Mile Drive with lush picnicking fields and patches of forest. Hiking trails, bike paths, and numerous gardens draw crowds year-round, particularly during summer festivals such as the Taste of Tacoma, in late June. The park begins at the north end of Pearl Street as you drive toward the Point Defiance Ferry Terminal, where vehicles depart for Vashon Island just across the Sound. A one-way road branches off the ferry lane, past a lake and picnic area, a rose garden, a spectacular 22-acre rhododendron garden, and a Japanese garden, finally winding down to the beach.

A half-mile past the gardens is **Owen Beach,** a driftwood-strewn stretch of pebbly sand near the ferry dock and a wonderful place for beach-combing and sailboat-watching. Kayak rentals and concessions are available in summer. Continue around the looping drive, which offers occasional views of the narrows. Cruise slowly to take in the scenes—and watch out for joggers and bikers. ✉ *5400 N. Pearl St.* ⊕ *www. metroparkstacoma.org/point-defiance-park.*

10

Point Defiance Zoo & Aquarium. One of the Northwest's finest collections of regional and international species, this winding and hilly site includes tigers, elephants, tapirs, and gibbons in the Asian Forest Sanctuary, where paw-print trails lead between lookouts so even the smallest tots can spot animals. The aquariums are also fun to explore, including a glass-walled, floor-to-ceiling shark tank; seahorse room; touch-tank marine area; and open-topped, two-level Pacific Northwest reef display. Other areas house such cold-weather creatures as beluga whales, Arctic foxes, polar bears, and penguins. Thirty-minute animal shows, run two to four times daily, let different creatures show off their skills. The fantastic playground area has friendly farm animals running between the slides, and seasonal special events include a Halloween trick-or-treat night and the famous nightly Zoolights holiday displays around Christmas. On weekends, weather permitting, camel rides are offered. ⊠ *Point Defiance Park, 5400 N. Pearl St.* ☎ *253/305–1000* ⊕ *www.pdza.org* ✉ *$17.95* ⊗ *Closed Nov.–mid-Dec., Jan. and Feb., Tues. and Wed.*

Ft. Nisqually. This restored Hudson's Bay Trading Post—a British outpost on the Nisqually Delta in the 1830s—was moved to Point Defiance in 1935. The compound houses a trading post, granary, blacksmith's shop, bakery, and officers' quarters. Docents dress in 1850s attire and demonstrate pioneer skills like weaving and loading a rifle. Queen Victoria's birthday in May is a big event, and eerie candlelight tours are offered several days in October. ⊠ *5400 N. Pearl St.* ☎ *253/591–5339* ⊕ *www.fortnisqually.org* ✉ *$8* ⊗ *Closed Oct.–Apr., Mon. and Tues.*

Tacoma Art Museum. Adorned in glass and steel, this Antoine Predock masterpiece wraps around a beautiful garden. Inside, you'll find paintings, ceramics, sculptures, and other creations dating from the 18th century to the present. Look for the many glass sculptures by Dale Chihuly—especially the magnificent, flame-color *Mille Fiori* (Thousand Flowers) glass garden. ⊠ *1701 Pacific Ave.* ☎ *253/272–4258* ⊕ *www. tacomaartmuseum.org* ✉ *$15* ⊗ *Closed Mon.*

Washington State History Museum. Adjacent to Union Station, and with the same opulent architecture, Washington's official history museum presents interactive exhibits and multimedia installations about the exploration and settlement of the state. Some rooms are filled with Native American, Inuit, and pioneer artifacts, while others display logging and railroad relics. The upstairs gallery hosts rotating exhibits, and summer programs are staged in the outdoor amphitheater. ⊠ *1911 Pacific Ave.* ☎ *253/272–3500, 888/238–4373* ⊕ *www.washingtonhistory.org* ✉ *$12* ⊗ *Closed Mon.*

WORTH NOTING

FAMILY **Children's Museum of Tacoma.** Fun activities for little ones take place at this hands-on, state-of-the-art museum where areas for exploration are broken down into a variety of "playscapes"—woods, water, voyager, Becka's Studio, invention, and reflection. Snacks are served in Café Play. Admission is "pay as you will." ⊠ *1501 Pacific Ave.* ☎ *253/627–6031* ⊕ *www.playtacoma.org* ✉ *Donation requested* ⊗ *Closed Mon. and Tues.*

Chihuly Bridge of Glass, Tacoma

Karpeles Manuscript Library Museum. Housed in the former American Legion hall and across from Wright Park, the museum showcases rare and unpublished letters and documents by notables who have shaped history. Themes of the rotating exhibits have included the correspondence from the family of Presidents John and John Quincy Adams and Einstein's theory of relativity. ⊠ *407 S. G St.* ☎ *253/383–2575* ⊕ *www. rain.org/~karpeles* ⬚ *Free.*

Tacoma-Narrows Bridge. A mile-wide waterway is the boundary between the Tacoma hills and the rugged bluffs of the Kitsap Peninsula. From the twin bridges that span it, the view plunges hundreds of feet down to roiling green waters, which are often busy with barge traffic or obscured by fog. The original bridge, "Galloping Gertie," famously twisted itself to death and broke in half during a storm in 1940—it's now the world's largest man-made reef, and is a popular dive site. Its mint-green replacement and a sister bridge opened in 2007. Note: the $6 toll is for eastbound cars only; westbound it's free from Tacoma into Gig Harbor. ⊠ *Hwy. 16 at N. Jackson Ave.*

FAMILY **Tacoma Nature Center at Snake Lake.** Comprising 71 acres of marshland, evergreen forest, and shallow lake that break up the urban sprawl of west Tacoma, the center shelters 20 species of mammals and more than 100 species of birds. The lake has nesting pairs of wood ducks, rare elsewhere in western Washington, and the interpretive center is a fun place for kids to look at small creatures, take walks and nature quizzes, and dress up in animal costumes. ⊠ *1919 S. Tyler St.* ☎ *253/591–6439* ⊕ *www.metroparkstacoma.org/tacomanaturecenter* ⬚ *Free, $3 per family donation suggested* ☉ *Center closed Sun.*

10

Union Station. This heirloom dates from 1911, when Tacoma was the western terminus of the Northern Pacific Railroad. Built by Reed and Stem, architects of New York City's Grand Central Terminal, the copper-domed, beaux arts–style depot shows the influence of the Roman Pantheon and Italian baroque style. The station houses federal district courts, but its rotunda contains a gorgeous exhibit of glass sculptures by Dale Chihuly. Since it's a highly guarded government facility, be prepared to walk through a metal detector and show photo ID. ✉ *1717 Pacific Ave.* ☎ *253/863–5173* 🌐 *www.unionstationrotunda.org* 🎟 *Free* 🕒 *Closed weekends.*

WHERE TO EAT

$$$ SEAFOOD
🍴 **Cliff House Restaurant.** For an unforgettable scene, witness the ocean panorama from this 1925 landmark restaurant's Rainier Room when there's a full moon. Entrées include Northwest seafood stew in a tomato-garlic broth and boneless rib-eye steak with a green-peppercorn demi-glace. **Known for:** Puget Sound and Mt. Rainier views; Northwest seafood stew; juicy steaks. [$] *Average main: $27* ✉ *6300 Marine View Dr.* ☎ *253/927–0400* 🌐 *www.cliffhousetacoma.com.*

$$ INTERNATIONAL
🍴 **Cooks Tavern.** This warmly lighted tavern in the historic North End operates under a clever and ambitious premise: every four months, the kitchen unveils a new menu dedicated to the cuisine of a different region of the Americas, from New Orleans to Montreal to Argentina. To keep fans with less adventurous tastes happy, the restaurant keeps a number of noteworthy dishes on every menu, including a burger topped with sharp cheddar, bacon, and fried egg and a few salads and appetizers. **Known for:** changing menu featuring a different cuisine every four months; breakfast served daily til 3 pm; trendy craft-beer bar, Brewers Row, next door. [$] *Average main: $18* ✉ *3201 N. 26th St.* ☎ *253/327–1777* 🌐 *www.cookstavern.com.*

$$$ SEAFOOD Fodor's Choice ★
🍴 **Duke's Chowder House.** One of several popular seafood restaurants along Ruston Way, overlooking Tacoma's picturesque Commencement Bay, Duke's is part of a regional chainlet that can be counted on for serving some of the freshest and most creative fare of the bunch—it's not just about the view here, although the tables on the patio do offer dazzling panoramas. Chowder fans having a tough time deciding what to try might want to order the "full fleet" sampler, with small servings of clam, lobster, crab bisque, chicken-corn, and Northwest seafood varieties. **Known for:** outdoor dining on Commencement Bay; chowder sampler; Dungeness crab cakes. [$] *Average main: $27* ✉ *3327 Ruston Way* ☎ *253/752–5444* 🌐 *www.dukeschowderhouse.com.*

$ NORTHERN ITALIAN
🍴 **Europa Bistro.** Set in the middle of the genial and hip Proctor retail and restaurant district, on the city's north side (not too far from Point Defiance), this charming, affordable neighborhood spot focuses on authentic northern Italian recipes. Regulars feast on traditional pan-fried zucchini with goat cheese and crostini, slow-roasted lamb over pappardelle noodles, seafood risotto, and thin-crust pizzas. **Known for:** great selection of Italian wines; seafood risotto; meatball pizza. [$] *Average main: $13* ✉ *2515 N. Proctor St.* ☎ *253/761–5660* 🌐 *www.europabistro.net* 🕒 *No lunch Sun.*

$$ ✕**Indochine.** The elegant, pan-Asian conglomeration of sounds, scents,
ASIAN and sights takes place in a sleekly modern yet darkly cozy space. The
Fodor's Choice taste-dazzling array of Thai, Chinese, Indian, and Japanese cuisines
★ includes curries, stir-fries, soups, and seafood. **Known for:** Oceans Five
seafood platter; honey-glazed-walnut prawns; spicy lemongrass prawn
soup. $ *Average main: $19* ✉ *1924 Pacific Ave.* ☎ *253/272–8200*
⊕ *www.indochinedowntown.com* ⊘ *Closed Mon.*

$$$ ✕**Over The Moon Cafe.** Tucked down an alley near Wright Park, the the-
PACIFIC ater district, and several popular antiques shops, this quirky and cozy
NORTHWEST neighborhood bistro serves first-rate Northwest-influenced Italian fare,
including bounteous salads and creative grills. It's worth seeking out
this art-filled space with exposed-brick walls for such delectable fare
as slow-cooked short-rib ragù over rigatoni and pan-seared, bourbon-
glazed salmon fillet. **Known for:** banana pie; lobster mac and cheese; artsy
pretheater crowd. $ *Average main: $25* ✉ *709 Opera Alley* ☎ *253/284–
3722* ⊕ *www.overthemooncafe.net* ⊘ *Closed Sun. and Mon.*

$$$ ✕**Pacific Grill.** With its clubby interior, huge wine list, and proximity to
MODERN downtown hotels and attractions, it's easy to see how this flashy res-
AMERICAN taurant is a favorite for special occasions and high-end business meals.
Here you can expect a menu of contemporary variations on seafood
and steak, including Columbia River steelhead with a maple-balsamic
glaze and New York steak with red-flannel hash and a red-wine sauce;
vegetarians shouldn't pass up the unusual roasted cauliflower "steak"
served with olive gremolata, tomatoes, orange, and capers. **Known for:**
bottomless drinks weekend brunch; smoked steelhead appetizer; filet
mignon. $ *Average main: $27* ✉ *1502 Pacific Ave.* ☎ *253/627–3535*
⊕ *www.pacificgrilltacoma.com.*

$ ✕**Red Hot.** The first thing you notice upon walking inside this bustling
HOT DOG tavern and hot-dog joint are the dozens of beer taps hanging from the ceil-
Fodor's Choice ing, each one representing a particular ale that's been poured here. Indeed,
★ this quirky spot is a must for beer lovers, with plenty of interesting vari-
eties on tap and available by the bottle, from Northwest craft brews to
Belgian Trappist tripels. **Known for:** the Hound Dog (with peanut butter
and bacon); late-night dining; lots of great beers on tap. $ *Average main:*
$6 ✉ *2914 6th Ave.* ☎ *253/779–0229* ⊕ *www.redhottacoma.com.*

$ ✕**Southern Kitchen.** Sure, it's awfully far north to be specializing in down-
SOUTHERN home Southern cooking, but this bustling, casual spot on Tacoma's
Fodor's Choice north side, a little west of Wright Park, serves remarkably authentic and
★ absolutely delicious soul food. In the morning, regulars swing by for
heaping plates of chicken-fried steak with grits and eggs, or homemade
biscuits and gravy. **Known for:** hand-battered fried catfish; chicken-fried
steak; jalapeño hush puppies. $ *Average main: $12* ✉ *1716 6th Ave.*
☎ *253/627–4282* ⊕ *www.southernkitchen-tacoma.com.*

$ ✕**Top of Tacoma.** This hillside neighborhood tavern just south of down-
AMERICAN town and the LeMay car museum makes a convivial option for lunch
(or weekend brunch), dinner, or cocktails, as the drinks selection is
extensive and the affordable food—from tacos to tofu—is a cut or two
above your typical pub grub. Favorites include crispy pork-belly tacos
with apple-cabbage slaw and tart cherries, Moroccan-style quinoa salad
with harrisa-agave vinaigrette and seared tofu, and a commendable

10

Reuben on rye bread. **Known for:** "hangover homies" (smothered home fries) at brunch; jukebox with plenty of old-school tunes; some of the best sandwiches in town. $ *Average main: $10* ⊠ *3529 McKinley Ave.* ☎ *253/272–1502* ⊕ *www.topoftacoma.com.*

WHERE TO STAY

$

B&B/INN

▦ **Chinaberry Hill.** Original fixtures and stained-glass windows are among the grace notes in this 1889 Queen Anne–style house on a tree-lined street, where accommodations come with shining wood floors, antique feather beds dressed in fine-quality linens, and ornate desks. **Pros:** wraparound porch with vast bay views; in the Stadium Historic District. **Cons:** creaks and quirks of a century-old mansion; 20- to 30-minute walk from downtown attractions. $ *Rooms from: $149* ⊠ *302 Tacoma Ave. N* ☎ *253/272–1282* ⊕ *www.chinaberryhill.com* ➷ *1 room, 4 suites, 1 cottage* ❑ *Breakfast.*

$$

HOTEL

▦ **Courtyard Marriott Tacoma Downtown.** Although set in the late-19th-century Waddell Building, this Marriott has spacious, modern rooms outfitted in bright Northwest colors with lots of 21st-century touches, and you'll find an upscale restaurant and bar. **Pros:** reliable chain hotel in historic building; steps from convention center and museums; full-service spa. **Cons:** rooms get street noise; can get little pricey for a midrange chain hotel; parking fee. $ *Rooms from: $189* ⊠ *1515 Commerce St.* ☎ *253/591–9100* ⊕ *www. marriott.com* ➷ *156 rooms, 6 suites* ❑ *Breakfast.*

$

B&B/INN

▦ **Green Cape Cod Bed & Breakfast.** At this 1929 house in a residential neighborhood only blocks from the historic Proctor shopping district rooms come with frilly linens and beautiful antiques. **Pros:** cozy, romantic rooms; lovely, historic neighborhood with several good restaurants within walking distance. **Cons:** need a car to get downtown. $ *Rooms from: $145* ⊠ *2711 N. Warner St.* ☎ *253/752–1977, 866/752–1977* ⊕ *www.greencapecod.com* ➷ *3 rooms* ❑ *Breakfast.*

$$

HOTEL

Fodor'sChoice

★

▦ **Hotel Murano.** Named for the Venetian island where some of the world's best glass is created, this big hotel with an intimate ambience centers around exhibits by world-famous glass artists and offers rooms done in black and white with fiery accents. **Pros:** stylish rooms with beautiful art; luxury amenities; top-flight service. **Cons:** no pool; parking fee. $ *Rooms from: $165* ⊠ *1320 Broadway Plaza* ☎ *253/238–8000, 888/862–3255* ⊕ *www.hotelmuranotacoma.com* ➷ *319 rooms, 10 suites* ❑ *Breakfast.*

$$$

HOTEL

Fodor'sChoice

★

▦ **Silver Cloud Inn.** Tacoma's lone waterfront hotel juts right out into the bay along picturesque Ruston Way and the historic Old Town area, with contemporary rooms and even swankier suites that have plush carpets, overstuffed chairs, fireplaces, and corner hot tubs that look right out over the water. **Pros:** water views from every room; Ruston Way walking paths and restaurants nearby; free parking and free Wi-Fi. **Cons:** area around hotel can get crowded on weekends; rates can get steep in summer, especially for suites. $ *Rooms from: $209* ⊠ *2317 N. Ruston Way* ☎ *253/272–1300, 866/820–8448* ⊕ *www.silvercloud.com* ➷ *90 rooms* ❑ *Breakfast.*

$$$$

B&B/INN

▦ **Thornewood Castle Inn and Gardens.** Spread over 4 lush acres along beautiful American Lake, this 27,000-square-foot, Gothic-Tudor-style mansion built in 1908 has hosted two American presidents (William Howard Taft and Theodore Roosevelt) and surrounds current guests with medieval-style stained-glass windows, gleaming wood floors, large mirrors, antiques, fireplaces, and hot tubs. **Pros:** castlelike ambience; lively events. **Cons:** one of the more expensive properties in the area; in a sort of no-man's-land between Tacoma and Fort Lewis; often fully booked on summer weekends for weddings. [$] *Rooms from: $265* ✉ *8601 N. Thorne La. SW, Lakewood* ✥ *12 miles south of Tacoma* ☎ *253/589–9052* 🌐 *www.thornewoodcastle.com* 🛏 *2 rooms, 7 suites, 3 apartments* 🍴 *Breakfast.*

NIGHTLIFE AND PERFORMING ARTS

NIGHTLIFE

Copper Door. Craft-brew lovers appreciate the 16 different rotating taps and more than 800 bottled beers at this hip yet unfussy bar in the historic Stadium District. The bar hosts the Barrel Aged Beer Festival each year in March. ✉ *12 N. Tacoma Ave.* ☎ *253/212–3708.*

Jazzbones. This classy no-cover, no-fuss, just-great-music joint is on the 6th Avenue strip, with live jazz on stage every night. There's a good restaurant here, too, serving eclectic Southern-inspired American food, and—a bit surprisingly—a popular sushi bar. ✉ *2803 6th Ave.* ☎ *253/396–9169* 🌐 *www.jazzbones.com.*

The Mix. Tacoma has a sizable, increasingly visible gay community, and this friendly, welcoming bar with a nice-size dance floor and fun karaoke parties is the top nightspot among LGBT folks. It's in the heart of the Theater District. ✉ *635 St. Helens Ave.* ☎ *253/383–4327* 🌐 *www.themixtacoma.com.*

Swiss Pub. This lively pub inside a historic building has microbrews on tap, pool tables, and bands on stage Thursday through Saturday. Monday brings free admission for live blues night, and there's karaoke on Wednesday. The place is best early in the evening before the bands start playing—it can get pretty loud and rambunctious in here as the evening goes on. ✉ *1904 S. Jefferson Ave.* ☎ *253/572–2821* 🌐 *www.theswisspub.com.*

Fodor's Choice ★ **1022 South.** You can't claim to have a sophisticated nightlife scene until someone in a vest is mixing artisanal cocktails, and 1022 South is Tacoma's top spot for fine drinks made with unusual infusions (nettles, yerba maté), house-made liqueurs and colas, and premium liquors with hipster cachet (Portland's Aviation gin, for example). Daily happy hour is 4 to 7 pm, and the kitchen produces nosh-worthy nibbles, from cheese plates to burgers. ✉ *1022 S. J St.* ☎ *253/627–8588* 🌐 *www.ten22southj.com.*

PERFORMING ARTS

Cultural activity in Tacoma centers on the outstanding—and historic—Broadway Center for the Performing Arts, which comprises four distinct venues, including the gorgeous 1918 Pantages Theater. One of the largest performing arts center in the Pacific Northwest, the venue hosts pop concerts, touring Broadway shows, Symphony Tacoma performances, and more.

Broadway Center for the Performing Arts. Cultural activity in Tacoma centers on this complex of performance spaces. ✉ *901 Broadway, between 10th and 11th Sts.* ☎ *253/591–5894, 800/291–7593* 🌐 *www.broadwaycenter.org.*

SHOPPING

Tacoma's top shopping districts are Antique Row, along Broadway at St. Helen's Street, where upscale shops sell everything from collectibles to vintage paraphernalia, and the Proctor District, in the north end, where many specialty shops do business.

OLYMPIA

30 miles southwest of Tacoma.

Olympia has been the capital of Washington since 1853, the beginning of city and state. It is small (population 48,000) for the capital city of a major state, but that makes it all the more pleasant to visit. The old and charming downtown area is compact and easy on the feet, stretching between Capitol Lake and the gathering of austere government buildings to the south, the shipping and yacht docks around glistening Budd Inlet to the west, the colorful market area capping the north end of town, and Interstate 5 running along the eastern edge. There are small, unexpected surprises all through town, from pretty, little half-block parks and blossoming miniature gardens to clutches of Thai and Vietnamese restaurants and antiques shops. The imposing state capitol, finished in 1928, is set above the south end of town like a fortress, framed by a skirt of granite steps. The monumental 287-foot-high dome is the fourth-tallest masonry dome in the world (only St. Peter's in Rome, St. Paul's in London, and St. Isaac's Cathedral in St. Petersburg rise higher).

GETTING HERE AND AROUND

From Seattle, take Interstate 5 south to Exit 105—this is an easy city to drive and park in, and a car is your best way around. Both Greyhound and Amtrak serve Olympia, but the Amtrak station is 8 miles away, so from Seattle, if you're not driving, taking the bus is actually more convenient, as the bus station is centrally located and the sights are clustered around downtown.

ESSENTIALS

Visitor Information Olympia Visitor and Convention Bureau. ✉ *103 Sid Snyder Ave. SW* ☎ *360/704–7544, 877/704–7500* ⊕ *www.visitolympia.com.*

EXPLORING

TOP ATTRACTIONS

Capitol Campus. These attractive grounds, sprawling around the buildings perched above the Capitol Lake bluffs, contain memorials, monuments, rose gardens, and Japanese cherry trees. The 1939 conservatory is open year-round on weekdays from 7 to 5:30 and also on weekends 11 to 4. Directly behind the legislative building, the modern state library has exhibits devoted to Washington's history. Free 45-minute tours (weekdays 10–3, weekends 11–3) from the visitor center take you around the area. If you want to see state government in action, the legislature is in session for 30 or 60 days from the second Monday in January, depending on whether it's an even- or odd-numbered year. ✉ *Capitol Way, between 10th and 14th Aves.* ☎ *360/902–8880 tour information* ⊕ *www.des.wa.gov* 🎟 *Free.*

FAMILY **Hands On Children's Museum.** This fun spot in a handsome, modern building just off Marine Drive overlooking East Bay is where children can touch, build, and play with all sorts of crafts and exhibits. Dozens of interactive, cleverly designed stations include an art studio and a special gallery for kids four and under. During the city's First Friday art walks the museum is open late, offers free admission after 5 pm, and stages special programs and events. ✉ *414 Jefferson St. NE* ☎ *360/956–0818* ⊕ *www.hocm.org* 💵 *$12.95.*

Fodor'sChoice **Nisqually National Wildlife Refuge.** More than 200 different bird species
★ along with a slew of reptiles, mammals, and amphibians thrive amid the marshes and grasslands of this 4,529-acre estuarial refuge on the delta formed by the Nisqually River's confluence with Puget Sound. Just 8 miles east of downtown Olympia, the tranquil space feels a world away from civilization and is laced with several miles of trails, some of them along boardwalks. Naturalists lead guided walks and give lectures on weekends from April through September, and a visitor center contains exhibits and a nature store. ✉ *100 Brown Farm Rd.* ☎ *360/753–9467* ⊕ *www.fws.gov/refuge/Billy_Frank_Jr_Nisqually* 💵 *$3* ⊗ *Visitor center closed Mon. and Tues.*

Percival Landing Waterfront Park. Framing nearly 4 acres of landscaped desert gardens and bird-watching areas, this lovely waterfront spot stretches along a 1-mile boardwalk through a beachy section of the Ellis Cove coastline. To the south are yachts bobbing in the water at the wooden docks and the waterfront Anthony's restaurant; to the north are the shipyards and cargo cranes; and to the east is the market. In the center is an open space with an outdoor stage for summer shows, music, and festivals. You can see it all from three stories up by climbing the winding steps of the viewing tower, where open benches invite visitors to relax and enjoy the outlook. ✉ *4th Ave. to Thurston Ave.* ☎ *360/753–8380* ⊕ *olympiawa. gov/community/parks/percival-landing* 💵 *Free.*

WORTH NOTING

Olympia Farmers Market. Neat, clean, and well run, this expanse of covered fruit, vegetable, pastry, and craft stalls at the north end of town includes organic produce. You'll also find all sorts of oddities such as ostrich eggs, button magnets, and glass sculptures. With several tiny ethnic eateries tucked in between the vendors, it's also a terrific place to grab a bite and then walk over to the waterfront. ✉ *700 N. Capitol Way* ☎ *360/352–9096* ⊕ *www.olympiafarmersmarket.com* 💵 *Free* ⊗ *Closed Mon.–Wed.; Nov. and Dec., weekdays; and Jan.–Mar. Sun.–Fri.*

The Olympic Flight Museum. Housed in a hangar at the Olympic Regional Airport south of town, this museum brings to life an ever-changing collection of vintage aircraft. Important pieces include a colorful P-51D Mustang, a sleek BAC-167 Strikemaster, and a serious-looking AH-1S Cobra helicopter. On the annual schedule are winter lectures, weekly tours, monthly flights, and the Olympic Airshow each June. The shop sells a model of just about everything you see on-site. ✉ *7637 Old Hwy. 99 SE* ☎ *360/705–3925* ⊕ *www.olympicflightmuseum.com* 💵 *$7* ⊗ *Closed Mon., Oct.–Apr.*

10

Priest Point Park. This leafy 314-acre tract is a beautiful section of protected shoreline and wetlands. Thick swaths of forest and glistening bay views are the main attractions, with picnic areas and playgrounds filling in the open spaces. The 3-mile **Ellis Cove Trail,** with interpretive stations, bridges, and nature settings, runs right through the Priest Point Park area and around the Olympia coast. ⊠ *East Bay Dr.* ☎ *360/753–8380* ⊕ *olympiawa.gov/community/parks/parks-and-trails/priest-point-park* ☜ *Free.*

222 Market. Olympia's foodie cred received a boost in 2015 with the opening of this artisanal marketplace just a couple of blocks east of Percival Landing and a short walk south of the city's renowned Farmers Market. The warren of boutique restaurants and food purveyors includes the long-running Bread Peddler bakery along with about 10 newer outlets specializing in everything from sustainable shellfish and bone broths to small-batch whiskey and premium gelato. There's also a florist and gourmet market. ⊠ *222 Capitol Way N* ⊕ *www.222market.com.*

FAMILY **Wolf Haven International.** Guided tours of this 80-acre wolf sanctuary are given every hour on the hour and run about 50 minutes, during which docents explain the recovery programs and visitors can view the wolves. You must join a tour. Note that it's worth taking a look at the website before visiting—the sanctuary has a few rules regarding conduct. Most importantly, parents should know that although the sanctuary can be a wonderful place for kids, it does not provide as much stimulation as a typical zoo and may bore kids with short attention spans. ⊠ *3111 Offut Lake Rd. SE* ⊹ *From Olympia, take I–5 south to Exit 99 and follow signs east for 7 miles* ☎ *800/448–9653* ⊕ *www.wolfhaven.org* ☜ *$12* ⊙ *Closed mid-Feb.–mid-Mar. and weekdays fall–spring.*

WHERE TO EAT

$$$ ✕**Dockside Bistro & Wine Bar.** The marina views are only part of the
PACIFIC appeal of this bright, modern bistro overlooking West Bay. It's the
NORTHWEST innovative, beautifully presented Asia-meets-Northwest cuisine that has foodies buzzing, not to mention friendly and efficient service and a stellar wine list. **Known for:** Pacific Northwest fare with Asian influences; bouillabaisse; views of West Bay. Ⓢ *Average main: $27* ⊠ *501 Columbia St. NW* ☎ *360/956–1928* ⊕ *www.docksidebistro.com* ⊙ *Closed Mon. No lunch Sun.*

$ ✕**Fish Tale BrewPub.** This long-running microbrewery and tavern in a
AMERICAN slightly industrial section of downtown has a bustling, open dining room with mounted fish on the walls and a quieter section of outdoor seating along the sidewalk. It's a funky and fun standby for big portions of pub standards—nachos, smoked wild salmon platters, black-bean burgers, fish-and-chips, and a much beloved Mudshark Porter dark-chocolate cheesecake. **Known for:** Mudshark Porter dark-chocolate cheesecake; nacho platters; plenty of interesting limited-release and seasonal ales. Ⓢ *Average main: $13* ⊠ *515 Jefferson St. SE* ☎ *360/943–3650* ⊕ *www. fishbrewing.com.*

$$ ✕**Mercato.** Tucked into a glitzy, glass-front office building on a sunny
MEDITERRANEAN corner across from the Farmers Market, the aptly named restaurant brings an Italian countryside ambience to this relaxed neighborhood. Specialties include the *piadina* sandwiches, slices of warmed

flatbread slathered with such cold fillings as smoked duck on spinach vinaigrette, along with thin-crust pizzas, creative pastas and risottos, and hearty grills. **Known for:** weekend brunch; three-course Sunday–Thursday $25 dinner special; gnocchi with smoked duck. $ Average main: $18 ⊠ 111 Market St. NE ☎ 360/528-3663 ⊕ www.mercatoristorante.com.

$ ✕ **New Moon Cafe.** This cheery, simple downtown breakfast and lunch
AMERICAN spot renowned for its house-made blackberry jam and funky vibe is a cooperative, owned entirely by its staff. The filling omelets, including the Northwestern (with smoked salmon, spinach, and cream cheese) and Benedicts are among the mainstays that keep regulars coming back, but the decadent blackberry French toast is the café's showstopper. **Known for:** blackberry French toast; smoked-salmon omelet; New Moon burger topped with avocado, feta, and mushrooms. $ Average main: $10 ⊠ 113 4th Ave. W ☎ 360/357-3452 ⊕ www.newmooncafe. coop ⊗ No dinner.

$ ✕ **Our Table.** Locally sourced, sustainable ingredients take center stage
MODERN in the artfully plated dishes at this otherwise simple-looking downtown
AMERICAN restaurant popular for its affordable breakfast, lunch, and dinner fare.
Fodor's Choice Fluffy house-made biscuits with sausage gravy and the hangtown fry
★ with local fried oysters, bacon, and house-made hot sauce are among noteworthy morning dishes. **Known for:** chocolate mousse; hangtown fry; duck-and-root-vegetable pâté. $ Average main: $13 ⊠ 406 4th Ave. E ☎ 360/932-6030 ⊕ www.ourtableolympia.com ⊗ Closed Tues. and Wed. No dinner Sun.

WHERE TO STAY

$$ 🏨 **Doubletree Olympia Hotel.** These polished rooms nestle right up to
HOTEL Budd Inlet just a couple of blocks from the Farmers Market and are done with plush fabrics in deep charcoals, golds, and beiges and come with such splashy bonuses as corner jetted tubs and chaise lounges. **Pros:** nicest rooms of any chain property in town; free parking; 24-hour pool and fitness center. **Cons:** pedestrian hotel appearance. $ Rooms from: $189 ⊠ 415 Capitol Way N ☎ 360/570-0555, 855/610-8733 ⊕ www.hilton.com ⤵ 102 suites ⓘ⊙ Breakfast.

$ 🏨 **Hotel RL Olympia by Red Lion.** Views of Capitol Lake, the capitol dome,
HOTEL and the surrounding hills are highlights of this recently rebranded and significantly upgraded hotel from which you can walk to many local sights. **Pros:** many rooms have water or park views; rooms have crisp, clean design; good value. **Cons:** popular for meetings and conventions (and can get noisy during these events). $ Rooms from: $149 ⊠ 2300 Evergreen Park Dr. ☎ 360/943-4000, 844/248-7467 ⊕ www.redlion. com/olympia ⤵ 193 rooms ⓘ⊙ Breakfast.

$ 🏨 **Swantown Inn & Spa.** Antiques and lace ornament every room of
B&B/INN this stylish, peak-roofed Victorian inn, built as a mansion in 1887 and then used for many years as a boardinghouse. **Pros:** 19th-century feel, but modern and business-friendly; on-site day spa. **Cons:** A 20- to 30-minute walk to downtown. $ Rooms from: $149 ⊠ 1431 11th Ave. SE ☎ 360/753-9123 ⊕ www.swantowninn.com ⤵ 3 rooms, 1 suite ⓘ⊙ Breakfast.

10

SHOPPING

Fodor's Choice ★ **Batdorf & Bronson Coffee Bar.** Here is a local roaster (also with branches in metro Atlanta, Georgia) that can stand up to the best of Seattle's coffeehouses. Several spacious and sleek shops, including this one across from the Farmers Market, pair the best beans with just-baked pastries and tasty sandwiches. The tasting room up the street at 200 Market is in the roastery. You can sample about a half-dozen of Batdorf's favorite blends Wednesday through Sunday from 9 to 4. ⊠ *111 Market St. NE* ☎ *360/528–5555* ⊕ *www.dancinggoats.com.*

MT. RAINIER ENVIRONS

The Cascade Mountains south of Snoqualmie Pass are more heavily eroded than those to the north and generally not as high. But a few peaks do top 7,000 feet, and two volcanic peaks are taller than any of the state's northern mountains. Mt. Adams is more than 12,000 feet high, and Mt. Rainier rises to more than 14,000 feet. The third of the southern peaks, Mt. St. Helens, blew its top in 1980, transforming it from 9,677 to 8,365 feet in elevation.

This is a rural part of the state with just a handful of fairly small towns that make good bases for visiting both Mt. Rainier and Mt. St. Helens—these include Ashford, which offers the only year-round access to and services near Mt. Rainier; the mountain village of Packwood, just below White Pass; and tiny Mossyrock, which lies between the alpine lakes of Riffe and Mayfield. Right on Interstate 5, about midway between Portland and Seattle, the town of Centralia—which has a historic downtown and a handful of antiques shops—makes a handy base or stopover. Seattle, Tacoma, and Olympia also make good bases if you're making just a day trip to Mt. Rainier, and Portland is close enough as a base for visiting Mt. St. Helens for the day. Here you'll find a few distinctive lodging and dining options, plus a plethora of chain properties just off the interstate.

ASHFORD

85 miles south of Seattle, 130 miles north of Portland.

Adjacent to the Nisqually (Longmire) entrance to Mount Rainier National Park, Ashford draws around 2 million visitors every year. Long a transit route for local aboriginal tribes, its more recent history began when it became a logging terminal on the rail line and developed into a tourism hub with lodges, restaurants, groceries, and gift shops along Highway 706.

GETTING HERE AND AROUND

Ashford is easiest to reach from Seattle via Interstate 5 southbound to Highway 7, then driving southeast to Highway 706. An alternate route is via Interstate 5 southbound to Highway 167, then continuing south to Highway 161 through Eatonville to Highway 7, then east to Highway 706. From Portland, follow Interstate 5 northbound, then head east on Highway 12 to Morton and north via Highway 7 to Highway 706.

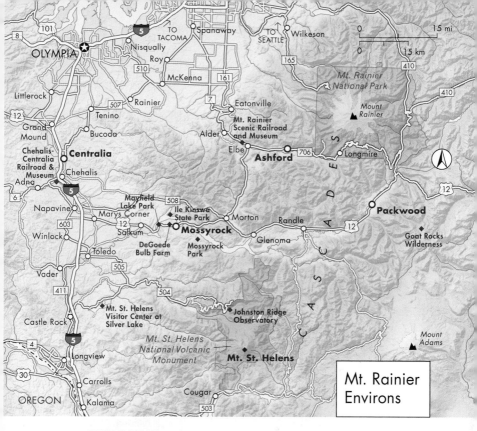

Mt. Rainier
Environs

10

EXPLORING

FAMILY **Mt. Rainier Scenic Railroad and Museum.** This trip takes you through lush forests and across scenic bridges, covering 14 miles of incomparable beauty. Trains depart from Elbe, 11 miles west of Ashford, then bring passengers to a lovely picnic area near Mineral Lake before returning. Seasonal theme trips, such as the Fall Leaves excursion and the Snowball Express, are also available. At Mineral Lake, guests can tour the museum containing old train memorabilia and artifacts, as well as exhibits on the area's old railroad camps, which served as the hub of logging operations by rail. ⊠ *54124 Mountain Hwy. E, Elbe* ☎ *360/569–7959, 888/783–2611* ⊕ *www.mtrainier-railroad.com* 🎟 *Rides $39–$49* ⊗ *Closed Nov.–Apr. (except for holiday excursions).*

WHERE TO EAT

$$ ✕ **Copper Creek Restaurant.** This good old-fashioned roadhouse, with
AMERICAN rough-hewn fir floors and knotty-pine walls, is nestled beneath soaring
FAMILY pine trees along the main road to Mt. Rainier from Eatonville. It's been
Fodor's Choice a favorite lunch and dinner stop since it opened in the 1940s, and these
★ days parkgoers still come by in droves to fill up on hearty, straightforward American comfort fare, such as biscuits and gravy in the morning, and bacon-and-blue-cheese burgers and wild Alaskan salmon with

MT. ST. HELENS

One of the most prominent peaks in the Northwest's rugged Cascade Range, Mount Saint Helens National Volcanic Monument affords visitors an up-close look at the site of the most destructive volcanic blast in U.S. history.

Just 55 miles northeast of Portland, and 155 miles southeast of Seattle, this once soaring, conical summit stood at 9,667 feet above sea level. Then, on May 18, 1980, a massive eruption launched a 36,000-foot plume of steam and ash into the air and sent nearly 4 million cubic yards of debris through the Toutle and Cowlitz river valleys. The devastating eruption leveled a 230-square-mile area, claiming 57 lives and more than 250 homes. The mountain now stands at 8,365 feet, and a horseshoe-shape crater—most visible from the north—now forms the scarred summit. A modern highway carries travelers to within about 5 miles of the summit, and the surrounding region offers thrilling opportunities for climbing, hiking, and learning about volcanology.

BEST TIME TO GO

It's best to visit from mid-May through late October, as the last section of Spirit Lake Highway, Johnston Ridge Observatory, and many of the park's forest roads are closed the rest of the year. The other visitor centers along the lower sections of the highway are open year-round, but overcast skies typically obscure the mountain's summit in winter.

PARK HIGHLIGHTS

Ape Cave. The longest continuous lava tube in the continental United States, Ape Cave is one of the park's outstanding attractions. Two routes traverse the tube. The lower route is an easy hour-long hike; the upper route is more challenging and takes about three hours. It's a good idea to bring a light source (although you can rent lanterns from the headquarters for $5) and warm clothing—temperatures in the cave don't rise above the mid-40s. In high season ranger-led walks are sometimes available; inquire at the **Apes' Headquarters** (*360/449-7800*), off Forest Service Road 8303, 3 miles north of the junction of Forest Roads 83 and 90. Although Ape Cave is open year-round, the headquarters closes from November through April. ⊠ *Cougar* ☎ *360/449-7800* ⊕ *www.fs.usda.gov/giffordpinchot.*

Johnston Ridge Observatory. The visitor center closest to the summit is named for scientist David Johnston, who was killed by the mountain's immense lateral blast, and stands at the end of the park's Spirit Lake Highway. Inside are fascinating exhibits on the mountain's geology, instruments measuring volcanic and seismic activity, and a theater that shows a riveting film that recounts the 1980 eruption. Several short trails afford spectacular views of the summit. ⊠ *2400 Spirit Lake Hwy., Toutle* ☎ *360/274-2140* ⊕ *www.fs.usda.gov/giffordpinchot* 🖼 *$8* ⊙ *Closed mid-May–early Nov.*

Spirit Lake Highway. Officially known as Highway 504, this winding road rises some 4,000 feet from the town of Castle Rock (just off I-5, Exit 49) to within about 5 miles of the Mt. St. Helens summit. Along this road are several visitor centers that interpret the region's geology and geography, and several turnouts afford views of the destruction wrought upon the Toutle and Cowlitz river valleys. Don't miss the **Mt. St. Helens Visitor Center at Silver Lake** (*Hwy. 504, 5 miles east of I-5, 360/274-0962, www.parks.wa.gov*) in Seaquest State Park, which shows video footage of the eruption, contains superb exhibits on the region's geologic beginnings, and houses a scale model of the mountain that you can actually climb through.

STAY THE NIGHT

Mt. St. Helens is in a remote area. You'll find a handful of chain motels in Kelso and Longview, about 10 to 15 miles south.

Patty's Place at 19 Mile House. For a memorable meal midway up Spirit Lake Highway, drop by this rustic roadhouse with a veranda overlooking the North Fork Toutle River—be sure to save room for the fresh-fruit cobblers. **Known for:** fruit cobblers; river setting. ⊠ *9440 Spirit Lake Hwy., Kid Valley* ☎ *360/274-8779* ⊙ *Closed Nov.–Apr.*

Lewis River B&B. In Woodland, 30 miles south of Castle Rock but right on Highway 503, the gateway for approaching great Mount St. Helens hiking from the south, the charming Lewis River B&B is a terrific lodging option. **Pros:** gorgeous, secluded setting; charming decor; delicious and filling breakfasts. **Cons:** a 40-minute drive from beginning of Highway 503. ⊠ *2339 Lewis River Rd., Woodland* ☎ *360/225-8630* ⊕ *www.lewisriverbedandbreakfast.com* 🛏 *7 rooms* 🍽 *Breakfast.*

10

blackberry vinaigrette in the evening. **Known for:** blackberry pie à la mode; biscuits and gravy; rustic, family-friendly vibe. Ⓢ *Average main: $16* ⊠ *35707 Hwy. 706* ☎ *360/569–2799* ⊕ *www.coppercreekinn.com* ⊙ *Closed Tues. and Wed. in winter.*

$ ✕ **Scaleburgers.** Once a 1939 logging-truck weigh station, the building
BURGER is now a popular restaurant serving homemade hamburgers, fries, and
FAMILY shakes. Eat outside on tables overlooking the hills and scenic railroad. **Known for:** views of scenic railroad and surrounding mountains; luscious milk shakes. Ⓢ *Average main: $9* ⊠ *54109 Mountain Hwy. E, Elbe* ✛ *11 miles west of Ashford* ☎ *360/569–2247* ▭ *No credit cards* ⊙ *Closed early Sept.–Mar. and weekdays in Apr. and May.*

WHERE TO STAY

$ ⊡ **Alexander's Lodge.** At this top-notch lodging just a mile from Mt.
B&B/INN Rainier's Nisqually entrance, antique furnishings and fine linens lend romance to rooms in the main building; there are also two adjacent guesthouses. **Pros:** luxurious amenities, especially considering moderate rates; on-site day spa; serving guests since 1912 and also home to one of the region's most popular restaurants. **Cons:** lots of breakables means it's not great for children. Ⓢ *Rooms from: $110* ⊠ *37515 Hwy. 706 E* ✛ *4 miles east of Ashford* ☎ *360/569–2300* ⊕ *www.alexanderslodge. com* ⊅ *16 rooms, 2 3-bedroom houses* ⍟ *Breakfast.*

$$ ⊡ **Nisqually Lodge.** Though these brightly updated accommodations a
HOTEL few miles west of Mount Rainier National Park are of the standard motel-room variety, crackling flames from the massive stone fireplace lend warmth and cheer to the great room. **Pros:** spacious rooms; central to mountain activities and just a few miles from park; the price is right. **Cons:** no frills. Ⓢ *Rooms from: $170* ⊠ *31609 Hwy. 706 E* ☎ *360/569–8804, 888/674–3554* ⊕ *www.whitepasstravel.com/nisquall* ⊅ *24 rooms* ⍟ *Breakfast.*

$$ ⊡ **Wellspring.** Deep in the woods outside Ashford, the accommodations
B&B/INN here include tastefully designed log cabins, a tree house, and a room in a greenhouse. **Pros:** unique lodging with a wide range of prices, depending on the room; some options good for groups; relaxing spa and hot soaking tubs. **Cons:** limited amenities; no cell service; no on-site assistance for guests. Ⓢ *Rooms from: $155* ⊠ *54922 Kernehan Rd.* ☎ *360/569–2514* ⊕ *www.wellspringspa.com* ⊅ *13 rooms* ⍟ *Breakfast.*

$ ⊡ **Whittaker's Bunkhouse Motel.** Inexpensive bunk spaces (available May–
HOTEL September) as well as large private rooms and a cottage are comfortable and come with a communal hot tub, a welcome amenity after a day of recreation. **Pros:** inexpensive; convenient; historical draw for mountain buffs. **Cons:** very basic; bunk room shares bathrooms; easy to hear noise from neighboring rooms. Ⓢ *Rooms from: $90* ⊠ *30205 Hwy. 706 E* ☎ *360/569–2439* ⊕ *www.whittakersbunkhouse.com* ⊅ *20 rooms, 1 12-bed bunk room, 1 cottage* ⍟ *No meals.*

Mt. Rainier was named after British admiral Peter Rainier in the late 18th century.

PACKWOOD

25 miles southeast of Ashford via Skate Creek Rd. (closed in winter).

Its location, between Mt. Rainier and Mt. St. Helens, makes this delightful mountain village on U.S. 12 an attractive destination for those who plan to explore the nearby wilderness areas.

GETTING HERE AND AROUND

From Seattle (about 120 miles away), take Interstate 5 south to Highway 167 near Renton, then south via Highway 161 through Eatonville and southeast on Highway 7 through Morton, then east on U.S. 12. Packwood is about 140 miles from Portland via Interstate 5 northbound to Exit 68, then 64 miles east via U.S. 12 (also called the White Pass Scenic Byway).

ESSENTIALS

Visitor Information Destination Packwood Association. ✉ *13011B U.S. 12* ☎ *360/494–2223* ⊕ *www.destinationpackwood.com.*

EXPLORING

Goat Rocks Wilderness. The crags in Gifford Pinchot National Forest, south of Mt. Rainier, are aptly named. You often see mountain goats here, especially when you hike into the backcountry. Goat Lake is a particularly good spot for viewing these elusive creatures. See the goats without backpacking by taking Forest Road 21 to Forest Road 2140, south from U.S. 12. The goats will be on Stonewall Ridge looming up ahead of you. ✉ *NF-21 and NF-2140, Randle* ☎ *360/891–5000* ⊕ *www.fs.usda.gov/giffordpinchot.*

WHERE TO EAT

$ BURGER FAMILY 🍴 **Cliff Droppers.** This casual burger joint with a small but decent beer list and an outdoor space draws hikers, skiers, families, and tourists on their way to Mt. Rainier and Gifford Pinchot National Forest. Fish-and-chips, vegan bean burgers, and BLTs share the menu with a variety of hearty meat patties, including some wild-game options (buffalo and elk burgers). **Known for:** jalapeño burger; wild-game burgers; fresh-berry milk shakes. [$] *Average main: $10* ✉ *12968 U.S. 12* ☎ *360/494–2055* 🕒 *Closed Mon.–Wed. in winter.*

WHERE TO STAY

$ HOTEL 🏨 **Cowlitz River Lodge.** A lodgelike construction and a large stone fireplace in the great room add some character—a good thing, since guest rooms have updated but fairly standard motel furniture and bedding. **Pros:** convenient location to scenic areas; knowledgeable staff. **Cons:** no pool; no restaurant; rooms are basic motel style. [$] *Rooms from: $129* ✉ *13069 U.S. 12* ☎ *360/494–4444, 888/305–2185* 🌐 *www.whitepasstravel.com/cowlitzriverlodge* 🛏 *31 rooms* 🍽 *Breakfast.*

$ HOTEL FAMILY 🏨 **Mountain View Lodge.** Rooms here have pine paneling, and some have log furniture, microwaves, and refrigerators; family suites have fireplaces and sleep six. **Pros:** roomy accommodations (some with kitchens); close to ski resort; friendly and helpful owners; rock-bottom rates. **Cons:** no restaurant on-site. [$] *Rooms from: $80* ✉ *13163 U.S. Hwy. 12* ☎ *360/494–5555, 877/277–7192* 🌐 *www.mtvlodge.com* 🛏 *22 rooms* 🍽 *No meals.*

MOSSYROCK

45 miles west of Packwood.

Another great outdoors destination, with opportunities for camping, fishing and boating in abundance, Mossyrock is a charming small town with two lakefront parks. The large lakes—Riffe and Mayfield—were created in the 1960s when dams were constructed for generating electricity, and Tacoma Power (which generates the power) stocks the lakes with fish. At Mayfield Lake there are also a state park and a privately owned marina and resort.

GETTING HERE AND AROUND

Mossyrock is reached from Portland or Seattle via Interstate 5, Exit 68, then 21 miles east via U.S. 12 (also called the White Pass Scenic Byway).

EXPLORING

DeGoede Bulb Farm. Just outside town, fields of tulips and other flowers grown at the DeGoede Bulb Farm provide a colorful backdrop along U.S. 12. Stroll through the manicured show gardens year-round. ✉ *409 Mossyrock Rd. W* ☎ *360/983–9000* 🌐 *www.degoedebulb.com* 🎟 *Free.*

Ike Kinswa State Park. This serene 454-acre preserve on the north side of Mayfield Lake is about 4 miles from Mossyrock. Many of the forested campsites provide a nice sense of seclusion, and some lake-view spots are situated for prime sunset views. Five cabins have electricity and bunk beds, but no bathrooms. There's year-round camping, two boat ramps, hiking trails, and fishing (including the challenging tiger muskie, stocked from a nearby hatchery). The park is named after a Cowlitz tribe that lived in this area; their burial grounds are nearby. ✉ *873 Harmony Rd. (Hwy. 122), Silver Creek* ☎ *360/983–3402* 🌐 *www.parks.wa.gov* 🎟 *$10 per vehicle.*

Mayfield Lake Park. At this park right off U.S. 12, 4 miles west of Mossyrock, you'll find a handy boat launch. The RV and tent camping sites are especially scenic, with lake views, forest settings, and even lakefront spots. Fish for trout, bass, and coho salmon. ✉ *180 Beach Rd.* ☎ *360/985–2364* 🌐 *www.mytpu.org/tacomapower* 🎟 *$5 per vehicle.*

Mossyrock Park. Fish, camp, and boat at this park on Riffe Lake, just a few miles east of town. The lake is stocked with cutthroat, rainbow, and brown trout, and coho salmon, steelhead, and bass. ✉ *202 Ajlune Rd.* ☎ *360/983–3900, 888/502–8690* 🌐 *www.mytpu.org/tacomapower* 🎟 *$5 per vehicle.*

WHERE TO STAY

$$ B&B/INN Fodor's Choice ★ 🏨 **Adytum Retreat.** The two suites here, equipped with fireplaces and all sorts of other amenities, are all about luxury in nature—set on a hill on nearly 16 acres of forested grounds, the castlelike home, with its stone front, towers, and 75 windows, faces Mayfield Lake and the valleys below. **Pros:** amazing views; beautiful grounds; unique amenities. **Cons:** a bit of a drive to restaurants and shopping. [$] *Rooms from: $200* ✉ *186 Skyview Dr.* ☎ *360/983–8008* 🌐 *www.adytumsanctuary.com* 🛏 *2 suites* 🍴 *Breakfast.*

CENTRALIA

Centralia is 35 miles northwest of Mossyrock.

Centralia (sen-*trail*-ya) was founded by George Washington, a freed slave from Virginia, who faced serious discrimination in several states and territories before settling here in 1852. The town has a well-maintained historic business district. In a park just off Interstate 5 stand the Borst Blockhouse (built during the 1855–56 Indian Wars) and the elegant Borst farmhouse. Centralia is an antiques-hunter's paradise, with some 350 dealers in several malls. It's also known for its numerous murals depicting the region's history. Pick up a brochure about the murals at the Centralia Train Depot. Six miles to the south is the sister city of Chehalis (sha- *hay*-liss), where there's a historical museum and the Chehalis–Centralia Steam Train.

GETTING HERE AND AROUND

Centralia is almost halfway between Seattle (85 miles north) and Portland (92 miles south) via Interstate 5, and coming by car is the only sensible option for anyone wanting to explore the area.

EXPLORING

FAMILY **Chehalis–Centralia Railroad & Museum.** Through scenic landscapes and over covered bridges, the authentic engines of the Chehalis–Centralia Steam Train will carry you on rails originally laid for logging. The line runs through farmland and rolling hills, and crosses several wooden bridges. There's a 13-mile round-trip ride and an 18-mile ride, plus dinner trains and special events. ✉ *1101 S.W. Sylvenus St., Chehalis* ☎ *360/748–9593* 🌐 *www.steamtrainride.com* 🎟 *$14–$17; dinner train $50* ⏲ *Closed weekdays and mid-Sept.–late May.*

WHERE TO EAT AND STAY

$ MEXICAN-MEXICAN Fodor's Choice ★ 🍴 **La Tarasca.** Fans of Michoacán-style Mexican food have been known to schedule their Portland–Seattle road trips to hit this festive but unfussy family-run restaurant for dinner. Authentic meals start with pickled carrots instead of chips and salsa, and favorite dishes include classic chicken mole and *carne en su jugo,* a heady soup of steak strips, bacon, onion, and cilantro, served with tortillas. **Known for:** capirotada (bread pudding); carne en su jugo soup; chicken mole. [$] *Average main: $13 ✉ 1001 W. Main St. ☎ 360/736–7756 ⏲ Closed Tues.*

$$ PACIFIC NORTHWEST Fodor's Choice ★ 🍴 **Mackinaw's Restaurant.** In a vintage redbrick building in downtown Chehalis, a 10-minute drive south of Centralia, you'll find the region's most sophisticated restaurant, where chef Laurel Khan produces consistently imaginative, fresh Pacific Northwest fare at reasonable prices. The seasonally driven menu changes daily but might feature a starter of grilled flatbread topped with Dungeness crab, herbed goat cheese, and tomato-pepper jam, followed by Parmesan-crusted whitefish with a light lemon-dill sauce, or sliced duck breast with a black-cherry-and-walnut reduction—it's pretty urbane fare for this laid-back, down-home part of Washington. **Known for:** extensive list of local beers and wines; Dungeness crab–and-goat-cheese flatbread. [$] *Average main: $20 ✉ 545 N. Market St., Chehalis ☎ 360/740–8000 🌐 www.mackinawsrestaurant.com ⏲ Closed Sun. and Mon. No lunch.*

$$$ RESORT FAMILY 🏨 **Great Wolf Lodge.** With nearly 400 spacious rooms, some with bunk beds and log-cabin-style forts geared to kids, this activity-focused, rustic-contemporary, lodge-style resort is the largest accommodation in the region. **Pros:** huge indoor water park and plenty of other activities for kids; easy access from freeway; the staff seem to have a good time. **Cons:** avoid this one if you're seeking a quiet, adults-oriented getaway; freeway setting; somewhat high rates. [$] *Rooms from: $209 ✉ 20500 Old Hwy. 99 SW ☎ 360/273–7718, 800/640–9653 🌐 www.greatwolf.com/grandmound 🛏 398 rooms 🍽 No meals.*

$ HOTEL 🏨 **McMenamins Olympic Club Hotel & Theater.** When it opened in 1908, the Olympic Club was an exclusive gentlemen's resort; now it's owned by microbrewery moguls the McMenamin brothers, and, along with European-style rooms with king, queen, or bunk beds and shared bathrooms down the hall, includes a restaurant, bar, pool hall, and vintage movie theater. **Pros:** restored historic facility complete with its own theater; inexpensive rates and restaurant. **Cons:** nearby train tracks may prove too noisy for light sleepers; shared bathrooms; small rooms. [$] *Rooms from: $75 ✉ 112 N. Tower Ave. ☎ 360/736–5164, 866/736–5164 🌐 www.mcmenamins.com 🛏 27 rooms with shared bath 🍽 No meals.*

THE SAN JUAN ISLANDS

WELCOME TO THE SAN JUAN ISLANDS

TOP REASONS TO GO

★ **Whale watch:** Spot whales and other marine life from a tour boat or sea kayak.

★ **Taste local flavors:** Talented chefs have turned Orcas and San Juan Islands into hot spots for sophisticated, locavore-driven cuisine.

★ **Gallery hop:** Dozens of acclaimed artists live year-round or seasonally in the San Juans, and you can find their work in studio galleries and group cooperatives throughout the islands.

★ **Indulge in a spa day:** Work out the kayaking or hiking kinks with a massage at the lovely seaside Rosario Resort and Spa on Orcas Island or Afterglow Spa at Roche Harbor on San Juan Island.

★ **Bike beautiful terrain:** Rent a bike and cycle the scenic, sloping country roads—Lopez Island has the gentlest terrain for this activity.

1 Lopez Island. The smallest, least populated, and most tranquil of the main islands is a largely rural and wonderfully restive place with a handful of charming cafés, a few inns, and traffic-free roads ideal for biking.

2 Orcas Island. The rugged and hilly terrain contains the highest point in the San Juans and is the largest in the archipelago, although the pace is easygoing and relaxed. The main village of Eastsound, however, contains a number of sophisticated restaurants and galleries, and you'll find several fine eateries, inns, and boutique resorts elsewhere on this verdant island.

3 San Juan Island. The political seat and commercial center of the archipelago, and the only one of the islands with direct ferry service to British Columbia, is home to the bustling town of Friday Harbor, which abounds with good shopping, cheery cafés, and a mix of midpriced and luxury inns and small hotels. Aside from cultural activities—including a national historic park, art museum, and sculpture garden—you'll enjoy fine beaches, great roads for biking, and marinas that rent kayaks and boats.

GETTING ORIENTED

Spending time on the San Juans is all about connecting with the sea, although there's plenty to see and do—especially on the two largest islands—away from the water, from mountain hiking to sophisticated gallery-hopping. A trip to the San Juans requires a bit of travel, planning, and expense, but visitors nevertheless flock here to spot whales, go kayaking, chill out in endearingly informal inns, and dine on creative, surprisingly urbane cuisine. The most popular boating activity is whale-watching, but each island has its share of parks, bluffs, and coastline to explore. The San Juan Islands are part of the same archipelago as the Gulf Islands of British Columbia—they're actually far closer to Victoria, BC, than they are to Seattle. The closest mainland Washington city is Anacortes, about 90 minutes north of Seattle.

Updated
by Andrew
Collins

The waters of the Pacific Northwest's Salish Sea, between mainland Washington and Vancouver Island, contain hundreds of islands, some little more than rocky reefs, others rising to nearly 2,500 feet. Among these, the San Juans are considered by many to be the loveliest.

About 100 miles northwest of Seattle, these romantic islands abound with breathtaking rolling pastures, rocky shorelines, and thickly forested ridges, and their quaint villages draw art lovers, foodies, and city folk seeking serenity. Inns are easygoing and well-appointed, and many restaurants are helmed by highly talented chefs emphasizing local ingredients.

Each of the San Juans maintains a distinct character, though all share in the archipelago's blessings of serene farmlands, unspoiled coves, blue-green or gray tidal waters, and radiant light. Offshore, seals haul out on sandbanks and orcas patrol the deep channels. You may see the occasional minke whale frolicking in the kelp, and humpback whales have become increasingly visible around the islands. You'll very rarely spy gray whales, which stick closer Washington's mainland.

There are 172 named islands in the archipelago. Sixty are populated (though most have only a house or two), and 10 are state marine parks, some of which are accessible only to nonmotorized craft—kayakers, canoes, small sailboats—navigating the Cascadia Marine Trail.

The San Juan Islands have valleys and mountains where eagles soar, and forests and leafy glens where the small island deer browse. Even a species of prickly pear cactus (*Opuntia fragilis*) grows here. Beaches can be of sand or shingle (covered in small pebbles). The islands are home to ducks and swans, herons and hawks, otters and whales. The main draw is the great outdoors, but there's plenty to do once you've seen the whales or hiked. Each island, even tiny Lopez, has at least one commercial center, where you'll find shops, restaurants, and history museums. Not surprisingly, many artists take inspiration from the dramatic surroundings, and each island has a collection of galleries; Friday Harbor even has an impressive sculpture park and art museum. Lavender and alpaca farms, spas and yoga studios, a whale museum and lighthouse tours—the San Juans have a little bit of everything.

THE SAN JUAN ISLANDS PLANNER

11

WHEN TO GO

This part of Washington has a mild, maritime climate. Winter temperatures average in the low 40s, while summer temps hover in the mid 70s. July and August are by far the most popular months to visit the three main islands—they can get busy during this time, with resorts, boating tours, and ferries often at capacity. To beat the crowds and avoid the worst of the wet weather, visit in late spring or early fall—September and early October can be fair and stunningly gorgeous, as can May and early June. Hotel rates are generally lower everywhere during these shoulder seasons—and even lower once often drizzly winter starts.

Orcas, Lopez, and San Juan islands are extremely popular in high season; securing hotel reservations in advance is essential. If you're bringing a car to the islands, be sure to book a ferry reservation well in advance. Or if you're traveling light and plan to stay put in one place in the islands, consider walking or biking on. Lot parking at Anacortes is $10 per day and $40 per week in summer and half that October–April.

FESTIVALS

Orcas Island Chamber Music Festival. This music festival comprises more than two weeks of "classical music with a view" in August. These concerts are immensely popular with chamber-music fans around the Pacific Northwest. ✉ *Orcas Island* ☎ *866/492–0003* ⊕ *www.oicmf.org.*

Savor the San Juans. Autumn has become increasingly popular thanks to the growth of this culinary festival, which runs about six weeks. It consists of an islands-wide series of events and gatherings celebrating local foods and beverages, including farm tours, film screenings, and harvest dinners. ☎ *360/378–3277* ⊕ *www.visitsanjuans.com/savor.*

GETTING HERE AND AROUND

AIR TRAVEL

Port of Friday Harbor is the main San Juan Islands airport, but there are also small airports on Lopez, Shaw, and Orcas Islands. Seaplanes land on the waterfront at Friday Harbor and Roche Harbor on San Juan Island; Rosario Resort, Deer Harbor, and West Sound on Orcas Island; and Fisherman Bay on Lopez Island. Daily scheduled flights link the San Juan Islands with mainland airports at Anacortes, Bellingham, and Lake Washington, Renton, and Boeing Field near Seattle. Some airlines also offer charter services.

If traffic and ferry lines really aren't your thing, consider hopping aboard a seaplane for the quick flight from Seattle. **Kenmore Air** offers several daily departures from Lake Union, Lake Washington, and Boeing Field, and from May through September **Friday Harbor Seaplanes** has up to four daily departures from Renton to Friday Harbor. Flying isn't cheap—around $130–$170 each way—but the scenic, hour-long flight is an experience in itself. Flights on **San Juan Airlines** from Bellingham and Anacortes run about $90 each way.

Air Contacts Friday Harbor Seaplanes. ☎ *277–1590, 690–0086* ⊕ *www.friday-harborseaplanes.com.* **Kenmore Air.** ☎ *425/486–1257, 866/435–9524* ⊕ *www.kenmoreair.com.* **San Juan Airlines.** ☎ *800/874–4434* ⊕ *www.sanjuanairlines.com.*

CAR TRAVEL

Most visitors arrive by car, which is the best way to explore these mostly rural islands comprehensively, especially if you plan on visiting for more than a couple of days. You can also park your car at the Anacortes ferry terminal ($10 per day or $40 per week high season, and half that fall through spring), as fares are cheaper and lines much shorter for passengers without cars. B&B owners can often pick guests up at the ferry terminal by prior arrangement, and you can rely on bikes and occasional taxis or on-island car or moped rentals (on San Juan and Orcas) for getting around. Also, in summer, a shuttle bus makes its way daily around San Juan Island and on weekends on Orcas and Lopez islands. From Seattle, it's a 90-minute drive via Interstate 5 north and Highway 20 west to reach Anacortes.

Island roads are narrow and often windy, with one or two lanes. Slow down and hug the shoulder when passing another car on a one-lane road. Expect rough patches, some unpaved lanes, deer and rabbits, bicyclists, and other hazards—plus the distractions of sweeping water views. There are a few car-rental agencies on San Juan and Orcas, with daily rates running about $60 to $100 in summer, and as much as 25% less off-season. You'll likely save money renting a car on the mainland, even factoring in the cost of ferry transport (which in high season is about $45 to $65 for a standard vehicle including driver, plus around $14 per passenger, depending on which island you're headed to).

Rental Car Contacts M and W Rental Cars. ⊠ *725 Spring St., Friday Harbor* ☎ *360/376–5266 Orcas, 360/378–2794 San Juan* ⊕ *www.sanjuanauto.com.* **Orcas Island Rental Cars.** ☎ *360/376–7433* ⊕ *www.orcasislandshuttle.com.* **Susie's Mopeds.** ⊠ *125 Nichols St., Friday Harbor* ☎ *360/378–5244, 800/532–0087* ⊕ *www.susiesmopeds.com.*

FERRY TRAVEL

The Washington State Ferries system can become overloaded during peak travel times. Thankfully, the company recently implemented a long-awaited reservations system, which makes it far easier to plan trips and avoid lines. Reservations are highly recommended, especially in summer and on weekends, although a small number of spaces on every sailing are always reserved for standby; always arrive at least 45 minutes ahead of your departure, and as much as two hours ahead at busy times if you don't have a reservation. You'll find information on the Washington State Ferries website on up-to-minute wait times as well as tips on which ferries tend to be the most crowded. It's rarely a problem to get a walk-on spot, although arriving a bit early to ensure you get a ticket is wise. *For more information, see Getting Here and Around in individual islands below.*

Ferry Contacts Washington State Ferries. ⊠ *2100 Ferry Terminal Rd., Anacortes* ☎ *206/464–6400, 888/808–7977* ⊕ *www.wsdot.wa.gov/ferries.*

RESTAURANTS

The San Juans have myriad small farms and restaurants serving local foods and fresh-harvested seafood, and culinary agritourism—visiting local farmers, growers, and chefs at their places of business—is on the rise.

HOTELS

With the exception of Lopez Island, which has just a handful of inns, accommodations in the San Juans are quite varied and tend be plush, if also expensive during the high summer season. Rosario Resort & Spa on Orcas Island and Roche Harbor Resort on San Juan Island are favorite spots for special-occasion splurges, and both islands have seen an influx of either new or luxuriously updated inns in recent years. These places often have perks like lavish breakfasts and on-site outfitters and tour operators. *Hotel reviews have been shortened. For full information, visit Fodors.com.*

WHAT IT COSTS IN U.S. DOLLARS			
$	**$$**	**$$$**	**$$$$**
Restaurants	under $16	$16–$22	$23–$30	over $30
Hotels	under $150	$150–$225	$226–$300	over $300

Restaurants prices are the average cost of a main course at dinner, or if dinner is not served, at lunch. Hotel prices are the cost of a standard double room in high season.

VISITOR INFORMATION

Look to the San Juan Islands Visitors Bureau for general information on all the islands—the website is very useful.

San Juan Islands Visitors Bureau. ✉ *The Technology Center, 640 Mullis St., Suites 210–211, Friday Harbor* ☎ *360/378–3277, 888/468–3701* ⊕ *www.visitsanjuans.com.*

LOPEZ ISLAND

45 mins by ferry from Anacortes.

Known affectionately as "Slow-pez," the closest significantly populated island to the mainland is a broad, bay-encircled bit of terrain set amid sparkling blue seas, a place where cabinlike homes are tucked into the woods, and boats are moored in lonely coves. Of the three San Juan Islands with facilities to accommodate overnight visitors, Lopez has the smallest population (approximately 2,200), and with its old orchards, weathered barns, and rolling green pastures, it's the most rustic and least crowded in the archipelago. Gently sloping roads cut wide curves through golden farmlands and trace the edges of pebbly beaches, while peaceful trails wind through thick patches of forest. Sweeping country views make Lopez a favorite year-round biking locale, and except for the long hill up from the ferry docks, most roads and designated bike paths are easy for novices to negotiate.

The only settlement is Lopez Village, really just a cluster of cafés and boutiques, as well as a summer market and outdoor theater, an upscale inn, a visitor information center, and a grocery store. Other attractions—such as seasonal berry-picking farms, small wineries, kitschy galleries, intimate restaurants, and one secluded bed-and-breakfast—are scattered around the island.

GETTING HERE AND AROUND

The Washington State Ferries crossing from Anacortes take about 45 minutes; round-trip peak-season fares are about $14 per person, $45 for a car and driver. One-hour flights from Seattle cost about $130 to $170 each way. You can get around the island by car (bring your own—there are no rentals) or bike; there are bike-rental facilities by the ferry terminal.

ESSENTIALS

Visitor Information Lopez Island Chamber of Commerce. ⊠ *Lopez Rd., at Tower Rd., Lopez* ☎ *360/468–4664* ⊕ *www.lopezisland.com.*

EXPLORING

Lopez Island Historical Museum. Artifacts from the region's Native American tribes and early settlers include some impressive ship and small-boat models and maps of local landmarks. You can also listen to fascinating digital recordings of early settlers discussing life on Lopez Island. ⊠ *Weeks Rd. and Washburn Pl., Lopez* ☎ *360/468–2049* ⊕ *www.lopezmuseum.org* ⊠ *Free* ⊘ *Closed Mon., Tues., and Oct.–Apr.*

Fodor'sChoice
★
Shark Reef Sanctuary. A quiet forest trail along beautiful Shark Reef leads to an isolated headland jutting out above the bay. The sounds of raucous barks and squeals mean you're nearly there, and eventually you may see throngs of seals and seagulls on the rocky islets across from the point. Bring binoculars to spot bald eagles in the trees as you walk, and to view sea otters frolicking in the waves near the shore. The trail starts at the Shark Reef Road parking lot south of the airport, and it's a 15-minute walk to the headland. ⊠ *Shark Reef Rd., Lopez* ✛ *2 miles south of Lopez Island Airport* ⊠ *Free.*

Spencer Spit State Park. Set on a spit along the Cascadia Marine Trail for kayakers, this popular spot for summer camping is on former Native American clamming, crabbing, and fishing grounds. A variety of campsites are available, from primitive tent sites to full hookups. This is one of the few Washington beaches where cars are permitted. ⊠ *521 A. Bakerview Rd., Lopez* ☎ *360/468–2251* ⊕ *www.parks. wa.gov/parks* ⊠ *$10.*

WHERE TO EAT AND STAY

$
AMERICAN
✕ Haven Kitchen & Bar. It's the rare kitchen that turns out such regionally diverse fare as Native American fry bread with honey, Spam musubi, made-to-order guacamole, and burrata with heirloom plum tomatoes, but this romantic restaurant in a handsome space with sweeping bay views prides itself in offering a little something for everyone. Prices are reasonable, too, and the eclecticism carries through to the well-curated wine, beer, and cocktail lists. **Known for:** Spam musubi appetizer; expansive flower-lined outdoor deck; well-crafted artisanal cocktails. $ *Average main: $14* ⊠ *9 Old Post Rd., Lopez* ☎ *360/468–3272* ⊕ *www.lopezhaven.com* ⊘ *Closed Sun.–Tues.*

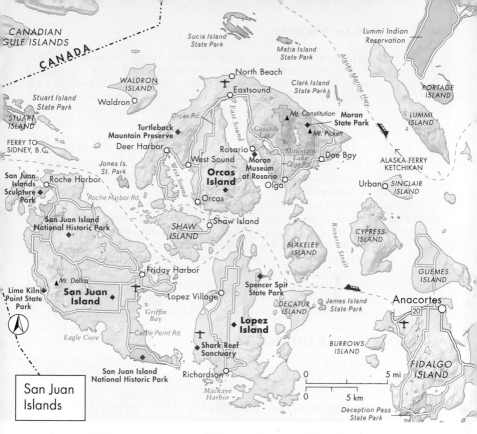

San Juan
Islands

$ ✗ **Holly B's Bakery.** Tucked into a small, cabinlike strip of businesses
BAKERY set back from the water, this cozy, wood-paneled bakery has been a
source of delicious fresh ham-and-Gruyere croissants, marionberry
scones, slices of pizza, and other savory and sweet treats since 1977.
Sunny summer mornings bring diners out onto the patio, where kids
play and parents relax. **Known for:** ginormous, decadent cinnamon
rolls; pizza by the slice; scones flavored with seasonal fruit. $ *Aver-
age main:* $6 ⊠ *Lopez Plaza, 211 Lopez Rd., Lopez* ☎ *360/468–2133*
⊕ *www.hollybsbakery.com* ▭ *No credit cards* ☉ *Closed Dec.–Mar.
No dinner.*

$ ✗ **Vita's Wildly Delicious.** At this gourmet market and wine shop (open
CAFÉ primarily during the daytime but until 8 pm on Friday), the proprietors create a daily-changing assortment of prepared foods and
some made-to-order items, such as Reuben panini sandwiches. Other
favorites include Dungeness crab cakes, hearty meat loaf, lobster
mac-and-cheese, and an assortment of tempting desserts. **Known for:**
Dungeness crab cakes; pretty garden-dining area; gourmet picnic supplies. $ *Average main:* $10 ⊠ *77 Village Rd., Lopez* ☎ *360/468–4268*
⊕ *www.vitasonlopez.com* ☉ *Closed Sun., Mon., and late fall–late
spring. No dinner.*

$$ ⚏ **Edenwild Inn.** Thoughtful and friendly owners Anthony and Crys-
B&B/INN tal Rovente operate this large Victorian-style farmhouse surrounded
by gardens and framed by Fisherman Bay. Spacious rooms are each
painted or papered in different pastel shades and furnished with simple
antiques; some have claw-foot tubs and brick fireplaces. **Pros:** bikes
and kayaks can be rented on-site; nice breakfast buffet using local
produce and homemade baked goods; handy location close to village
restaurants. **Cons:** no TVs in rooms. $\boxed{\$}$ *Rooms from: $195* ✉ *132
Lopez Rd., Lopez* ☎ *360/468–3238* ⊕ *www.edenwildinn.com* ➲ *9
rooms* ⑩*Breakfast.*

$$ ⚏ **Mackaye Harbor Inn.** This former sea captain's house, built in 1904,
B&B/INN rises two stories above the beach at the southern end of the island and
Fodor's Choice accommodates guests in cheerfully furnished rooms with golden-oak
★ and brass details and wicker furniture; three have views of MacKaye
Harbor. **Pros:** fantastic water views; mountain bikes (free) and kayaks
(reasonable daily fee) available; friendly and attentive hosts. **Cons:** on
far end of the island; several miles from the ferry terminal and airport;
some bathrooms are across the hall from rooms. $\boxed{\$}$ *Rooms from: $175*
✉ *949 MacKaye Harbor Rd., Lopez* ☎ *360/468–2253, 888/314–6140*
⊕ *www.mackayeharborinn.com* ➲ *4 rooms, 1 suite* ⑩*Breakfast.*

SPORTS AND THE OUTDOORS

BIKING

Bike rental rates start at around $7 an hour and $30 a day. Reservations
are recommended, particularly in summer.

Lopez Bicycle Works. At the marina 4 miles from the ferry, this full-service
operation can bring bicycles to your door or the ferry. In addition to
cruisers and mountain bikes, the shop also rents tandem and recumbent
bikes. ✉ *2847 Fisherman Bay Rd., Lopez* ☎ *360/468–2847* ⊕ *www.
lopezbicycleworks.com.*

Village Cycle. This aptly named full-service rental and repair shop is in
the heart of Lopez Village. ✉ *214 Lopez Rd., Lopez* ☎ *360/468–4013*
⊕ *www.villagecycles.net.*

SEA KAYAKING

Cascadia Kayaks. This company rents kayaks for half days or full days
The outfitter also organizes half-day, full-day, and two- to three-day
guided tours. Hour-long private lessons are available, too, if you need a
little coaching before going out on your own. ✉ *135 Lopez Rd., Lopez*
☎ *360/468–3008* ⊕ *www.cascadiakayaks.com.*

Lopez Island Sea Kayak. Open May–September at Fisherman Bay, this
outfitter has a huge selection of kayaks, both plastic and fiberglass
touring models. Rentals are by the hour or day, and the company
can deliver kayaks to any point on the island for an additional fee.
✉ *2845 Fisherman Bay Rd., Lopez* ☎ *360/468–2847* ⊕ *www.lope-
zkayaks.com.*

ORCAS ISLAND

75 mins by ferry from Anacortes.

Orcas Island, the largest of the San Juans, is blessed with wide, pastoral valleys and scenic ridges that rise high above the neighboring waters. (At 2,409 feet, Orcas's Mt. Constitution is the highest peak in the San Juans.) Spanish explorers set foot here in 1791, and the island is actually named for one of these early visitors, Juan Vicente de Güemes Padilla Horcasitas y Aguayo—not for the black-and-white whales that frolic in the surrounding waters. The island was also the home of Native American tribes, whose history is reflected in such places as Pole Pass, where the Lummi people used kelp and cedar-bark nets to catch ducks, and Massacre Bay, where in 1858 a tribe from southeast Alaska attacked a Lummi fishing village.

Today farmers, fishermen, artists, retirees, and summer-home owners make up the population of about 4,500. Houses are spaced far apart, and the island's few hamlets typically have just one major road running through them. Low-key resorts dotting the island's edges are evidence of the thriving local tourism industry, as is the gradual but steady influx of urbane restaurants, boutiques, and even a trendy late-night bar in the main village of Eastsound. The beauty of this island is beyond compare; Orcas is a favorite place for weekend getaways from the Seattle area any time of the year, as well as one of the state's top settings for summer weddings.

The main town on Orcas Island lies at the head of the East Sound channel, which nearly divides the island in two. More than 20 small shops and boutiques here sell jewelry, pottery, and crafts by local artisans, as well as gourmet edibles, from baked goods to chocolates.

GETTING HERE AND AROUND

The Washington State Ferries crossing from Anacortes to Orcas Village, in the island's Westsound area, takes about 75 minutes; peak-season round-trip fares are about $14 per person, $55 for a car and driver. One-hour flights from Seattle cost about $130 to $170 each way. Planes land at Deer Harbor, Eastsound, Westsound, and at the Rosario Resort and Spa.

The best way to get around the island is by car—bikes will do in a pinch, but the hilly, curvy roads that generally lack shoulders make cycling a bit risky. Most resorts and inns offer transfers from the ferry terminal.

ESSENTIALS

Visitor Information Orcas Island Chamber of Commerce & Visitor Center.
⊠ *65 N. Beach Rd.* ☎ *360/376–2273* ⊕ *www.orcasislandchamber.com.*

EXPLORING

Moran Museum at Rosario. This 1909 mansion that forms the centerpiece of Rosario Resort was constructed as the vacation home of Seattle shipping magnate and mayor Robert Moran. On the second floor is this fascinating museum that spans several former guest rooms and includes old photos, furniture, and memorabilia related to the Moran family, the resort's history, and the handsome ships built by Moran and his brothers. A highlight is the music room, which contains an incredible two-story 1913 aeolian pipe organ and an ornate, original Tiffany chandelier. Renowned musician Christopher Peacock discusses the resort's history and performs on the 1900 Steinway grand piano daily (except Sunday) at 4 pm in summer, and on Saturday at 4 the rest of the year. The surrounding grounds make for a lovely stroll, which you might combine with lunch or a cocktail in one of the resort's water-view restaurants. ⊠ *1400 Rosario Rd.* ☎ *360/376–2222* ⊕ *www. rosarioresort.com/museum* ⊠ *Free.*

NEED A BREAK ✕ **Brown Bear Baking.** You might make it a point to get to this wildly popular village bakery by late morning—come midafternoon, many of the best treats are sold out. Delectables here include flaky almond-coated bear paw pastries, rich croque monsieur sandwiches, hubcap-sized "Sasquatch" cookies, Tuscan olive bread, and moist blueberry muffins. **Known for:** almond-coated bear paw pastries; alfresco dining on the patio. ⊠ *29 N. Beach Rd.* ☎ *360/855–7456* ⊕ *www.facebook.com/ brownbearbaking.*

FAMILY
Fodor's Choice
★
Moran State Park. This pristine patch of wilderness comprises 5,252 acres of hilly, old-growth forests dotted with sparkling lakes, in the middle of which rises the island's highest point, 2,409-foot Mt. Constitution. A drive to the summit affords exhilarating views of the islands, the Cascades, the Olympics, and Vancouver Island, and avid hikers enjoy the strenuous but stunning 7-mile round-trip trek from rippling Mountain Lake to the summit (some 38 miles of trails traverse the entire park). The observation tower on the summit was built by the Civilian Conservation Corps in the 1930s. In summer, you can rent boats to paddle around beautiful Cascade Lake. ⊠ *Mt. Constitution Rd.* ☎ *360/376–2326* ⊕ *www.parks.wa.gov/parks* ⊠ *$10.*

Orcas Island Historical Museum. Surrounded by Eastsound's lively shops and cafés, this museum comprises several reassembled and relocated late-19th-century pioneer cabins. An impressive collection of more than 6,000 photographs, documents, and artifacts tells the story of the island's Native American and Anglo history, and in an oral-history exhibit longtime residents of the island talk about how the community has evolved over the decades. The museum also operates the 1888 Crow Valley Schoolhouse, which is open on summer Wednesdays and Saturdays; call the museum for hours and directions. ⊠ *181 N. Beach Rd.* ☎ *360/376–4849* ⊕ *www.orcasmuseum.org* ⊠ *$5* ⊘ *Closed Oct.–May, Sun.–Tues.*

Fodor's Choice
★
Turtleback Mountain Preserve. A more peaceful, less crowded hiking and wildlife-watching alternative to Moran State Park, this 1,576-acre expanse of rugged ridges, wildflower-strewn meadows, temperate rain forest, and lush wetlands is one of the natural wonders of the archipelago. Because the San Juan County Land Bank purchased this land in 2006, it will be preserved forever for the public to enjoy. There are 8 miles of well-groomed trails, including a steep trek up to 1,519-foot-elevation Raven Ridge and a windy hike to Turtlehead

Point, a soaring bluff with spectacular views west of San Juan Island and Vancouver Island beyond that—it's an amazing place to watch the sunset. You can access the preserve either from the North Trailhead, which is just 3 miles southwest of Eastsound on Crow Valley Road, or the South Trailhead, which is 3 miles northeast of Deer Harbor off Wild Rose Lane—check the website for a trail map and detailed directions. ✉ *North Trailhead parking, Crow Valley Rd., just south of Crow Valley Schoolhouse* ☎ *360/378–4402* ⊕ *www.sjclandbank. org/turtle_back.html* 💰 *Free.*

WHERE TO EAT

$$
PACIFIC
NORTHWEST
Fodor'sChoice
★

✗ **Doe Bay Cafe.** Most of the tables in this warmly rustic dining room at Doe Bay Resort overlook the tranquil body of water for which the café is named. This is a popular stop for brunch or dinner before or after hiking or biking in nearby Moran State Park—starting your day off with smoked-salmon Benedict with Calabrian-chili hollandaise sauce will provide you with plenty of fuel for recreation. **Known for:** locally sourced and foraged ingredients; smoked-salmon Benedict; funky, rustic vibe. $ *Average main: $21* ✉ *107 Doe Bay Rd.* ☎ *360/376–8059* ⊕ *www.doebay.com* ⊘ *Closed Tues. and Wed. Limited hrs Oct.–May; call ahead.*

$$
PIZZA
Fodor'sChoice
★

✗ **Hogstone's Wood Oven.** An intimate, minimalist space with large windows and just a handful of tables, this hip locavore-minded pizza joint serves wood-fired pies with creative toppings—consider the one with new potatoes, crispy pork fat, chickweed, cultured cream, and uncured garlic. The bounteous, farmers'-market-sourced salads are another strength, and the wine list, with varietals from the Northwest and Europe, is exceptional. **Known for:** wildly inventive pizzas with unusual toppings; extensive wine list; long wait on the weekend. $ *Average main: $20* ✉ *460 Main St.* ☎ *360/376–4647* ⊕ *www.hogstone. com* ⊘ *Closed Tues. and Wed. (and some additional days in winter; call first). No lunch.*

$$$
PACIFIC
NORTHWEST

✗ **Inn at Ship Bay.** This restaurant at this stylish, contemporary inn just a mile from Eastsound offers among the most memorable dining experiences on the island. Tucked into a renovated 1869 farmhouse, the dining room and bar serve food that emphasizes local, seasonal ingredients. **Known for:** outstanding wine list; house-made sourdough bread made from a century-old starter yeast. $ *Average main: $26* ✉ *326 Olga Rd.* ☎ *360/376–5886* ⊕ *www.innatshipbay.com* ⊘ *Closed Sun. and Mon. and mid-Dec.–mid-Mar. No lunch.*

$
ASIAN

✗ **The Kitchen.** Seating at this casual, affordable Asian restaurant adjacent to the distinctive boutiques of Prune Alley is in a compact dining room or, when the weather is nice, at open-air picnic tables in a tree-shaded yard. The pan-Asian food here is filling and simple, using local seafood and produce, with plenty of vegetarian options. **Known for:** hearty ramen and Thai noodle soups; chocolate-ginger cookies for dessert; nice selection of craft brews on tap. $ *Average main: $8* ✉ *249 Prune Alley* ☎ *360/376–6958* ⊕ *www.thekitchenorcas.com* ⊘ *Closed Sun.*

$$$$ PACIFIC NORTHWEST
🍴 **Mansion Restaurant.** For a special-occasion dinner (or lunch on weekends), it's worth the drive to this grandly romantic dining room inside the historic main inn at Rosario Resort, where you'll be treated to polished service, sweeping bay views, and exquisitely plated seasonal Northwest cuisine. You might start with the house-made rabbit pâté with dried apples and candied pecans, followed by either the signature bouillabaisse in a Pernod-tomato broth or pan-roasted filet mignon rossini (topped with duck-liver mousse). **Known for:** lovely views of Cascade Bay; bouillabaisse; less expensive fare by the same chef in the adjacent Moran Lounge. [$] *Average main: $31* ✉ *1400 Rosario Rd.* ☎ *360/376–2222* 🌐 *www.rosarioresort.com* 🕓 *No lunch Mon.–Thurs.*

$$ MEXICAN FAMILY
🍴 **Mijitas.** A bustling family-friendly Mexican restaurant with a cozy dining room and a sprawling shaded garden patio is helmed by Raul Rios, who learned to cook during his years growing up outside Mexico City. The flavorful food here isn't entirely authentic—expect of mix of Mexican and Mexican-American dishes, many featuring local ingredients. **Known for:** sweet, tangy margaritas; expansive garden patio; braised short ribs with blackberry-mole sauce. [$] *Average main: $19* ✉ *310 A St.* ☎ *360/376–6722* 🕓 *No lunch.*

$$ MODERN AMERICAN
🍴 **Roses Bakery & Cafe.** Set inside a cheerfully renovated former Eastsound fire station, this bustling café known for its house-baked breads and an impressive selection of artisanal gourmet groceries (from cheeses to fine wines) is also a fine spot for breakfast or lunch. The fare is French-Italian influenced but using local ingredients: try the croque monsieur or house-cured gravlax in the morning. **Known for:** rhubarb galette with fennel ice cream; outstanding assortment of cheese, sweets, and wines to go; thin-crust pizzas with interesting toppings. [$] *Average main: $19* ✉ *382 Prune Alley* ☎ 🌐 *www.rosesbakerycafe.com* 🕓 *No dinner.*

WHERE TO STAY

$$ B&B/INN
🏨 **All Dream Cottages and Kingfish Inn.** Spacious units in this atmospheric 1902 house are equipped with a king or queen bed, private bath, and all the serenity a guest could ever want, while four lovely cottages come with plenty of privacy and beautiful views. **Pros:** decor is tasteful and contemporary; good café; water views. **Cons:** somewhat small bathrooms in some rooms; although on the lesser-visited shore of West Sound, the rooms do get some noise from road and busy marina; two-night minimum. [$] *Rooms from: $198* ✉ *Crow Valley Rd., at Deer Harbor Rd.* ☎ *360/376–2500* 🌐 *www.kingfishinn.com* 🕓 *Closed early Jan.–mid-Feb.* 🛏 *3 rooms, 1 suite, 4 cottages* 🍽 *Breakfast.*

$$ B&B/INN
🏨 **Inn on Orcas Island.** Innkeepers Jeremy Trumble and John Gibbs welcome guests to their handsome, contemporary, adults-only inn, with spacious, plush rooms in the main house and two in separate outbuildings. **Pros:** among the most opulent accommodations on the island; serene setting; delicious breakfasts (and fresh-baked chocolate-chip cookies); overlooking the northern tip of Deer Harbor and within walking distance of the community's bustling marina. **Cons:** 20-minute drive from Eastsound shopping and dining. [$] *Rooms from: $225* ✉ *114 Channel Rd.* ☎ *360/376–5227* 🌐 *www.theinnonorcasisland.com* 🛏 *1 room, 3 suites, 2 cottages* 🍽 *Breakfast.*

Rosario Point at Rosario Resort, on Orcas Island in the San Juans

$ HOTEL Fodor's Choice ★ 🏨 **Outlook Inn.** This nice range of accommodations in the center of Eastsound includes small budget-oriented rooms with twin beds and shared bathrooms, rooms with queen or double beds, and rambling bay-view suites with gas fireplaces, kitchenettes, and two-person Jacuzzi tubs. **Pros:** steps from Eastsound dining and shops (and great restaurant on-site); superfriendly and helpful staff; broad mix of rates. **Cons:** in-town location can be a little noisy; only some rooms have water view; least expensive rooms have shared bath. [$] *Rooms from: $99* ✉ *171 Main St.* ☎ *360/376–2200, 888/688–5665* 🌐 *www.outlookinn.com* 🛏 *24 rooms, 14 with shared bath, 16 suites* 🍴 *No meals.*

$$ RESORT FAMILY Fodor's Choice ★ 🏨 **Rosario Resort and Spa.** Shipbuilding magnate Robert Moran built this Arts and Crafts–style waterfront mansion in 1909, and it is now the centerpiece of a 40-acre resort that comprises several different buildings with sweeping views of Cascade Bay and Rosario Point—accommodations range from moderately priced standard guest rooms to deluxe one- and two-bedroom suites with fireplaces, decks, and full kitchens. **Pros:** gorgeous, peaceful location; management continues to make improvements and upgrade the rooms; first-rate spa and several dining options. **Cons:** often busy with weddings and special events. [$] *Rooms from: $164* ✉ *1400 Rosario Rd.* ☎ *360/376–2222, 800/562–8820* 🌐 *www.rosarioresort.com* 🛏 *16 rooms, 51 suites* 🍴 *No meals.*

$$ B&B/INN 🏨 **Turtleback Farm Inn.** Eighty acres of meadow, forest, and farmland in the shadow of Turtleback Mountain surround these pleasant and homey rooms in the carefully restored late-19th-century green-clapboard farmhouse and the newer cedar Orchard House. **Pros:** lovely grounds to stroll through; peaceful location, smartly furnished rooms. **Cons:** not near the water; two-night minimum in high season; some

rooms are quite cozy. [$] *Rooms from: $165* ✉ *1981 Crow Valley Rd.* ☎ *360/376–3914, 800/376–4914* 🌐 *www.turtlebackinn.com* 🛏 *11 rooms* 🍴 *Breakfast.*

$$ RESORT FAMILY 🏨 **West Beach Resort.** This old-school cottage compound with a dazzling beachfront location on the island's northwest shore, just a 10-minute drive from Eastsound, is a good value for families and groups of friends—most of these compact, rustic cottages sleep four to six guests, and all have kitchens. **Pros:** many cabins are right on the beach; great for families and groups; good value, especially considering these water views. **Cons:** furnishings in some cottages are a bit dated and basic; no restaurants within walking distance. [$] *Rooms from: $169* ✉ *190 Waterfront Way* ☎ *360/376–2240, 877/937–8224* 🌐 *www.westbeachresort.com* 🛏 *21 cottages* 🍴 *No meals.*

NIGHTLIFE

Fodor's Choice ★ **The Barnacle.** This quirky hole-in-the-wall bar with an insider-y, speakeasy vibe is across the lawn from the Kitchen restaurant, and has developed a cult following for its sophisticated, well-made craft cocktails—many infused with house-made bitters and local herbs and berries—and interesting wines. On this quiet, early-to-bed island, it's a nice late-night option. Light tapas are served, too. ✉ *249 Prune Alley* ☎ *206/679–5683.*

Island Hoppin' Brewery. Set in an otherwise inauspicious industrial area near the airport, this craft brewery and taproom (open nightly till 9 pm) has quickly earned a reputation throughout the archipelago—and even on the mainland as far away as Seattle—for well-made beers, including the faintly citrusy Elwha Rock IPA and the silky Old Salts Brown Ale. Smoked salmon, cheese and crackers, and a few other snacks are sold in the homey taproom. ✉ *33 Hope La.* ☎ *360/376–6079* 🌐 *www.islandhoppinbrewery.com.*

SPORTS AND THE OUTDOORS

BIKING

Mountain bikes rent for about $30 per day or $100 per week. Tandem, recumbent, and electric bikes rent for about $50 per day.

Wildlife Cycles. This trusty shop rents bikes and can recommend great routes all over the island. ✉ *350 N. Beach Rd.* ☎ *360/376–4708* 🌐 *www.wildlifecycles.com.*

BOATING AND SAILING

Kruger Escapes. Three-hour day adventures and sunset cruises around the islands are offered on two handsome sailboats that were both designed and formerly used for racing. The boats are also available for multiday charters. ✉ *Orcas Island* ☎ *360/201–0586* 🌐 *www.krugerescapes.com.*

Orcas Boat Rentals. You can rent a variety of sailboats, outboards, and skiffs for full- and half-day trips, as well as book custom charter cruises, with this company. ✉ *5164 Deer Harbor Rd.* ☎ *360/376–7616* 🌐 *www.orcasboatrentals.com.*

West Beach Resort Marina. This is a good option for renting motorized boats, kayaks and canoes, and fishing gear on the island's northwest shore. The resort is also a popular spot for divers, who can fill their tanks here. ✉ *190 Waterfront Way* ☎ *360/376–2240, 877/937–8224* ⊕ *www.westbeachresort.com.*

SEA KAYAKING

All equipment is usually included in a rental package or tour. Three-hour trips cost around $80; and day tours, $110 to $135.

Orcas Outdoors Sea Kayak Tours. This outfitter offers one-, two-, and three-hour journeys, as well as day trips, overnight tours, and rentals. ✉ *Orcas Ferry Landing* ☎ *360/376–4611* ⊕ *www.orcasoutdoors.com.*

Shearwater Kayak Tours. This established company holds kayaking classes and runs three-hour, day, and overnight tours from Rosario, Deer Harbor, West Beach, and Doe Bay resorts. ✉ *138 N. Beach Rd.* ☎ *360/376–4699* ⊕ *www.shearwaterkayaks.com.*

WHALE-WATCHING

Cruises, which run about four hours, are scheduled daily in summer and once or twice weekly at other times. The cost is around $90 to $110 per person, and boats hold 20 to 40 people. Wear warm clothing and bring a snack.

Deer Harbor Charters. This eco-friendly tour company (the first in the San Juans to use biodiesel) offers whale-watching cruises around the island straits, with departures from both Deer Harbor Marina and Rosario Resort. Outboards and skiffs are also available, as is fishing gear. ✉ *Deer Harbor Rd.* ☎ *360/376–5989, 800/544–5758* ⊕ *www.deerharborcharters.com.*

Eclipse Charters. In addition to tours that search around Orcas Island for whale pods and other sea life, this charter company offers lighthouse tours. ✉ *Orcas Island Ferry Landing* ☎ *360/376–6566* ⊕ *www.orcasislandwhales.com.*

SHOPPING

Crow Valley Gallery. This colorful gallery in Eastsound's village exhibits beautiful and distinctive ceramics, metalworks, blown glass, and sculptures. ✉ *296 Main St.* ☎ *360/376–4260* ⊕ *www.crowvalley.com.*

Darvill's Bookstore. This island favorite, with a coffee bar and a couple of cozy seats with panoramic views of the water, specializes in literary fiction and nautical literature. ✉ *296 Main St.* ☎ *360/376–2135* ⊕ *www.darvillsbookstore.com.*

Kathryn Taylor Chocolates. This sweet sweetshop in Eastsound village sells the creative bonbons (pistachio-fig, black raspberry) of Kathryn Taylor. It's also a good stop for ice cream and Stumptown coffee drinks. ✉ *68 N. Beach Rd.* ☎ *360/376–1030* ⊕ *www.kathryntaylorchocolates.com.*

Fodor'sChoice
★ **Orcas Island Artworks.** Stop by this cooperative gallery to see the impressive displays pottery, sculpture, jewelry, art glass, paintings, and quilts by resident artists. Following a devastating fire in 2013, the gallery has

reopened in its original beautifully restored 1937 barn in the village of Olga. Catkin Café serves tasty breakfast and lunch fare. ✉ *11 Point Lawrence Rd.* ☎ *360/376–4408* ⊕ *www.orcasartworks.com.*

Fodor's Choice **Orcas Island Pottery.** A stroll through the historic house, outbuildings, ★ and gardens of this enchanting arts complex on a bluff overlooking President Channel and Waldron Island is more than just a chance to browse beautiful pottery—it's a great spot simply to relax and soak up the views. More than a dozen regular and guest potters exhibit and sell their wares here, everything from functional dinnerware and mugs to fanciful vases and wall hangings. ✉ *338 Old Pottery Rd.* ☎ *360/376– 2813* ⊕ *www.orcasislandpottery.com.*

SAN JUAN ISLAND

45 mins by ferry from Orcas Island, 75–90 mins by ferry from Anacortes or Sidney, BC (near Victoria).

San Juan is the cultural and commercial hub of the archipelago that shares its name. Friday Harbor, the county seat, is larger and both more vibrant and crowded than any of the towns on Orcas or Lopez, yet San Juan still has miles of rural roads, uncrowded beaches, and rolling woodlands. It's easy to get here, too, making San Juan the preferred destination for travelers who have time to visit only one island.

Several different Coast Salish tribes first settled on San Juan, establishing encampments along the north end of the island. North-end beaches were especially busy during the annual salmon migration, when hundreds of tribal members would gather along the shoreline to fish, cook, and exchange news. Many of the indigenous early inhabitants were killed by smallpox and other imported diseases in the 18th and 19th centuries. Smallpox Bay was where tribal members plunged into the icy water to cool the fevers that came with the disease.

The 18th century brought explorers from England and Spain, but the island remained sparsely populated until the mid-1800s. From the 1880s Roche Harbor and its newspaper were controlled by lime-company owner and Republican bigwig John S. McMillin, who virtually ran this part of the island as a personal fiefdom from 1886 until his death in 1936. Friday Harbor ultimately emerged as the island's largest community. The town's main street, rising from the harbor and ferry landing up the slopes of a modest hill, hasn't changed much in the past few decades, though the cafés, inns, and shops have become increasingly urbane.

GETTING HERE AND AROUND

With ferry connections from both Anacortes and Sidney, BC (on Vancouver Island, near Victoria), San Juan is the most convenient of the islands to reach, and the island is easily explored by car; public transportation and bicycles also work, but require a bit more effort. However, if you're staying in Friday Harbor, you can get from the ferry terminal to your hotel as well as area shops and restaurants easily on foot.

11

AIR TRAVEL

One-hour flights from Seattle to San Juan Airport, Friday Harbor, or Roche Harbor cost about $130 to $170 each way.

BUS TRAVEL

San Juan Transit & Tours operates shuttle buses daily from mid-May to mid-September. Hop on at Friday Harbor, the main town, to get to all the island's significant points and parks, including the San Juan Vineyards, Krystal Acres Alpaca Farm, Lime Kiln Point State Park, and Snug Harbor and Roche Harbor resorts. Different buses call on different stops, so be sure to check the schedule before you plan your day. Tickets are $5 one-way, or $15 for a day pass. From mid-June through mid-September, the Friday Harbor Jolly Trolley offers trips around the island—also stopping at all of they key attractions—in an old-fashioned trolley-style bus; tickets cost $20 and are good for the entire day.

Contact **Friday Harbor Jolly Trolley.** ☎ *360/298–8873* ⊕ *www.fridayharbor-jollytrolley.com.* **San Juan Transit & Tours.** ✉ *Cannery Landing, Friday Harbor* ☎ *360/378–8887* ⊕ *sanjuantransit.com.*

BOAT AND FERRY TRAVEL

The Washington State Ferries crossings from Anacortes to Friday Harbor takes about 75 to 90 minutes; round-trip fares in high season are about $14 per person, $65 for a car and driver. It's about the same distance from Sidney, BC, on Vancouver Island—this service is available twice daily in summer and once daily spring and fall (there's no BC service in winter). Round-trip fares are about $25 per person, $85 for car and driver. Clipper Navigation operates the passenger-only *San Juan Clipper* jet catamaran service between Pier 69 in Seattle and Friday Harbor. Boats leave Seattle daily mid-June–early September, Thursday–Monday mid-May–mid-June, and weekends early September–early October at 8:15 am and return from Friday Harbor at 5 pm; reservations are strongly recommended. The journey costs $80 to $100 round-trip, depending on the day and whether you purchase in advance (which is cheaper). Clipper also offers optional whale-watching excursions, which can be combined ferry passage.

Contacts **Clipper Navigation.** ☎ *206/448–5000, 800/888–2535* ⊕ *www.clippervacations.com.*

ESSENTIALS

The San Juan Island Chamber of Commerce has a visitor center (open daily 10 to 4) in Friday Harbor where you can grab brochures and ask for advice.

Visitor Information **San Juan Island Chamber of Commerce.** ✉ *165 1st St., Friday Harbor* ☎ *360/378–5240* ⊕ *www.sanjuanisland.org.*

EXPLORING

TOP ATTRACTIONS

FAMILY
Fodor's Choice
★

Lime Kiln Point State Park. To watch whales cavorting in Haro Strait, head to these 36 acres on San Juan's western side just 9 miles from Friday Harbor. A rocky coastal trail leads to lookout points and a little, white, 1919 lighthouse. The best period for sighting whales is from the end of April through September, but resident pods of orcas regularly cruises past the point. This park is also a beautiful spot to soak in a summer sunset, with expansive views of Vancouver Island and beyond. ⊠ *1567 Westside Rd.* ☏ *360/378–2044* ⊕ *www.parks.wa.gov/parks* ⊠ *$10* ☉ *Interpretive center closed mid-Sept.–late May.*

FAMILY

Pelindaba Lavender Farm. Wander a spectacular 20-acre valley smothered with endless rows of fragrant purple-and-gold lavender blossoms. The oils are distilled for use in therapeutic, botanical, and household products, all created on-site. The farm hosts the very popular San Juan Island Lavender Festival in mid- to late July. If you can't make it to the farm, stop at the outlet in the Friday Harbor Center at 150 1st Street, where you can buy their products and sample delicious lavender-infused baked goods, ice cream, and beverages. ⊠ *33 Hawthorne La., Friday Harbor* ☏ *360/378–4248, 866/819–1911* ⊕ *www.pelindabalavender. com* ⊠ *Free* ☉ *Closed Nov.–Apr.*

FAMILY
Fodor's Choice
★

Roche Harbor. It's hard to believe that fashionable Roche Harbor at the northern end of San Juan Island was once the most important producer of builder's lime on the West Coast. In 1882 John S. McMillin gained control of the lime company and expanded production. But even in its heyday as a limestone quarrying village, Roche Harbor was known for abundant flowers and welcoming accommodations. McMillin transformed a bunkhouse into private lodgings for his invited guests, who included such notables as Teddy Roosevelt. The guesthouse is now the Hotel de Haro, which displays period photographs and artifacts in its lobby. The staff has maps of the old quarry, kilns, and the Mausoleum, an eerie Greek-inspired memorial to McMillin.

McMillin's heirs operated the quarries and plant until 1956, when they sold the company to the Tarte family, who developed it into an upscale resort (but no longer own it)—the old lime kilns still stand below the bluff. Locals say it took two years for the limestone dust to wash off the trees around the harbor. McMillin's former home is now a restaurant, and workers' cottages have been transformed into comfortable visitors' lodgings. With its rose gardens, cobblestone waterfront, and well-manicured lawns, Roche Harbor retains the flavor of its days as a hangout for McMillin's powerful friends—especially since the sheltered harbor is very popular with well-to-do pleasure boaters. ⊠ *End of Roche Harbor Rd.* ⊕ *www.rocheharbor.com.*

FAMILY
Fodor's Choice
★

San Juan Island National Historic Park. Fortifications and other 19th-century military installments commemorate the Pig War, in which the United States and Great Britain nearly went into battle over their respective claims on the San Juan Islands. The dispute began in 1859 when an American settler killed a British settler's pig, and escalated until roughly 500 American soldiers and 2,200 British soldiers with five warships were poised for battle. Fortunately, no blood was spilled, and the disagreement was finally settled in 1872 in the Americans' favor, with Kaiser Wilhelm I of Germany as arbitrator.

The park comprises two separate areas on opposite sides of the island. English Camp, in a sheltered cove of Garrison Bay on the northern end, includes a blockhouse, a commissary, and barracks. A popular (though steep) hike is to the top of Young Hill, from which you can get a great view of northwest side of the island. American Camp, on the southern end, has a visitor center and the remains of fortifications; it stretches along driftwood-strewn beaches. Many of the American Camp's walking trails are through prairie; in the evening, dozens of rabbits emerge from their warrens to nibble in the fields. Great views greet you from the top of the Mt. Finlayson Trail—if you're lucky, you might be able to see Mt. Baker and Mt. Rainier along with the Olympics. From June to August you can take guided hikes and see reenactments of 1860s-era military life. ⊠ *Park headquarters, 125 Spring St., American Camp, 6 miles southeast of Friday Harbor; English Camp, 9 miles northwest of Friday Harbor, Friday Harbor* ☎ *360/378–2240* ⊕ *www.nps.gov/sajh* 🖾 *Free* ☉ *American Camp visitor center closed mid-Dec.–Feb. English Camp visitor center closed early Sept.–late May.*

San Juan Islands Museum of Art. Previously known as the Visual Arts Museum, this facility now generally referred to as the SJIMA presents rotating art shows and exhibits with an emphasis on island and Northwest artists, including the highly touted Artists' Registry Show in winter, which features works by nearly 100 San Juan Islands artists. The museum has been in its sleek, angular, contemporary permanent building since 2014. ⊠ *540 Spring St., Friday Harbor* ☎ *360/370–5050* ⊕ *www.sjima.org* 🖾 *$10* ☉ *Closed Tues.–Thurs.*

FAMILY **San Juan Islands Sculpture Park.** At this serene 20-acre park near Roche Harbor, you can stroll along five winding trails to view more than 150 colorful, in many cases large-scale sculptures spread amid freshwater and saltwater wetlands, open woods, blossoming fields, and rugged terrain. The park is also a haven for birds; more than 120 species nest and breed here. It's a great spot for picnicking, and dogs are welcome. ⊠ *Roche Harbor Rd., just before entrance to Roche Harbor Resort, Roche Harbor* ⊕ *www.sjisculpturepark.com* 🖾 *$5.*

WORTH NOTING

FAMILY **Krystal Acres Alpaca Farm.** Kids and adults love admiring the more than 70 alpacas from South America at this sprawling 80-acre ranch on the west side of the island. The shop in the big barn displays beautiful, high-quality clothing and crafts, all handmade from alpaca hair. ⊠ *152 Blazing Tree Rd., Friday Harbor* ☎ *360/378–6125* ⊕ *www.krystalacres. com* 🖾 *Free.*

FAMILY **Whale Museum.** A dramatic exterior mural depicting several types of whales welcomes you into a world filled with models of whales and whale skeletons, recordings of whale sounds, and videos of whales. Head around to the back of the first-floor shop to view maps of the latest orca pod trackings in the area. ⊠ *62 1st St. N, Friday Harbor* ☎ *360/378–4710* ⊕ *www.whalemuseum.org* 🖾 *$6.*

WHERE TO EAT

$$$ ✕ **Backdoor Kitchen.** This local favorite has become well-known beyond
ECLECTIC the San Juans, thanks to the stellar service and inventive, globally
Fodor's Choice inspired cuisine and craft cocktails. As the name might indicate, it's
★ a bit hard to find, tucked in an elegant courtyard a few blocks uphill
from the water. **Known for:** "noodle Bowl Monday" lunch specials;
some of the best pan-Asian dishes on the island; relaxing and scenic
outdoor dining in a landscaped courtyard. $ Average main: $23 ⊠ 400b
A St., Friday Harbor ☎ 360/378–9540 ⊕ www.backdoorkitchen.com
⊗ Closed Mon., Tues., and additional days in winter; call off-season.
No lunch Tues.–Sun.

$$ ✕ **Cask and Schooner.** This convivial pub decked out with nautical
AMERICAN trappings and steps from the ferry terminal serves reliably filling,
tasty, English-inspired pub fare with contemporary twists. Among
the popular dishes are spicy braised short ribs with mashed potatoes and horseradish crème and a lamb burger with tomato chutney, watercress, and feta. **Known for:** convivial ambience; excellent
brunch; strong selection of craft beers. $ Average main: $21 ⊠ 1
Front St., Friday Harbor ☎ 360/378–2922 ⊕ www.caskandschooner.
com ⊗ Closed Tues.

$$ ✕ **Downriggers.** This snazzy, contemporary, seafood-driven restaurant
PACIFIC overlooking the harbor is helmed by one of the most celebrated chefs
NORTHWEST in the islands, Aaron Rock. The light-filled dining room is a terrific spot
to watch boats and ferries come and go while sampling such tempting
fare as Penn Cove mussels and pan-seared sockeye salmon with sweet-
corn grits, and caramel-chicken and ginger-spiced waffles drizzled with
warm honey. **Known for:** pub fare with creative twists; extensive list
of craft cocktails; Asian-inspired chicken and waffles. $ Average main:
$21 ⊠ 10 Front St., Friday Harbor ☎ 360/378–2700 ⊕ www.downrig-
gerssanjuan.com.

$ ✕ **Ernie's Cafe.** Ask a local for the best lunch recommendation in town,
ECLECTIC and you may be surprised by the answer—plenty of folks will send you
to this casual diner at the airport, fun as much for watching planes
take off and land as for the laid-back, friendly vibe and delicious,
casual fare. You'll find a few Asian-fusion dishes on the menu, includ-
ing Korean-style *bulgogi* (grilled marinated beef), and hearty noodle
bowls, plus diner classics like hefty cheeseburgers, breakfast sand-
wiches, and flaky popovers. **Known for:** popovers at breakfast; sev-
eral Korean-inspired dishes; watching airplanes. $ Average main: $10
⊠ 744 Airport Circle Dr., Friday Harbor ☎ 360/378–6605 ⊗ Closed
weekends. No dinner.

$ ✕ **The Market Chef.** Only 50 yards from the ferry holding area, this café
CAFÉ makes fantastic sandwiches (try the roast-beef-and-rocket version,
which is served on a house-baked roll with spicy chili aioli). The soups
and deli items—including a decadent macaroni and cheese—are also
top-notch. **Known for:** mac and cheese; picnic and to-go lunches. $ Av-
erage main: $9 ⊠ 225 A St., Friday Harbor ☎ 360/378–4546 ⊗ Closed
weekends. No dinner.

$$$
PACIFIC
NORTHWEST
Fodor's Choice
★

✕**Restaurant at Friday Harbor House.** Creativity and dedication to local ingredients are hallmarks of this stylish, contemporary restaurant that serves daily brunch and dinner most evenings. The brunch burger, topped with a fried egg and green-tomato-and-bacon jam, and breakfast poutine with duck confit and cheese curds make for decadent starts to your day. **Known for:** brunch served every day; excellent wine and cocktail lists; panoramic views of Friday Harbor. $ *Average main: $26* ✉ *Friday Harbor House, 130 West St., Friday Harbor* ☎ *360/378–8455* ⊕ *www.fridayharborhouse.com* ◷ *No dinner Tues. and Wed.*

WHERE TO STAY

$$
HOTEL

Birdrock Hotel. The range of spiffy lodging options ranges from affordably priced if compact rooms that have private baths down the hall to downright cushy two-bedroom suites with gas fireplaces, spacious sitting rooms, pitched ceilings, and terrific harbor views. **Pros:** handy downtown Friday Harbor location; tasteful, unfussy furnishings; great value. **Cons:** central location means some street noise and crowds. $ *Rooms from: $188* ✉ *35 1st St., Friday Harbor* ☎ *360/378–5848, 800/352–2632* ⊕ *www.birdrockhotel.com* ⟿ *10 rooms, 5 suites* ⦿❘ *Breakfast.*

$$$$
HOTEL
Fodor's Choice
★

Friday Harbor House. At this bluff-top getaway with floor-to-ceiling windows, sleek, modern wood furnishings and fabrics in beige hues fill the rooms, all of which have gas fireplaces, deep jetted tubs, and at least partial views of the marina, ferry landing, and San Juan Channel below (be sure to request a marina-view room at booking). **Pros:** great views; excellent restaurant; steps from downtown shopping and dining. **Cons:** limited views from some rooms; among the priciest hotels in the San Juan Islands. $ *Rooms from: $309* ✉ *130 West St., Friday Harbor* ☎ *360/378–8455, 866/722–7356* ⊕ *www.fridayharborhouse.com* ⟿ *23 rooms* ⦿❘ *Breakfast.*

$$
HOTEL
Fodor's Choice
★

Island Inn at 123 West. There's a pretty striking mix of accommodation styles at this cosmopolitan complex that tumbles down a hillside overlooking Friday Harbor, from intimate Euro-style rooms that lack exterior windows to expansive suites with water views to ginormous bilevel penthouses with two bedrooms, private decks, gorgeous full kitchens, and astounding views. **Pros:** penthouse suites are great for luxurious family getaways; Euro-style standard rooms are a good deal; handy in-town location. **Cons:** suites are quite spendy; standard rooms have no outlooks. $ *Rooms from: $209* ✉ *123 West St., Friday Harbor* ☎ *360/378–4400, 877/512–9262* ⊕ *www.123west.com* ⟿ *5 rooms, 11 suites* ⦿❘ *No meals.*

$$$
B&B/INN

Kirk House Bed and Breakfast. Rooms are all differently decorated in this 1907 Craftsman bungalow, the summer home of steel magnate Peter Kirk: the Garden Room has a botanical motif, the sunny Trellis Room is done in soft shades of yellow and green, and the Arbor Room has French doors leading out to the garden. **Pros:** gorgeous house full of stained glass and other lovely details; within walking distance of town. **Cons:** occasional noise from nearby airport; a couple of the rooms are on the small side. $ *Rooms from: $245* ✉ *595 Park St., Friday Harbor* ☎ *360/378–3757, 800/639–2762* ⊕ *www.kirkhouse.net* ⟿ *4 rooms* ⦿❘ *Breakfast.*

$$$ RESORT Fodor's Choice ★ 🏨 **Roche Harbor Resort.** This sprawling resort, with several types of accommodations ranging from historic hotel rooms to luxurious contemporary waterfront suites, occupies the site of the lime works that made John S. McMillin his fortune in the late 19th century. **Pros:** lots of different options for families and groups; very convenient for boaters; beautiful grounds; gorgeous full-service spa. **Cons:** condos have less character and are away from the waterfront; a bit isolated from the rest of the island if you don't have a car; the least expensive rooms in Hotel de Haro have shared baths. [$] *Rooms from: $239* ✉ *248 Reuben Memorial Dr., Roche Harbor* ☎ *360/378–2155, 800/451–8910* 🌐 *www.rocheharbor.com* 🛏 *16 rooms, 18 suites, 9 cottages, 20 condos* 🍴 *No meals.*

$$$ RESORT FAMILY 🏨 **Snug Harbor Resort.** At this popular cottage resort and marina on the northwest side of the island, all of the units were completely rebuilt in 2014 with tall windows overlooking the water, high ceilings, well-equipped kitchens, knotty-pine wood paneling, gas fireplaces, and private decks. **Pros:** beautiful, contemporary decor; quiet location; nice views of the harbor. **Cons:** no pets; 20-minute drive from Friday Harbor; expensive. [$] *Rooms from: $299* ✉ *1997 Mitchell Bay Rd., Friday Harbor* ☎ *360/378–4762* 🌐 *www.snugresort.com* 🛏 *17 cottages* 🍴 *No meals.*

SPORTS AND THE OUTDOORS

BEACHES

San Juan County Park. You'll find a wide gravel beachfront at this park 10 miles west of Friday Harbor, overlooking waters where orcas often frolic in summer, plus grassy lawns with picnic tables and a small campground. **Amenities:** parking (free); toilets. **Best for:** walking. ✉ *380 Westside Rd., Friday Harbor* ☎ *360/378–8420* 🌐 *www.co.san-juan.wa.us.*

South Beach at American Camp. This 2-mile public beach on the southern end of the island is part of San Juan Island National Historical Park. **Amenities:** parking (free); toilets. **Best for:** solitude; walking. ✉ *Off Cattle Point Rd.* 🌐 *www.nps.gov/sajh.*

BIKING

You can rent standard, mountain, and BMX bikes for $40 to $50 per day or about $200 to $240 per week. Tandem, recumbent, and electric-assist bikes rent for about $55 to $80 per day.

Discovery Adventure Tours. The noted Friday Harbor outfitter (aka Discovery Sea Kayaks) also rents conventional road bikes and electric-assist bikes. ✉ *260 Spring St., Friday Harbor* ☎ *360/378–2559, 866/461–2559* 🌐 *www.discoveryadventuretours.com.*

Island Bicycles. This full-service shop rents bikes. ✉ *380 Argyle Ave., Friday Harbor* ☎ *360/378–4941* 🌐 *www.islandbicycles.com.*

BOATING AND SAILING

At public docks, high-season moorage rates are $1 to $2 per foot (of vessel) per night.

Port of Friday Harbor. The marina at the island's main port offers guest moorage, vessel assistance and repair, bareboat and skippered charters, overnight accommodations, and wildlife- and whale-watching cruises. ✉ *204 Front St., Friday Harbor* ☎ *360/378–2688* 🌐 *www.portfridayharbor.org.*

Roche Harbor Marina. The marina at Roche Harbor Resort has a fuel dock, pool, grocery, and other guest services. ✉ *248 Reuben Memorial Dr., Roche Harbor* ☎ *360/378–2155* ⊕ *www.rocheharbor.com.*

Snug Harbor Resort Marina. This well-located marina adjoins a popular, upscale small resort. It provides van service to and from Friday Harbor and rents small powerboats. ✉ *1997 Mitchell Bay Rd., Friday Harbor* ☎ *360/378–4762* ⊕ *www.snugresort.com.*

SEA KAYAKING

You'll find many places to rent kayaks in Friday Harbor, as well as outfitters providing classes and tours. Be sure to make reservations in summer. Three-hour tours run about $75 to $100, day tours cost around $110 to $125, and overnight tours start around $175 per day. Equipment is always included in the cost.

Crystal Seas Kayaking. Sunset trips and multisport tours that might include biking, kayaking, yoga, and camping are among the options with this respected guide company. ✉ *40 Spring St., Friday Harbor* ☎ *360/378–4223, 877/732–7877* ⊕ *www.crystalseas.com.*

Discovery Sea Kayaks. This outfitter offers both sea-kayaking adventures, including sunset trips and multiday excursions, and whale-watching paddles. ✉ *260 Spring St., Friday Harbor* ☎ *360/378–2559, 866/461–2559* ⊕ *www.discoveryseakayak.com.*

San Juan Kayak Expeditions. This reputable company has been running kayaking and camping tours in two-person kayaks since 1980. ✉ *85 Front St., Friday Harbor* ☎ *360/378–4436* ⊕ *www.sanjuankayak.com.*

Sea Quest Expeditions. Kayak eco-tours with guides who are trained naturalists, biologists, and environmental scientists are available through this popular outfitter. ✉ *Friday Harbor* ☎ *360/378–5767, 888/589–4253* ⊕ *www.sea-quest-kayak.com.*

WHALE-WATCHING

Whale-watching expeditions typically run three to four hours and cost around $100–$120 per person. Note that tours departing from San Juan Island typically get you to the best whale-watching waters faster than those departing from the mainland. ■TIP➜ For the best experience, look for tour companies with small boats that carry under 30 people. Bring warm clothing even if it's a warm day.

Fodor's Choice **Maya's Legacy Whale Watching.** These informative tours on small, modern, and speedy boats ensure great views for every passengers; departures are from Friday Harbor and Snug Harbor Marina. ✉ *14 Cannery Landing, Friday Harbor* ☎ *360/378–7996* ⊕ *www.sanjuanislandwhale-watch.com.*

San Juan Excursions. Whale-watching cruises are offered aboard a converted 1941 U.S. Navy research vessel. ✉ *40 Spring St., Friday Harbor* ☎ *360/378–6636, 800/809–4253* ⊕ *www.watchwhales.com.*

San Juan Island Whale & Wildlife Tours. Tours from Friday Harbor leave daily at noon and are led by highly knowledgeable marine experts. ✉ *1 Front St., Friday Harbor* ☎ *360/298–0012* ⊕ *www.sanjuanisland-whales.com.*

Western Prince Whale & Wildlife Tours. Narrated whale-watching tours last three to four hours. ⊠ *1 Spring St., Friday Harbor* ☎ *360/378–5315, 800/757–6722* ⊕ *www.orcawhalewatch.com.*

SHOPPING

Friday Harbor is the main shopping area, with dozens of shops selling a variety of art, crafts, and clothing created by residents, as well as a bounty of island-grown produce.

Arctic Raven Gallery. The specialty here is Northwest native art, including scrimshaw and wood carvings. ⊠ *130 S. 1st St., Friday Harbor* ☎ *360/378–3433* ⊕ *www.arcticravengalleryfridayharbor.com.*

San Juan Island Farmers Market. From April through October, this open-air market with more than 30 vendors selling local produce and crafts takes place at Friday Harbor Brickworks on Saturdays from 10 to 1. The market is also open once or twice a month on Saturdays in winter; check the website for the schedule. ⊠ *150 Nichols St., Friday Harbor* ⊕ *www.sjifarmersmarket.com.*

San Juan Vineyards. This winery 3 miles north of Friday Harbor has a tasting room and gift shop, and organizes such special events as a harvest festival in October and November barrel tastings. Noteworthy varietals here include Chardonnay, Riesling, Merlot, and Cabernet Franc. ⊠ *3136 Roche Harbor Rd., Friday Harbor* ☎ *360/378–9463* ⊕ *www.sanjuanvineyards.com.*

Waterworks Gallery. This respected gallery represents about 30 eclectic, contemporary artists, from painters to jewelers. ⊠ *315 Argyle Ave., Friday Harbor* ☎ *360/378–3060* ⊕ *www.waterworksgallery.com.*

OLYMPIC
NATIONAL PARK

WELCOME TO OLYMPIC NATIONAL PARK

TOP REASONS TO GO

★ **Exotic rain forest:**
A rain forest in the Pacific Northwest? Indeed, Olympic National Park is one of the few places in the world with this unique temperate landscape.

★ **Beachcombing:** Miles of rugged, spectacular coastline hemmed with sea stacks and tidal pools edge the driftwood-strewn shores of the Olympic Peninsula.

★ **Nature's hot tubs:**
A dip in Sol Duc's natural geothermal mineral pools offers a secluded spa experience in the wooded heart of the park.

★ **Lofty vistas:** The hardy can hike up meadowed foothill trails or climb the frosty peaks throughout the Olympics—or just drive up to Hurricane Ridge for endless views.

★ **A sense of history:**
American Indian history is key to this region, where eight tribes have traditional ties to the park lands—there's 12,000 years of human history to explore.

1 Coastal Olympic.
Here the Pacific smashes endlessly into the rugged coastline, carving out some of the park's most memorable scenes in the massive, rocky sea stacks and islets just offshore. Back from the water are beaches and tide pools full of sea stars, crabs, and anemones.

Neah Bay

112

Sekiu
Clallam Bay

112

Pysht

S T R A I T   O F

Ozette

113

Storm King Station

Lake Crescent

Lake Ozette

101

SOL DUC VALLEY

Eagle
Sol Duc

NPS/USFS Information Station

Forks

29

R U G G E D   R I D G E

1

Mora

110

Hoh River Rain Forest

La Push

Second Beach

Third Beach

Visitor Center

101

Pelton Peak

Kalaloch

Kalaloch Information Station

Queets

Queets

Quinault Rain Forest

2

Lake Quinault

0   10 mi

0   10 km

USFS/NPS Information Station

Amanda Park

101

2 The Rain Forest.
Centered on the Hoh, Queets, and Quinault river valleys, this is the region's most unique landscape. Fog-shrouded Douglas firs and Sitka spruces, some more than 300 feet tall, huddle in this moist, pine-carpeted area, shading fern- and moss-draped cedars, maples, and alders.

3 The Mountains. Craggy gray peaks and snow-covered summits dominate the skyline. Low-level foliage and wildflower meadows make for excellent hiking in the plateaus. Even on the sunniest days, temperatures are brisk. Some roads are closed in winter months.

4 Alpine Meadows.
In midsummer, the swath of colors is like a Monet canvas spread over the landscape, and wildlife teems among the honeyed flowers. Trails are never prettier, and views are crisp and vast.

12

GETTING ORIENTED

The Olympic Peninsula's elegant snowcapped and forested landscape is edged on all sides by water: to the north the Strait of Juan de Fuca separates the United States from Canada, a network of Puget Sound bays laces the east, the Chehalis River meanders along the southern end, and the massive gray Pacific Ocean guards the west side.

KEY	
🏃	Ranger Station
⛺	Campground
🌲	Picnic Area
🍴	Restaurant
🏠	Lodge
🚶	Trailhead
🚻	Restrooms
⇶	Scenic Viewpoint
-----	Walking/Hiking Trails

Updated by
Shelley Arenas

A spellbinding setting is tucked into the country's far northwestern corner, within the heart-shape Olympic Peninsula. Edged on all sides by water, the forested landscape is remote and pristine, and works its way around the sharpened ridges of the snowcapped Olympic Mountains. Big lakes cut pockets of blue in the rugged blanket of pine forests, and hot springs gurgle up from the foothills. Along the coast the sights are even more enchanting: wave-sculpted boulders, tidal pools teeming with sea life, and tree-topped sea stacks.

OLYMPIC PLANNER

WHEN TO GO

Summer, with its long stretches of sun-filled days, is prime touring time for Olympic National Park. June through September are the peak months; Hurricane Ridge, the Hoh Rain Forest, Lake Crescent, and Ruby Beach are bustling by 10 am.

Late spring and early autumn are also good bets for clear weather; anytime between April and October, you'll have a good chance of fair skies. Between Thanksgiving and Easter, it's a toss-up as to which days will turn out fair; prepare for heavy clouds, rain showers, and chilly temperatures, then hope for the best.

Winter is a great time to visit if you enjoy isolation. Locals are usually the only hardy souls during this time, except for weekend skiers heading to the snowfields around Hurricane Ridge. Many visitor facilities have limited hours or are closed from October to April.

FESTIVALS AND EVENTS

FEBRUARY
FAMILY
Chocolate on the Beach Festival. Venues in the North Beach towns of Seabrook, Moclips, and Pacific Beach host this annual celebration of chocolate the last weekend of February. Activities include classes, contests, demonstrations, and dining and sampling events. ⊠ *Pacific Beach* ⊕ *www.chocolateonthebeachfestival.com.*

MAY
Irrigation Festival. For more than a century, the people of Sequim have been celebrating the irrigation ditches that brought life-giving water here. Highlights of the 10-day festival include a beauty pageant, logging demonstrations, arts and crafts, a classic car show, a strongman competition, parades, and a picnic. ⊠ *Sequim* ☎ *360/461–6511* ⊕ *www. irrigationfestival.com.*

JUNE–
AUGUST
Centrum Summer Arts Festival. This summerlong lineup of concerts and workshops is held at Fort Worden State Park, a 19th-century Army base near Port Townsend. ⊠ *Port Townsend* ☎ *360/385–3102* ⊕ *www. centrum.org.*

JUNE–
SEPTEMBER
Olympic Music Festival. A variety of classical concerts are performed in a renovated barn on weekends from July through early September; picnic on the farm while you listen. ☎ *360/385–9699 office, 360/838–3006 tickets* ⊕ *www.olympicmusicfestival.org.*

JULY
Forks Old-Fashioned Fourth of July. A salmon bake, parade, demolition derby, arts-and-crafts exhibits, kids' activities, and plenty of fireworks mark Forks's weekend-long celebration. ⊠ *Forks* ☎ *360/374–2531, 800/443–6757* ⊕ *www.forkswa.com.*

Sequim Lavender Festival. The third weekend in July, a street fair and free self-guided farm tours celebrate Sequim's many fragrant lavender fields. ⊠ *Sequim* ☎ *360/681–3035* ⊕ *www.lavenderfestival.com.*

SEPTEMBER
Wooden Boat Festival. Hundreds of antique boats sail into Port Townsend for the weekend; there's also live music, education programs, and demonstrations. ⊠ *Port Townsend* ☎ *360/385–3628* ⊕ *www.wood-enboat.org.*

PLANNING YOUR TIME

OLYMPIC IN ONE DAY

Start at the **Lake Quinault Lodge,** in the park's southwest corner. From here, drive a half hour into the Quinault Valley via **South Shore Road.** Tackle the forested **Graves Creek Trail,** then head up **North Shore Road** to the Quinault Rain Forest Interpretive Trail. Next, head back to U.S. 101 and drive to **Ruby Beach,** where a shoreline walk presents a breathtaking scene of sea stacks and sparkling, pink-hued sands.

Forks, and its **Timber Museum,** are your next stop; have lunch here, then drive 20 minutes to the beach at **La Push.** Next, head to **Lake Crescent,** around the corner to the northeast, where you can rent a boat, take a swim, or enjoy a picnic next to the sparkling teal waters. Drive through **Port Angeles** to **Hurricane Ridge;** count on an hour's drive from bottom to top if there aren't too many visitors. At the ridge, explore the visitor center or hike the 3-mile loop to **Hurricane Hill,** where you can see over the entire park north to Vancouver Island and south past Mt. Olympus.

GETTING HERE AND AROUND

You can enter the park at a number of points, but because the park is 95% wilderness, access roads do not penetrate far. The best way to get around and to see many of the park's top sites is on foot.

AIR TRAVEL

Seattle–Tacoma International Airport is the nearest airport to Olympic National Park. It's roughly a two-hour drive from the park.

BOAT TRAVEL

Ferries provide another unique (though indirect) link to the Olympic area from Seattle; contact **Washington State Ferries** (☎ *800/843–3779, 206/464–6400* ⊕ *www.wsdot.wa.gov/ferries*) for information.

BUS TRAVEL

Grays Harbor Transit runs buses Monday through Saturday from Aberdeen and Hoquiam to Amanda Park, on the west end of Lake Quinault. Jefferson Transit operates a Forks–Amanda Park route Monday through Saturday.

Bus Contacts Grays Harbor Transit. ☎ *360/532–2770, 800/562–9730* ⊕ *www.ghtransit.com.* **Jefferson Transit.** ☎ *800/371–0497, 360/385–4777* ⊕ *www.jeffersontransit.com.*

CAR TRAVEL

U.S. 101 essentially encircles the main section of Olympic National Park, and a number of roads lead from the highway into the park's mountains and toward its beaches. You can reach U.S. 101 via Interstate 5 at Olympia, via Route 12 at Aberdeen, or via Route 104 from the Washington state ferry terminals at Bainbridge or Kingston.

PARK ESSENTIALS

ADMISSION FEES AND PERMITS

Seven-day vehicle admission is $25; an annual pass is $50. Individuals arriving on foot, bike, or motorcycle pay $10. An overnight wilderness permit, available at visitor centers and ranger stations, is $7 per person per night. An annual wilderness camping permit costs $45. Fishing in freshwater streams and lakes within Olympic National Park does not require a Washington state fishing license; however, anglers must acquire a salmon-steelhead catch record card when fishing for those species. Ocean fishing and harvesting shellfish require licenses, which are available at sporting-goods and outdoor-supply stores.

ADMISSION HOURS

Six park entrances are open 24/7; gate kiosk hours (for buying passes) vary according to season and location, but most are staffed during daylight hours. Olympic National Park is in the Pacific time zone.

CELL-PHONE RECEPTION

Note that cell reception is sketchy in wilderness areas. There are public telephones at the Olympic National Park Visitor Center, Hoh River Rain Forest Visitor Center, and lodging properties within the park— Lake Crescent, Kalaloch, and Sol Duc Hot Springs. Fairholme General Store also has a phone.

RESTAURANTS

The major resorts are your best bets for eating out in the park. Each has a main restaurant, café, and/or kiosk, as well as casually upscale dinner service, with regional seafood, meat, and produce complemented by a range of microbrews and good Washington and international wines. Reservations are either recommended or required.

Outside the park, small, easygoing cafés and bistros line the main thoroughfares in Sequim, Port Angeles, and Port Townsend, offering cuisine that ranges from hearty American-style fare to more eclectic local flavor.

HOTELS

Major park resorts run from good to terrific, with generally comfortable rooms, excellent facilities, and easy access to trails, beaches, and activity centers. Midsize accommodations, like Sol Duc Hot Springs Resort, are often shockingly rustic—but remember, you're here for the park, not for the rooms.

The towns around the park have motels, hotels, and resorts for every budget. For a full beach-town vacation experience, base yourself in a home or cottage in the coastal community of Seabrook (near Pacific Beach). Sequim and Port Angeles have many attractive, friendly B&Bs, plus lots of inexpensive chain hotels and motels. Forks is basically a motel town, with a few guesthouses around its fringes.

Hotel reviews have been shortened. For full information, visit Fodors.com.

WHAT IT COSTS				
	$	$$	$$$	$$$$
Restaurants	under $12	$12–$20	$21–$30	over $30
Hotels	under $100	$100–$150	$151–$200	over $200

Restaurant prices are the average cost of a main course at dinner, or if dinner is not served, at lunch. Hotel prices are the lowest cost of a standard double room in high season, excluding taxes and service charges.

VISITOR INFORMATION

Park Contact Information Olympic National Park. ⊠ *Olympic National Park Visitor Center, 3002 Mount Angeles Rd., Port Angeles* ☎ *360/565–3130* ⊕ *www.nps.gov/olym.*

VISITOR CENTERS

Hoh Rain Forest Visitor Center. Pick up park maps and pamphlets, permits, and activities lists in this busy, woodsy chalet; there's also a shop and exhibits on natural history. Several short interpretive trails and longer wilderness treks start from here. ⊠ *Hoh Valley Rd., Forks* ✚ *31 miles south of Forks* ☎ *360/374–6925* ⊕ *www.nps.gov/olym/ planyourvisit/visitorcenters.htm* ۩ *Closed Jan., Feb., and weekdays off-season.*

Hurricane Ridge Visitor Center. The upper level of this visitor center has exhibits and nice views; the lower level has a gift shop and snack bar. Guided walks and programs start in late June. In winter, find details

GOOD READS

- Robert L. Wood's *Olympic Mountains Trail Guide* is a great resource for both day hikers and those planning longer excursions.

- Craig Romano's *Day Hiking Olympic Peninsula: National Park/ Coastal Beaches/Southwest Washington* is a detailed guide to day hikes in and around the national park.

- Stephen Whitney's *A Field Guide to the Cascades and Olympics* is an excellent trailside reference, covering more than 500 plant and animal species found in the park.

- The park's newspaper, the *Olympic Bugler*, is a seasonal guide for activities and opportunities in the park. You can pick it up at the visitor centers.

- A handy online catalog of books, maps, and passes for northwest parks is available from Discover Your Northwest (⊕ *www.discovernw.org*).

on the surrounding ski and sledding slopes and take guided snowshoe walks. ⊠ *Hurricane Ridge Rd.* ☎ *360/565–3131 for road conditions* ⊕ *www.nps.gov/olym/planyourvisit/visitorcenters.htm* ⊙ *Operating hrs/days vary off-season.*

Olympic National Park Visitor Center. This modern, well-organized facility, staffed by park rangers, provides everything: maps, trail brochures, campground advice, weather forecasts, listings of wildlife sightings, educational programs and exhibits, information on road and trail closures, and a gift shop. ⊠ *3002 Mount Angeles Rd., Port Angeles* ☎ *360/565–3130* ⊕ *www.nps.gov/olym/planyourvisit/ visitorcenters.htm.*

South Shore Quinault Ranger Station. The National Forest Service's ranger station near the Lake Quinault Lodge has maps, campground information, and program listings. ⊠ *353 S. Shore Rd., Quinault* ☎ *360/288– 2525* ⊕ *www.fs.usda.gov/main/olympic/home* ⊙ *Weekends early Sept.–late May.*

Wilderness Information Center (WIC). Located behind Olympic National Park Visitor Center, this facility provides all the information you'll need for a trip in the park, including trail conditions, safety tips, and weather bulletins. The office also issues camping permits, takes campground reservations, and rents bear-proof food canisters. ⊠ *3002 Mount Angeles Rd., Port Angeles* ☎ *360/565–3100* ⊕ *www.nps.gov/olym/planyourvisit/wic.htm* ⊙ *Closed Mon.–Thurs. off-season.*

EXPLORING

Most of the park's attractions are found either off U.S. 101 or down trails that require hikes of 15 minutes or longer. The west-coast beaches are linked to the highway by downhill tracks; the number of cars parked alongside the road at the start of the paths indicates how crowded the beach will be.

12

SCENIC DRIVES

Fodor's Choice ★ **Port Angeles Visitor Center to Hurricane Ridge.** The premier scenic drive in Olympic National Park is a steep ribbon of curves, which climbs from thickly forested foothills and subalpine meadows into the upper stretches of pine-swathed peaks. At the top, the visitor center at Hurricane Ridge has some spectacular views over the heart of the peninsula and across the Strait of Juan de Fuca. A mile past the visitor center, there are picnic tables in open meadows with photo-worthy views of the mountains to the east. Hurricane Ridge also has an uncommonly fine display of wildflowers in spring and summer. In winter, vehicles must carry chains and the road is usually open Friday–Sunday only (call first to check conditions). ⊠ *Olympic National Park* ⊕ *www.nps.gov/olym.*

HISTORIC SITES

La Push. At the mouth of Quileute River, La Push is the tribal center of the Quileute Indians. In fact, the town's name is a variation on the French *la bouche,* which means "the mouth." Offshore rock spires known as sea stacks dot the coast here, and you may catch a glimpse of bald eagles nesting in the nearby cliffs. ⊠ *Rte. 110, 14 miles west of Forks, La Push* ⊕ *www.nps.gov/olym/planyourvisit/upload/mora.pdf.*

Lake Ozette. The third-largest glacial impoundment in Washington anchors the coastal strip of Olympic National Park at its north end. The small town of Ozette, home to a coastal tribe, is the trailhead for two of the park's better one-day hikes. Both 3-mile trails lead over boardwalks through swampy wetland and coastal old-growth forest to the ocean shore and uncrowded beaches. ⊠ *Ozette* ⊹ *At end of Hoko-Ozette Rd., 26 miles southwest of Hwy. 112 near Sekiu* ☎ *360/565–3130 Ozette Ranger Station* ⊕ *www.nps.gov/olym/planyourvisit/visiting-ozette.htm.*

SCENIC STOPS

Fodor's Choice ★ **Hoh River Rain Forest.** South of Forks, an 18-mile spur road links Highway 101 with this unique temperate rain forest, where spruce and hemlock trees soar to heights of more than 200 feet. Alders and big-leaf maples are so densely covered with mosses they look more like shaggy prehistoric animals than trees, and elk browse in shaded glens. Be prepared for precipitation: the region receives 140 inches or more each year. ⊠ *Olympic National Park* ⊹ *From Hwy. 101, at about 20 miles north of Kalaloch, turn onto Upper Hoh Rd. 18 miles east to Hoh Rain Forest Visitor Center* ☎ *360/374–6925* ⊕ *www.nps.gov/olym/planyourvisit/visiting-the-hoh.htm.*

12

Fodor's Choice ★ **Hurricane Ridge.** The panoramic view from this 5,200-foot-high ridge encompasses the Olympic range, the Strait of Juan de Fuca, and Vancouver Island. Guided tours are given in summer along the many paved and unpaved trails, where wildflowers and wildlife such as deer and marmots flourish. ⊠ *Hurricane Ridge Rd., 17 miles south of Port Angeles* ☎ *360/565–3130 visitor center* ⊕ *www.nps.gov/olym/planyourvisit/ visiting-hurricane-ridge.htm* ⊗ *Closed when road is closed.*

Kalaloch. With a lodge and restaurant, a huge campground, miles of coastline, and easy access from the highway, this is a popular spot. Keen-eyed beachcombers may spot sea otters just offshore; they were reintroduced here in 1970. ⊠ *Hwy. 101, 32 miles northwest of Lake Quinault, Kalaloch* ☎ *360/565–3130 visitor center* ⊕ *www.nps.gov/ olym/planyourvisit/visiting-kalaloch-and-ruby-beach.htm.*

Lake Crescent. Visitors see Lake Crescent as Highway 101 winds along its southern shore, giving way to gorgeous views of teal waters rippling in a basin formed by Tuscan-like hills. In the evening, low bands of clouds caught between the surrounding mountains often linger over its reflective surface. ⊠ *Hwy. 101, 16 miles west of Port Angeles and 28 miles northeast of Forks* ☎ *360/565–3130 visitor center* ⊕ *www.nps. gov/olym/planyourvisit/visiting-lake-crescent.htm.*

Lake Quinault. This glimmering lake, 4½ miles long and 300 feet deep, is the first landmark you'll reach when driving the west-side loop of U.S. 101. The rain forest is thickest here, with moss-draped maples and alders, and towering spruce, fir, and hemlock. Enchanted Valley, high up near the Quinault River's source, is a deeply glaciated valley that's closer to the Hood Canal than to the Pacific Ocean. A scenic loop drive circles the lake and travels around a section of the Quinault River. ⊠ *Hwy. 101, 38 miles north of Hoquiam* ☎ *360/288–2525 Quinault Rain Forest ranger station* ⊕ *www.nps.gov/olym/planyourvisit/visiting-quinault.htm.*

Second and Third Beaches. During low tide these flat, driftwood-strewn expanses are perfect for long afternoon strolls. Second Beach, accessed via an easy forest trail through Quileute lands, opens to a vista of Pacific Ocean and sea stacks. Third Beach offers a 1¼-mile forest hike for a warm-up before reaching the sands. ⊠ *Hwy. 101, 32 miles north of Lake Quinault* ☎ *360/565–3130 visitor center* ⊕ *www.nps.gov/olym.*

Sol Duc. Sol Duc Valley is one of those magical places where all the Northwest's virtues seem at hand: lush lowland forests, sparkling river scenes, salmon runs, and serene hiking trails. Here, the popular Sol Duc Hot Springs area includes three attractive sulfuric pools ranging in temperature from 98°F to 104°F. ⊠ *Sol Duc Rd.* ⊕ *South of U.S. 101, 12 miles past west end of Lake Crescent* ☎ *360/565–3130 visitor center* ⊕ *www.nps.gov/olym/planyourvisit/visiting-the-sol-duc-valley.htm.*

Staircase. Unlike the forests of the park's south and west sides, Douglas fir is the dominant tree on the east slope of the Olympic Mountains. Fire has played an important role in creating the majestic forest here, as the Staircase Ranger Station explains in interpretive exhibits. ⊠ *Olympic National Park* ⊕ *At end of Rte. 119, 15 miles from U.S. 101 at Hoodsport* ☎ *360/565–3130 visitor center* ⊕ *www.nps.gov/olym/planyourvisit/visiting-staircase.htm.*

CLOSE UP

Plants and Wildlife in Olympic

Along the high mountain slopes hardy cedar, fir, and hemlock trees stand tough on the rugged land; the lower montane forests are filled with thickets of silver firs; and valleys stream with Douglas firs and western hemlock. The park's famous temperate rain forests are on the peninsula's western side, marked by broad western red cedars, towering red spruces, and ferns festooned with strands of mosses and patchwork lichens. This lower landscape is also home to some of the Northwest's largest trees: massive cedar and Sitka spruce near Lake Quinault can measure more than 700 inches around, and Douglas firs near the Queets and Hoh rivers are nearly as wide.

These landscapes are home to a variety of wildlife, including many large mammals and 15 creatures found nowhere else in the world. Hikers often come across Roosevelt's elk, black-tailed deer, mountain goats, beavers, raccoons, skunks, opossums, and foxes; Douglas squirrels and flying squirrels populate the heights of the forest. Less common are black bears (most prevalent from May through August); wolves, bobcats, and cougar are rarely seen. Birdlife includes bald eagles, red-tailed hawks, osprey, and great horned owls. Rivers and lakes are filled with freshwater fish, while beaches hold crabs, sea stars, anemones, and other shelled creatures. Get out in a boat on the Pacific to spot seals, sea lions, and sea otters—and perhaps a pod of porpoises, orcas, or gray whales.

Beware of jellyfish around the shores—beached jellyfish can still sting. In the woods, check for ticks after every hike and after each shower. Biting nasties include black flies, horseflies, sand fleas, and the ever-present mosquitoes. Yellow-jacket nests populate tree hollows along many trails; signs throughout the Hoh Rain Forest warn hikers to move quickly through these sections. If one or two chase you, remain calm and keep walking; these are just "guards" making sure you're keeping away from the hive. Poison oak is common, so familiarize yourself with its appearance. Bug repellent, sunscreen, and long pants and sleeves will go a long way toward making your experience more comfortable.

SPORTS AND THE OUTDOORS

BIKING

The rough gravel car tracks to some of the park's remote sites were meant for four-wheel-drive vehicles, but can double as mountain-bike routes. The Quinault Valley, Queets River, Hoh River, and Sol Duc River roads have bike paths through old-growth forest. Graves Creek Road, in the southwest, is a mountain-bike path; Lake Crescent's north side is also edged by the bike-friendly Spruce Railroad Trail. More bike tracks run through the adjacent Olympic National Forest. Note that U.S. 101 has heavy traffic and isn't recommended for cycling, although the western side has broad roads with beautiful scenery and can be biked off-season. Bikes are not permitted on foot trails.

TOURS AND OUTFITTERS

All Around Bikes. This bike, gear, and repair shop is a great resource for advice on routes around the Olympic Peninsula. Bike rentals cost $30 per half day, $50 all day, and $60 for 24 hours. ✉ *150 W. Sequim Bay Rd., Sequim* ☎ *360/681–3868* ⊕ *www.allaroundbikes.com.*

Sound Bike & Kayak. This sports outfitter rents and sells bikes, kayaks, and related equipment. Kayak rentals run $15 per hour and $50 per day. Bikes rent for $10 per hour and $45 per day. ✉ *120 E. Front St., Port Angeles* ☎ *360/457–1240* ⊕ *www.soundbikeskayaks.com.*

12

CLIMBING

At 7,980 feet, Mt. Olympus is the highest peak in the park and the most popular climb in the region. To attempt the summit, climbers must register at the Glacier Meadows Ranger Station. Mt. Constance, the third-highest Olympic peak at 7,743 feet, has a well-traversed climbing route that requires technical experience; reservations are recommended for the Lake Constance stop, which is limited to 20 campers. Mt. Deception is another possibility, though tricky snows have caused fatalities and injuries in the last decade.

Climbing season runs from late June through September. Note that crevasse skills and self-rescue experience are highly recommended. Climbers must register with park officials and purchase wilderness permits before setting out. The best resource for climbing advice is the Wilderness Information Center in Port Angeles.

TOURS AND OUTFITTERS

Mountain Madness. Adventure through the rain forest to the glaciated summit of Mt. Olympus on a five-day trip, offered several times per year by Mountain Madness. ☎ *800/328–5925, 206/937–8389* ⊕ *www. mountainmadness.com* 🖾 *From $1350 for 5-day climb.*

FISHING

There are numerous fishing possibilities throughout the park. Lake Crescent is home to cutthroat and rainbow trout, as well as petite kokanee salmon; Lake Cushman, Lake Quinault, and Ozette Lake have trout, salmon, and steelhead. As for rivers, the Bogachiel and Queets have steelhead salmon in season. The glacier-fed Hoh River is home to chinook salmon April to November, and coho salmon from August through November; the Sol Duc River offers all five species of salmon. Rainbow trout are found in the Dosewallips, Elwha, and Skykomish rivers. Other places to go after salmon and trout include the Duckabush, Quillayute, Quinault, and Salmon rivers. A Washington state punch card is required during salmon-spawning months; fishing regulations vary throughout the park. Licenses are available from sporting-goods and outdoor-supply stores.

TOURS AND OUTFITTERS

Bob's Piscatorial Pursuits. This company, based in Forks, offers salmon and steelhead fishing trips around the Olympic Peninsula from mid-September through May. ✉ *Forks* ☎ *866/347–4232* ⊕ *www.piscatorialpursuits.com* 🖾 *From $225 per person for 2 people; $340 for 1 person.*

HIKING

Know your tides, or you might be trapped by high water. Tide tables are available at all visitor centers and ranger stations. Remember that a wilderness permit is required for all overnight backcountry visits.

EASY

FAMILY

Fodor's Choice

★

Hoh River Trail. From the Hoh Visitor Center, this rain-forest jaunt takes you into the Hoh Valley, wending its way for 17½ miles alongside the river, through moss-draped maple and alder trees and past open meadows where elk roam in winter. *Easy.* ⊠ *Olympic National Park* ✛ *Trailhead: Hoh Visitor Center, 18 miles east of U.S. 101* ⊕ *www.nps. gov/olym/planyourvisit/hoh-river-trail.htm.*

Hurricane Ridge Meadow Trail. A ¼-mile alpine loop, most of it wheelchair accessible, leads through wildflower meadows overlooking numerous vistas of the interior Olympic peaks to the south and a panorama of the Strait of Juan de Fuca to the north. *Easy.* ⊠ *Olympic National Park* ✛ *Trailhead: Hurricane Ridge Rd., 17 miles south of Port Angeles* ⊕ *www.nps.gov/olym/planyourvisit/visiting-hurricane-ridge.htm.*

MODERATE

FAMILY

Cape Alava Trail. Beginning at Ozette, this 3-mile boardwalk trail leads from the forest to wave-tossed headlands. *Moderate.* ⊠ *Ozette* ✛ *Trailhead: end of Hoko-Ozette Rd., 26 miles south of Hwy. 112, west of Sekiu* ⊕ *www.nps.gov/olym/planyourvisit/visiting-ozette.htm.*

Graves Creek Trail. This 6-mile-long moderately strenuous trail climbs from lowland rain forest to alpine territory at Sundown Pass. Due to spring floods, a fjord halfway up is often impassable in May and June. *Moderate.* ⊠ *Olympic National Park* ✛ *Trailhead: end of S. Shore Rd., 23 miles east of U.S. 101* ⊕ *www.nps.gov/olym.*

FAMILY

Fodor's Choice

★

Sol Duc River Trail. The 1½-mile gravel path off Sol Duc Road winds through thick Douglas fir forests toward the thundering, three-chute Sol Duc Falls. Just off the road, below a wooden platform over the Sol Duc River, you'll come across the 70-foot Salmon Cascades. In late summer and autumn, thousands of salmon negotiate 50 miles or more of treacherous waters to reach the cascades and the tamer pools near Sol Duc Hot Springs. The popular 6-mile **Lovers Lane Loop Trail** links the Sol Duc falls with the hot springs. You can continue up from the falls 5 miles to the **Appleton Pass Trail,** at 3,100 feet. From there you can hike on to the 8½-mile mark, where views at the High Divide are from 5,050 feet. *Moderate.* ⊠ *Olympic National Park* ✛ *Trailhead: Sol Duc Rd., 12 miles south of U.S. 101* ⊕ *www.nps.gov/olym/planyourvisit/sol-duc-river-trail.htm.*

DIFFICULT

High Divide Trail. A 9-mile hike in the park's high country defines this trail, which includes some strenuous climbing on its last 4 miles before topping out at a small alpine lake. A return loop along High Divide wends its way an extra mile through alpine territory, with sensational views of Olympic peaks. This trail is only for dedicated, properly equipped hikers who are in good shape. *Difficult.* ⊠ *Olympic National Park* ✛ *Trailhead: end of Sol Duc River Rd., 13 miles south of U.S. 101* ⊕ *www.nps.gov/olym/planyourvisit/high-divide-loop.htm.*

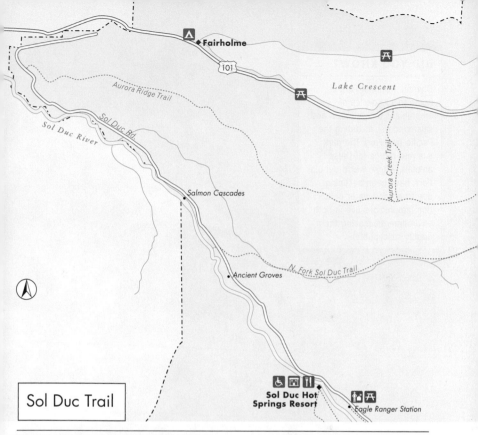

Sol Duc Trail

KAYAKING AND CANOEING

Lake Crescent, a serene expanse of teal-color waters surrounded by deep-green pine forests, is one of the park's best boating areas. Note that the west end is for swimming only; no speedboats are allowed here.

Lake Quinault has boating access from a gravel ramp on the north shore. From U.S. 101, take a right on North Shore Road, another right on Hemlock Way, and a left on Lakeview Drive. There are plank ramps at Falls Creek and Willoughby campgrounds on South Shore Drive, 0.1 mile and 0.2 mile past the Quinault Ranger Station, respectively.

Lake Ozette, with just one access road, is a good place for overnight trips. Only experienced canoe and kayak handlers should travel far from the put-in, since fierce storms occasionally strike—even in summer.

TOURS AND OUTFITTERS

Fairholme General Store. Kayaks and canoes on Lake Crescent are available to rent from $20 per hour to $55 for eight hours. The store is at the lake's west end, 27 miles west of Port Angeles. ✉ *221121 U.S. 101, Port Angeles* ☎ *360/928-3020* ⊘ *Closed after Labor Day–Apr. and Mon.–Thurs. in May.*

Lake Crescent Lodge. You can rent canoes and kayaks here for $20 per hour and $55 per half day. Two-hour guided kayak tours are offered and include instructions; they cost $55 in a single kayak and $75 in a double kayak. ⊠ *416 Lake Crescent Rd.* ☎ *360/928–3211* ⊕ *www. olympicnationalparks.com* ⊘ *Closed Jan.–Apr.*

12

Log Cabin Resort. This resort, 17 miles west of Port Angeles, has paddle-boat, kayak, canoe, and paddleboard rentals for $20 per hour and $55 per day. The dock provides easy access to Lake Crescent's northeast section. ⊠ *3183 E. Beach Rd., Port Angeles* ☎ *360/928–3325* ⊕ *www. olympicnationalparks.com* ⊘ *Closed Oct.–mid-May.*

Rainforest Paddlers. This company takes kayakers down the Lizard Rock and Oxbow sections of the Hoh River and rafters on both the Hoh and Sol Duc rivers. They also offer river rafting and kayak rentals. ⊠ *4883 Upper Hoh Rd., Forks* ☎ *360/374–5254, 866/457–8398* ⊕ *www.rainforestpaddlers.com* ⛵ *Tours from $44; kayak rentals from $11/hr.*

RAFTING

Olympic has excellent rafting rivers, with Class II to Class V rapids. The Elwha River is a popular place to paddle, with some exciting turns. The Hoh is better for those who like a smooth, easy float.

TOURS AND OUTFITTERS

Olympic Raft and Kayak. Based in Port Angeles, this rafting outfit offers trips on the Sol Duc and Hoh rivers, and on the restored Elwha River when conditions allow. It also offers half-day kayaking trips on the Salish Sea, launching from a county park in Port Angeles. ⊠ *123 Lake Aldwell Rd., Port Angeles* ☎ *888/452–1443* ⊕ *www.raftandkayak.com* ⛵ *From $65.*

WINTER SPORTS

Hurricane Ridge is the central spot for winter sports. Miles of downhill and Nordic ski tracks are open late December through March, and a ski lift, towropes, and ski school are open 10 to 4 weekends and holidays. A snow-play area for children ages eight and younger is near the Hurricane Ridge Visitors Center. Hurricane Ridge Road is open Friday through Sunday in the winter season; all vehicles are required to carry chains.

TOURS AND OUTFITTERS

Hurricane Ridge Visitor Center. Rent snowshoes and ski equipment here December through March. ⊠ *Hurricane Ridge Rd., Port Angeles* ☎ *360/565–3131 road condition information* ⊕ *www.nps.gov/olym/ planyourvisit/hurricane-ridge-in-winter.htm* ⊘ *Closed Mon.–Thurs.*

WHERE TO EAT

$$$ AMERICAN 🍴 **Creekside Restaurant.** A tranquil country setting and ocean views at Kalaloch Lodge's restaurant create the perfect backdrop for savoring Pacific Northwest dinner specialties like grilled salmon, fresh shellfish, and vegan lasagne. Tempting seasonal desserts include local berry tart in summer and organic winter squash bread pudding in winter; warm vegan chocolate brownies are enjoyed year-round. [$] *Average main: $24* ✉ *157151 Hwy. 101, Forks* ☎ *866/662–9928, 360/962–2271* 🌐 *www.thekalalochlodge.com/dine.aspx.*

$$$ AMERICAN 🍴 **Lake Crescent Lodge.** Part of the original 1916 lodge, the fir-paneled dining room overlooks the lake; you won't find a better spot for sunset views. Dinner entrées include wild salmon, thyme roasted halibut, grilled steak, pork shank, and roasted chicken breast; the lunch menu features elk cheeseburgers, inventive salads, and a variety of sandwiches. [$] *Average main: $29* ✉ *416 Lake Crescent Rd., Port Angeles* ☎ *360/928–3211* 🌐 *www.olympicnationalparks.com/stay/dining/lake-crescent-lodge.aspx* ⏲ *Closed Jan.–Apr.*

$$$ AMERICAN 🍴 **The Springs Restaurant.** The main Sol Duc Hot Springs Resort restaurant is a rustic, fir-and-cedar-paneled dining room surrounded by trees. In summer big breakfasts are turned out daily 7:30 to 10; dinner is served between 5 and 9, and features comfort foods like pan-roasted salmon, chicken with garlic mashed potatoes, short ribs, burgers, fish-and-chips, mac and cheese, and sandwiches. [$] *Average main: $21* ✉ *12076 Sol Duc Rd., at U.S. 101, Port Angeles* ☎ *360/327–3583* 🌐 *www.olympicnationalparks.com/stay/dining/sol-duc-hot-springs-resort-.aspx* ⏲ *Closed Nov.–late Mar.*

PICNIC AREAS

All Olympic National Park campgrounds have adjacent picnic areas with tables, some shelters, and restrooms, but no cooking facilities. The same is true for major visitor centers, such as Hoh Rain Forest. Drinking water is available at ranger stations, interpretive centers, and inside campgrounds.

East Beach Picnic Area. Set on a grassy meadow overlooking Lake Crescent, this popular swimming spot has six picnic tables and vault toilets. ✉ *East Beach Rd., Port Angeles* ✣ *At far east end of Lake Crescent, off Hwy. 101, 17 miles west of Port Angeles.*

Rialto Beach Picnic Area. Relatively secluded at the end of the road from Forks, this is one of the premier day-use areas in the park's Pacific coast segment. This site has 12 picnic tables, fire grills, and vault toilets. ✉ *Rte. 110, 14 miles west of Forks, Forks.*

WHERE TO STAY

$$$ HOTEL FAMILY Fodor's Choice ★ 🏨 **Kalaloch Lodge.** Overlooking the Pacific, Kalaloch has cozy lodge rooms with sea views and separate cabins along the bluff. **Pros:** ranger tours; clam digging; supreme storm-watching in winter. **Cons:** no Internet and most units don't have TVs; some rooms are two blocks from main lodge; limited cell-phone service. [$] *Rooms from: $189* ✉ *157151 U.S. 101, Forks* ☎ *360/962–2271, 866/662–9928* 🌐 *www.thekalalochlodge.com* 🛏 *20 rooms, 46 cabins* 🍽 *No meals.*

CLOSE UP

Best Campgrounds in Olympic

12

Note that only a few places take reservations; if you can't book in advance, you'll have to arrive early to get a place. Each site usually has a picnic table and grill or fire pit, and most campgrounds have water, toilets, and garbage containers; for hookups, showers, and laundry facilities, you'll have to head into the towns. Firewood is available from camp concessions, but if there's no store you can collect dead wood within 1 mile of your campsite. Dogs are allowed in campgrounds, but not on most trails or in the backcountry. Trailers should be 21 feet long or less (15 feet or less at Queets Campground) though a few campgrounds can accommodate up to 35 feet. There's a camping limit of two weeks. Nightly rates run $15–$22 per site.

If you have a backcountry pass, you can camp virtually anywhere throughout the park's forests and shores. Overnight wilderness permits are $7 per person per night and are available at visitor centers and ranger stations. Note that when you camp in the backcountry, you must choose a site at least ½ mile inside the park boundary.

Kalaloch Campground. Kalaloch is the biggest and most popular Olympic campground, and it's open all year. Its vantage of the Pacific is unmatched on the park's coastal stretch. ⊠ *U.S. 101, ½ mile north of Kalaloch Information Station, Olympic National Park* ☎ *877/444–6777 for reservations.*

Lake Quinault Rain Forest Resort Village Campground. Stretching along the south shore of Lake Quinault, this RV campground has many recreation facilities, including beaches, canoes, ball fields, and horseshoe pits. The 31 RV sites, which rent for $35 per night, are open year-round but bathrooms are closed in winter. ⊠ *3½ miles east of U.S. 101, South Shore Rd., Lake Quinault* ☎ *360/288–2535, 800/255–6936* ⊕ *www.rainforestresort.com.*

Mora Campground. Along the Quillayute estuary, this campground doubles as a popular staging point for hikes northward along the coast's wilderness stretch. ⊠ *Rte. 110, 13 miles west of Forks* ☎ *No phone.*

Ozette Campground. Hikers heading to Cape Alava, a scenic promontory that is the westernmost point in the lower 48 states, use this lakeshore campground as a jumping-off point. ⊠ *Hoko-Ozette Rd., 26 miles south of Hwy. 112* ☎ *No phone.*

Sol Duc Campground. Sol Duc resembles virtually all Olympic campgrounds save one distinguishing feature—the famed hot springs are a short walk away. ⊠ *Sol Duc Rd., 11 miles south of U.S. 101* ☎ *877/444–6777 for reservations.*

Staircase Campground. In deep woods away from the river, this campground is a popular jumping-off point for hikes into the Skokomish River Valley and the Olympic high country. ⊠ *Rte. 119, 16 miles northwest of U.S. 101* ☎ *No phone.*

$$$ 🛏 **Lake Crescent Lodge.** Deep in the forest at the foot of Mt. Storm King,
HOTEL   this 1916 lodge has a variety of comfortable accommodations, from
basic rooms with shared baths to spacious two-bedroom fireplace cot-
tages. **Pros:** gorgeous setting; free wireless access in the lobby. **Cons:**
no laundry; Roosevelt Cottages often are booked a year in advance for
summer stays. $ *Rooms from: $195* ✉ *416 Lake Crescent Rd., Port
Angeles* ☎ *360/928–3211, 888/896–3818* ⊕ *www.olympicnational-
parks.com* ⊘ *Closed Jan.–Apr., except Roosevelt fireplace cabins open
weekends* ⇋ *30 motel rooms, 17 cabins, 5 lodge rooms with shared
bath* ⎟⊘⎜ *No meals.*

$$$$ 🛏 **Lake Quinault Lodge.** On a lovely glacial lake in Olympic National For-
HOTEL   est, this beautiful early-20th-century lodge complex is within walking
distance of the lakeshore and hiking trails in the spectacular old-growth
forest. **Pros:** hosts summer campfires with s'mores; family-friendly
ambience; year-round pool and sauna. **Cons:** no TV in some rooms;
some units are noisy and not very private. $ *Rooms from: $229* ✉ *345
South Shore Rd., Quinault* ☎ *360/288–2900, 888/896–3818* ⊕ *www.
olympicnationalparks.com* ⇋ *92 rooms* ⎟⊘⎜ *No meals.*

$$ 🛏 **Log Cabin Resort.** This rustic resort has an idyllic setting at the north-
HOTEL   east end of Lake Crescent with lodging choices that include A-frame
FAMILY   chalet units, standard cabins, small camper cabins, motel units, and RV
sites with full hookups. **Pros:** boat rentals available on-site; convenient
general store; pets allowed in some cabins. **Cons:** cabins are extremely
rustic; no plumbing in the camper cabins; no TVs. $ *Rooms from:
$111* ✉ *3183 E. Beach Rd., Port Angeles* ☎ *888/896–3818, 360/928–
3325* ⊕ *www.olympicnationalparks.com* ⊘ *Closed Oct.–late May* ⇋ *4
rooms, 23 cabins, 22 RV sites, 4 tent sites* ⎟⊘⎜ *No meals.*

$$$$ 🛏 **Sol Duc Hot Springs Resort.** Deep in the brooding forest along the Sol
HOTEL   Duc River and surrounded by 5,000-foot-tall mountains, the main draw
of this remote 1910 resort is the pool area, with soothing mineral baths
and a freshwater swimming pool. **Pros:** nearby trails; peaceful setting;
some units are pet-friendly. **Cons:** units are dated; no air-conditioning, TV, or Internet access; pools get crowded. $ *Rooms from: $207*
✉ *12076 Sol Duc Hot Springs Rd.* ☎ *888/896–3818* ⊕ *www.olympic-
nationalparks.com* ⊘ *Closed Nov.–late Mar.* ⇋ *32 cabins, 1 suite, 17
RV sites* ⎟⊘⎜ *No meals.*

OLYMPIC PENINSULA AND WASHINGTON COAST

WELCOME TO OLYMPIC PENINSULA AND WASHINGTON COAST

TOP REASONS TO GO

★ **Soak up the scene in Port Townsend:** Washington's Victorian seaport is home to artists, boat lovers, and foodies and a variety of annual festivals celebrating their passions, everything from wooden boats and films to fiddle tunes, jazz, and blues.

★ **Get wet:** From hiking in the moss-drenched Hoh Rain Forest, bodysurfing at Pacific Ocean beaches, soaking in thermal pools at Sol Duc Hot Springs, or simply getting caught in a good Pacific Northwest rain, you're sure to get wet.

★ **Follow the light:** Lighthouses and their histories beckon—from Point Wilson at Fort Worden, one of the state's best loved parks, to Grays Harbor and many points in between.

★ **Meet the Makah:** Exhibits at the impressive Makah Cultural Center complex display authentic scenes of early life in the Northwest.

★ **Enjoy the great outdoors at Hurricane Ridge:** Drive to the top of this spectacular ridge for splendid summer hikes and winter snow sports.

1 Northeastern Olympic Peninsula. On the northeastern tip by the restored Victorian seaport of Port Townsend, this part of the peninsula is less remote than its northwestern counterpart. Here, the protected waters of Hood Canal meet the Strait of Juan de Fuca, providing a backdrop for boatbuilding, bird-watching, sailing and—at the turn of the 19th century—shanghaiing. Farther west, bucolic farmland abounds in the rain shadow surrounding Sequim. Port Angeles provides a launchpad for skiing, snowboarding, hiking, and biking at Hurricane Ridge, one of the most easily accessible parts of Olympic National Park.

2 Northwestern Olympic Peninsula. Driftwood-strewn secluded beaches and dense old-growth forests, featuring enormous ferns and moss-dripping evergreens, rule the rain-soaked west end. Marked by waterfalls, rivers, mountain lakes, and lodges, this part of the peninsula is home to Cape Flattery, the most northwesterly edge of the contiguous United States, and the old logging town of Forks, the setting for the fictional *Twilight* series.

3 Washington Coast. The communities along this stretch of Pacific coastline range from the new Cape Cod–style homes in the master-planned development of Seabrook, where bikes and flip-flops provide the preferred means of transportation, to Ocean Shores and Westport, guarding the entry to Grays Harbor. Tucked inside are the historic lumber and fishing towns of Hoquiam and Aberdeen, hometown of Nirvana front man Kurt Cobain and home port of the *Lady Washington*. The state's official ship offers dockside tours as well as sail training.

4 Long Beach Peninsula. Bookended by two state parks and bounded in part by the Pacific Ocean and the Columbia River, this narrow stretch of land offers a series of ocean-side retreats, oyster farms, cranberry bogs, and beach after beach to comb. Kite flying, kayaking, horseback riding, clam digging, and winter-storm watching are also popular pastimes. At the southern tip, Cape Disappointment is anything but, with two lighthouses, stunning views, 8 miles of hiking trails, and the Lewis and Clark Interpretative Center.

Cape Flattery

Neah Bay

Ozette Lake

La Push

Olympic National Park

PACIFIC OCEAN

0   20 mi

0   20 km

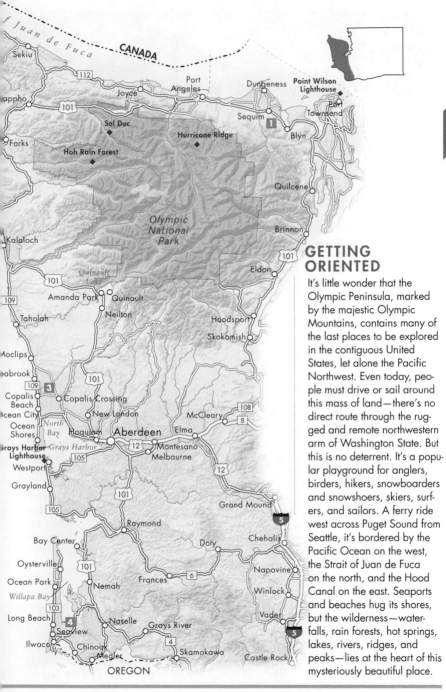

13

GETTING ORIENTED

It's little wonder that the Olympic Peninsula, marked by the majestic Olympic Mountains, contains many of the last places to be explored in the contiguous United States, let alone the Pacific Northwest. Even today, people must drive or sail around this mass of land—there's no direct route through the rugged and remote northwestern arm of Washington State. But this is no deterrent. It's a popular playground for anglers, birders, hikers, snowboarders and snowshoers, skiers, surfers, and sailors. A ferry ride west across Puget Sound from Seattle, it's bordered by the Pacific Ocean on the west, the Strait of Juan de Fuca on the north, and the Hood Canal on the east. Seaports and beaches hug its shores, but the wilderness—waterfalls, rain forests, hot springs, lakes, rivers, ridges, and peaks—lies at the heart of this mysteriously beautiful place.

Updated
by Adriana
Janovich

Wilderness envelops most of the Olympic Peninsula, an unrefined and enchanting place that promises craggy, snowcapped peaks, pristine evergreen forests, and driftwood-covered coastlines. This is a wonderland where the scent of saltwater and pine hang in the air and the horizon sometimes seems to make the entire world appear to be shades of blue and green. Historic lighthouses, seaports, and tidal pools trim its shores and a majestic mountain range rises up from its heart.

The Olympic Mountains form the core of the peninsula, skirted by saltwater on three sides. The area's highest point, Mt. Olympus, stands nearly 8,000 feet above sea level. It's safeguarded in the 922,000-acre Olympic National Park *(see Chapter 12)*, along with much of the extraordinary interior landscape. Several thousand acres more are protected in the Olympic National Forest. The peninsula also encompasses seven Native American reservations, five wilderness areas, five national wildlife refuges, the world's largest unmanaged herd of Roosevelt elk, and some of the wettest and driest areas in the coastal Pacific Northwest. The mountains catch penetrating Pacific storms, bringing an average annual rainfall of about 140 inches to the lush western river valleys and rain forests. The drier northeastern slopes of the peninsula's rain shadow see about 16 inches of precipitation per year, creating an ideal climate for the lavender that's grown commercially here.

Most residents live on the edges of the peninsula, anchored at its southwestern corner by Grays Harbor, named for Captain Robert Gray—in 1792, he became the first European American to enter the harbor. From there, the coast extends north to Cape Flattery and Neah Bay on the Makah Indian Reservation, then stretches to the Victorian seaport of Port Townsend, on the tip of the Quimper Peninsula, a narrow, crooked elbow of land at the northeastern end of the larger land mass. Rugged terrain and few roads limit interior accessibility to backpackers and climbers. But the 330-mile outer loop of U.S. 101 offers breathtaking forest, ocean, and mountain vistas as well as rest stops at a variety of colorful outposts along the way.

OLYMPIC PENINSULA AND WASHINGTON COAST PLANNER

13

WHEN TO GO

Visitors trek to the Olympic Peninsula year-round, but summer is prime touring time for this outdoors-lovers' paradise. June through September, when it's least likely to rain, is busiest. Beaches, campgrounds, and downtown areas bustle during the sun-filled summer months, and festivals attract additional crowds. This is also the time of peak lodging rates.

Early and late spring and fall are likely to be less crowded, and in many cases the shoulder season also promises less expensive hotel rates. Anytime between April and October, there's a good chance of clear skies, even if temperatures dip. The rest of the year, prepare for heavy clouds, rain showers, and chilly temperatures.

Accommodations tend to fill up year-round on festival and holiday weekends. Some museums and other tourist attractions close or operate on a limited schedule in winter, when unrelenting storms pound Washington's Pacific coast. Mid-October through mid-March, pummeling waves crash into sea stacks and outcroppings, and wind speeds of up to 60 mph send rain spitting sideways. Winter-storm watchers, weekend skiers and snowboarders heading to Hurricane Ridge, and locals are usually the only hardy souls around this time of the year. For some, that—coupled with off-season lodging rates—is a draw.

FESTIVALS AND EVENTS

The region has a number of festivals and events that are worth planning for.

Great Port Townsend Bay Kinetic Sculpture Race. Since 1983, contestants have been racing human-powered contraptions through sand, mud, neighborhoods, and saltwater in the hope of winning the most coveted prize: the Mediocrity Award for finishing in the middle of the pack. The race takes place the first full weekend in October. Festivities include safety tests, a parade, and a "Kween Koronation Kostume Ball" on Saturday night. ⊠ *Port Townsend* ⊕ *ptkineticrace.org.*

Irrigation Festival. Sequim has been celebrating the introduction of irrigation water to its once-parched prairie since 1896. The fest, held in May, features an antique-car show, art show, logging show, street fair, pageant, parade, dance, community breakfast, and Strongman Showdown, in which competitors put their muscles to the test in events like the arm-over-arm truck pull, log press, and car lift. ⊠ *Sequim* ☎ *360/683–6197 Sequim Dungeness Valley Chamber of Commerce* ⊕ *www.irrigationfestival.com.*

Olympic Music Festival. From July through September, concertgoers can enjoy chamber music at the Wheeler Theater in Fort Worden State Park. ✉ *Inside Fort Worden State Park, 25 Eisenhower Way, Port Townsend* ☎ *360/385–9699 festival office, 800/838–3006 tickets* ⊕ *www.olympicmusicfestival.org.*

Port Townsend Film Festival. Founded in 1999 by Rocky Friedman, owner and operator of the town's 1907 Rose Theatre, this mid-September fest (first held in 2000) features onstage discussions with Hollywood stars, a variety of documentary and narrative films, and the ever-popular outdoor screenings on Taylor Street in front of the movie house. More than 80 films are screened at seven venues throughout the three-day festival. ✉ *Port Townsend* ☎ *360/379–1333* ⊕ *www.ptfilmfest.com.*

Sequim Lavender Festival. A street fair and free self-guided farm tours celebrate Sequim's many fragrant lavender fields in mid-July. ✉ *Sequim* ☎ *360/681–3035* ⊕ *www.lavenderfestival.com.*

Wooden Boat Festival. Hundreds of wooden boats sail into the Bay of Port Townsend each September for a weekend of demonstrations, presentations, tours, and sea shanties. Believed to be the largest gathering of its kind on the West Coast, the festival is sponsored by the Wooden Boat Foundation, part of the Northwest Maritime Center, which holds on-the-water programming for adults and youths all year. ✉ *Port Townsend* ☎ *360/385–3628* ⊕ *www.nwmaritime.org/wooden-boat-foundation/wooden-boat-festival.*

GETTING HERE AND AROUND

AIR TRAVEL

Port Angeles is the major northern gateway to the Olympic Peninsula, while Olympia is the major entry point in the south. Kenmore Air connects Port Angeles with Boeing Field, near Seattle. Fairchild International Airport, the largest on the Olympic Peninsula, is 6 miles southwest of Port Angeles off U.S. 101 (take Airport Road north from U.S. 101). Jefferson County Airport, a small charter-flight base, is 4 miles southwest of Port Townsend off Highway 19.

Contacts Fairchild International Airport. ✉ *1402 Fairchild International Airport Rd., Port Angeles* ☎ *360/417-3433 airport manager, 866/435-9524 Kenmore Air* ⊕ *www.portofpa.com.* **Jefferson County International Airport.** ✉ *310 Airport Rd., Port Townsend* ☎ *360/385-0656* ⊕ *www.portofpt.com.*

AIRPORTS AND TRANSFERS

Olympic Bus Lines, a Greyhound affiliate, transports passengers twice daily from Port Angeles, Discovery Bay, and Port Townsend to Sea-Tac Airport ($49) and downtown Seattle ($39).

Contacts Olympic Bus Lines. ☎ *360/417-0700, 800/457-4492* ⊕ *www.olympicbuslines.com.*

BOAT AND FERRY TRAVEL

Washington State Ferries offer the most direct route from Seattle to the Olympic Peninsula. Fares vary seasonally. Walk-ons pay less than vehicles with a driver and other passengers. A ferry from Whidbey Island takes travelers to downtown Port Townsend.

Nearby ferry terminals in Edmonds, Kingston, and Bremerton also provide access to the Olympic Peninsula. From Port Angeles, travelers can reach Victoria, British Columbia, on the M.V. *Coho,* which makes 1½-hour Port Angeles–Victoria crossings four times daily from mid-May through mid-October and twice daily the rest of the year (except when it's docked for maintenance, from mid-January through mid-March). Rates are $62 per car and driver, $17.50 per passenger, and $6.50 per bike; travelers can reserve ahead online or by telephone for an additional fee. *Coho,* operated by Black Ball Transport, departs from the ferry terminal at the foot of Laurel Street.

Contacts Black Ball Ferry Line. ☎ *360/457–4491 in Port Angeles, 250/386–2202 in Victoria, 888/993–3779 toll-free ⊕ www.cohoferry.com.*

13

CAR TRAVEL

U.S. 101, the main thoroughfare around the Olympic Peninsula, is a two-lane, well-paved highway. Rural back roads are blacktop or gravel, and tend to have potholes and get washed out during rains. In winter, landslides and wet weather frequently close roads. Highway 112 heads west from U.S. 101 at Port Angeles to Neah Bay. Highway 113 winds north from U.S. 101 at Sappho to Highway 112. Highway 110 travels west from U.S. 101 at Forks to La Push. Highway 109 leads west from U.S. 101 at Hoquiam to Copalis Beach, Moclips, and Taholah. Highway 8 heads west from Olympia and connects with U.S. 12, which travels west to Aberdeen. From the Hood Canal Bridge, State Routes 19 and 20 branch off State Route 104 to Port Townsend, Discovery Bay, and Sequim.

RESTAURANTS

Port Townsend reigns as the foodie capital of the Olympic Peninsula, where Pacific Northwest coastal cuisine prevails. For a small town, it features an impressive collection of casual yet upscale dining options, some with sweeping bay views. Influences include Mediterranean, Latin, and Southern American cooking. Many restaurants and pubs offer straight-from-the-farm organic herbs and vegetables as well as locally crafted artisanal breads and cheeses and, of course, shellfish and salmon from local waters.

The entire Olympic Culinary Loop—from Port Townsend, Sequim, Port Angeles, and Forks to the Long Beach Peninsula (⊕ *www.olympicculinary-loop.com*)—is best known for its seafood, fresh from local bays and inlets or wild caught in the Pacific Ocean by local fishermen. Many restaurants along the route feature fish-and-chips, chowders, oyster or salmon burgers, crab cakes, cioppino, clams, and mussels. The peninsula also offers many family-friendly and down-home eateries, from hearty burger and breakfast joints to authentic Thai, Japanese, and Mexican restaurants.

HOTELS

The Olympic Peninsula offers an array of lodging options, from Cape Cod–style cottages and rustic cabins to midrange motels, timber-lined lodges, and Victorian-mansions-turned-bed-and-breakfasts. Many offer beach access or views of the water or mountains—or both. It's most difficult to find rooms during holidays and festivals. Winter and shoulder seasons typically offer the most economical prices. Skiers, snowboarders, and day hikers headed to Hurricane Ridge might opt to use Port

Angeles as their home base. For gourmands, history buffs, and maritime enthusiasts, Port Townsend offers numerous Victorian-themed B&Bs and hotels as well as inns and motels with bay views. Those seeking peace and quiet might consider accommodations in Sequim. The Washington Coast and Long Beach Peninsula are the best destinations for winter-storm watchers and beachcombers. *Hotel reviews have been shortened. For full information, visit Fodors.com.*

WHAT IT COSTS IN U.S. DOLLARS				
	$	$$	$$$	$$$$
Restaurants	under $16	$16–$22	$23–$30	over $30
Hotels	under $150	$150–$200	$201–$250	Over $250

Restaurant prices are the average cost of a main course at dinner, or if dinner is not served, at lunch. Hotel prices are the lowest cost of a standard double room in high season.

VISITOR INFORMATION

Contacts Discover Your Northwest. ⊠ *Olympic National Park Visitor Center, 3002 Mt. Angeles Rd., Port Angeles* ☎ *360/565–3195* ⊕ *www.discovernw. org.* **North Olympic Peninsula Visitor and Convention Bureau.** ⊠ *618 S. Peabody St., Suite F, Port Angeles* ☎ *360/452–8552, 800/942–4042* ⊕ *www. olympicpeninsula.org.* **Olympic National Forest.** ⊠ *1835 Blacklake Blvd. SW, Olympia* ☎ *360/956–2400 Olympia Office, 360/765–2200 Hood Canal Ranger District, Quilcene, 360/374–6522 Pacific Ranger District North, Forks, 360/288–2525 Pacific Ranger District South, Quinault* ⊕ *www.fs.usda.gov/ olympic.* **Olympic National Park.** ⊠ *3002 Mt. Angeles Rd., (visitor center), Port Angeles* ☎ *360/565–3130 visitor information, 360/565–3131 road and weather hotline* ⊕ *www.nps.gov/olym.*

NORTHEASTERN OLYMPIC PENINSULA

The northeastern shelf of the Olympic Peninsula is easily accessible, making it a favorite getaway for Seattleites and other Washingtonians who live along the urban corridor that follows the north–south ribbon of Interstate 5. The restored Victorian seaport of Port Townsend at the peninsula's northeastern tip is a mere hour-and-45-minute drive from Seattle, including a scenic half-hour ferry ride across Puget Sound. The town is small—some 9,000 people live here—but it's teeming with activity. With its thriving arts scene, main street lined with galleries and boutiques, rich maritime heritage, upscale eateries, and variety of festivals, PT—as locals call it—offers plenty to do. Travelers could easily spend an entire weekend in this town alone. But, farther west, past Discovery Bay, bucolic farmland abounds in the rain shadow surrounding Sequim, home of the Olympic Game Farm and Dungeness Spit, a 5-mile sandy finger of shoreline topped with a wide, wishbone-shaped beach that juts into the Strait of Juan de Fuca. An 1857 lighthouse, which allows families to serve as lighthouse keepers for a week at a time, stands guard at the north end of the wishbone. At the western edge of this corner of the peninsula, Port Angeles provides a launchpad for skiing, snowboarding, hiking, and biking at Hurricane Ridge, one of the most easily accessible parts of Olympic National Park. It also offers ferry service to Victoria, British Columbia, sweeping views of the Strait of Juan de Fuca, and a chance for *Twilight* fans to relive some of their favorite scenes, including dinner at La Bella Italia, the restaurant that served as the backdrop for Bella and Edward's first date.

PORT TOWNSEND

99 miles north from Olympia.

On a peninsula—the small, crooked arm of the Quimper on the northeastern tip of the larger, torch-shaped Olympic—Port Townsend is a place where the modern meets the Victorian, maritime trades meet the arts, and the sun sets over the water. Its inhabitants are a collection of artists, writers, retirees, musicians, mariners, and "shed boys," a term coined in the early 2000s for the mostly single men who live here off the grid. For all of them Port Townsend remains a city of dreams. These knit-cap and Carhartt-wearing residents are well traveled and highly educated. It's not unusual to find waitresses, bartenders, and students at the boat school who have willingly given up more lucrative positions in larger cities to live here, in the most picturesque gateway to the Olympic Peninsula.

Ship captains from around the world once sailed into this port, known for its parlors of ill repute, saloons, shanghaiing, and other mid-19th century waterfront shenanigans. In fact, it was developed into two separate urban centers: the waterfront, which catered to hard-drinking sailors and other adventurers, and uptown, on the cliff above the bay, where merchants and permanent residents lived and raised their families away from the riffraff. The refined Victorian-era women who once shunned Water Street, the main drag through downtown, would likely want to be seen there now. The once rough-and-tumble thoroughfare has given way to art galleries and antiques stores, trendy boutiques, coffeehouses, pubs, upscale eateries, and public docks.

GETTING HERE AND AROUND

From Downtown Seattle, Port Townsend is reached via the Washington State Ferries to Bainbridge Island, then north on State Route 305, north on State Route 3, west on State Route 104, and north on State Route 19, which connects to State Route 20 and takes travelers into town. From Edmonds (north of Seattle via Interstate 5), take the Washington State Ferries to Kingston, then travel west via Highway 104 and north via State Route 19. Both routes run roughly an hour and 45 minutes, not including ferry waits. From Olympia and points south, there are two routes northbound: U.S. 101 and Highway 14. Both take about two hours.

GUIDED TOURS

Port Townsend Walking Tours. The Jefferson County Historical Society conducts hour-long walking tours of Port Townsend on weekends from June through September for $10. ✉ *540 Water St.* ☎ *360/385–1003* ⊕ *www.jchsmuseum.org.*

ESSENTIALS

Visitor Information Jefferson County Chamber of Commerce and Visitor Information Center. ⊠ *2409 Jefferson St.* ☎ *360/385–7869 administrative office, 360/385–2722 visitor information office, 888/365–6978 visitor information office* ⊕ *jeffcountychamber.org.*

EXPLORING

FAMILY **Chetzemoka Park.** A lovely gazebo is the hallmark of this gem of a city park, a perfect place to picnic perched atop a bluff overlooking Admiralty Inlet. The 6 well-maintained acres also feature a pond, footbridge, swings, other playground equipment, and a whimsical, trellis-covered pathway that teems with blooms in spring. The Port Townsend Summer Band performs concerts in the park. Access the sliver of beach below via a short footpath. ⊠ *Jackson and Blaine Sts.* ☎ *360/379–5096 Public Works* ⊕ *www.cityofpt.us/parks.htm.*

Fire Bell Tower. Set high along the bay-side bluffs, the tower is recognizable by its pyramid shape and red paint job. Built in 1890 to hold a 1,500-pound brass alarm bell, the 75-foot wooden structure was once the key alert center for local volunteer firemen. A century later it's considered one of the state's most valuable historic structures. Reach the tower by climbing the steep set of stairs behind Haller Fountain at the end of Taylor Street. The tenth-of-an-acre plot also holds a park bench and five parking spots. ⊠ *Jefferson and Tyler Sts.* ☎ *360/385–1003 Jefferson County Historical Society* ⊕ *www.jchsmuseum.org.*

FAMILY **Fort Worden State Park.** With hiking trails, restored—and rentable—Victorian officers' houses, and pre–World War I-era bunkers, this historic 434-acre park provides myriad outdoor activities along with a step back in time. Built on Point Wilson in 1896 to guard the mouth of Puget Sound, the old fort is now a magical place for both children and adults to explore. A sandy beach leads to the graceful 1913 Point Wilson Lighthouse. Memory's Vault, hidden in the hill above the inlet, features works from local poet Sam Hamill as well as a place to contemplate. Touch tanks at Port Townsend Marine Science Center on the pier offer an up-close look at sea life. The fort also hosts kayaking tours, conferences, camping, an artillery museum, and music festivals in an old military balloon-hangar-turned-performing-arts-pavilion. ⊠ *200 Battery Way* ☎ *360/344–4400 accommodations* ⊕ *www.fortworden.org* ⊠ *Day pass: $10 per vehicle; annual Discovery Pass $30 (valid at all state parks).*

Northwest Maritime Center. The myriad traditions and trades of the Pacific Northwest's seafaring history are explained here, with special emphasis on the importance of Port Townsend as one of only three Victorian-era seaports on the country's register of National Historic Sites. It's the core of the Point Hudson district and the center of operations for the Wooden Boat Foundation, which stages the annual Wooden Boat Festival each September. The center has interactive exhibits, hands-on sailing training, boatbuilding workshops, a wood shop, and a pilot house where you can test navigational tools. The boardwalk, pier, and beach that front the buildings are the perfect points to launch a kayak or watch sloops and schooners gliding along the bay. The chandlery features a variety of nautical gifts and gear, from brass fittings and rigging supplies to galley wares, illustrated knot books, and boats in a bottle. In a well-lighted back corner overlooking the bay, Velocity Coffee Bar sells espresso and baked goods from 6:30 am to 5 pm Monday through Saturday. ✉ *431 Water St.* ☎ *360/385–3628, 360/379–5383 coffee shop* 🌐 *www.nwmaritime.org* 🎟 *Free.*

Port Townsend Marine Science Center. Along the waterfront at Fort Worden State Park, the center is divided into two sections. The marine lab and aquarium building, in a former World War II military storage facility at the end of a pier, houses numerous aquarium displays, as well as touch tanks with sea stars, crabs, and anemones. The separate, onshore Natural History Exhibit Center is filled with displays detailing the region's geography and marine ecology. Beach walks, nature camps, cruises, and day camps run throughout the summer, and there's a Low Tide Festival each July. Open weekends only during fall and winter; the marine center is closed in winter. ✉ *520 Battery Way* ☎ *360/385–5582, 800/566–3932* 🌐 *www.ptmsc.org* 🎟 *$5* 🕒 *Closed weekdays in fall and winter; marine center closed in winter.*

13

WHERE TO EAT

$$$ ECLECTIC Fodor's Choice ★ 🍴 **Alchemy Bistro & Wine Bar.** This upscale eatery overlooking Haller Fountain offers a blend of Italian, Spanish, and French favorites alongside Pacific Northwest fare, including succulent salmon, oysters, and mussels. Entrées include a selection of salads, seafood, and pastas as well as the often-requested Drunken Rabbit, slow-cooked in red wine with garlic, carrots, and onions. **Known for:** elegant European-inspired fare; sophisticated feel; craft cocktails. [$] *Average main: $24* ✉ *842 Washington St.* ☎ *360/385–5225* 🌐 *www.alchemybistroandwinebar.com.*

$ AMERICAN 🍴 **Blue Moose Cafe.** Comfortable, cozy, and a bit off-the-wall, this is one of the best places in Port Townsend to go for a generous, hearty, and unfussy breakfast or lunch. It's popular with locals—especially sailors and shipwrights who work in the surrounding Port Townsend Boat Haven. **Known for:** "This Ain't No Atkins Special" with biscuits, thick gravy, and corned-beef hash; local hot spot. [$] *Average main: $12* ✉ *311 Haines Pl., in Port Townsen Boat Haven* ☎ *360/385–7339* 💳 *No credit cards* 🕒 *No dinner.*

$ CONTEMPORARY 🍴 **Cellar Door.** The entrance to this subterranean space can be difficult to spot—at the bottom of a Tyler Street staircase. There you'll find a sophisticated yet casual wine and cocktail bar that melds vintage Victorian with a rustic-industrial feel and sense of whimsy (concrete floors, reclaimed wood, antiques). **Known for:** high-quality craft cocktails; late-night libations. [$] *Average main: $13* ✉ *940 Water St., entrance on Tyler St.* ☎ *360/385–6959* 🌐 *www.cellardoorpt.com.*

$ AMERICAN 🍴 **Courtyard Café.** This homey mom-and-pop coffee-and-baked-goods shop sells thick-crusted, overstuffed, house-made berry and fruit pies, cinnamon rolls, muffins, and other assorted pastries and breads. Order at the deli-style counter and take treats to go, or seat yourself and enjoy the family-friendly, cozy café, which serves hearty breakfasts and lunches like a skillet scramble; corned beef and hash; spinach, mushroom, and cheese quiche; soups; salads; and a wide selection of amply filled sandwiches. **Known for:** hearty sandwiches; homemade pies and pastries. [$] *Average main: $10* ✉ *230 Quincy St.* ☎ *360/379–3355* 🌐 *www.courtyardcafept.com* 🕒 *Closed Tues. No dinner.*

$$$ SEAFOOD 🍴 **Doc's Marina Grill.** Enjoy a view of boats bobbing in the marina while filling up on seafood, the specialty at this waterfront eatery, where the feel is light and bright and the decor is modern. The menu features smoked-salmon mac and cheese, salmon piccata, and herb-crusted ahi tuna along with a few nonfish items, such as the popular chicken-cheddar club sandwich. **Known for:** steamed mussels and clams; fish-and-chips; seafood soups such as crab, cioppino, and clam chowder. [$] *Average main: $24* ✉ *141 Hudson St., Point Hudson Marina* ☎ *360/344–3627* 🌐 *www.docsgrill.com.*

$$ ECLECTIC 🍴 **Fountain Café.** Artwork lines the walls of the small, eclectic café tucked inside a historic clapboard building a block off the main drag, where seafood and pasta dishes carry Mediterranean, Moroccan, Italian, and Pacific Northwest influences. Start with panfried oysters or mussels and clams in a pesto-Chardonnay broth. **Known for:** warm gingerbread with vanilla custard and whipped cream; locally famous clam chowder; buffalo frogs' legs. [$] *Average main: $18* ✉ *920 Washington St.* ☎ *360/385–1364* 🌐 *www.fountaincafept.com.*

$ JAPANESE 🍴 **Hanazono Asian Noodle.** The regular menu at this small, long, thin, authentic Japanese noodle house includes three types of egg noodles—ramen, *yakisoba*, and *champon*—as well as rice, soba and udon noodles in a variety of soups, stir-fries, and salads. The restaurant also serves sushi rolls, *donburi* (rice bowl dish), bento, and daily specials. **Known for:** authentic Japanese cuisine; house-made gyoza; beef pho. [$] *Average main: $11* ✉ *225 Taylor St.* ☎ *360/385–7622* 🌐 *hanazonoasiannoodle.com* 🕒 *Closed Mon.*

$$ ITALIAN 🍴 **Lanza's Ristorante.** Intimate and romantic, this small Uptown eatery has been a local institution for 30 years and exudes the warmth of Italy with welcoming and gracious staff, generous portions, and authentic, old-country recipes. Share the ample antipasto platter while waiting for pizza or pasta, from classic spaghetti and meatballs to ravioli Florentine, penne with sausage, mushrooms and spinach, and a rich, creamy linguine luna. **Known for:** hearty Italian cuisine; rich and creamy linguine luna; decadent tiramisu. [$] *Average main: $19* ✉ *1020 Lawrence St.* ☎ *360/379–1900* 🌐 *www.lanzaspt.com* 🕒 *Closed Sun. and Mon. No lunch.*

$$ MODERN AMERICAN 🍴 **Owl Sprit Cafe.** Tucked into a small space on a side street on the edge of downtown, this cozy and eclectic little gem uses locally sourced, organic ingredients in its variety of grilled sandwiches, burgers, burritos, and pasta dishes. A colorful owl mural on the back wall watches over the dining room, full of plants, patterned tablecloths, and local works of art. **Known for:** hand-cut haystack onion rings; juice bar. [$] *Average main: $16* ✉ *218 Polk St.* ☎ *360/385–5275* 🌐 *www.owlsprit.com* 🕒 *Closed Sun. and Mon. No breakfast.*

$$$ PACIFIC NORTHWEST 🍴 **Silverwater Cafe.** On the first floor of the 1889 Elks' Lodge building, this established restaurant—opened a hundred years after the Lodge in 1989—pairs elegant surroundings with a sophisticated menu with entrées such as pan-seared halibut in a slightly sweet hazelnut-cream sauce, cilantro-ginger-lime jumbo prawns, or lavender-pepper ahi. Dessert offers such delicacies as Northwest blackberry pie, raspberry white-chocolate cheesecake, and the signature coconut flan—caramel-topped custard with a wisp of coconut flavoring. **Known for:** elegant Pacific

Northwest cuisine; signature coconut flan. $ *Average main: $25* ✉ *237 Taylor St.* ☎ *360/385–6448* ⊕ *www.silverwatercafe.com.*

$$$
BISTRO
Fodor's Choice
★

✕ **Sweet Laurette Café and Bistro.** Paris meets the Pacific Northwest in this Uptown bistro, where classic French bistro fare meets contemporary, farm-to-table flair. Chef-owner Laurette Feit—known by her nickname, Lolo—sources her ingredients, including grass-fed beef, organic eggs, and wild king salmon, from local farmers and fishermen. **Known for:** cozy French-inspired feel; generous brunch in the lavender-lined courtyard; buttery pastries. $ *Average main: $26* ✉ *1029 Lawrence St.* ☎ *360/385–4886* ⊕ *www.sweetlaurette.com* ⊘ *Closed Mon. and Tues.*

$
PIZZA

✕ **Tin Brick.** Enter this bright and family-friendly underground pizza place from a sidewalk staircase across from the **Rose Theatre** and you'll promptly forget you're in a basement. Gourmet, thin-crust, wood-fired pies range from classics like the Margherita and caprese to Buffalo chicken and cheesesteak. **Known for:** wood-fired pizza; Philly cheesesteak sandwiches. $ *Average main: $13* ✉ *232 Taylor St.* ☎ *360/379–4181.*

$$
PIZZA

✕ **Waterfront Pizza.** This popular longtime pizza place is a Port Townsend institution known for its sourdough crust, generously covered with all kinds of toppings. Try the Waterfront, with sausage, pepperoni, mushrooms, and olives, in the small, upstairs dining room overlooking the town's main street, or order a slice to go at the walk-up counter on the ground floor and enjoy it on the small beach nearby. **Known for:** sourdough crust; pizza by the slice from the walk-up window. $ *Average main: $18* ✉ *951 Water St.* ☎ *360/385–6629.*

WHERE TO STAY

$
B&B/INN
Fodor's Choice
★

🛏 **Ann Starrett Mansion.** Gables, turrets, and gingerbread trim decorate this glorious 1889 mansion, built by a wealthy contractor for his young bride and now a boutique hotel decorated with florals and antiques. **Pros:** sweeping views; a short walk to downtown and uptown restaurants and shops; a chance to experience Victorian elegance. **Cons:** no breakfast; no elevator. $ *Rooms from: $139* ✉ *744 Clay St.* ☎ *360/385–3205, 800/321–0644 for reservations* ⊕ *www.starrettmansion.com* ⟿ *10 rooms* |◯| *No meals.*

$$
B&B/INN

🛏 **Bishop Victorian Hotel.** This brick inn abounds with 19th-century charm and thoughtful service, and most of the one- and two-bedroom suites, adorned with floral fabrics, antiques, and authentic brass features, have garden, mountain, or water views, as well as fireplaces. **Pros:** Victorian flair with contemporary conveniences; a stone's throw from the waterfront, restaurants, boutiques, and coffee shops; congenial staff; some kitchenettes. **Cons:** no elevator. $ *Rooms from: $170* ✉ *714 Washington St.* ☎ *360/385–6122, 800/824–4738* ⊕ *www.bishopvictorian.com* ⟿ *16 rooms* |◯| *Breakfast.*

$
HOTEL

🛏 **Manresa Castle.** This expansive, imposing, hillside mansion, built in 1892 for Port Townsend's first mayor, has lots of Victorian character—wood trim, antique furniture, high ceilings, patterned wallpaper, and lace curtains covering tall windows—and some sweeping views of the bay. **Pros:** staying in a real slice of history. **Cons:** somewhat a spooky vibe (ask the staff about reported ghost sightings). $ *Rooms from: $109* ✉ *651 Cleveland St.* ☎ *360/385–5750, 800/732–1281* ⊕ *www.manresacastle.com* ⟿ *39 rooms* |◯| *Breakfast.*

13

$

B&B/INN

Fodor's Choice

★

⌖ **Old Consulate Inn.** Perched on a bluff above the bay, this elegant, red, turreted Victorian mansion with a sweeping veranda and parklike gardens features well-appointed view rooms, three with claw-foot tubs and one that's dog-friendly. **Pros:** gourmet breakfast; gorgeous grounds and views; quiet; a real stepping-back-in-time experience. **Cons:** no children under 14; no elevator. $ *Rooms from: $125* ⌗ *313 Walker St.* ☎ *360/385–6753, 800/300–6753* ⊕ *www.oldconsulate.com* ⌇ *8 rooms* ⧈ *Breakfast.*

$

B&B/INN

⌖ **Palace Hotel.** In a former bordello that retains its 19th-century grandeur, light-filled rooms, many named for the women who used to work here, feature 14-foot ceilings and elegant period furnishings like hand-carved dressers, wrought-iron bed frames, and big claw-foot bathtubs. **Pros:** a feeling of participating in a bit of Port Townsend's history; a stone's throw from restaurants, boutiques, and bars. **Cons:** might not suit travelers who don't appreciate Victorian charm. $ *Rooms from: $89* ⌗ *1004 Water St.* ☎ *360/385–0773, 800/962–0741* ⊕ *www.palacehotelpt.com* ⌇ *19 rooms* ⧈ *No meals.*

$

B&B/INN

⌖ **The Swan Hotel.** Tucked at the end of the downtown thoroughfare, this balcony-encased, four-story hotel features well-lighted, airy rooms with gorgeous sea views or, on the north side, overlooking the Point Hudson Marina. **Pros:** central location; majestic views; comfortable and cozy; suite is good for small groups. **Cons:** no breakfast; small, often crowded parking lot, with an alternative lot a few blocks away. $ *Rooms from: $130* ⌗ *216 Monroe St.* ☎ *360/379–1840, 800/824–4738* ⊕ *www. theswanhotel.com* ⌇ *13 rooms* ⧈ *No meals.*

$

HOTEL

⌖ **Tides Inn and Suites.** The multistory, peak-roofed inn resembles an expansive beach house, and it's set on the water near the ferry dock with a nice variety of lodgings, from small, basic, cabin-type budget rooms in the inn to more spacious units with mini-refrigerators, microwaves, jetted tubs, and balconies in the suites. **Pros:** beach locale, with beautiful bay views; reasonable price; one of the few hotels in town with an elevator. **Cons:** need to book far in advance for festivals and summer weekends; three rooms don't have a sea view. $ *Rooms from: $89* ⌗ *1807 Water St.* ☎ *360/385–0595, 800/822–8696* ⊕ *www.tides-inn. com* ⌇ *44 rooms* ⧈ *Breakfast.*

$

HOTEL

⌖ **Washington Hotel.** With its keyless entry and modern interiors, this small boutique hotel on the second floor of a historic building in the heart of downtown caters to the stylish, independent traveler. **Pros:** stylish city feel in a small-town environment; central location. **Cons:** no lobby; not the best choice for travelers who require 24-hour concierge services. $ *Rooms from: $130* ⌗ *825 Washington St.* ☎ *360/774–0213* ⊕ *washingtonhotelporttownsend.com* ⌇ *4 rooms* ⧈ *No meals.*

NIGHTLIFE

Port Townsend Brewing Company. Boatyard workers and beer enthusiasts congregate at this casual and cozy Boat Haven brewery to enjoy a pint and bowl of peanuts (don't worry about dropping the spent shells on the floor). There's an outdoor beer garden during warmer months. Proprietors Kim and Guy Sands opened the brewery in 1997 with only two beers. Ten brews are on now the menu, including the award-winning Boatyard Bitter, Port Townsend Pale Ale, and Hop Diggidy, a classic Northwest-style IPA. The brewery closes early evening, so nightlife seekers might want to make this one of their first stops. ✉ *330 10th St.* ☎ *360/385–9967* 🌐 *www.porttownsendbrewing.com.*

Pourhouse. This gathering place for local and out-of-town beer enthusiasts features a dozen rotating taps, 200 bottles and cans of beer and hard cider, and wines by the glass. The waterfront beer garden offers sweeping views of Port Townsend Bay and nearby harbor along with picnic tables, a pétanque court, and a concrete table for table tennis. Some snacks—like charcuterie or cheese plates—are served, you can bring your own takeout, or order from one of the many in-town eateries that will deliver full meals; menus are available in the taproom. Most Friday and Saturday nights in summer, there's live music outside in the "Impound Lot." ✉ *2231 Washington St.* ☎ *360/379–5586* 🌐 *www.ptpourhouse.com.*

13

Sirens. The upper floor of a historic sandstone building on Port Townsend's main street provides breathtaking bay views and regularly books West Coast rockabilly, alternative country, blues, jazz, and rock bands on weekends. Fiddlers jam here Tuesday nights, and Wednesday open-mike nights are a local tradition. Microbrews and handcrafted cocktails quench thirst, and there's a menu of hearty Pacific Northwest–inspired pub food, from pastas and burgers to salads and innovative seafood dishes. If there's a free table, opt to sit on the back upper or lower deck overlooking the water. There is a $5 cover charge some weekend nights for music. ✉ *832 Water St.* ☎ *360/379–1100* 🌐 *www.sirenspub.com.*

$ WINE BAR 🍴 **Starlight Room.** This third-floor room in the Silverwater Cafe, a collaboration with the next-door Rose Theatre, allows moviegoers aged 21 and over the chance to watch a film and enjoy wine (by the glass or bottle), beer, a cocktail, dessert, or an array of Mediterranean antipasti. [$] *Average main: $10* ✉ *237 Taylor St.* ☎ *360/385–6448 café, 360/385–1089 movie info* 🌐 *www.rosetheatre.com/starlight-room.*

SHOPPING

Port Townsend brims with antiques stores, art galleries, clothing boutiques, consignment shops, vintage and New Age-y bookstores, and upscale maritime, kitchen, home design, and gift shops. Water and Washington Streets, which run parallel to the bay, are lined with storefronts. So are their block-long offshoots, cut off by the cliff that separates downtown from uptown. More stores are located uptown on Lawrence Street near an enclave of Victorian houses. To reach them, walk up the Terrace Steps behind Haller Fountain at Washington and Taylor streets. Along the way, plenty of pubs, coffeehouses, and eateries provide tired shoppers a place to revive and rest their feet.

Conservatory Coastal Home. With an array of upscale, seaside luxe-living essentials and soy candles (hand-poured on-site in small batches in scents like sailcloth, fog, moss, and water) this high-ceilinged, brick-walled home-design and gift boutique smells as good and it looks. A variety of air plants in recycled glass terrariums are always in stock. Look for furniture fashioned from reclaimed wood, nautical-themed throw pillows, jewelry, and seashells. ✉ *639 Water St.* ☎ *360/385–3857* 🌐 *www.conservatorycoastalhome.com.*

get-a-bles. An eclectic range of supplies makes this little shop as interesting and fun as the name suggests. There are eat-a-bles and drink-a-bles—sandwiches, cheese, pickles, pretzels, nuts, hard cider, soda, and beer—and gift-a-bles such as locally roasted coffee, gourmet salts, handmade sugar scrubs and soaps, toys, and flasks. ⊠ *810 Water St.* ☎ *360/385–5560* ⊕ *www.getablespt.com.*

Green Eyeshade. This well-stocked kitchen and gift shop features a wide array of linens, glassware, dishes, jewelry, wine accessories, candles, knickknacks, and gourmet gadgets. ⊠ *720 Water St.* ☎ *360/385–3838.*

Maestrale. East meets West in this specialty shop that imports fabrics, furniture, jewelry, and other handicrafts from India, Indonesia, Thailand, Nepal, and China. ⊠ *821 Water St.* ☎ *360/385–5565* ⊕ *maestraleimports.com.*

Mt. Townsend Creamery. Watch cheese makers at work while sampling artisanal offerings like the ale-washed Off Kilter or popular Seastack. The creamery, founded in 2007, uses cows' milk from a single, local herd to make nearly a dozen different kinds of cheese. ⊠ *338 Sherman St.* ☎ *360/379–0895* ⊕ *www.mttownsendcreamery.com* ☾ *Closed Mon. and Tues.*

Pane d'Amore. Pick up a baguette, chocolate-chip cookie, or cinnamon bun at this top-notch bakery, tucked into a small storefront in the heart of the Uptown district. ⊠ *617 Tyler St.* ☎ *360/385–1199* ⊕ *panedamore.com.*

Perfect Season. You'll find a little bit of everything here, including things for the home, pottery, planters, bath and baby items, books, birdhouses, and antiques. ⊠ *1046 Water St.* ☎ *360/385–9265* ⊕ *www.theperfectseason.com.*

Port Townsend Antique Mall. Three dozen dealers at the two-story Port Townsend Antique Mall sell merchandise ranging from pricey Victorian collectors' items to cheap flea-market kitsch. ⊠ *802 Washington St.* ☎ *360/379–8069* ⊕ *www.ptantiquemall.com.*

Port Townsend Farmers' Market. Port Townsend is proud of its farm-to-table food movement and visitors can witness and share in the region's bounty at its vibrant farmers' market. Approximately 70 vendors, including some 40 farmers, showcase their fare—fresh produce, flash-frozen salmon, artisanal foods and baked goods, crafts, and handmade soaps and salves. The market is open Saturday (9 to 2) April–December on Tyler Street and Wednesday (2 to 6) mid-June to mid-September on Polk Street. ⊠ *Tyler St. and Lawrence St.* ☎ *360/379–9098* ⊕ *www.jcfmarkets.org.*

William James Bookseller. Used and out-of-print books covering all fields—with an emphasis on nautical, regional history, and art titles—are arrayed from floor to ceiling of this jam-packed gem of a bookstore. For rare books, visit the store's Rare Book Annex two blocks away on Water Street. ⊠ *829 Water St.* ☎ *360/385–7313* ⊕ *www.williamjamesbookseller.com.*

SPORTS AND THE OUTDOORS

BIKING

The nearest place to go biking is Fort Worden State Park, but you can range as far afield as Fort Flagler, the lower Dungeness trails (no bikes are allowed on the spit itself), or across the water to Whidbey Island.

The Broken Spoke. This bike retail, repair, and rental shop in the heart of downtown promotes cycling at all levels. ⊠ *630 Water St.* ☎ *360/379–1295* ⊕ *www.thebrokenspokept.blogspot.com.*

P. T. Cyclery. Mountain bikes are available for rent here, and the shop repairs flats and can advise you on where to start your journey. ⊠ *252 Tyler St.* ☎ *360/385–6470* ⊕ *www.ptcyclery.com.*

BOAT CRUISES

Puget Sound Express. This family-run company runs summer speedboat connections between Port Townsend and Friday Harbor from May through September. Boats depart from Port Townsend at 9, arriving in Friday Harbor at noon; the return trip departs from Friday Harbor at 2:30 and arrives back in Port Townsend at 5. Four-hour guaranteed-sighting whale-watching trips depart from Friday Harbor at 10 and 2:30 May–late September to view orcas (killer whales) and at 10 from mid-March–April to see migrating gray whales. Whale-watching trips are subject to a minimum number of passengers. ⊠ *227 Jackson St., at Point Hudson Marina* ☎ *360/385–5288* ⊕ *www.pugetsoundexpress. com* ☝ *Trips and tours from $85.*

KAYAKING

FAMILY **Port Townsend Paddlesports.** This small, family-owned kayak, bicycle, and paddleboard (and beach umbrella) rental company is located next to the beach in Fort Worden State Park. Group or private tours can also be arranged here. ⊠ *Fort Worden State Park, 532 Battery Way E* ✛ *On the beach* ☎ *360/379–3608* ⊕ *www.ptpaddlesports.com.*

SEQUIM

31 miles west of Port Townsend.

Sequim (pronounced *skwim*), incorporated in 1913, is a pleasant old mill town and farming center between the northern foothills of the Olympic Mountains and the southeastern stretch of the Strait of Juan de Fuca. With lots of sunshine, lovely views, and neat, quiet blocks, it's also a popular place to retire. Sequim's walkable downtown, marked by a historic grain elevator, features a variety of gift and other shops. A few miles to the north is the shallow and fertile Dungeness Valley, which enjoys some of the lowest rainfall in western Washington. Fragrant purple lavender flourishes in local fields. East of town, scenic Sequim Bay is home to the John Wayne Marina. The actor, who navigated local waters aboard his yacht, *Wild Goose,* donated land for the marina in 1975, four years before his death.

The Dungeness National Wildlife Refuge

GETTING HERE AND AROUND

Sequim is about two hours from Seattle, via the Seattle–Bainbridge Island or Edmonds–Kingston ferries and U.S. 101. It's served by Clallam Transit to local Olympic Peninsula towns, and Olympic Bus Lines to Silverdale, Seattle, and Sea-Tac International Airport.

Contacts Clallam Transit. ☎ *360/452–4511, 800/858–3747* ⊕ *www.clallamtransit.com.* **Olympic Bus Lines.** ☎ *360/417–0700, 800/457–4492* ⊕ *www.olympicbuslines.com.*

ESSENTIALS

Visitor Information Sequim-Dungeness Valley Chamber of Commerce. ✉ *1192 E. Washington St.* ☎ *360/683–6197, 800/737–8462* ⊕ *www.sequimchamber.com.*

EXPLORING

FAMILY

Fodor's Choice

★

Dungeness Spit. Curving 5½ miles into the Strait of Juan de Fuca, the longest natural sand spit in the United States is a wild, beautiful section of shoreline. More than 30,000 migratory waterfowl stop here each spring and fall, but you'll see plenty of birdlife any time of year. The entire spit is part of the **Dungeness National Wildlife Refuge.** Access it through the **Dungeness Recreation Area,** which serves as a portal to the shoreline. ✉ *554 Voice of America Rd.* ✛ *Entrance 3 miles north from U.S. 101, 4 miles west of Sequim* ☎ *360/457–8451 wildlife refuge* ⊕ *www.clallam.net/parks/dungeness.html* 🗐 *$3 per family.*

New Dungeness Lighthouse. At the end of the Dungeness Spit is the towering white 1857 New Dungeness Lighthouse; tours are available, though access is limited to those who can hike or kayak out 5 miles to the end of the spit. Guests also have the opportunity to serve as lighthouse keepers for a week at a time. An adjacent, 66-site camping area, on the bluff above the Strait of Juan de Fuca, is open year-round. ⊠ *Sequim ✢ Entrance 3 miles north of Hwy. 101 via Kitchen Dick Rd.* ☎ *360/683–6638* ⊕ *www.newdungenesslighthouse.com.*

FAMILY **Olympic Game Farm.** This 200-acre property—part zoo, part safari—is Sequim's biggest attraction after the Dungeness Spit. For years, the farm's exclusive client was Walt Disney Studios, and many of the animals here are the offspring of former movie stars. On the hour-long, drive-through tour, which covers some 84 acres of the picturesque property, be prepared to see large animals like buffalo surround your car and lick your windows. You'll also see zebras, llamas, lynx, lions, elk, Tibetan yak, emu, bobcat, Siberian and Bengal tigers, and Kodiak and black bears, among other animals. Facilities also include an aquarium, studio barn with movie sets, snack kiosk, and a gift shop. Guests are allowed to feed uncaged animals (with wheat bread only), except for the buffalo and elk at the entrance gates, but must stay in their vehicles. Even sunroofs must remain locked. ⊠ *1423 Ward Rd.* ☎ *360/683–4295, 800/778–4295* ⊕ *www.olygamefarm.com* ⊡ *Drive-through tour $13–$15 per person in vehicle.*

Railroad Bridge Park. Set along a beautifully serene, 25-acre stretch of the Dungeness River, the park is centered on a lacy ironwork bridge that was once part of the coastal line between Port Angeles and Port Townsend. Today the park shelters a pristine river environment. The River Walk hike-and-bike path leads from the River Center educational facility, on the banks of the Dungeness, into the woods, and a horseback track links Runnion Road with the waterway. In summer, families picnic at the River Shed pavilion, students participate in science programs at the Dungeness River Audubon Society office, and locals come to watch performances at the River Stage amphitheater. There are free guided bird walks every Wednesday morning from 8:30 to 10:30. You'll find the park 2 miles west of town, and a five-minute drive from the coast. ⊠ *2151 Hendrickson Rd.* ☎ *360/681–4076* ⊕ *www.dungenessrivercenter.org* ⊡ *Free.*

Sequim Farmers Market. You'll find honey, lavender, sea glass jewelry, pottery, and locally grown produce in abundance at this Saturday market, a tented affair with lots of color and live music, open from 9 to 3 between early May and late October. ⊠ *Cedar St., between Seal St. and 2nd Ave.* ☎ *360/582–6218* ⊕ *www.sequimmarket.com.*

WHERE TO EAT

$$ ✕ **Alder Wood Bistro.** An inventive menu of local and organic dishes ECLECTIC makes this one of the most popular restaurants in Sequim. Pizzas from the wood-fired oven include creative combinations, such as one featuring oyster, shiitake, and cremini mushrooms, bacon, morel crème fraîche, caramelized onions, mozzarella, and finished with mixed greens. **Known for:** wood-fired oysters and mussels; wood-fired pizza; wood-fired apple pie. $ *Average main: $20* ⊠ *139 W. Alder St.* ☎ *360/683–4321* ⊕ *www. alderwoodbistro.com* ⊗ *Closed Sun.–Wed.*

13

$$ ✕ **Dockside Grill.** With tremendous views of John Wayne Marina and
PACIFIC Sequim Bay, this is a fun place to watch boats placidly sail by. The casual
NORTHWEST yet elegant menu includes Dungeness crab fritters, steamed clams, cedar-
plank salmon, bouillabaisse, cioppino, and pasta. **Known for:** steak
and seafood with a spectacular waterfront view. Ⓢ *Average main: $20*
✉ *2577 W. Sequim Bay Rd.* ☎ *360/683–7510* ⊕ *www.docksidegrill-
sequim.com* ☽ *Closed Mon. and Tues.*

$$ ✕ **Nourish.** The greenhouse-enclosed restaurant and patio café overlook
PACIFIC one of the region's oldest lavender and herb farms and feature an ever-
NORTHWEST evolving, seasonally inspired menu, specializing in the garden-to-plate
experience. Chicken potpie, lamb, elk, beef or beet burgers on Brazilian
cheese buns, and smoked portobello and cauliflower lasagna are specialties. **Known for:** fresh farm-to-table fare; gorgeous garden views;
interesting smoothies. Ⓢ *Average main: $22* ✉ *101 Provence View La.*
☎ *360/797–1480* ⊕ *www.nourishsequim.com* ☽ *Closed Mon.*

$ ✕ **Oak Table Café.** Carefully crafted breakfasts and lunches are the
AMERICAN focus of this well-run, family-friendly eatery, a Sequim institution since
Fodor's Choice 1981. Breakfast is served throughout the day, and on Sunday, when
★ the large, well-lighted dining room is especially bustling, it's the only
meal. **Known for:** Eggs Nicole with eggs and veg on a croissant with
hollandaise sauce; the humongous apple pancake filled with fresh fruit.
Ⓢ *Average main: $13* ✉ *292 W. Bell St.* ☎ *360/683–2179* ⊕ *www.oak-
tablecafe.com* ☽ *No dinner.*

WHERE TO STAY

$$$ ⛉ **Holiday Inn Express & Suites Sequim.** Modern rooms done in soothing
HOTEL green-and-tan Pacific Northwest color schemes come with lots of perks,
including an indoor pool, hot tub, fitness center, and 24-hour business
center. **Pros:** easily accessible from the highway; next door to café;
contemporary decor. **Cons:** not right in town center; some complaints
about high summer rates and noise. Ⓢ *Rooms from: $215* ✉ *1441 E.
Washington St.* ☎ *360/681–8756, 800/315–2621* ⊕ *www.hiexpress.
com* ⇆ *96 rooms* ⦿⧘ *Breakfast.*

$$$ ⛉ **Red Caboose Getaway.** Vintage metal railcars form the centerpiece
B&B/INN of this bed-and-breakfast, where guests can experience the romance
Fodor's Choice of the rails and sleep in luxury cabooses, each with a different theme.
★ **Pros:** memorable style and experience; great for railroad aficionados.
Cons: no children under 12. Ⓢ *Rooms from: $222* ✉ *24 Old Coy-
ote Way* ☎ *360/683–7350* ⊕ *www.redcaboosegetaway.com* ⇆ *6 suites*
⦿⧘ *Breakfast.*

PORT ANGELES

17 miles west of Sequim.

Sprawling along the hills above the deep-blue Strait of San Juan de Fuca,
Port Angeles is the crux of the Olympic Peninsula's air, sea, and land
links. The once largely blue-collar logging and fishing town is capped
off at the water's edge by a gathering of hotels, restaurants, shops, and
attractions, all set around the modern marina and the sandy swath of
Hollywood Beach. With a population of about 19,000, the town is
the largest on the Olympic Peninsula and a major gateway to Olympic

National Park. Summer foot traffic is shoulder-to-shoulder downtown with hopefuls rushing to ferries, vacationers strolling the waterfront, locals relaxing at outdoor cafés, and *Twilight* fans retracing steps of their favorite characters (Port Angeles served as a backdrop for several scenes in the popular series). Other fans flock here, too; Port Angeles is the last place writer Raymond Carver lived, and it remains home to his widow, the poet Tess Gallagher, who was born here.

It didn't start out this way, though, as the seasonal crowds have only been a phenomenon since the 1950s. The area was first settled by the Hoh, Makah, Quileute, Quinault, and S'Klallam tribes, and others had little reason to visit until a Greek navigator named Apostolos Valerianus—aka Juan de Fuca—sailed into the strait in 1610. In 1791 Spanish explorer Juan Francisco de Eliza followed him and named it Puerto de Nuestra Señora de Los Angeles, or Port of Our Lady of the Angels. George Vancouver shortened the name to Port Angeles in 1792, and the site was settled by pioneers in 1856. In the century that followed, Port Angeles became a timber-mill town, a military base, and a key regional fishing port.

GETTING HERE AND AROUND

Port Angeles is about two hours from Seattle via the Seattle–Bainbridge Island and Edmonds–Kingston ferries and Highway 104; it's about 17 miles west of Sequim on U.S. 101. It's served by Clallam Transit to local Olympic Peninsula towns, and Olympic Bus Lines to Silverdale, Seattle, and Sea-Tac airport. Kenmore Air runs flights between Port Angeles and Boeing Field, near Seattle.

Contacts Clallam Transit. ☎ *360/452–4511, 800/858–3747* 🌐 *www.clallamtransit.com.* **Olympic Bus Lines.** ☎ *360/417–0700, 800/457–4492* 🌐 *www.olympicbuslines.com.*

ESSENTIALS

Visitor Information Port Angeles Regional Chamber of Commerce. ✉ *121 E. Railroad Ave.* ☎ *360/452–2363 visitor center* 🌐 *www.portangeles.org.*

EXPLORING

Port Angeles Fine Arts Center. This small, sophisticated museum is inside the former home of late artist and publisher Esther Barrows Webster, one of Port Angeles's most energetic and cultured citizens; displays are modern, funky, and intriguing. Outside, Webster's Woods Art Park is dotted with oversize sculptures set before a vista of the city and harbor. Exhibitions emphasize the works of emerging and well-established Pacific Northwest artists. ✉ *1203 E. Lauridsen Blvd.* ☎ *360/457–3532* 🌐 *www.pafac.org* 🎟 *Free* ⏰ *Closed Oct.–Mar.*

WHERE TO EAT

$$$$ FRENCH

🍴 **C'est Si Bon.** The interior design as well as the food is far more Euro-savvy than is typical on the Olympic Peninsula. A fanciful dining room is done up in bold red hues, with crisp white linens, huge oil paintings, and glittering chandeliers; the spacious solarium takes an equally formal approach. **Known for:** a little piece of Paris in Port Angeles. [$] *Average main: $32* ✉ *23 Cedar Park Rd.* ☎ *360/452–8888* 🌐 *www.cestsibon-frenchcuisine.com* ⏰ *Closed Mon. No lunch.*

$$ SEAFOOD 🍴 **Dupuis Restaurant.** This kitschy little log cabin, painted a cheery yellow, served as a tavern in the 1920s and still evokes the feeling of a bygone era. Seafood dominates the menu; look for grilled local fish, like king salmon, as well as steamed crabs, crab cakes, panfried oysters, oyster stew, seafood gnocchi, and prawns with pesto and pasta. **Known for:** quality steak and seafood; evoking a sense of nostalgia. [$] *Average main: $20* ✉ *256861 U.S. 101* ☎ *360/457–8033* ⏰ *Closed Sun. and Mon. No lunch.*

WHERE TO STAY

$$ B&B/INN Fodor's Choice ★ 🏨 **Colette's Bed & Breakfast.** A contemporary oceanfront mansion set on a 10-acre sanctuary of gorgeous gardens offers more space, service, and luxury than any other property in the area, with water-view suites that have fireplaces, patios, and two-person spa tubs. **Pros:** water views extend to Victoria, BC; discreet personal service. **Cons:** does not cater to families. [$] *Rooms from: $195* ✉ *339 Finn Hall Rd.* ✣ *10 miles east of town* ☎ *360/457–9197, 888/457–9777* 🌐 *www.colettes.com* 🛏 *5 suites* 🍽 *Breakfast.*

$$ B&B/INN 🏨 **Domaine Madeleine.** Perched on a bluff above the Strait of Juan de Fuca, the luxurious accommodations here have either impressionist or Asian accents, fireplaces, and water and mountain views. **Pros:** colorful waterfront lodgings; abundant wildlife; well-appointed rooms. **Cons:** no children under 12; the gourmet breakfast costs extra. [$] *Rooms from: $180* ✉ *146 Wildflower La.* ✣ *8 miles east of town* ☎ *360/457–4174* 🌐 *www.domainemadeleine.com* 🛏 *5 rooms* 🍽 *No meals.*

$ B&B/INN 🏨 **Five Seasuns Bed & Breakfast.** Just steps from town, within award-winning gardens, this cozy 1926 inn overlooks the mountains and the bay and offers elegant rooms, each with the theme of a time of year: the four seasons plus an Indian summer. **Pros:** lovely garden setting close to town; gourmet breakfast; well-appointed rooms. **Cons:** on a busy street; no children under 12; strict 14-day cancellation policy. [$] *Rooms from: $145* ✉ *1006 S. Lincoln St.* ☎ *360/452–8248* 🌐 *www.seasuns.com* 🛏 *5 rooms* 🍽 *Breakfast.*

$ HOTEL 🏨 **Quality Inn Uptown.** South of Port Angeles, at the green edge of the Olympic Mountain foothills, this no-frills choice has a great thing going for it: a stunning panorama of mountain and harbor views. **Pros:** central location; great views. **Cons:** basic interior design and amenities; somewhat dated; no elevators. [$] *Rooms from: $143* ✉ *101 E. 2nd St.* ☎ *360/457–9434* 🌐 *www.qualityinnportangeles.com* 🛏 *51 rooms* 🍽 *Breakfast.*

$$$ B&B/INN Fodor's Choice ★ 🏨 **Sea Cliff Gardens Bed & Breakfast.** A gingerbread-style porch fronts this antiques-furnished waterfront Victorian home on 2 acres of landscaped grounds; all of the exquisitely appointed guest rooms have fireplaces and panoramic water views through large picture windows. **Pros:** sumptuous accommodations with stunning views; gorgeous flower gardens; romantic setting. **Cons:** a bit off the beaten path. [$] *Rooms from: $225* ✉ *397 Monterra Dr.* ☎ *360/452–2322* 🌐 *www.seacliffgardens.com* 🛏 *5 suites* 🍽 *Breakfast.*

SPORTS AND THE OUTDOORS

BEACHES

FAMILY **Ediz Hook.** At the western end of Port Angeles, this 3-mile-long natural sand spit protects the harbor from big waves and storms. The Hook is a fine place to take a walk along the water and watch shore- and seabirds, and to spot the occasional seal, orca, or gray whale. It's also a popular dive spot. From downtown, take Front Street west and follow it as it meanders past the shuttered lumber mill. **Amenities:** toilets. **Best for:** walking; sunset. ⌧ *Ediz Hook Rd., off west end of Marine Dr.*

13

KAYAKING

Olympic Raft & Kayak. White-water and scenic float trips are conducted on the Hoh and Elwha Rivers, and the Sound Dive Center has scuba-certification classes, dive equipment, and tours around the region, including Lake Crescent. ⌧ *123 Lake Aldwell Rd.* ☎ *360/452–1443* ⊕ *www.raftandkayak.com.*

NORTHWESTERN OLYMPIC PENINSULA

It takes travelers more time to reach the remote, rugged, and rain-soaked west end of the Olympic Peninsula, but unspoiled beaches, old-growth forests, and mountain lakes make for a spectacular geographic pilgrimage. This is where the forest meets the ocean and the wilderness runs into the water. It's lush, green, and wet, a land of fallen trees, ferns, moss-covered rocks, sea stacks, saltwater spray, and smoked salmon. Surfers seek out the coastline near Neah Bay, immortalized in Robert Sullivan's 2000 book *A Whale Hunt,* documenting the Makah Nation's quest to reclaim its cultural heritage. Artifacts from an ancient fishing village at the tribe's museum and cultural center offer an opportunity to learn about the people whose ancestors lived for thousands of years off the land and sea. Nearby, in the old logging town of Forks, fans still celebrate the setting of the fictional *Twilight* series, and Cape Flattery offers views from the most northwesterly edge of the contiguous United States.

NEAH BAY

15 miles northwest of Sekiu.

One of the oldest villages in Washington, Neah (pronounced *nee*-ah) Bay is surrounded by the Makah Reservation at the northwestern tip of the Olympic Peninsula. It's a quiet, seldom-visited seaside settlement of one-story homes, espresso stands, and bait shops stretched along about a mile of gravelly coastal road, which parallels the glistening, boat-filled bay. Stroll along the docks to watch boot-clad fishermen and shaggy canines motoring out on warped and barnacled vessels, and peer into the oil-stained water for views of anemones, shellfish, and sea lions. The rocky bulkhead rises behind the marina; look beyond that to view sunsets and Cape Flattery, the northwesternmost point in the contiguous United States.

Explorer James Cook named the cape in 1778 when his ship missed the fog-smothered Strait of Juan de Fuca and landed here instead. In 1792 Spanish mariners established a short-lived fort, the first European settlement in what is now Washington State. The local Makah tribe is more

Makah Indian art

closely related to the Nootka of Vancouver Island, just across the water, than to any Washington tribe. Like their ancestors, they embark on whale hunts by canoe, a right guaranteed by treaty, although fleets of kayaks skimming through the calm bay are all you're likely to see during your visit.

GETTING HERE AND AROUND

Neah Bay is quite remote, accessed only by Highway 112 west of Sekiu (about a half-hour drive).

EXPLORING

FAMILY
Fodor's Choice
★

Makah Cultural and Research Center. Thousands of Makah art pieces and artifacts, many eons old, fill a space done in low lights and rich timbers and divided into an easy route of intriguing exhibits. The centerpiece is a full-size cedar longhouse, complete with handwoven baskets, fur skins, cattail wool, grass mats on the bed planks, and a background of tribal music. Another section houses full-size whaling and seal-hunting canoes and weapons. Other areas show games, clothing, crafts, and relics from the ancient Ozette Village mudslide. The small shop stocks a collection of locally made art pieces, books, and crafts; plan to spend some time looking around. ⊠ *1880 Bayview Ave.* ☎ *360/645–2711* ⊕ *www.makahmuseum.com* ✉ *$5.*

Makah National Fish Hatchery. Here visitors can view chinook salmon as they make their way over fish ladders to the hatchery's spawning area. Spawning months are October through December, and the salmon are released in late April. Smaller numbers of coho and chum salmon as well as steelhead trout also populate the hatchery. Call to find out the best times to see hatchery activity. From Neah Bay, follow signs south for 7 miles. ⊠ *897 Hatchery Rd.* ☎ *360/645–2521* ⊕ *www.fws.gov/makahnfh* ✉ *Free.*

WHERE TO STAY

$
B&B/INN

🛏 **Inn at Neah Bay.** This three-story, sky-gray chalet above the Strait of Juan de Fuca offers a range of basic but comfortable accommodations, each with different decor. **Pros:** there's a fire pit and barbecue grill for guests; owners also run a charter-fishing and marine-tour service; well suited for anglers, budget travelers, and families. **Cons:** no children under 12. $ Rooms from: $115 ✉ 1562 Hwy. 112, Sekiu ☎ 360/374–2225 ⊕ www.theinnatneahbay.com ⇄ 4 rooms ❍ Breakfast.

13

FORKS

49 miles south of Neah Bay.

The former logging town of Forks is named for two nearby river junctions: the Bogachiel and Calawah Rivers merge west of town, and a few miles farther they are joined by the Soleduck to form the Quileute River, which empties into the Pacific at the Native American village of La Push. Forks is a small, quiet gateway town for Olympic National Park's Hoh River valley unit. The surrounding countryside is exceptionally green, with an annual precipitation of more than 100 inches. As the setting for the popular *Twilight* movie series, the town has become a favorite destination for fans in recent years, and Bella's Birthday Weekend, in October, has plenty of *Twilight*-related events.

GETTING HERE AND AROUND

From the Seattle area, Forks is about 3½ hours via the Seattle–Bainbridge Island and Edmonds–Kingston ferries and U.S. 101 west; it's about an hour past Port Angeles. Coming from the south, U.S. 101 north from Aberdeen to Forks takes about two hours. Clallam Transit runs from Forks to Port Angeles and other north peninsula towns. West Jefferson Transit provides service between Forks and Lake Quinault, including a stop at Kalaloch.

GUIDED TOURS

Peak 6 Tours and Gift Shop. At this tucked-away shop, you'll find gear and information for hiking, biking, camping, climbing, and sightseeing on the Olympic Peninsula. Guided hikes cost about $50 per day. ✉ 4883 Upper Hoh Rd. ☎ 360/374–5254.

ESSENTIALS

Visitor Information Forks Chamber of Commerce. ✉ 1411 S. Forks Ave. ☎ 360/374–2531, 800/443–6757 ⊕ www.forkswa.com.

EXPLORING

Big Cedar. Thought to be the world's largest, this monumental cedar tree stands 178 feet tall and is 19 feet 5 inches in diameter. Area loggers left it standing when they realized just how enormous it really was. The tree is off Nolan Creek Road. From U.S. 101, turn right onto Highway N1000 for 1.3 miles, then turn right onto N1100 for 2.4 miles. Turn right again onto N1112 for 0.4 miles, and then turn right once more for 0.1 miles. ✉ Forks.

WHERE TO EAT

$ ✕ **Forks Coffee Shop.** This modest diner on the highway in downtown
DINER   Forks serves home-style, classic American fare—from giant pancakes
and Sol Duc scrambles (eggs, sausage, hash browns, and veggies tum-
bled together) to soups, salads, and hot and cold sandwiches, which
the waitstaff will bag for pickup if you're on the run. Dinner specials
come with free trips to the salad bar and include entrées like baby back
ribs and grilled Hood Canal oysters. **Known for:** no-frills but generous
portions; house-made pie; sack lunches to go. $ *Average main: $10*
✉ *241 Forks Ave.* ☎ *360/374–6769.*

$ ✕ **Plaza Jalisco.** Desert colors, ceramic bells, hand-painted masks, and
MEXICAN   hand-knit blankets decorate the small, airy dining room, where locals
gather to down heaping plates of rice, beans, and meat-filled burritos.
Frothy and potent margaritas are the big draw on weekends. **Known
for:** hearty Mexican fare and margaritas. $ *Average main: $9* ✉ *90 N.
Forks Ave.* ☎ *360/374–3108.*

WHERE TO STAY

$$ ⊡ **Manitou Lodge.** If seclusion, quiet, and relaxation are what you seek,
B&B/INN   visit this cedar lodge in the rain forest, where five lodge rooms of vary-
ing sizes and two suites in the adjacent cottage have cedar paneling,
handmade quilts, driftwood headboards, and oak furnishings; the large
Sacagawea room even has a fireplace. **Pros:** well-appointed rooms fea-
ture local flair; breakfast comes in a basket; variety of lodging options,
some family-friendly. **Cons:** no TV, phones, or cell-phone service,
though there is Wi-Fi; a little off the beaten path. $ *Rooms from: $159*
✉ *813 Kilmer Rd.* ☎ *360/374–6295, 360/374–7495* ⊕ *www.manitou-
lodge.com* ⇱ *9 rooms* ⊙| *Breakfast.*

WASHINGTON COAST

The communities along this stretch of Pacific coastline range from
quiet and secluded getaways to busy beach towns, especially during
the summer months when highways in and out of towns can become
congested with vacationers. Pacific Beach and Moclips to the north
are a little more remote and less crowded than their southern coun-
terparts. Ocean Shores is one of the busier beaches, with horseback
riders, kite flyers, go-carts, dune buggies, and beachcombers all com-
peting for space. Although the sun shines here in summer, it gets gusty
on the beach at any time of year, so don't forget your windbreaker
and polar fleece.

COPALIS BEACH

74 miles west of Olympia.

A Native American village for several thousand years, this small coastal
town at the mouth of the Copalis (pronounced coh-*pah*-liss) River was
settled by European Americans in the 1890s. The beach here is known
locally for its innumerable razor clams, which can be gathered by the
thousands each summer, and for its watchtowers, built between 1870
and 1903 to spot and stalk sea otters—the animals are now protected

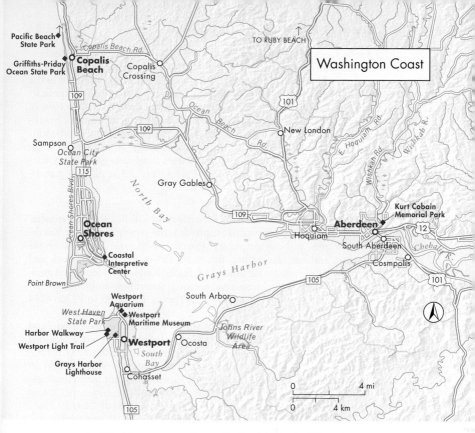

by Washington state law. The first oil well in the state was dug here in 1901, but it proved to be unproductive. However, some geologists still claim that the continental shelf off the Olympic Peninsula holds major oil reserves.

GETTING HERE AND AROUND

Copalis Beach is about 30 miles from Aberdeen, via Highway 109. Bus service is provided by Grays Harbor Transit.

Contact Grays Harbor Transit. ☎ 360/532–2770, 800/562–9730 ⊕ www.ghtransit.com.

EXPLORING

Griffiths-Priday Ocean State Park. You can hike or ride horses in this 364-acre marine park stretching more than a mile along both the Pacific Ocean and the Copalis River. A boardwalk crosses low dunes to the broad, flat beach. The Copalis Spit section of the park is a designated wildlife refuge for thousands of snowy plover and other birdlife. There is no camping at this park, but there's plenty of picnicking, bird-watching, mountain biking, fishing, clamming, kite flying, and beachcombing. ⊠ 3119 Hwy. 109 ☎ 360/902–8844 ⊕ www.parks. wa.gov/parks ⌁ Day pass $10 per vehicle; annual Discovery Pass $30 (valid at all state parks).

Pacific Beach State Park. Between Copalis Beach and the town of Moclips, this is a lovely spot for walking, surf-perch fishing, and razor-clam digging. There's also excellent fishing for sea-run cutthroat trout in the Moclips River—but be careful not to trespass onto Native American land, as the Quinault Reservation starts north of the river. The 10-acre park has developed tent and RV sites, as well as a few primitive beach-front campsites. **Amenities:** parking (free); toilets. **Best for :** solitude; sunset; walking. ⊠ *49 2nd St., Pacific Beach* ⊹ *Hwy. 109 S, 5 miles north of Copalis Beach* ☎ *360/276–4297* ⊕ *www.parks.wa.gov* ⊠ *Day pass $10 per vehicle; annual Discovery Pass $30 (valid at all state parks); camping $12–$45.*

WHERE TO EAT AND STAY

$$
PACIFIC
NORTHWEST

✕ **Mill 109 Restaurant and Pub.** A perch atop a hillside in the master-planned beach community of Seabrook is the setting for Pacific Northwest entrées and contemporary American pub fare. Look for ample burgers and hot sandwiches, fish tacos, fish-and-chips, and thick and creamy clam chowder for lunch and dinner. **Known for:** modern American and Pacific Northwest fare; seafood; gastropub ambience. Ⓢ *Average main: $18* ⊠ *5 W. Myrtle La., Pacific Beach* ☎ *360/276–4884* ⊕ *www.mill109.com.*

$
RESORT

🛏 **Sandpiper Beach Resort.** These no-frills studios and one-, two-, and three-bedroom suites, all but one with a fireplace, are on a secluded beach 3 miles south of Moclips, and are great for getting away from it all and immersing yourself in nature. **Pros:** spacious lodgings; right on the beach; affordable; gorgeous ocean views. **Cons:** not for technology-dependent folks; no on-site restaurant; some walls are paper-thin; decor and furnishings are a bit dated. Ⓢ *Rooms from: $109* ⊠ *4159 Hwy. 109, Pacific Beach* ☎ *360/276–4580, 800/567–4737* ⊕ *www.sandpiper-resort.com* ↪ *31 rooms* ⦿⎮ *No meals.*

$$$$
RENTAL
FAMILY
Fodor'sChoice
★

🛏 **Seabrook Cottage Rentals.** Crushed seashells line pathways throughout this charming collection of some 300 Cape Cod–style homes, more than half of which are available to rent. **Pros:** recreational activities and beach within walking distance; homes are new with many amenities; some are pet-friendly. **Cons:** ongoing construction; added cleaning fees; limited services outside of village. Ⓢ *Rooms from: $279* ⊠ *4275 Ste. Rte. 109, Pacific Beach* ☎ *360/276–0265, 877/779–9990* ⊕ *www.seabrookcottagerentals.com* ↪ *150 cottages* ⦿⎮ *No meals.*

SPORTS AND THE OUTDOORS

Ruby Beach. Named for the rosy fragments of garnet that color its sands, this is one of the peninsula's most beautiful stretches of coastline. A short trail leads to the wave-beaten sands, where sea stacks, caves, rock cairns, tidal pools, and bony driftwood make it a favorite place for beachcombers, artists, and photographers. It's 28 miles south of Forks, off U.S. 101. **Amenities:** toilets. **Best for:** sunset; walking. ⊠ *Kalaloch* ⊕ *www.wta.org/go-hiking/hikes/ruby-beach.*

OCEAN SHORES

13

10 miles south of Copalis Beach.

Ocean Shores, a long stretch of resorts, restaurants, shops, and attractions, sits on the northern spit that encloses Grays Harbor. The whole area was planned by housing developers in the 1960s, and with its broad, flat, white beach, shallow surf, and sunset panoramas, it's been a favorite seaside getaway since. Come summer, dune buggies and go-carts buzz up and down the sand road, weaving around clusters of horses trotting tourists over the dunes. Colorful kites flap overhead, dogs romp in the waves, and tide pools are filled with huge orange Dungeness crabs, live sand dollars, and delicate snails, to the delight of small children. It's no tropical haven, however, as summer can bring chilly breezes, and the water never warms up much for swimming—jackets are mandatory even in July. A fog of sea mist often blows in during the late afternoon, and in winter massive thunderstorms billow onto land directly before the line of coastal hotels. An indoor pool and in-room fireplace are coveted amenities year-round in this cool climate, and well worth the added expense.

GETTING HERE AND AROUND

Ocean Shores is the closest developed ocean-beach town to Seattle; it's about a 2½-hour drive via Interstate 5 south to Olympia then west via U.S. 101 and north via Highway 109. The traffic through Aberdeen and Hoquiam can slow to a crawl on busy summer weekends; try especially to avoid heading back east on Sunday or holiday afternoons. Grays Harbor Transit serves the community locally.

Contact Grays Harbor Transit. ☎ *360/532–2770, 800/562–9730* ⊕ *www.ghtransit.com.*

ESSENTIALS

Visitor Information Ocean Shores/North Beach Chamber of Commerce. ✉ *873 Point Brown Ave. NW, Suite 1* ☎ *360/289–2451* ⊕ *www.oceanshores.org.*

EXPLORING

Coastal Interpretive Center. A great stormy-day educational spot for families, the center highlights the seaside environment, local history, and Native American traditions. Displays include tsunami debris, artifacts from the founding of the city, and Native American basketry. Reproduction seabirds, whale bones, and a vast shell collection let you examine the shoreline wildlife up close. ✉ *1033 Catala Ave. SE* ☎ *360/289–4617* ⊕ *www.interpretivecenter.org* 🎟 *Free* 🕑 *Closed weekdays Feb.–Apr. 1.*

WHERE TO EAT

$$
AMERICAN
✕ **Alec's by the Sea.** Conveniently set between the town and beach, this family-run place has been serving seafood for two decades. The best dishes are made with the ocean's bounty that's caught locally, such as steelhead, razor clams, and Grays Harbor oysters. **Known for:** razor clam chowder; prime rib; family atmosphere. 💲 *Average main: $17* ✉ *131 E. Chance a la Mer Blvd.* ☎ *360/289–4026.*

$ SEAFOOD 🍴 **Bennett's Fish Shack.** This is unfussy, family-friendly, casual coastal dining. Look for crowd-pleasers like the crab cakes, clam chowder, hand-breaded halibut, and fish tacos. **Known for:** halibut fish-and-chips; family atmosphere; no frills. [$] *Average main: $15* ✉ *105 W. Chance a la Mer* ☎ *360/289–2847* 🌐 *www.bennettsdining.com.*

$$ IRISH 🍴 **Galway Bay Irish Restaurant, Pub and Gifts.** Steak and traditional Irish fare are served at this dimly lit eatery, anchored by a corner fireplace and decorated with old church pews. The fare is decidedly Irish: beef in Guinness stew, soda bread, corned beef, steak in a Bailey's reduction, and a Blarney burger with Swiss cheese on a warm bun. Jameson and Bushmills line the top shelf of the back bar, along with a variety of other Irish whiskeys. **Known for:** authentic Irish feel; hosting the largest Irish music festival in the region. [$] *Average main: $20* ✉ *880 Point Brown Ave. NE* ☎ *360/289–2300* 🌐 *www.galway-bayirishpub.com.*

$$ SEAFOOD 🍴 **Mike's Steak and Seafood Restaurant.** Wander through the small, roadside seafood stand out front to see what's cooking at this humble-looking must-stop before sitting down in the adjacent restaurant. Everything served is fresh caught, and salmon is smoked on the premises. **Known for:** fresh, high-quality seafood. [$] *Average main: $18* ✉ *830 Point Brown Ave. NE* ☎ *360/289–0532* 🌐 *www.oceanshores-seafood.com.*

$ AMERICAN 🍴 **Ocean Beach Roasters.** Espresso, beer, and a variety of sweet baked goods—including memorable cinnamon rolls and lemon bars—are available; for lunch, there are soups, quiches, and hearty sandwiches, like capicola with fresh mozzarella, spinach, and pesto, and turkey croissants with provolone, spinach, and Roma tomatoes. The shop roasts its own coffee beans and also offers tapas and wine tastings. **Known for:** coffee, pastries, and other quick bites; wine tasting. [$] *Average main: $6* ✉ *841 Point Brown Ave.* ☎ *360/289–3100* 🌐 *ocean-beachroasters.com* ⏰ *No dinner.*

WHERE TO STAY

$ RESORT 🏨 **Quinault Beach Resort & Casino.** A half mile of dunes and wild beach grasses surrounds this enormous resort, where shades of green, gray, and gold appear throughout the rooms, all with 10-foot ceilings, gas fireplaces, and twin bathroom sinks. **Pros:** grand rooms; upscale setting; on-site spa and dining. **Cons:** gambling crowds can be rowdy. [$] *Rooms from: $144* ✉ *78 Hwy. 115* ☎ *360/289–5001, 888/461–2214* 🌐 *www.quinaultbeachresort.com* 🛏 *158 rooms* 🍽 *No meals.*

$ HOTEL 🏨 **Shilo Inn.** Framed by a Pacific Ocean seascape to the west and a dune-covered state park to the south, this all-suites hotel houses guests in large, modern units that include a living area, fireplace, and a balcony overlooking the beach. **Pros:** great location; spacious lodgings; lots of amenities. **Cons:** lots of tourists, families, and groups make hallways noisy late and early; rates spike during summer and special events. [$] *Rooms from: $99* ✉ *707 Ocean Shores Blvd.* ☎ *360/289–4600, 800/222–2244* 🌐 *www.shiloinns.com* 🛏 *113 rooms* 🍽 *No meals.*

SPORTS AND THE OUTDOORS

Ocean Shores Beaches. Six miles of wide, public, sandy beaches line a peninsula trimmed by the Pacific Ocean on the west and Grays Harbor on the east. With five access roads, it's possible to find secluded sections along the state's most visited beach destination. Highest tides occur in July and December, the latter when winter storm watching is at its peak. Motor vehicles are allowed on **City Beach,** a popular place for clam digging and kite flying. **Ocean City State Park,** a 170-acre oceanfront park 2 miles north in Hoquiam, has year-round camping. Several hotels and resorts line the beach, including **Quinault Beach Resort & Casino** and **Shilo Inn;** trails provide access. **Amenities:** food and drink; parking; showers; toilets. **Best for:** solitude; sunrise; sunset; walking. ⊠ *Sand Dune Ave. SW and off Duck Lake Dr. SE* ☎ *360/289–2451* ⊕ *oceanshores.org.*

13

ABERDEEN

4 miles east of Hoquiam.

The pretty town of Aberdeen, on Grays Harbor at the mouth of the Chehalis River, is known for its lovely harbor, spread glittering and gray along the west edge of town, where the bay bobs with sailboats and speed cruisers. Vast swaths of lumberyards are broken up by towering cranes, which transport the massive timbers onto immense metal barges. Forested hills serve as a backdrop to town, promising a picturesque entry into the Olympic Peninsula to the north. The town is also dotted with the classic, century-old mansions built by shipping and timber barons of the 20th century. Walking tours provide looks at some of the largest and most beautiful homes as well as local highlights from some of the town's best-known former residents, including Bill Boeing and Kurt Cobain.

GETTING HERE AND AROUND

Aberdeen is 4 miles east of Hoquiam and is served by Grays Harbor Transit.

Contact Grays Harbor Transit. ☎ *360/532–2770, 800/562–9730* ⊕ *www.ghtransit.com.*

EXPLORING

Kurt Cobain Memorial Park. This pocket park, dedicated in 2011 along the muddy banks of the Wishkah River, pays homage to grunge legend and Nirvana front man Kurt Cobain, who grew up in a modest home two blocks from here. A guitar sculpture, lyrics to "Something in the Way," and other remembrances—like an empty instrument-stand sculpture identified as the musician's air guitar—mark the quiet spot that fans still seek out more than 20 years after the rock star's death. Some leave messages on the park bench and picnic table as well as under the bridge. ⊠ *E. 2nd St., under Young Street Bridge.*

Lady Washington. Tall, billowing white sails in the harbor mark the presence of this replica of the 1750s coastal freighter from Boston that in 1792, under the command of famous explorer Captain Robert Gray, was the first American vessel to reach the northwest American coast.

The replica was famously converted into the multimasted HMS *Interceptor* sloop for the 2003 Disney movie *Pirates of the Caribbean: Curse of the Black Pearl.* Its main base is the Grays Harbor Historic Seaport, but you'll find the vessel at local coastal towns throughout the region, where it's open for self-guided tours. Three-hour cruises include the hands-on "Adventure Sail" and a mock "Battle Sail" war between two vessels, and if you're at least 18 you can volunteer as a deckhand for multiday trips. The free **Seaport Learning Center,** a 214-acre site spread across the harbor and surrounding wetlands, runs tours on two historic longboats, and schedules monthly boatbuilding, rope-climbing, and marine-trade programs for families and students. ✉ *712 Hagara St.* ☎ *360/532–8611, 800/200–5239* 🌐 *historicalseaport.org* 🎫 *Tours $5; sailings $42–$79.*

Morrison Riverfront Park Walk. For a general look at the lay of Aberdeen, follow this 1½-mile-long, paved walkway to the 40-foot-wide Compass Rose mosaic, inlaid at the confluence of the Wishkah and Chehalis rivers. ✉ *1404 Sargent Blvd.*

WHERE TO EAT AND STAY

$ ITALIAN 🍴 **Amoré Pizza and Pasta.** Pizza comes in three sizes—small, medium, and large—at this Italian eatery across the street from the historic D&R Theatre in the heart of downtown Aberdeen. Jumbo cheese or spinach ravioli, seafood risotto, amply stuffed calzones, and chicken or veal marsala or piccata round out the menu. Starters include a pound of steamed clams. **Known for:** tomato-basil soup decorated with an artful pesto "A.". [$] *Average main: $15* ✉ *116 W. Heron St.* ☎ *360/533–2442.*

$ AMERICAN 🍴 **Billy's.** This bar and grill used to be the most popular saloon and brothel in town, and the restaurant has a collection of prints recalling those bawdy days. Even the establishment's name was taken from the saloon's notorious original owner, Billy Ghol. **Known for:** Billy's Belt Buster burger; offering a taste of the town's colorful past. [$] *Average main: $11* ✉ *322 E. Heron St.* ☎ *360/533–7144.*

$$ PACIFIC NORTHWEST 🍴 **Rediviva.** *Rediviva* means renewed or revived, and much of the material—wood, metal, and glass—in the interior has been repurposed for an effect that is intimate, elegant, rustic yet refined, modern, and somewhat nautical. Edison-style lighting and blown-glass floats mix with steel cable in what is perhaps the most cosmopolitan eatery around the region, where the focus is on fresh, seasonal, and locally sourced ingredients from the Olympic Peninsula and the Washington Coast. **Known for:** rustic-elegant ambience; fresh, local, and thoughtful Pacific Northwest cuisine; creative craft cocktails. [$] *Average main: $22* ✉ *118 E. Wishkah St.* ☎ *360/637–9259* 🌐 *redivivarestaurant.com* 🕒 *Closed Sun. and Mon.*

$ B&B/INN 🏨 **A Harbor View Inn.** You can see the harbor from every room in this 1905 Colonial Revival–style mansion with old-fashioned rooms, three with fireplaces, where handmade quilts cover king-size beds with antique headboards. **Pros:** special packages available; gourmet breakfast served in the sunroom overlooking the harbor; feeling of stepping back in time. **Cons:** not for those who don't enjoy an abundance of Victoriana. [$] *Rooms from: $129* ✉ *111 W. 11th St.* ☎ *360/533–7996, 877/533–7996* 🌐 *www.aharborview.com* 🛏 *4 rooms, 1 suite* 🍽 *Breakfast.*

WESTPORT

21 miles southwest of Aberdeen.

Westport is a bay-front fishing village on the southern spit that helps protect the entrance to Grays Harbor from the fury of the Pacific Ocean. Numerous charter companies based here offer salmon, lingcod, rockfish, and albacore fishing trips, as well as whale-watching tours. If you're not taking a cruise, you can stand on Westport's beach to look for gray whales migrating southward in November and December, toward their breeding grounds in Baja California, and northward in April and May, toward their feeding grounds in the Bering Sea. The serene beach is perfect for walking, surfing, or kite flying—although it's too dangerous for swimming and too cold for sunbathing. In winter it's one of the best spots on the coast to watch oncoming storms.

13

GETTING HERE AND AROUND

Westport is about a half-hour southwest of Aberdeen via Highway 105. Grays Harbor Transit serves the town.

Contact Grays Harbor Transit. ☎ *360/532–2770, 800/562–9730* ⊕ *www.ghtransit.com.*

ESSENTIALS

Visitor Information Westport-Grayland Chamber of Commerce. ⊠ *2985 S. Montesano St.* ☎ *360/268–9422, 800/345–6223* ⊕ *www.westportgrayland-chamber.org.*

EXPLORING

FAMILY **Westport Aquarium.** Exhibits of local marine life include a wolf eel, an octopus, and a dog shark. Touch tanks let you feel shells, starfish, anemones, and other sea creatures. You can even hand-feed two seals. ⊠ *321 Harbor St.* ☎ *360/268–7070* ⊕ *westportaquarium.weebly.com* 🖭 *$5.50* ☉ *Closed Sun.–Fri. in winter.*

Westport Light Trail. A 2½-mile-long paved promenade, sometimes called the Dunes Trail, winds along the sandy beach between Grays Harbor Lighthouse and West Haven State Park. ⊠ *Ocean Ave.* ⊕ *www.wta.org/ go-hiking/hikes/westport-light-trail.*

Westport Maritime Museum. A former Coast Guard station houses displays of historic photos, equipment, clothing, and other relics from the life-saving service and such local industries as fishing, logging, and cranberry farming. Exhibits include a collection of sea-mammal bones, and the 17-foot-tall Destruction Island Lens, a lighthouse beacon that was built in 1888 and weighs almost 6 tons. The octagonal **Grays Harbor Lighthouse,** a 107-foot structure built in 1898, is the tallest on the Washington coast. It stands near the museum and adjacent to Westport Light State Park, a day-use area with picnic tables and a beach. A tour of the lighthouse base is included with museum admission; it costs extra to climb to the top. ⊠ *2201 Westhaven Dr.* ☎ *360/268–0078* ⊕ *www. westportmaritimemuseum.com* 🖭 *$5, includes lighthouse base (extra $5 to climb to top)* ☉ *Closed Dec. and Jan.*

WHERE TO STAY

$ **🛏 Chateau Westport Motel.** These large, affordable rooms (some with
HOTEL fireplaces and kitchenettes) are near the dunes and are perfect for families who want a base near the beach. **Pros:** great location. **Cons:** rooms
facing parking lot can be noisy; two-night minimum stay some holiday
weekends. $ *Rooms from: $129 ⊠ 710 Hancock Ave.* ☎ *360/268–9101,
800/255–9101 ⊕ www.chateauwestport.com ⤳ 108 rooms* ⦿ *Breakfast.*

SPORT AND THE OUTDOORS

Westport Beaches. At the southern mouth of Grays Harbor, **Westhaven
State Park** encompasses some 80 acres, including oceanfront and easy
pedestrian access to the beach. A 1½-mile concrete boardwalk crosses
the dunes, connecting Westhaven with the 212-acre **Westport Light State
Park,** adjacent to the historic Westport Lighthouse, built in 1898. Farther south, the 172-acre **Twin Harbors State Park** provides another stretch
of Pacific coastline, popular for clamming, bird-watching, and beachcombing. **Amenities:** parking (fee); showers; toilets. **Best for:** solitude;
sunrise; sunset; walking. ⊠ *St. Park Access Rd., off N. Montesano St.*
☎ *360/268–9422 ⊕ www.westportwa.com.*

LONG BEACH PENINSULA

Long Beach Peninsula stretches north from Cape Disappointment,
where the mighty Columbia River meets the stormy waters of the Pacific
Ocean. The peninsula has vast stretches of sand dunes, friendly beach
towns, dank cranberry bogs, and forests and meadows. To the east the
peninsula shelters Willapa Bay, once known as Shoalwater Bay because
it runs almost dry at low tide. It's a prime oyster habitat, producing
more of the creatures than any other estuary in the country.

Seas beneath the cliffs of Cape Disappointment are so turbulent that
several explorers, from James Cook to George Vancouver, mistook
the river's mouth for surf breaking on a wild shore. Many ships have
crossed (and many have come to grief) here since American sea captain Robert Gray sailed into the river on May 11, 1792, and named
it after his ship.

The 28-mile-long, uninterrupted stretch of sand that runs along the
peninsula's ocean shore is a great place to beachcomb. Don't even think
about swimming here, however. Though surfers in wet suits brave the
waves in some areas, the water is too cold and the surf too rough for
most people; hypothermia, shifting sands underfoot, and tremendous
undertows account for several drownings each year.

The peninsula is a great place to hike, bike, and bird-watch. Lakes and
marshes attract migrating birds, among them trumpeter swans. Long
Island, in southeastern Willapa Bay, has a stand of old-growth red cedar
trees, home to spotted owls, marbled murrelets (a western seabird), elks,
and black bears. The island is accessible only by private boat (the boat
ramp is on the bay's eastern shore).

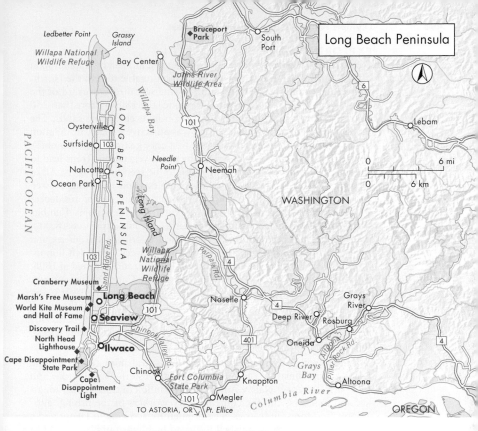

GETTING HERE AND AROUND

The Long Beach peninsula is a little more than three hours from Seattle via Interstate 5 south to Olympia and then southwest via U.S. 101. From Portland, the drive takes about 2¼ hours via Interstate 5 north to Kelso then west via Highway 30. Pacific Transit buses serve the towns of Aberdeen, Bay Center, Chinook, Ilwaco, Long Beach, Nahcotta, Naselle, Ocean Park, Oysterville, South Bend, Surfside, Raymond, and Astoria, Oregon.

Contact Pacific Transit. ☎ 360/642-9418 ⊕ www.pacifictransit.org.

ILWACO

170 miles southwest of Seattle, 109 miles northwest of Portland, OR.

Ilwaco (ill- *wah*-co) has been a fishing port for thousands of years, first as a Native American village and later as an American settlement. A 3-mile scenic loop winds past Cape Disappointment State Park (formerly Fort Canby State Park) to North Head Lighthouse and through the town. The colorful harbor is a great place for watching gulls and boats. Lewis and Clark camped here before moving their winter base to the Oregon coast at Fort Clatsop.

EXPLORING

FAMILY Fodor's Choice ★ **Cape Disappointment State Park.** The cape, named in 1788 by Captain John Meares, an English fur trader who had been unable to find the Northwest Passage, and treacherous sandbar—the so-called graveyard of the Pacific—has been the scourge of sailors since the 1800s. More than 250 ships have sunk after running aground on its ever-shifting sands. The 1,882-acre park overlooking the cape was an active military installation until 1957. Emplacements for the guns that once guarded the Columbia's mouth remain, some of them hidden by dense vegetation. Trails lead to stunning beaches and eagles can sometimes be seen on the cliffs. All of the park's 220 campsites have stoves and tables; some have water, sewer, and electric hookups. The park also has three lightkeepers' residences (houses) available for rent, as well as 14 yurts and three cabins. Exhibits at the park's **Lewis & Clark Interpretive Center** tell the tale of the duo's 8,000-mile round-trip expedition. Displays include artwork, journal entries, and other items that elaborate on the Corps of Discovery, which left Illinois, in 1804, arrived at Cape Disappointment in 1805, and returned in 1806. A ½-mile-long path from the center leads to the Cape Disappointment Lighthouse. Built in 1856, it's the oldest lighthouse on the West Coast that's still in use. ✉ *Robert Gray Dr.* ✣ *2½ miles southwest of Ilwaco off U.S. 101* ☎ *360/642–3029, 360/642–3078* 🌐 *www.parks.wa.gov* 🎟 *Day pass $10 per vehicle, annual Discovery Pass $30 (valid at all state parks); Interpretive center $5; lighthouse tours $2.50; campsites $20–$45.*

Columbia Pacific Heritage Museum. Dioramas and miniatures of Long Beach towns illustrate the history of southwestern Washington, and other displays cover Native Americans; the influx of traders, missionaries, and pioneers; and the contemporary workers of the fishing, agriculture, and forest industries. The original Ilwaco Freight Depot and a Pullman car from the Clamshell Railroad highlight rail history. ✉ *115 S.E. Lake St., off U.S. 101* ☎ *360/642–3446* 🌐 *columbiapacificheritagemuseum.org* 🎟 *$5; free on Thurs.* 🕒 *Closed Sun. and Mon.*

North Head Lighthouse. Built in 1898, this lighthouse was needed to help skippers sailing from the north, who couldn't see the Cape Disappointment Lighthouse. Stand high on a bluff above the pounding surf here, amid the windswept trees, for superb views of the Long Beach Peninsula. Lodging is available in the Lighthouse Keepers' Residence. ✉ *North Head Lighthouse Rd.* ✣ *2 miles from Cape Disappointment via Spur 100 Rd.* ☎ *360/642–3029* 🌐 *www.parks.wa.gov/241/North-Head-Lighthouse* 🎟 *$2.50.*

WHERE TO EAT AND STAY

$ DINER 🍴 **Portside Café.** This local favorite, painted the color of sea glass and located two blocks from the dock and boat launch, is known for its big breakfasts and hearty lunches of biscuits and gravy, French toast on fresh-baked bread, chicken-fried steak, BLTs, soups, and pies—all of them homemade. Pizza is also on the menu, along with burgers and platter cakes, pancakes the size of a platter. **Known for:** generous, homemade breakfast and lunch fare. [$] *Average main: $12* ✉ *303 1st Ave. S.* ☎ *360/642–3477* 🕒 *No dinner.*

$$ B&B/INN 🏨 **China Beach Retreat.** Between the port of Ilwaco and Cape Disappointment State Park, this secluded and comfortable B&B filled with antiques, original art, and handcrafted furniture is surrounded by serene wetlands

Cape Disappointment State Park

and has wonderful views of Baker's Bay and the mouth of the Columbia River. **Pros:** secluded, back-to-nature setting; tide-flat views will keep bird-watchers enthralled. **Cons:** breakfast served at sister property, Shelburne Inn, 5 miles away (but it's sumptuous and complimentary). [$] *Rooms from: $199* ✉ *222 Robert Gray Dr.* ☎ *360/642–2442* 🌐 *www.chinabeachretreat.com* 🛏 *3 rooms, 1 cottage* 🍴 *Breakfast.*

SPORTS AND THE OUTDOORS

FISHING AND WHALE-WATCHING

Gray whales pass the Long Beach Peninsula twice a year: December to February, on their migration from the Arctic to their winter breeding grounds in Californian and Mexican waters, and March to May, on the return trip north. The view from the **North Head Lighthouse** is spectacular. **■ TIP→ The best time for sightings is in the morning, when the water is calm and overcast conditions reduce the glare.** Look on the horizon for a whale blow—the vapor, water, or condensation that spouts into the air when the whale exhales. If you spot one blow, you're likely to see others: whales often make several shorter, shallow dives before a longer dive that can last as long as 10 minutes.

The fish that swim in the waters near Ilwaco include salmon, rock cod, lingcod, flounder, perch, sea bass, and sturgeon. Charters generally cost from $100 to $200 per person.

Port of Ilwaco. Free tide charts are available from the port; check the website for information about fishing season and clam-digging dates. ✉ *165 Howerton Ave.* ☎ *360/642–3143* 🌐 *www.portofilwaco.com.*

SEAVIEW

3 miles north of Ilwaco.

Seaview, an unincorporated town, has 750 year-round residents and several homes that date from the 1800s. The Shelburne Inn, built in 1896, is on the National Register of Historic Places. In 1892 U.S. Senator Henry Winslow Corbett built what's now the Sou'wester Lodge.

WHERE TO EAT AND STAY

$$
PACIFIC
NORTHWEST
Fodor'sChoice
★

✕ **42nd Street Cafe and Bistro.** Inspired and creative yet unpretentious, this cozy, cheerful place serves gourmet comfort food at its best. Look for small plates such as fried-green tomatoes, Dungeness crab beignets, and Willapa Bay clams steamed in Hefeweizen, and dinner entrées such as ravioli stuffed with butternut squash and Gorgonzola, eight-hour pot roast, and lemon, crab, and shrimp fettuccine. **Known for:** food comes with a money-back guarantee; excellent service. $ *Average main: $20 ⊠ 4201 Pacific Hwy. ☎ 360/642–2323 ⊕ www.42ndstreetcafe.com ⊘ Closed Mon. and Tues.*

$
B&B/INN
Fodor'sChoice
★

☷ **Shelburne Inn.** A white picket fence and lovely gardens surround a Victorian hotel that's been continuously operating since it was built in 1896 and offers distinctly decorated rooms, full of fresh flowers, antiques, fine-art prints, wrought-iron beds, vintage wardrobes, and a variety of colors and patterns. **Pros:** excellent breakfast; historical appeal; attentive service. **Cons:** no in-room phones or TVs; some rooms are rather small. $ *Rooms from: $149 ⊠ 4415 Pacific Way ☎ 360/642–2442, 800/466–1896 ⊕ www.theshelburneinn.com ⤴ 14 rooms ⦿ Breakfast.*

$
RESORT

☷ **Sou'wester Lodge and Cabins.** For a bohemian and iconic Pacific Northwest experience, try these eclectic accommodations—beach cottages, a fleet of vintage travel trailers just behind the beach, three large bedrooms, or second-floor suites converted from space that once housed a ballroom—at the 1892 summer retreat of Henry Winslow Corbett, a Portland magnate and U.S. senator. **Pros:** one-of-a-kind lodgings; interesting history; good for bohemian and budget travelers; involved and attentive owner. **Cons:** not for luxury seekers; some rooms don't have private baths. $ *Rooms from: $103 ⊠ 3728 J Pl. ☎ 360/642–2542 ⊕ www.souwesterlodge.com ⤴ 23 rooms.*

LONG BEACH

½ mile north of Seaview.

Long Beach bears a striking resemblance to Brooklyn's Coney Island in the 1950s. Along its main drag, which stretches southwest from 10th Street to Bolstadt Street, you'll find everything from cotton candy and hot dogs to go-karts and bumper cars.

EXPLORING

Cranberry Museum. Here, visitors can learn about more than a century of cranberry cultivation in this area, take a self-guided walking tour through the bogs, try some cranberry tea, and buy cranberry products to take home. ⊠ *2907 Pioneer Rd. ☎ 360/642–5553 ⊕ www.cranberry-museum.com ☒ Free ⊘ Museum closed mid-Dec.–Mar. Walking tours available all year.*

FAMILY **Discovery Trail.** Created to memorialize Lewis and Clark's explorations here in 1805–06, the 8½-mile Discovery Trail traces the explorers' moccasin steps from Ilwaco to north Long Beach, overlooking sandy dunes and beachfront. Access the trail from the beach parking lots on Sid Snyder Drive or Bolstad Street in Long Beach. Parking is also available at the Beard's Hollow lot in Cape Disappointment State Park. ✉ *Long Beach* ☎ *800/451–2542, 360/642–3900* 🌐 *www.funbeach.com.*

FAMILY **Long Beach Boardwalk.** The ½-mile-long wooden boardwalk runs through the dunes parallel to the beach, and is a great place for strolling, bird-watching, or just sitting and listening to the wind and the roar of the surf. It's ¼ mile west of downtown, between Bolstad Avenue and Sid Snyder Drive. ✉ *Long Beach* 🌐 *funbeach.com.*

FAMILY **Marsh's Free Museum.** If you've got kids in your group, or simply an appreciation of oddities, be sure to visit this quirky museum that's best known for "Jake the Alligator Man." Marsh's is filled with plenty of other curiosities, like real shrunken heads, skeletons, and an eight-legged lamb. ✉ *400 S. Pacific Ave.* ☎ *360/642–2188* 🌐 *www.marshsfreemuseum.com* 🎟 *Free.*

World Kite Museum and Hall of Fame. Each August Long Beach hosts the Washington State International Kite Festival; the community is also home to the Northwest Stunt Kite Championships, a competition held each June. At the only U.S. museum focused solely on kites and kiting, you can view an array of kites and learn about kite making and history. ✉ *303 Sid Snyder Dr. SW* ☎ *360/642–4020* 🌐 *www.kitefestival.com* 🎟 *$5* ⏲ *Hrs vary seasonally; call ahead.*

WHERE TO EAT AND STAY

$$ SEAFOOD 🍴 **Dooger's Seafood and Grill.** Locals will urge you to eat here—listen to them. The ample portions of all kinds of seafood come with potatoes, shrimp-topped salad, and garlic toast. **Known for:** ample servings; locals' favorite. [$] *Average main: $22* ✉ *900 Pacific Hwy. S* ☎ *360/642–4224* 🌐 *doogersseafood.com.*

$ RENTAL FAMILY 🏨 **Anchorage Cottages.** Along a western ridge of the Long Beach Peninsula, these cozy cottages with fireplaces and unobstructed views of the dunes have been accommodating beach getaways since the early 1950s. **Pros:** pretty gardens and courtyard; affordable; near the beach. **Cons:** not very private; town is a mile away; two-night minimum during high season. [$] *Rooms from: $89* ✉ *2209 Boulevard Ave. N* ☎ *800/646–2351, 360/642–2351* 🌐 *www.theanchoragecottages.com* 🛏 *10 cottages* 🍽 *No meals.*

$$ B&B/INN 🏨 **Boreas Bed and Breakfast.** Antiques and books fill this vintage 1920s beach house, where rooms have balconies or decks and ocean views, a jetted spa tub sits in an enclosed glass-and-cedar gazebo overlooking the ocean, and a private path leads through the dunes to the shore. **Pros:** great breakfast; helpful innkeepers; on the Lewis and Clark Trail. **Cons:** no bathtubs in three rooms; not for families. [$] *Rooms from: $179* ✉ *607 N. Ocean Beach Blvd.* ☎ *360/642–8069, 888/642–8069* 🌐 *www.boreasinn.com* 🛏 *5 suites, 3 with shower only* 🍽 *Breakfast.*

$ **Breakers Motel and Condominiums.** Each of the contemporary one- and
RESORT   two-bedroom condominiums here has a private balcony or patio, and
FAMILY   many also have fireplaces and exceptional views of the dunes and the
surf. **Pros:** very family-friendly, with lots of activities. **Cons:** units are
individually owned, so style and quality differs. $ *Rooms from: $139*
⊠ *210 26th St. NW* ☎ *360/642–4414, 800/219–9833* ⊕ *www.break-
erslongbeach.com* ⊅ *144 rooms* ⊙ *No meals.*

$ **Our Place at the Beach.** This older, pet-friendly motel is both quiet
HOTEL   and convenient, and styles vary from basic, budget accommodations
with a queen bed to family suites that sleep eight and have kitchens.
Pros: cheerful, accommodating staff; reasonably priced; five-minute
walk from the beach, restaurants, and shops. **Cons:** thin walls and
somewhat dated interiors in some units. $ *Rooms from: $74* ⊠ *1309
S. Ocean Beach Blvd.* ☎ *360/642–3793, 800/538–5107* ⊕ *www.our-
placelongbeach.weebly.com* ⊅ *26 rooms* ⊙ *Breakfast.*

SPORTS AND THE OUTDOORS
BEACHES
Long Beach. The Long Beach Peninsula consists of 28 continuous miles
of broad sandy beach, which fills with kite flyers, sand-castle builders,
sunbathers, bicyclists, horseback riders, and drivers during summer
months. Watch out for horses, cars, and other motor vehicles—some
sections are open for driving year-round, while other parts don't allow
it in summer; the speed limit on the sand is 25 mph. Bonfires are also
allowed. Bring a windbreaker—strong gusts are common near the
water, which remains consistently frigid throughout the year. **Amenities:**
toilets. **Best for:** solitude; sunrise; sunset; walking. ⊠ *Long Beach* ✛ *West
off State Rte. 103* ☎ *360/642–2400* ⊕ *funbeach.com.*

GOLF
Peninsula Golf Course. There are two 9-hole, par-33 courses here, on
Long Beach's northern edge. ⊠ *9604 Pacific Hwy.* ☎ *360/642–2828*
⊕ *peninsulagolfcourse.com.*

HORSEBACK RIDING
Back Country Wilderness Outfitters. One- and two-hour horseback rides are
offered here for $30 per hour. ⊠ *409 Sid Snyder Dr.* ☎ *360/642–2576*
⊕ *www.backcountryhorseadventures.wordpress.com.*

14

NORTH CASCADES
NATIONAL PARK

1414

141414

WELCOME TO NORTH CASCADES NATIONAL PARK

TOP REASONS TO GO

★ **Pure wilderness:** Spot bald eagles, deer, elk, and other wildlife on nearly 400 miles of mountain and meadow hiking trails.

★ **Majestic glaciers:** The North Cascades are home to several hundred moving ice masses, more than half of the glaciers in the United States.

★ **Splendid flora:** A bright palette of flowers blankets the hillsides in midsummer, while October's colors paint the landscape in vibrant autumn hues.

★ **Thrilling boat rides:** Lake Chelan, Ross Lake, and the Stehekin River are the starting points for kayaking, white-water rafting, and ferry trips.

★ **19th-century history:** Delve into the state's farming, lumber, and logging pasts in clapboard towns and homesteads around the park.

1 North Unit. The park's creek-cut northern wilderness, centered on snowy Mt. Challenger, stretches north from Highway 20 over the Picket Range toward the Canadian border. It's an endless landscape of pine-topped peaks and ridges.

2 South Unit. Hike lake-filled mountain foothills in summer to take in vistas of blue skies and flower-filled meadows. Waterfalls and wildlife are abundant here.

3 Ross Lake National Recreation Area. Drawing a thick line from British Columbia all the way down to the North Cascades Scenic Highway, placid Ross Lake is edged with pretty bays that draw swimmers and boaters.

4 Lake Chelan National Recreation Area. Ferries cruise between small waterfront villages along this pristine waterway, while kayakers and hikers follow quiet trails along its edges. This is one of the Northwest's most popular summer escapes, with nature-bound activities and rustic accommodations.

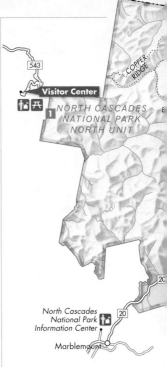

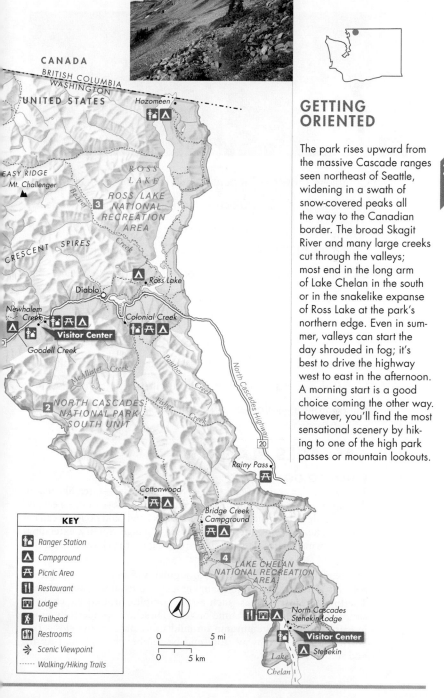

GETTING ORIENTED

14

The park rises upward from the massive Cascade ranges seen northeast of Seattle, widening in a swath of snow-covered peaks all the way to the Canadian border. The broad Skagit River and many large creeks cut through the valleys; most end in the long arm of Lake Chelan in the south or in the snakelike expanse of Ross Lake at the park's northern edge. Even in summer, valleys can start the day shrouded in fog; it's best to drive the highway west to east in the afternoon. A morning start is a good choice coming the other way. However, you'll find the most sensational scenery by hiking to one of the high park passes or mountain lookouts.

CANADA
BRITISH COLUMBIA
WASHINGTON
UNITED STATES
Hozomeen

EASY RIDGE
Mt. Challenger

ROSS LAKE

ROSS LAKE NATIONAL RECREATION AREA

CRESCENT SPIRES

Beaver Creek

Ross Lake

Diablo

Newhalem Creek
Visitor Center
Goodell Creek

Colonial Creek

McAllister Creek

Panther Creek

Fisher Creek

North Cascades Highway

20

NORTH CASCADES NATIONAL PARK SOUTH UNIT

Rainy Pass

Cottonwood

Stehekin R.

Bridge Creek Campground

LAKE CHELAN NATIONAL RECREATION AREA

North Cascades Stehekin Lodge

Visitor Center

Stehekin

Lake Chelan

KEY

- 🧍 Ranger Station
- ▲ Campground
- 🪧 Picnic Area
- 🍴 Restaurant
- 🏠 Lodge
- 🚶 Trailhead
- 🚻 Restrooms
- 🔭 Scenic Viewpoint
- ----- Walking/Hiking Trails

0   5 mi
0   5 km

Updated by
Shelley Arenas

Countless snow-clad mountain spires dwarf narrow glacial valleys in this 505,000-acre expanse of the North Cascades, which encompasses three diverse natural areas. North Cascades National Park is the core of the region, flanked by Lake Chelan National Recreation Area to the south and Ross Lake National Recreation Area to the north; all are part of the Stephen T. Mather Wilderness Area. It's a spectacular gathering of snowy peaks, glacial meadows, plunging canyons, and cold deep-blue lakes. Traditionally the lands of several American Indian tribes, it's fitting that it's still completely wild—and wildlife filled.

NORTH CASCADES PLANNER

WHEN TO GO

The spectacular, craggy peaks of the North Cascades—often likened to the Alps—are breathtaking anytime. Summer is peak season, especially along the alpine stretches of Highway 20; weekends and holidays can be crowded. Summer is short and glorious in the high country, extending from snowmelt (late May to July, depending on the elevation and the amount of snow) to early September.

The North Cascades Highway is a popular autumn drive in September and October, when the changing leaves put on a colorful show. The lowland forest areas, such as the complex around Newhalem, can be visited almost any time of year. These are wonderfully quiet in early spring or late autumn on mild rainy days. Snow closes the North Cascades Highway from mid-November through mid-April, and sometimes longer.

PLANNING YOUR TIME
NORTH CASCADES IN ONE DAY

The **North Cascades Highway,** with its breathtaking mountain and meadow scenery, is one of the most memorable drives in the United States. Although many travelers first head northeast from Seattle into the park and make this their grand finale, if you start from Winthrop, at the south end of the route, traffic is lighter and there's less morning fog. Either way, the main highlight is **Washington Pass,** the road's highest point, where an overlook affords a sensational panorama of snow-covered peaks.

Rainy Pass, where the road heading north drops into the west slope valleys, is another good vantage point. Old-growth forest begins to appear, and after about an hour you reach **Gorge Creek Falls overlook** with its 242-foot cascade. Continue west to Newhalem and stop for lunch, then take a half-hour stroll along the **Trail of the Cedars.** Later, stop at the **North Cascades Visitor Center** and take another short hike. It's an hour drive down the Skagit Valley to Sedro-Woolley, where bald eagles are often seen along the river in winter.

14

GETTING HERE AND AROUND
AIR TRAVEL

The nearest commercial airports are in Bellingham to the northwest and in Wenatchee south of Chelan.

CAR TRAVEL

Highway 20, the North Cascades Highway, splits the park's north and south sections. The gravel Cascade River Road, which runs southeast from Marblemount, peels off Highway 20; Sibley Creek/Hidden Lake Road (USFS 1540) turns off Cascade River Road to the Cascade Pass trailhead. Thornton Creek Road is another rough four-wheel-drive track. For the Ross Lake area in the north, the unpaved Hozomeen Road (Silver–Skagit Road) provides access between Hope, British Columbia, and Silver Lake and Skagit Valley provincial parks. From Stehekin, the Stehekin Valley Road continues to High Bridge and Car Wash Falls—although seasonal floods may cause washouts. Note that roads are narrow and some are closed seasonally, many sights are off the beaten path, and the scenery is so spectacular that, once you're in it, you'll want to make more than a day trip.

PARK ESSENTIALS
PARK FEES AND PERMITS

There are no entrance fees to the national park and no parking fees at trailheads on park land. A Northwest Forest Pass, required for parking at Forest Service trailheads, is $5 per vehicle for a calendar day or $30 for a year. A free wilderness permit is required for all overnight stays in the backcountry; these are available in person only. Dock permits for boat-in campgrounds are also $5 per day. Car camping is $16 per night at Colonial Creek, Goodell Creek, and Newhalem Creek campgrounds during the summer (when water and other services are available) and free off-season; free at the primitive Gorge Lake and Hozomeen campgrounds. Passes and permits are sold at visitor centers and ranger stations around the park area.

PARK HOURS

The park never closes, but access is limited by snow in winter. Highway 20 (North Cascades Highway), the major access to the park, is partially closed from mid-November to mid-April, depending on snow levels.

CELL-PHONE RECEPTION

Cell-phone reception in the park is unreliable. Public telephones are found at the North Cascades Visitor Center and Skagit Information Center in Newhalem, and the Golden West Visitor Center and North Cascades Stehekin Lodge in Stehekin.

EDUCATIONAL OFFERINGS

Seattle City Light Information and Tour Center. Based at a history museum that has exhibits about the onset of electric power through the Cascade ranges, Seattle's public electric company offers tours and programs during summer. Several trails start at the building, and the group offers sightseeing excursions on Diablo Lake in partnership with the North Cascades Institute, Thursday through Monday in summer by advance reservation, and afternoon cruises on summer weekends. The tour includes a visit to the Diablo Dam. Free 45-minute walking tours through the historic town of Newhalem are offered daily from July through Labor Day. ⊠ *Milepost 120, North Cascades Hwy., Newhalem* ☎ *360/854–2589* ⊕ *www.skagittours.com* 🖅 *Walking tour free, afternoon boat tour $20, day boat tour $40 (includes lunch)* ⊘ *Closed Oct.–Apr.*

RANGER PROGRAMS

In summer, rangers conduct programs at the visitor centers, where you also can find exhibits and other park information. At the North Cascades Visitor Center (in Newhalem) you can learn about rain-forest ecology, while at the Golden West Visitor Center (in Stehekin) there's an arts-and-crafts gallery as well as audiovisual and children's programs. Check center bulletin boards for schedules.

RESTAURANTS

There are no formal restaurants in North Cascades National Park, just a lakeside café at the North Cascades Environmental Learning Center.

HOTELS

Accommodations in North Cascades National Park are rustic, cozy, and comfortable. Options range from plush Stehekin lodges and homey cabin rentals to spartan Learning Center bunks and campgrounds. *Hotel reviews have been shortened. For full information, visit Fodors.com.*

WHAT IT COSTS			
$	$$	$$$	$$$$
Restaurants under $12	$12–$20	$21–$30	over $30
Hotels under $100	$100–$150	$151–$200	over $200

Restaurant prices are the average cost of a main course at dinner or, if dinner is not served, at lunch. Hotel prices are the lowest cost of a standard double room in high season, excluding taxes and service charges.

TOURS

FAMILY
Fodor's Choice
★

North Cascades Environmental Learning Center. Come here for information on park hiking, wildlife watching, horseback riding, climbing, boat rentals, and fishing, as well as classroom education and hands-on nature experiences. Guided tours staged from the center include lake and dam tours, mountain climbs, pack-train excursions, and guided canoe trips on Diablo Lake. Other choices range from forest ecology and backpacking trips to writing and art retreats. Family getaway weekends in summer are a fun way to unplug from technology and introduce kids to nature. There's also a research library, a dock on Diablo Lake, an amphitheater, and overnight lodging. The center is operated by the North Cascades Institute, in partnership with the National Parks Service and Seattle City Light. ☒ *1940 Diablo Dam Rd., Diablo* ☎ *360/854–2599 Headquarters, 206/526–2599 Environmental Learning Center* ⊕ *www.ncascades.org* ☒ *Day programs from $65; overnight lodging (including meals) from $210 per couple.*

14

VISITOR INFORMATION

Park Contact Information **North Cascades National Park.** ☒ *810 Rte. 20, Sedro-Woolley* ☎ *360/854–7200* ⊕ *www.nps.gov/noca.*

VISITOR CENTERS

Golden West Visitor Center. Rangers here offer guidance on hiking, camping, and other activities, as well as audiovisual and children's programs and bike tours. There's also an arts-and-crafts gallery. Maps and concise displays explain the layered ecology of the valley, which encompasses in its length virtually every ecosystem in the Northwest. Campers can pick up free backcountry permits. Note that access to Stehekin is by boat or trail only. ☒ *Stehekin Valley Rd., Stehekin* ✛ *¼ mile north of Stehekin Landing* ☎ *509/699–2080* ⊕ *www.nps.gov/noca/planyourvisit/visitor-centers.htm* ☉ *Closed Oct.–May.*

North Cascades Visitor Center. The main visitor facility for the park complex has extensive displays on the surrounding landscape. Learn about the history and value of old-growth trees, the many creatures that depend on the rain-forest ecology, and the effects of human activity on the ecosystem. Park rangers frequently conduct programs; check bulletin boards for schedules. ☒ *Milepost 120, North Cascades Hwy., Newhalem* ☎ *206/386–4495* ⊕ *www.nps.gov/noca/planyourvisit/visitorcenters.htm* ☉ *Closed Nov.–Apr. and weekdays in early May and Oct.*

EXPLORING

SCENIC DRIVES

North Cascades Highway. Also known as Highway 20, this classic scenic route first winds through the green pastures and woods of the upper Skagit Valley, the mountains looming in the distance. Beyond Concrete, a former cement-manufacturing town, the highway climbs into the mountains, passes the Ross and Diablo dams, and traverses Ross Lake National Recreation Area. Here several pull-outs offer great views of the lake and the surrounding snowcapped peaks. From June to September, the meadows are covered with wildflowers, and from late September through October, the mountain slopes flame with fall foliage. The pinnacle point of this stretch is 5,477-foot-high Washington Pass: look east, to where the road descends quickly into a series of hairpin curves between Early Winters Creek and the Methow Valley. Remember, this section of the highway is closed from roughly November to April, depending on snowfall, and sometimes closes temporarily during the busy summer season due to mudslides from storms. From the Methow Valley, Highway 153 takes the scenic route along the Methow River's apple, nectarine, and peach orchards to Pateros, on the Columbia River; from here, you can continue east to Grand Coulee or south to Lake Chelan. ⊕ *www.cascadeloop.com.*

> **PLANTS AND WILDLIFE IN NORTH CASCADES**
>
> Bald eagles are present year-round along the Skagit River and the lakes—in December, hundreds flock to the Skagit to feed on a rare winter salmon run, and remain through January. Spring and early summer bring black bears to the roadsides in the high country. Deer and elk can often be seen in early morning and late evening, grazing and browsing at the forest's edge. Other mountain residents include beaver, marmots, pika, otters, skunks, opossums, and smaller mammals, as well as forest and field birds.

SPORTS AND THE OUTDOORS

HIKING

⚠ Black bears are often sighted along trails in the summer; do not approach them. Back away carefully, and report sightings to the Golden West Visitor Center. Cougars, which are shy of humans and well aware of their presence, are rarely sighted in this region. Still, keep kids close and don't let them run too far ahead or lag behind on a trail. If you do spot a cougar, pick up children, have the whole group stand close together, and make yourself look as large as possible.

EASY

FAMILY **Happy Creek Forest Walk.** Old-growth forests are the focus of this kid-friendly boardwalk route, which loops just less than a ½ mile through the trees right off the North Cascades Highway. Interpretive signs provide details about flora along the way. *Easy.* ⊠ *North Cascades National Park* ✛ *Trailhead: at milepost 135, North Cascades Hwy.* ⊕ *www.nps.gov/noca.*

Rainy Lake Trail. An easy and accessible 1-mile paved trail leads to Rainy Lake, a waterfall, and glacier-view platform. *Easy.* ⊠ *North Cascades National Park* ✛ *Trailhead: off Hwy. 20, 38 miles east of visitor center at Newhalem* ⊕ *www.nps.gov/noca.*

Trail of the Cedars. Just less than a ½ mile long, this trail winds its way through one of the finest surviving stands of old-growth western red cedar in Washington. Some of the trees on the path are more than 1,000 years old. *Easy.* ⊠ *Newhalem* ✛ *Trailhead: near North Cascades Visitor Center, milepost 120, Hwy. 20* ⊕ *www.nps.gov/noca/planyourvisit/newhalem-area-trails.htm.*

MODERATE

Fodor's Choice
★
Cascade Pass. This extremely popular 3¾-mile, four-hour trail is known for stunning panoramas from the great mountain divide. Dozens of peaks line the horizon as you make your way up the fairly flat, hairpin-turn track, the scene fronted by a blanket of alpine wildflowers from July to mid-August. Arrive before noon if you want a parking spot at the trailhead. *Moderate.* ✉ *North Cascades National Park* ✛ *Trailhead: at end of Cascade River Rd., 14 miles from Marblemount* ⊕ *www.nps. gov/noca/planyourvisit/cascade-pass-trail.htm.*

Diablo Lake Trail. Explore nearly 4 miles of waterside terrain on this route, which is accessed from the Sourdough Creek parking lot. An excellent alternative for parties with small hikers is to take the Seattle City Light Ferry one way. *Moderate.* ✉ *North Cascades National Park* ✛ *Trailhead: at milepost 135, Hwy. 20* ⊕ *www.nps.gov/noca.*

14

KAYAKING

The park's tangles of waterways offer access to remote areas inaccessible by road or trail; here are some of the most pristine and secluded mountain scenes on the continent. Bring your own kayak and you can launch from any boat ramp or beach; otherwise, companies in several nearby towns and Seattle suburbs offer kayak and canoe rentals, portage, and tours. The upper basin of Lake Chelan (at the park's southern end) and Ross Lake (at the top edge of the park) are two well-known kayaking expanses, but there are dozens of smaller lakes and creeks between. The Stehekin River also provides many kayaking possibilities.

TOURS AND OUTFITTERS

Ross Lake Resort. The resort rents kayaks, motor boats, canoes, and fishing equipment, and offers portage service for exploring Ross Lake. A water-taxi service is also available; the resort is not accessible by road. ✉ *503 Diablo St., Rockport* ☎ *206/386–4437* ⊕ *www.rosslakeresort.com.*

Stehekin Valley Ranch. Kayak tours of the upper estuary of Lake Chelan are offered daily at 8:45 am. ✉ *Stehekin Valley Rd., Stehekin* ✛ *3½ miles from Stehekin Landing* ☎ *509/682–4677, 800/536–0745* ⊕ *www. stehekinvalleyranch.com* ▣ *$40.*

RAFTING

June through August is the park's white-water season, and rafting trips run through the lower section of the Stehekin River. Along the way take in views of cottonwood and pine forests, glimpses of Yawning Glacier on Magic Mountain, and placid vistas of Lake Chelan.

TOURS AND OUTFITTERS

North Cascades River Expeditions. June through October, North Cascades River Expeditions focuses on regional rivers; trips are offered on the Upper Skagit year-round. ☎ *800/634–8433* ⊕ *www.riverexpeditions. com* ▣ *From $65.*

FAMILY **Orion River Expeditions.** Introductory family-oriented floats are offered in August on the Skagit River for ages six and up. More lively white-water tours run on other area rivers April through September. ☎ *509/548–1401, 800/553–7466* ⊕ *www.orionexp.com* ✉ *From $70.*

FAMILY **Wildwater River Guides.** Half-day rafting excursions on the Skagit River depart from Goodell Creek Campground near Newhalem, March through September. The mild waters are great for beginners and families. ✉ *Goodell Creek Campground, Newhalem* ☎ *509/470–8558, 800/522–9453* ⊕ *www.wildwater-river.com* ✉ *$69.*

WHERE TO EAT

$$ ✕ **Restaurant at Stehekin Valley Ranch.** Meals in the rustic log ranch house,
AMERICAN served at polished wood tables, include buffet dinners of steak, ribs,
FAMILY hamburgers, fish, salad, beans, and dessert. Note that breakfast is served 7 to 9, lunch is noon to 1, and dinner is 5:30 to 7. **Known for:** hearty meals; fresh berries, fruit, and produce; communal dining. $ *Average main: $20* ✉ *Stehekin Valley Rd., 9 miles north of Stehekin Landing, Stehekin* ☎ *509/682–4677, 800/536–0745* ⊕ *www.stehekinvalleyranch.com* ☻ *Closed Oct.–mid-June.*

$ ✕ **Stehekin Pastry Company.** As you enter this lawn-framed timber cha-
CAFÉ let, you're immersed in the tantalizing aromas of a European bakery. Glassed-in display cases are filled with trays of homemade baked goods, and the pungent espresso is eye-opening. **Known for:** fruit pie; pastry. $ *Average main: $7* ✉ *Stehekin Valley Rd., Stehekin* ✛ *About 2 miles north of Stehekin Landing* ☎ *509/682–7742* ⊕ *www.stehekinpastry.com* ☻ *Closed mid-Oct.–mid-May.*

WHERE TO STAY

$$ ⊡ **North Cascades Lodge at Stehekin.** Crackling fires and Lake Chelan
HOTEL views are provided both in standard rooms in the Alpine House, with its shared lounge and lakeside deck, and in larger rooms in the Swiss Mont building, with private decks overlooking the water. **Pros:** on the water; recreation center with pool table; tent-to-tent hiking excursions; kayaking. **Cons:** no air-conditioning; TV is only available in the recreation building; limited Internet service and no cell-phone service. $ *Rooms from: $134* ✉ *955 Stehekin Valley Rd., Stehekin* ☎ *509/682–4494* ⊕ *www.lodgeatstehekin.com* ⇆ *28 rooms, 1 house* ⦿ *No meals.*

$$$$ ⊡ **Stehekin Valley Ranch.** Alongside pretty meadows at the edge of pine
ALL-INCLUSIVE forest, this rustic ranch is a center for hikers and horseback riders, who
FAMILY stay in barnlike cabins with cedar paneling, tile floors, and a private bath, or canvas-roof tent cabins with bunk beds, kerosene lamps, and shared bathrooms. **Pros:** easy access to recreation; playground and outdoor game fields; hearty meals included. **Cons:** no bathrooms in tent cabins; many repeat guests so book early. $ *Rooms from: $270* ✉ *Stehekin Valley Rd., Stehekin* ✛ *9 miles north of Stehekin Landing* ☎ *509/682–4677, 800/536–0745* ⊕ *stehekinvalleyranch.com* ☻ *Closed Oct.–mid-June* ⇆ *7 tent cabins (shared bathroom), 8 cabins* ⦿ *All meals.*

NORTH CENTRAL WASHINGTON

WELCOME TO NORTH CENTRAL WASHINGTON

TOP REASONS TO GO

★ **Winter sports:** The nonprofit Methow Valley Sport Trails Association maintains 120 miles of groomed trails in the North Cascades during winter, when the region is also busy with snowmobiling, heli-skiing, snowshoeing, and other winter sports.

★ **Summer sports:** The groomed trails of winter are used for mountain biking, trail running, and hiking when the snow melts. Mountain lakes, ridges, and rivers also provide a perfect playground.

★ **Cascade Loop:** Visitors to the North Cascades don't have to be athletic. This scenic byway circles through the mountains, offering some 400 miles of stunning sights.

★ **The Old West:** With its wagon wheels, wooden sidewalks, false fronts, and hitching posts, riverside Winthrop gives a glimpse into frontier days.

★ **The Old World:** The Bavarian-style mountain town of Leavenworth lights up for the holidays, Oktoberfest, and its annual accordion festival.

1 North Cascades.
West of Washington Pass, Highway 20 winds around the northern shore of Diablo Lake and southern tip of Ross Lake, continuing through the former cement-manufacturing town of Concrete and fertile Skagit Valley pastures. The route offers breathtaking views of snowcapped peaks, summer wildflowers, and fall foliage. Snowfall closes the pass from November to April, cutting the valley off from Okanogan County, which includes Old West–style Winthrop and the river-front town of Twisp in the Methow Valley.

2 Central Cascades.
This picturesque region encompasses not only the resort town and fjord-like Lake Chelan, but also the Bavarian-style village of Leavenworth and Wenatchee, self-proclaimed "Apple Capital of Washington," surrounded by orchards. Bordered by the Columbia River to the east, this stretch offers the ultimate in outdoor experiences, from boating and mountain biking to hiking and fishing, as well as plenty of outposts at which to relax and recoup.

GETTING ORIENTED

Former logging towns, nestled in the shadow of Mt. Baker to the north, line the upper ring of the Cascade Loop, encircling a vast series of national forests fanning north and east from Seattle. The ridges and valleys of the Cascade Range form the heart of this region, a mecca for skiers, snowshoers, whitewater river rafters, campers, hikers, mountain bikers, and other adventurers drawn to its natural beauty. Fjordlike Lake Chelan reaches into the wilderness from the eastern edge of the loop. The alpine area is anchored by the orchards surrounding Wenatchee to the southeast, where the Columbia River forms a natural border between north-central and eastern Washington.

15

Updated
by Adriana
Janovich

Wilderness embraces much of north-central Washington, replete with old timber towns, cascading creeks, glacial peaks, and low-hanging valleys dusted with wildflowers. The region's natural beauty creates a feeling of journeying to an out-of-the-way, rural retreat. This is the quintessential Great Outdoors, a place of snowcapped summits, sparkling lakes, evergreen forests, and—despite a road closure that walls off the east and west in winter—surprising accessibility.

Because of the depth of their glaciated valleys, the North Cascades are uncommonly reachable. One of the most popular drives in the state encircles the region, from the old lumber towns of Sedro-Woolley and Marblemount to the northwest, over Washington Pass to Mazama, where the family-run country store is a must-stop for a bowl of soup and baked goods, through the riverside stops of Twisp and Winthrop to the northeast. Both towns boast riverfront brewpubs with live music on summer weekends as well as good selections of craft beer. Farther south, the resort community of Chelan, on the southern tip of a pristine, 50-mile, glacier-fed lake of the same name, chalks up some 300 days of sunshine per year. The lake stretches 1½ miles at its widest and descends 1,486 feet at its deepest. Bavarian-style Leavenworth, 23 miles northwest of Wenatchee, bustles with shopping and a variety of festivals, including an annual Oktoberfest celebration.

Most permanent residents live along the loop, on ranches and orchards and in pocket-sized towns, all gateways to the northern ridges of the Cascade Range. In winter, these peaks, which climb 4,000 to 9,000 feet and higher, have the greatest measured snowfall in North America—more than 80 feet in high places on the western slopes. Washington Pass closes in November, cutting off the Cascade Loop until April, but the region remains accessible via Interstate 90. Still, when Highway 20 reopens in spring, travelers on both sides line up, waiting to be among the first to travel back over the byway.

NORTH CENTRAL WASHINGTON PLANNER

WHEN TO GO

With its evergreen foothills, impressive peaks, and general accessibility, the North Cascades—often likened to the Alps—is a popular destination year-round. Skiers, snowboarders, and snowshoers come here from December through March, relaxing après-ski in the area's lodges, small hotels, and bed-and-breakfasts. With Washington Pass closed, however, winter visitors have to take alternative routes, making some otherwise easily accessible destinations and accommodations seem out-of-the-way. Still, almost all lowland forest areas and valleys can be visited any time of year. Summer peak season extends from snowmelt (late May through July, depending on elevation) to early September. Many annual visitors to Lake Chelan book lodging for the following summer before leaving. Weekends and holidays can get crowded with hikers, backpackers, boaters, anglers, white-water rafters, and other outdoors enthusiasts.

In the fall, when the North Cascades glow with crimson, saffron, and rust-colored foliage against a backdrop of its evergreen trees, the Cascade Loop is a popular route. Leaf-peepers who don't mind the rainy days of late autumn can enjoy otherwise mild temperatures and a quieter drive. Early spring also offers peace and quiet as well as the promise of alpine air. Many hotels and other lodging options offer economical shoulder-season pricing.

FESTIVALS AND EVENTS

If you want to match your visit up with a local event, there are highlights in each season.

Christkindlmarkt and Christmas Lighting Festival. Old-world holiday traditions blend with modern rituals to turn downtown Leavenworth into a glittering holiday wonderland, complete with carriage rides, carols, arts and crafts, tree lighting, children's activities, and other festivities. ⊠ *Leavenworth* ☎ *509/548–5807 Leavenworth Chamber of Commerce* ⊕ *www.christkindlmarktleavenworth.com.*

Lake Chelan Winterfest Fire and Ice. Held during two weekends in mid-January, this festival features a chili cook-off, music, winter ale tasting, a fun run, ice slide, wine walk, polar bear dip, children's activities, and ice sculpture. ⊠ *Chelan* ☎ *509/682–3503 Lake Chelan Chamber of Commerce* ⊕ *www.lakechelanwinterfest.com.*

Leavenworth International Accordion Celebration. Sponsored by the Northwest Accordion Society, this mid-June fest features jam sessions, competitions, concerts, workshops, vendors, and free accordion lessons. ⊠ *Leavenworth* ⊕ *www.accordioncelebration.org.*

Maifest. Enjoy traditional German dancing, including an intricate old-world maypole dance, as well as a lederhosen contest and parade in the flower-decked Bavarian-style village of Leavenworth. As the name suggests, it takes place in May. ⊠ *Leavenworth* ☎ *509/548–5807* ⊕ *www.leavenworth.org.*

Oktoberfest. Show off your "chicken dance" and other oom-pah moves in Leavenworth at one of the most exuberant stateside celebrations of this German beer festival, complete with German food, German music, German dancing and, of course, beer. Needless to say, it's in October. Lodging fills up fast this festive weekend; some participants book rooms a year in advance. ✉ *Leavenworth* ☎ *509/548–5807 Leavenworth Chamber of Commerce* ⊕ *www.leavenworthoktoberfest.com.*

Winthrop Rhythm and Blues Fest. The Blues Ranch, 1 mile west of Winthrop, hosts this nonprofit, volunteer-run July music festival—an outdoor Methow Valley tradition. ✉ *Winthrop* ☎ *509/997–3837* ⊕ *www. winthropbluesfestival.com.*

GETTING HERE AND AROUND

AIR TRAVEL

In addition to the regular commercial service to and from Seattle, small craft make it easy to get around this far-flung region.

Catlin Flying Service. This Twisp-based company offers direct flights to Chelan, Winthrop, and Seattle's Boeing Field. Private flights, including scenic mountain flights, are also available for up to five passengers. ✉ *Box 427, Twisp* ☎ *509/429–2697* ⊕ *www.catlinflyingservice.com.*

Pangborn Memorial Airport. Commercial flights from Sea-Tac International Airport to Wenatchee's airport are available through Horizon Air. ✉ *1 Pangborn Dr., East Wenatchee* ☎ *509/884–2494* ⊕ *www.flywenatchee.com.*

CAR TRAVEL

From the Skagit Valley towns of Mount Vernon and Burlington, about 65 miles north of Seattle on Interstate 5, take Highway 20, the North Cascades Highway, east through Sedro-Woolley, Concrete, and Marblemount. From April to November, when Washington Pass is open, continue to Winthrop and Twisp, then use State Route 153 to get to Chelan, and U.S. 97—with a short jaunt on U.S. 2 heading west—to get to Leavenworth and Wenatchee. An hour and a half to the south, U.S. 97 connects with Interstate 90 at Ellensburg, about an hour and 45 minutes from Seattle.

From Seattle, take Interstate 90 to U.S. 97 to Wenatchee and Leavenworth—with a short jaunt on U.S. 2 heading east—to Chelan. From there, State Route 153 takes travelers north to Highway 20 through Twisp and Winthrop, and—from April to November—west over Washington Pass, through Marblemount, Concrete, Sedro-Woolley, and Burlington, where it connects with Interstate 5, Washington's main north–south artery.

RESTAURANTS

This region has a good range of dining options, from American pub fare to fine dining, and many incorporate locally grown and produced ingredients, including organic produce, beef, chicken, eggs, and artisanal breads and cheeses. Around the region, there are low-key, affordable, and unpretentious eateries—coffee shops, bakeries, brewpubs, diners, and restaurants.

Wenatchee is the largest city in the North Cascades and features the most variety when it comes to dining. It's home to the most ethnically diverse cuisine in the region, including several Mexican restaurants as well as Italian, Thai, Japanese, Chinese, and others. The self-proclaimed "Apple Capital of Washington," this is the place to try the fruit in a variety of forms, sweet and savory.

Bavarian-themed Leavenworth offers a number of restaurants specializing in traditional German fare as well as Pacific Northwest cuisine and American pub fare. Wine enthusiasts might want to make a stop in the Lake Chelan region, home to some two dozen wineries. Craft-beer lovers won't want to miss the riverfront breweries in both Winthrop and Twisp.

HOTELS

Accommodations in the North Cascades range from rustic cabins and basic motels to charming bed-and-breakfasts, riverside inns, intimate hotels, and upscale mountain resorts, most featuring first-rate hospitality. Many also have picturesque mountain, lake, or river views. Book well in advance for holiday and summer weekends, particularly during festivals and events. Winter and shoulder seasons tend to feature lower prices. Look for package deals online at many establishments. *Hotel reviews have been shortened. For full information, visit Fodors.com.*

15

WHAT IT COSTS IN U.S. DOLLARS			
$	**$$**	**$$$**	**$$$$**
Restaurants under $16	$16–$22	$23–$30	over $30
Hotels under $150	$150–$200	$201–$250	over $250

Restaurant prices are the average cost of a main course at dinner or, if dinner is not served, at lunch. Hotel prices are the lowest cost of a standard double room in high season.

NORTH CASCADES

This is a backpacker's paradise, the perfect place to take a hike, enjoy winter snow sports, and go white-water rafting or fishing. In fall, the changing leaves provide a colorful backdrop along the Cascade Loop, one of the state's most popular scenic byways. In summer, the valleys and slopes are blanketed with wildflowers. The towns of Twisp and Winthrop—the latter with an appealing Old West feel—provide launch pads to the great outdoors, easily accessible from every corner of this gorgeous region, marked by snowcapped peaks and low-hanging valleys.

GLACIER

113 miles north of Seattle.

The canyon village of Glacier, just outside the Mount Baker–Snoqualmie National Forest boundary, has a few shops, cafés, and lodgings. Highway 542 winds east from Glacier into the forest through an increasingly steep-walled canyon. It passes 170-foot-high Nooksack Falls, about 5 miles east of Glacier, and travels up the north fork of the Nooksack River and the slopes of Mt. Baker to a ski area, which is bright with huckleberry patches and wildflowers in summer.

CANADA

North Cascades

Mt. Baker-Snoqualmie National Forest

542

9 542 Glacier

Mt. Redoubt 8,970 ft

Mt. Challenger 8,207 ft

Ross L.

Ross Lake National Recreation Area

Mt. Shuksan 9,131 ft

North Cascades National Park

Okanogan National Forest

Bellingham

Mt. Baker 10,778 ft

Lake Whatcom Railway

Baker Lake

Lake Shannon

Bacon Pk. 7,070 ft

Newhalem

Klawatti Pk. 8,485 ft

Burlington Sedro-Woolley

Concrete

20 Marblemount

20

Winthrop

Mount Vernon

9

Skagit R.

Twisp R. 20

Twisp

N. Fk. Stillaguamish R.

530

Stehekin R.

Glacier Peak Wilderness

Stehekin

WASHINGTON

Wenatchee National Forest

53

Arlington

Mount Baker-Snoqualmie National Forest

Stillaguamish R.

Lake Chelan

Everett

Glacier Peak 10,541 ft

Snohomish

Gold Bar

Monroe

Index

Mount Baker-Snoqualmie National Forest

Chelan

2

Skykomish R.

Wenatchee Lake

2

ALT 97 97

S. Fk. Skykomish R.

2

Stevens Pass

Columbia R.

2

Puget Sound

99

Seattle

5

0   15 mi
0   15 km

Alpine Lakes Wilderness

TO ELLENSBURG TO WENATCHEE

CASCADE RANGE

Sauk R.

Suiattle R.

GETTING HERE AND AROUND

Glacier is about two hours and 15 minutes from Seattle. Take Interstate 5 north to Exit 230 at Burlington; go east 6 miles on Highway 20 then north via Highway 9, then northeast via Highway 542.

EXPLORING

Mount Baker–Snoqualmie National Forest. A vast forest, including much of the mountain and forest land around North Cascades National Park, this national forest has many trails, but because the snowline is quite low in Washington State, the upper ridges and mountains are covered by snow much of the year. This makes for a short hiking, climbing, and mountain-biking season, usually from mid-July to mid-September or early October—but winter brings skiing and snowmobiling. The wildflower season is also short, but it's spectacular; expect fall color by late August or early September. The 10,778-foot-high, snow-covered volcanic dome of **Mt. Baker** is visible from much of Whatcom County and from as far north as Vancouver and as far south as Seattle. ⊠ *Ranger Station: 1405 Emens Ave. N, Darrington* ☎ *360/783–6000 Everett office, 800/627–0062 toll-free, 360/436–1155 Darrington Ranger District office, 206/470–4060 Outdoor Recreation Information* ⊕ *www.fs.fed.us/r6/mbs* ⊡ *$10 per car for day pass, $30 for annual pass.*

WHERE TO STAY

$ B&B/INN 🏨 **Kale House Bed & Breakfast.** The charming home, which gleams with polished wood, has large windows overlooking knobby apple trees and a comfortable fireplace lounge. **Pros:** small and inviting; lovely gardens; lots of art. **Cons:** no children or pets. [$] *Rooms from: $125* ✉ *201 Kale St., Everson* ☎ *360/966–7027* 🌐 *www.kalehouse.net* 🛏 *2 rooms* 🍴 *Breakfast.*

$ RENTAL 🏨 **The Logs at Canyon Creek.** Choose from rustic, timber-lined two-bedroom cabins with full kitchens and rock fireplaces and three-bedroom cedar chalet vacation homes fully equipped with such amenities as a hot tub, pool table, DVD player, and dishwasher. **Pros:** your home in the woods; great ski access; children and pets welcome. **Cons:** a long drive from civilization; three-night minimum stay in summer; extra charge for children and pets. [$] *Rooms from: $135* ✉ *7577 Canyon View Dr., Deming* ✥ *3½ miles northwest of Glacier off Mt. Baker Hwy.* ☎ *360/599–2711* 🌐 *www.thelogs.com* 🛏 *5 cabins, 3 chalets* 🍴 *No meals.*

15

SPORTS AND THE OUTDOORS

Mt. Baker Ski Area. Snowboard and ski downhill or cross-country from roughly November to the end of April. The area set a world snowfall record in winter 1998–99. Ski and snowboard equipment is available to rent. ✉ *Glacier* ✥ *17 miles east of Glacier at end of Hwy. 542* ☎ *360/734–6771, 360/671–0211 snow reports* 🌐 *mtbaker.us* 🎟 *Lift ticket $54 weekdays, $59 weekends and holidays.*

SEDRO-WOOLLEY

42 miles southwest of Glacier.

On its way east from Interstate 5, Highway 20 skirts Burlington and Sedro-Woolley, the latter a former mill and logging town now considered the gateway to the Cascades. Fronted by a huge black steam engine, the settlement has a bit of an old downtown and a smattering of Tar Heel culture, as it was settled by pioneer loggers and farmers from North Carolina. It also has an institute that arranges trips into North Cascades National Park, and a nearby park headquarters.

GETTING HERE AND AROUND

Sedro-Woolley is about one hour, 20 minutes from Seattle via Interstate 5 north to Burlington (Exit 230), then 5 miles east via Highway 20.

ESSENTIALS

Visitor Information Sedro-Woolley Chamber of Commerce. ✉ *810 Metcalf St.* ☎ *360/855–1841* 🌐 *www.sedro-woolley.com.*

EXPLORING

FAMILY **Lake Whatcom Railway.** The steam-powered train makes 1½-hour jaunts through the woods 11 miles north of Sedro-Woolley. Excursions run in July and August and for special events, such as Christmas train rides with Santa in December. The schedule changes seasonally. ✉ *Hwy. 9, Wickersham* ☎ *360/441–0719* 🌐 *www.lakewhatcomrailway.com* 🎟 *$25.*

WINTHROP

128 miles east of Sedro-Woolley.

Before the cowboys came, the Methow Valley was a favorite gathering place for Native American tribes, who dug the plentiful and nutritious bulbs and hunted deer while their horses fattened on the tall native grasses. For wayward pioneers who came later, the cool, glacier-fed streams provided welcome relief on hot summer days, and the rich fields were a starting point for vast crops and orchards. The 1800s saw the burgeoning riverside settlement of Winthrop grow into a cattle-ranching town, whose residents inspired some of Owen Wister's colorful characters in his novel *The Virginian*. In 1972, inspired by Leavenworth's Bavarian theme, Winthrop business owners enacted a plan to restore its Old West feel, and many of the original, turn-of-the-20th-century buildings still stand.

Getting to town through the Washington countryside is a picturesque drive, with endless vistas of golden meadows, neatly sown crop fields, and rustic old barn frames. In winter the land is a crisp blanket of glittering frost; in summer little fruit-and-vegetable stands pop up along the back roads. Massive tangles of blackberry bushes produce kumquat-size fruit you can eat right off the vines, and the pungent aroma of apples pervades the breezes in autumn. Flat roads, small towns, incredible views, and plenty of camping spots make this the perfect weekend wandering territory by bike, car, or motorcycle.

GETTING HERE AND AROUND

When the North Cascades Highway is open, Winthrop can be reached via that scenic route; it takes about three hours, 45 minutes from Seattle. The rest of the year, it will take about an extra hour via Stevens Pass (U.S. 2) or Snoqualmie Pass (Interstate 90 then Highway 970 to Highway 2) to Wenatchee then north via Highways 97, 153, and 20. From Spokane, Winthrop is about 3½ hours west via Highway 2, then Highways 174, 17, 97, 153, and 20.

ESSENTIALS

Visitor Information **Winthrop Chamber of Commerce.** ✉ *202 Hwy. 20* ☎ *509/996–2125* 🌐 *www.winthropwashington.com.*

WHERE TO EAT

$$$$ PACIFIC NORTHWEST Fodor's Choice ★ 🍴 **Dining Room at Sun Mountain Lodge.** A sylvan hilltop overlooking the Methow Valley sets the scene for an extraordinary dining experience featuring upscale Pacific Northwest cuisine with local and often organic ingredients. Exquisite flavors match the artful presentation and elegant yet unpretentious lodgelike atmosphere. **Known for:** sophisticated Pacific Northwest fare; sweeping mountain views; extensive wine list. [$] *Average main: $38* ✉ *604 Patterson Lake Rd.* ☎ *509/996–4707, 800/572–0493* 🌐 *www.sunmountainlodge.com/dining* 🕒 *Closed Sun.–Thurs. in winter and spring; closed 2 wks in Nov. and early spring. No lunch.*

$$ BURGER 🍴 **Kelly's at Wesola Polana.** Steven Kelly, a transplant from Ireland, serves hearty American pub grub and Peruvian- and Asian-inspired fare alongside an impressive selection of beer and wine. Dishes feature

Sun Mountain Lodge

seasonal local ingredients and offer sustenance for winter skiers and summer hikers and cyclists heading for the miles of groomed trails that run past the place (trail passes are available here). **Known for:** pub grub; ethnic fare; easy access to groomed trails. [$] *Average main: $16* ✉ *18381 Hwy. 20* ☎ *509/996–9804* 🌐 *www.kellys-wesolapolana.com* 🕓 *Closed Mon.–Wed. No lunch.*

$ AMERICAN

🍴 **Old Schoolhouse Brewery.** Located in a long red building designed to resemble an old one-room schoolhouse, this craft brewpub sits between the town's main drag and the Chewuch River. While waiting for big burgers or a succulent pork sandwich, sip an Epiphany Pale, Hooligan Stout, or Renegade IPA. **Known for:** fantastic craft beer; festive atmosphere; hearty pub grub. [$] *Average main: $13* ✉ *155 Riverside Ave.* ☎ *509/996–3183* 🌐 *www.oldschoolhousebrewery.com.*

WHERE TO STAY

$$$ RESORT FAMILY Fodor's Choice ★

🏨 **Freestone Inn.** At the heart of the 120-acre, historic Wilson Ranch, amid more than 2 million acres of forest, this upscale mountain retreat embraces the pioneer spirit in spacious rooms, suites, and wood-paneled cabins snuggled up to Early Winters Creek. **Pros:** gorgeous scenery; myriad activities; close to North Cascades National Park (17 miles west). **Cons:** limited cell-phone and TV service; some resort amenities may be limited in shoulder season. [$] *Rooms from: $239* ✉ *31 Early Winters Dr., Mazama* ✥ *About 14 miles northwest of Winthop* ☎ *509/996–3906, 800/639–3809* 🌐 *www.freestoneinn.com* 🛏 *34 rooms* 🍽 *No meals.*

$ RENTAL Fodor's Choice ★ **Rolling Huts.** Designed as a modern alternative to camping by Seattle architect Tom Kundig, these six raised cabins in an alpine-river-valley meadow with mountain views accommodate up to four guests and have an industrial, boxcarlike appearance and unfussy interiors. **Pros:** gorgeous views; serene setting; interesting architecture. **Cons:** limited cell-phone service; portable toilets and water faucets outside each hut. [$] *Rooms from: $145* ✉ *18381 Hwy. 20, Mazama* ✣ *About 14 miles northwest of Winthrop on State Rte. 20* ☎ *509/996–4442* 🌐 *www.rollinghuts.com* 🛏 *6 huts* 🍴 *No meals.*

$$$$ RESORT Fodor's Choice ★ **Sun Mountain Lodge.** The stunning North Cascades and all its attractions are the stars of this outdoor-oriented resort replete with luxurious accommodations, spectacular mountain views, and a range of activities that make it a year-round destination, whether the peaks are covered in snow or wildflowers. **Pros:** stunning setting; a wide array of outdoor activities year-round; panoramic views; award-winning dining; warm hospitality. **Cons:** limited cell service; roundabout route from Seattle in winter. [$] *Rooms from: $265* ✉ *604 Patterson Lake Rd.* ☎ *509/996–2211, 800/572–0493* 🌐 *www.sunmountainlodge.com* 🕓 *Closed 2 wks in early Nov. and Mar.–early Apr.* 🛏 *112 rooms* 🍴 *Breakfast.*

$$$ HOTEL Fodor's Choice ★ **Twisp River Suites.** These chic, comfortable, and contemporary rooms and condominium-style suites with thoughtful extras hug the banks of the Twisp River, lined by ponderosa pine and frequented by bald eagles. **Pros:** riverfront views; sleek and modern mountain feel; next door to a popular brewpub. **Cons:** not much to do in the little town of Twisp. [$] *Rooms from: $209* ✉ *140 W. Twisp Ave., Twisp* ☎ *509/997–0100, 855/784–8328* 🌐 *www.twispriversuites.com* 🛏 *16 rooms* 🍴 *Breakfast.*

SPORTS AND THE OUTDOORS

MULTISPORT OUTFITTERS

North Cascades Mountain Guides. This outfitter provides guided backcountry-skiing and rock-climbing excursions for single and multiple days, as well as mountaineering courses, international expeditions, and more. ✉ *48 Lost River Rd., Mazama* ☎ *509/996–3194* 🌐 *www.ncmountainguides.com.*

HIKING

Methow Valley Ranger District. Miles of hiking trails, including the famed Pacific Crest Trail, abound in the wilderness surrounding Winthrop. The ranger district has information about trails and conditions in the Okanogan-Wenatchee National Forest. ✉ *24 W. Chewuch Rd.* ☎ *509/996–4003* 🌐 *www.fs.usda.gov/okawen/.*

RAFTING

Outdoor Adventures. Beginning and experienced paddlers are welcome on rafting trips through the rapids of the Wenatchee River during spring and summer. Half-day excursions are $79. ✉ *The River House, 444 Ave. A, Index* ☎ *800/282–4043* 🌐 *outdooradventurecenter.com.*

SKIING

Methow Valley Sport Trails Association. The Methow Valley boasts one of the most extensive groomed cross-country ski trail systems in the country. Fat bikes and snowshoes are also allowed. When there's no snow, the trails are open to dirt bikers and are said to be some of the best for dirt biking in the state. ✉ *309 Riverside Ave.* ☎ *509/996–3287 office, 509/996–3860 trail conditions* ⊕ *www.methowtrails.org.*

North Cascade Heli-Skiing. If they can afford it, experienced skiers looking for fresh powder can get dropped off in virgin, backcountry snow by a helicopter for one day of runs ($1,200) or three days in a row ($3,200). Three- or four-night yurt trips are also available ($1,250 and $1,400), as are custom trips. ✉ *Freestone Inn, 31 Early Winters Dr., Mazama* ☎ *509/996–3272* ⊕ *www.heli-ski.com.*

CENTRAL CASCADES

Lake Chelan, with its sparkling glacier-fed waters, is one of Washington's longtime favorite destinations. Temperatures soar at this mountain lake in the summer, when vacationers flock to its shores. To the south, the Bavarian-style town of Leavenworth hosts numerous festivals, along with outdoor fun and plenty of bratwurst. Wenatchee, known for the apples plucked from its local orchards, and Cashmere, with its candied aplets and cotlets, anchor the region's southeast corner. Like its North Cascades neighbor, this area is also good for hiking, backpacking, fishing, rafting, skiing, and other winter snow sports.

15

CHELAN

181 miles east of Seattle.

Lake Chelan, a sinewy, 50½-mile-long fjord—Washington's deepest lake—works its way from the town of Chelan, at its south end, to Stehekin, in North Cascades National Park at the far northeast edge. The scenery is unparalleled, the flat blue water encircled by plunging gorges, with a vista of snow-slathered mountains beyond. No roads access the lake except for the shoreline around Chelan, so a floatplane or boat is needed to see the whole thing. Resorts dot the warmer eastern shores. South of the lake, 9,511-foot Bonanza Peak is the tallest nonvolcanic peak in Washington.

Today Chelan serves as the favorite beach resort of western Washingtonians. In summer Lake Chelan is one of the hottest places in Washington, with temperatures often soaring above 100°F. The mountains surrounding the fjordlike lake rise from a height of about 4,000 feet near Chelan to 8,000 and 9,000 feet at the head of the lake.

GETTING HERE AND AROUND

From Seattle it takes about three hours, 15 minutes to reach Chelan by either Highway 2 (Stevens Pass) or Interstate 90 (Snoqualmie Pass) then north via Highway 97. From Spokane it's about three hours via Highways 2 and 17.

ESSENTIALS

Visitor Information Lake Chelan Chamber of Commerce. ✉ *216 E. Woodin Ave.* ☎ *509/682–3503* ⊕ *www.lakechelan.com.*

Stehekin River Valley

EXPLORING

Fodor's Choice **Lake Chelan.** Best known as a summer vacation spot, this narrow
★ fjord—Washington's largest natural lake—offers a reason to visit all
year: its striking scenery. The views include sparkling blue water with
snowcapped peaks in the distance. The lake offers swimming, boating,
fishing, and a chance to soak up the sun. Access to the shore is fairly
limited, but the lake makes for a beautiful backdrop throughout the
region. ⊠ *U.S. 97A* ☎ *509/682–3503* ⊕ *www.lakechelan.com.*

Lake Chelan Boat Co. The *Lady of the Lake II* makes journeys from
May to October, departing Chelan at 8:30 and returning at 6 ($40.50
round-trip). The *Lady Express*, a speedy catamaran, runs between Stehekin, Holden Village, the national park, and Lake Chelan year-round;
schedules vary with the seasons. Tickets are $61 round-trip May to
October and $40.50 round-trip the rest of the year. The vessels also
can drop off and pick up at lakeshore trailheads. ⊠ *1418 Woodin Ave.*
☎ *509/682–4584, 888/682–4584* ⊕ *ladyofthelake.com.*

Lake Chelan State Park. Right on the lake and 9 miles west of Chelan on
the opposite (less crowded) shore, this 127-acre park with 6,000 feet of
shoreline is a favorite hangout for folks from the cool west side of the
Cascades who want to soak up some sun. There are docks, a boat ramp,
RV sites with full hookups, and lots of campsites for those who prefer
a less "citified" approach to camping. ⊠ *7544 S. Lakeshore Rd.* ✛ *U.S.
97A, west to S. Shore Dr. or Navarre Coulee Rd.* ☎ *360/902–8844,
509/687–3710* ⊕ *www.parks.wa.gov* ☒ *Day pass $10 per vehicle,
annual Discovery Pass $30 (valid at all state parks), camping $20–$45*
☉ *Closed Labor Day–Memorial Day.*

Twenty-Five Mile Creek State Park. Directly north of Lake Chelan State Park, this park also abuts the lake's western shore. It has many of the same facilities as the Chelan park, including a modern marina that offers easier access to the lake's upper reaches, and because it's the more remote of the two, it's often less crowded. ✉ *20530 S. Lakeshore Rd.* ☎ *509/687–3610, 888/226–7688* 🌐 *www.parks.wa.gov* 🕒 *Closed Nov.–Mar.*

WHERE TO STAY

$$$$ RESORT FAMILY 🏨 **Campbell's Resort.** This long-established lakeshore landmark has 8 acres of landscaped grounds and 1,200 feet of pristine sandy beachfront, and every room has a balcony or patio with lake views. **Pros:** lots of activities as well as tranquil spaces; private beach; lake and mountain views; low off-season rates. **Cons:** very busy high season. [$] *Rooms from: $300* ✉ *104 W. Woodin Ave.* ☎ *509/682–2561, 800/553–8225* 🌐 *www.campbellsresort.com* 🛏 *170 rooms* 🍴 *No meals.*

$$$$ RENTAL FAMILY 🏨 **The Lake House at Chelan.** Just across the street from lakeshore Don Morse Park you'll find these sophisticated and impeccable condominium-style rental units with one or three bedrooms and full modern kitchens, fireplaces, and decks or patios. **Pros:** modern and immaculate; family-friendly; year-round pool; reasonable shoulder and off-season rates; secured underground parking. **Cons:** some traffic noise from State Route 150, which fronts the property; no restaurant or bar on-site. [$] *Rooms from: $299* ✉ *402 W. Manson Hwy.* ☎ *509/293–5982, 800/347–8182* 🌐 *www.lakehousechelan.com* 🛏 *40 condominiums* 🍴 *No meals.*

$$$ HOTEL Fodor's Choice ★ 🏨 **Lake View Hotel.** Overlooking a riverfront park in the heart of Chelan's historic downtown, this boutique hotel has deluxe rooms done in warm, earthen tones accented by high ceilings, wrought-iron balconies, skylights, and lake and river views. **Pros:** sophisticated feel; prime location; well-kept rooms. **Cons:** not suitable for families; no on-site parking; harsh cancellation fee. [$] *Rooms from: $225* ✉ *104 E. Woodin Ave.* ☎ *509/682–1334* 🌐 *chelanhotel.com* 🛏 *13 rooms* 🍴 *No meals.*

WENATCHEE

39 miles southwest of Chelan.

Wenatchee (we- *nat*-chee), the county seat of Chelan County, is an attractive city in a shallow valley at the confluence of the Wenatchee and Columbia Rivers. Surrounded by orchards, Wenatchee is known as the "Apple Capital of Washington." Downtown has many old commercial buildings as well as apple-packing houses where visitors can buy locally grown apples by the case (at about half the price charged in supermarkets). The paved Apple Valley Recreation Loop Trail runs on both sides of the Columbia River. It crosses the river on bridges at the northern and southern ends of town and connects several riverfront parks. The Wenatchee section is lighted until midnight.

The town was built on an ancient Wenatchi tribal village, which may have been occupied as long as 11,000 years ago, as archaeological finds of Clovis hunter artifacts suggest. (The Clovis hunters, also known as Paleo-Indians, were members of the oldest tribes known to have inhabited North America.)

GETTING HERE AND AROUND

Horizon Air serves Wenatchee's Pangborn Memorial Airport. Amtrak's Empire Builder, which runs from Chicago to Seattle, stops in Wenatchee; Greyhound Bus Lines serves the town, too. From Seattle it's about a 2½-hour drive to Wenatchee via Highway 2 or Interstate 90 and Highway 97; from Spokane it takes about three hours via Highway 2 or Interstate 90.

ESSENTIALS

Visitor Information Wenatchee Chamber of Commerce and Visitor Center. ⊠ *1 S. Wentachee Ave.* ☎ *509/662–2116, 800/572–7753* ⊕ *wenatchee.org.*

EXPLORING

Aplets and Cotlets/Liberty Orchards Co., Inc. Surrounded by snowcapped mountain peaks 11 miles northwest of Wenatchee, Cashmere is one of Washington's oldest towns, founded by Oblate missionaries back in 1863, when the Wenatchi and their vast herds of horses still roamed free over the bunch grasslands of the region. Today Cashmere is the apple, apricot, and pear capital of the Wenatchee Valley. Aplets and Cotlets/Liberty Orchards Co., Inc. was founded by two Armenian brothers who escaped the massacres of Armenians by Turks early in the 20th century. When a marketing crisis hit the orchards in the 1920s, the brothers remembered dried-fruit confections from their homeland, re-created them, and named them aplets (made from apples) and cotlets (made from apricots). Free samples are offered during the 15-minute tour of the plant. If production isn't taking place, be sure to watch the video in the candy shop, which displays memorabilia and usually has specially priced confections. ⊠ *117 Mission Ave., Cashmere* ☎ *509/782–2191* ⊕ *www.libertyorchards.com* ☜ *Free* ۞ *Closed weekends Jan.–Mar.*

OFF THE BEATEN PATH

Ohme Gardens. At this lush green oasis, high atop bluffs near the confluence of the Columbia and Wenatchee Rivers, visitors can commune with a blend of native rocks, ferns, mosses, pools, waterfalls, rock gardens, and conifers. Herman Ohme purchased the land in 1929 as a private family retreat and developed the gardens—now owned and managed by Chelan County—for his wife, Ruth. The couple nurtured the gardens until Herman died in 1971. ⊠ *3327 Ohme Rd.* ✛ *North of Wenatchee near U.S. 2 at U.S. 97A* ☎ *509/662–5785* ⊕ *www.ohmegardens.com* ☜ *$8* ۞ *Closed mid-Oct.–mid-May.*

Okanogan-Wenatchee National Forest. More than 4 million acres of pines extend from the eastern slopes of the Cascades to the crest of the Wenatchee Mountains and north to Lake Chelan. Camping, hiking, boating, fishing, hunting, and picnicking are popular activities. ⊠ *215 Melody La.* ☎ *509/664–9200* ⊕ *www.fs.usda.gov/okawen* ☜ *$5 daily parking pass, or $30 Northwest Forest Pass.*

Rocky Reach Dam. There's a museum and visitor center here, as well as picnic tables and landscaped grounds. The Gallery of the Columbia has the pilothouse of the late-19th-century Columbia River steamer *Bridgeport,* Native American tools and replica dwellings, and loggers' and railroad workers' tools. The Gallery of Electricity has exhibits making a case for why dams are good for us. ⊠ *U.S. 97A N* ✛ *About 10 miles north of Wenatchee* ☎ *509/663–7522* ⊕ *www.chelanpud.org/visitor-center.html* ☜ *Free* ۞ *Visitor center closed Dec.–Mar.*

Wenatchee Valley Museum & Cultural Center. Displays include local Native American and pioneer artifacts, the story of the Washington apple industry, and the 1931 landing of the first-ever flight across the Pacific. Children enjoy the hands-on area and the model railway. There are also Northwest artist exhibits. ✉ *127 S. Mission St.* ☎ *509/888–6240* ⊕ *www.wvmcc.org* ✉ *$5; free 1st Fri. of month* ⊗ *Closed Sun. and Mon.*

WHERE TO EAT

$ ✕ **Anjou Bakery.** Located on the edge of a pear orchard 11 miles outside
BAKERY Wenatchee, this easily accessible bakeshop boasts an industrial–vintage–
Fodor's Choice farmhouse feel and the best breads and pastries in the region—from
★ bread pudding and almond meringue cookies to lemon cheesecake, muffins, and a rustic apricot or pear Danish. Enjoy an espresso or European-style sandwich (baguette, butter, cured meats, cheeses) at a picnic table indoors or on the sunny patio anchored by a modern, concrete water feature and lots of lavender. **Known for:** decadent pastry; excellent bread. ⓈⓈ *Average main: $6* ✉ *3898 Old Monitor Rd., Cashmere* ☎ *509/782–4360* ⊗ *Closed Mon.–Wed.*

$ ✕ **Badger Mountain Brewing.** A large window lets guests sneak a peek at
PIZZA the brewing operation while quenching their thirst with some two dozen taps and enjoying pizza, chicken wings, and other pub grub. **Known for:** chicken wings (6- and 12-packs); house-made root beer; eight signature ales. Ⓢ *Average main: $10* ✉ *1 Orondo Ave.* ☎ *509/888–2234* ⊕ *www.badgermountainbrewing.com* ⊗ *Closed Sun. and Mon.*

$ ✕ **Bob's Classic Restaurant and Distillery.** A classic hot-pink car on a pedes-
BURGER tal in the parking lot beckons diners to this longtime burger joint, where
FAMILY another car is positioned to look as though it's coming through the roof. This casual, sometimes noisy eatery serves up a variety of burgers with fries and onion rings, plus prime rib, teriyaki skewers, overstuffed sandwiches, and wraps, salads, and pasta dishes. **Known for:** American pub fare; classic automobile-inspired decor. Ⓢ *Average main: $10* ✉ *110 2nd St.* ☎ *509/663–3954* ⊕ *www.bobsclassicrestaurant.com.*

$$ ✕ **Garlini's Napoletana.** This casually elegant and romantic longtime
ITALIAN Italian eatery is known for its pastas and wood-fired pizzas. Start with steamed clams, bruschetta, or tomato-Gorgonzola bisque before a main course such as cannelloni, lasagna, chicken Milanese, and other standards. **Known for:** wood-fired pizza; classic Italian pasta dishes. Ⓢ *Average main: $18* ✉ *212 5th St.* ☎ *509/884–1707* ⊕ *garlinisrestaurant.com.*

$ ✕ **McGlinn's Public House.** This popular public house, with its exposed-
AMERICAN brick walls and high, wood-beam ceilings, goes beyond traditional pub fare (that's available, too) with an ample variety of starters, specialty salads, pastas, and entrées like wild Alaskan salmon and steak. Wash it all down with one of the craft beers on tap. **Known for:** upscale pub fare; craft beer. Ⓢ *Average main: $15* ✉ *111 Orondo Ave.* ☎ *509/663–9073* ⊕ *www.mcglinns.com.*

$ ✕ **Riverside Pub at Columbia Valley Brewing Company.** Burgers are the food
AMERICAN of choice at this pub across the road from the Columbia River. Stuffed with spinach, mushrooms, and caramelized onions (Popeye's Favorite), or turkey, dried cranberries, and cream cheese (the Bird Brain), or

15

topped with bacon and cheddar, they're accompanied by dozens of beers on tap. **Known for:** creative burgers; dozens of tap beers. $ *Average main: $10* ⊠ *538 Riverside Dr.* ☎ *509/888–9993.*

$ **✕ Saddle Rock Pub and Brewery.** Pizzas are the specialty at this brewpub,
AMERICAN   where you can choose from a variety of toppings or order the "You're the Brewer" and create your own. Choose from 12 rotating taps and an array of pub grub (sandwiches, wraps, and appetizers such as meatballs, breadsticks, and nachos). **Known for:** specialty pizza; craft brews. $ *Average main: $12* ⊠ *25 N. Wenatchee St.* ☎ *509/888–4790* ⊕ *www. saddlerockbrewery.com* ☾ *Closed Sun.*

$$$ **✕ Shakti's.** The small, two-level restaurant and bar has twinkling white
ECLECTIC   lights that create a romantic ambience, and an eclectic menu that offers several pasta dishes as well as steak and seafood. A charming garden is open during the warmer months for patio dining. **Known for:** elegant Italian-inspired dinner fare; romantic setting. $ *Average main: $26* ⊠ *218 N. Mission St.* ☎ *509/662–3321* ⊕ *www.shaktisfinedining.com* ☾ *Closed Sun. No lunch.*

$ **✕ Spring Lotus.** This small, casual, and popular Vietnamese, Chinese, and
ASIAN   Thai restaurant, located in a strip mall, is known for its friendly service and delicious food. Specialties include pad thai and several chicken dishes, including crispy garlic chicken, orange chicken, and chicken pho. **Known for:** pho; curry dishes; noodle dishes. $ *Average main: $12* ⊠ *1050 Springwater St.* ☎ *509/662–8898.*

$$$$ **✕ The Windmill.** The comfortable old roadhouse, topped by a wind-
AMERICAN   mill and built in 1931, is all about home-style food, particularly steak; famous entrées include whiskey pepper steak (pepper-coated New York strip sautéed, flamed with whiskey, and finished with mushrooms in a rich demi-glace), slow-roasted prime rib, and marinated tenderloin chunks, flamed with cognac. Seafood isn't to be overlooked, either; try the salmon with herbed butter and white wine, jumbo tempura prawns, or prawn sauté. **Known for:** steak; seafood; weekend brunch; house-made pies. $ *Average main: $35* ⊠ *1501 N. Wenatchee Ave.* ☎ *509/665–9529* ⊕ *www.thewindmillrestaurant.com* ☾ *No lunch.*

WHERE TO STAY

$ **⚏ Coast Wenatchee Center Hotel.** A skywalk links these tidy and comfort-
HOTEL   able rooms to a convention center, a bonus for travelers on business, but there are enough facilities and amenities, including indoor and outdoor pools, to appeal to vacationing families, too. **Pros:** convenient access to local sights and activities; suites have kitchenettes. **Cons:** standard hotel atmosphere. $ *Rooms from: $139* ⊠ *201 N. Wenatchee Ave.* ☎ *509/662–1234, 800/716–6199* ⊕ *www.wenatcheecenter.com* ⌦ *147 rooms* ⍾◎ *Breakfast.*

$$ **⚏ Warm Springs Inn & Winery.** This 1917 mansion, set amid 10 acres of
B&B/INN   gardens, offers elegant, well-appointed rooms filled with art and antiques. **Pros:** charming, quiet setting; wine tasting; lots of fun and romantic additions available to customize stay. **Cons:** wedding bookings fill rooms far in advance; no children under 12; strict cancellation policy. $ *Rooms from: $180* ⊠ *1611 Love La.* ☎ *509/662–5863* ⊕ *www.warmspringsinn. com* ⌦ *6 rooms* ◎ *Breakfast* ⌐ *Add a picnic for two, champagne, prosecco and chocolates, mimosas and more for an additional cost.*

SHOPPING

FodorsChoice **Pybus Public Market.** Located in a renovated warehouse along the
★ Columbia River, this market offers specialty food products, fresh produce from nearby farms, artisanal cheeses, seafood, coffee, gelato,
and charcuterie, as well as a few restaurants and gift shops. It's been
likened to an eastern Washington version of the much larger and older
Pike Place Market in Seattle. ✉ *7 N. Worthen Ave.* ☎ *509/888–3900*
⊕ *www.pybuspublicmarket.org.*

SPORTS AND THE OUTDOORS

SKIING

Mission Ridge Ski Area. Four lifts, 33 downhill runs, powder snow, and
some 30 miles of marked cross-country trails make Mission Ridge one
of Washington's most popular ski areas. There's a 2,100-foot vertical
drop, and the snowmaker scatters whiteness from the top to bottom
slopes during the season. Snowboarding is allowed. Lift tickets cost $63
per day. ✉ *7500 Mission Ridge Rd.* ☎ *509/663–6543, 800/374–1693
snow conditions* ⊕ *www.missionridge.com.*

15

LEAVENWORTH

23 miles northwest of Wenatchee, 118 miles northeast of Seattle.

Leavenworth is a favorite weekend getaway for Seattle folks, and it's
easy to see why: the charming (if occasionally *too* cute) Bavarian-style
village, home to good restaurants and attractive lodgings, is a hub for
some of the Northwest's best skiing, hiking, rock climbing, rafting,
canoeing, and snowshoeing.

A railroad and mining center for many years, Leavenworth fell on
hard times around the 1960s, and civic leaders, looking for ways to
capitalize on the town's setting in the heart of the Central Cascade
Range, convinced shopkeepers and other businesspeople to maintain a
gingerbread-Bavarian architectural style in their buildings. Today, even
the Safeway supermarket and the Chevron gas station adhere to the
theme. Restaurants prepare Bavarian-influenced dishes, candy shops
sell Swiss-style chocolates, and stores and boutiques stock music boxes,
dollhouses, and other Bavarian items.

GETTING HERE AND AROUND

From Seattle, Leavenworth can be reached by either of Washington's
most developed mountain passes—Stevens (Highway 2) or Snoqualmie
(Interstate 90, then a short jog up Highway 97/Blewett Pass); either
takes about 2½ hours. From Spokane, traveling west via Highway 2
takes about 3½ hours. Amtrak's Empire Builder makes daily trips from
Spokane and Seattle to Leavenworth, and Greyhound Bus Lines also
serves the town.

ESSENTIALS

Visitor Information Leavenworth Chamber of Commerce. ✉ *940 Hwy. 2,
Suite B* ☎ *509/548–5807* ⊕ *leavenworth.org.*

EXPLORING

Leavenworth Upper Valley Museum. Located on the banks of the Wenatchee River, the century-old River Haus, once the home of the town banker, now evokes pioneer days in the Cascades. Exhibits highlight the lives and times of the Field family, as well as local Native American tribes and other prominent residents of Leavenworth and the Upper Wenatchee Valley. The riverside grounds, where Arabian stallions were once put to graze, now host Audubon programs that take advantage of plentiful bird sightings. ⊠ *347 Division St.* ☎ *509/548–0728* ⊕ *www.uppervalleymuseum.org* ⊠ *$3* ☉ *Closed Mon.–Wed.*

Nutcracker Museum and Shop. Nearly 6,000 modern and antique nutcrackers—some of them centuries old—are displayed in the upstairs museum and sold downstairs in a popular shop that stocks nutcrackers of all sizes and in the likeness of all kinds of characters. ⊠ *735 Front St.* ☎ *509/548–4573, 800/892–3989* ⊕ *www.nutcrackermuseum.com and www.nussknackerhaus.com* ⊠ *$5.*

FAMILY **Red Tail Canyon Farm.** Arrange for group hay rides aboard a horse-drawn wagon through a peaceful valley and tree farm from April through October (10-person minimum, $150, reservations required). The experience can include a barbecue cookout, too. In winter, sleigh rides are offered through the woods, and you can warm up with hot cocoa by a campfire afterward ($20 per person). ⊠ *11780 Freund Canyon Rd.* ☎ *509/548–4512, 800/678–4512* ⊕ *www.redtailcanyon-farmleavenworth.com.*

FAMILY **Waterfront Park.** Hiking trails and bird-watching abound at this pretty city park, located along the banks of the Wenatchee River just steps from downtown shops and restaurants. ⊠ *Commercial St.* ✦ *From corner of 8th and Commercial Sts., follow Commercial St. downhill to find trail* ⊕ *cityofleavenworth.com.*

WHERE TO EAT

$$ ✕ **Andreas Keller Restaurant.** Merry "oompah" music bubbles out from
GERMAN marching accordion players at this fun-focused dining hub, where the theme is "Germany without the Passport." Laughing crowds lap up strong, cold brews and feast on a selection of wursts—bratwurst, knackwurst, weisswurst, and mettwurst—Polish sausage, Wiener schnitzel, and schnitzel cordon bleu, all nestled into heaping sides of sauerkraut, tangy German potato salad, and thick, dark rye bread. Get a taste of it all with the sampler plate—and save room for the knockout apple strudel. **Known for:** old-world ambience; German sausage. $ *Average main: $19* ⊠ *829 Front St.* ☎ *509/548–6000* ⊕ *www.andreaskellerrestaurant.com.*

$$ ✕ **Bären Haus.** The cuisine at this spacious, noisy, and often crowded
GERMAN beer hall–style room may not be haute, but the generous servings will
FAMILY appeal to hungry travelers. Fill up on basic American and German fare in the large dining room, located in a historic corner building with a high ceiling and exposed brick walls. **Known for:** German fare; beer hall–style dining. $ *Average main: $17* ⊠ *208 9th St.* ☎ *509/548–4535* ⊕ *www.barenhaus.com.*

Holiday season in Leavenworth

$ MODERN MEXICAN 🍴 **Carlos 1800 Mexican Grill and Cantina.** At this light, bright, and casual spot the usual fare includes tacos, enchiladas, burritos, and fajitas, as well as entrées with a Yucatecan influence, such as green mole and *pipian* sauce (made from pumpkin and sesame seeds, peanuts, and chili peppers). The specialty is *conchinita pibil,* or pork marinated in achiote paste and sour-orange juice, then cooked in a banana leaf, but prawn dishes and fish tacos are also popular. **Known for:** authentic Mexican cuisine; marinated pork. [$] *Average main: $14* ✉ *633 Front St.* ☎ *509/888–0265* 🕒 *Closed Mon.–Wed.*

$ GERMAN 🍴 **Gustav's Grill and Beer Garden.** Traditional Bavarian pub food meets Pacific Northwest cuisine at this Leavenworth landmark, topped with a distinctive onion dome and anchored by a large river-rock fireplace. Munch on German sausage, an array of gourmet burgers, sandwiches, and salads. **Known for:** one of the best decks in town; friendly atmosphere. [$] *Average main: $10* ✉ *617 Hwy. 2* ☎ *509/548–4509* 🌐 *gustavsleavenworth.com.*

$ AMERICAN 🍴 **Icicle Brewing Company.** Enjoy a cold Bootjack IPA, Dirtyface Amber, or Priebe Porter at a picnic table in the lively beer garden overlooking the town's main drag. Inside, check out stainless-steel fermentation tanks or play a board game while you quench your thirst. **Known for:** craft beer; convivial beer garden. [$] *Average main: $10* ✉ *935 Front St.* ☎ *509/548–2739* 🌐 *www.iciclebrewing.com.*

$ AMERICAN 🍴 **The Loft.** The decor is nothing special, but this small, casual, second-floor lounge stands out because it's one of the few downtown spots open nightly past 11. There are 19 beers on tap, specialty cocktails, and plenty of pub grub. **Known for:** late-night libations; live music. [$] *Average main: $10* ✉ *815 Front St.* ☎ *509/888–0231.*

$$ ✕ **Mozart's Restaurant.** This intimate upstairs eatery specializing in Euro-
ECLECTIC pean and Pacific Northwest cuisine resembles an old-world town house,
Fodor's Choice capturing the essence of gemütlichkeit (coziness) in the way the small
★ dining rooms are decorated and the drapes are cut. Start, perhaps, with
cold-smoked Norwegian salmon on a potato pancake, followed by a
"symphony of schnitzels" (veal or pork topped with a choice of sauces)
or rainbow trout fillet with toasted almond butter. **Known for:** intimate
setting; elegant cuisine. $ *Average main: $22* ✉ *829 Front St., upstairs*
☎ *509/548–0600* ⊕ *www.mozartsrestaurant.com* ☾ *No lunch weekdays.*

$ ✕ **Munchen Haus.** Bratwurst, beef franks, and brews abound at this
GERMAN outdoor Bavarian grill and beer garden, tucked into a cozy corner in
FAMILY downtown and perfect for travelers on a tight budget. The atmosphere
is laid-back, friendly, and welcoming to families. **Known for:** budget-
friendly German fare; outdoor picnic-table dining. $ *Average main: $6*
✉ *709 Front St.* ☎ *509/548–1158* ⊕ *www.munchenhaus.com.*

$$ ✕ **Pavz Cafe Bistro.** This cozy, long, narrow room has only eight tables
ECLECTIC and serves up an eclectic mix of Pacific Northwest and European fare—
Fodor's Choice from seafood, steak, and pasta to soups, salads, and sandwiches. But
★ the signature dishes here are the savory and sweet crepes: portobello
mushroom topped with blue cheese, cream sauce, and walnuts, and
spicy Italian with sausage, roasted red peppers, basil, ricotta, and four
cheeses—it's thick and baked, resembling lasagna—as well as hazel
nougat, mango, strawberry and more. **Known for:** sweet and savory
crepes; elegant Pacific Northwest cuisine; cozy ambience. $ *Average
main: $19* ✉ *833 Front St.* ☎ *509/548–2103* ⊕ *pavzcafe.com.*

$$ ✕ **South.** An innovative menu of modern, Latin-inspired dishes provides
LATIN AMERICAN a nice—and spicy—change from all the Bavarian food in town. Enjoy
sweet-potato-and-roasted-poblano-chili enchiladas, Yucatán chicken
rojo (marinated in achiote and citrus), and Oaxacan black mole with
chicken or pork, and be sure to take a trip to the salsa bar. **Known
for:** elevated Latin cuisine; craft cocktails. $ *Average main: $18* ✉ *913
Front St.* ☎ *509/888–4328* ⊕ *www.southrestaurants.com.*

$$$ ✕ **Visconti's.** This castlelike establishment provides fine Italian dining
ITALIAN paired with one of the region's most extensive wine lists. Whet your
Fodor's Choice appetite with an antipasti platter of cheeses and house-made salamis
★ and sausages, then move on to such pastas as clam linguine or bone-in
rib-eye steak and wild Alaskan sockeye salmon. **Known for:** house-
cured meats; house-made gelato; elegant Italian cuisine; extensive wine
list. $ *Average main: $25* ✉ *636 Front St.* ☎ *509/548–1213* ⊕ *www.
viscontis.com.*

WHERE TO STAY

$$$ ⛺ **Abendblume Pension.** Wonderful views of the mountains and Leav-
B&B/INN enworth Valley are afforded from each room's private balcony, and
the many fireplaces and carved-wood walls and ceilings of this Bavar-
ian-style country chalet give it an authentic alpine feel. **Pros:** very
romantic; Bavarian breakfast is authentic and ample; exceptional hos-
pitality. **Cons:** fills up quickly during festivals; strict cancellation policy.
$ *Rooms from: $249* ✉ *12570 Ranger Rd.* ✛ *¾ mile from downtown*
☎ *509/548–4059, 800/669–7634* ⊕ *www.abendblume.com* ⤵ *7 rooms*
⦿*Breakfast.*

$$ HOTEL

🏨 **Bavarian Lodge.** The well-appointed rooms of this warm, inviting, and highly rated hotel come with modern, lodge-style furnishings and an ample complimentary breakfast of waffles, biscuits and gravy, ham and potatoes, and more. **Pros:** across the street from downtown shopping and restaurants; year-round pool and two hot tubs; on-site dining and live music at Woodsman Pub. **Cons:** located on what can be a busy thoroughfare through town. [$] *Rooms from: $179* ✉ *810 Hwy. 2* ☎ *888/717–7878* 🌐 *www.bavarianlodge.com* 🛏 *54 rooms* 🍴 *Breakfast.*

$ HOTEL FAMILY

🏨 **Enzian Inn.** Accommodations are fairly standard, but the hotel has a distinctive alpine feeling, complete with an alphorn performance each morning at breakfast, and extensive facilities including indoor and outdoor pools and hot tubs and a spa. **Pros:** very close to downtown shopping and restaurants; plenty of amenities. **Cons:** only frequent guests can book rooms for the annual Christmas Lighting Festival; extra charge for children six and older. [$] *Rooms from: $130* ✉ *590 Hwy. 2* ☎ *509/548–5269, 800/223–8511* 🌐 *www.enzianinn.com* 🛏 *104 rooms* 🍴 *Breakfast.*

15

$$ RESORT FAMILY

🏨 **Icicle Village Resort.** This nearly 7-acre, easily accessible resort has an array of amenities, including two outdoor pools, and attractive rooms and suites decorated with modern, mountain-chic flair. **Pros:** lots of on-site activities; very kid-friendly; full, hot breakfast buffet included, even for condominium guests; some rooms are dog-friendly; bicycles available to borrow. **Cons:** no room service (the restaurant offers takeout); nearly a mile walk along the highway to downtown shops and restaurants. [$] *Rooms from: $199* ✉ *505 Hwy. 2* ☎ *800/961–0162, 509/888–2776* 🌐 *www.iciclevillage.com* 🛏 *121 rooms, 27 condominiums* 🍴 *Breakfast.*

$$ HOTEL FAMILY

🏨 **Linderhof Inn.** One of the best-value lodgings in town offers rooms that are basic yet modern and comfortable, with all of the usual amenities and a bit of chintz added for character. **Pros:** seasonal pool; across the street from town and shopping; rooms all have microwaves; family-friendly. **Cons:** prices increase during Christmas, Oktoberfest, and festivals. [$] *Rooms from: $155* ✉ *690 U.S. 2* ☎ *509/548–5283, 800/828–5680* 🌐 *www.linderhof.com* 🛏 *34 rooms* 🍴 *Breakfast* ☞ *Many holiday and summer weekends require a 2-night stay.*

$$$$ B&B/INN

🏨 **Mountain Home Lodge.** This contemporary mountain inn, where peeled-pine and vine-maple furniture fills the rooms, is built of sturdy cedar and redwood and sits on a 20-acre alpine meadow with breathtaking Cascade Mountains views. **Pros:** pristine luxury; high-quality sports and activities; thoughtful extras like binoculars and wine. **Cons:** tough winter transportation; some rooms on the small side. [$] *Rooms from: $390* ✉ *8201 Mountain Home Rd.* ✥ *3 miles south of Leavenworth* ☎ *509/548–7077, 800/414–2378* 🌐 *www.mthome.com* 🛏 *10 rooms, 2 cabins* 🍴 *Breakfast; All meals.*

$$ B&B/INN Fodor's Choice ★

🏨 **Pension Anna.** These rooms in the heart of town are decorated with sturdy imported alpine furniture, fresh flowers, and cozy comforters. **Pros:** hearty breakfast; very European feel; nice location. **Cons:** no elevator; some guests have complained about noisy plumbing. [$] *Rooms from: $169* ✉ *926 Commercial St.* ☎ *509/548–6273, 800/509–2662* 🌐 *www.pensionanna.com* 🛏 *17 rooms* 🍴 *Breakfast.*

$$$ B&B/INN

🏨 **Run of the River.** This intimate, relaxed mountain inn stands on the banks of the Icicle River near Leavenworth, placing the rustic rooms, with timber furnishings, private outside entrances, and decks, close to nature. **Pros:** close to nature; generous, hearty breakfasts; lots of outdoor activities. **Cons:** a bit off the beaten path. [$] *Rooms from: $249* ✉ *9308 E. Leavenworth Rd.* ☎ *509/548–7171, 800/288–6491* 🌐 *www.runoftheriver.com* 🛏 *6 rooms, 1 lodge* 🍴 *Breakfast.*

$$$$ RESORT Fodor's Choice ★

🏨 **Sleeping Lady Mountain Resort.** Fall asleep on a hand-hewn log bed under a down comforter along the banks of Icicle Creek at this quiet and scenic retreat in the heart of the Cascade Mountains, where lodge-like rooms are light and airy, with lots of wood accents. **Pros:** plenty of activities as well as peace and quiet; spectacular setting and scenery; spa, fitness room, seasonal pool, and hot tub. **Cons:** 10-minute drive to downtown; no TVs (which may be a plus). [$] *Rooms from: $300* ✉ *7375 Icicle Rd.* ☎ *509/548–6344* 🌐 *www.sleepinglady.com* 🛏 *58 rooms* 🍴 *Some meals.*

SHOPPING

The Cheesemonger's Shop. Pick up a snack or the makings of a picnic at this lively basement-level cheese shop, where applewood-smoked cheddar is the number one seller, and you'll be offered a sample as soon as one of the mongers makes eye contact. ✉ *819 Front St.* ☎ *509/548–9011, 877/888–7389* 🌐 *www.cheesemongersshop.com.*

Danish Bakery. The sweet buttery scent wafting from this long and narrow shop lures customers for the almond kringle, Bavarian waffles, and custard-filled pastries. ✉ *731 Front St.* ☎ *509/548–7514.*

Homefires Bakery. Tucked inside a back corner of Dan's Food Market, which is easily accessible off the highway and offers ample parking, this homey little bakery turns out delicious breads, muffins, cookies, cakes, and pastries. Take a cinnamon roll or berry pie—and espresso—to go. You can satisfy your sweet tooth here daily from 6 am to 10 pm. ✉ *1329 U.S. 2* ☎ *509/548–7362* 🌐 *homefiresbakery.com.*

The Oil and Vinegar Cellar. In this basement-level specialty shop sample gourmet salts; aged balsamic vinegars in flavors like fig, honey ginger, pecan praline, and garlic cilantro; and infused olive oils such as basil, blood orange, garlic mushroom, and rosemary. ✉ *633 Front St.* ☎ *509/470–7684* 🌐 *www.oilandvinegarcellar.com.*

Schocolat. Tucked in the back of the high-end home-decor and gourmet-kitchen store **Ganz Klasse,** which offers handcrafted wooden cutting boards, table linens, and porcelain pieces, **Schocolat** sells fine handcrafted chocolates in flavors like Raspberry Crown, with raspberry puree and Chambord; Earl Grey, with double bergamot tea; and Golden Cinnamon, with milk chocolate ganache, gold flecks, and Goldschläger Swiss cinnamon schnapps. ✉ *834 Front St.* ☎ *509/548–7274* 🌐 *www.schocolat.com.*

SPORTS AND THE OUTDOORS
HIKING

The Leavenworth Ranger District has more than 320 miles of scenic trails, among them Hatchery Creek, Icicle Ridge, the Enchantments, Tumwater Canyon, Fourth of July Creek, Snow Lake, Stuart Lake, and Chatter Creek. Both of the following sell the Northwest Forest Pass ($5 day pass; $30 annual pass), which is required year-round for parking at trailheads and for camping in the upper Chiwawa Valley.

Lake Wenatchee Ranger Station. Updates on trails and fire closures are available here spring through fall. ✉ *22976 Hwy. 207 ✛ 9 miles north of the Coles Corner junction with Hwy. 2* ☎ *509/763–3103* ⊕ *www.leavenworth.com/Activities_hiking.htm.*

Leavenworth Ranger District. Contact this district office for information on area hikes. ✉ *600 Sherburne St.* ☎ *509/548–2550* ⊕ *www.fs.usda.gov.*

HORSEBACK RIDING
Eagle Creek Ranch. Take 2-, 3- or 5-mile horse rides ($25 to $45) at this ranch. Seasonal sleigh rides are also available ($16–$35). ✉ *7951 Eagle Creek Rd. ✛ 8 miles northwest of Leavenworth* ☎ *509/548–7798* ⊕ *www.eaglecreek.ws.*

Icicle Outfitters & Guides. You can enjoy 2- to 4-mile trail rides ($30–$60 per person), daylong rides with lunch ($185), and even two- to seven-day custom deluxe pack trips (starting at $200 per person per day). In winter, there are sleigh rides ($18.50). ✉ *7373 Icicle Creek Rd.* ☎ *800/497–3912, 509/669–1518* ⊕ *www.icicleoutfitters.com.*

Mountain Springs Lodge. Horseback rides from 50 minutes to all day long ($27–$135) are offered here, as well as daytime sleigh rides ($25), moonlight dinner sleigh rides ($75), breakfast sleigh rides ($40), and snowmobile tours lasting one to five hours ($70–$250), including a moonlight dinner ride ($189). In summer, there's ziplining ($75 for two hours and five lines, $95 for three hours and nine lines). ✉ *19115 Chiwawa Loop Rd.* ☎ *509/763–2713, 800/858–2276* ⊕ *www.mtsprings.com.*

SKIING
More than 20 miles of cross-country ski trails lace the Leavenworth area. Skiers and snowboarders from the Seattle area often make the drive over the mountains for the downhill runs at Stevens Pass.

Leavenworth Ski Hill. In winter enjoy a Nordic ski jump, snowboarding, tubing, and really great downhill and cross-country skiing here. In summer, come for the wildflowers or to catch the Leavenworth Summer Theatre's production of *The Sound of Music*. The ski hill is 1 mile north of downtown Leavenworth. The Play All Day Pass is $32; there's also a Nordic Day Pass ($18), an Alpine Day Pass ($18), a Snowshoe Pass ($10), and a Tubing Pass ($20). ✉ *Ski Hill Dr.* ☎ *509/548–5477* ⊕ *www.skileavenworth.com.*

Loup Loup Ski Bowl. Lift tickets at this small ski area, where you can downhill or telemark ski, cost $48 on weekends or holidays, and $42 on weekdays. ✉ *Off Hwy. 20, Twisp ✛ 20 miles east of town* ☎ *509/557–3401 office, 509/557–3405 conditions* ⊕ *www.skitheloup.com.*

15

Stevens Pass. There's snowboarding and cross-country skiing here as well as 37 major downhill runs and slopes for skiers of every level. Lift tickets cost $67 ($74 during peak weekends). Summer weekends, it's open for biking. ⊠ *U.S. 2, Summit Stevens Pass, Skykomish ✢ 51 miles west of Leavenworth* ☎ *206/812–4510* ⊕ *www.stevenspass.com.*

WHITE-WATER RAFTING

Rafting is popular from March to July; the prime high-country runoff occurs in May and June. The Wenatchee River, which runs through Leavenworth, is considered one of the best white-water rivers in the state—a Class III on the International Canoeing Association scale.

Alpine Adventures. Challenging white-water and relaxing river floats through spectacular scenery are the options here. A Wenatchee River white-water trip with lunch costs $84; a scenic Wenatchee River float (lunch included) is $79. The Methow River drift is $89. An Icicle River run (no lunch) is $49 and fills up fast. ⊠ *Leavenworth* ☎ *800/723–8386, 509/470–7762* ⊕ *www.alpineadventures.com.*

Blue Sky Outfitters. Half- and full-day rafting trips on the Methow and Wenatchee Rivers are offered by this outfitter. They also have snowshoe tours, wine tours, and combination snowshoe-and-wine (or beer) tours in Leavenworth, as well as white-water-and-wine (or beer) tours in Wenatchee. Private rafting trips are available, too. ⊠ *Cashmere Riverside Park, Riverside Dr., Cashmere* ☎ *206/938–4030, 800/228–7238* ⊕ *www.blueskyoutfitters.com.*

Leavenworth Outdoor Center. Rent tubes, rafts, kayaks, paddleboards, and bicycles at this shop, which provides a shuttle to the launch point along the Wenatchee River, and even outfits your pet pooch with a life jacket for a float downstream. ⊠ *321 9th St.* ☎ *509/548–8823* ⊕ *www. leavenworthoutdoorcenter.com.*

Osprey Rafting Co. This outfitter offers 4½-hour trips on the Wenatchee River for $78.56, which includes wet suits and booties, transportation, and a barbecue lunch; there's a two-hour "happy hour" trip ($55.46) for travelers short on time. ⊠ *9342 Icicle Rd.* ☎ *509/548–6800, 800/743–6269, 509/264–1088 Paddleshack* ⊕ *www.ospreyrafting.com.*

MOUNT RAINIER
NATIONAL PARK

WELCOME TO MOUNT RAINIER NATIONAL PARK

TOP REASONS TO GO

★ **The mountain:** Some say Mt. Rainier is the most magical mountain in America. At 14,411 feet, it is a popular peak for climbing, with more than 10,000 attempts per year—nearly half of which are successful.

★ **The glaciers:** About 35 square miles of glaciers and snowfields encircle Mt. Rainier, including Carbon Glacier and Emmons Glacier, the largest glaciers by volume and area, respectively, in the continental United States.

★ **The wildflowers:** More than 100 species of wildflowers bloom in the park's high meadows; the display dazzles from midsummer until the snow flies.

★ **Fabulous hiking:** More than 240 miles of maintained trails provide access to old-growth forest, river valleys, lakes, and rugged ridges.

★ **Unencumbered wilderness:** Under the provisions of the 1964 Wilderness Act and the National Wilderness Preservation System, 97% of the park is preserved as wilderness.

1 Longmire. Inside the Nisqually Gate explore Longmire historic district's museum and visitor center, ruins of the park's first hotel, or the nature loop. Nearby, delicate footbridges span the thundering Christine and Narada falls.

2 Paradise. The park's most popular destination is famous for wildflowers in summer and skiing in winter. Skyline Trail is one of many hiking routes that crisscross the base of the mountain; the larger of the two park lodges is also here.

3 **Ohanapecosh.** Closest to the southeast entrance and the town of Packwood, the giant old-growth trees of the Grove of the Patriarchs are a must-see. Another short trail around nearby Tipsoo Lake has great views.

4 **Sunrise and White River.** This side of the park is easy to visit in summer if you enter from the east side, but it's a long drive from the southwest entrance. Sunrise is the highest stretch of road in the park and a great place to take in the alpenglow—reddish light on the peak of the mountain near sunrise and sunset. Mt. Rainier's premier mountain-biking area, White River, is also the gateway to more than a dozen hiking trails.

5 **Carbon River and Mowich Lake.** Near the Carbon River Entrance Station is a swath of temperate forest, but to really get away from it all, follow the windy gravel roads to remote Mowich Lake.

GETTING ORIENTED

The jagged white crown of Mt. Rainier is the showpiece of the Cascades and the focal point of this 337-square-mile national park. The most popular destination in the park, Paradise, is in the southern region; Ohanapecosh, the Grove of the Patriarchs, and Tipsoo Lake are in the southeastern corner. Mount Rainier National Park's eastern and northern areas are dominated by wilderness. The snowy folds of the Cascade mountain range stretch out from this Washington park; Seattle is roughly 50 miles north and the volcanic ruins of Mount St. Helens 100 miles south.

16

Map labels

Huckleberry Creek

SOURDOUGH MOUNTAINS

SUNRISE RIDGE

410

Sunrise
Visitor Center

4 White River Entrance
White River

White River

Mather Memorial Parkway

Pacific Crest Trail

GOAT ISLAND MOUNTAIN

GOVERNORS RIDGE

410

410

Tipsoo Lake

123

Wonderland Trail

COWLITZ DIVIDE

3

0   2 mi
0   2 km

Grove of the Patriarchs
Stevens Canyon Entrance

Visitor Center

123
TO
PACKWOOD

Updated by
Shelley Arenas

Like a mysterious, white-clad chanteuse, veiled in clouds even when the surrounding forests and fields are bathed in sunlight, Mt. Rainier is the centerpiece of its namesake park. The impressive volcanic peak stands at an elevation of 14,411 feet, making it the fifth-highest peak in the lower 48 states. Nearly 2 million visitors a year enjoy spectacular views of the mountain and return home with a lifelong memory of its image.

The mountain holds the largest glacial system in the contiguous United States, with more than two dozen major glaciers. On the lower slopes you find silent forests made up of cathedral-like groves of Douglas fir, western hemlock, and western red cedar, some more than 1,000 years old. Water and lush greenery are everywhere in the park, and dozens of thundering waterfalls, accessible from the road or by a short hike, fill the air with mist.

MOUNT RAINIER PLANNER

WHEN TO GO

Rainier is the Puget Sound's weather vane: if you can see it, skies will be clear. Visitors are most likely to see the summit July through September. Crowds are heaviest in summer, too, meaning the parking lots at Paradise and Sunrise often fill before noon, campsites are reserved months in advance, and other lodgings are reserved as much as a year ahead.

True to its name, Paradise is often sunny during periods when the lowlands are under a cloud layer. The rest of the year, Rainier's summit gathers flying-saucer-like lenticular clouds whenever a Pacific storm approaches; once the peak vanishes from view, it's time to haul out rain gear. The rare periods of clear winter weather bring residents up to Paradise for cross-country skiing.

PLANNING YOUR TIME
MT. RAINIER IN ONE DAY
The best way to get a complete overview of Mt. Rainier in a day is to enter via Nisqually and begin your tour by browsing in **Longmire Museum.** When you're done, get to know the environment in and around Longmire Meadow and the overgrown ruins of Longmire Springs Hotel on the ½-mile **Trail of the Shadows** nature loop.

From Longmire, Highway 706 East climbs northeast into the mountains toward Paradise. Take a moment to explore two-tiered **Christine Falls,** just north of the road 1½ miles past Cougar Rock Campground, and the cascading **Narada Falls,** 3 miles farther on; both are spanned by graceful stone footbridges. Fantastic mountain views, alpine meadows crosshatched with nature trails, a welcoming lodge and restaurant, and the excellent **Jackson Memorial Visitor Center** combine to make lofty Paradise the primary goal of most park visitors. One outstanding (but challenging) way to explore the high country is to hike the 5-mile round-trip **Skyline Trail** to Panorama Point, which rewards you with stunning 360-degree views.

Continue eastward on Highway 706 East for 21 miles and leave your car to explore the incomparable, 1,000-year-old **Grove of the Patriarchs.** Afterward, turn your car north toward White River and **Sunrise Visitor Center,** where you can watch the alpenglow fade from Mt. Rainier's domed summit.

GETTING HERE AND AROUND
AIR TRAVEL
Seattle–Tacoma International Airport, 15 miles south of downtown Seattle, is the nearest airport to the national park.

CAR TRAVEL
The Nisqually entrance is on Highway 706, 14 miles east of Route 7; the Ohanapecosh entrance is on Route 123, 5 miles north of U.S. 12; and the White River entrance is on Route 410, 3 miles north of the Chinook and Cayuse passes. These highways become mountain roads as they reach Rainier, winding up and down many steep slopes, so cautious driving is essential: use a lower gear, especially on downhill sections, and take care not to overheat brakes by constant use. These roads are subject to storms any time of year and are repaired in the summer from winter damage and washouts.

Side roads into the park's western slope are narrower, unpaved, and subject to flooding and washouts. All are closed by snow in winter except Highway 706 to Paradise and Carbon River Road, though the latter tends to flood near the park boundary. (Route 410 is open to the Crystal Mountain access road entrance.)

Park roads have a maximum speed of 35 mph in most places, and you have to watch for pedestrians, cyclists, and wildlife. Parking can be difficult during peak summer season, especially at Paradise, Sunrise, Grove of the Patriarchs, and at the trailheads between Longmire and Paradise; arrive early if you plan to visit these sites. All off-road-vehicle use—4X4 vehicles, ATVs, motorcycles, snowmobiles—is prohibited in Mount Rainier National Park.

16

PARK ESSENTIALS
PARK FEES AND PERMITS
The entrance fee of $25 per vehicle and $10 for those on foot, motorcycle, or bicycle is good for seven days. Annual passes are $50. Climbing permits are $46 per person per climb or glacier trek. Wilderness camping permits must be obtained for all backcountry trips, and advance reservations are highly recommended.

PARK HOURS
Mount Rainier National Park is open 24/7 year-round, but with limited access in winter. Gates at Nisqually (Longmire) are staffed year-round during the day; facilities at Paradise are open daily from late May to mid-October; and Sunrise is open daily July to early September. During off-hours you can buy passes at the gates from machines that accept credit and debit cards. Winter access to the park is limited to the Nisqually entrance, and the Jackson Memorial Visitor Center at Paradise is open on weekends and holidays in winter. The Paradise snow-play area is open when there is sufficient snow.

CELL-PHONE RECEPTION
Cell-phone reception is unreliable throughout much of the park, although access is clear at Paradise, Sunrise, and Crystal Mountain. Public telephones are at all park visitor centers, at the National Park Inn at Longmire, and at Paradise Inn at Paradise.

EDUCATIONAL OFFERINGS
RANGER PROGRAMS
FAMILY **Junior Ranger Program.** Youngsters ages 6 to 11 can pick up an activity booklet at a visitor center and fill it out as they explore the park. When they complete it, they can show it to a ranger and receive a Mount Rainier Junior Ranger badge. ⊠ *Visitor centers, Mt. Rainier National Park* ☎ *360/569–2211* ⊕ *www.nps.gov/mora/learn/kidsyouth/index. htm* ⊠ *Free with park admission.*

FAMILY **Ranger Programs.** Park ranger-led activities include **guided snowshoe walks** in the winter (most suitable for those older than eight) as well as **evening programs** during the summer at Longmire/Cougar Rock, Ohanapecosh, and White River campgrounds, and at the Paradise Inn. Evening talks may cover subjects such as park history, its flora and fauna, or interesting facts on climbing Mt. Rainier. There are also daily guided programs that start at the Jackson Visitor Center, including meadow and vista walks, tours of the Paradise Inn, a morning ranger chat, and evening astronomy program. ⊠ *Visitor centers, Mt. Rainier National Park* ☎ *360/569–2211* ⊕ *www.nps.gov/mora/planyourvisit/ rangerprograms.htm* ⊠ *Free with park admission.*

RESTAURANTS
A limited number of restaurants are inside the park, and a few worth checking out lie beyond its borders. Mt. Rainier's picnic areas are justly famous, especially in summer, when wildflowers fill the meadows. Resist the urge to feed the yellow pine chipmunks darting about.

HOTELS

The Mt. Rainier area is remarkably bereft of quality lodging. Rainier's two national park lodges, at Longmire and Paradise, are attractive and well maintained. They exude considerable history and charm, especially Paradise Inn, but unless you've made summer reservations a year in advance, getting a room can be a challenge. Dozens of motels, cabin complexes, and private vacation-home rentals are near the park entrances; while they can be pricey, the latter are convenient for longer stays. *Hotel reviews have been shortened. For full information, visit Fodors.com.*

WHAT IT COSTS

	$	$$	$$$	$$$$
Restaurants	under $12	$12–$20	$21–$30	over $30
Hotels	under $100	$100–$150	$151–$200	over $200

Restaurant prices are the average cost of a main course at dinner, or if dinner is not served, at lunch. Hotel prices are the lowest cost of a standard double room in high season, excluding taxes and service charges.

16

VISITOR INFORMATION

Park Contact Information Mount Rainier National Park. ⊠ *55210 238th Ave. East, Ashford* ☎ *360/569–2211, 360/569–6575* ⊕ *www.nps.gov/mora.*

VISITOR CENTERS

Jackson Memorial Visitor Center. High on the mountain's southern flank, this center houses exhibits on geology, mountaineering, glaciology, and alpine ecology. Multimedia programs are staged in the theater; there's also a snack bar and gift shop. This is the park's most popular visitor destination, and it can be quite crowded in summer. ⊠ *Hwy. 706 E, 19 miles east of Nisqually park entrance, Mt. Rainier National Park* ☎ *360/569–6571* ⊕ *www.nps.gov/mora/planyourvisit/paradise.htm* ☺ *Weekdays mid-Oct.–Apr.*

Longmire Museum and Visitor Center. Glass cases inside this museum preserve the park's plants and animals, including a stuffed cougar. Historical photographs and geographical displays provide a worthwhile overview of the park's history. The adjacent visitor center has some perfunctory exhibits on the surrounding forest and its inhabitants, as well as pamphlets and information about park activities. ⊠ *Hwy. 706, 10 miles east of Ashford, Longmire* ☎ *360/569–6575* ⊕ *www.nps.gov/ mora/planyourvisit/longmire.htm.*

Sunrise Visitor Center. Exhibits at this center explain the region's sparser alpine and subalpine ecology. A network of nearby loop trails leads you through alpine meadows and forest to overlooks that have broad views of the Cascades and Rainier. The visitor center has a snack bar and gift shop. ⊠ *Sunrise Rd., 15 miles from the White River park entrance, Mt. Rainier National Park* ☎ *360/663–2425* ⊕ *www.nps.gov/mora/planyourvisit/sunrise.htm* ☺ *Mid-Sept.–June.*

EXPLORING

SCENIC DRIVES

Chinook Pass Road. Route 410, the highway to Yakima, follows the eastern edge of the park to Chinook Pass, where it climbs the steep, 5,432-foot pass via a series of switchbacks. At its top, take in broad views of Rainier and the east slope of the Cascades. The pass usually closes for the winter in November. ⊠ *Mt. Rainier National Park* ⊕ *www.wsdot. wa.gov/traffic/passes/chinook-cayuse.*

Mowich Lake Road. In the northwest corner of the park, this 24-mile mountain road begins in Wilkeson and heads up the Rainier foothills to Mowich Lake, traversing beautiful mountain meadows along the way. Mowich Lake is a pleasant spot for a picnic. The road is open mid-July to mid-October. ⊠ *Mt. Rainier National Park* ⊕ *www.nps.gov/mora/ planyourvisit/carbon-and-mowich.htm* ☉ *Closed mid-Oct.-mid-July.*

Paradise Road. This 9-mile stretch of Highway 706 winds its way up the mountain's southwest flank from Longmire to Paradise, taking you from lowland forest to the ever-expanding vistas of the mountain above. Visit early on a weekday if possible, especially in peak summer months, when the road is packed with cars. The route is open year-round though there may be some weekday closures in winter. From November through April, all vehicles must carry chains. ⊠ *Mt. Rainier National Park* ⊕ *www.nps.gov/mora/planyourvisit/paradise.htm.*

Sunrise Road. This popular (and often crowded) scenic road to the highest drivable point at Mt. Rainier carves its way 11 miles up Sunrise Ridge from the White River Valley on the northeast side of the park. As you top the ridge there are sweeping views of the surrounding lowlands. The road is open late June to early October. ⊠ *Mt. Rainier National Park* ⊕ *www.nps.gov/mora/planyourvisit/sunrise.htm* ☉ *Usually closed Oct.–June.*

HISTORIC SITES

National Park Inn. Even if you don't plan to stay overnight, you can stop by year-round to view the architecture of this inn, built in 1917 and on the National Register of Historic Places. While you're here, relax in front of the fireplace in the lounge, stop at the gift shop, or dine at the restaurant. ⊠ *Longmire Visitor Complex, Hwy. 706, 10 miles east of Nisqually entrance, Longmire* ☎ *360/569–2411* ⊕ *www.mtrainier-guestservices.com/accommodations/national-park-inn.*

SCENIC STOPS

Christine Falls. These two-tiered falls were named in honor of Christine Louise Van Trump, who climbed to the 10,000-foot level on Mt. Rainier in 1889 at the age of nine, despite having a crippling nervous-system disorder. ⊠ *Next to Hwy. 706, about 2½ miles east of Cougar Rock Campground, Mt. Rainier National Park.*

Fodor's Choice
★

Grove of the Patriarchs. Protected from the periodic fires that swept through the surrounding areas, this small island of 1,000-year-old trees is one of Mount Rainier National Park's most memorable features. A 1½-mile loop trail heads through the old-growth forest of Douglas fir, cedar, and hemlock. ⊠ *Rte. 123, west of the Stevens Canyon entrance, Mt. Rainier National Park* ⊕ *www.nps.gov/mora/planyourvisit/ohanapecosh.htm.*

Narada Falls. A steep but short trail leads to the viewing area for these spectacular 168-foot falls, which expand to a width of 75 feet during peak flow times. In winter the frozen falls are popular with ice climbers. ⊠ *Along Hwy. 706, 1 mile west of the turnoff for Paradise, 6 miles east of Cougar Rock Campground, Mt. Rainier National Park* ⊕ *www.nps.gov/mora/planyourvisit/longmire.htm.*

FAMILY

Tipsoo Lake. The short, pleasant trail that circles the lake—ideal for families—provides breathtaking views. Enjoy the subalpine wildflower meadows during the summer months; in early fall there is an abundant supply of huckleberries. ⊠ *Off Cayuse Pass east on Hwy. 410, Mt. Rainier National Park* ⊕ *www.nps.gov/mora/planyourvisit/sunrise.htm.*

SPORTS AND THE OUTDOORS

16

MULTISPORT OUTFITTERS

RMI Expeditions. Reserve a private hiking guide through this highly regarded outfitter, or take part in its one-day mountaineering classes (mid-May through late September), where participants are evaluated on their fitness for the climb and must be able to withstand a 16-mile round-trip hike with a 9,000-foot gain in elevation. The company also arranges private cross-country skiing and snowshoeing guides. ⊠ *30027 Hwy. 706 E, Ashford* ☎ *888/892–5462, 360/569–2227* ⊕ *www.rmiguides.com* 🖫 *From $1087 for 4-day package.*

Whittaker Mountaineering. You can rent hiking and climbing gear, skis, snowshoes, snowboards, and other outdoor equipment at this all-purpose Rainier Base Camp outfitter, which also arranges for private cross-country skiing and hiking guides. ⊠ *30027 SR 706E, Ashford* ☎ *800/238–5756, 360/569–2982* ⊕ *www.whittakermountaineering.com.*

BIRD-WATCHING

Be alert for kestrels, red-tailed hawks, and, occasionally, golden eagles on snags in the lowland forests. Also present at Rainier, but rarely seen, are great horned owls, spotted owls, and screech owls. Iridescent rufous hummingbirds flit from blossom to blossom in the drowsy summer lowlands, and sprightly water ouzels flutter in the many forest creeks. Raucous Steller's jays and gray jays scold passersby from trees, often darting boldly down to steal morsels from unguarded picnic tables. At higher elevations, look for the pure white plumage of the white-tailed ptarmigan as it hunts for seeds and insects in winter. Waxwings, vireos, nuthatches, sapsuckers, warblers, flycatchers, larks, thrushes, siskins, tanagers, and finches are common throughout the park.

HIKING

Although the mountain can seem remarkably benign on calm summer days, hiking Rainier is not a city-park stroll. Dozens of hikers and trekkers annually lose their way and must be rescued—and lives are lost on the mountain each year. Weather that approaches cyclonic levels can appear quite suddenly, any month of the year. All visitors venturing far from vehicle access points, with the possible exception of the short loop hikes listed here, should carry day packs with warm clothing, food, and other emergency supplies.

EASY

Nisqually Vista Trail. Equally popular in summer and winter, this trail is a 1¼-mile round-trip through subalpine meadows to an overlook point for Nisqually Glacier. The gradually sloping path is a favorite venue for cross-country skiers in winter; in summer, listen for the shrill alarm calls of the area's marmots. *Easy.* ⊠ *Mt. Rainier National Park* ✤ *Trailhead: at Jackson Memorial Visitor Center, Rte. 123, 1 mile north of Ohanapecosh, at high point of Hwy. 706* ⊕ *www.nps.gov/mora/planyourvisit/day-hiking-at-mount-rainier.htm.*

Sunrise Nature Trail. The 1½-mile-long loop of this self-guided trail takes you through the delicate subalpine meadows near the Sunrise Visitor Center. A gradual climb to the ridgetop yields magnificent views of Mt. Rainier and the more distant volcanic cones of Mt. Baker, Mt. Adams, and Glacier Peak. *Easy.* ⊠ *Mt. Rainier National Park* ✤ *Trailhead: at Sunrise Visitor Center, Sunrise Rd., 15 miles from White River park entrance* ⊕ *www.nps.gov/mora/planyourvisit/sunrise.htm.*

Trail of the Shadows. This ¾-mile loop is notable for its glimpses of meadowland ecology, its colorful soda springs (don't drink the water), James Longmire's old homestead cabin, and the foundation of the old Longmire Springs Hotel, which was destroyed by fire around 1900. *Easy.* ⊠ *Mt. Rainier National Park* ✤ *Trailhead: at Hwy. 706, 10 miles east of Nisqually entrance* ⊕ *www.nps.gov/mora/planyourvisit/day-hiking-at-mount-rainier.htm.*

MODERATE

Fodor's Choice
★

Skyline Trail. This 5-mile loop, one of the highest trails in the park, beckons day-trippers with a vista of alpine ridges and, in summer, meadows filled with brilliant flowers and birds. At 6,800 feet, Panorama Point, the spine of the Cascade Range, spreads away to the east, and Nisqually Glacier tumbles downslope. *Moderate.* ⊠ *Mt. Rainier National Park* ✤ *Trailhead: Jackson Memorial Visitor Center, Rte. 123, 1 mile north of Ohanapecosh at high point of Hwy. 706* ⊕ *www.nps.gov/mora/planyourvisit/skyline-trail.htm.*

Van Trump Park Trail. You gain an exhilarating 2,200 feet on this route while hiking through a vast expanse of meadow with views of the southern Puget Sound. The 5¾-mile track provides good footing, and the average hiker can make it up and back in five hours. *Moderate.* ⊠ *Mt. Rainier National Park* ✤ *Trailhead: Hwy. 706 at Christine Falls, 4½ miles east of Longmire* ⊕ *www.nps.gov/mora/planyourvisit/van-trump-trail.htm.*

DIFFICULT

FodorsChoice **Wonderland Trail.** All other Mt. Rainier hikes pale in comparison to
★ this stunning 93-mile trek, which completely encircles the mountain.
The trail passes through all the major life zones of the park, from the
old-growth forests of the lowlands to the alpine meadows and goat-
haunted glaciers of the highlands—pick up a mountain-goat sighting
card from a ranger station or visitor center if you want to help in the
park's effort to learn more about these elusive animals. Wonderland is
a rugged trail; elevation gains and losses totaling 3,500 feet are common in a day's hike, which averages 8 miles. Most hikers start out from
Longmire or Sunrise and take 10–14 days to cover the 93-mile route.
Snow lingers on the high passes well into June (sometimes July); count
on rain any time of the year. Campsites are wilderness areas with pit
toilets and water that must be purified before drinking. Only hardy,
well-equipped, and experienced wilderness trekkers should attempt this
trip, but those who do will be amply rewarded. Wilderness permits are
required, and reservations are strongly recommended. *Difficult.* ⊠ *Mt.
Rainier National Park* ✢ *Trailheads: Longmire Visitor Center, Hwy.
706, 17 miles east of Ashford; Sunrise Visitor Center, Sunrise Rd., 15
miles west of White River park entrance* ⊕ *www.nps.gov/mora/plany-
ourvisit/the-wonderland-trail.htm.*

16

MOUNTAIN CLIMBING

Climbing Mt. Rainier is not for amateurs; each year, adventurers die on
the mountain, and many become lost and must be rescued. Near-cata-
strophic weather can appear quite suddenly, any month of the year. If
you're experienced in technical, high-elevation snow, rock, and ice-field
adventuring, Mt. Rainier can be a memorable adventure. Climbers can
fill out a climbing card at the Paradise, White River, or Carbon River
ranger stations and lead their own groups of two or more. Climbers
must register with a ranger before leaving and check out on return. A
$46 annual climbing fee applies to anyone heading above 10,000 feet
or onto one of Rainier's glaciers. During peak season it is recommended
that climbers make their camping reservations ($20 per site) in advance;
reservations are taken by fax and mail beginning in mid-March on a
first-come, first-served basis (find the reservation form at ⊕ *www.nps.
gov/mora/planyourvisit/climbing.htm*).

SKIING AND SNOWSHOEING

Mt. Rainier is a major Nordic ski center for cross-country and telemark
skiing. Although trails are not groomed, those around Paradise are
extremely popular. If you want to ski with fewer people, try the trails
in and around the Ohanapecosh–Stevens Canyon area, which are just
as beautiful and, because of their more easterly exposure, slightly less
subject to the rains that can douse the Longmire side, even in the dead
of winter. Never ski on plowed main roads, especially around Paradise—the snowplow operator can't see you. Rentals aren't available on
the eastern side of the park.

Mount Rainier, Looking North

MOUNT RAINIER

Columbia Crest 14,411 ft
Liberty Cap 14,122 ft
Point Success 14,153 ft
Gibraltar Rock 12,660 ft
Little Tahoma Peak 11,138 ft
Disappointment Cleaver
Ingraham Glacier
CATHEDRAL ROCKS
Camp Muir 10,188 ft
Anvil Rock 9,584 ft
Paradise Glaciers
McClure Rock 7,385 ft
Unicorn Peak 6,917 ft
Muir Snowfield
Nisqually Glacier
Panoramic Point 6,800 ft
Alta Vista
Paradise
Louise Lake
The Castle
Reflection Lakes
TATOOSH RANGE
Skyline Trail
Henry M. Jackson Memorial Visitor Center
Pinnacle Peak 6,562 ft
Plummer Peak 6,370 ft
Lane Peak 6,012 ft
Wahpenayo Peak 6,231 ft
Chutla Peak
Eagle Peak 5,958 ft
SUNSET AMPHITHEATER
St. Andrews Rock 10,992 ft
Wilson Glacier
Van Trump Glaciers
SUCCESS CLEAVER
WAPOWETY CLEAVER
Kautz Glacier
Success Glacier
South DIVIDE
Van Trump Park
CUSHMAN CREST
Mildred Point
PUYALLUP CLEAVER
Tahoma Glacier
GLACIER ISLAND
SUCCESS
Pyramid Glaciers
Tahoma Glacier
PYRAMID PARK
Pyramid Peak 6,937 ft
Tokaloo Rock 7,684 ft
EMERALD RIDGE
Iron Mountain 6,283 ft
Cougar Rock
PYRAMID RIDGE
Rampart Ridge Trail
Wonderland Trail
Creek
RAMPART
THE RAMPARTS
Longmire

KEY
Paved Roads
Hiking Trails
Climbing Routes

Deep snows make Mt. Rainier a snowshoeing pleasure. The Paradise area, with its network of trails, is the best choice. The park's east-side roads, Routes 123 and 410, are unplowed and provide other good snowshoeing venues, although you must share the main routes with snowmobilers.

Paradise Snowplay Area and Nordic Ski Route. Sledding on flexible sleds (no toboggans or runners), inner tubes, and plastic saucers is allowed only in the Paradise snow-play area adjacent to the Jackson Visitor Center. The area is open when there is sufficient snow, usually from late December through mid-March. The easy, 3½-mile Paradise Valley Road Nordic ski route begins at the Paradise parking lot and follows Paradise Valley/Stevens Canyon Road to Reflection Lakes. Equipment rentals are available at Whittaker Mountaineering in Ashford or at the National Park Inn's General Store in Longmire. ✉ *Adjacent to Jackson Visitor Center at Paradise, Mt. Rainier National Park* ☎ *360/569–2211* 🌐 *www.nps.gov/mora/planyourvisit/winter-recreation.htm.*

TOURS AND OUTFITTERS

General Store at the National Park Inn. The store at the National Park Inn in Longmire rents cross-country ski equipment and snowshoes. It's open daily in winter, depending on snow conditions. ✉ *National Park Inn, Longmire* ☎ *360/569–2411* 🌐 *www.mtrainierguestservices.com/activities-and-events/winter-activities/cross-country-skiing.*

WHERE TO EAT

$$$ ECLECTIC 🍴 **National Park Inn Dining Room.** Photos of Mt. Rainier taken by top photographers adorn the walls of this inn's large dining room, a bonus on the many days the mountain refuses to show itself. Meals are simple but tasty: pot roast with mashed potatoes, seared halibut, cedar-plank trout, and blackberry cobbler à la mode. [$] *Average main: $22* ✉ *Hwy. 706, Longmire* ☎ *360/569–2411* 🌐 *www.mtrainierguestservices.com.*

$ AMERICAN FAMILY 🍴 **Paradise Camp Deli.** Grilled meats, sandwiches, salads, and soft drinks are served daily from May through early October and on weekends and holidays during the rest of the year. [$] *Average main: $9* ✉ *Jackson Visitor Center, Paradise Rd. E, Paradise* ☎ *360/569–6571* 🌐 *www.mtrainierguestservices.com* ⏲ *Closed weekdays early Oct.–Apr.*

$$$ AMERICAN 🍴 **Paradise Inn.** Where else can you enjoy Sunday brunch in a historic, heavy-timbered lodge halfway up a mountain? Tall windows provide terrific views of Rainier, and the warm glow of native wood permeates the large dining room, where hearty Pacific Northwest fare is served. [$] *Average main: $24* ✉ *E. Paradise Rd., near Jackson Visitor Center, Paradise* ☎ *360/569–2275* 🌐 *www.mtrainierguestservices.com* ⏲ *Closed Oct.–late May.*

$ AMERICAN FAMILY 🍴 **Sunrise Day Lodge Food Service.** A cafeteria and grill serve inexpensive hamburgers, chili, and hot dogs from July through September. [$] *Average main: $9* ✉ *Sunrise Rd., 15 miles from White River park entrance, Mt. Rainier National Park* ☎ *360/663–2425* 🌐 *www.mtrainierguestservices.com* ⏲ *Closed Oct.–June.*

PICNIC AREAS

Park picnic areas are usually open only from late May through September.

Sunrise Picnic Area. Set in an alpine meadow that's filled with wildflowers in July and August, this picnic area provides expansive views of the mountain and surrounding ranges in good weather. ⊠ *Sunrise Rd., 11 miles west of White River entrance, Mt. Rainier National Park* ⊕ *www. nps.gov/mora/planyourvisit/sunrise.htm* ⊗ *Road to Sunrise usually closed Oct.–June.*

WHERE TO STAY

$$$
B&B/INN
National Park Inn. A large stone fireplace warms the common room of this country inn, the only one of the park's two inns that's open year-round. **Pros:** classic ambience; open all year. **Cons:** jam-packed in summer; must book far in advance; some rooms have shared bath. $ *Rooms from: $177* ⊠ *Longmire Visitor Complex, Hwy. 706, 6 miles east of Nisqually entrance, Longmire* ☎ *360/569–2275, 855/755–2275* ⊕ *www.mtrainierguestservices.com* ⊅ *25 rooms, 18 with bath* ⎮⊙⎮ *No meals.*

$$$
HOTEL
FodorsChoice
★
Paradise Inn. With its hand-carved Alaskan cedar logs, burnished parquet floors, stone fireplaces, Indian rugs, and glorious mountain views, this 1917 inn is a classic example of a National Park lodge. **Pros:** central to trails; pristine vistas; nature-inspired details. **Cons:** rooms are small and basic; many rooms have shared bathrooms; no elevators, a/c, cell service, or Wi-Fi. $ *Rooms from: $182* ⊠ *E. Paradise Rd., near Jackson Visitor Center, Paradise* ☎ *360/569–2275, 855/755–2275* ⊕ *www. mtrainierguestservices.com* ⊗ *Closed mid-Oct.–mid-May* ⊅ *121 rooms* ⎮⊙⎮ *No meals.*

WASHINGTON WINE COUNTRY

Yakima River Valley

WELCOME TO WASHINGTON WINE COUNTRY

TOP REASONS TO GO

★ **Sip fine wine:** Yakima Valley may be the state's finest wine region, with more than 100 wineries producing excellent yields.

★ **Stay at a spectacular mountain lodge:** The Lodge at Suncadia is one of Washington's premier resorts. Golfers, cross-country skiers, hikers, and families will enjoy this terrific lodge in the beautiful Cascade Mountains.

★ **Mine Washington history:** The former mining towns of Roslyn and Cle Elum honor their hardscrabble pasts with the Coal Mines Trail, which winds past several old mine sites, and the Roslyn Museum, which displays vintage equipment.

★ **Take a hike:** From the Manastash Ridge and Boulder Cave trails to the more leisurely Yakima Greenway and Cowiche Canyon trail, opportunities for trekking abound in this region.

★ **Authentic Mexican fare:** From hand-folded tamales to tacos with freshly made tortillas, authentic Mexican food abounds throughout the Yakima Valley.

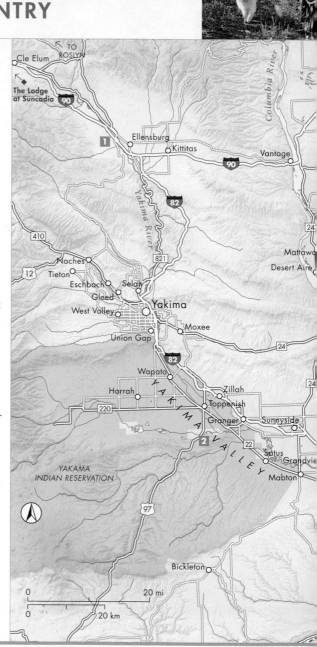

1 **Northern Yakima River Valley.** Just 80 miles from Seattle over the Cascade Mountains, the historic mining towns of Roslyn and Cle Elum offer quaint shops and one very plush resort. Golf, fishing, hiking, biking, cross-country skiing, and more are readily available in this region. As you follow the Yakima River down past Ellensburg to Yakima, you'll see how irrigation turns a virtual desert into one of the most agriculturally rich regions in the nation. Yakima is the shopping and entertainment hub of the region.

2 **Southern Yakima River Valley.** From Yakima, which touts itself as the gateway to wine country, visitors can choose from more than 100 wineries, as well as fresh fruits and vegetables of all kinds. The area is one of the most agriculturally diverse in the country, with some outstanding restaurants. History is rich here as well. The Yakama Indian Reservation occupies much of the land, and the history of its people can be seen in several museums around the region, including the museum at the Yakama Nation Cultural Center in Toppenish.

GETTING ORIENTED

The Yakima River Valley encompasses a region of south-central Washington that starts just east of Snoqualmie Pass in the Kittitas Valley. It includes the forested eastern slopes and the foothills of the Central Cascades, from Chinook and White Pass all the way down through the Yakima Valley near Benton City. Two interstates meet in Ellensburg. Interstate 90 links Seattle to Cle Elum and Ellensburg before heading east toward Spokane. Interstate 82 branches south off Interstate 90 just east of Ellensburg, and runs through the Yakima Valley to the so-called Tri-Cities (Richland, Pasco, and Kennewick). U.S. 97 is the primary link from Ellensburg north (Wenatchee, Canada's Okanagan Valley) and from Yakima south toward central Oregon.

17

Updated
by Adriana
Janovich

The Yakima River binds a region of great contrasts. Snowcapped volcanic peaks and evergreen-covered hills overlook a natural shrub steppe turned green by irrigation. Famed throughout the world for its apples and cherries, its wine and hops, this fertile landscape is also the ancestral home of the Yakama people from whom it takes its name.

The river flows southeasterly from its source in the Cascade Mountains near Snoqualmie Pass. Between the college town of Ellensburg, at the heart of the Kittitas Valley, and Yakima, the region's largest city, the river cuts steep canyons through serried, sagebrush-covered ridges before merging with the Naches River. Then it breaks through Union Gap to enter its fecund namesake, the broad Yakima Valley. Some 200 miles from its source, the river makes one final bend around vineyard-rich Red Mountain before joining the mighty Columbia River at the Tri-Cities.

Broad-shouldered Mt. Adams is the sacred mountain of the Yakama people. The 12,276-foot-tall mountain marks the western boundary of their reservation, second largest in the Pacific Northwest. As they have for centuries, wild horses run free through the Yakama Nation and can be seen feeding along Highway 97 south of Toppenish. Deer and elk roam the evergreen forests, eagles and ospreys soar overhead.

Orchards and vineyards dominate Yakima Valley's agricultural landscape. Cattle and sheep ranching initially drove the economy; apples and other produce came with the engineering of irrigation canals and outlets in the 1890s. The annual asparagus harvest begins in April, followed by cherries in June; apricots and peaches ripen in early to midsummer. Hops are ready by late August and exported throughout the world for the brewing of beer; travelers may see the bushy vines spiraling up fields of twine. The apple harvest runs from late summer through October.

The valley's real fame, however, rests on its wine grapes, which have a growing reputation as among the best in the world. Concord grapes were first planted here in the 1960s, and they still take up large tracts of land. But vinifera grapes, the noble grapes of Europe, now dominate the local wine industry. Merlot and white Burgundies boosted the region, and Syrah is often regarded as the grape of the future. Expect to find fine Cabernet, Grenache, Riesling, Chardonnay, Gewürztraminer, Sémillon, Sauvignon Blanc, Chenin Blanc, and Muscat, as well as such lesser-known varietals as Sangiovese, Nebbiolo, and Lemberger.

WASHINGTON WINE COUNTRY PLANNER

WHEN TO GO

Much of the area is considered semiarid shrub steppe, with annual rainfall of just 8 inches a year. But in winter, in the higher elevations, it is quite common to have snow on the ground from November until March. This is a decidedly four-season region, with wet, cool, windy springs, beautiful warm summer days, and gorgeous falls with colors to match those of any Northeastern state. Best time to visit is April through October, unless, of course, you're looking to ski, snowboard, or snowmobile.

The main wine-tasting season begins in late April and runs to the end of the fall harvest in November. Winery hours vary in winter, when you should call ahead before visiting. The Yakima Valley Winery Association (⊕ *wineyakimavalley.org*) publishes a map-brochure that lists wineries with tasting-room hours. Most are owned and managed by unpretentious enthusiasts, and their cellar masters are often on hand to answer questions.

GETTING HERE AND AROUND

AIR TRAVEL

Although major airlines serve the region's two airports, most people fly into Seattle or Portland, Oregon, and drive to the area.

Both Yakima and the Tri-Cities are served by Horizon. The Tri-Cities are also served by Delta and United. *For detailed information on airlines that service the region, see Air Travel in Travel Smart.*

Airports Tri-Cities Regional Airport. ⊠ *3601 N. 20th Ave., Pasco* ☎ *509/547-6352* ⊕ *www.flytricities.com.* **Yakima Air Terminal.** ⊠ *2300 W. Washington Ave., 4 miles southeast of downtown, Yakima* ☎ *509/575-6149* ⊕ *www.yakimaairterminal.com.*

Transfers Airporter Shuttle. ☎ *866/235-5247* ⊕ *www.airporter.com.*

Airport Transportation Diamond Cab. ☎ *509/453-3113.*

CAR TRAVEL

The Yakima Valley Highway, which turns into Wine Country Road just south of Sunnyside, is a reliable, off-the-beaten-track alternative to Interstate 82 for wine-country visits; but it can be slow, especially through towns, or if farm machinery is on the road. Because of unmarked turns and other potential hazards, it's wise to stick to the freeway after dark. Gas stations in towns, and at major freeway intersections, are typically open well after dark.

17

Major car rental companies in the area include **Avis** (☎ *509/469–4543 Yakima*), **Budget** (☎ *509/248–6767 Yakima*), **Enterprise** (☎ *509/494–7111 Yakima, 509/925–5040 Ellensburg*), and **Hertz** (☎ *509/452–9965 Yakima*). Hertz and Budget are available at Yakima Air Terminal.

RESTAURANTS

National fast-food chains, local eateries, and some fine-dining restaurants can be found scattered throughout the region, or sometimes right alongside one another. As a huge agricultural area, the Yakima Valley supplies many of its local restaurants with fresh fruits and vegetables in season. Yakima Valley wines are a staple at virtually all the fine-dining establishments. Pacific Northwest seafood (particularly salmon) is another staple. South-central Washington also has a fair share of Mexican food, from taco trucks to family-run Mexican restaurants.

HOTELS

Two major freeways, Interstate 90 and Interstate 82, pass through the cities of Ellensburg and Yakima, where you'll find the highest concentration of lodgings. A few independent motels are available, but the majority are independently operated under familiar chain names. At the far northeastern end of the region sits Suncadia Resort, offering possibly the finest accommodations in the area. Several bed-and-breakfasts are also available, particularly in the lower Yakima Valley, near the plethora of wineries. It is always prudent to call ahead for reservations, but the busiest tourist times include the third week in April, for Spring Barrel Tasting, and from Memorial Day through Labor Day. *Hotel reviews have been shortened. For full information, visit Fodors.com.*

WHAT IT COSTS IN U.S. DOLLARS			
$	**$$**	**$$$**	**$$$$**
Restaurants	under $16	$16–$22	$23–$30	over $30
Hotels	under $150	$150–$200	$201–$250	over $250

Restaurant prices are the average cost of a main course at dinner or, if dinner is not served, at lunch. Hotel prices are the lowest cost of a standard double room in high season.

TOURS

Bus companies, such as A & A Motorcoach, and limo services, including Moonlit Ride, conduct charter tours of the Yakima area.

Tour Contacts A & A Motorcoach. ✉ *2410 S. 26th Ave., Yakima* ☎ *509/575–3676* ⊕ *www.aamotorcoach.com.* **Moonlit Ride Limousine.** ✉ *3908 River Rd., Yakima* ☎ *509/575–6846* ⊕ *www.moonlitride.com.*

VISITOR INFORMATION

Wine Yakima Valley Association. ☎ *509/965–5201, 800/258–7270* ⊕ *wineyakimavalley.org.*

Yakima Valley Visitor Information Center. ✉ *101 N. Fair Ave., at Exit 34 off I–82, Yakima* ☎ *509/573–3388, 800/221–0751* ⊕ *www.visityakima.com.*

NORTHERN YAKIMA RIVER VALLEY

In the upper Kittitas Valley, tucked between the Cascade Mountains to the west and the rugged, snowcapped Sawtooth Mountains to the east, visitors will find the newest in championship golf courses, resort amenities, and fine dining. Plentiful shops, restaurants, museums, and outdoor activities make this one of the most diverse regions of the state. The old-time coal-mining towns of Roslyn and Cle Elum are being discovered by more and more travelers seeking good food, fun, and relaxation. The college town of Ellensburg, home of the annual Ellensburg Rodeo on Labor Day, offers a variety of entertainment, restaurants, and hotels. Through it all runs the Yakima River, the lifeblood of this agricultural region, and one of Washington's best trout-fishing rivers.

The city of Yakima is the region's hub, offering all kinds of shopping, and, thanks to a newly refurbished downtown core, many new restaurants, wineries, and nightlife options. Thousands of acres of orchards, producing cherries, apricots, peaches, pears, plums, nectarines, and apples, surround the city. In spring and summer, outdoors enthusiasts flock here to hike, bike, canoe, raft, swim, and fish. Winter-sports enthusiasts delight in the multitude of cross-country skiing, snowshoeing, and snowmobiling options, along with downhill skiing at White Pass.

17

CLE ELUM AND ROSLYN

86 miles southeast of Seattle.

A former railroad, coal, and logging town, Cle Elum (pronounced "klee *ell*-um") now caters to travelers stopping for a breath of air before or after tackling Snoqualmie Pass. Outside town is the ever-growing, world-class Suncadia Resort, one of Washington's finest destination resorts. It's actually closer to Roslyn, a former coal-mining town just 3 miles northwest of Cle Elum. Roslyn gained notoriety as the stand-in for the fictional Alaskan village of Cicely on the 1990s TV show *Northern Exposure*. Today, Cicely's Gift Shop on the town's main drag sells memorabilia, and the radio-station set can be viewed a block away at the old Northwestern Improvement Co. building. Roslyn is also notable for its 26 ethnic cemeteries, established by communities of miners in the late 19th and early 20th centuries and clustered on a hillside west of town.

GETTING HERE AND AROUND

Cle Elum is hard to miss; it's just off Interstate 90. Exit 80 will get you to Suncadia Resort as well as Roslyn. Exit 84 will put you at the west end of Cle Elum, placing you in the business district if you're approaching from Seattle and points west. Exit 85 will deliver you into the eastern boundaries of Cle Elum, but will also put you directly in the business district. Most of the amenities are found within the city limits of Cle Elum and Roslyn.

WHERE TO EAT

$ CAFÉ Fodor's Choice ★ 🍴 **Basecamp Books and Bites.** Part bookstore, part café, part coffee shop, this little gem features a simple but seasonal menu, with fresh fare from grilled sandwiches and soups to breakfast offerings, and espresso brewed on a beautiful teal La Marzocco machine. There's a craft-cocktail bar in the basement, too. **Known for:** fun literary atmosphere; strong espresso. [$] *Average main: $14* ✉ *110 W. Pensylvania Ave.* ☎ *509/649–3821* 🌐 *www.basecampbooks.com* 🕒 *No dinner Sun. and Mon.*

$ BAKERY Fodor's Choice ★ 🍴 **Cle Elum Bakery.** A local institution, this establishment has been doing business from the same spot since 1906. Fresh-baked loaves of bread and delectable treats from fresh-baked doughnuts and pastries to a fabulous sticky bun–cinnamon roll are available daily. **Known for:** sticky bun–cinnamon rolls; torchetti (Italian sugar cookies); all kinds of doughnuts. [$] *Average main: $5* ✉ *501 E. 1st St.* ☎ *509/674–2233* 🕒 *No dinner.*

$$ ITALIAN 🍴 **MaMa Vallone's Steak House and Inn.** Set in a building constructed in 1906, the rustic Western look makes the perfect backdrop for this cozy restaurant that once was a boardinghouse for unmarried miners. In addition to steaks and prime rib, many Italian family recipes are featured on the menu. **Known for:** steak and prime rib; Italian family recipes; bagna cauda. [$] *Average main: $20* ✉ *302 W. 1st St.* ☎ *509/674–5174* 🌐 *mamavallones.wixsite.com/cleelum* 🕒 *No lunch.*

$ CAFÉ 🍴 **Red Bird Cafe.** Red vintage tables and chairs await diners at this charming café on the first floor of a blue-and-red-painted house built in 1906 near the town center. Look for hoagie sandwiches, scratch-made soups, salads, and baked goods. **Known for:** Glondo sandwich with eggs and locally cured meat; Bird's Nest Stacker with ham, bacon, Havarti, and two eggs on toast. [$] *Average main: $10* ✉ *102 E. Pennsylvania Ave.* ☎ *509/649–3209* 🕒 *No dinner.*

$ AMERICAN 🍴 **Roslyn Brewing Co.** This small craft brewery offers five selections mostly reminiscent of old-world German-style beer: Roslyn Dark Lager, Brookside Pale Lager, Roslyn India Pale Lager, Roslyn Red Lager, and Roslyn Belgian Ale. Look for a beer garden and house-made root beer, named for one of the old mine sites, too. **Known for:** craft beer; house-made root beer. [$] *Average main: $5* ✉ *208 Pennsylvania Ave.* ☎ *509/649–2232* 🌐 *roslynbrewery.com* 🕒 *Closed Mon.–Wed.*

$ PACIFIC NORTHWEST 🍴 **Roslyn Cafe.** Perhaps best known for its camel mural, which figured prominently in the intro of the popular 1990s show *Northern Exposure*, this eclectic corner café features fresh and hearty Pacific Northwest fare. Look for the Salmon La Sac omelet, named for a nearby area, with house-smoked sockeye salmon and cream cheese; Coal Miner breakfast with two eggs, home fries, and a choice of meat and toast; and the banh mi burger, a twist on the classic Vietnamese sandwich, among other handhelds, salads, and appetizers. **Known for:** famous camel mural; ample breakfasts and burgers. [$] *Average main: $10* ✉ *201 W. Pennsylvania Ave.* ☎ *509/649–2763* 🌐 *theroslyncafe.com* 🕒 *Closed Tues. and Wed.*

$$ PIZZA 🍴 **Village Pizza.** This popular pizza place in the heart of Roslyn can get super busy; consider making a reservation or taking a pie to go. If you can get a table, make like a local and drizzle honey on the crust. **Known for:** old Trivial Pursuit cards at every table; no frills. [$] *Average main: $20* ✉ *105 W. Pennsylvania Ave.* ☎ *509/649–2992* 🕒 *Closed Mon. and Tues. No lunch.*

WHERE TO STAY

$ HOTEL **Econo Lodge-Cle Elum Mountain Inn.** Interiors are simple, but the large rooms are well kept and provide home-away-from-home comfort with amenities such as in-room refrigerators and microwaves. **Pros:** clean, affordable rooms; kitchenettes are an added convenience; convenient location on the main drag. **Cons:** no-frills motel; no pool. [$] *Rooms from: $79* ✉ *906 E. 1st St.* ☎ *509/674–2380, 888/674–3975* 🌐 *www.choicehotels.com* 🛏 *43 rooms* 🍴 *Breakfast.*

$ B&B/INN **Huckleberry House.** Set on a hill overlooking Roslyn's main street, this charming inn with a wraparound porch is a short walk from the heart of town and local eateries and watering holes. **Pros:** picturesque perch; cozy and conveniently located. **Cons:** some guests complain about late-night noise. [$] *Rooms from: $100* ✉ *301 Pennsylvania Ave.* ☎ *509/649–2900* 🌐 *www.huckleberryhouse.com* 🛏 *3 rooms* 🍴 *No meals.*

$ B&B/INN **Iron Horse Inn Bed and Breakfast.** This former boardinghouse for rail workers (1909–74) is now a comfortable country inn full of railroad memorabilia. **Pros:** memorable railroad-themed lodging experience; on the National Registry of Historic Places; adjacent to Iron Horse State Park. **Cons:** some rooms share bathrooms. [$] *Rooms from: $80* ✉ *526 Marie Ave., South Cle Elum* ☎ *509/674–5939, 800/228–9246* 🌐 *www.ironhorseinnbb.com* 🛏 *11 rooms, 8 with bath* 🍴 *Breakfast.*

$$$$ RESORT FAMILY Fodor's Choice ★ **The Lodge at Suncadia.** Set on a ridge overlooking the Cle Elum River, with spectacular views of the pine-covered Cascade Mountains, this world-class resort blends beautifully with its quintessential Pacific Northwest surroundings. **Pros:** intimate and upscale environment; golf, fly-fishing, cross-country skiing, snowshoeing, and hiking just minutes away; amenities abound for adults and children alike; sweeping mountain and forest views. **Cons:** costs can quickly add up for a family visit. [$] *Rooms from: $268* ✉ *3320 Suncadia Trail* ☎ *509/649–6400, 866/904–6300* 🌐 *www.suncadia.com* 🛏 *254 rooms* 🍴 *No meals.*

SHOPPING

Owens Meats. The Owens family established this marvelous smokehouse in 1887 and has been running it ever since. No processed meats here—just the freshest smoked and cured meats around, including beef jerky that is addictive. Twenty-four-hour meat machines scattered throughout the area, including at this store, mean you'll never have to go without. ✉ *502 E. 1st St.* ☎ *509/674–2530* 🌐 *www.owensmeats.com.*

ELLENSBURG

24 miles southeast of Cle Elum.

This university town is one of the state's friendliest and most easy-going places. "Modern" Ellensburg had its origin in a July 4 fire that engulfed the original city in 1889. Almost overnight, Victorian brick buildings rose from the ashes; many still stand, though their functions have changed. Stroll downtown to discover art galleries, comfortable cafés, an old-fashioned hardware store, and one antiques shop after another.

One of central Washington's biggest events is the Ellensburg Rodeo, held Labor Day weekend. On the national circuit since the 1920s, the rodeo has a year-round headquarters on Main Street, where you can buy tickets and souvenirs. You can also get a bird's-eye view of the rodeo grounds from Reed Park, in the 500 block of North Alder Street.

GETTING HERE AND AROUND

Ellensburg is adjacent to Interstate 90, with two exits that will take you right to gas, fast food, and lodging. Follow Main Street north and it will put you into the heart of downtown and Central Washington University.

ESSENTIALS

Visitor Information Kittitas County Chamber of Commerce. ⊠ *609 N. Main St.* ☏ *509/925–2002, 888/925–2204* ⊕ *www.kittitascountychamber.com.*

EXPLORING

TOP ATTRACTIONS

Central Washington University. The nearly 11,000 students here enjoy a pleasant, tree-shaded campus marked by formidable redbrick architecture. On the 8th Avenue side are several handsome buildings dating from the university's founding in 1891 as the State Normal School. Near the center of campus is a serene Japanese garden. The Sarah Spurgeon Gallery, in Randall Hall, features the work of regional and national artists as well as students and faculty. ⊠ *400 E. University Way* ☏ *509/963–1111* ⊕ *www.cwu.edu* ⊠ *Free.*

Clymer Museum of Art. Half the museum houses a collection of works by painter John Clymer (1907–89), an Ellensburg native who was one of the most widely published illustrators of the American West, focusing his oils and watercolors of wildlife and native cultures. The other half features other well-known and aspiring Western and wildlife artists. ⊠ *416 N. Pearl St.* ☏ *509/962–6416* ⊕ *www.clymermuseum.org* ⊠ *Free* ⊙ *Closed 1st 2 wks of Jan.*

Ginkgo Petrified Forest and Wanapum State Parks. Separated by Interstate 90, 28 miles east of Ellensburg on the Columbia River, are two state parks. Ginkgo Petrified Forest State Park preserves a fossil forest of ginkgoes and other trees. A 3-mile-long trail leads from the interpretive center (open weekends only during shoulder season; open by appointment only November–March). Wanapum State Park, 3 miles south, has camping and river access for boaters. ⊠ *I–90 east to Exit 136, Vantage* ☏ *509/856–2700* ⊕ *www.parks.wa.gov* ⊠ *Free; $10 vehicle pass, camping from $30.*

WORTH NOTING

FAMILY **Dick and Jane's Spot.** The home of artists Jane Orleman and her late husband Dick Elliott is a continuously growing whimsical sculpture: a collage of 20,000 bottle caps, 1,500 bicycle reflectors, and other bits. Their masterpiece stands on private property near downtown, but it's still possible to see the recycled creation from several angles; be sure to sign the guestbook mounted on the surrounding fence. ⊠ *101 N. Pearl St.* ☏ *509/925–3224* ⊕ *www.reflectorart.com.*

Grant PUD Visitor Center. Native American and pioneer artifacts are exhibited here as well as displays on modern hydroelectric power. The center is in Beverly, 36 miles from Ellensburg. ✉ *14352 Hwy. 243 S* ☎ *509/793–1501* 🌐 *www.grantpud.org/recreation/educational/grant-pud-visitor-center* 🎟 *Free* 🕒 *Closed weekends Oct.–Apr.*

FAMILY **Olmstead Place State Historical Park.** This park and 217-acre working farm encompasses the grounds of an original pioneer farm built in 1875. A 1-mile interpretive trail links eight buildings, including a barn and schoolhouse. During harvest time, the park holds threshing bees, demonstrating historic farming practices. ✉ *N. Ferguson Rd.* ✥ *½ mile south of Kittitas Hwy., 4 miles east of Ellensburg* ☎ *509/925–1943* 🌐 *www.parks.wa.gov* 🎟 *$10 per vehicle.*

WHERE TO EAT

$ PIZZA 🍴 **Cornerstone Pie.** Set near the CWU campus and decorated with repurposed, reclaimed, and even historical artifacts, this casual place with a great porch revolves around one central piece, a wood-fire pizza oven. Out of that oven come pies and grinders with a focus on local and seasonal ingredients. **Known for:** wood-fired pizza; Pacific Northwest craft beer on tap. [$] *Average main: $13* ✉ *307 E. 5th Ave.* ☎ *509/933–3600* 🌐 *www.cornerstonepie.com* 🕒 *No lunch.*

$$ AMERICAN 🍴 **Dakota Cafe.** This modern café with a Western touch in the heart of downtown is a popular spot for lunches of hearty sandwiches, soups, and salads as well as dinners of pasta and entrées such as lemon-rosemary chicken and steak with chimichurri sauce. Fresh-baked pastries are also available. **Known for:** daily quiche; ample sandwiches; elegant dinner fare. [$] *Average main: $16* ✉ *417 N. Pearl St.* ☎ *509/925–4783* 🌐 *www.dakotacafe.net* 🕒 *Closed Sun.*

$ AMERICAN 🍴 **Iron Horse Brewery Pub.** At this casual, hip pub you can have A Date with Kevin Bacon—bacon-wrapped dates stuffed with blue cheese and almonds—or some spent-grain beer bread. Then try a kale-and-spinach Caesar salad, bratwurst, or Korean short ribs with spicy kimchi. **Known for:** elevated pub fare; menu with a sense of humor; Quilter's Irish Death dark ale. [$] *Average main: $9* ✉ *412 N. Main St.* ☎ *509/933–3134* 🌐 *www.ironhorsebrewery.com.*

$ AMERICAN 🍴 **The Palace Cafe.** Hungry travelers and locals have enjoyed good food here since 1892, and now choose from a solid menu with standard varieties of steaks, burgers, chicken, and pasta, served in a Western setting. The specialty is a prawn strawberry salad, and the chicken linguine is excellent, as are the ample breakfasts. **Known for:** generous breakfasts; burgers, steaks, and classic American diner fare; prawn strawberry salad. [$] *Average main: $15* ✉ *323 Main St.* ☎ *509/925–2327* 🌐 *www.thepalacecafe.net.*

$ AMERICAN FAMILY 🍴 **Red Horse Diner.** Step back in time to a 1930s-era service station that's been converted into a diner, serving up specialty sandwiches, shakes, and more. While you wait for your burger and fries, check out the hundreds of old metal signs and advertisements that enhance the vintage appeal of this classic burger joint. **Known for:** burgers, fries, and milk shakes; authentic vintage feel and appeal. [$] *Average main: $10* ✉ *1518 W. University Way* ☎ *509/925–1956.*

$ AMERICAN 🍴 **Starlight Lounge.** Weekend nights when CWU is in session are lively at this three-room restaurant and bar in a historical downtown building. Sip a signature Dammit Doris—orange, raspberry, and vanilla vodkas muddled with cherries and a kiss of sweet-and-sour mix—and join the fun, or come in earlier for the fantastic steak quesadilla, a variety of handhelds, or entrées such as herb-roasted chicken or blackened salmon fillet. **Known for:** a bevy of craft cocktails; casual but sophisticated dinner fare. [$] *Average main: $12* ✉ *402 N. Pearl St.* ☎ *509/962–6100* 🌐 *starlight-lounge.com.*

$ AMERICAN 🍴 **The Tav.** This no-frills watering hole is a longtime favorite with locals and CWU students alike for its budget burgers and fries, nachos, and deep-fried mozzarella sticks, and the best jukebox in town. Previous diners have left their mark, carving their names into the wooden tables and brick walls. **Known for:** Super Mother and other burgers; deep-fried appetizers; popular dive bar that won't break the bank. [$] *Average main: $6* ✉ *117 W. 4th Ave.* ☎ *509/925–3939.*

$$ CONTEMPORARY Fodor's Choice ★ 🍴 **Valley Cafe.** Meals at this vintage art deco diner consist of Mediterranean bistro-style salads, pastas, and other plates. Featured dinner entrées include pork tenderloin, seared ahi tuna, and chicken marsala. **Known for:** authentic 1930s feel and appeal; elegant cuisine; superb wine list. [$] *Average main: $22* ✉ *105 W. 3rd Ave.* ☎ *509/925–3050* 🌐 *valleycafeellensburg.com.*

$$ AMERICAN Fodor's Choice ★ 🍴 **Yellow Church Café.** Built in 1923 as a Lutheran church, this cheery, yellow house of culinary worship now offers seating in the nave or choir loft. Soups, salads, sandwiches, pastas, and home-baked goods are served, as well as dinner specials. **Known for:** divine and friendly atmosphere; busy weekend breakfast; elevated Pacific Northwest dinner fare. [$] *Average main: $20* ✉ *111 S. Pearl St.* ☎ *509/933–2233* 🌐 *www.theyellowchurchcafe.com.*

WHERE TO STAY

$ HOTEL 🏨 **Best Western Plus Ellensburg Hotel.** A spacious and contemporary hotel conveniently located one block off Ellensburg's main north–south arterial offers travelers plenty of elbow room in rooms with separate sitting areas and lots of amenities and services. **Pros:** pool; free breakfast. **Cons:** a bit more expensive than the competition. [$] *Rooms from: $102* ✉ *211 W. Umptanum Rd.* ☎ *509/925–4244, 866/925–4288* 🌐 *www.bestwestern.com* 🛏 *55 rooms* 🍽 *Breakfast.*

YAKIMA

38 miles south of Ellensburg.

The gateway to Washington wine country is sunny Yakima (pronounced *yak*-imah), home to more than 90,000 people within the city limits and another 25,000 in the surrounding area. Spread along the west bank of the Yakima River just south of its confluence with the Naches River, Yakima is a bustling community with lovely parklands and a downtown in the midst of revitalization. Downtown street improvements with period lighting, trees, and planters have created a fresh new "old" feel.

Yakima was settled in the late 1850s as a ranching center where Ahtanum Creek joins the Yakima River, on the site of earlier Yakama tribal villages at present-day Union Gap. When the Northern Pacific Railroad established its terminal 4 miles north in 1884, most of the town literally picked up and moved to what was then called "North Yakima."

Yakima's Mission-style Northern Pacific Depot (1912) is the highlight of its historic North Front Street. Four blocks east is the ornate Capitol Theatre, built in 1920. The former vaudeville and silent-movie hall is now a performing arts center. Opposite is Millennium Plaza, a public art installation that celebrates the importance of water to the Yakima Valley. Residents and visitors alike enjoy year-round natural beauty in the heart of Yakima, thanks to the city's ongoing restoration and preservation of the Yakima Greenway. The nature area and trails stretch from Selah Gap to Union Gap, and west along the Naches River.

Yakima is also home to the Central Washington State Fair, the original state fair of Washington. Drawing more than 300,000 people from all over the Northwest, the annual fair, held in late September, is the showcase for the agricultural bounty of the area and provides big-name entertainment and all the unique and delicious "fair" fare.

GETTING HERE AND AROUND
Yakima can be reached via air and road. The Yakima Air Terminal offers commercial flights to and from Seattle daily, and also welcomes private flights from all over. Interstate 82 from Ellensburg to the Tri-Cities and beyond runs right through the city limits. Highways 12 and 410, known as White and Chinook Pass, pass on either side of Mt. Rainier and connect with Interstate 82 at Yakima, as does Highway 97, which brings travelers from Oregon and points south.

Yakima is the only city in the region with a public transportation system.

Yakima Transit. Buses operate weekdays 6:15 am to 6:45 pm, Saturday from 8:45 to 6:45, and Sunday from 8:45 to 4 on 11 routes, at half-hour intervals on weekdays and hourly on weekends. The one-way fare is $1. ☎ 509/575–6175 ⊕ yakimatransit.org.

ESSENTIALS
Visitor Information Yakima Valley Visitors and Convention Bureau.
✉ 10 N. 8th St. ☎ 800/221–0751 ⊕ www.visityakima.com.

EXPLORING
TOP ATTRACTIONS
Gilbert Cellars. In downtown Yakima's historic district, this tasting room serves up selections from the family vineyards, specializing in blends of Rhone and Bordeaux varietals and an unoaked Chardonnay. Look for the top-selling Allobroges and Left Bank red blends as well as small plates such as bacon-wrapped dates, Marcona almonds, and a cheese platter to accompany your favorite vintage. The location makes Gilbert Cellars an ideal place to meet before a night on the town, or to enjoy a glass of wine after dinner. First Fridays, there's usually live music in the basement. ✉ 5 N. Front St. ☎ 509/249–9049 ⊕ www.gilbertcellars. com ▢ Tastings $6.

17

Fodor's Choice ★ **Tieton Cider Works Cider Bar.** Six hand-crafted ciders are typically on tap at this North Yakima cidery—from cranberry to dry hopped, apricot, apple, and more. In warmer weather, try out the bocce ball court and enjoy live music from the outdoor stage. ✉ *619 W. J St.* ☎ *509/571–1430* 🌐 *tietonciderworks.com* 🕒 *Closed Mon. and Tues.*

Fodor's Choice ★ **Treveri Cellars.** Some of the best handcrafted sparkling wines in the country come from these family-owned cellars on a hillside just south of Yakima. Enjoy valley views while sipping sparkling rosé, Riesling, Gewürztraminer, and the extraordinary Syrah Brut. ✉ *71 Gangl Rd., Wapato* ☎ *509/877–0925* 🌐 *www.trevericellars.com.*

Yakima Area Arboretum. Just off Interstate 82, this parklike swath features hundreds of different plants, flowers, and trees. A Japanese garden and a wetland trail are highlights. The arboretum sits alongside the Yakima River and the 10-mile-long Yakima Greenway, a paved path that links a series of riverfront parks. ✉ *1401 Arboretum Dr., off Nob Hill Blvd.* ☎ *509/248–7337* 🌐 *www.ahtrees.org* 🎫 *Free.*

FAMILY **Yakima Valley Museum.** Exhibits here focus on Yakama native, pioneer, and 20th-century history, ranging from horse-drawn vehicles to a "neon garden" of street signs. Highlights include a fully operating 1930s-style soda fountain and a model of Yakima native and Supreme Court Justice William O. Douglas's Washington, D.C., office. Other visiting and rotation exhibits are also scheduled throughout the year. ✉ *2105 Tieton Dr.* ☎ *509/248–0747* 🌐 *www.yakimavalleymuseum.org* 🎫 *$5* 🕒 *Closed Sun. and Mon.*

WORTH NOTING

Naches Heights Vineyard. Just a few miles west of Yakima, this winery is located in one of Washington's newest wine-growing areas. Set among organic and biodynamic vineyards at an elevation of 1,780 feet, the tasting room has ample seating inside, where you may catch some live music while contemplating their wines. The winery features blends in both red and white. ✉ *1857 Weikel Rd., south of Hwy. 12* ☎ *855/648–9463* 🌐 *www.nhvwines.com* 🕒 *Closed Mon.–Thurs. in winter.*

WHERE TO EAT

$ MEXICAN 🍴 **Antojitos Mexicanos.** Never mind that it's located in a remodeled Dairy Queen; this is hands down the best and most popular Mexican food in Yakima. There are no frills here, but the service is fast and friendly, the food is hearty and authentic, and the portions are ample. **Known for:** wide selection of house-made salsas; fresh tortillas; pozole. [$] *Average main: $12* ✉ *3512 Summitview Ave.* ☎ *509/248–2626* 🕒 *Closed Mon.*

$$$ CONTEMPORARY Fodor's Choice ★ 🍴 **Cowiche Canyon Kitchen and Icehouse Bar.** Named for the hiking trail that runs through an old railway route in a canyon west of Yakima, this award-winning restaurant offers contemporary, elevated takes on American classics like no other place in town. Lauded for its architecture and design as well as its menu, this is a must-stop for its lemony, smoky, grilled-artichoke appetizer, chicken and melt-in-your-mouth dumplings, steamed clams in apple-and-squash broth, and excellent craft cocktails. **Known for:** upscale and modern American fare; extensive selection of regional and local beer; award-winning architecture and design. [$] *Average main: $24* ✉ *202 E. Yakima Ave.* ☎ *509/457–2007* 🌐 *www.cowichecanyon.com.*

Yakima Valley vineyard

$$$ ITALIAN 🍴 **Gasperetti's.** John Gasperetti's restaurant keeps an elegant low profile in a high-traffic area north of downtown. Hearty pasta dishes share the menu with meat or seafood entrées with organically grown local produce and daily specials; Thursday's crab cannelloni is particularly popular. **Known for:** upscale fare and atmosphere in an unlikely location; popular with local foodies; a Yakima institution since 1966. [$] *Average main: $24* ✉ *1013 N. 1st St.* ☎ *509/248–0628* 🌐 *www.gasperettisrestaurant.com* 🕒 *Closed Sun. No lunch Sat.*

$ MEXICAN 🍴 **Los Hernandez Tamales.** From this humble shop come some of the region's best tamales—shredded chicken and pork and, during spring, asparagus and cheese. You'll probably want to order more than one. **Known for:** tamales; springtime asparagus-and-cheese tamales. [$] *Average main: $2* ✉ *3706 Main St., Union Gap* ☎ *509/457–6003.*

$ AMERICAN FAMILY 🍴 **Miner's Drive-In.** This Yakima icon (actually located in Union Gap) is a must-visit for many travelers—particularly entire sports teams—coming to or through town. It's an authentic 1940s hamburger joint that has expanded from a traditional drive-in to a family sit-down diner with menu items from salads to fish-and-chips and burgers. **Known for:** old-fashioned burger-joint ambience; big burgers; gets crowded and lively during youth sports seasons. [$] *Average main: $10* ✉ *2415 S. 1st St., Union Gap* ☎ *509/457–8194.*

$ AMERICAN FAMILY 🍴 **The Soda Fountain at Yakima Valley Museum.** Soda jerks at the Yakima Valley Museum's café make shakes and sundaes plus soups, hot dogs, and sandwiches while a period Wurlitzer spins 1930s big-band records. **Known for:** milk shakes, malts, sundaes, and ice-cream cones; vintage look and feel. [$] *Average main: $8* ✉ *Yakima Valley Museum, 2105 Tieton Dr.* ☎ *509/457–9810* 🌐 *yakimavalleymuseum.org/soda.cfm* 🕒 *Closed Sun.*

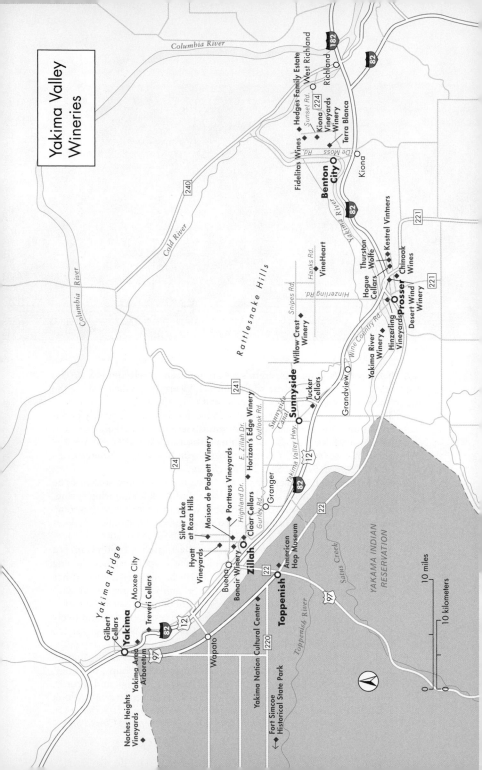

$ ✕ **White House Cafe.** This charming Craftsman-style hillside home serves
CAFÉ scrumptious salads, sandwiches,and egg dishes with lovely garnishes
Fodor'sChoice and, often, a dusting of powdered sugar. Sit in the dining, living, or
★ sun room—or, when the weather's nice, in the garden out back—and
relish dining in the vintage home. **Known for:** vintage charm; charming
gift shop off the dining room. $ *Average main: $13* ⊠ *3602 Kern Rd.*
☏ *509/469–2644 café, 509/910–0961* ⊕ *www.whitehouseinyakima.
com* ☺ *No dinner.*

WHERE TO STAY

$$ ⊡ **Birchfield Manor.** These luxurious accommodations, set on a plateau
B&B/INN just east of Yakima, include an old manor that houses a restaurant and
five traditionally furnished upstairs rooms, while a newer, more private
cottage contains rooms with such amenities as steam-sauna showers
and gas fireplaces. **Pros:** a distinctive experience for this region; good
restaurant on-site. **Cons:** a little off the beaten path; limited restaurant
hours. $ *Rooms from: $170* ⊠ *2018 Birchfield Rd.* ✣ *Just south of
Hwy. 24* ☏ *509/452–1960, 800/375–3420* ⊕ *www.birchfieldmanor.
com* ⌇ *11 rooms* ♟⃝ *Breakfast.*

$ ⊡ **Hilton Garden Inn.** Modern, spacious, and comfortably furnished
HOTEL rooms in the heart of downtown offer some of the city's finest upscale
lodgings. **Pros:** one block from the convention center and walking dis-
tance to shops and restaurants; restaurant and 24-hour pantry on-site;
indoor pool; Ummelina spa. **Cons:** in the midst of the concrete jungle;
the fitness center overlooks the city's main drag and there are no privacy
blinds. $ *Rooms from: $129* ⊠ *402 E. Yakima Ave.* ☏ *509/454–1111*
⊕ *hiltongardeninn3.hilton.com* ⌇ *114 rooms* ♟⃝ *Breakfast.*

$ ⊡ **Hotel Maison.** This elegant and formidable boutique hotel, Yakima's
HOTEL newest, was built in 1911 as a Masonic temple, and hints of its heri-
Fodor'sChoice tage can be seen throughout the building, which boasts some of the
★ city's most contemporary and stylish accommodations. **Pros:** located in
the downtown core, within walking distance of shops and restaurants;
complimentary glass of wine upon arrival; stylish modern furnishings.
Cons: none of the rooms have bathtubs. $ *Rooms from: $129* ⊠ *321
E. Yakima Ave.* ☏ *509/571–1900* ⊕ *www.thehotelmaison.com* ⌇ *36
rooms* ♟⃝ *Breakfast.*

$$ ⊡ **North Park Lodge.** Outdoorsy designs combine with overstuffed
HOTEL leather and handsome wood furniture, lending a rustic appeal to these
accommodations. **Pros:** quiet and affordable, with plenty of room for
the family; indoor pool. **Cons:** 8 miles from Yakima. $ *Rooms from:
$172* ⊠ *659 N. Wenas Rd., Selah* ☏ *509/698–6000* ⊕ *www.northpark-
lodge.com* ⌇ *53 rooms* ♟⃝ *Breakfast.*

$ ⊡ **Rosedell Bed and Breakfast.** This neoclassical manor, completed in 1909
B&B/INN by A.E. Larson, one of Yakima's earliest entrepreneurs, for his wife,
Rose, remains one of the city's most luxurious residences. **Pros:** memorable mansion with a sense of history; well-appointed rooms. **Cons:** a
1½-mile trek to downtown shops and restaurants. $ *Rooms from: $125*
⊠ *1811 W. Yakima Ave.* ☏ *509/961–2964* ⊕ *www.rosedellbb.com* ⌇ *4
rooms* ♟⃝ *Breakfast.*

17

SPORTS AND THE OUTDOORS

GOLF

Apple Tree Golf Course. This beautiful course, cut through the apple orchards of west Yakima, is rated among the state's top 10. The signature hole on the course is Number 17, shaped like a giant apple surrounded by a lake. ⊠ *8804 Occidental Rd.* ☎ *509/966–5877* ⊕ *www.appletreeresort. com* ⚑ *Weekdays $29–$58, weekends $35–$73; $16 for cart* ▲ *18 holes, 6900 yards, par 72.*

SKIING

White Pass Ski Area. A full-service ski area 50 miles west of Yakima toward Mt. Rainier is the home mountain of Olympic medalists Phil and Steve Mahre. Eight lifts serve 47 trails on a vertical drop of 1,500 feet from the 6,000-foot summit. Here you'll find condominiums, a gas station, grocery store, and snack bar. Open woods are popular with cross-country skiers and summer hikers. ⊠ *48935 U.S. 12* ☎ *509/672– 3101* ⊕ *www.skiwhitepass.com.*

NIGHTLIFE AND PERFORMING ARTS

Fodor's Choice ★
Bale Breaker Brewing Company. This brewery is situated in the middle of hop fields first planted in 1932 by the great-grandparents of the three siblings who now own it. Their hop-forward brews are made with hops that grow right out the back door. On a sunny day, enjoy the signature Field 41 pale ale, Topcutter IPA, and Bottomcutter double IPA in the grassy outdoor seating area, complete with lawn games, or just hang out in the taproom. Weekends often bring live music and food trucks serving a variety of cuisine. ⊠ *1801 Birchfield Rd.* ☎ *509/424–4000* ⊕ *www.balebreaker.com.*

Mickey's Pub and Orion Cinema. At this pub inside a downtown cinema, you can opt to watch a film and push a call button for seat-side service, including beer, or just sit in the pub and skip the movie—but maybe not the popcorn. Burgers, sandwiches, salads, and personal pizzas fill the menu. Some weekend nights there's live music in the bar. ⊠ *202 E. Chestnut Ave.* ☎ *509/248–0245* ⊕ *www.mickeyspubyakima.com.*

Sports Center Yakima. Find this longtime Yakima hangout on the town's main drag by its signature neon sign showing a sportsman pointing a rifle into the air. Inside, the restaurant serves up a variety of burgers, sandwiches, and shareables such as pork shanks, nachos, and calamari. Weekend nights, a DJ gives the pub a clubby vibe. ⊠ *214 E. Yakima Ave.* ☎ *509/453–4647* ⊕ *www.sportscenteryakima.com.*

SHOPPING

FAMILY
Fodor's Choice ★
Johnson Orchards. This company has been growing and selling fruit— including cherries, peaches, apples, and pears—to the public on this site since 1904. One of the best things about this orchard is that it's in town—the city of Yakima grew up around it, so no need to drive far into the countryside to buy fresh-picked fruit. Plus, there's a bakeshop on-site. ⊠ *4906 Summitview Ave.* ☎ *509/966–7479* ⊕ *johnsonorchardsfruit.com* ⊙ *Closed Tues., Wed., and Sun. in winter.*

Valley Mall. Central Washington's largest shopping center has all kinds of specialty shops and three major department stores: Sears, Kohls, and Macy's. Twigs is a popular place to rest tired feet and grab a martini after shopping. The area surrounding the mall is the main retail area for the region, featuring several national retailers within a mile radius. Sportsmen and -women flock to the Cabela's outdoors store. ⊠ *2529 Main St., Union Gap* ✢ *Off I–82, Exit 36* ☎ *509/453–8233* ⊕ *www. shopatvalleymall.com.*

Fodor's Choice
★

Yakima Farmers' Market. This vibrant and bustling but small downtown market features live music, street food, and items ranging from artisanal breads and fresh-cut flowers to locally grown fruits and vegetables. It takes place Sunday from May through October. At other times, roadside stands and farms throughout the Yakima Valley welcome visitors. Best bets for roadside produce are west of town on Highway 12, and south on Highway 97. ⊠ *Yakima Ave. and 3rd St.* ⊕ *yakimafarmersmarket.org.*

SOUTHERN YAKIMA RIVER VALLEY

The lower Yakima Valley encompasses hundreds of thousands of acres both on and off the Yakama Indian Reservation and includes several small towns. Agriculture is the name of the game in this part of the lower valley, where everything from apples to zucchinis are grown. Throughout the summer visitors buy or pick all kinds of fresh vegetables and fruits. In early May the asparagus grows to cutting height, and soon after that it's time for the cherries to be harvested. Basically, it's one harvest after the next, culminating with apples in late October. Growing conditions also make this area the hot spot for wine-grape growing, and where there are grapes, there are wineries. The vines of some 70 wineries now carpet the Yakima Valley, with many of the best wines in the country coming from these vintners. The history of this region stretches back hundreds of years from the time of the Native American Yakama people and early white settlers. Much of this history can be seen in several museums around the region, including the museum at the Yakama Nation Cultural Center in Toppenish.

17

ZILLAH

15 miles southeast of Yakima.

The south-facing slopes above Zillah, a tiny town named after the daughter of a railroad manager, are covered with orchards and vineyards. Several wineries are in or near the community; more are near Granger, 6 miles southeast.

GETTING HERE AND AROUND
The outskirts of Zillah, which is growing to include many new businesses, sits right on Interstate 82, southeast of Yakima. Downtown Zillah is just up the hill a half mile or so.

EXPLORING
TOP ATTRACTIONS
Bonair Winery. The Puryear family began commercial wine production in their native Yakima Valley in 1985. Their tasting room, reminiscent of a European chalet, sits among vineyards near a duck pond, and was voted one of Washington's best places for a kiss. At the tasting room, you'll likely meet owners Gail Puryear and his wife, the "wine

goddess" Shirley, as well as winemaker Bill Mechem, who's worked for the family since 2005. Bonair makes Cabernets, Cabernet Francs, Chardonnays, Gewürztraminer port, Merlots, and Rieslings, and sells some snack foods. Plan to picnic on the grounds. ⊠ *500 S. Bonair Rd.* ☎ *509/829–6027* ⊕ *www.bonairwine.com.*

Claar Cellars. This family-owned estate winery has a tasting room right off Interstate 82 and enjoys one of the highest visitor numbers of any Yakima Valley winery. Claar produces a variety of wines, including some ice wines, Sangiovese, and rare varieties such as Corneauxcopia (a blended variety) and Fouled Anchor Port, which includes cherries, raisins, honey, and maple syrup. The winery also produces traditional Merlots, Cabernets, Chardonnays, Sauvignon Blancs, and Rieslings. The grapes come from vineyards in the White Bluffs region, quite a distance from the vineyards. ⊠ *1001 Vintage Valley Pkwy.* ☎ *509/829–6810* ⊕ *www.claarcellars.com.*

Hyatt Vineyards. Leland and Linda Hyatt's 97 acres of estate vineyards have long been well respected locally for Merlot and Cabernet Sauvignon, and lately those wines have been attracting national attention. Their late-harvest Riesling is also worth tasting. The tasting room is well appointed, the staff has wide knowledge of local viniculture, and the spacious, well-manicured grounds are nice for picnicking. On clear days there are spectacular views of the Yakima Valley, Mt. Adams, and the Cascade Mountains. ⊠ *2020 Gilbert Rd.* ⊹ *Off I–82, Exit 52* ☎ *509/829–6333* ⊕ *www.hyattvineyards.net.*

Fodor's Choice ★ **Portteus Vineyards.** One of the early Yakima Valley wineries, established in 1981, Portteus is beloved by red-wine drinkers. Production includes Cabernet Sauvignon and Franc, Merlot, Malbec, Syrah, Zinfandel, and port—as well as a robust Chardonnay. The family-run tasting room is often staffed by the second generation of the Portteus family. Grapes are grown at 1,440-foot elevation on 47 acres above Zillah. ⊠ *5201 Highland Dr.* ☎ *509/829–6970* ⊕ *www.portteus.com.*

WORTH NOTING

Horizon's Edge Winery. With a spectacular view of the Yakima Valley, Mt. Adams, and Mt. Rainier, it is easy to see where Horizon's Edge got its name. The winery makes sparkling wine, Chardonnay, Pinot Noir, Merlot, Cabernet Sauvignon, and Muscat Canelli. ⊠ *4530 E. Zillah Dr., east of Yakima Valley Hwy.* ☎ *509/829–6401* ⊕ *www.horizonsedgewinery.com* ⊗ *Closed Tues. and Wed.*

Maison de Padgett Winery. This small family winery produces specialized handcrafted wines in a beautiful setting with pillars and porticos reminniscent of old-world architecture and adjoining European-style gardens. It's perfect for weddings or simply sipping wine during warm weather. Groups of 10 or more should call ahead. ⊠ *2231 Roza Dr., at Highland Dr.* ☎ *509/829–6412* ⊕ *www.maisondepadgettwinery.com.*

Silver Lake at Roza Hills. Bands serenade picnickers on summer weekends on what the winery calls their "viniferanda," above their historic estate high in the Rattlesnake Hills. With both a large deck and well-manicured lawn with a soothing fountain, visitors are afforded

Desert Wind Winery, Prosser

views of the Cabernets, Merlots, Chardonnays, Rieslings, and other vintages in production in the valley below. Sundays in August bring live music and salmon dinners, and the tasting room offers spectacular vineyard views as well. ✉ *1500 Vintage Rd., off Highland Dr.* ☎ *509/829–6235* 🌐 *www.silverlakewinery.com* ⏲ *Closed Tues. and Wed. in Nov.–Apr.*

WHERE TO EAT AND STAY

$ MEXICAN 🍴 **El Porton.** Authentic, affordable Mexican fare is what you get at this no-frills but friendly establishment. Savory seafood dishes such as *mariscos al mojo de ajo* (sautéed prawns with mushrooms and garlic) are favorites, and traditional offerings such as beef or chicken burritos and enchiladas round out the menu. **Known for:** budget-friendly, authentic Mexican fare; large portions. [$] *Average main: $14* ✉ *905 Vintage Valley Pkwy., Exit 52 off I–82* ☎ *509/829–9100.*

$ HOTEL 🏨 **Best Western Plus Vintage Valley Inn.** Large, comfortable rooms, a business center, gym, and an indoor pool and spa make this stop just a few steps from Claar Cellars ideal for wine lovers and families alike. **Pros:** right on the freeway, and the only motel within miles; indoor heated pool, spa, and gym; good breakfast included in the rate. **Cons:** potential traffic noise. [$] *Rooms from: $110* ✉ *911 Vintage Valley Pkwy.* ☎ *509/829–3399, 800/501–5433* 🌐 *www.vintagevalleyinn.com* 🛏 *40 rooms* 🍽 *Breakfast.*

TOPPENISH

17 miles southeast of Yakima.

This intriguing small town with a rustic Old West sensibility lies within the Yakama Reservation and blends history and culture, art and agriculture. You can't miss the 70 colorful murals that adorn the facades and exterior walls of businesses and homes. Commissioned since 1989 by the Toppenish Mural Association and done in a variety of styles by regional artists, they commemorate the town's history and Western spirit. Tours in a horse-drawn covered wagon leave from the association's office on Toppenish Avenue.

GETTING HERE AND AROUND

Jump on Highway 97 out of Yakima, and the four-lane road will take you through Wapato and right to Toppenish. Or follow the signs from Interstate 82 at Zillah. From Oregon and points south Highway 97 also brings you right to Toppenish over Satus Pass.

ESSENTIALS

Visitor Information Toppenish Chamber of Commerce. ✉ *504 S. Elm St.* ☎ *509/865–3262, 800/863–6375* ⊕ *www.visittoppenish.com.*

EXPLORING

FAMILY **American Hop Museum.** The Yakima Valley grows about 78% of the nation's hops, and the industry's story is well told at this museum. Exhibits describe the history, growing process, and unique biology of the plant, a primary ingredient in beer. ✉ *22 S. B St.* ☎ *509/865–4677* ⊕ *www. americanhopmuseum.org* 🎫 *$3* ⊗ *Closed Mon., Tues., and Oct.–Apr.*

FAMILY **Fort Simcoe Historical State Park.** The residential quarters of an 1856 army fort, located on some 200 acres about 30 miles west of Toppenish, look like a Victorian summer retreat. Exhibits focus on relations between the Yakama people—in the heart of whose reservation the fort stands—and American settlers. The Military Days celebration in May features reenactments. There's wildlife viewing, especially bird-watching, all year as well as 45 picnic tables and four sheltered picnic areas. ✉ *5150 Ft. Simcoe Rd.* ☎ *509/874–2372* ⊕ *www.parks.wa.gov* 🎫 *Free.*

FAMILY **Yakama Nation Cultural Center.** This six-building complex has a fascinating museum of tribal history and culture, including costumes, basketry, beadwork, and reconstructions of traditional lodges. Tribal dances and other cultural events are often staged in the Heritage Theater; the complex also includes a gift shop and library. ✉ *Buster Dr. at U.S. 97* ☎ *509/865–2800* ⊕ *www.yakamamuseum.com* 🎫 *$6.*

SUNNYSIDE

14 miles southeast of Zillah.

The largest community in the lower Yakima Valley and the hometown of astronaut Bonnie Dunbar, Sunnyside runs along the sunny southern slopes of the Rattlesnake Hills. Not the most charming town in the valley, it has a few wineries and dining and lodging options, making it a convenient stopover.

GETTING HERE AND AROUND

Interstate 82 runs right past Sunnyside as it threads its way down through the lower Yakima Valley. Three exits put you at either end and in the middle of Sunnyside.

EXPLORING

Tucker Cellars. The Tucker family came to the Yakima Valley as sharecroppers during the Great Depression, became successful farmers, and were among the first to grow vinifera grapes on a commercial scale. Dean and Rose Tucker founded the winery in 1981; today the family operation is run by the third generation. Plantings include Riesling, Pinot Noir, Gewürztraminer, Chenin Blanc, Chardonnay, and Muscat Canelli. Attached to the tasting room is the family's produce stand, which sells some of the Yakima Valley's best seasonal fruits and vegetables. There's also a picnic area. ✉ *70 Ray Rd.* ☎ *509/837–8701* 🌐 *www.tuckercellars.net.*

WHERE TO EAT AND STAY

$ MEXICAN 🍴 **El Conquistador.** The menu at this brightly colored restaurant ranges from burritos, fajitas, tacos, and enchiladas mole to shrimp sautéed with green peppers and onions and served with a tangy salsa. Egg dishes are also on the menu, as are authentic Mexican salads and soups. **Known for:** authentic Mexican fare; locals' favorite. [$] *Average main: $12* ✉ *214 S. 6th St.* ☎ *509/839–2880.*

$ AMERICAN Fodor's Choice ★ 🍴 **Snipes Mountain Microbrewery & Restaurant.** In an imposing log structure that resembles a hunting or ski lodge, the lower valley's oldest and largest brewpub features fare ranging from burgers and wood-fired pizzas to pasta dishes, fresh king salmon cooked on an alder plank, prime rib, and rack of lamb. Head brewer Ryan Wattenbarger makes handcrafted beers such as the Coyote Moon brown ale using locally grown hops. **Known for:** wood-fired pizza and calzone; craft beer brewed on-site. [$] *Average main: $15* ✉ *905 Yakima Valley Hwy.* ☎ *509/837–2739* 🌐 *snipesmountain.com.*

$ B&B/INN 🏨 **Sunnyside Inn Bed & Breakfast.** At this two-house inn, built in 1919 as a doctor's residence and office, many of the 13 rooms have whirlpool tubs and private entrances; several also include small sunrooms. **Pros:** in the heart of wine country; a short drive to several different wineries; free Wi-Fi in rooms. **Cons:** immediate surroundings are not the most appealing. [$] *Rooms from: $95* ✉ *800–804 E. Edison Ave.* ☎ *509/839–5557, 800/221–4195* 🌐 *www.sunnysideinn.com* 🛏 *13 rooms* 🍽 *Breakfast.*

PROSSER

13 miles southeast of Sunnyside.

On the south bank of the Yakima River, Prosser feels like small-town America of the 1950s. The seat of Benton County since 1905, it has a 1926 courthouse. In 2005, Prosser's Horse Heaven Hills, on the Columbia River's north slope, became Washington's seventh federally recognized wine region.

GETTING HERE AND AROUND

On the lower end of the Yakima Valley, Prosser sits alongside Interstate 82 as it works its way to Benton City and then on to the Tri-Cities (Richland/Kennewick/Pasco). Two exits put you at either end of town.

ESSENTIALS

Visitor Information Prosser Chamber of Commerce. ✉ *1230 Bennett Ave.* ☎ *509/786–3177, 866/343–5101* ⊕ *www.prosserchamber.com.*

EXPLORING

TOP ATTRACTIONS

Fodor'sChoice
★
Desert Wind Winery. This expansive tasting room housed in an elegant Southwestern-style building featuring a vast patio overlooking the Yakima River is one of the highlights of any wine tour in the valley. Tasters will delight in Sémillon, Barbera, Ruah, Viognier, and various other unique wine selections. Just off Interstate 82, this family-owned winery also includes a luxurious four-room inn as well as a gift shop with Yakima Valley food products and gift items. ✉ *2258 Wine Country Rd.* ☎ *509/786–7277* ⊕ *www.desertwindwinery.com.*

Hogue Cellars. Founded in 1982, Hogue Cellars is one of the largest wineries in the state and has earned numerous awards for its wines. The gift shop carries the winery's famous pickled beans and asparagus as well as Cabernet Sauvignon, Merlot, Chenin Blanc, Rieslings, and Fume Blanc, among other wines. ✉ *Prosser Wine and Food Park, 2800 Lee Rd.* ☎ *509/786–6108* ⊕ *www.hoguecellars.com.*

Kestrel Vintners. Although visiting this winery, in the Port of Benton's Prosser Wine and Food Park, doesn't necessarily rank as a great sensory pleasure, tasting the wines does. Kestrel is one of the Yakima Valley's premium wineries and makes mainly reds (Cabernet Sauvignon, Merlot, Syrah), as well as some white (Chardonnay, Viognier), from grapes—some of them estate grown—that are deliberately stressed to increase the intensity of their flavors. The tasting room sells cheeses and deli items to go with the wines. Look for its signature Lady in White and Lady in Red series. ✉ *Prosser Wine and Food Park, 2890 Lee Rd.* ☎ *509/786–2675* ⊕ *www.kestrelwines.com.*

WORTH NOTING

Chinook Wines. This small house winery is run by Kay Simon and Clay Mackey, vintners known for their dry wines, including Merlot, Chardonnay, Sémillon, and Sauvignon Blanc. The tasting room is within the original farm buildings, and there's a shady picnic area outside. ✉ *Wittkopf Loop at Wine Country Rd.* ☎ *509/786–2725* ⊕ *www.chinookwines.com* ⊗ *Closed Nov.–Apr.*

Hinzerling Vineyards. The place that's billed as the valley's first winery specializes in dessert and appetizer wines, including port, sherry, and Muscat. Vintner Mike Wallace was one of the state's wine pioneers: he planted his first Prosser-area vines in 1972, and established the small winery in 1976. ✉ *1520 Sheridan Ave., at Wine Country Rd.* ☎ *509/786–2163* ⊕ *www.hinzerling.com.*

Thurston Wolfe. Established in 1987, one of the region's most highly regarded wineries features Wade Wolfe's unusual blends of specialty wines, including a white Pinot Gris–Viognier, for instance, and a red mix of Zinfandel, Syrah, Lemberger, and Touriga. One of their popular varieties is Sweet Rebecca, an orange Muscat. ✉ *Prosser Wine and Food Park, 588 Cabernet Ct.* ☎ *509/786–3313* ⊕ *www.thurstonwolfe.com* ⊗ *Hrs vary; call ahead.*

Hogue Cellars, Prosser

VineHeart. This pleasant boutique winery offers a buttery Riesling, a raspberry-toned Sémillon, a Lemberger, and a Sangiovese, as well as Zinfandel, Cabernet Sauvignon, and Syrah. ⊠ *44209 N. McDonald Rd.* ✢ *7 miles northeast of Prosser* ☎ *509/973–2993* ⊕ *www.vineheart.com* ☽ *Closed Tues. and Wed.*

Willow Crest Winery. David Minick founded his small winery in 1995 and offers a Tuscan-themed tasting room that pours its own award-winning Syrah, as well as Cabernet Franc and Pinot Gris. ⊠ *Vintners Village, 590 Merlot Dr.* ☎ *509/786–7999* ⊕ *www.willowcrestwinery. com* ☽ *Closed Tues. and Wed.*

Yakima River Winery. Another of the pioneer wineries in the valley, established by John and Louise Rauner in 1977, specializes in barrel-aged reds and a memorable port. ⊠ *143302 N. River Rd.* ✢ *1½ miles south of Wine Country Rd.* ☎ *509/786–2805.*

BENTON CITY

16 miles east of Prosser.

The Yakima River zigzags north, making a giant bend around Red Mountain and the West Richland district before pouring into the Columbia River. Benton City—which, with a mere 3,000 residents, is hardly a city—is on a bluff west of the river facing vineyard-cloaked Red Mountain. High-carbonate soil, a location in a unique high-pressure pocket, and geographical anomalies have led to this district's being given its own appellation. You can access the wineries from Highway 224.

GETTING HERE AND AROUND

You'll find Benton City just off Interstate 82 about halfway between Prosser and Richland. One exit takes off from the interstate and funnels traffic into the little town and to Highway 224.

EXPLORING

Fodor's Choice
★ **Fidelitas Wines.** This craft winery with sweeping views specializes in Bordeaux varietals and high-end, award-winning wines. The tasting room is modern, bright, and airy, and outdoor seating areas provide a spectacular backdrop for indulging in rich red wines. ⊠ *51810 N. Sunset Rd.* ☎ *509/588–3469* ⊕ *www.fidelitaswines.com.*

Hedges Family Estate. This spectacular hillside château winery dominates upper Red Mountain and produces robust red wines. The estate blends, Cabernet Sauvignon, Cabernet Franc, Merlot, Syrah, and reserve blends are superb. ⊠ *53511 N. Sunset Rd.* ☎ *509/588–3155* ⊕ *www.hedges-familyestate.com* ☽ *Closed Dec.–Mar. and weekdays Apr.–Nov.*

Kiona Vineyards Winery. John Williams planted the first grapes on Red Mountain in 1975, made his first wines in 1980, and produced the first commercial Kiona Lemberger, a light German red, in the United States. Today Williams's 10,000-square-foot tasting room features a 180-degree view of Red Mountain and the Rattlesnake Hills. Kiona also produces premium Riesling, Chenin Blanc, Chardonnay, Cabernet Sauvignon, Merlot, Syrah, Sangiovese, and dessert wines. You can picnic on the patio; in addition to the wines, a range of meats and cheeses can be purchased. ⊠ *44612 N. Sunset Rd.* ☎ *509/588–6716* ⊕ *www.kionawine.com.*

Fodor's Choice
★ **Terra Blanca.** It's named for the calcium carbonate in its soil—Terra Blanca is Latin for "white earth"—and from this unique soil grow wine grapes that produce such specialties as Syrah, Merlot, Cabernet Sauvignon, and Chardonnay. This award-winning picturesque estate winery offers sweeping views of the Red Mountain region, providing a beautiful backdrop for photos. ⊠ *34715 N. Demoss Rd.* ☎ *509/588–6082* ⊕ *www.terrablanca.com.*

SPOKANE AND EASTERN WASHINGTON

WELCOME TO SPOKANE AND EASTERN WASHINGTON

TOP REASONS TO GO

★ **Historic lodgings:** Take a step back in time. Visit the historic hotels and inns in Spokane, Walla Walla, and Dayton, which have been updated with modern amenities and high-tech touches, yet retain the flavor of yesteryear.

★ **Natural wonders:** Get off the beaten path to experience the unique waters of Soap Lake, see the cliffs and canyons along the Columbia River, and hike in national forests.

★ **Wineries:** Explore the many wineries in Walla Walla, Tri-Cities, and Spokane.

★ **Family attractions:** Slip in a little education on your family vacation by visiting pioneer museums, then play at water parks and Spokane's sprawling Riverfront Park.

★ **Big sporting events:** Join over 40,000 runners in one of the largest timed running races in the nation—Spokane's annual 12K Bloomsday Run. And take to the streets for the biggest 3-on-3 basketball tournament in the world, Spokane's annual Hoopfest.

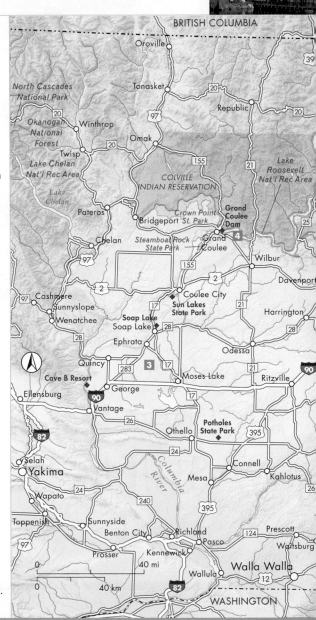

1 Southeastern Washington. In the wide-open areas of the Walla Walla and Columbia Valleys, hillsides are covered with rows of grapevines and wind turbines. Lodging, restaurants, museums, and wine-tasting opportunities can be found in Walla Walla and the Tri-Cities. Farther east are historic Dayton and the college town of Pullman.

2 Spokane. The second-largest city in Washington is home to one of the state's best hotels, the restored Davenport, and several other historic lodgings. There are numerous restaurants, from fine dining to family-friendly; a fun kids' museum and science museum, and an interesting history museum; and two especially notable parks (Manito, with its duck pond and Japanese Garden, and Riverfront, with lots of activities for the whole family).

3 East Central Washington. Venture off the main highway to discover the stunning Cave B Resort by the Columbia River, see pioneer-history displays in Ephrata, and experience the healing waters of Soap Lake, before heading back on Interstate 90 through Moses Lake.

4 Northeastern Washington. Travelers to this region will find the "Eighth Technological Wonder of the World"—the Grand Coulee Dam—which features a daily laser-light show in summer. Further exploration brings you to the Colville and Okanogan national forests, and the small towns of Grand Coulee, Coulee City, Omak, and Colville.

GETTING ORIENTED

The main route through eastern Washington is Interstate 90. Coming from the west, as you leave the Cascade Mountains and its foothills behind, the terrain turns to desert and sagebrush, before crossing over the Columbia River and reaching the irrigated areas where fields of crops grow. In this area's barren, dry lands a new type of farming has emerged—wind farms with giant turbines that transform the landscape and provide electricity. The southeast part of the state offers a more verdant setting—rolling hills and fields where rain helps produce abundant crops of grains and wine grapes. The northeast part of the state is flanked by three mountain ranges (Selkirk, Okanogan, and Kettle River), which are considered foothills of the Rocky Mountains; this area is rich with lakes, rivers, cliffs, and meadows, and home to diverse wildlife.

18

Updated by
Shelley Arenas

The Columbia Plateau was created by a series of lava flows that were later deeply cut by glacial floods. Because its soil is mostly made up of alluvial deposits and windblown silt (known to geologists as loess), it's very fertile. But little annual rainfall means that its vast central section—more than 30,000 square miles from the foothills of the Cascades and the northeastern mountains east to Idaho and south to Oregon—has no forests. In fact, except for a few scattered pine trees in the north, oaks in the southwest, and willows and cottonwoods along creeks and rivers, it has no trees.

This treeless expanse is part of an even larger steppe and desert region that runs north into Canada and south to California and the Sea of Cortez. There is water, however, carried from the mountains by the great Columbia and Snake Rivers and their tributaries. Irrigation provides the region's cities with shrubs, trees, and flowers, and its fields bear a great variety of crops: asparagus, potatoes, apples, peaches, alfalfa, sweet corn, wheat, lentils, and much more. This bounty of agriculture makes the region prosperous, and provides funds for symphony halls and opera houses, theaters, art museums, and universities.

Southeast of the Columbia Plateau lies a region of rolling hills and fields. Farmers of the Palouse region and of the foothills of the Blue Mountains don't need to irrigate their fields, as rain here produces record crops of wheat, lentils, and peas. It's a blessed landscape, flowing green and golden under the sun in waves of loam. In the Walla Walla Valley the traditional crops of wheat and sweet onions remain, but more than 1,800 acres of grapes now supply more than 100 wineries that have opened in the past few decades. The region is not only fertile, it is historically significant as well. The Lewis and Clark expedition passed through the Palouse in 1805, and Walla Walla was one of the earliest settlements in the Inland Northwest.

The northeastern mountains, from the Okanogan to the Pend Oreille Valley, consist of granite peaks, glaciated cliffs, grassy uplands, and sunlit forests. Few Washingtonians seem to know about this region's attractions, however. Even at the height of the summer its roads and trails are rarely crowded.

The hidden jewel of these mountains is the Sanpoil River Valley, which is a miniature Yosemite Valley, with vertical rock walls rising 2,000–3,000 feet straight from the river, their height accentuated by the narrowness of the canyon. The valley has no amenities, and is still in the possession of its original owners, the Native Americans of the Colville Reservation, who have preserved its beauty. These wild highlands have few visitor facilities. Towns in the Okanogan Valley and the regional metropolis of Spokane, on the fringes of the region, offer more services.

SPOKANE AND EASTERN WASHINGTON PLANNER

WHEN TO GO

Eastern Washington has four distinct seasons, with generally very hot summers and sometimes very snowy winters. Recreational activities are geared to the specific season, with several downhill ski resorts open for skiing and snowboarding, and Nordic skiing available in the national forests, too. In summer, water activities on the lakes and rivers are popular, and there are many places to pursue hiking, backpacking, cycling, and fishing. Eastern Washington rarely feels crowded, though popular campgrounds may fill in summer. Lodging rates tend to be higher between Memorial Day and Labor Day, so visiting off-season can reduce costs. Spring and fall are both beautiful seasons to explore the region. In smaller towns certain attractions are open only from May through September, so call ahead to plan visits to sights. Also call well in advance to make reservations during college special-event weekends in Pullman and Walla Walla.

18

FESTIVALS AND EVENTS

The region's rich bounty of viniculture and agriculture is celebrated with festivals throughout the year.

Bloomsday. On the first Sunday of May, more than 40,000 runners course 12 km (7½ miles) through downtown Spokane and the northwest part of the city. ✉ *Spokane* ☎ *509/838–1579* ⊕ *www.bloomsdayrun.org.*

Farmer Consumer Awareness Day. Farms and processing plants in Quincy throw an open house for a weekend every mid-September so consumers can get a closer look at where their food comes from. There are exhibits, a farmers' market, food booths, tours of farms, processors, and geology sites, and lots of other events. ✉ *Quincy* ☎ *509/787–2140* ⊕ *www.quincyfarmerconsumer.com.*

Green Bluff Growers Festivals. The association of small farms and food stands in Green Bluff (about 20 miles northeast of downtown Spokane) presents several festivals as orchard fruits come into season. Strawberries are celebrated in late June and early July, while the Cherry Festival runs two weekends in July, the Peach Festival mid-August through Labor Day, and the Apple Festival weekends from late September through late October. ⊠ *Hwy. 2 and Green Bluff Rd., Colbert* ⊕ *www. greenbluffgrowers.com.*

Hoopfest. The last weekend in June, basketball mania descends on downtown Spokane as Hoopfest comes to town, a mega tournament with nearly 7,000 teams and 27,000 players playing 3-on-3 basketball on 450 courts over 40 city blocks. It's the world's largest event of its type, with more than 225,000 fans in attendance. ⊠ *Spokane* ☎ *509/624–2414* ⊕ *www.spokanehoopfest.net.*

Pig Out in the Park. Locals and tourists flock to Riverfront Park over Labor Day to gorge on yummy food and nonstop live music. ⊠ *Riverfront Park, 507 N. Howard St., Spokane* ☎ *509/879–0826* ⊕ *www. spokanepigout.com.*

Spokane Lilac Festival. Parades and other events honor the flower that gives Spokane the moniker "Lilac City." ⊠ *Spokane* ☎ *509/535–4554* ⊕ *www.spokanelilacfestival.org.*

Walla Walla Wine Festivals. The Walla Walla Valley Wine Alliance coordinates Spring Release Weekend, the first weekend in May; Celebrate Walla Walla Wines, for a weekend in mid-June; Fall Release Weekend, the first weekend in November; and Holiday Barrel Tasting, the first weekend in December. Events include wine tasting, tours, winemaker dinners, music, and arts festivals. ⊠ *Walla Walla* ☎ *509/526–3117* ⊕ *www.wallawallawine.com.*

GETTING HERE AND AROUND
AIR TRAVEL
Spokane International Airport is the main hub for air travel in eastern Washington. Smaller airports include Pullman, Tri-Cities, Walla Walla, and Lewiston, Idaho (across the border from Clarkston). Spokane International Airport is served by Alaska, American, Delta, Southwest, and United; the Tri-Cities Airport is served by Alaska, Allegiant, Delta, and United. Alaska serves the smaller regional airports.

Contacts Lewiston-Nez Perce County Airport. ⊠ *406 Burrell Ave., Lewiston* ☎ *208/746–7962* ⊕ *www.golws.com.* **Spokane International Airport.** ⊠ *9000 W. Airport Dr., Spokane* ☎ *509/455–6455* ⊕ *www.spokaneairports.net.* **Tri-Cities Airport.** ⊠ *3601 N. 20th Ave., Pasco* ☎ *509/547–6352* ⊕ *www.flytricities.com.*

CAR TRAVEL
Interstate 90 is the most direct route from Seattle to Spokane over the Cascade Mountains (Snoqualmie Pass). U.S. 2 (Stevens Pass), an alternate route, begins north of Seattle near Everett, and passes through Wenatchee and Coulee City. South of Interstate 90, U.S. 395 leads to the Tri-Cities from the east; the Tri-Cities can also be accessed via Interstate 82 from the west. Past the Tri-Cities, continue on Interstate 82 then U.S. 12 to reach Walla Walla. U.S. 195 traverses southeastern Washington to Pullman. Leave U.S. 195 at Colfax, heading southwest on Highway 26 and then 127, and finally U.S. 12 to Dayton and Walla Walla. Gas stations along the main highways cater to truckers, and some are open 24 hours.

RESTAURANTS

Local diners and cafés are great spots for getting a hearty breakfast of traditional favorites like farm-fresh eggs or biscuits and gravy. Somewhat surprisingly, several of the small towns have outstanding dining options, too. At many restaurants there's an emphasis on locally grown, organic foods. With the region's many farms, it's easy to source produce, grains, poultry, meat, and dairy items, and some restaurants have their own gardens on-site for the freshest produce of all. Spokane has a good diversity of cuisines and some highly acclaimed restaurants, but up-and-coming Walla Walla is also becoming a hot spot for foodies and wine lovers.

HOTELS

Family-owned motels and budget chains are prevalent in small towns like Colville, Grand Coulee, Moses Lake, Omak, Pullman, and Soap Lake. Many of these properties have updated their amenities to include modern touches such as flat-screen TVs; others can feel dated, but at least the prices are reasonable, except during special events when demand spikes create rate hikes. Several pleasant bed-and-breakfasts with friendly innkeepers are found in Spokane, Walla Walla, Dayton, and Uniontown (near Pullman), but with no more than six suites at each it's usually necessary to call ahead for a reservation. There are several historic hotels built in the early 1900s and restored in recent years that are definitely worth visiting in Spokane, Walla Walla, and Dayton. The Inn at Abeja, just outside Walla Walla on a historic farm site, offers unique, high-end lodging. A stay at the Cave B Resort by the Columbia River—in one of its cliff houses, cavern rooms, or luxury yurts—is a recommended destination experience, too. *Hotel reviews have been shortened. For full information, visit Fodors.com.*

18

WHAT IT COSTS IN U.S. DOLLARS			
$	**$$**	**$$$**	**$$$$**
Restaurants	under $16	$16–$22	$23–$30	over $30
Hotels	under $150	$150–$200	$201–$250	over $250

Restaurant prices are the average cost of a main course at dinner, or if dinner is not served, at lunch. Hotel prices are the lowest cost of a standard double room in high season.

SOUTHEASTERN WASHINGTON

The most populated area in this region is the Tri-Cities—Pasco, Kennewick, and Richland. Each town has its own character, but their proximity makes it easy to access an array of services and attractions like local wineries and pleasant riverfront parks. The town of Walla Walla has a historic downtown shopping district with innovative restaurant choices, wine-tasting rooms, elegant B&Bs, and the impressive Marcus Whitman Hotel. Just outside town, wineries in bucolic country settings are as enjoyable for picnickers as for serious wine connoisseurs. If you continue east and north on quiet two-lane highways you'll discover Dayton, another historic small town, and Pullman, home of Washington State University.

RICHLAND

202 miles southeast of Seattle, 145 miles southwest of Spokane.

Richland is the northernmost of the three municipalities along the bank of the Columbia River known as the Tri-Cities (the others are Pasco and Kennewick). Founded in the 1880s, Richland was a pleasant farming village until 1942, when the federal government built a nuclear reactor on the nearby Hanford Nuclear Reservation. The Hanford site was instrumental in the building of the Tri-Cities, and still plays a major role in the area's economy. In recent years this has also become a major wine-producing area. You can find more than 100 wineries within a 50-mile radius, many with tasting rooms.

GETTING HERE AND AROUND

The Tri-Cities Airport in Pasco is served by Alaska, Allegiant, Delta, and United. Taxis and rental cars are available there. Some hotels also offer an airport shuttle. Greyhound Bus Lines and Amtrak's Empire Builder both stop in Pasco. Ben Franklin Transit serves all three cities. By car, Interstate 82 is the main east–west highway; from Ritzville or Spokane, take Highway 395 to reach the Tri-Cities; from Ellensburg and Yakima, take Highway 82 south and east.

Contact Ben Franklin Transit. ☎ 509/735–5100 ⊕ www.bft.org.

ESSENTIALS

Visitor Information City of Richland. ☎ 509/942–7390 ⊕ www.ci.richland. wa.us. **Tri-Cities Visitor and Convention Bureau.** ✉ 7130 W. Grandridge Blvd., Suite B, Kennewick ☎ 800/254–5824, 509/735–8486 ⊕ www.visittri-cities.com.

EXPLORING

Barnard Griffin Winery and Tasting Room. Owners Rob Griffin and Deborah Barnard offer a variety of fine wines, including excellent Merlot and Cabernet. The Kitchen at Barnard Griffin features farm-to-table cuisine to enjoy with wine pairings; there's live music some nights, too. The art gallery adds class to the wine-tasting experience. ✉ 878 Tulip La. ☎ 509/627–0266 ⊕ www.barnardgriffin.com ⊗ Wine bar closed Sun. and Mon.

Bookwalter Winery. Next door to Barnard Griffin Winery, Bookwalter produces red wines aged in French oak barrels and whites that are 100% stainless-steel fermented. The classic Merlot is celebrated. Blends are prevalent in both reds and whites. The on-site restaurant, Fiction, features small plates like prosciutto flatbread with pears, five types of salad, and heartier fare such as steaks, burgers, and salmon. ✉ 894 Tulip La. ☎ 509/627–5000 ⊕ www.bookwalterwines.com ✍ $10 tasting fee; applied to wine purchase $35 or more.

The REACH (*The Hanford Reach Interpretive Center*). Here's the place to learn about the Hanford Reach National Monument, an area that encompasses the Hanford Reach of the Columbia River and greater Columbia Basin and surrounds the former site of the Hanford Nuclear Reservation. The interpretive center highlights the region's history, culture, science and technology, natural resources and agriculture, and arts. The exhibit area has permanent exhibits on the Columbia Basin

Project's irrigated agriculture, the history of the atomic age and Hanford's contribution to ending World War II, and the Columbia River's role in producing electrical power. Special events include tours, classes, and culinary events highlighting the area's wineries and agriculture. The 18-acre setting on the Columbia River includes outdoor exhibits, a nature trail, and a stage where concerts are held in the summer. ✉ *1943 Columbia Park Trail* ☎ *509/943–4100* 🌐 *www.visitthereach.org* 🎟 *$8* 🕒 *Closed Sun. and Mon.*

WHERE TO EAT AND STAY

$$$ SEAFOOD 🍴 **Anthony's at Columbia Point.** For years the Anthony's chain has been known for fine waterfront dining in western Washington; this Anthony's on the Columbia River waterfront continues the tradition. Seafood is the specialty—from fish-focused appetizers, including panfried Willapa Bay oysters and fresh Puget Sound mussels, to entrées with Dungeness crab (whole, in fettuccine, or in crab cakes), Idaho rainbow trout, Alaskan weathervane scallops, and char-grilled Alaskan halibut. **Known for:** weekday sunset four-course dinners; Northwest and Alaska seafood; moorage for boating guests. [$] *Average main: $28* ✉ *550 Columbia Point Dr.* ☎ *509/946–3474* 🌐 *www.anthonys.com.*

$ AMERICAN 🍴 **Atomic Ale Brewpub and Eatery.** The staff is friendly at this small, casual brewpub, which serves several house-brewed beers to go with the delicious wood-fired pizzas, sandwiches (the hot grinder is a specialty), salads, and soups. Local memorabilia is displayed throughout the restaurant, and the history of the Hanford nuclear plant is depicted in photos on the walls. **Known for:** red-potato soup made with in-house brew; yummy desserts; local nuclear-history theme. [$] *Average main: $16* ✉ *1015 Lee Blvd.* ☎ *509/946–5465* 🌐 *www.atomicalebrewpub.com.*

18

$ HOTEL 🏨 **Red Lion Hotel Richland Hanford House.** The best of these standard-issue motel-style rooms overlook the Columbia River, and all have access to the riverfront park and trails along the levee. **Pros:** nice location; free airport shuttle; seasonal outdoor pool. **Cons:** older hotel, though some rooms have been updated; can get noisy with larger groups and teams. [$] *Rooms from: $149* ✉ *802 George Washington Way* ☎ *509/946–7611, 844/248–7467* 🌐 *www.redlion.com* 🛏 *149 rooms* 🍽 *Breakfast.*

$ HOTEL FAMILY 🏨 **Shilo Inn Suites Hotel.** Rooms are simple in style yet they come with coffeemakers, microwaves, refrigerators, and fold-down ironing units, making them convenient for both business and leisure guests. **Pros:** excellent value; convenient riverfront location. **Cons:** rooms by outdoor pool can be noisy; property needs updating; no elevators. [$] *Rooms from: $114* ✉ *50 Comstock St.* ☎ *509/946–4661, 800/222–2244* 🌐 *www.shiloinns.com* 🛏 *164 rooms* 🍽 *Breakfast.*

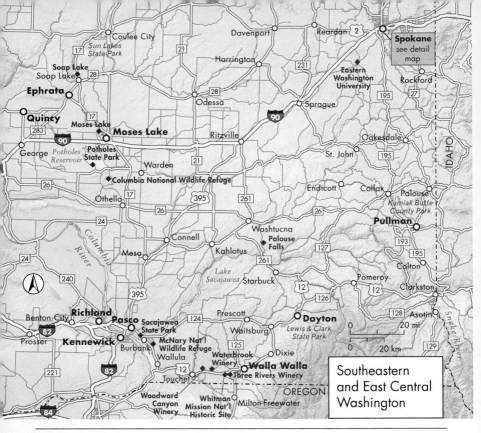

Southeastern and East Central Washington

PASCO

10 miles east of Richland.

Tree-shaded Pasco, a college town and the Franklin County seat, is an oasis of green on the Columbia River near a site where the Lewis and Clark expedition made camp in 1805. The city began as a railroad switchyard and now has a busy container port. The neoclassical Franklin County Courthouse (1907) is worth a visit for its fine marble interior.

The Pasco Basin has first-rate vineyards and wineries and some of the state's most fertile land. You can purchase the regional bounty at the farmers' market, held downtown every Wednesday and Saturday morning during the growing season.

GETTING HERE AND AROUND

The Tri-Cities Airport is in Pasco; Alaska, Allegiant, Delta, and United operate there. Taxis and rental cars are both available, and some hotels offer an airport shuttle. Ben Franklin Transit serves all three cities. By car, Interstate 82 is the main east–west highway; from Ritzville or Spokane, take Highway 395 to reach the Tri-Cities; from Ellensburg and Yakima, take Interstate 82 south and east.

ESSENTIALS

Visitor Information City of Pasco. ☎ 509/544–3080 ⊕ *www.pasco-wa.gov.*

EXPLORING

Franklin County Historical Museum. Here you'll find numerous items illustrating local history, including Native American artifacts. Revolving exhibits have featured the Lewis and Clark expedition, the railroad, World War II, agriculture, and aviation. ⊠ *305 N. 4th Ave.* ☎ *509/547–3714* ⊕ *www.franklincountyhistoricalsociety.org* ⊘ *Closed Sat.–Mon.*

Sacajawea State Park. At the confluence of the Snake and Columbia Rivers, this park occupies the site of Ainsworth, a railroad town that flourished from 1879 to 1884. It's named for the Shoshoni woman who guided the Lewis and Clark expedition over the Rocky Mountains and down the Snake River. The 284-acre day-use park has an interpretive center and a large display of Native American tools. A beach, boat launch, picnic area, and children's playground round out the facilities; sand dunes, marshes, and ponds are great for watching wildlife. ⊠ *2503 Sacajawea Park Rd.* ✛ *Off U.S. 12, 5 miles southeast of Pasco* ☎ *509/545–2361* ⊕ *parks.state.wa.us/575/Sacajawea* ✉ *Day pass $10 per vehicle; annual Discovery Pass $30 (valid at all state parks)* ⊘ *Closed Nov.–Mar.*

WHERE TO STAY

$ 🖥 **Red Lion Hotel Pasco.** Most of these functional rooms, in three separate
HOTEL   wings of low-rise buildings, have either a patio or balcony, and the out-
FAMILY   door pool area and spacious, open lobby are attractive. **Pros:** some rooms have been renovated; rooms are spacious; wine bar and restaurant open evenings. **Cons:** large convention hotel; rooms near highway can be noisy; inconsistent service. $ *Rooms from: $149* ⊠ *2525 N. 20th St.* ☎ *509/547–0701, 844/248–7467* ⊕ *www.redlion.com* ↩ *289 rooms* ❍| *No meals.*

KENNEWICK

3 miles southwest of Pasco, directly across the Columbia River.

In its 100-year history, Kennewick (*ken*-uh-wick) evolved from a railroad town to a farm-supply center and then to a bedroom community for Hanford workers and a food-processing capital for the Columbia Basin. The name Kennewick translates as "grassy place," and Native Americans had winter villages here long before Lewis and Clark passed through. Arrowheads and other artifacts aside, the 9,000-year-old skeleton of Kennewick Man was studied by scientists at the University of Washington to determine whether its features are Native American or, as some claim, Caucasian. Nearly two decades after its discovery, it was finally confirmed to be Native American and turned over to tribes for burial.

GETTING HERE AND AROUND

The Tri-Cities Airport is in nearby Pasco, served by Alaska, Allegiant, Delta, and United. Taxis and rental cars are available and some hotels offer an airport shuttle. Ben Franklin Transit serves all three cities. By car, Interstate 82 is the main east–west highway; from Ritzville or Spokane, take Highway 395 to reach the Tri-Cities; from Ellensburg and Yakima, take Interstate 82 south and east.

ESSENTIALS

Visitor Information City of Kennewick. ☎ *509/585–4200* ⊕ *www.go2kennewick.com.*

18

EXPLORING

TOP ATTRACTIONS

Badger Mountain Vineyard. A beautiful view of the valley and wine made without pesticides or preservatives is what you'll find here. Badger Mountain was the first wine-grape vineyard in Washington State to be certified organic. ✉ *1106 N. Jurupa St.* ☎ *800/643–9463* 🌐 *www.badgermtnvineyard.com.*

FAMILY **Columbia Park.** Adjacent to the Columbia River, this is one of Washington's great parks. Its 4½-mile-long riverfront has boat ramps, a golf course, picnic areas, playgrounds (including an aquatic one), train ride, ropes course, and family fishing pond. In summer, hydroplane races are held here. ✉ *Columbia Trail Dr., between U.S. 240 and Columbia River* ☎ *509/585–4293* 🌐 *www.go2kennewick.com.*

FAMILY **McNary National Wildlife Refuge.** More than 200 species of birds have been identified here, and many waterfowl make it their winter home. But the 15,000 acres of water and marsh, croplands, grasslands, trees, and shrubs are most enjoyable in spring and summer. The Environmental Education Center features hands-on exhibits. A self-guided 2-mile trail winds through the marshes, and a cabinlike blind hidden in the reeds allows you to watch wildlife up close. Other recreation includes boating, fishing, hiking, and horseback riding. ✉ *64 Maple Rd., Burbank* ✥ *¼ mile east of U.S. 12, south of Snake River Bridge* ☎ *509/546–8300* 🌐 *www.fws.gov/refuge/McNary.*

WORTH NOTING

East Benton County Historical Museum. The entire entryway to the museum is made of petrified wood. Photographs, agricultural displays, petroglyphs, and a large collection of arrowheads interpret area history. Kennewick's oldest park, Keewaydin, is across the street. ✉ *205 Keewaydin Dr.* ☎ *509/582–7704* 🌐 *www.ebchs.org* 🎟 *$5* ⏲ *Closed Sun. and Mon.*

Ice Harbor Lock and Dam. At 103 feet, the single-lift locks here are among the world's highest. ✉ *2763 Monument Dr., Burbank* ✥ *About 12 miles southeast of Kennewick* ☎ *509/547–7781* 🌐 *www.nww.usace.army.mil/Locations/District-Locks-and-Dams/Ice-Harbor-Lock-and-Dam/* ⏲ *Closed Nov.–Mar.*

WHERE TO EAT AND STAY

$$$$ AMERICAN 🍴 **The Cedars.** A perch right on the edge of the Columbia River provides beautiful views and a 200-foot dock for boaters coming to dine; a deck is open seasonally and is popular as an after-work gathering place in summer. The menu includes top-quality steaks, pasta, poultry, and shellfish, as well as several kinds of fresh fish, including salmon, halibut, swordfish, and ahi tuna. **Known for:** views from every table; meals include chowder or salad bar; delicious dessert choices. [$] *Average main: $32* ✉ *355 Clover Island Dr.* ☎ *509/582–2143* 🌐 *www.cedarskennewick.com* ⏲ *No lunch.*

$ HOTEL FAMILY 🏨 **Red Lion Columbia Center.** Talk about convenience: these well-kept, up-to-date rooms, all with microwaves and refrigerators, are next to a regional shopping mall and a few blocks from the convention center. **Pros:** handy location; good value; seasonal pool. **Cons:** no elevators;

Walla Walla's cute revitalized downtown

rooms are dated but under renovation. $ *Rooms from: $124* ✉ *1101 N. Columbia Center Blvd.* ☎ *509/783–0611, 800/733–5466* ⊕ *www. redlion.com* ⤳ *153 rooms* 🍽 *No meals.*

WALLA WALLA

52 miles southeast of Kennewick.

A successful downtown restoration has earned Walla Walla high praise. The heart of downtown, at 2nd and Main Streets, looks as pretty as it did 60 years ago, with beautifully maintained old buildings and newer structures designed to fit in. Walla Walla's Main Street is the winner of the "Great American Main Street Award" from the National Trust for Historic Preservation. Residents and visitors come here to visit shops, wineries, cafés, and restaurants.

Walla Walla, founded in the 1850s on the site of a Nez Perce village, was Washington's first metropolis. As late as the 1880s its population was larger than that of Seattle. Walla Walla occupies a lush green valley below the rugged Blue Mountains. Its beautiful downtown boasts old residences, green parks, and the campus of Whitman College, Washington's oldest institution of higher learning.

West of town, the green Walla Walla Valley—famous for asparagus, sweet onions, cherries, and wheat—has emerged as Washington's premier viticultural region. Tall grain elevators mark Lowden, a few miles west of Walla Walla, a wheat hamlet that now has several wineries.

GETTING HERE AND AROUND

Coming from points west, Walla Walla is reached via Interstate 82 east of the Tri-Cities, then Highway 12, which is still a two-lane highway in places but has recently been expanded west of Walla Walla and into the town. From Spokane and the northeast, travel is all by two-lane highway, going south on Highway 195 to Colfax, then southwest via Highways 26 and 127 to Highway 12, then continuing south through Dayton and Waitsburg. Horizon Air runs two daily flights (one on Saturday) each way between Walla Walla and Seattle.

Contacts Walla Walla Regional Airport. ⊠ *45 Terminal Loop Rd.* ☎ *509/525–3100* ⊕ *www.wallawallaairport.com.*

ESSENTIALS

Visitor Information Walla Walla Valley Chamber of Commerce. ⊠ *29 E. Sumach St.* ☎ *509/525–0850* ⊕ *www.wwvchamber.com.*

EXPLORING

TOP ATTRACTIONS

FAMILY **Fort Walla Walla Museum.** On 15 acres at Fort Walla Walla Park, a 17-building pioneer village depicts the region's life in the 1800s, and five halls house military, agricultural, textile, and transportation exhibits. ⊠ *755 Myra Rd.* ☎ *509/525–7703* ⊕ *www.fwwm.org* ☞ *$8.*

L'Ecole No. 41. Housed in the lower floors of a circa-1915 schoolhouse, this winery produces outstanding Sémillon and Merlot, among other wines. The tasting room is in one of the old classrooms, and details like chalkboards and books add to the ambience. ⊠ *41 Lowden School Rd., Lowden* ☎ *509/525–0940* ⊕ *www.lecole.com.*

Sinclair Estate Vineyards. This downtown tasting room for one of Walla Walla's newest wineries offers Syrah, Merlot, and Chardonnay. The elegant tasting room includes a grand piano and live music on Friday evening, with no cover charge. ⊠ *109-B E. Main St.* ☎ *509/876–4300* ⊕ *www.sinclairestatevineyards.com.*

Three Rivers Winery. This winery just off U.S. 12 and surrounded by vineyards produces premium Cabernet Sauvignon, Merlot, Malbec, Sauvignon Blanc, Chardonnay, and Riesling. It has a nice tasting room, a gift shop, summer concerts, and a 3-hole golf course. ⊠ *5641 Old Hwy. 12* ☎ *509/526–9463, 866/485–7566* ⊕ *www.threeriverswinery.com.*

Waterbrook Winery. The tasting room, part of a facility on 75 acres, has an indoor-outdoor feel, with a spacious patio and outdoor fireplace, hillside views, and natural landscaping and ponds. Waterbrook is best known for Merlot, Chardonnay, and Cabernet. ⊠ *10518 W. U.S. Hwy. 12* ☎ *509/522–1262* ⊕ *www.waterbrook.com.*

FAMILY **Whitman Mission National Historic Site.** This is a reconstruction of Waiilatpu Mission, a Presbyterian outpost established on Cayuse lands in 1836. The park preserves the foundations of the mission buildings, a short segment of the Oregon Trail, and, on a nearby hill, the graveyard where the Native American victims of an 1847 measles epidemic and subsequent uprising are buried. ⊠ *328 Whitman Mission Rd.* ✛ *7 miles west of downtown* ☎ *509/522–6360, 509/522–6357 visitor info* ⊕ *www.nps.*

gov/whmi ⏲ *Visitor center closed Dec. and Jan., and Mon. and Tues. in Oct., Nov., and Feb.–mid-May.*

Woodward Canyon Winery. Lovers of fine wines make pilgrimages to this winery, 12 miles west of Walla Walla, for the superb Cabernet Sauvignon, Chardonnay, and Merlot. The winery occasionally produces other varietals and also has a second label, Nelms Road, that focuses on younger and more affordable red wines. ✉ *11920 W. U.S. 12, Lowden* ☎ *509/525–4129* 🌐 *www.woodwardcanyon.com.*

WORTH NOTING

Canoe Ridge Vineyards. Owned by Precept Wine, this vineyard produces Merlot, Cabernet Sauvignon, Chardonnay, rosé, and a red blend. The tasting room is in Walla Walla's historic Engine House. ✉ *1102 W. Cherry St.* ☎ *509/525–1843* 🌐 *www.canoeridgevineyard.com* ⏲ *Closed Tues. and Wed.*

FAMILY **Pioneer Park.** Planted with native and exotic flowers and trees, this turn-of-the-20th-century park has a fine aviary. It was originally landscaped by sons of Frederick Law Olmsted, who designed New York City's Central Park. ✉ *E. Alder St. and Division St.* 🌐 *www.wallawallawa.gov.*

Seven Hills Winery. Here, owner Casey McClellan makes well-balanced Cabernet Sauvignon, Malbec, Merlot, and several white wines, too. The winery is in Walla Walla's historic Whitehouse-Crawford building. ✉ *212 N. 3rd Ave.* ☎ *509/529–7198, 877/777–7870* 🌐 *www.sevenhillswinery.com.*

Whitman College. Large, tree-lined lawns surround the many beautiful 19th-century stone and brick structures of the Whitman College campus. The school began as a seminary in 1859 and became a college in 1883. ✉ *345 Boyer Ave.* ☎ *509/527–5111* 🌐 *www.whitman.edu.*

18

WHERE TO EAT

$ CAFÉ 🍴 **Olive Marketplace & Cafe.** Between pouring its first cup of coffee at 8 am and the last glass of wine before closing at 9 pm, this two-level casual downtown café serves reasonably priced and varied items. The breakfast menu ranges from classics like eggs Benedict to contemporary dishes like pork-belly sweet-potato hash, while the all-day menu includes hearty meals like adobo-braised beef enchiladas, along with sandwiches, salads, and soups. **Known for:** live music and wine tasting on Thursday; prime-rib night on Wednesday; house-made bread and delectable desserts. [$] *Average main: $15* ✉ *21 E. Main St.* ☎ *509/526–0200* 🌐 *www.olivemarketplaceandcafe.com.*

$$$ ITALIAN 🍴 **T. Maccarones.** Italian food with a very contemporary flare is the draw at "T-Mac's," along with the neighborly feel of the small, two-level restaurant that has become a local favorite. The menu focuses on bold flavors and fresh, local, and organic ingredients for dishes like cioppino, seared sockeye salmon, and braised beef and pork ragout. **Known for:** mac and cheese, made with truffle oil; fried brussels sprouts salad; braised meats. [$] *Average main: $28* ✉ *4 N. Colville St.* ☎ *509/522–4776* 🌐 *www.tmaccarones.com* ⏲ *No lunch weekends.*

$$$ AMERICAN Fodor's Choice ★ 🍴 **Whitehouse-Crawford Restaurant.** In a former wood mill, this fine-dining restaurant has gained a reputation for quality and excellence, thanks to chef-owner Jamie Guerin. Local is the watchword here, where hamburgers are made with grass-fed beef from Blue Valley Meats, and more than a dozen nearby purveyors supply produce, cheese, meat, eggs, and coffee. **Known for:** cool building and ambience; prix-fixe menu only during slower season; more casual dining at bar. [$] *Average main: $30* ✉ *55 W. Cherry St.* ☎ *509/525–2222* 🌐 *www.whitehousecrawford.com* 🕒 *Closed Tues. No lunch.*

WHERE TO STAY

$$ B&B/INN 🏨 **Green Gables Inn.** One block from the Whitman College campus, this 1909 Arts and Crafts–style mansion sits among flowering plants and shrubs on a quaint, tree-lined street and offers charming guest rooms individually decorated with Victorian antiques. **Pros:** mini-refrigerators in rooms; pretty setting; on-site chef makes delicious gourmet breakfasts. **Cons:** two-night minimum stay on weekends; no children under 12 except in Carriage House. [$] *Rooms from: $179* ✉ *922 Bonsella St.* ☎ *509/876–4373* 🌐 *www.greengablesinn.com* 🛏 *4 rooms, 1 suite* 🍽 *Breakfast.*

$$$$ B&B/INN Fodor's Choice ★ 🏨 **Inn at Abeja.** Thirty-five acres of gardens, lawns, and vineyards surround this turn-of-the-20th-century farm; the high-end details of the incredibly stylish, beautifully furnished guest cottages and suites, attentive and friendly service, and gated entrance all contribute to an experience of serene, relaxing, secluded luxury. **Pros:** beautiful grounds; spacious accommodations, some with kitchens; private tours of the on-site winery, which is not open to the public. **Cons:** closed from early December through February; book early as it fills up fast, especially with repeat guests; 30-day cancellation policy. [$] *Rooms from: $295* ✉ *2014 Mill Creek Rd.* ☎ *509/522–1234* 🌐 *www.abeja.net/inn* 🕒 *Closed early Dec.–Feb.* 🛏 *7 rooms* 🍽 *Breakfast.*

$$ B&B/INN 🏨 **Inn at Blackberry Creek.** Central, yet with a secluded feel, this 1906 Kentucky farmhouse-style home with cozy, traditionally furnished accommodations sits on a 2-acre lot in a residential area, with Blackberry Creek running through the backyard. **Pros:** wonderful breakfast with several choices; rooms are very well stocked with lots of extras; hosts are warm and friendly. **Cons:** very popular but only four rooms, so book ahead for special wine-event weekends; no children under 12. [$] *Rooms from: $169* ✉ *1126 Pleasant St.* ☎ *509/522–5233, 877/522–5233* 🌐 *www.innatblackberrycreek.com* 🛏 *4 rooms* 🍽 *Breakfast.*

$$ HOTEL Fodor's Choice ★ 🏨 **Marcus Whitman Hotel.** This 1928 hotel is *the* landmark in downtown Walla Walla, and guest quarters include spacious two-room parlor suites and spa suites in the historic tower building—adorned with Renaissance-style Italian furnishings and lots of amenities, these rooms are well worth the splurge. **Pros:** range of accommodations available; downtown location; full breakfast buffet and parking included. **Cons:** no pool; no bathtubs in historic rooms. [$] *Rooms from: $179* ✉ *6 W. Rose St.* ☎ *509/525–2200, 866/826–9422* 🌐 *www.marcuswhitmanhotel.com* 🛏 *133 rooms* 🍽 *Breakfast.*

DAYTON

31 miles northeast of Walla Walla.

The tree-shaded county seat of Columbia County is the kind of Currier & Ives place many people conjure up when they imagine the best qualities of rural America. This tidy town has 117 buildings listed on the National Register of Historic Places, including the state's oldest railroad depot and courthouse.

GETTING HERE AND AROUND

Dayton is northeast of Walla Walla via Highway 12. From the Spokane area, take Highway 195 to Colfax, then veer southwest via Highways 26 and 127 before reaching Highway 12 and continuing into the town.

EXPLORING

Dayton Historical Depot Society. At Washington's oldest standing depot, the society houses exhibits illustrating the history of Dayton and surrounding communities. ✉ *222 E. Commercial Ave.* ☎ *509/382–2026* 🌐 *www.daytonhistoricdepot.org* 🕒 *Closed Sun.–Tues.*

OFF THE BEATEN PATH

Palouse Falls State Park. Just north of its confluence with the Snake River, the Palouse River gushes over a basalt cliff higher than Niagara Falls and drops 198 feet into a steep-walled basin. Those who are surefooted can hike to an overlook above the falls, which are at their fastest during spring runoff in March. Just downstream from the falls at the Marmes Rock Shelter, remains of the earliest-known inhabitants of North America, dating back 10,000 years, were discovered by archaeologists. The park has 11 primitive campsites, open year-round, but with no water September through April. ✉ *Palouse Falls Rd. and Ste. Rte. 261* ✥ *38 miles north of Dayton* ☎ *509/646–9218* 🌐 *parks.state.wa.us/559/Palouse-Falls* 🎟 *Day pass $10 per vehicle; annual Discovery Pass $30 (valid at all state parks); campsites $12.*

18

WHERE TO EAT AND STAY

$$ AMERICAN

🍴 **Weinhard Café and Bakery.** The past seems to echo through this restaurant, which is across the street from the Weinhard Hotel in what was once a pharmacy. The menu changes frequently to highlight seasonal specialties and local purveyors; some signature items include the chef's salad, rib-eye steak, and dark chocolate cake. **Known for:** great variety of baked desserts and breads; Thursday spaghetti night. [$] *Average main: $19* ✉ *258 E. Main St.* ☎ *509/382–1681* 🌐 *www.weinhardcafe.com* 🕒 *Closed Sun. and Mon.*

$ HOTEL

🏨 **Weinhard Hotel.** Echoes of the Old West ring through this hotel, built as a saloon and lodge in the late 1800s by the nephew of beer baron Henry Weinhard, and where rooms have modern amenities but period antiques. **Pros:** friendly, attentive service; rooms have refrigerators; complimentary fruit and chocolates. **Cons:** some street noise from rooms that face highway; no elevator. [$] *Rooms from: $129* ✉ *235 E. Main St.* ☎ *509/382–4032* 🌐 *www.weinhard.com* 🛏 *15 rooms* 🍽 *Breakfast.*

PULLMAN

75 miles south of Spokane.

This funky, liberal town—home of Washington State University—is in the heart of the rather conservative Palouse agricultural district. The town's freewheeling style can perhaps be explained by the fact that most of the students come from elsewhere in Washington.

The Palouse River, the upper course of which flows though the town, is an exception among Washington rivers: because of the high erosion rate of the light Palouse loess soils it usually runs muddy, almost like a gruel during floods (most Washington rivers run clear, even after major storms). The 198-foot-high Palouse Falls farther downstream, near Washtucna, dramatically drop as a thin sheet of water into a steep box canyon.

GETTING HERE AND AROUND

Alaska flies into the local airport, where taxis and rental cars are available to get you to your destination. Most of the hotels have free airport shuttles, too. Pullman is reached via Highway 195, about 75 miles from Spokane.

Pullman-Moscow Regional Airport. ✉ *3200 Airport Complex N* ☎ *509/338–3223* ⊕ *www.flypuw.com.*

ESSENTIALS

Visitor Information Pullman Chamber of Commerce. ✉ *415 N. Grand Ave.* ☎ *509/334–3565, 800/365–6948* ⊕ *www.pullmanchamber.com.*

EXPLORING

Kamiak Butte County Park. The 3,640-foot-tall butte is part of a mountain chain that was here long before the lava flows of the Columbia basin erupted millions of years ago. The park has great views of the Palouse hills and Idaho's snowcapped peaks to the east, as well as seven primitive campsites, a picnic area, and a 1-mile trail to the top of the butte. ✉ *902 Kamiak Butte Park Rd., Palouse* ✛ *12 miles north of Pullman* ☎ *509/397–6238* ⊕ *www.whitmancounty.org* 🖾 *Free; campsite $15.*

Washington State University. Opened in 1892 as the state's agriculture school, Washington State University today sprawls almost all the way to the Idaho state line. To park on campus, pick up a parking pass in the Security Building on Wilson Road. ✉ *1 S.E. Stadium Way* ☎ *509/335–3564* ⊕ *www.wsu.edu.*

Ferdinand's. On weekdays between 9:30 and 4:30, you can pop into Ferdinand's, an ice-cream and cheese shop in the food-science building, to buy Aged Cougar Gold, a cheddar-type cheese in a can. Ice cream is made daily from milk from the university's dairy cows. ✉ *2035 N.E. Ferdinand's La.* ☎ *509/335–2141* ⊕ *creamery.wsu.edu* ⊗ *Closed weekends, holidays, school breaks.*

Museum of Art. The small Museum of Art has lectures as well as exhibitions that might include turned-wood art, Native American art, or landscaping displays. ✉ *WSU Fine Arts Center, Wilson Rd. and Stadium Way* ☎ *509/335–1910* ⊕ *museum.wsu.edu* ⊗ *Closed Sun. and Mon.; also closed Sat. in summer.*

Charles R. Conner Museum of Zoology. This museum has the finest collection of stuffed birds and mammals and preserved invertebrates in the Pacific Northwest; more than 700 are on display. ✉ *Abelson Hall, Library Rd. and College Ave.* ☎ *509/335–3515* 🌐 *sbs.wsu.edu/connermuseum.*

WHERE TO EAT AND STAY

$ ITALIAN 🍴 **Basilio's Italian Café.** In the heart of downtown, Basilio's serves up such classics as pasta, lasagna, and chicken parmigiana in addition to an assortment of sandwiches and pizzas. Order at the counter then snag a table at the sidewalk seating area for a view of scenic downtown Pullman. **Known for:** very affordable; outdoor seating. [$] *Average main: $9* ✉ *337 E. Main St.* ☎ *509/334–7663* 🌐 *www.basiliospullman.com.*

$ PIZZA 🍴 **Sella's Calzone and Pastas.** Made daily from scratch, the calzones are always fresh at this cozy storefront and include the most popular, Coug (pepperoni, mushrooms, and black olives), followed by the Gourmet (artichoke hearts, sun-dried tomatoes, and pesto sauce). Pizzas, sandwiches, pastas, and salads are also served. **Known for:** really good pizza; affordable daily lunch specials. [$] *Average main: $10* ✉ *1115 E. Main St.* ☎ *509/334–1895* 🌐 *www.sellascalzone.com.*

$ B&B/INN 🏨 **Churchyard Inn.** Registered as a national and state historic site, this 1905 Flemish-style inn, 15 miles southeast of Pullman in Uniontown, was once a parish house for the adjacent church; some of the homey, traditionally furnished rooms have views of the countryside, and one suite has its own kitchen. **Pros:** welcoming and helpful innkeeper; interesting history; quiet and scenic. **Cons:** no a/c or TVs in most rooms. [$] *Rooms from: $125* ✉ *206 St. Boniface St., Uniontown* ☎ *509/229–3200* 🌐 *www.churchyardinn.com* 🛏 *7 rooms* 🍽 *Breakfast.*

$ HOTEL FAMILY 🏨 **Holiday Inn Express.** You can count on this member of the national chain for cleanliness, comfortable beds, and friendly service, and all rooms include a refrigerator, microwave, and flat-screen TV. **Pros:** near a walking/biking trail; board games to borrow in lobby; indoor pool. **Cons:** no restaurant on-site; rates go up on college event weekends. [$] *Rooms from: $130* ✉ *1190 S.E. Bishop Blvd.* ☎ *509/334–4437, 877/859–5095* 🌐 *www.holidayinnexpress.com* 🛏 *130 rooms* 🍽 *Breakfast.*

SPOKANE

75 miles north of Pullman, 282 miles east of Seattle.

Washington's second-largest city, Spokane (spo- *can,* not spo- *cane*) takes its name from the Spokan tribe of Salish Native Americans. It translates as "Children of the Sun," a fitting name for this sunny city. It's also a city of flowers and trees, public gardens, parks, and museums. Known as the "Capital of the Inland Empire," Spokane is the cultural and financial center of the Inland Northwest.

Spokane began as a Native American village at a roaring waterfall where each autumn salmon ascended in great numbers. American settlers built a sawmill at the falls in 1873. Several railroads arrived after 1881, and Spokane soon became the transportation hub of eastern Washington. In 1885 Spokane built the first hydroelectric plant west of

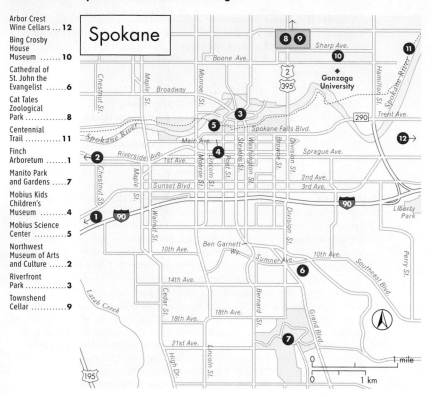

the Mississippi. Downtown boomed after the fire of 1889, as the city grew rich from mining ventures in Washington, Idaho, and Montana, and from shipping the wheat grown on the Palouse hills.

Until they were cleared away for the 1974 World's Fair, bridges and railroad trestles hid Spokane's magnificent falls from view. Today they form the heart of downtown's Riverfront Park, and the city rises from the falls in a series of broad terraces to the valley's rim. Urban parks are among Spokane's assets. The dry, hot summers here make it easy to plan golf, fishing, and hiking excursions; long, snowy winters provide nearly five months to enjoy skiing, snowboarding, and sledding.

GETTING HERE AND AROUND
AIRPORT TRANSFERS

Many hotels offer a free airport shuttle service. Spokane Transit runs between the airport and downtown, every half hour 6:40 am–6:40 pm (then hourly until 11 pm) weekdays, and hourly on weekends: 6:40 am–9:25 pm Saturday and 8:40–6:40 Sunday; the 20-minute bus ride costs $1.75. Wheatland Express has shuttle service between the Spokane Airport and Pullman and Moscow, Idaho. Reservations are recommended; the cost is $38 one way. City Cab serves the Spokane area. Metered fares run about $2.60 a mile. A taxi ride from the Spokane airport to downtown costs about $25.

Contacts **City Cab.** ☎ 509/455–3333 ⊕ www.spokanecitycab.com. **Spokane Transit Authority.** ☎ 509/328–7433 ⊕ www.spokanetransit.com. **Wheatland Express.** ☎ 509/334–2200 ⊕ www.wheatlandexpress.com.

BUS TRAVEL

Spokane has an extensive local bus system. The fare is $1.75; exact change or a token is required. Pick up schedules, maps, and tokens at the bus depot or the Plaza, the major downtown transfer point.

Contacts **The Plaza.** ✉ Bus Shop at the Plaza, 701 W. Riverside Ave. ☎ 509/456–7277 ⊕ www.spokanetransit.com.

CAR TRAVEL

Spokane can be reached by Interstate 90 from the east or west. U.S. 395 runs north from Spokane to Colville and the Canadian border. Downtown Spokane is laid out along a true grid: streets run north–south, avenues east–west; many are one way. Spokane's heaviest traffic is on Interstate 90 between Spokane and Spokane Valley on weekday evenings. Metered parking is available on city streets; there are also several downtown lots.

TRAIN TRAVEL

Amtrak's Empire Builder runs daily between Spokane and Seattle and between Spokane and Portland, stopping at points in between (including Ephrata and Pasco). Reservations are recommended. Round-trip fares vary depending on season; $120 is an average fare between Seattle and Spokane.

ESSENTIALS

Visitor Information **Spokane Area Visitors Information.** ✉ Visitor Center, River Park Square, 808 W. Main ☎ 509/624–1341, 888/776–5263 ⊕ www.visitspokane.com.

18

EXPLORING

TOP ATTRACTIONS

Cathedral of St. John the Evangelist. This architectural masterpiece, considered one of America's most important and beautiful Gothic cathedrals, was constructed in the 1920s with sandstone from Tacoma and Boise and limestone from Indiana. The cathedral's renowned 49-bell carillon has attracted international guest musicians. ✉ 127 E. 12th Ave. ☎ 509/838–4277 ⊕ www.stjohns-cathedral.org.

FAMILY
Fodor's Choice
★

Centennial Trail. This trail—which starts near Nine Mile Falls, northwest of Spokane, then runs through downtown, along Riverfront Park, and then stretches east to the Idaho border—is perfect for a hike, bike, or run. Roughly 40 miles long, the path follows the Spokane River. ✉ Along Spokane River ⊕ spokanecentennialtrail.org.

FAMILY
Fodor's Choice
★

Manito Park and Gardens. A pleasant place to stroll in summer, this 90-acre park has a formal Renaissance-style garden, conservatory, Japanese garden, duck pond, and rose and perennial gardens. A café is open daily in summer and Friday–Sunday in the off-season. Snowy winters find its hills full of sledders and its frozen pond packed with skaters. ✉ 1702 S. Grand Blvd. ☎ 509/625–6200 ⊕ my.spokanecity.org/parksrec/ ☉ Japanese Garden closed Nov.–Mar.

FAMILY **Mobius Kids Children's Museum.** Spokane's museum for children is in the lower level of River Park Square and has six interactive galleries for hands-on learning. Exhibits include a miniature city with safety education features, an art studio, a science exhibit called Geotopica, a forest-themed play area for infants and toddlers, and a stage with theater equipment and costumes. A partner facility, Mobius Science Center, is across the street. ⊠ *808 W. Main Ave.* ☎ *509/321–7121* ⊕ *www.mobiusspokane.org* ⊠ *$8; $10 combined same-day admission with Mobius Science Center* ☉ *Closed Mon.*

FAMILY **Mobius Science Center.** The museum moved into the historic Washington Water Power building in 2016, a smaller site than its previous location, and features a variety of visiting exhibits. It also includes some permanent interactive science and technology exhibits that change every three to five years as technology advances. Special events, camps, and educational programs are also offered. ⊠ *331 N. Post St.* ☎ *509/321–7133* ⊕ *www.mobiusspokane.org* ⊠ *$8; $10 combined same-day admission with Mobius Kids Children's Museum* ☉ *Closed Mon.*

FAMILY **Northwest Museum of Arts and Culture.** Affectionately referred to as the MAC, the museum is in an impressive six-level glass-and-wood structure. It has an audiovisual display and artifacts that trace Spokane's history as well as a fine Native American collection that includes baskets and beadwork of the Plateau nation. Wander the adjacent Victorian, the Campbell House, to admire the interior or view mining-era exhibits; guided tours are offered four times a day except Saturday (register in advance when you arrive at the museum). ⊠ *2316 W. 1st Ave.* ☎ *509/456–3931* ⊕ *www.northwestmuseum.org* ⊠ *$15; $7.50 on Tues.* ☉ *Closed Mon.*

FAMILY
Fodor's Choice
★
Riverfront Park. The 100-acre park is what remains of Spokane's Expo '74. Sprawling across several islands in the Spokane River, near the falls, the park was developed from old railroad yards, where the stone clock tower of the former Great Northern Railroad Station, built in 1902, stands in sharp architectural contrast to the Expo '74 building. One of the modernist buildings houses an IMAX theater, and the performing arts center occupies the former Washington State pavilion. A children's train chugs around the park in summer, and a 1909 carousel, hand-carved by master builder Charles I.D. Looff, is a local landmark. Another icon here is the giant red slide shaped like a Radio Flyer wagon. For a great view of the river and falls, walk across Port Street Bridge. Other attractions include a sky ride over Spokane Falls and a minigolf course. A major park redevelopment began in 2016; park enhancements include a new recreational ice-skating rink opening in fall 2017 and new carousel building scheduled to open in early 2018. ⊠ *507 N. Howard St.* ☎ *509/625–6600* ⊕ *www.spokaneriverfrontpark.com* ⊠ *Park free, fees for some attractions.*

WORTH NOTING

Arbor Crest Wine Cellars. On the grounds of the eclectic 1924 mansion of Royal Riblet, the inventor of a square-wheel tractor and the poles that hold up ski lifts, you can sample Arbor Crest wines, enjoy the striking view of the Spokane River 450-feet below, or meander through the impeccably kept grounds (the house isn't open to tours). Enjoy Sunday-evening concerts (5:30 pm–sunset) outside from mid-May through September; in winter there's live music by the fireside in the Wine Bar on Friday and Saturday nights (5:30–7:30). Local musicians perform Thursday evenings in summer, too. Arbor Crest's wines include Cabernet Sauvignon, Cliff House Red, Chardonnays from the Columbia Valley and more. ✉ *4705 N. Fruithill Rd.* ☎ *509/927–9463* 🌐 *www.arborcrest.com.*

Bing Crosby House Museum. Crooner Bing Crosby grew up in Spokane in a Craftsman-style house built in 1911 by his father and uncles. The house museum has hundreds of items (out of the thousands in Gonzaga University's Crosby Collection) on display, including his Oscar for the film *Going My Way*, his gold records, and other memorabilia from his life. ✉ *508 E Sharp Ave.* ☎ *509/313–3847* 🌐 *researchguides.gonzaga.edu/bingcrosbyhouse* 🕒 *Closed Sun.*

OFF THE BEATEN PATH

Cat Tales Zoological Park. Among the large cats living at this zoo are lions, tigers, ligers (a combination of lion and tiger), leopards, pumas, and lynxes. Guided tours give background information on the animals. There's also a petting zoo. ✉ *17020 N. Newport Hwy., Mead* ⊕ *12 miles north of I–90* ☎ *509/238–4126* 🌐 *www.cattales.org* 🎟 *$10* 🕒 *Closed Mon.*

Finch Arboretum. This mile-long green patch along Garden Springs Creek has an extensive botanical garden with more than 2,000 labeled trees, shrubs, and flowers. Follow the walking tour on well-manicured paths along the creek, or follow your whim—depending on the season—through flowering rhododendrons, hibiscus, magnolias, dogwoods, hydrangeas, and more. ✉ *3404 W. Woodland Blvd.* ☎ *509/363–5466* 🌐 *my.spokanecity.org/urbanforestry/programs/finch-arboretum.*

Townshend Cellar. A drive to the Green Bluff countryside leads wine lovers to this small winery and its tasting room. It's won awards for its Cabernet Sauvignon, and also produces Merlot, Chardonnay, Syrah, and several blends, offering more than 20 wines. Huckleberries from nearby Idaho are used in sparkling wine. ✉ *8022 E. Greenbluff Rd., Colbert* ⊕ *13 miles northeast of Spokane* ☎ *509/238–1400* 🌐 *www.townshendcellar.com* 🕒 *Closed Mon.–Thurs.*

EN ROUTE

Eastern Washington University. The tree-shaded Cheney campus has six original buildings that are on the National Register of Historic Places, but most of the 300-acre campus consists of post–World War II concrete-and-glass structures. ✉ *526 5th St., Cheney* ⊕ *About 20 miles west of Spokane* ☎ *509/359–6200* 🌐 *www.ewu.edu.*

18

WHERE TO EAT

$$ ECLECTIC

🍴 **The Blackbird.** Inside the historic Broadview Dairy building, this gastropub has a casual, industrial setting, welcoming outdoor patio, and exceptional food. There's a southern influence found in menu items like the weekend brunch's shrimp and grits, as well as a focus on meats smoked on-site, charcuterie, and wood-grilled burgers and steaks. **Known for:** bacon-fat popcorn, topped with brown sugar and sea salt; happy hour with $5 drink specials and $3 snacks; more than 30 beers and ciders on tap. [$] *Average main: $18* ✉ *905 N. Washington* ☎ *509/392–4000* 🌐 *www.theblackbirdspokane.com.*

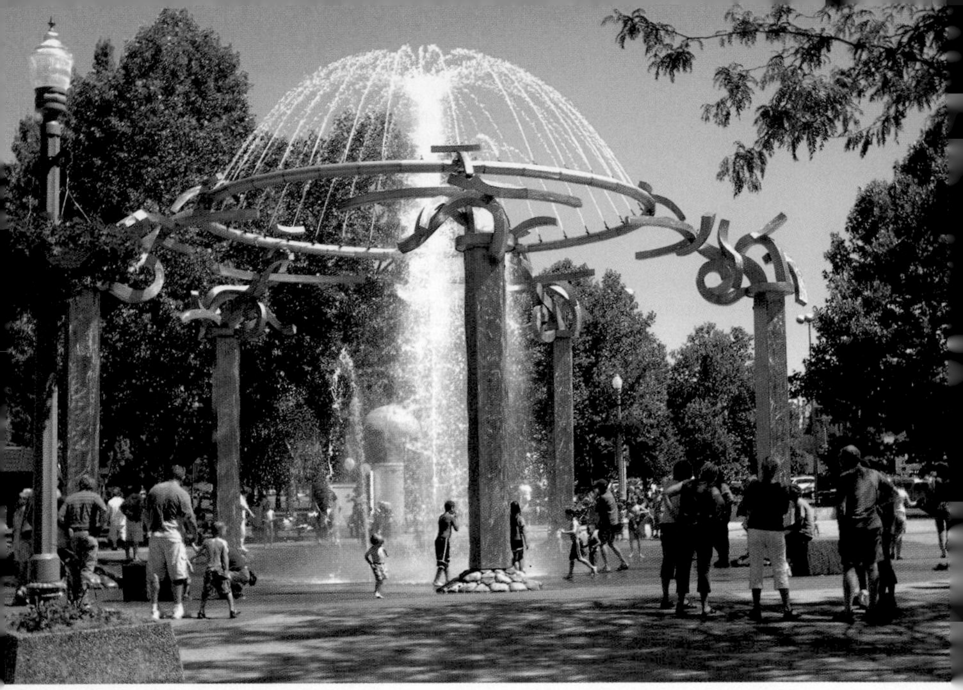

Riverfront Park

$$ SOUTHERN FAMILY

🍴 **Casper Fry.** Spokane's South Perry District has been revitalized in recent years, and this restaurant is one of the reasons why. With food quality and ambience that would fit right into a hip Seattle or Portland foodie neighborhood, the menu includes such comfort foods as cast-iron-skillet mac and cheese, buttermilk fried chicken, blackened catfish, po' boys, and shrimp and grits. **Known for:** barrel-aged cocktails and an impressive list of whiskeys; charcoal-burning Josper oven. [$] *Average main: $19* ✉ *928 S. Perry* ☎ *509/535–0536* 🌐 *www.casperfry.com* 🕒 *Closed Mon.*

$$$ SEAFOOD FAMILY Fodor's Choice ★

🍴 **Clinkerdagger.** In a former flour mill with great views of the Spokane River, Clink's has been a Spokane institution since 1974, and a favorite for special occasions. The seafood, steaks, and prime rib are excellent; the Maytag blue cheese salad and beer-battered fish-and-chips are both popular at lunch. **Known for:** excellent happy hour; surf-and-turf dinner combos; creative cocktails. [$] *Average main: $30* ✉ *621 W. Mallon Ave.* ☎ *509/328–5965* 🌐 *www.clinkerdagger.com* 🕒 *No lunch Sun.*

$ AMERICAN

🍴 **Elk Public House.** This casual eatery in the relaxed Browne's Addition neighborhood, west of downtown, serves pub food such as grilled lamb sandwiches, burgers, soft tacos, salads, and a spicy gumbo, together with a good selection of microbrews, most from the Northwest. A copper bar stands along one wall, backed by a mirror, giving the interior a saloonlike appearance. **Known for:** hipster vibe, but families welcome, too; was featured on TV's "Diners, Drive-Ins, and Dives"; nice patio for outdoor dining. [$] *Average main: $12* ✉ *1931 W. Pacific Ave.* ☎ *509/363–1973* 🌐 *www.wedonthaveone.com.*

$ ✕ **Frank's Diner.** Right off the Maple Street Bridge, this is the state's old-
DINER   est railroad-car restaurant; built as an observation car in 1906, it has
FAMILY   original light fixtures, stained-glass windows, and mahogany details.
Fodor'sChoice   Breakfast is the specialty here, with large portions and unique items
★   like Creole Benedict with lobster and crab. **Known for:** fun setting and
very popular—there's often a wait; menu is inventive. $ *Average main:*
$10 ✉ *1516 W. 2nd Ave.* ☎ *509/747–8798* ⊕ *www.franksdiners.com.*

$$$ ✕ **Latah Bistro.** Tucked into a strip mall in south Spokane near Qual-
ECLECTIC   chan Golf Course, this neighborhood restaurant serves a diverse menu
that changes frequently. Some standards include glazed pork tender-
loin, seared scallops, spinach salad with hot bacon, pizzas baked in a
wood-burning oven, and rich desserts. **Known for:** well-priced Sunday
brunch; diverse wine list. $ *Average main: $25* ✉ *4241 S. Cheney–*
Spokane Rd. ☎ *509/838–8338* ⊕ *www.latahbistro.com* ☾ *No lunch*
Sat., brunch on Sun. only.

$$$ ✕ **Luna.** You'll find inventive approaches to classics here, from a Kobe
ECLECTIC   burger to citrus-cured salmon, as well as small plates and wood-fired
pizza. Weekend brunch has sweet treats like beignets with chocolate
sauce as well as many savory offerings, including butternut-squash
hash, smoked-salmon scramble, and brisket hash and peppers. **Known**
for: rose terrace and courtyard dining in summer; extensive wine list;
fabulous desserts. $ *Average main: $30* ✉ *5620 S. Perry St.* ☎ *509/448–*
2383 ⊕ *www.lunaspokane.com.*

$ ✕ **Mary Lou's Milk Bottle.** Built in 1933, this restaurant is shaped like
AMERICAN   a gigantic milk bottle; since 1978 the eatery has been selling home-
FAMILY   made ice cream. Fries are made from hand-cut potatoes, buns are
made in-house, and burgers, sandwiches, salads, and soup (in winter
only) round out the menu. **Known for:** huckleberry shakes; reasonable
prices; kitschy building. $ *Average main: $7* ✉ *802 W. Garland Ave.*
☎ *509/325–1772* ▭ *No credit cards* ☾ *No dinner Sun.*

$$$ ✕ **Milford's Fish House.** This brick and terra-cotta-tile structure was built
SEAFOOD   in 1925, and the terrazzo floor and tin ceiling are relics of that era.
The interior's exposed-brick walls and wood details, lit by candles,
create a romantic environment in which to enjoy the wide array of
seafood dishes and steaks. **Known for:** panfried oysters; calamari; well-
priced seasonal desserts. $ *Average main: $29* ✉ *719 N. Monroe St.*
☎ *509/326–7251* ⊕ *www.milfordsfishhouse.com* ☾ *No lunch.*

$$$ ✕ **Mizuna Restaurant.** Fresh flowers and redbrick walls lend color and
ECLECTIC   charm to this downtown eatery, where a patio is open for outdoor dining
May through September. Grilled swordfish is served with cumin-dusted
fingerling potatoes, Oregon rack of lamb comes with sautéed kale, and
local produce is the inspiration for such scrumptious vegetarian fare
as white-cheddar-and-apple salad. **Known for:** many vegan, vegetarian, and gluten-free options; cheese plate gets rave reviews; Northwest
wines. $ *Average main: $29* ✉ *214 N. Howard St.* ☎ *509/747–2004*
⊕ *www.mizuna.com* ☾ *No lunch Sun.*

$ ✕ **Post Street Ale House.** Adjacent to The Davenport Lusso, this casual
AMERICAN   eatery offers standard pub fare like fish-and-chips, burgers, sausage
dogs, and several kinds of pasta and salads. Starters include the signature fried pickles, deviled eggs, and bar food like nachos, sliders, and

18

wings. **Known for:** late-night munchies; quick service. $ *Average main: $14* ⊠ *1 N. Post St.* ☎ *509/789–6900* ⊕ *www.davenporthotelcollection. com/our-hotels/the-davenport-lusso/dining/.*

$$$
FRENCH
FAMILY
Fodor's Choice
★

✕ **Sante Restaurant and Charcuterie.** The focus here is spectacular French cuisine that isn't too rich and saucy and that uses sustainably and locally produced food. The charcuterie board brings to mind an outdoor picnic, with cheese, jam, mustard, and a baguette; pâté made of chicken liver is also accompanied by a baguette. **Known for:** presliced charcuterie for sale by the pound; excellent baked goods from the owners' Common Crumb Bakery; outstanding brunch; kids' menu includes green eggs and ham. $ *Average main: $25* ⊠ *404 W. Main St.* ☎ *509/315–4613* ⊕ *www.santespokane.com.*

$$
AMERICAN
FAMILY

✕ **Steelhead Bar & Grille.** This casual pub-style eatery, housed in one of Spokane's many older brick buildings, has an urban contemporary vibe, with lots of burnished-metal artwork by local artists. Sandwiches and burgers make this a handy place for lunch; kebabs, steak, fish-and-chips, and (of course) steelhead are heartier fare at dinner. **Known for:** half-pound bison burger; chocolate desserts. $ *Average main: $18* ⊠ *218 N. Howard St.* ☎ *509/747–1303* ⊕ *www.steelheadbarandgrille.com.*

$
AMERICAN

✕ **The Wandering Table.** For the adventurous, chef-owner Adam Hegsted will create your meal based on what is in season, and is likely to include some of the house standards, such as deviled eggs with maple-bacon filling, fried brussels sprouts, spaghetti-stuffed meatballs, and albacore tuna ceviche. These and other small plates make this a popular spot for both a light lunch and tapas-style dinner. **Known for:** more than a dozen items for just $3 during happy hour (3–5 pm); multicourse meals uniquely created each day for a fixed price; most food locally sourced. $ *Average main: $16* ⊠ *1242 W. Summit Pkwy.* ☎ *509/443–4410* ⊕ *www.thewanderingtable.com* ⊘ *No lunch Sun. and Mon.*

WHERE TO STAY

$$
HOTEL

▦ **The Davenport Grand.** The newest hotel in the Davenport Collection, and Spokane's largest, is right across from the INB Performing Arts Center and Riverfront Park and features business-friendly, large, modern rooms. **Pros:** across the street from convention center; nice views from upper floors; discounted rates are often available. **Cons:** no pool; no bathtubs; hotel can be noisy when crowded. $ *Rooms from: $189* ⊠ *333 W Spokane Falls Blvd.* ☎ *800/918–9344, 509/458–3330* ⊕ *www. davenporthotelcollection.com* ⌨ *716 rooms* ⦿|*No meals.*

$$
HOTEL

▦ **The Davenport Lusso.** European furnishings and many modern amenities, including flat-screen TVs, provide an intimate and elegant getaway, enhanced by the Italian marble floor, archways, and fountains of the lobby. **Pros:** small and intimate; access to amenities at flagship sister property nearby; attentive service. **Cons:** no minibars; some rooms face an alley and other buildings; room lighting is subdued. $ *Rooms from: $159* ⊠ *808 W. Sprague Ave.* ☎ *509/747–9750, 800/899–1482* ⊕ *www. davenporthotelcollection.com* ⌨ *48 rooms* ⦿|*No meals.*

$$
HOTEL
FAMILY

▦ **The Davenport Tower.** This 21-floor modern tower has contemporary-style rooms decorated in a fun safari theme, and its lively Safari Room Grill restaurant offers great happy-hour deals and early dinner specials. **Pros:** across the street from the historic original Davenport Hotel; very affordable in off-season; comfortable beds. **Cons:** rooms can be noisy from other guests and nearby train tracks; no mini-refrigerators. [$] *Rooms from: $169* ✉ *111 S. Post St.* ☎ *509/789–6965, 800/918–9342* 🌐 *www.davenporthotelcollection.com* 🛏 *328 rooms* 🍴 *No meals.*

$$ HOTEL FAMILY Fodor's Choice ★ 🏨 **The Historic Davenport Hotel.** One of four unique Davenport properties in Spokane, this is the oldest and best; more than a century old, it was restored in the early 2000s, reopening with beautiful accommodations featuring hand-carved mahogany furniture and fine Irish linens, marble bathrooms with big soaking tubs and separate showers, and stunning ballrooms and public spaces. **Pros:** historical restoration is a marvel to see; abundant resortlike amenities; though independently owned, booking is through Marriott. **Cons:** some guests have noted service issues. [$] *Rooms from: $189* ✉ *10 S. Post St.* ☎ *509/455–8888, 800/899–1482* 🌐 *www.davenporthotel.com* 🛏 *284 rooms* 🍴 *No meals.*

$$ HOTEL FAMILY 🏨 **Hotel RL Spokane at the Park.** This large Red Lion hotel got a hip makeover in 2016, including an open stage in the colorful lobby where guests can enjoy live performances by locals and mingle with other guests, redecorated rooms with wood floors and modern minimalist furniture, and a bistro-style restaurant. **Pros:** pool area is popular with families; free summer outdoor concerts Friday and Saturday evenings; great location next to river and walking trail through Riverfront Park; free use of bikes. **Cons:** new check-in procedure can be confusing; no in-room coffeemakers (guests can get free espresso drink at coffee bar); no room service, but takeout can be ordered from restaurant. [$] *Rooms from: $180* ✉ *303 W. North River Dr.* ☎ *509/326–8000, 800/733–5466* 🌐 *www.redlion.com* 🛏 *402 rooms* 🍴 *No meals.*

$ B&B/INN 🏨 **Marianna Stolz House.** Across from Gonzaga University on a tree-lined street, this American foursquare home built in 1908 is listed on Spokane's historical register and is decorated with leaded-glass china cabinets, Renaissance Revival armchairs, and original dark-fir woodwork. **Pros:** convenient location; friendly innkeeper. **Cons:** shared bathroom for some rooms; minimum stay for some dates. [$] *Rooms from: $115* ✉ *427 E. Indiana Ave.* ☎ *509/483–4316, 800/978–6587* 🌐 *www.mariannastoltzhouse.com* 🛏 *4 rooms, 2 with bath* 🍴 *Breakfast.*

$$ HOTEL FAMILY 🏨 **Oxford Suites.** Located on the north side of the Spokane River, this three-story hotel of well-equipped studio suites is convenient to downtown and Riverfront Park, as well as the Spokane Arena and Gonzaga University. **Pros:** 24-hour store and guest laundry are nice conveniences; electric-vehicle charging station; free shuttle to downtown and airport. **Cons:** two-night minimum most weekends; need to book ahead for popular events. [$] *Rooms from: $155* ✉ *115 W. North River Dr.* ☎ *509/353–9000, 800/774–1877* 🌐 *www.oxfordsuitesspokane.com* 🛏 *125 rooms* 🍴 *Breakfast.*

NIGHTLIFE AND PERFORMING ARTS

NIGHTLIFE

The Observatory. This bar, which opened in late 2015, received the local news weekly's "best new nightspot" award in its first year. It's known for craft cocktails, some made with fresh-squeezed juice; a menu of charcuterie, cheese, and sandwiches that tops out at $10; and great service. Live music happens weekly. ✉ *15. S. Howard St.* ☎ *509/598–9833* ⊕ *www.observatoryspokane.com.*

The Ridler Piano Bar. Every Thursday through Saturday pianists duke it out on the ivories, playing both popular and offbeat tunes—and, of course, they take requests. Open-mike night is held every Tuesday and there's karaoke Sunday nights. ✉ *718 W. Riverside Ave.* ☎ *509/822–7938* ⊕ *www.ridlerpiano.bar.*

PERFORMING ARTS

The Bing Crosby Theater. Formerly the Clemmer theater, the Bing, built in 1915, is one of America's few remaining palace-style theaters. It was renamed for hometown hero Bing Crosby; he performed skits here in between the showing of silent films. In addition to a varied roster from comedy to music, it also hosts the Bing Crosby Holiday Film Festival every December, which highlights some of Crosby's best films from his storied career. ✉ *901 W. Sprague Ave.*

FAMILY **The Garland Theater.** Spokane's only independent movie theater, the Garland has "bottomless bags" of popcorn, booze, and grub (slow-roasted pork shoulder, pasta in a five cheese sauce, and more) that you can take into the cinema. Catch a second-run flick here with the locals and bring the kids to the free morning showings. ✉ *924 W. Garland Ave.* ☎ *509/327–2509* ⊕ *garlandtheater.com* ☐ *$5.*

The Knitting Factory Concert House. National acts, ranging from Tech N9ne to Social Distortion, are hosted in this 1,500-seat venue. ✉ *919 W. Sprague Ave.* ☎ *509/244–3279* ⊕ *sp.knittingfactory.com.*

Spokane Civic Theatre. The long-running community theater presents musicals and dramas on two stages from September through June. ✉ *1020 N. Howard St.* ☎ *509/325–2507* ⊕ *www.spokanecivictheatre.com.*

Spokane Symphony. Classical and pops concerts are presented from September through May in the newly restored historic Martin Woldson Theater at The Fox, plus special events such as the *Nutcracker* at the INB Performing Arts Center, free outdoor concerts at city parks in summer, and chamber music in the Davenport Hotel. ✉ *Fox Theater, 1001 W. Sprague* ☎ *509/624–1200* ⊕ *www.spokanesymphony.org/.*

SHOPPING

Boo Radley's. Part curiosity shop, part vintage toy store, this eclectic spot is great for unusual gifts or to spend some time browsing. Original and creative toys, cards, games, T-shirts, masks and statuettes are just some of the treasures you'll find here. ✉ *232 N. Howard St.* ☎ *509/456–7479* ⊕ *www.instagram.com/boo_radleys_spokane/.*

Flour Mill. When it was built in 1895, the mill was a huge technical innovation. Today it's home to shops, restaurants, and an event center. The mill sits virtually atop the falls, north of the river. ⊠ *621 W. Mallon Ave.*

River Park Square. Upscale shopping here includes Nordstrom, an Apple Store, Williams-Sonoma, Pottery Barn, The North Face, and other national retailers—more than 40 stores in all. Several restaurants are here or nearby, and there's a 20-screen movie theater. ⊠ *808 W. Main St.* ⊕ *www.riverparksquare.com.*

SPORTS AND THE OUTDOORS

GOLF

Hangman Valley. This 18-hole, par-72 course, has greens fees of $32 weekdays, $36 weekends. ⊠ *2210 E. Hangman Valley Rd.* ☎ *509/448–1212* ⊕ *www.spokanecounty.org/1141/Hangman-Valley.*

Indian Canyon. On the slope of a basalt canyon, this 18-hole course has great views of North Spokane and Mt. Spokane. The greens fees are $33 Monday through Thursday, $36 Friday through Sunday. ⊠ *1000 S. Assembly* ☎ *509/747–5353* ⊕ *my.spokanecity.org/golf/courses/indian-canyon/.*

Liberty Lake. This course is near MeadowWood, so avid golfers can visit both and play 36 holes. The greens fees are $32 weekdays, $36 weekends. ⊠ *24403 E. Sprague Ave., Liberty Lake* ☎ *509/255–6233* ⊕ *www.spokanecounty.org/1210/Liberty-Lake.*

MeadowWood. This is a Scottish-style course that has been ranked in Washington's top 10 municipal courses. Greens fees are $32 weekdays, $36 weekends. ⊠ *24501 E. Valleyway Ave., Liberty Lake* ☎ *509/255–9539* ⊕ *www.spokanecounty.org/1234/MeadowWood.*

HIKING

The hills around Spokane are laced with trails, almost all of which connect with 37-mile-long **Centennial Trail,** which winds along the Spokane River. Beginning in Nine Mile Falls, northwest of Spokane, the well-marked trail ends in Idaho. Maps are available at the visitor center at 201 West Main Street. Northwest of downtown at **Riverside State Park,** a paved trail leads through a 17-million-year-old fossil forest in Deep Creek Canyon. From there it's easy to get to the western end of the Centennial Trail by crossing the suspension bridge at the day-use parking lot; trails heading both left and right will lead to the Centennial.

SKIING

49° North. An hour north of Spokane in the Colville National Forest, this is a 2,325-acre family-oriented resort. Lift tickets cost $51 to $58; snowboards and ski package rentals are $33. ⊠ *U.S. 395, 3311 Flowery Trail Rd., Chewelah* ☎ *509/935–6649* ⊕ *www.ski49n.com.*

Mt. Spokane. This modest downhill resort, 28 miles northeast of downtown Spokane, has a 2,000-foot drop and 10 miles of groomed cross-country ski trails. Snowshoeing and tubing are also options. There's night skiing Wednesday–Saturday. Lift tickets cost $41 to $55. A Discover Pass is required on all vehicles ($10 for one day or $30 annually) and is valid at all Washington state parks. A

18

Sno-Park permit is also required for parking at Nordic skiing trailheads. ⊠ *29500 N. Mt. Spokane Park Dr., Mead* ☎ *509/238–2220* ⊕ *www.mtspokane.com.*

EAST CENTRAL WASHINGTON

If you travel along the Interstate at 70-plus mph, it might seem that this area is mainly a lot of crop fields and a single town with a big lake. But slow the pace a bit and get off the beaten path to discover family-friendly activities in Moses Lake, including a lively water park and lakefront park for swimming on hot summer days. North in the town of Ephrata, local history is depicted in a pioneer village. Soap Lake is a body of water like no other, with bubbly, mineral-rich water that has been purported to have healing effects for more than a century. Closer to the Columbia River just west of Quincy, the award-winning Gorge Amphitheatre hosts concerts through the summer. Adjacent to the Gorge is the not-to-be-missed Cave B Resort, which has luxurious accommodations, fabulous river and canyon views, an estate winery, pool, spa, fine dining, and upscale yurts.

MOSES LAKE

105 miles west of Spokane.

The natural lake from which this sprawling town takes its name seems to be an anomaly in the dry landscape of east-central Washington. But ever since the Columbia Basin Project took shape, there's been water everywhere. Approaching Moses Lake from the west on Interstate 90, you'll pass lushly green irrigated fields; to the east lie vast stretches of wheat. The lakes of this region have more shorebirds than Washington's ocean beaches. Potholes Reservoir is an artificial lake that supports as much wildlife as does the Columbia Wildlife Refuge. The Winchester Wasteway, west of Moses Lake, is a great place to paddle a kayak or canoe and watch birds as you glide along the reedy banks. The airfield north of town was once a major Air Force base, and now serves as a training facility for airline pilots.

GETTING HERE AND AROUND

Moses Lake straddles Interstate 90; it's about 100 miles from Spokane and 175 miles from Seattle. To the north, Highway 17 connects Moses Lake to Ephrata and points north, including Soap Lake and Coulee City.

ESSENTIALS

Visitor Information Moses Lake Area Chamber of Commerce. ⊠ *324 S. Pioneer Way* ☎ *509/765–7888, 800/992–6234* ⊕ *www.moseslake.com.*

EXPLORING

Columbia National Wildlife Refuge. A great number of birds are attracted to this reserve: hawks, falcons, golden eagles, ducks, sandhill cranes, herons, American avocets, black-necked stilts, and yellow-headed and red-winged blackbirds. The refuge is also home to beavers, muskrats, badgers, and coyotes. ⊠ *Othello* ✛ *7 miles northwest of Othello via McMahon Rd. to Morgan Lake Rd.; about 20 miles southeast of Moses Lake* ☎ *509/546–8300* ⊕ *www.fws.gov/refuge/columbia/* 🎫 *Free.*

Moses Lake. Claw-shaped, 38-foot-deep, 18-mile-long Moses Lake is filled by Crab Creek—which originates in the hills west of Spokane—with three side branches known as Parker Horn, Lewis Horn, and Pelican Horn. The city of Moses Lake sprawls over the peninsulas formed by these "horns," and can therefore be a bit difficult to get around. This is the state's second-largest lake. ✉ *Hwy. 17* ✣ *Off I–90.*

Moses Lake Museum and Art Center. Fossils collected all over North America, including prehistoric land and marine animals, are exhibited here. Regional artists are also featured. ✉ *Moses Lake Civic Center, 401 S. Balsam St.* ☎ *509/764–3830* 🌐 *www.cityofml.com* 🕒 *Closed Sun.*

Potholes State Park. This park is 25 miles southwest of Moses Lake on the west side of O'Sullivan Dam. Camping and boating, as well as fishing for trout, perch, and walleye, are popular diversions. ✉ *6762 Hwy. 262 E, Othello* ☎ *509/346–2759, 888/226–7688 campsite reservations* 🌐 *parks.state.wa.us/568/Potholes* 🎫 *Day pass $10 per vehicle; annual Discovery Pass $30 (valid at all state parks); campsite $25–$45, cabins $69–$79.*

FAMILY **Surf 'n Slide Water Park.** This is a great place to cool off from the hot central Washington sunshine, with an Olympic-sized pool, two 200-foot waterslides, a tube slide, a "baby octopus" slide, and diving boards. ✉ *McCosh Park, 401 W. 4th Ave.* ☎ *509/764–3805* 🌐 *www.cityofml.com* 🎫 *$12* 🕒 *Closed after Labor Day–Memorial Day weekend.*

WHERE TO EAT AND STAY

$$$ AMERICAN 🍴 **Michael's on the Lake.** In the late afternoon golden rays of sunlight wash over the dining room and deck at this lakeside restaurant, where you can indulge in prime rib or Parmesan-crusted halibut over linguine, or enjoy lighter soups and sandwiches, and share small plates and unique appetizers like ginger-chicken lettuce wraps and fried brussels sprouts. Small plates include mahimahi tacos and lobster mac and cheese. **Known for:** half-price appetizers during daily happy hours; decadent desserts; more than a dozen salads. [$] *Average main: $24* ✉ *910 W. Broadway Ave.* ☎ *509/765–1611* 🌐 *www.michaelsonthelake.com.*

$$ HOTEL FAMILY 🏨 **Comfort Suites.** Spacious and comfortable rooms, considered suites because there's a sitting area separate from the beds, shine with modern style and conveniences. **Pros:** clean and modern; nice pool; friendly service. **Cons:** no restaurant; prices steep during some events. [$] *Rooms from: $180* ✉ *1700 E. Kittleson Rd.* ☎ *509/765–3731, 877/424–6423* 🌐 *www.comfortsuitesmoseslake.com* 🛏 *60 suites* 🍽 *Breakfast.*

SHOPPING

Moses Lake Farmers Market. Vendors come here each Saturday from May–October to sell fresh produce and handmade arts and crafts. ✉ *McCosh Park (next to aquatic center), Dogwood St.* ☎ *509/750–7831* 🌐 *www.moseslakefarmersmarket.com.*

QUINCY

34 miles northwest of Moses Lake.

On the fences along Interstate 90 to Gorge and north on Highway 281 to Quincy, crop-identification signs highlight what the Quincy Valley is known for: agriculture. From Thanksgiving to New Year's Eve, these same fields are filled with Christmas motion-light displays, powered by electricity from farmers' irrigation lines—a delightful sight for highway travelers in the dark winter nights. Agriculture hasn't always been king in this area. Though the rich soils attracted many settlers after the railroad made the region accessible in the early 1900s, several serious droughts proved that Mother Nature could not be relied on to water the crops consistently. In the mid-1930s the federal government began to assist with irrigation plans, and by the early 1950s the first systems were in place.

Today the area has 200,000 irrigable acres growing corn, alfalfa, wheat, potatoes, seed, apples, and more. An annual Farmer Consumer Awareness Day is held the second Saturday of September, with farm tours, entertainment, food, arts and crafts, and plenty of fresh produce. Tourism is also growing here, with visitors from across the state and beyond coming to summer concerts at the Gorge Amphitheatre, touring wineries between Quincy and Wenatchee, and hiking and climbing near the Columbia River.

GETTING HERE AND AROUND

Quincy is 11 miles north of Interstate 90's Exit 149, via Highway 281. It's about two hours, 45 minutes from Seattle and two hours, 30 minutes from Spokane.

EXPLORING

Gorge Amphitheatre. This 27,500-seat amphitheater has won accolades as best outdoor concert venue due to its fine acoustics and stunning vistas of the Columbia River—a setting compared to the Grand Canyon's. Set in one of the sunniest parts of the state, the concert season runs from May to September. Concertgoers often overnight at the adjacent campground or at motels and hotels in Quincy, Moses Lake, and Ellensburg. ✉ *754 Silica Rd. NW, George* ☎ *509/785–6262.*

WHERE TO EAT AND STAY

$ CAFÉ FAMILY 🍴 **The Grainery.** The spacious, brightly decorated, country-cozy café features espresso and baked goods to start the day and a wide selection of paninis and deli sandwiches, served with salad or chips and a mini-cookie, for lunch. Menu items change to reflect what's in season, such as the strawberry summer salad and hearty vegetable soups. **Known for:** scrumptious pastries baked in-house; soups and salads featuring local produce. [$] *Average main: $9* ✉ *101 E St. SE* ☎ *509/797–7240* 🌐 *www.grainerycafe.biz* 🕘 *Closed Sun.; also closed Sat. seasonally. No dinner.*

$$$ RESORT Fodor's Choice ★ 🏨 **Cave B Estate Winery and Resort.** Washington's first destination winery resort is built on (and into) ancient basalt cliffs 900 feet above the Columbia River; its 15 cliff houses, cavern (with 12 rooms), and inn are all designed to blend into the natural environment and offer

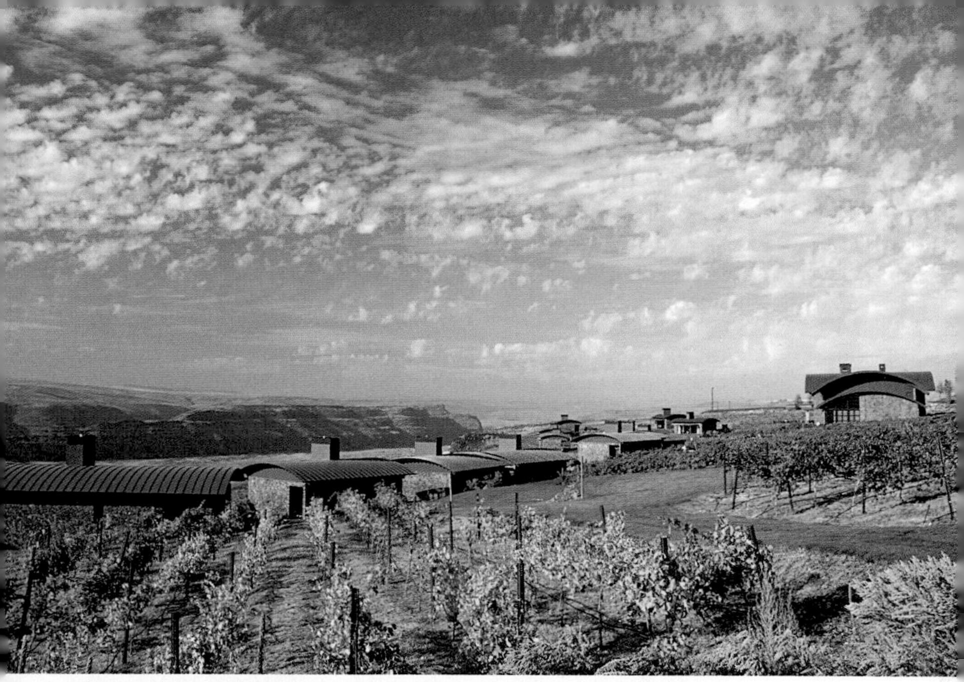

Cave B Estate Winery and Resort

casually elegant, comfortable accommodations with fireplaces, soaking tubs, and other luxuries. **Pros:** fantastic place to stargaze; secluded; gorgeous accommodations. **Cons:** expensive during Gorge Amphitheatre events; no local meal options besides on-site restaurant. [$] *Rooms from: $229* ✉ *344 Silica Rd. NW* ☎ *509/787–8000, 888/785–2283* 🌐 *www.cavebinn.com* 🕒 *Closed mid-Dec.–early Feb.; yurts closed Nov.–Mar.* 🛏 *30 rooms, 25 yurts* 🍴 *No meals.*

18

EPHRATA

18 miles northeast of Quincy.

Ephrata (e-*fray*-tuh), a pleasant, small farm town and the Grant County seat, is in the exact center of Washington. It was settled quite early because its abundant natural springs made it an oasis in the dry steppe country of the Columbia Basin. Native Americans visited the springs, as did cattle drovers after American ranchers stocked the open range. Ephrata began to grow after the Great Northern Railroad established a terminal here in 1892. Cattlemen took advantage of the railroad to round up and ship out thousands of wild horses that roamed the range. The last great roundup was held in 1906, when the remaining 2,400 horses of a herd that once numbered some 25,000 were corralled and shipped off.

GETTING HERE AND AROUND

Ephrata is about 20 miles north of Moses Lake via Highway 17. Continuing north on the highway leads to the town of Soap Lake, then past state parks, up to Coulee City.

EXPLORING

FAMILY **Grant County Historical Museum and Village.** More than 30 pioneer-era buildings have been brought here from other parts of Grant County. They include a blacksmith forge, saloon, barbershop, and printing office. ✉ *742 Basin St. N.* ☎ *509/754–3334* 🎫 *$3.50* 🕒 *Closed Wed.*

Soap Lake. The water is high in dissolved carbonates, sulfates, and chlorides, and the lake has long been famous for its mineral waters and therapeutic mud baths; in fact it was called the "World's Greatest Medical Marvel" nearly a century ago. Yet the eponymous small town has never quite succeeded as a modern-day resort—perhaps because the miraculous waters have been heavily diluted by irrigation waters. But agriculture is much more profitable anyway, and many other beautiful recreation areas are nearby. ✉ *Soap Lake* ✥ *6 miles north of Ephrata* 🌐 *www.soaplakecoc.org.*

WHERE TO STAY

$ B&B/INN FAMILY 🏨 **Inn at Soap Lake.** At this inn opened in 1915 during Soap Lake's heyday as a destination for health treatments, most rooms have a soaking tub with the natural mineral-rich water on tap, along with contemporary furnishings and modern amenities. **Pros:** beautifully landscaped gardens; private beach has lounge chairs; cozy lobby. **Cons:** two-week cancellation policy; registration desk is not staffed, but management is on-site. [$] *Rooms from: $110* ✉ *226 Main Ave. E, Soap Lake* ☎ *509/246–1132, 800/557–8514* 🌐 *soaplakeresort.com/accommodation/the-inn-at-soap-lake/* 🛏 *20 rooms, 8 cottages* 🍴 *No meals.*

$$ HOTEL FAMILY 🏨 **Notaras Lodge.** The spacious rooms at this four-building lodge on the shore of Soap Lake are individually decorated; all have a rustic log-style construction. **Pros:** room style is very unusual and fun; helpful staff; interesting grounds. **Cons:** not all rooms have lake views. [$] *Rooms from: $158* ✉ *236 Main Ave. E, Soap Lake* ☎ *509/246–0462, 800/557–8514* 🌐 *www.soaplakeresort.com/accommodation/notaras-lodge/* 🛏 *15 rooms* 🍴 *No meals.*

NORTHEASTERN WASHINGTON

A technological marvel, the Grand Coulee Dam took nearly a decade to build in the 1930s. Its fascinating history is on display at the year-round visitor center, where tours are also available. The dam created a 150-mile-long lake; several campgrounds surround it and recreational activities abound. Farther north, the Colville and Okanogan National Forests comprise three mountain ranges that are foothills of the Rockies. These wild areas teem with wildlife and natural beauty, yet remain pristine and uncrowded. The small towns of Omak and Colville provide basic services for travelers.

COULEE DAM NATIONAL RECREATION AREA

60 miles northeast of Ephrata, 239 miles northeast of Seattle, 87 miles northwest of Spokane.

Grand Coulee Dam is the one of the world's largest concrete structures. At almost a mile long, it justly deserves the moniker "Eighth Technological Wonder of the World." Beginning in 1932, 9,000 men excavated 45 million cubic yards of rock and soil and dammed the Grand Coulee, a gorge created by the Columbia River, with 12 million cubic yards of concrete—enough to build a sidewalk the length of the equator. By the time the dam was completed in 1941, 77 men had perished and 11 towns were submerged under the newly formed Roosevelt Lake. The waters backed up behind the dam turned eastern Washington's arid soil into fertile farming land, but not without consequence: salmon-fishing stations that were a source of food and spiritual identity for Native Americans were destroyed. Half the dam was built on the Colville Indian Reservation on the north shore of the Columbia; the Colville tribes later received restitution in excess of $75 million from the U.S. government.

In 1946 most of Roosevelt Lake and the grassy and pine woodland hills surrounding it were designated the Coulee Dam National Recreation Area. Crown Point Vista, about 5 miles west of Grand Coulee on Highway 174, may have the best vantage for photographs of the dam, Roosevelt Lake, Rufus Woods Lake (below the dam), and the town of Coulee Dam.

After nightfall from Memorial Day weekend through September the dam is transformed into an unlikely entertainment complex by an extravagant, free laser-light show. After 25 years of the same show, a new one called "One River, Many Voices" debuted in 2014 with a more contemporary, high-tech style and oral histories of the dam project. The audio portion is broadcast on 90.1 FM. Show up early to get a good seat. The show starts at 10 pm Memorial Day weekend through July, 9:30 pm in August, and 8:30 pm in September.

18

GETTING HERE AND AROUND

From Ephrata, take Highway 17 north to reach Grand Coulee. From the Spokane area, U.S. 2 to Highway 174 is the most direct route.

ESSENTIALS

Visitor Information Grand Coulee Dam Area Chamber of Commerce. ⊠ *17 Midway Ave., Grand Coulee* ☎ *509/633–3074* ⊕ *www.grandcouleedam.org.*

EXPLORING

Colville Indian Reservation. Highway 155 passes through the Colville Indian Reservation, one of the largest reservations in Washington, with about 7,700 enrolled members of the Colville Confederated Tribes. This was the final home for Chief Joseph and the Nez Perce, who fought a series of fierce battles with the U.S. Army in the 1870s after the U.S. government enforced a treaty that many present-day historians agree was fraudulent. Chief Joseph lived on the Colville reservation until his death in 1904. There's a memorial to him off Highway 155 east of the town of Nespelem, 17 miles north of the dam; four blocks away (two east and two north) is his grave. You can drive through the reservation's undeveloped landscape, and except for a few highway signs you'll feel like you've time-traveled to pioneer days. The **Colville Tribal Museum** (*512 Mead Way, Coulee Dam, 509/633–0751, open daily 8:30–5*) is worth a visit. ⊠ *Coulee Dam* ⊕ *www.colvilletribes.com.*

FAMILY **Grand Coulee Dam Visitor Center.** Colorful displays about the dam, a 13-minute film on the site's geology and the dam's construction, and information about the 30-minute laser-light show (held nightly from Memorial Day weekend through September) are here. The U.S. Bureau of Reclamation, which oversees operation and maintenance of the dam, conducts tours April through October, weather and maintenance schedules permitting. You can also pick up a self-guided historical walking tour that will take you from the visitor center through the old part of town, across the bridge, and into the old engineers' town. ⊠ *Hwy. 155, Coulee Dam* ✛ *South of Coulee Dam* ☎ *509/633–9265* ⊕ *www.usbr. gov/pn/grandcoulee.*

Lake Roosevelt National Recreation Area. The 150-mile-long lake was created by the Columbia River when it was backed up by Grand Coulee Dam. Several Native American villages, historic sites, and towns lie beneath the waters. ⊠ *Headquarters, 1008 Crest Dr., Coulee Dam* ☎ *509/754–7800* ⊕ *www.nps.gov/laro* ⊠ *Free; camping $18 May– Sept., $9 Oct.–Apr.*

Steamboat Rock State Park. Here, a 2,200-foot-high flat-topped lava butte rises 1,000 feet above Banks Lake, the 31-mile-long irrigation reservoir filled with water from Lake Roosevelt by giant pumps and siphons. Water is distributed from the south end of the lake throughout the Columbia Basin. The state park has campsites, three cabins, a swimming area, and boat ramps. In summer it's popular with boaters and anglers, and in winter there's Nordic skiing, snowshoeing, and ice fishing. ⊠ *51052 Hwy. 155, Electric City* ✛ *16 miles north of Coulee City* ☎ *360/633–1304, 888/226–7688* ⊕ *parks.state.wa.us/590/Steamboat-Rock* ⊠ *Day pass $10 per vehicle; annual Discovery Pass $30 (valid at all state parks); campsites $25–$45, cabins $$69–79.*

Fodor's Choice ★ **Sun Lakes-Dry Falls State Park.** A high point in the coulee, this park has campgrounds, picnic areas, boat rentals, and a state-run golf course that attracts visitors year-round; in summer the lakes bristle with boaters. From the bluffs on U.S. 2, west of the dam, you can get a great view over this enormous canyon. To the north, the banks of the lake are hemmed in by cliffs. At Dry Falls, the upstream erosion of the canyon caused by the floods stops. Below Dry Falls, steep, barren cliffs—some 1,000 feet high—rise from green meadows, marshes, and blue lakes bordered by trees. Most of the water is irrigation water seeping through the porous rock, but the effect is no less spectacular. Eagles and ravens soar along the cliffs, while songbirds, ducks, and geese hang out in the bottomlands.

South of the Sun Lakes, the landscape turns even wilder. The coulee narrows and the cliffs often look like they are on fire, an illusion created by the bold patterns of orange and yellow lichens. The waters of the lakes change, too. The deep blue waters of the small lakes below

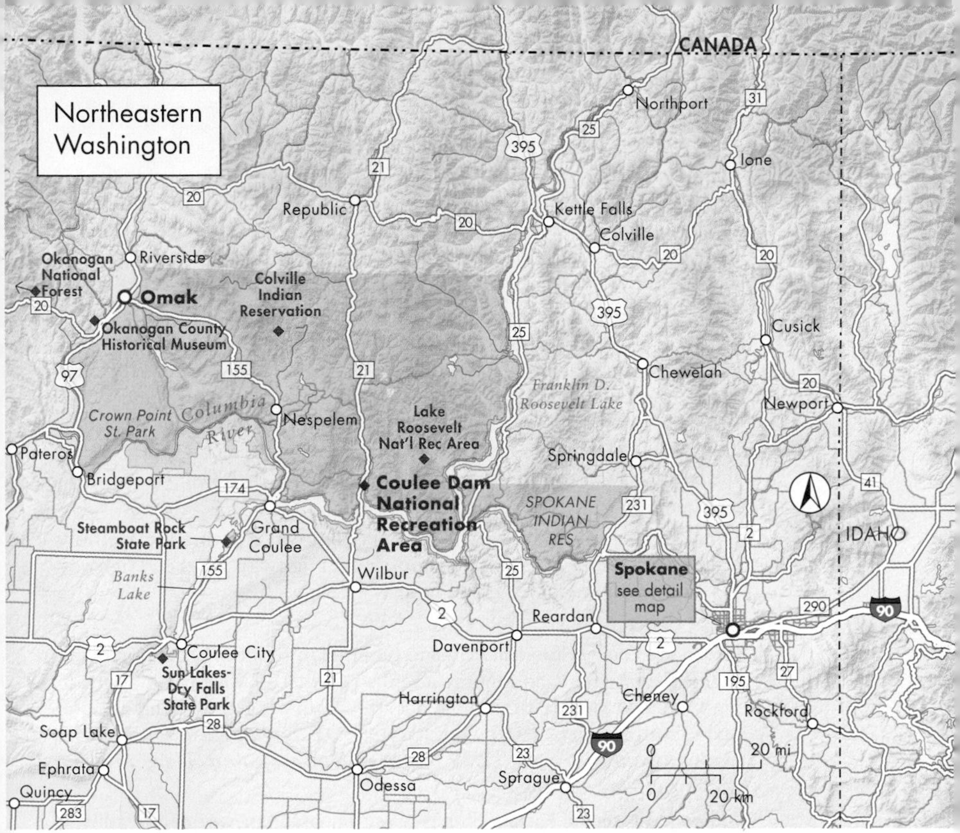

Dry Falls are replaced by lapis lazuli in the Sun Lakes and turn milky farther south. Presentations at the park's interpretive center at Dry Falls survey the area's geology, and an excellent film describes the great floods. ✉ *34875 Park Lake Rd. NE, Coulee City* ☎ *360/902–8844, 888/226–7688* 🌐 *parks.state.wa.us/298/Sun-Lakes-Dry-Falls* 🎟 *Day pass $10 per vehicle; annual Discovery Pass $30 (valid at all state parks); camping $25–$45.*

WHERE TO EAT AND STAY

$ DINER 🍴 **Flo's Cafe.** One mile south of the dam, this diner dishes up heaps of local color along with loggers' food: biscuits and gravy, corned-beef hash, hamburgers, chicken-fried steak, and chef's salads. Flo's is open for breakfast but closes at 1, so look elsewhere if you want a late lunch. **Known for:** local gathering spot; hearty meals. [$] *Average main: $9* ✉ *316 Spokane Way, Grand Coulee* ☎ *509/633–3216* ⏲ *No dinner.*

$ HOTEL 🏨 **Columbia River Inn.** The well-appointed rooms all have private decks at this inn across the street from Grand Coulee Dam, with easy access to hiking trails and fishing. **Pros:** rooms have microwaves and refrigerators; pretty location; reliable Wi-Fi. **Cons:** basic rooms on the small side; some visitors have complained about a/c noise. [$] *Rooms from: $118* ✉ *10 Lincoln St., Coulee Dam* ☎ *509/633–2100, 800/633–6421* 🌐 *www.columbiariverinn.com* 🛏 *35 rooms* 🍽 *No meals.*

OMAK

52 miles northwest of Grand Coulee Dam.

Omak is a small mill and orchard town in the beautifully rustic Okanogan Valley of north-central Washington. Lake Omak to the southeast, on the Colville Reservation, is part of an ancient channel of the Columbia River, which ran north prior to the last ice age before turning south at Omak in what is now the lower Okanogan Valley.

For years Omak has been criticized by animal lovers for its mid-August Omak Stampede and Suicide Race. During the annual event, which started as a rodeo in 1933, wild horses race down a steep bluff and across the Okanogan River. Some horses have been killed and riders seriously injured. Many of the riders are from the Colville Reservation, and elders defend the race as part of Native American culture. Despite the detractors, more spectators attend the event each year.

GETTING HERE AND AROUND

Omak can be reached from the west via Highway 20 from the Methow Valley area. From Ephrata, head north via Highway 17, then Highway 97. From Grand Coulee Dam, take WA 155N.

EXPLORING

FAMILY **Okanogan County Historical Museum.** Okanogan pioneer life is portrayed in the displays here, and there's a replica of an Old West town. Outside are Okanogan's oldest building, a 19th-century log cabin, and antique farm equipment. ✉ *1410 2nd Ave. N, Okanogan* ☎ *509/422–4272* 🌐 *okanoganhistory.org* 🎫 *$2* 🕒 *Closed after Labor Day; reopens Memorial Day weekend.*

Okanogan National Forest. This is a region of open woods, meadows, and pastoral river valleys in the Okanogan highlands. There's lots of wildlife: deer, black bears, coyotes, badgers, bobcats, cougars, grouse, hawks, and golden eagles. Campgrounds are scattered throughout the region. There are 11 Sno-Parks with groomed trails for snowmobilers, and open areas for cross-country skiing. Ski areas are at Loup Loup Pass (Nordic and alpine) and Sitzmark (alpine only). ✉ *Forest Headquarters, 215 Melody La., Wenatchee* ☎ *509/664–9200* 🌐 *www.fs.usda.gov/okawen* 🎫 *Free; permits required at Sno-Parks.*

WHERE TO EAT AND STAY

$$ ECLECTIC Fodor's Choice ★ 🍴 **Breadline Cafe.** For more than 35 years, Breadline has been a top dining destination in the Okanogan Valley for hearty servings of eclectic items. The menu features local organic produce, locally raised natural Angus beef, crepes, seafood, and a variety of breads. **Known for:** kitschy antique decor; Saturday buffet brunch; bread bar and bakery treats; varied menu of international cuisines. [$] *Average main: $18* ✉ *102 S. Ash St.* ☎ *509/826–5836* 🌐 *www.breadlinecafe.com* 🕒 *Closed Sun. and Mon. No breakfast Tues.–Fri.*

$ HOTEL 🏨 **Omak Inn.** At this motel just off U.S. 97, all rooms are "mini-suites," with a separate sitting area, and there's a small patio and an expansive lawn for relaxing in the summer. **Pros:** most rooms have microwaves and refrigerators; close to restaurants. **Cons:** room style is basic; no elevator. [$] *Rooms from: $80* ✉ *912 Koala Dr.* ☎ *509/826–3822, 800/204–4800* 🛏 *64 rooms* 🍽 *Breakfast.*

VANCOUVER AND VICTORIA

WELCOME TO VANCOUVER AND VICTORIA

TOP REASONS TO GO

★ **Stanley Park:** The views, the activities, and the natural wilderness beauty here are quintessential Vancouver.

★ **Granville Island:** Ride the miniferry across False Creek to the Granville Island Public Market, where you can shop for delicious lunch fixings; eat outside when the weather's fine.

★ **Museum of Anthropology at the University of British Columbia:** The phenomenal collection of First Nations art and cultural artifacts, and the incredible backdrop, make this a must-see.

★ **The Journey here:** Yes, getting here is one of the best things about Victoria: whether by ferry meandering past the Gulf or San Juan Islands, by floatplane (try to travel at least one leg this way), or on a whale-watching boat, getting to Victoria from the mainland is memorable.

★ **Butchart Gardens:** Nearly a million and a half visitors can't be wrong—these lavish gardens north of town live up to the hype.

1 **Vancouver.** Many people say that Vancouver is the most gorgeous city in North America, and situated as it is, between mountains and water, it's hard to disagree. The Vancouver area actually covers a lot of ground, but the central core—Downtown, Gastown, Yaletown, Chinatown, Stanley Park, and Granville Island—is fairly compact. An excellent public transportation system makes getting around a snap. When in doubt, remember that the mountains are north.

2 **Victoria.** British Columbia's capital city, Victoria, is a lovely, walkable city with waterfront paths, lovely gardens, fascinating museums, and splendid 19th-century architecture. In some senses remote, it's roughly midway between Vancouver and Seattle and about three hours by car and ferry from either city.

Powell River

East Cove

101

Strait of Georgia

Parksville

Nan

VANCOUVER ISLAND

Lake Cowichan

0   15 miles
0   15 kilometers

Pacific Rim National Park

Port Renfrew

14

Juan de Fuca Strait

112

British
Columbia

GETTING ORIENTED

Most of Vancouver is on a peninsula, which makes it compact and easy to explore on foot. To get your bearings, use the mountains as your "true north" and you can't go too far wrong.

Victoria, at the southern tip of Vancouver Island, is farther south than most of Canada, giving it the mildest climate in the country, with virtually no snow and less than half the rain of Vancouver.

The names can get confusing so here's what to remember: the city of Victoria is on Vancouver Island (not Victoria Island). The city of Vancouver is on the British Columbia mainland, not on Vancouver Island, or on Victoria Island (which isn't in British Columbia but rather way up north, spanning parts of Nunavut and the Northwest Territories).

19

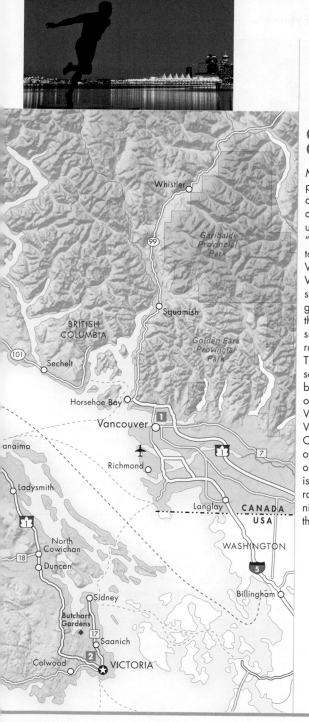

Updated by
Chloë Ernst,
Jennifer Foden,
Sue Ker-
naghan, Chris
McBeath,
Lesley Mirza,
and Christina
Newberry

Set on Canada's West Coast, Vancouver and Victoria blend urban sophistication and multicultural vitality with spectacular settings near mountains, ocean, and rain forest.

Both cities are famously livable: Vancouver gleams with towering sky-scrapers; the smaller Victoria charms with its historic waterfront. To see the appeal, stroll and bike in Vancouver's Stanley Park, eat fresh seafood, sip cocktails, browse boutiques, and visit renowned museums and gardens. Sure, it rains out here, but take a cue from the laid-back locals in their chic, all-weather clothes. Vancouver is a delicious jux-taposition of urban sophistication and on-your-doorstep wilderness adventure. The mountains and seascape make the city an outdoor play-ground for hiking, skiing, kayaking, cycling, and sailing—and so much more—while the cuisine and arts scenes are equally diverse, reflect-ing the makeup of Vancouver's ethnic (predominantly Asian) mosaic. Victoria, British Columbia's photogenic capital, is a walkable, livable seaside city of fragrant gardens, waterfront paths, engaging museums, and beautifully restored 19th-century architecture. In summer, the Inner Harbour—Victoria's social and cultural center—buzzes with visiting yachts, horse-and-carriage rides, street entertainers, and excursion boats heading out to visit pods of friendly local whales.

VANCOUVER

More than 8 million visitors each year come to Vancouver, Canada's third-largest metropolitan area. Because of its peninsula location, traf-fic flow is a contentious issue. Vancouver is wonderfully walkable, especially in the Downtown core. The mild climate, exquisite natural scenery, and relaxed outdoor lifestyle keep attracting residents, and the number of visitors is increasing for the same reasons. People often get their first glimpse of Vancouver when catching an Alaskan cruise, and many return at some point to spend more time here.

PLANNING

MAKING THE MOST OF YOUR TIME

If you don't have much time in Vancouver, you'll probably still want to spend at least a half day in Stanley Park. A couple of hours at the Granville Island Public Market are also a must—plan to have breakfast or lunch, and, if you have time, check out the crafts stores. Walking the Downtown core is a great way to get to know the city. Start at Canada Place and head east to Gastown and Chinatown; that's a good half day. Then head north to Yaletown, perhaps for a glass of wine and dinner. If you're traveling with children, make sure to check out Science World, Grouse Mountain, and the Capilano Suspension Bridge or Lynn Canyon. For museums, adults and older children love the displays of Northwest Coast First Nations art at the Museum of Anthropology. The Bill Reid Gallery also has an impressive collection of aboriginal art.

GETTING HERE AND AROUND

Central Vancouver is extremely walkable, and the public transit system—a mix of bus, ferry, and SkyTrain (a fully automated rail system)—is efficient and easy to use. The hop-on, hop-off Vancouver Trolley buses circle the city in a continuous loop and are a great way to see the sites—especially on a rainy day; the same company runs the seasonal Stanley Park Shuttle.

Contacts Vancouver Trolley Company. ☎ *604/801–5515* ⊕ *www.vancouver-trolley.com.*

BUS AND RAPID-TRANSIT TRAVEL

TransLink, Metro Vancouver's public transport system, includes bus service, a rapid transit system called SkyTrain, and a 400-passenger commuter ferry (SeaBus) that connects Downtown to the North Shore.

TransLink offers an electronic Compass Card system for single-fare tickets or stored-value cards, to be purchased at station vending machines before boarding. You "tap in" your ticket or card to the electronic reader when you board the SkyTrain or SeaBus; you "tap out" when you exit, which subtracts the fare from your card (you only have to "tap in" on buses). Cash fares (exact change required) can only be used for bus travel (single-fare tickets and stored-value cards are good for bus travel as well); SkyTrain and SeaBus fares must be purchased from machines (correct change isn't necessary). All fares are valid for 90 minutes and allow travel in any direction on the buses, SkyTrain, or SeaBus. Your Compass Card or single fare ticket must be carried with you as proof of payment. SkyTrain and SeaBus fares are based on zones (bus travel is considered one zone) and whether you have a stored-value Compass Card or single fare ticket: one zone (C$2.75 single fare, C$2.10 stored-value), two zones (C$4 single fare, C$3.15 stored-value), or three zones (C$5.50 single fare, C$4.20 stored-value). Fares go down in zones two and three in off-peak hours. Travel within the Vancouver city limits is a one-zone trip; traveling between Vancouver and the North Shore or from Vancouver to Richmond is two zones. You can also buy a day pass (on a Compass Card or single fare ticket) if you're planning to use the system frequently in one day (C$11 single/cash fare, C$9.75 stored-value, good all day across all zones).

19

A stored-value Compass Card does have its price: a C$6 refundable deposit. However, at a savings of 65 cents per ride in zone one (versus the single fare ticket), it'll pay off in just 10 rides. You can also get your deposit back if you return your card to the Customer Service Centre at Stadium-Chinatown Station. Also, note: all SkyTrain rides leaving YVR airport add a C$5 fee to your fare. If you're traveling to the airport, the same fee does not apply.

■**TIP→** SkyTrain is convenient for transit between Downtown, BC Place Stadium, Pacific Central Station, Science World, and Vancouver International Airport. SeaBus is the fastest way to travel between Downtown and the North Shore (there are bus connections to Capilano Suspension Bridge and Grouse Mountain). There is also a free shuttle from Canada Place to Capilano Suspension Bridge and Grouse Mountain in the summer.

Contacts TransLink. ☎ *604/953–3333* ⊕ *www.translink.ca.*

FERRY TRAVEL
Twelve- and 20-passenger Aquabus Ferries and False Creek Ferries bypass busy bridges and are a key reason why you don't need a car in Vancouver. Both of these are private commercial enterprises—not part of the TransLink system—that provide passenger services between key locales on either side of False Creek. Single-ride tickets range from C$3.25 to C$5.50 depending on the route; day passes are C$15. Aquabus Ferries connections include The Village (Science World and the Olympic Village), Plaza of Nations, Yaletown, Spyglass Place, Stamp's Landing, David Lam Park, Granville Island, and the Hornby Street dock. False Creek Ferries provides service between all of these stops (with the exception of the Hornby Street dock), and instead stops at the Aquatic Centre on Beach Avenue and the Maritime Museum in Kitsilano. The large SeaBus ferries (via TransLink, *see above*) travel between Waterfront Station and Lonsdale Quay in North Vancouver.

EXPLORING VANCOUVER

The city's Downtown core includes the main business district between Robson Street and the Burrard Inlet harbor front; the West End that edges up against English Bay; Stanley Park; trendy Yaletown; and Gastown and Chinatown, which are the oldest parts of the city. Main Street, which runs north–south, is roughly the dividing line between the east and west sides. The entire Downtown district sits on a peninsula bordered by English Bay and the Pacific Ocean to the west; by False Creek to the south; and by Burrard Inlet, the city's working port, to the north, where the North Shore Mountains loom.

DOWNTOWN AND THE WEST END
Vancouver's compact Downtown juxtaposes historic architecture with gleaming brand-new buildings. There are museums and galleries to visit, as well as top-notch shopping, most notably along Robson Street, which runs into the city's West End. The harbor front, with the green-roofed convention center, has a fabulous water's edge path all the way to Stanley Park—walk along here to get a feel for what Vancouver is all about.

DOWNTOWN

Fodor's Choice
★

Bill Reid Gallery. Named after one of British Columbia's preeminent artists, Bill Reid (1920–98), this small aboriginal gallery is as much a legacy of Reid's works as it is a showcase of current First Nations artists. Displays include wood carvings, jewelry, print, and sculpture, and programs often feature artist talks and themed exhibitions such as basket weaving. Reid is best known for his bronze statue *The Spirit of Haida Gwaii, The Jade Canoe*—measuring 12 feet by 20 feet; it is displayed at the Vancouver International Airport, and its image was on the back of Canadian $20 bills issued between 2004 and 2012. More Bill Reid pieces are at the Museum of Anthropology. ⊠ *639 Hornby St., Downtown* ☎ *604/682–3455* ⊕ *www.billreidgallery.ca* ✉ *C$10* ⊗ *Closed Mon. and Tues., Oct.–May.*

Olympic Cauldron. A four-pronged sculpture towering more than 30 feet, the Olympic Cauldron is next to the Vancouver Convention Centre's West Building. In 2010, when Vancouver hosted the Winter Olympic and Paralympic Games, it burned with the Olympic flame and it's relit occasionally, for Canada Day and other special events. The Cauldron overlooks the Burrard Inlet on Jack Poole Plaza, which is named for the Canadian businessman who led the bid to bring the Olympics to Vancouver. Sadly, Poole died of cancer just one day after the flame for the Olympic torch relay was lit in Olympia, Greece, at the start of its journey to Vancouver. ⊠ *Foot of Thurlow St., at Canada Pl., Downtown.*

Robson Street. Running from the Terry Fox Plaza outside BC Place Stadium down to the West End, Robson is Vancouver's busiest shopping street, where fashionistas hang out at see-and-be-seen sidewalk cafés, high-end boutiques, and chain stores. Most of the designer action takes place between Jervis and Burrard streets and that's also where you can find buskers and other entertainers in the evenings. ⊠ *Downtown* ⊕ *www.robsonstreet.ca.*

19

Vancouver Art Gallery. Canadian painter Emily Carr's haunting evocations of the British Columbian hinterland are among the attractions at western Canada's largest art gallery. Carr (1871–1945), a grocer's daughter from Victoria, BC, fell in love with the wilderness around her and shocked middle-class Victorian society by running off to paint it. Her work accentuates the mysticism and danger of BC's wilderness, and records the diminishing presence of native cultures during that era (there's something of a renaissance now). The gallery, which also hosts touring historical and contemporary exhibitions, is housed in a 1911 courthouse that Canadian architect Arthur Erickson redesigned in the early 1980s as part of the Robson Square redevelopment. Stone lions guard the steps to the park-like Georgia Street side (often the site of festivals and other events); the main entrance is accessed from Robson Square or Hornby Street. ⊠ *750 Hornby St., Downtown* ☎ *604/662–4719* ⊕ *www.vanartgallery.bc.ca* ✉ *C$24; higher for some exhibits; by donation Tues. 5–9.*

WEST END

Robson Street, Vancouver's prime shopping boulevard, runs from Downtown into the West End, a partly residential and partly commercial district. The West End has Vancouver's prettiest streetscapes and harks back to the early 1930s when it housed the affluent middle class:

trees are plentiful, gardens are lushly planted, and homes and apartment buildings exude the character of that era. There are lots of restaurants and cafés along the main arteries: Robson, Denman, and Davie streets.

STANLEY PARK

Fodor's Choice ★ A 1,000-acre wilderness park, only blocks from the Downtown section of a major city, is a rare treasure and Vancouverites make use of it to bike, walk, jog, in-line skate, and go to the beach.

Prospect Point. At 211 feet, Prospect Point is the highest point in the park and provides striking views of the Lions Gate Bridge (watch for cruise ships passing below), the North Shore, and Burrard Inlet. There's also a year-round souvenir shop, a snack bar with terrific ice cream, and a restaurant. From the seawall, you can see where cormorants build their seaweed nests along the cliff ledges. ⊠ *Stanley Park.*

Fodor's Choice ★ **Stanley Park Seawall.** Vancouver's seawall path includes a 9-km (5½-mile) paved shoreline section within Stanley Park. It's one of several car-free zones in the park and it's popular with walkers and cyclists. If you have the time (about a half day) and the energy, strolling the entire seawall is an exhilarating experience. It extends an additional mile east past the marinas, cafés, and waterfront condominiums of Coal Harbour to Canada Place in downtown, so you could start your walk or ride from there. From the south side of the park, the seawall continues for another 28 km (17 miles) along Vancouver's waterfront to the University of British Columbia, allowing for a pleasant, if ambitious, day's bike ride. Along the seawall, cyclists must wear helmets and stay on their side of the path. Within Stanley Park, cyclists must ride in a counterclockwise direction. The seawall can get crowded on summer weekends, but inside the park is a 28-km (17-mile) network of peaceful walking and cycling paths through old- and second-growth forest. The wheelchair-accessible Beaver Lake Interpretive Trail is a good choice if you're interested in park ecology. Take a map—they're available at the park-information booth and many of the concession stands—and don't go into the woods alone or after dusk. ⊠ *Stanley Park.*

Totem poles. Totem poles are an important art form among native peoples along British Columbia's coast. These nine poles—eight carved in the latter half of the 20th century, and one created in 2009—include replicas of poles originally brought to the park from the north coast in the 1920s, as well as poles carved specifically for the park by First Nations artists. The several styles of poles represent a cross section of BC native groups, including the Kwakwaka'wakw, Haida, and Nisga'a. The combination of carved animals, fish, birds, and mythological creatures represents clan history. An information center near the site has a snack bar, a gift shop, and information about BC's First Nations. ⊠ *Brockton Point, Stanley Park.*

FAMILY
Fodor's Choice ★ **Vancouver Aquarium.** Massive floor-to-ceiling windows let you get face-to-face with sea otters, sea lions, dolphins, and harbor seals at this award-winning research and educational facility. In the Amazon Gallery you walk through a rain-forest jungle populated with piranhas, caimans, and tropical birds; in summer, hundreds of free-flying butterflies add to the mix. The Tropic Zone is home to exotic freshwater and saltwater life, including clown fish, moray eels, and black-tip reef sharks. Other displays,

many with hands-on features for kids, show the underwater life of coastal British Columbia and the Canadian Arctic. Sea lion and dolphin shows, as well as dive shows (where divers swim with aquatic life, including sharks) are held daily. Be sure to check out the stingray touch pool, as well as the "4-D" film experience (it's a multisensory show that puts mist, smell, and wind into the 3-D equation). For an extra fee, you can help the trainers feed and train otters, belugas, and sea lions. There's also a café and a gift shop. Be prepared for lines on weekends and school holidays. In summer, the quietest time to visit is before 11 am or after 4 pm; in other seasons, the crowds are smaller before noon or after 2 pm. ✉ *845 Avison Way, Stanley Park* ☎ *604/659–3474* ⊕ *www.vanaqua.org* ⌨ *C$36.*

GASTOWN AND CHINATOWN

Historic Gastown and adjacent Chinatown are full of character. They're favorite destinations for visitors and residents alike, and easily explored together. Both neighborhoods are experiencing gentrification as historic buildings get a new lease on life.

GASTOWN

Steam Clock. An underground steam system, which also heats many local buildings, supplies the world's first steam clock—possibly Vancouver's most-photographed attraction. On the quarter hour a steam whistle rings out the Westminster chimes, and on the hour a huge cloud of steam spews from the apparatus. The ingenious design, based on an 1875 mechanism, was built in 1977 by Ray Saunders of Landmark Clocks to commemorate the community effort that saved Gastown from demolition. Fun fact: yes, the clock does use steam power, but three electric motors help it run, too. ✉ *Water St. at Cambie St., Gastown.*

CHINATOWN

Dr. Sun Yat-Sen Chinese Garden. The first authentic Ming Dynasty–style garden outside China, this small garden was built in 1986 by 52 Chinese artisans from Suzhou. No power tools, screws, or nails were used in the construction. It incorporates design elements and traditional materials from several of Suzhou's centuries-old private gardens. Guided tours (45 minutes long), included in the ticket price, are conducted on the hour between mid-June and the end of August (call ahead or check the website for off-season tour times); these are valuable for understanding the philosophy and symbolism that are central to the garden's design. Covered walkways make this a good rainy-day choice. A concert series, including classical, Asian, world, jazz, and sacred music, plays on Thursday evenings in July and August. The free public park next door is a pleasant place to sit, but lacks the context that you get with a tour of the Sun Yat-Sen garden. ✉ *578 Carrall St., Chinatown* ☎ *604/662–3207* ⊕ *www.vancouverchinesegarden.com* ⌨ *C$14* ⊘ *Closed Mon., Nov.–Apr.* Ⓜ *Stadium-Chinatown.*

YALETOWN

Yaletown is one of Vancouver's most fashionable areas and one of the most impressive urban-redevelopment projects in North America. The brick warehouses were turned into apartment buildings and offices, and the old loading docks are now terraces for cappuccino bars and trendy restaurants. There are brewpubs, day spas, retail and wholesale fashion outlets, and shops selling upscale home decor.

19

GRANVILLE ISLAND

Fodor's Choice ★ An indoor food market and a thriving diversity of artist studios as well as performing arts spaces, specialty shops (there's not a chain store or designer label in sight), and a busy marina make Granville Island one of Vancouver's top attractions. Explore at your leisure but try to plan your expedition over a meal, since the market is an excellent place for breakfast, lunch, snacks, and shopping.

The mini Aquabus ferries are a favorite (and the most adorable) way to get to Granville Island (it's about a two-minute ride). They depart from the south end of Hornby Street (about a 15-minute walk from Downtown Vancouver) and take passengers across False Creek to the Granville Island Public Market. The larger False Creek ferries leave every five minutes for Granville Island from a dock behind the Vancouver Aquatic Centre, on Beach Avenue. Still another option is to take a 10-minute ride on a TransLink bus: from Waterfront Station or stops on Granville Street, take Bus 50 to the edge of the island.

FAMILY Fodor's Choice ★ **Granville Island Public Market.** The dozens of stalls in this 50,000-square-foot building sell locally grown fruits and vegetables direct from the farm and farther afield; other stalls stock crafts, chocolates, artisanal cheeses and pastas, fish, meat, flowers, and exotic foods. On Thursday in summer, farmers sell fruit and vegetables from trucks outside. At the north end of the market, you can pick up a snack, lunch, or coffee from one of the many prepared-food vendors. The Market Courtyard, on the waterside, has great views of the city and is also a good place to catch street entertainers—be prepared to get roped into the action, if only to check the padlocks of an escape artist's gear. Weekends can get madly busy. ⊠ *1689 Johnston St., Granville Island* ☎ *604/666–6655* ⊕ *www.granvilleisland.com.*

THE WEST SIDE

The West Side, the set of diverse neighborhoods just south of Downtown, has some of Vancouver's best gardens and natural sights as well as some chic shopping. "Kits," as the locals refer to Kitsilano, though, is really where all the action is: the once-hippie neighborhood has evolved into an upscale district of shops, restaurants, museums, and one of the city's best people-watching beaches.

KITSILANO

FAMILY **H.R. MacMillan Space Centre.** The interactive exhibits and high-tech learning systems at this museum include a Virtual Voyages ride, where visitors can take a simulated space journey (definitely not for those afraid of flying); GroundStation Canada, showcasing Canada's achievements in space; and the Cosmic Courtyard, full of hands-on space-oriented exhibits including a moon rock and a computer program that shows what you would look like as an alien. You can catch daytime astronomy shows or evening music-and-laser shows at the **H.R. MacMillan Planetarium.** ⊠ *Vanier Park, 1100 Chestnut St., Kitsilano* ☎ *604/738–7827* ⊕ *www.spacecentre.ca* ☑ *C$18.*

Museum of Vancouver. Vancouver's short-but-funky history comes to life at this seaside museum. The 1930s gallery remembers some poignant episodes involving the Japanese internment during WWII, as well as local stories of the war effort. The 1950s Gallery has a 1955

Ford Fairlane Victoria and a Seeburg select-o-matic jukebox. The 1960s-theme Revolution Gallery revisits the city's days as the hippie capital of Canada: visitors can hear local bands from the '60s and poke around a re-created communal house. The museum regularly mounts intriguing temporary exhibits and hosts lectures and other public events. ⊠ *Vanier Park, 1100 Chestnut St., Kitsilano* ☎ *604/736–4431* ⊕ *www.museumofvancouver.com* ☒ *C$15.*

POINT GREY

Fodor's Choice
★
Museum of Anthropology. Part of the University of British Columbia, the MOA has one of the world's leading collections of Northwest Coast First Nations art. The Great Hall has dramatic cedar poles, bentwood boxes, and canoes adorned with traditional Northwest Coast–painted designs. On clear days, the gallery's 50-foot-tall windows reveal a striking backdrop of mountains and sea. Another highlight is the work of the late Bill Reid, one of Canada's most respected Haida artists. In *The Raven and the First Men* (1980), carved in yellow cedar, he tells a Haida story of creation. Reid's gold-and-silver jewelry work is also on display, as are exquisite carvings of gold, silver, and argillite (a black shale found on Haida Gwaii, also known as the Queen Charlotte Islands) by other First Nations artists. The museum's visible storage section displays, in drawers and cases, contain thousands of examples of tools, textiles, masks, and other artifacts from around the world. The Koerner Ceramics Gallery contains 600 pieces from 15th- to 19th-century Europe. Behind the museum are two Haida houses, set on the cliff over the water. Free guided tours—given several times daily (call or check the website for times)—are immensely informative. For an extra C$5 you can rent a VUEguide—an electronic device that senses where you are in the museum and shows relevant artist interviews, archival footage, and photographs of the artifacts in their original contexts, on a handheld screen. The MOA also has an excellent book and fine-art shop, as well as a café. To reach the museum by transit, take any UBC-bound bus from Granville Street downtown to the university bus loop, a 15-minute walk (or 10-minute ride on shuttle bus, C$18 or C$20) from the museum. Pay parking is available in the Rose Garden parking lot, across Marine Drive from the museum. A UBC Museums and Gardens Pass will save you money if you're planning to visit several attractions at UBC. ⊠ *University of British Columbia, 6393 N.W. Marine Dr., Point Grey* ☎ *604/822–5087* ⊕ *www.moa.ubc.ca* ☒ *C$18; Tues. 5–9 C$10* ☉ *Closed Mon. mid-Oct.–mid-May.*

19

FAMILY **University of British Columbia Botanical Garden.** Ten thousand trees, shrubs, and rare plants from around the world thrive on this 70-acre research site on the university campus, which edges on Pacific Spirit Park. The complex feels as far away from the city as you can get, with forested walkways through an Asian garden, a garden of medicinal plants, and an alpine garden with some of the world's rarest plants. A Walk in the Woods is a 20-minute loop that takes you through more than 1,000 species of coastal plant life. The garden gift store is one of the best of its kind. One-hour guided tours, free with garden admission, are offered on certain days; call or check the website for schedule. A UBC Museums and Gardens Pass will save you money if you're planning

The exhibits outside the museum, on the cliffs overlooking the water, are part of the attraction of the Museum of Anthropology.

to visit several attractions at UBC. ⊠ *6804 S.W. Marine Dr., Point Grey* ☎ *604/822–4208* ⊕ *www.botanicalgarden.ubc.ca* ✉ *C$9; C$13 includes admission to Nitobe Memorial Garden; C$20 includes Greenheart Canopy Walkway; C$24 includes Nitobe Memorial Garden and Greenheart Canopy Walkway* ☉ *Closed Nov.–Mar.*

CAMBIE CORRIDOR

FAMILY **Queen Elizabeth Park.** Lavish sunken gardens (in a former stone quarry), a rose garden, and an abundance of grassy picnicking spots are just a few of the highlights at this 52-hectare (130-acre) park. Poised at the highest point in the city, there are 360-degree views of Downtown. Other park facilities include 18 tennis courts, pitch and putt (an 18-hole putting green), and a restaurant. On summer evenings there's free outdoor dancing on the Plaza—everything from Scottish country dance to salsa, for all ages and levels. In the **Bloedel Conservatory** you can see tropical and desert plants and 100 species of free-flying tropical birds in a glass geodesic dome—the perfect place to be on a rainy day. To reach the park by public transportation, take the Canada Line to King Edward station; from there, it's a six-block walk to the edge of the park (and a hike up the hill to appreciate the views). Cambie Bus 15, which runs south along Cambie Street from the Olympic Village SkyTrain station, will drop you a little closer, at the corner of 33rd and Cambie. Park activities make for a great family excursion, and unlike Stanley Park with its acres of rain forest, Queen Elizabeth Park is all about the flowers. ⊠ *Cambie St. at 33rd Ave., Cambie* ☎ *604/873–7000* ⊕ *www. vancouver.ca/parks* ✉ *Conservatory C$6.75.*

FAMILY **VanDusen Botanical Garden.** An Elizabethan maze, a formal rose garden, a meditation garden, and a collection of Canadian heritage plants are among the many displays at this 55-acre site. The garden is also home to five lakes, a garden shop, a library, and the Truffles Fine Foods Café (serving breakfast, lunch, and afternoon tea). Special events throughout the year include a spectacular Christmas-theme Festival of Lights every December. From Downtown, catch the Oak Bus 17 directly to the garden entrance; alternatively, ride the Canada Line to Oakridge/41st, then take the UBC Bus 41 to Oak Street, and walk four blocks north to the garden. Queen Elizabeth Park is a 1-km (½-mile) walk away, along West 37th Avenue. Because this was once a golf course, pathways make this garden extremely wheelchair accessible ⌧ *5251 Oak St., at W. 37th Ave., Cambie* ☎ *604/257–8335 garden, 604/267–8335 restaurant* ⊕ *www.vandusengarden.org* ⌧ *C$11.25 Apr.–Sept.; C$8.25 Oct.–Mar.*

THE EAST SIDE

Vancouver's East Side, which spans the area from Ontario Street east to the suburb of Burnaby, was originally a working-class district. These days, as real estate prices across the city have continued to climb, many artists, young families, and professional people have moved east, and this half of the metropolitan area now mixes multicultural residential communities, art galleries, theaters, and an eclectic assortment of restaurants.

MAIN STREET

FAMILY **Science World.** In a gigantic shiny dome on the False Creek waterfront, this hands-on science center encourages children to participate in interactive exhibits and demonstrations about the natural world, the human body, and other science topics. Exhibits change throughout the year, so there's always something new to see; there's an Omnimax theater, too. Adjacent to the museum, the Ken Spencer Science Park is an outdoor exhibit area focusing on environmental issues. Science World is an easy walk (or miniferry ride) from Yaletown; the Main Street-Science World SkyTrain station is on its doorstep, and there's plenty of parking. ⌧ *1455 Quebec St., Mt. Pleasant* ☎ *604/443–7440* ⊕ *www.scienceworld.ca* ⌧ *C$25.75 Science World, C$31.75 Science World and Omnimax theater* ⊙ *Closed Mon., Sept.–June.*

19

NORTH SHORE

The North Shore and its star attractions—the Capilano Suspension Bridge, Grouse Mountain, Lonsdale Quay, and, farther east, the lovely hamlet of Deep Cove—are just a short trip from Downtown Vancouver. The North Shore is where people come to kayak up fjords, and hike, ski, and explore the forest and mountainous terrain. The two main communities on the North Shore are North Vancouver and West Vancouver.

NORTH VANCOUVER

FAMILY
Fodor's Choice
★

Capilano Suspension Bridge. At Vancouver's oldest tourist attraction (the original bridge was built in 1889), you can get a taste of rain-forest scenery and test your mettle on the swaying, 450-foot cedar-plank suspension bridge that hangs 230 feet above the rushing Capilano River. Across the bridge is the Treetops Adventure, where you can walk along 650 feet of cable bridges suspended among the trees. If you're even braver, you can follow the **Cliffwalk,** a series of narrow cantilevered bridges and walkways hanging out over the edge of the canyon. Without crossing the bridge, you can enjoy the site's viewing decks, nature trails, totem park, and carving center (where you can watch First Nations carvers at work), as well as history and forestry exhibits. There's also a massive gift shop in the original 1911 teahouse, and a restaurant. May through October, guides in 19th-century costumes conduct free tours on themes related to history, nature, or ecology, while fiddle bands, First Nations dancers, and other entertainers keep things lively. In December, more than 250,000 lights illuminate the canyon during the Canyon Lights winter celebration. Catch the attraction's free shuttle service from Canada Place; it also stops along Burrard and Robson streets. ✉ *3735 Capilano Rd., North Vancouver* ☎ *604/985–7474* ⊕ *www.capbridge.com* ✆ *C$39.95.*

FAMILY
Fodor'sChoice
★

Grouse Mountain. North America's largest aerial tramway, the **Skyride** is a great way to take in the city, sea, and mountain vistas (be sure to pick a clear day or evening). The Skyride makes the 2-km (1-mile) climb to the peak of Grouse Mountain every 15 minutes. Once at the top you can watch a half-hour video presentation at the Theatre in the Sky (it's included with your Skyride ticket). Other mountaintop activities include, in summer, lumberjack shows, chairlift rides, walking tours, hiking, falconry demonstrations, and a chance to visit the grizzly bears in the mountain's wildlife refuge. For an extra fee you can also try zip-lining and tandem paragliding, tour the wind turbine that tops the mountain, or take a helicopter flight. In winter you can ski, snowshoe, snowboard, ice-skate on a mountaintop pond, or take Sno-Cat-drawn sleigh rides. A stone-and-cedar lodge is home to snack shops, a pub-style bistro, and a high-end restaurant, all with expansive city views. The Grouse Grind— a hiking trail up the face of the mountain—is one of the best workouts on the North Shore. Depending on your fitness level, allow between 40 minutes and two hours to complete it (90 minutes is an average time). Then you can take the Skyride down. The BCMC Trail is a less crowded, slightly longer alternative. From late May through September, you can catch a free shuttle to Grouse Mountain from Canada Place. ✉ *6400 Nancy Greene Way, North Vancouver* ☎ *604/980–9311* ⊕ *www.grouse-mountain.com* ✆ *Skyride and many activities C$43.95.*

OFF THE
BEATEN
PATH

Lynn Canyon Park. With a steep canyon landscape, a temperate rain forest complete with waterfalls, and a suspension bridge (circa 1912) 166½ feet above raging Lynn Creek, this 616-acre park provides thrills to go with its scenic views. There are many hiking trails, including a popular one that ends at a waterfall where you can swim. Lynn Canyon Park's on-site Ecology Centre distributes maps of area hiking trails, waterfalls, and pools as well as information about the local flora and fauna. There's also a gift shop and a café here. To get to the park, take the Lions Gate Bridge and Capilano Road, go east on Highway 1, take the Lynn Valley Road exit, and turn right on Peters Road. From Downtown Vancouver, you can take the SeaBus to Lonsdale Quay, then Bus 228 or 229 from the quay; both stop near the park. ■ TIP➜ **The suspension bridge here is shorter than the Capilano Suspension Bridge (130 feet versus 450 feet at Capilano) so the experience is less thrilling, but also less touristy.** ✉ *3663 Park Rd., at end of Peters Rd., North Vancouver* ☎ *604/990–3755 Ecology Centre, 604/984–9311 café* ⊕ *www.dnv.org/ecology* ✆ *Ecology Centre by donation, suspension bridge free.*

WHERE TO EAT

From inventive neighborhood bistros to glamorous Downtown dining rooms to ethnic restaurants that rival those in the world capitals, Vancouver has a diverse array of gastronomic options. Many cutting-edge establishments are perfecting what we call Modern Canadian fare, which—at the western end of the country—incorporates regional seafood (notably salmon, halibut, and spot prawns) and locally grown produce. Vancouver is all about "localism," with many restaurants emphasizing the provenance of their ingredients and embracing products that hail from within a 100-mile-or-so radius of the city, or at least from within BC.

With at least 40% of the region's population of Asian heritage, it's no surprise that Asian eateries abound in Vancouver. From mom-and-pop noodle shops, curry houses, and corner sushi bars to elegant and upscale dining rooms, cuisine from China, Taiwan, Hong Kong, Japan, and India (and to a lesser extent, from Korea, Thailand, Vietnam, and Malaysia) can be found all over town.

Listed alphabetically within neighborhoods. Use the coordinate at the end of each listing (✥ B2) to locate a property on the Where to Eat in Vancouver map.

WHAT IT COSTS IN CANADIAN DOLLARS

	$	$$	$$$	$$$$
At Dinner	under C$13	C$13–C$20	C$21–C$30	over C$30

Prices in the restaurant reviews are for an average main course or equivalent combination of smaller dishes at dinner, or if dinner is not served, at lunch.

19

DOWNTOWN AND THE WEST END

DOWNTOWN

$$$ BELGIAN 🍴 **Chambar.** In this hip eatery, classic Belgian dishes are reinvented with flavors from North Africa and beyond. The *moules* (mussels) are justifiably popular, either steamed in white wine or sauced with exotic smoked chilies, cilantro, and coconut cream. **Known for:** moules frites; Belgian beer; specialty meats. [$] *Average main: C$30* ✉ *568 Beatty St., Downtown* ☎ *604/879–7119* 🌐 *www.chambar.com.*

$$ JAPANESE 🍴 **Hapa Izakaya.** Serving small plates designed for sharing, this spirited Japanese tapas bar is known for the mackerel dish, seared table-side with a blowtorch. Also worth trying are the *ebi mayo* (tempura shrimp with spicy mayonnaise), the *ishi-yaki* (a Korean-style stone bowl filled with rice, pork, and vegetables), and anything on the daily fresh sheet. **Known for:** table-seared mackerel; daily fresh sheet; Japanese tapas. [$] *Average main: C$14* ✉ *909 W. Cordova St., Downtown* ☎ *604/420–4272* 🌐 *www.hapaizakaya.com* 🕒 *No lunch weekends.*

$ ECLECTIC 🍴 **Japadog.** There might be other places in the world that sell Japanese-style hot dogs but the phenomenon is so very multiculti Vancouver and this storefront is the sit-down spin-off of a wildly successful food cart with a loyal following. Bratwurst and wieners are topped

STANLEY PARK

Stanley Park

PARK LN.

Stanley Park Dr.

CHILCO ST.

GILFORD ST.

DENMAN ST.

BIDWELL ST.

CARDERO ST.

NICOLA ST.

BROUGHTON ST.

JERVIS ST.

BUTE ST.

THURLOW ST.

W. Georgia St.

Melville St.

Alberni St.

Robson St.

Haro St.

Barclay St.

Nelson St.

Comox St.

Harwood St.

Burnaby St.

Davie St.

Pendrell St.

Beach Ave.

English Bay

WEST END

DOWNTOWN

Nelson Park

Helmcken St.

Davie St.

Drake St.

Pacific St.

Beach Ave.

Sunset Beach Park

McNicol Ave.

Vanier Park

Maple St.

Cypress St.

KITSILANO

Burrard St. Bridge

GRANVILLE ISLAND

Granville St. Bridge

KEY

SkyTrain

Ⓜ — Station
— Expo Line
— Canada Line

🚢 SeaBus

❶ *Exploring Sights*

① *Hotels & Restaurants*

0 _____ 1/4 mi
0 _____ 1/4 km

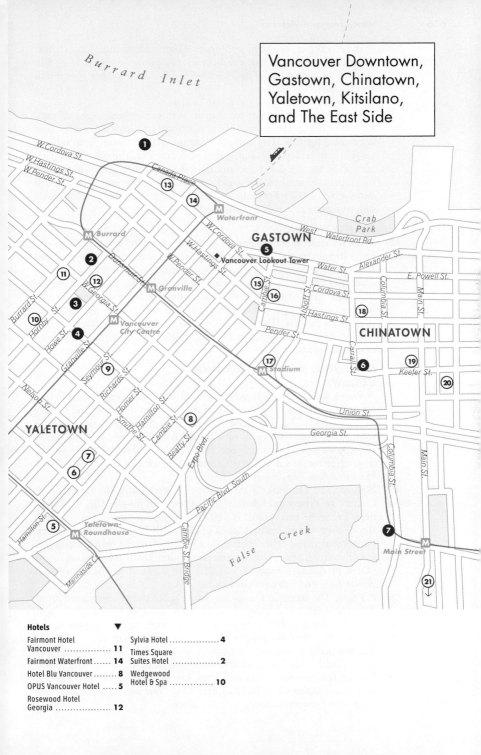

Vancouver Downtown, Gastown, Chinatown, Yaletown, Kitsilano, and The East Side

Burrard Inlet

W. Cordova St.
W. Hastings St.
W. Pender St.
Canada Place

GASTOWN

Waterfront
W. Cordova St.
W. Hastings St.
■ Vancouver Lookout Tower
Water St.
West Waterfront Rd.
Alexander St.
E. Powell St.

Crab Park

Burrard
Dunsmuir St.
W. Pender St.
W. Georgia St.
Granville
Cordova St.
Abbott St.
Hastings St.
Columbia St.
Main St.

CHINATOWN

Burrard St.
Hornby St.
Howe St.
Granville St.
Vancouver City Centre
Pender St.
Carrall St.
Keefer St.

Seymour St.
Richards St.
Homer St.
Hamilton St.
Cambie St.
Stadium
Union St.
Georgia St.
Columbia St.
Main St.

Nelson St.
Smithe St.
Beatty St.
Expo Blvd.

YALETOWN

Hamilton St.
Yaletown-Roundhouse
Pacific Blvd. South
Marinaside Cr.
Cambie St. Bridge
False Creek
Main Street

with teriyaki sauce, nori, and other Asian condiments. **Known for:** Japanese hot dogs; Asian condiments. Ⓢ *Average main: C$6* ✉ *530 Robson St., Downtown* ☎ *604/569–1158* ⊕ *www.japadog.com* ⊟ *No credit cards.*

WEST END

$$
JAPANESE

✕ **Kingyo.** Behind its ornate wooden door, this *izakaya* occupies the stylish end of the spectrum, with a carved wood bar, lots of greenery, and sexy mood lighting. The intriguing Japanese small plates, from salmon carpaccio to grilled miso-marinated pork cheeks to the spicy *tako-wasabi* (octopus), are delicious, and the vibe is bustling and fun. **Known for:** Japanese small plates; shochu and sake; stylish room. Ⓢ *Average main: C$13* ✉ *871 Denman St., West End* ☎ *604/608–1677* ⊕ *www. kingyo-izakaya.ca* ⊟ *No credit cards.*

STANLEY PARK

$$$
CANADIAN

✕ **The Teahouse in Stanley Park.** The former officers' mess at Ferguson Point in Stanley Park is a prime location for water views by day, and for watching sunsets at dusk. The Pacific Northwest menu is not especially innovative but its broad appeal will please those looking for local fish, rack of lamb, steaks, and a host of other options, including gluten-free pasta. **Known for:** tasting boards; lovely patio; Pacific Northwest cuisine. Ⓢ *Average main: C$30* ✉ *7501 Stanley Park Dr., Stanley Park* ✛ *At Ferguson Point* ☎ *604/669–3281* ⊕ *www.vancouverdine.com/teahouse.*

GASTOWN AND CHINATOWN

GASTOWN

$
DELI

✕ **Meat & Bread.** At this trendy sandwich shop, you simply wait in line (there's nearly always a queue) and choose from the short daily menu of sandwiches. The rich and crispy house-made porcetta (Italian-style roast pork) with salsa verde on a freshly baked ciabatta bun is a must-try. **Known for:** house-made porchetta; communal table; hearty soups. Ⓢ *Average main: C$9* ✉ *370 Cambie St., Gastown* ☎ *604/566–9003* ☾ *Closed Sun. No dinner.*

$$
MIDDLE EASTERN

✕ **Nuba.** You can make a meal of *meze*—appetizers like falafel, tabbouleh, or crispy cauliflower served with tahini—at this subterranean Lebanese restaurant. If you're looking for something heartier, the kitchen serves roast chicken glazed with honey and red pepper, lamb kebabs, and other meat dishes but much of the menu is vegetarian friendly. **Known for:** vegetarian dining; Lebanese cuisine; small plates. Ⓢ *Average main: C$20* ✉ *207B W. Hastings St., Gastown* ☎ *604/668–1655* ⊕ *www.nuba.ca.*

$$$
ASIAN FUSION
Fodor's Choice
★

✕ **Pidgin.** The menu in this glossy white space draws inspiration from Asia for inventive sharing plates that are some of Vancouver's most exciting eating options. From the ever-changing menu, you might choose spicy shishito peppers topped with Parmesan and pine nuts, charred octopus with dashi eggplant puree, or a Chinese-style "dan dan" noodle salad with shaved kohlrabi standing in for the pasta. **Known for:** inventive sharing plates; creative cocktails; bold flavors. Ⓢ *Average main: C$25* ✉ *350 Carrall St., Gastown* ☎ *604/620–9400* ⊕ *www.pidginvancouver.com* ☾ *No lunch.*

CHINATOWN

$$ CHINESE

🍴 **Bao Bei.** Start with an eclectic Chinatown storefront, stir in funky Asian-flavored cocktails, then add a creative take on traditional Chinese dishes, and the result is this hip and happening hangout. Load up your table with nibbles like Chinese pickles and steamed prawn, scallop, and chive dumplings or tapas-size dishes like *shao bing* (sesame flatbread with cumin-scented lamb, pickled red onion, cilantro, and chilis), *mantou* (steamed buns stuffed with pork belly and preserved turnip), or steelhead trout with kabocha cumin gnocchi, rapini, and shiso butter clam sauce. **Known for:** Asian-inspired cocktails; creative Chinese tapas. [$] *Average main: C$15* ✉ *163 Keefer St., Chinatown* ☎ *604/688–0876* 🌐 *www.bao-bei.ca* 💳 *No credit cards* 🕒 *No lunch.*

$$ ECLECTIC

🍴 **The Union.** At this casually cool restaurant and lounge whose tagline could be "Asia's greatest hits," the sharing plates and fun cocktails have elements from Japan to India and everywhere in between. Start with a Banga a cocktail in a jar, then choose Thai papaya salad, a Vietnamese *banh mi* (sandwich), or Indonesian *nasi goreng* (fried rice). **Known for:** pan-Asian menu; refreshing cocktails. [$] *Average main: C$15* ✉ *219 Union St., Chinatown* ☎ *604/568–3230* 🌐 *www.theunionvancouver.ca* 🕒 *No lunch weekdays.*

YALETOWN

$$$$ SEAFOOD Fodor's Choice ★

🍴 **Blue Water Cafe & Raw Bar.** Executive chef Frank Pabst focuses his menu on both popular and lesser-known local seafood (including frequently overlooked varieties like mackerel or herring) at his widely heralded, fashionable fish restaurant. You can dine in the warmly lighted interior or outside on the former loading dock that's now a lovely terrace. **Known for:** seafood-centric menu; top-notch sushi; great local wine list. [$] *Average main: C$36* ✉ *1095 Hamilton St., Yaletown* ☎ *604/688–8078* 🌐 *www.bluewatercafe.net* 🕒 *No lunch.*

GRANVILLE ISLAND

$$$ MODERN CANADIAN

🍴 **Edible Canada Bistro.** At this contemporary bistro with a patio for people-watching, you can sample foods from BC and across Canada. Smaller appetites might gravitate toward the elk tartare with truffle salt aioli, while hungrier travelers can sup on wild salmon with bacon-glazed greens. **Known for:** Canadian cuisine; duck-fat fries; seasonal menus. [$] *Average main: C$24* ✉ *1596 Johnston St., Granville Island* ☎ *604/682–6681* 🌐 *www.ediblecanada.com.*

THE WEST SIDE

KITSILANO

$$$$ MODERN CANADIAN Fodor's Choice ★

🍴 **Bishop's.** Before "local" and "seasonal" were all the rage, this highly regarded restaurant was serving West Coast cuisine with an emphasis on organic regional produce. Menu highlights include starters like tuna tartare with pickled garlic scapes and arugula seed pods, while Haida Gwaii halibut with broccoli puree, roasted cauliflower, and crispy potato, and heritage pork with clams are among the tasty main dishes. **Known for:** impeccable service; extensive local wine list; West Coast cuisine. [$] *Average main: C$39* ✉ *2183 W. 4th Ave., Kitsilano* ☎ *604/738–2025* 🌐 *www.bishopsonline.com* 🕒 *Closed Mon. No lunch.*

19

$$$ MODERN CANADIAN

🍴 **Fable.** The name doesn't have to do with fairy tales: it's about "farm to table," which encapsulates the philosophy of this bustling Kitsilano bistro. The idea is creative comfort food, and while the menu looks straightforward—wild BC salmon, smoked duck breast—it's full of surprising plot twists. **Known for:** inventive menu; local ingredients. [$] *Average main: C$25* ✉ *1944 W. 4th St., Kitsilano* ☎ *604/732–1322* 🌐 *www.fablekitchen.ca.*

$ SEAFOOD Fodor's Choice ★

🍴 **Go Fish.** If the weather's fine, head for this seafood stand on the seawall overlooking the docks beside Granville Island. The menu is short—highlights include fish-and-chips, grilled salmon or tuna sandwiches, and fish tacos—but the quality is first-rate. **Known for:** seaside location; fish and chips; long queues. [$] *Average main: C$10* ✉ *Fisherman's Wharf, 1505 W. 1st Ave., Kitsilano* ☎ *604/730–5040* 🕓 *Closed Mon. No dinner.*

SOUTH GRANVILLE

$$$$ MODERN CANADIAN Fodor's Choice ★

🍴 **Farmer's Apprentice.** Book ahead to nab one of the 30 or so seats in this cozy bistro, where chef-owner David Gunawan and his team in the open kitchen craft wildly creative "vegetable forward" set menus. It's not a vegetarian restaurant, but fresh local produce plays starring roles both the "omnivore" (C$55) and "herbivore" (C$50) menus, each featuring six courses that change daily to feature seasonal ingredients like garlic ramps, heirloom tomatoes, and black garlic. **Known for:** six-course menus; seasonal ingredients; great vegetarian dining. [$] *Average main: C$55* ✉ *1535 W. 6th Ave., South Granville* ☎ *604/620–2070* 🌐 *www.farmersapprentice.ca* 🕓 *No lunch weekdays.*

$$$ INDIAN

🍴 **Vij's.** Long lauded as Vancouver's most innovative Indian restaurant, this dining destination, run by genial proprietor Vikram Vij and his ex-wife Meeru Dhalwala, uses local ingredients to create exciting takes on South Asian cuisine. Dishes such as lamb "popsicles" in a creamy curry or BC rainbow trout served with a wheat berry pilaf are far from traditional but are beautifully executed. **Known for:** pan-Indian cuisine; rooftop patio; warm, welcoming service. [$] *Average main: C$30* ✉ *3106 Cambie St., Cambie* ☎ *604/736–6664* 🌐 *www.vijs.ca* 🕓 *No lunch.*

CAMBIE CORRIDOR

$$$$ JAPANESE Fodor's Choice ★

🍴 **Tojo's.** Hidekazu Tojo is a sushi-making legend in Vancouver, with thousands of special preparations stored in his creative mind. In this bright modern, high-ceilinged space, complete with a separate sake lounge, the prime perch is at the sushi bar, a convivial ringside seat for watching the creation of edible art. **Known for:** omakase; top-notch sushi; sake lounge. [$] *Average main: C$36* ✉ *1133 W. Broadway, Cambie* ☎ *604/872–8050* 🌐 *www.tojos.com* 🕓 *Closed Sun. No lunch.*

THE EAST SIDE

MAIN STREET

$ CAFÉ

🍴 **Forty Ninth Parallel Café.** Locally run 49th Parallel Coffee Roasters sources and roasts their own coffees, which they feature at their flagship café on Main Street. It's always packed with neighborhood denizens and shoppers enjoying the top-notch brews and the house-made Lucky's Doughnuts, which come in flavors from simple vanilla-glazed to salted caramel to decadent triple chocolate. **Known for:** direct-sourced coffee; exceptional doughnuts. [$] *Average main: C$5* ✉ *2902 Main St., Mt. Pleasant* ☎ *604/872–4901* 🌐 *www.49thparallelroasters.com.*

WHERE TO STAY

Vancouver is a pretty compact city, but each neighborhood has a distinct character and its own style of accommodations options. From hip boutique hotels to historic bed-and-breakfasts to sharp-angled glass-and-mirror towers, there are lodging choices for every style and budget. You can choose to be in the center of the shopping action on Robson Street, among the gracious tree-lined boulevards near Stanley Park, or in close proximity to the pulsing heart of the city's core.

Most hotels let children under 18 stay free in their parents' room, though you may be charged extra for more than two adults. Parking runs about C$25 to C$40 per day at Downtown hotels, and can be free outside the Downtown core. Watch out for phone and Internet charges, which can add up. You'll also be charged a 1.5% accommodations tax, a 10% Provincial Sales Tax (PST), and a 5% Goods and Services Tax (GST) for a total levy of 16.5%.

Hotel reviews have been shortened. For full information, visit Fodors.com. Hotels are listed alphabetically within neighborhoods. Use the coordinate at the end of each listing (⊕ B2) to locate a property on the Where to Stay in Vancouver map.

WHAT IT COSTS IN CANADIAN DOLLARS

	$	$$	$$$	$$$$
Hotels	under C$125	C$125–C$195	C$196–C$300	over C$300

Prices in the reviews are the lowest cost of a standard double room in high season.

DOWNTOWN AND THE WEST END

DOWNTOWN

$$$$ HOTEL **Fairmont Hotel Vancouver.** The copper roof of this 1939 château-style hotel dominates Vancouver's skyline, and the elegantly restored property is considered the city's gracious grande dame—aptly referred to as the Castle in the City. **Pros:** full-service spa; great location for shopping; stunning architecture. **Cons:** "standard" room sizes vary greatly; pricey parking. [$] *Rooms from: C$419* ✉ *900 W. Georgia St., Downtown* ☎ *604/684–3131, 866/540–4452* 🌐 *www.fairmont.com/hotelvancouver* 🛏 *557 rooms* 🍴 *No meals.*

$$$$ HOTEL Fodor's Choice ★ **Fairmont Waterfront.** Stunning views of the harbor, mountains, and Stanley Park from the floor-to-ceiling windows of the guest rooms are one of the highlights of this luxuriously modern 23-story hotel across the street from Vancouver's cruise-ship terminal. **Pros:** harbor views; proximity to the waterfront; inviting pool terrace. **Cons:** long elevator queues; busy lobby lounge. [$] *Rooms from: C$459* ✉ *900 Canada Pl. Way, Downtown* ☎ *866/540–4509* 🌐 *www.fairmont.com/waterfront-vancouver* 🛏 *513 rooms* 🍴 *No meals.*

$$$$
HOTEL
Fodor's Choice
★

Rosewood Hotel Georgia. One of Vancouver's newer hotels, the classy Rosewood is also one of the city's most historic properties: the 1927 Georgian Revival building once welcomed such prestigious guests as Elvis Presley and Katharine Hepburn. **Pros:** at the center of the city's action; top-rated spa; iconic restaurant. **Cons:** expensive valet parking; restaurant can get very busy. *Rooms from: C$425 ⊠ 801 W. Georgia St., Downtown ☎ 604/682–5566, 888/767–3966 ⊕ www.rosewoodhotels.com/en/hotelgeorgia ⊅ 156 rooms ¡○¡ No meals.*

$$$$
HOTEL
Fodor's Choice
★

Wedgewood Hotel & Spa. A member of the exclusive Relais & Châteaux Group, the luxurious, family-owned Wedgewood is all about pampering. **Pros:** personalized service; great location close to shops; Bacchus Lounge is a destination in its own right. **Cons:** small size means it books up quickly. *Rooms from: C$398 ⊠ 845 Hornby St., Downtown ☎ 604/689–7777, 800/663–0666 ⊕ www.wedgewoodhotel.com ⊅ 83 rooms ¡○¡ No meals.*

WEST END

$$$
HOTEL
FAMILY

Sylvia Hotel. This Virginia-creeper-covered 1912 heritage building is continually popular because of its affordable rates and near-perfect location: a stone's throw from the beach on scenic English Bay, two blocks from Stanley Park, and a 20-minute walk from Robson Street. **Pros:** beachfront location; close to restaurants; a good place to mingle with the locals. **Cons:** older building; parking can be difficult; walk to Downtown is slightly uphill. *Rooms from: C$199 ⊠ 1154 Gilford St., West End ☎ 604/681–9321, 877/681–9321 ⊕ www.sylviahotel.com ⊅ 120 rooms ¡○¡ No meals.*

$$
HOTEL
FAMILY
Fodor's Choice
★

Times Square Suites Hotel. You can't get much closer to Stanley Park than this chic but understated all-suites hotel near plenty of restaurants. **Pros:** next to Stanley Park; good location for restaurants; roof deck for guest use. **Cons:** on a very busy intersection. *Rooms from: C$159 ⊠ 1821 Robson St., West End ☎ 604/684–2223 ⊕ www.timessquaresuites.com ⊅ 42 rooms ¡○¡ No meals.*

YALETOWN

$$$
HOTEL

Hotel BLU Vancouver. A designer blend of comfort, high-tech, and, especially, eco-friendly features, Hotel BLU Vancouver could almost be called "Hotel Green" because of the focus on sustainability. **Pros:** close to theaters and sports arenas; free guest laundry; indoor pool and sauna. **Cons:** only suites and lofts have bathtubs; sports crowds swarm the neighborhood on event days. *Rooms from: C$275 ⊠ 177 Robson St., Yaletown ☎ 604/620–6200, 855/284–2091 ⊕ www.hotelbluvancouver.com ⊅ 75 rooms ¡○¡ No meals.*

$$$$
HOTEL
Fodor's Choice
★

OPUS Vancouver Hotel. Groundbreakingly trendy when it opened in 2002, the OPUS continues to reinvent itself and live up to the motto of being a "place to be not just a place to stay." The design team created a set of online fictitious characters, then decorated the rooms to suit each "persona." Guests are matched with room styles using the Lifestyle Concierge. **Pros:** great Yaletown location, right by rapid transit; funky and hip vibe; the lobby bar is a fashionable meeting spot. **Cons:** trendy nightspots nearby can be noisy at night; expensive and limited parking. *Rooms from: C$399 ⊠ 322 Davie St., Yaletown ☎ 604/642–6787, 866/642–6787 ⊕ www.opushotel.com ⊅ 96 rooms ¡○¡ No meals.*

WEST SIDE

KITSILANO

$$ B&B/INN Fodor's Choice ★ 🏨 **Corkscrew Inn.** This restored 1912 Craftsman-style house near the beach in Kitsilano combines the comforts of a B&B with a quirky tribute to the humble corkscrew: guests are encouraged to explore the small wine paraphernalia museum. **Pros:** great local neighborhood; delicious breakfast. **Cons:** not Downtown; a 15-minute bus ride to the Canada Line airport connection. [$] *Rooms from: C$130* ✉ *2735 W. 2nd Ave., Kitsilano* ☎ *604/733–7276, 877/737–7276* 🌐 *www.corkscrewinn.com* 🛏 *5 rooms* 🍴 *Breakfast.*

NIGHTLIFE

Vancouver might be best-known for its outdoors activities but this hip city delivers plenty of entertainment once the sun goes down. Look for modern craft breweries, wine bars showcasing wines from the nearby Okanagan Valley, and some excellent music venues.

DOWNTOWN AND THE WEST END

BARS

Fodor's Choice ★ **Tap & Barrel.** The 360-degree views from this convention center patio take in Stanley Park, the seaplane terminal, and the North Shore Mountains. You can sit inside, amid the wooden casks of wine, but waiting for a seat on the deck is worth it if the weather even hints at sunshine. There's another location—and similarly large patio—on False Creek (*1 Athlete's Way*). ✉ *1055 Canada Pl., Downtown* ☎ *604/235–9827* 🌐 *www.tapandbarrel.com.*

Uva Wine & Cocktail Bar. At street level in the century-old Moda Hotel, Uva puts a modern spin on the Italian wine bar concept, with bold decor and sleek furnishings. The well-dressed crowd comes for the not-too-wild atmosphere, often for a drink before heading to one of nearby Granville Street's performance venues. ✉ *Moda Hotel, 900 Seymour St., Downtown* ☎ *604/632–9560* 🌐 *www.uvavancouver.com.*

DANCE CLUBS

Commodore Ballroom. This 1929 dance hall has been restored to its art deco glory, complete with massive dance floor and state-of-the-art sound system. Indie rock bands and renowned DJs play here most nights. ✉ *868 Granville St., Downtown* ☎ *604/739–4550, 855/985–5000 tickets* 🌐 *www.commodoreballroom.com.*

GASTOWN AND CHINATOWN

BARS

Alibi Room. If beer is your thing, head to Alibi, which specializes in pairing beer with your meal. Kegs of microbrews from around BC and beyond are the pride and joy here and it's known for having one of the best selections of craft beers in Vancouver. There are also organic wines and a few fun cocktails if you're not feeling beer-inclined. ✉ *157 Alexander St., Gastown* ☎ *604/623–3383* 🌐 *www.alibi.ca.*

Fodor's Choice ★ **The Diamond.** At the top of a narrow staircase above Maple Tree Square, the Diamond occupies the second floor of one of the city's oldest buildings. A cool hangout and cocktail lounge, the venue serves a mix of historic tipples and inventive house concoctions. There's a daily, and very welcoming, after-work happy hour. ⊠ *6 Powell St., at Carrall St., Gastown* ⊕ *www.di6mond.com.*

The Keefer Bar. The Keefer Bar has fully capitalized on its Chinatown connection, using ingredients sourced from local herbalists (magnolia bark anyone?)—ginseng, tea-based tinctures, or astragalus root, for example. Small plates of Asian dishes make good nibbling. The decor is dark and red, with hanging cylindrical neon lights that layer a sultry, hidden vibe over nights of live music and DJs. ⊠ *135 Keefer St., Chinatown* ☎ *604/688–1961* ⊕ *www.thekeeferbar.com.*

YALETOWN
BARS
Opus Bar. Traveling executives in suits and film industry creatives sip martinis (or perhaps a cocktail made with bourbon and blood oranges) while scoping out the room, on the ground floor of the Opus Hotel. During the day, it's a sleek café. ⊠ *Opus Hotel, 350 Davie St., Yaletown* ☎ *604/642–0557* ⊕ *www.opusbar.ca.*

Yaletown Brewing Company. In a renovated warehouse with a glassed-in brewery turning out several tasty beers, this always-crowded gastropub and patio has a lively singles scene and reliable happy hour. Even though it's super popular it still feels like a neighborhood place. ⊠ *1111 Mainland St., Yaletown* ☎ *604/681–2739* ⊕ *www.mjg.ca/yaletown.*

GRANVILLE ISLAND
BARS
The Sandbar. With a seafood restaurant, a wine bar, and live music nightly (piano Sunday to Thursday; rotating acts Friday and Saturday) in the Teredo Lounge, this venue has something for everyone. There are televised sports on game days. For dramatic views over False Creek, reserve a table on the rooftop patio in the summer. ⊠ *1535 Johnson St., Granville Island* ☎ *604/669–9030* ⊕ *www.vancouverdine.com/sandbar.*

THE WEST SIDE
BARS
Kits Beach Boathouse. A summer visit to Vancouver isn't complete without an afternoon enjoying cocktails on this rooftop patio overlooking sand-court volleyball matches at Kits Beach. At other times of the year, the views of the vivid sunsets and dramatic winter storms are exceptional, though you may want to retreat behind the floor-to-ceiling windows to sip in comfort. ⊠ *1305 Arbutus St., Kitsilano* ☎ *604/738–5487* ⊕ *www. boathouserestaurants.ca/locations/#kitsilano.*

EAST SIDE
BARS
Brassneck Brewery. Long, lean, and creatively wood-paneled, this is among a fresh crop of Main Street breweries leading the craft beer resurgence. The brewery operations dictate the layout, and the tasting room's communal tables attract a dedicated after-work crowd for pints, growler fills, and food truck eats. A visit can be combined with other breweries nearby—such as Main Street Brewing Co. (*261 E. 7th Ave.*) and Steel Toad Brewery (*97 E. 2nd Ave.*)—to create a self-made pub crawl. ⊠ *2148 Main St., Mt. Pleasant* ☎ *604/259–7686* ⊕ *www.brassneck.ca.*

Cascade Room. Named after the signature beer the Vancouver Brewery once produced on this very spot, the Cascade Room is a usually busy Main Street lounge. The cocktail menu is lengthy, with a focus on classics. ⊠ *2616 Main St., at Broadway, Mt. Pleasant* ☎ *604/709–8650* ⊕ *www.thecascade.ca.*

SPORTS AND THE OUTDOORS

Blessed with a mild climate, fabulous natural setting, and excellent public-use facilities, Vancouverites, unsurprisingly, are an outdoorsy lot. The Downtown peninsula of Vancouver is entirely encircled by a seawall along which you can walk, in-line skate (which is still quite popular in Vancouver), cycle, or otherwise propel yourself for more than 22 km (13½ miles), with plenty of picturesque jumping on and off points.

You'll find rental equipment and tour operators in Vancouver for every imaginable outdoor activity, from tandem bikes for Stanley Park trails to stand-up paddleboards on Granville Island. Yoga studios seem to be around every corner and hiking trails materialize just at the end of the road. Hotel concierges can recommend the best wilderness trails just as easily as they can top sushi spots. To buy or rent gear, head to the Mountain Equipment Co-op, a local institution (⇨ *see Shopping*).

BEACHES

Greater Vancouver is well endowed with beaches but the waters are decidedly cool, with summer water temperatures ranging from 12 to 18°C (54 to 64°F). Aside from kids and the intrepid, most stick to quick dips, sunbathing, or wearing a wet suit for water activities.

English Bay Beach. The city's best-known beach, English Bay, lies just to the east of Stanley Park's southern entrance. A long stretch of golden sand, a waterslide, volleyball courts, kayak rentals, and food trucks keep things interesting all summer. Known locally for being gay-friendly, it draws a diverse crowd. Special events include summer Celebration of Light fireworks and a New Year's Day swim. **Amenities:** food and drink; lifeguards; parking (fee); toilets; water sports. **Best for:** atmosphere; partiers; sunset; swimming; walking. ⊠ *1700 Beach Ave., between Gilford and Bidwell Sts., West End* ☎ *604/665–3424* ⊕ *www.vancouver. ca/parks-recreation-culture/english-bay-beach.aspx.*

Fodor's Choice ★ **Kitsilano Beach.** West of the southern end of the Burrard Bridge, Kits Beach is the city's busiest beach—Frisbee tossers, beach volleyball players, and sleek young people are ever present. Facilities include a playground, restaurant, concession stand, and tennis courts. **Kitsilano Pool** is here: at 137.5 meters (451 feet), it's the longest pool in Canada and one of the few heated saltwater pools in the world (open May to September). Just steps from the sand, the Boathouse on Kits Beach serves lunch, dinner, and weekend brunch inside and on its big ocean-view deck. There's also a take-out concession at the same site. Inland from the pool, the Kitsilano Showboat, an outdoor amphitheater hosts music and dance performances during the summer. **Amenities:** food and drink; lifeguards; parking (fee); toilets; water sports. **Best for:** atmosphere; sunrise; sunset; swimming; walking. ⊠ *2305 Cornwall Ave., Kitsilano* ☎ *604/731–0011* ⊕ *www.vancouver.ca/parks-recreation-culture/kitsilano-beach.aspx.*

19

Fodor's Choice
★
Stanley Park Beaches. There are two fine beaches accessed from Stanley Park, with other unnamed sandy spots dotted along the seawall. The most popular with families is **Second Beach,** which has a playground and large heated pool with slides. **Third Beach** is a little more removed than the other central beaches. It has a larger stretch of sand, fairly warm water, and unbeatable sunset views. It's a popular evening picnic spot. **Amenities:** food and drink; lifeguards; parking (fee); toilets. **Best for:** sunset; swimming; walking. ⊠ *7495 Stanley Park Dr., Stanley Park* ⊕ *www.vancouver.ca/parks-recreation-culture/third-beach.aspx.*

BIKING

Vancouver's most popular bike path is the 9-km (5½-mile) **Stanley Park Seawall,** which follows the park's perimeter, hugging the harbor along the way. The views of Lions Gate Bridge and the mountains to the north are breathtaking. The path connects at both ends with the city's longer seawall path, if you feel like making a day of it. Rent your bike near the entrance to Stanley Park, in the West End, as there are no rentals once you're inside the park.

For biking on city streets, Downtown Vancouver's "separated bike lanes" have made biking even easier—most bike lanes have a barrier between them and the traffic. Especially useful ones are along Hornby and Dunsmuir streets. These lanes are in addition to the city's many bikeways, identified by green bicycle signs. There are detailed maps and other information on the website operated by the City of Vancouver (⊕ *www.vancouver.ca/streets-transportation/biking-and-cyclists.aspx*). Cycling maps are also available from most bike shops and bike-rental outlets. Helmets are required by law, and a sturdy lock is essential.

Fodor's Choice
★
Seawall. The paved bike paths of Vancouver's 22-km (13½-mile) seawall start Downtown at Canada Place, go around Stanley Park, and follow False Creek to Kitsilano. ⊠ *Downtown* ⊕ *www.vancouver.ca/parks-recreation-culture/seawall.aspx.*

FAMILY **Bayshore Bike Rentals.** If you're starting your ride near Stanley Park, try this friendly store. It has a wide range of bikes as well as bike trailers for kids, and in-line skates. ⊠ *745 Denman St., West End* ☎ *604/688–2453* ⊕ *www.bayshorebikerentals.ca.*

Spokes Bicycle Rentals. Near Stanley Park, Spokes has a wide selection of mountain bikes, tandem bikes, and children's bikes. Everything from hourly to weekly rentals are available. Helmets, locks, and route maps are complimentary. ⊠ *1798 W. Georgia St., West End* ☎ *604/688–5141* ⊕ *www.spokesbicyclerentals.com.*

ECOTOURS AND WILDLIFE VIEWING

Given a temperate climate and forest, mountain, and marine environments teeming with life, it's no surprise that wildlife-watching is an important pastime and growing business in and around Vancouver.

Fodor's Choice
★
Sewell's Marina. This marina near the protected waters of Howe Sound runs year-round, two-hour ecotours of the surrounding marine and coastal mountain habitat. Sightings range from swimming seals to soaring eagles. High-speed rigid inflatable hulls are used. They also offer

guided and self-driven salmon-fishing charters in Howe Sound and to the mouths of the Capilano and Fraser rivers. ⊠ *6409 Bay St., West Vancouver* ☎ *604/921–3474* ⊕ *www.sewellsmarina.com.*

WHALE-WATCHING

Between April and October pods of orca whales migrate through the Strait of Georgia, near Vancouver. The area is also home to year-round pods of harbor seals, elephant seals, minke whales, porpoises, and a wealth of birdlife, inlcuding bald eagles. Other migrating whales include humpbacks and grays.

Prince of Whales. This established operator runs half-day trips from Vancouver's Coal Harbour waterfront across the Strait of Georgia to Victoria, in season. ⊠ *The Westin Bayshore, 1601 Bayshore Dr., West End* ☎ *888/383–4884* ⊕ *www.princeofwhales.com.*

Wild Whales Vancouver. Boats leave Granville Island in search of orca pods in the Strait of Georgia, often traveling as far as Victoria. Rates are C\$135 for a three- to seven-hour trip in either an open or glass-domed boat (trip lengths depend on where the whales are hanging out on a particular day). Each boat leaves once daily, April through October, conditions permitting. ⊠ *1806 Mast Tower Rd., Granville Island* ☎ *604/699–2011* ⊕ *www.whalesvancouver.com.*

HIKING

With its expansive landscape of mountains, inlets, alpine lakes, and approachable glaciers, as well as low-lying rivers, hills, dikes, and meadows, southwestern British Columbia is a hiker's paradise. For easy walking and hiking, you can't beat Stanley Park in Downtown Vancouver but for more strenuous hiking, there are fabulous parks not far away. With their photo-worthy profile, the North Shore Mountains may appear benign, but this is a vast and rugged territory filled with natural pitfalls and occasionally hostile wildlife.

HIKING TRAILS

FAMILY
Fodor's Choice
★
Capilano River Regional Park. About 26 km (16 miles) of hiking trails explore in and around Capilano Canyon—where the Capilano River is flanked by old-growth forest. There is also a salmon hatchery that's open to the public. Trailheads are off Capilano Road in North Vancouver (near Capilano Suspension Bridge) and near Ambleside Beach. ⊠ *4500 Capilano Park Rd., North Vancouver* ☎ *604/224–5739.*

FAMILY
Grouse Grind. Vancouver's most famous, or infamous, hiking route, the Grind, is about a 3-km (about 2-mile) climb straight up 853 meters (2,799 feet) to the top of Grouse Mountain. Thousands do it annually, but climbers are advised to be experienced and in excellent physical condition. The route is open daily during daylight hours, from spring through autumn (conditions permitting). Or you can take the Grouse Mountain Skyride to the top 365 days a year; a round-trip ticket is C\$43.95. Hiking trails in the adjacent Lynn Headwaters Regional Park are accessible from the gondola, including **Goat Mountain Trail.** ⊠ *Grouse Mountain, 6400 Nancy Greene Way, North Vancouver* ☎ *604/980–9311* ⊕ *www.grousemountain.com.*

19

GUIDED HIKING TOURS

Novice hikers and serious walkers can join guided trips or do self-guided walks of varying approach and difficulty. **Grouse Mountain** hosts several daily "eco-walks" along easy, meandering paths, including a discussion of flora and fauna and a visit to the Refuge for Endangered Wildlife. They're free with admission to Grouse Mountain Skyride.

FAMILY **Stanley Park Ecology Centre.** A calendar of guided nature walks and discovery sessions is filled with fun, kid-friendly options. Despite its urban access, Stanley Park offers incredible wildlife diversity—from the namesake rodents in Beaver Lake to a rookery of great blue herons near the tennis courts. The organization also operates the Stanley Park Nature House on the shores of Lost Lagoon. ⊠ *Alberni St. at Chilco St., Stanley Park* ✛ *Southeast corner of Lost Lagoon* ☎ *604/257–8544, 604/718–6522* ⊕ *www.stanleyparkecology.ca* ⊠ *Free.*

WINTER SPORTS

SKIING, SNOWBOARDING, SNOWSHOEING, AND SNOW-TUBING

Fodor's Choice ★ **Cypress Mountain Ski Resort.** Just 30 minutes from Downtown, the ski facilities at Cypress Mountain include six quad or double chairs, 53 downhill runs, and a vertical drop of 610 meters (2,001 feet). The resort has a snow-tubing area and snowshoe tours. This is also a major cross-country skiing area. Summer activities at Cypress Mountain include hiking, geocaching, wildlife viewing, and mountain biking. ⊠ *Cypress Provincial Park, 6000 Cypress Bowl Rd., West Vancouver* ☎ *604/926–5612* ⊕ *www.cypressmountain.com.*

FAMILY **Grouse Mountain Ski Resort.** A 15-minute drive from Downtown Vancouver, the Skyride gondola takes skiers up to the ski resort on a slope overlooking the city. The views are fine on a clear day, but at night they're spectacular, and the area is known for its night skiing. Facilities include two quad chairs, 26 skiing and snowboarding runs, and several all-level freestyle-terrain parks. There's a choice of upscale and casual dining in a handsome stone-and-timber lodge. Summer activities at Grouse Mountain include hiking, disc golf, zip-lining (in winter, too), wildlife viewing, and taking in sky-high views from inside The Eye of the Wind turbine. ⊠ *6400 Nancy Greene Way, North Vancouver* ☎ *604/980–9311, 604/986–6262 snow report* ⊕ *www.grousemountain.com.*

SKATING RINKS

FAMILY **Robson Square Ice Rink.** Rent skates and lace them up tight to enjoy this free ice-skating rink in the city center. It's the best of indoor and outdoor skating combined—with a glass dome covering the open-air rink. The season runs December through February. ⊠ *800 Robson St., Downtown* ☎ *604/646–3553* ⊕ *www.robsonsquare.com* ⊠ *Free.*

SHOPPING

Art galleries, ethnic markets, gourmet-food shops, and high-fashion boutiques abound in Vancouver. Shopping here is more unique than in many other North American cities because of the prevalence of Asian and First Nations influences in crafts, home furnishings, and foods. In the art scene, look for First Nations and other aboriginal art, from souvenir trinkets to stellar contemporary art; many galleries showcasing First Nations artists are in Gastown. Area artisans also create a variety of fine crafts, exhibiting and selling their wares at Granville Island galleries.

DOWNTOWN AND THE WEST END

BOOKS

MacLeod's Books. One of the city's best antiquarian and used-book stores, this jam-packed shop is a treasure trove of titles from mainstream to wildly eclectic. ⊠ *455 W. Pender St., Downtown* ☎ *604/681–7654.*

CLOTHING: MEN'S AND WOMEN'S

Fodor'sChoice ★ **lululemon athletica.** Power-yoga devotees, soccer moms, and anyone who likes casual, comfy clothes covets the fashionable, well-constructed workout wear with the stylized "A" insignia from this Vancouver-based company. In addition to this flagship location, there are several branches around town, including one at 2113 West 4th Avenue in Kitsilano. A new lululemon lab at 50 Powell Street in Gastown showcases the latest athleisure lines. ⊠ *970 Robson St., Downtown* ☎ *604/681–3118* ⊕ *www.lululemon.com.*

Fodor'sChoice ★ **Roots.** For outdoorsy clothes that double as souvenirs (many sport maple-leaf logos), check out these Canadian-made sweatshirts, leather jackets, and other comfy casuals for men, women and kids. In addition to this Downtown flagship store, there's a smaller branch down the street at 1153 Robson Street, branches on South Granville Street and on West 4th Avenue in Kitsilano, and a number of outlet stores, called Roots 73, in the suburbs. ⊠ *1001 Robson St., West End* ☎ *604/683–4305* ⊕ *www.roots.com.*

DEPARTMENT STORES

Hudson's Bay. A Canadian institution (though it's now American-owned), the Bay was founded as part of the fur trade in the 17th century. There's a whole department selling the signature tricolor blankets and other Canadiana. On the lower level, the Topshop and Topman boutiques carry imports from the trendy British retailer. ⊠ *674 Granville St., at Georgia St., Downtown* ☎ *604/681–6211* ⊕ *www.thebay.com.*

GASTOWN AND CHINATOWN

ART AND ANTIQUES

Fodor'sChoice ★ **Hill's Native Art.** This highly respected store has Vancouver's largest selection of First Nations art. The main floor is crammed with souvenirs, keepsakes, and high-quality pieces, including carvings, masks, and drums. If you think that's impressive, head upstairs for one-of-a-kind collector pieces and limited editions. ⊠ *165 Water St., Gastown* ☎ *604/685–4249* ⊕ *www.hills.ca.*

SHOES AND ACCESSORIES

Fodor'sChoice ★ **John Fluevog.** You might have seen John Fluevog shops in New York and Los Angeles, but did you know that these funky shoes were created by a Vancouverite? The Gastown location is worth a look for the store itself, with its striking glass facade and soaring ceilings. There's another branch Downtown at 837 Granville Street. ⊠ *65 Water St., Gastown* ☎ *604/688–6228* ⊕ *www.fluevog.com.*

19

YALETOWN
CLOTHING: MEN'S AND WOMEN'S

Fine Finds Boutique. It's hard to predict what you'll find in this pretty little shop—it's a fun spot to browse for cute women's clothing, jewelry, and accessories. ⊠ *1014 Mainland St., Yaletown* ☎ *604/669–8325* ⊕ *www. finefindsboutique.com.*

GRANVILLE ISLAND
ART AND ANTIQUES

Circle Craft. This artist co-op sells finely crafted textiles, wood pieces, jewelry, ceramics, and glass works. Chosen by juried selection, the artists are all local to British Columbia and all their work must be made by hand. ⊠ *Net Loft, 1–1666 Johnston St., Granville Island* ☎ *604/669–8021* ⊕ *www.circlecraft.net.*

FOOD AND WINE

Artisan Sake Maker. You can learn all about sake (Japanese rice wine), and sample the locally made product, at Vancouver's own sake brewery. ⊠ *1339 Railspur Alley, Granville Island* ☎ *604/685–7253* ⊕ *www. artisansakemaker.com.*

Edible Canada. Tucked behind the Edible Canada bistro, this little shop sells jams, sauces, chocolates, and dozens of other edible items from around the country. It's a great place to find gifts for foodie friends. ⊠ *1596 Johnston St., Granville Island* ☎ *604/682–6675* ⊕ *www.ediblecanada.com.*

MARKETS

Fodor's Choice ★ **Granville Island Public Market.** Locals and visitors alike crowd this indoor market that's part farm stand, part gourmet grocery, and part upscale food court. The stalls are packed with locally made sausages, exotic cheeses, just-caught fish, fresh produce, baked goods, and prepared foods from handmade fudge to frothy cappuccinos. This is definitely the place to come for lunch. If the sun is out, you can dine on your purchases out on the waterfront decks. The crowds can get crazy, though, so avoid weekends if possible (or come early). ⊠ *1689 Johnston St., Granville Island* ☎ *604/666–6655* ⊕ *www.granvilleisland.com/ public-market.*

THE WEST SIDE
ART AND ANTIQUES

MOA Shop. The Museum of Anthropology gift shop carries an excellent selection of Northwest Coast jewelry, carvings, and prints, as well as books on First Nations history and culture. ⊠ *University of British Columbia, 6393 N.W. Marine Dr., Point Grey* ☎ *604/827–4810* ⊕ *www.moa.ubc.ca.*

BOOKS

Fodor's Choice ★ **Barbara-Jo's Books to Cooks.** Local-chef-turned-entrepreneur Barbara-Jo McIntosh spreads the good-food word with scores of cookbooks, including many by Vancouver- and BC–based chefs, as well as wine books, memoirs, and magazines. The store also hosts special events, recipe demos, and classes in its sparkling demonstration kitchen—they're a tasty way to explore local cuisine. ⊠ *1740 W. 2nd Ave., Kitsilano* ☎ *604/688–6755* ⊕ *www.bookstocooks.com* ☺ *Closed Sun.*

Wanderlust. Travelers and armchair travelers love this shop, which feeds everyone's wanderlust. There are thousands of travel books and maps, as well as luggage, gear, and accessories. ⊠ *1929 W. 4th Ave., Kitsilano* ☎ *604/739–2182* ⊕ *www.wanderlustore.com.*

FOOD

Chocolate Arts. Looking for a present for a chocolate lover? Check out the chocolates in First Nations motifs, specially designed by Robert Davidson, one of Canada's premier artists. This delicious shop and café, where you can refuel with a hot chocolate, some bonbons, or some house-made ice-cream, is a short walk from Granville Island. ⊠ *1620 W. 3rd Ave., Kitsilano* ☎ *604/739–0475, 877/739–0475* ⊕ *www.chocolatearts.com.*

Fodor'sChoice ★ **Les Amis du Fromage.** If you love cheese, don't miss the mind-boggling array of selections from BC, the rest of Canada, and elsewhere at this family-run shop of delicacies. The extremely knowledgeable staff encourage you to taste before you buy. Yum. The fromagerie is located between Granville Island and Kitsilano Beach—useful to keep in mind if you're assembling a seaside picnic. There's a second location at 843 East Hastings Street on Vancouver's East Side. ⊠ *1752 W. 2nd Ave., Kitsilano* ☎ *604/732–4218* ⊕ *www.buycheese.com.*

THE EAST SIDE

OUTDOOR EQUIPMENT

Fodor'sChoice ★ **MEC (Mountain Equipment Co-op).** Vancouver's go-to outdoor store since the 1970s, MEC stocks a good selection of high-performance clothing and equipment for hiking, cycling, climbing, and kayaking, and for just looking good while hanging around outdoors. You can rent sports gear here, too. A one-time C$5 membership is required for purchases or rentals. ⊠ *130 W. Broadway, Mt. Pleasant* ☎ *604/872–7858* ⊕ *www.mec.ca.*

VICTORIA

19

Despite its role as the provincial capital, Victoria was largely eclipsed, economically, by Vancouver throughout the 20th century. This, as it turns out, was all to the good, helping to preserve Victoria's historic Downtown and keeping the city largely free of skyscrapers and highways. For much of the 20th century, Victoria was marketed to tourists as "The Most British City in Canada," and it still has more than its share of Anglo-themed pubs, tea shops, and double-decker buses, but these days, Victorians prefer to celebrate their combined indigenous, Asian, and European heritage, and the city's stunning wilderness backdrop. Locals do often venture out for afternoon tea, but they're just as likely to nosh on dim sum or tapas. The outdoors is ever present here. You can hike, bike, kayak, sail, or whale-watch straight from the city center, and forests, beaches, offshore islands, and wilderness parklands lie just minutes away.

At the southern tip of Vancouver Island, Victoria dips slightly below the 49th parallel. That puts it farther south than most of Canada, giving it the mildest climate in the country, with virtually no snow and less than half the rain of Vancouver.

The city's geography, or at least its place names, can cause confusion. Just to clarify: the city of Victoria is on Vancouver Island (not Victoria Island). The city of Vancouver is on the British Columbia mainland, not on Vancouver Island. At any rate, the city of Vancouver didn't even exist in 1843 when Victoria, then called Fort Victoria, was founded as the westernmost trading post of the British-owned Hudson's Bay Company.

PLANNING

WHEN TO GO
Victoria has the warmest, mildest climate in Canada: snow is rare and flowers bloom in February. Summers are mild, too, rarely topping 75°F. If you're here for dining, shopping, and museums, winter is a perfectly nice time for a visit: it's gray and wet, and some minor attractions are closed, but hotel deals abound. If your focus is the outdoors—biking, hiking, gardens, and whale-watching—you need to come with everyone else, between May and October. That's when the streets come to life with crafts stalls, street entertainers, blooming gardens, and the inevitable tour buses. It's fun and busy but Victoria never gets unbearably crowded.

MAKING THE MOST OF YOUR TIME
You can see most of the sights in Downtown Victoria's compact core in a day, although there's enough to see at the main museums to easily fill two days. You can save time by prebooking tea at the Empress Hotel and buying tickets online for the Royal British Columbia Museum. You should also save at least half a day or a full evening to visit Butchart Gardens.

An extra day allows for some time on the water, either on a whale-watching trip—it's fairly easy to spot orcas in the area during summer—or on a Harbour Ferries tour, with stops for tea at Point Ellice House or fish-and-chips at Fisherman's Wharf. You can also explore the shoreline on foot, following all, or part, of the 7-mile waterfront walkway.

GETTING HERE AND AROUND
It's easy to visit Victoria without a car. Most sights, restaurants, and hotels are in the compact walkable core, with bikes, ferries, horse-drawn carriages, double-decker buses, step-on tour buses, taxis, and pedicabs on hand to fill the gaps. For sights outside the core—Butchart Gardens, Hatley Castle, Scenic Marine Drive—tour buses are your best bet if you don't have your own vehicle. Bike paths lace Downtown and run along much of Victoria's waterfront, and long-haul car-free paths run to the ferry terminals and as far west as Sooke. Most buses and ferries carry bikes.

AIR TRAVEL
Air Canada, Pacific Coastal Airlines, and WestJet fly to Victoria from Vancouver International Airport. Alaska Airlines (under its Horizon Air division) flies between Seattle and Victoria. Victoria International Airport is 25 km (15 miles) north of Downtown Victoria. The flight from Vancouver to Victoria takes about 25 minutes. There is

floatplane service to Victoria's Inner Harbour in Downtown Victoria with Harbour Air Seaplanes. Harbour Air also flies from Whistler to Downtown Victoria, May–September. Kenmore Air has daily floatplane service from Seattle to Victoria's Inner Harbour. Helijet has helicopter service from Downtown Vancouver and Vancouver International Airport to Downtown Victoria.

BOAT AND FERRY TRAVEL

BC Ferries has daily service between Tsawwassen, about an hour south of Vancouver, and Swartz Bay, at the end of Highway 17 (the Patricia Bay Highway), about 30 minutes north of Victoria. Sailing time is about 1½ hours. An excellent option combines four hours of whale-watching with travel between Vancouver and Victoria, offered by the Prince of Whales. The 74-passenger boat leaves the Westin Bayshore Hotel in Downtown Vancouver daily at 9 am (June–mid-September), arriving in Victoria at 1 pm; there are also departures from Victoria's Inner Harbour at 1:45 pm (one-way C$200).

The Victoria Harbour Ferry serves the Inner Harbour; stops include the Fairmont Empress, Chinatown, Point Ellice House, the Delta Victoria Ocean Pointe Resort, and Fisherman's Wharf. Fares start at C$5. Boats make the rounds every 15 to 20 minutes. They run 10 to 9 from mid-May through mid-September and 11 to 5 from March through mid-May and mid-September to late October. The ferries don't run from November through February. The 45-minute harbor tours cost C$22, and gorge cruises cost C$26. At 10:45 am on summer Sundays, the little ferries perform a water ballet set to classical music in the Inner Harbour.

Contacts Victoria Harbour Ferry. ☎ *250/708–0201* ⊕ *www.victoriaharbourferry.com.*

EXPLORING VICTORIA

19

Victoria is small and easily explored. A walk around Downtown, starting with the museums and architectural sights of the Inner Harbour, followed by a stroll up Government Street to the historic areas of Chinatown and Old Town, covers most of the key attractions, though seeing every little interesting thing along the way could easily take two days. Most visitors also make time for the Butchart Gardens, a stunning exhibition garden 20 minutes by car north on the Saanich Peninsula.

DOWNTOWN

Home to the vast majority of Victoria's sights, hotels, and eateries, Downtown *is* Victoria for most visitors. At its heart is the Inner Harbour. Busy with yachts, passenger ferries, whale-watching boats, and floatplanes, and framed by such iconic buildings as the Fairmont Empress hotel, this pedestrian-friendly area is busy with horse-and-carriage rides, street entertainers, tour buses, and, yes, tourists—all summer long. The south shore of the harbor, extending to the Dallas Road waterfront and Beacon Hill Park, is known as James Bay. Two key sites, the Parliament Buildings and the Robert Bateman Centre, are here, but if you stroll just a block south, you'll find a peaceful residential district of modest historic homes, and such interesting historic sites as Emily Carr House. North of the Inner Harbour, a straight shot up Government Street leads to some great shopping and to more historic areas: Bastion Square, Market Square, and Chinatown. Founded in 1858, Victoria's Chinatown, along Fisgard Street between Government and Store streets, is the oldest such district in Canada. At just two square blocks, it's much smaller than Vancouver's but still pleasant to stroll through, particularly as hip boutiques and eateries have moved into the district. If you enter from Government Street, you'll pass under the elaborate Gate of Harmonious Interest, made of Taiwanese ceramic tiles and decorative panels.

Emily Carr House. One of Canada's most celebrated artists and a respected writer, Emily Carr (1871–1945) lived in this extremely proper, wooden Victorian house before she abandoned her middle-class life to live in the wilds of British Columbia. Carr's own descriptions, from her autobiography *Book of Small,* were used to restore the house. Art on display includes reproductions of Carr's work—visit the Art Gallery of Greater Victoria or the Vancouver Art Gallery to see the originals. ⊠ *207 Government St., James Bay, Downtown* ☎ *250/383–5843* ⊕ *www.emily-carr.com* ✍ *C$6.75.*

Fairmont Empress. Opened in 1908 by the Canadian Pacific Railway, the Empress is one of the grand château-style railroad hotels that grace many Canadian cities. Designed by Francis Rattenbury, who also designed the Parliament Buildings across the way, the solid Edwardian grandeur of the Empress has made it a symbol of the city. The elements that made the hotel an attraction for travelers in the past—old-world architecture, ornate decor, and a commanding view of the Inner Harbour—are still here although they exude a fresh, contemporary air. Nonguests can reserve ahead for afternoon tea (the dress code is smart casual) in the chandelier-draped Tea Lobby, meet for Pimm's cocktails or enjoy superb Pacific Northwest cuisine at the Q Lounge and Restaurant, or enjoy a treatment at the hotel's Willow Stream spa. In summer, lunch, snacks, and cocktails are served on the veranda overlooking the Inner Harbour. ⊠ *721 Government St., Downtown* ☎ *250/384–8111, 250/389–2727 tea reservations* ⊕ *www.fairmont.com/empress* ✍ *Free; afternoon tea C$63.*

FAMILY **Fisherman's Wharf.** This favorite nautical spot is only a 20-minute walk from downtown, along a waterfront path just west of the Inner Harbour. Or you can get here by hopping aboard one of the many Victoria Harbour Ferries. You can watch fishers unload their catches and admire the various vessels, or picnic in the shoreside park. If you stroll the docks and walk among the colorful houseboats, you'll come across several floating shacks where you can buy ice cream, fish tacos, and live crabs, take kayak tours, buy tickets for whale-watching cruises, or join a pirate-themed boat tour. Other booths sell fish to feed the harbor seals who often visit the quay (you can even watch them on the underwater "seal cam"). The busiest vendor is Barb's, an esteemed fish-and-chips spot that is open only in the summer, from May through October. ⊠ *Corner of Dallas Rd. and Erie St., James Bay, Downtown* ⊕ *fishermanswharfvictoria.com.*

More than 3,300 lights outline Victoria's Parliament Buildings; like the Fairmont Empress hotel, the buildings have a prominent position in the Inner Harbor, and were designed by the same architect: Francis Rattenbury.

Parliament Buildings. Officially the British Columbia Provincial Legislative Assembly Buildings, these massive stone structures are more popularly referred to as the Parliament Buildings. Designed by Francis Rattenbury (who also designed the Fairmont Empress Hotel) when he was just 25 years old, and completed in 1897, they dominate the Inner Harbour. Atop the central dome is a gilded statue of Captain George Vancouver (1757–98), the first European to sail around Vancouver Island. A statue of Queen Victoria (1819–1901) reigns over the front of the complex. More than 3,300 lights outline the buildings at night. The interior is lavishly done with stained-glass windows, gilt moldings, and historic photographs, and in summer actors play historic figures from British Columbia's past. When the legislature is in session, you can sit in the public gallery and watch British Columbia's democracy at work (custom has the opposing parties sitting 2½ sword lengths apart). Free, informative, 30- to 45-minute tours run every 20 to 30 minutes in summer and several times a day in the off-season (less frequently if school groups or private tours are coming through). Tours are obligatory on summer weekends (mid-May until Labor Day) and optional the rest of the time. ⊠ *501 Belleville St., James Bay, Downtown* ☎ *250/387–3046* ⊕ *www.leg.bc.ca* ✉ *Free.*

FAMILY
Fodor's Choice
★

Royal British Columbia Museum. This excellent museum, one of Victoria's leading attractions, traces several thousand years of British Columbian history. Especially strong is its First Peoples Gallery, home to a genuine Kwakwaka'wakw big house, an intriguing exhibit on First Nations languages, and a dramatically displayed collection of masks and other artifacts. Special exhibits, usually held between mid-May and mid-November, attract crowds despite the higher admission prices. You can skip (sometimes very long) ticket lines by booking online. In front of the museum, at Government and Belleville streets, is the **Netherlands Centennial Carillon.** With 62 bells, it's the largest bell tower in Canada; the Westminster chimes ring out every hour, and free recitals are occasionally held on Sunday afternoon. The Native Plant Garden at the museum's entrance showcases 400 indigenous plant species. Behind the main building, bordering Douglas Street, are the grassy lawns of **Thunderbird Park,** home to 10 totem poles (carved replicas of originals that are preserved in the museum). One of the oldest houses in BC, **Helmcken House** (*open late May–early Sept., daily noon–4*) was built in 1852 for pioneer doctor and statesman John Sebastian Helmcken. Inside are displays of the family's belongings, including the doctor's medical tools. Behind it is **St. Ann's School House,** built in 1858. One of British Columbia's oldest schools, it is thought to be Victoria's oldest building still standing. Both buildings are part of the Royal British Columbia Museum. ⊠ *675 Belleville St., Downtown* ☎ *250/356–7226, 888/447–7977 museum, 877/480–4887 IMAX theater* ⊕ *www.royalbcmuseum.bc.ca* 🖾 *C$24, IMAX theater C$11.95; combination ticket C$33.95.*

BRENTWOOD BAY

Fodor'sChoice ★ **Butchart Gardens.** This stunning 55-acre garden and National Historic Site has been drawing visitors since it was started in a limestone quarry in 1904. Highlights include the dramatic 70-foot Ross Fountain, the formal Japanese garden, and the intricate Italian garden complete with a gelato stand. Kids will love the old-fashioned carousel and will likely enjoy the 45-minute miniboat tours around Tod Inlet. From mid-June to mid-September the gardens are illuminated at night with hundreds of hidden lights. In July and August, jazz, blues, and classical musicians play at an outdoor stage each evening and fireworks draw crowds every Saturday night. The wheelchair- and stroller-accessible site is also home to a seed-and-gift shop, a plant identification center, two restaurants (one offering traditional afternoon tea), and a coffee shop; you can even call ahead for a picnic basket on fireworks nights. To avoid crowds, come at opening time, in the late afternoon or evening (except ultrabusy fireworks Saturday evenings), or between September and June, when the gardens are still stunning and admission rates are reduced. The grounds are especially magical at Christmas, with themed lighting and an ice rink. The gardens are a 20-minute drive north of Downtown; parking is free but fills up on fireworks Saturdays. You can get here by city Bus #75 from Douglas Street in Downtown Victoria, but service is slow and infrequent. **CVS Tours** (*877/578–5552 www.cvstours.com*) runs shuttles from Downtown Victoria. ⊠ *800 Benvenuto Ave., Brentwood Bay* ☎ *250/652–5256, 866/652–4422* ⊕ *www.butchartgardens.com* 🖾 *C$32* ☞ *Rates are lower between Sept. and mid-June.*

Butchart Gardens

SIDNEY
23 km (14 miles) north of Victoria on Hwy. 17.

Sidney, short for Sidney-by-the-Sea, is an inviting seaside town just 30 minutes north of Victoria. Home to the Washington State Ferry terminal (vessels travel to Anacortes via the San Juan Islands), and just five minutes south of the BC Ferries terminal, it's worth a stop or even a weekend visit. The streets are lined with independent shops, including a wealth of bookstores—so many, in fact, that Sidney has earned a place as Canada's only official Booktown (⊕ *www.sidneybooktown. ca*). Sidney's parklike waterfront, which houses a marine ecology center as well as cafés, restaurants, and a wheelchair-accessible waterfront path, is a launching point for kayakers, whale-watchers, and ecotour boats heading out to explore the Gulf Islands National Park Reserve offshore.

FAMILY **Shaw Ocean Discovery Centre.** A simulated ride underwater in a deep-sea elevator is just the beginning of a visit to this fun and educational marine interpretive center. Devoted entirely to the aquatic life and conservation needs of the Salish Sea—the waters south and east of Vancouver Island—the small but modern center displays local sea life, including luminous jellyfish, bright purple starfish, wolf eels, rockfish, and octopi. Hands-on activities and touch tanks delight kids, who also love the high-tech effects, including a floor projection that ripples when stepped on and a pop-up tank you can poke your head into. ⊠ *9811 Seaport Pl., Sidney* ☎ *250/665–7511* ⊕ *www.oceandiscovery.ca* ⊠ *C$15* ⌖ *Last admission 30 mins before closing.*

WHERE TO EAT

Victoria has a tremendous number and variety of restaurants for such a small city; this fact, and the glorious pantry that is Vancouver Island—think local fish, seafood, cheese, and organic fruits and veggies—keeps prices down (at least compared to Vancouver) and standards up. Restaurants in the region are generally casual. Smoking is banned in all public places, including restaurant patios, in Greater Victoria and on the Southern Gulf Islands. Victorians tend to dine early—restaurants get busy at 6 and many kitchens close by 9. Pubs, lounges, and the few open-late places mentioned here are your best options for an after-hours nosh.

Afternoon tea is a Victoria tradition, as is good coffee—despite the Starbucks invasion, there are plenty of fun and funky local caffeine purveyors around town.

Use the coordinate (⊕ B2) at the end of each listing to locate a site on the corresponding map.

WHAT IT COSTS IN CANADIAN DOLLARS

	$	$$	$$$	$$$$
Restaurants	under C$13	C$13–C$20	C$21–C$30	over C$30

Prices in the restaurants reviews are the average cost of a main course or equivalent combination of small dishes at dinner or, if dinner is not served, at lunch.

DOWNTOWN

$$$ PACIFIC NORTHWEST Fodor's Choice ★ 🍴 **Aura.** When an award-winning chef names "imagination" as his most treasured possession, you know the food here is likely to be creative, if not exquisite. The seasonal menu uses primarily local ingredients, revealing Asian influences. **Known for:** waterfront patio; local wine list; stylish dining room. [$] *Average main: C$29* ✉ *Inn at Laurel Point, 680 Montreal St., James Bay, Downtown* ☎ *250/414–6739* 🌐 *www.aurarestaurant.ca.*

$$ SEAFOOD FAMILY 🍴 **Barb's Fish & Chips.** Funky Barb's, a tin-roofed takeout shack, floats on the quay at Fisherman's Wharf, west of the Inner Harbour off St. Lawrence Street. Halibut, salmon, oysters, mussels, crab, burgers, and chowder are all prepared fresh. **Known for:** fresh seafood; harborside picnic tables. [$] *Average main: C$15* ✉ *Fisherman's Wharf, St. Lawrence St., James Bay, Downtown* ☎ *250/384–6515* 🌐 *www.barbsplace.ca* 🕒 *Closed Nov.–early Mar.*

$$$ SEAFOOD 🍴 **Blue Crab Seafood House.** Fresh-daily seafood and expansive harbor views make this airy James Bay hotel restaurant a popular lunch and dinner spot. Signature dishes include a crab cake starter, a scallop-and-prawn sauté, cedar plank salmon, and bouillabaisse in coconut green curry, but check the tempting daily specials on the blackboard as well. **Known for:** fresh seafood; harbor views; local wine list. [$] *Average main: C$30* ✉ *Coast Harbourside Hotel and Marina, 146 Kingston St., James Bay, Downtown* ☎ *250/480–1999* 🌐 *www.bluecrab.ca.*

$$$ FRENCH Fodor's Choice ★ 🍴 **Brasserie L'École.** French-country cooking shines at this informal Chinatown bistro, and the historic room—once a schoolhouse for the Chinese community—evokes a timeless brasserie, from the patina-rich fir floors to the chalkboards above the slate bar listing the day's oyster, mussel, and steak options. Owner Sean Brennan, one of the city's better-known chefs, works with local farmers and fishermen to source the best seasonal, local, and organic ingredients. **Known for:** seasonal menus; French-country fare. [$] *Average main: C$25* ✉ *1715 Government St., Downtown* ☎ *250/475–6260* 🌐 *www.lecole.ca* 🕒 *Closed Sun. and Mon. No lunch.*

$$$$ MODERN CANADIAN Fodor's Choice ★ 🍴 **Café Brio.** This intimate yet bustling Italian villa–style room has long been a Victoria favorite, mainly because of its Mediterranean-influenced atmosphere and cuisine, which is prepared primarily with locally raised ingredients. The menu changes almost daily, but you might find local rockfish paired with peperonata (sweet roasted red onion and heirloom tomato syrup), maple-glazed quail, or even an apricot dessert soup. **Known for:** house-made charcuterie; 400-label wine list; seasonal dishes. [$] *Average main: C$31* ✉ *944 Fort St., Downtown* ☎ *250/383–0009, 866/270–5461* 🌐 *www.cafe-brio.com* 🕒 *No lunch. Closed Jan.*

$$ CANADIAN FAMILY 🍴 **Mo:Lé.** A good choice for vegans, this brick-lined Chinatown café has plenty of wholesome, organic, local fare for meat eaters, too. All-day breakfasts of free-range eggs, locally made sausages, and organic spelt griddle cakes fuel a postparty, preyoga crowd. **Known for:** vegan-friendly menu; all-day breakfast; sandwiches and wraps. [$] *Average main: C$14* ✉ *554 Pandora St., Downtown* ☎ *250/385–6653* 🌐 *www.molerestaurant.ca* 🕒 *No dinner.*

$$$ MODERN CANADIAN Fodor's Choice ★ 🍴 **Olo Restaurant.** Victoria's foodies rave about this small Chinatown bistro that serves up some of the city's most innovative fare, simply yet superbly. Many items like the smoked salmon and pasta are crafted in-house, and the locally sourced menu changes often and items often have a French flair. **Known for:** grass-fed beef; basil ice cream; weekend brunch. [$] *Average main: C$25* ✉ *509 Fisgard St., Downtown* ☎ *250/590–8795* 🌐 *www.olorestaurant.com.*

$$ SEAFOOD 🍴 **Red Fish Blue Fish.** If you like your fish both yummy *and* ecologically friendly, look no further than this former shipping container on the pier at the foot of Broughton Street. From the soil-topped roof and biodegradable packaging to the sustainably harvested local seafood, this waterfront takeout shop minimizes its ecological footprint. **Known for:** local wild salmon; barbecued oysters; top-notch fish and chips. [$] *Average main: C$13* ✉ *1006 Wharf St., Downtown* ☎ *250/298–6877* 🌐 *www.redfish-bluefish.com* 🕒 *No dinner. Closed Nov.–mid-Feb.*

WHERE TO STAY

Victoria has a vast range of accommodations, with what seems like whole neighborhoods dedicated to hotels. Options range from city resorts and full-service business hotels to midpriced tour-group haunts and family-friendly motels, but the city is especially known for its lavish B&Bs in beautifully restored Victorian and Edwardian mansions. Outlying areas, such as Sooke and Saanich, pride themselves on destination spa resorts and luxurious country inns, though affordable lodgings can be found there, too.

WHAT IT COSTS IN CANADIAN DOLLARS			
$	$$	$$$	$$$$
Hotels	under C$126	C$126–C$195 C$196–C$300 over C$300

Prices in the hotel reviews are the lowest cost of a standard double room in high season.

Hotel reviews have been shortened. For full information, visit Fodors. com. Use the coordinate (⊕ B2) at the end of each listing to locate a site on the corresponding map.

DOWNTOWN

$$$$ ▦ **Fairmont Empress.** Opened in 1908, this harborside château and
HOTEL city landmark has aged gracefully. **Pros:** central location; professional
Fodor's Choice service; great spa and restaurant. **Cons:** small- to average-size rooms
★ and bathrooms; pricey. $ *Rooms from: C$349* ⊠ *721 Government St., Downtown* ☎ *250/384–8111, 866/540–4429 central reservations* ⊕ *www.fairmont.com/empress* ⇆ *436 rooms, 41 suites* ⏐⊙⏐ *No meals.*

$$$ ▦ **Hotel Grand Pacific.** The city's biggest and best health club (with a
HOTEL 25-meter indoor lap pool, yoga classes, squash courts, and state-of-the-art equipment), a great spa, complimentary bikes to ride, and a prime Inner Harbour location appeal to savvy regulars, including Seattleites stepping off the ferry across the street. **Pros:** great health club and spa; concierge; complimentary Wi-Fi. **Cons:** standard hotel decor in some rooms. $ *Rooms from: C$240* ⊠ *463 Belleville St., James Bay, Downtown* ☎ *250/386–0450, 800/663–7550* ⊕ *www.hotelgrandpacific.com* ⇆ *258 rooms, 46 suites* ⏐⊙⏐ *No meals.*

$$$ ▦ **Inn at Laurel Point.** A seaside Japanese garden, a museum-quality art col-
HOTEL lection, and water views from every room make this Asian-inspired independent hotel on the Inner Harbour's quiet south shore a favorite among Victoria regulars. **Pros:** views; quiet, parklike setting; terrific on-site dining. **Cons:** 10-minute walk from Downtown. $ *Rooms from: C$239* ⊠ *680 Montreal St., James Bay, Downtown* ☎ *250/386–8721, 800/663–7667* ⊕ *www.laurelpoint.com* ⇆ *135 rooms, 65 suites* ⏐⊙⏐ *No meals.*

ROCKLAND

$$$ ▦ **Abbeymoore Manor.** This 1912 mansion has the wide verandas, dark
B&B/INN wainscoting, and high ceilings of its era, but the attitude is informal and
Fodor's Choice welcoming, from the superhelpful hosts to the free snacks to the coffee
★ on tap all day. **Pros:** good value; friendly hosts; excellent service. **Cons:** a mile from the Inner Harbour; often booked in advance. $ *Rooms from: C$219* ⊠ *1470 Rockland Ave., Rockland* ☎ *250/370–1470, 888/801– 1811* ⊕ *www.abbeymoore.com* ⇆ *5 rooms, 2 suites* ⏐⊙⏐ *Breakfast.*

BRENTWOOD BAY

$$$ ▦ **Brentwood Bay Resort & Spa.** Every room has a private ocean-view
RESORT patio or balcony at this adult-oriented boutique resort in a tiny sea-
Fodor's Choice side village. **Pros:** magnificent setting; close to Butchart Gardens; free
★ Wi-Fi. **Cons:** pricey rates; 30-minute drive from Downtown. $ *Rooms from: C$295* ⊠ *849 Verdier Ave., Brentwood Bay* ☎ *250/544–2079, 888/544–2079* ⊕ *www.brentwoodbayresort.com* ⇆ *30 rooms, 3 suites, 2 villas* ⏐⊙⏐ *No meals.*

SIDNEY

$$$ HOTEL [icon] **Sidney Pier Hotel & Spa.** Stylish and ecologically friendly, this glass-and-stone boutique hotel on the parklike waterfront has helped introduce Sidney to more travelers. **Pros:** lovely views; eco-friendly vibe; free airport and ferry shuttle in summer; pet friendly. **Cons:** 30 minutes from Downtown; no pool. [$] *Rooms from: C$199* ✉ *9805 Seaport Pl., Sidney* ☎ *250/655–9445, 866/659–9445* 🌐 *www.sidneypier.com* 🛏 *46 rooms, 9 suites* 🍴 *No meals.*

NIGHTLIFE AND PERFORMING ARTS

Victoria isn't the busiest destination after dark. But there are two important local sources to help visitors keep on top of the happenings, whether they're looking for a quiet pint, a music festival, or a night on the town. One is a monthly digest of arts and nightlife; the other is the local tourist office, which also sells tickets.

NIGHTLIFE

DOWNTOWN

BARS **Canoe Brewpub.** One of Victoria's biggest and best pub patios overlooks the Gorge, the waterway just north of the Inner Harbour. The interior of the former power station has been stylishly redone with high ceilings, exposed bricks, and wood beams. There's a wide range of in-house brews, top-notch bar snacks, and an all-ages restaurant. Live music from Thursday to Saturday adds to its happening vibe. ✉ *450 Swift St., Downtown* ☎ *250/361–1940* 🌐 *www.canoebrewpub.com.*

Clive's Classic Lounge. Leading Victoria's cocktail renaissance, the bartenders at this classic lounge in the Chateau Victoria Hotel make their own syrups and bitters and use fresh juices in their traditional and contemporary drinks. Try one of their interesting liquor flights. ✉ *Chateau Victoria Hotel, 740 Burdett Ave., Downtown* ☎ *250/361–5684* 🌐 *www.clivesclassiclounge.com.*

Swans Brewpub. A stunning array of First Nations masks and other artworks hangs from the open rafters in this popular Downtown brewpub, where jazz, blues, and swing bands play nightly. ✉ *506 Pandora Ave., Downtown* ☎ *250/361–3310* 🌐 *www.swanshotel.com.*

MUSIC CLUBS **Hermann's Jazz Club.** Dinner, dancing, and live jazz, blues, and Dixie are on the menu at this venerable Downtown restaurant and jazz club. ✉ *753 View St., Downtown* ☎ *250/388–9166* 🌐 *www.hermannsjazz.com.*

PERFORMING ARTS

MUSIC

Summer in the Square. Free jazz, classical, and folk concerts; cultural events; and more run all summer at Centennial Square, which is next to City Hall. Free lunchtime concerts are offered Tuesday to Thursday from noon to 1, from July through September. ✉ *Centennial Sq., Pandora Ave. at Douglas St., Downtown* ☎ *250/361–0500* 🌐 *www.victoria.ca/cityvibe.*

Victoria Jazz Society. Watch for music events hosted by this group, which also organizes the annual TD Victoria International JazzFest in late June and the Vancouver Island Blues Bash in early September. ✉ *Victoria* ☎ *250/388–4423* 🌐 *www.jazzvictoria.ca.*

19

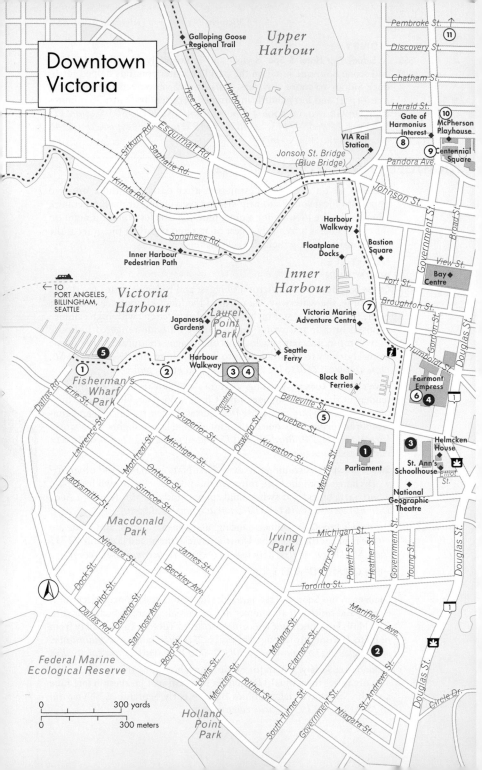

Downtown Victoria

Upper Harbour

Pembroke St. ↑

Discovery St.

Chatham St.

Galloping Goose
Regional Trail

Tree Rd.

Harbour Rd.

Esquimalt Rd.

Sitkum Rd.

Saghalie Rd.

Kimta Rd.

Songhees Rd.

Inner Harbour
Pedestrian Path

Jonson St. Bridge
(Blue Bridge)

VIA Rail
Station

Herald St.

Gate of
Harmonious
Interest ⑧

McPherson
Playhouse ⑩

⑪

⑨ Centennial
Square

Pandora Ave.

Johnson St.

Harbour
Walkway

Floatplane
Docks

Bastion
Square

Government St.

Broad St.

View St.

Bay
Centre

Inner
Harbour

Fort St.

Broughton St.

Gordon St.

Douglas St.

⑦

TO
PORT ANGELES,
BILLINGHAM,
SEATTLE

Victoria
Harbour

Japanese
Gardens

Laurel
Point
Park

Harbour
Walkway

Victoria Marine
Adventure Centre

Seattle
Ferry

Humboldt St.

Fairmont
Empress

⑤

①

Fisherman's
Wharf
Park

②

③ ④

Black Ball
Ferries

⑥ ④

Dallas Rd.

Erie St.

Belleville St.

Quebec St.

⑤

Helmcken
House

Pendral St.

St. Ann's
Schoolhouse

③

Lawrence St.

Superior St.

Oswego St.

Kingston St.

Menzies St.

Parliament ①

Elliot
St.

Montreal St.

Michigan St.

Onterio St.

Simcoe St.

National
Geographic
Theatre

Macdonald
Park

Ladysmith St.

Irving
Park

Michigan St.

Niagara St.

James St.

Beckley Ave.

Parry St.

Powell St.

Heather St.

Government St.

Young St.

Toronto St.

Douglas St.

Dock St.

Pilot St.

Oswego St.

San Jose Ave.

Dallas Rd.

Boyd St.

Medana St.

Clarence St.

Marifield Ave.

②

St. Andrews St.

Douglas St.

Circle Dr.

Federal Marine
Ecological Reserve

Lewis St.

Menzies St.

Rithet St.

South Turner St.

Government St.

Niagara St.

Holland
Point
Park

0 ————— 300 yards

0 ————— 300 meters

KEY

🛈 *Tourist information*

⛴ *Ferry*

- - - *Pedestrian trail*

1 *Exploring sights*

① *Hotels & Restaurants*

SPORTS AND THE OUTDOORS

BIKING

Victoria is a bike-friendly town with more bicycle commuters than any other city in Canada. Bike racks on city buses, bike lanes on Downtown streets, and tolerant drivers all help, as do the city's three long-distance cycling routes, which mix car-free paths and low-traffic scenic routes.

BIKE ROUTES

Galloping Goose Regional Trail. Following an old rail bed, this 55-km (35-mile) route officially starts at the Vic West end of Johnson Street Bridge, which connects Downtown Victoria to Vic West. The multiuse trail runs across old rail trestles and through forests west to the town of Sooke, finishing just past Sooke Potholes Provincial Park. Just north of Downtown it links with the Lochside Regional Trail to the BC Ferries terminal at Swartz Bay, creating a nearly continuous 55-mile car-free route. It has earned many accolades, deservedly so. ⊠ *Johnson St. Bridge, Vic West* ☎ *250/478–3344* ⊕ *www.crd.bc.ca/ parks* ⊡ *Free.*

Lochside Regional Trail. This fairly level, mostly car-free route follows an old rail bed for 29 km (18 miles) past farmland, wineries, and beaches from the ferry terminals at Swartz Bay and Sidney to Downtown Victoria. It joins the Seaside Touring Route at Cordova Bay and meets the Galloping Goose Trail just north of Downtown Victoria. ⊠ *Sidney* ☎ *250/478–3344* ⊕ *www.crd.bc.ca/parks.*

Victoria Seaside Touring Route. Starting at the corner of Government and Belleville streets on the Inner Harbour, this 39-km (24-mile) route along city streets and coastal roads, marked with bright yellow signs, leads past Fisherman's Wharf and along the Dallas Road waterfront to Beacon Hill Park. It then follows the seashore to Cordova Bay, where it connects with Victoria's other two long-distance routes: the Lochside and Galloping Goose regional trails. ⊠ *Government St. at Belleville St., Inner Harbour, Downtown.*

BIKE RENTALS AND TOURS

Cycle BC Rentals. This centrally located shop rents bikes for adults and children, as well as bike trailers, motorcycles, and scooters. ⊠ *685 Humboldt St., Downtown* ☎ *250/380–2453, 866/380–2453* ⊕ *www.cyclebc.ca.*

Cycletreks. Besides renting bikes, this company runs bike tours of Victoria, multiday trips to the Gulf Islands, and vineyard tours of the Saanich Peninsula and the Cowichan Valley. Their self-guided trips include bikes, maps, and a ride to Butchart Gardens or the end of the Galloping Goose or Lochside trail so that you can pedal back. ⊠ *1000 Wharf St., Downtown* ☎ *250/386–3147* ⊕ *www.cycletreks.com.*

HIKING AND WALKING

Victoria is one of the most pedestrian-friendly cities in North America. Waterfront pathways make it possible to stroll virtually all around Victoria's waterfront. For some interesting self-guided walks around the city's historic areas, check out ⊕ *www.victoria.ca/tours* or pick up a free walking-tour map at the city's visitor information center. Though popular with cyclists, the area's long-distance paths are also great for long walks. For views and elevation, check out the trail networks in the area's many provincial and regional parks.

Mount Douglas Park. Trails through the forest to the 260-meter (853-foot) summit of Mt. Douglas reward hikers with a 360-degree view of Victoria, the Saanich Peninsula, and the mountains of Washington State. ⊠ *Off Cedar Hill Rd., Saanich* ☎ *250/475–5522* ⊕ *www.saanich.ca.*

WHALE-WATCHING

The following companies provide whale-watching excursions from Victoria.

FAMILY **Orca Spirit Adventures.** This company offers year-round tours with both Zodiacs and covered vessels. Boats are equipped with hydrophones and all guides are marine biologists. In summer a three-hour tour starts at C$115. It offers free hotel pickup/drop-off service. ⊠ *950 Wharf St., Victoria* ☎ *250/383–8411, 888/672–6722* ⊕ *www.orcaspirit.com.*

FAMILY **Prince of Whales.** Victoria's biggest whale-watching company offers a whole range of marine excursions, from three-hour boat or Zodiac tours from Victoria, to five-hour trips that include a stop at Butchart Gardens, to one-way or round-trip crossings between Vancouver and Victoria; all sailings have naturalists on board. Zodiac trips cost C$120 and leave year-round; covered boat sailings on the *Ocean Magic II* are C$120 and run from April to October; and Victoria to Butchart Garden trips run from late May to late September (the C$150 fare includes admission to the gardens). The company's Vancouver to Victoria crossings, running from late May to late September on the 94-passenger *Salish Sea Dream,* are a great time-saver, combining a sailing to or from Victoria with a whale-watching trip. A stop at the Butchart Gardens or return flights by floatplane or helicopter are options, too. The most popular trip, billed as The Ultimate Day Trip, includes a whale-watching trip from Vancouver to Victoria, a stop in Downtown Victoria, a bus transfer to Butchart Gardens, and a sunset sailing back to Vancouver. This C$310 trip runs daily from late May to late September. The company's Victoria office is on the Inner Harbour Causeway, below the Visitor Info Centre. ⊠ *812 Wharf St., Lower Causeway Level, Downtown* ☎ *250/383–4884, 888/383–4884* ⊕ *www.princeofwhales.com.*

19

SHOPPING

In Victoria, as in the rest of British Columbia, the most popular souvenirs are First Nations arts and crafts, which you can pick up at shops, galleries, street markets, and—in some cases—directly from artists' studios. Look for silver jewelry and cedar boxes carved with traditional images and, especially around Duncan (in the Cowichan Valley), the thick hand-knit sweaters made by the Cowichan people. BC wines, from shops in Victoria or directly from the wineries, make good souvenirs, as most are unavailable outside the province. Shopping in Victoria is easy: virtually everything is in the Downtown area on or near Government Street stretching north from the Fairmont Empress hotel.

DOWNTOWN
AREAS AND MALLS
Chinatown. Exotic fruits and vegetables, children's toys, wicker fans, fabric slippers, and other Chinese imports fill the shops along Fisgard Street. Fan Tan Alley, a narrow lane off Fisgard Street, has more nouveau-hippie goods, with a record store and yoga studio tucked in among its tiny storefronts. ⊠ *Downtown.*

Lower Johnson Street. This row of candy-color Victorian-era shopfronts in LoJo (Lower Johnson) is Victoria's hub for independent fashion boutiques. Storefronts—some closet size—are filled with local designers' wares, funky boutiques, and shops selling ecologically friendly clothes of hemp and organic cotton. ⊠ *Johnson St., between Government and Store Sts., Downtown.*

SPECIALTY STORES
Artina's. Canadian-made jewelry—all handmade, one-of-a-kind pieces—fills the display cases at this unique jewelry shop. ⊠ *1002 Government St., Downtown* ☎ *250/386–7000* ⊕ *www.artinas-jewellery.com.*

Cowichan Trading. First Nations jewelry, art, moccasins, and Cowichan sweaters are the focus at this long-established outlet. ⊠ *1328 Government St., Downtown* ☎ *250/383–0321* ⊕ *www.cowichantrading.com.*

Hill's Native Art. Of the many First Nations stores you'll come across, Hill's is one of the best, offering everything from affordable souvenirs to original First Nations totems, masks, and jewelry as well as Inuit sculptures. ⊠ *1008 Government St., Downtown* ☎ *250/385–3911* ⊕ *www.hills.ca.*

Munro's Books. Move over, Chapters: this beautifully restored 1909 former bank now houses one of Canada's best-stocked independent bookstores. Deals abound in the remainders bin. ⊠ *1108 Government St., Downtown* ☎ *250/382–2464* ⊕ *www.munrobooks.com.*

Fodor's Choice
★   **Silk Road.** Tea aspires to new heights in this chic emporium. Shelves are stacked with more than 300 intriguing varieties; some you can enjoy in flights at an impressive tasting bar, and others have been restyled into aromatherapy remedies and spa treatments, including a green tea facial, which you can try out in the tiny spa downstairs. ⊠ *1624 Government St., Downtown* ☎ *250/704–2688* ⊕ *www.silkroadtea.com.*

TRAVEL SMART PACIFIC NORTHWEST

GETTING HERE AND AROUND

∎ AIR TRAVEL

It takes about 5 hours to fly nonstop to Seattle or Portland from New York, 4 hours from Chicago, and 2½ hours from Los Angeles. Flights from New York to Vancouver take about 6 hours nonstop; from Chicago, 4½ hours nonstop; and from Los Angeles, 3 hours nonstop. Flying from Seattle to Portland takes just under an hour; flying from Portland to Vancouver takes an hour and 15 minutes; and from Seattle to Vancouver about 45 minutes.

Airlines and Airports AirlineandAirport-Links.com. ⊕ www.airlineandairportlinks.com.

Airline Security Issues Transportation Security Administration. ☎ 866/289–9673 ⊕ www.tsa.gov.

AIRPORTS

The main gateways to the Pacific Northwest are Portland International Airport (PDX), Sea-Tac International Airport (SEA), and Vancouver International Airport (YVR).

Airport Information Portland International Airport (PDX). ☎ 503/460–4234, 877/739–4636 ⊕ www.flypdx.com. **Sea-Tac International Airport (SEA).** ☎ 206/787–5388, 800/544–1965 ⊕ www.portseattle.org/seatac. **Vancouver International Airport (YVR).** ☎ 604/207–7077 ⊕ www.yvr.ca.

FLIGHTS

Many international carriers serve the Pacific Northwest with direct flights. These include Air France, All Nippon Airways, British Airways, Cathay Pacific, Emirates, Icelandair, Japan Airlines, and Lufthansa. Vancouver has the most connections with international cities, but Seattle's a close second. U.S. carriers serving the area include Alaska Airlines, American, Delta, and United. JetBlue has daily direct flights from New York's JFK Airport, Logan International in Boston, and Los Angeles's Long Beach Airport to both Seattle and Portland. Virgin America has daily direct flights to Seattle from San Francisco and Los Angeles (LAX). Frontier Airlines Skywest (via Delta), and United Express provide frequent service between cities in Washington, Oregon, Idaho, Montana, and California. Southwest Airlines has frequent nonstop service to Seattle and Portland from cities in California, Nevada, Arizona, and Texas, as well as Baltimore, Chicago, and some other parts of the country. The major regional carrier in western Canada is Air Canada (and its subsidiary, Air Canada Express), which has flights from Seattle and Portland to Vancouver and Victoria, along with many direct flights between Vancouver and major U.S. cities outside the Northwest.

Airline Contacts Air Canada/Air Canada Express. ☎ 888/247–2262 ⊕ www.aircanada. com. **Alaska Airlines.** ☎ 800/252–7522 ⊕ www.alaskaair.com. **American Airlines.** ☎ 800/433–7300 ⊕ www.aa.com. **Delta Airlines.** ☎ 800/221–1212 ⊕ www.delta. com. **Frontier Airlines.** ☎ 801/401–9000 ⊕ www.flyfrontier.com. **Japan Airlines.** ☎ 800/525–3663 ⊕ www.jal.com. **jetBlue.** ☎ 800/538–2583 ⊕ www.jetblue.com. **Southwest Airlines.** ☎ 800/435–9792 ⊕ www. southwest.com. **United Airlines.** ☎ 800/864–8331 ⊕ www.united.com. **Virgin America.** ☎ 877/359–8474 ⊕ www.virginamerica.com.

∎ BOAT AND FERRY TRAVEL

Ferries play an important part in the transportation network of the Pacific Northwest. Some are the sole connection to islands in Puget Sound and to small towns and islands along the west coast of British Columbia. Each day ferries transport thousands of commuters to and from work in the coastal cities. Always comfortable, convenient, and providing spectacular views, ferries are also one of the best ways for you to get a feel for the region and its ties to the sea.

Generally, the best times for travel are 9–3 and after 7 pm on weekdays. In July and August you may have to wait hours to take a car aboard one of the popular ferries, such as those to the San Juan Islands. Walk-on space is almost always available; if possible, leave your car behind. Reservations aren't taken for most domestic routes in Washington.

WASHINGTON AND OREGON

Washington State Ferries carries millions of passengers and vehicles each year on 10 routes between 20 points on Puget Sound, the San Juan Islands, and Sidney, British Columbia. Onboard services vary depending on the size of the ferry, but many ships have a cafeteria, vending machines, newspaper and tourist-information kiosks, arcade games, and restrooms with family facilities. There are discounted fares in off-peak months.

Black Ball Transport's MV *Coho* makes daily crossings year-round from Port Angeles, WA, to Victoria. The *Coho* can carry 800 passengers and 100 cars across the Strait of Juan de Fuca in 1½ hours. Clipper Vacations operates the passenger-only *Victoria Clipper* jet catamaran service between Seattle and Victoria year-round and between Seattle and the San Juan Islands May through September. ■TIP→ Victoria Clipper fares are less expensive if booked at least one day in advance, tickets for children under 12 are discounted, and some great package deals are often available online (be sure to ask about any other promotions or deals, too).

Contacts **Black Ball Transport.** ☎ 250/386–2202 in Victoria, 360/457–4491 in Port Angeles, 888/993–3779 ⊕ www.cohoferry. com. **Clipper Vacations.** ☎ 206/448–5000 in Seattle, 250/382–8100 in Victoria, 800/888–2535 ⊕ www.clippervacations.com. **King County Water Taxi.** ☎ 206/477–3979 ⊕ kingcounty.gov/transportation/kcdot/WaterTaxi. **Washington State Ferries.** ☎ 800/843–3779 automated line in WA and BC, 888/808–7977 WA and BC reservations, 206/464–6400 ⊕ www.wsdot.wa.gov/ferries.

BRITISH COLUMBIA

British Columbia Ferries operates passenger and vehicle service between the mainland and Victoria and elsewhere. Most ferries take reservations.

Information **British Columbia Ferries.** ☎ 250/386–3431 in Victoria, 888/223–3779 ⊕ www.bcferries.com.

SIGHTSEEING

Argosy cruising vessels make sightseeing, dinner, weekend brunch, and special-event cruises around Elliott Bay, Lake Union, Lake Washington, the Ballard Locks, and other Seattle waterways.

From Portland, the *Portland Spirit, Willamette Star,* and *Crystal Dolphin* make sightseeing and dinner cruises on the Willamette and Columbia Rivers. The high-speed *Explorer* takes day trips from Portland to the Columbia River, and offers a one-way option for cyclists to return via a 45-mile historic highway route. Departing from Cascade Locks, Oregon (45 minutes east of Portland), the stern-wheeler *Columbia Gorge* cruises the Columbia River.

Information **Argosy Cruises.** ☎ 206/623–1445, 888/623–1445 ⊕ www.argosycruises. com. **Portland Spirit River Cruises.** ☎ 503/224–3900 ⊕ www.portlandspirit.com.

▌ BUS TRAVEL

Greyhound services the Washington–Oregon region. BoltBus service runs between Vancouver, Bellingham, Seattle, and Portland and features sleek new buses with Wi-Fi, extra legroom, reserved seating, and power outlets. Experience Oregon in Eugene operates charter bus services and scheduled sightseeing tours that last from a few hours to several days. Greyhound serves many towns in Washington, Oregon, and British Columbia, and provides frequent service on popular runs. Quick Shuttle runs buses from Sea-Tac Airport, Downtown Seattle, and Bellingham to various Vancouver spots and hotels.

Pacific Coach Lines runs multiple daily buses between Vancouver and Victoria, including a ferry ride across the Strait of Georgia, and between Vancouver and Whistler Village. The company also has connections from Vancouver International Airport and Downtown Vancouver.

Bus Information BoltBus. ☎ *877/265–8287* ⊕ *www.boltbus.com.* **Experience Oregon.** ☎ *541/342–2662, 888/342–2662* ⊕ *www. experienceoregon.com.* **Greyhound Lines.** ☎ *800/231–2222, 214/849–8100 outside U.S., 800/661–8747 in Canada* ⊕ *www.greyhound. com.* **Pacific Coach Lines.** ☎ *800/661–1725, 604/662–7575 in Vancouver* ⊕ *www.pacific-coach.com.* **Quick Shuttle.** ☎ *800/665–2122, 604/940–4428 in Vancouver* ⊕ *www.quick-coach.com.*

SIGHTSEEING

Gray Line operates a few day trips from Portland, Victoria, and Vancouver, including tours to Multnomah Falls and the Columbia River Gorge, Willamette Valley, Whistler Village, and Vancouver and Victoria attractions, and schedules a variety of popular in-city hop-on hop-off bus tours.

Gray Line. ☎ *855/624–4298 toll-free Portland, 503/241–7373 local Portland, 604/451–1600 local Vancouver, 877/451–1777 toll-free Vancouver, 250/385–6553 local Victoria, 855/385–6553 toll-free Victoria* ⊕ *www.grayline.com.*

▌ CAR TRAVEL

Driver's licenses from other countries are valid in the United States and Canada. International driving permits (IDPs)—available from the American and Canadian automobile associations and Canada's National Auto Club, and, in the United Kingdom, from the Automobile Association, Royal Automobile Club, and some post office branches—are a good idea. Valid only in conjunction with your regular driver's license, these permits are universally recognized; having one may spare you from difficulties with local authorities.

Bookstores, gas stations, convenience stores, and rest stops sell maps (about $5) and multiregion road atlases (about $14). Along larger highways, roadside stops with restrooms, fast-food restaurants, and sundries stores are well spaced. Police and tow trucks patrol major highways and lend assistance.

TRAVEL TIMES FROM SEATTLE BY CAR	
Portland	3–3½ hours
Vancouver	2½–3 hours
Victoria	2½–3 hour drive to Vancouver; 1½-hour ferry ride from Vancouver
Mount Rainier National Park (Paradise or Longmire entrances)	2½ hours
North Cascades National Park	3–3½ hours
Olympic National Park	2½ hours to Port Angeles; 1 hour from Port Angeles to Hurricane Ridge
Mt. St. Helens	3–3½ hours
Spokane	4½–5 hours
Yakima Valley	2–2½ hours

TRAVEL TIMES FROM PORTLAND BY CAR	
Bend	3½–4 hours
Crater Lake National Park	4½–5 hours
Columbia River Gorge/Mt. Hood	1½ hours
Willamette Valley	1½–2 hours

BORDER CROSSING

See also Passports in Essentials below.

You will need a valid passport to cross the border; passport cards and enhanced driver's licenses are also accepted for land and sea crossings only. In addition, drivers must carry owner registration and proof of insurance coverage, which is compulsory in Canada. The Canadian Non-Resident Inter-Provincial Motor Vehicle Liability Insurance Card, available from any U.S. insurance company, is accepted as evidence of financial responsibility in Canada. If you are driving a car that is not registered in your name, carry a letter from the owner that authorizes your use of the vehicle.

The main entry point into British Columbia from the United States by car is on Interstate 5 at Blaine, Washington, 30 miles south of Vancouver. Three highways enter British Columbia from the east: Highway 1, or the Trans-Canada Highway; Highway 3, or the Crowsnest Highway, which crosses southern British Columbia; and Highway 16, the Yellowhead Highway, which runs through northern British Columbia from the Rocky Mountains to Prince Rupert. From Alaska and the Yukon, take the Alaska Highway (from Fairbanks) or the Klondike Highway (from Skagway or Dawson City).

Border-crossing procedures are usually quick and simple. Every British Columbia border crossing is open 24 hours (except the one at Aldergrove, which is open from 8 am to midnight). The Interstate 5 border crossing at Blaine, Washington (also known as the Douglas, or Peace Arch, border crossing), is one of the busiest border crossings between the United States and Canada. An alternate route, the Pacific Highway border crossing (also known as the "truck crossing"), is just east of the Peace Arch crossing and serves all vehicles, not just trucks. For updated information on border wait times, check local radio traffic reports and watch for electronic signs on the main highways.

CAR RENTALS

■TIP➜ Make sure that a confirmed reservation guarantees you a car. Agencies sometimes overbook, particularly for busy weekends and holiday periods.

Unless you only visit Seattle, Portland, and Vancouver, you will need to rent a car for at least part of your trip. It's possible to get around the big cities by public transportation and taxis, but once you go outside city limits, your options are limited. National lines like Greyhound do provide service between major towns, and Amtrak has limited service between points in Washington, Oregon, and British Columbia (allowing you to get from, say, Seattle to Portland, by train), but it is nearly impossible to get to and around the major recreation areas and national parks of each state without your own wheels. For example, there is no public transportation from Seattle to Mount Rainier National Park.

Rates in Seattle begin at $31 a day ($168 per week) for an economy car. This does not include the 17.3% tax. The tax on rentals at Sea-Tac Airport, which includes an airport concession fee, is more than 30%, so try to rent from a Downtown branch, where base rental rates are often lower, too. Rates in Portland begin at $33 a day and $168 a week, not including the 17% tax. Rates in Vancouver begin at about C$20 a day or C$115 a week, usually including unlimited mileage. Note that summer rates in all cities can be absurd (up to $75 per day for a compact); book as far in advance as possible, and if you find a good deal, grab it. Car rentals in British Columbia also incur a 12% sales tax. An additional 17% Concession Recovery Fee, charged by the airport authority for retail space in the terminal, is levied at airport locations.

All the major agencies are represented in the region. If you're planning to cross the U.S.–Canadian border with your rental car, discuss it with the agency to see what's involved.

In the Pacific Northwest you must be 21 to rent a car. Car seats are compulsory for infants and toddlers; older children are required to sit in booster seats until they are eight years old or 4 feet, 9 inches tall. (In British Columbia, children up to 40 pounds or 18 kilos in weight must use a child seat; booster seats are required for children up to nine years old or 145 cm tall.) In the United States nonresidents need a reservation voucher, passport, driver's license, and insurance for each driver.

ROAD CONDITIONS

Winter driving can present challenges. In coastal areas the mild, damp climate contributes to frequently wet roadways. Snowfalls generally occur in low-lying Portland, Seattle, and Vancouver only once or twice a year, but when snow does fall, traffic grinds to a halt and roadways become treacherous and stay that way until the snow melts.

Tire chains, studs, or snow tires are essential equipment for winter travel in mountain areas. If you're planning to drive into high elevations, be sure to check the weather forecast beforehand. Even the main-highway mountain passes can close because of snow conditions. In winter state and provincial highway departments operate snow-advisory telephone lines that give pass conditions.

ROADSIDE EMERGENCIES

Contacts Oregon State Police. ☎ *503/378–3720* ⊕ *www.oregon.gov/OSP.* **Washington State Patrol.** ☎ *911 for emergencies* ⊕ *www.wsdot.wa.gov.*

∎ TRAIN TRAVEL

Amtrak, the U.S. passenger rail system, has daily service to the Pacific Northwest from the Midwest and California. The Empire Builder takes a northern route through Minnesota and Montana from Chicago to Spokane, from which separate legs continue to Seattle and Portland. The Coast Starlight begins in Los Angeles; makes stops throughout California, western Oregon, and Washington; and terminates in Seattle.

The Amtrak Cascades trains travel between Seattle and Vancouver and between Seattle, Portland, and Eugene. The trip from Seattle to Portland takes roughly 3½ hours and costs $26–$63 for a coach seat each way; this is a pleasant alternative to a mind-numbing drive down Interstate 5. The trip from Seattle to Vancouver takes roughly 4½ hours and costs $32–$75 one-way. The Empire Builder's northern leg between Seattle and Spokane takes eight hours and costs $45–$121 each way. The southern leg travels between Portland and Spokane (7½ hours, $45–$121 one-way), with part of the route running through the Columbia River Gorge. From Portland to Eugene, the trip is just under three hours; the cost is $21–$50.

∎**TIP→** Book Amtrak tickets at least a few days in advance, especially if you're traveling between Seattle and Portland on summer weekends.

Contact Amtrak. ☎ *800/872–7245* ⊕ *www.amtrak.com.*

ESSENTIALS

▌ ACCOMMODATIONS

The lodgings we list are the cream of the crop in each price category. Prices are for a standard double room in high season and excluding tax and service charges. Seattle room tax is 15.6%. Elsewhere in Washington it ranges from 10% to 16%. Portland room tax is 11.5% (13.5% at hotels with 50 or more rooms) while elsewhere in Oregon it ranges from 7% to 12%. Vancouver room tax is 16% with elsewhere in British Columbia ranging from 13% to 15%. Most hotels and other lodgings require you to give your credit-card details before they will confirm your reservation.

BED-AND-BREAKFASTS

The Pacific Northwest is known for its vast range of bed-and-breakfasts, which are found everywhere from busy urban areas to casual country farms and coastal retreats. Many B&Bs here provide full gourmet breakfasts, and some have kitchens that guests can use. Other popular amenities to ask about are fireplaces, jetted bathtubs, outdoor hot tubs, and area activities.

The regional B&B organizations listed here can provide information on reputable establishments.

Reservation Services Airbnb. ⊕ *www. airbnb.com.* **American Bed & Breakfast Association.** ⊕ *www.abba.com.* **BBCanada. com.** ⊕ *www.bbcanada.com.* **British Columbia Bed and Breakfast Innkeepers Guild.** ⊕ *www.bcsbestbnbs.com.* **British Columbia Bed and Breakfasts.** ⊕ *www.bcbbonly.com.* **The Canadian Bed and Breakfast Guide.** ☎ *905/641–8484* ⊕ *www.canadianbandb-guide.ca.* **Oregon Bed and Breakfast Guild.** ☎ *800/944–6196* ⊕ *www.obbg.org.* **Washington Bed and Breakfast Guild.** ☎ *253/987–6619* ⊕ *www.wbbg.com.*

HOTELS

When booking a room, always call the hotel's direct number (if one is available) rather than the central reservations number—you'll often get a better price.

Deals can often be found at hotel websites. Always ask about special packages or corporate rates. Many properties offer special weekend rates, sometimes up to 50% off regular prices. However, these deals are usually not extended during peak summer months, when hotels are normally full. All hotels listed have private bath unless otherwise noted.

▌ CUSTOMS AND DUTIES

You're always allowed to bring goods of a certain value back home without having to pay any duty or import tax. But there's a limit on the amount of tobacco and liquor you can bring back duty-free, and some countries have separate limits for perfumes; for exact figures, check with your customs department. The values of so-called "duty-free" goods are included in these amounts. When you shop abroad, save all your receipts, as customs inspectors may ask to see them as well as the items you purchased. If the total value of your goods is more than the duty-free limit, you'll have to pay a tax (most often a flat percentage) on the value of everything beyond that limit.

U.S. Information U.S. Customs and Border Protection. ☎ *877/227–5511* ⊕ *www.cbp.gov.*

Information in Canada Canada Border Services Agency. ☎ *204/983–3500, 800/461–9999 toll-free within Canada* ⊕ *www. cbsa-asfc.gc.ca.*

▌ EATING OUT

Pacific Northwest cuisine highlights regional seafood and locally grown, organic produce, often prepared in styles that reflect an Asian influence (Seattle, Victoria, and Vancouver have large Asian populations) or incorporate European (often French or Italian) influences. *See our Flavors of the Pacific Northwest feature at the beginning of this book.*

The restaurants we list are the cream of the crop in each price category. Please note that restaurant prices listed as "Average Cost" indicate the price of a main course at dinner; or if dinner is not served, at lunch.

MEALS AND MEALTIMES

Unless otherwise noted, the restaurants listed here are open daily for lunch and dinner.

PAYING

Credit cards—Visa and MasterCard, in particular—are widely accepted in most restaurants, especially in Seattle, Portland, and Vancouver. Debit cards are widely accepted in coffeehouses, delis, and grocery stores.

WINES, BEER, AND SPIRITS

Oregon, Washington, and British Columbia all have thriving wineries, and many restaurants in major cities and many small towns, and even in wilderness areas, take their wine lists very seriously. Most of Washington's vineyards are east of the Cascades in the south-central part of the state; you'll also find more than 100 wineries in Woodinville, near Seattle. Oregon's wineries mostly lie in the valleys between the southern Cascades and the coast. British Columbia wine-making has become increasingly prominent, with many wineries in the Okanagan Valley. The Washington State Wine Commission (⊕ *www.washingtonwine.org*) and the Oregon Wine Board (⊕ *www.oregonwine. org*) both maintain websites with facts, history, and information on local wineries. The British Columbia Wine Institute's website (⊕ *www.winebc.com*) has facts and information on individual wineries.

Oregon has more than 200 microbreweries, and Washington has no shortage of excellent local microbrews. Both states have festivals and events celebrating their brews—Seattle's Fremont neighborhood has its own Oktoberfest. The website for the Washington Brewers Guild (⊕ *www. washingtonbeer.com*) has info on breweries in the state and events throughout

the Pacific Northwest. The Oregon Brewers Guild (⊕ *www.oregoncraftbeer.org*) also has links to breweries and information on events.

You must be 21 to buy alcohol in Washington and Oregon. The legal drinking age in British Columbia is 19.

▐ MONEY

Prices listed for sights and attractions are for adults. Substantially reduced fees are almost always available for children, students, and senior citizens.

CURRENCY AND EXCHANGE

The units of currency in Canada are the Canadian dollar (C$) and the cent, in almost the same denominations as U.S. currency ($5, $10, $20, 5¢, 10¢, 25¢, etc.). Canada stopped distributing pennies in 2013. C$1 and C$2 coins (known as a "loonie," because of the loon that appears on the coin, and a "toonie," respectively) are used in lieu of bills. Check with a bank or other financial institution for the current exchange rate. A good way to be sure you're getting the best exchange rate is by using your credit card or ATM/debit card. The issuing bank will convert your bill at the current rate, though foreign transaction fees may still be added.

▐ PASSPORTS

All people traveling by air between the United States and Canada are required to present a passport to enter or reenter the United States. To enter Canada (or more precisely, to reenter the United States from Canada) by land or sea you need to present either a valid passport or a U.S. Passport Card—sort of a "passport lite" that is only valid for land or sea crossings from Canada, Mexico, the Caribbean, or Bermuda. Enhanced drivers licenses, issued by Washington and other border states, can also be used for land or sea crossings.

For more information on border crossings, see Car Travel.

U.S. passports are valid for 10 years. You must apply in person if you're getting a passport for the first time; if your previous passport was lost, stolen, or damaged; or if your previous passport has expired and was issued more than 15 years ago or when you were under 16. All children under 18 must appear in person to apply for or renew a passport. Both parents must accompany any child under 14 (or send a notarized statement with their permission) and provide proof of their relationship to the child.

The cost to apply for a new passport is $135 for adults, $105 for children under 16; renewals are $110. Allow up to six weeks for processing, both for first-time passports and renewals. For an expediting fee of $60, you can reduce this time to about three weeks. If your trip is less than two weeks away, you can get a passport even more rapidly by going to a passport office with the necessary documentation. Private expediters can get things done in as little as 48 hours, but charge hefty fees for their services.

U.S. Passport Information U.S. Department of State. ☎ 877/487-2778 ⊕ passports. state.gov.

Canadian Passports Passport Canada. ✉ Passport Canada Program, Gatineau ☎ 819/997-8338, 800/567-6868 toll-free Canada and U.S. ⊕ www.cic.gc.ca/english/ passport/.

U.S. Passport and Visa Expediters American Passport. ☎ 800/455-5166 ⊕ www. americanpassport.com. **Travel Document Systems.** ☎ 202/638-3800, 800/874-5100 ⊕ www.traveldocs.com. **Travel the World Visas.** ☎ 202/223-8822, 866/886-8472 ⊕ www.world-visa.com.

▌SAFETY

The most dangerous element of the Northwest is the great outdoors. Don't hike alone, and make sure you bring enough water plus basic first-aid items. If you're not an experienced hiker, stick to tourist-friendly spots like the more accessible parts of the national parks; if you have to drive 30 miles down a Forest Service road to reach a trail, it's possible you might be the only one hiking on it.

▌TAXES

Oregon has no sales tax, although many cities and counties levy a tax on lodging and services. Room taxes, for example, vary from 7% to 13.5%. The state retail sales tax in Washington is 6.5%, but there are also local taxes that can raise the total tax to almost 10%, depending on the goods or service and the municipality; Seattle's retail sales tax is 9.5%. A Goods and Services Tax (GST) of 5% applies on virtually every transaction in Canada except for the purchase of basic groceries.

In British Columbia an additional Provincial Sales Tax (PST) of 7% applies to most goods and services.

▌VISITOR INFORMATION

British Columbia Tourism Vancouver Island. ✉ 65 Front St., Suite 501, Nanaimo ☎ 250/754-3500 ⊕ www.vancouverisland. travel. **Tourism Vancouver Visitor Centre.** ✉ Plaza Level, 200 Burrard St., Vancouver ☎ 604/683-2000 ⊕ www.tourismvancouver. com. **Tourism Victoria.** ✉ Visitors Centre, 812 Wharf St., Victoria ☎ 250/953-2033, 800/663-3883 ⊕ www.tourismvictoria.com.

Oregon Travel Oregon. ☎ 800/547-7842 ⊕ www.traveloregon.com. **Travel Portland.** ✉ Visitor Info Center, 701 S.W. 6th, Portland ☎ 503/275-8355, 877/678-5263 ⊕ www. travelportland.com.

Washington Seattle Convention and Visitors Bureau. ☎ 866/732-2695 visitor information, 206/461-5840 main office ⊕ www.visitseattle.org. **Washington Tourism Alliance.** ☎ 800/544-1800 ⊕ www.experiencewa.com.

INDEX

PHOTO CREDITS

Front cover: Image Source / Alamy [Description: Mount Hood and Trillium Lake, Oregon]. **Back cover, from left to right:** Natalia Bratslavsky; Rachell Coe/Shutterstock; San Juan Safaris. **Spine:** Jo Ann Snover/Shutterstock. 1, Arthit Kaeoratanapattama / Shutterstock. 2-3, Jeanne Hatch/iStockphoto. 5, Liem Bahneman/Shutterstock. **Chapter 1: Experience the Pacific Northwest:** 8-9, mlwphoto / Shutterstock. 16 (left), Christopher Boswell/Shutterstock. 16 (top right), moohaha/Flickr. 16 (bottom center), Elena Korenbaum/iStockphoto. 16 (bottom right), Brian Holsclaw/Flickr. 17 (top left), The High Desert Museum. 17 (top center), James Hornung/Shutterstock. 17 (bottom left), Neta Delgany/iStockphoto. 17 (bottom center), Chuck Pefley/Alamy. 17 (right), Norman Eder/iStockphoto. 18 (left), neelsky/Shutterstock. 18 (top right), moohaha/Flickr. 18 (bottom center), Rimasz/Dreamstime.com. 18 (bottom right), thinair/iStockphoto. 19 (top left), Jdanne | Dreamstime.com. 19 (bottom left), Pike Place Market. 19 (bottom center), Tim Thompson. 19 (right), Victor Maschek / Shutterstock. 20 (left), Kenji Nogai21. 20 (top right), Lissandra Melo/Shutterstock. 20 (bottom center), Natalia Bratslavsky/Shutterstock. 20 (bottom right), WordRidden/Flickr. 21 (top left), Steve Rossett/Shutterstock. 21 (top center) Natalia Braslavsky/Shutterstock. 21 (right), fotofriends/Shutterstock. 21 (bottom left), Michel Teiten/Wikipedia.com. 21 (bottom center) Royal BC Museum. 39, Stuart Westmorland/age fotostock. 41, Thomas Kitchin & Vict/age fotostock. 42, San Juan Safaris. 43, Sylvain Grandadam/age fotostock. **Chapter 2: Portland:** 45, Torsten Kjellstrand/Travel Portland. 46, -b-/Flickr. 48, Karen Massier/Stockphoto. 57, Strekoza2 | Dreamstime.com. 64, Joshuaraineyphotography | Dreamstime.com. 67, Appalachianviews | Dreamstime.com. **Chapter 3: The Oregon Coast:** 103, Glebtarro | Dreamstime.com. 104, scaredy_kat/Flickr. 105, Oksana Perkins/iStockphoto. 106, Tom Wald/iStockphoto. 107 (bottom), John Norris/Flickr. 107 (top), Scott Catron/wikipedia.org. 108, Pacific Northwest USCG/Flickr. 136, Oregon Coast Aquarium. 145, Greg Vaughan. **Chapter 4: Willamette Valley and Wine Country:** 157, Dennis Frates / Alamy. 158, Don Hankins/Flickr. 160, Craig Sherod. 168, Greg Vaughn. 176, Jason Tomczak. 176-77, Greg Vaughn. 178, Fox Hill Vineyards. 179 (left), Jason Tomczak. 179 (right), REX HILL, Newberg, OR. 180 (top), Ponzi Vineyards. 180 (bottom), Vercingetorix Vineyards. 181 (left), Adelsheim Vineyard. 181 (center), Box Hill. 181 (right), Norman Eder/iStockphoto. 183 (left), Pennar-Ash Wine Cellars. 183 (center), Polara Studio. 183 (right), Dundee Bistro. 194, Jpldesigns | Dreamstime.com. 200, Oregonlass | Dreamstime.com. **Chapter 5: The Columbia River Gorge and Mt. Hood:** 207, William Blacke/iStockphoto. 210, Rigucci | Dreamstime.com. 216, zschnepf/Shutterstock. 218 and 225, GregVaughn. **Chapter 6: Central Oregon:** 239, Livingstonatlarge | Dreamstime.com. 240, Robert O. Brown Photography/iStockphoto. 241, JonDissed/Flickr. 242, Sunriver Resort. 249, Svetlana55 | Dreamstime.com. 253, Sunriver Resort. **Chapter 7: Crater Lake National Park:** 261, William A. McConnell. 263, Michael Rubin/iStockphoto. 264, Vivian Fung/Shutterstock. **Chapter 8: Southern Oregon:** 273, Greg Vaughn. 274, Michael Dunn-I/Flickr. 276, Paula C. Caudill. 293, Viviansviews | Dreamstime.com. **Chapter 9: Seattle:** 301, José Fuste Raga / age fotostock. 303, Stephen Finn/Shutterstock. 304, Gregory Olsen/iStockphoto. 311, Mariusz S. Jurgielewicz/Shutterstock. 313, jeffwilcox/Flickr. 316-317, Mark B. Bauschke/Shutterstock. 316 (bottom), Charles Amundson/Shutterstock. 318 (top), The Tasting Room. 318 (bottom left), piroshky bakery. 318 (bottom right), Beecher's Handmade Cheese. 319 (left), Phillie Casablanca/Flickr. 319 (center), Nick Jurich of flashpd.com. 319 (right), eng1ne/Flickr. 359, Richard Cummins / age fotostock. **Chapter 10: Washington Cascade Mountains and Valleys:** 365, Carlos Arguelles/Shutterstock. 367, Rodefeld/Flickr. 368, Mrs. Flinger/Flickr. 374, John Carlson. 391, Richard Cummins / age fotostock. 399, amanderson2/Flickr. 410, neelsky/Shutterstock. 411 (bottom), Bill Perry/Shutterstock. 411 (top), Donald A. Swanson/USGS. 413, tusharkoley/Shutterstock. **Chapter 11: San Juan Islands:** 417, Edmund Lowe Photograph/Shutterstock. 418, funflow/Shutterstock. 419, Monica Wieland/Shutterstock. 420, yel02/Flickr. 431, Jdanne | Dreamstime.com. **Chapter 12: Olympic National Park:** 443, E+/iStockphoto. 444, Washington State Tourism. 446, Andrey Lukashenkov/Shutterstock. 452, Lindsay Douglas/Shutterstock. 458, Superstock/age fotostock. **Chapter 13: Olympic Peninsula and Washington Coast:** 463, Sylvia Grandadam/age fotostock. 466, cdrin/Shutterstock. 480, UnGePhoto/Shutterstock. 486, Konrad Wothe / age fotostock. 499, Alan Majchrowicz / age fotostock. **Chapter 14: North Cascades National Park:** 503, LoweStock / iStockphoto. 504, Washington-State Tourism. 505, Iwona Erskine-Kellie/Flickr. 506, Alan Kearney/age fotostock. **Chapter 15: North Central Washington:** 513 and 514, Bill Perry/Shutterstock. 515, Pierdelune/Shutterstock. 516, Bill Perry/Shutterstock. 523, Sun Mountain Lodge. 526, brewbooks/Flickr. 533, Natalia Bratslavsky/Shutterstock. **Chapter 16: Mount Rainier National Park:** 539, chinana, Fodors.com member. 541 (top and bottom), Washington State Tourism. 542, Pat Leahy/Flickr. 552-53, zschnep/Shutterstock. **Chapter 17: Washington Wine Country:** 555, Bruce Block/iStockphoto. 556, Jackie Johnston. 557, Desert Wind Winery. 558, Hogue Cellars. 569, waterfordyork/Stockphoto. 575, Lynn Hawlett. 579, Hogue Cellars. **Chapter 18: Spokane and Eastern Washington:** 581, Inge Johnsson / Alamy. 582, Mark Wagner/wikipedia.org. 584, James Hawley/Flickr. 593, Danita Delimont / Alamy. 604, Jame Hawley/Flickr. 613, Cave B Inn at Sangcliffe. **Chapter 19: Vancouver and Victoria:** 619, Dan Breckwoldt/shutterstock. 620, Natalia Bratslavsky/Shutterstock. 621, Xuanlu Wang/Shutterstock. 622, ABC Pics/Shutterstock. 630, SuperStock / age fotostock. 653, North Light Images / age fotostock. 655, Xuanlu Wang/Shutterstock. **About Our Writers:** All photos are courtesy of the writer except for the following: Shelley Arenas, courtesy of Jannie Anderson; Kimberley Bowker, courtesy of Tim Gallivan; Andrew Collins, courtesy of Fernando Nocedal; Adriana Janovich, courtesy of John Guenther; AnnaMaria Stephens, courtesy of KJ Stephens; Christine Vovakes, courtesy of Michael Vovakes.

ABOUT OUR WRITERS

Shelley Arenas grew up in eastern Washington and returns there often from her home in Seattle to escape city traffic and visit family and friends. She has been a regular contributor to *Fodor's Pacific Northwest* and other guidebooks for more than a decade, along with co-authoring a book about Seattle for families. She updated the Olympic National Park, Mt. Rainier National Park, North Cascades National Park, Spokane and Eastern Washington, and Travel Smart chapters for this edition.

Margot Bigg is a freelance travel writer and editor based in Portland, Oregon. She's lived and worked all over the world, most recently in India, where she worked at *Time Out Magazine* and contributed to the last three editions of *Fodor's Essential India*. Though now back in the States, she continues to contribute to a variety of Indian publications, including local editions of *Rolling Stone* and *National Geographic Traveler*, as well as U.S. publications ranging from *Sunset Magazine* to *VICE*. Margot updated the Willamette Valley chapter for this edition.

Andrew Collins, a former Fodor's editor, updated Experience Pacific Northwest, Portland, Oregon Coast, Columbia River Gorge and Mt. Hood, Crater Lake National Park, Southern Oregon, Washinton Cascade Mountains and Valleys, and The San Juan Islands chapters this edition. A resident of both Portland and Mexico City who travels frequently throughout the Northwest, he has authored more than a dozen guidebooks, and is editor in chief of three magazines, including *The Pearl* (about Portland's hip Pearl District). He also writes about restaurants, art, and design for *Four Seasons Magazine* and travel for *New Mexico Magazine*; teaches food writing and travel writing for Gotham Writers' Workshop; and has contributed to *Travel + Leisure, Sunset,* and dozens of other periodicals.

A travel writer since 2006, **Chloë Ernst** most often explores her British Columbia backyard—freelancing for Fodor's, Google Trips, ZAGAT, and travelandleisure. com. Though she loves Vancouver's hiking trails and breweries, Chloë has a special affinity for long ferry journeys and out-of-the-way places. Her adventures have taken her to abandoned Alaskan gold mines and along jungle roads in Bolivia. Find more about these and other journeys at ⊕ *www.chloeernst.com.*

Jennifer Foden is an award-winning freelance writer and editor who relocated from Toronto to Vancouver—for the mountains. She writes about travel, sustainability, social justice, architecture, and food and drink for a variety of publications. When she's not working with words, she's traveling, watching sports, or Face Timing her niece and nephew.

A newspaper internship first lured Seattle native **Adriana Janovich** to Port Townsend, Washington nearly 20 years ago. Now a food, travel, and lifestyles writer and editor in the Inland Northwest, she loved revisiting her old haunts—and discovering some new ones—for the Olympic Peninsula and Washington Coast, North Central Washington, and Washington Wine Country chapters this edition. She also teaches journalism at Whitworth University in Spokane.

Lauren Kelley received a BA in English Writing from the University of Redlands before moving to Seattle in 2012. Currently a freelance writer, Lauren lives with her boyfriend in their cozy city loft that doubles as her office. Her favorite place she's traveled? Mallorca, Spain. Lauren updated Seattle Shopping.

 Freelance writer **Sue Kernaghan** has written about British Columbia for dozens of publications and websites around the world, including several editions of *Fodor's Vancouver and Victoria*. A fourth-generation British Columbian, she now lives and writes on Salt Spring Island.

Kade Krichko is a journalist and photographer who turned chasing curiosity into his profession. He is fluent in one language, but has gotten lost in many others. Despite the occasional lack of direction, he always finds his way back to the mountains. Kade updated the Seattle Sports and Outdoors section.

 Award-winning freelance travel writer **Chris McBeath's** more than 25 years in the tourism industry have given her an insider's eye about what makes a great vacation. British Columbia is her home, so whether routing through backcountry or discovering a hidden-away inn, Chris has combined history, insight, and anecdotes into her contribution to this book. Many of Chris's articles can be found at ⊕ *www. greatestgetaways.com*; her destination videos are available on YouTube.

 Born in Canada and raised in the UK, **Lesley Mirza** was introduced to the pleasure of travel at an early age by her globetrotting parents. Now back in Canada, and living in Vancouver, BC, with her husband and two senior pugs, Lesley works as a freelance writer, penning travel and lifestyle stories for a variety of publications.

 Christina Newberry is a freelance writer and editor based in Vancouver. When she's not traveling the world in search of a great story, Christina can be found exploring the sights, sounds and tastes of Vancouver's unique neighborhoods, happily playing tourist in her own hometown.

 Conor Risch is a Seattle-based writer. When he's not enjoying Seattle's food, drinks, and live music offerings, he's somewhere outside, exploring the natural beauty of the Pacific Northwest. Or watching sports. Conor updated the Seattle Nightlife and Performing Arts.

 Jonathan Shadel is a writer based in Portland, Oregon, where he currently works as senior editor for MEDI-America Publishing. His features and essays appear in the *Washington Post, The Atlantic CityLab*, and *VICE*, among many other publications. A self-described gastronome and coffee snob, Shadel writes frequently about food and drink for *Barista, Fresh Cup,* and other foodie magazines. His favorite assignments have him eating and drinking around his adopted home state of Oregon. He updated the Eastern and Central Oregon chapters in this guide.

 AnnaMaria Stephens is a Seattle-based freelance writer who covers travel, design, food, and more. She's a fan of everything her city has to offer, from the coffee and culture to the countless views of mountains and water. She also firmly believes that Seattle's spectacular summers are worth a few months of drizzle. AnnaMaria updated Seattle Exploring, Where to Stay, and Side Trips.

Naomi Tomky lives and writes in Seattle, where she's the city's biggest cheerleader and most enthusiastic eater. She writes about Seattle's food scene for local and national publications and received the Association of Food Journalist's Best Food and Travel Award for 2016. Naomi updated Seattle Where to Eat.